THIRD EDITION

Architecture
Drafting and Design

Donald E. Hepler • Paul I. Wallach

McGraw-Hill Book Company
New York St. Louis San Francisco Dallas Auckland Bogotá Düsseldorf
Johannesburg London Madrid Mexico Montreal New Delhi Panama
Paris São Paulo Singapore Sydney Tokyo Toronto

Editor: Hal Lindquist
Editing Supervisors: Faye Allen and Mary Naomi Russell
Design Supervisor: Jim Darby
Production Supervisors: Renee Guilmette, Ted Agrillo, and Suzanne LanFranchi

Design: Aspen Hollow Art Service
Cover Photo: Pedro A. Noa
Cover Design: Cathy Gallagher

Library of Congress Cataloging in Publication Data

Hepler, Donald E
Architecture: drafting and design.

Includes index.
1. Architectural drawing. 2. Architectural design. I. Wallach, Paul I., joint author. II. Title.
NA2700.H4 1977 720'.28 76-19073
ISBN 0-07-028291-9

Contents

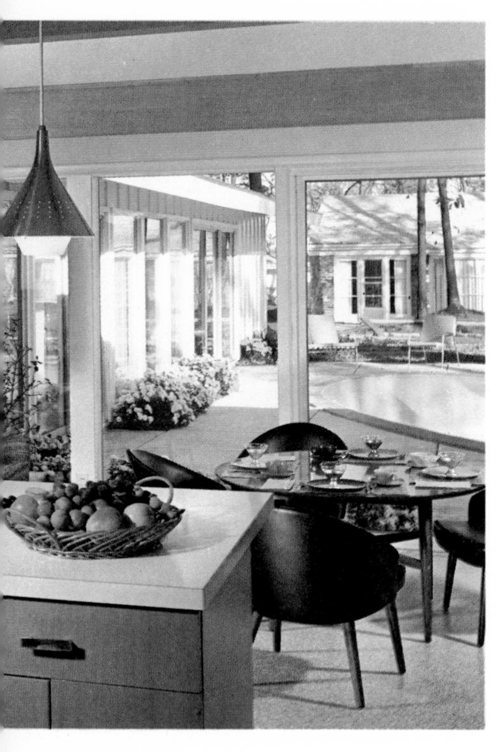

About the Authors

Donald E. Hepler completed his undergraduate work at California State College, California, Pennsylvania, and his graduate work at the University of Pittsburgh. He joined Admiral Homes, Inc., as an architectural draftsman and later joined the architectural staffs of Rust Engineering; Patterson, Emerson, and Comstock, Engineers; and Union Switch and Signal Company. After serving as an officer with the United States Army Corps of Engineers, he became head of the Industrial Arts Department, Avonworth High School, Pittsburgh, Pennsylvania. He later joined the faculty of California State College as Associate Professor of Industrial Arts. Working for the McGraw-Hill Book Company since 1961, he is presently Editor in Chief for Trade and Technical Publishing in the Gregg Division.

Paul I. Wallach received his undergraduate education at the University of California at Santa Barbara and did his graduate work at Los Angeles State College. He has acquired extensive experience in the drafting, designing, and construction phases of architecture. He has traveled extensively in Europe and the Far East and has studied and taught for several years in Europe. He taught architecture and drafting for 27 years in California at both the secondary school and community college levels.

A Word about Metrication

The metric system of measurement is being introduced in this third edition of ARCHITECTURE: DRAFTING AND DESIGN even though most architectural work is not being designed in metric units. The introduction of the metric system as a secondary system of measure is done so that the student may get a feel for the new measurement system which is to come.

Because standards for building materials and modular units have not yet been established, the metric dimensions used are not necessarily those which will become standard. Usually the dimensions are conversions of present standards. In the future, as standards are established, other editions of this text will reflect those changes.

We hope that the use of metrics will be found to be practical. We have not converted every dimension nor have we metricated every problem. The metric equivalents for the most part are approximate and not exact, in the hopes of being practical. For example, in asking a student to design a room of 100 square feet, the exact metric equivalent is 9.290 square meters, but as a practical approach 10 square meters is used. Similarly, the equivalent for 48 inches is given as 1220 rather than 1219 millimeters, for convenience.

As a guide to accuracy, meters are carried to one decimal place for approximate sizes and to three decimal places for accurate dimensions. Millimeters are rounded to the nearest sensible unit ending in 0 or 5 for approximate dimensions and rounded to the nearest millimeter for accurate sizes.

Please note that we are following the metric practice of using a space rather than a comma to separate numbers of five digits or more at three-digit intervals.

Any comments or suggestions for metric use in future editions are welcome.

THE EDITOR

Preface

ARCHITECTURE: DRAFTING AND DESIGN is designed as a first course in architectural drafting and design. Since a study of mechanical drawing normally precedes a course in architecture, only the principles and practices that are essentially related to architectural drafting are presented in this book.

This edition of ARCHITECTURE: DRAFTING AND DESIGN is divided into five parts: Part One, *The Design Process;* Part Two, *Basic Architectural Plans;* Part Three, *Technical Architectural Plans;* Part Four, *Architectural Support Services;* and Part Five, *Appendix.*

Part One, *The Design Process,* covers the basic elements of planning various areas of a structure and combining these areas into a composite, functional plan.

Part Two, *Basic Architectural Plans,* includes the basic techniques and procedures used in preparing architectural floor plans, elevations, and pictorial drawings. Information about the metric scale and computer-aided graphics is included in this part.

Part Three, *Technical Architectural Plans,* shows how to prepare the many technical architectural plans that are necessary for a complete and detailed description of a basic design.

Part Four, *Architectural Support Services,* covers the activities in which an architectural draftsman may participate but which are not directly related to the drafting function.

Part Five, *Appendix,* includes reference material on architectural terms, related mathematics, and career information.

ARCHITECTURE: DRAFTING AND DESIGN is organized to be presented consecutively from Part One through Part Four. Other sequences of study may be more suitable for classes with different emphases. When the basic emphasis is placed on developing fundamental architectural drafting skills and techniques, Part Two may be studied first. Classes that are specifically oriented to the construction phase of architecture may find Part Three a logical point of departure.

All the illustrations have been selected and prepared to reinforce and amplify the principles and procedures described in the text. Whenever possible, each principle and practice has been reduced to its most elementary form and, for easy comprehension, has been directly related to the student's own environment.

Progression within each section and unit is from the simple to the complex, from the familiar to the abstract. The problems that appear at the end of each unit are organized to provide the maximum amount of flexibility. Most units include problems that range from the simplest, which can be completed in a few minutes, to the complex, which require considerable research and application of the principles of architectural drafting and design.

Since communication in the field of architectural drafting and design depends largely on understanding the vocabulary of architecture, new terms, abbreviations, and symbols are defined when they first appear and are reinforced throughout the rest of the text.

The practice of architecture functions through a utilization of the basic principles of mathematics and science. The correlation of basic scientific and mathematical concepts with architectural principles has been presented wherever appropriate.

Primarily, the residence is used to illustrate the application of the various architectural plans and techniques. Other structures also are used as examples, when suitable.

In this edition, illustrations have been replaced and updated, and new illustrations have been added. To help the student more fully understand the basic principles and applications of good design, 96 pages are in full color.

In addition to expanding and updating existing units, this edition adds completely new units on the metric scale, computer-aided graphics, and line techniques, and it includes a complete set of plans showing their interrelationships.

The authors gratefully acknowledge Jay Helsel and John Seals for their help in redesigning and redrawing many of the illustrations for this edition and also thank Richard Pollman and Wendy Talcott for the use of the many Home Planners, Inc. designs.

Celotex Corp.

Greek use of post and lintel construction.

Introduction

Architecture had its beginning when early humans first fashioned caves or lean-to shelters for their families. Architectural drafting and design began when these people first drew the outline of a shelter in the sand or dirt and planned in advance the use of existing materials. Thus, an architect uses the knowledge gained from past centuries when designing a building today.

HISTORY

The history of architectural design is directly related to the great movements of history. For example, architecture has relied heavily upon the advancements of science and mathematics. From these advancements have come new building materials and methods. New engineering developments and new building materials have brought about more changes in architectural design in the last 30 years than have occurred in all the preceding history of architecture. Yet many of the basic principles of modern architecture, such as bearing-wall construction and skeleton-frame construction, have been known for centuries.

Even today architectural structures are divided into two basic types, the bearing-wall and the skeleton-frame. The bearing wall has walls that are solid and that support themselves and the roof.

BEARING WALL

Most early architecture, such as the Egyptian and Grecian structures, used the bearing wall for support. In fact, one of the first major problems in architectural drafting and design involved the bearing wall. The problem was simply how to provide an opening in a supporting wall without taking away the support. One of the first solutions to this problem was

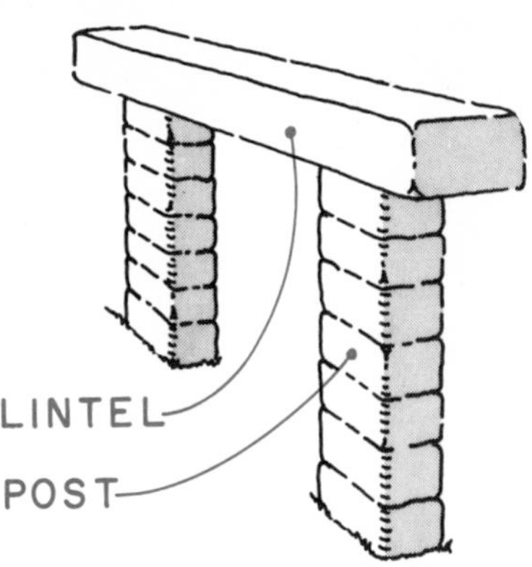

Post and lintel construction.

The basic orders of architecture.

the development of the post and the lintel. In this type of construction, posts large enough to support the lintel were used to support the rest of the wall and the roof.

The ancient Greeks used post and lintel construction to erect many of their beautiful buildings. Most ancient people used stone as their primary building material. The great weight of the stone limited the application of post and lintel construction. Furthermore, stone post and lintel construction could not support wide openings. Therefore, many posts were placed close together to provide the needed support. The Greeks developed many styles of columns and gave names to their parts. The various styles of column designs were known as *orders*. These orders of architecture developed by the Greeks were known as the *Doric*, the *Ionic*, and the *Corinthian* orders. Later the Romans developed the *Composite* and the *Tuscan* orders.

Since the Greek climate was well suited to open-air construction, the Greeks used the post and lintel technique to great advantage. The Parthenon is a classic example of Greek use of the post and lintel.

Oriental architects also made effective use of the post and lintel. They were able to construct buildings with larger openings under the lintel because they used lighter materials. The use of lighter materials resulted in the development of a style of architecture which was very light and graceful. The oriental post and lintel technique was also used extensively for gates and entrances.

Interior posts designed by Aztec architects were spaced close together.

Celotex Corp.

The Arch

The Romans began a new trend in the design of wall openings when they developed the arch. The arch is different from the post and lintel because it can span greater areas without sup-

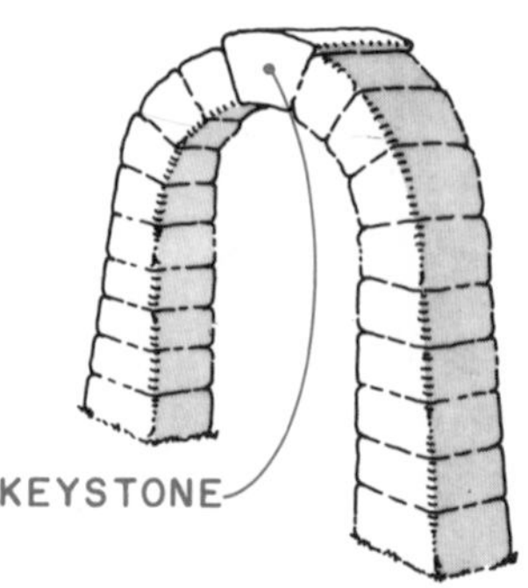

A keystone supports both sides of an arch, which must also be supported at its base.

Celotex Corp.

An early oriental application of post and lintel construction.

Celotex Corp.

Ancient Siamese temples featured the dome.

port. This advantage of the arch is due to its being made of small pieces of stone. The principle of the arch is that each stone is supported by leaning on the keystone in the center.

The Vault

The simple arch led to the development of the vault. The *vault* is simply a series of arches which forms a continuous covering. This development allowed the use of the arch as a passageway rather than just as an opening in a wall. The barrel vault and the cross vault were popular Roman construction devices. The cross vault is the intersection of two barrel vaults.

The Dome

The dome is a further refinement of the arch. The *dome* is made of arches so arranged that the bases make a circle and the tops meet in the middle of the ceiling. The Romans felt that the dome developed a feeling of power. Hence, domes were used extensively on religious and governmental structures.

The barrel vault is a series of arches.

The Gothic Arch

Gothic architecture originated in France. It spread throughout Western Europe between 1160 and 1530. With its development came another variation of the arch—the pointed arch. The pointed arch became very popular in Gothic cathedrals because it created a sense of reaching and aspiring by its emphasis on vertical lines. Construction of the pointed arch posed the same problem as did conventional arches, that of spreading at the bottom. But instead of just supporting the arch at the bottom, a new device known as a *buttress* was developed. Buttresses were gradually moved up the walls and resulted in the development of the *flying buttress.*

The flying buttress helps to support thin walls and many windows.

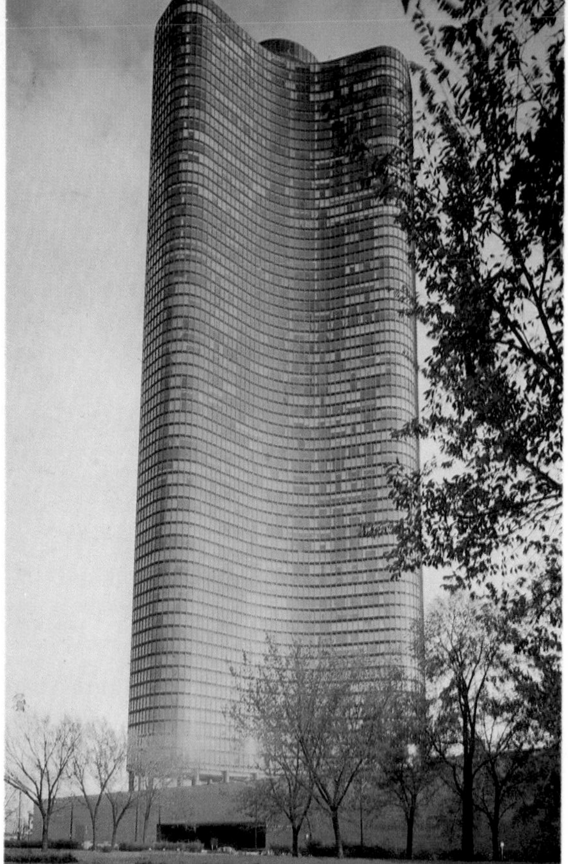

Glaverbel

Glass provided the architects of Lake Point Tower in Chicago with great freedom in design.

New applications of wood in architecture.

California Redwood Association

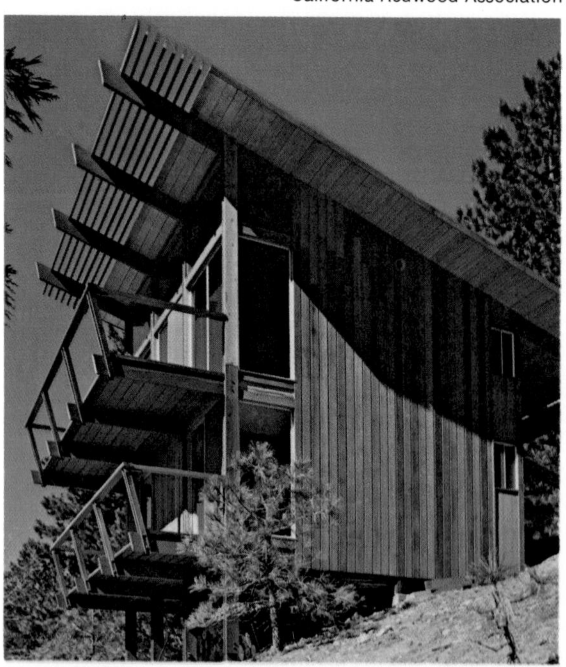

TECHNOLOGICAL ADVANCES

Bearing-wall construction is still used extensively in modern architecture. The use of modern building materials, such as reinforced and prestressed concrete, enables the architect to span greater areas. This allows a greater flexibility in design. Because of the development of new materials and new building methods, we can design and build structures that are larger, lighter, safer, and more functional than ever before.

NEW MATERIALS

Advancements in architecture through the ages have been greatly affected by the availability of building materials. As recently as American colonial times, builders had only wood, stone, and ceramic materials with which to work. Early American architecture reflects the use of these materials. But with the development of steel, aluminum, structural glass, prestressed concrete, wood laminates, and plastics, buildings can be designed in sizes and shapes never before possible.

Many new materials are really old materials used in new applications. Sometimes they are old materials manufactured in a different way. For example, glass is not a new material, but the development of structural glass, glass blocks, corrugated glass, and thermal glass has given the architect much greater freedom in the use of this material.

Wood is also a classic building material. It is one of the oldest materials used in construction. Yet the development of new structural wood forms, plywoods, and laminates has revolutionized the structural use of wood. The manufacture of stressed skin panels, boxed beams, curved panels, folded roof plates, and laminated beams has opened new horizons for the use of wood.

Among the new architectural materials is plastic. The development of vinyl and laminated plastic has provided the architect with a wide range of new materials with which to work. The material that has contributed most to architectural change has been steel. Without the use of steel, construction of most of our

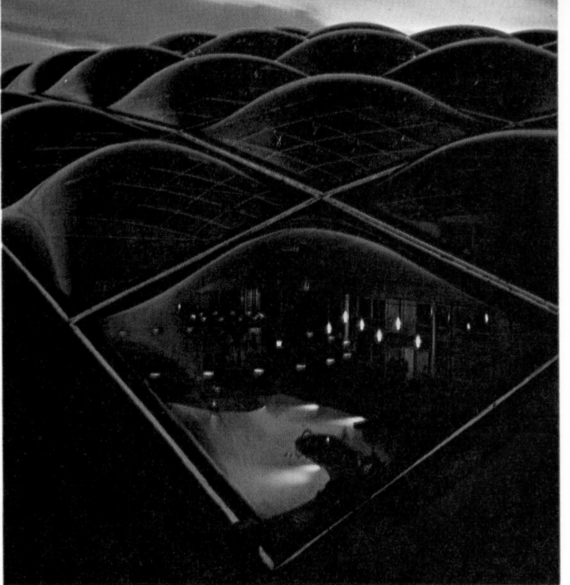

Rohm & Haas Company

Plastics are among the newest architectural materials, as shown in these skylights.

PPG Industries, Inc.

This building combines skeleton-frame and bearing-wall construction.

large high-rise buildings would be impossible. Even smaller structures can now be built on locations and in shapes that were impossible without the structural stability of steel.

The manufacture of aluminum into lightweight, durable sheets and structural shapes has also contributed greatly to design flexibility. But it is another old material, concrete, that has changed the basic nature of structural design. New uses of concrete are factory-made reinforced and prestressed structural shapes. The shapes are used for floors, roofs, and walls. These developments have provided the architect with still other tools for structural design.

Today's architects now have the opportunity to design the framework of a building of steel. In the same building, they are free to use large glass sheets for walls, prestressed concrete for floors, aluminum for casements, plastics for skylights, wood for cabinets, and a wide variety of other material combinations. Thus, the development of each new material complements another.

NEW CONSTRUCTION METHODS

The development of new materials is usually not possible without the development of new construction methods. For example, large glass panels could not have been used in the eighteenth century even if they were available, because no large-span lintel-support system had been developed. Only when both new materi-

An example of cantilever construction.

PPG Industries, Inc.

PPG Industries, Inc.

An example of curtain-wall construction.

als and new methods exist is the architect free to design with complete flexibility.

Present-day structures usually incorporate some combination of old and new. In a modern building, examples of the old post and lintel method may be used in conjunction with skeleton-frame, curtain-wall, or cantilevered construction.

One of the earliest methods developed to utilize modern materials is the skeleton frame. This type of building has an open frame to which a wall covering is attached. The frame provides the primary support, and the covering provides the needed shelter. The development of light, strong, and diversified framing materials and wall coverings has led to the popularization of the skeleton frame in modern architecture. The skeleton frame is now commonly used in family dwellings and in the construction of commercial buildings. When steel is used for the skeleton, the skeleton frame is known as *steel-cage construction.*

The use of the skeleton frame, as opposed to bearing-wall construction, has opened new horizons for architects. They can now design a structure without direct vertical-line support. In this type of construction, called *cantilevered construction,* the loads are supported at only one end. Cantilever construction is well suited to steel because unsupported steel beams can be extended farther without sagging than can any other material.

Because loads in steel-cage construction are not supported by the outside wall, curtain walls are possible. In this type of construction, also known as *curtain-wall construction,* a steel cage is erected, forming the shape of the building. The curtain wall, or skin, is added last. This curtain has no structural relationship to the stability of the building; it acts only as a protection from the weather. Therefore, the curtain wall may be made of materials with little or no structural value, such as glass, sheet metal, or plastic.

Triangular cross-bracing is used on the Alcoa Building in San Francisco.

Aluminum Company of America

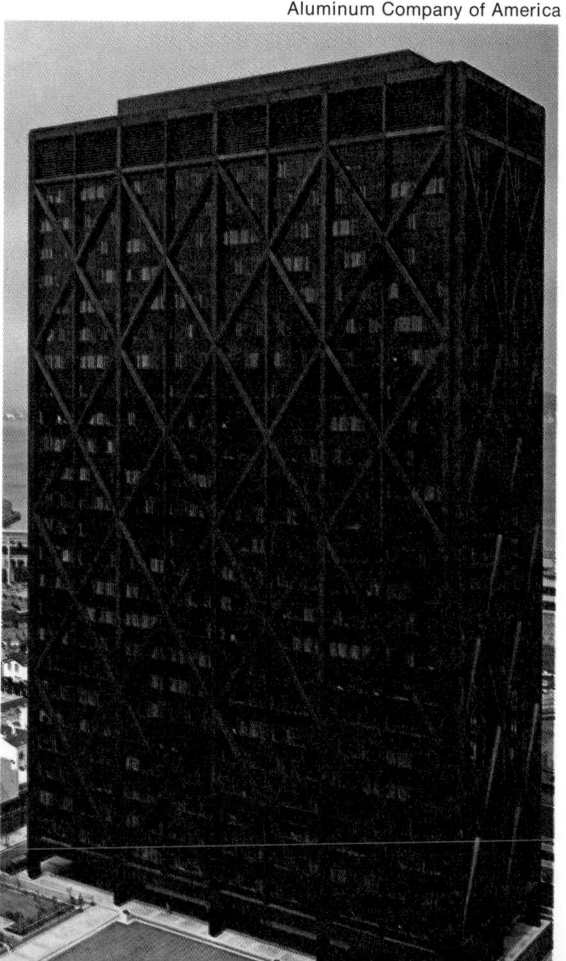

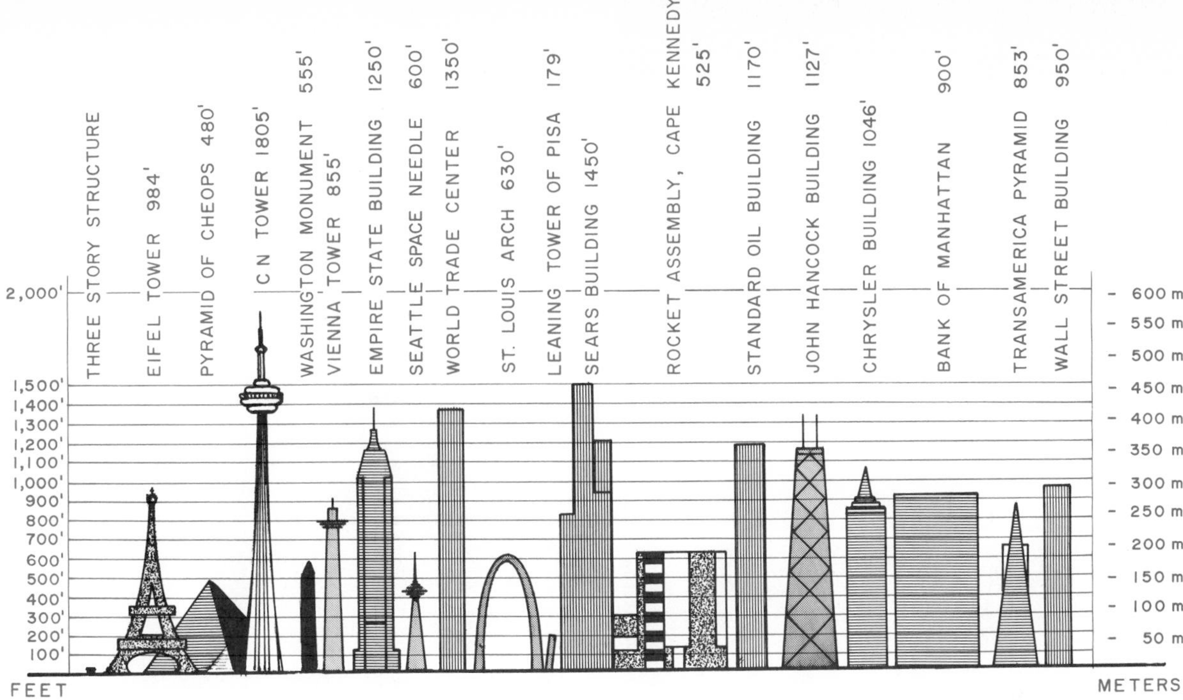

Comparison of the tallest structures from around the world.

Triangular architectural shapes are not new. Early Egyptians recognized that the triangle provided the strongest rigidity with the fewest number of members. Today we are using new triangular principles to provide structural stability to several of our largest buildings. Unlike conventional curtain-wall construction, in which the wall is applied to a steel frame, some buildings have an exposed structural steel frame, eliminating all vertical columns from the skin to the core. These truss walls direct all building loads around the structure and downward triangularly. The Alcoa building in San Francisco also introduces a triangular cross-bracing system which provides stability against wind and earthquakes. The U.S. Steel building is built in a triangular plan with supporting steel columns standing out 3 feet from the building wall.

United States Steel Corporation

The U.S. Steel Building in Pittsburgh is built on a triangular plan.

One of the most spectacular achievements of our technological explosion is the use of new materials and new methods to design and build structures of unprecedented size. The Sears Tower is now the tallest building in the world. Frank Lloyd Wright's proposed mile-high skyscraper is now a structural possibility. Today, architects cannot only design buildings of enormous size but can do so for locations unthought of years ago. Further advancements in transportation systems and refinements in structural engineering will make it possible to build in locations that are unacceptable today.

One of the most significant advancements to take place in the past several years is the design and construction of architectural components. Components may or may not contain

The use of modular components has revolutionized construction methods.

Celotex Corp.

Transportation of components and materials was extremely difficult in A.D. 987.

new materials, but they do allow the builder to construct parts of the building away from the site. As more components are developed, construction changes from fabrication on the site to assembly of component parts on the site. The development of component systems does not necessarily change the nature of design, but it does change the way in which architects may design, because components will provide them with more complete tools.

TODAY AND TOMORROW

Because of the development of new materials and methods of construction, the architect can often be free from the use of traditional materials and methods. An architect becomes a coordinator of the activities of the structural engineer, electrical engineer, acoustical engineer, sociologist, interior decorator, and so forth. As the role of the architect as a coordinator is increased, the relationship between art and technology will be refined. This will enable all types of buildings to be technically accurate and aesthetically acceptable.

No one can predict the future of architecture. It will certainly be related to the development of new materials, new construction methods, and sociological changes.

Designing a structure that will last is a great challenge. The architect, the designer, and the builder must keep abreast of technological changes and advancements in architectural engineering and building design. This is true whether they are designing a residence, designing a large building, or planning a completely different kind of structure. In any case, today's architect must understand people, their habits, their needs, their activities, and their desires. The architect, designer, or draftsman must also be capable of working with shapes, materials, colors, and proportions in order to design aesthetically pleasing structures. Architectural science and engineering must be understood in order to produce buildings that are structurally sound. The architect must be able to arrange and balance space in order to create buildings that are functionally appropriate.

PART ONE

Before a set of architectural plans can be prepared, the building must be thought out and a rough design decided upon. In creating the design, the designer must progress logically, step by step through the design process. The first step in this process is to divide plans into various areas according to their specific function. The designer must become familiar with the activities that will occur in each area. A school would be divided into such areas as administrative, classroom, service, and physical-activity areas. In the same way, a house is divided into three major areas for planning purposes: the living area, the service area, and the sleeping area.

Areas constitute the main divisions of a structure. Areas are broken into subdivisions called *rooms.* These subdivisions are related to the basic function of the area. Part One provides the principles, practices, information, and specific steps necessary to arrange rooms and areas so as to create the basic elements of an architectural plan.

The Design Process

SECTION 1

Designing and Planning

This section provides background information that is needed prior to the design of a structure. It involves a study of architects and architectural styles. It also covers the important environmental factors of orientation, density, and ecological planning which must be considered prior to the finalization of an architectural plan.

UNIT 1

Architectural Styles

Architectural styles have evolved through the years as a result of new developments in building materials and new demands of the culture. Styles of the past reflect the culture of the past. Styles of the present reflect our current living habits and needs. Architectural styles of the future will be largely determined by advancements in technology and changes in our living habits.

Our architectural heritage is largely derived from European and early American architecture. The oriental influence has become significant in some parts of the country.

EUROPEAN STYLES

The English, French, Italians, and Spanish have had the most significant influence on our architecture.

English Architecture

The English Tudor style of architecture originated in England during the fifteenth century. Tudor homes featured high-pitched gable roofs, small windows, shallow dormers, Norman towers, and tall chimneys which extended high above the roof line.

The Elizabethan, or half-timbered, style is an adaptation of the Tudor style. It is characterized by the use of mortar set between timbers. Figure 1–1 shows a modern adaptation of the Elizabethan style of architecture from which many of our modern styles are derived.

Home Planners, Inc.

Fig. 1–1. Elizabethan style.

Home Planners, Inc.

Fig. 1–2. French chateau style.

French Architecture
French provincial architecture was brought to this continent when the French settled Quebec. French provincial architecture can be identified by the mansard roof. This roof design was developed by the French architect François Mansard. On the French provincial home this roof is high-pitched, with steep slopes and rounded dormer windows projecting from the sides. Figure 1–2 shows an example of French architecture of the chateau style.

Southern European Architecture
Spanish architecture was brought to this country by Spanish colonials who settled the Southwest. Spanish architecture is characterized by low-pitched roofs of ceramic tile and stucco exterior walls. A distinguishing feature of almost every Spanish home is a courtyard patio. Two-story Spanish homes contain open balconies enclosed in grillwork. One-story Spanish homes were the forerunners of the present ranch-style homes that first developed in southern California.

Italian architecture is very similar to Spanish architecture. One distinguishing feature is the use of columns and arches at a loggia entrance, and windows of balconies opening onto a loggia roof. A *loggia* is an open gallery covered by a roof. The use of classical mouldings around first-floor windows also helps to distinguish the Italian style from the Spanish.

EARLY AMERICAN

Early colonists came to the New World from many different cultures and were familiar with many different styles of architecture.

New England
The colonists who settled the New England coastal areas were influenced largely by English styles of architecture. Lack of materials, time, and equipment greatly simplified their adaptation of these styles. One of the most popular of the New England styles was the *Cape Cod.* This is a one-and-one-half story gabled-roof house with dormers. It has a central front entrance, a large central chimney, and exterior walls of clapboard or bevel siding. Double-hung windows are fixed with shutters, and the floor plan is symmetrical. Cold New England winters influenced the development of many design features such as shutters, small window areas, double chimneys and enclosed breezeways. Figure 1–3 shows an example of a New England colonial-style home.

Dutch Colonial
Gambrel roofs characterized many small farm buildings in Germany. A *gambrel roof* is a double-pitched roof with projecting overhangs. Many of the German settlers who later settled New York and Pennsylvania made the gambrel roof a part of the Dutch colonial style of architecture.

Home Planners, Inc.

Fig. 1–3. New England colonial style.

© Walt Disney Productions

Fig. 1–4. Examples of Mid-Atlantic colonial style.

Mid-Atlantic Colonial

The availability of brick, a seasonal climate, and the influence of the architecture of Thomas Jefferson led to the development of the early American style of architecture illustrated in Fig. 1–4. The style was formal, massive, and ornate. In colonial days, buildings from Virginia to New Jersey were designed in this manner. It was an adaptation of many urban English designs.

Southern Colonial

When the early settlers migrated to the South, warmer climates and outdoor living activities led them to develop the Southern colonial style of architecture. As the house became the center of plantation living, the size was increased, and often a second story was added. Two-story columns were used to support the front-roof overhang and the symmetrical gabled roof (Fig. 1–5).

Ranch Style

As settlers moved West, architectural styles were changed to meet their needs. The availability of space eliminated the need for second floors. This same amount of space could then be spread horizontally rather than vertically, which resulted in a rambling plan (Fig. 1–6). The Spanish influence also led to the popularization of the Western ranch, which utilized a U-shaped plan with a patio in the center.

Victorian

The Industrial Revolution in this country provided architects and builders with machinery and equipment which could be used to construct very intricate millwork items. Since living habits had changed little, this new-found technology was used by adding decoration to a building. Intricate finials, lintels, parapets, balconies, and cornices were added to structures (Fig. 1–7). Ornate aspects of Victorian architec-

Fig.1–5. Southern colonial home.

Home Planners, Inc.

Potlatch Corp.

Fig. 1–6. Western ranch style of architecture.

ture (gingerbread) were designed into homes until recent years.

Modern

The development of lighter, stronger building materials combined with the need to produce inexpensive structures in less time led to the evolution of simple functional designs, as shown in Fig. 1–8.

THE PRESENT

Louis Sullivan wrote, "Our architecture reflects us as truly as a mirror." Modern architecture is now reflecting our freedom, our functionalism, and our technological advances. Modern architects are working to achieve even more functionalism, freedom, and technological refinements in the art and science of architecture.

Functionalism

Louis Sullivan's "form follows function" idea has now been accepted by most modern architects. Few items can find their way into an architectural design without performing some specific function. Most modernists feel this is the line of distinction between architecture and sculpture. Architecture performs a function; a piece of sculpture does not. It may exist and be admired for its aesthetic qualities alone.

The concept of functionalism in architecture has led to extreme applications of simplicity in design. Simplicity and functionalism complement each other.

Louis Sullivan is one of the first architects to reach upward with steel construction. The Wainwright Building (1890), St. Louis, and the Guaranty Building (1894), Buffalo, were the first structures to show the potentials of metal-frame construction. These first skyscraper office buildings showed the external skeleton of the metal framing. Sullivan made many refinements in the development of large metal-framed structures.

Library of Congress

Fig. 1–7. A home in the Victorian style of architecture.

Home Planners, Inc.

Fig. 1–8. An example of modern design.

Fig. 1–9. A model at the Guggenheim Museum in New York City is an example of Frank Lloyd Wright's unconventional use of space.

Frank Lloyd Wright is considered the greatest American architect. He believed that architecture should be organic—that the materials, function, form, and surroundings in nature should be completely coordinated. The designs of his homes are X-, L-, and T-shaped, with open areas throughout the living areas. The elevations are low and horizontal. The

Wright showed his genius by continually developing new styles and trends in architecture. Wright believed that even the basic shapes of floor plans should be more diversified with the development of new and more flexible building materials. Frank Lloyd Wright demonstrated for 60 years that interior space can be much richer and much more interesting than a box. When you see any corner of a square room, without looking around you know what the remainder of the room is like. Not so when the squareness is removed. Frank Lloyd Wright constantly attempted to avoid the box and to accomplish his goal of greater freedom and less static space. Even today, more diversified shapes are finding their way onto the architectural scene (Fig. 1–9).

Freedom

Freedom of expression, freedom in the use of space, and structural freedom in design characterize modern architecture.

Charles le Corbusier was one of the leading exponents of freedom in architectural design. He felt that we must no longer challenge nature with our architecture but rather work with nature. The house, he said, should be looked upon as a machine for living in, or as a tool as serviceable as a typewriter.

Characteristics of his work are free-standing support, independence of the wall from the frame, the open plan, the free facade, and the roof garden.

Eduardo Torroja used great imaginative powers working with reinforced and prestressed concrete. Using the forms of folded, undulating, or warped shapes, he designed structures possessing fluid continuity, beauty, and freedom. He said that complete freedom of expression can be achieved by using flexible materials which allow the architect to express his ideas with freedom and independence.

Relationships

Relating the areas of the structure to each other and to its environment have become well-established principles of modern architecture.

Eero Saarinen proved that functional form does not have to be rigid and boxlike. His designs of the Yale Hockey Rink and the Trans World Airlines Terminal at J. F. Kennedy International Airport in New York (Fig. 1–10) have the appearance of gigantic pieces of sculpture. Both are gracefully molded, with rhythmically curving and flowing lines. His concrete shell structures create spaces of expressionistic quality with a perfect understanding and use of space. It is a dramatic departure by Saarinen from the regularity of the conventional styles. He also advanced the importance of relationships in stating, "Always design a thing by considering it in its next largest context—a

Trans World Airlines

Fig. 1–10. Trans World Airlines Terminal at John F. Kennedy International Airport.

Pan American Airlines Photo

Fig. 1–11. Brasilia is a planned city.

dish on a table, a table in a room, a room in a house, a house in a neighborhood, a neighborhood in a city." Saarinen practiced this concept. His designing pursuits have included the design of furniture as well as buildings. His designs for the General Motors Technical Center and the Dulles International Terminal were created with great freedom in the use of space.

Oscar Niemeyer, the designer of Brasilia, believes that architectural freedom should be expressed through a conquest of space. Brasilia is a classic example of relating large areas to each other. It is the only city in the world that has been designed to be built at one time. Hence, space could be controlled without the hazards of evolution that normally accompany the growth of cities (Fig. 1–11).

Technology

Technological advances now allow architects to build large structures of light materials (Fig. 1–12), to erect buildings quickly, and to design the utmost in structural safety into buildings.

Ludwig Mies van der Rohe, the architect of steel, believed that when technology reaches its full development in any culture, it immediately transcends into architecture. His plans are characterized by cubic simplicity. They are masterpieces of precise engineering. They depend on proportion, fitness of material used, and mechanical precision of the finish of the material for beauty.

PPG Industries, Inc.

Fig. 1–12. A building made of steel aluminum, glass, concrete, wood, and plastics.

Walter Gropius believed that in the design of structures, experts from various fields must be consulted. The work of designers, engineers, sociologists, and builders is to be coordinated by the architect. He thought that the design of a structure is complex and that no one person can be aware of all the aspects that must be considered for the final design.

Minoru Yamasaki designs reflect his attitude that architecture should provide serenity and quiet. Yamasaki's building style is the covering of a wall by an apparently textile-like fabric which hides the structural members. His designs also feature umbrella walls of textured building blocks, axial planes, high natural lighting, and beautiful gardens and pools.

Robert Buckminster Fuller has been acclaimed for his geodesic domes. The domes are a product of much research and mathematical calculations. They are based on triangular sec-

Rohm & Haas Company

Fig. 1–13. Buckminster Fuller's Geodesic Dome.

American-Saint Gobain Corp.

Fig. 1–14. Sample of Edward D. Stone's use of grillwork.

tions called *tetrahedrons.* The domes are strong, yet lightweight. They can be constructed in a comparatively short time from almost any building materials. One of his largest domes is at Baton Rouge, Louisiana. It has a diameter of 384 feet (Fig. 1–13).

The Romanticists

Many architects favor the attempt to bring back to architecture some of the traditional elements of ornament that have been a part of the great classic monuments of the past.

Edward D. Stone designed the United States Embassy Building in New Delhi in a romantic style. He promoted the international style of functional architecture with his design of the Museum of Modern Art in New York City. He changed his original style of pure functionalism to become one of the leaders of romanticism. An example of Stone's ornamental elements is the use of the patterned screen wall, called a *grille.* He designs his grilles from bricks, metal screens, and tiles, as shown in Fig. 1–14.

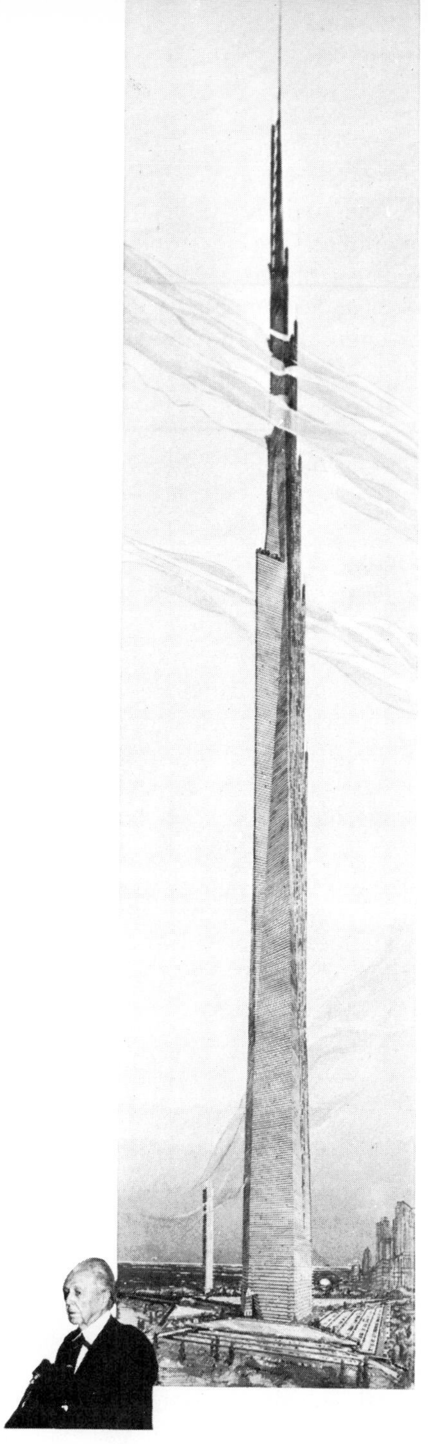

Architectural Record

Fig. 1–15. Frank Lloyd Wright's proposed mile-high skyscraper.

THE FUTURE

No one can accurately predict what the future of architecture will bring. The future will certainly be related to the development of new

Fig. 1–16. Buckminster Fuller's proposed geodesic dome over Manhattan.

materials, new construction methods, and sociological changes.

Size

As technology develops, buildings could increase to sizes previously thought impossible. Figure 1–15 shows Frank Lloyd Wright's proposal for a mile-high skyscraper. Ten such structures, Wright said, would take care of the working office staff of all New York City. Six would suffice for Chicago. The structure's tremendous weight would not rest on a flat surface, as with conventional buildings. It would be distributed equally around a deep-sunk taproot, a sharp wedge descending approximately a thousand feet (one-fifth of the structure's height) into solid bedrock. The proposed skyscraper would tower far above the largest structures of today.

Who can say what will be possible? The prospect of building a geodesic dome over central Manhattan, as shown in Fig. 1–16, certainly seems impossible, but a flight to the moon seemed impossible a few years ago. Within the span of a lifetime, technology has advanced from the horse and buggy era to the space age.

Ford Motor Company

Fig. 1–17. Advancements in technology have opened up endless possibilities in using new locations.

Location

In the future, structures could be built on locations that would now be unthought of. The house perched on the rim of the Grand Canyon, shown in Fig. 1–17, may not be practical for typical home life, but it is within the realm of technical possibility at the present time. Advancements in transportation methods and refinement in the engineering of structures will make even more locations feasible.

Shapes

For centuries, architectural development has been hampered through the use and overuse of the square and the cube as the basis for our structures. Architects are just now realizing the possibilities of using other shapes such as the triangle, the pyramid (Fig. 1–18), the circle, and the sphere. The development of stronger, more versatile materials and new construction techniques should enable buildings to be built that are completely functional without reference to any basic geometric form. Even the basic shapes of floor plans should be more diversified with the development of new and more flexible building materials, as shown in Fig. 1–19.

Components

The development of components should allow custom-designed structures to be erected on the site. This practice would practically eliminate on-the-job construction work. Construction would then merely be the assembly of the component parts in a unique design, just as an automobile is constructed of many different, interchangeable parts. What houses will look like in 10, 20, 30, or 100 years is an interesting question to ponder. Figure 1–20 shows Buckminster Fuller's concept of the Garden of Eden. It is not a house; it is a controlled environment. Indeed, houses as are now known may become museum pieces or merely illustrations of architectural history.

Population Mobility

With increased mobility of the population, custom designing becomes more and more difficult. Building for resale becomes more and

Fig. 1–18. Use of the pyramid in residential design.

Potlatch Corp.

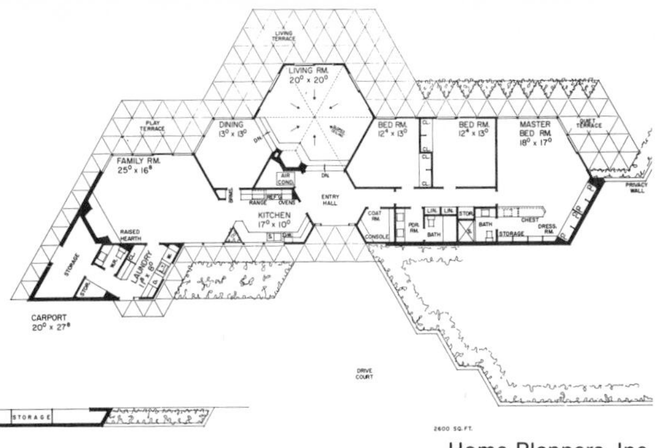

Home Planners, Inc.

Fig. 1–19. Flexibilities can be achieved by altering the normal rectangular floor-plan pattern.

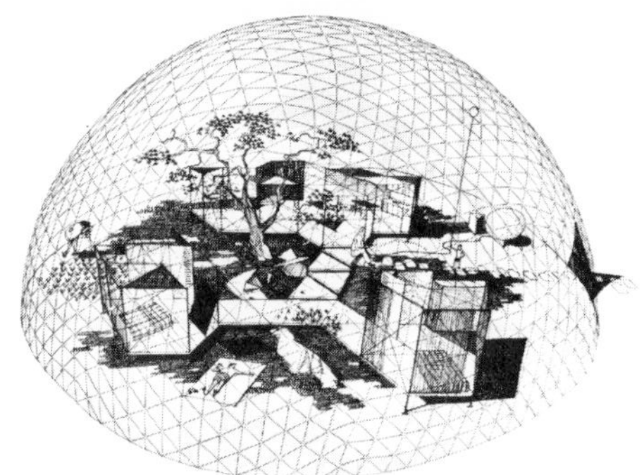

Fig. 1–20. Buckminster Fuller's Garden of Eden.

more important. Therefore, designs that will permit the rearranging of partitions and fixtures may be developed to meet the unique needs of the householder.

With more leisure time anticipated in the future, more emphasis will be placed on recreational activities within or about the home.

The City

The team approach to the design of commercial buildings such as hotels, motels, air terminals, and schools will be intensified in the future. The importance of planning whole cities, or at least whole sections of cities, based on sociological needs will become more and more evident. With growing suburbanization and exurbanization, cities are now in need of complete redevelopment (Fig. 1–21).

The role of the architect as a coordinator in these activities will be increased. The relationship between art and technology will be refined to enable all types of buildings to be technically appropriate and aesthetically acceptable.

PROBLEMS

1. **Name three advancements we might expect in the field of architecture in the next 10 years.**
2. **What effect will the mobility of our population have on the future of architecture?**
3. **What effect does the team approach have on the design of commercial buildings?**
4. **Sketch your ideas for a house of the future.**
5. **Identify past styles of architecture used on buildings in your community.**

Newman Schmidt and John R. Shrader Photo

Fig. 1–21. Redevelopment of Pittsburgh's Golden Triangle.

UNIT 2

Design Factors

Design activities may be formal or informal. Informal design occurs when a product is made by the designer without the use of a plan. Formal design involves the complete preparation of a set of working drawings. The working drawings are then used in constructing the product. Buildings are designed formally. A complete set of working drawings must be prepared before the actual construction begins. Therefore, the major design activity in architectural work occurs during the preparation of sketches, plans, and detailed drawings.

CREATIVE DESIGN

Buildings should be designed creatively. In other words, the design should be an expression of the ideas of the creator.

Ideas in the creative stage may be recorded by sketching basic images. These sketches are then revised until the basic ideas are crystallized. First sketches rarely produce a finished design. Usually, many revisions are necessary, as shown in Fig. 2–1.

Many designers make a habit of never throwing away a sketch. They resketch the problem on successive sheets of paper (usually a pad of graph paper). Often the fifth sketch may reveal the solution to a problem in the tenth sketch. The ideas may not be combined in a functional design until perhaps 20 or 30 sketches have been made.

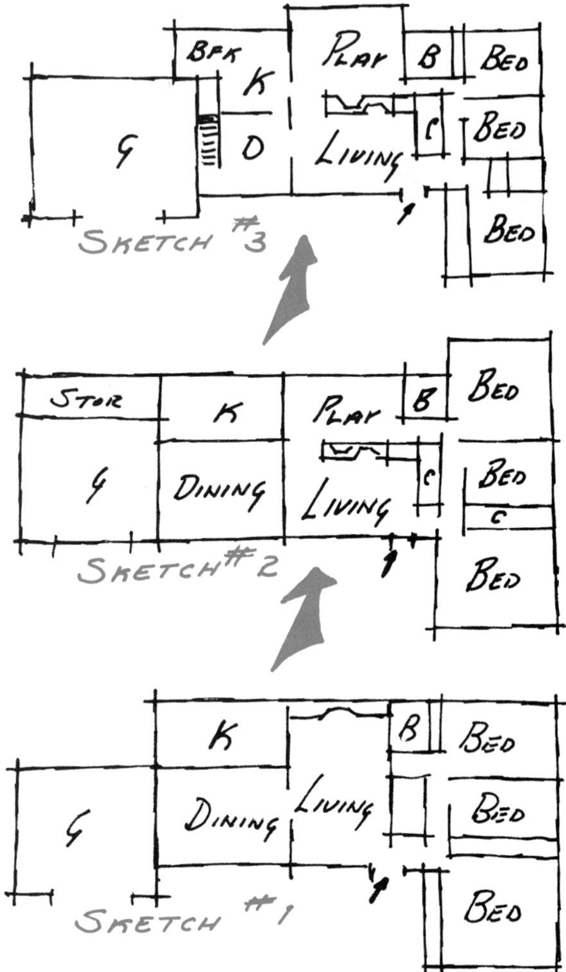

Fig. 2–1. Sketches are used to revise and alter a plan.

TECHNICAL DESIGN

A basic idea, regardless of how creative and imaginative, is useless unless the design can be successfully built. Technical designing involves the transfer of basic sketches into architectural working drawings.

Every useful building must perform a specific function. Every part of the structure should also be designed to perform a specific function. The retractable roof on Pittsburgh's Civic Auditorium is designed to perform a dual function (Fig. 2–2). It provides an open-air theater in good weather and provides protection during bad weather.

AESTHETIC DESIGN

Today's buildings not only must be functional but must be aesthetically designed as well. The

Molitor Photo

Fig. 2–2. Pittsburgh's Civic Auditorium.

© Walt Disney Productions

Fig. 2–3. Open and projecting form.

term *aesthetic* refers to beauty. When the appearance of a building appeals to our senses, it is beautiful. Thus beauty is the aesthetic part of design. Today the aesthetic part of design is important.

ELEMENTS OF DESIGN

Every building should contain the six basic elements of design in some combination. These basic elements are form, space, light and shadow, texture, line, and color.

Form
The form of the building is its shape. The form may appear closed and solid or closed and volume-containing. It may be open and projecting, as shown in the building in Fig. 2–3. The form of a structure should be determined by its function.

Space
Space surrounds form and is contained within it. The design can create a feeling of space; it should not create the impression that every form is surrounded by other forms and those forms by yet other forms. The continuous ceiling shown in Fig. 2–4 creates an expanded impression of space.

Light and Shadow
Light reflects from the surface of a form. Shadows appear in areas that light cannot reach. Light and shadow both give a sense of depth to the building. Areas around windows and doors and areas under roof overhangs appear darker, since these parts are shadowed. The relationship of light and dark areas should be planned accordingly. The designer of the building shown in Fig. 2–5 has used the element of light and shadow to create an impressive effect.

Fig. 2–4. Expansion of visual space through a continuous ceiling.

Texture
Building materials such as concrete, stone, and brick have rough and dull surfaces. Others such as glass, aluminum, and plastics are relatively smooth. A balance between these two types of textures should be worked for in every building. The designer must be careful not to

S. C. Johnson & Son, Inc.

Fig. 2–5. Use of light and shadow to create a dramatic effect.

include too many different textures of a similar nature. For this reason, brick and stone are usually not combined. The texture of wood is emphasized in Fig. 2–6.

Line

The elements of line can produce a sense of movement within the object or a greater sense of length or height. The lines of the building shown in Fig. 2–7 emphasize the horizontal aspects of this design. The major lines of most buildings include the ground line, eave line, roof line, and the pattern of any other large areas within the building, such as the window lines.

Fig. 2–6. Emphasis on wood texture.

Western Wood Products Association

Home Planners, Inc.

Fig. 2–7. Horizontal line emphasis.

Color

Color is either a part of the building material, or it must be added to the material. If possible, the natural color of building materials should be used. In using color, the designer should create a scheme to emphasize one color and to add contrasting colors for variety. The use of too many colors is as bad as the lack of the use of color.

Bold colors, such as red, tend to advance. Pale colors (pastels) tend to recede (Fig. 2–8).

PRINCIPLES OF DESIGN

The basic principles of design show how the designer uses the elements of design in creating a building. The six basic principles of design are unity, repetition, rhythm, variety, emphasis, and balance.

Fig. 2–8. Bold colors advance; pale colors recede.

Armstrong Cork Company

PPG Industries, Inc.

Fig. 2–9. An example of unity in design.

Frank Lloyd Wright, architect; Guerrero Photo

Fig. 2–10. Curved, horizontal lines provide repetition in this Frank Lloyd Wright design.

Unity

Unity is the sense of wholeness in the design. Every building should appear complete. No parts should appear as appendages or afterthoughts. In the building in Fig. 2–9, the designer has achieved unity through the use of a consistent line throughout the building.

Repetition

Unity is often achieved through repetition. Curved lines, spaces, and textures are repeated throughout the design to tie the structure together aesthetically and to achieve unity, as shown in Fig. 2–10.

Rhythm

When lines, planes, and surface treatments are repeated in a regular sequence, a sense of rhythm is achieved. The windows in Fig. 2–11 give a sense of rhythm to the building.

Variety

Without variety, a building may become dull and tiresome to the viewer. Too much rhythm, too much repetition, too much unity ruin a sense of variety. Light, shadow, and color are used to achieve variety. The light-textured surface of the kitchen counters make a good contrast to the dark cabinets in Fig. 2–12.

Emphasis

The principle of emphasis is used by the designer to draw attention to any given area of the subject. Emphasis may be achieved by color, form, texture, or line. The corner towers of the building shown in Fig. 2–13 are emphasized by form and texture. They are larger than other areas of the building. They are also of a different texture from other parts of the building. These features also create emphasis in light and color, since the sun will strike and reflect from the surfaces differently.

Balance

Balance is the achievement of equilibrium in design. Buildings may be *formally* balanced if they are symmetrical (Fig. 2–14). Buildings are *informally* balanced if there is variety in the space relationship and yet a harmonious distribution of space, form, line, color, and light and shade. The building shown in Fig. 2–15 is informally balanced.

Fig. 2–11. Window panels provide rhythm in this building.

PPG Industries, Inc.

Frigidaire Division, General Motors Corporation

Fig. 2–12. Different cabinet and counter textures provide variety in this design.

PPG Industries, Inc.

Fig. 2–13. Emphasis is provided by form and texture in the corner towers.

DESIGN SEQUENCE

Proceeding logically from a basic idea to a final design is often a long process. Rough ideas are recorded in sketches. The sketches are refined and changed. The basic form is established. Elements of light and shadow, texture, line, and color are combined in the most appropriate relationship.

The effects of unity, repetition, rhythm, variety, emphasis, and balance must be achieved without sacrificing the functional or technical aspect of the design.

PROBLEMS

1. **Sketch the front elevation of the house shown in Fig. 2–16. Convert the front-elevation design to a formally balanced elevation.**
2. **Sketch the houses shown in Fig. 35–4 to provide more emphasis on one phase of the design.**
3. **Sketch the houses shown in Fig. 35–8 to improve the light and shadow patterns and to provide more unity of texture and line in the design.**
4. **List the major color you would use to decorate each room in your home. List two supporting colors you would use for contrast or variety.**
5. **Follow the steps shown in Fig. 2–1 to achieve a creative design of your own.**
6. **Define these terms: *technical design, creative design, aesthetic, informal design, formal design, function, form, space, light, shadow, texture, line, color, beauty, repetition, variety, emphasis, informal balance, formal balance.***

Deeter–Ritchey–Sippel

Fig. 2–14. A formal balanced house.

Home Planners, Inc.

Fig. 2–15. An informally balanced house.

Home Planners, Inc.

Fig. 2–16. Convert the front elevation to a formally balanced design.

UNIT 3

Orientation

The orientation of a building is the relationship of the building to its environment. The building must be suitably oriented to the site, the lot, the sun, and the prevailing winds (Fig. 3–1). A well-oriented home is designed to take full advantage of the good features of these exterior conditions (Fig. 3–2).

Fig. 3–1. A building must be oriented to the lot and site.

SOLAR ORIENTATION

A structure should be oriented to provide maximum control and use of the rays of the sun. Solar orientation is becoming increasingly important with the extensive use of larger glass areas. In the Northern Hemisphere, the south and west sides of a structure are warmer than the east and north sides. The north side is always cooler because it is shaded (Fig. 3–3). The south side of the building has almost constant exposure to the sun.

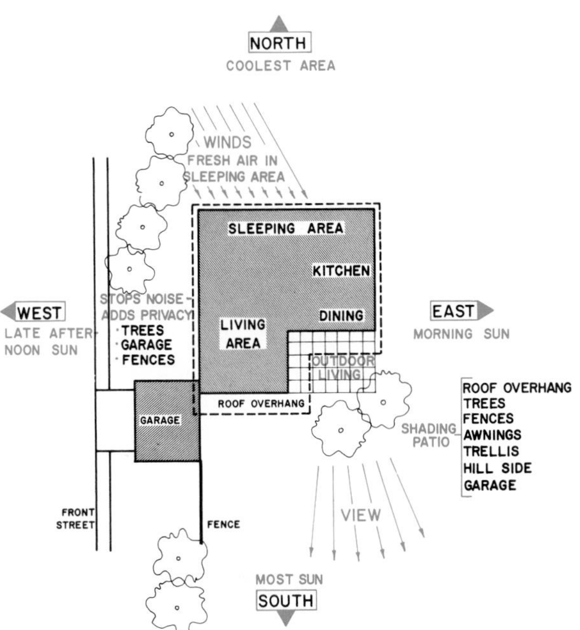

Fig. 3–2. All exterior conditions must be considered.

Ideally, the building should be oriented to absorb as much winter heat as possible and to repel excessive summer heat. For perfect sun orientation, a rotating house such as the one shown in Fig. 3–4 is ideal since the structure will rotate to take full advantage of the sun's position at any time of day. In this design, services such as water, electricity, and telephone enter the house through a central shaft within the stairwell. They are distributed to the revolving areas through a swing valve and a communicator.

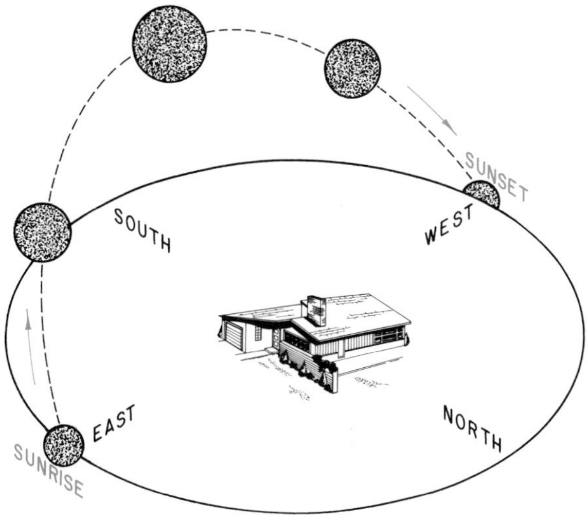

Fig. 3–3. The north side is always shaded.

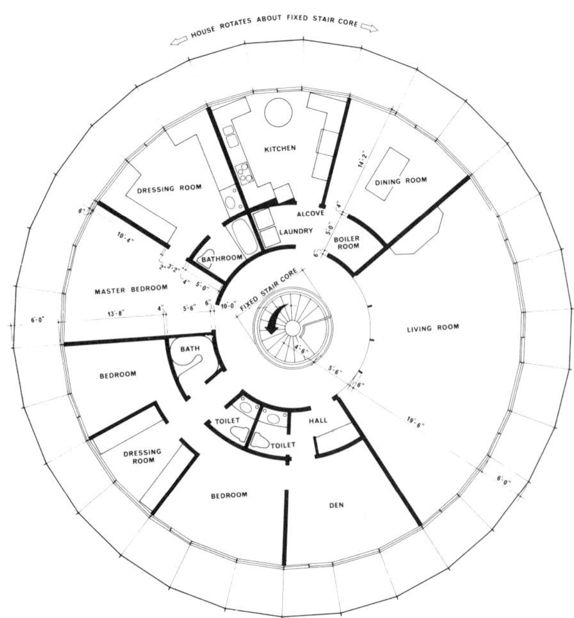

Richard Foster, Architect

Fig. 3–4. Richard Foster's rotating house. Elevation and floor plan.

Overhang Protection
The angle of the sun differs in summer and in winter (Fig. 3–5). Roof overhangs should be designed with a length and angle that will shade the window in summer and allow the sun to enter during winter months.

Room Locations
Rooms should be located either to absorb the heat of the sun through glass or to be *baffled,* or walled from the heat of the sun, Rooms should also be located so that they can make the maximum use of sunlight. Generally, sunshine should be available in the kitchen in mornings and should reach the living areas in the afternoon. Kitchens and dining rooms placed on the south or east side of the house are desirable. Living areas placed on the south or west side of the house to obtain afternoon exposure are usually desirable. The north side is the most appropriate side for placing sleeping areas, since it provides the greatest darkness in the morning and evening for sleeping and is also the coolest side. North light is consistent and has little glare.

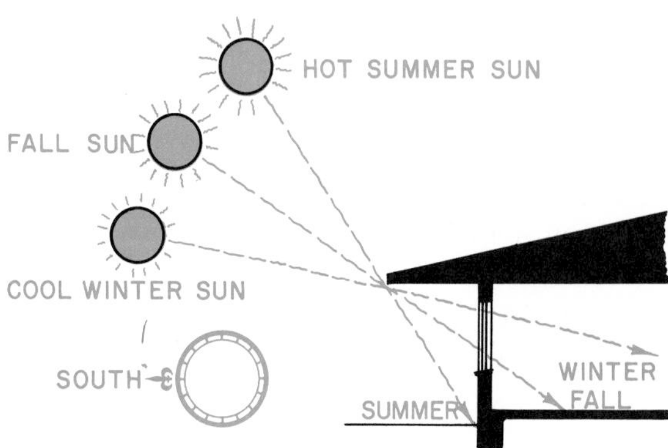

Fig. 3–5. Sun angles in the summer, fall, and winter.

WIND

In some areas, wind or heavy breezes may be menacing to outdoor living activities. Efforts should be made to preserve large trees. Trees are not only effective as wind baffles but provide necessary shade. Prevailing winds also can be baffled by the use of shelters and shrubbery.

NOISE

Insulation will help reduce excessive noise from the outside. However, locating rooms requiring quiet on the side away from the source of noise is also effective.

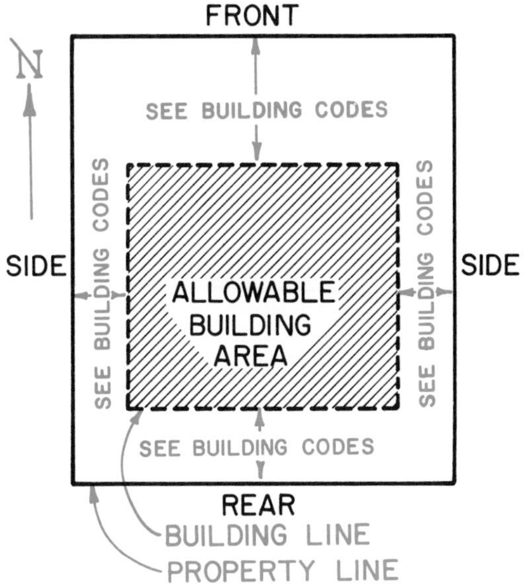

Fig. 3–6. The position of a building is restricted by building codes.

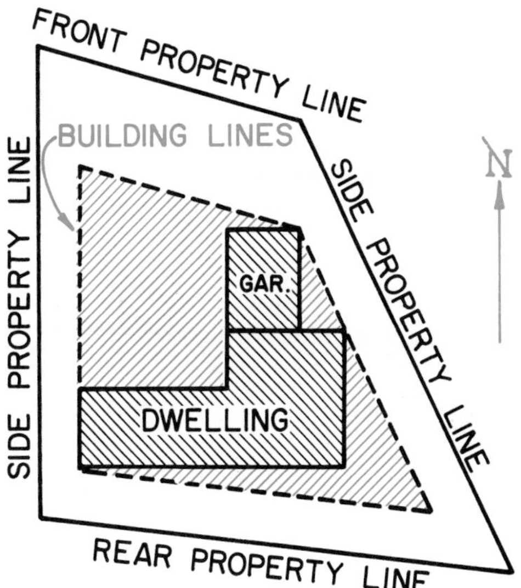

Fig. 3–7. A permissible building area.

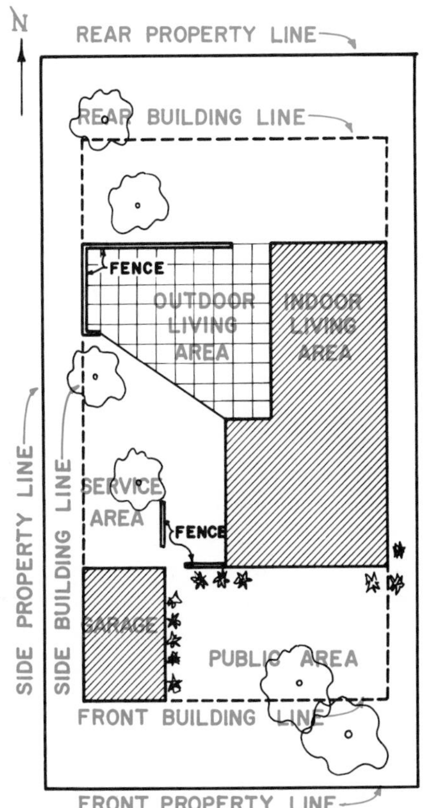

Fig. 3–8. The three areas of a lot are the public area, the private area, and the service area.

LOT

The size of the lot affects the flexibility of choice in locating the house. Building codes restrict the placement of the house on the lot. Some building codes require that the house be placed no closer than 10′ (3 meters) to the property line. Other codes require a distance of 50′ (15 m) or more. Building codes also restrict the distance from the house to the street (Fig. 3–6). A line drawn parallel to the property line on all sides represents the *building line.* The area within the building line is the area in which the building can be located (Fig. 3–7). On small lots, there is often little flexibility in orienting the home. On larger lots, the possibility of using a variety of positions is greater.

Lots may be divided into three areas according to function: the private area, the public area, and the service area (Fig. 3–8). The private area includes the house and outdoor living space. A southern exposure is usually desirable for the outdoor living area.

The public area is the area of the lot viewed from the street. This area is usually at the front of the house and should provide off-street parking and access to the main entrance.

The service area of the lot should be adjacent to the service area of the home. The placement of the home on the lot determines the relative size and relationship of these areas.

Hedrich-Blessing

Fig. 3–9. Frank Lloyd Wright always sought to relate a building structurally and aesthetically to the site.

RELATIONSHIP OF HOUSE TO SITE

A lot may be hilly, rugged, and rocky, or it may be smooth and level. Whatever the shape of the terrain, the house should be designed as an integral part of the site. It should not appear as an appendix to the land. It should appear as a desirable, functional improvement of the site.

Frank Lloyd Wright probably did more than any other architect to popularize the desirability of relating the home to the site. He called this principle *organic architecture.* One of the most profound examples of organic architecture is *Falling Water,* at Bear Run, Pennsylvania (Fig. 3–9). The bold use of the site, with cantilevered decks extending over a waterfall, produces a dramatic effect that has rarely if ever been equaled. Cantilevered slabs are anchored in the hillside, relating the building structurally to its setting.

Figure 3–10 shows another house that has been effectively related to the contour of the lot. In this case the relationship is developed and reinforced by the use of materials related to the site. In addition, cantilevered wood decks project over the slope of the lot and provide shelter for the first level. Figure 3–11 shows how a large structure is carefully oriented to its site. Models such as this provide an excellent aid in the determination of site orientation.

A house may be compatible with one lot and site and yet appear out of place in another location. Split-level homes, for example, are designed for sloping lots where an entrance can be provided on each level, and each level is used functionally to its maximum. The placement of the split-level home on a flat lot does not use the house or the lot effectively. If com-

Home Planners, Inc.

Fig. 3–10. A house effectively related to the contour of the land.

Fig. 3–11. The use of a model to check orientation.

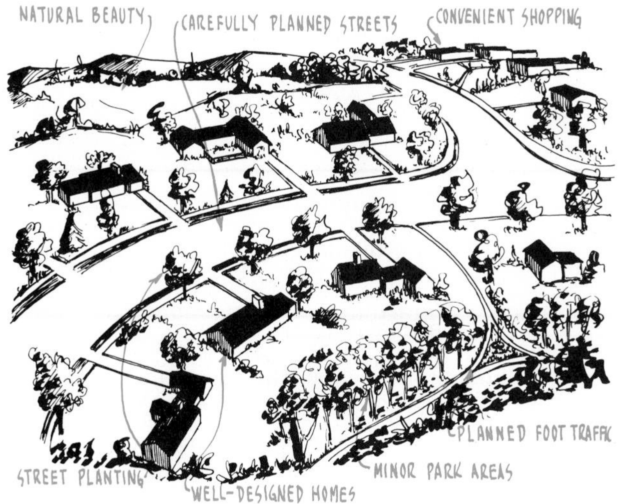

Fig. 3–12. Features of a well-planned neighborhood.

plete integration of indoor and outdoor living areas is to be achieved, a house and lot must be designed as part of the same plan.

RELATIONSHIP OF SITE TO NEIGHBORHOOD

A house which is ideally suited to a lot may not fit the neighborhood. The architect must be certain that the needs of the home owner are consistent with the characteristics of the neighborhood. Features of the neighborhood such as availability of parks and playgrounds, consistency of home design, proximity to shopping areas, and the preservation of natural beauty must be matched to the needs of the prospective homeowner (Fig. 3–12).

RELATIONSHIP OF NEIGHBORHOOD TO COMMUNITY

Not only must the house be related to the site and the site related to the neighborhood, but the neighborhood must be related to the community. Features of the community which must be considered include the availability and quality of schools, theaters, playgrounds, houses of worship, parking facilities, shopping centers, highway access, automobile service, police and fire protection, and traffic patterns.

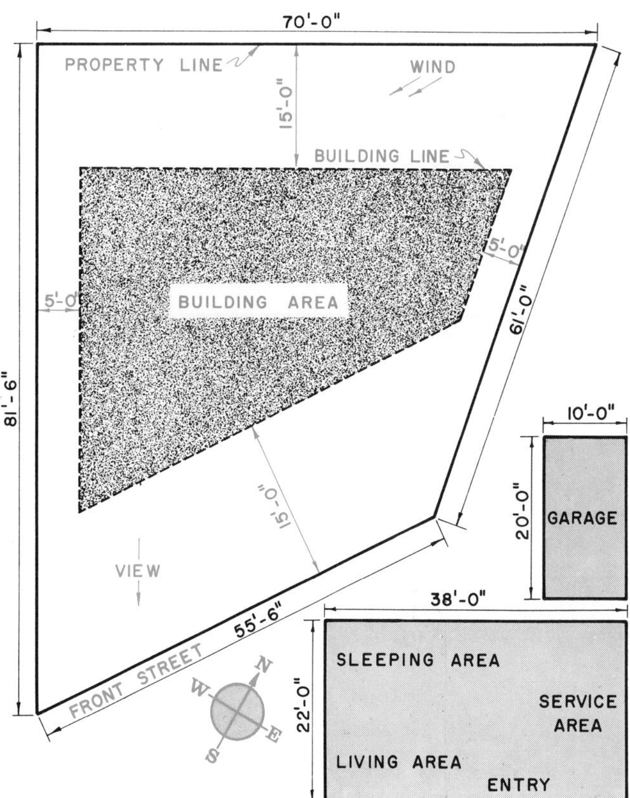

Fig. 3–13. Place this house and garage on the lot.

PROBLEMS

1. **Sketch a 75′ × 110′ property. Prepare a template of a house to the same scale and place it on the property in the most desirable location.**
2. **Sketch the lot layout shown in Fig. 3–13. Place templates of the house and garage on this lot in the most desirable position. Also sketch the position of driveways, walks, and other landscape features you would add to this design. Sketch adjacent lots and show their key landscape features.**
3. **Prepare templates of the rooms in Fig. 6–10. Combine these in a workable floor plan and place the templates on a 100′ × 100′ level lot.**
4. **Define the following terms: *solar orientation, site, lot, overhang, wind baffle, building line, public area, private area, service area, organic architecture, split level.***

UNIT 4

Density Planning

Density in architectural terms is the relationship of the number of residential structures and people to a given amount of space. The density factor is usually referred to as the number of people or families per acre, square mile, or governmental unit such as town, village, borough, or county. For example, a town may have a density of 10 families per acre or 50 families per square mile.

People have always tended to cluster into communities for protection and to share common facilities (Fig. 4–1). The development of transportation has enabled today's people to live in semi-isolation without sacrificing conveniences or safety (Fig. 4–2). Yet most people work with others and prefer to live in close proximity to others while striving for maximum privacy in their homes. This desire to live close to others, maintain and enjoy common conveniences, and yet have a high degree of privacy makes density planning very difficult and complex.

Average Density

In large geographical areas such as countries or cities, the density pattern may vary greatly among different parts of the area. For this reason the *average density* of a large geographical area is not as significant as the average density of smaller areas. For example, the average density of the area shown in Fig. 4–3A is the same as the average density of the area shown in Fig. 4–3B. However, the *density patterns* are significantly different. The number of people living in a large geographical area cannot always be controlled, but planning the most effective density patterns can provide the best possible use of the available land for the maximum number of people who may eventually use it.

Planning Philosophies

There are several basic approaches to density planning. The first and most common is to restrict the size of each building lot through zoning ordinances. This method automatically restricts the number of families allowed in a specific area. Zoning laws also indicate which areas can be used for industrial, commercial, or residential construction. Within residential zoned areas there may also be restrictions concerning the number of multiple-family dwellings or the size and capacity of apartment

Celotex Corp.

Fig. 4–1. Ancient Indians practiced density planning.

Potlatch Corp.

Fig. 4–2. People can live in semi-isolation because of good transportation.

Fig. 4–4. Apartment living is one solution to density problems.

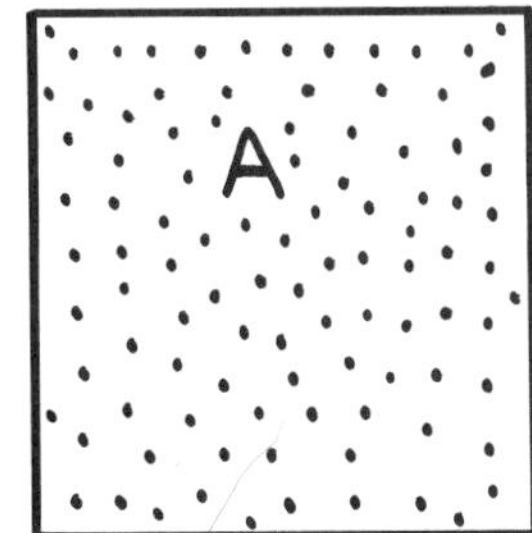

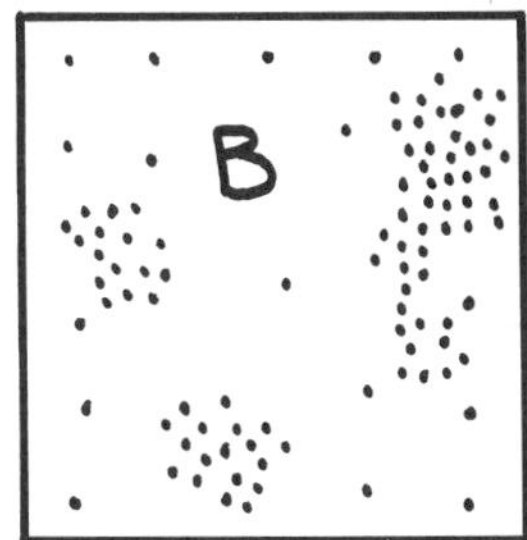

Fig. 4–3. Area A has the same average density as area B.

buildings. These restrictions are primarily designed to avoid overcrowding of local school, transportation, and recreational facilities.

The second approach is to cluster residents into fewer structures such as high-rise apartments (Fig. 4–4) or row houses (Fig. 4–5). Transportation, shopping centers, schools, theaters, golf courses, swimming pools, and tennis courts should then be planned adjacent to housing units.

The third approach is actually a combination of plans. It involves zoning part of the area for single-family residences, specifying other areas for row houses, and reserving some areas for high-rise apartments. The amount of space planned for each type of structure depends on the average density desired.

Fig. 4–5. Row houses or townhouses provide individual housing units in dense areas.

Simpson Lumber Co.

REDEVELOPMENT

Often, undesirable density patterns develop as a result of population growth or shifts. This occurs especially in older communities. When undesirable density patterns develop, the best corrective action is to redevelop the area. Redevelopment can either be short-term or long-range. Short-term redevelopment involves completely razing buildings and substituting new housing units, parks, and shopping centers in their place. Long-range redevelopment is the changing of the density pattern of an area over a long period of time but according to a predetermined building plan and time schedule.

NEIGHBORHOOD PLANNING

The smallest residential unit involving density planning is the neighborhood. The next largest unit, the community, is a combination of neighborhoods. Cities are combinations of communities. Regions are a combination of interrelated cities, communities, and neighborhoods. A residence isolated from a neighborhood must be planned to include facilities for its own transportation, recreation, security, and maintenance (see Fig. 4–2). The high-rise apartment is a vertically oriented neighborhood and must provide neighborhood facilities for its inhabitants. A neighborhood is a series of homes, whether arranged vertically, as in a high-rise apartment, or connected, as in row houses, located on several acres, as in some rural areas, or on small lots, as in most cities. Figure 4–6 shows the alternatives in planning a one-acre neighborhood under many density requirements. Figure 4–7 shows how a geographical area can be planned for 4, 6, 8, and 14 houses per acre. The houses used in each of these plans must be carefully designed for lot size and location in relation to other property. Designing areas with heavy population concentrations is more difficult than designing areas that are thinly populated. However, by using the best combination of plans shown in Fig. 4–6 and by practicing effective overall location and traffic patterns as shown in Fig. 4–8,

6–8 PERSONS

18–24 PERSONS

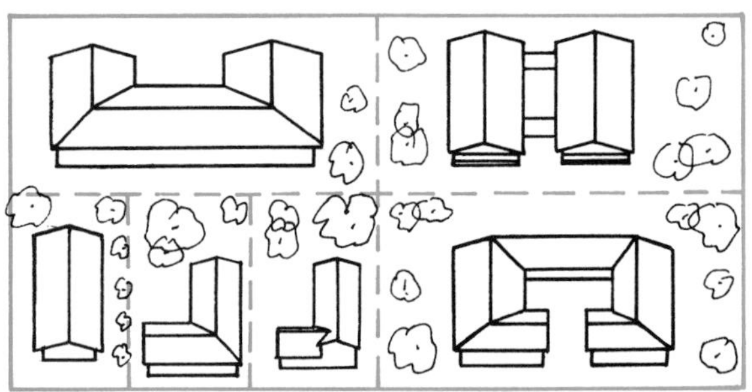

70–100 PERSONS

150–1000 PERSONS

Fig. 4–6. Alternatives in planning a neighborhood.

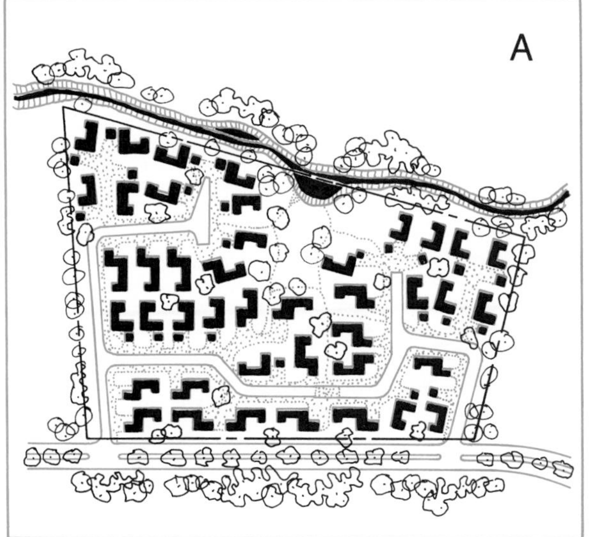

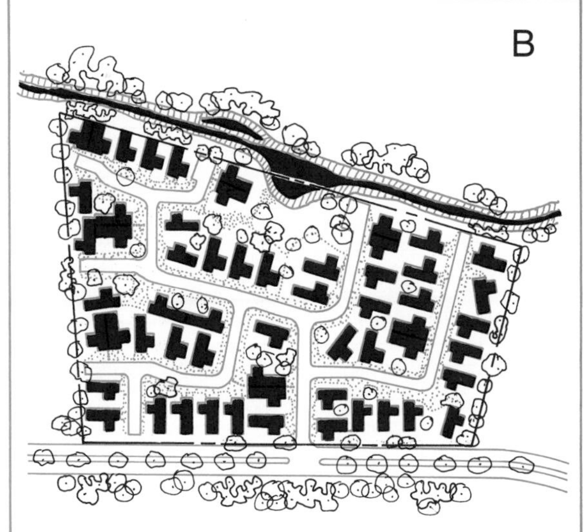

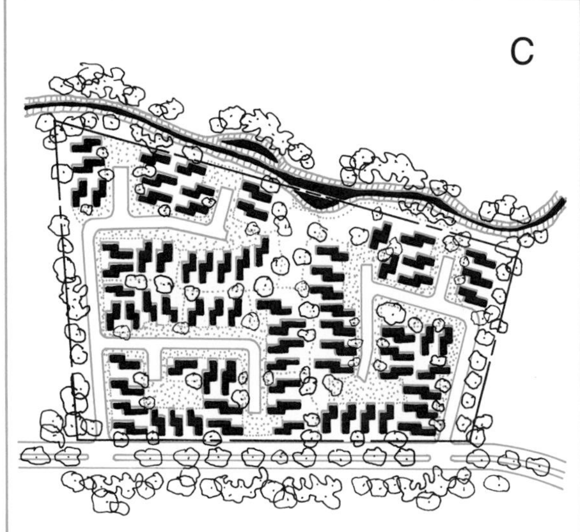

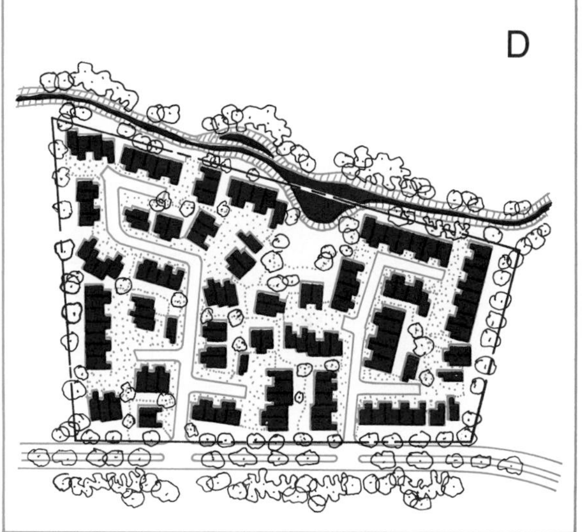

Fig. 4–7. Use of an area for different density levels: (A) Four houses per acre, (B) six houses per acre, (C) eight houses per acre, and (D) sixteen houses per acre.

residents can achieve the maximum effect with the minimum of expenses according to their needs and life-style requirements.

COMMUNITY PLANNING

Most cities and towns were not planned; they developed without a plan. Thus most architectural activity in the area of community planning relates to efforts to control and direct future growth according to a master long-range plan. City plans are defined according to the geometric form produced on a map of the area. Each form has its distinct advantages and disadvantages, depending on the terrain, density, and future growth patterns anticipated in the cultural and economic needs of the area (Fig. 4–9). Architectural plans of the future must provide for the implementations of technological advances in construction and transportation and must accommodate the enormous rate of growth change anticipated for in cities and towns.

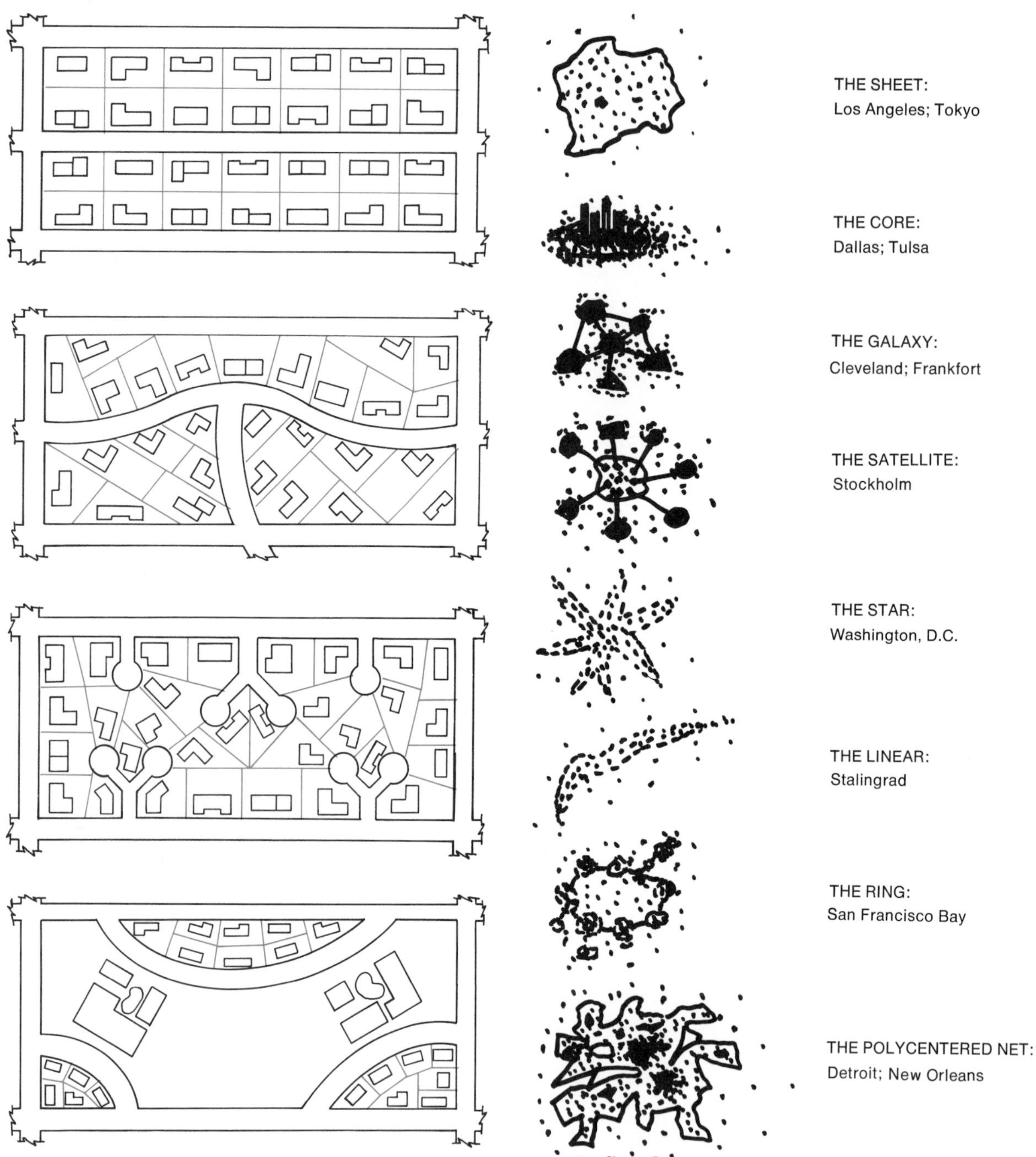

Fig. 4–8. Layout and traffic patterns must be changed for different densities.

Architecture of Towns and Cities. McGraw-Hill Book Company

Fig. 4–9. City forms.

PROBLEMS

1. **What are the local zoning ordinances in your community? How can they be improved?**
2. **Redesign a square-mile area around your home to provide better density balance.**
3. **Define these terms: *density, average density, density patterns, zoning.***

UNIT 5

Ecology and Planning

There are four billion people on the earth today. That is twice as many as a century ago. This population increase combined with the shift from an agrarian to an industrial society over the last century has led to the creation of environmental problems previously unknown. The ever-increasing material needs of our technological economy have created enormous pollution problems that must be resolved if humanity is to survive to enjoy the fruits of its own inventiveness. Designers must plan for the reduction or elimination of pollutants. The preservation of natural ecological balances should be a prime requirement in the creation of every design. Architectural creations must be designed to preserve our supply of clean air, pure water, and fertile land. At the same time, sound levels must be controlled. The aesthetic qualities of good design must also be maintained.

AIR POLLUTION

Air is polluted by industrial wastes discharged into the air. Some pollutants are nontoxic and are not suspended in the air for long periods of time. They present an annoyance but usually do not endanger life. Other materials such as sulfur oxides and organic gases composed of hydrocarbons, nitrous oxides, and carbon monoxide are extremely dangerous to both animal and plant life. These pollutants are emitted primarily as by-products of manufacturing plants, heating devices, and vehicular exhaust. Eco-

Fig. 5–1. Reflective insulating units in the century building in San Antonio provide illumination and heat in cool weather, yet rejects 90 percent of the sun's heat during hot seasons.

C-E Glass

Fig. 5–2. The results of removing trees and foliage from building tracts is bare-looking houses.

logically sensitive designers can do much to reduce pollution by planning heavy traffic patterns away from heavily populated areas. They can also plan or specify electronic air filters or other solid-waste removal systems to eliminate particles before they become airborne. They can develop and design buildings with energy conservation features. Conserving energy not only diminishes pollution because of decreased fuel consumption but also helps conserve fuel supplies and reduce operating costs of buildings. Major methods of energy conservation in the design of buildings include the maximum use of thermal insulation, recessed and shielded windows, heat-recovery–heat-storage systems, and low-watt lighting systems. Solar energy and heat-recovery systems such as the one shown in Fig. 5–1 can provide all of or part of a building's energy needs, depending on the climate and location of the structure. This is done by collecting heat through absorption, storing the heat, and then recovering the heat through exhaust devices and redistributing the heat where and when needed.

WATER POLLUTION

Water is polluted by sewage and by industrial chemicals and agricultural wastes being dumped into bodies of water. These wastes include pathogens, unstable organic solids, mineral compounds, plant nutrients, and agricultural insecticides. Water pollution results in the destruction of marine life. It presents very serious potential health hazards to animal and human life.

Architectural planning can help reduce water pollution through the design of sewage treatment systems in conjunction with each new construction. Plans may also provide for the removal of industrial waste without exhausting them into waterways and by topographically eliminating excessive run-off of topsoil into rivers and streams.

LAND POLLUTION

Land is polluted by the discharge of solid and liquid wastes on land surfaces or by the removal of topsoil, vegetation, or trees from large tracts of land (Fig. 5–2). Figure 5–3 shows several site developments as they relate to their topography. Land pollutants come from industrial waste, agricultural waste, residential waste, and garbage. When these pollutants exist in excessive quanties, they create health hazards, contribute to soil erosion, cause unpleasant odors, or overwork sewage-treatment plants.

Architectural plans to reduce land pollution include recycling waste material, compacting waste material to reduce volume, providing for sanitary landfills, and a minimum removal of vegetation, especially trees.

SOUND POLLUTION

Pollution caused by excessive sound levels may not be seen, but it can be measured. Scientists have proved that constant excessive sound from motors, horns, aircraft, and even radios can cause irritation in some people.

Planning buildings with ample noise-buffer space, acoustical wall panels, maximum use of buffer foliage or carefully controlled vehicular traffic patterns can help reduce noise to acceptable levels.

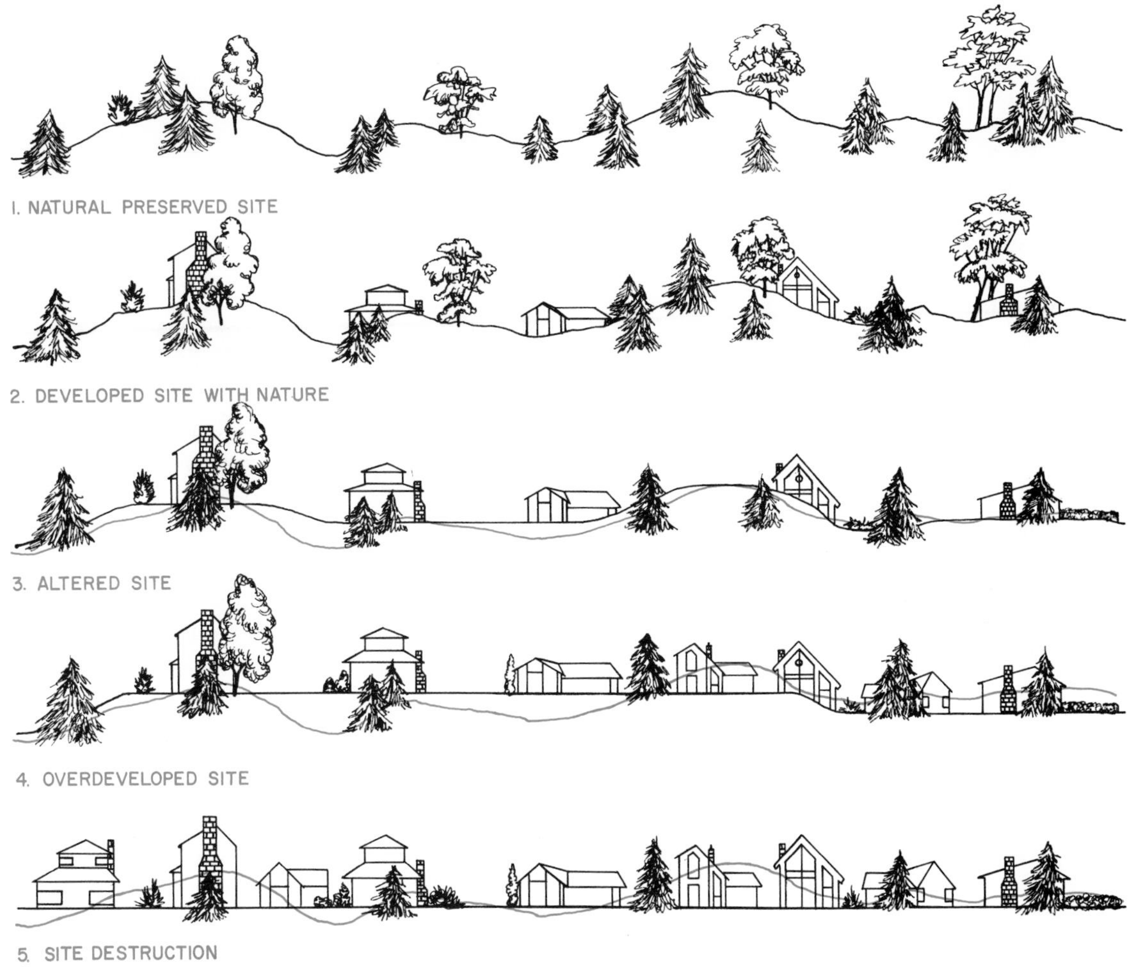

Fig. 5–3. Stages and types of site development.

VISUAL POLLUTION

Many air, water, and land pollutants such as unsanitary garbage dumps, treeless land tracts, and smog are visually undesirable. Other pollutants such as junkyards, exposed power lines, and large billboards do not create health or safety hazards but are aesthetically objectionable and should be avoided in the architectural design process.

PROBLEMS

1. **Find buildings in your area which are designed to control pollution.**
2. **Find buildings in your area that emit pollutants into the air or water or on the land. List ways of correcting these conditions.**
3. **Define these terms: *air pollution, solar energy, electronic filter, water pollution, sanitary landfill, erosion, industrial waste.***

SECTION 2

Living Area

Your first impression of a home is probably the image you retain of the living area. In fact, this is the only area of the home that most strangers observe. The living area is just what the name implies, the area where most of the living occurs. It is here the family entertains, relaxes, dines, listens to music, watches television, enjoys hobbies, and participates in other recreational activities.

The total living area is divided into smaller areas (rooms) which are designed to perform specific living functions. The subdivisions of most living areas may include the living room, dining room, recreation or game room, family room, patio, entrance foyer, den or study, and guest lavatories. Other specialized rooms, such as the library, music room, or sewing room, are often included as part of the living area of large houses that have the space to devote to such specialized functions. In smaller homes, many of the standard rooms combine two or more rooms. For example, the living room and dining room are often combined. In extremely small homes, the living room constitutes the entire living area and provides all the facilities normally assigned to other rooms in the living area. Although the subdivisions of the living area are called *rooms,* they are not always separated by a partition or a wall. Nevertheless, they perform the function of a room, whether there is a complete separation, a partial separation, or no separation.

Potlach Corp.

When rooms are completely separated by partitions and doors, the plan is known as a *closed plan.* When partitions do not divide the rooms of an area, the arrangement is called an *open plan.*

In most two-story dwellings the living area is normally located on the first floor. However, in split-level homes or one-story homes with functional basements, part of the living area may be located on the lower level.

UNIT 6

The Living Room

The living room is the center of the living area in most homes. In small homes the living room may represent the entire living area. Hence, the function, location, decor, size, and shape of the living room are extremely important and affect the design, functioning, and appearance of the other living-area rooms.

FUNCTION

The living room is designed to perform many functions. The exact function depends on the living habits of the occupants. In the home it is often the entertainment center, the recreation center, the library, the music room, the TV

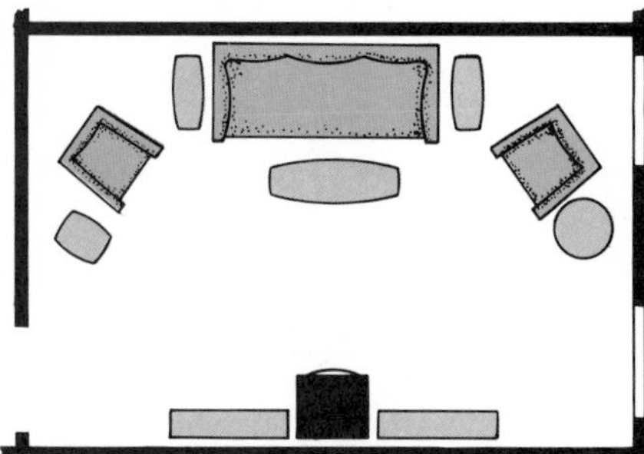

Fig. 6–1. A living room specifically planned for television viewing.

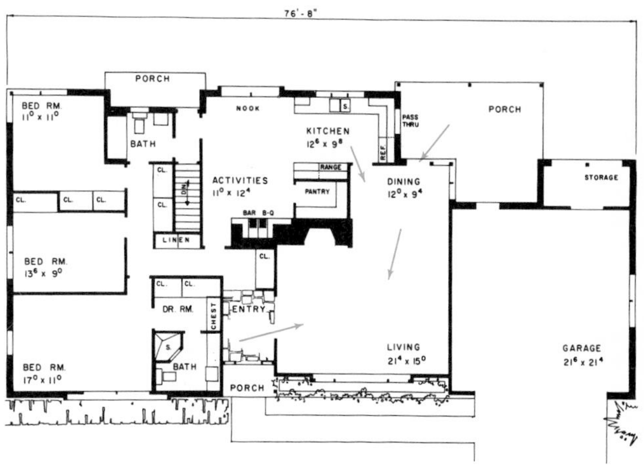

Home Planners, Inc.

Fig. 6–2. A centrally located living room.

center, the reception room, the social room, the study, and occasionally the dining center. In small dwellings the living room often becomes a guest bedroom. If the living room is to perform all or some of these functions, then it should be designed accordingly. The shape, size, location, decor, and facilities of the room should be planned to provide for each activity. For example, if the living room is to be used for television viewing, it will be planned differently from a living room without television. Figure 6–1 shows some of the considerations in planning a room for TV viewing.

Many of the facilities normally associated with the living room can be eliminated if a separate, special-purpose room exists for that activity. For example, if television viewing is restricted to a recreation room, then planning for TV in the living room can be eliminated. If a den or study is provided for reading and for storing books, facilities for the use of large numbers of books in the living room can be eliminated. Regardless of the exact activities anticipated, the living room should always be planned as a functional, integral part of the home. The living room is planned for the comfort and convenience of the family and guests.

LOCATION

The living room should be centrally located. It should be adjacent to the outside entrance, but the entrance should not lead directly into the living room. In smaller residences the entrance may open into the living room, but whenever possible this arrangement is to be avoided. The living room should not be a traffic access to the sleeping and service area of the house. Since the living room and dining room function together, the living room should also be adjacent to the dining room. Figure 6–2 shows the central location of a living room and its proximity to other rooms of the living area.

Open Plan

In an open-plan living area, the living room, dining room, and entrance may be part of one open area, as shown in Fig. 6–3. The living room may be separated from other rooms by means of a divider without doors, such as the storage wall shown in Fig. 6–4. In Fig. 6–5, the

Bethlehem Steel Corp.

Fig. 6–3. An open-plan living room.

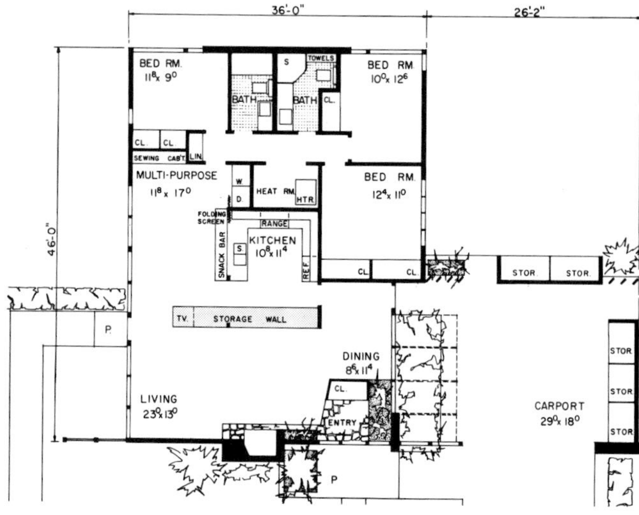

Home Planners, Inc.

Fig. 6–4. The storage wall separates the living room from the kitchen without enclosing the room.

Rittling Corporation

Fig. 6–5. A fireplace can be used to separate the living room from the dining room without isolation.

living room is separated from the dining room by a fireplace. In Fig. 6–6 the wrought-iron grill provides partial separation of the living room and foyer. Often a separation is accomplished by placing the living room on a different level (Fig. 6–7). Separation may also be achieved by the use of area rugs and furniture placement, as shown in Fig. 6–8. Of course, these features do not separate the rooms visually, but they do effect a functional separation.

When an open plan is desired and yet the designer wants to provide some means of closing off the room completely, sliding doors or folding doors can be used (Fig. 6–9).

Closed Plan

In a closed plan, the living room would be completely closed from the other rooms by means of walls. Access would be through doors, arches, or relatively small openings in partitions (Fig. 6–10).

DECOR

There is no one way to design and decorate a room. The decor depends primarily on the tastes, habits, and personalities of the people who will use the room. If the residents' tastes

Fig. 6–6. A living room separated from the foyer by a wrought iron screen.

Weyerhaeuser Company

Fig. 6–7. A living room separated from adjacent rooms by level.

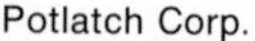

Potlatch Corp.

Thomas Industries Inc.

Fig. 6–8. A living room separated by furniture clusters and area-defining rugs.

Fig. 6–9. In the open plan, folding doors provide privacy when needed.

Rolscreen Company

are modern, the wall, ceiling, and floor treatments should be consistent with the clean, functional lines of modern architecture and modern furniture, as shown in Fig. 6–11. If the residents prefer colonial or period-style architecture, then this theme should be reflected in the decor of the room.

The living room should appear inviting, comfortable, and spacious, This appearance can be accomplished by an effective use of color and lighting techniques and by the tasteful selection of wall, ceiling, and floor-covering materials. The selection and placement of func-

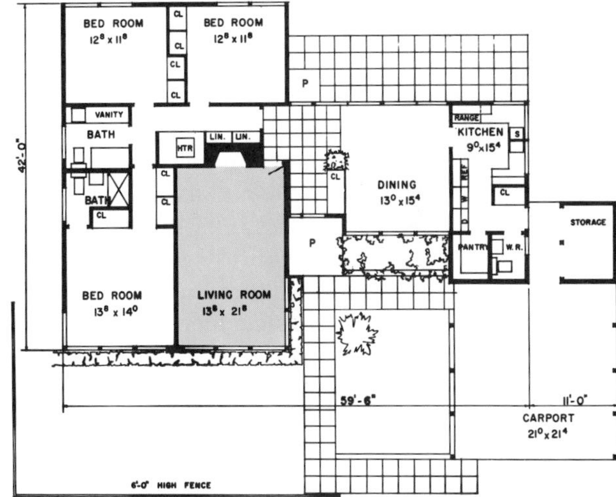

Home Planners, Inc.

Fig. 6–10. A closed-plan living room.

Fig. 6–11. A contemporary-style living room.

Armstrong Cork Company

Weyerhaeuser Company

Fig. 6–12. The living room should appear inviting, comfortable, and spacious.

PPG Industries, Inc.

Fig. 6–13. Mirrors can help create a spacious effect.

tional, well-designed furniture also helps the appearance. All these techniques have been combined to create a most desirable total impression in the living room shown in Fig. 6–12. Decorating a room is much like selecting clothing. The color, style, and materials should be selected to minimize faults and to emphasize good points. Figure 6–13 shows that the use of mirrors and floor-to-ceiling drapes along with proper furniture placement can create a spacious effect in a relatively small room.

Walls

The design and placement of doors, windows, and chimneys along the walls of the living room can change the entire appearance of the room. The kind of wall-covering material used can also affect the appearance. Wall coverings are selected from a variety of materials, including plaster, gypsum wallboard, wood paneling, brick, stone, and glass. Sometimes furniture is built into the walls. Fireplaces, windows, doors, or openings to other areas should be designed as integral parts of the room. They should not appear as afterthoughts.

Notice the difference between the two designs in Fig. 6–14A and B. Figure 6–14A shows a wall, fireplace, and opening designed as a functional part of the room. Figure 6–14B shows the same room with door openings, fireplaces, and wall treatments placed on the wall without reference to other parts of the room.

Orientation

The living room should be oriented to take full advantage of the position of the sun and the most attractive view. Since the living room is used primarily in the afternoon and evening, it should be located to take advantage of the afternoon sun.

Windows

When a window is placed in a living-room wall, it should become an integral part of that wall. The view from the window or windows becomes part of the living-room decor, especially when landscape features are near and are readily observable, as in Fig. 6–15. When planning windows, consider also the various seasonal changes in landscape features.

Fig. 6–14A. A functionally designed open-plan living-room wall.

Fig. 6–14B. A closed-plan living room.

Scholz Homes, Inc.

Fig. 6–15. The outdoors can become part of the living-room decor.

Although the primary function of a window is twofold, to admit light and to provide a pleasant view of the landscape, there are many conditions under which only the admission of light is desirable. If the view from the window is unpleasant or is restricted by other buildings, translucent glass, which primarily admits light, as shown in Fig. 6–16, can be incorporated into the plan.

Translucent drapes, as shown in Fig. 6–17, can also be used to admit light while providing a semivisual separation. Window placement in apartment buildings cannot always be altered. However, the location and orientation of the living room must be planned to provide the most desirable furniture arrangement in designing apartment buildings (Fig. 6–18).

Fireplace

The primary function of a fireplace is to provide heat, but it is also a permanent decorative feature. The fireplace and accompanying masonry should maintain a clean, simple line consistent with the decor of the room and of the wall where they are placed. In Fig. 6–19, the fireplace and chimney masonry is the entire wall. Consequently, it becomes the focal point of the room. The corner fireplace shown in Fig. 6–20 is used to divide the library area of the living room from the conversational area. The fireplace shown in Fig. 6–21 is used as the major separation between the living room and the dining room.

The external appearance of the house must be considered in locating the fireplace, because the location of the fireplace in the room determines the position of the chimney on the roof. This does not mean that the outside of the house should be designed first. But it does mean that the outside appearance must be considered in designing and locating features of the house that appear inside and outside. Examples to be considered are fireplaces, doors, and windows.

Fig. 6–16. Translucent glass admits light while it subdues images.

PPG Industries, Inc.

Fig. 6–17. The use of translucent drapes for semiprivacy.

Hedrich-Blessing

Hedrich-Blessing

Fig. 6–18. The view from an apartment must be considered in planning the placement and orientation of the living room.

Floors

The living-room floor should reinforce and blend with the color scheme, textures, and overall style of the living room. Exposed hardwood flooring, room-size carpeting, wall-to-wall carpeting, throw rugs, and sometimes polished flagstone are appropriate for living-room use.

Ceilings

Most conventional ceilings are flat surfaces covered with plaster. New building materials, such as laminated beams and arches, and new construction methods now enable architects to design ceilings that conserve building materials and utilize previously wasted space. An example of an open-beam ceiling is shown in Fig. 6–22. Figure 6–23A shows two optional methods of producing cathedral ceilings either in double-pitch or in single-pitch style. The cathedral ceiling makes a room appear more spacious, through the addition of more area. Compare the space provided by the cathedral ceilings shown in Fig. 6–23A with the space available in the conventional ceiling shown in Fig. 6–23B.

Home Planners, Inc.

Fig. 6–20. A corner fireplace.

Home Planners, Inc.

Fig. 6–21. A fireplace used as a divider between the living room and the dining room.

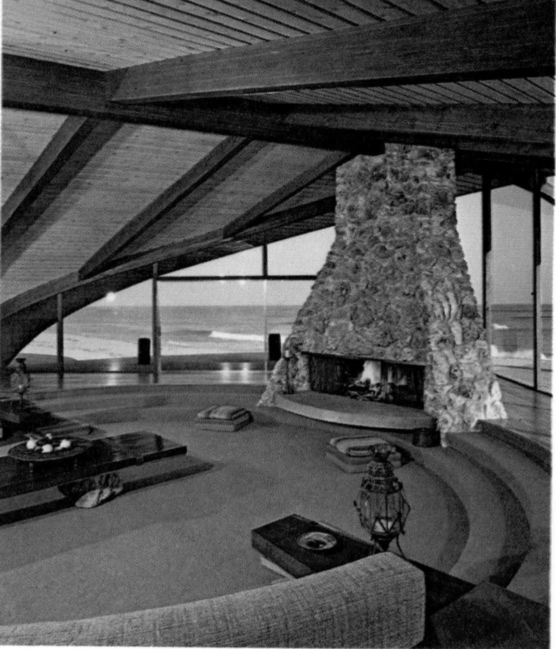

Potlatch Corp.

Fig. 6–19. This fireplace design is an integral part of the room.

Fig. 6–22. An open-beam ceiling.

Richard Gross

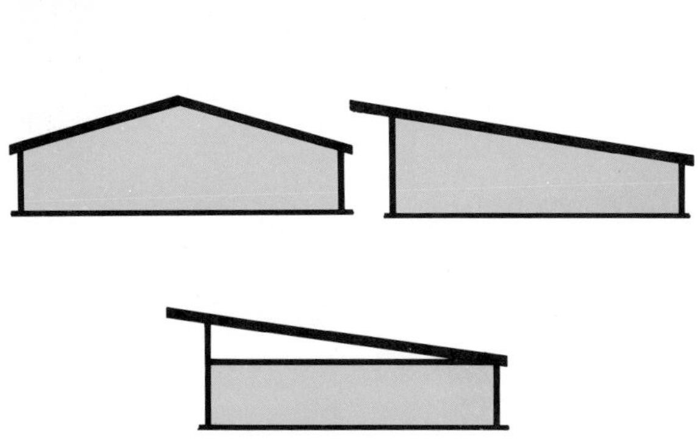

Fig. 6–23A. Cathedral ceilings help make the room look more spacious.
Fig. 6–23B. A conventional ceiling.

Fred W. Farish

Fig. 6–24. General lighting and local lighting should be used to illuminate a room.

Lighting

Living-room lighting is divided into two types, general lighting and local lighting. General lighting is designed to illuminate the entire room through the use of ceiling fixtures, wall spots, or cove lighting. Local lighting is provided for a specific purpose, such as reading, drawing, or sewing. Local lighting can be supplied by table lamps, wall lamps, pole lamps, or floor lamps. Note the two types of lighting in Fig. 6–24.

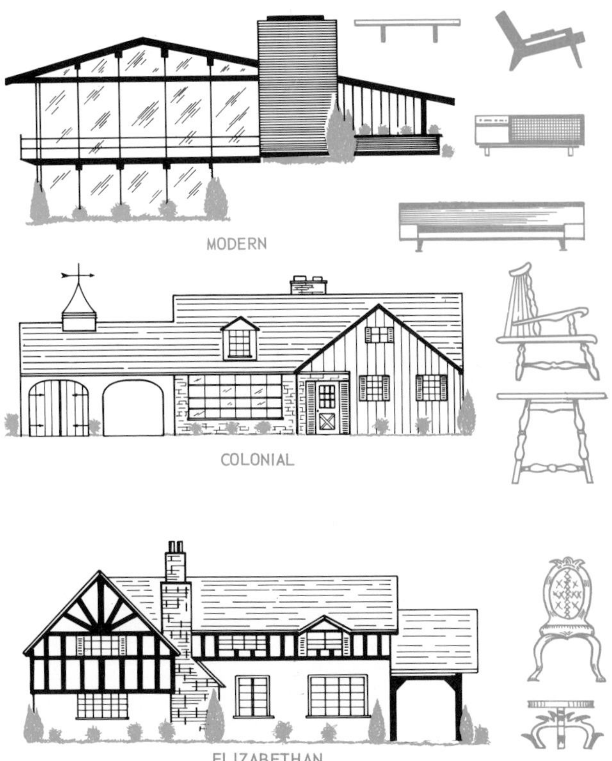

Fig. 6–25. Furniture styles should be related to the type of architecture used.

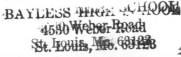

Furniture

Furniture for the living room should reflect the motif and architectural style of the home. If the architectural style of the home is modern, the furniture should be modern. If the home is colonial, the furniture should be colonial. If the home is of some period style, the furniture should reflect the furniture style of that period. Figure 6–25 shows the relationship between the various furniture styles and architectural styles. The mixing of modern and period furniture styles should be avoided.

Furniture should not only be consistent in period and style but should also be related in texture and design. All the furniture in the living room should be of same kind of wood. If walnut is used for built-in furniture, in the paneling, and in the trim, walnut should be repeated in the other furniture in the room. Avoid mixing furniture of different kinds of wood, such as oak, walnut, and mahogany. Wood furniture should be finished in the same type of finish throughout the room, such as all glossy, all semiglossy, all flat or all satin finish.

A special effort should be made to have built-in furniture maintain lines consistent with the remaining wall treatment. Notice how the built-in music center in Fig. 6–26 and the built-in book shelves in Fig. 6–27 eliminate the need for other pieces of furniture in the room. Each blends functionally into the total decor of the room. The furniture for the living room is

Fig. 6–26. **Built-in furniture saves space.**

Armstrong Cork Company

Fig. 6–27. **Built-in book shelves conserve floor space.**

chosen to fit the living needs of the residents. The size, shape, and layout of the room should be designed to accommodate the furniture. Figure 6–28A shows a living room of adequate size which functions well with the necessary furniture. Figure 6–28B shows a room with a size and shape not adequate for the furniture. This latter design is a result of establishing the size and shape of the room without considering the size and number of pieces of furniture to be used.

SIZE AND SHAPE

One of the most difficult aspects of planning the size and shape of a living room, or any other room, is to provide sufficient wall space for the effective placement of furniture. Continuous wall space is needed for the placement of many articles of furniture, especially musical equipment, bookcases, chairs, and couches.

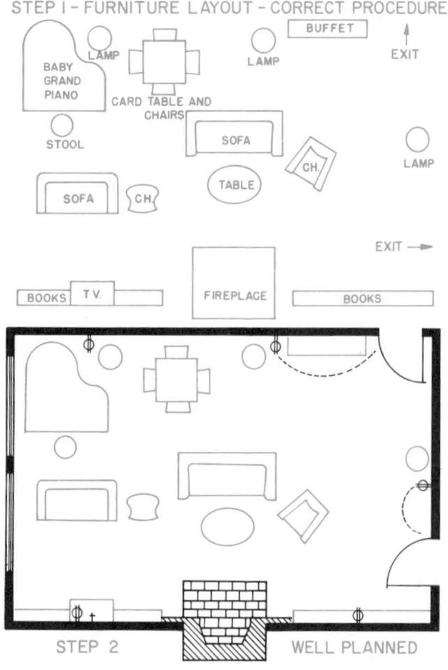

Fig. 6–28A. **A living room planned to accommodate the necessary furniture.**

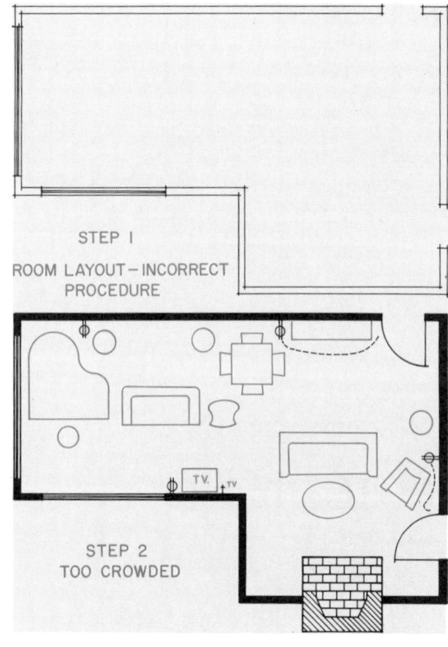

Fig. 6–28B. **A living room of inadequate size for the furniture needed.**

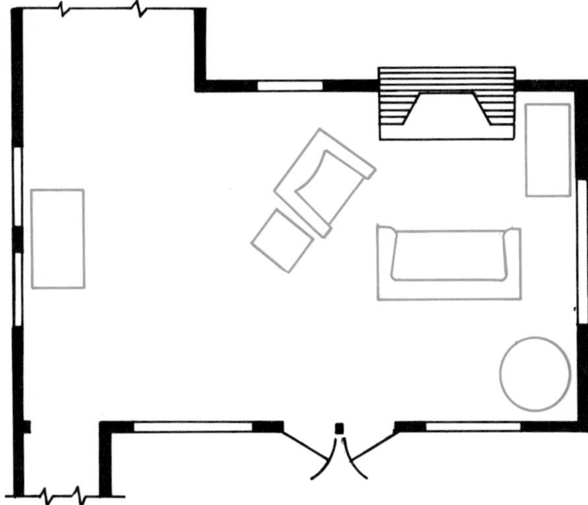

Fig. 6–29A. A living room with inadequate wall space.

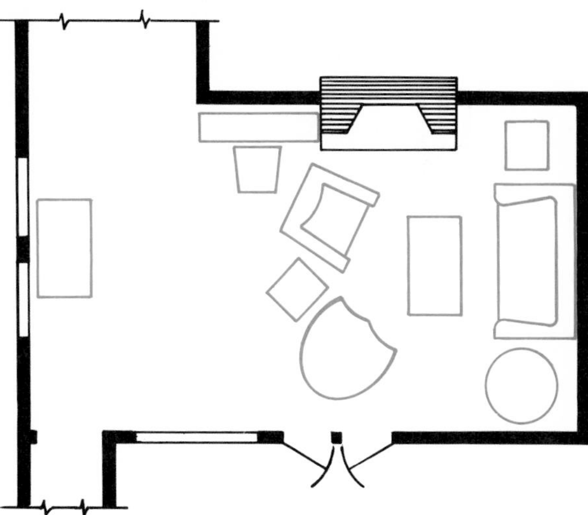

Fig. 6–29B. A living room with ample wall space for furniture placement.

The placement of fireplaces, doors, or openings to other rooms should be planned to conserve as much wall space for furniture placement as possible. Figure 6–29A shows a living room with practically no wall space for furniture placement. Figure 6–29B shows the same room with the wall space adjusted to provide the needed space for furniture placement.

Rectangular rooms are generally easier to plan and to place furniture in than are square rooms. However, the designer must be careful not to establish a proportion that will break the living room into several conversational areas, as shown in Fig. 6–30 at A. This design has actually resulted in the merging of two separate rooms into one. The arrangement shown in Fig. 6–30 at B is much more desirable, since it integrates the total activities of the room without separation.

Living rooms vary greatly in size. A room 12 by 18 feet (12′ × 18′) (3.7 × 5.5 meters) would be considered a small or minimum-sized living room. A living room of average size would be approximately 16′ × 20′ (4.9 × 6.1 m), and a very large or optimum-sized living room would be 20′ × 26′ (6.1 × 7.9 m) or more.

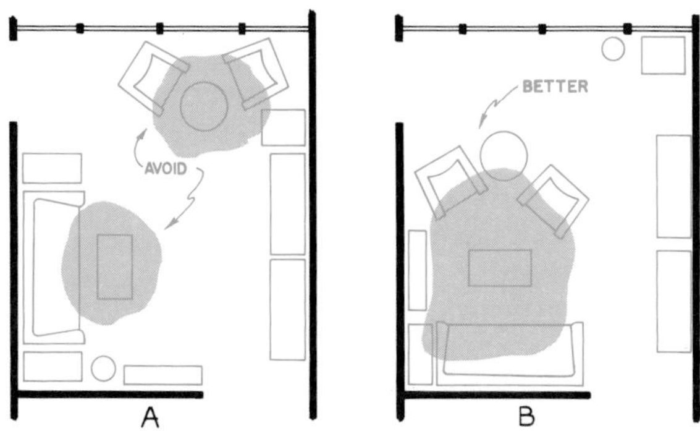

Fig. 6–30. Avoid breaking the room into several isolated conversation areas.

PROBLEMS

1. Sketch an open-plan living room. Indicate the position of windows, fireplace, foyer, entrance, and dining room.
2. Sketch a closed-plan living room. Show the position of adjacent rooms.
3. Sketch one wall of the living room you designed for Problem 2. Use Fig. 6–14B as a guide.
4. List the furniture you would include in your living room. Cut out samples of this furniture from catalogs or newspapers. Be consistent in style, choosing either contemporary or period-style furniture.
5. Determine the best size for a living room to accommodate these pieces of furniture: a couch, a television set, a stereo, a baby grand piano, a bookcase, a chaise lounge, a coffee table, a fireplace, two chairs.
6. Define the following terms: *closed plan, open plan, decor, living area, living room, local lighting, general lighting.*

UNIT 7

The Dining Room

The dining facilities designed for a residence depend greatly on the dining habits of the occupants. The dining room may be large and formal, or the dining area may consist of a dining alcove, as shown in Fig. 7–1. It may also be a breakfast nook in the kitchen. Large homes may contain dining facilities in all these areas.

FUNCTION

The function of a dining area is to provide a place for the family to gather for breakfast, lunch, or dinner in both casual and formal situations. When possible, a separate dining area potentially capable of seating from eight to twelve persons for dinner should be provided in addition to breakfast or dinette facilities. Contrast the formal dining area shown in Fig. 7–1 with the informal dining facilities shown in the dining area in Fig. 7–2.

Fig. 7–1. A dining alcove in the living area.

California Redwood Association

Scholz Homes, Inc.

Fig. 7–2. An informal dining area.

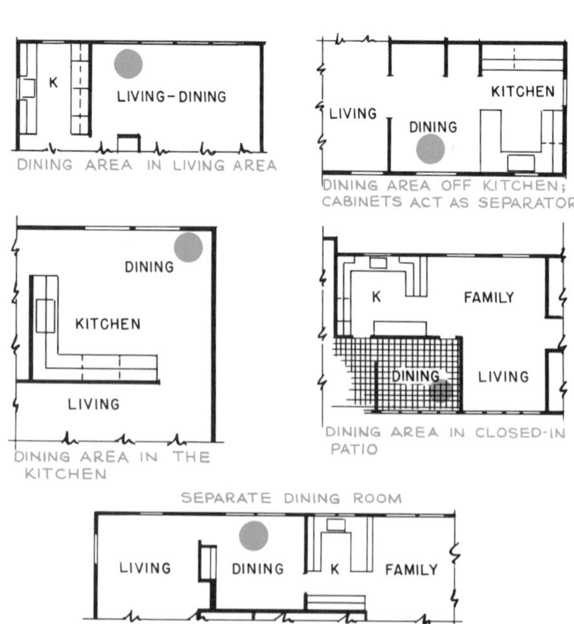

Fig. 7–3. Plans showing the location of dining facilities in many different areas.

Potlatch Corp.

Fig. 7–4. A dining area located in the kitchen.

California Redwood Association, Architect: James D. Morton

Fig. 7–5. A dining area located in a living room.

LOCATION

Dining facilities can be located in many different areas, depending on the capacity needed and the type of plan. In the closed plan, a separate dining room is usually provided. In an open plan, many different dining locations are possible (Fig. 7–3). Open-area dining facilities are provided in the kitchen shown in Fig. 7–4. In Fig. 7–5 the living room houses the dining area.

Relation to Kitchen

Regardless of the exact position of the dining area, it must be placed adjacent to the kitchen. The ideal dining location is one that requires few steps from the kitchen to the dining table. However, the preparation of food and other kitchen activities should be baffled from direct view from the dining area.

Relation to Living Room

If dining facilities are not located in the living room, they should be located next to it. Family and guests normally enter the dining room from the living room and use both rooms jointly.

The nearness of the dining room to the kitchen, and to the living room, requires that it be placed between the kitchen and the living area. The dining room in the closed plan shown in Fig. 7–6 is located in this manner.

Separation

Complete separation should be possible between the kitchen and the dining room. The area between the living room and the dining room may be entirely open, partially baffled, or completely closed off. Sometimes the separation of the dining room and the living room is accomplished by level or by dividing the rooms with a common fireplace, as shown in Fig. 7–7.

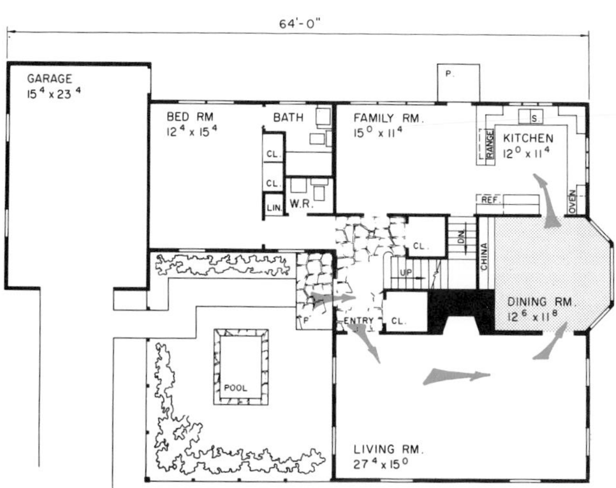

Home Planners, Inc.

Fig. 7–6. The dining room is located between the living room and the kitchen.

Home Planners, Inc.

Fig. 7–7. The see-through fireplace separates the dining area from the living room.

Masonite Corporation

Fig. 7–8. A partial wall without a door makes this an open plan.

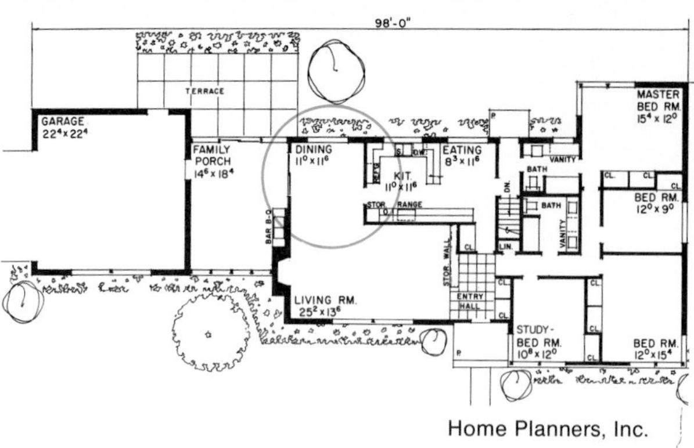

Home Planners, Inc.

Fig. 7–9. An open dining-room plan.

Another method of separating the dining area in an open plan is through the use of partial partitions, as shown in Fig. 7–8. Compare these semi-isolated arrangements with the completely open dining areas shown in Figs. 7–9 and 7–10.

Outside Dining Facilities

There is often a need for dining facilities on or adjacent to the patio, as shown in Fig. 7–11. The porch or patio should be near the kitchen and directly accessible to it. Locating the patio or dining porch directly outside the dining room or kitchen wall provides maximum use of the facilities. This minimizes the inconvenience of using outside dining facilities (Fig. 7–12).

DECOR

The decor of the dining room should be consistent with the rest of the house and specifically relate in style to the other parts of the living area. This relationship is especially desirable in the open plan, in which the dining area is integrated with the rest of the living area. Floor, wall, and ceiling treatment should be the same in the dining area as in the living area.

If a dining porch or a dining patio is used, its decor must also be considered part of the dining-room decor. This is because the outside dining area is viewed from the inside. Notice how the view of the courtyard in Fig. 7–13 is brought to the inside by the use of window walls directly next to the dining area.

Fig. 7–10. An open dining area.

Armstrong Cork Company

Fig. 7–11. Dining facilities located adjacent to the patio.

Julius Shulman

Western Wood Products Association

Fig. 7–12. Dining facilities may be moved to a porch in fair weather.

American-Saint Gobain Corp.

Fig. 7–13. Consider the view when locating the dining area.

Dividers

If semi-isolation is desired, partial divider walls can be used effectively. These dividers may be planter walls, glass walls, half walls of brick or stone, paneled walls, fireplaces, or grillwork. Figure 7–14 shows the effective use of arches to provide semi-isolation for the dining area. The dining area shown in Fig. 7–15 is separated by level.

Lighting

Controlled lighting can greatly enhance the decor of the dining room. General illumination which can be subdued or intensified can provide the right atmosphere for almost any occasion. Lighting is controlled by a rheostat which is commonly known as a *dimmer switch.*

In addition to general illumination, local lighting should be provided for the table either by a direct ceiling spot light or by a hanging lamp (Fig. 7–16). A hanging lamp can be adjusted down for local dining lighting and up for general illumination when the dining facilities are not in use.

Fig. 7–14. The use of arches to provide semi-isolation.

SIZE AND SHAPE

The size and shape of the dining area are determined by the size of the family, the size and number of pieces of furniture, and the clearances and traffic areas between furniture.

Maximum Planning

The dining area should be planned for the largest group that will dine in it regularly. There is

Fig. 7–15. The use of levels to separate the dining area.

Julius Shulman

Scholz Homes, Inc.

Fig. 7–16. The use of local lighting over the dining table.

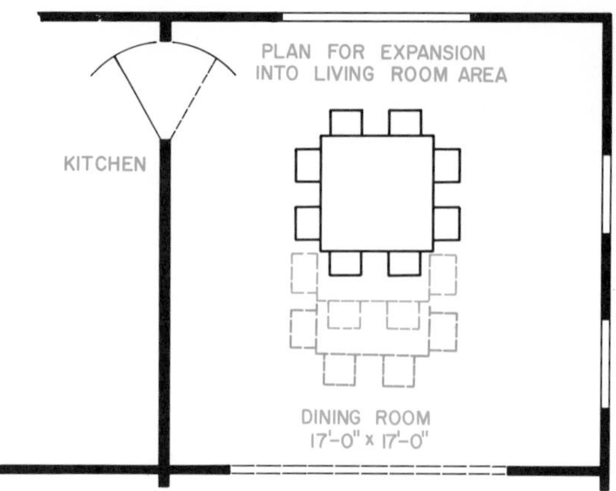

Fig. 7–17. A dining area planned for maximum expansion.

little advantage in having a dining-room table that expands, if the room is not large enough to accommodate the expansion. One advantage of the open plan is that the dining facilities can be expanded in an unlimited manner into the living area, as shown in Fig. 7–17. Thus, the living area temporarily becomes part of the dining area.

Furniture
The dining room should be planned to accommodate the furniture. Dining-room furniture may include an expandable table, side chairs, armchairs, buffet, server or serving cart, china closet, and serving bar. In most situations a rectangular dining room will accommodate the furniture better than a square room. Figure 7–18 shows a typical furniture placement for a dining room.

Clearance
Regardless of the furniture arrangement, a minimum space of 2′ (610 millimeters) should be allowed between the chair and the wall or furniture when the chair is pulled to the out position. This allowance will permit serving traffic behind chairs and will permit entrance to and exit from the table without difficulty. A distance of 27 inches (27″) (690 mm) per person should be allowed at the table. This spacing is accomplished by allowing 27″ (690 mm) from the center line of one chair to the center line of another, as shown in Fig. 7–19.

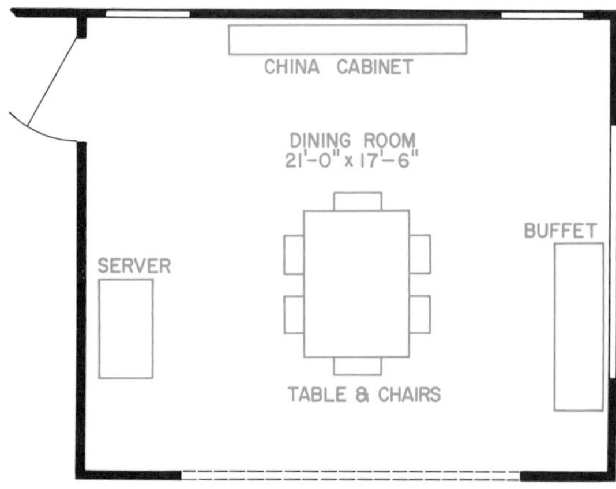

Fig. 7–18. Typical furniture placement in a dining room.

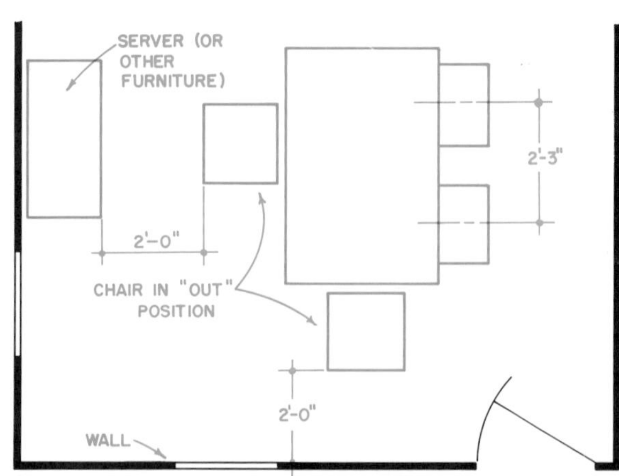

Fig. 7–19. Dining-room clearances.

Recommended Sizes

A dining room that would accommodate the minimum amount of furniture—a table, four chairs, and a buffet—would be approximately 10′ × 12′ (3.0 × 3.7 m). A minimum-sized dining room which would accommodate a dining table, six or eight persons, a buffet, a china closet, and a server would be approximately 12′ × 15′ (3.7 × 4.6 m). A more nearly optimum-sized dining room would be 14′ × 18′ (4.3 × 5.5 m) or larger. A room of this size would accommodate practically any size gathering.

Armstrong Cork Company

Fig. 7–20. Draw a floor plan of this dining room.

PROBLEMS

1. **Sketch a dining room to include the following furniture: dining table to accommodate six, buffet, china closet. Indicate the relationship to the living room, and provide access to a patio.**
2. **Sketch a plan for an informal dining area directly adjacent to the kitchen.**
3. **Sketch an open-plan dining area. Show the relationship of this area to the living room.**
4. **Sketch a separate dining room. Indicate the position of adjacent rooms.**
5. **Add a dining porch to the plan shown in Fig. 7–6.**
6. **Sketch a plan of the dining area shown in Fig. 7–10. Convert this to a closed plan.**
7. **Redesign the dining area of your own home.**
8. **Indicate the position of local lighting and general lighting on one of the plans you have designed.**
9. **Sketch a dining room to scale, showing the position of all furniture you would like to include in the dining room of a house of your own design.**
10. **Draw a floor plan of the dining room shown in Fig. 7–20. Show lighting and placement of furniture.**
11. **Define the following terms: *buffet, china closet, server, rheostat, dining porch, dining patio, formal dining, casual dining.***

UNIT 8

The Family Room

Several years ago the term *family room* did not exist in the architectural vocabulary. The trend toward more informal living because of more leisure time has influenced the popularity of the family room. Today the majority of homes are designed to include a family room.

FUNCTION

The purpose of the family room is to provide facilities for family-centered activities. It is designed for the entire family, children and adults alike.

Only in extremely large residences is there sufficient space for a separate sewing room, children's playroom, hobby room, or music room. The modern family room often performs the functions of all these rooms. The children's area in the family room in Fig. 8–1 provides facilities for a variety of children's activities The area of the family room in Fig. 8–2 is designed primarily for watching television and pursuing chess as a hobby.

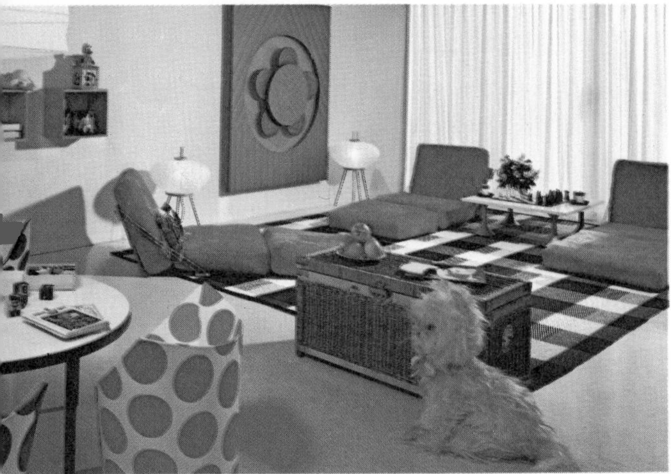

Lisanti, Inc.

Fig. 8–1. A children's area in the family room.

LOCATION

Activities in the family room often result in the accumulation of hobby materials and clutter. Thus, the family room is often located in an area accessible from, but not visible from, the rest of the living area.

It is quite common to locate the family room adjacent to the kitchen, as shown in Fig. 8–3. This location revives the idea of the old country kitchen in which most family activities were centered.

Fig. 8–2. A family room designed for television viewing and chess.

Armstrong Cork Company

When the family room is located adjacent to the living room or dining room, it becomes an extension of these rooms for social affairs. In this location, the family room is often separated from the other rooms by folding doors, screens, or sliding doors. The family room shown in Fig. 8–4 is located next to the kitchen and yet is accessible from the living room when the folding door is open.

Another popular location for the family room is between the service area and the living area. The family room shown in Fig. 8–5 is located between the garage, the kitchen, and the entrance. This location is especially appropriate when some service functions, such as home-workshops facilities, are assigned to the family room.

DECOR

The family room is also known as the *activities room* or *multiactivities room*. Decoration of this room should provide a vibrant atmosphere. Ease of maintenance should be one of the chief considerations in decorating the family room.

Furniture

Family-room furniture should be informal and suited to all members of the family. The use of

Olson-Spencer & Associates

Fig. 8–3. A family room located adjacent to the kitchen.

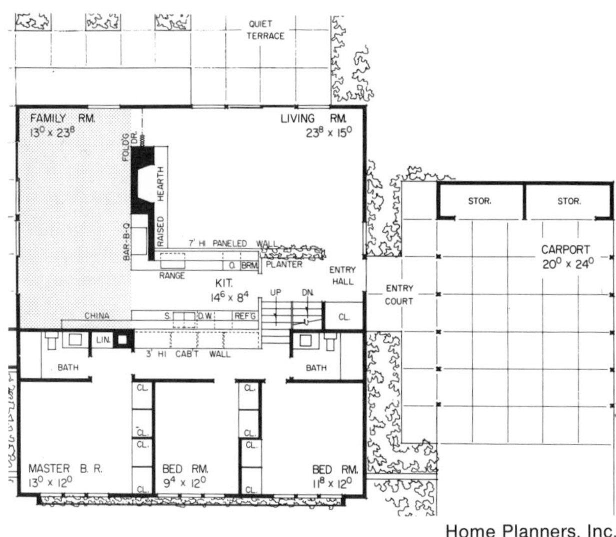

Home Planners, Inc.

Fig. 8–4. A family room accessible from the kitchen and living room.

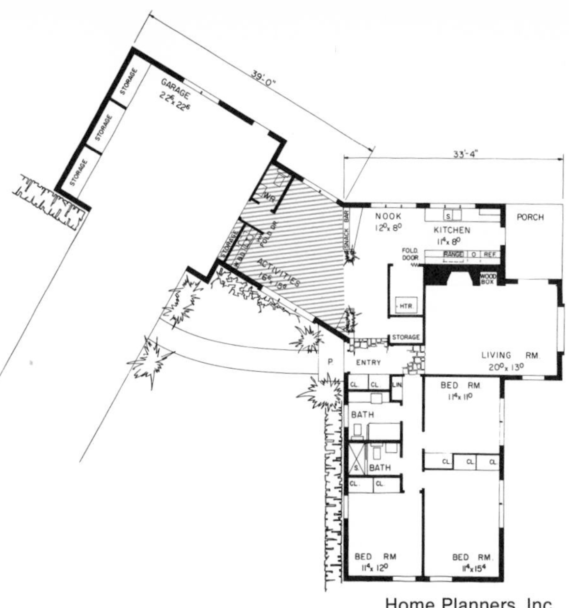

Home Planners, Inc.

Fig. 8–5. A family room located near the service area.

plastics, leather, and wood provides great flexibility in color and style and promotes easy maintenance.

Floors

Floors should be resilient. Linoleum or tile made of asphalt, rubber, or vinyl will best resist the abuse normally given a family-room floor. If rugs are used, they should be the kind that will stand up under rough treatment. They should also be washable.

Walls

Soft, easily damaged materials such as wallpaper and plaster should be avoided for the family room. Materials such as tile and paneling are most functional. Chalkboards, bulletin boards, built-in cupboards, and toy-storage cabinets should be used when appropriate. Work areas that fold into the wall when not in use conserve space and may perform a dual function if the cover wall can also be used as a chalkboard or a bulletin board.

Storage

Since a variety of hobby and game materials will be used in the family room, sufficient space must be provided for the storage of these materials. Figure 8–6 shows the use of built-in storage facilities, including cabinets, closets, and drawer storage.

Ceilings

Acoustical ceilings are recommended to keep the noise of the various activities from spreading to other parts of the house. This feature is especially important if the family room is located on a lower level.

Fig. 8–6. Plan for adequate storage in the family room.

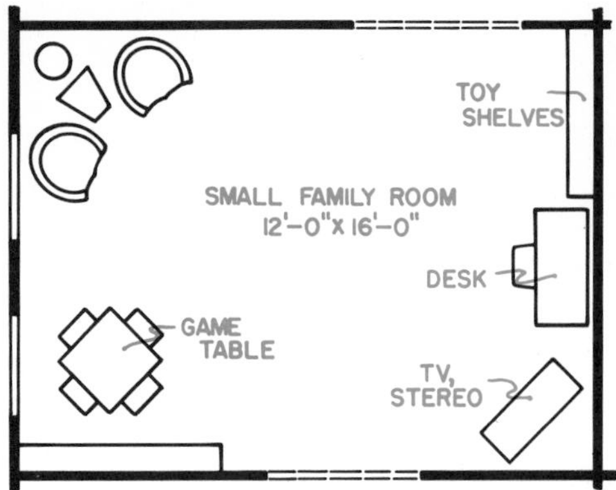

Fig. 8–7. A minimum-sized family room.

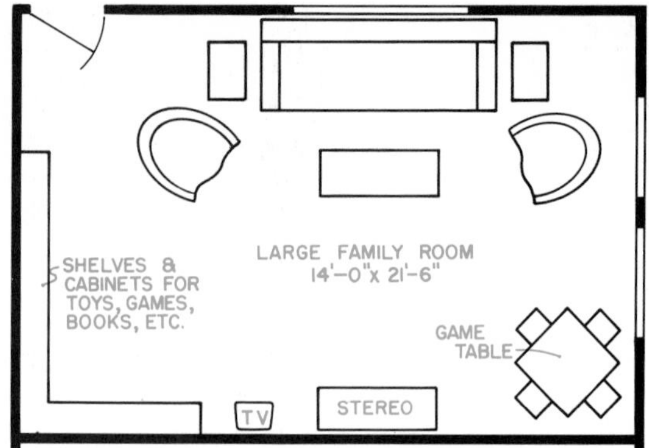

Fig. 8–8. An optimum-sized family room.

SIZE AND SHAPE

The size and shape of the family room depends directly on the equipment needed for the activities the family will pursue in this room. The room may vary from a minimum-sized room, as shown in Fig. 8–7, to the more optimum-sized family room shown in Fig. 8–8. This room contains practically all the equipment almost any family would need in the family room. Included are a sewing machine, a hobby table, bulletin boards, drawing boards, easels, a television set, a studio couch, chalkboards, a bookcase, a desk, a children's desk, a children's play table, a children's toy box, storage cabinets, a motion-picture screen, and a serving bar. Most family-room requirements lie somewhere between the two extremes shown.

PROBLEMS

1. **Sketch a family room you would like to include in a home of your own design. Include the location of all furniture and facilities.**
2. **Determine the size and shape of a family room to accommodate the following activities: television viewing, sewing, knitting, model-building, slide-viewing, dancing, eating.**
3. **Design a family room primarily for children's activities.**
4. **Design a family room that doubles as a guest bedroom.**
5. **Define the following terms: *sewing room, children's playroom, hobby room, music room, family room, multiactivities, linoleum, asphalt tile, rubber tile, vinyl tile, acoustical ceiling.***

UNIT 9

The Recreation Room

The recreation room (game room, playroom) is exactly what the name implies. It is a room for play and recreation. It includes facilities for participation in recreational activities.

FUNCTION

The design of the recreation room depends on the number and arrangement of the facilities needed for the various pursuits. Activities for which many recreation rooms are designed include billiards, chess, checkers, ping-pong, darts, television watching, eating, and dancing. For example, the recreation room shown in Fig. 9–1 has been designed around three activity areas: the ping-pong area, the chess area, and the television and conversation area. Designing the recreation room around a music center, as shown in Fig. 9–2, is also very practical.

Armstrong Cork Company

Fig. 9–1. The design of the recreation room depends on the number of activities planned.

The function of the recreation room often overlaps that of the family room. Overlapping occurs when a multipurpose room is designed to provide for recreational activities such as ping-pong and billiards and also includes facilities for more sedentary family activities such as sewing, knitting, model-building, and other hobbies.

LOCATION

The recreation room is frequently located in the basement in order to use space that would otherwise be wasted. Basement recreation rooms often provide more space for the use of large equipment, such as Ping-Pong tables, billiard tables, and shuffleboard. Figure 9–3 shows a basement recreation room with a fireplace located directly beneath the living-room fireplace on the upper level. The most important reason why recreation rooms are often located in the basement of older homes, however, is because the basement is the only available space which can be converted into a recreation room. An example of the conversion of the basement of an older home into a well-planned recreation room is shown in Figs. 9–4A and B.

American Plywood Association

Fig. 9–2. A recreation room designed around a music center.

Armstrong Cork Company

Fig. 9–3. This recreation-room fireplace is located directly below the living-room fireplace.

Armstrong Cork Company

Fig. 9–4A. A typical basement before conversion.

Armstrong Cork Company

Fig. 9–4B. A basement converted to a recreation room.

When the recreation room is located on the ground level, its function can be expanded to the patio or terrace, as shown in Fig. 9–5. Regardless of the level, the recreation room should be located away from the quiet areas of the house.

Often the recreation room can actually be separated from the main part of the house. This separation is possible when the recreation room is included as part of the garage or carport design, as shown in Fig. 9–6. When a separate location such as this is selected, some sheltered access should be provided from the house to the recreation area.

DECOR

Designers take more liberties in decorating the recreation room than any other room. They do so primarily because the active, informal atmosphere which characterizes the recreation room lends itself readily to unconventional furniture, fixtures, and color schemes. Bright warm colors can reflect a party mood. Furnishings and accessories can accent a dramatic central theme. The designer of the recreation room shown in Fig. 9–7 has developed a restful, quietly dignified atmosphere through the use of an oriental decor. The designer of the recreation room shown in Fig. 9–8 has created a festive yet casual atmosphere using a winter sports theme.

Regardless of the central theme, recreation-room furniture should be comfortable and easy to maintain. The same rules apply to recreation room walls, floors, and ceilings as apply to those of the family room. Floors should be hard-surfaced and easy to maintain. Walls should be paneled or covered

Fig. 9–5. Whenever possible, the recreation room should be located adjacent to the patio.

Julius Shulman

Fig. 9–6. A recreation room included as part of the garage design.

Condon-King Company

Fig. 9–7. A quiet, restful recreation room.

Armstrong Cork Company

Fig. 9–8. A recreation room decorated in a winter sports theme.

with some easily maintained material. Acoustical (soundproofed) ceilings are recommended if the recreation room is located in the basement or on a lower level.

SIZE AND SHAPE

The size and shape of the recreation room depend on whether the room occupies an area on the main level or whether it occupies basement space. If basement space is used, the only restrictions on the size are the other facilities that will also occupy space in the basement, such as the laundry, the workshop, or the garage. Figure 9–9 shows a recreation room which occupies a rather large basement area which would otherwise be wasted space. Figure 9–10 shows a relatively small recreation room located on the main level of the house. The size of most recreation rooms ranges between these two extremes.

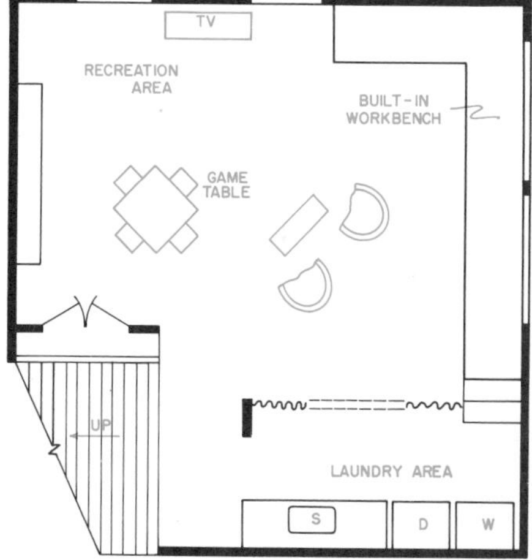

Fig. 9–9. A recreation room occupying a large area.

PROBLEMS

1. **Sketch a plan of a recreation room you would include in a house of your own design.**
2. **Sketch a plan for a recreation room, including facilities for billiards, chess, shuffleboard, and television watching.**
3. **Determine the size and shape of a recreation room to accommodate the following furniture: television set, stereo, chaise lounge, studio couch, two lounge chairs, soft-drink bar and stools, bookcase, billiard table.**
4. **Define the following terms: *game room, playroom, recreation room.***

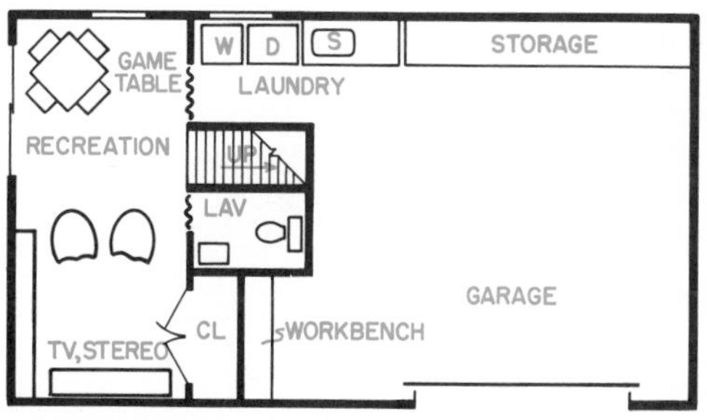

Fig. 9–10. A small recreation room.

UNIT 10

Porches

A porch is a covered platform leading into an entrance of a building. Porches are commonly enclosed by glass, screen, or post and railings. A porch is not the same as a patio. The porch is attached structurally to the house, whereas a patio is placed directly on the ground. The porch on the house shown in Fig. 10–1 is connected to a balcony that extends around the perimeter of the house and covers the patio below. Balconies and decks are actually elevated porches.

FUNCTION

Porches serve a variety of functions. Some are used for dining and some for entertaining and relaxing. Others are furnished and function like patios for outdoor living. Still others provide an additional shelter for the entrance to a house or patio. The primary function of a porch depends on the structure and purpose of the building to which it is attached. For example, the porch in Fig. 10–2 provides outdoor living facilities and access to motel rooms. The condominium porch shown in Fig. 10–3 is designed as an outdoor private extension to the living room. The porch in Fig. 10–4 is planned to provide maximum appreciation of an ocean view.

Verandas

Southern colonial homes such as the one in Fig. 10–5 were designed with large porches, or verandas, extending around several sides of the home. Outdoor plantation life centered on the veranda, which was very large.

Balconies

A balcony is a porch suspended from an upper level of a structure. It usually has no accesss from the outside. Balconies often provide an extension to the living area or a private extension to a bedroom.

The house shown in Fig. 10–6 is distinguished by several types of balconies. The

Fig. 10–1. This porch extends into a perimeter balcony.
California Redwood Association

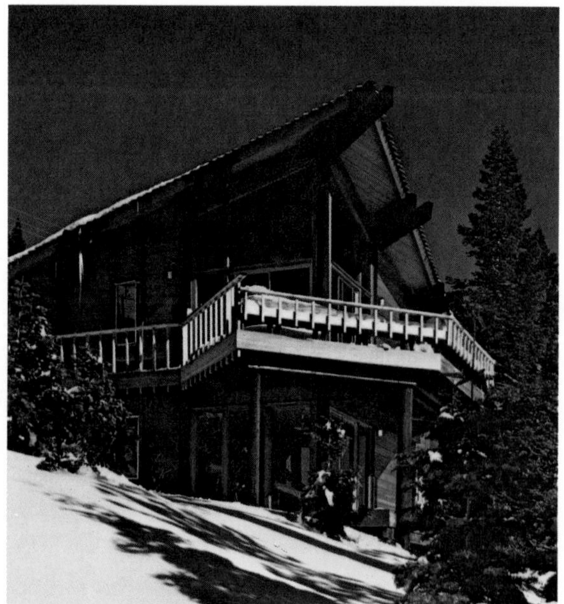

Fig. 10–2. A porch used to connect motel units.
Western Wood Products Association

Western Wood Products Association

Fig. 10–3. A condominium porch designed for privacy.

Potlatch Corp.

Fig. 10–4. A porch designed with a view.

upper balcony is supported by cantilevered beams and provides an extension which covers the porch below. The porch in turn shelters a patio below it. Hillside lots lend themselves to vertical plans and provide maximum flexibility in using outdoor living facilities.

Spanish- and Italian-style architecture is characterized by numerous balconies. The return of the balcony to popularity has been influenced and accelerated by new developments in building materials. These materials permit large areas to be suspended. The balcony in the house shown in Fig. 10–7A is cantilevered (supported only at one end) on wood joists that extend beyond the exterior wall. The flooring provides lateral support for the joists, as shown in Fig. 10–7B.

Oil by Margaret de Loo

Fig. 10–5. A southern colonial home with a veranda.

Fig. 10–6. The upper balcony of this house provides protection for the porch and patio below.

Western Wood Products Association

Fig. 10–7A. A cantilevered porch (left).
Fig. 10–7B. Cantilever supports (right).

Western Wood Products Association

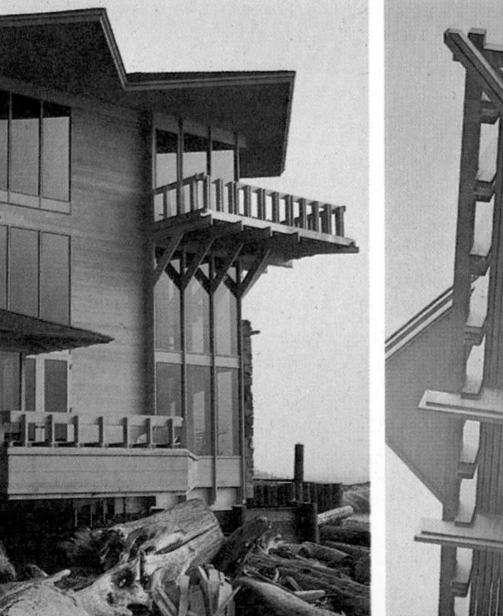

The principle of cantileverage, or suspension in space, can also be used to a greater extent with steel construction. An example is shown in the balcony which overhangs the patio in Fig. 10–8.

Stoop

The stoop is a projection from a building, similar to a porch. However, a stoop does not provide sufficient space for any activities. It provides only shelter and an access to the entrance of the building.

The Modern Porch

Only in the last several years has the porch been functionally designed and effectively utilized for outdoor living. The classic front porch and back porch which characterized most homes built in this country during the 1920s and 1930s were designed and used merely as places in which to sit. Little effort was made to use the porch for any other activities. A porch for a modern home should be designed for the specific activities anticipated for it. The form of the porch should be determined by its function.

LOCATION

Since the porch is an integral part of the total house design, it must be located where it will function best. The porch in Fig. 10–9 becomes a functional extension of the living area when in use. A porch can be made consistent with the rest of the house by extending the lines of the roof to provide sufficient *overhang*, or projection (Fig. 10–10).

Fig. 10–10. This porch is an integral part of the exterior design.

Rocky Mountain National Park

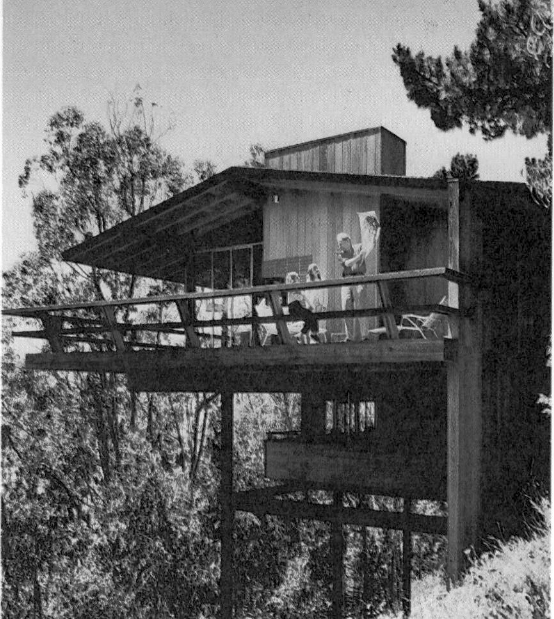

Fig. 10–8. Steel members make large cantilevered distances possible.

Fig. 10–9. This porch is an extension of the living room located on the right.

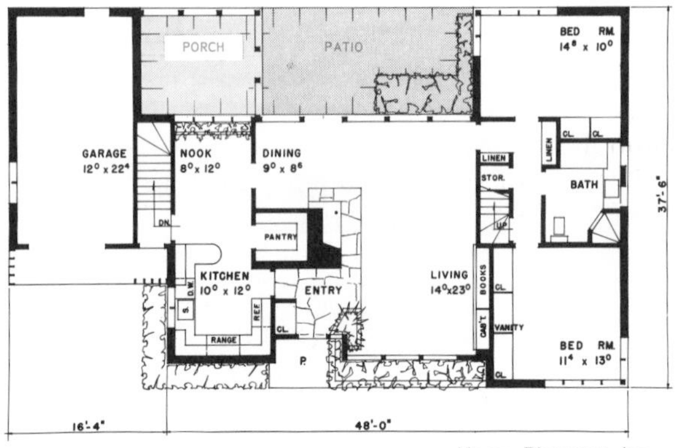

Home Planners, Inc.

Fig. 10–11. Location of a dining porch.

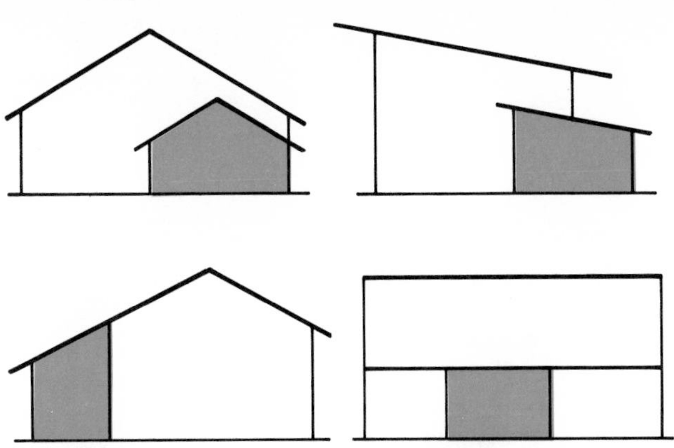

Fig. 10–12. The lines of the porch should be consistent with the major lines of the house.

Western Wood Products Association

Fig. 10–13. The use of vertical strips to provide semiprivacy, safety, and wind baffling.

PPG Industries, Inc.

Fig. 10–14. Glass windscreens protect this porch from wind and sand.

A dining porch should be located adjacent to either the dining room or the kitchen. The dining porch shown in Fig. 10–11 can be approached from the dining room through the terrace. This arrangement makes possible the use of the nook, dining room, patio, or porch for dining purposes with little traffic difficulty. Locating the porch between two walls of the house in this manner is also economical, since only two sides must be enclosed.

The porch should be located to provide the maximum in flexibility. A porch which can function for dining and other living activities is desirable. The primary functions of the porch should be considered when orienting the porch with the sun. If much daytime use is anticipated and direct sunlight is desirable, a southern exposure should be planned. If little sun is wanted during the day, a northern exposure would be preferable. If morning sun is desirable, an eastern exposure would be best, and for the afternoon sun, a western exposure.

DECOR

The porch should be designed as an integral and functional part of the total structure. A blending of roof styles and major lines of the porch roof and house roof is especially important (Fig. 10–12). A similar consistency should characterize the vertical columns or support members of the porch. Figure 10–12 shows some relationships that can be established to prevent the tacked-on look and to ensure uniformity in design.

Various materials and methods can be used as deck railing, depending on the degree of privacy or sun and wind protection needed. For example, the sides of the porch shown in Fig. 10–3 provide complete privacy but also block out ventilation. The sides of the porch shown in Fig. 10–13 provide adequate ventilation but also offer semiprivacy and safety. Railings on elevated porches such as this should be designed at a height above 3 feet (915 mm) to discourage the use of the top rail as a place to sit.

Porch furniture should withstand deterioration in any kind of weather. Covering material should be waterproof, stain-resistant, and washable. Protection from wind and rain should be planned. Note how the use of glass on the porch shown in Fig. 10–14 blocks out wind-driven sand and yet allows maximum sun exposure.

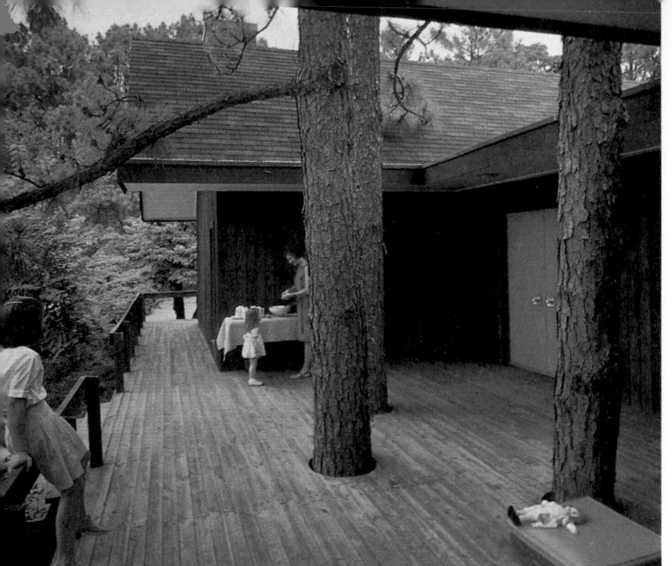

Frank Lotz Miller

Fig. 10–15. A large porch.

Western Wood Products Association

Fig. 10–16A. A small porch at ground level.

SIZE AND SHAPE

Porches range in size from the very large veranda to rather modest-sized stoops, which provide only shelter and a landing surface for the main entrance. Figure 10–15 shows a large porch which extends across the entire front of the house. Figure 10–16A shows the effective use of a small porch at ground level, and Fig. 10–16B shows how a small elevated porch can be designed to extend the living area outdoors. A porch approximately 6′ × 8′ (1.8 × 2.4 m) is considered a minimum size. An 8′ × 12′ (2.4 × 3.7 m) porch is about average. Porches larger than 12′ × 18′ (3.7 × 5.5 m) are considered rather large.

The shape of the porch depends greatly upon how the porch can be integrated into the overall design of the house.

Home Planners, Inc.

Fig. 10–16B. A small, elevated porch.

PROBLEMS

1. **Add a porch to the floor-plan sketch shown in Fig. 37–16. Show the exact width and length, and list the materials you recommend for the deck, roof, and enclosure.**
2. **Add a porch to the sketch shown in Fig. 36-9.**
3. **Add a porch to a floor plan of your own design.**
4. **From catalogs, newspapers, and magazines, cut out pictures of porch furniture you would choose for your own porch.**
5. **Draw or sketch a floor plan of the porch shown in Fig. 10-17. Design and draw access areas to the lake and show which rooms are adjacent to the porch.**
6. **Define the following terms: *veranda, balcony, cantilever, stoop.***

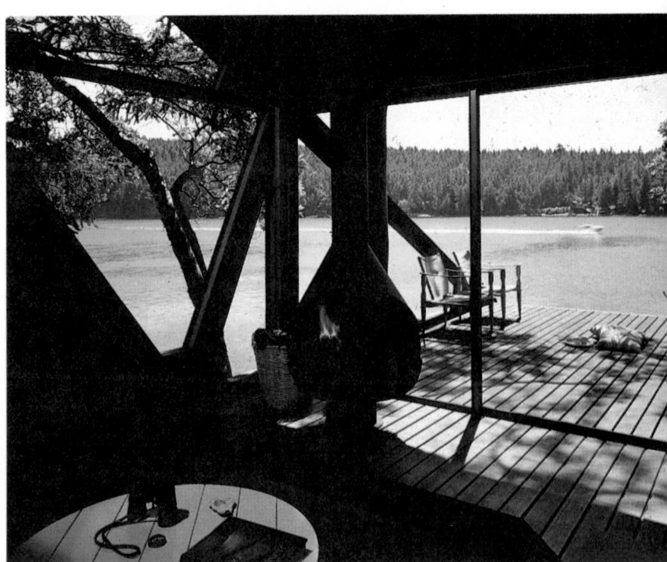

Stanmar, Inc.

Fig. 10–17. Draw a plan of this porch and show access to the lake.

UNIT 11

Patios

A *patio* is a covered surface adjacent or directly accessible to the house. The word *patio* comes from the Spanish word for courtyard. Courtyard living was an important aspect of Spanish culture, and courtyard design was an important part of early Spanish architecture.

FUNCTION

The patio at various times may perform outdoors all the functions that the living room, dining room, recreation room, kitchen, and family room perform indoors.

The patio is often referred to by other names, such as *loggia, breezeway,* and *terrace.*

Patios can be divided into three main types according to function: living patios, play patios, and quiet patios. The home shown in Fig. 11–1 contains all three kinds of patios.

LOCATION

Patios should be located adjacent to the area of the home to which they relate. They should also be somewhat secluded from the street or from neighboring residences.

Living Patio

Living patios should be located close to the living room or the dining room. When dining is anticipated on the patio, access should be provided from the kitchen or dining room.

Play Patio

It is often advantageous to provide a play patio for use by children and for physical activities not normally associated with the living terrace. The play terrace sometimes doubles as the service terrace and can conveniently be placed adjacent to the service area. Notice the location of the play terrace in Fig. 11–1. It is related directly to the service area and also to the family room in the living area.

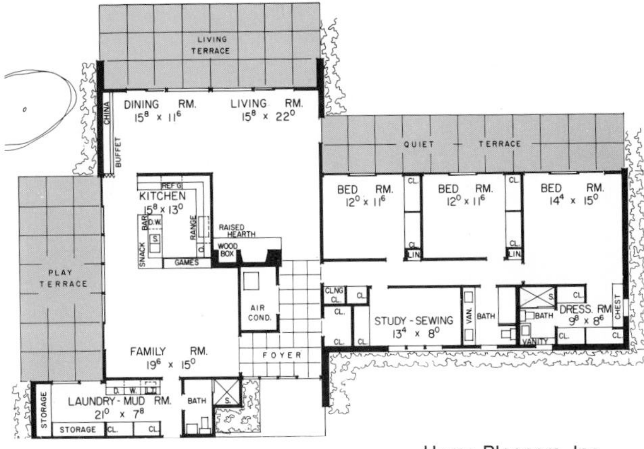

Home Planners, Inc.

Fig. 11–1. This plan includes three types of patios.

Quiet Patio

The quiet patio can actually become an extension of the bedroom. It can be used for relaxation or even sleeping. The quiet terrace shown in Fig. 11–1 can be entered from the bedrooms or the living area. This type of patio should be secluded from the normal traffic of the home. Often the design of the house will allow these separately functioning patios to be combined in one large, continuous patio. This kind of patio is shown in Fig. 11–2. Here the play room, living room, master bedroom, and kitchen all have access to the patio.

Fig. 11–2. A continuous patio.

Southern California Gas Company

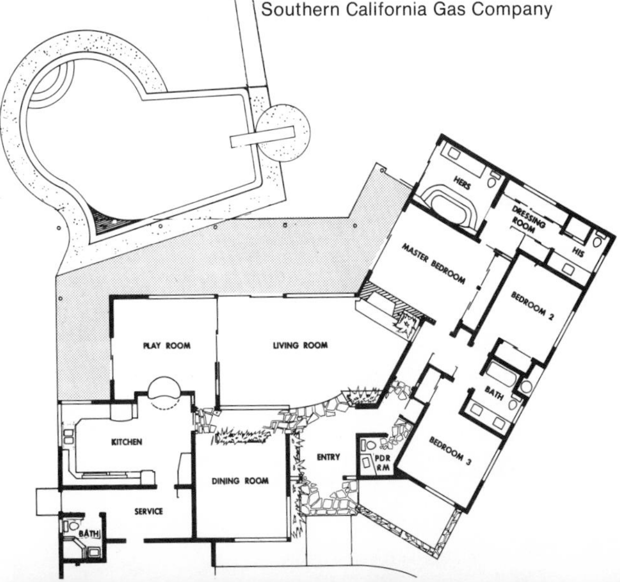

PPG Industries, Inc.

Fig. 11–3A. A living-area patio viewed from the interior.

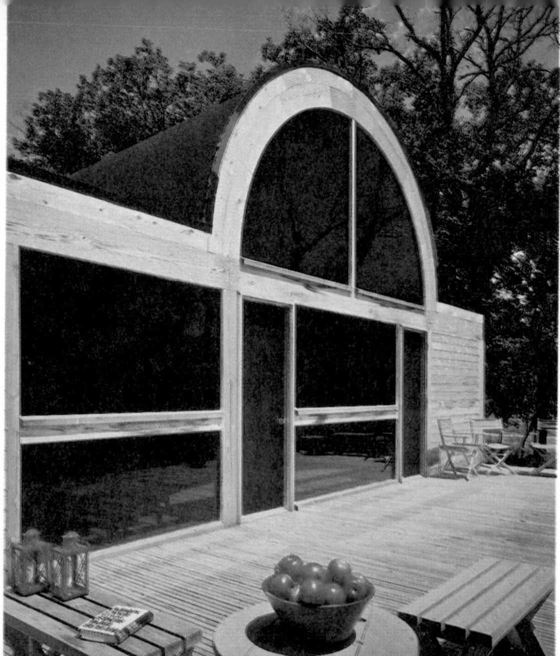

PPG Industries, Inc.

Fig. 11–3B. The living-area patio viewed from the exterior.

Placement
Patios can be conveniently placed at the end of a building, as the living terrace is placed in Fig. 11–1. They may be placed between corners of a house as in the play terrace and quiet terrace in Figs. 11–1 and 11–3A and B. Patios may be wrapped around the side of the house, as shown in Fig. 11–2, or they may be placed in the center of a U-shaped house or in a courtyard. The courtyard patio shown in Fig. 11–4 offers complete privacy from all sides.

Separate Patios
In addition to the preceding locations, the patio is often located completely apart from the house. When a wooded area, a particular view, or a terrain feature is of interest, the patio can be placed away from the house. When it is located in this manner, it should be readily accessible, as shown in Fig. 11–5.

Orientation
When the patio is placed on the north side of the house, the house itself can be used to shade the patio. If sunlight is desired, the patio should be located on the south side of the house. The planner should take full advantage of the most pleasing view and should restrict the view of undesirable sights.

DECOR

The materials used in the deck, cover, baffles, and furniture of the patio should be consistent

Fig. 11–4. A courtyard patio.

Shakertown

Fig. 11–5. A separated patio.

California Redwood Association

Julius Shulman

Fig. 11-6. A wood-slat patio deck.

Olympic Stains

Fig. 11-7. A brick-surface patio.

with the lines and materials used in the rest of the home. Patios should not appear to be designed as an afterthought but should appear and function as an integral part of the total design.

Patio Deck

The deck (floor) of the patio should be constructed from materials that are permanent and maintenance-free. Flagstone, redwood, concrete, and brick are among the best materials for use on patio decks. Wood slats such as those shown in Fig. 11–6 provide for drainage between the slats and also create a warm appearance. However, they do require some maintenance.

Brick-surface patio decks are very popular because bricks can be placed in a variety of arrangements to adapt to practically any shape or space. The area between the bricks may be filled with concrete, gravel, sand, or grass (Fig. 11–7).

A concrete deck is effective when a smooth, unbroken surface is desired. Patios where bouncing-ball games are played, or where pool-side cover is desired, can use concrete advantageously (Fig. 11–8).

Patio Cover

Patios need not be covered if the house is oriented to shade the patio during the times of the day when shade is normally desired. Since a patio is designed to provide outdoor living, too much cover can defeat the purpose of the patio. Coverings can be an extension of the roof structure, as shown in Fig. 11–9. They may be graded or tilted to allow light to enter when

Scholtz Homes, Inc.

Fig. 11-8. A concrete-deck patio.

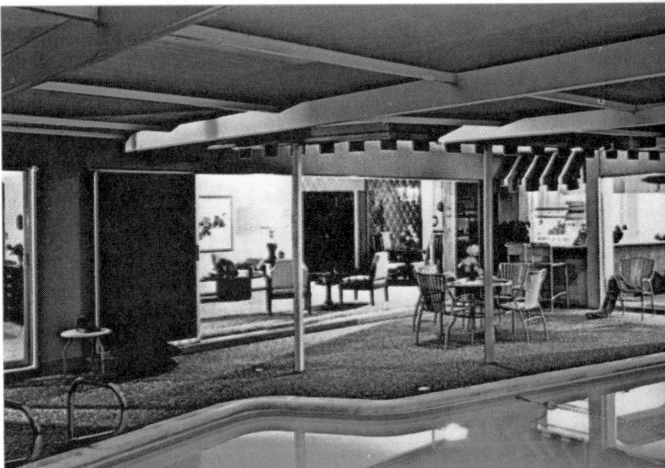

PPG Industries, Inc.

Fig. 11-9. A roof extension used as a pool and patio cover.

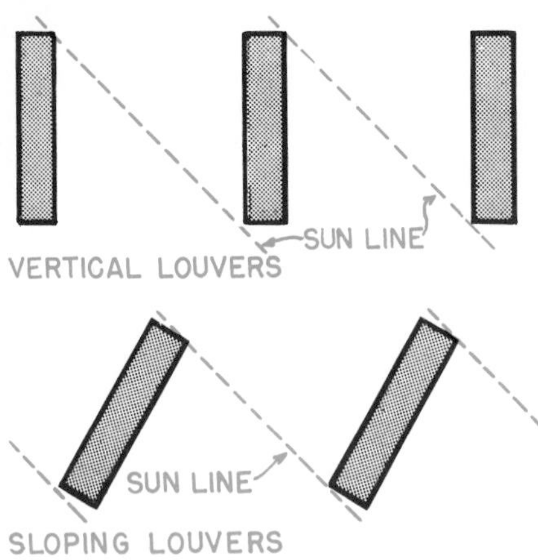

Fig. 11–10. The angle and spacing of louvers is important in sun screening.

California Redwood Association

Fig. 11–11. A louvered patio cover.

the sun is high and to block the sun's rays when the sun is lower. The graded effect can be obtained by placing louvers spaced straight or slanted to admit the high sun and block the low sun, as shown in Fig. 11–10. Figure 11–11 shows a louvered patio supported by posts which rest in a garden area. The center portion of the cover is solid, and the outer part is slotted.

Plastic, glass fiber, and other translucent materials used to cover patios admit sunlight and yet provide protection from the direct rays of the sun. Translucent covers also provide shelter from rain. When translucent covering is used, it is often desirable to have only part of the patio covered. This arrangement provides sun for part of the patio and shade for other parts (Fig. 11–12). Balconies may also be used effectively to provide shelter for a patio as shown in Fig. 11–13.

California Redwood Association

Fig. 11–12. A translucent overhang helps protect this patio.

Fig. 11–13. A balcony used to provide patio shelter.

PPG Industries, Inc.

Fig. 11–14. A patio with a fence used as a wall.

Julius Shulman

California Redwood Association

Fig. 11–15. A slatted baffle wall provides privacy but admits light and air.

New Homes Guide

Fig. 11–16. A baffle wall used to separate the patio from the service entrance.

Walls and Baffles

Patios are designed for outdoor living, but outdoor living need not be public living. Some privacy is always desirable. Solid walls can often be used effectively to baffle the patio from a street view, from wind, and from the low rays of the sun (Fig. 11–14). Baffling devices include solid fences, slatted fences, concrete blocks, post and rails, brick or stone walls, and hedges or other shrubbery.

A solid baffle wall is often undesirable because it restricts the view, eliminates the circulation of air, and makes the patio appear smaller. Figure 11–15 shows a baffle wall used to provide privacy for the patio without restricting circulation of air. The baffle wall in Fig. 11–16 is used to separate the patio from the service entrance without restricting the view.

In mild climates, completely enclosing a patio by solid walls can help make the patio function as another room. In such an enclosed patio, some opening should be provide to allow light and air to enter. The grillwork openings on the wall shown in Fig 11–17A and 11–17B provide an effective and aesthetically pleasing solution to this problem.

Occasionally nature provides its own baffle through a rise in the landscape, as shown in Fig. 11–18. This condition is highly desirable and should be taken advantage of, if sufficient drainage away from the house and patio can be maintained.

Fig. 11–17A. A semi-isolated patio.
Fig. 11–17B. Plan of the semi-isolated patio.

Home Planners, Inc.

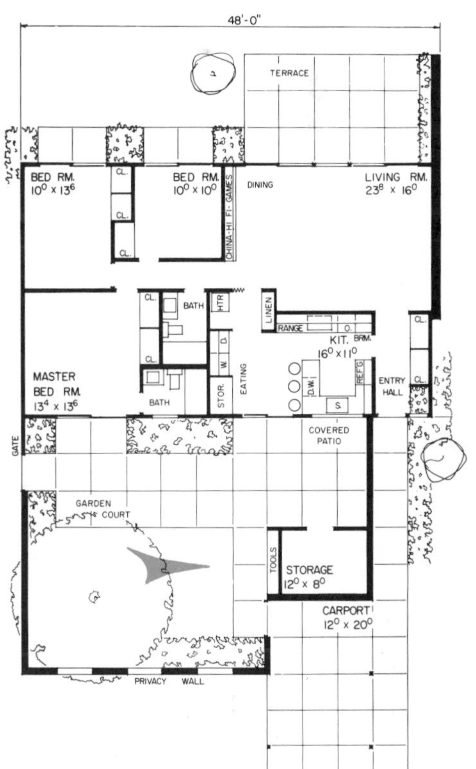

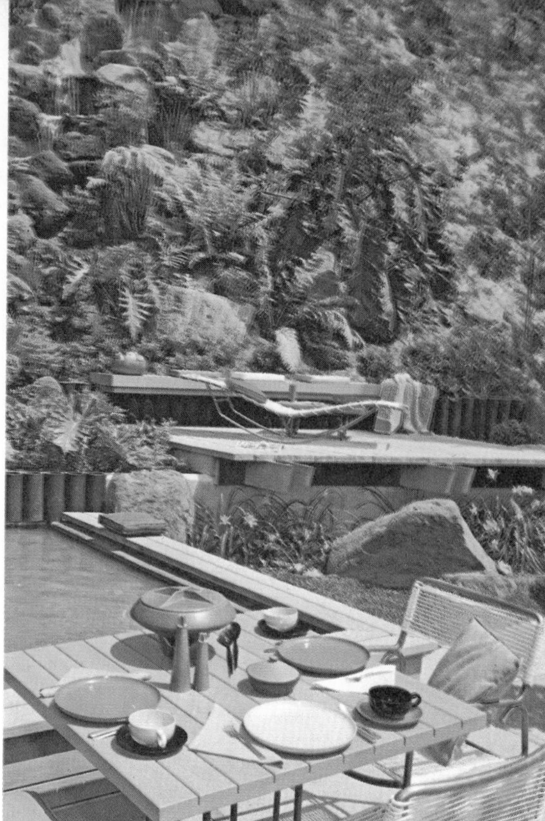

Paul J. Peart, Landscape Architect

Fig. 11–18. A natural patio baffle.

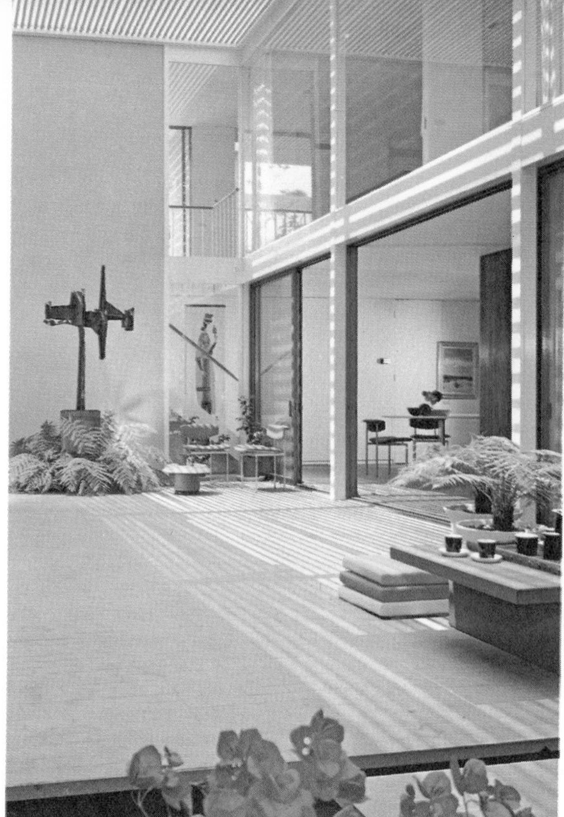

Julius Shulman

Fig. 11–19. The patio at midday.

Western Wood Products Association

Fig. 11–20. The patio should also be designed for nighttime use.

Day and Night Decor

To be totally effective, the patio should be designed for both daytime and nighttime use. Figure 11–19 shows a typical midday use of the patio. Figure 11–20 shows some of the possibilities for nighttime utilization. Correct use of general and local lighting can make the patio useful for many hours each day. If the walls between the inside areas of the house and the patio are designed as in Fig. 11–20, much light from the inside can be utilized on the patio. Figure 11–21 shows some of the specific types of lights and lighting that can be used to illuminate patios at night.

SIZE AND SHAPE

Patios may be as small as the garden terrace shown in Fig. 11–22 or as spacious as the courtyard patio shown in Fig. 11–23. The primary function will largely determine the size. The Japanese garden has no furniture and is designed primarily to provide a baffle and a beautiful view. The courtyard patio is designed for many uses.

Western Wood Products Association

Fig. 11–21. Examples of types of patio lighting.

California Redwood Association

Fig. 11–22. A small garden patio.

Activities should be governed by the amount of space needed for equipment. Equipment and furnishings normally used on patios include picnic tables and benches, lounge chairs, serving carts, game apparatus, and barbecue pits (Fig. 11–24). The placement of these items and the storage of games, apparatus, and fixtures should determine the size of the patio. Patios vary more in length than in width since patios may extend over the entire length of the house. A patio 12′ × 12′ (3.7 × 3.7 m) is considered a minimum-sized patio. Patios with dimensions of 20′ × 30′ (6.0 × 9.1 m) or more are not uncommon but are certainly considered large. When a pool is designed for a home, it becomes an integral part of the patio. The poolside and the entire area around the pool function as a patio (Fig. 11–25).

Fig. 11–23. A spacious courtyard patio.

Home Planners, Inc.

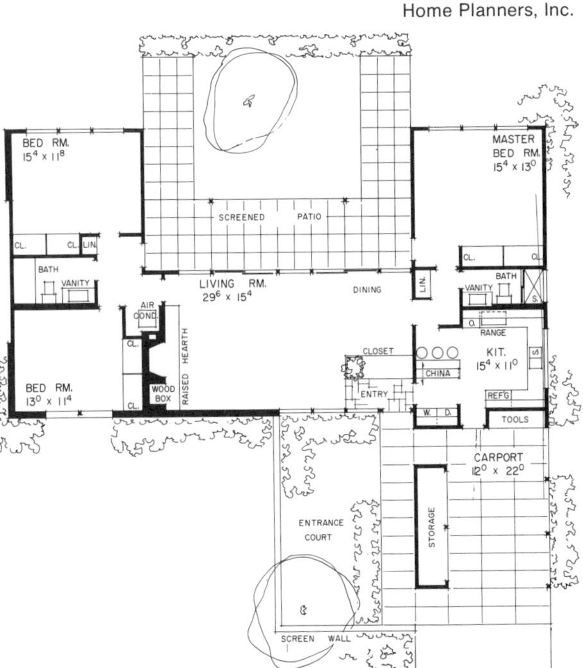

Fig. 11–24. Barbeque equipment incorporated into a patio design.

Frigidaire Division, General Motors Corporation

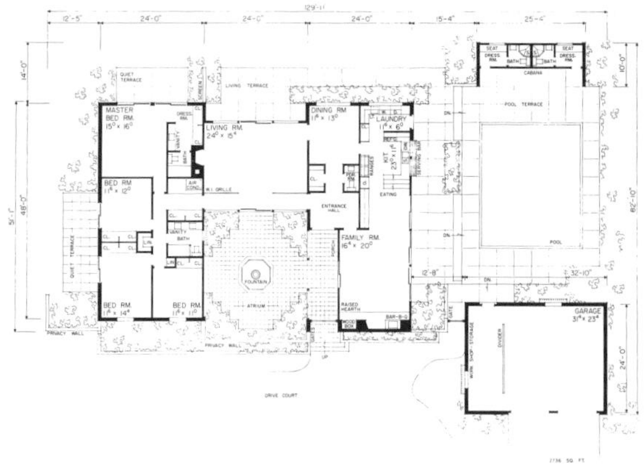

Libbey-Owens-Ford Company

Fig. 11–25. A pool integrated into the patio design.

PPG Industries, Inc.

Fig. 11–26. The patio and pool design can be blended together.

Many pool shapes now available allow the designer to blend the pool into the size and shape of the patio. Notice how the shape of the pool in Fig. 11–26 extends to the patio and continues around it.

When designing and locating a pool, the location of the filter, heater (if used), electrical plumbing, and filter lines must be planned. Since the filter runs continuously it should be located as far from the patio as possible without the use of excessively long plumbing, electrical, and filter supply lines. Figure 11–27 shows the location of this equipment in relationship to the pool and patio.

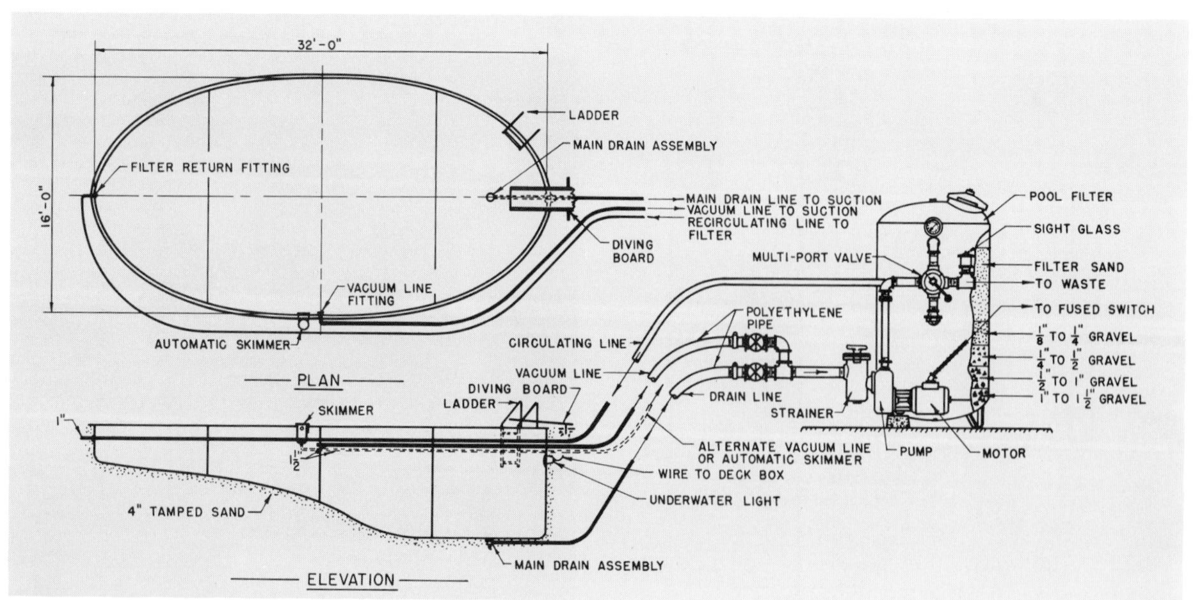

Lancer Pool Corporation

Fig. 11–27. Filtering-system equipment must be included in plans.

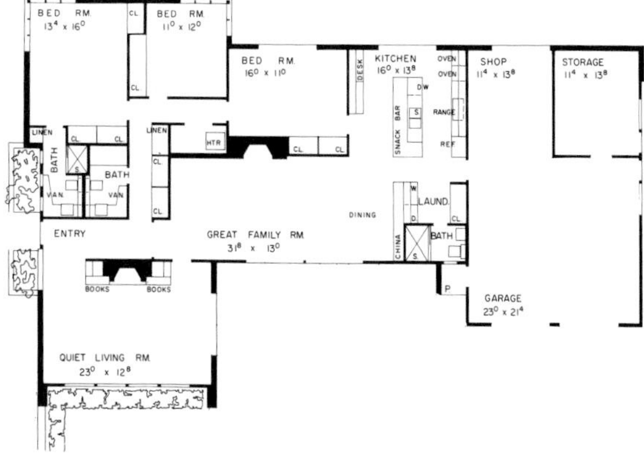

Home Planners, Inc.

Fig. 11–28. Add patios to this plan.

Western Wood Products Association

Fig. 11–29. Design a baffle and cover for this patio.

PROBLEMS

1. **Sketch a baffle wall for the exposed patio shown in Fig. 11–29.**
2. **What type of covering would you recommend for the patio shown in Fig. 11–29?**
3. **Design a covering for the patio shown in Fig. 11–29. Sketch a top view of your solution.**
4. **Choose an interesting pool shape and incorporate it in the patio design shown in Fig. 11–23.**
5. **Add a patio design to the floor-plan layout shown in Fig. 11–28.**
6. **Plan a patio for a house of your own design. Sketch the basic scheme and the facilities.**
7. **Define the following terms: *patio, loggia, breezeway, terrace, play patio, quiet patio, living patio, flagstone, redwood, concrete, patio deck, patio baffles.***

UNIT 12

Lanais

Lanai is the Hawaiian word for porch. However, the word lanai is now used to refer to a covered exterior passageway.

FUNCTION

Large lanais are often used as patios, although their main function is to provide shelter for the traffic accesses on the exterior of a building. Lanais are actually exterior hallways.

Lanais which are located parallel to exterior walls are usually created by extending the roof overhang to cover a traffic area, as shown in Fig. 12–1. Figure 12–2 shows a typical lanai plan which eliminates the need for more costly interior halls. Lanais are used extensively in commercial buildings, especially in warmer climates, as shown in Fig. 12–3.

LOCATION

In residence planning, a lanai can be used most effectively to connect opposite areas of a home. Lanais are commonly located between the

Fig. 12–1. A lanai created by a roof overhang.

garage and the kitchen, the patio and the kitchen or the living area, and the living area and the service area. U-shaped houses such as the one shown in Fig. 12–4 are especially suitable for using lanais because of the natural connection of the extremes of the U.

When lanais are carefully located they can also function as sheltered access from inside areas to outside facilities such as patios (Fig. 12–5) or pools (Fig. 12–6) or outdoor cooking areas, as shown in Fig. 12–7. A covered or partially covered patio is also considered a lanai when it doubles as a major access from one area

Western Wood Products Association

Fig. 12–3. Commercial use of a lanai.

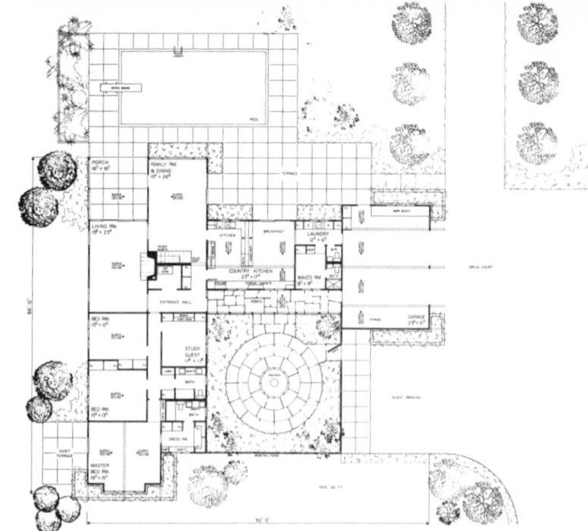

Fig. 12–2A. A typical lanai plan.

Fig. 12–2B. View of the lanai shown in A.

Home Planners, Inc.

Fig. 12–4. A lanai used in a U-shaped plan.

Fig. 12–5. A patio used as a lanai.

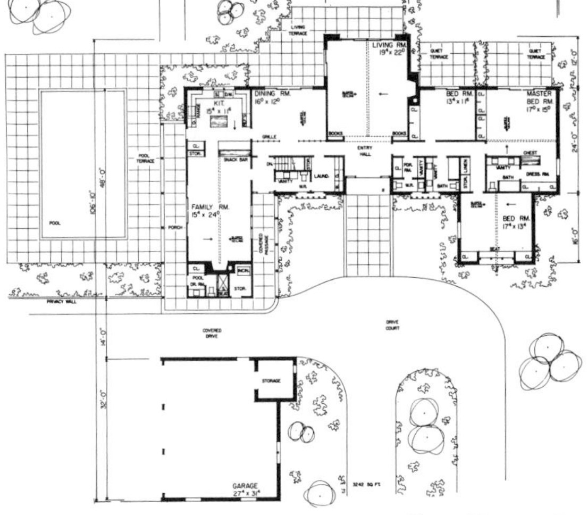

Home Planners, Inc.

Fig. 12–6. A lanai connecting the living areas and the pool.

California Redwood Association

Fig. 12–9. A semienclosed lanai.

Home Planners, Inc.

Fig. 12–7. An outdoor cooking area connected by a lanai.

Fig. 12–8. A large patio and overhang create a lanai.

Rendering by George Parenti for the Masonite Corp.

Fig. 12–10. A marquee is a type of lanai.

of a structure to another. The patio shown in Fig. 12–8 functions in this manner. A lanai can also be semienclosed, as shown in Fig. 12–9, and provide not only traffic access but also privacy and sun and wind shielding. When lanais are used to connect the building with the street, they actually function as marquees (Fig. 12–10).

Western Wood Products Association

Fig. 12–11. A lanai porch created with roof overhang.

DECOR

The lanai should be a consistent, integral part of the design of the structure. The lanai cover may be an extension of the roof overhang (Fig. 12–11) or may be supported by columns, as shown in Fig. 12–12. If glass is placed between the columns as shown in Fig. 12–13, the lanai becomes an interior hallway rather than an exterior one. This separation is sometimes the only difference between a lanai and an interior hall.

It is often desirable to design and locate the lanai to provide access from one end of an extremely long building to the other end, as shown in Fig. 12–14. The lines of this kind of lanai strengthen and reinforce the basic lines of the building. The columns supporting the roof overhang in Fig. 12–14 also provide a visual boundary to the lanai without obstructing the view from within.

If a lanai is to be utilized extensively at night, effective lighting must be provided. Light from within is used when drapes are open, but additional lighting fixtures are used when drapes are closed. This lanai is a balcony which connects opposite areas by extending around two sides of the house.

Bethlehem Steel Corp.

Fig. 12–12. A lanai supported by columns.

Nestle Alimentana

Fig. 12–13. An enclosed lanai functions as an interior hallway.

Fig. 12–14. A large commercial lanai.

Libbey-Owens-Ford Company

Julius Shulman

Fig. 12–15. A large residential lanai.

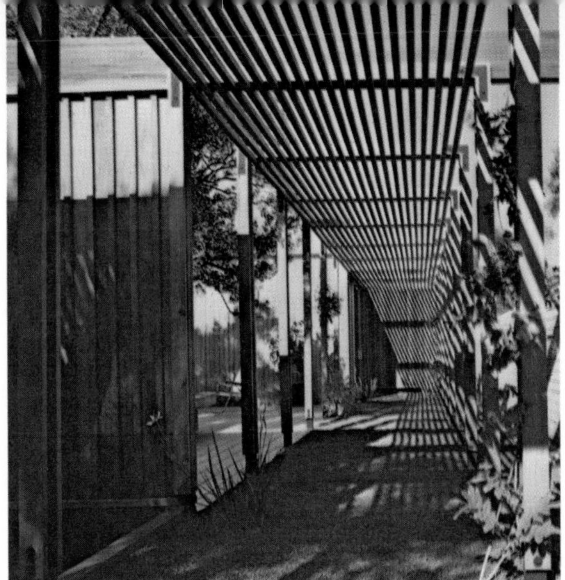

California Redwood Association

Fig. 12–16. A long lanai connecting several buildings.

SIZE AND SHAPE

Lanais may extend the full length of a building and may be designed for maximum traffic loads, as shown in Fig. 12–15. They may be as small as the area under a 2′ or 3′ (610 or 915 mm) roof overhang. However, a lanai at least 4′ (1220 mm) wide is desirable. The length and type of cover is limited only by the location of areas to be covered. For example, the lanai shown in Fig. 12–16 extends a very long distance between buildings.

PROBLEMS

1. **Draw the outline of a lanai you would plan for a home of your own design.**
2. **Add a lanai to the plan shown in Fig. 6–2.**
3. **Add a lanai to the plan shown in Fig. 6–10.**
4. **Resketch the plan shown in Fig. 6–4. Using dotted lines, sketch the outline of a lanai you would add to this plan.**
5. **Sketch a floor plan of your own home. Add a lanai to connect two of the areas, such as the sleeping and living areas.**
6. **Define the following terms: *lanai cover, roof overhang, exterior hallway.***

UNIT 13

Traffic Areas

When an architect plans a commercial structure such as the World Trade Center (Fig. 13–1), traffic volume and patterns must be considered for both vehicular and pedestrian traffic. Traffic both inside and outside the building must be considered. Traffic areas for employees, visitors, and deliveries into and out of the building must be allocated using a minimum amount of space. Special considerations such as the heliport on top of the U.S. Steel building (Fig. 13–2) must also be incorporated into the plan. Planning the traffic areas of a residence is not as complex because of the small number of people involved. Nevertheless, the same basic principle of efficient space allocation prevails. The traffic areas of the home provide passage from one room or area to another. The main traffic areas of a residence include the halls, entrance foyers, stairs, lanais, and areas of rooms that are part of the traffic pattern.

TRAFFIC PATTERNS

Traffic patterns of a residence should be carefully considered in the design of the room

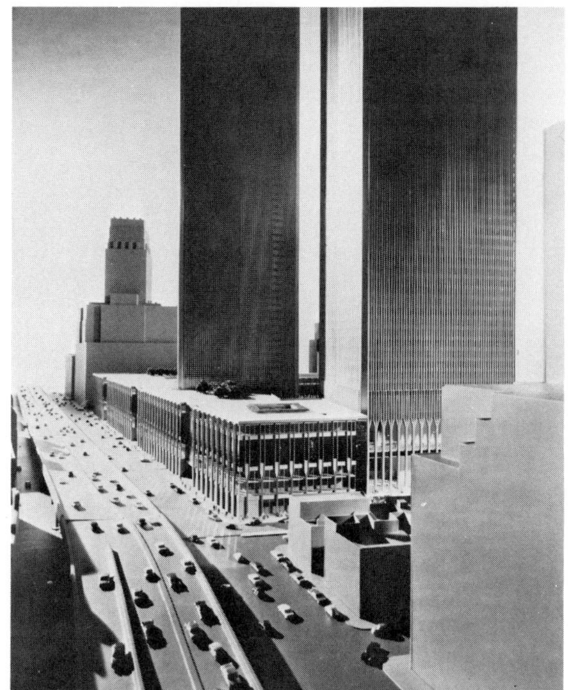

Port Authority of New York and New Jersey

Fig. 13–1. Commercial traffic patterns.

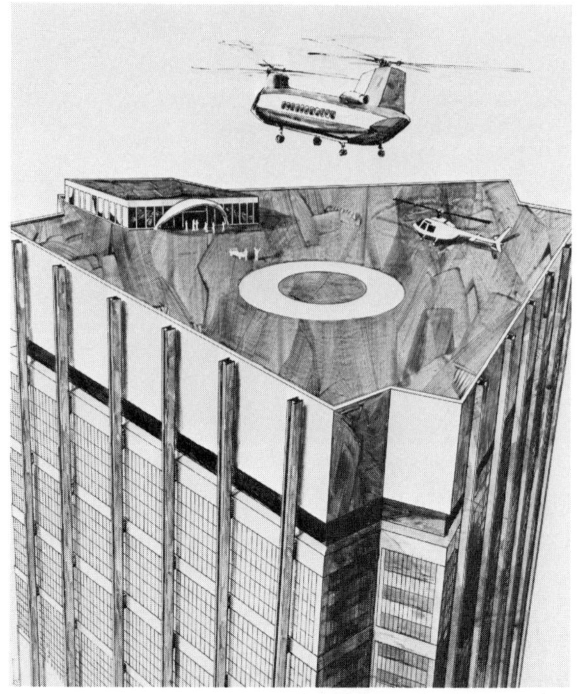

United States Steel Corporation

Fig. 13–2. Special traffic needs must be considered by the architect.

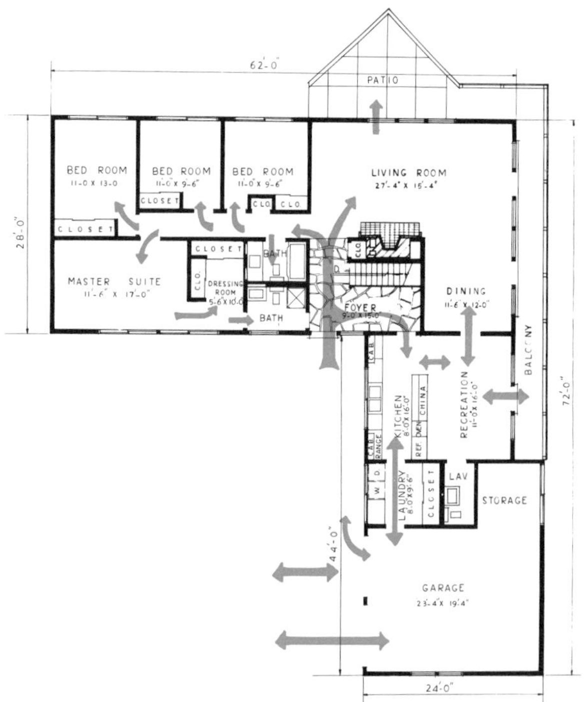

Home Planners, Inc.

Fig. 13–3. An efficient traffic pattern.

layout. A minimum amount of space should be devoted to traffic areas. Extremely long halls and corridors should be avoided. They are difficult to light and actually provide no living space. Traffic patterns that require passage through one room to get to another should also be avoided, especially in the sleeping area.

The traffic pattern shown in the plan in Fig. 13–3 is efficient and functional. It contains a minimum amount of wasted hall space without creating a boxed-in appearance. It provides access to each of the areas without passing through other areas. The arrows clearly show that the sleeping area, living area, and service area are accessible from the entrance without passage through other areas. In this plan the service entrance provides access to the kitchen from the carport and other parts of the service area.

One method of determining the effectiveness of the traffic pattern of a house is to imagine yourself moving through the house by placing your pencil on the floor plan and tracing your route through the house as you perform your daily routine. If you trace through a

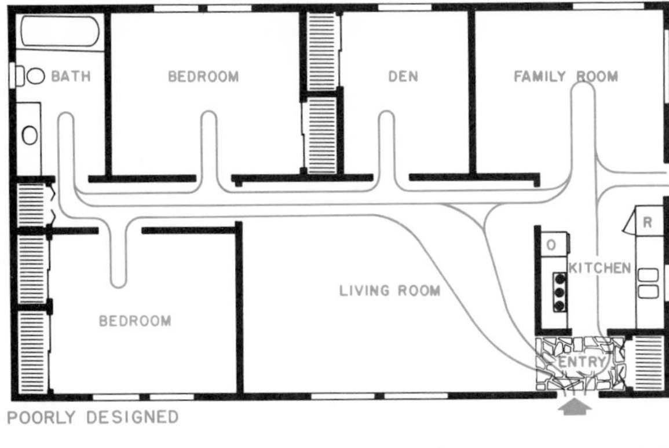

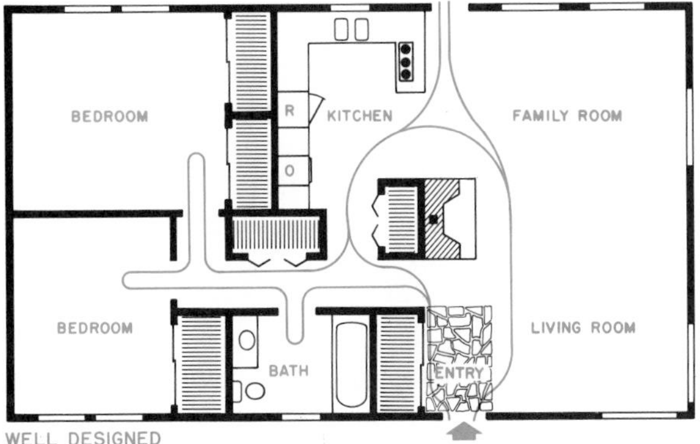

Fig. 13–4. The difference between a poorly designed and a well-designed traffic pattern.

Fig. 13–5. A traffic area with light and level variations.

whole day's activities, including those of other members of the household, you will be able to see graphically where the heaviest traffic occurs and whether the traffic areas have been planned effectively. Figure 13–4 shows the difference between a poorly designed traffic pattern and a well-designed traffic pattern.

HALLS

Halls are the highways and streets of the home. They provide a controlled path which connects the various areas of the house. Halls should be planned to keep to a minimum or eliminate the passage of traffic through rooms. Long, dark, tunnel-like halls should be avoided. Halls should be well lighted, light in color and texture, and planned with the decor of the whole house in mind. The hall shown in Fig. 13–5 is extremely long; however, it is broken by level, by open partitions, and by light variations.

One method of channeling hall traffic without the use of solid walls is with the use of dividers. Planters, half-walls, louvered walls, and even furniture can be used as dividers. Figure 13–6 shows the use of furniture components in dividing the living area from the hall. This arrangement enables both the hall and the living room to share ventilation, light, and heat.

Another method of designing halls and corridors as an integral part of the area design is with the use of movable partitions. The Japa-

United States Plywood Corporation

Fig. 13–6. The use of furniture components in separating traffic areas.

Fig. 13–7. The use of movable partitions to separate traffic areas.

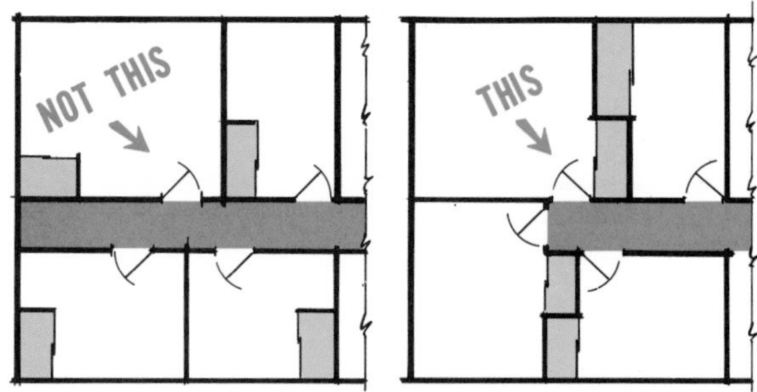

Fig. 13–8. Principles of efficient hall design.

nese scheme of placing these partitions between the living area and a hall is shown in Fig. 13-7. In some Japanese homes this hall actually becomes a lanai when the partition between the living area and the hall is closed and the outside wall is opened. Figure 13–8 shows some of the basic principles of efficient hall design.

STAIRS

Stairs are inclined hallways. They provide access from one level to another. Stairs may lead directly from one area to another without a change of direction, they may turn 90 degrees (90°) by means of a landing, or they may turn 180° by means of landings. Figure 13–9 shows four basic types of stairs and the amount of space utilized by each type.

With the use of newer, stronger building materials and new techniques, there is no longer any reason for enclosing stairs in walls that restrict light and ventilation (Fig. 13–10). Stairs can now be supported by many different devices. The stairs in Fig. 13–11 are center-supported and therefore do not need side walls or other supports. Even when vertical supports are necessary or desirable, completely closing in the wall is not mandatory. Figure 13–12 shows stairs supported by exposed steel rods which maintain the open plan without sacrificing support or safety. These stairs are supported by hanging one side of the tread from steel rods. Combining open-stair assemblies with windows provides the maximum amount of light, especially when the windows in the open area extend through several levels, as shown in Fig. 13–13.

Fig. 13–9. Basic types of stairs.

National Lumber Manufacturers Association

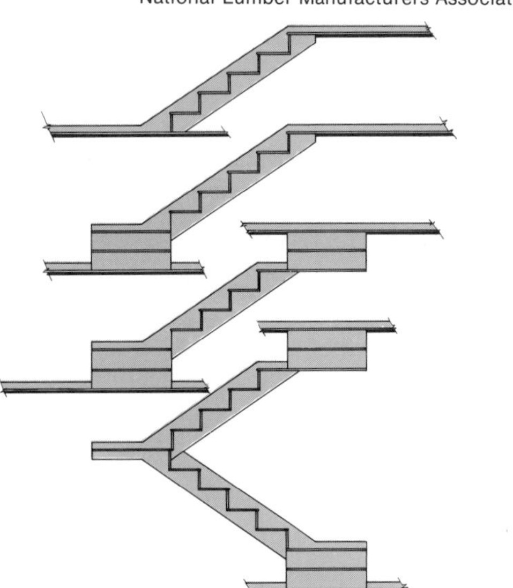

Fig. 13–10. An exposed stair system.

Armstrong Cork Company

Fig. 13–11. Center-supported stairs.

Armstrong Cork Company

Fig. 13–12. These stairs are hung from steel rods.

SPACE REQUIREMENTS

There are many variables to consider in designing stairs. The *tread* width, the *riser* width, the width of the stair opening, and the headroom all help to determine the total length of the stairwell.

The *tread* is the horizontal part of the stair, the part upon which you walk. The average width of the tread is 10″ (250 mm). The riser is the vertical part of the stair. The average riser height is 7¼″ (185 mm). Figure 13–14 shows the importance of correct tread and riser design.

The overall width of the stairs is the length or distance across the treads. A minimum of 3′ (915 mm) should be allowed for the total stair width. However, a width of 3′—6″ (1070 mm) or even 4′ (1220 mm) is preferred (Fig. 13–15).

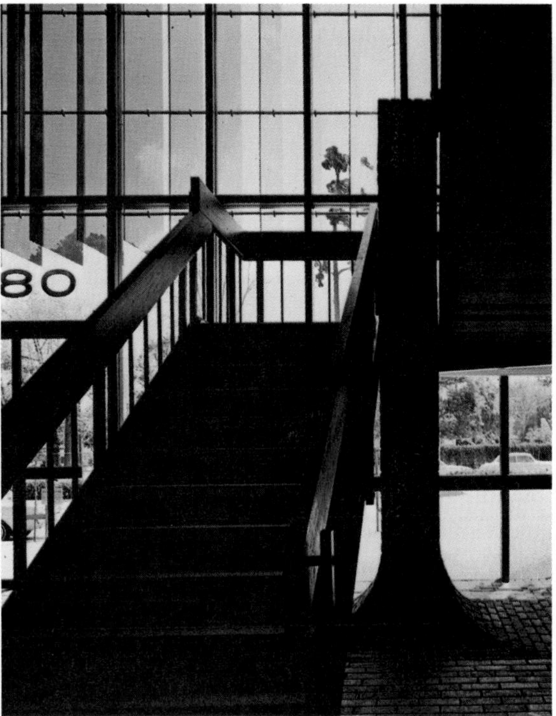

Rohm & Haas Company

Fig. 13–13. When possible, use natural light to illuminate stairwells.

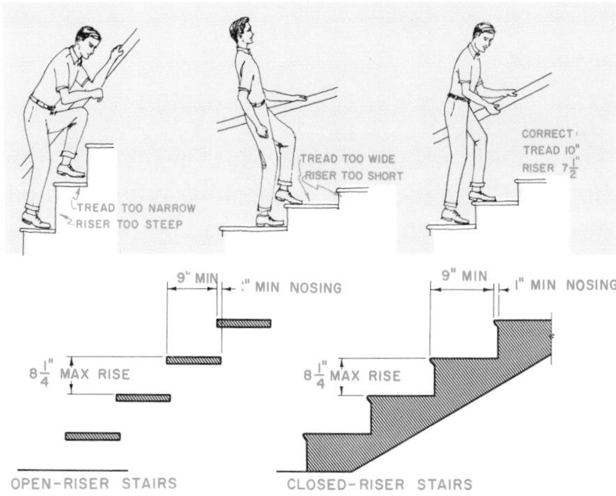

Fig. 13–14. Correct tread and riser design is important.

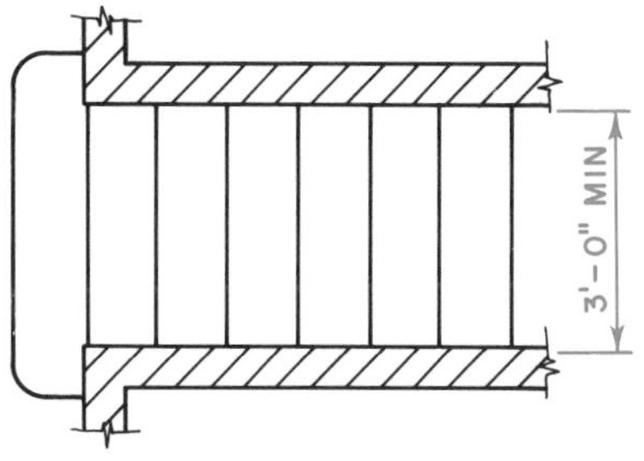

Fig. 13–15. Minimum width of stairs.

Fig. 13–16. Minimum headroom clearance.

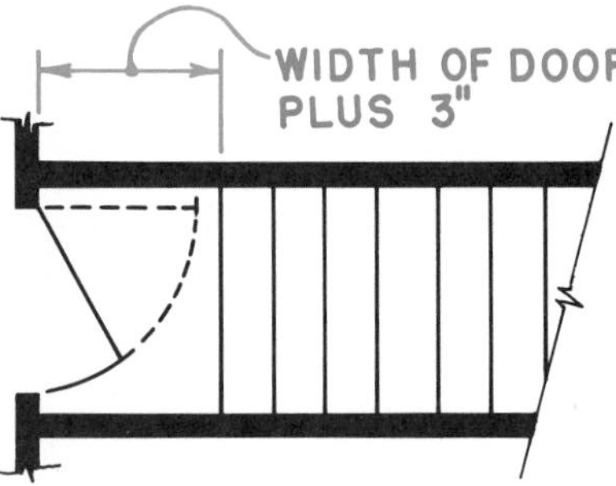

Fig. 13–17. Landing dimensions are critical.

Headroom is the vertical distance between the top of each tread and the top of the stairwell ceiling. A minimum headroom distance of 6′—6″ (1.9 m) should be allowed. However, distances of 7′ (2.1 m) are more desirable (Fig. 13–16).

Landing dimensions are also critical. Figure 13–17 shows some allowances for landings when used to turn a stairway 90° and 180°. More clearance must be allowed where a door opens on a landing.

PROBLEMS

1. **Sketch the floor plan shown in Fig. 11–1. Redesign the traffic pattern to eliminate passing directly through the living room to get to the sleeping area.**
2. **Sketch the plan shown in Fig. 11–2. Move the entrance to another location to provide more central access to each of the areas without passing through the others.**
3. **Resketch the plan shown in Fig. 11–23 in order to shorten the long hall in the bedroom area.**
4. **Sketch the floor plan of your own home. Redesign the entrance and halls to make this pattern more efficient.**
5. **Define the following terms: *traffic pattern, halls, corridors, main traffic areas, movable partitions, center-supported stairs, tread, riser, minimum stair width, headroom, landing.***

UNIT 14

Entrances

Entrances are divided into several different types: the main entrance, the service entrance, and the special-purpose entrance. The entrance is composed of an outside waiting area (porch, marquee, lanai), a separation (door), and an inside waiting area (foyer, entrance hall).

FUNCTION

Entrances provide for and control the flow of traffic into and out of a building. Different types of entrances have somewhat different functions.

Main Entrance

The main entrance provides access to the house, through which guests are welcomed and from which all major traffic patterns radiate. The main entrance should be readily identifiable by a stranger. It should provide shelter to anyone awaiting entrance. The entrance of the house shown in Fig. 14–1 has two walkways. The one on the right leads to the street; the one on the left leads to the driveway and garage.

Some provision should be made in the main-entrance wall for the viewing of callers from the inside. This can be accomplished

California Redwood Association

Fig. 14–1. A main entrance with a walk leading to the street and to the driveway.

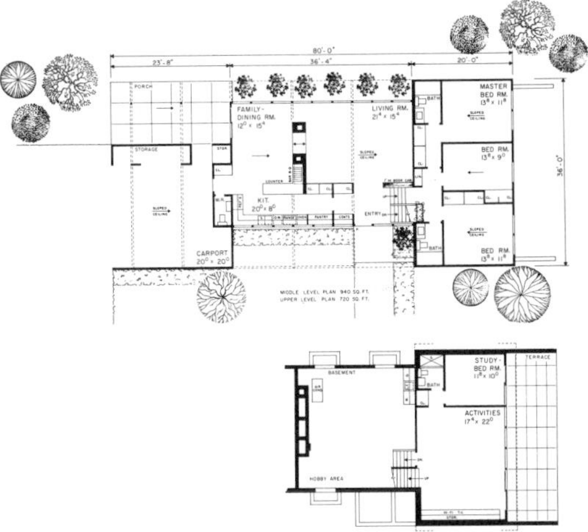

Home Planners, Inc.

Fig. 14–2. Side windows provide a view of the entrance from the inside.

through the use of side panels, lights (panes) in the door, or windows (Fig. 14–2) which face the side of the entrance.

The main entrance should be planned to create a desirable first impression (Fig. 14–3). A direct view of other areas of the house from the foyer should be baffled but not sealed off. This result is often accomplished by placing the access to the other rooms at the rear or to one side of the entrance foyer. Also, a direct view of exterior parking areas should be baffled from view as shown in Fig. 14–4.

The entrance foyer should include a closet for the storage of outside clothing and bad-weather gear. This foyer closet should have a capacity which will accommodate both family and guests. The foyer closet shown in Fig. 14–5 is located at a convenient distance from the entrance door.

Service Entrance

The service entrance provides access to the house through which supplies can be delivered to the service areas without going through other parts of the house. It should also provide access to parts of the service area (garage, laundry, workshop) for which the main entrance is inappropriate and inconvenient.

Fig. 14–3. A decorative support used in an entrance foyer.

Western Wood Products Association

Western Wood Products Association

Fig. 14–4. Undesirable areas (parking) should be baffled visually from the entrance.

Fig. 14–5. The foyer should include storage facilities.

Special-Purpose Entrances

Special-purpose entrances and exits do not provide for outside traffic. Instead they provide for movement from the inside living area of the house to the outside living areas. A sliding door from the living area to the patio is a special-purpose entrance. It is not an entrance through which street, drive, or sidewalk traffic would have access. Figure 14–6 shows the difference between special-purpose entrances, main entrance, and service entrances.

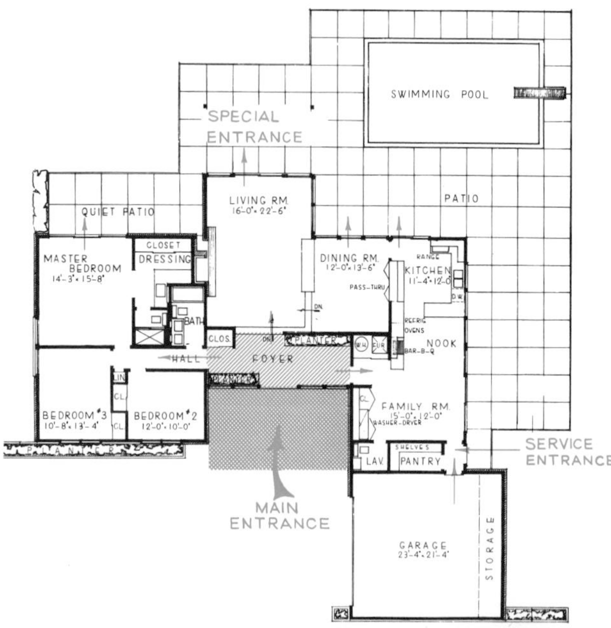

Scholz Homes, Inc.

Fig. 14–6. The basic types of entrances.

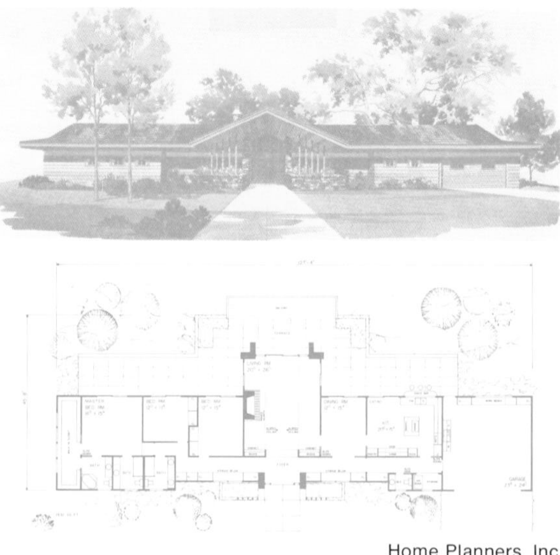

Home Planners, Inc.

Fig. 14–7. The main entrance should be centrally located.

PPG Industries, Inc.

Fig. 14–8. The entrance adjacent to a quiet patio.

Western Wood Products Association

Fig. 14–9. A first impression is an important feature of an entrance.

LOCATION

The main entrance should be centrally located to provide easy access to each area. It should be conveniently accessible from driveways, sidewalks, or street (Fig. 14–7).

The service entrance should be located close to the drive and garage. It should be placed near the kitchen or food-storage areas.

Special-purpose entrances and exits are often located between the bedroom and the quiet patio, between the living room and the living patio (Fig. 14–8), and between the dining room or kitchen and the dining patio. Figure 14–6 shows the functional placement of all these entrances.

DECOR

The entrance should create a desirable first impression. It should be easily identifiable yet an integral part of the architectural style (Fig. 14–9).

Consistency of Style

The total design of the entrance should be consistent with the overall design of the house. The design of the door, the side panel, and the deck and cover should be directly related to the lines of the house. The lines of the entrances shown at the left in Fig. 14–10 are designed as integral parts of the exterior. The lines of the entrance shown at the right in Fig. 14–10 are unrelated to the major building lines of the structure.

The entrance shown in Fig. 14–11A, B, and C is a good example of entrance design involving all the principles of location, style consistency, lighting utilization, and size and shape effectiveness. Figure 14–11A shows a

Fig. 14–10. Left—an entrance with lines related to the lines of the structure. Right—an entrance with lines unrelated to the lines of the structure.

Scholz Homes, Inc.

Fig. 14–11A. A close view of related entrance lines (upper left).
Fig. 14–11B. Entrance lines related to the remainder of the home (lower).
Fig. 14–11C. The foyer of the entrance shown in A and B is consistent in design with the outside (upper right).

close view of the entrance, Fig. 14–11B shows the location of the entrance in reference to the entire front of the house, and Fig. 14–11C shows an interior view of the entrance foyer.

Open Planning

The view from the main entrance to the living area should be baffled without creating a boxed-in appearance. The foyer should not appear as a dead end. The extensive use of glass, effective lighting, and carefully placed baffle walls can create an open and inviting impression. This is accomplished in the entrance shown in Fig. 14–12 by the use of window walls, double doors, roof-overhang extension, and baffle walls which extend the length of the foyer. Open planning between the entrance foyer and the living areas can also be accomplished by the use of louvered walls or planter walls. These provide a break in the line of sight but not a complete separation. Sinking or elevating the foyer or entrance approach as shown in Fig. 14–13 also provides the desired separation without isolation.

Flooring

The outside portion of the entrance should be weather-resistant stone, brick, or concrete. If a

American-Saint Gobain Corp.

Fig. 14–12. A maximum-sized open-plan entrance and foyer.

PPG Industries, Inc.

Fig. 14–13. An elevated entrance.

porch is used outside the entrance, a wood deck will suffice. The foyer deck should be easily maintained and be resistant to mud, water, and dirt brought in from the outside. Asphalt, vinyl or rubber tile, stone, flagstone, marble, and terrazzo are most frequently used for the foyer deck. The use of a different material in the foyer area helps to define the area when no other separation exists.

Foyer Walls

Paneling, masonry, planters, murals, and glass are used extensively for entrance foyer walls. The walls of the exterior portion of the entrance should be consistent with the other materials used on the exterior of the house.

Lighting

An entrance must be designed to function day and night. General lighting, spot lighting, and all-night lighting (Fig. 14–14) are effective for this purpose. Lighting can be used to accent distinguishing features or to illuminate the pattern of a wall, which actually provides more light by reflection and helps to identify and accentuate the entrance at night.

Fig. 14–14. Effective use of outside entrance lighting.

PPG Industries, Inc.

Western Wood Products Association

Fig. 14–15. Natural lighting used in a foyer.

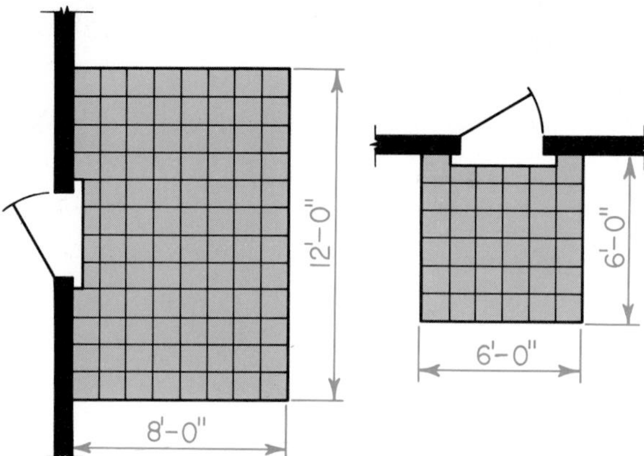

Fig. 14–16. The entrance area on the left has optimum dimensions. The entrance on the right has minimum dimensions.

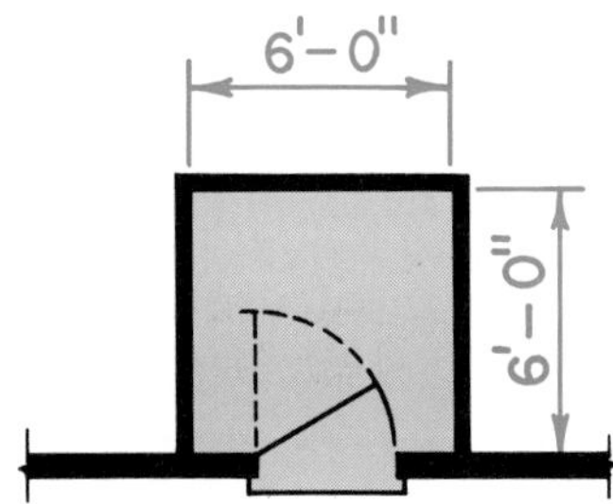

Fig. 14–17. A minimum-sized foyer.

Natural lighting as shown in Fig. 14–15 is also effective in lighting entrance areas during daylight hours.

SIZE AND SHAPE

The size and shape of the areas inside and outside the entrance depend on the budget and the type of plan. Foyers are not bounded by solid walls in the open plan.

The Outside

The outside, covered portion of the entrance should be large enough to shelter several people at one time. Sufficient space should be allowed on all sides, exclusive of the amount of space needed to open storm doors which open to the outside. Outside shelter areas range in size from the minimum arrangement shown at the right in Fig. 14–16 to the more generous size shown at the left in Fig. 14–16.

The Inside

The inside of the entrance foyer should be sufficiently large to allow several people to enter at the same time, remove their coats, and store them in the closet. A 6′ × 6′ (1.8 × 1.8 m) foyer, as shown in Fig. 14–17 is considered minimum for this function. A foyer 8′ × 10′ (2.4 × 3.0 m) is average, but a more desirable size is 8′ × 15′ (2.4 × 4.6 m), as shown in Fig. 14–18.

Figure 14–18 also shows a foyer arrangement which allows for the swing of the door, something which must be taken into consideration in determining the size of the foyer. If the foyer is too shallow, passage will be blocked when the door is open, and only one person may enter at a time. Figure 14–11C shows a foyer that is near the optimum size. It is not extremely deep, but it does extend a great distance on either side. This allows sufficient traffic to pass. It also allows sufficient movement around the doors when they are opened.

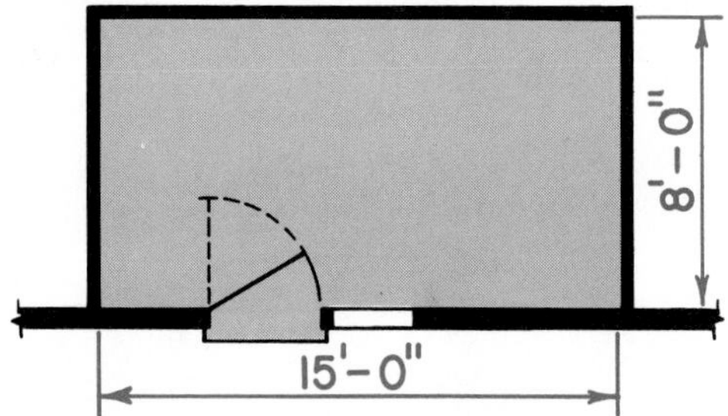

Fig. 14–18. An optimum-sized foyer.

Foyers are normally rectangular because they lead to several areas of the home. They do not need much depth in any one direction. The ideal entry includes:

1. Adequate room to handle traffic flow
2. Access to all three areas of a home
3. A closet
4. Bath access for guests
5. Consistent decor
6. Outside weather protection
7. Effective lighting day and night

PROBLEMS

1. Redesign the entrance shown in Fig. 14–11B, adding sufficient shelter space that will be consistent with the main lines of the house.

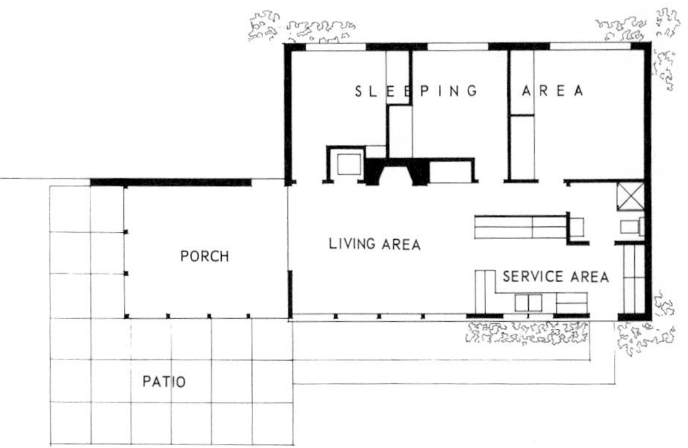

Fig. 14–19. Add a foyer to this living area.

2. List the characteristics of foyer design in the foyer shown in Fig. 6–2.

3. Sketch the foyer layout for the plan shown in Fig. 14–18. Indicate the position of the foyer closet.

4. Plan a foyer for the living area shown in Fig. 14–19. Label the materials you select for the outside deck, overhang, access walk, foyer floor, and foyer walls.

5. Define the following terms: ***main entrance, service entrance, foyer, special-purpose entrances, open planning.***

UNIT 15

The Den

The den or study can be designed for many different purposes, depending on the living habits of its occupants.

FUNCTION

The den may function basically as a reading room, writing room, hobby room, or professional office. For the teacher, writer, or clergyman, the study may be basically a reading room, such as the one shown in Fig. 15–1. For the engineer, architect, draftsman, or artist, the den or study may function primarily as a studio and may include such facilities as those shown in the study in Fig. 15–2.

The den or study often doubles as a guest room. Quite often the children's bedroom must provide facilities normally included in a study such as desk, bookcase, and typewriter (Fig. 15–3).

The den is often considered part of the sleeping area since it may require placement in a quiet part of the house. It also may function primarily in the living area, especially if the study is used as a professional office by a physi-

Armstrong Cork Company

Fig. 15-1. This study is basically a reading room.

Louis Rens Photo; Interiors Magazine

Fig. 15-2. This study was planned for drawing and designing activities.

Armstrong Cork Company

Fig. 15-3. This study doubles as a bedroom.

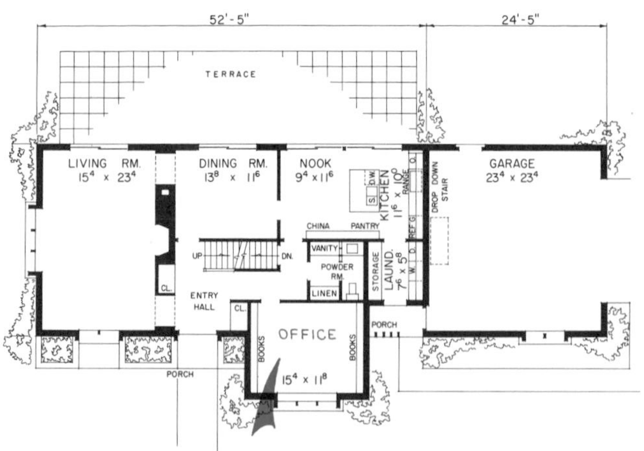

Home Planners, Inc.

Fig. 15-4. A study used as a professional office.

cian or an insurance agent whose clients call at home. Figure 15–4 shows a professional study or office located near the main entrance hall and accessible from the main entrance and also from a side entrance directly from the garage.

LOCATION

If a study doubles as an office, it should be located in an accessible area. However, if it is to serve a private use, then it can be located in the basement or attic, utilizing otherwise wasted space.

DECOR AND LIGHTING

The decor of the study should reflect the main activity and should allow for well-diffused general lighting and glareproof local lighting. Notice the open effect achieved in Fig. 15-5 by the row of windows above eye level. They admit the maximum amount of light without exposing distracting eye-level images from the outside.

As in the recreation room, a central theme may be used in the decoration of the study. The people who used the study shown in Fig.

Bethlehem Steel Corp.

Fig. 15–5. High windows admit light but block the view.

Fig. 15–6. A quiet restful study.

15–6 obviously enjoyed reading. Notice how the architect has created an inviting atmosphere for reading by providing the warmth of a fireplace, adequate bookshelf space, and the natural light from a skylight.

SIZE AND SHAPE

The size and shape of the den, study, or office will vary greatly with its function. Size and shape will depend on whether one or two persons expect to use the room privately or whether it should provide a meeting place for business clients. Studies range in size from just enough space for a desk and chair in a small corner, as shown in Fig. 15–7, to a large amount of space with a diversity of furnishings, such as the study shown in Fig. 5–8. This illustration shows a study with the maximum number of furnishings, including a desk and chair, lounge chair, studio couch, file cabinets, bookcases, storage space, and coffee table.

Armstrong Cork Company

Fig. 15–7. A small study corner.

PROBLEMS

1. **Sketch a plan for a den in a home of your own design.**
2. **Sketch a plan for a den for your own home.**
3. **Sketch a plan for a den to accommodate the following facilities: desk, chair, bookcases, drafting table, lounge.**
4. **Sketch a plan for a den which will double as a guest bedroom.**
5. **Define the following terms: *den, study, living area, sleeping area, guest room, professional office, central theme.***

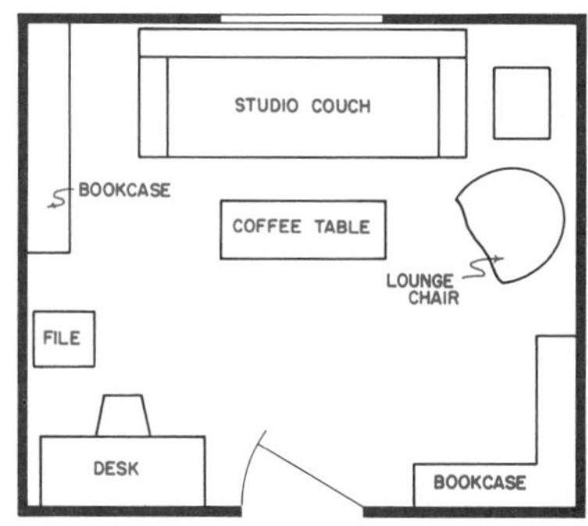

Fig. 15–8. An optimum-sized study.

SECTION 3

Service Area

The service area includes the kitchen, laundry, garage, workshops, storage centers, and utility room. Since a great number of different activities take place in the service area, it should be designed for the greatest efficiency. The service area includes facilities for the maintenance and servicing of the other areas of the home. The functioning of the living and the sleeping areas is greatly dependent upon the efficiency of the service area.

Frigidaire Division, General Motors Corporation

UNIT 16

The Kitchen

A well-planned kitchen is efficient, attractive, and easy to maintain. To design an efficient kitchen, the designer must consider the function, basic shape, decor, size, and location of equipment (Fig. 16–1).

FUNCTION

The preparation of food is the basic function of the kitchen. However, the kitchen may also be used as a dining area and as a laundry.

Fig. 16–1. A functional, well-planned kitchen.

Hotpoint Division, General Electric Company

DESIGNING FOR EFFICIENCY

The proper placement of appliances, storage cabinets, and furniture is important in planning efficient kitchens. Locating appliances in an efficient pattern eliminates much wasted motion (Fig. 16–2). An efficient kitchen is divided into three areas: the storage and mixing center, the cleaning and preparation center, and the cooking center.

Fig. 16–2. A well-planned kitchen should be efficient.

Hotpoint Division, General Electric Company

Storage and Mixing Center

The refrigerator is the major appliance in the storage and mixing center. The refrigerator may be free-standing, built-in, or suspended from a wall. The storage and mixing center also includes cabinets for the storage of utensils and ingredients used in cooking and baking, as well as a counter-top work area.

Preparation and Cleaning Center

The sink is the major appliance in the preparation and cleaning center. Sinks are available in one- and two-bowl models with a variety of cabinet arrangements and counter-top and drainboard areas. The preparation and cleaning center may also include a waste-disposal unit, an automatic dishwasher, a waste compactor (Fig. 16–3), and cabinets for storing brushes, towels, and cleaning supplies.

Cooking Center

The range and oven are the major appliances in the cooking center. The range and oven may be combined into one appliance, or the burners may be installed in the counter top and the oven built into the wall. The cooking center should also include counter-top work space, as well as storage space for minor appliances and cooking utensils that will be used in the area. The cooking center must have an adequate supply of electrical outlets for the many minor appliances used in cooking.

Figure 16–4 shows the size requirements for the storage or installation of many minor appliances that may be located in the various centers.

Fig. 16–3. A waste compactor.

Whirlpool Corporation

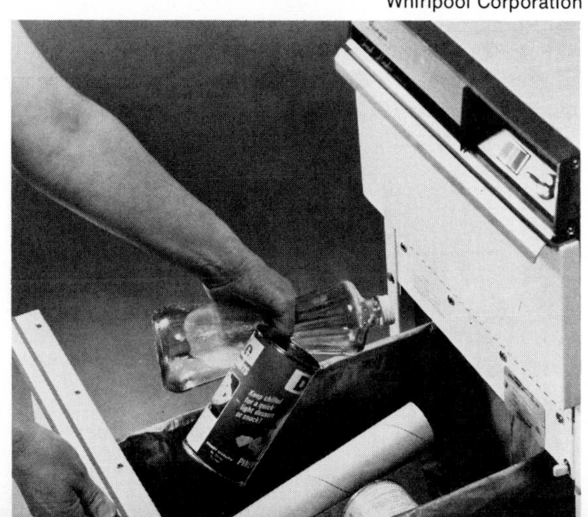

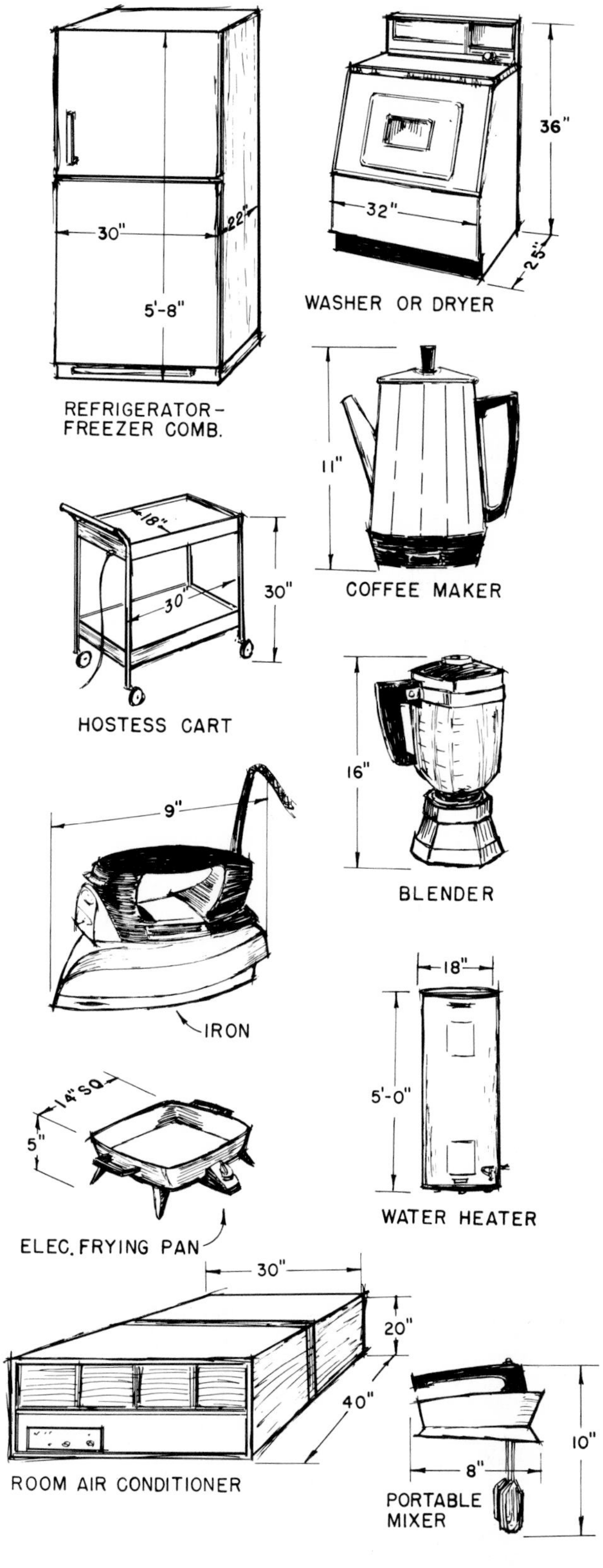

Fig. 16–4. Sizes of common appliances.

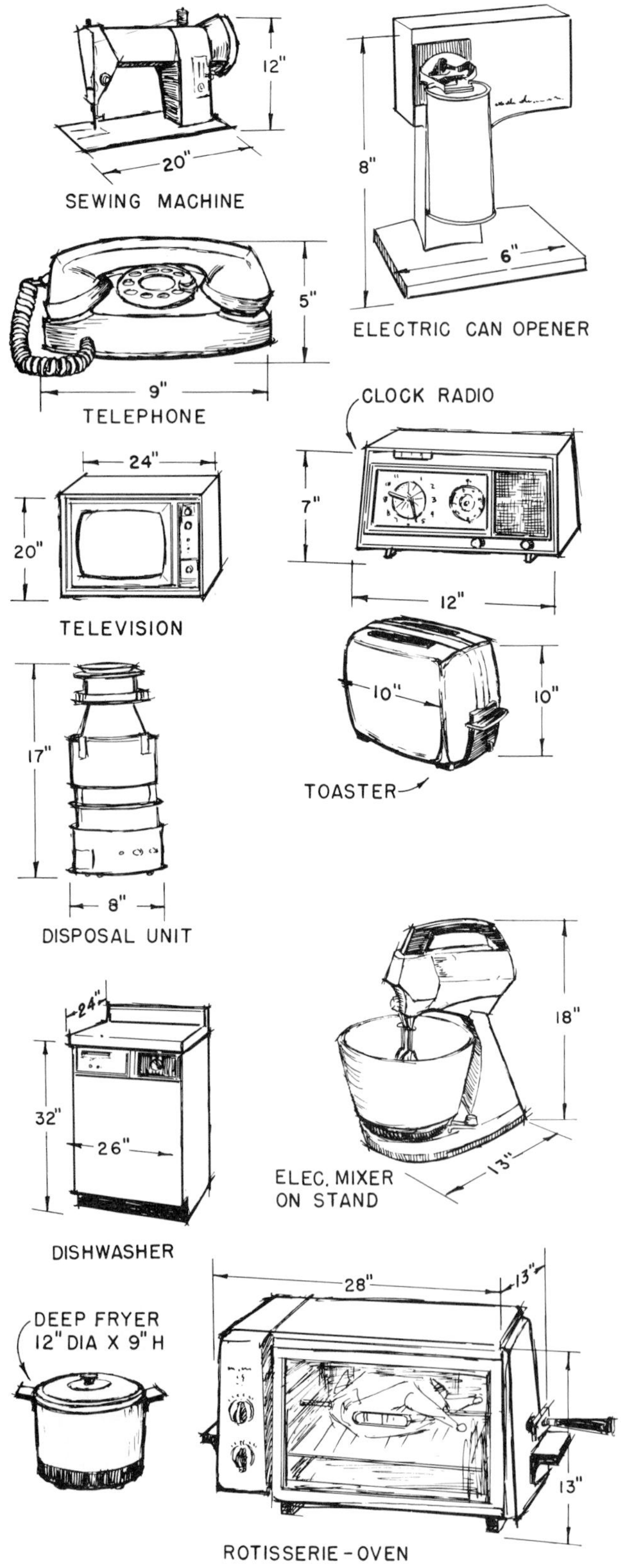

SEWING MACHINE 12" 20"
ELECTRIC CAN OPENER 8" 6"
TELEPHONE 5" 9"
CLOCK RADIO 7" 12"
TELEVISION 24" 20"
TOASTER 10" 10"
DISPOSAL UNIT 17" 8"
ELEC. MIXER ON STAND 18" 13"
DISHWASHER 24" 32" 26"
DEEP FRYER 12" DIA X 9" H
ROTISSERIE - OVEN 28" 13" 13"

Fig. 16–4 (Continued). Appliance sizes.

Frigidaire Division, General Motors Corporation

Fig. 16–5. The length of the work triangle should be between 12 feet (3.7 m) and 22 feet (6.7 m).

Work Triangle
If you draw a line connecting the three centers of the kitchen, a triangle is formed (Fig. 16–5). This is called the *work triangle.* The perimeter of an efficient kitchen work triangle should be between 12′ and 22′ (3.7 and 6.7 m).

BASIC SHAPES

The position of the three areas on the work triangle may vary greatly. However, the most efficient arrangements usually fall into the following categories.

U-Shaped Kitchen
The U-shaped kitchen, as shown in Fig. 16–6, is a very efficient arrangement. The sink is located at the bottom of the U, and the range and the refrigerator are at the opposite ends. In this

Hotpoint Division, General Electric Company

Fig. 16–6. A U-shaped kitchen.

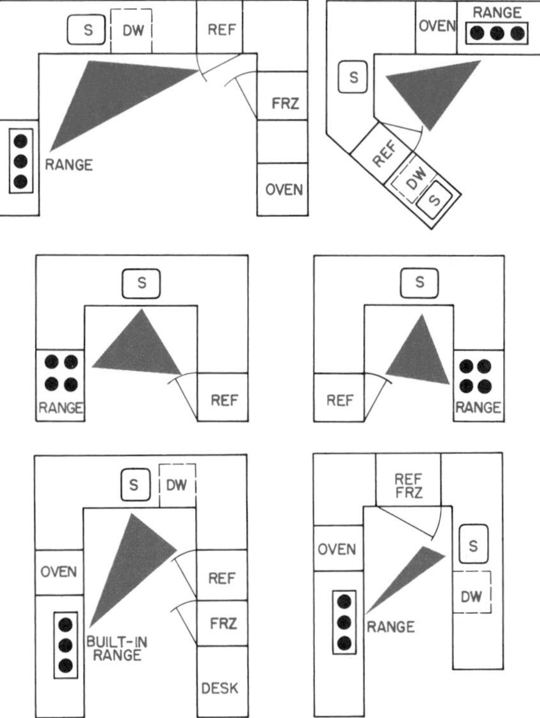

Fig. 16–7. Six arrangements for a U-shaped kitchen.

Fig. 16–9. Four arrangements for a peninsula kitchen.

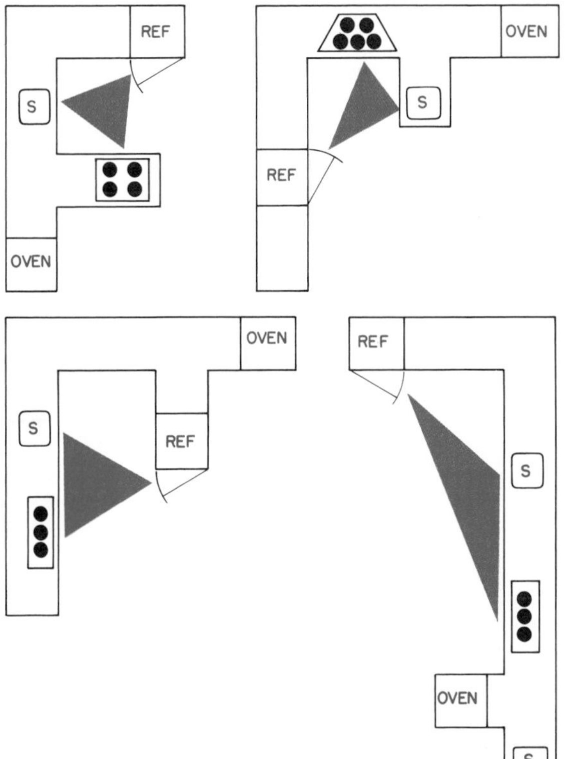

Formica Corporation

Fig. 16–8. A peninsula kitchen.

arrangement, traffic passing through the kitchen is completely separated from the work triangle. The open space in the U between the sides may be 4′ or 5′ (1.2 or 1.5 m). This arrangement produces a very efficient but small kitchen. Figure 16–7 shows various U-shaped-kitchen layouts and the resulting work triangles.

Peninsula Kitchen

The peninsula kitchen (Fig. 16–8) is similar to the U kitchen. However, one end of the U is not enclosed with a wall. The cooking center is often located in this peninsula, and the peninsula is often used to join the kitchen to the dining or family room. Figure 16–9 shows various arrangements of peninsula kitchens and the resulting work triangles.

L-shaped Kitchen

The L-shaped kitchen (Fig. 16–10) has continuous counters and appliances and equipment on two adjoining walls. The work triangle is not in

Fig. 16–10. L-shaped kitchens permit a large area of open floor space.

Superior Kitchens, Inc.

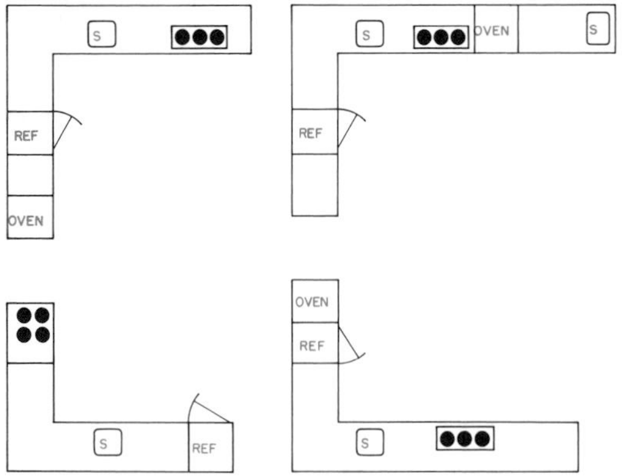

Fig. 16–11. Four arrangements for an L-shaped kitchen.

the traffic pattern. The remaining space is often used for other kitchen facilities, such as dining or laundry facilities. If the walls of an L-shaped kitchen are too long, the compact efficiency of the kitchen is destroyed. Figure 16–11 shows several L-shaped kitchens and the work triangles that result from these arrangements.

Corridor Kitchen

The two-wall corridor kitchens shown in Fig. 16–12 are very efficient arrangements for long, narrow rooms. A corridor kitchen is unsatisfactory, however, if considerable traffic passes through the work triangle. A corridor kitchen produces one of the most efficient work triangles of all the arrangements.

General Electric Company

Fig. 16–13. A one-wall kitchen.

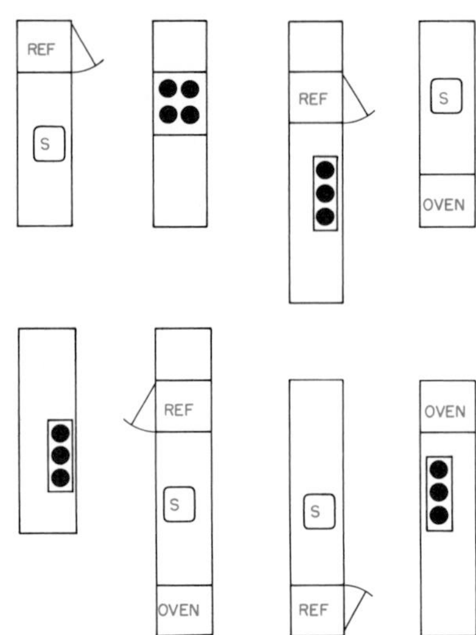

Fig. 16–12. Four arrangements for a corridor kitchen.

One-Wall Kitchen

A one-wall kitchen is an excellent plan for small apartments, cabins, or houses in which little space is available. The work centers are located in one line and produce a very efficient arrangement (Fig. 16–13). However, in planning the one-wall kitchen, the designer must be careful to avoid having the wall too long and must provide adequate storage facilities. Figure 16–14 shows several one-wall-kitchen arrangements.

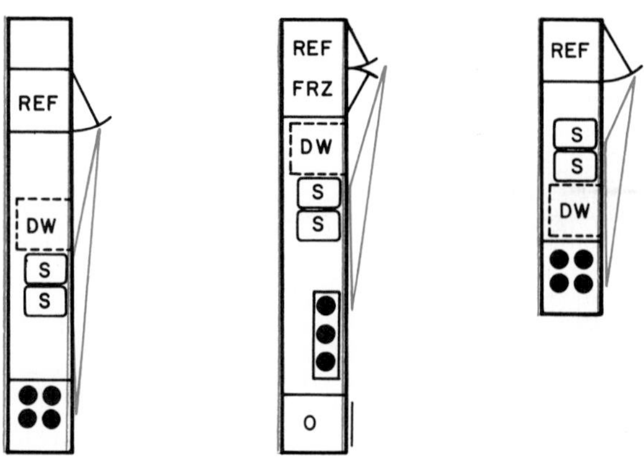

Fig. 16–14. Three arrangements for a one-wall kitchen.

Frigidaire Division, General Motors Corporation

Fig. 16–15. A sink island kitchen.

Island Kitchen

The island, which serves as a separator for the different parts of the kitchen, usually has a range top or sink, or both, and is accessible on all sides. Other facilities that are sometimes located in the island are the mixing center, work table, buffet counter, extra sink (Fig. 16–15), and snack center. See Fig. 16–16. Figure 16–17 shows an example of an island with a range and dining facilities.

Family Kitchen

The family kitchen is an open kitchen using any of the basic plans. Its function is to provide a meeting place for the entire family in addition to providing for the normal kitchen functions. Family kitchens are normally divided into two sections. One section is for food preparation, which includes the three work centers; the other section includes a dining area and family-room facilities, as shown in Fig. 16–18.

Family kitchens must be rather large to accommodate these facilities. An average size for a family kitchen is 15 feet (4.6 m) square. Figure 16–19 shows several possible arrangements for family kitchens.

Southern California Gas Company

Fig. 16–17. A range island kitchen.

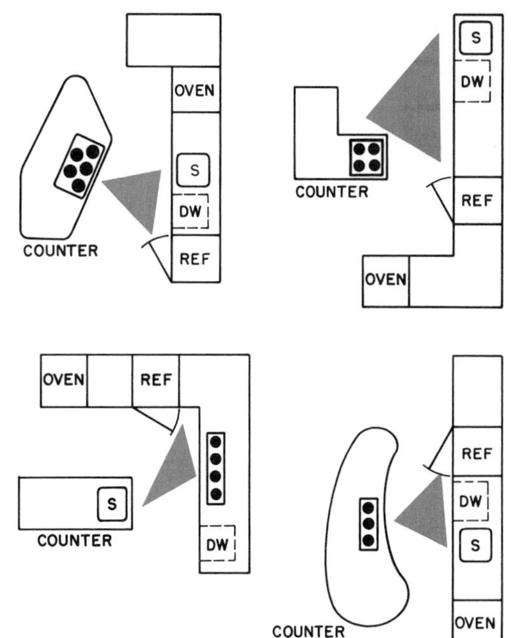

Fig. 16–16. Four island-kitchen arrangements.

Frigidaire Division, General Motors Corporation

Fig. 16–18. This family kitchen is designed for a variety of activities.

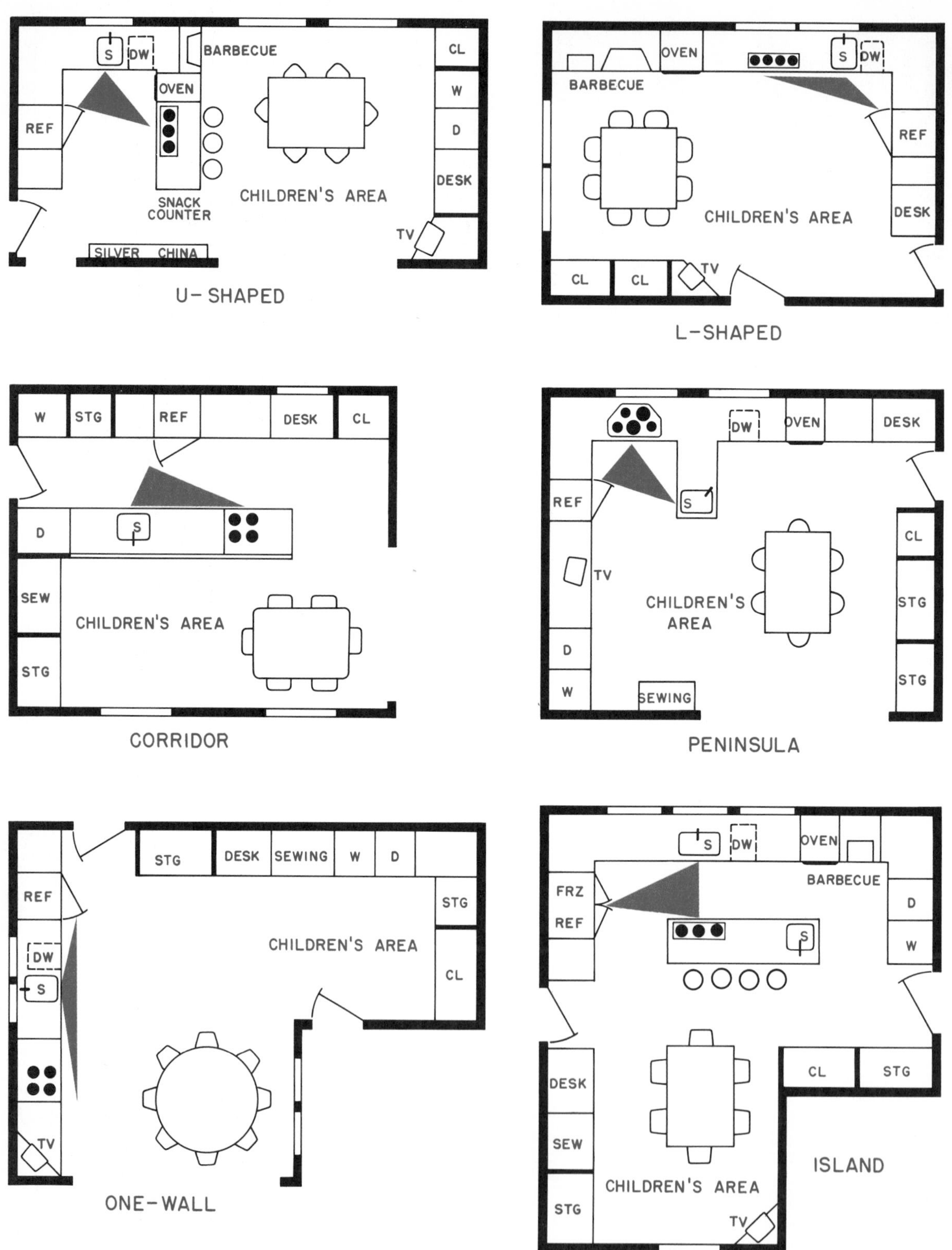

Fig. 16–19. Six family-kitchen plans.

Consoweld Corporation

Fig. 16–20. A colonial kitchen decor.

Consoweld Corporation

Fig. 16–21. A modern kitchen decor.

DECOR

Even though kitchen appliances are of contemporary design, some homemakers prefer to decorate kitchens with a period or colonial motif. The design of the cabinets, floors, walls, and accessory furniture must therefore be accented to give the desired effect. Compare the colonial kitchen shown in Fig. 16–20 with the modern kitchen shown in Fig. 16–21. You will notice that it is somewhat easier to design the lines of the modern kitchen in harmony with the lines of the major appliances. However, front panels can be added to some appliances to make them conform to the style and color scheme of the kitchen. The kitchen shown in Fig. 16–20 is a colonial version of the kitchen shown in Fig. 16–21.

Regardless of the style, kitchen walls, floors, counter tops, and cabinets should require a minimum amount of maintenance. Materials that are relatively maintenance-free include stainless steel, stain-resistant plastic, ceramic tile, washable wall coverings, washable paint, asphalt vinyl tile, and laminated plastic counter tops.

LOCATION

Since the kitchen is the core of the service area, it should be located near the service entrance and near the waste-disposal area. The children's play area should also be visible from the kitchen, and the kitchen must be adjacent to the dining area and outdoor eating areas.

KITCHEN PLANNING GUIDES

The following guides for kitchen planning provide a review of the more important factors to consider in designing efficient and functional kitchens:

1. The traffic lane is clear of the work triangle.
2. The work areas include all necessary appliances and facilities.
3. The kitchen is located adjacent to the dining area.
4. The kitchen is located near the children's play area.
5. The view from the kitchen is cheerful and pleasant.
6. The centers include (a) the storage center, (b) the preparation and cleaning center, and (c) the cooking center.
7. The work triangle measures less than 22′ (6.7 m).
8. Electrical outlets are provided for each work center.
9. Adequate storage facilities are available in each work center (Fig. 16–22).
10. Shadowless and glareless light is provided and is concentrated on each work center.
11. Adequate counter space is provided for meal preparation.
12. Ventilation is adequate.
13. The oven and range are separated from the refrigerator by at least one cabinet.
14. Doors on appliances swing away from the work-counter area (Fig. 16–23).
15. Lapboard heights are 26″ (660 mm) (Fig. 16–24).

Frigidaire Division, General Motors Corporation

Fig. 16–22. A kitchen designed with adequate storage.

16. Working heights for counters are 36″ (915 mm) (Fig. 16–25).
17. Working heights for tables are 30″ (760 mm) (Fig. 16–24).
18. The combination of base cabinets, wall cabinets, and appliances provides a consistent standard unit without gaps or awkward depressions or extensions.

DRAWING KITCHENS

In planning and drawing kitchen floor plans, use template planning techniques and procedures as outlined in Unit 31. However, once basic dimensions are established or if room di-

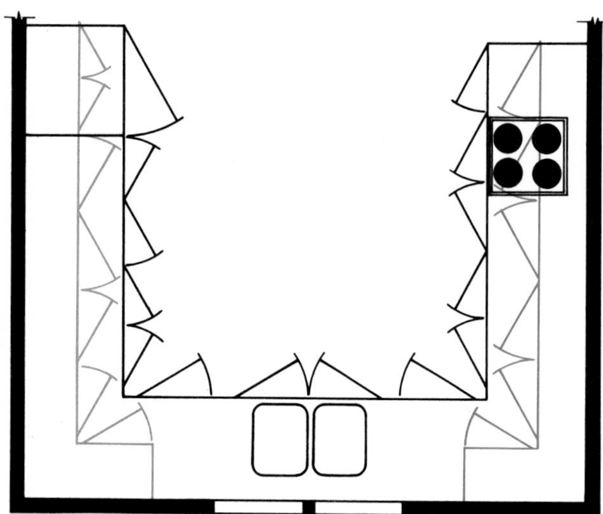

Fig. 16–23. Cabinet doors should open away from the work area.

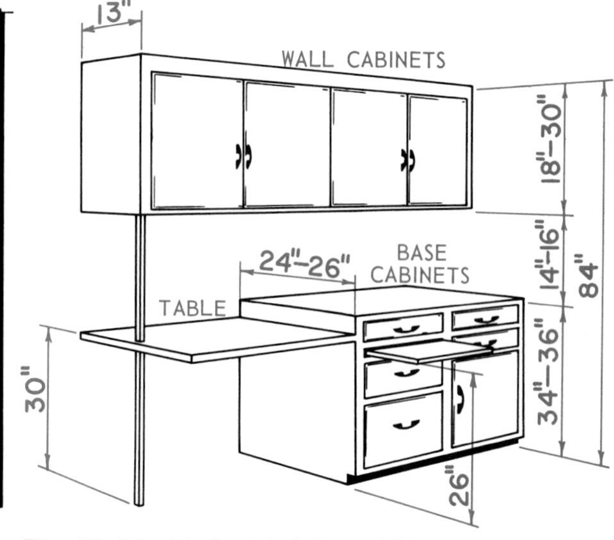

Fig. 16–24. Typical heights of kitchen working surfaces.

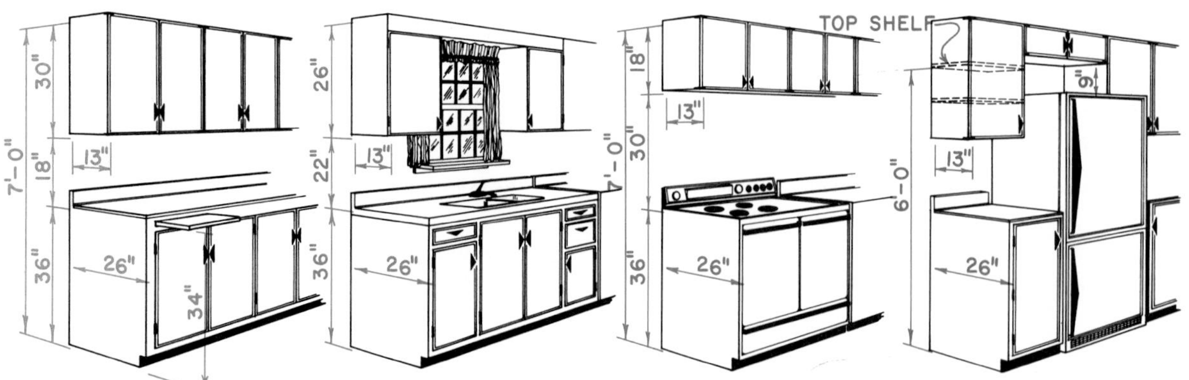

Fig. 16–25. Typical heights of kitchen cabinets.

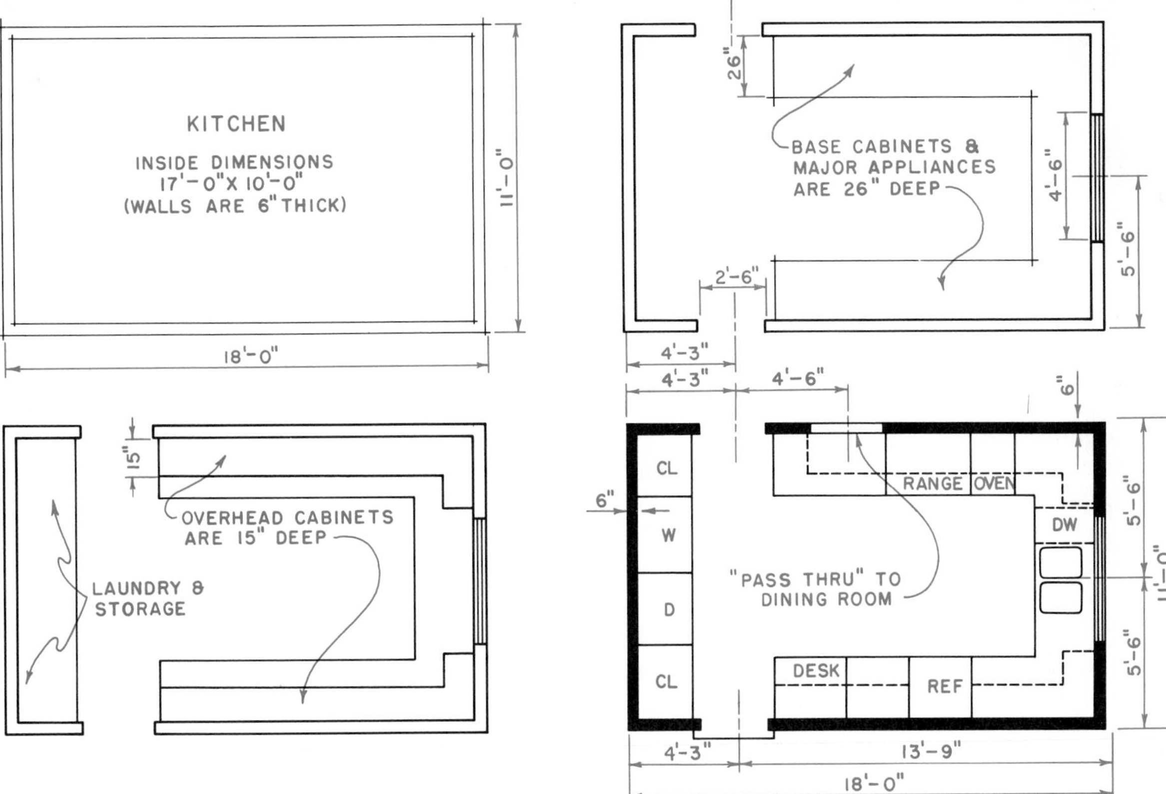

Fig. 16–26. Basic steps in drawing kitchen plans.

mensions are predetermined, follow the steps outlined in Fig. 16–26 in drawing a kitchen floor plan.

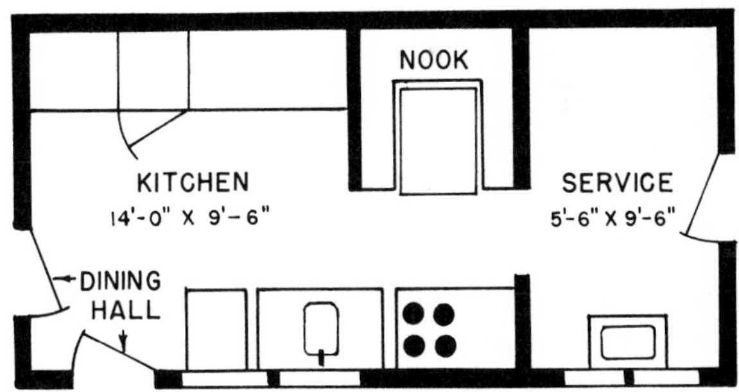

Fig. 16–27. Remodel this kitchen.

PROBLEMS

1. Sketch a floor plan of the peninsula kitchen shown in Fig. 16–8, using the scale ¼″ = 1′—0″.
2. Sketch an elevation drawing of the two walls of the L-shaped kitchen shown in Fig. 16–10, using the scale ¼″ = 1′—0″.
3. Sketch a floor plan of the island kitchen shown in Fig. 16–17. Show the position of the dining area in relation to this kitchen, using the scale ¼″ = 1′—0″.
4. Remodel the kitchen shown in Fig. 16–27. Change door arrangements and dining facilities as needed.
5. Sketch a floor plan of the kitchen in your own home. Prepare a revised sketch to show how you would propose to redesign this kitchen. Make an attempt to reduce the size of the work triangle.
6. Sketch a floor plan of a kitchen you would include in a house of your own design, using the scale ¼″ = 1′—0″.
7. Define the following terms: *work triangle, U-shape, peninsula, L-shape, corridor, island, family kitchen, storage and mixing center, planning and preparation center, cooking center, major appliances, minor appliances, base cabinet, wall cabinet, counter top, service area.*

UNIT 17

The Utility Room

The utility room may include facilities for washing, drying, ironing, sewing, and storing household cleaning equipment. It may contain heating and air-conditioning equipment or even a pantry for storing foods. Other names for this room are *service room, all-purpose room,* and *laundry room* (Fig. 17–1).

If the utility room is used for heating and air-conditioning, space must be planned for the furnace, heating and air-conditioning ducts, hot-water heater, and any related equipment such as humidifiers or air purifiers.

Frigidaire Division, General Motors Corporation

Fig. 17–1. Two main functions of a utility room include washing and drying clothes.

SHAPE AND SIZE

The shapes and sizes of utility rooms differ, as shown in Fig. 17–2. The average floor space required for appliances, counter, and storage area is 100 square feet (10 m^2). However, this size may vary according to the budget or needs of the household.

STYLE AND DECOR

Style and decor in a utility room depend on the function of the appliances, which are themselves an important factor in the appearance of the room. Simplicity, straight lines, and continuous counter spaces produce an orderly effect and permit work to progress easily. Such features also make the room easy to clean.

An important part of the decor is the color of the paint used for walls and cabinet finishes. Colors should harmonize with the colors used on the appliances. All finishes should be washable. The walls may be lined with sound-absorbing tiles or wood paneling.

The lighting in a utility room should be carefully planned so that it will be 48″ (1220 mm) above the equipment used for washing, ironing, and sewing (Fig. 17–3). However, the lighting fixtures placed above the preparation area and laundry sinks can be further from the work-top area, as shown in Fig. 17–3.

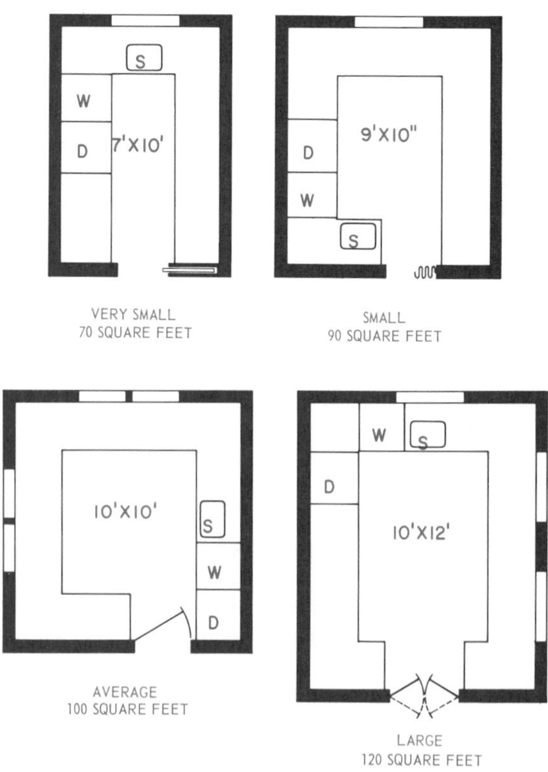

Fig. 17–2. The size of a utility room varies according to the budget and needs of the family.

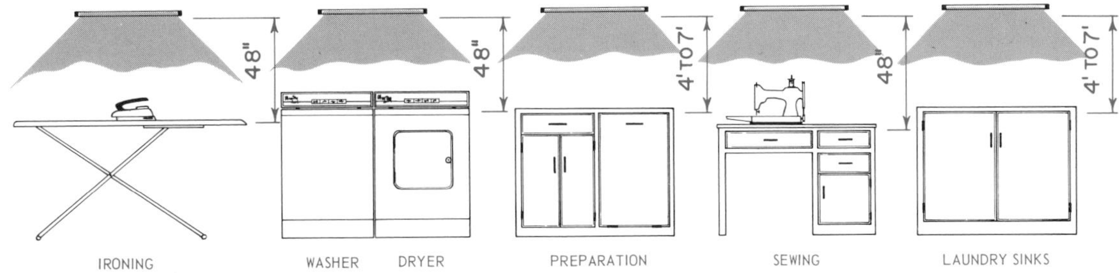

Fig. 17–3. The lighting for a utility room must be carefully planned.

THE LAUNDRY AREA

The laundry area is only one part of the utility room, but it is usually the most important center. To make laundry work as easy as possible, the appliances and working spaces in a laundry area should be located in the order in which they will be used. Such an arrangement will save time and effort. There are four steps in the process of laundering. The equipment needed for each of these steps should be grouped so that the person doing the laundry can proceed from one stage to the next in an orderly and efficient way (Fig. 17–4).

Receiving and Preparing Laundry

The first step in laundering—receiving and preparing the items—requires hampers or bins, as well as counters on which to collect and sort the articles. Near this equipment there should be storage facilities for laundry products such as detergents, bleaches, and stain removers (Fig. 17–5).

Washing

The next step, the actual washing, takes place in the area containing the washing machine and laundry tubs or sink. Figure 17–6 shows the equipment used in this area.

Fig. 17–4. The appliances and working spaces should be arranged in the order in which they are used.

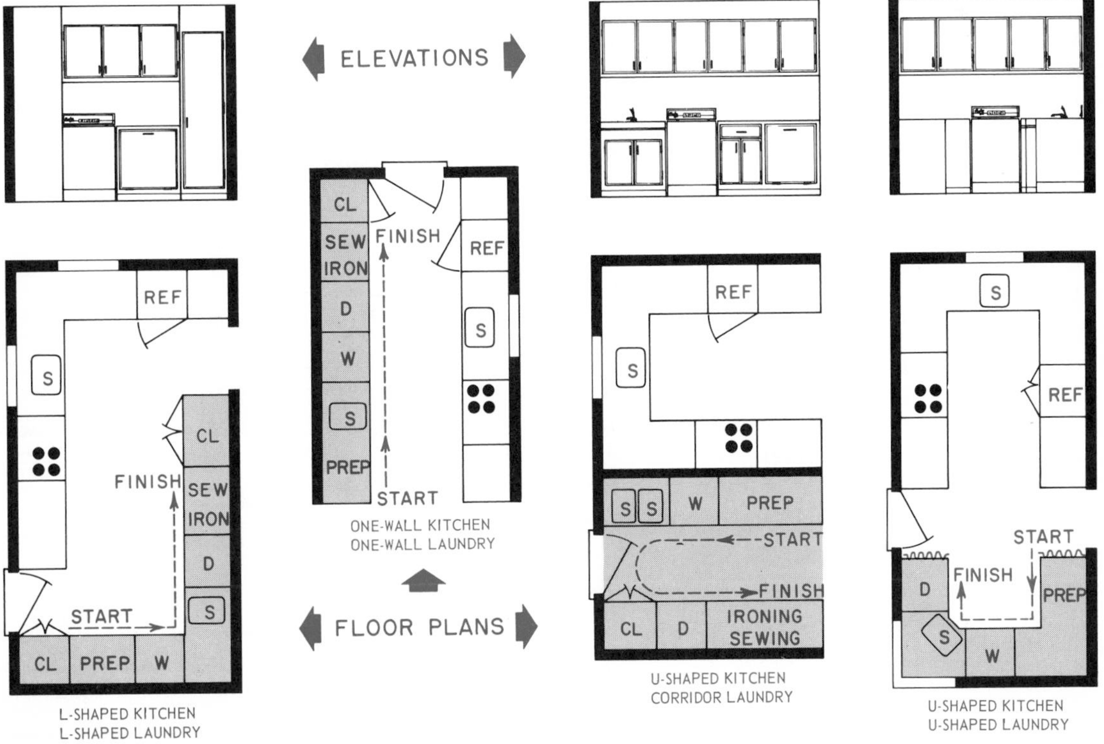

Fig. 17–5. The reception and preparation area.

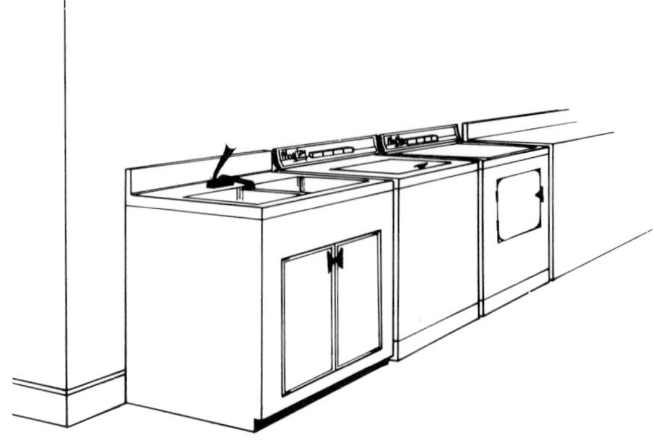

Fig. 17–6. The washing area.

Drying
The equipment needed for this stage of the work includes a dryer, indoor drying lines, and space to store clothespins, as shown in Fig. 17–7. Figure 17–8 shows a compact but complete washing and drying center.

Ironing and Storage
For the last part of the process, the required equipment consists of an iron and a board or an automatic ironer, a counter for sprinkling and folding, a rack on which to hang finished ironing, and facilities for sewing and mending, as shown at the right in Fig. 17–7. If a sewing machine is included, it may be portable, or it may fold into a counter or wall.

Fig.17–7. The major components needed for drying.

LOCATION

Separate Laundry Area
The location of the laundry area in a utility room is desirable because all laundry functions, including repairs, are centered in one place. A further advantage of the separate room is that laundering is kept well apart from the preparation of foods (Fig. 17–9).

Space is not always available for a utility room, however, and the laundry appliances and space for washing and drying may need to be located in some other area (Fig. 17–10A). Wherever it is placed, the equipment in the laundry unit should be arranged in the order in which the work must be done.

Fig. 17–8. This compact laundry center combines a cabinet, a shoulder-high dryer, and an automatic washer.

Frigidaire Division, General Motors Corporation

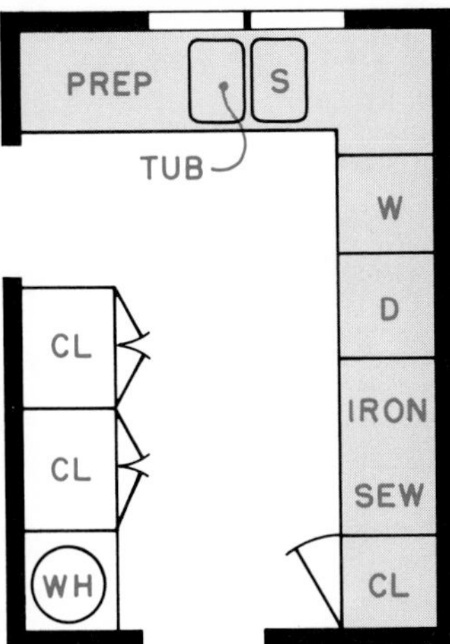

Fig. 17–9. **Plan of a separate laundry area.**

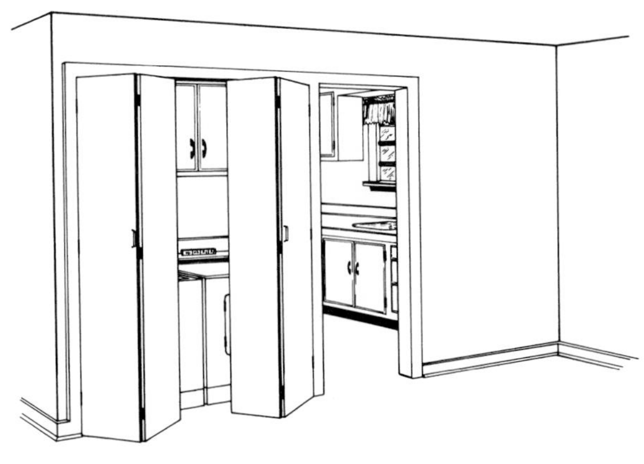

Fig. 17–10A. **An alternate location for the washer and dryer.**

The Kitchen

Placing the laundry unit in the kitchen has some advantages. The unit is in a central location and is near a service entrance. Plumbing facilities are near. The sink may be used as a laundry tub, and the drainboards may be used as counters for sprinkling and folding.

Other Locations

Laundry appliances may be located in a closet (Fig. 17–10B), on a service porch, in a basement, or in a garage or carport. The service porch, basement, garage or carport provides less expensive floor space than other parts of the house.

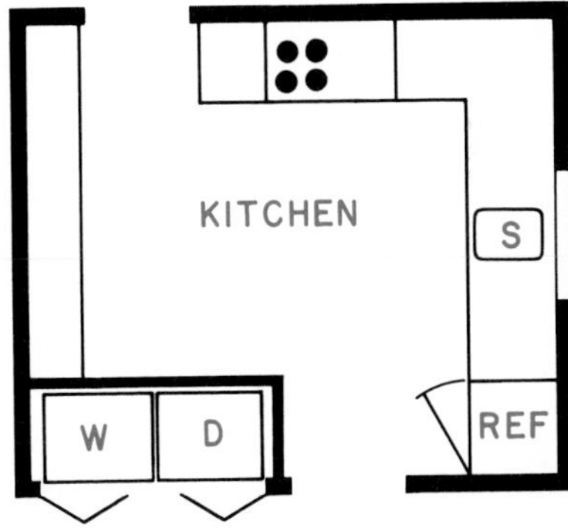

Fig. 17–10B. **The plan of the alternate laundry location from Fig. 17–10A. Being near the kitchen will minimize plumbing problems.**

PROBLEMS

1. **Sketch a complete laundry floor plan from that shown in Fig. 17–1. Show positions of appliances and equipment.**
2. **Design a utility room with a complete laundry within an area of 100 square feet, or 10 m^2 if working with a metric scale.**
3. **Define the following terms: *utility room, laundry area, hamper, water heater.***

UNIT 18

Garages and Carports

Storage of the automobile occupies a large percentage of the available space of the house or property. Garages and carports must therefore be designed with the greatest care to ensure maximum utilization of space.

GARAGE

A *garage* is a structure designed primarily to shelter an automobile. It may be used for many secondary purposes such as a workshop or for

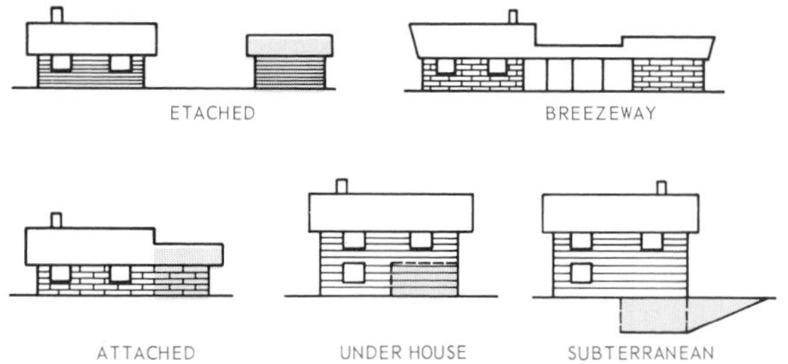

Fig. 18–1. Possible locations for the garage.

storage space. A garage may be connected with the house (integral) or it may be a separate building (detached). Figure 18–1 shows several possible garage locations.

CARPORT

A *carport* is a garage with one or more of the exterior walls removed. It may consist of a freestanding roof completely separate from the house, or it may be built against the existing walls of the house (Figs. 18–2 and 18–3). Carports are most acceptable in mild climates where complete protection from cold weather is not needed. A carport offers protection primarily from sun and precipitation.

The garage and the carport both have distinct advantages. The garage is more secure and provides more shelter. However, carports lend themselves to open-planning techniques and are less expensive than garages.

DESIGN

The lines of the garage or carport should be consistent with the major building lines of the

Fig. 18–2. A carport provides only overhead protection.

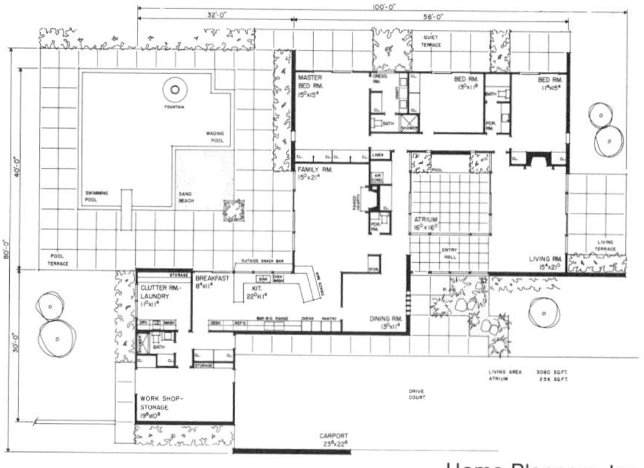

Home Planners, Inc.

Fig. 18–3. A carport attached to a ranch home.

Scholz Homes, Inc.

Fig. 18–4. The garage style must be integrated with the house style.

Fig. 18–5. A breezeway provides protection for a detached garage.

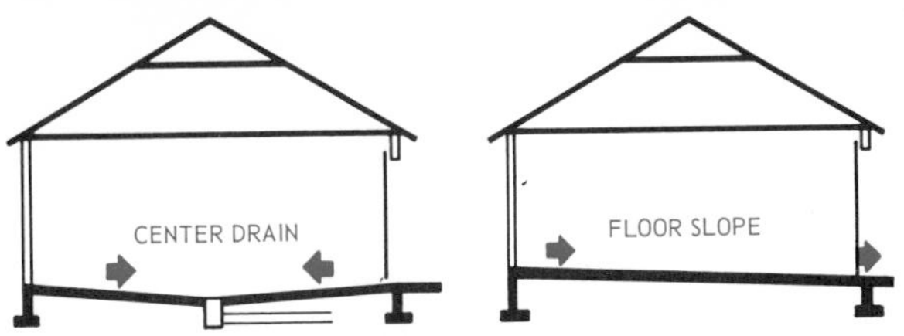

Fig. 18–6. Proper drainage is important for the garage.

house. The style of the garage should be consistent with the style of architecture used in the house (Fig. 18–4).

The garage or carport must never appear as an afterthought. Often a patio, porch, or breezeway is planned between the garage and the house to integrate a detached garage with the house (Fig. 18–5). A covered walkway from the garage or carport to the house should be provided if the garage is detached.

The garage floor must be solid and easily maintained. A concrete slab 3″ or 4″ (75 or 100 mm) thick provides the best deck for a garage or carport. The garage floor must have adequate drainage either to the outside or through drains located inside the garage (Fig. 18–6). A vapor barrier consisting of waterproof materials under the slab should be provided. The driveway should be of asphalt or concrete construction, preferably with welded-wire fabric to maintain rigidity (Fig. 18–7).

The design of the garage door greatly affects the appearance of the garage. Several types of garage doors are available. These include the two-leaf swinging, overhead, four-leaf swinging, and sectional roll-up doors (Fig. 18–8). Several electronic devices are available for opening the door of the garage from the car (Fig. 18–9).

SIZE

The size and number of automobiles and the additional facilities needed for storage or workshop use should determine the size of the garage (Fig. 18–10).

The dimensions of a single-car garage range between 11′ × 19′ (3.4 × 5.8 m) and 13′ × 25′ (4.0 × 7.6 m). A 16′ × 25′ (4.9 × 7.6 m) garage is more desirable if space is needed for benches, mowers, tools, and the storage of children's vehicles. A full double garage is 25′ × 25′ (7.6 × 7.6 m).

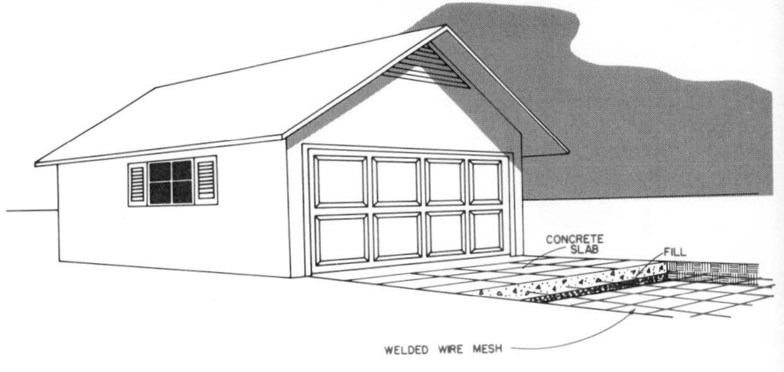

Fig. 18–7. Steel-wire mesh in the concrete will help keep the pavement and garage floor from cracking.

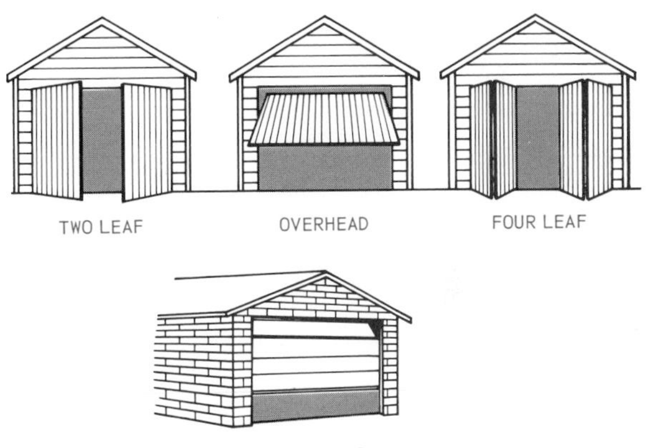

Fig. 18–8. Four common types of garage doors.

Berry Doors

Fig. 18–9. A garage door controlled with a radio signal.

A two-car garage does not cost twice as much as a one-car garage. However, if the second half is added at a later date, the cost will more than double.

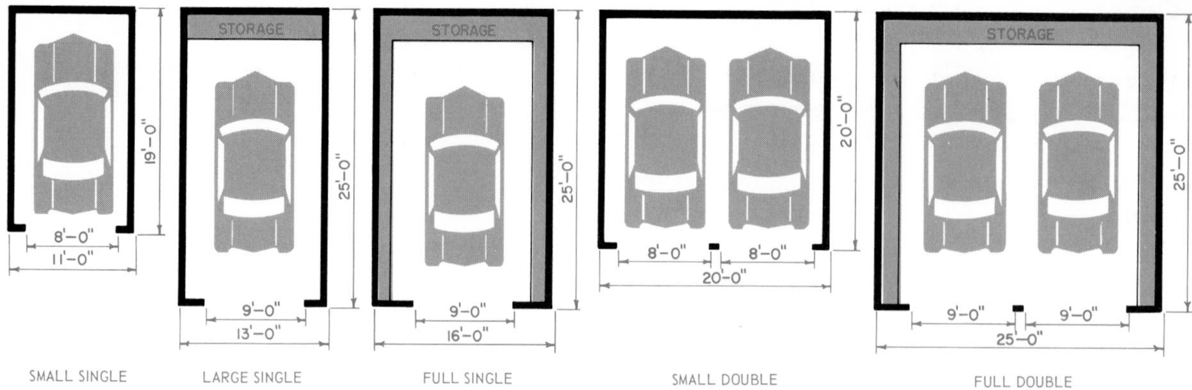

Fig. 18–10. Typical garage sizes.

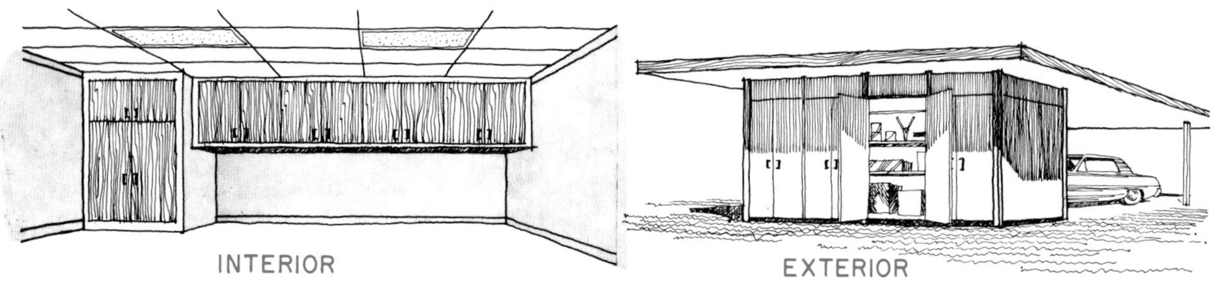

Fig. 18–11. Plans for storage space in the garage or carport.

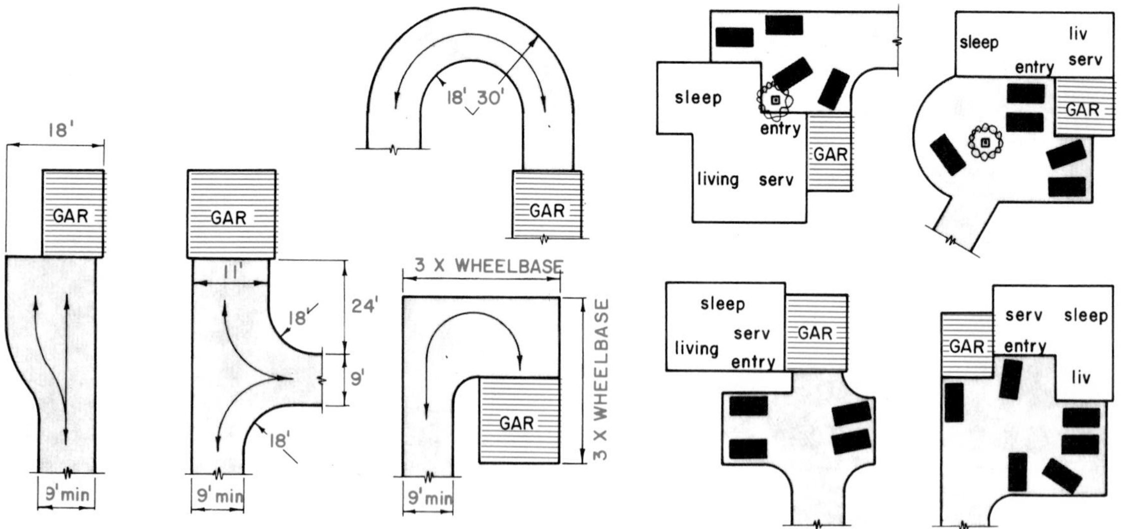

Fig. 18–12. Apron arrangements for parking and turning.

STORAGE

Storage is often an additional function of most garages. The storage space over the hood of the car should be utilized effectively (Fig. 18–11). Cabinets should be elevated from the floor several inches to eliminate moisture and to facilitate cleaning the garage floor. Garden-tool cabinets can be designed to open from the outside of the garage.

DRIVEWAY

A driveway can be planned for purposes other than providing access to the garage and temporary parking space for guests. By adding a wider space to an apron at the door of the garage, an area can be provided for car washing and polishing and for a hard, level surface for children's games. Aprons are often needed to provide space for turning the car in order to eliminate backing out onto a main street (Fig. 18–12).

The driveway should be accessible to all entrances, and the garage should provide easy access to the service area of the home. Sufficient space in the driveway should be provided for parking of guests' cars.

Driveways should be designed at least several feet wider than the track of the car (approximately 7′ or 2.1 m). However, slightly wider driveways are desirable (Fig. 18–13).

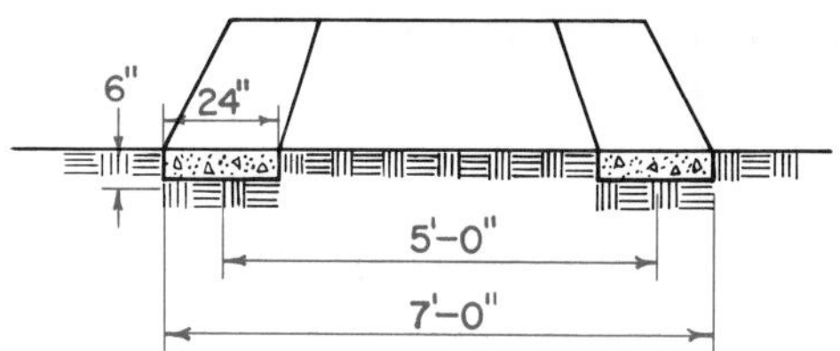

Fig. 18–13. A typical driveway width.

PROBLEMS

1. **Sketch the floor plan from Fig. 18–2, and design a garage, apron, and driveway for each.**
2. **Sketch a front elevation for a small single garage, using the scale ¼″ = 1′—0″.**
3. **Sketch a full double garage, and draw in storage, laundry, and workbench.**
4. **Convert a large double garage to a recreation and entertainment area. Sketch the layout.**
5. **Sketch a two-car garage plan. Show the following storage facilities: storage wall, outside storage, boat slung from ceiling, laundry area, gardening equipment, storage over the hood of the cars.**
6. **Define these architectural terms: *garage, carport, breezeway, subterranean, apron, integral garage, detached garage.***

UNIT 19

Home Work Area

The home work area is designed for activities ranging from hobbies to home-maintenance work (Fig. 19–1). The home work area may be located in part of the garage, in the basement, in a separate room, or in an adjacent building (Fig. 19–2).

LAYOUT

Power tools, hand tools, workbench space, and storage should be systematically planned. A workbench complete with vise is needed in every home work area. The average workbench is 36″ (915 mm) high. A movable workbench is appropriate when large projects are to be constructed. A *peninsula workbench* provides

Lisanti, Inc.

Fig. 19–1. The home work area is often used for home maintenance and hobby work.

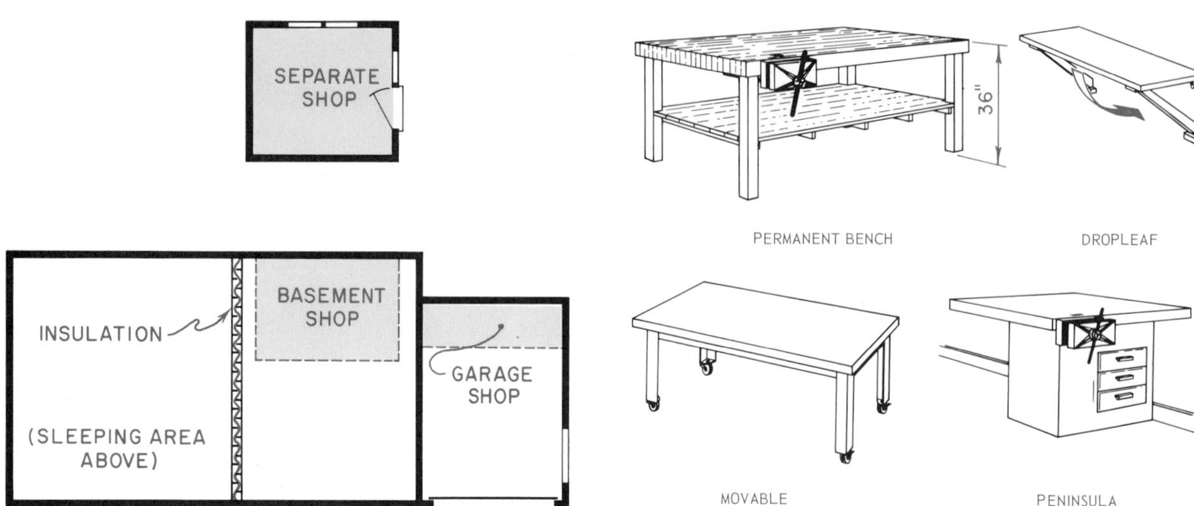

Fig. 19–2. The home workshop may be located in the garage, basement, or a separate building.

Fig. 19–3. Types of workbenches.

three working sides and storage compartments on three sides. A dropleaf workbench is excellent for work areas where a minimum amount of space is available (Fig. 19–3).

Hand Tools

Some hand tools are basic to all types of hobbies or home-maintenance work. These basic tools include a claw hammer, carpenter's square, files, hand drills, screwdrivers, planes, pliers, chisels, scales, wrenches, saws, a brace and bit, mallets, and clamps.

Power Tools

Although power tools are not absolutely necessary for the performance of most home workshop activities, they do make the performance of many tasks easier and quicker. Some of the more common power tools used in home workshops include electric drills, jigsaws, routers, band saws, circular saws, radial-arm saws, jointers, belt sanders, lathes, and drill presses. Placement of equipment should be planned to provide the maximum amount of work space. Figure 19–4 suggests clearances necessary for safe and efficient machine operation.

Multipurpose Machines

Multipurpose machines are machines that can perform a variety of operations. The multipurpose tool shown in Fig. 19–5 has many attachments which are used to convert its function. Multipurpose equipment is popular for use in

Fig. 19–4. Machinery must be spaced for proper clearances.

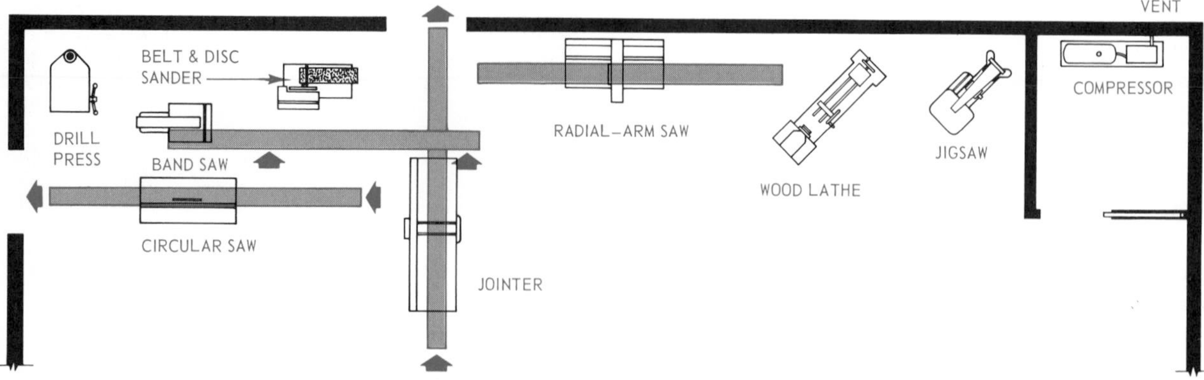

Shopsmith

Fig. 19–5. A multipurpose tool.

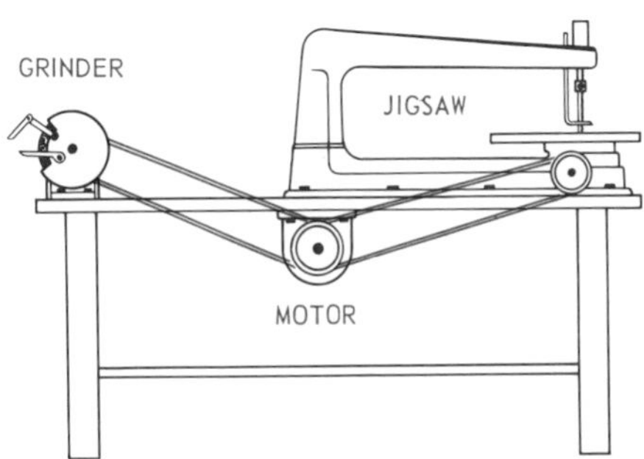

Fig. 19–6. One motor can drive machines.

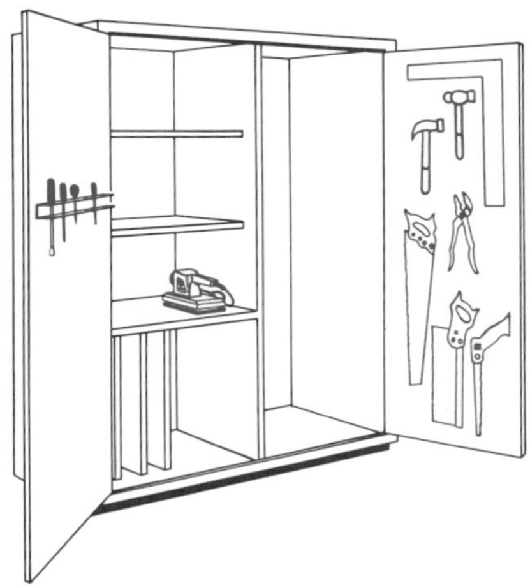

Fig. 19–7. Closed storage facilities are the safest for tools.

the home workshop since the purchase of only one piece of equipment is necessary and the amount of space needed is relatively small, compared with the amount of space needed for a variety of machines.

Tools and equipment needed for working with large materials should be placed where the material can be easily handled. Separate-drive motors can be used to drive more than one piece of power equipment, in order to conserve motors (Fig. 19–6). Separate electrical circuits for lights and power tools should be included in the plans for the home workshop area.

STORAGE FACILITIES

Maximum storage facilities in the home work area are essential. Hand tools may be stored in cabinets which keep them dust-free and safe (Fig. 19–7), or hung on perforated hardboard, as shown in Fig. 19–8. Tools too small to be hung should be kept in special-purpose drawers, and any inflammable finishing material, such as turpentine or oil paint, should be stored in metal cabinets.

SIZE AND SHAPE

The size of the work area depends on the size and number of power tools and equipment, the amount of workbench area, and the amount of tool and material storage facilities provided.

Better Homes and Gardens

Fig. 19–8. Perforated hardboards can be used for hanging tools.

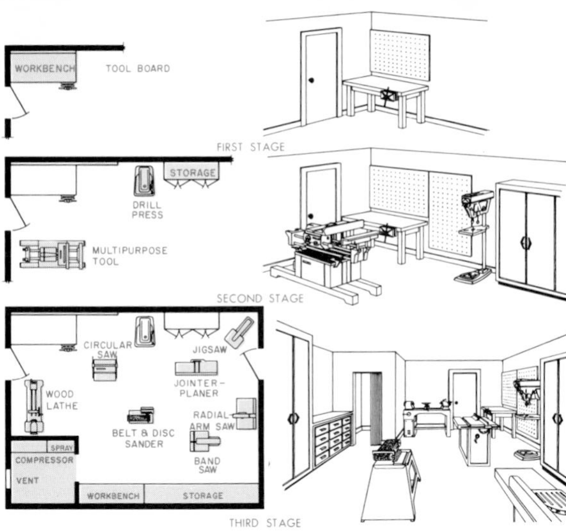

Fig. 19–9. A three-stage development of a workshop.

The size of the work area should be planned for maximum expansion, even though only a workbench or a few tools may be available when the area is first occupied. Therefore, space for the maximum amount of facilities should be planned and located when the area is designed. As new equipment is added, it will fit appropriately into the basic plan (Fig. 19–9).

The designer must anticipate the type and number of materials for which storage space will be needed and design the storage space accordingly.

DECOR

The work area should be as maintenance-free as possible. Glossy paint or tile retards an accumulation of shop dust on the walls. Exhaust fans eliminate much of the dust and the gasses produced in the shop. The shop floor should be of concrete or linoleum for easy maintenance. Abrasive strips around machines will eliminate the possibility of slipping. Do not locate noisy equipment near the children's sleeping area. Interior walls and ceilings should be soundproofed by offsetting studs and adding adequate insulation to produce a sound barrier (Fig. 19–10).

Light and color are most important factors in designing the work area. Pastel colors, which reduce eye strain, should be used for the general color scheme of the shop. Extremely light colors that produce glare, and extremely dark colors that reduce effective illumination, should be avoided. Adopting one of the major paint manufacturers' color systems for color coding will help to create a pleasant atmosphere in the shop and will also help to provide the most efficient and safest working conditions.

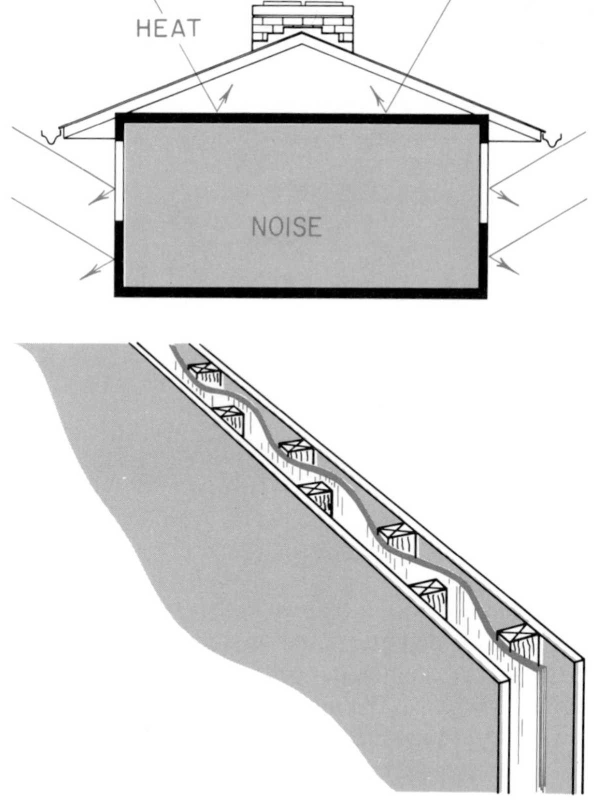

Fig. 19–10. Insulation stops disturbing noises from entering other parts of the house.

General lighting should be provided in the shop to a level of 100 footcandles (1076 lux) on machines and worktable tops.

PROBLEMS

1. **Design a small work area to fit into a single garage that will also house a car (see Unit 18).**
2. **Design a work area to fill one side of a double garage (see Unit 18).**
3. **Design a work area in a double garage for an activity other than woodworking (ceramics, jewelry, metalworking, or automotive repairs, for example). Show what tools and work areas are necessary.**
4. **Define the following architectural terms: *dehumidifier, workbench, perforated hardboard, flammable, hand tools, power tools, multipurpose tools.***

UNIT 20

Storage Areas

Storage areas should be provided for general storage and for specific storage within each room (Fig. 20–1). Areas that would otherwise be considered wasted space should be used as general storage areas. Parts of the basement, attic, or garage often fall into this category (Fig. 20–2). Effective storage planning is necessary to provide storage facilities within each room that will create the least amount of inconvenience in securing the stored articles. Articles that are used daily or weekly should be stored in or near the room where they will be used (Fig. 20–3). Articles that are used only seasonally should be placed in more permanent general storage areas.

STORAGE FACILITIES

Storage facilities, equipment, and furniture used for storage within the various rooms of the house are divided into the following categories (Fig. 20–4):

Wardrobe Closets

A *wardrobe closet* is a shallow clothes closet built into the wall. The minimum depth for the wardrobe is 24″ (610 mm). If this closet is more than 30″ (760 mm) deep, you will be unable to reach the back of the closet. Swinging or sliding doors should expose all parts of the closet to your reach. A disadvantage of the wardrobe closet is the amount of wall space needed for the doors (Fig. 20–5).

Walk-In Closets

Walk-in closets are closets large enough to walk into. The area needed for this type of closet is an area equal to the amount of space needed to hang clothes plus enough space to walk and turn. Although some area is wasted in

Fig. 20–1. Locations of storage areas.

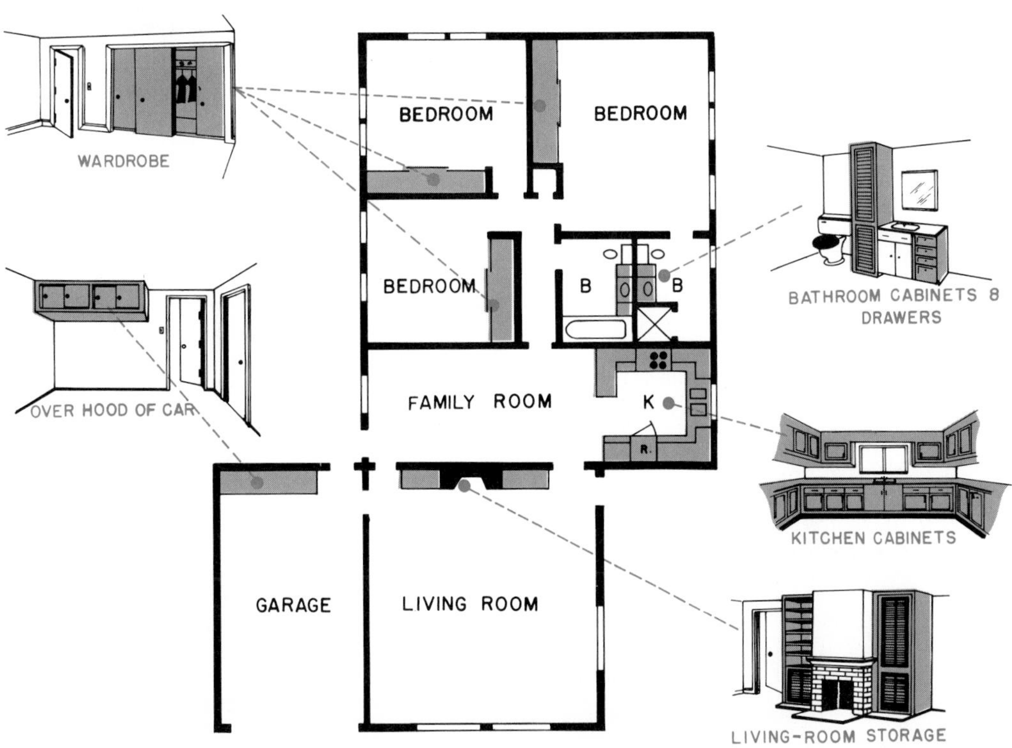

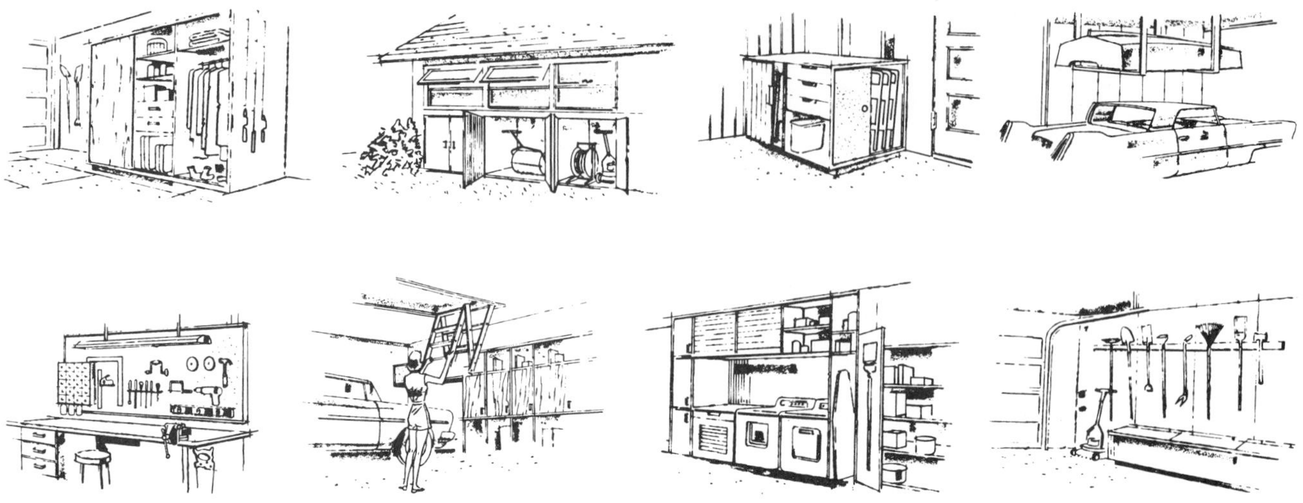

Fig. 20–2. Typical storage areas in most homes.

the passage, the use of the walk-in closet does provide more wall area for furniture placement, since only one door is needed (Fig. 20–6).

Wall Closets

A *wall closet* is a shallow closet in the wall holding cupboards, shelves, and drawers. Wall closets are normally 18″ (460 mm) deep, since this size provides access to all stored items without using an excessive amount of floor area (Fig. 20–7). Figure 20–8 is an example of wall storage with wardrobe closets on each side.

Pella Rollscreen Co.

Fig. 20–3. Room storage must be provided for objects used every day.

Fig. 20–4. Types of storage facilities.

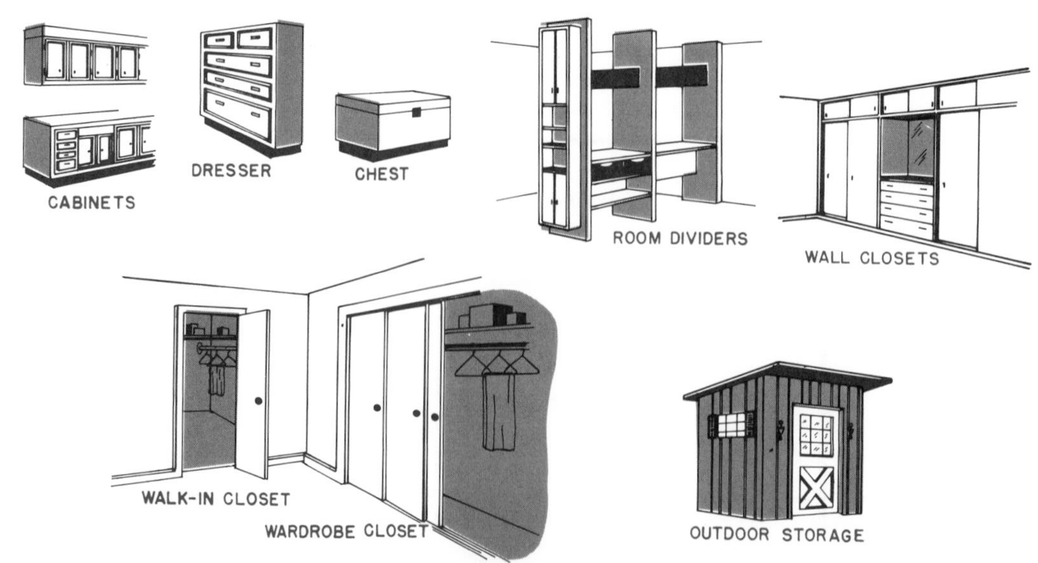

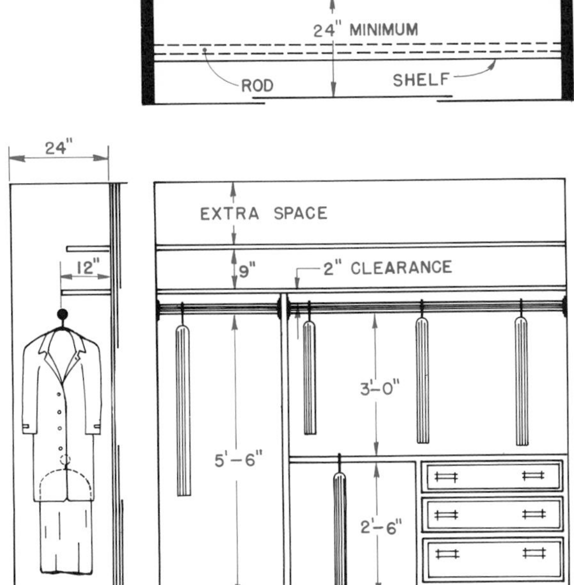

Fig. 20–5. Dimensions for wardrobe closets.

Protruding closets that create an offset in a room should be avoided. Often by filling the entire wall between two bedrooms with closet space it is possible to design a square or rectangular room without the use of offsets (Fig. 20–9). Doors on closets should be sufficiently wide to allow easy accessibility. Swing-out doors have the advantage of providing extra storage space on the back of the door. However, space must be allowed for the swing. For this reason, sliding doors are usually preferred. All

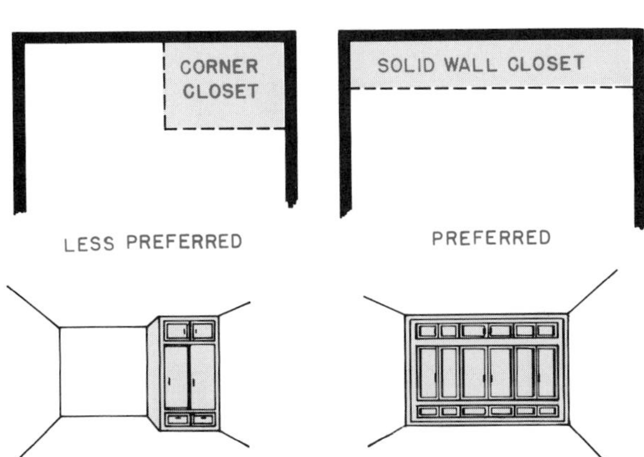

Fig. 20–9. Avoid closets that create offsets.

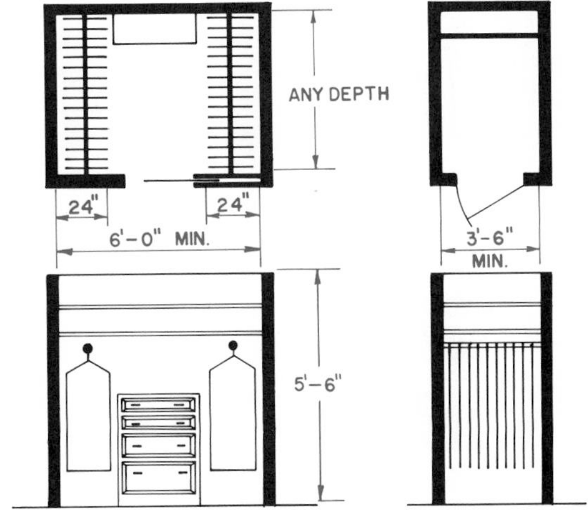

Fig. 20–6. Dimensions for walk-in closets.

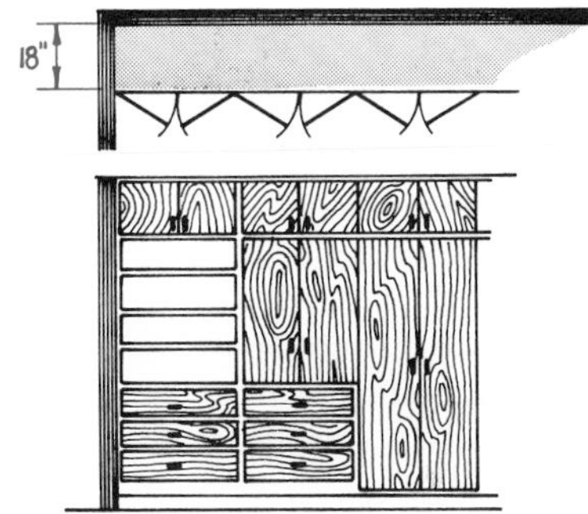

Fig. 20–7. Wall storage uses a minimum of floor space.

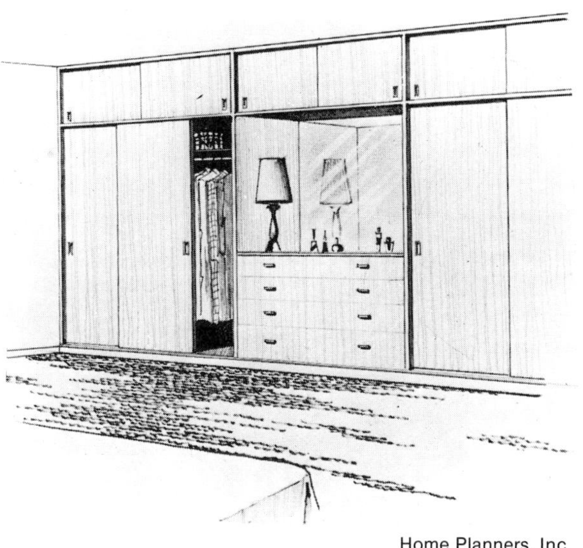

Home Planners, Inc.

Fig. 20–8. Built-in closets and drawer storage.

Douglas Fir Plywood Association

Fig. 20–10. Room dividers can be used for storage.

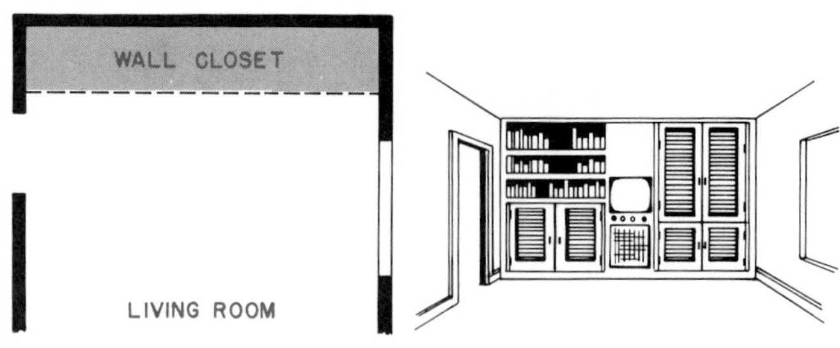

Fig. 20–11. Built-in wall cabinets.

closets, except very shallow linen closets, should be provided with lighting.

Chests and Dressers

Chests and dressers are free-standing pieces of furniture used for storage, generally in the bedroom. They are available in a variety of sizes, usually with shelves and drawers.

Room Dividers

A room divider often doubles as a storage area, especially when a protruding closet divides several areas. Room dividers often extend from the floor to the ceiling or may only be several feet high. Many room dividers include shelves and drawers that open from both sides (Fig. 20–10).

LOCATION

Different types of storage facilities are necessary for areas of the home, depending on the type of article to be stored. The most appropriate types of storage facilities for each room in the house are as follows:

Living room: room divider, built-in wall cabinets (Fig. 20–11), bookcases, window seats
Dining area: room divider, built-in wall closet
Family room: built-in wall storage, window seats
Recreation room: built-in wall storage (Fig. 20–12)
Porches: under porch stairs, walk-in closet
Patios: sides of barbecue, separate building
Outside: closets built into the side of the house (see Fig. 20–2)

Armstrong Cork Company

Fig. 20–12. Rec-room storage.

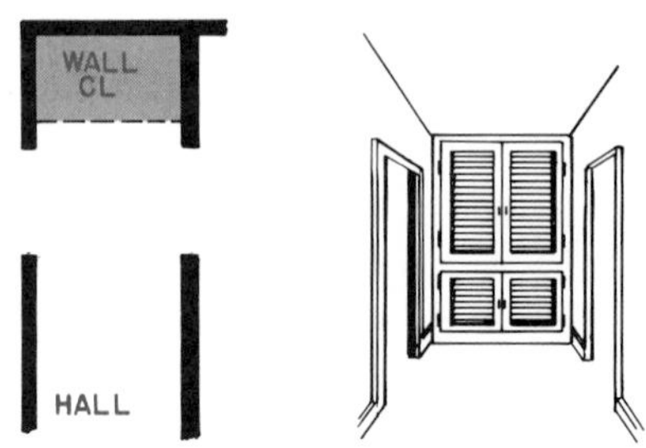

Fig. 20–13. Built-in hall storage.

Home Planners, Inc.

Fig. 20–14. Hall storage.

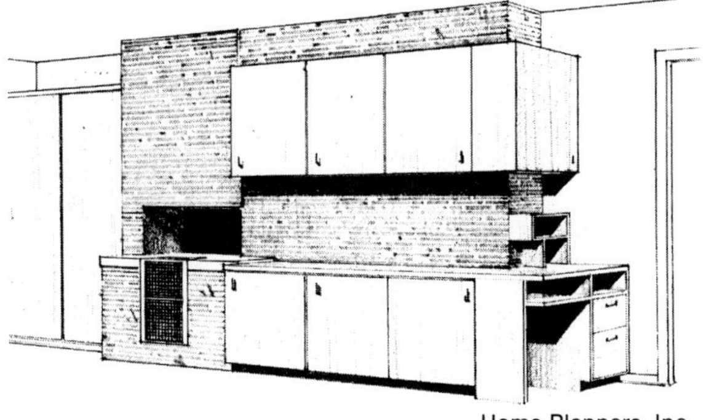

Home Planners, Inc.

Fig. 20–15. Kitchen storage.

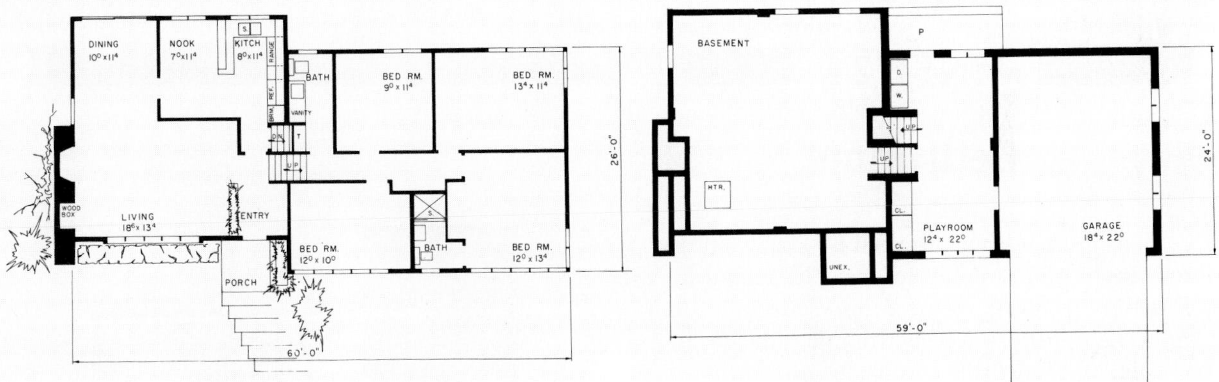

Fig. 20–16. Sketch and label storage areas on this plan.

Home Planners, Inc.

Halls: solid built-in wall closets, ends of blind halls (Fig. 20–13)

Entrance: room divider, wardrobe, walk-in closet (Fig. 20–14)

Den: built-in wall closet, window seats, bookcases

Kitchen: wall and floor cabinets, room divider, wall closets (Fig. 20–15)

Utility room: cabinets on floor and walls

Garage: cabinets over hood of car, wall closets along sides, added construction on the outside of the garage (see Fig. 20–2)

Work area: open tool board, wall closets, cabinets

Bedroom: walk-in closet, wardrobe closet, under bed, foot of bed, head of bed, built-in cabinets and shelves, dressers, chests

Bathroom: cabinets on floor and ceiling, room dividers

PROBLEMS

1. **Draw the floor plan in Fig. 20–16, using the scale ¼″ = 1′—0″. Add all needed storage space.**
2. **Draw the floor plan in Fig. 32–7A, using the scale ¼″ = 1′—0″. Add all the needed storage space.**
3. **Draw the floor plan in Fig. 32–10, using the scale ¼″ = 1′—0″. Add all needed storage space.**
4. **How many square feet of storage area are there in Fig. 20–16? Is this at least 7 percent of the area of the house?**
5. **Add storage facilities to the first and second floor of the house shown in Fig. 33–21. Sketch your solution and label each storage area.**

SECTION 4

Sleeping Area

One-third of our time is spent in sleeping. Because of its importance, the sleeping area should be planned to provide facilities for maximum comfort and relaxation. The sleeping area is usually located in a quiet part of the house and contains bedrooms, baths, dressing areas, and nurseries.

Thomas Industries, Inc.

UNIT 21

Bedrooms

Houses are usually classified by size according to the number of bedrooms; for example, a three-bedroom home, or a four-bedroom home. In a home there are bedrooms, master bedrooms, and nursery rooms, according to the size of the family.

FUNCTION

The primary function of a bedroom is to provide facilities for sleeping. Some bedrooms may also provide facilities for writing, reading, sewing, listening to music, or generally relaxing.

NUMBER OF BEDROOMS

Ideally, each member of the family should have his or her own private bedroom. A family with no children may require only one bedroom. However, two bedrooms are usually desirable, in order to provide one for guest use (Fig. 21–1). Three-bedroom homes are most popular because they provide a minimum of accommodation for a family with one boy and one girl. As a family enlarges, boys can share one bedroom and girls can share the other. With only two bedrooms, this is not possible.

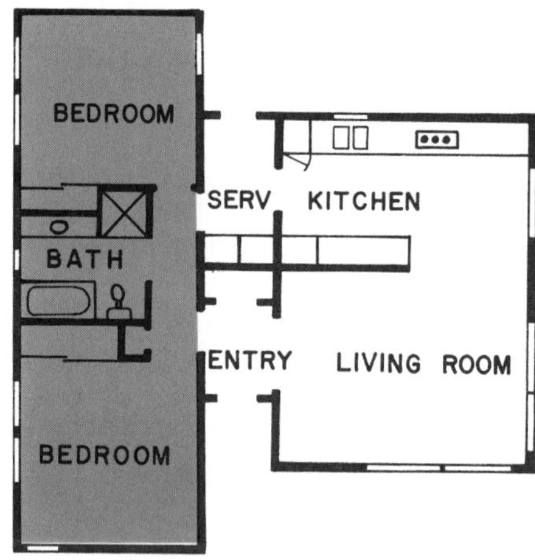

Fig. 21–1. The sleeping area should be away from the activity area of the home.

SIZES AND SHAPES

The size and shape of a bedroom depend upon the amount of furniture needed. A minimum-sized bedroom would accommodate a single bed, bedside table, and dresser. In contrast, a complete master bedroom might include a double bed or twin beds, bedside stands, dresser, chest of drawers, lounge chair, dressing area, and adjacent master bath (Fig. 21–2).

Crane Co.

Fig. 21–2. An example of a dressing area adjacent to the master bedroom.

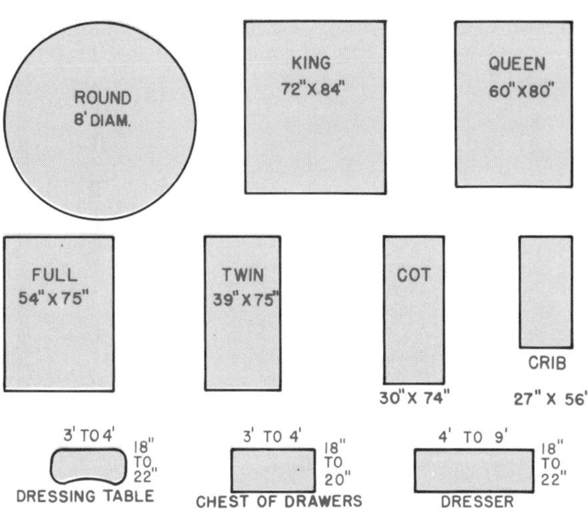

Fig. 21–3. Typical bedroom furniture sizes.

Space Requirements

The type and style of furniture included in the bedroom should be chosen before the size of the bedroom is established. The size of the furniture should determine the size of the room, and not the reverse. Average bedroom furniture sizes are shown in Fig. 21–3. The wall space needed for twin beds is 8′-6″ (2.6 m). A full bed with a night stand requires 6′ (1.8 m) of wall space (Fig. 21–4).

A small bedroom would average from 90 to 100 square feet (8 to 10 m^2) (Fig. 21–5), an average bedroom from 100 to 150 square feet (10 to 15 m^2) (Fig. 21–6), and a large bedroom over 200 square feet (20 m^2) (Fig. 21–7).

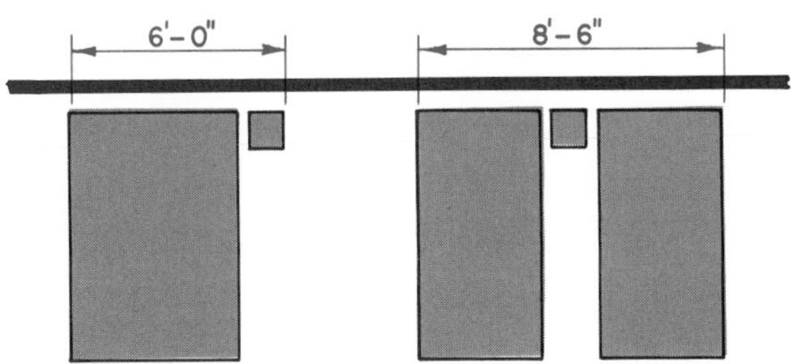

Fig. 21–4. Much wall space is needed for bedroom furniture.

Wall Space

Since wall space is critical in the placement of furniture in the bedroom, the designer must plan for maximum wall space. One method of conserving wall space for bedroom furniture

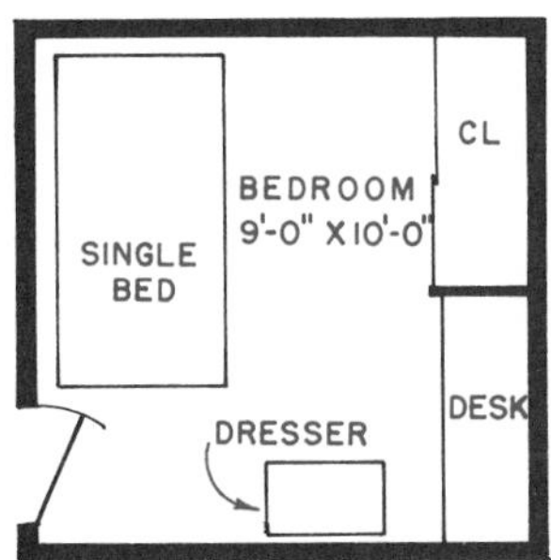

Fig. 21–5. A small bedroom.

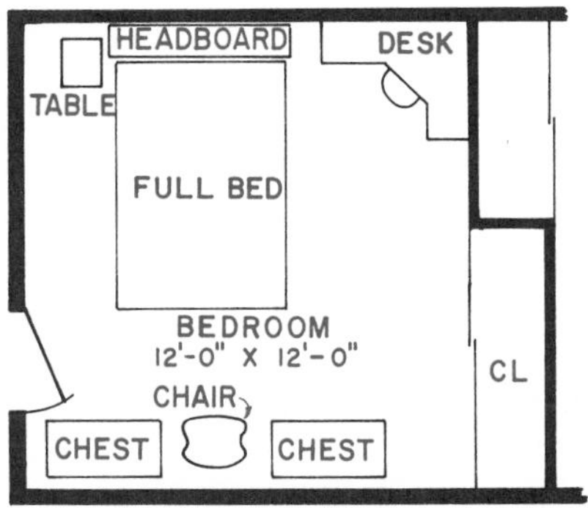

Fig. 21–6. An average-sized bedroom.

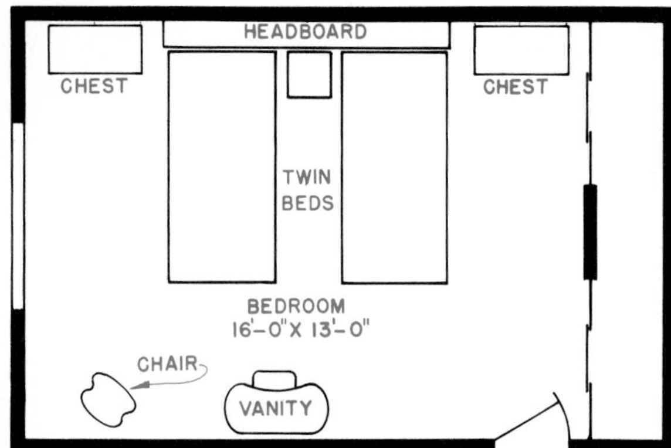

Fig. 21–7. A large bedroom.

placement is by using high windows. High shallow windows allow furniture to be placed underneath, and they also provide some privacy for the bedroom.

Bedroom Doors
Unless it has doors leading to a patio, the bedroom will normally have only one access door from the inside. Entrance doors, closet doors, and windows should be grouped to conserve wall space whenever possible. Separating these doors slightly will spread out the amount of unusable wall space by eliminating long stretches of unused wall space. Sliding doors for closets and for entrance doors help to conserve valuable wall space in bedrooms. If swinging doors are used, the door should always swing into the bedroom and not into the hall (Fig. 21–8).

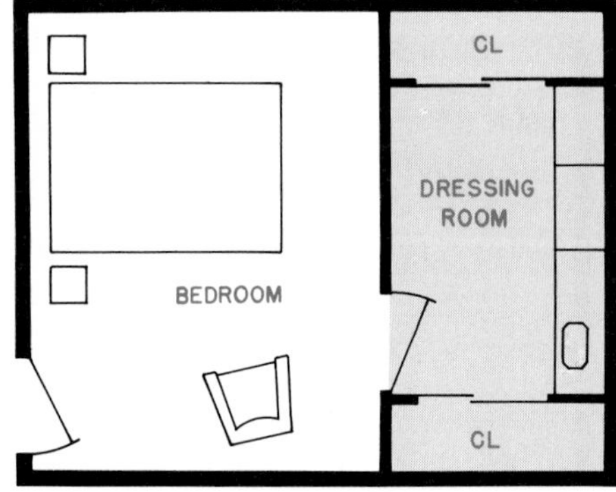

Fig. 21–9. A dressing area.

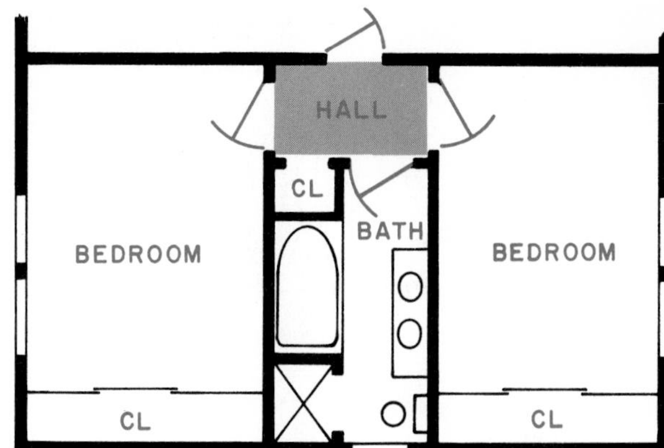

Fig. 21–8. Bedroom doors should not open into halls.

DRESSING AREAS

Dressing areas are sometimes separate rooms or an alcove or a part of the room separated by a divider (Fig. 21–9).

NOISE CONTROL

Since noise contributes to fatigue, it is important to plan for the elimination of as much noise as possible from the bedroom area (Fig. 21–10). The following guides for noise control will help you design bedrooms that are quiet and restful:

1. The bedroom should be in the quiet part of the house, away from major street noises.
2. Carpeting or soft cork wall panels helps to absorb many noises.
3. Rooms above a bedroom should be carpeted.
4. Floor-to-ceiling draperies help to reduce noise.
5. Acoustical tile in the ceiling is effective in reducing noise.
6. Trees and shrubbery outside the bedroom help deaden sounds.
7. The use of insulating glass in windows and sliding doors helps to seal off the bedroom.
8. The windows of an air-conditioned room should be kept closed during hot weather. Air conditioning eliminates much noise and aids in keeping the bedroom free from dust and pollen.

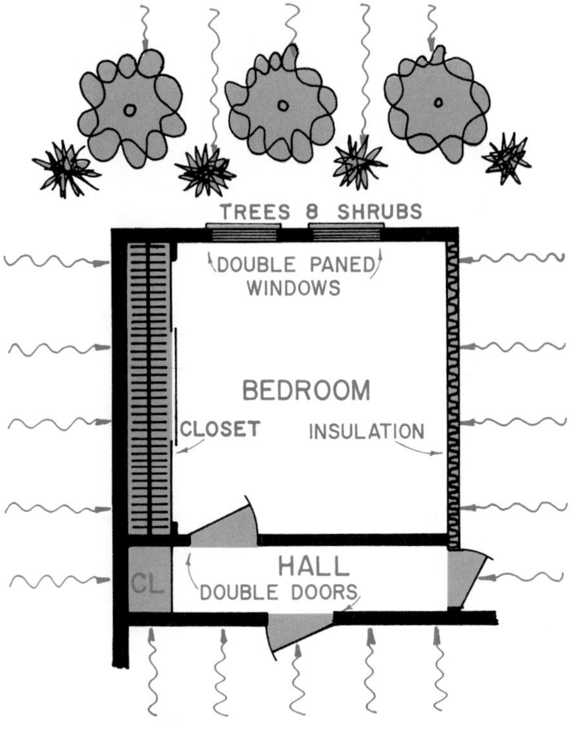

Fig. 21–10. Some methods of bedroom noise control.

9. Air is a good insulator; therefore, closets provide additional buffers which eliminate much noise coming from other rooms.
10. In extreme cases when complete soundproofing is desired, fibrous materials in the walls may be used, and studs may be offset to provide a sound buffer.
11. Placing rubber pads under appliances such as refrigerators, dishwashers, washers, and dryers often eliminates much vibration and noise throughout the house.

STORAGE SPACE

Storage space in the bedroom is needed primarily for clothing and personal accessories. Storage areas should be easy to reach, easy to maintain, and large. Walk-in closets or wardrobe closets should be built in for hanging clothes (Fig. 21–11). Care should be taken to eliminate offset closets. Balancing offset closets from one room to an adjacent bedroom helps solve this problem. Providing built-in storage facilities also helps in overcoming awkward

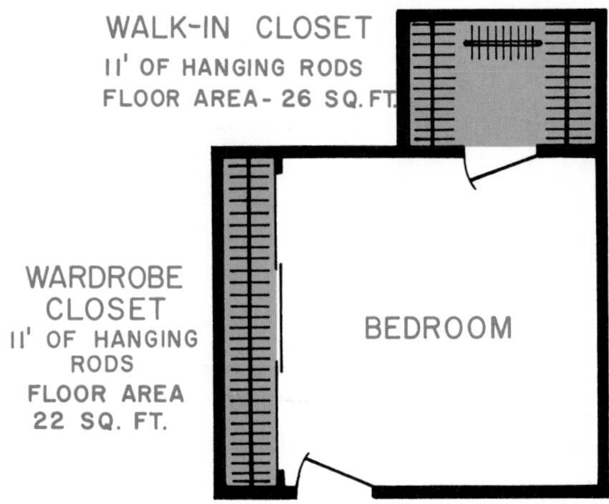

Fig. 21–11. Hanging rods are best for storing clothing.

Fig. 21–12. Built-in storage helps eliminate offsets.

offsets, as shown in Fig. 21–12. Except for the storage space provided in dressers, chests, vanities, and dressing tables, most storage space should be provided in the closet. Double rooms (Fig. 21–13) allow for maximum storage, yet provide flexibility and privacy as the family expands.

VENTILATION

Proper ventilation is necessary and is conducive to sound rest and sleep. Central air conditioning and humidity control provide constant levels of temperature and humidity and are an efficient method of providing ventilation and air circulation. When air conditioning is avail-

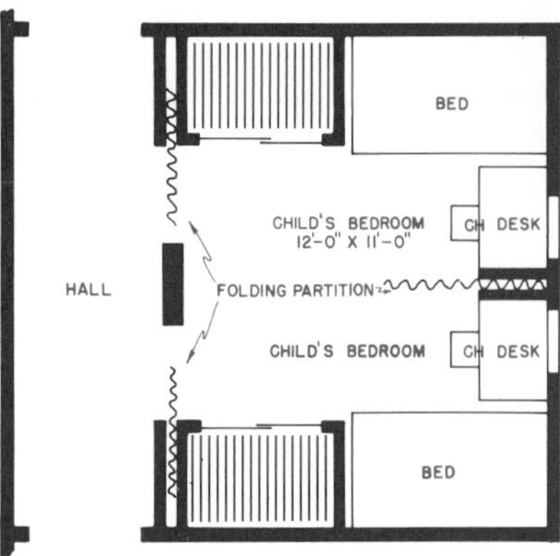

Fig. 21–13. A convertible double room.

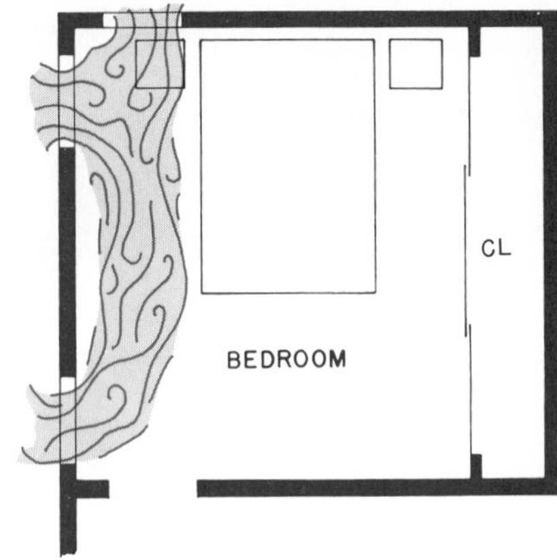

Fig. 21–14. Cross-ventilation which does not pass over the bed is desirable.

able, the windows and doors may remain closed. Without air conditioning, windows and doors must provide the ventilation. Bedrooms should have cross-ventilation. However, the draft must not pass over the bed (Fig. 21–14). High ribbon windows provide light, privacy, and cross-ventilation without causing a draft on the bed. Jalousie windows are also very effective, since they direct the air flow upward (Fig. 21–15).

NURSERIES

Children's bedrooms and nurseries need special facilities. They must be planned to be comfortable, quiet, and sufficiently flexible to change as the child grows and matures (Fig. 21–16). Storage shelves and rods in closets should be adjustable so that they may be raised as the child becomes taller. Light switches should be placed low, with a delay switch which allows the light to stay on for some time after the switch has been thrown.

Chalkboards and bulletin boards help make the child's room usable. Adequate facili-

Fig. 21–15. Louvered or jalousie windows direct air circulation upward.

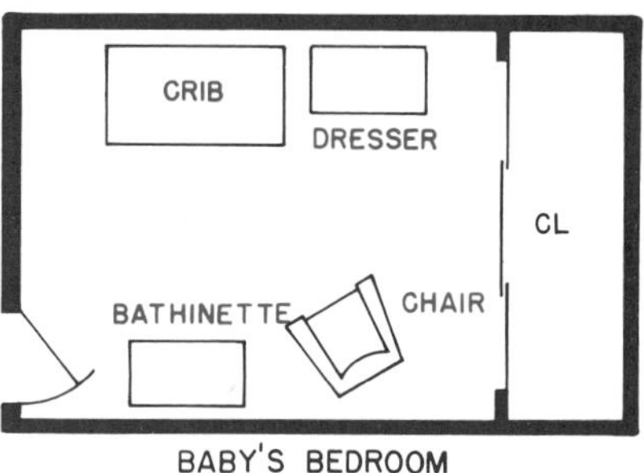

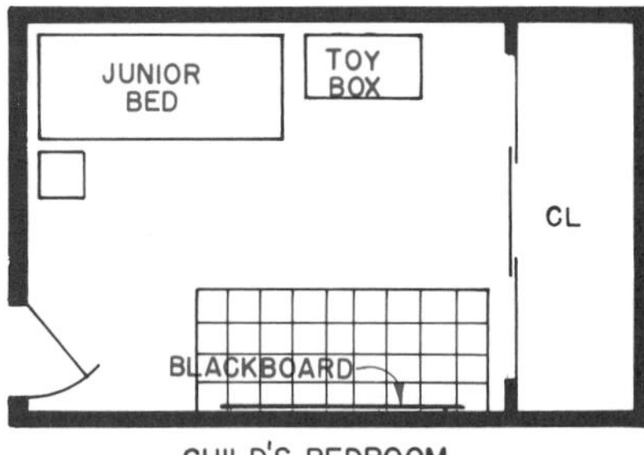

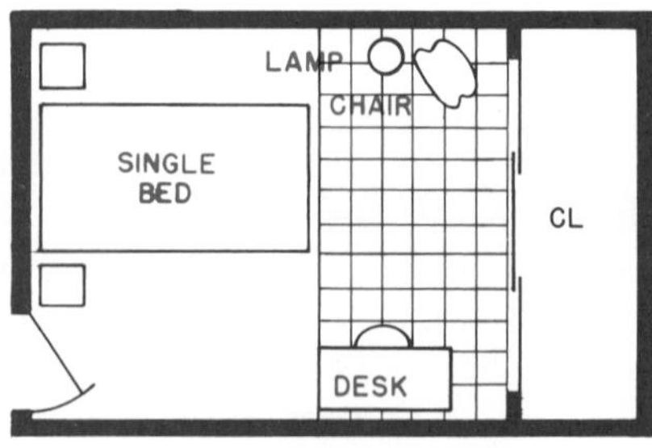

Fig. 21–16. Bedroom furnishings must change as children grow older.

Formica Corporation

Fig. 21–17. Study facilities must be provided for school-age children.

ties for study and some hobby activities should be provided, such as a desk and work table (Fig. 21–17). Storage space for books, models, and athletic equipment is also desirable.

DECOR

Bedrooms should be decorated in quiet, restful tones. Matching or contrasting bedspreads, draperies, and carpets help accent the color scheme. Uncluttered furniture with simple lines also helps to develop a restful atmosphere in the bedroom.

PROBLEMS

1. **Design a bedroom, 100 square feet (or 10 m^2) in size, for a very young child.**

Fig. 21–19. Draw a floor plan of this bedroom.

Armstrong Cork Company

LIVING ROOM
BATH
HALL
SUN PORCH
11′-0″ x 7′-6″
BEDROOM
13′-6″ x 11′-0″
BEDROOM
13′-0″ x 16′-0″
CL
CL

Fig. 21–18. Redesign the sleeping area for a family of four.

2. **Design a bedroom, 150 square feet (or 15 m^2) in size, for a teenager.**
3. **Design a master bedroom which is 200 square feet (or 20 m^2) in size.**
4. **List five things which make a bedroom comfortable for you. Draw the furniture and show its placement to illustrate your list.**
5. **How could you make your own bedroom more comfortable?**
6. **A family composed of a mother, a father, and a baby bought a home with the bedroom area shown in Fig. 21–18. The family has expanded and now consists of the mother, the father, and two teenagers. Redesign their bedroom area to fit their needs. Additional area may be added to the exterior of the house.**
7. **Draw a floor plan for a bedroom for two boys as suggested in Fig. 21–19.**
8. **The bath shown in Fig. 21–20 adjoins a master bedroom. Sketch or draw a floor plan of a master bedroom suite using this bath.**
9. **Define these architectural terms: *alcove, insulation, acoustical tile, cross-ventilation.***

Fig. 21–20. Draw or sketch a floor plan of a master-bedroom suite including this master bath.

Kohler Co.

UNIT 22

Baths

The design of the bathroom requires careful planning, as does every other room in the house. The bath must be planned to be functional, attractive, and easily maintained (Fig. 22–1).

Armstrong Cork Company

Fig. 22–1. A functional and attractive bathroom.

FUNCTION

In addition to the normal functions of the bath, facilities may also be included for dressing, exercising, sunning, and laundering (Fig. 22–2). Designing the bath involves the appropriate placing of fixtures; providing for adequate ventilation, lighting, and heating; and planning efficient runs for plumbing pipes.

Ideally it would be advisable to provide a bath for each bedroom, as in Fig. 22–3. Usually this provision is not possible, and a central bath is designed to meet the needs of the entire family (Fig. 22–4). A bath for general use and a bath adjacent to the master bedroom are a desirable compromise (Fig. 22–5). When it is impossible to have a bath with the master bedroom (Fig. 22–6), the general bath should be accessible from all bedrooms in the sleeping area. A bath may also function as a dressing room (Fig. 22–7). In this case, a combination bath and dressing room with space for clothing storage can be placed between the bathroom and the bedroom.

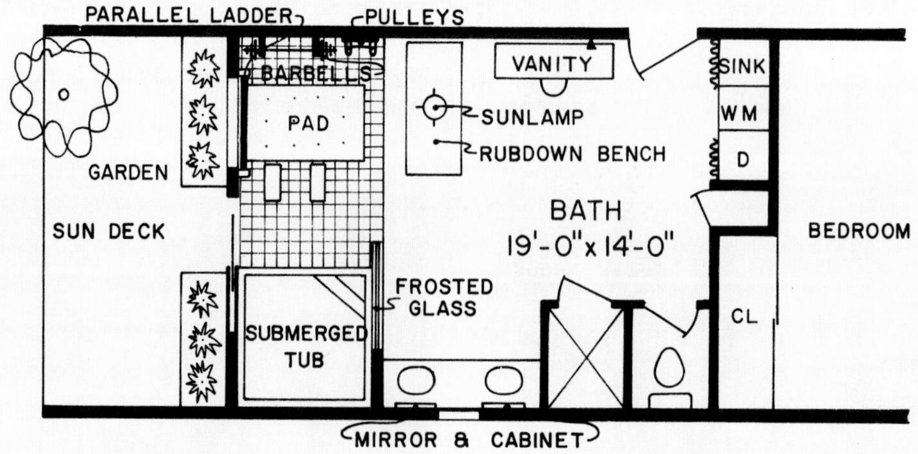

Fig. 22–2. A bath may be designed for many functions.

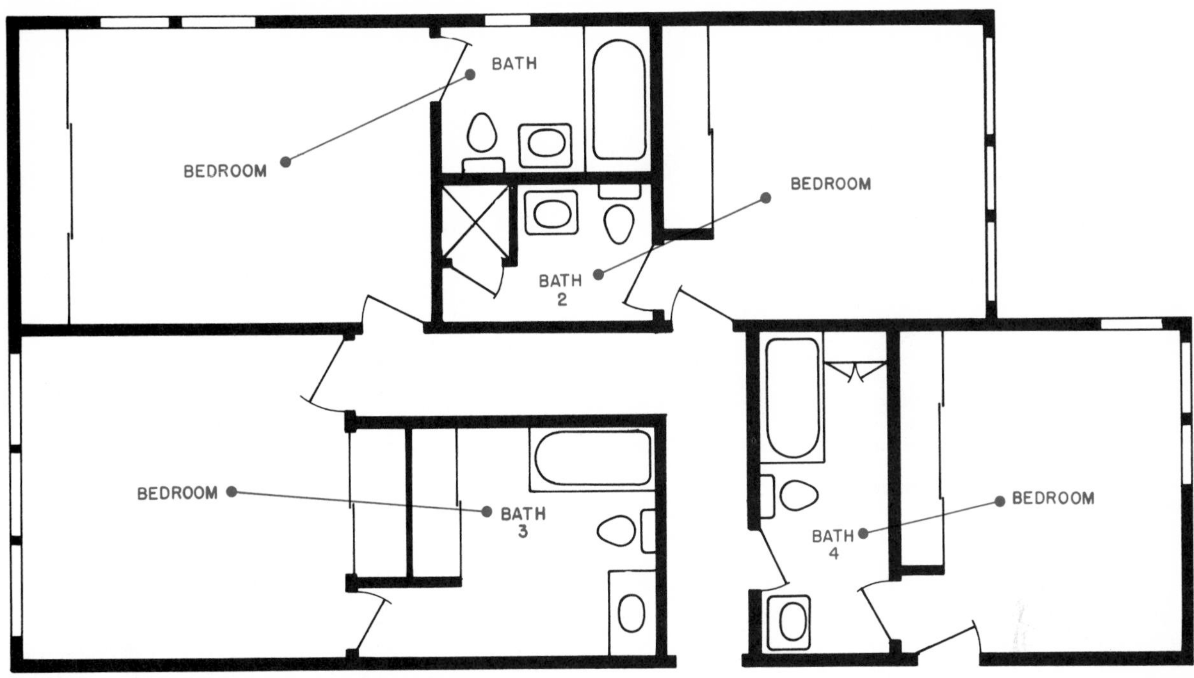

Fig. 22–3. A bath for each bedroom would be ideal.

Fig. 22–4. A central bath serves the entire family.

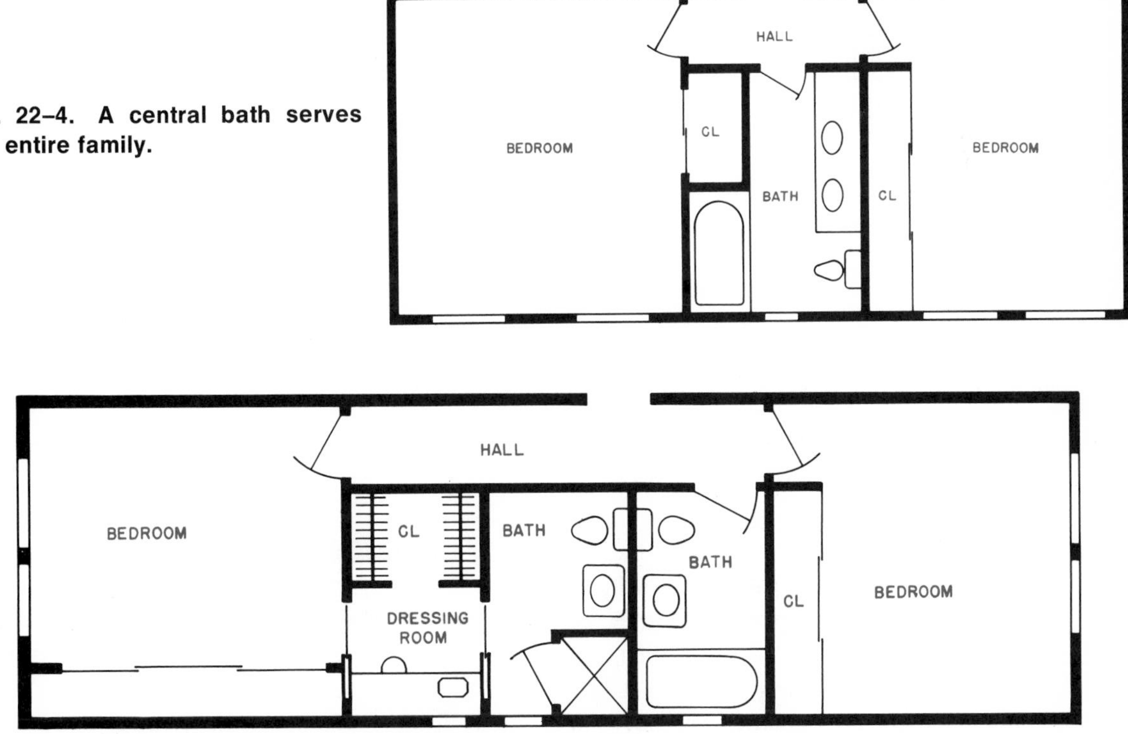

Fig. 22–5. A bath for the master bedroom and another bath for other bedrooms is a convenient arrangement.

Southern California Edison Co.

Fig. 22–6. A master bedroom bath.

Fixtures
The three basic fixtures included in most bathrooms are a lavatory, water closet, and tub or shower. The efficiency of the bath is greatly dependent upon the effectiveness of the arrangement of these three fixtures. Mirrors should be located a distance from the tub to prevent fogging. Sinks should be well lighted and free from traffic. If sinks are placed 18″ (460 mm) from other fixtures, they need no separate plumbing lines. The water closet needs a minimum of 15″ (380 mm) from the center to the side wall or other fixtures (Fig. 22–8). Tubs and showers are available in a great variety of sizes and shapes. Square, rectangular, or sunken-pool tubs allow flexibility in fixture arrangement.

Ventilation
Baths should have either natural ventilation from a window or forced ventilation from an exhaust fan. Care should be taken to place windows in a position where they will not cause a draft on the tub or interfere with privacy.

Lighting
Lighting should be relatively shadowless in the area used for grooming (Fig. 22–9). Shadowless general lighting can be achieved by the use of fluorescent tubes on the ceiling, covered with glass or plastic panels, as shown in Fig. 22–10. Skylights, as shown in Fig. 22–11, can also be used for general illumination if the bath is without outside walls.

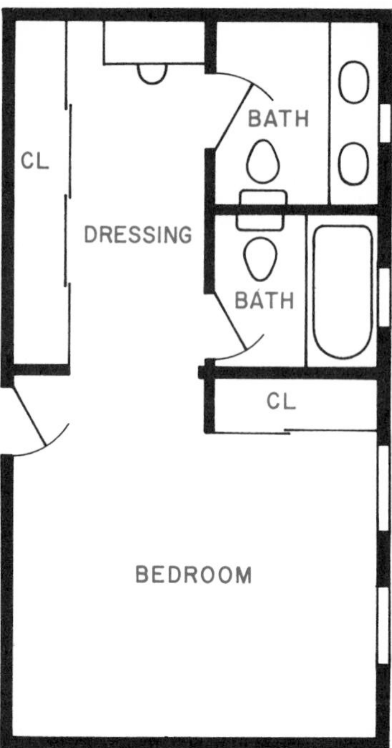

Fig. 22–7. A bedroom with a compartment bath and dressing area.

Heating
Heating in the bath is most important to prevent chills. In addition to the conventional heating outlets, an electric heater or heat lamp is often used to provide instant heat. It is advisable to have the source of heat under the window to eliminate drafts. All heaters should be properly ventilated.

Plumbing Lines
The plumbing lines that carry water to and from the fixtures should be concealed and minimized as much as possible. When two

Fig. 22–8. Water-closet spacing.

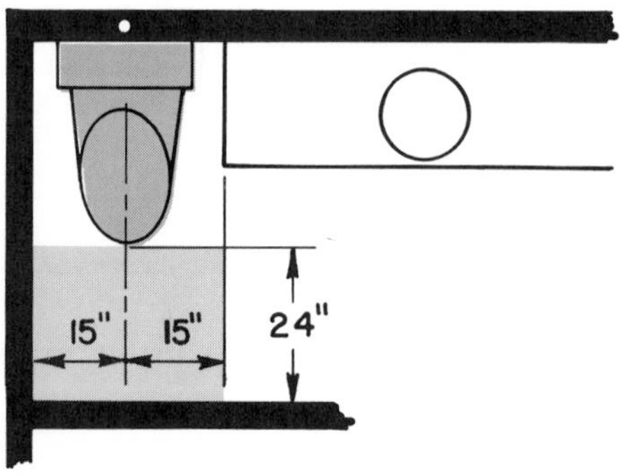

General Electric Company

Fig. 22–9. Shadowless lighting is desirable.

C. R. Campbell Home

Fig. 22–10. Continuous fluorescent tubes under frosted glass help to diffuse light.

bathrooms are placed side by side, placing the fixtures back to back on opposite sides of the plumbing wall results in a reduction of the length of plumbing lines (Fig. 22–12). In multiple-story dwellings, the length of plumbing lines can be reduced and a common plumbing wall used if the baths are placed directly above each other. When a bath is placed on a second floor, a plumbing wall must be provided through the first floor for the soil and water pipes.

Layout

There are two basic types of bathroom layout, the compartment and the open plan. In the *compartment plan,* partitions (sliding doors, glass dividers, louvers, or even plants) are used to divide the bath into several compartments, one housing the water closet, another the lavatory area, and the third the bathing area (Fig. 22–13). In the *open plan,* all bath fixtures are completely visible.

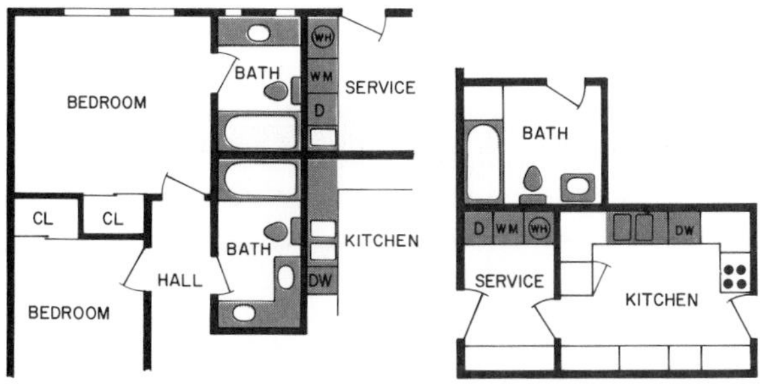

Fig. 22–12. Fixture arrangements that compact plumbing lines.

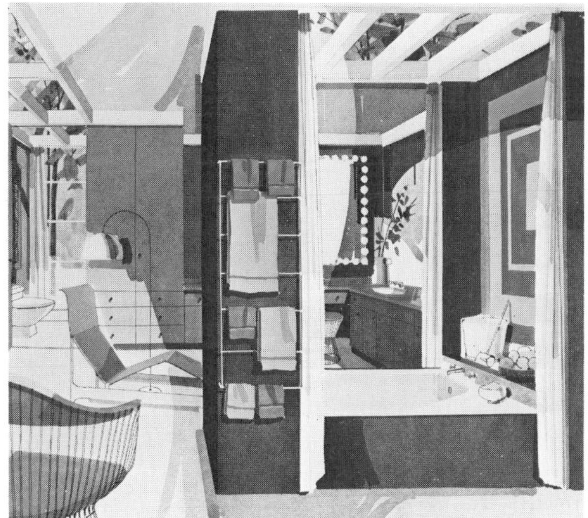

Consoweld Corp.

Fig. 22–11. Skylights used for bath illumination.

Consoweld Corp.

Fig. 22–13. A compartment bath.

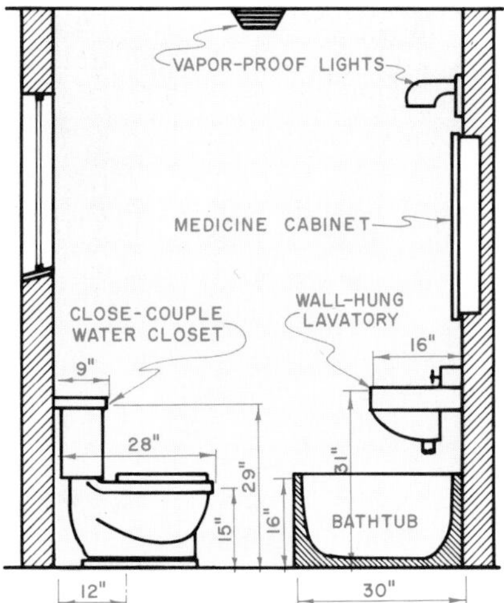

Fig. 22–14. Typical fixture sizes.

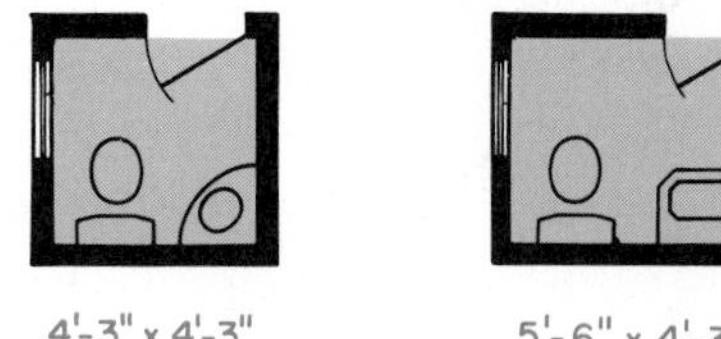

Fig. 22–15. Minimum-sized baths.

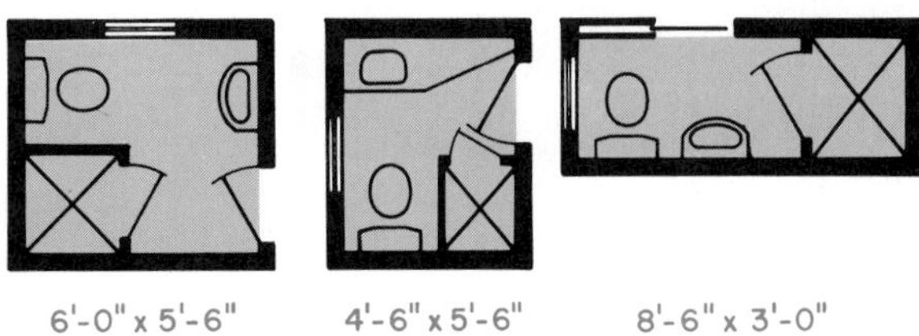

Fig. 22–16. Small baths.

A bath designed for, or used partially by, children should include a low or tilt-down mirror, benches for reaching the lavatory, low towel racks, and shelves for personal items and bath toys.

SIZE AND SHAPE

The size and shape of the bath are influenced by the spacing of basic fixtures, the number of auxiliary functions requiring additional equipment, the arrangement or compartmentalization of areas, and the relationship to other rooms in the house.

Furniture
Typical fixture sizes, as shown in Fig. 22–14, greatly influence the ultimate size of the bath. Figure 22–15 shows minimum-sized baths. Figure 22–16 shows small baths. Figure 22–17 shows average baths, and Fig. 22–18 shows large baths. Regardless of the size, these baths contain the three basic fixtures: lavatory, tub or shower, and water closet.

The sizes given here refer to complete baths and not to half-baths, which include only a lavatory and water closet. Half-baths are used in conjunction with the living area and therefore are not designed for bathing.

Accessories
In addition to the three basic fixtures, the following accessories are often included in a bath designed for optimum use:

exhaust fan
sunlamp
heat lamp
instant wall heater
medicine cabinet
extra mirrors
magnifying mirror

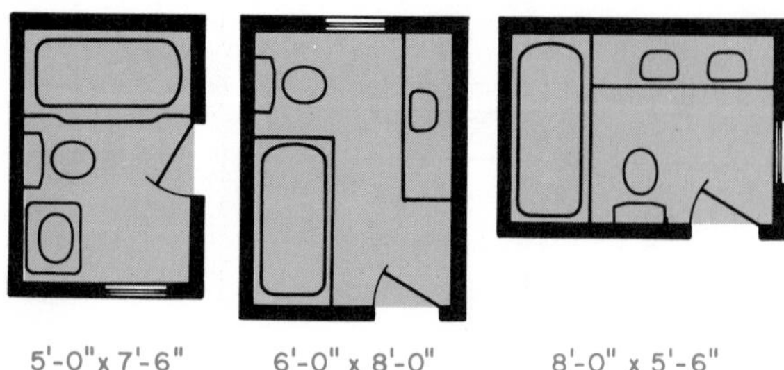

Fig. 22–17. Average-sized baths.

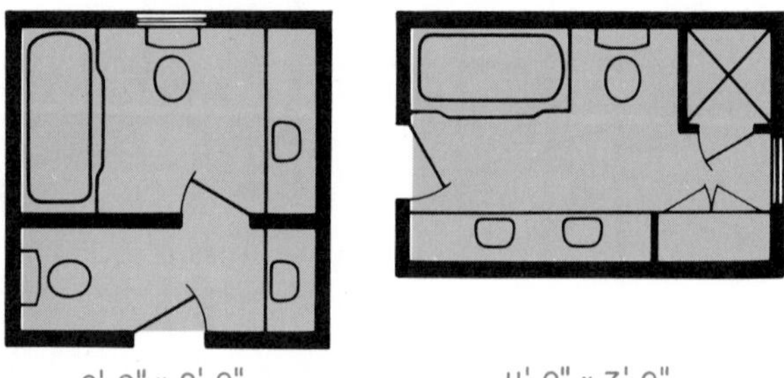

Fig. 22–18. Large baths.

American Standard, Inc.

Fig. 22–19. A bath designed with many extra features.

Kohler Co.

Fig. 22–20. Waterproof materials should be used in the bath.

extra counter space
dressing table
whirlpool bath
foot-pedal control for water
single-mixing, one-control faucets
facility for linen storage
clothes hamper
bidet

Figure 22–19 shows a bath with many of these extra features.

DECOR

The bath should be decorated and designed to provide the maximum amount of light and color. Materials used in the bath should be water-resistant, easily maintained, and easily sanitized (Fig. 22–20). Tiles, linoleum, marble, plastic laminate, and glass are excellent materials for bathroom use. If wallpaper or wood paneling is used, it should be waterproof. If plastered or dry-wall construction is exposed, a gloss or semigloss paint should be used on the surface.

Fixtures and accessories should match in color. Fixtures are now available in a variety of colors. Matching counter tops and cabinets are also available.

Baths need not be small boxes with plumbing fixtures. With new building materials and products, bathrooms can be designed in an infinite number of arrangements and decors, as shown in Fig. 22–21.

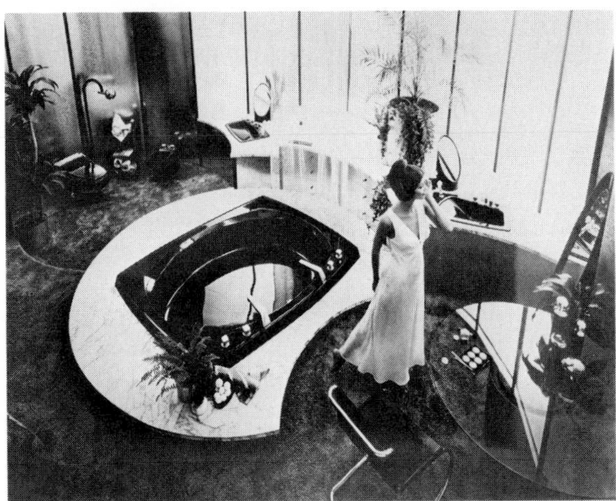

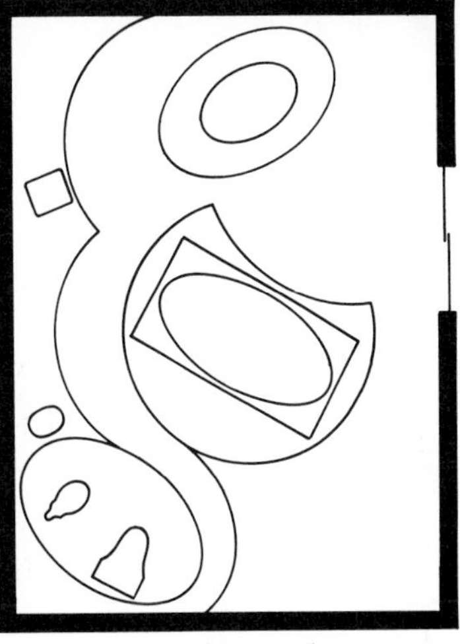

11'-0" x 15'-0"

Kohler Co.

Fig. 22–21. A bathroom designed with unusual space relationships.

American Standard, Inc.

Fig. 22–22. A precast shower unit.

Universal-Rundle Corp.

Fig. 22–23. A precast shower and tub unit.

New materials and components are now available which enable the designer to plan bathrooms with modular units that range from one-piece molded showers and tubs, as shown in Figs. 22–22 and 22–23, to entire bath modules, as shown in Fig. 22–24. In these units, plumbing and electrical wiring are connected after the unit is installed.

Today's bathroom need not be strictly functional and sterile in decor. Bathrooms can be planned and furnished in a variety of styles. Figures 22–25 through 22–29 show examples of a variety of bathroom decors and motifs.

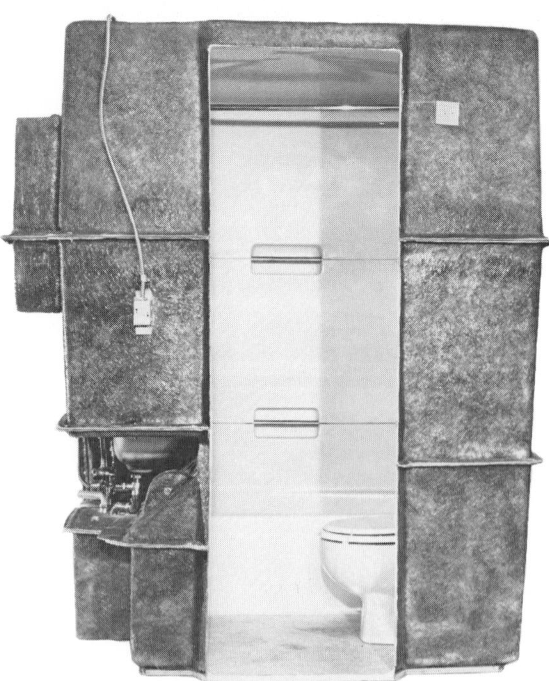

Crane Co.

Fig. 22–24. A precast total bath unit.

American Standard, Inc.

Fig. 22–25. Roman decor.

American Standard, Inc.

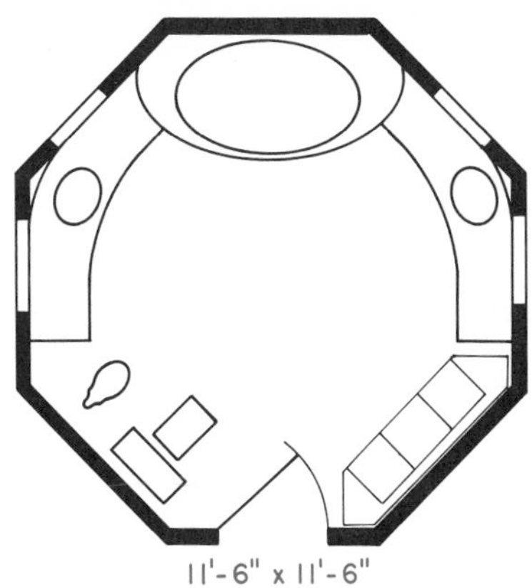

Fig. 22–26. Oriental decor.

American Standard, Inc.

Fig. 22–27. Classical decor.

Kohler Co.

Fig. 22–28. Early American decor.

Kohler Co.

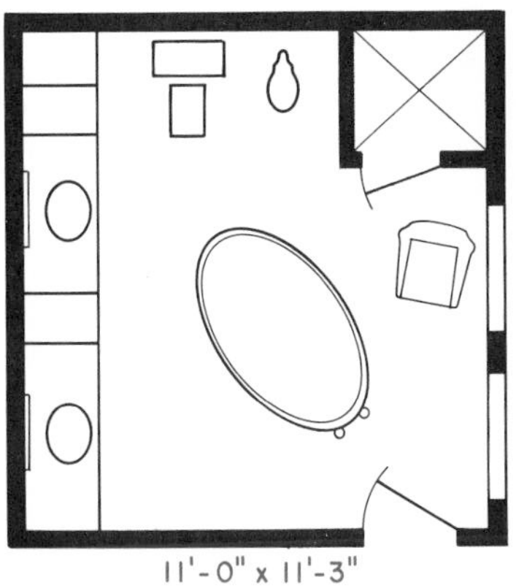

Fig. 22–29. Gay Nineties decor.

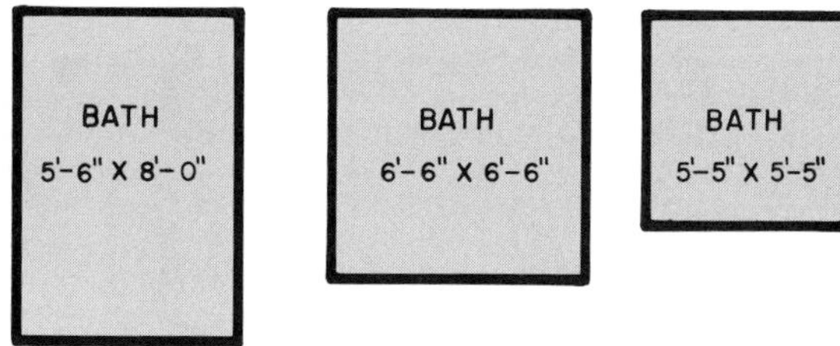

Fig. 22–30. Add fixtures to these plans.

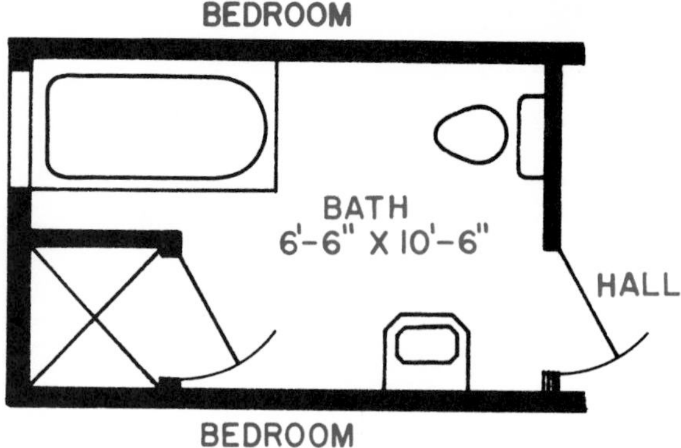

Fig. 22–31. Remodel this bath.

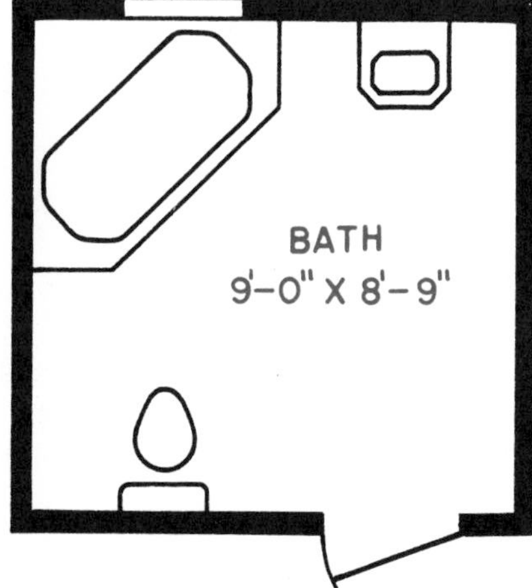

Fig. 22–32. Remodel this bath.

Potlatch Corp.

Fig. 22–33. Sketch a plan for this bath.

PROBLEMS

1. Make a plan for adding fixtures to Fig. 22–30.
2. Draw a plan for remodeling the bath in Fig. 22–31, making the room more efficient.
3. Draw a plan for remodeling the bath in Fig. 22–32, making the room more efficient.
4. Design one bedroom and bath in an area of 12′ × 17′ (or 3.6 × 5.2 m).
5. Sketch or draw a floor plan of the bath shown in Fig. 22–33.
6. Design two bedrooms and a bath in an area 13′ × 34′ (or 4.0 × 10.4 m).
7. Design two bedrooms and a bath or a master bedroom with bath in an area of 1000 square feet (or 100 m^2).
8. Redesign the floor plan shown in Fig. 6–2. Add two bedrooms and expand the bath facilities to accommodate these rooms.
9. Define these architectural terms: *water closet, lavatory, fixture, open bath, sunken tub, shower stall, square tub, rectangular tub.*

PART TWO

The general design of a structure is interpreted through several basic architectural plans. These include floor plans, elevations, and pictorial drawings. *Floor plans* show the arrangement of the internal parts of the design. *Elevations* graphically describe the exterior design. *Pictorial drawings* are prepared to show how the structure will appear when complete. In Part Two you will learn how to prepare these basic architectural drawings.

Basic Architectural Plans

SECTION 5

Drafting Techniques

Most of the drafting skills and techniques used in architectural work are similar to those you have learned in mechanical drawing courses. However, there are some drafting procedures that are somewhat different. These involve the use of line techniques, templates, lettering practices, time-saving devices, and dimensioning practices. The differences are primarily due to the large size of most architectural drawings and to the great speed with which architectural plans must be prepared. For these reasons architectural drawings contain many abbreviated techniques.

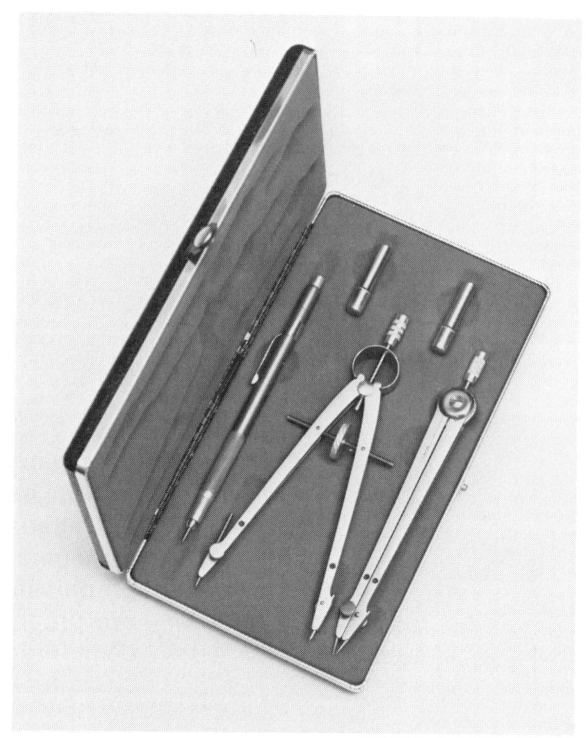

Vemco

UNIT 23

Architectural Line Weights

Architects use various line weights to emphasize or deemphasize areas of a drawing. Architectural draftsmen also use different line weights. Architectural line weights are standardized in order to make possible the consistent interpretation of architectural drawings. Figure 23–1 shows some of the common types of lines and line weights used on architectural drawings. You should learn the name of the line, the number of the pencil used to make the line, and the technique used to draw the line.

ALPHABET OF LINES

Hard pencils, as shown in Fig. 23–2, are used for architectural layout work. Medium pencils are used for most final lines, and soft pencils are used for lettering, cutting-plane lines, and shading pictorial drawings. Figure 23–2 shows a comparison of the various types of pencils and the lines they produce.

Floor-Plan Lines

Figure 23–3 shows some of the common lines used on architectural floor plans.

Object, or *visible, lines* are used to show the main outline of the building, including exterior walls, interior partitions, porches, patios, driveways, and walls. These lines should be the outstanding lines on the drawing.

Dimension lines are thin unbroken lines upon which building dimensions are placed. Figure 23–4 shows dimension lines with several types of arrow heads.

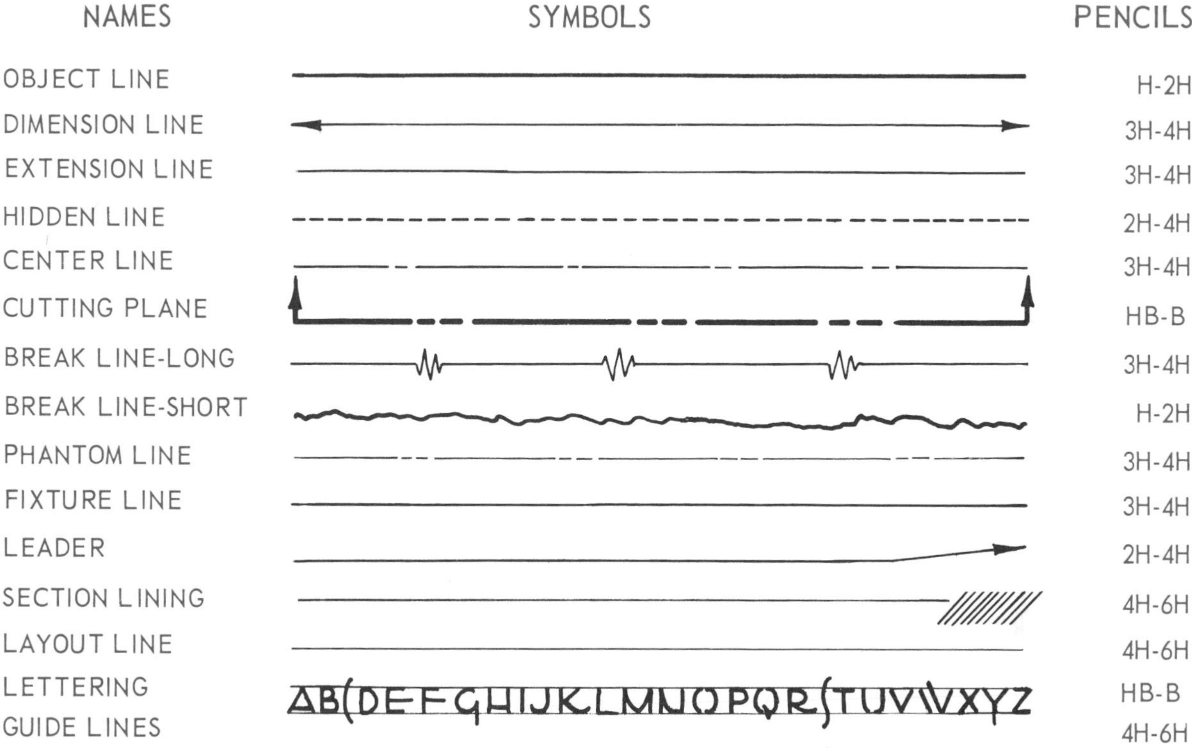

NAMES
SYMBOLS
PENCILS
OBJECT LINE
H-2H
DIMENSION LINE
3H-4H
EXTENSION LINE
3H-4H
HIDDEN LINE
2H-4H
CENTER LINE
3H-4H
CUTTING PLANE
HB-B
BREAK LINE-LONG
3H-4H
BREAK LINE-SHORT
H-2H
PHANTOM LINE
3H-4H
FIXTURE LINE
3H-4H
LEADER
2H-4H
SECTION LINING
4H-6H
LAYOUT LINE
4H-6H
LETTERING
ABCDEFGHIJKLMNOPQRSTUVWXYZ
HB-B
GUIDE LINES
4H-6H

Fig. 23–1. Architectural line weights.

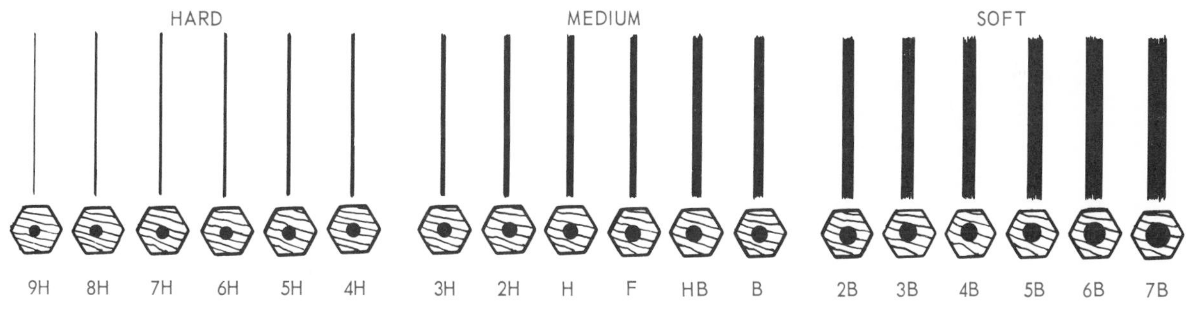

Fig. 23–2. Cross sections of pencils and matching lines used for architectural drawings.

Extension lines extend from the building to permit dimensioning. They are drawn very lightly to eliminate confusion with the building outlines.

Hidden lines are used to show areas which are not visible on the surface but which exist behind the plane of projection. Hidden lines are also used in floor plans to show objects *above* the floor section, such as wall cabinets, arches, and beams.

Center lines denote the center of symmetrical objects such as exterior doors and windows. These lines are usually necessary for dimensioning purposes.

Cutting-plane lines are very heavy lines used to denote an area to be sectioned, because it would interfere with other lines on the drawing. In this case, the only part of the line drawn is the extreme end of the line.

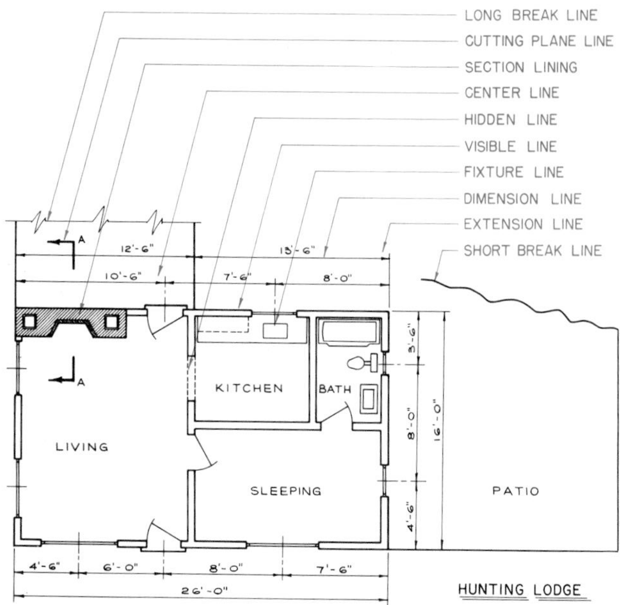

Fig. 23–3. Types of lines used on floor plans.

Break lines are used when an area cannot or should not be drawn entirely. A ruled line with freehand breaks is used for long, straight breaks. A wavy, uneven freehand line is used for smaller, irregular breaks.

Phantom lines are used to indicate alternate positions of moving parts, adjacent positions of related parts, and repeated detail.

Fixture lines outline the shape of kitchen, laundry, and bathroom fixtures, or built-in furniture. These lines are light to eliminate confusion with object lines.

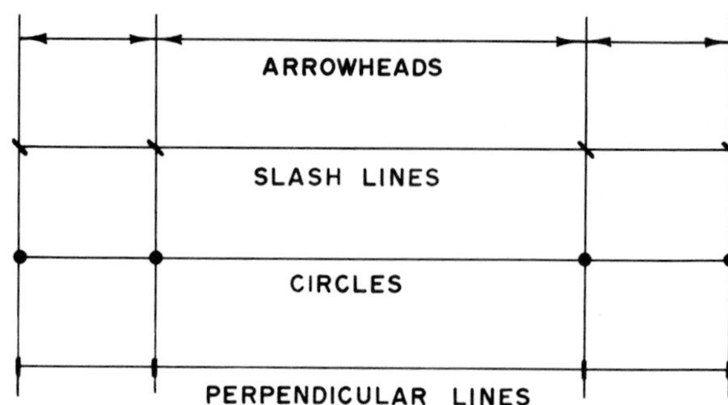

Fig. 23–4. Dimension lines with alternative arrowheads.

Leaders are used to connect a note or dimension to part of the building. They are drawn lightly and sometimes are curved to eliminate confusion with other lines.

Section lines are used to draw the section lining in sectional drawings. A different material symbol is used for each building material. The section lining is drawn lighter than the object lines.

Elevation Lines

Figure 23–5 shows the application of the lines used on architectural elevation drawings. The technique and weight of each of the lines are exactly the same as those for the lines used on floor plans except that they are drawn on a vertical plane.

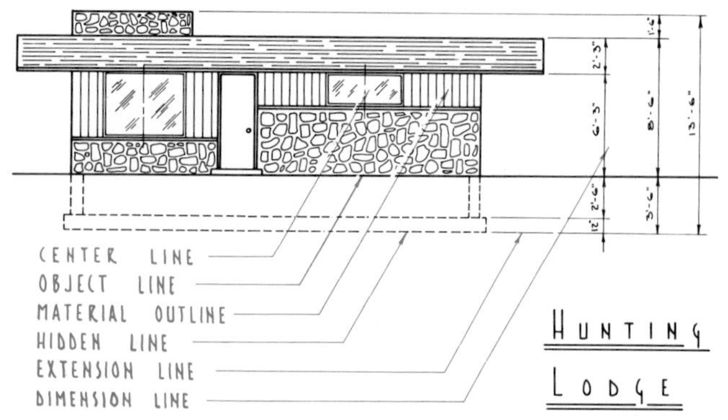

Fig. 23–5. Types of lines used on elevation drawings.

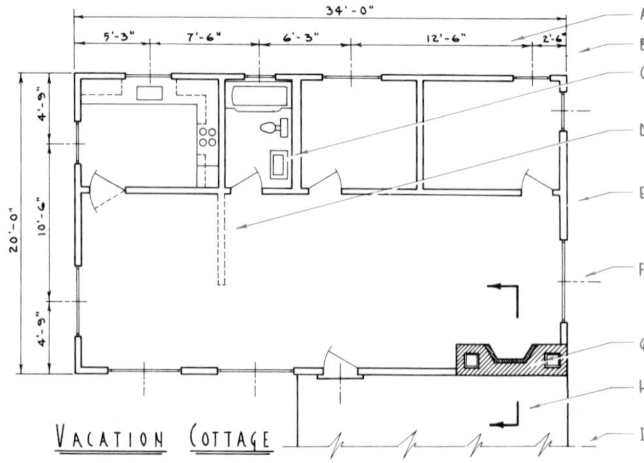

Fig. 23–6. Identify these types of lines.

PAPER

Since the type of paper on which the line is drawn will greatly affect the line weight, different pencils may be necessary. Weather conditions, such as temperature and humidity, also greatly affect the line quality. During periods of high humidity, harder pencils must be employed.

PROBLEMS

1. **Identify the types of lines indicated by the letters in Fig. 23–6.**
2. **List the grade of pencil you would use to draw each of the lines shown in Figs. 23–3 and 23–4.**
3. **Practice drawing each of the lines shown in Fig. 23–1, using your T square and triangle.**
4. **Draw an object line, a dimension line, and a cutting-plane line on several different surfaces, such as tracing paper, tracing cloth, vellum, bond paper, and illustration board. Compare the results.**
5. **Define these terms: *line weights, alphabet of lines, hard lead, soft lead, object lines, dimension lines, extension lines, hidden lines, center lines, cutting-plane lines, break lines, phantom lines, fixture lines, leaders, section lines, elevation lines.***

UNIT 24

The Architect's Scale

The architect's scale is the trademark of the architect, just as the stethoscope is the universal trademark of the physician. The architect's scale is used not only for preparing drawings, as shown in Fig. 24–1A, but also is used in a variety of related architectural jobs such as bidding, estimating and specification writing (Fig. 24–1B), and model building.

Bond Ryder Associates

Fig. 24–1A. An architect using an architect's scale.

REDUCED SCALE

The architect's scale is used to reduce the size of a structure so that it can be drawn on paper of standard size; or it is used to enlarge a detail that may be too small to interpret or to dimension accurately.

Divisions

Architect's scales are either open-divided or fully divided. In *fully divided scales* each main unit on the scale is fully subdivided throughout the scale. On *open-divided scales*, only the main units of the scale are graduated, with a fully subdivided extra unit at each end, as shown in Fig. 24–2. The main function of an architect's scale is to enable the architect, designer, and draftsman to think in relation to

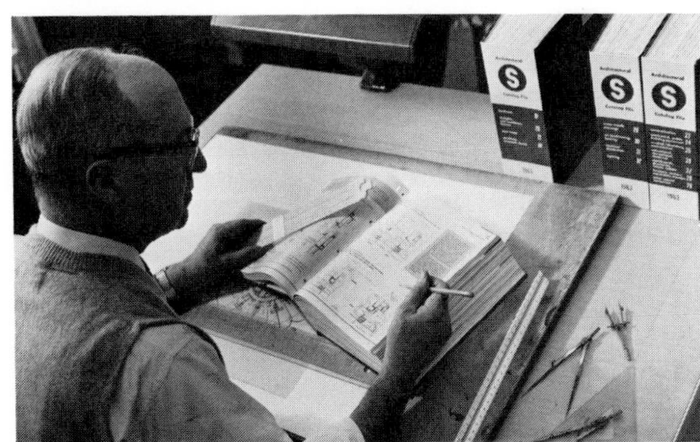

Sweet's Division, McGraw-Hill Information Systems Company

Fig. 24–1B. The architect's scale is used in checking drawings for bidding, estimating, and specification writing.

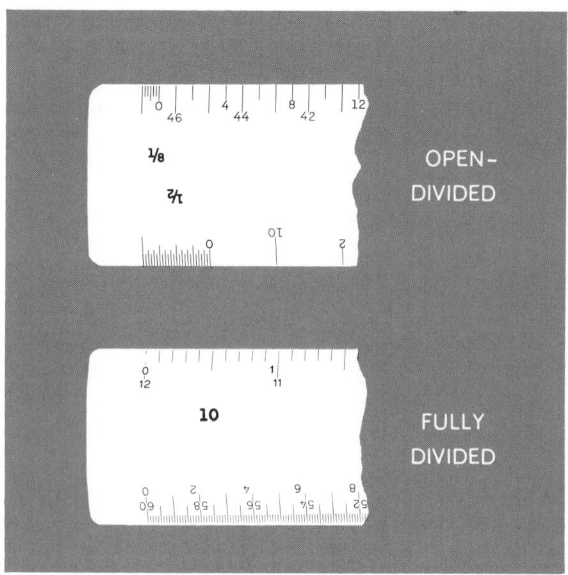

Fig. 24–2. Kinds of divisions on architect's scales.

the actual size of the structure and to convert these measurements into smaller values for illustration purposes. For example, when a drawing is prepared to a reduced scale in which 1′ (12″) is actually drawn 1/4″ long, the architect does not think of this 1/4″ line as representing ¼″ but as actually being 1′ long on the reduced scale, as shown in Fig. 24–3.

TYPES

Architect's scales are of either the bevel or the triangular style, as shown in Fig. 24–4. You will notice that the triangular scale has 6 sides

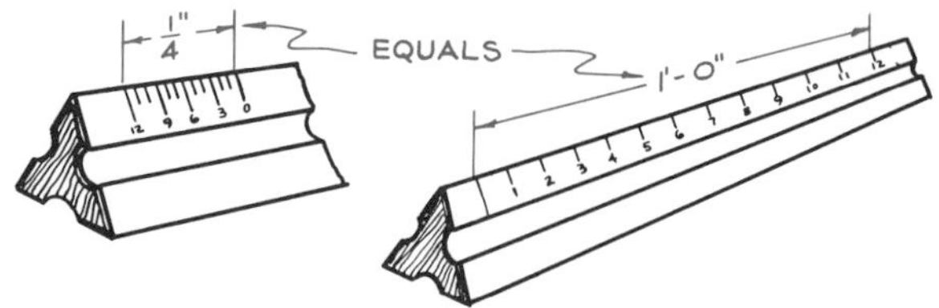

Fig. 24–3. On a drawing ¼″ may represent 1′—0″.

which will accommodate 11 different scales. These scales are a full scale of 12″ graduated 16 parts to an inch and 10 other open-divided scales which include ratios of 3/32, 1/8, 3/16, 1/4, 3/8, 1/2, 3/4, 1, 1 1/2, and 3. Two scales are located on each face. One scale reads from left to right. The other scale, which is twice as large, reads from right to left. For example, the 1/4″ scale and, half of this, the 1/8″ scale are placed on the same face. Similarly, the 3/4″ scale and the 3/8″ scale are placed on the same face but are read from different directions. Be sure you are reading in the correct direction when using an open-divided scale. Otherwise your measurement could be wrong, since the second row of numbers read from the opposite side at half scale, or twice the scale, as seen in Fig. 24–5.

The architect's scale can be used to make the divisions of the scale equal 1′ or 1″. For example, in the 1/2″ scale shown in Fig. 24–6, this 1/2″ represents 1″. The same scale in Fig. 24–7 is shown representing 1′. Therefore 1/2″ can equal 1″ or 1′.

Since buildings are large, most major architectural drawings use a scale which relates the parts of an inch to a foot. Architectural details such as cabinet construction and joints

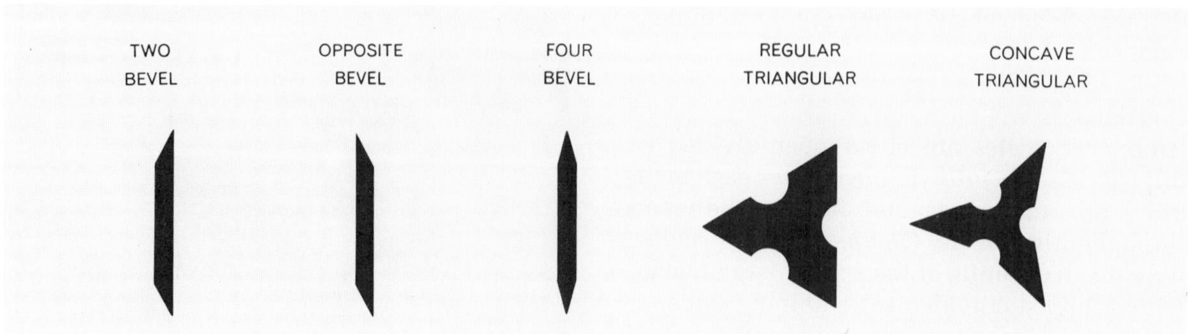

Fig. 24–4. Styles of architect's scales.

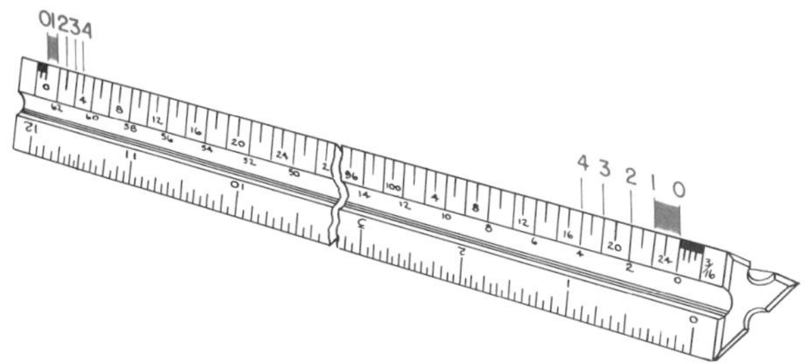

Fig. 24–5. **The scale that reads from right to left is twice as large as the scale that reads from left to right.**

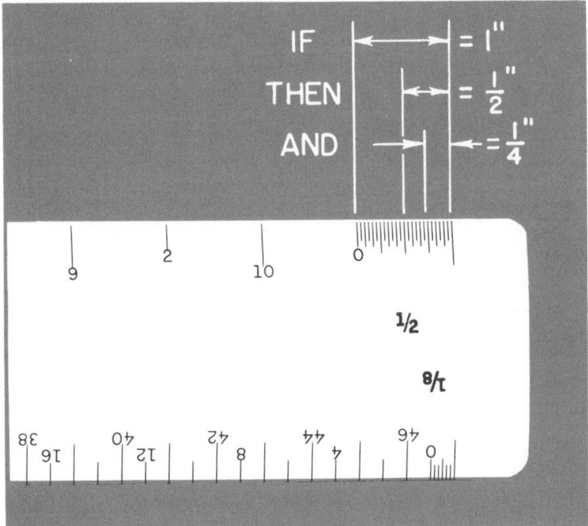

Fig. 24–6. If ½″ equals 1″, then ¼″ equals ½″, and ⅛″ equals ¼″.

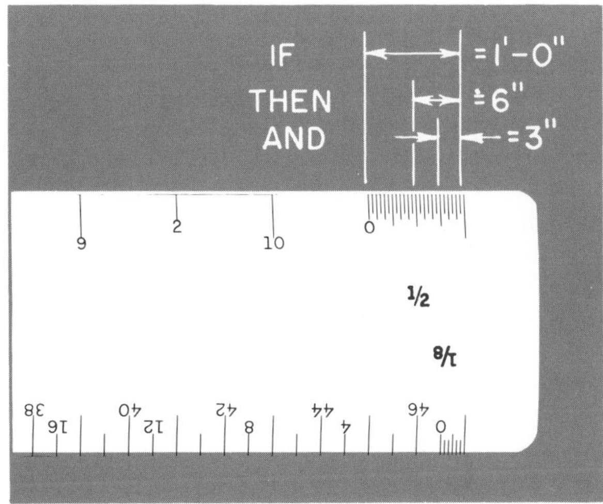

Fig. 24–7. If ½″ equals 1′—0″, then ¼″ equals 6″, and ⅛″ equals 3″.

often use the parts of an inch to represent 1″. In either case, on open-divided scales the divided section at the end of the scale is not a part of the numerical scale. When measuring with the scale, start with the zero line, not with the fully divided section. Always start with the number of feet you wish to measure and then add the additional inches in the subdivided area. For example, in Fig. 24–8 the distance of 4′—11″ is derived by measuring from the line 4 to 0, then 11″ past 0, since each of the lines in the subdivided parts equals 1″. On smaller scales these lines may equal only 2″. On larger scales they may equal ½″. Figure 24–9 shows a further application of this use of the architect's scale. You will notice that the dimensioned distance of 8′—0″ extends from the 8 to the 0 on the scale, and the 6″ wall is shown as one-half of the subdivided foot on the end. Likewise you can read the distance of 2′—0″ on the ¼″ scale shown in this illustration.

Scale Selection

The selection of the proper scale is sometimes difficult. If the structure to be drawn is extremely large, a small scale must be used. Small structures can be drawn to a larger scale, since they will not take up as much space on the drawing sheet. Most floor plans, elevations, and foundation plans of residences are drawn

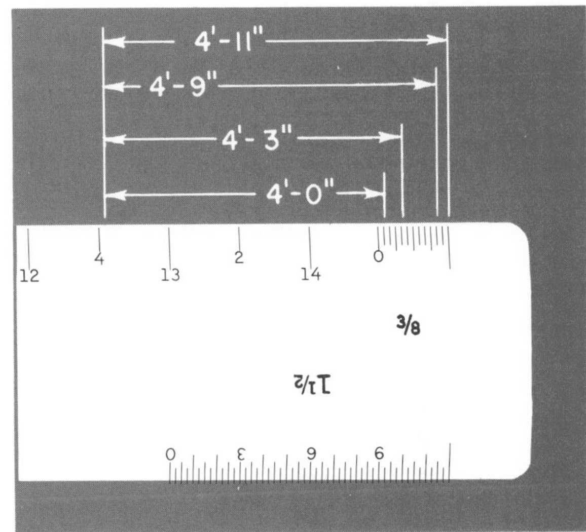

Fig. 24–8. Subdivisions at the end of an open-divided scale are used for inch measurement.

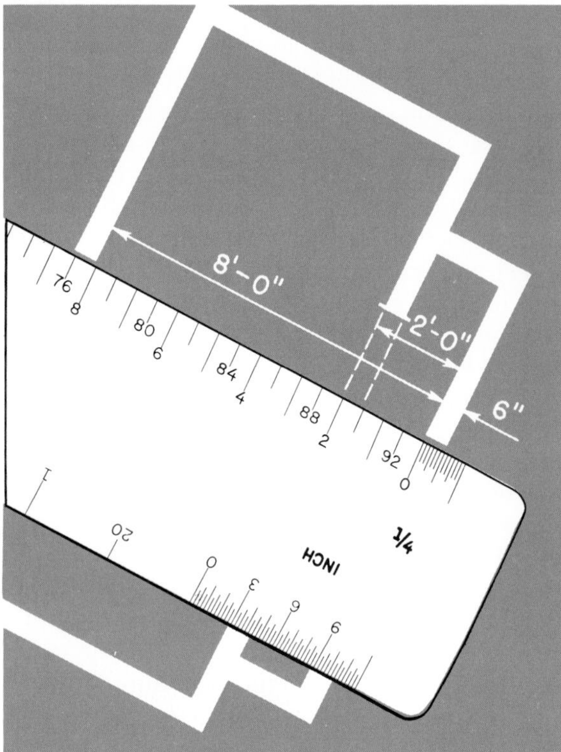

Fig. 24–9. **Subdivisions of the architect's scale can be used to indicate overall dimensions and subdimensions.**

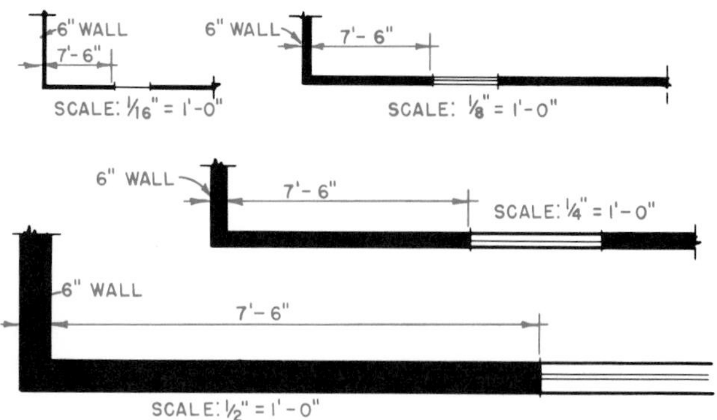

Fig. 24–10. Comparison of a similar wall drawn to several different scales.

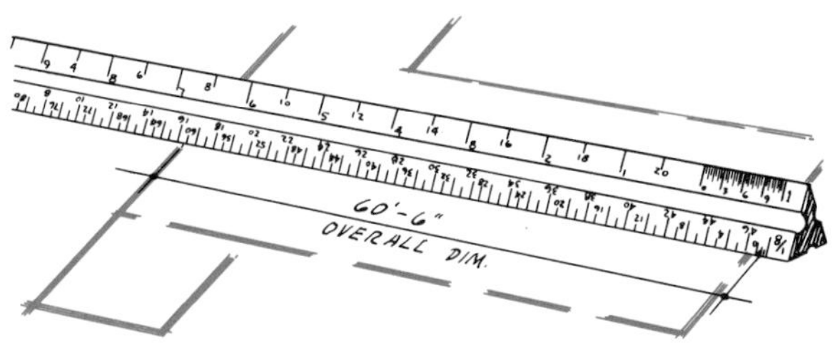

Fig. 24–11. Establish overall dimensions first.

to $\frac{1}{4}''$ scale, whereas construction details pertaining to these drawings are often drawn to $\frac{1}{2}''$, $\frac{3}{4}''$, or even $1'' = 1'$. Remember that as the scale changes, not only does the length of each line increase or decrease but also the width of the various wall thicknesses increases or decreases. The actual appearance of a typical corner wall drawn to $\frac{1}{16}'' = 1'$—$0''$, $\frac{1}{8}'' = 1'$—$0''$, $\frac{1}{4}'' = 1'$—$0''$, and $\frac{1}{2}'' = 1'$—$0''$ is shown in Fig. 24–10. You can see that the wall drawn to the scale of $\frac{1}{16}'' = 1'$—$0''$ is small and that a great amount of detail would be impossible. The $\frac{1}{2}'' = 1'$—$0''$ wall would probably cover too large an area on the drawing if the building were very large. Therefore, the $\frac{1}{4}''$ and $\frac{1}{8}''$ scales are the most popular for this type of work.

USE OF THE SCALE

The architect's scale is only as accurate as its user. In using the scale, do not accumulate distances. That is, always lay out overall dimensions first (Fig. 24–11). The width and the length will be correct and their position will not change if you are slightly off in measuring any of the subdivisions that make up the overall dimension. Furthermore, if your overall dimensions are correct, you will find it easier to check your subdimensions, since if one is off, another will also be incorrect.

Figure 24–12 shows the comparative distances used to measure $1'$—$9''$ as it appears on various architect's scales. All these scales represent $1'$—$9''$ as a reduced size. This same comparison would exist if we related the scales to $1''$ rather than $1'$. In this case, a distance of $1\frac{3}{4}''$ would have the same line length as $1'$—$9''$ on the foot representation. The $\frac{3}{32}''$, $\frac{3}{16}''$, $\frac{1}{8}''$, $\frac{1}{4}''$, $\frac{3}{8}''$, $\frac{1}{2}''$, and $\frac{3}{4}''$ scales represent a distance smaller than full size ($1\frac{3}{4}''$). The $1\frac{1}{2}''$ and $3''$ scales represent a distance $1\frac{1}{2}$ and 3 times as large as the full scale. Figure 24–13 shows the same comparison, using a distance of $5'$—$6''$ on the foot-equivalent scale. If an inch-equivalent scale were used, the distance shown would be $5\frac{1}{2}''$ in each case.

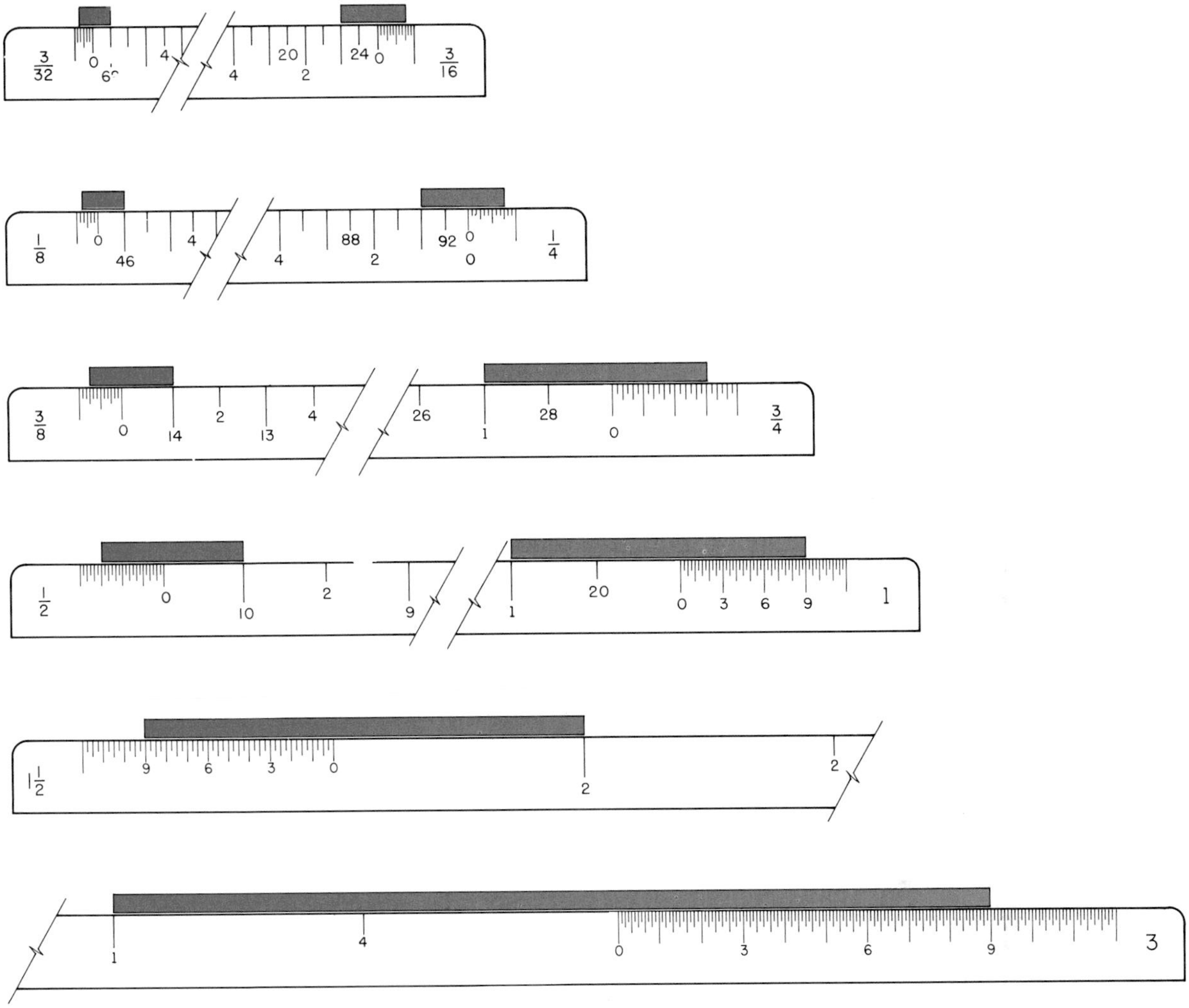

Fig. 24–12. The distance 1′—9″ as it appears on different architect's scales.

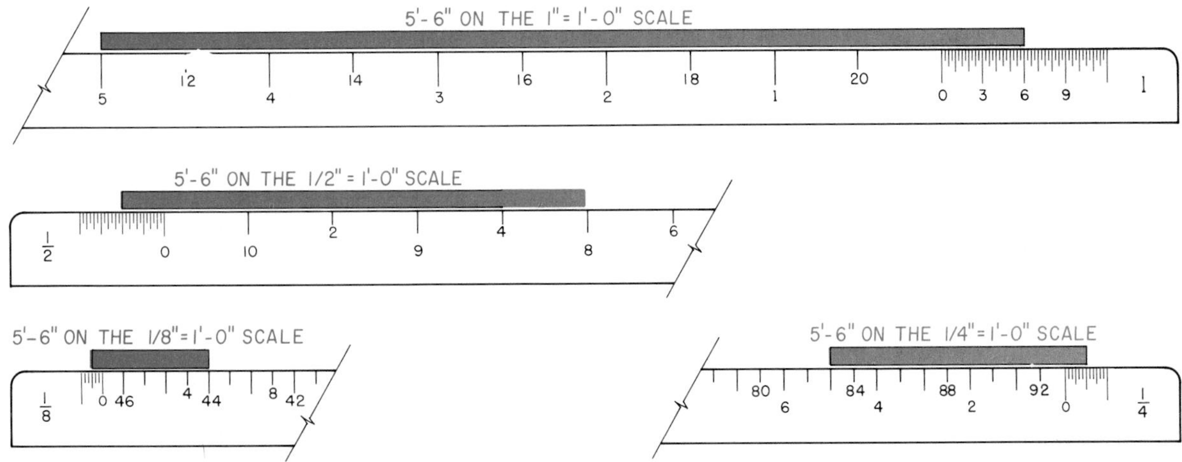

Fig. 24–13. The distance 5′—6″ shown on several architect's scales.

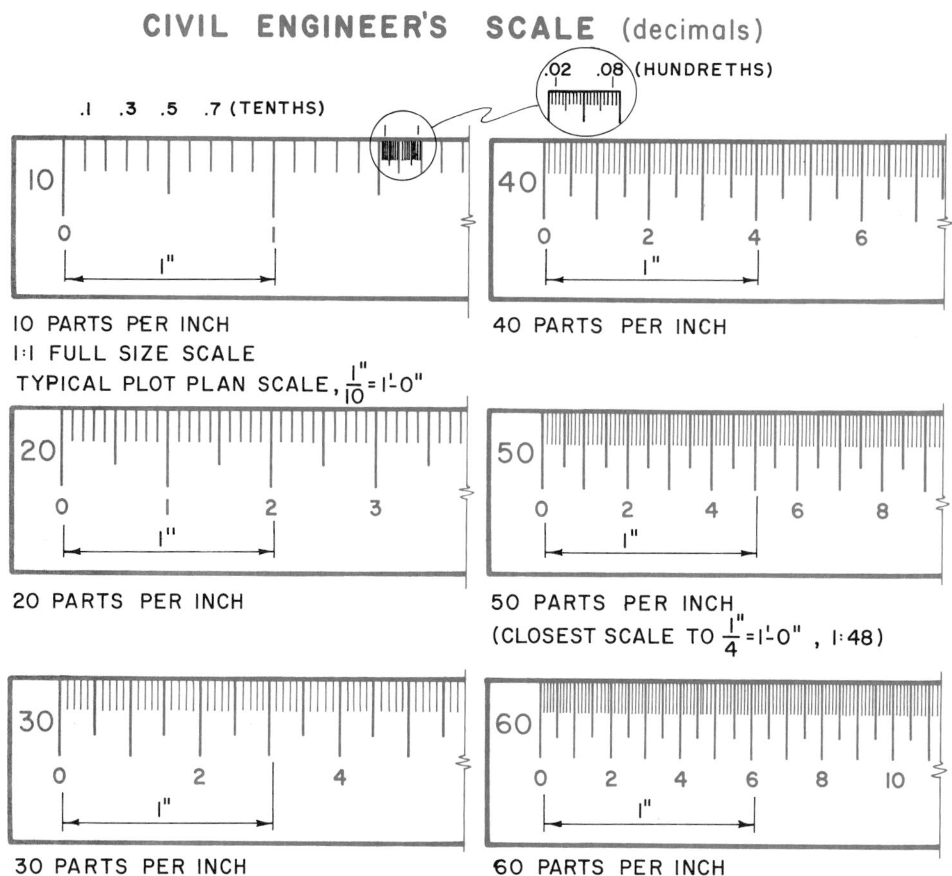

Fig. 24–14. The civil engineer's scale.

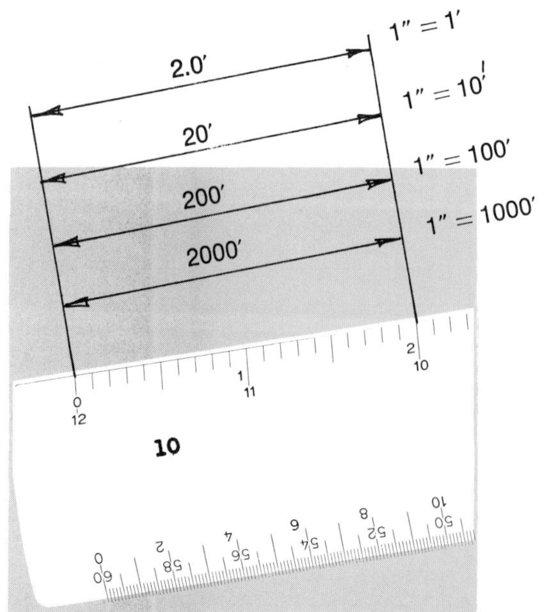

Fig. 24–15. Use of the civil engineer's scale divided by tenths.

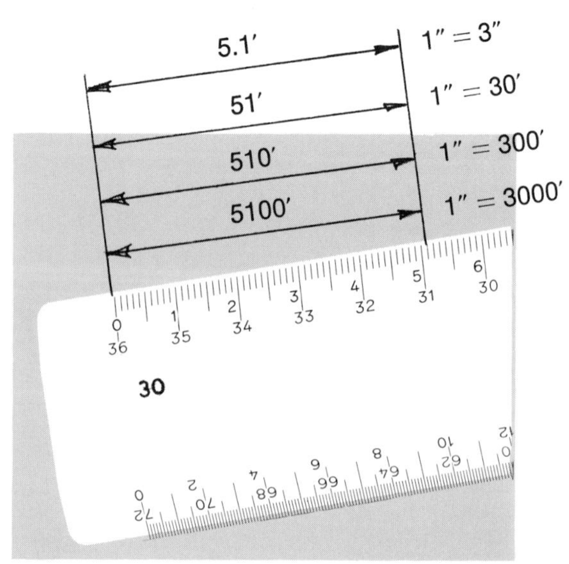

Fig. 24–16. Use of the civil engineer's scale divided by thirtieths.

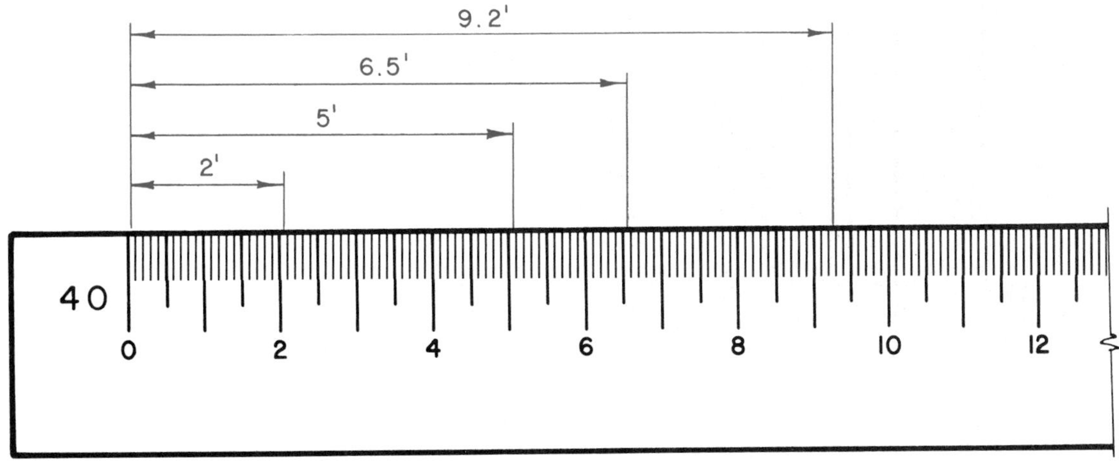

Fig. 24–17. Use of civil engineer's decimal dimensions for architectural drawing. The scale of 1″ = 4′ is the same as ¼″ = 1′—0″.

Civil Engineer's Scale

The civil engineer's scale is often used for plot plans, surveys, and landscape plans. Each scale divides the inch into decimal parts. These parts are 10, 20, 30, 40, 50, and 60 parts per inch (Fig. 24–14). Each one of these units can represent any distance, such as an inch, foot, yard, or mile, depending on the final drawing size. Typical use of this scale is shown in Figs. 24–15 and 24–16. The civil engineer's scale can also be used to draw floor plans. The scale $^1/_4$″ = 1′—0″ (1:48 ratio) is the same as 1″ = 4′ (1:48 ratio) (Fig. 24–17).

Full Architect's Scale

The full side of the architect's scale is useful in dividing any area into an equal number of parts by following these steps.

Scale the distance available, as shown in Fig. 24–18. Next, place the zero point of the architect's scale on one side line. Then count off the correct number of spaces, using any convenient unit, such as 1″ or $^1/_2$″. Place the last unit mark on the line opposite the zero point line. In Fig. 24–18 the 8-inch mark is used since 1-inch divisions are the most convenient. Mark each division and draw the dividing lines. Measure the horizontal distance between the lines to find the actual spacing; then multiply by the number of spaces to check your work.

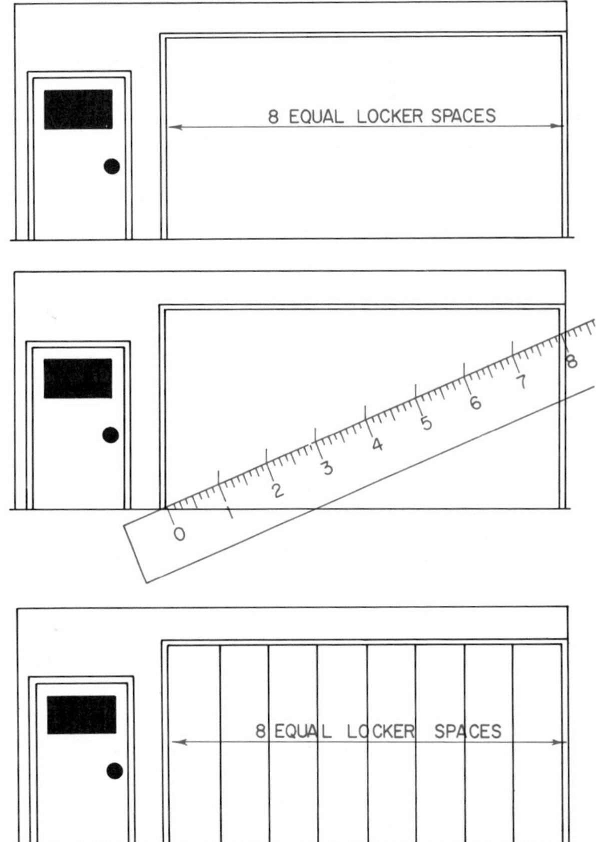

Fig. 24–18. Dividing an area into an equal number of parts.

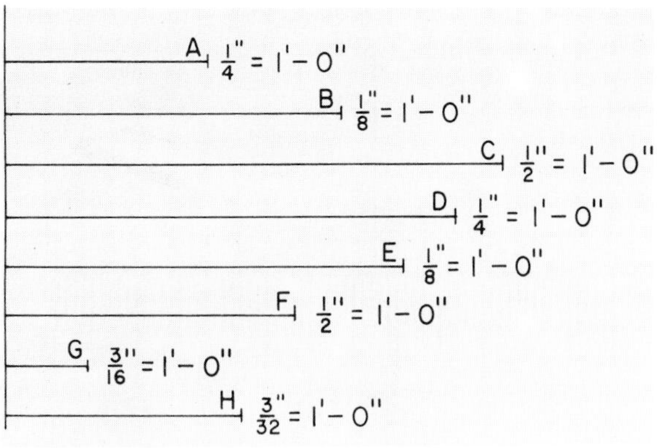

A $\frac{1}{4}'' = 1'-0''$

B $\frac{1}{8}'' = 1'-0''$

C $\frac{1}{2}'' = 1'-0''$

D $\frac{1}{4}'' = 1'-0''$

E $\frac{1}{8}'' = 1'-0''$

F $\frac{1}{2}'' = 1'-0''$

G $\frac{3}{16}'' = 1'-0''$

H $\frac{3}{32}'' = 1'-0''$

Fig. 24–19. Measure these distances.

PROBLEMS

1. **Measure the distances indicated on the horizontal lines, using the scale indicated in Fig. 24–19.**
2. **Measure the distances between the following letters in Fig. 24–20, using the $^1/_4'' = 1'$–$0''$ scale: AB, AL, DE, EJ, KO, ST, FT, CK, EP.**
3. **Measure the same distances shown in Problem 2, using the $^1/_8'' = 1''$ scale.**
4. **Answer the following questions concerning the plan shown in Fig. 24–21:**
   a. **What is the overall length of the building?**
   b. **What are the dimensions of bedroom 1, including the closets?**
   c. **What is the length of the stairwell opening?**
   d. **What are the dimensions of bedroom 2?**
   e. **Determine the length of dimensions A through G.**
5. **Define these terms:** ***open-divided, fully divided, architect's scale, decimal scale, triangular scale, reduced scale, division, inch-equivalent scale, foot-equivalent scale, full scale.***

Fig. 24–20. Measure the distances between the letters.

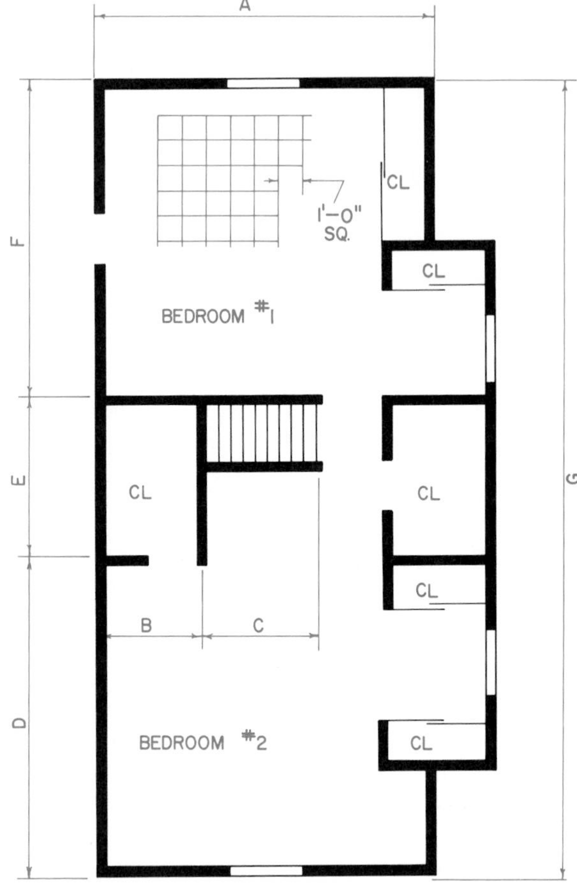

Fig. 24–21. List the sizes of each room shown in this plan.

UNIT 25

Metric Scale

The basic units of measure in the metric system are the *meter* (m) for distance, the *kilogram* (kg) for mass (weight), and the *liter* (l) for volume. Since most measurements used on architectural drawings are distances, multiples or subdivisions of the meter are most commonly used.

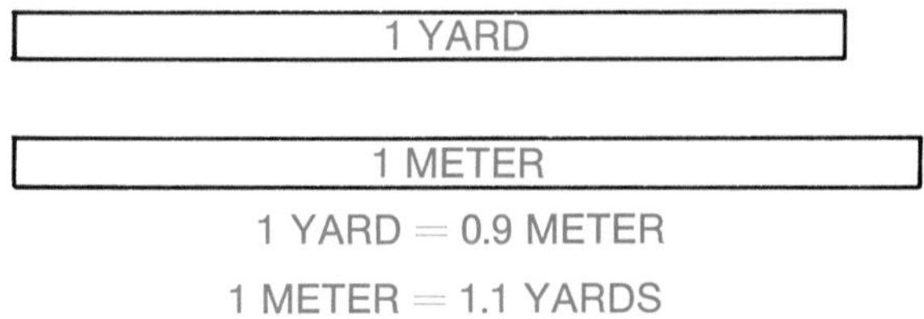

Fig. 25–1. The meter is slightly longer than a yard.

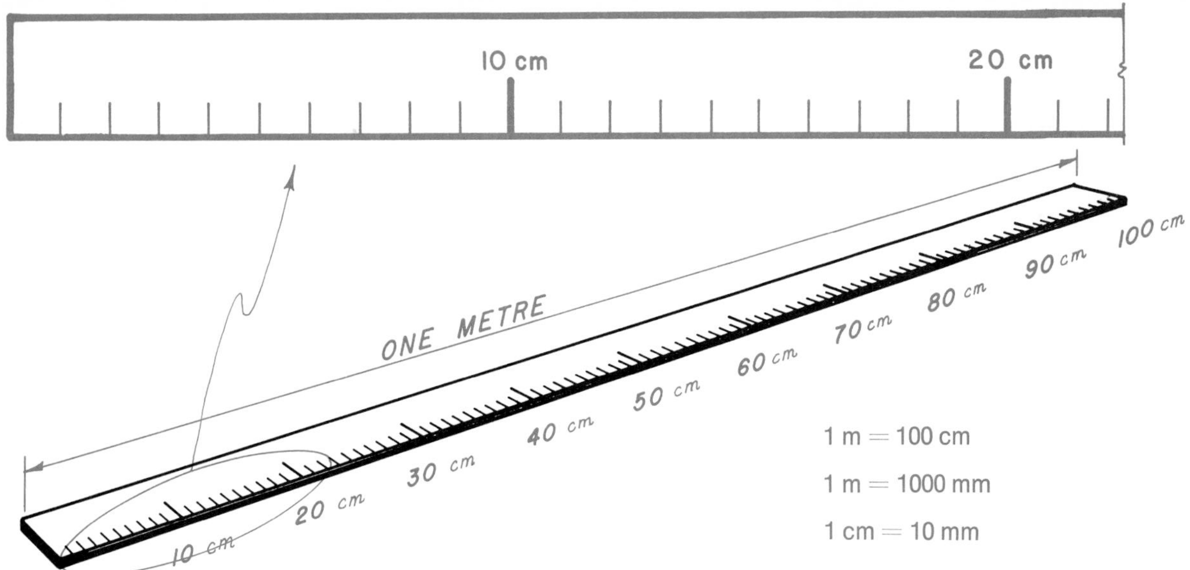

Fig. 25–2. A centimeter is one one-hundredth of a meter.

PREFIXES

The meter (Fig. 25–1) is a base unit of one. To eliminate the use of many zeros, prefixes are used to change the base (meter) to larger or smaller amounts by units of 10.

Prefixes which represent multiples of meters are deka-, hecto-, and kilo-. A dekameter equals 10 meters. A hectometer equals 100 meters. A kilometer equals 1000 meters. The most useful multiple of the meter is the kilometer.

Prefixes which represent subdivisions of meters are deci-, centi-, and milli-. A decimeter equals one-tenth (0.1) of a meter. A centimeter equals one one-hundredth (0.01) of a meter (Fig. 25–2). A millimeter equals one one-thousandth (0.001) of a meter (Fig. 25–3). The

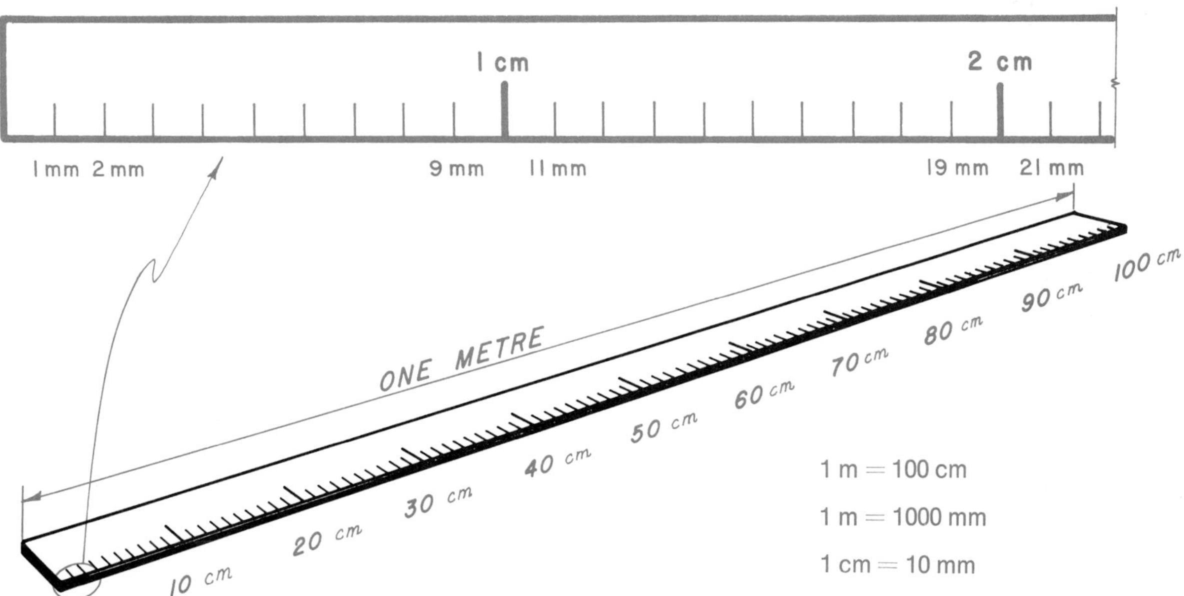

Fig. 25–3. A millimeter is one one-thousandth of a meter.

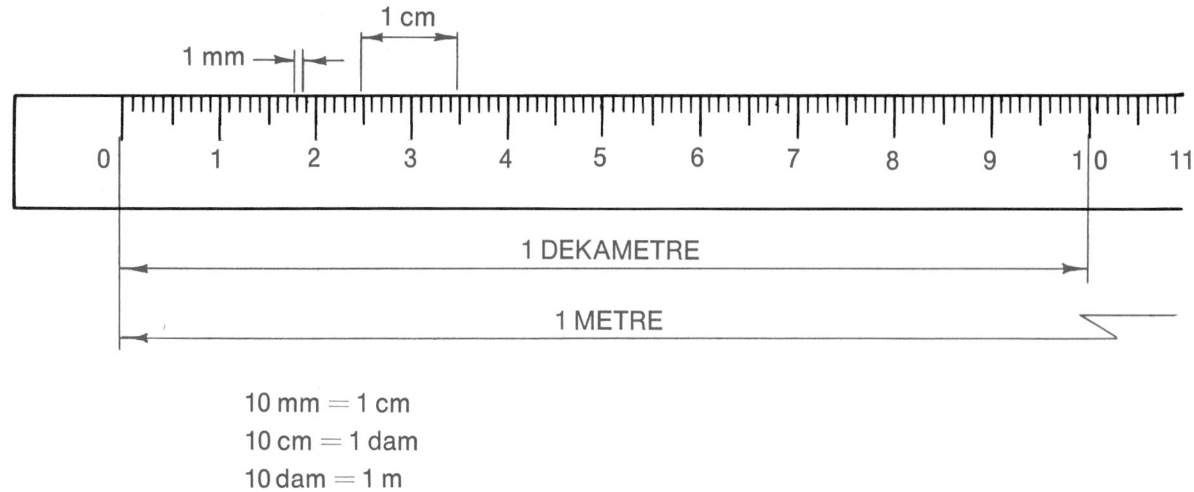

10 mm = 1 cm
10 cm = 1 dam
10 dam = 1 m

Fig. 25–4. A meter scale subdivided into millimeters.

most useful subdivisions of a meter are the centimeter and the millimeter.

Figure 25–4 shows a portion of a meter scale. The numbers on the scale mark every tenth line and represent centimeters. Each line represents millimeters. Note that there are 10 millimeters between each centimeter.

Table 25–1 gives many of the most useful metric prefixes and shows the relationship of these prefixes to the meter. The prefixes may be applied to all base metric units except mass.

Table 25–1. PREFIXES CHANGE THE BASE UNIT BY INCREMENTS OF 10

	PREFIX	SYMBOL	+ METER =	
$1000 = 10^3$	kilo	k	kilometer	km
$100 = 10^2$	hecto	h	hectometer	hm
$10 = 10^1$	deka	da	dekameter	dam
$0.1 = 10^{-1}$	deci	d	decimeter	dm
$0.01 = 10^{-2}$	centi	c	centimeter	cm
$0.001 = 10^{-3}$	milli	m	millimeter	mm

Table 25–2. THE METRIC SYSTEM USES FEWER BASE UNITS THAN THE CUSTOMARY SYSTEM

METRIC SYSTEM

LENGTH	MASS-WEIGHT	CAPACITY	TEMPERATURE	ELECTRIC CURRENT	TIME
Meter	Gram	Liter	Celsius	Ampere	Second

CUSTOMARY SYSTEM

LENGTH	MASS-WEIGHT	CAPACITY	TEMPERATURE	ELECTRIC CURRENT	TIME
Inch Foot Yard Fathom Rod Furlong Mile	Ounce Pound Ton Grain Dram	Teaspoon Tablespoon Fluid ounce Cup Pint Quart Gallon Barrel Peck Bushel	Fahrenheit	Ampere	Second Minute Hour

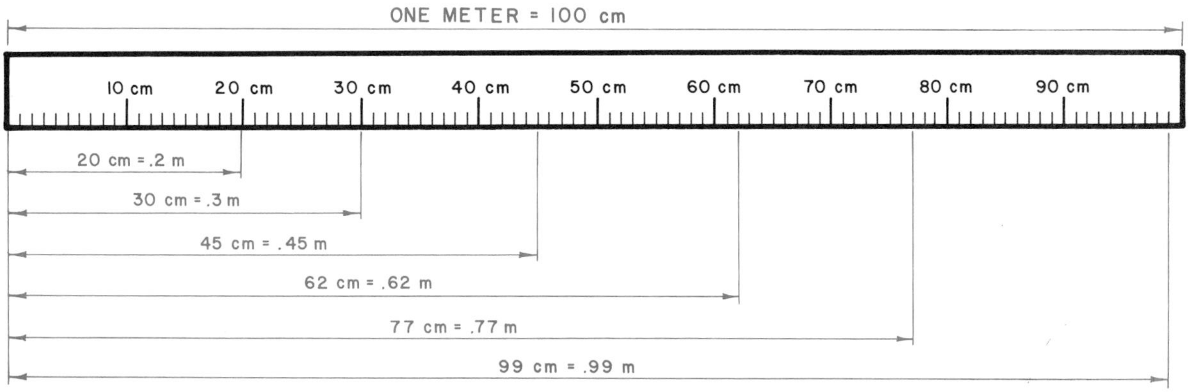

ONE METER = 100 cm

10 cm 20 cm 30 cm 40 cm 50 cm 60 cm 70 cm 80 cm 90 cm

20 cm = .2 m

30 cm = .3 m

45 cm = .45 m

62 cm = .62 m

77 cm = .77 m

99 cm = .99 m

Fig. 25–5. Most dimensions are in meters and decimal parts of a meter.

This is because the base unit for mass is a multiple unit, the kilogram. The prefixes are applied to the gram for mass units. This consistent use of prefixes for distance, mass, and volume makes the metric system much easier to use than our customary system. The number of metric base units is fewer, making it easier to remember. Table 25–2 compares the number of base units in the metric system with those in the customary system.

There are prefixes which extend the range upward to 10^{12} (tera) and downward to 10^{-18} (atto). These very large and very small units are used primarily for scientific notations in areas such as astronomy and microbiology.

In the United States there is a disagreement as to how to spell meter. Many people are in favor of an American spelling, **meter,** as is used in this book. Many other people, including those in industries that are using the metric system, prefer to spell it **metre.** All English-speaking countries using the metric system except the United States have adopted the metre spelling. Both spellings are correct, and until one spelling becomes more popular in the United States than the other, you should know that meter and metre mean the same thing. This is also true for liter and litre.

METRIC DIMENSIONS

Linear metric sizes used on basic architectural drawings such as floor plans and elevations are expressed in meters and decimal parts of a meter, as shown in Fig. 25–5. Dimensions on these plans are usually carried to three decimal points, as shown in Figs. 25–6A and B. Small detail drawings usually use millimeters, which eliminates the use of decimal points, as shown in Fig. 25–7.

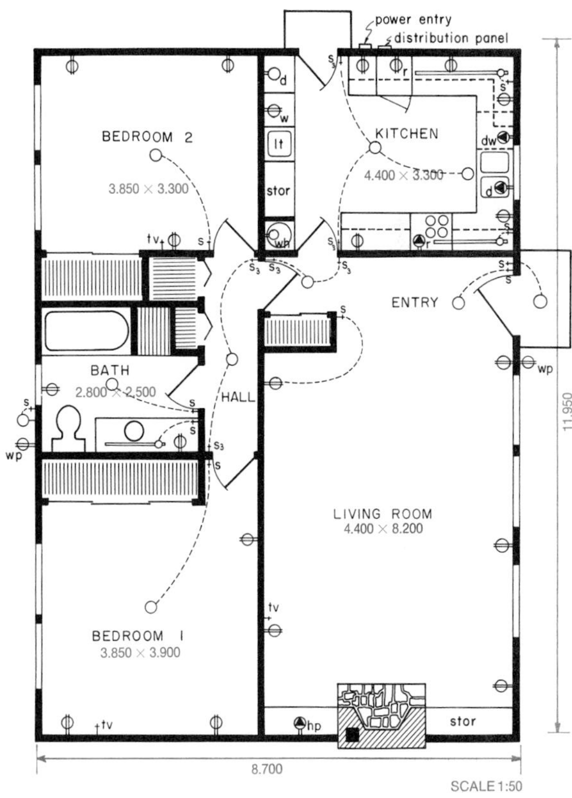

Fig. 25–6A. Room sizes shown in meters to three decimal points.

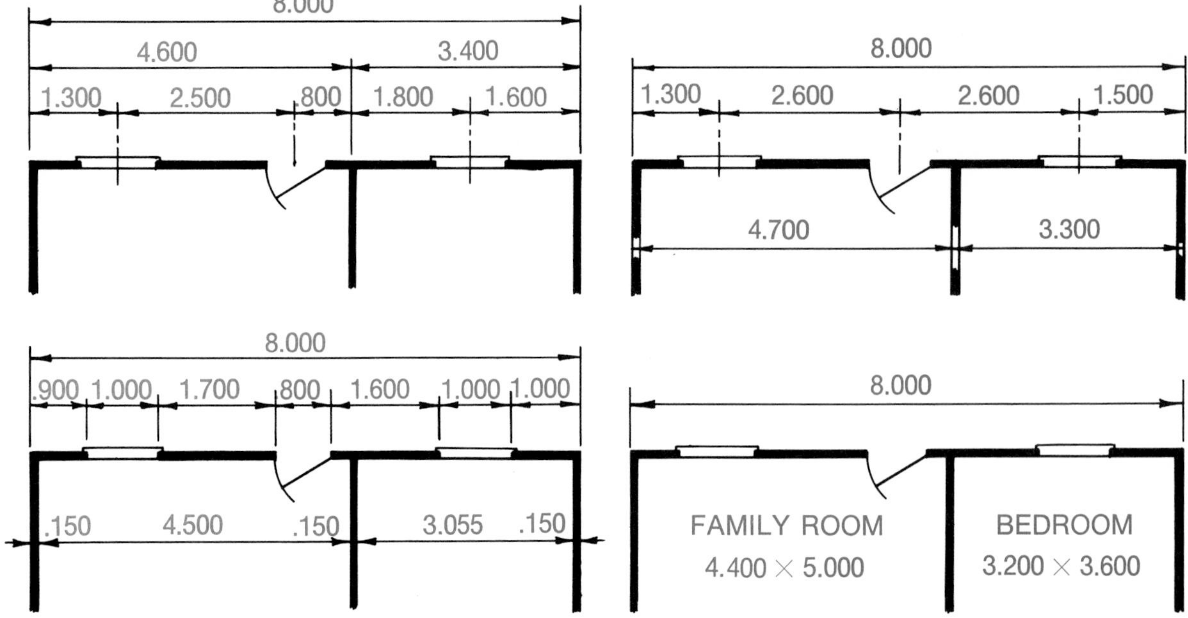

Fig. 25–6B. Examples of dimensions in meters to three decimal points.

METRIC DRAWING RATIOS

Metric scales such as those shown in Figs. 25–8 and 25–9 are used in the same manner as the architect's scale is used to prepare reduced-size drawings. Metric scales, however, use ratios in increments of 10 rather than the fractional ratios of 12 used in architect's scales. Just as with fractional scales, the ratio chosen depends on the size of the drawing compared to the full

Fig. 25–7. The millimeter is used for detail dimensioning.

Fig. 25–8. A metric scale showing two ratios.

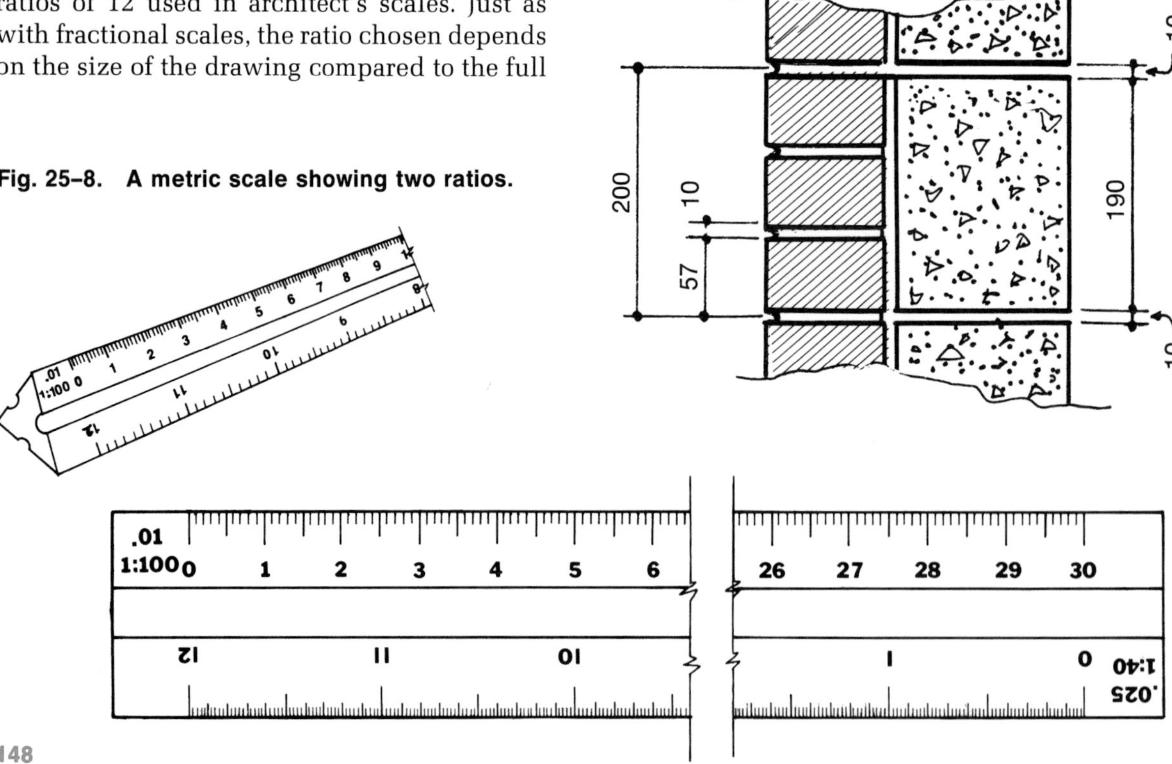

Table 25-3. ARCHITECTURAL USE OF METRIC RATIOS

USE	RATIO	COMPARISON TO 1 METER
CITY MAP	1:2500 1:1250	(0.4 mm equals 1 m) (0.8 mm equals 1 m)
PLAT PLANS	1:500 1:200	(2 mm equals 1 m) (5 mm equals 1 m)
PLOT PLANS	1:100 1:80	(10 mm equals 1 m) (12.5 mm equals 1 m)
FLOOR PLANS	1:75 1:50 1:40	(13.3 mm equals 1 m) (20 mm equals 1 m) (25 mm equals 1 m)
DETAILS	1:20 1:10 1:5	(50 mm equals 1 m) (100 mm equals 1 m) (200 mm equals 1 m)

size of the object. Table 25–3 shows some common metric ratios and the various types of architectural drawings for which they are used. It is important to prepare *all* drawings in a set using metric ratios or to prepare all drawings in a set using the customary fractional system. Do not mix metric and customary units. If approximate conversion from one system to the other is necessary, Table 25–4 can be used. When accurate conversion from customary to metric units is necessary, consult a handbook or use ANSI Z210.1-1973 METRIC PRACTICE GUIDE.

As metrication becomes more widely used in the United States, building materials will be manufactured in metric sizes. Table 25–5, 25–6, and 25–7 show metric sizes of construction lumber and sheet lumber which will probably become standard.

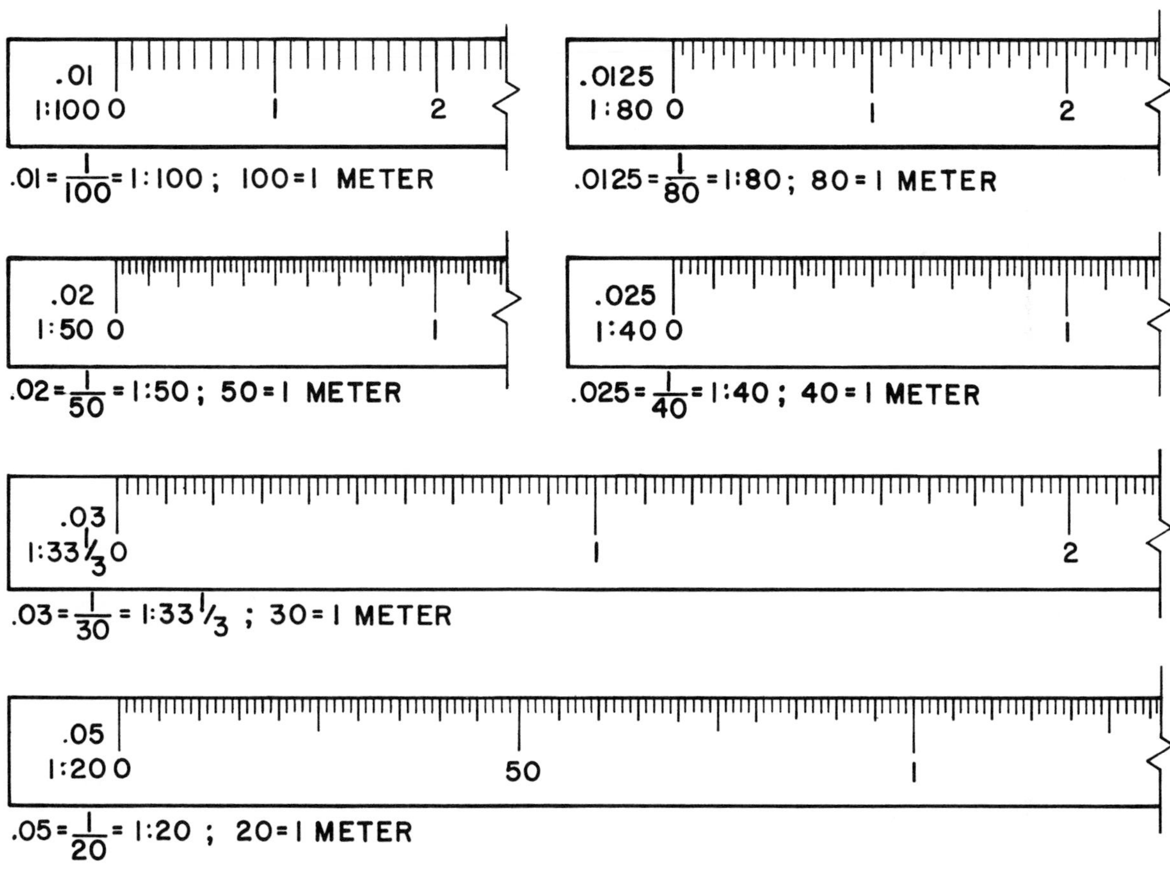

Fig. 25–9. Typical metric ratios.

Table 25-4. APPROXIMATE METRIC UNITS COMPARED TO SIMILAR CUSTOMARY UNITS

	WHEN YOU KNOW:	YOU CAN FIND:	IF YOU MULTIPLY BY:
LENGTH	inches	millimeters	25.4
	feet	centimeters	30.48
	yards	meters	0.9
	miles	kilometers	1.6
	millimeters	inches	0.04
	centimeters	inches	0.4
	meters	yards	1.1
	kilometers	miles	0.6
AREA	square inches	square centimeters	6.5
	square feet	square meters	0.09
	square yards	square meters	0.84
	square miles	square kilometers	2.6
	acres	square hectometers (hectares)	0.4
	square centimeters	square inches	0.16
	square meters	square yards	1.2
	square kilometers	square miles	0.4
MASS	ounces	grams	28.0
	pounds	kilograms	0.45
	short tons	megagrams (metric tons)	0.9
	grams	ounces	0.035
	kilograms	pounds	2.2
	megagrams (metric tons)	short tons	1.1
LIQUID VOLUME	ounces	milliliters	30.0
	pints	liters	0.47
	quarts	liters	0.95
	gallons	liters	3.8
	milliliters	ounces	0.034
	liters	pints	2.1
	liters	quarts	1.06
	liters	gallons	0.26
TEMPERATURE	degrees Fahrenheit	degrees Celsius	$^5/_9$ (after subtracting 32)
	degrees Celsius	degrees Fahrenheit	$^9/_5$ (then add 32)

Table 25-5. PROBABLE STANDARD LENGTHS OF CONSTRUCTION LUMBER IN METERS

1.8 m	3.0 m	4.2 m	5.4 m
2.1 m	3.3 m	4.5 m	5.7 m
2.4 m	3.6 m	4.8 m	6.0 m
2.7 m	3.9 m	5.1 m	6.3 m

Table 25-6. PROBABLE STANDARD LUMBER SHEET SIZES IN MILLIMETERS

SIZE (mm)
1800 × 1200
2400 × 1200
2700 × 1200
3000 × 1200
3600 × 1200
2400 × 900

PROBLEMS

1. **Measure common objects, such as your book, desk, and room, using a metric scale. Record your results. Compare your measurements with customary measurements.**
2. **Measure the lines shown in Fig. 24-20 in metric units.**
3. **Change the dimensions on Fig. 34-3 to metric units.**
4. **Draw a complete set of plans using metric units.**
5. **Define the following terms: *meter, kilogram, liter, millimeter, kilometer, prefix, centimeter, metric system, customary system, ratio.***

Table 25-7. PROBABLE STANDARD SIZES OF CONSTRUCTION LUMBER IN MILLIMETERS

THICKNESS, mm	WIDTH, mm								
16 x	75	100	125	150					
19 x	75	100	125	150					
22 x	75	100	125	150					
25 x	75	100	125	150	175	200	225	250	300
32 x	75	100	125	150	175	200	225	250	300
36 x	75	100	125	150					
38 x	75	100	125	150	175	200	225		
40 x	75	100	125	150	175	200	225		
44 x	75	100	125	150	175	200	225	250	300
50 x	75	100	125	150	175	200	225	250	300
63 x		100	125	150	175	200	225		
75 x		100	125	150	175	200	225	250	300
100 x		100		150		200		250	300
150 x				150		200			300
200 x						200			
250 x								250	
300 x									300

UNIT 26

Drafting Instruments

A course in mechanical drawing usually precedes a course in architectural drawing. Therefore only the procedures, practices, and techniques which specifically relate to the use of instruments for architectural drafting are presented in this unit.

T SQUARE

The T square is used primarily as a guide for drawing horizontal lines and for guiding the triangle when drawing vertical and inclined lines. The T square is also the most useful instrument for drawing extremely long lines that deviate from the horizontal plane. Common T-square lengths for use in architectural drafting are 18″, 24″, 30″, 36″, and 42″.

T squares must be held tightly against the edge of the drawing board, and triangles must be held firmly against the T square to ensure accurate horizontal and vertical lines. Since only one end of the T square is held against the drawing board, considerable sag occurs when extremely long T squares are not held securely.

Horizontal Lines

Horizontal lines are always drawn with the aid of some instrument such as the T square, parallel slide, or drafting machine. In drawing horizontal lines with the T square, hold the head of the T square firmly against the left working

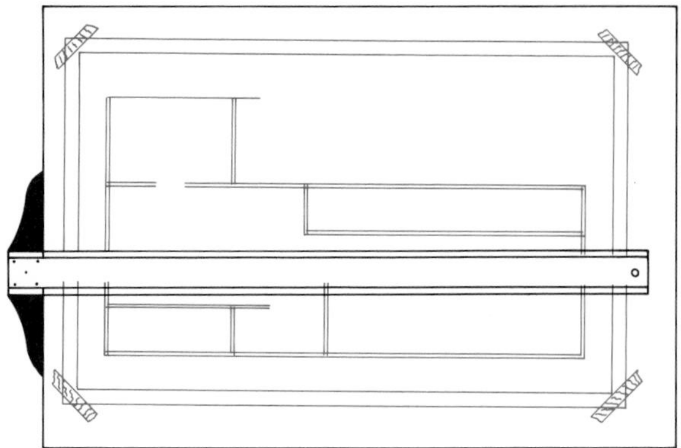

Fig. 26–1. A T square placed on a drawing board.

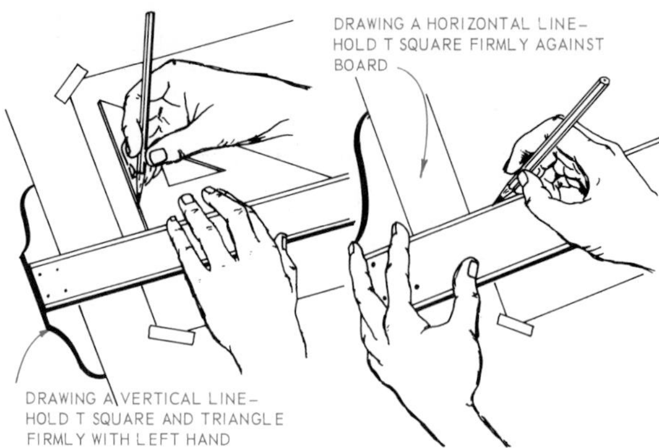
DRAWING A HORIZONTAL LINE–
HOLD T SQUARE FIRMLY AGAINST
BOARD
DRAWING A VERTICAL LINE–
HOLD T SQUARE AND TRIANGLE
FIRMLY WITH LEFT HAND

Fig. 26–2. Drawing horizontal and vertical lines with a T square and triangle.

edge of the drawing board (if you are right-handed). This procedure keeps the blade in a horizontal position to draw horizontal lines from left to right. Figure 26–1 shows the T square placed on the drawing board in the correct manner for drawing floor plans and elevations. Figure 26–2 shows the correct method of drawing horizontal lines by the use of the T square.

Vertical Lines

Triangles are used with the T square for drawing vertical or inclined lines. The 8″, 45° triangle and the 10″, 30°—60° triangle are preferred for architectural work. Figure 26–2 shows the correct method of drawing vertical lines by the use of the T square and triangle.

PARALLEL SLIDE

The parallel slide performs the same function as the T square. It is used as a guide for drawing horizontal lines and as a base for aligning triangles in drawing vertical lines.

Extremely long lines are common in many architectural drawings such as floor plans and elevations. Since most of these lines should be drawn continuously, the parallel slide is used extensively by architectural draftsmen.

The parallel slide is anchored at both sides of the drawing board, as shown in Fig. 26–3. This attachment eliminates the possibility of sag at one end, which is a common objection to the use of the T square.

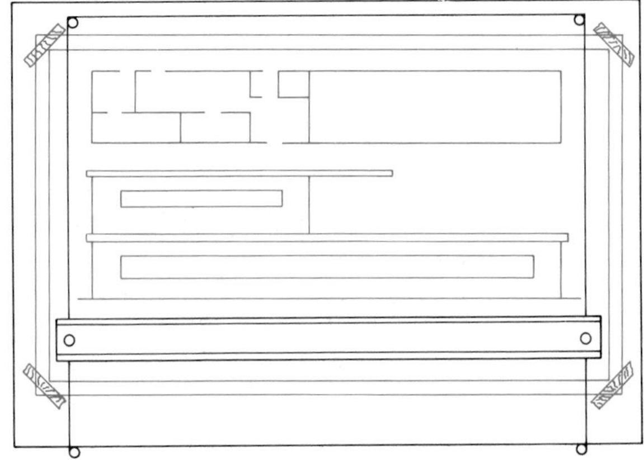

Fig. 26–3. A parallel slide used on a drawing board.

In using the parallel slide the drawing board can be tilted to a very steep angle without causing the slide to fall to the bottom of the board. If the parallel slide is adjusted correctly, it will stay in the exact position in which it is placed.

DRAFTING MACHINE

Use of the drafting machine eliminates the need for the architect's scale, triangle, T square, or parallel slide. A drafting machine consists of a head to which two scales are attached (Fig. 26–4). These scales (arms) of the drafting machine are graduated like other architect's scales. They are usually made of aluminum or plastic. The two scales are attached to the head

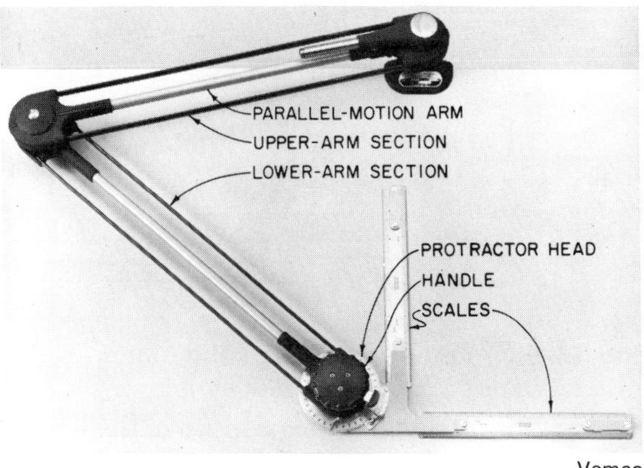

Fig. 26–4. A drafting machine.

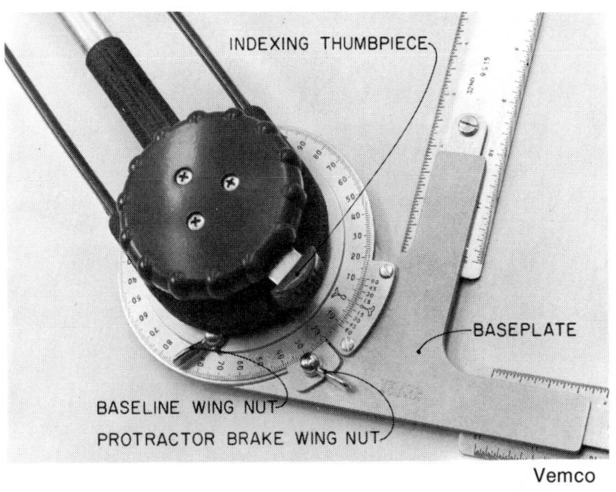

Fig. 26–5. Location of the indexing thumbpiece.

of the drafting machine perpendicular to each other. The horizontal scale performs the function of a T square or parallel slide in drawing horizontal lines. The vertical scale performs the function of a triangle in drawing vertical lines.

The head of the drafting machine can be rotated so that either of the scales can be used to draw lines at any angle. When the indexing thumbpiece, as shown in Fig. 26–5, is depressed and then released, the protractor head of the drafting machine will lock into position every 15°. Figure 26–6 shows the intervals at which the scales will index from a horizontal line. If the indexing thumbpiece remains depressed, the protractor head can be aligned to any degree. The protractor brake wing nut is used to lock the head in position. If accuracy in minutes is desired, the *vernier scale* (Fig. 26–7) is used to set the protractor head at the desired angle. In this case, the vernier clamp is used to lock the head in the exact position when the desired setting is achieved.

The drafting machine is used to the greatest advantage in architectural work for the preparation of architectural detail drawings. It is sometimes unsatisfactory for large floor plans and elevations which require long horizontal or vertical lines. However, a drafting machine mounted on a vertical slide, as shown in Fig. 26–8, is very effective for large drawings, provided they do not require continuous long lines.

For every position of the head of the drafting machine, there are two possible posi-

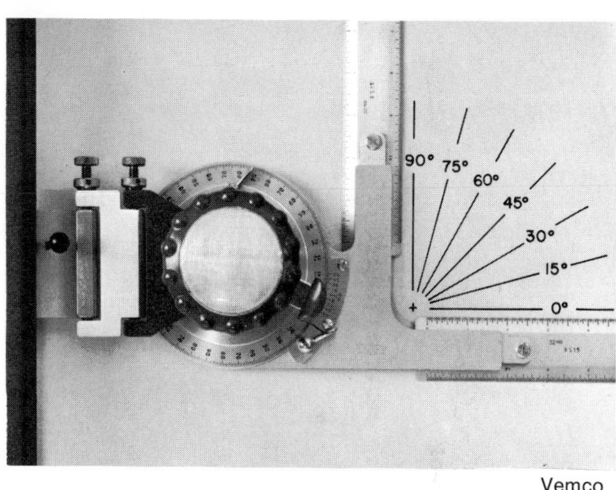

Fig. 26–6. Angles at which the scales will lock.

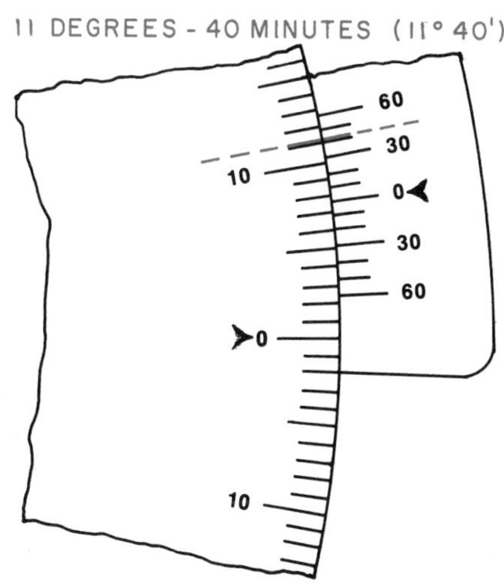

Fig. 26–7. Use of the vernier scale.

Bruning Division, Addressograph Multigraph Corporation

Fig. 26–8. A drafting machine mounted on a vertical slide.

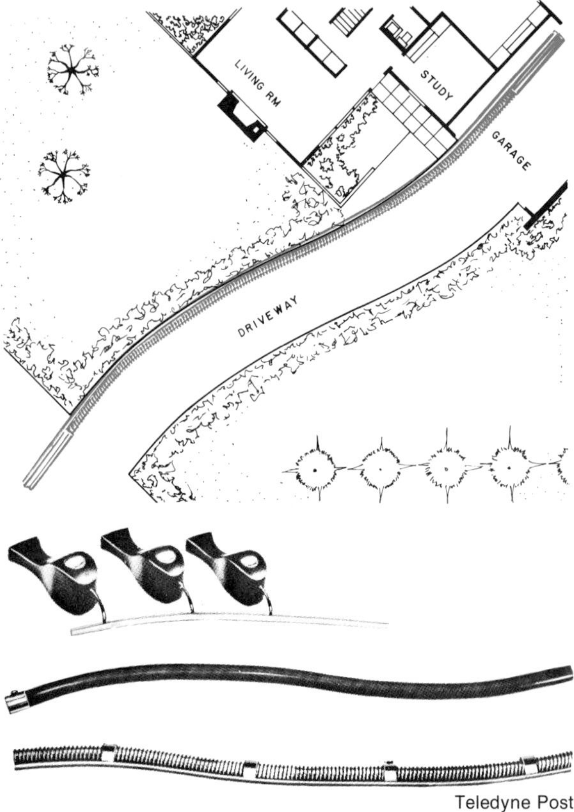

Teledyne Post

Fig. 26–10. Use of the flexible rule.

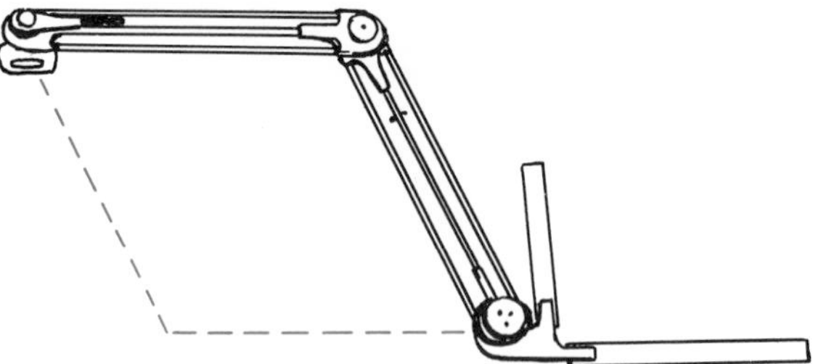

Fig. 26–9. Alternative position of the arm.

tions of the elbow. If some position of the lower arm covers the vernier scales, shifting the elbow to the position shown in Fig. 26–9 will avoid this difficulty.

FLEXIBLE RULE

Many architectural drawings contain irregular lines which must be repeated. Flexible rules, such as those shown in Fig. 26–10, are used to repeat irregular curves that have no true radius or series of radii.

Triangles are used to draw vertical and inclined lines. The 45° triangle is frequently used to draw miter lines that are used to turn angles of buildings, as shown in Fig. 26–11. Triangles are used also to draw various symbols. Figure 26–11 shows the use of the 30°—60° triangle in drawing a door symbol.

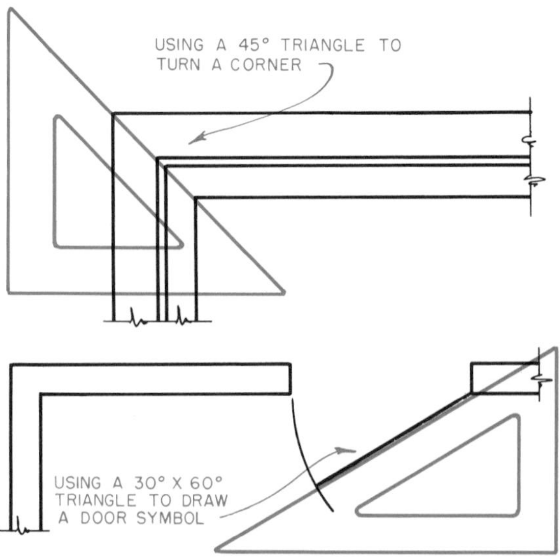

Fig. 26–11. Use of triangles.

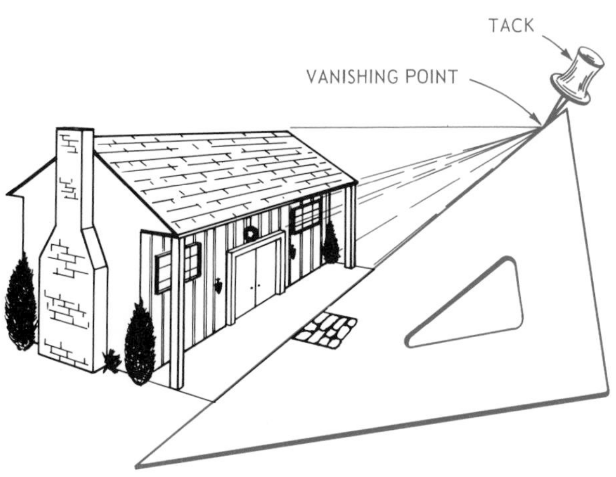

Fig. 26–12. Projecting lines to a vanishing point.

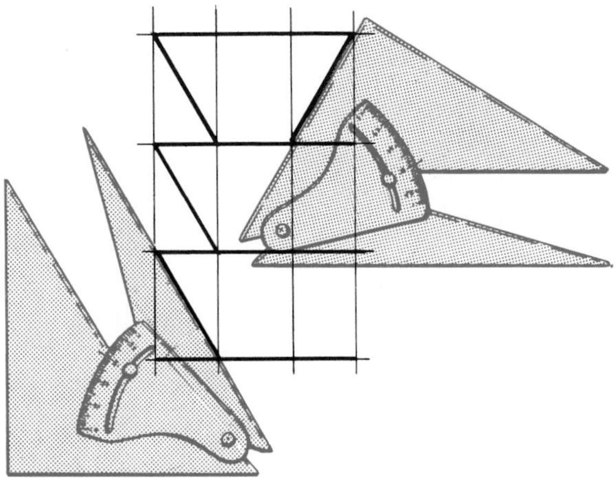

Fig. 26–13. An adjustable triangle is used for angles of any number of degrees.

Triangles (and inverted T squares) are often used to project perspective lines from vanishing points, as shown in Fig. 26–12. The adjustable triangle is used to draw angles that cannot be laid out by combining the 45° and 30°—60° triangles. Figure 26–13 shows an application of the adjustable triangle.

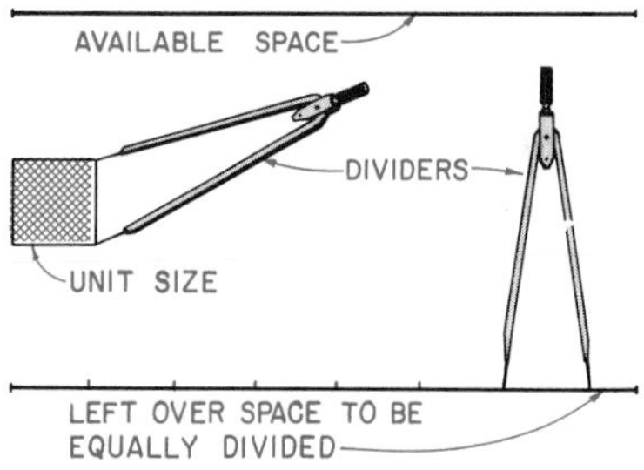

Fig. 26–14. The use of dividers in dividing areas.

DIVIDERS

Dividing an area into an equal number of parts is a common task performed by architectural draftsmen. In addition to the architect's scale (see Unit 24), the dividers are used for this purpose. To divide an area equally, first adjust the dividers until they appear to represent the desired division of the area. Then place one point at the end of the area and step off the distance with the dividers. If the divisions turn out to be too short, increase the opening on the dividers by trial and error. Repeat the process until the line is equally divided. If the divisions are too long, decrease the setting. Figure 26–14 shows the use of dividers in dividing an area into an equal number of parts.

Dividers are also used frequently to transfer dimensions and to enlarge or reduce the size of a drawing. Figure 26–15 shows the use of dividers to double the size of a floor plan. This work is done by setting the dividers to the distances on the plan and then stepping off the distance twice on the new plan.

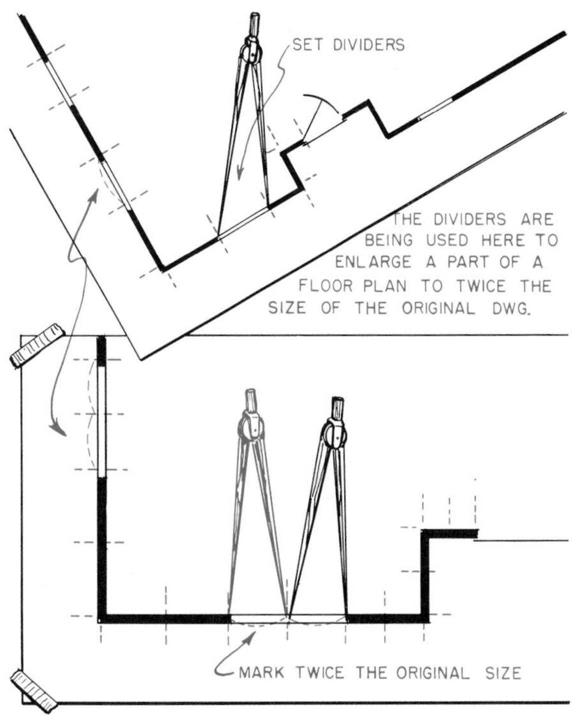

Fig. 26–15. The use of dividers to enlarge an area.

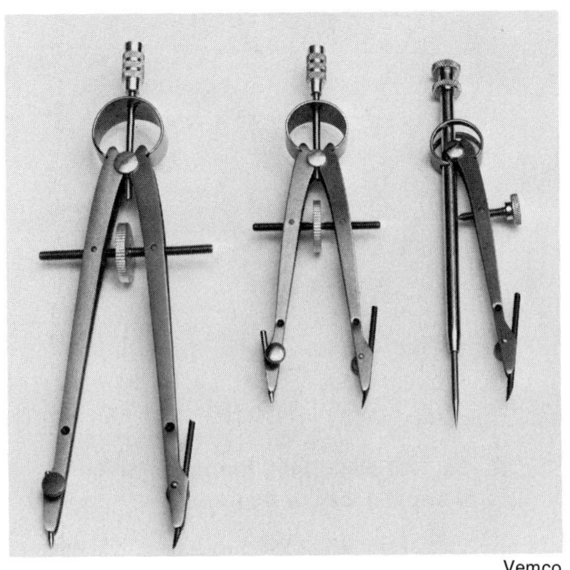
Vemco

Fig. 26–16. A variety of compasses.

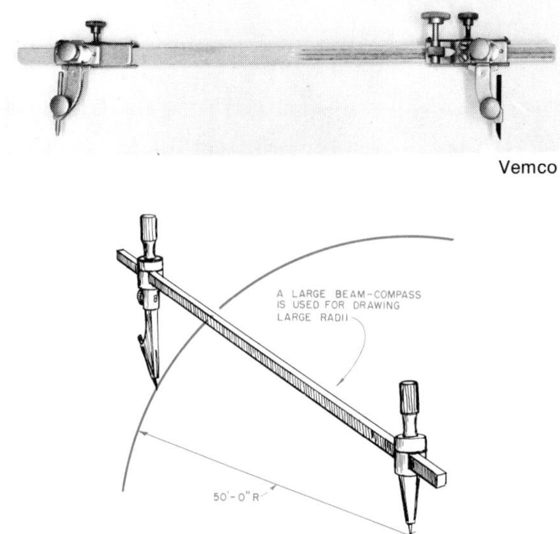
Vemco
A LARGE BEAM-COMPASS IS USED FOR DRAWING LARGE RADII
50'-0"R

Fig. 26–17. The use of a large beam-compass.

COMPASS

A compass is used on architectural drawings to draw circles, arcs, radii, and parts of many symbols. Small circles are drawn with a bow pencil compass (Fig. 26–16). The bow is set to the desired radius, holding the stem between the thumb and forefinger and rotating the compass with a clockwise forward motion and forward inclination.

Large circles on architectural drawings, such as those used to show the radius of driveways, walks, patios, and stage outlines, are drawn with a large beam-compass, as shown in Fig. 26–17.

PROBLEMS

1. **Using a T square and triangle, parallel slide and triangle, or drafting machine, draw the floor plan shown in Fig. 33–15.**
2. **Using drafting instruments and an architect's scale, draw the elevation shown in Fig. 38–1 to the scale ¼″ = 1′—0″. Add horizontal dimensions.**
3. **With a flexible rule, lay out the driveway shown in Fig. 32–12, using a scale of ⅛″ = 1′—0″.**
4. **Define the following terms: *T square, 45° triangle, 60° triangle, vertical lines, horizontal lines, parallel slide, drafting machine, flexible rule, dividers, compass.***

UNIT 27

Computer-Aided Drafting Systems

Speed and accuracy in producing finished drawings is important. Through computer-aided drafting methods, finished drawings are produced in a fraction of the time required by traditional methods. The computer performs complicated computations, giving architects and engineers more time for creative design. The use of a computer also allows fast and accurate checking of a design at any time in its development. The sequence of producing

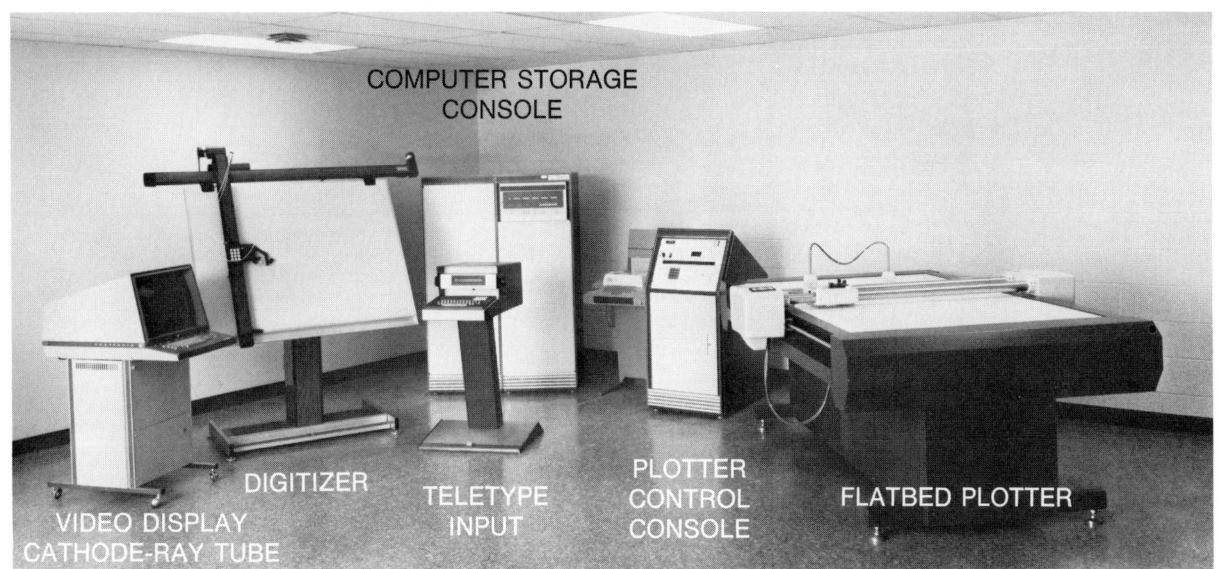

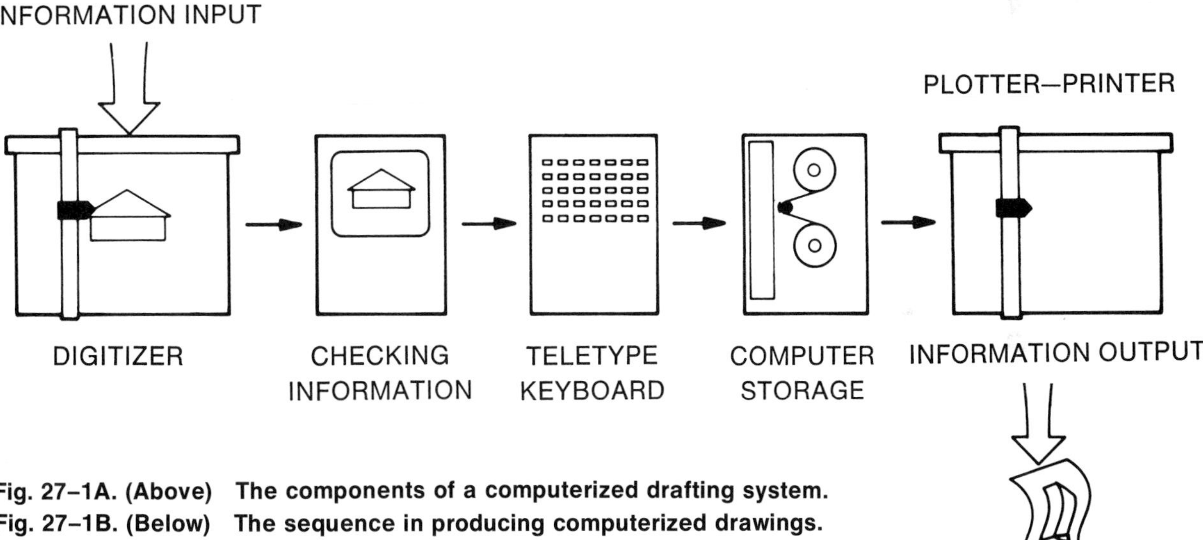

Fig. 27–1A. (Above) The components of a computerized drafting system.
Fig. 27–1B. (Below) The sequence in producing computerized drawings.

architectural drawings with a computer-aided system is shown in Fig. 27–1A and B.

With appropriate information fed into the computer, the system can perform the following functions:

- mirror reversals of drawings
- combine and change symbols
- revolve a drawing or part of a drawing
- recall any stored information
- locate any information anywhere on drawings
- change scale sizes
- plan with modular building units
- plan with orientation factors

INPUT

To graphically record data into the computer memory bank, the designer works with a digitizer. The digitizer has an arm that moves in two directions on the *x*-axis and the *y*-axis (Fig. 27–2). It may also be a cathode ray tube (CRT) and a light pen (Fig. 27–3). Additional input can be fed into the computer with a free-cursor digitizer which will move in any direction (Fig. 27–4). The input source may be from a keyboard, teletypewriter, premade computer pro-

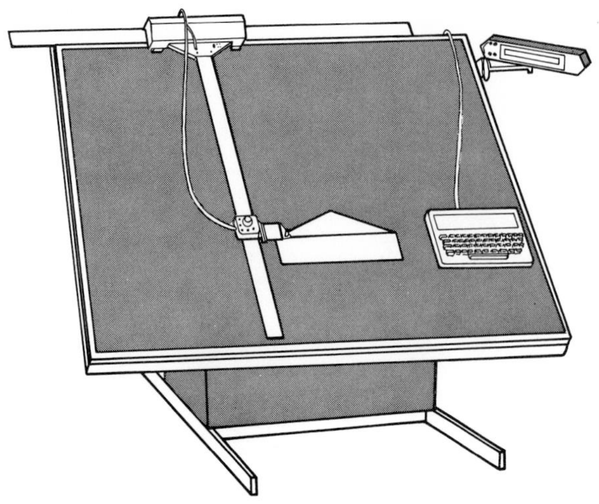

Fig. 27–2. A digitizer moves in two direction on an *x-y* axis.

Fig. 27–3. A CRT and light-pen digitizer.

gram, or tablet digitizer (Fig. 27–5). The digitizer changes graphic information (lines) into numbered coordinates (digits) which can be stored in the computer. When a designer uses the system in the sequence shown in Fig. 27–6, a table of standard architectural symbols is created by making a rough sketch of each symbol on the digitizer. These symbols are then fed into the computer. The designer then positions the digitizer follower at the location of each symbol on a sketch and records the coordinates with the symbol on the keyboard. The lines on the drawing are then connected, and necessary information and dimensions are added. When the design is thought to be satisfactory, it can be checked and stored in the computer.

Designing is also simplified by use of a large bank of repeated architectural details and data that is entered into the computer memory files and coded for recall. This information consists of architectural symbols such as those for windows, doors, electrical fixtures, walls, standard room sizes, stairs, furniture, roof styles, building and structural materials, and general architectural line work. The information would also contain engineering data.

The digitizer converts rough sketches, drawings, layouts, and artwork into coordinate information that is stored in the computer. This information can be recalled on command (Fig. 27–7). Recalled drawings may also be presented in various positions (Fig. 27–8).

Computer Vision Corp.

Fig. 27–4. The free-cursor digitizer moves in all directions.

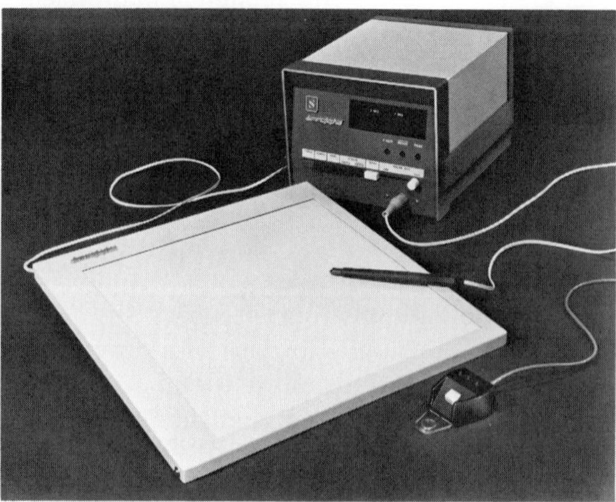

Summagraphic Corp.

Fig. 27–5. A tablet digitizer.

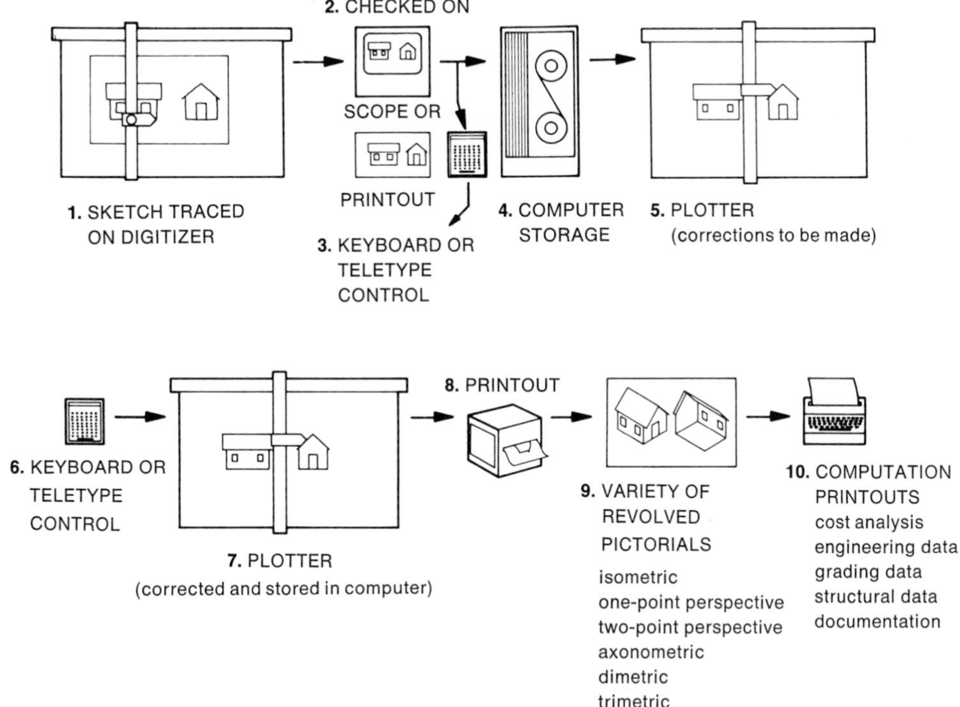

Fig. 27–6. The sequence of producing a variety of data.

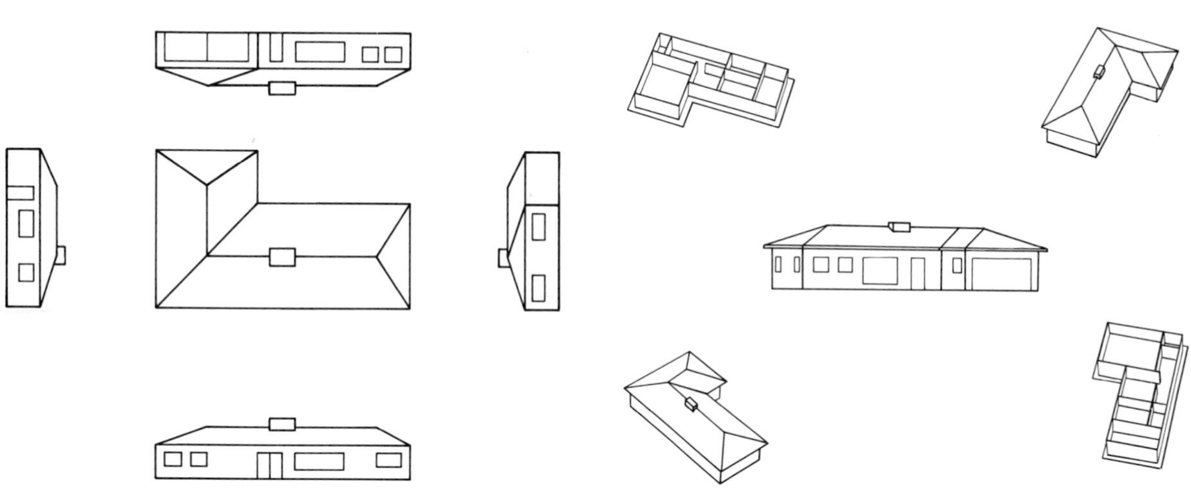

Fig. 27–7. Information of these views was stored in the computer in coordinate form. They were drawn (recalled) on command.

Fig. 27–8. Drawings can also be recalled in various positions.

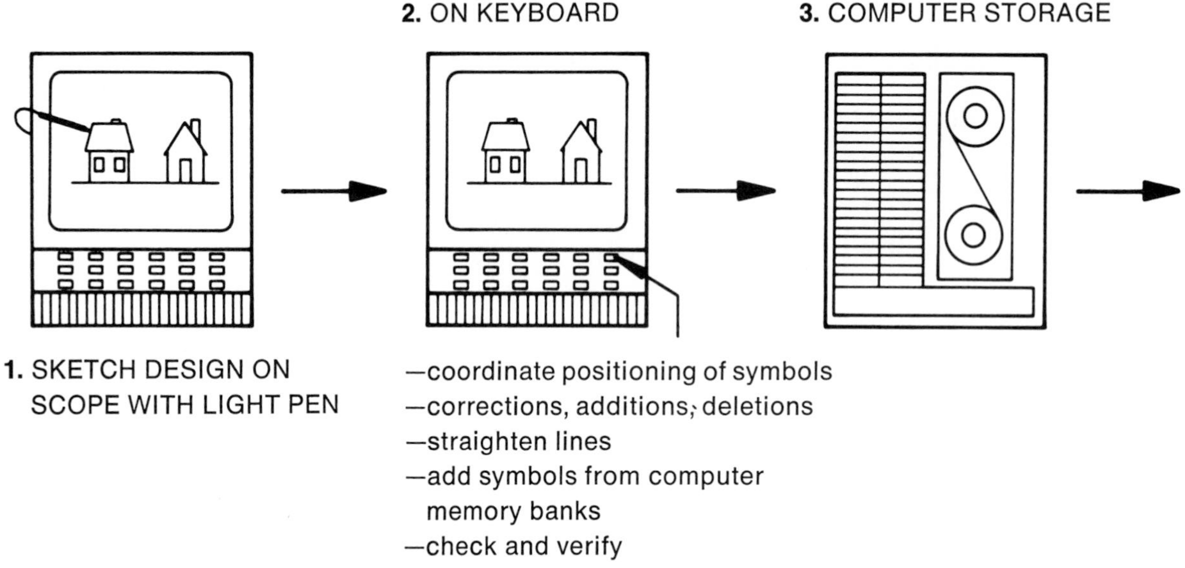

Fig. 27–10. The use of a CRT and light pen for input.

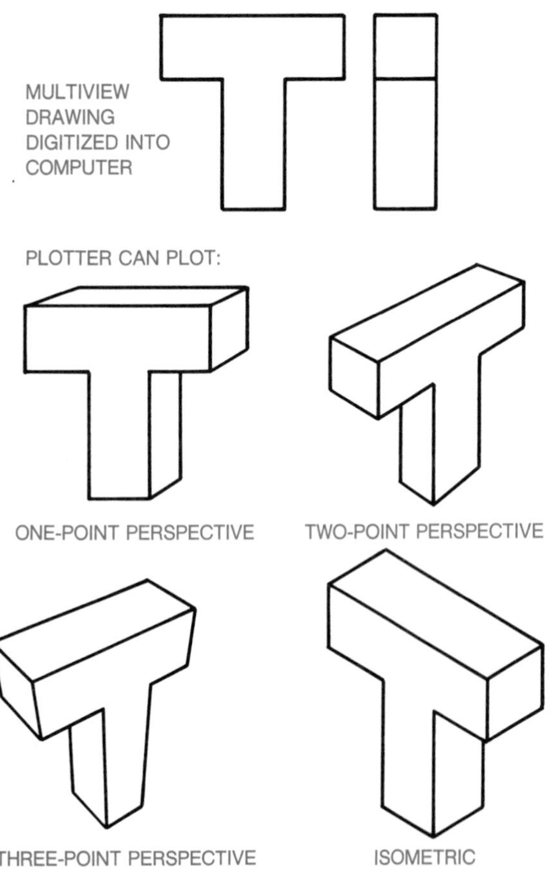

Fig. 27–9. Different types of perspective drawings can be produced from the same input.

A printout or a video display may be used to verify and check the accuracy of the symbols or design. Input information from paper tapes, magnetic tapes, magnetic discs, magnetic drums, or punch cards is stored in the computer memory banks. This information is stored as temporary or as permanent data. At any time during the development of a design, changes can be made. The graphic display of the input can be edited, added to, deleted, or repositioned. Checking a design is made easier when the design can be rotated and viewed in different positions. The stored library of digitized standard symbols provides for fast layout and for corrections or changes that a designer must make. Different types of perspective drawings can also be generated from a working drawing (Fig. 27–9).

When designing with a computerized scope (CRT) and light pen (Fig. 27–10), the process is the same as with the digitizer, except that all original sketching is done directly on the CRT with the light pen. All stored symbols can be called up and positioned with the light pen. The design work is all done directly on the scope. When the designer is satisfied with the design and has made all changes and verifications, the design is recorded into the computer memory bank for future recall or changes.

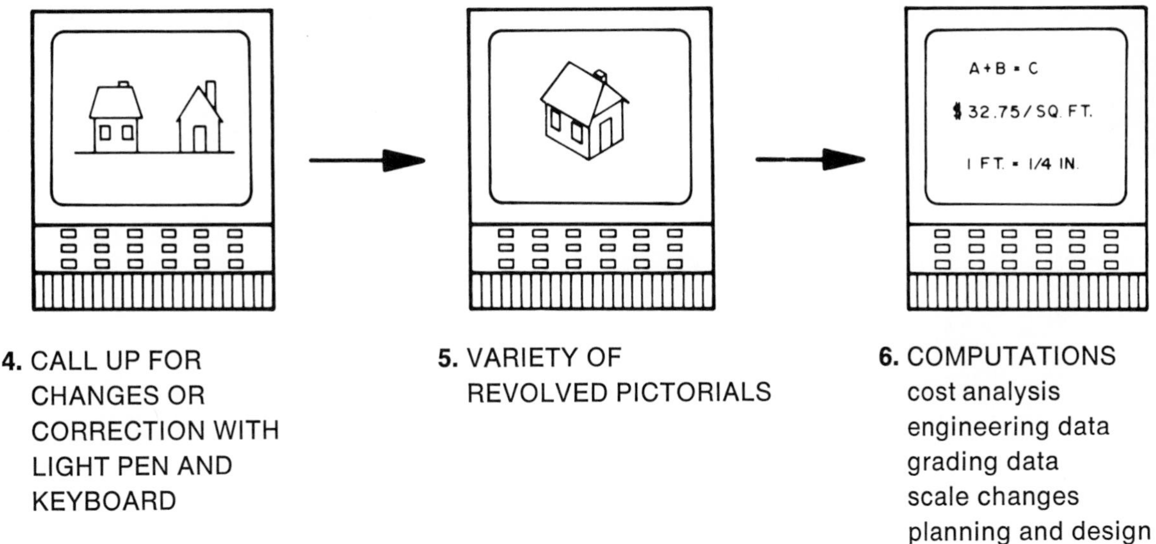

Fig. 27–10. Continued.

COMPUTER

The computer is called the *graphics control center*. All input information is digitized into the computer (Fig. 27–11). That is, the information is translated into electric pulses and magnetic currents, which is a language the computer understands. The computer has the capability to modify the data on immediate recall. This information provides automated artwork as sketches are translated into commands accepted by the automated drafting machine. All information stored can be called for and generated by the computer controls.

Auto-trol Corp.

Fig. 27–11. The computer is the graphics control center.

GRAPHICS OUTPUT

The plotter or automatic drafting machine produces the graphic output. There are two basic types of plotters, the flatbed (Fig. 27–12) and the drum plotter (Fig. 27–13). The plotter follows instruction from the computer to produce the artwork, maps, data reductions, changes, or pictorial or revolved drawings. Output may be produced by electric typewriters, bar printers, high-speed chain printers, cathode ray scope, or printouts.

COMPUTERIZED LAND DRAWINGS

Drawings of land surfaces are of great value to the civil engineer and landscape architect. To produce computerized drawings of land surfaces, the computer operator feeds contour

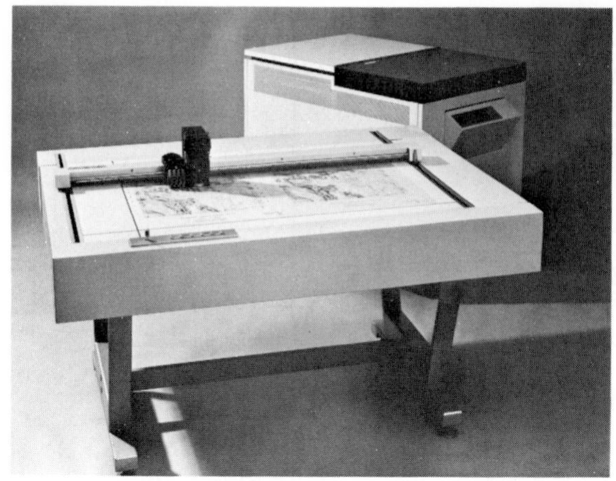

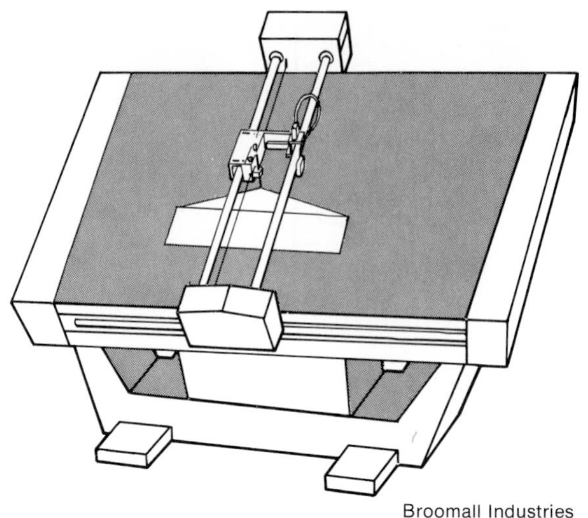

Fig. 27–12. **A flatbed plotter.**

Broomall Industries

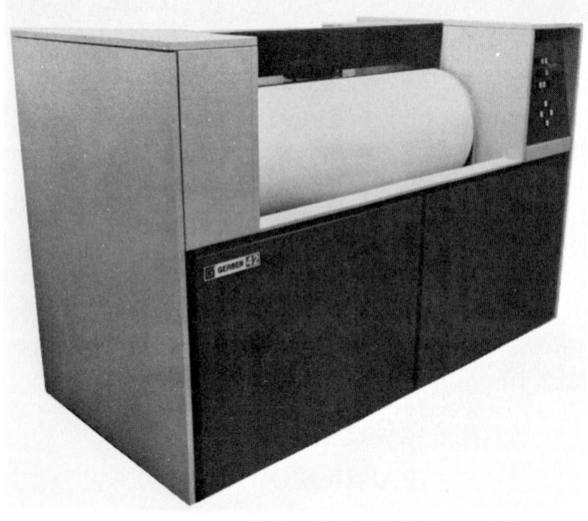

Gerber Scientific Instrument Company

Fig. 27–13. A drum plotter.

points into the computer. The operator can then receive output information from the computer on cut analysis, fill analysis, contour maps (Fig. 27–14), cross sections, drainage maps, slope maps, grid perspectives (Fig. 27–15), presentation grids, and perspective land maps (Fig. 27–16). In addition the computer can perform such mathematical computations as volume of earth to be moved or filled and time and cost of earth-moving operations.

OTHER ARCHITECTURAL USES

Computer-aided drafting systems can provide a perspective drawing (Fig. 27–17) of a building from a digitized floor plan and elevation. It can

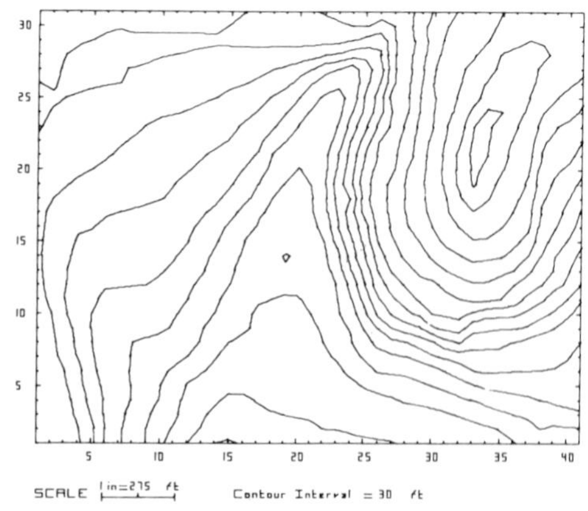

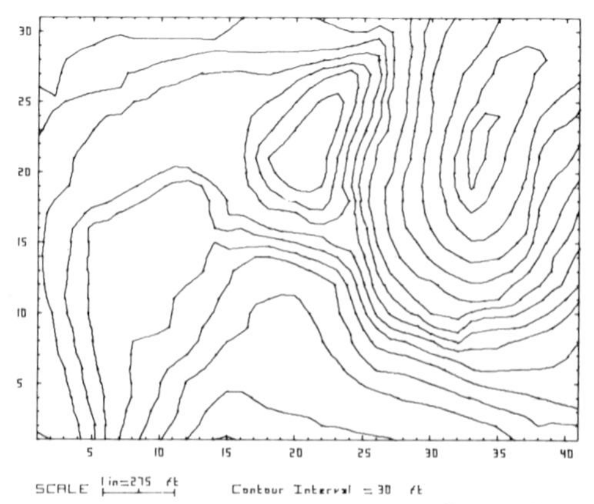

Comarc Design Systems

Fig. 27–14. Computer-drawn contour maps.

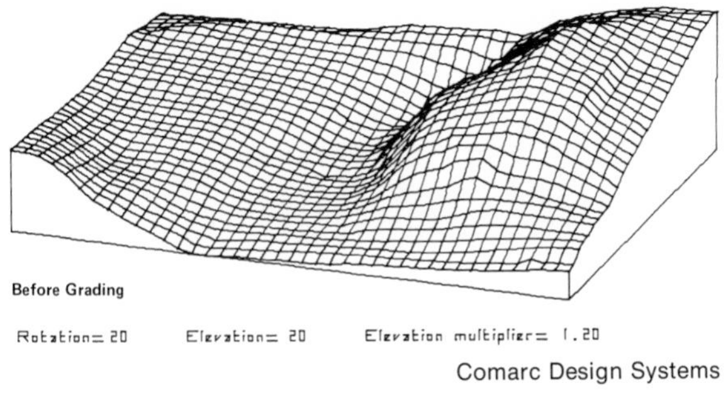

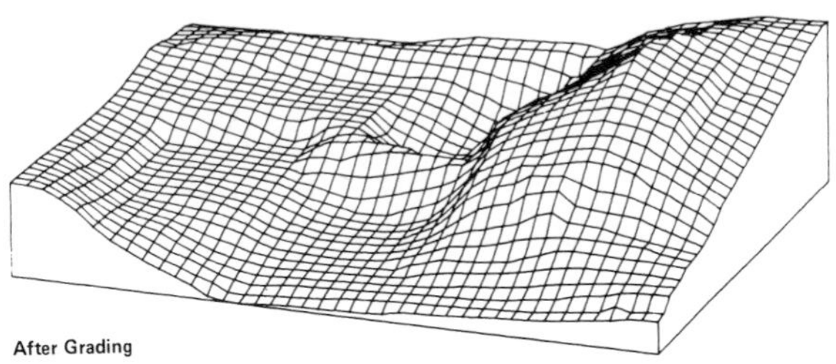

Fig. 27–15. **Computer-drawn grid perspectives.**

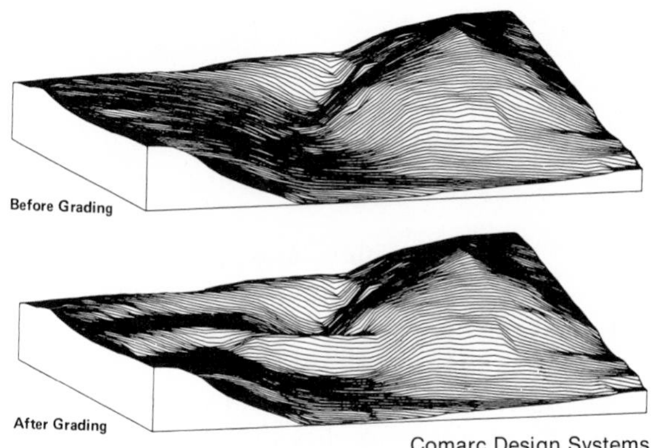

Fig. 27–16. Computer-drawn contour land maps.

Calcomp

Fig. 27–17. Perspective view drawn by a computer system.

Calcomp

Fig. 27–18. Computer drawn plat plan.

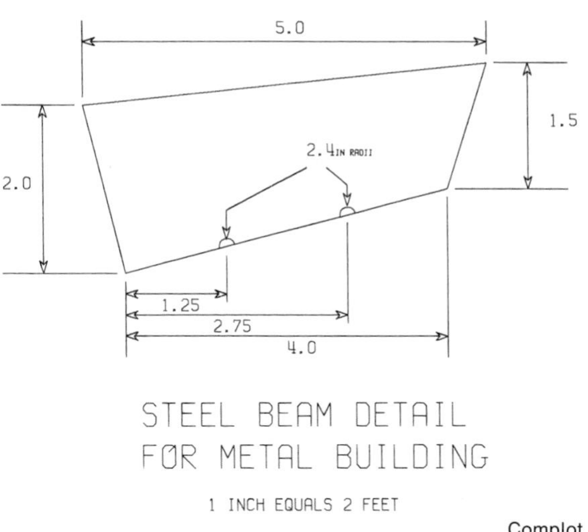

Complot

Fig. 27–19. Computer-generated engineering data.

also redraw a plot plan from an original (Fig. 27–18) or record engineering data on a drawing, as shown in Fig. 27–19.

PROBLEMS

1. **List the steps in the development of a computerized drawing from a rough sketch.**
2. **Define the following terms: *software, hardware, digitizer, plotter, input, printout.***

UNIT 28

Timesavers

Architectural drawings must frequently be prepared quickly because construction often begins immediately upon completion of the working drawings. Under these conditions, speed in the preparation of drawings is of utmost importance. For this reason many timesaving devices are employed by architectural draftsmen. The purpose of these timesaving devices is to eliminate unnecessary time on the drawing board without sacrificing the quality of the drawing.

ARCHITECTURAL TEMPLATES

Templates are pieces of paper, cardboard, metal, or plastic. Openings in the template are shaped to represent the outline of various symbols and fixtures. A symbol or fixture is traced on the drawing by following the outline with a pencil. This procedure eliminates the repetitious task of measuring and laying out the symbol each time it is to be used on the drawing.

General-Purpose Templates

Templates such as the one shown in Fig. 28–1 have openings that represent many different types of symbols and fixtures. This template is positioned to be used to outline a door symbol. Many other types of general-purpose templates are shown in Fig. 28–2.

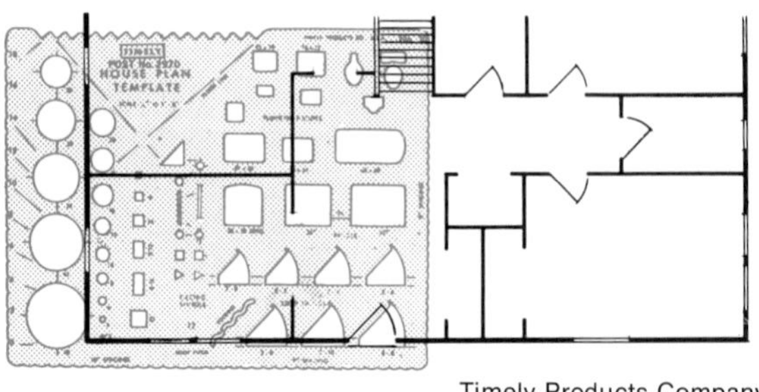

Timely Products Company

Fig. 28–1. Floor-plan symbols.

Special-Purpose Templates

Many architectural templates, such as those shown in Fig. 28–3, are used to draw only one type of symbol. Special templates are available for doors, windows, landscape features, electrical symbols, plumbing symbols, furniture, structural steel, outlines, lettering, and circle and ellipse guides. Figure 28–4 shows how a special landscape template is used to draw landscape symbols on a drawing. When symbols contain many intersecting lines, templates often provide only the basic outline. The detailing is completed by freehand methods. The landscape symbols shown in Fig. 28–4 are completed in this manner.

Each part of the symbol is drawn by using a different opening in the template. For example, in using the template shown in Fig. 28–5, the center part of the template is employed to outline the window. The horizontal lines are then added by using the openings at the right of the template as shown. The vertical lines are added by using the opening at the bottom of the template.

When the major axis of a symbol is to be aligned with the lines of the drawing, it is necessary to use a T square, drafting machine, or parallel slide as a guide. This alignment is

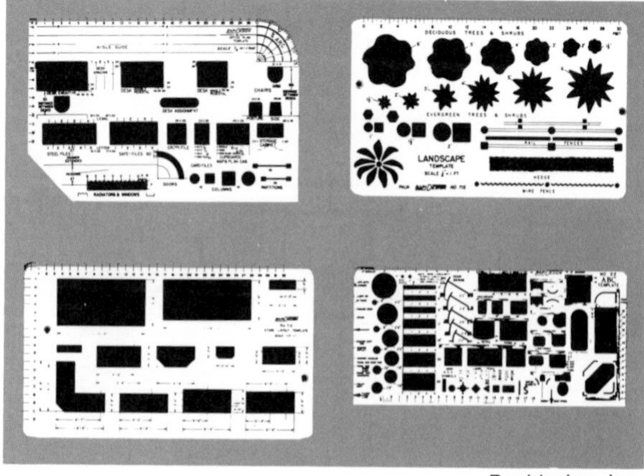

Rapidesign, Inc.

Fig. 28–2. General-purpose architectural templates.

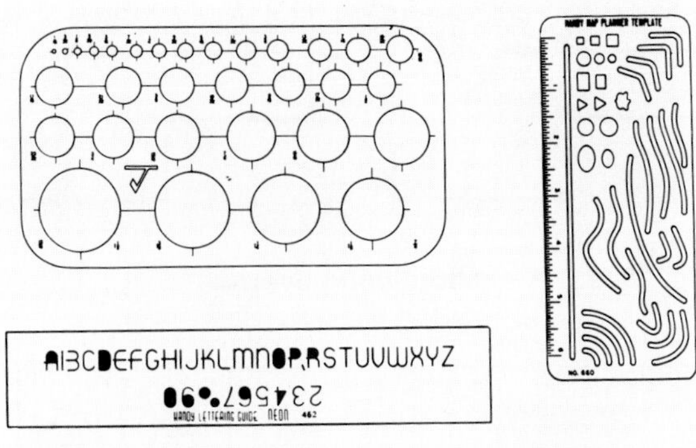

Rapidograph, Inc.

Fig. 28–3. Special-purpose templates.

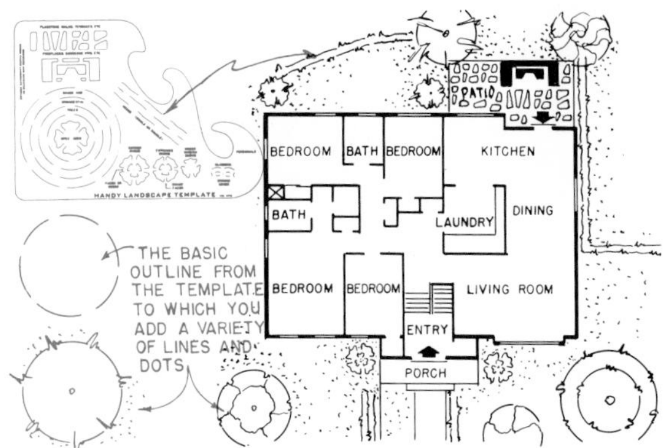

Fig. 28–4. The use of a landscape template.

made by resting one true edge of the template against the blade of the T square, parallel slide, or drafting machine. This procedure is also necessary to ensure the alignment of symbols that are repeated in an aligned pattern.

OVERLAYS

An overlay is any sheet that is placed over the original drawing. The information placed on the overlay becomes part of the interpretation of the original drawing.

Temporary Overlays
Most overlays are made by drawing on transparent material such as acetate, tracing cloth, or vellum. Overlays are used in the design process to add to or change features of the original drawing without marking the drawing.

Overlays are also used to add to a drawing features which would normally complicate the original drawing. Lines that would become hidden and many other details can be made clear by preparing this information on an overlay. Figure 28–6 shows the use of an acetate overlay in locating a building on a lot. The building can be moved to any position on the overlay until the final location is established. It can then be added to the original drawing.

Timely Products Company

Fig. 28–5. Steps in using a window template.

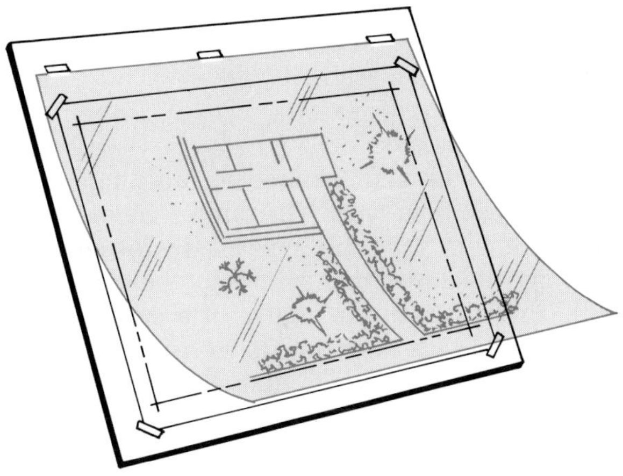

Fig. 28–6. The use of an acetate overlay.

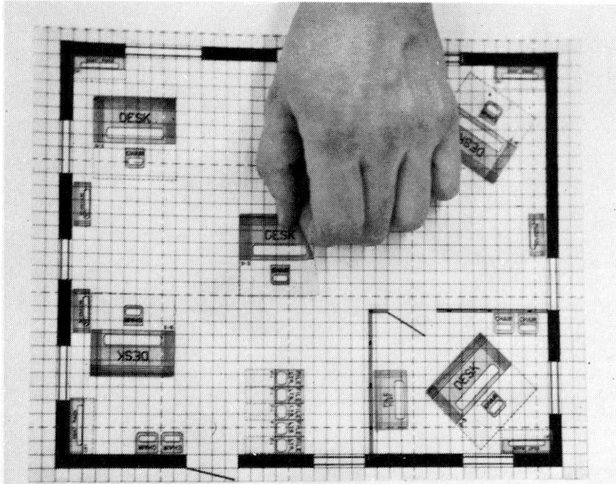

Chart-Pak, Inc.

Fig. 28–7. A permanent overlay.

Permanent Overlays
Overlays which adhere to the surface of the drawing, such as the overlay shown in Fig. 28–7, save much drawing-board time. Attaching a preprinted symbol or fixture by this method is considerably faster than drawing it, even if a template is used.

In addition to fixture and symbol overlays, continuous material symbols are often used on architectural drawings. Figure 28–8 shows the use of a section-lining overlay on architectural drawings. These overlays are self-adhering and can be cut to any desired size or shape.

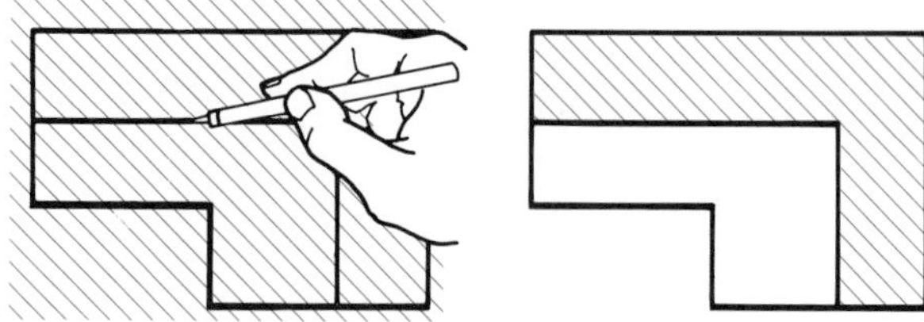

Fig. 28–8. A section-lining overlay.

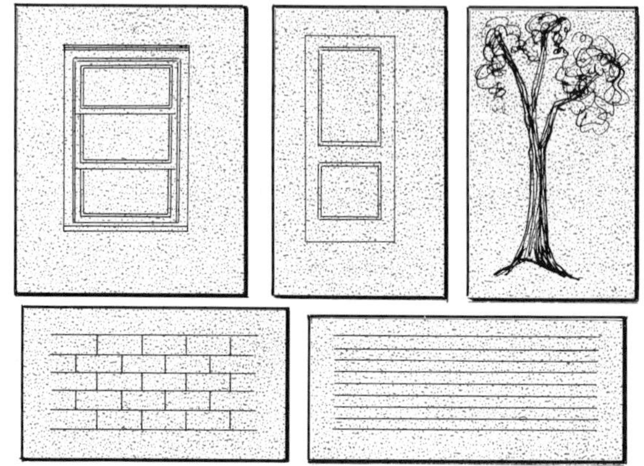

Fig. 28–9. Examples of common architectural underlays.

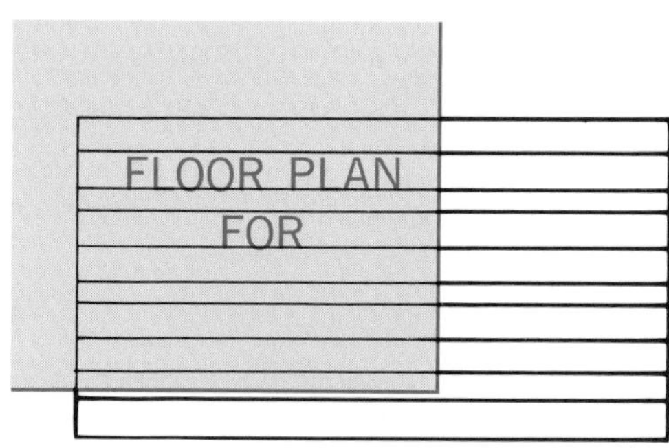

Fig. 28–10. A lettering-guideline underlay.

UNDERLAYS

Underlays are drawings or parts of drawings which are placed under the original drawing and traced on the original.

Symbol Underlays
Many symbols and features of buildings are drawn more than once. The same style of door or window or the same type of tree or shrubbery may be drawn many times by the architectural draftsman in the course of a day. It is a considerable waste of time to measure and lay out these features each time they are to be drawn. Therefore, many draftsmen prepare a series of underlays of the features repeated most often on their drawings. Figure 28–9 shows several underlays commonly used on architectural drawings. Underlays are commonly prepared for doors, windows, fireplaces, trees, walls, and stairs.

Lettering Underlays
Lettering guidelines, as shown in Fig. 28–10, are frequently prepared on underlays. When the guidelines are placed under the drawing, the draftsman may trace the line from the original drawing, thus eliminating the measurement of each line. If the underlay remains

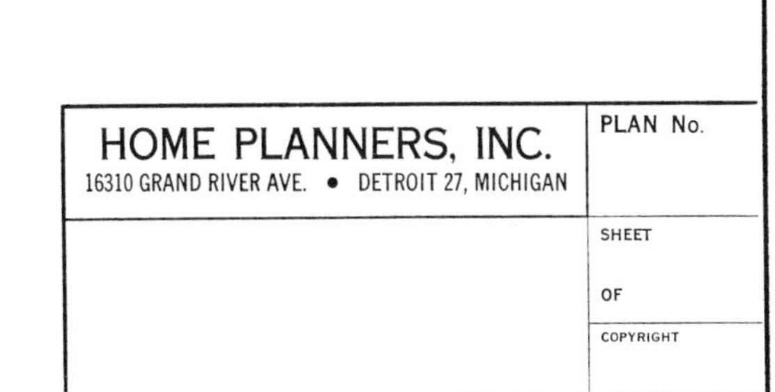

Fig. 28–11. A title-block underlay.

under the drawing while it is being lettered, the guideline on the drawing can be considerably lighter so that the draftsman does not need to erase heavy guidelines. The spacing of other lines, such as crosshatching and brick-symbol lines, is also prepared on underlays.

Drawing paper preprinted with title blocks is a considerable timesaver (Fig. 28–11). However, when printed title blocks are not available, the title-block underlay is often used to save valuable layout time and to ensure the correct spacing of lettering.

Use of Underlays

Underlays are master drawings. To be effective, they must be prepared to the correct scale and carefully aligned. The underlay is first positioned under the drawing and aligned with light guidelines (Fig. 28–12); then it is traced on the drawing. The underlay can now be removed or moved to a new location to trace the symbol or feature again if necessary. Architects use master underlays many times.

Underlays do not necessarily replace the use of instruments or scales in original design work. They are most effective when symbols are continually repeated. Figure 28–13 shows a comparison of the use of the scale, dividers, and underlay in laying out wall thicknesses. The use of the underlay in this case is only possible after the original wall dimensions have been established by the use of the scale.

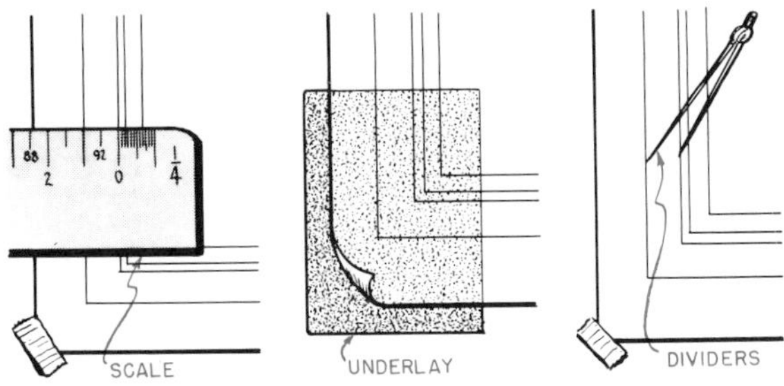

Fig. 28–13. The scale, an underlay, or dividers may be used to lay out wall thickness.

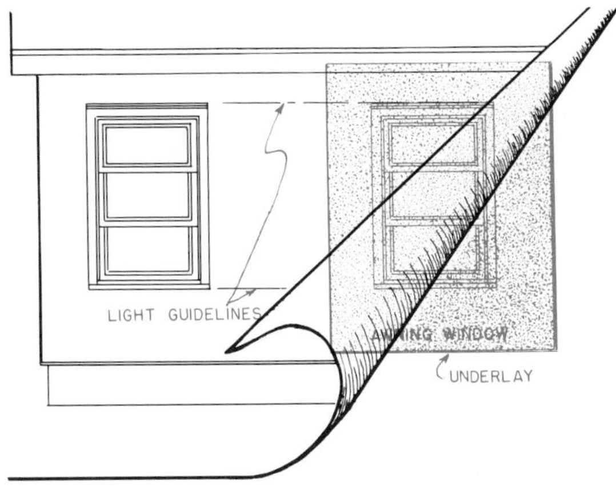

Fig. 28–12. The correct positioning of an underlay.

GRIDS

Grid sheets are used under the tracing paper as underlays and are removed after the drawing is finished, or the drawing is prepared on nonreproducible grid paper. Nonreproducible grid paper does not reproduce when the original drawing is copied through photographic processes. Figure 28–14 shows an original drawing complete with nonreproducible grid lines and the print from this drawing without grid lines.

Squared Paper

Squared (graph) paper is available in graduations of 4, 8, 16, and 32 squares per inch. Squared paper is also available in decimal-divided increments of 10, 20, and 30 or more squares per inch. Decimal-divided squared paper is used for the layout of survey and plot plants. Metric graph paper is ruled in millimeters.

Pictorial Grids

Grids prepared with isometric angles and preplotted to perspective vanishing points are

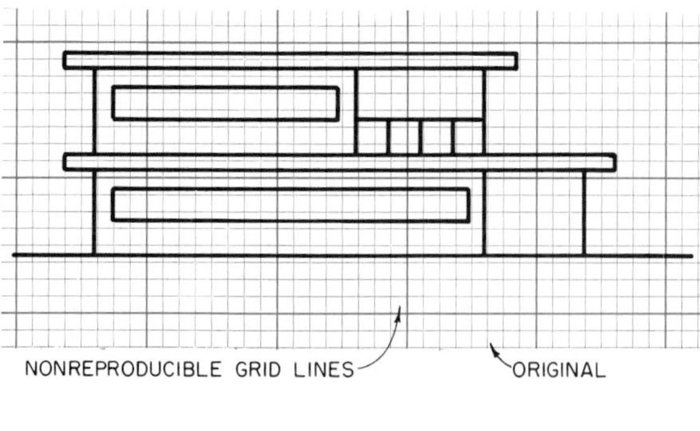

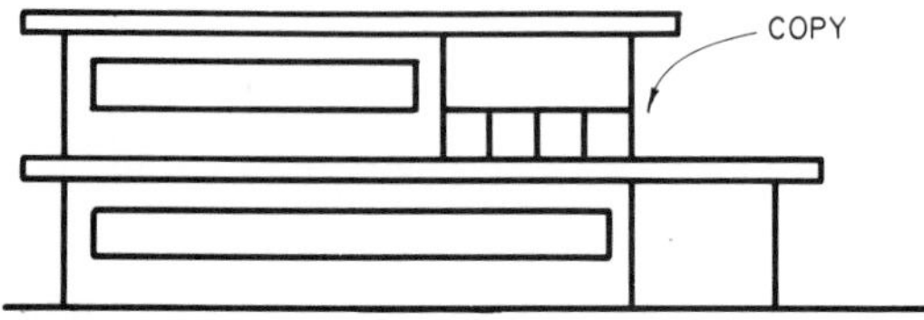

Fig. 28–14. An example of the use of nonreproducible grid paper.

used for pictorial illustrations. *Perspective* and *isometric* grid paper are available with many angles of projection (Fig. 28–15).

Perspective grids can be obtained with the vanishing point placed at various intervals from the station point and with the horizon placed in various locations, as shown in Fig. 28–16.

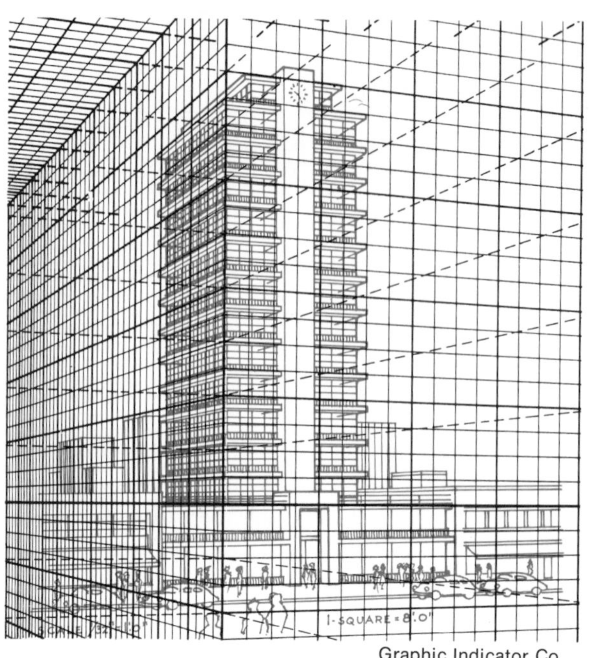

Graphic Indicator Co.

Fig. 28–15. The use of a prepared perspective grid paper.

TAPE

Many types of manufactured tape can be substituted for lines and symbols on architectural drawings.

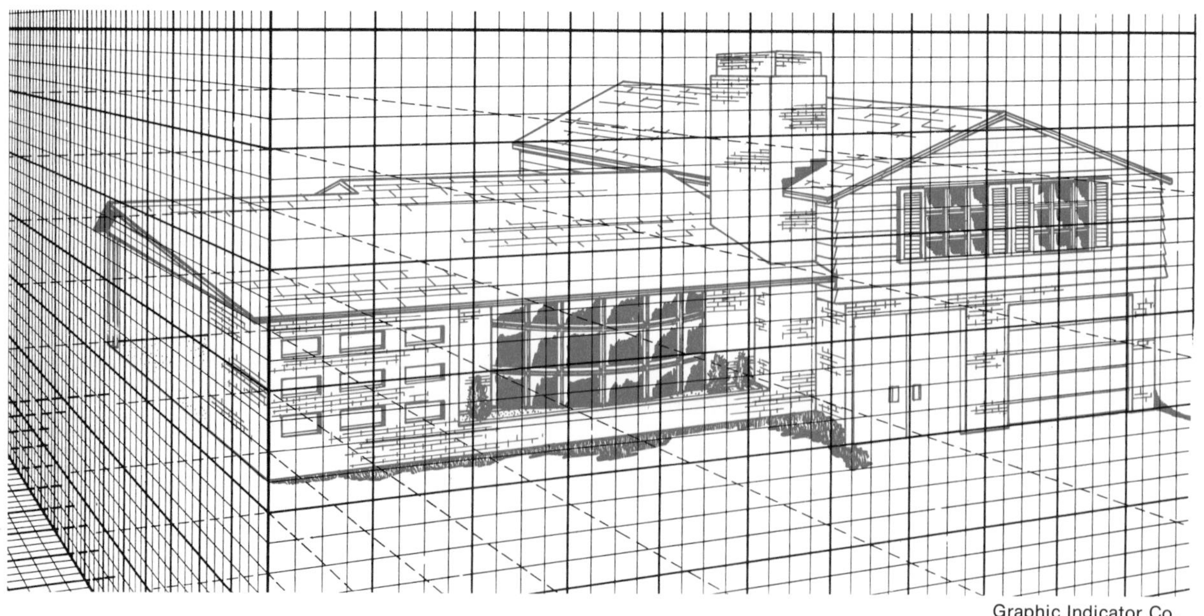

Graphic Indicator Co.

Fig. 28–16. A drawing may be projected in many locations.

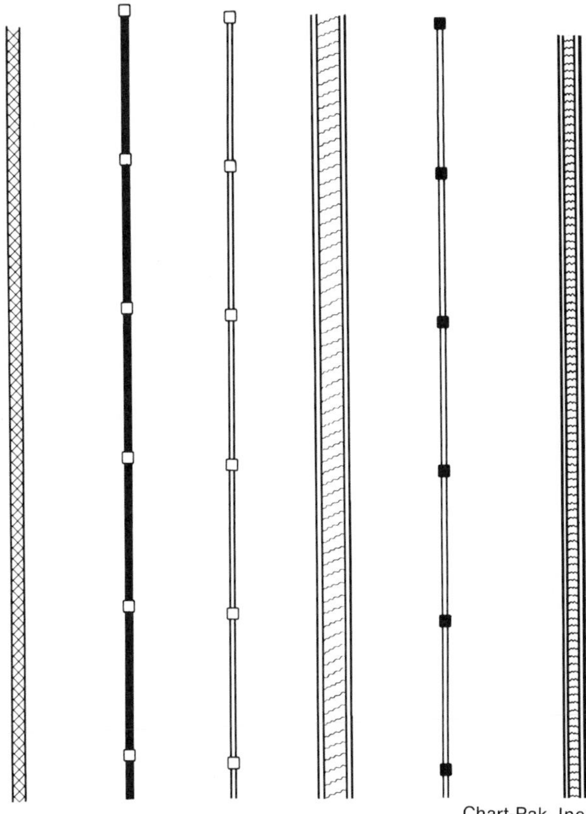

Chart-Pak, Inc.

Fig. 28–17. Architectural symbol tape.

Pressure-Sensitive Tape

Tape with printed symbols and special lines is used to produce lines and symbols that otherwise would be difficult and time-consuming to construct. Figure 28–17 shows some of the various symbols and lines available in this kind of tape. A special roll-on applicator enables the draftsman to draw lines by using tape, as shown in Fig. 28–18. This method is used extensively on overlays (Fig. 28–19). Figure 28–20 shows another application of this kind of tape.

Matte-Surface Tape

Temporary changes can be added to a drawing by drawing the symbol, note, or change on translucent matte-surface tape. If the drawing is changed, the tape can be removed and a new symbol added, or the symbol can be made permanent. The proposed closet wall in Fig. 28–21 was prepared on transparent tape. If the arrangement is unsatisfactory, the tape can be removed without destroying the drawing.

Bond Ryder Associates

Fig. 28–18. Rolling on pressure-sensitive tape.

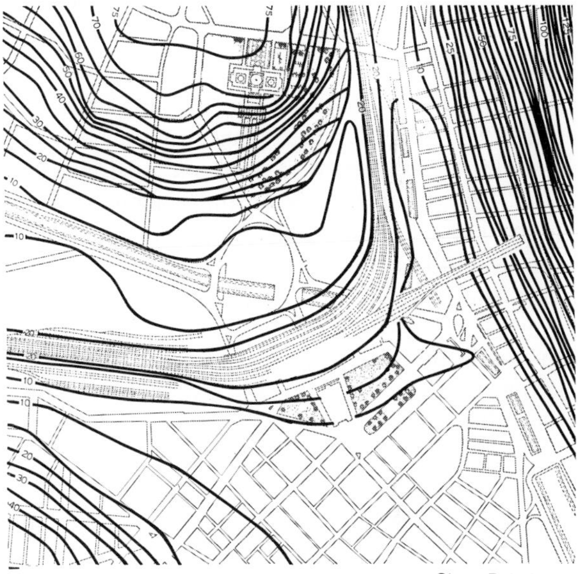

Chart-Pak, Inc.

Fig. 28–19. Pressure-sensitive tape used on a map overlay.

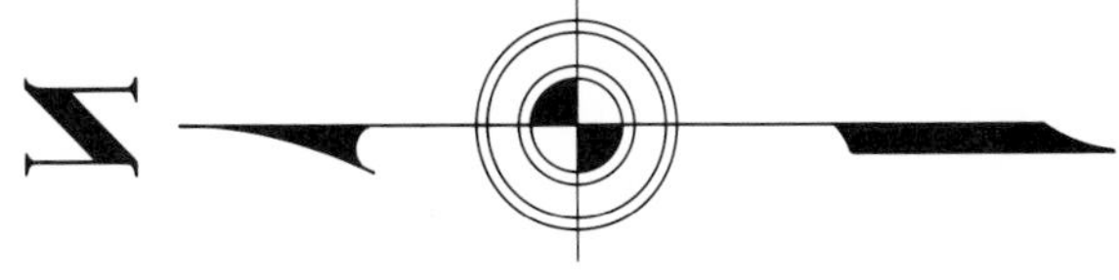

Fig. 28–20. Reverse uses of pressure-sensitive tape.

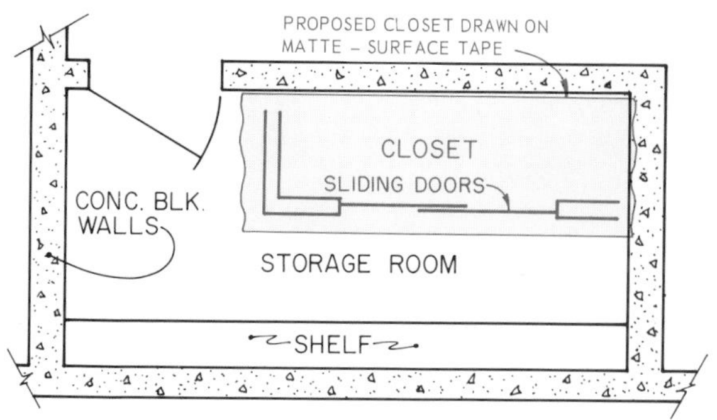

Fig. 28–21. A trial layout prepared on a matte-surface tape.

Masking Tape

Masking tape has other timesaving uses besides its use to attach the drawing to the drawing board. Strips of masking tape help ensure the equal length of lines when ruling many close lines. Strips of tape are placed on the drawing to mask the areas not to be lined. The lines are then drawn on the paper and extended on the tape. When the tape is removed, the ends of the lines are even and sharp, as shown in Fig. 28–22. This procedure eliminates the careful starting and stopping the pencil stroke with each line.

Since masking tape will pull out some graphite, a piece of paper can be placed on drawings to perform the masking function for large areas. If a small area is to remain unlined, sometimes it is easier to line through the surface and erase the small area with an erasing shield.

ABBREVIATIONS

Stenographers use shorthand to speed and condense their work. Architects also use shorthand. Architects' shorthand consists of symbols and abbreviations. When a symbol does not describe an object completely, a word or phrase must be used. Words and phrases can occupy much space on a drawing. Abbreviations therefore should be used to minimize this space. Refer to Section 26 for a list of architectural abbreviations.

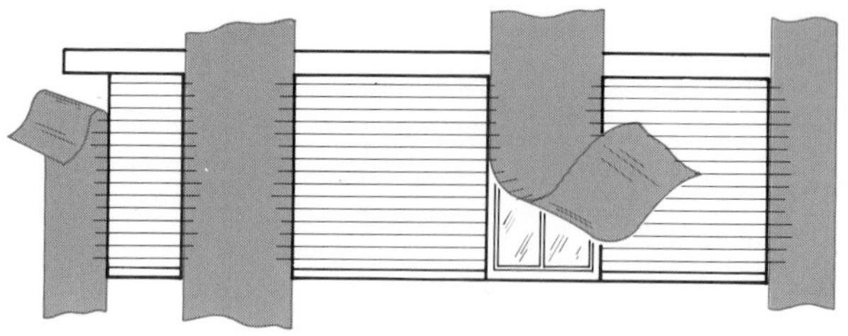

Fig. 28–22. The use of masking-out areas.

RUBBER STAMPS

For architectural symbols that are often repeated, the use of rubber stamps is effective and timesaving. Stamps can be used with any color ink, or stamps can be used in faint colors to provide an outline which may then be rendered with pencil or ink. Rubber stamps are used most often for symbols which do not require precise positioning on the drawing, such as landscape features, people, and cars. However, stamps may be used for furniture outlines and sometimes for labels. Figure 28–23 shows some common symbols used on rubber stamps.

BURNISHING PLATES

Burnishing plates are embossed sheets which have raised areas representing an outline of a symbol or texture lines. The plates are placed under a drawing; then a soft pencil is rubbed over the surface of the drawing. This creates lines on the drawing over the raised portions of the plate. The use of burnishing plates allows the draftsman to create consistent texture lines throughout a series of drawings with a minimum use of time.

PHOTOGRAPHIC REPRODUCTION

Often a section of a drawing needs to be changed, or a design element needs to be repeated on many drawings. The entire drawing need not be redrawn, nor must the design element be drawn repeatedly on each drawing. The section to be redrawn or repeated can be drawn once, attached to the drawing, and then the entire drawing can be reproduced through photographic processes.

PROBLEMS

1. **Prepare an underlay for a fireplace.**
2. **Prepare a title-strip underlay with the following information: your name, school or company, drawing number, teacher or supervisor, title of drawing series, title of specific drawing.**
3. **Prepare a lettering-guide underlay for 1/8", 1/4", and 3/16" letters.**
4. **Identify the following abbreviations: CL, FTG, HB, FL. See Section 26.**
5. **Redraw and add fixtures to the bathroom layouts shown in Fig. 22–30.**
6. **Redraw and add fixtures to the kitchen shown in Fig. 33–31, using a template.**
7. **Add doors to the plan shown in Fig. 28–4, using a door template.**
8. **Add landscape features to the plan shown in Fig. 33–3, using a landscape-plan template.**
9. **Define the following terms: *template, general-purpose template, special-purpose template, overlay, temporary overlay, permanent overlay, underlay, lettering underlay, pictorial bridge, bridge, squared paper, graph paper, perspective, grid, modular grid, pressure-sensitive tape, matte-surface tape, masking tape, architectural abbreviations, burnishing plates.***

Fig. 28–23. Examples of common rubber-stamp symbols.

UNIT 29

Architectural Lettering

Architectural lettering differs greatly from lettering used on engineering drawings because most architectural drawings are shown to a client. Architectural drawings not only must be correct and meaningful but must look attractive to the client.

PURPOSE

Figure 29–1 shows a plan without any lettering. This plan does not communicate a complete description of the size and function of the various components. All labels, notes, dimensions, and descriptions must be legibly lettered on architectural drawings if they are to function as an effective means of graphic communication.

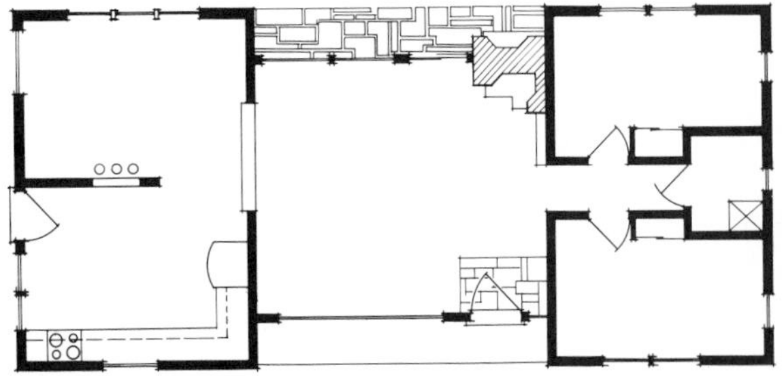

Fig. 29–1. A plan without lettering.

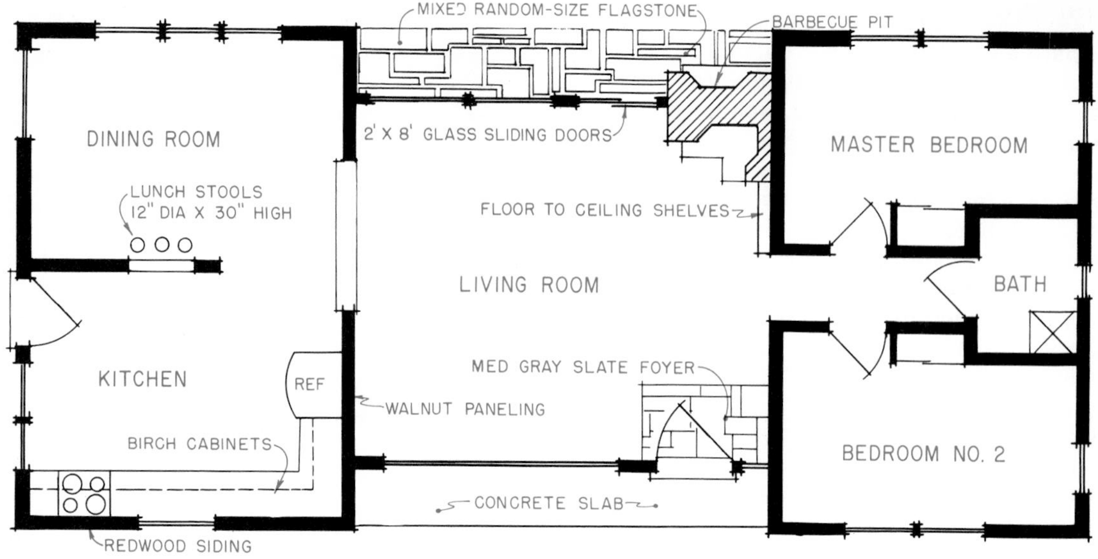

Fig. 29–2. The same plan with lettering added.

Legible, well-formed letters and numerals do more for a drawing than merely aid in communication. Effective lettering helps give the drawing a finished and professional look. Poor lettering is the mark of an amateur. The plan shown in Fig. 29-2 is more easily interpreted and appears more professional because lettering was used.

STYLES

Because architectural designs are somewhat personalized, many lettering styles have been developed by various architects. Nevertheless, these personalized styles are all based on the American National Standard Alphabet shown in Fig. 29–3.

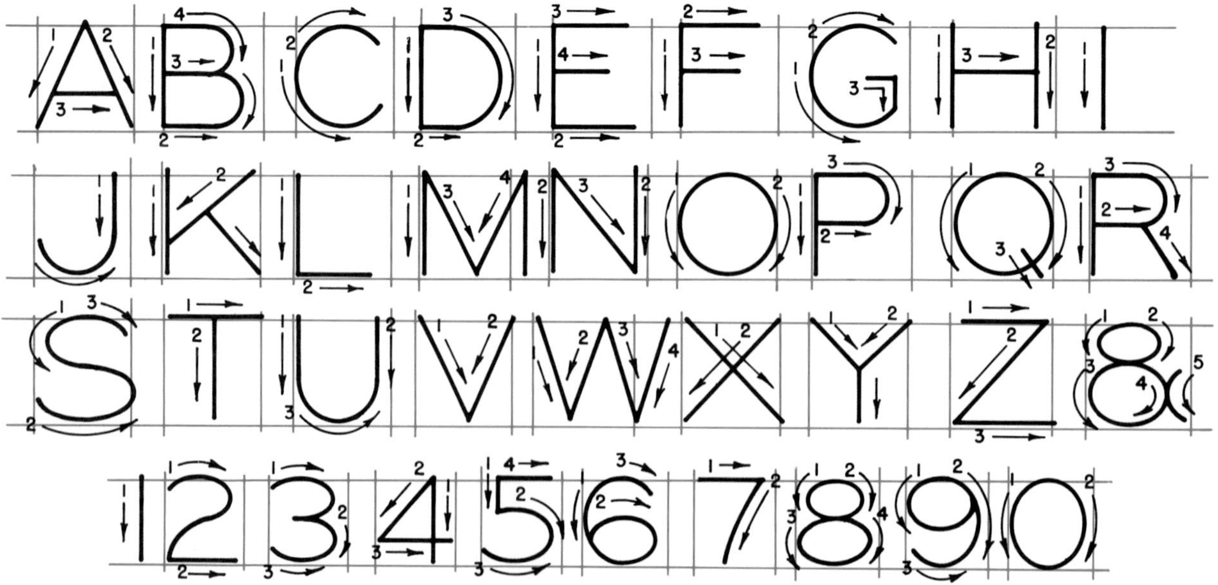

Fig. 29–3. The American National Standard Alphabet.

RULES FOR ARCHITECTURAL LETTERING

Much practice is necessary to develop the skills necessary to letter effectively. Although architectural lettering styles may be very different, all professional draftsmen follow certain basic rules of lettering. If you follow these rules you will develop accuracy, consistency, and speed in lettering your drawings.

1. Always use guidelines in lettering. Notice what a difference guidelines make in the lettering shown in Fig. 29–4.
2. Choose one style of lettering, and practice the formation of the letters of that style until you master it. Figure 29–5 compares the effect of using a consistent style with that of using an inconsistent style. Each letter in the inconsistent style may be correct, but the effect is undesirable.
3. Make letters bold and distinctive. Avoid a delicate, fine touch.
4. Make each line quickly from the beginning to the end of the stroke. See the difference between letters drawn quickly and those drawn slowly in Fig. 29–6.
5. Practice with larger letters (about 1/4″ or 6 mm), and gradually reduce the size until you can letter effectively at 1/16″, or 2 mm.
6. Practice spacing by lettering words and sentences, not alphabets. Figure 29–7 shows the effect of uniform and even spacing of letters.
7. Form the habit of lettering whenever possible—as you take notes, address envelopes, or write your name.
8. Practice only the capital alphabet. Lowercase letters are rarely used in architectural work.
9. Do not try to develop speed at first. Make each stroke quickly, but take your time between letters and between strokes until you have mastered each letter. Then gradually increase your speed. You will soon be able to letter almost as fast as you can write script.
10. If your lettering has a tendency to slant in one direction or the other, practice making a series of vertical and horizontal lines, as shown in Fig. 29–8.
11. If slant lettering is desired, practice slanting the horizontal strokes approxi-

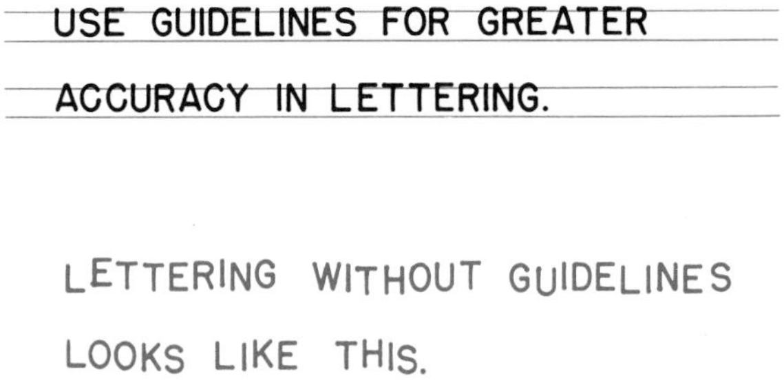

USE GUIDELINES FOR GREATER
ACCURACY IN LETTERING.

LETTERING WITHOUT GUIDELINES
LOOKS LIKE THIS.

Fig. 29–4. Always use guidelines when lettering.

CONSISTENT STYLE
CONSISTENT STYLE
INCONSISTENT STYLE

Fig. 29–5. Always use a consistent lettering style.

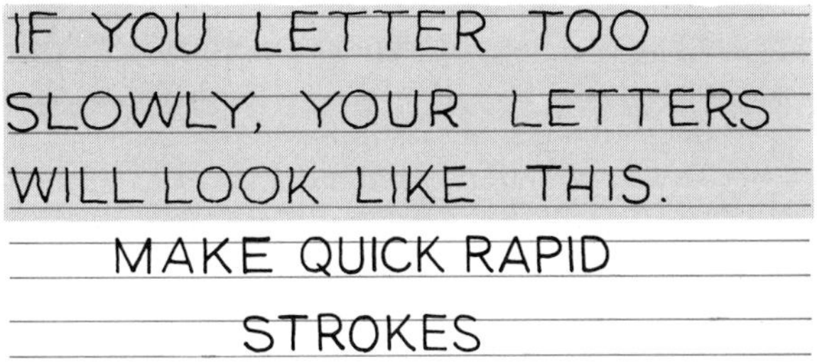

IF YOU LETTER TOO
SLOWLY, YOUR LETTERS
WILL LOOK LIKE THIS.
MAKE QUICK RAPID
STROKES

Fig. 29–6. Make each letter stroke quickly.

UNIFORM SPACING
UNEVEN SPACING

Fig. 29–7. Uniform spacing of letters is important.

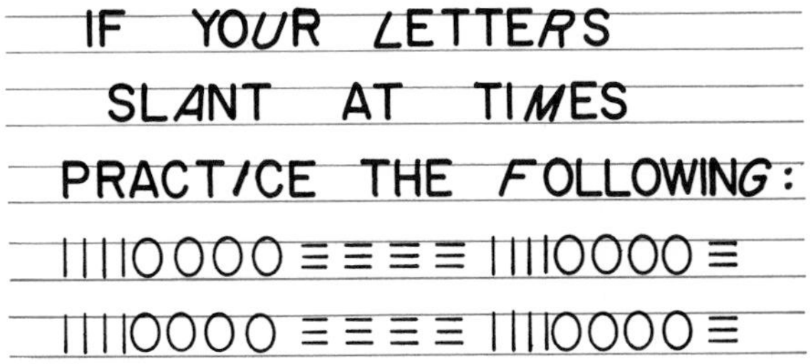

IF YOUR LETTERS
SLANT AT TIMES
PRACTICE THE FOLLOWING:
IIIIOOOO ≡≡≡≡ IIIIOOOO ≡
IIIIOOOO ≡≡≡≡ IIIIOOOO ≡

Fig. 29–8. Practice making horizontal and vertical lines.

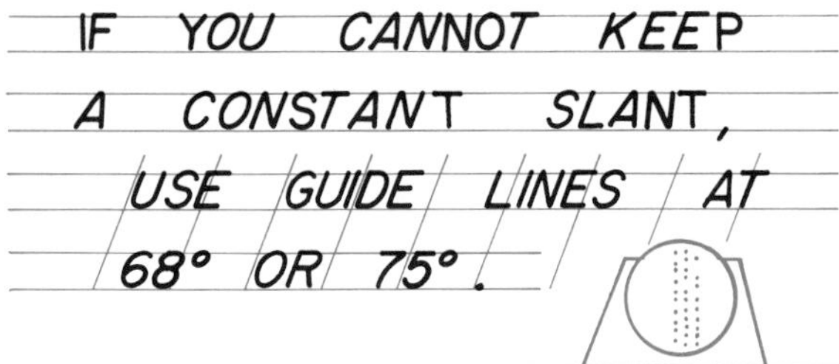

Fig. 29–9. Maintain the same degree of slant if slant lettering is used.

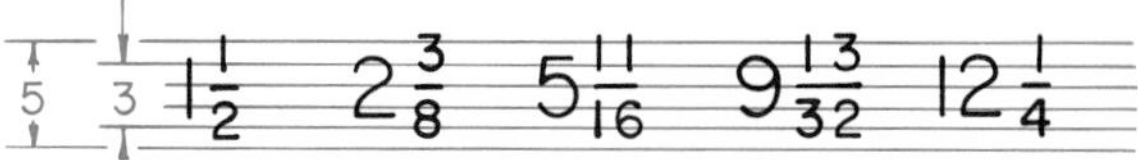

Fig. 29–10. Proper fraction proportions.

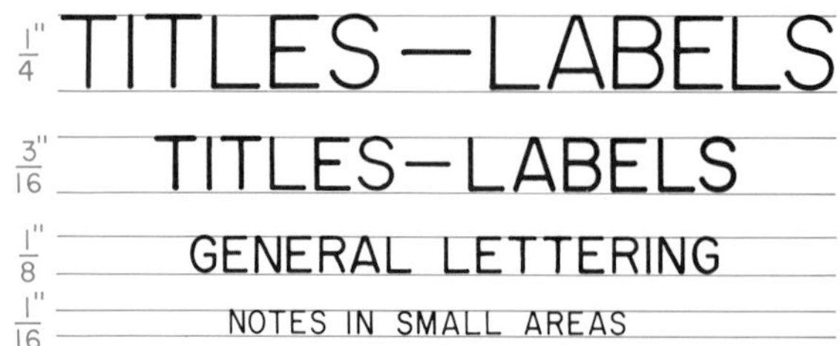

Fig. 29–11. Lettering height should relate to the importance of the label size.

mately 68°. The problem with most slant lettering, as shown in Fig. 29–9, is that it is difficult to maintain the same degree of slant continually. The tendency is for more and more slant to creep into the style.

12. Letter the drawing last to avoid smudges and overlapping with other areas of the drawing. This procedure will enable you to space out your lettering and to avoid lettering through important details.
13. Use a soft pencil, preferably an HB or F. A soft pencil will glide and is more easily controlled than a hard pencil.
14. Numerals used in architectural drawing should be adapted to the style, just as the alphabet is adapted. Fractions also should be made consistent with the style. Fractions are $1^2/_3$ times the height of the whole number. The numerator and the denominator of a fraction are each $^2/_3$ of the height of the whole number, as shown in Fig. 29–10. Notice also that in the expanded style, the fraction is slashed to conserve vertical space. The fraction takes the same amount of space as the whole number. (See rule 5, Fig. 34–3.)
15. The size of the lettering should be related to the importance of the labeling (Fig. 29–11).
16. If drawings are to be microfilmed, use microfont lettering (Fig. 29–12).
17. Specialized lettering templates can also be used (Fig. 29–13).

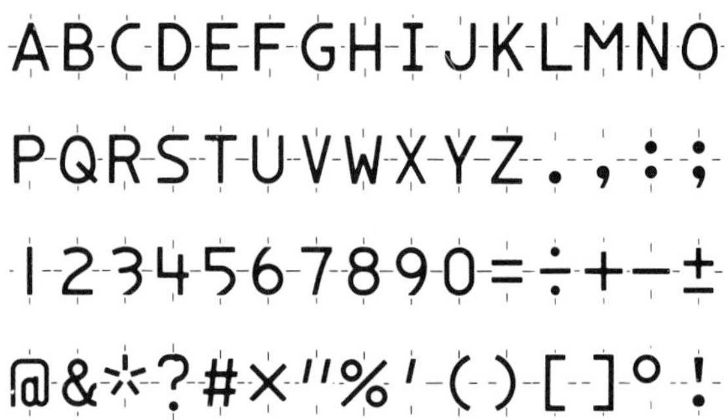

Fig. 29–12. Lettering used for drawings which are to be microfilmed.

Teledyne Post

Fig. 29–13. A common lettering template.

PROBLEMS

1. **Letter your name and your complete address, using an expanded lettering style.**
2. **Letter your name and your complete address, using a condensed style.**
3. **Letter the preceding rules for lettering, using any style you choose.**
4. **Letter the names and addresses of four of your friends in 1/4″, 3/16″, 3 mm, and 1/16″ lettering.**
5. **Letter the name of your town, county, and state.**
6. **Define the following terms: *American National Standard Alphabet, condensed style, expanded style, consistent style, vertical strokes, horizontal strokes, lettering pencil, slant lettering.***

UNIT 30

Line Techniques

In addition to the precise technical line work used on floor plans and elevations, other line techniques are used to create realism in architectural drawings. Some of the line techniques used are variation in the distance between lines or dots, variation in the width of lines, blending of lines, and use of gray tones or solid black areas (Fig. 30–1). These techniques are used to show materials, texture, contrast between areas, or light and shadow patterns. Some common combinations of line patterns are shown in Fig. 30–2 and the use of these techniques to show texture on a perspective drawing is shown in Fig. 30–3.

Varying the interval between lines drawn with pencil or pen can show texture, light, and density patterns, as shown in Fig. 30–4. When less precise line identification is desired, the use of wash-drawing (water-color) techniques

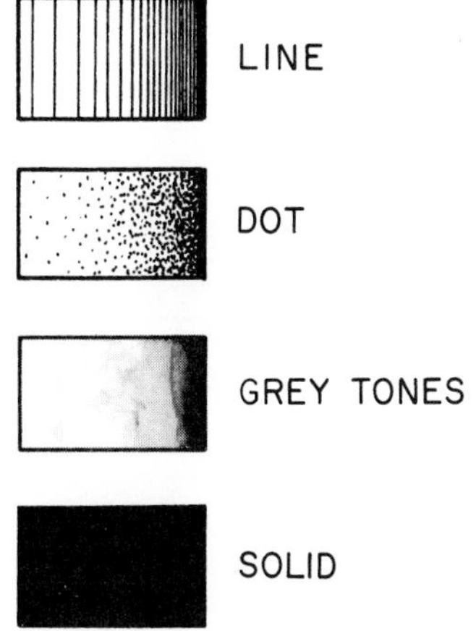

Fig. 30–1. Some types of line techniques.

Fig. 30–2. Examples of line-pattern combinations.

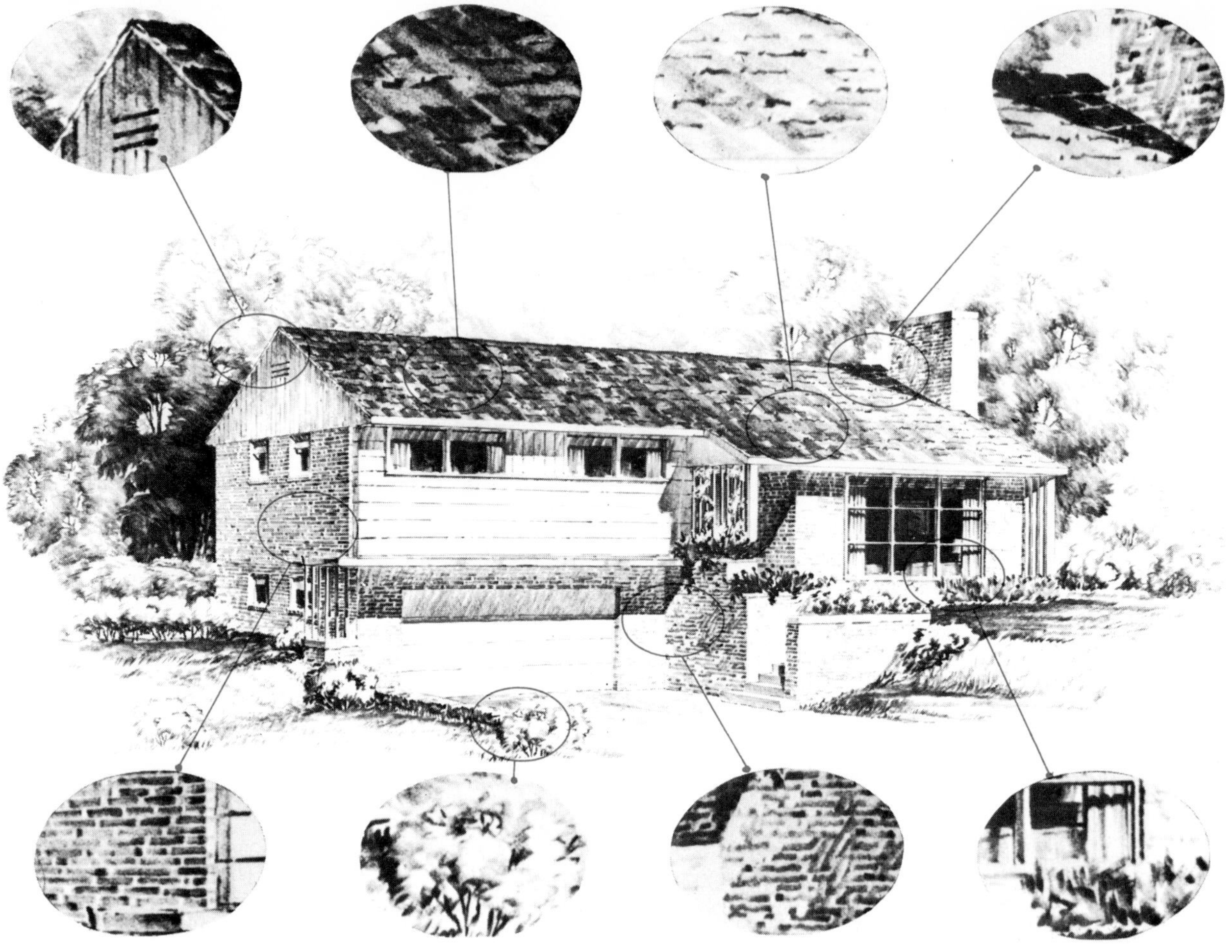

Home Planners, Inc.

Fig. 30–3. Methods of illustrating textures.

Fig. 30–4. Line-rendering techniques.

is effective. The drawing shown in Fig. 30–5 is a wash drawing. The drawing shown in Fig. 30–6 is rendered using a combination of wash techniques over a line drawing.

Floor plans and elevation drawings are prepared primarily for the builder. These drawings must be accurately scaled and dimensioned. However, some floor plans and elevation drawings are rendered to provide the pro-

Scholz Homes, Inc.

Fig. 30–5. Wash-drawing technique.

Home Planners, Inc.

Fig. 30–6. Combination of line and wash technique.

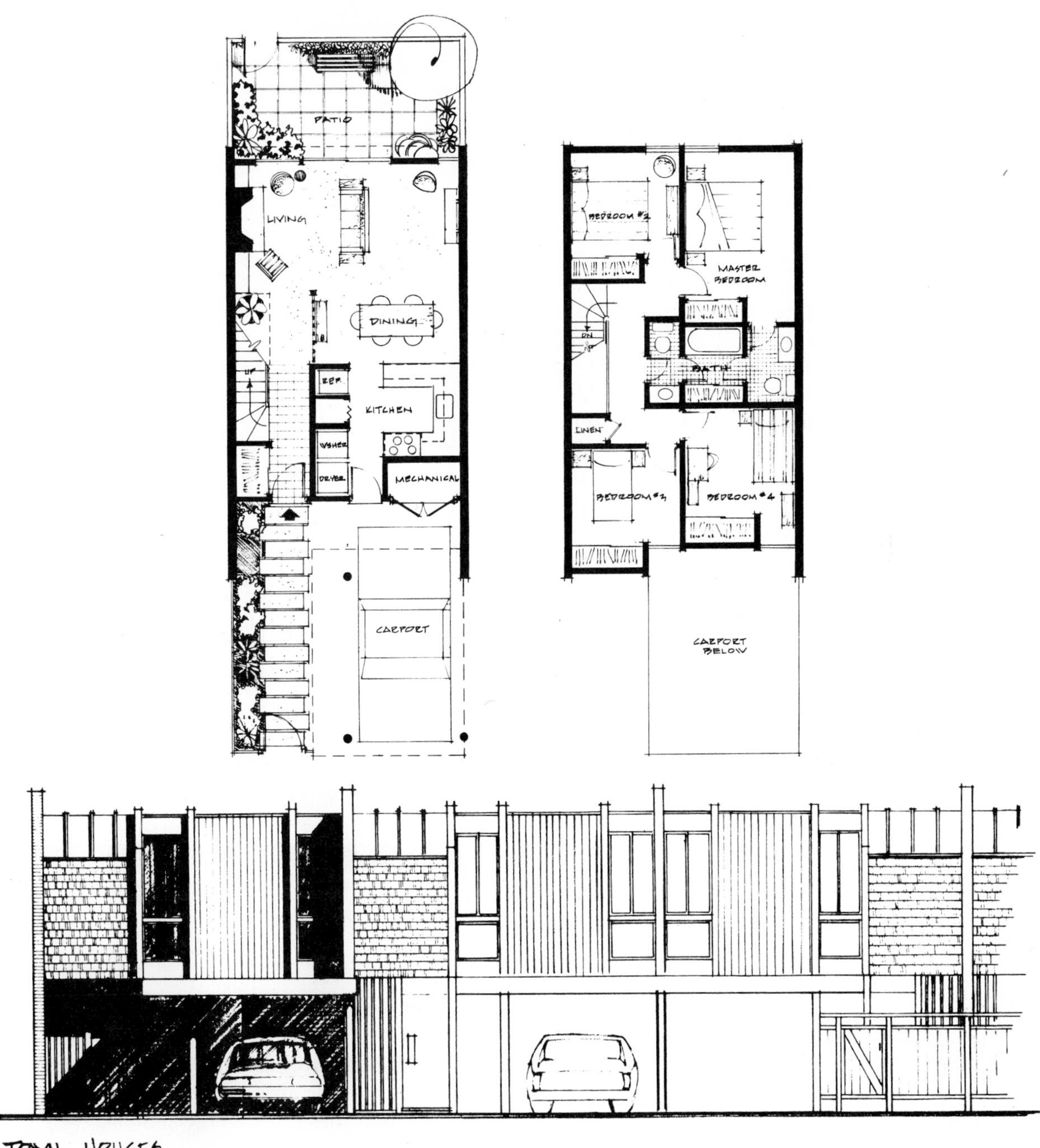

TOWN HOUSES

John Seals, Architect

Fig. 30–7. Presentation drawings.

spective customer with a better idea of the final appearance of the building. Figure 30–7 shows a presentation floor plan and elevation. These plans have no dimensions but include items such as plantings, floor surfaces, and material textures not usually found on floor plans or elevations used for construction purposes.

PROBLEMS

1. **Add material texture to the floor plan shown in Fig. 32–18.**
2. **Add texture to the surfaces of the elevation shown in Fig. 37–14.**
3. **Define these terms: *line, tone, wash drawing, presentation drawing.***

SECTION 6

Drawing Floor Plans

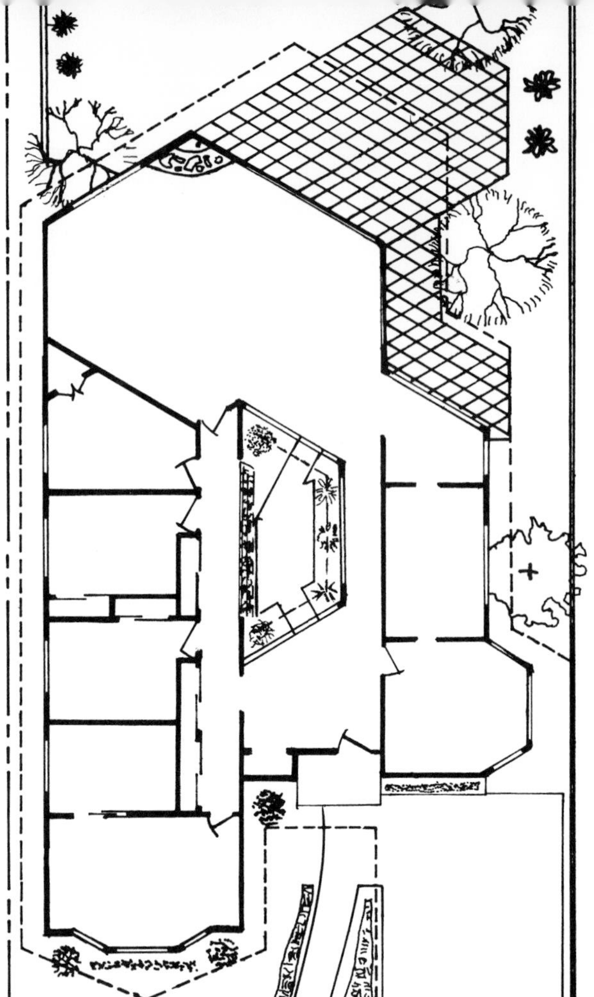

The most commonly used architectural drawing is the floor plan. The floor plan is a drawing of the outline and partitions of a building as you would see them if the building were cut horizontally about 4′ (or for practical purposes 1 m) above the floor line. The floor plan provides more specific information about the design of the building than any other plan. To design a floor plan that will be accurate and functional, the designer must determine what facilities will be included in the various areas of the building. These various areas must be combined into an integrated plan. Only then can a final floor plan be prepared which includes a description and sizes of all the materials and areas contained in the design. The floor plan is used as a base for the projection of other drawings.

UNIT 31

Room Planning

Not long ago the outside of most homes was designed before the inside. A basic square, rectangle, or series of rectangles was established to a convenient overall size and then rooms were fitted into these forms.

Today the inside of most homes is designed before the outside, and the outside design is determined by the size and relationship of the inside areas. This is known as designing from the inside out.

BASIC REQUIREMENTS

In designing from the inside out, the architect evolves the plan from basic room requirements. By learning about the living habits and tastes of the occupants, the architect determines what facilities are required for each room. In this way the furniture, fixtures, and amount of space that will be appropriate for the activities are provided for.

SEQUENCE OF DESIGN

When designing from the inside out, the home planner first determines what furniture and fixtures are needed. Next the amount and size of furniture must be determined. The style selected will greatly affect the dimensions of the furniture.

After the furniture dimensions are established, furniture templates can be made and ar-

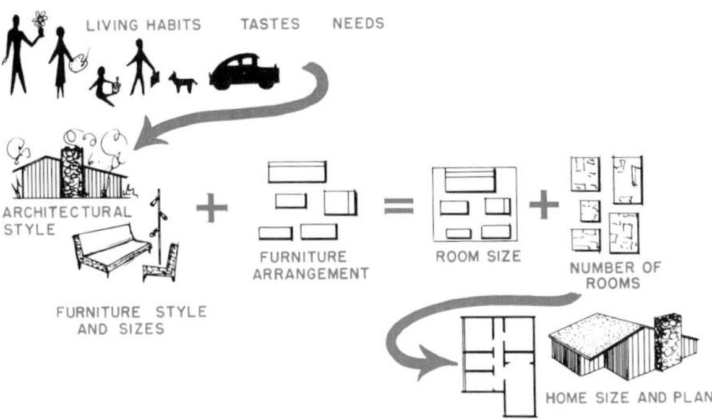

Fig. 31–1. The importance of room planning in arriving at the overall design.

ranged in functional patterns. Room sizes can then be established by drawing a perimeter around the furniture placements.

When the room sizes are determined, rooms can be combined into areas, and areas into the total floor plan. Finally the outside is designed by projecting the elevations from the floor plan. Figure 31–1 shows the importance of room planning in the overall sequence of planning a home.

FURNITURE

Furniture styles vary greatly in size and proportion. Sizes of furniture therefore cannot be decided on until the style is chosen. The furniture style should be consistent with the style of architecture (Fig. 31–2).

Selection

Furniture should be selected according to the needs of the occupants (Fig. 31–3 at A and B). A piano should be provided for someone interested in music. A great amount of bookcase space must be provided for the avid reader. The artist, draftsman, or engineer may require drafting equipment in the den or study. A good starting point in room planning is to list the uses to be made of each room. Then make a list of furniture needed for each of these activities. For example: I want to *watch television;* therefore, I need a *television set* and a *lounge chair.* I want to *read;* therefore, I need a *lounge chair,* a *reading lamp,* and a *bookcase.* I want to *listen to records;* therefore, I need a *stereo* or a *hi-fi.*

From these requirements a rather comprehensive list of needed furniture can be com-

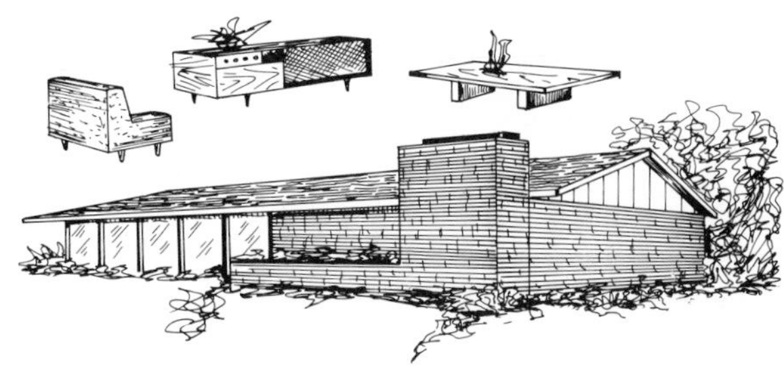

Fig. 31–2. Furniture style should be consistent with the architectural style.

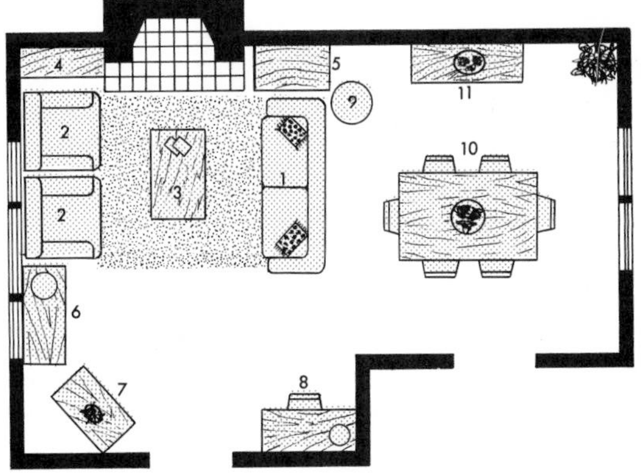

COMBINATION LIVING-DINING ROOM

1 - CHESTERFIELD	7 - TV CONSOLE
2 - LOUNGE CHAIR	8 - DESK
3 - COFFEE TABLE	9 - FLOOR LAMP
4 - BOOKCASE	10 - DINING ROOM TABLE AND 6 CHAIRS
5 - END TABLE	11 - BUFFET
6 - STEREO	

Fig. 31–3A. Living needs determine the amount of furniture.

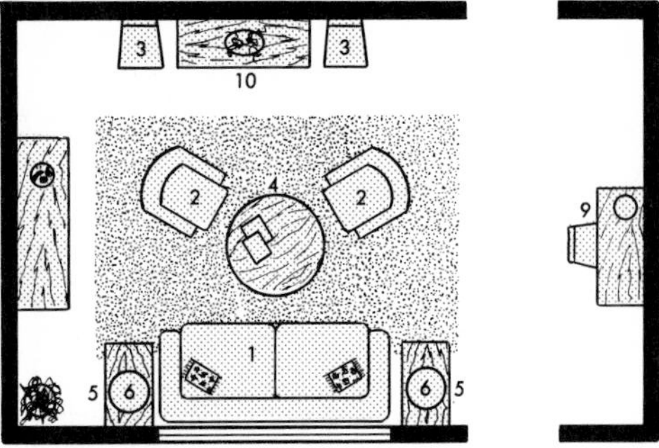

FURNITURE GROUPING AROUND COFFEE TABLE

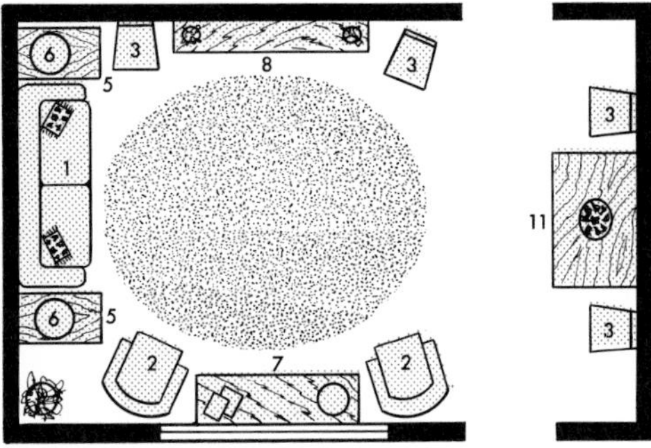

MULTIPURPOSE LIVING ROOM

1 - CHESTERFIELD
2 - LOUNGE CHAIR
3 - CHAIR
4 - COFFEE TABLE
5 - END TABLE
6 - LAMP
7 - STEREO
8 - BUILT-IN CABINET
9 - DESK AND CHAIR
10 - BUFFET
11 - FOLDING TABLE

Fig. 31–3B. Life-style determines the furniture arrangement.

piled. When the exact style is determined, the width and length of each piece of furniture can also be added to the list, as shown below.

Living Room

1 couch 34″ × 100″ (864 × 2540 mm)
2 armchairs 30″ × 36″ (762 × 914 mm)
1 chaise 28″ × 60″ (711 × 1524 mm)
1 TV 26″ × 24″ (660 × 610 mm)
1 hi-fi 24″ × 56″ (610 × 1422 mm)
1 bookcase 15″ × 48″ (381 × 1219 mm)
1 floor lamp 6″ × 14″ 152 × 356 mm)
1 coffee table 18″ × 52″ (457 × 1321 mm)
2 end tables 14″ × 30″ (356 × 762 mm)
1 baby grand piano 60″ × 80″ (1524 × 2032 mm)

Dining Room

1 dining table 44″ × 72″ (1118 × 1829 mm)
2 armchairs 28″ × 36″ (711 × 914 mm)
4 chairs 26″ × 36″ (660 × 914 mm)
1 china closet 18″ × 42″ (457 × 1067 mm)
1 buffet 26″ × 56″ (660 × 1422 mm)

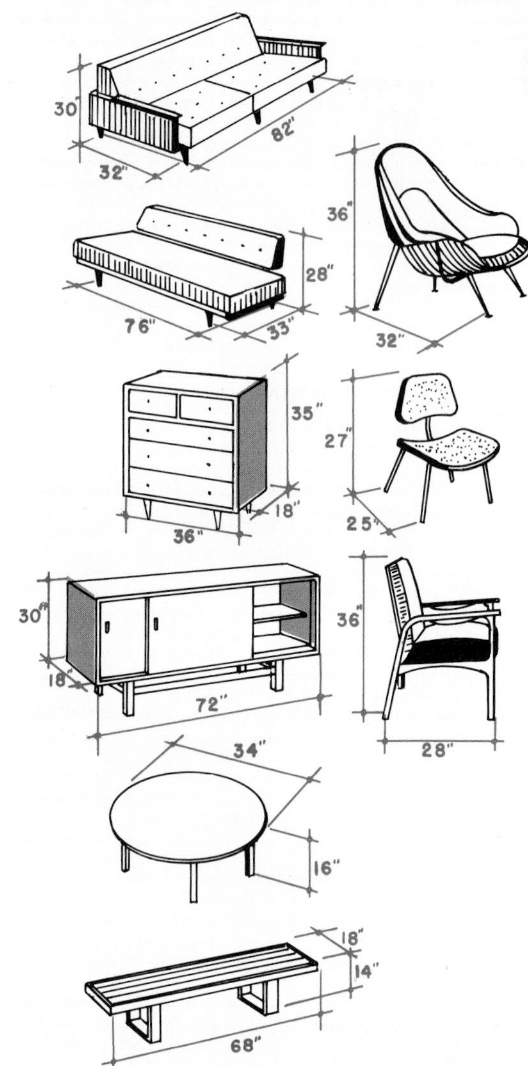

Fig. 31–4. Some typical furniture dimensions.

Similar lists should be prepared for the kitchen, bedrooms, nursery, bath, and all other rooms where furniture is required. Figure 31–4 shows some typical furniture dimensions which can be included with the furniture lists.

Furniture Templates

Arranging and rearranging furniture in a room is heavy work. It is much easier to arrange furniture by the use of templates (Fig. 31–5). *Furniture templates* are thin pieces of paper, cardboard, plastic, or metal which represent the width and length of pieces of furniture. They are used to determine exactly how much floor space each piece of furniture will occupy. One

Fig. 31-5. Templates represent the width and length of each piece of furniture.

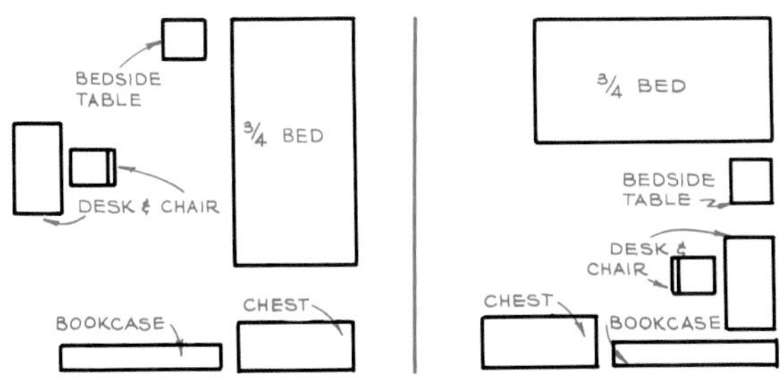

Fig. 31-7. Room dimensions should be determined by arrangement and number of pieces of furniture.

template is made for each piece of furniture on the furniture list.

Templates are always prepared to the scale that will be used in the final drawing of the house. The scale most frequently used on floor plans is 1/4″ = 1′—0″. Scales of 3/16″ = 1′—0″ and 1/8″ = 1′—0″ are sometimes used.

Wall-hung furniture, or any projection from furniture, even though it does not touch the floor, should be included as a template because the floor space under this furniture is not usable for any other purpose.

Templates show only the width and length of furniture and the floor space covered (Fig. 31-6). Table 31-1 shows common furniture sizes which can be used as a guide in constructing furniture templates.

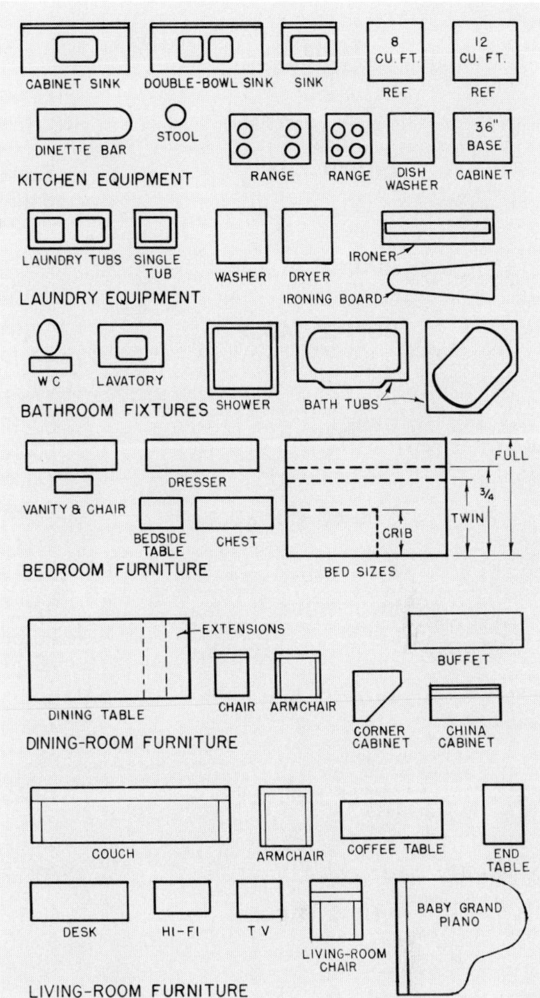

Fig. 31-6. Typical furniture templates.

ROOM ARRANGEMENTS

Furniture templates are placed in the arrangement that will best fit the living pattern anticipated for the room. Space must be allowed for free flow of traffic and for opening and closing doors, drawers, and windows. Figure 31-7 shows furniture templates placed in several different arrangements before the room dimensions are established.

Determining Room Dimensions

After a suitable furniture arrangement has been established, the room dimensions can be determined by drawing an outline around the furniture, as shown in Fig. 31-8.

Table 31-1. COMMON FURNITURE SIZES

ITEM	LENGTH, INCHES (mm)	WIDTH, INCHES (mm)	HEIGHT, INCHES (mm)
COUCH	72(1829)	30(762)	30(762)
	84(2134)	30(762)	30(762)
	96(2438)	30(762)	30(762)
LOUNGE	28(711)	32(813)	29(737)
	34(864)	36(914)	37(940)
COFFEE TABLE	36(914)	20(508)	17(432)
	48(1219)	20(508)	17(432)
	54(1372)	20(508)	17(432)
DESK	50(1270)	21(533)	29(737)
	60(1524)	30(762)	29(737)
	72(1829)	36(914)	29(737)
STEREO CONSOLE	36(914)	16(406)	26(660)
	48(1219)	17(432)	26(660)
	62(1575)	17(432)	27(660)
END TABLE	22(559)	28(711)	21(533)
	26(660)	20(508)	21(533)
	28(711)	28(711)	20(508)
TV CONSOLE	38(965)	17(432)	29(737)
	40(1016)	18(457)	30(762)
	48(1219)	19(483)	30(762)
SHELF MODULES	18(457)	10(254)	60(1524)
	24(610)	10(254)	60(1524)
	36(914)	10(254)	60(1524)
	48(1219)	10(254)	60(1524)
DINING TABLE	48(1219)	30(762)	29(737)
	60(1524)	36(914)	29(737)
	72(1829)	42(1067)	28(711)
BUFFET	36(914)	16(406)	31(787)
	48(1219)	16(406)	31(787)
	52(1321)	18(457)	31(787)
DINING CHAIRS	20(508)	17(432)	36(914)
	22(559)	19(483)	29(737)
	24(610)	21(533)	31(787)
	DIAMETER, INCHES (mm)		**HEIGHT, INCHES (mm)**
DINING TABLE (ROUND)	36(914)		28(711)
	42(1067)		28(711)
	48(1219)		28(711)

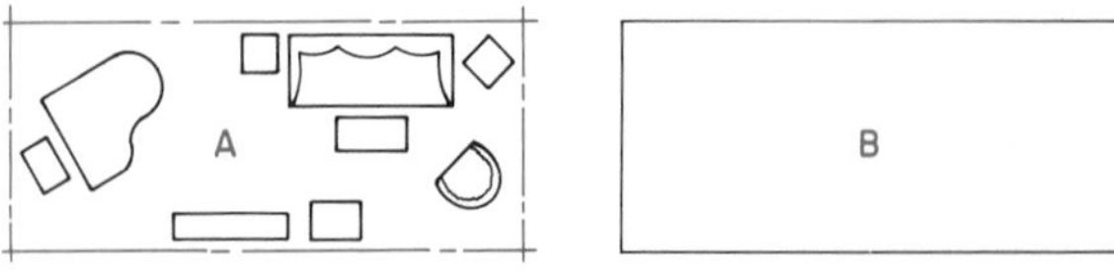

Fig. 31-8. The preferred method of determining room dimensions.

Room templates are made by cutting around the outline of the room. Figure 31–9 shows some typical room templates constructed by cutting around furniture template arrangements.

Table 31–2. ROOM SIZES FOR SMALL, AVERAGE, AND LARGE HOMES

	LIVING ROOM, FT^2/m^2	DINING ROOM, FT^2/m^2	KITCHEN, FT^2/m^2	BEDROOMS, FT^2/m^2	BATH, FT^2/m^2
SMALL HOME	200/18.5	155/14.4	110/10.2	140/13.0	40/3.7
AVERAGE HOME	250/24.2	175/16.2	135/12.5	170/15.7	70/6.5
LARGE HOME	300/27.8	195/18.1	165/15.3	190/17.6	100/9.3

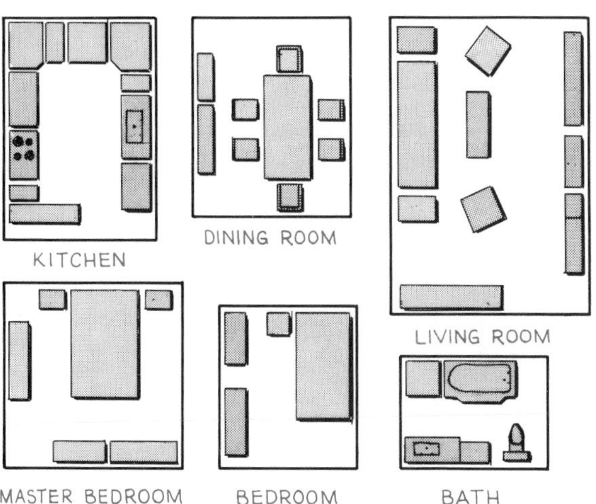

Fig. 31–9. Typical placement of furniture templates.

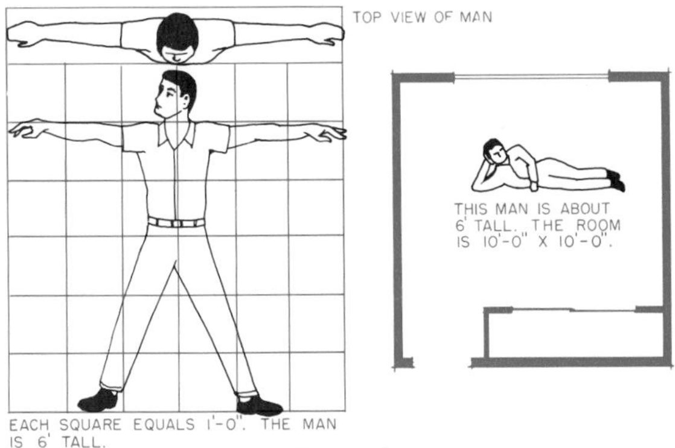

Fig. 31–10. Comparative size of a room with the size of its inhabitants.

Common Room Sizes

Determining what room sizes are desirable is only one aspect of room planning. Since the cost of the home is largely determined by the size and number of rooms, room sizes must be adjusted to conform to the acceptable price range. Table 31–2 shows sizes for each room in large, medium, and small dwellings. These dimensions represent only average widths and lengths. Even in large homes where perhaps no financial restriction exists, room sizes are limited by the size of building materials. Furthermore, a room can become too large to be functional for the purpose intended.

Checking Methods

It is sometimes difficult to visualize the exact amount of real space that will be occupied by furniture or that should be allowed for traffic through a given room. One device used to give the layman a point of reference is a template of a human figure, as shown in Fig. 31–10. With this template you can imagine yourself moving through the room to check the appropriateness of furniture placement and the adequacy of traffic allowances.

The experienced architect and homeplanner does not always go through the procedure of cutting out furniture templates and arranging them into patterns to arrive at room sizes. But the architect uses templates frequently to recheck designs. Until you are completely familiar with furniture dimensions and the sizes of building materials, the use of the procedures outlined here is recommended.

PROBLEMS

1. Rearrange the following steps in their proper order in room planning:
 a. Make list of furniture needed.
 b. Choose furniture style.
 c. Choose home style.
 d. Determine living habits.
 e. Make furniture templates.
 f. Determine room dimensions.
 g. Arrange furniture templates.
 h. Determine sizes of furniture.

2. **Choose a style of furniture suitable for use in your home. Visit a furniture store and sketch examples of furniture suitable for a modern, a colonial, and a period house.**
3. **Define your living needs and activities. List each piece of furniture needed for each room in order to fulfill these needs. Example:**

Living Habit	***Furniture Needed***
Watching TV	**TV set**
Playing Ping-Pong	**Ping-Pong table**
Writing	**Desk, chair**

4. **Make a list of furniture you would need for a home you might design. The list should include the number of pieces and size (width and length) of each piece of furniture.**
5. **Make a furniture template (¼″ = 1′—0″) for each piece of furniture you would include in a home of your design.**
6. **Start a scrapbook of furniture styles by selecting examples from current magazines.**
7. **Define the following terms: *furniture template, furniture dimensions, room dimensions, furniture style.***

UNIT 32

Floor-Plan Design

The architect or designer develops and records ideas through preliminary sketches which are later transformed into final working drawings. These ideas are directly translated into sketches that may approximate the final design. The architect knows through experience how large each room or area must be made to perform its particular function. He or she can mentally manipulate the relationships of areas and record design ideas through the use of sketches. This skill is attained after much experience.

LEARNING DESIGN PROCEDURES

Until you have gained much experience in designing floor plans, you may have difficulty in creating floor plans by the same methods professionals use. In the beginning you should rely on more tangible methods of designing.

The information in this unit outlines the procedures you should use in developing floor-plan designs. These procedures represent real activities which relate to the mental activities of a professional designer. Figure 32–1 shows the sequence of these design activities in developing a floor plan. You will notice that the sequence includes the development of room templates through the use of furniture templates, as described in Unit 31. These room templates

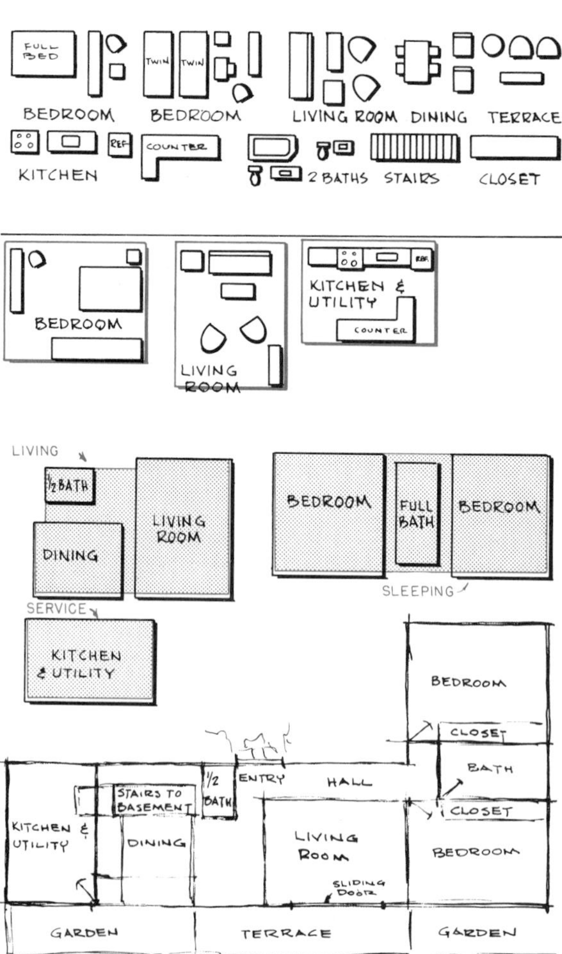

Fig. 32–1. Preliminary rough sketches of floor plans are prepared from template layouts of the living, service, and sleeping areas.

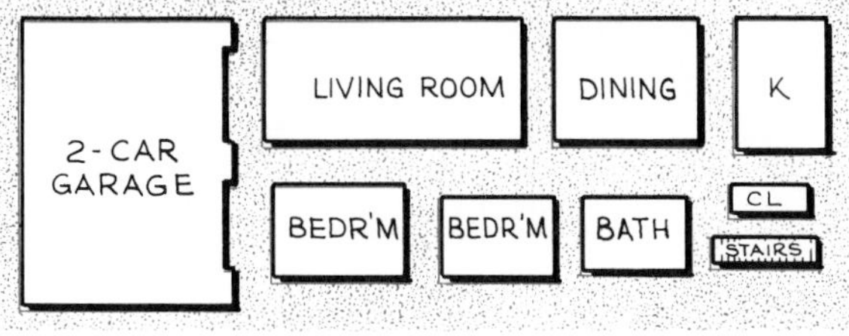

Fig. 32–2. Room templates prepared for floor-plan-design use.

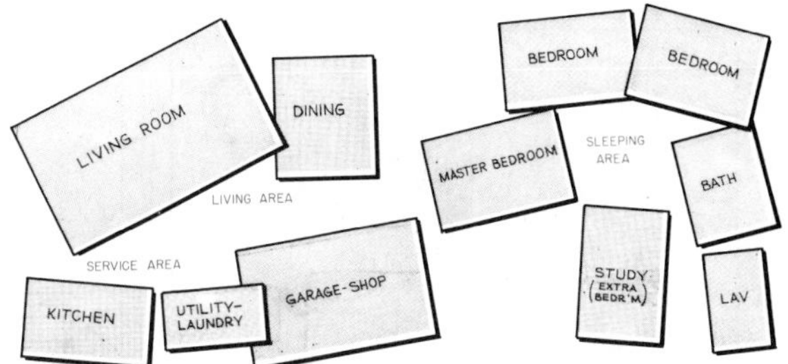

Fig. 32–3. Room templates divided into areas.

become the building blocks used in floor-plan designing. The room templates are arranged, rearranged, and moved into various patterns until the most desirable plan is achieved. Think of these room templates as pieces of a jigsaw puzzle which are manipulated to produce the final picture. Figure 32–2 shows a typical set of room templates prepared for use in floor-plan design.

PLANNING WITH ROOM TEMPLATES

A residence or any other building is not a series of separate rooms, but a combination of several activity areas. In the design of floor plans, room templates are first divided into area classifications, as shown in Fig. 32–3. The templates are then arranged in the most desirable plan for each area (Fig. 32–4). Next the area arrangements are combined in one plan (Fig. 32–5). The position of each room is then sketched and revised to achieve unity.

As you combine areas, you will need to rearrange and readjust the position of individual rooms. At this time you should consider the traffic pattern, compass direction, street location, and relationship to landscape features. Space must be allowed for stairways and halls. Figure 32–6 shows some common allowances for stairwells and halls on the floor plan. Unless closets have been incorporated in the room template, adequate space must also be provided for storage spaces.

Rooms and facilities such as the recreation room, laundry, workshop, and heating equipment are often placed in the basement. The designer must be sure that the floor plan developed provides sufficient space on the lower level for these facilities. In two-story houses, the sleeping area is usually placed on the level above the ground floor. Templates should also be developed for rooms on this level, but they must be adjusted to conform to the sizes established for the first level.

FLOOR-PLAN SKETCHING

Preparing a layout for a room template is only a preliminary step in designing the floor plan. The template layout shows only the desirable size, proportion, and relationship of each room to the entire plan.

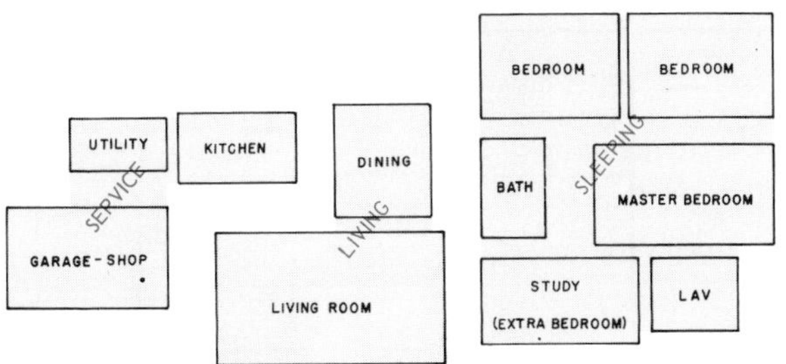

Fig. 32–4. Templates arranged into area plans.

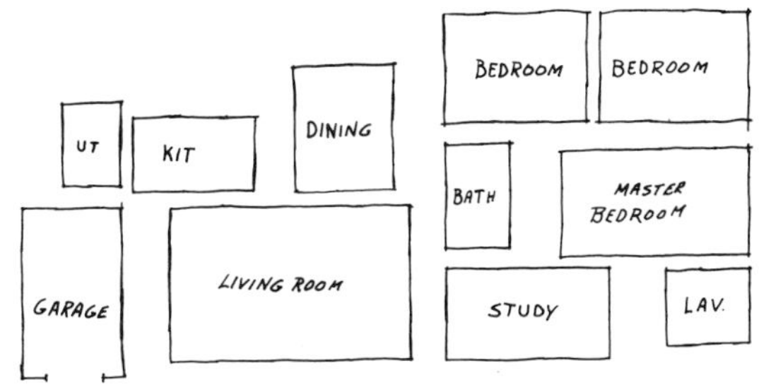

Fig. 32–5. Area templates combined into one plan.

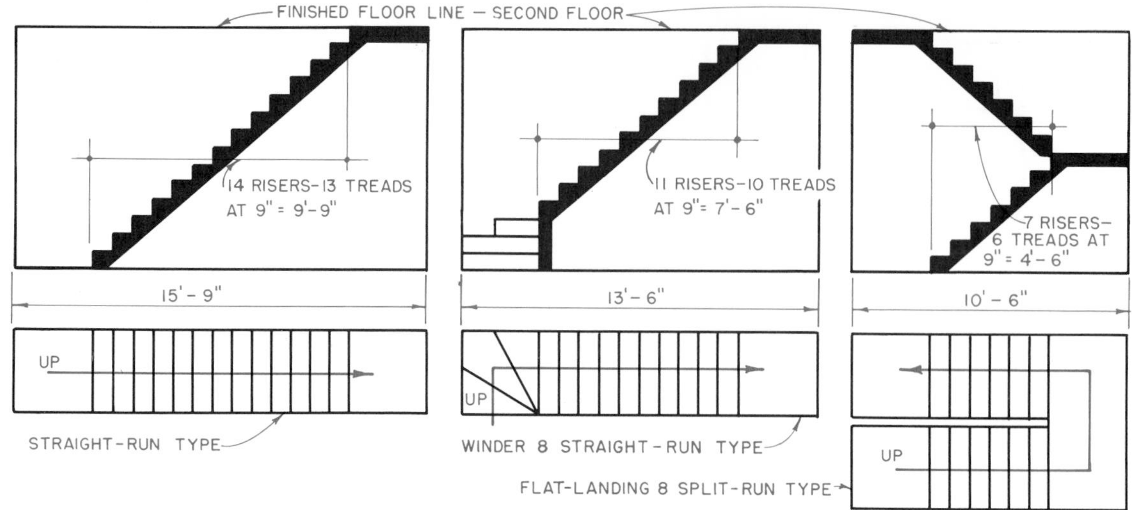

Fig. 32–6. Space must be allowed for halls and stairways.

Preliminary Sketching

Template layouts such as the one shown in Fig. 32–5 usually contain many irregularities and awkward corners because room dimensions were established before the overall plan was completed. These offsets and indentations can be smoothed out by increasing the dimensions of some rooms and changing slightly the arrangement of others. These alterations are usually made by sketching the template layout, as shown in Fig. 32–7A. At this time features such as fireplaces, closets, and divider walls can be added where appropriate.

Think of this first floor-plan sketch as only the beginning. Many sketches are usually necessary before the designer achieves an acceptable floor plan. In successive sketches such as the one shown in Fig. 32–7B, the design should be refined further. Costly and unattractive offsets and indentations can be eliminated. Modular sizes can be established that will facilitate the maximum use of standard building materials and furnishings. The exact positions and sizes of doors, windows, closets, and halls can be determined.

Refinement of the design is done by resketching until a satisfactory sketch is reached, as shown in Fig. 32–7C. Except for very minor changes, it is always better to make a series of sketches than to erase and change the original sketch. Many designers use tracing paper to trace the acceptable parts of the design and then change the poor features on the new sheet. This procedure also provides the designer with a record of the total design process. Early

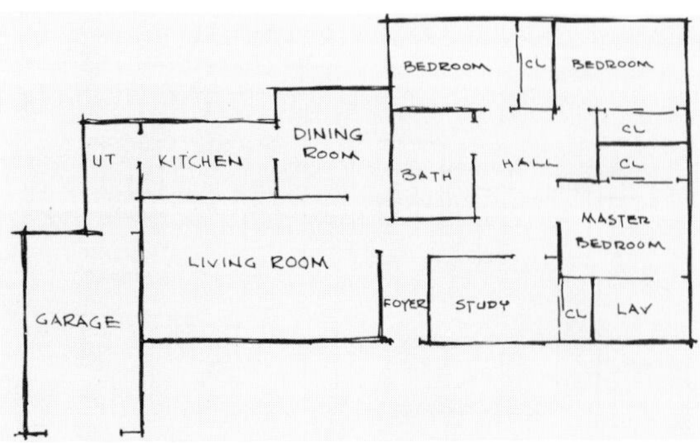

Fig. 32–7A. A preliminary sketch.

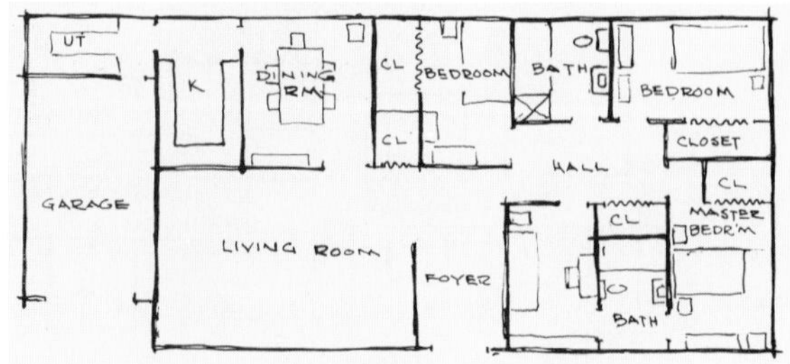

Fig. 32–7B. A refined sketch.

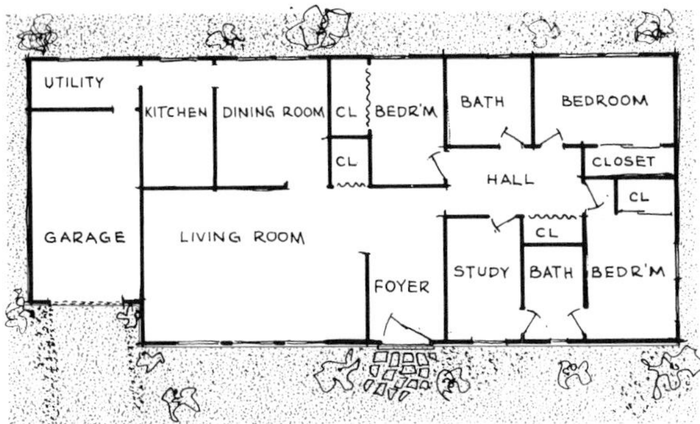

Fig. 32–7C. A final sketch.

sketches sometimes contain solutions to problems that develop later in the final design. Final sketches can still be improved as shown in Fig. 32–8.

Plan Variations

Many different room arrangements are possible within the same amount of space. Figure 32–9 shows two methods of rearranging and redistributing space to overcome poor design features.

Final Sketching

Single-line sketches such as those shown in Fig. 32–7 are satisfactory for basic planning purposes. However, they are not adequate for establishing final sizes. A final sketch (Fig. 32–10) should be prepared on cross-section paper to provide a better description of wall thicknesses and to include property features. This sketch should include the exact position

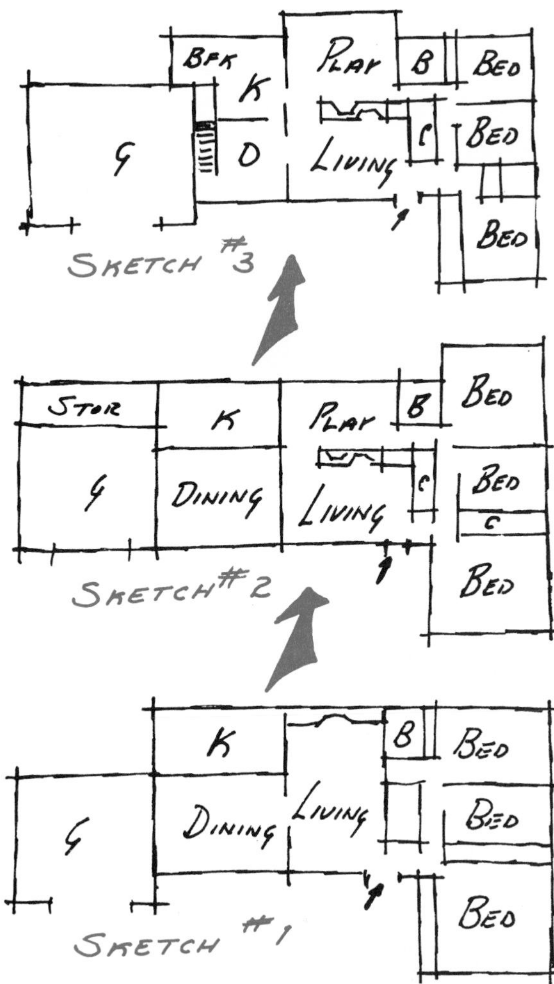

Fig. 32–8. Revisions may be made to final sketches.

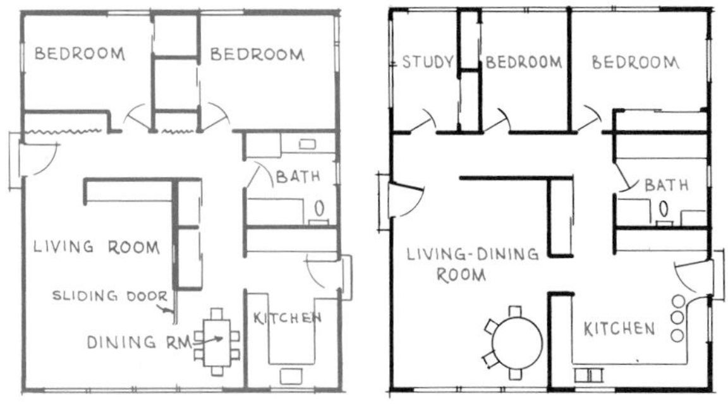

Fig. 32–9. Many different room arrangements are possible within the same amount of space.

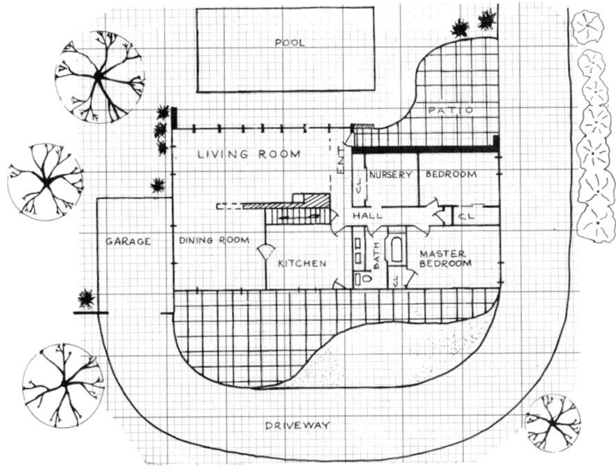

Fig. 32–10. A final sketch prepared on cross-section paper.

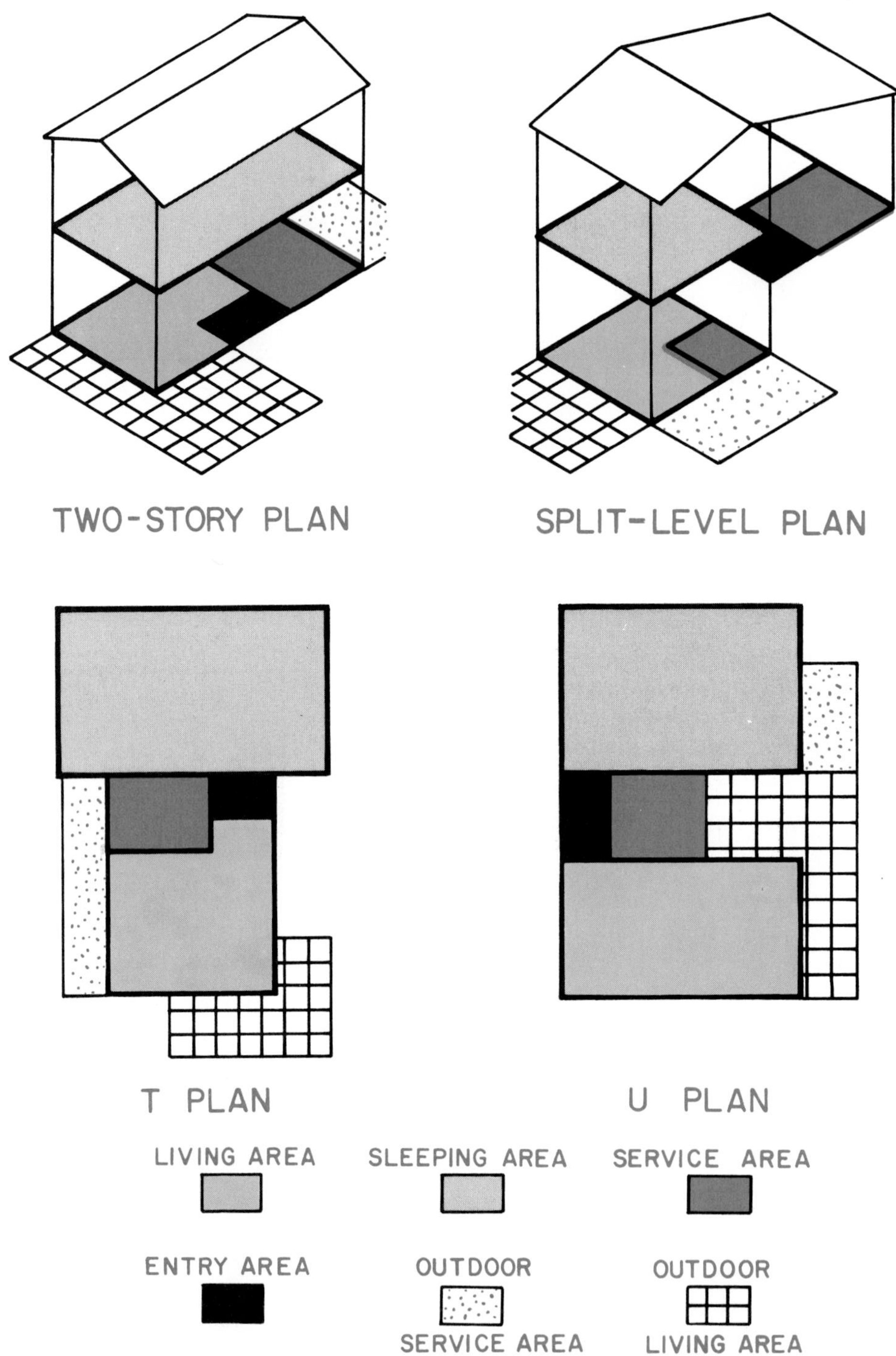

Fig. 32–11. Many different plans are possible within the same amount of space.

of doors, windows, and partitions. It should also include the location of shrubbery, trees, patios, walks, driveways, courts, pools, and gardens. Figure 32–11 shows the many plan variations possible by combining basic geometric shapes on different levels. Notice how the areas are arranged to achieve the most convenient plan.

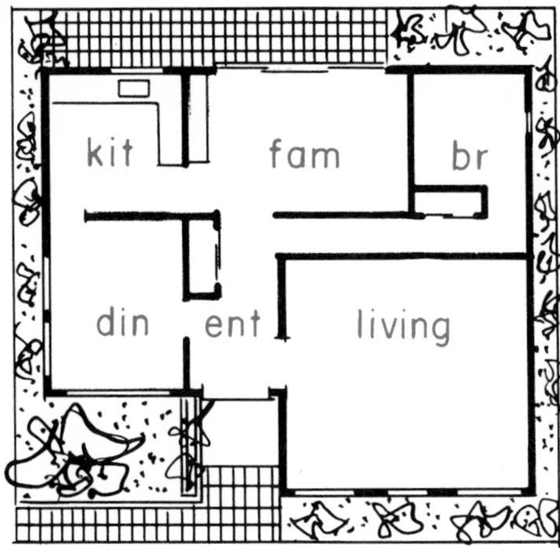

Fig. 32–12. A closed plan.

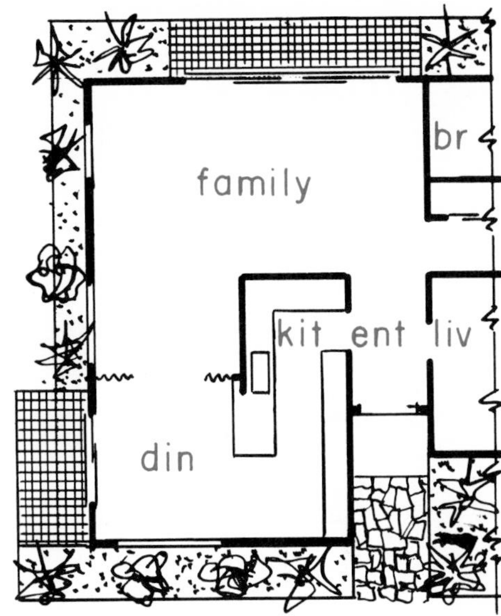

Fig. 32–13. An open plan.

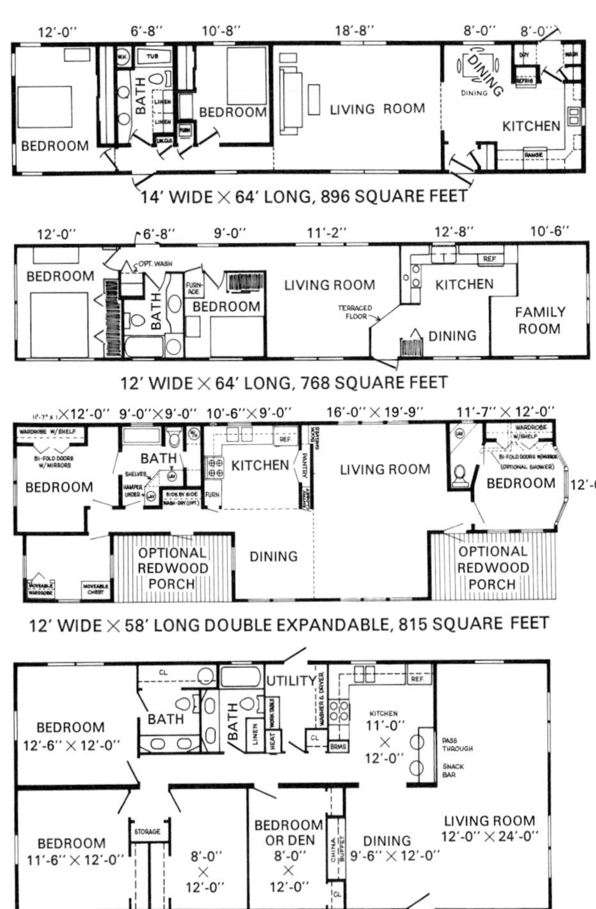

Fig. 32–14. A mobile-home design must fit within the limits of the overall size.

OPEN PLANNING

When the rooms of a plan are divided by solid partitions, doors, or arches, the plan is known as a *closed plan*. A closed plan is shown in Fig. 32–12. If the partitions between the rooms of an area are eliminated, such as in Fig. 32–13, then the plan is known as an *open plan*.

The open plan is used mostly and to best advantage in the living area. Here the walls that separate the entrance foyer, living room, dining room, activities room, and recreation room can be removed or partially eliminated. These open areas are created to provide a sense of spaciousness, to aid lighting efficiency, and to increase the circulation of air through the areas.

Obviously not all the areas of a residence lend themselves well to open-planning techniques. For example, a closed plan is almost always used in the sleeping area.

The floor plan for an open plan is developed in the same manner as for a closed plan. However, in the open plan the partitions are often replaced by dividers or by variations in level to set apart the various functions.

When designing floor plans for modular units such as apartments or mobile homes (Fig. 32–14), the designer must develop a plan within predetermined dimensional limits.

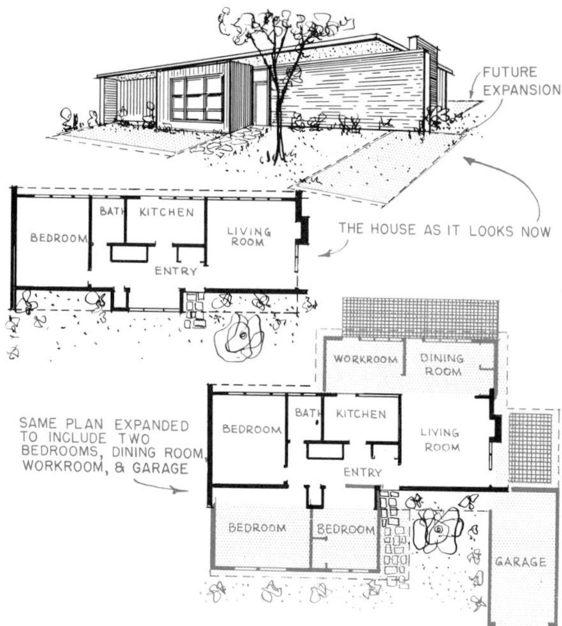

Fig. 32–15. An expandable plan.

EXPANDABLE PLANS

Because of limitations of time or money, it is sometimes desirable to construct a house over a long period of time. When the complete construction is delayed, the house should be built in several steps. The basic part of the house can be constructed first. Then additional rooms (usually bedrooms) can be added in future years as the need develops.

When future expansion of the plan is anticipated, the complete floor plan should be drawn before the initial construction begins, even though the entire plan may not be complete at that time. If only part of the building is planned and built, and a later addition is made, the addition will invariably look tacked on. This appearance can be avoided by designing the floor plan for expansion, as shown in Fig. 32–15.

PROBLEMS

1. **Prepare room templates and use them to make a functional arrangement for the living area, service area, and sleeping area of a house.**
2. **Arrange templates for a sleeping area, service area, and living area in a total composite plan.**

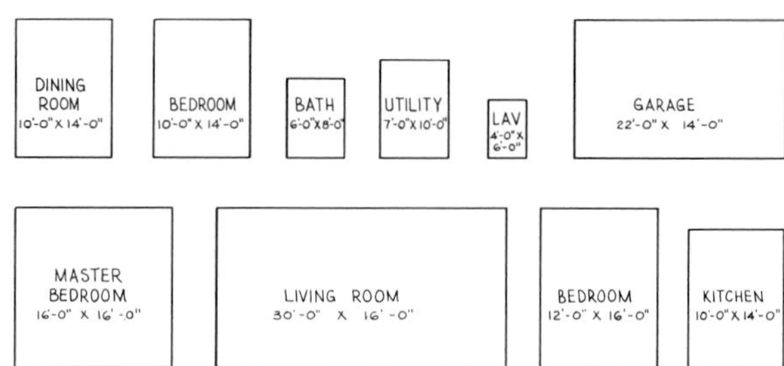

Fig. 32–16. Arrange these templates into a suitable floor plan.

Fig. 32–17. Convert this closed plan to an open plan.

3. **Make a floor-plan sketch of the arrangement you completed in Problem 2. Have your instructor criticize this sketch, and then you revise it according to the recommendations.**
4. **After you have completed a preliminary line sketch, prepare a final sketch complete with wall thicknesses, overall dimensions, driveways, walks, and shrubbery. Use Fig. 32–10 as a guide.**

5. Arrange the templates found in Fig. 32–16 in a floor-plan arrangement. Make a sketch of this arrangement, and revise the sketch until you arrive at a suitable plan.
6. Make room templates of each room in your own home. Rearrange these templates according to a remodeling plan, and make a sketch.
7. Convert the floor plan shown in Fig. 32–17 to an open plan. Sketch your solution.
8. Define the following terms: *room template, floor-plan sketching, sketch, template layout, final sketching, open planning, closed plan, expandable plan.*

UNIT 33

Complete Floor Plan

A floor plan is a drawing of the outline and partitions of a building as you would see them if the building were cut (sectioned) horizontally about 4′ (1.2 m) above the floor line, as shown in Fig. 33–1. There are many types of floor plans, ranging from very simple sketches to completely dimensioned and detailed floor-plan working drawings. (See the special floor-plan symbols which are shown in these sections: 7, elevation symbols; 9, location-plan symbols; 13, electrical symbols; 14, air-conditioning symbols; and 15, plumbing symbols.)

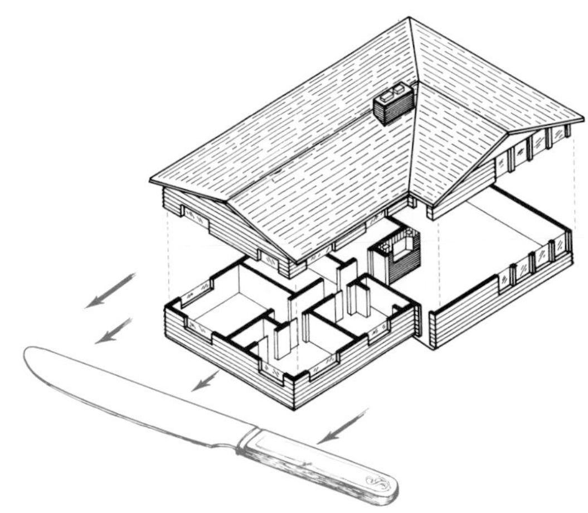

Fig. 33–1. A floor plan is a section view cut through the building 4 feet (1.2 m) above the floor line.

TYPES OF FLOOR PLANS

Some of the various types of floor plans commonly prepared for interpretation by the layman are the single-line drawing (Fig. 33–2), the abbreviated plan (Fig. 33–3), and the pictorial floor plan (Fig. 33–4). Bird's-eye views such as the one shown in Fig. 33–5 are often prepared to convey a sense of depth to the viewer. Pictorial plans such as that shown in

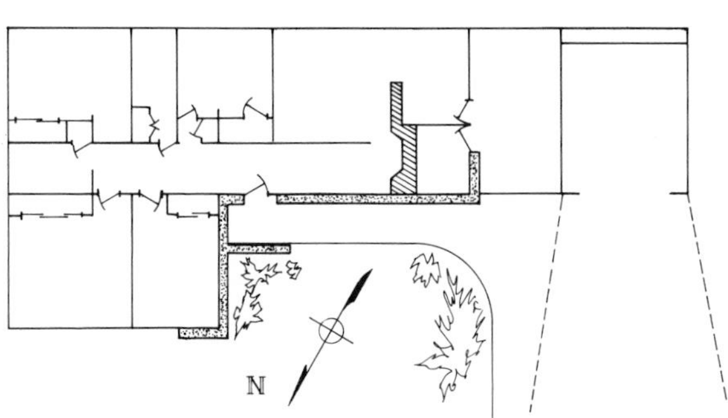

Fig. 33–2. A single-line floor plan.

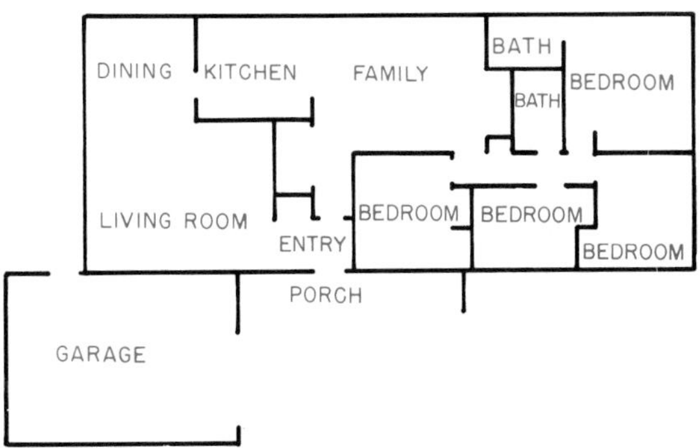

Fig. 33–3. An abbreviated floor plan.

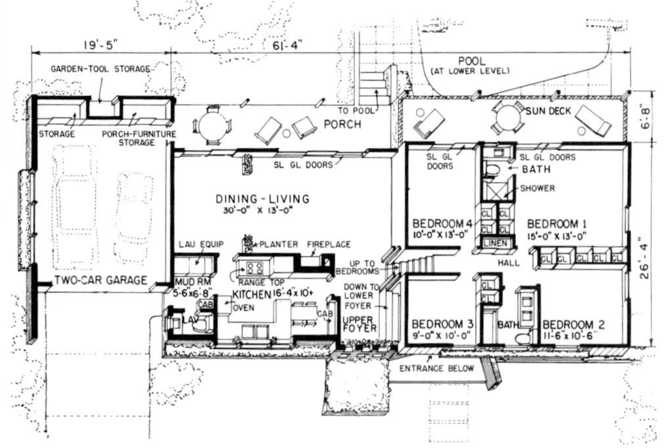

Master Plan Service, Inc.

Fig. 33–4. A pictorial floor plan.

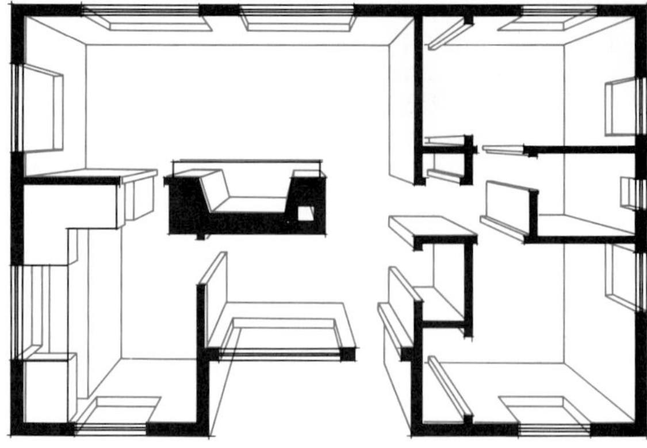

Fig. 33–5. A bird's-eye-view floor plan.

Fig. 33–6 are often prepared to show the relationship among various areas of the lot.

These plans are satisfactory for general use. However, a completely dimensioned floor plan is necessary to show the amount of detail necessary for construction purposes.

Floor-plan sketches such as those shown in Figs. 33–2 through 33–6 are sufficient for rough layout and preliminary design purposes but are not accurate or complete enough to be used as working drawings. An accurate floor plan, complete with dimensions and material symbols, must be prepared. When a plan of this type is developed, the contractor can interpret the desires of the designer without consultation. The prime function of a working-drawing floor plan is to communicate information to the contractor. A complete floor plan eliminates many misunderstandings between the designer and the builder. The builder's judgment must be used to fill in the omitted details if an incomplete floor plan is prepared. The function of the designer is transferred to the builder when this happens.

FLOOR-PLAN SYMBOLS

Architects substitute symbols for materials and fixtures, just as stenographers substitute shorthand for words. It is obviously more convenient and timesaving to draw a symbol of a material than to repeat a description every time that material is used. It would be impossible to describe all construction materials used on

Fig. 33–6. A flat pictorial floor plan.

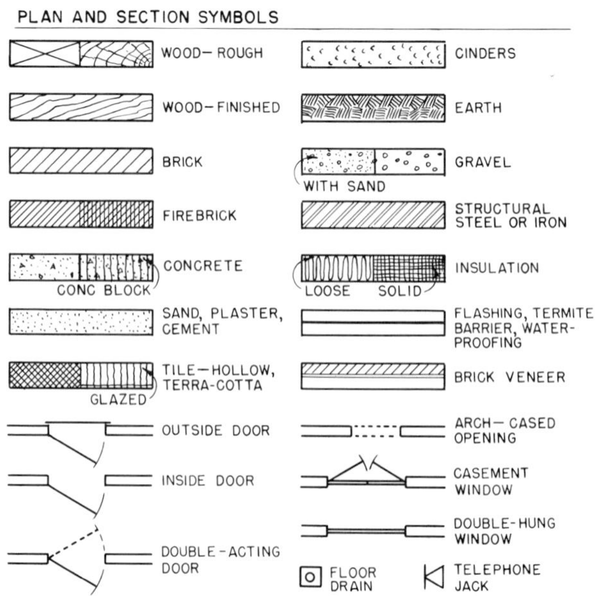

Fig. 33–7. Common floor-plan symbols.

floor plans, such as fixtures, doors, windows, stairs, and partitions, without the use of symbols. Figures 33–7 through 33–14 show common floor-plan symbols. Figure 33–15 shows the application of some of these symbols to a floor plan.

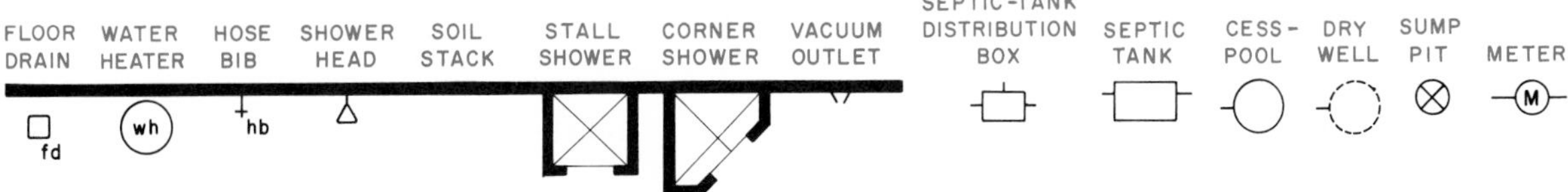

Fig. 33–8. Sanitation-facilities symbols.

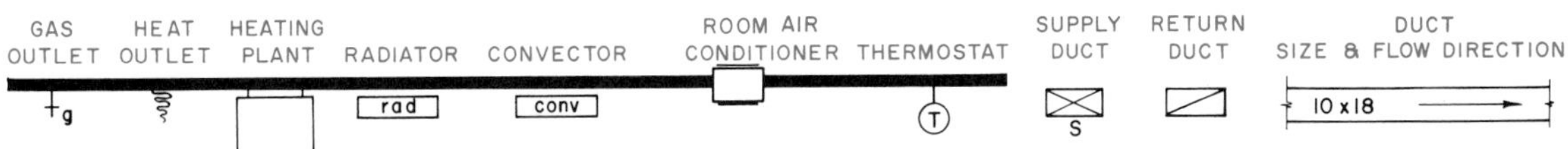

Fig. 33–9. Heating and air-conditioning floor-plan symbols.

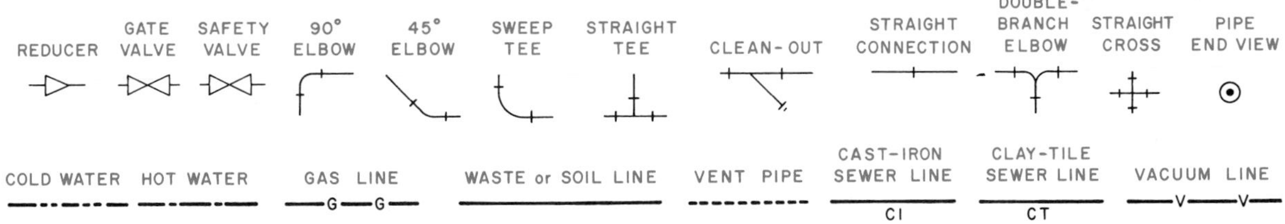

Fig. 33–10. Plumbing floor-plan symbols.

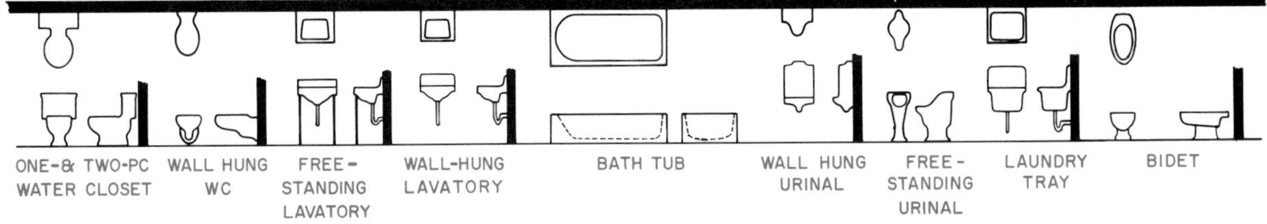

Fig. 33–11. Lavatory-fixture symbols.

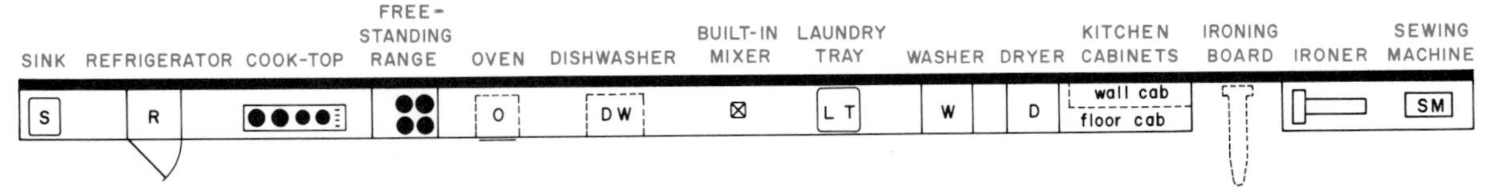

Fig. 33–12. Kitchen and laundry symbols.

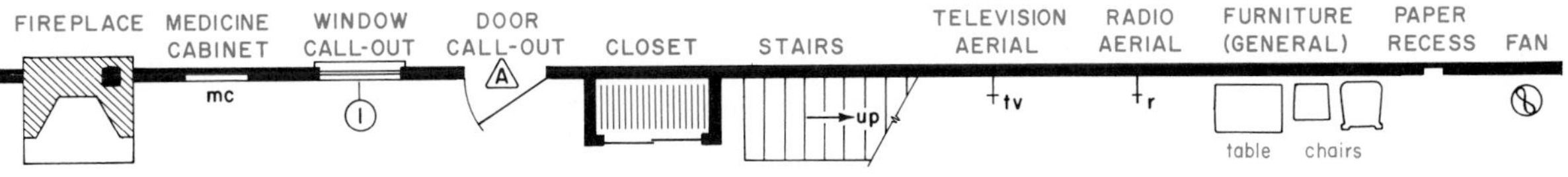

Fig. 33–13. Built-in-components symbols.

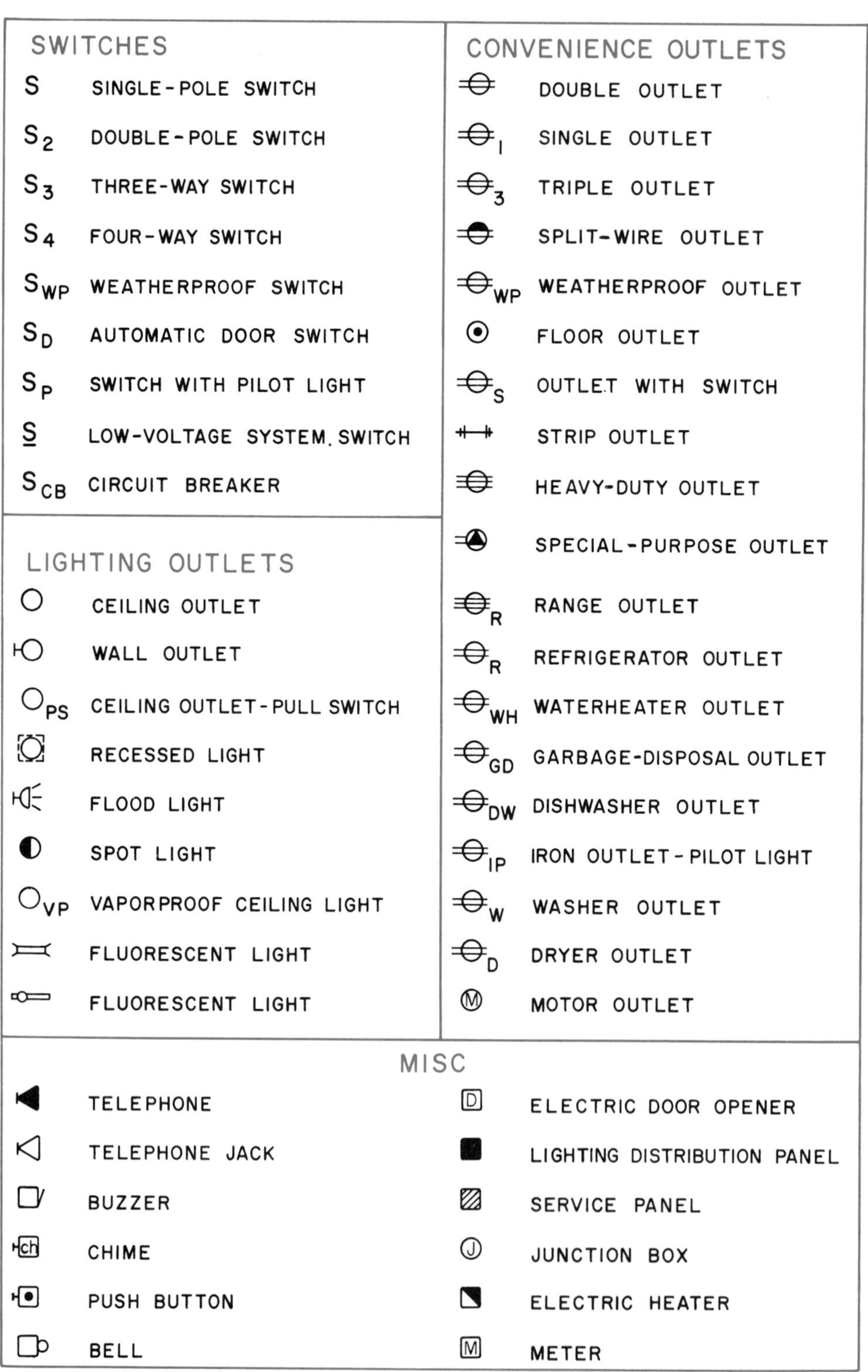

SWITCHES
S SINGLE-POLE SWITCH
S2 DOUBLE-POLE SWITCH
S3 THREE-WAY SWITCH
S4 FOUR-WAY SWITCH
SWP WEATHERPROOF SWITCH
SD AUTOMATIC DOOR SWITCH
SP SWITCH WITH PILOT LIGHT
S LOW-VOLTAGE SYSTEM. SWITCH
SCB CIRCUIT BREAKER
LIGHTING OUTLETS
CEILING OUTLET
WALL OUTLET
PS CEILING OUTLET-PULL SWITCH
RECESSED LIGHT
FLOOD LIGHT
SPOT LIGHT
VP VAPORPROOF CEILING LIGHT
FLUORESCENT LIGHT
FLUORESCENT LIGHT
CONVENIENCE OUTLETS
DOUBLE OUTLET
1 SINGLE OUTLET
3 TRIPLE OUTLET
SPLIT-WIRE OUTLET
WP WEATHERPROOF OUTLET
FLOOR OUTLET
S OUTLET WITH SWITCH
STRIP OUTLET
HEAVY-DUTY OUTLET
SPECIAL-PURPOSE OUTLET
R RANGE OUTLET
R REFRIGERATOR OUTLET
WH WATERHEATER OUTLET
GD GARBAGE-DISPOSAL OUTLET
DW DISHWASHER OUTLET
IP IRON OUTLET-PILOT LIGHT
W WASHER OUTLET
D DRYER OUTLET
M MOTOR OUTLET
MISC
TELEPHONE
TELEPHONE JACK
BUZZER
ch CHIME
PUSH BUTTON
BELL
D ELECTRIC DOOR OPENER
LIGHTING DISTRIBUTION PANEL
SERVICE PANEL
J JUNCTION BOX
ELECTRIC HEATER
M METER

Fig. 33–14. Electrical symbols for floor plans.

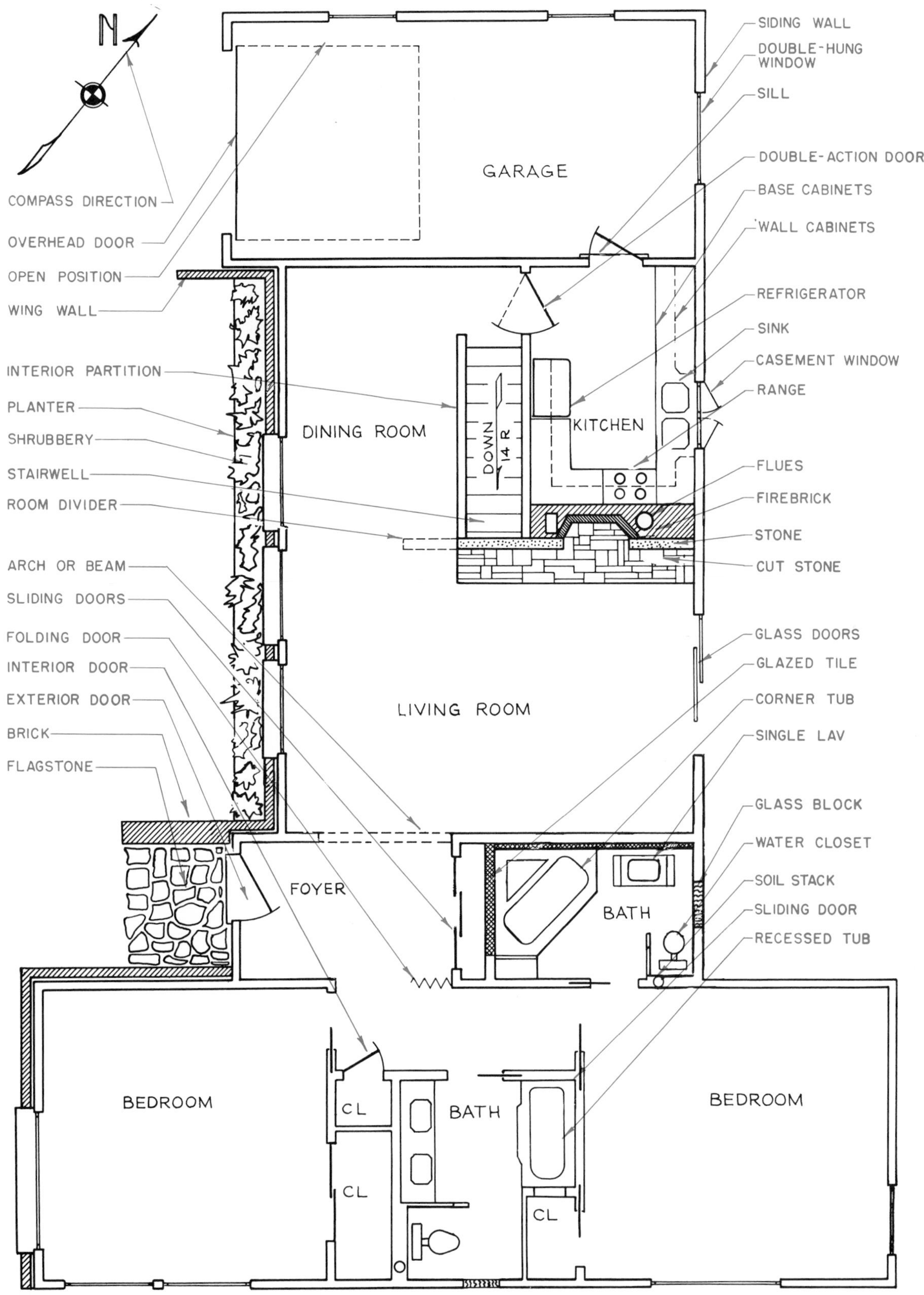

Fig. 33–15. The application of floor-plan symbols.

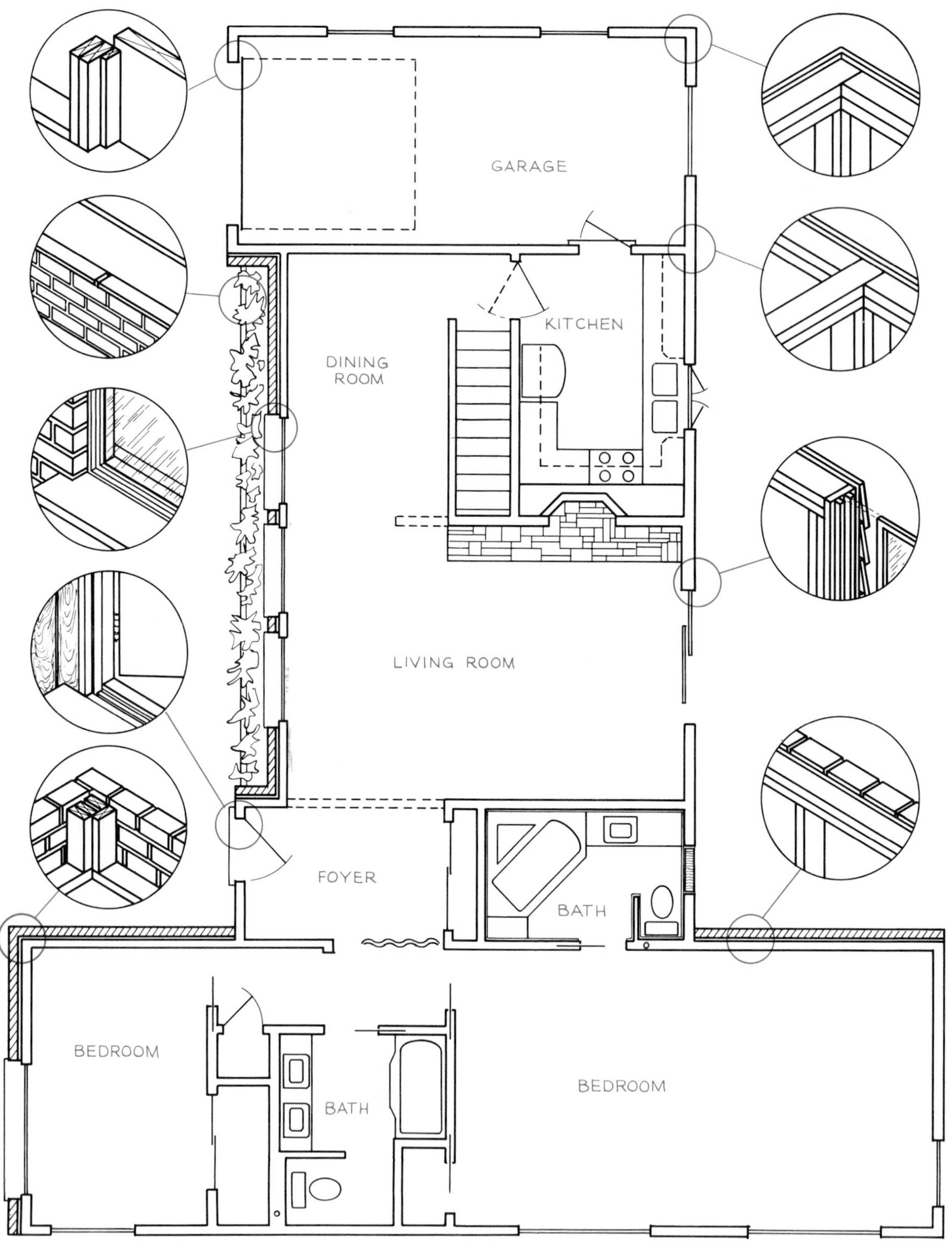

Fig. 33–16. Methods of showing construction details on a floor plan.

Although architectural symbols are standardized, some variations of symbols are used in different parts of the country. Figures 33–16

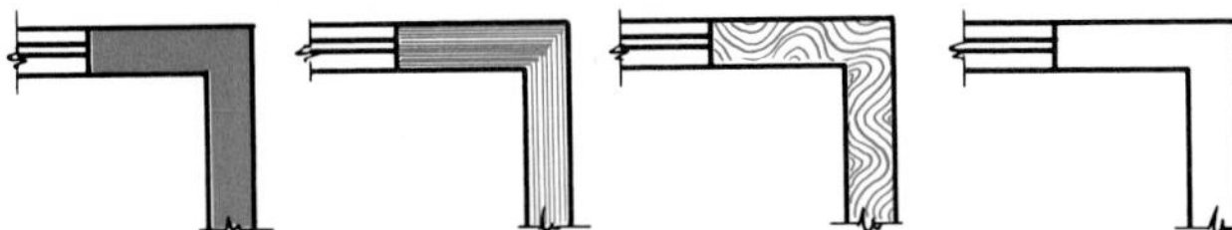

Fig. 33–17. Methods of showing wall construction on a floor plan.

and 33–17 show several methods architects use for drawing construction details and the outside walls of frame buildings.

Learning and remembering floor-plan symbols will be easier if you associate each symbol with the actual material or facility it represents. For example, as you learn the telephone-jack symbol, you should associate this symbol with the actual appearance of the telephone jack, as shown in Fig. 33–18.

Floor-plan symbols often represent the exact appearance of the floor-plan section as viewed from above, but sometimes this representation is not possible. Many floor-plan symbols are too intricate to be drawn to the scale 1/4″ = 1′—0″ or 1/8″ = 1′—0″. Therefore, many details are eliminated on the floor-plan symbols. Figure 33–19 shows the construction method and the symbol used to depict the various materials on the floor plan. Figure 33–19 also shows details of walls for which only the outlines are shown on the accompanying floor plan.

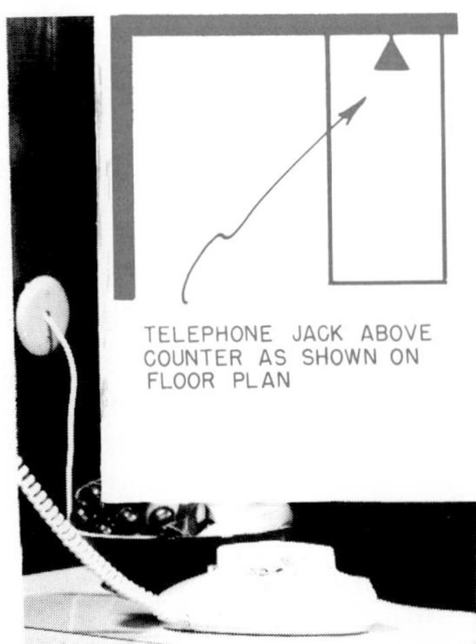

Western Electric Company

Fig. 33–18. A solid triangle is used to denote a telephone jack.

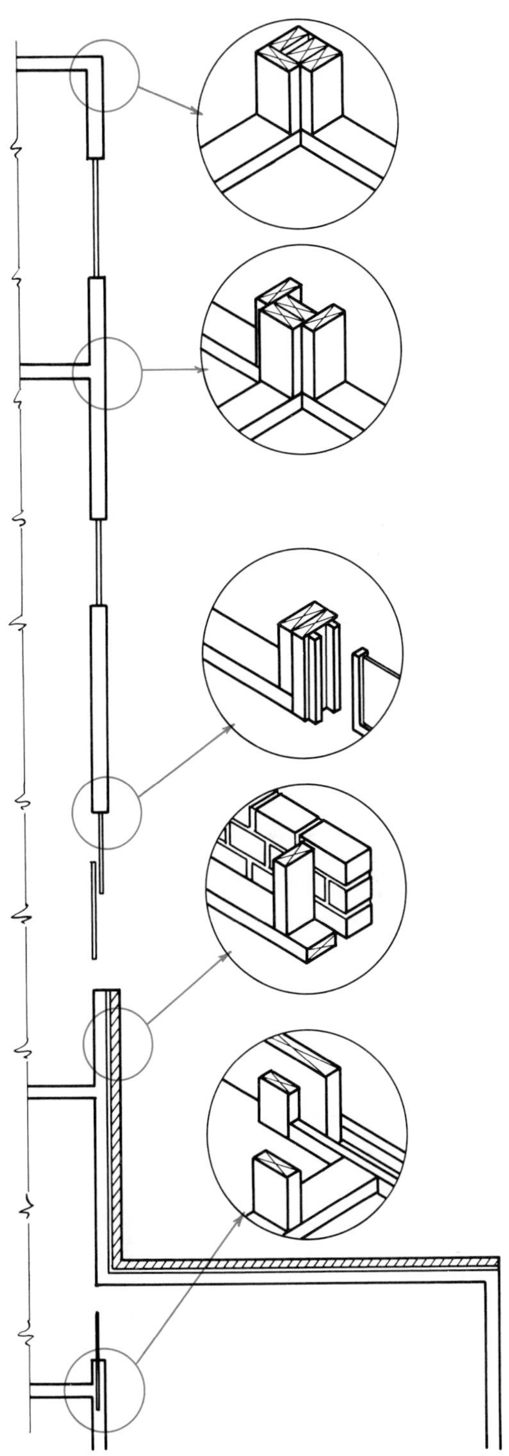

Fig. 33–19. Construction details that are represented by floor-plan symbols.

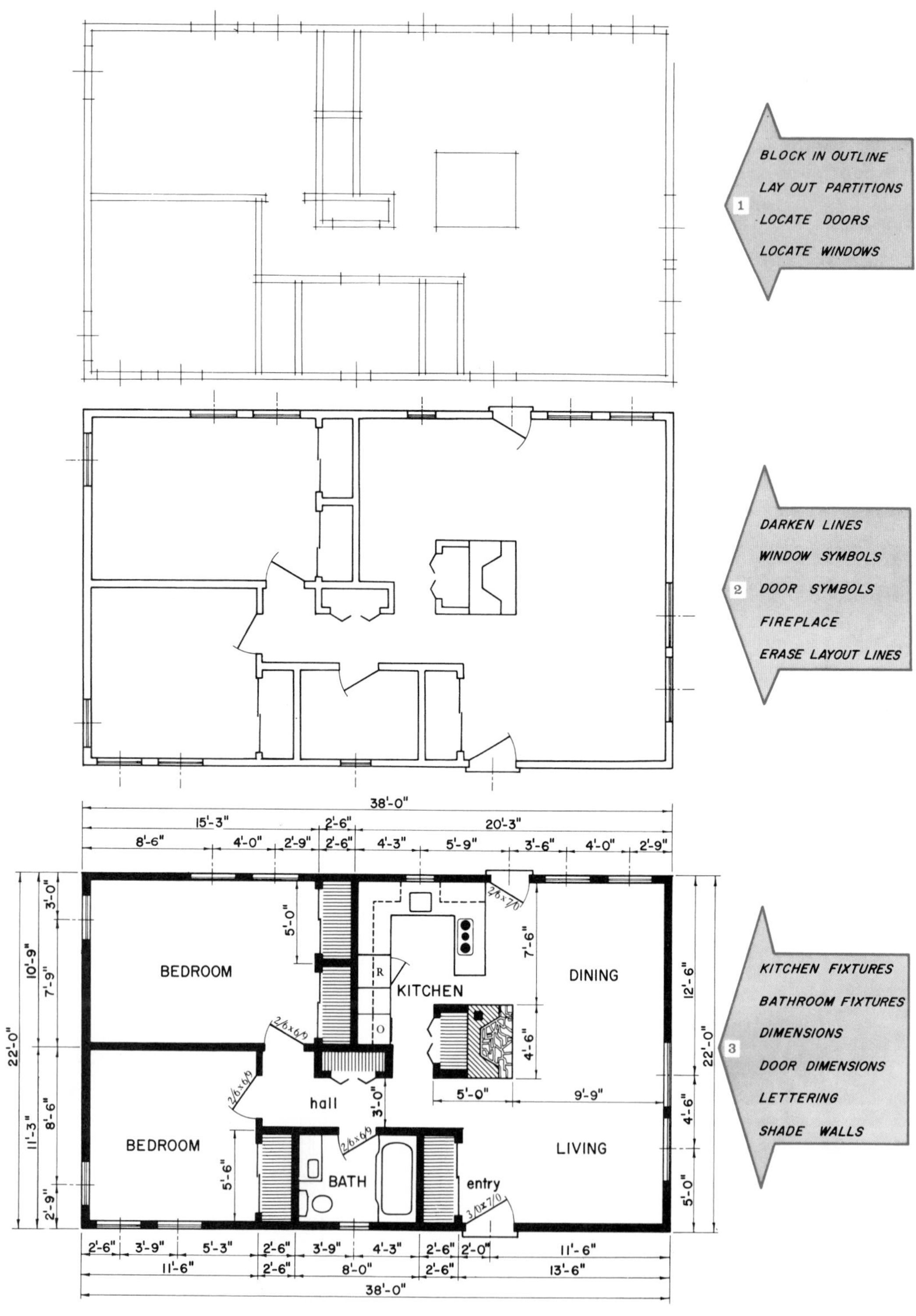

Fig. 33–20. The sequence of drawing floor plans.

STEPS IN DRAWING FLOOR PLANS

For maximum speed, accuracy, and clarity, the following steps, as illustrated in Fig. 33–20, should be observed in laying out and drawing floor plans:

1. Block in the overall dimensions of the house and add the thickness of the outside walls with a very hard pencil (6H).
2. Lay out the position of interior partitions with a 6H pencil.
3. Locate the position of doors and windows by center line and by their widths.
4. Darken the object lines with a 2H pencil.
5. Add door and window symbols with a 2H pencil.
6. Add symbols for stairwells.
7. Erase extraneous layout lines if they are too heavy. If they are extremely light, they can remain.
8. Draw the outlines of kitchen and bathroom fixtures.
9. Add the symbols and sections for any masonry work, such as fireplaces and planters.
10. Dimension the drawing (see Unit 34).

SECOND-FLOOR PLAN

Bilevel, two-story, one-and-one-half-story, and split-level homes require a separate floor plan for each additional level. This floor plan is prepared on tracing paper placed directly over the first-floor plan to ensure alignment of walls and bearing partitions. When the major outline has been traced, the first-floor plan is removed. Figure 33–21 shows the method of projecting a second-floor plan from the first-floor plan. Alignment of features such as stairwell openings, outside walls, plumbing walls, and chimneys is critical in preparing the second-floor plan. Figure 33–22 shows a typical second-floor plan of a one-and-one-half-story house with the roof line broken. This drawing, in addition to revealing the second-floor plan, shows the outline of the roof. In this plan, dotted lines are used to show the outline of the building under the roof.

Figure 33–23 shows a second-floor plan of a two-story house. In this plan there is no break

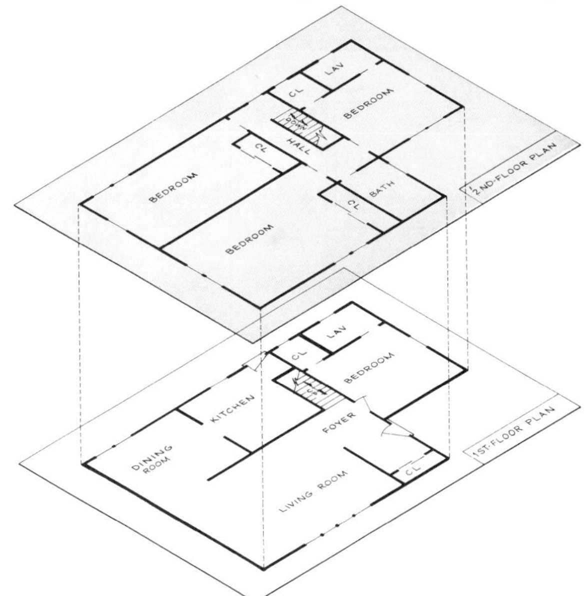

Fig. 33–21. Projection of the second-floor plan.

since the first-floor plan is the same size as the second-floor plan. This plan is usually prepared by tracing over the first-floor outline.

ALTERNATIVE PLANS

A technique frequently used to alter or adapt the appearance of the house and the location of various rooms is the practice of reversing a floor plan. Figure 33–24 shows a floor plan with its reversed counterpart. This reversal is accomplished by turning the floor plan upside down and tracing the mirror image of the floor plan to provide either a right-hand or a left-hand plan.

PROBLEMS

1. **Draw a complete floor plan, using a sketch of your own design as a guide, and using the scale 1/4″ = 1′—0″.**
2. **Draw a complete floor plan from the sketch shown in Fig. 33–25, using the scale 1/4″ = 1′—0″.**
3. **Measure the rooms in your home. Draw a complete floor plan of your home, using the scale 1/4″ = 1′—0″ or 1/8″ = 1′—0″.**
4. **After making a floor-plan sketch of your home, revise this sketch to show how you would propose to remodel your home. Then make a complete floor-plan drawing of the remodeled design, using the scale 1/4″ = 1′—0″ or 1/8″ = 1′—0″.**

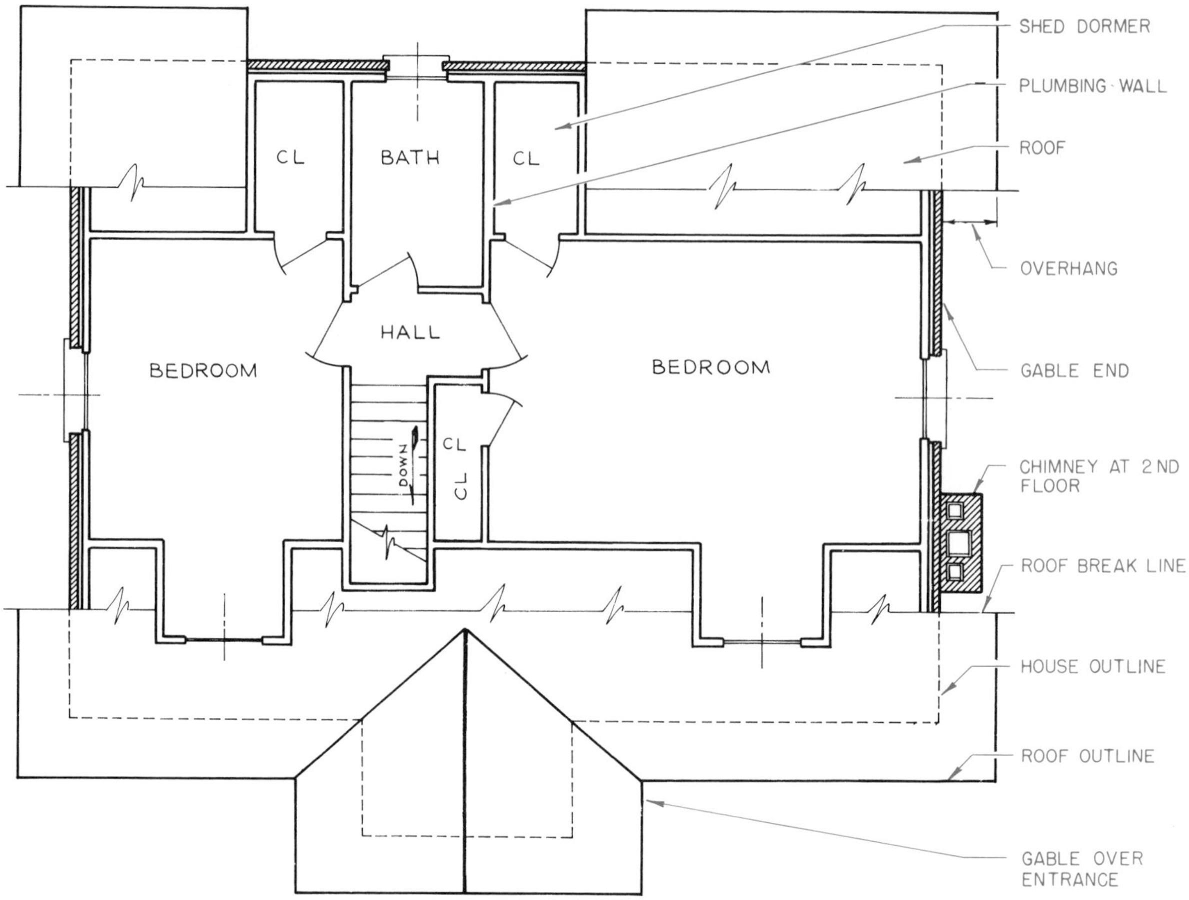

SHED DORMER
PLUMBING WALL
ROOF
OVERHANG
GABLE END
CHIMNEY AT 2ND FLOOR
ROOF BREAK LINE
HOUSE OUTLINE
ROOF OUTLINE
GABLE OVER ENTRANCE
CL
BATH
CL
HALL
BEDROOM
BEDROOM
DOWN
CL
CL

Fig. 33–22. A one-and-one-half-story second-floor plan.

BED RM.
16⁰x 13⁴
BATH
S
BED RM.
15⁰x 13⁴
CL.
CL.
SHELVES
CL.
CL.
STOR.
DN
LIN
CFDAR CL
CL.
CL.
BATH
CL.
CL.
BED RM.
10⁸x 13⁴
BED RM.
11⁶x 13⁴

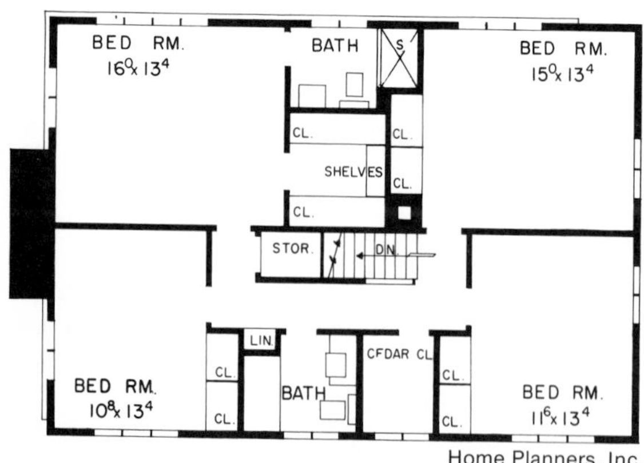

Home Planners, Inc.

Fig. 33–23. A full second-floor plan.

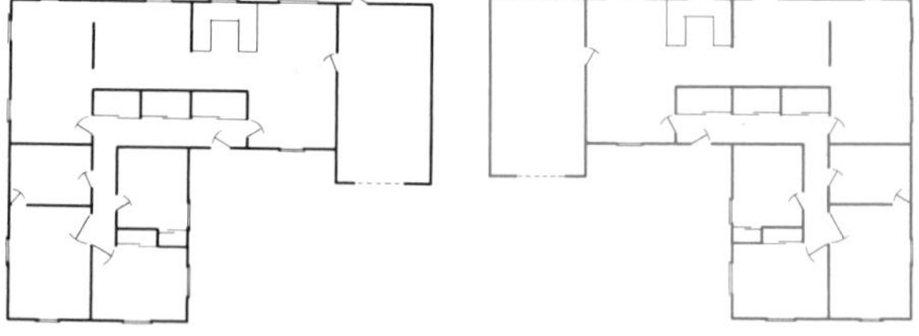

Fig. 33–24. A reversed plan.

5. **Draw the second-floor plan of your own home, using the scale 1/4″ = 1′—0″.**
6. **Identify the symbols shown in Fig. 33–26.**
7. **Draw a complete floor plan, using the sketch shown in Fig. 33–27 as a guide. Make any alterations necessary to adapt the cabin to your own needs, as a hunting cabin or seaside lodge, for example.**
8. **Draw a complete floor plan, using the sketch shown in Fig. 33–28 as a guide.**
9. **Draw a complete floor plan from the abbreviated plan shown in Fig. 33–29.**
10. **Identify the symbols shown in Fig. 33–30.**
11. **Define these terms: *floor plan, single-line floor plan, pictorial floor plan, bird's-eye view, floor-plan symbols, second-floor plan, alternative plan, plumbing wall, right-hand plan, left-hand plan.***

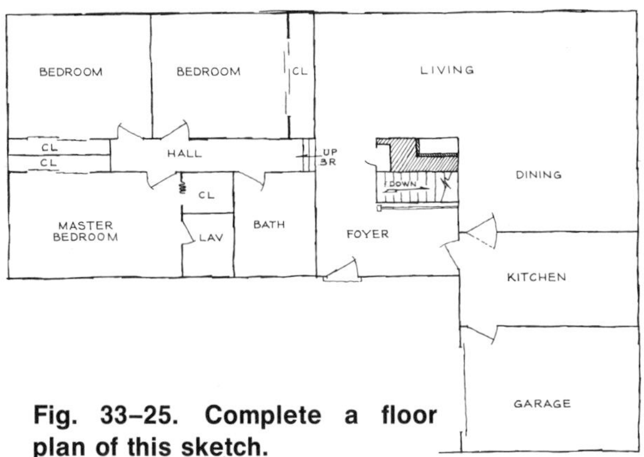

Fig. 33–25. Complete a floor plan of this sketch.

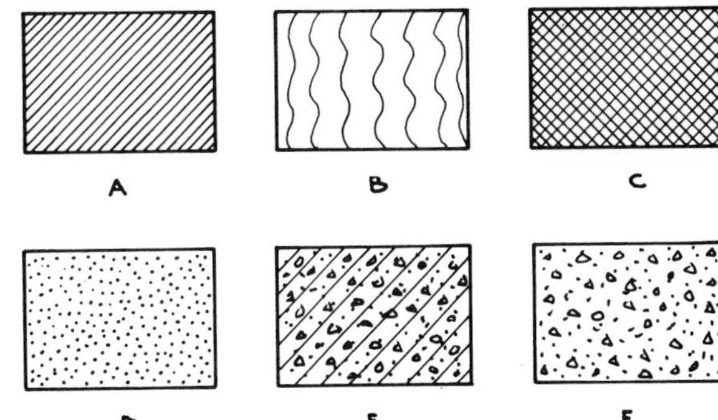

Fig. 33–26. Identify these symbols.

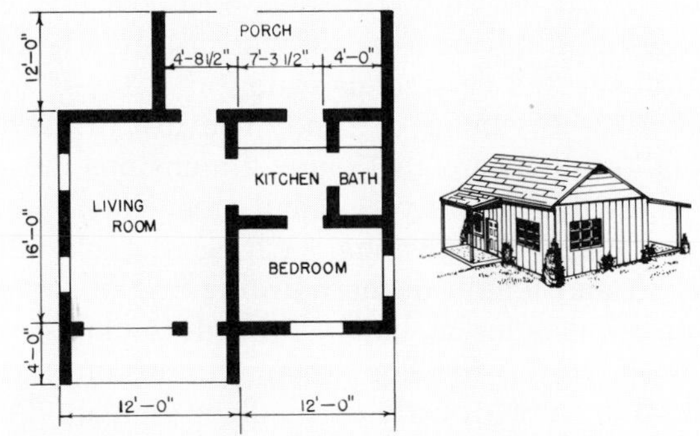

Fig. 33–27. Draw a complete floor plan of this cabin.

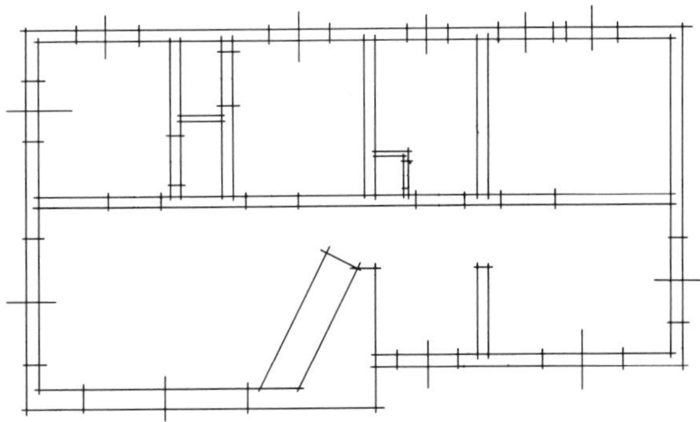

Fig. 33–28. Draw a complete floor plan using this layout as a guide.

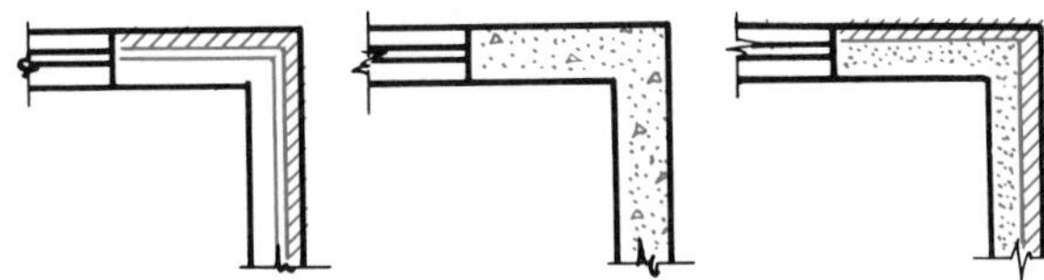

Fig. 33–30. Identify these symbols.

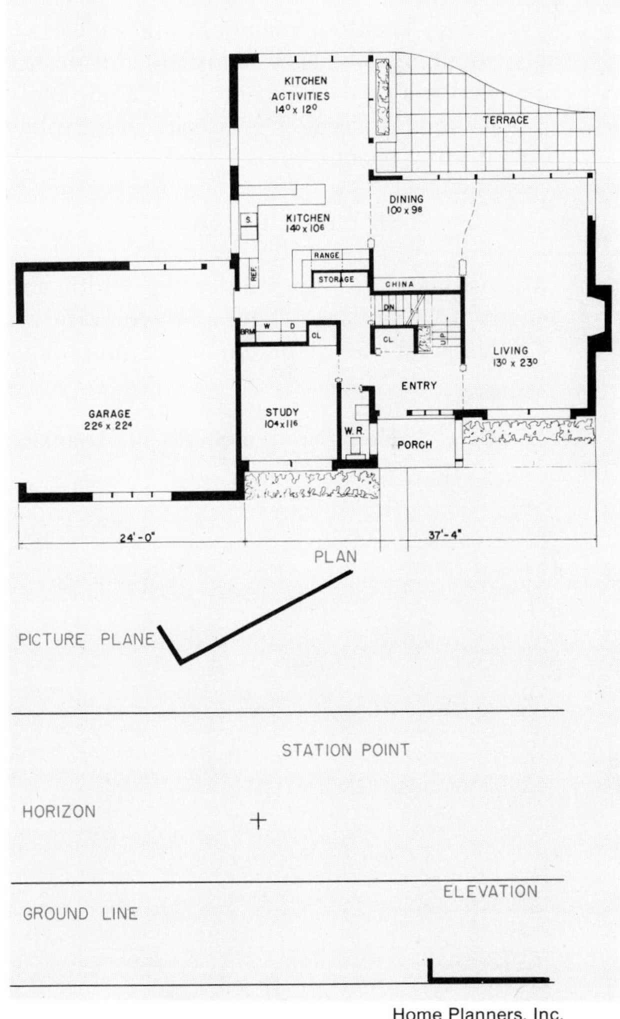

Home Planners, Inc.

Fig. 33–29. Draw a complete floor plan of this abbreviated plan.

UNIT 34

Floor-Plan Dimensioning

In colonial times, simple cabins could be built without architectural plans and without established dimensions. The outline of the house and the position of each room could be determined experimentally by pacing off approximate distances. The owner could then erect the dwelling, using existing materials and adjusting sizes and dimensions as necessary. The owner acted in the capacities of architect, designer, contractor, carpenter, and materials manufacturer.

Today, building materials are so varied, construction methods so complex, and design requirements so demanding that a completely dimensioned drawing is necessary to complete any building exactly as designed.

SIZE DESCRIPTION

Dimensions show the builder the width and length of the building. They show the location of doors, windows, stairs, fireplaces, and planters. Just as symbols and notes show exactly what materials are to be used in the building, dimensions show the sizes of materials and exactly where they are to be located.

Dimensioning architectural drawings differ from dimensioning mechanical drawings in many ways and for many reasons. Dimensioning practices often vary among designers. Several common methods of dimensioning floor plans are shown in Fig. 34–1. Because a large building must be drawn on a relatively small sheet, a very small scale (¼″ = 1′—0″ or ⅛″ = 1′—0″) must be used. The use of such small scale means that many dimensions must be crowded into a very small area. Therefore, only major dimensions such as the overall width and length of the building and of separate rooms, closets, halls, and wall thicknesses are shown on the floor plan. Dimensions too small to show directly on the floor plan are described either by a note on the floor plan or by separate, enlarged details. Enlarged details are

Fig. 34–1. Some different methods of dimensioning floor plans.

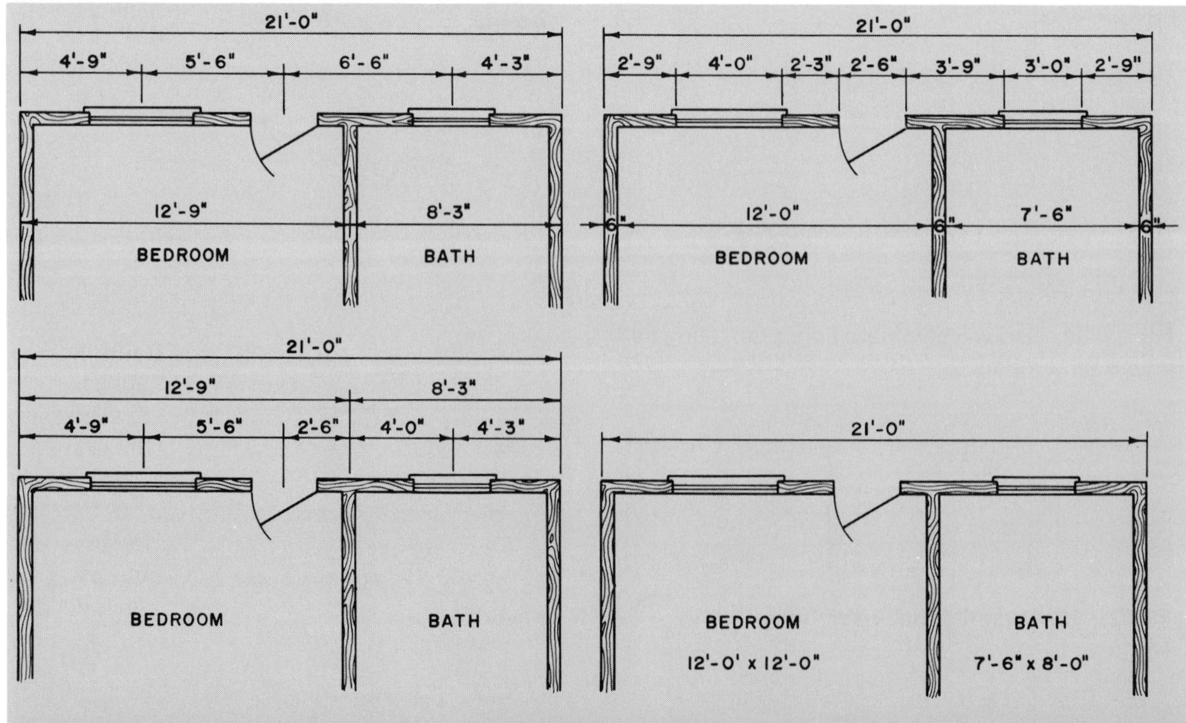

sometimes merely enlargements of some portion of the floor plan. They may also be an allied section indexed to the floor plan. Separate details are usually necessary to interpret adequately the dimensioning of fireplaces, planters, built-in cabinets, door and window details, stair-framing details, or any unusual construction methods.

Complete Dimensions

The number of dimensions included on a floor plan depends largely on how much freedom of interpretation the architect wants to give to the builder. If complete dimensions are shown on the plan, a builder cannot deviate greatly from the original design. However, if only a few dimensions are shown, then the builder must determine many of the sizes of areas, fixtures, and details. When you rely on a builder to provide dimensions, you place the builder in the position of a designer. A good builder is not expected to be a good designer. Supplying adequate dimensions will eliminate the need for guesswork.

Limited Dimensions

A floor plan with only limited dimensions is shown in Fig. 34–2. This type of dimensioning, which shows only the overall building dimensions and the width and length of each room, is sufficient to summarize the relative sizes of the building and its rooms for the prospective owner. These dimensions are not sufficient for building purposes.

A floor plan must be completely dimensioned (Fig. 34–3) to ensure that the house will be constructed precisely as designed. These dimensions convey the exact wishes of the architect and owner to the builder, and little tolerance is allowed the contractor in interpreting the size and position of the various features of this plan. The exact size of each room, closet, partition, door, or window is given.

RULES FOR DIMENSIONING

Many construction mistakes result from errors in architectural drawings. Most errors in architectural drawing result from mistakes in dimensioning. Dimensioning errors are therefore costly in time, efficiency, and money. Familiarization with the following rules for dimensioning floor plans will eliminate much confusion and error. These rules are illustrated by the numbered arrows in Fig. 34–3.

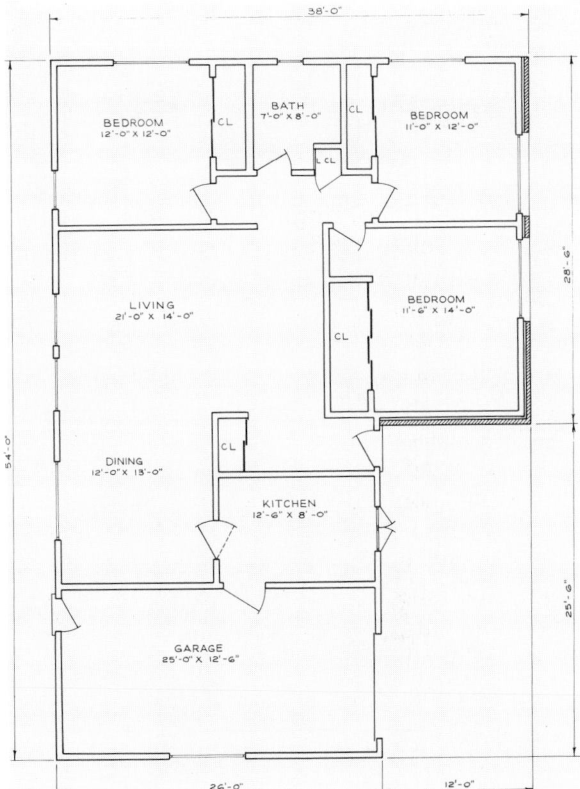

Fig. 34–2. A floor plan with a minimum of dimensioning.

1. Architectural dimension lines are unbroken lines with dimensions placed above the line. Arrowheads of several styles are optional (Fig. 34–4).
2. Foot and/or inch marks are used on all architectural dimensions.
3. Dimensions over 1′ are expressed in feet and inches.
4. Dimensions less than 1′ are shown in inches.
5. A slash is often used with fractional dimensions to conserve vertical space.
6. Dimensions should be placed to read from the right or from the bottom of the drawing.
7. Overall building dimensions are placed outside the other dimensions.
8. Line and arrowhead weights for architectural dimensioning are the same as those used in dimensioning mechanical drawings.

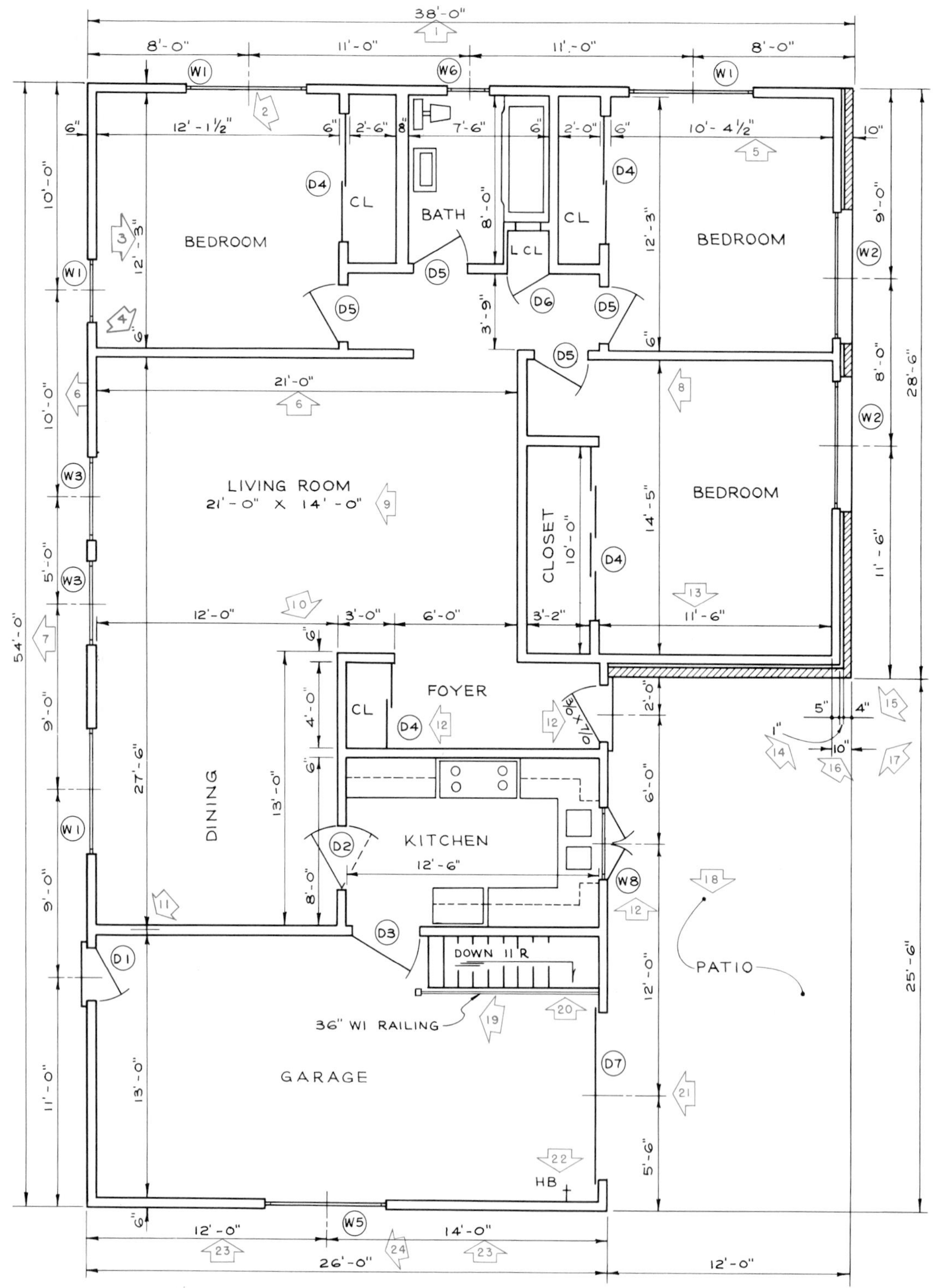

Fig. 34–3. Rules for dimensioning architectural floor plans.

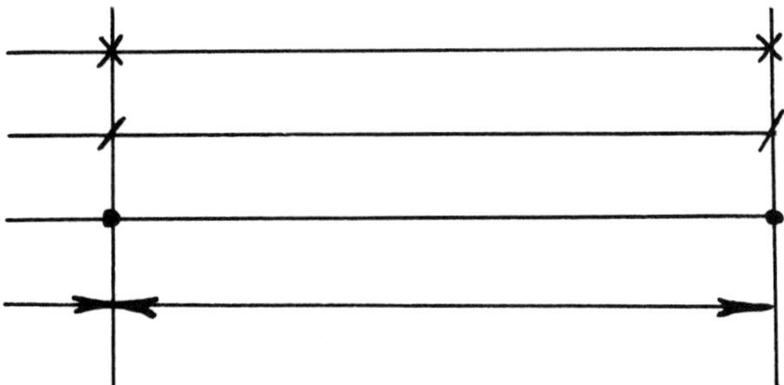

Fig. 34–4. Different styles of arrowheads used on dimension lines.

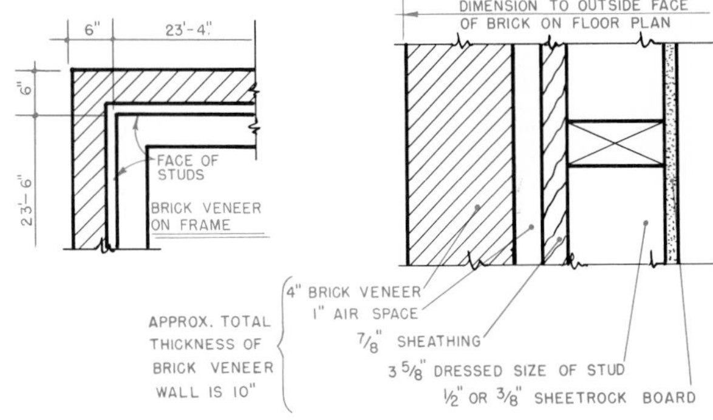

Fig. 34–5. Brick or stone dimensions must be added to the framing dimensions.

9. Room sizes may be shown by stating width and length.
10. When the area to be dimensioned is too small for the numerals, they are placed outside the extension lines.
11. Rooms are sometimes dimensioned from center lines of partitions; however, rule 13 is preferred.
12. Window and door sizes may be shown directly on the door or window symbol or may be indexed to a door or window schedule.
13. Rooms are dimensioned from wall to wall, exclusive of wall thickness.
14. Curved leaders are often used to eliminate confusion with other dimension lines.
15. When areas are too small for arrowheads, dots may be used to indicate dimension limits.
16. The dimensions of brick or stone veneer must be added to the framing dimension (Fig. 34–5).
17. When the space is small, arrowheads may be placed outside the extension lines.
18. A dot with a leader refers to the large area noted.
19. Dimensions that cannot be seen on the floor plan or those too small to place on the object are placed on leaders for easier reading.
20. In dimensioning stairs, the number of risers is placed on a line with an arrow indicating the direction (down or up).
21. Windows, doors, pilasters, beams, and areaways are dimensioned to their center lines.
22. Use abbreviations when symbols do not show clearly what is intended.
23. Subdimensions must add up to overall dimensions (14′—0″ + 12′—0″ = 26′—0″).
24. Architectural dimensions always refer to the actual size of the building regardless of the scale of the drawing. The building in Fig. 34–3 is 38′—0″ wide.
25. When framing dimensions are desirable, rooms are dimensioned by distances between studs in the partitions (Fig. 34–6).
26. Since building materials vary somewhat in size, first establish the thickness of each component of the wall and partition, such as furring thickness, panel thickness, plaster thickness, stud thickness, brick and tile thicknesses. Add these thicknesses together to establish the total wall thickness. Common thicknesses of wall and partition materials are shown in Fig. 34–7.

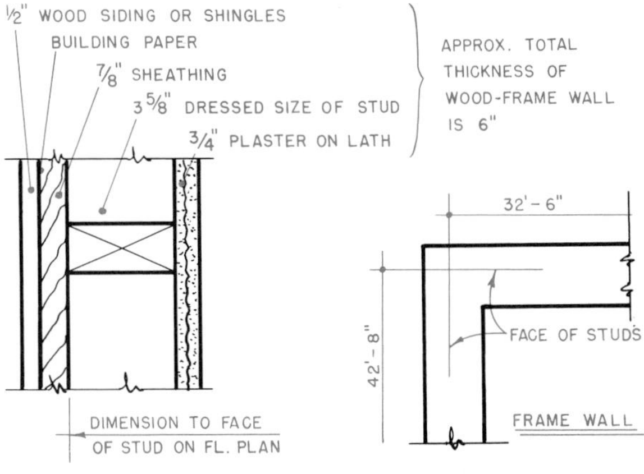

Fig. 34–6. When framing dimensions alone are desired, the dimensions should read to the face of the stud.

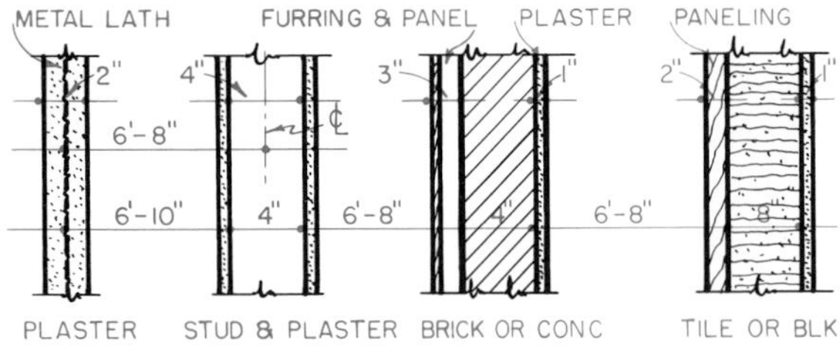

Fig. 34–7. Methods of dimensioning various wall and partition thicknesses.

All other rules of floor-plan dimensioning adhere to the American National Standard Drafting Manual.

MODULAR CONSTRUCTION

Buildings to be erected with modular components must be designed within modular limits. In dimensioning by the modular system, building dimensions are expressed in standard sizes. This procedure ensures the proper fitting of the various components. Planning rooms to accommodate standard materials also saves considerable labor, time, and material. The modular system of coordinated drawings is based on a standard grid placed on the width, length, and height of a building, as shown in Fig. 34–8.

In modular designing, an effort is made to establish all building dimensions (width, length, and height) to fall on some 4″ module, if the building material can be selected to conform to this module. As new building materials are developed, their sizes are established to conform to modular sizes. However, many building materials do not conform to the 4″ grid, and therefore the dimensioning procedure must be adjusted accordingly. Dimensions that align with the 4″ module are known as *grid dimensions*. Dimensions that do not align with the 4″ module are known as *non-grid dimensions*.

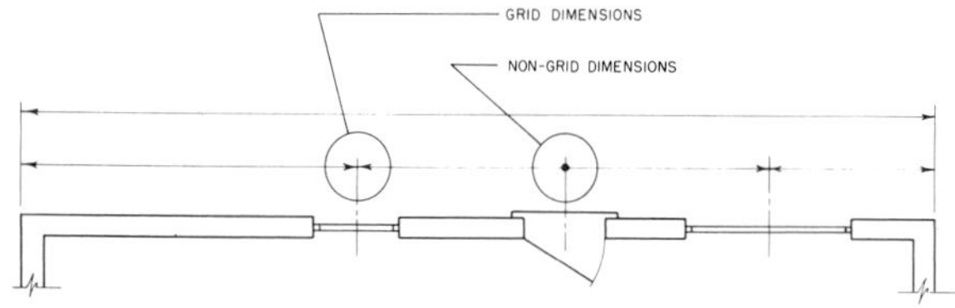

Fig. 34–9. Modular dimensioning methods.

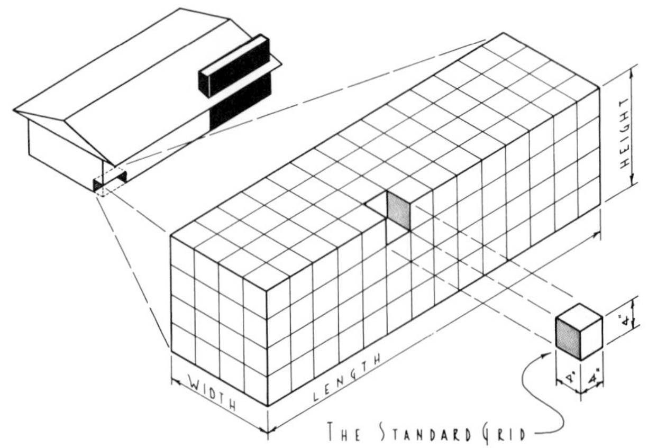

Fig. 34–8. A modular grid.

Figure 34–9 shows the two methods of indicating grid dimensions and non-grid dimensions. Grid dimensions are shown by conventional arrowheads, and non-grid dimensions are shown by dots instead of arrowheads on the dimension lines.

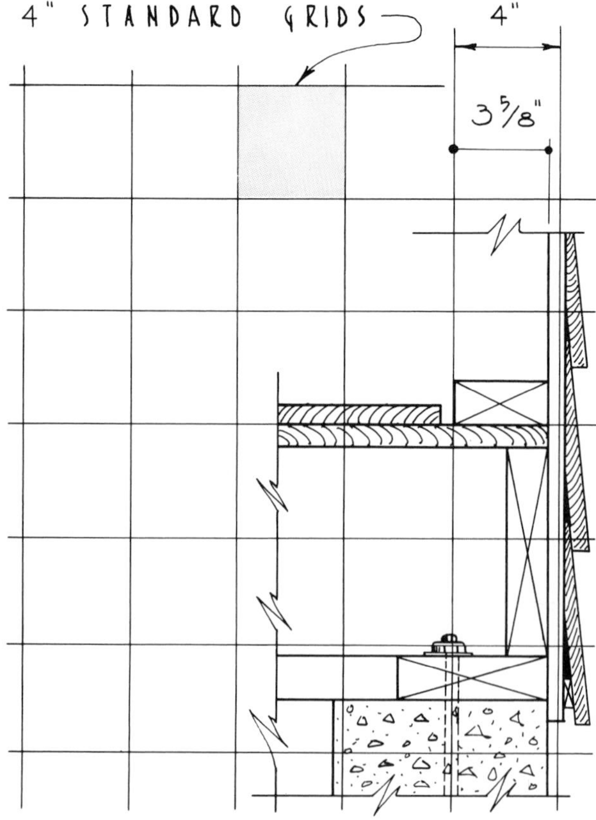

Fig. 34–10. Modular dimensions, as applied to detail drawings.

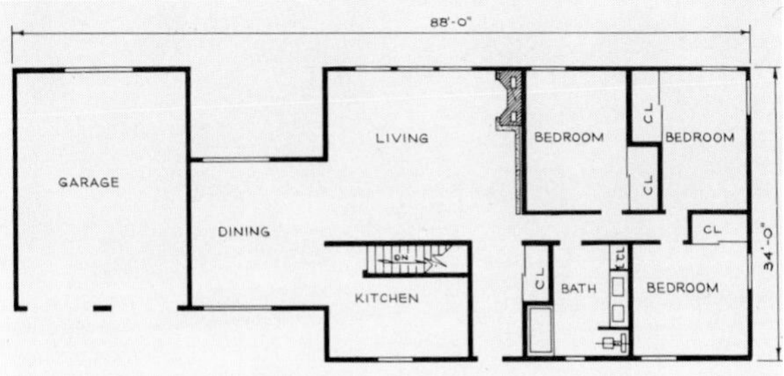

Fig. 34–11. Dimension this floor plan.

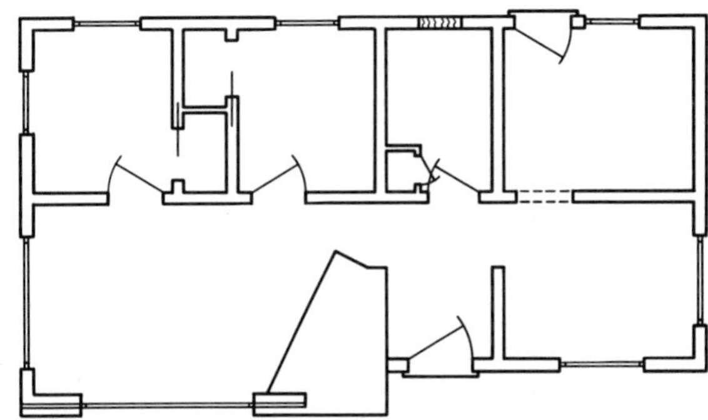

Fig. 34–13. Draw a floor plan of this house, complete with dimensions.

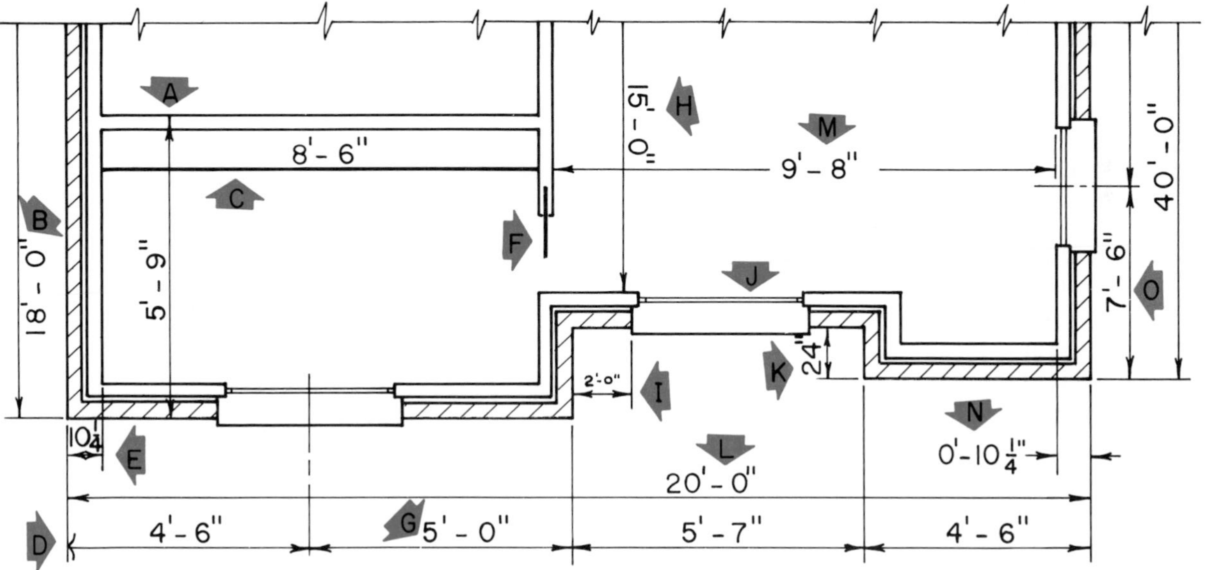

Fig. 34–12. Find the dimensioning errors shown by the letters.

In many detail drawings it is possible to eliminate the placement of some dimensions by placing the grid lines directly on the drawing, as shown in the detail given in Fig. 34–10. When the 4″ grid lines coincide exactly with the material lines, no dimensions are needed, since each line represents 4″ and any building material that is an increment of 4″ is reflected by placement on this grid. Other dimensions that do not coincide, such as the 3⅝″ stud dimension shown in Fig. 34–10, must be dimensioned by conventional methods.

PROBLEMS

1. **Dimension a floor plan that you have completed for a previous assignment.**
2. **Sketch or draw and dimension the floor plan shown in Fig. 34–11, using the scale ¼″ = 1′—0″.**
3. **Dimension the floor plan shown in Fig. 34–11 by the modular method.**
4. **Find the dimensioning errors in Fig. 34–12. List the dimensioning rule violated in each case. (Example: L violates rule 7.)**
5. **Draw and dimension the floor plan of your own home.**
6. **Sketch or draw the floor plan shown in Fig. 34–13 and completely dimension your plan.**
7. **Define the following terms: *dimension line, fractional dimensions, overall dimensions, center lines, extension lines, leader lines, subdimensions, framing dimensions, modular dimensioning, grid dimensions, non-grid dimensions.***

SECTION 7

Elevation Drawings

The main features of the interior of a building are shown on the floor plan. The main features of the outside of a building are shown on elevation drawings. *Elevation drawings* are orthographic drawings of the exterior of a building. They are prepared to show the design, materials, dimensions, and final appearance of the exterior of a building.

UNIT 35

Elevation Design

Designing the elevation of a structure is only one part of the total design process. However, this is the part of the building that most people see, and it is the part they use to judge the entire structure.

RELATIONSHIP WITH THE FLOOR PLAN

Since a structure is designed from the inside out, the design of the floor plan normally precedes the design of the elevation. The complete design process requires a continual relationship between the elevation and the floor plan through the entire process.

Much flexibility is possible in the design of elevations, even in those designed from the same floor plan. Figure 35–1 shows the development of two different elevations from the same basic floor plan. When the location of doors, windows, and chimneys has been established on the floor plan, the development of an attractive and functional elevation for the structure still depends on the factors of roof style, overhang, grade-line position, and relationship of windows, doors, and chimneys to the building line. Figure 35–1 clearly shows that choosing a desirable elevation design is not an automatic process which follows the floor-plan design, but a development which calls on the imagination.

The designer should keep in mind the fact that only horizontal distances can be established on the floor plan and that the vertical heights, such as heights of windows and doors, must be shown on the elevation. As these vertical heights are established, the appearance of the outside and the functioning of the heights as they affect the internal functioning of the house must be considered, as shown in Fig. 35–2.

FUNDAMENTAL SHAPES

The basic architectural style of a building is more closely identified with the design of the elevation than with any other factor. Consequently the selection of the basic type of structure must be compatible with the architectural style of the elevation. The elevation design can be changed to create the appearance of different architectural styles if the basic building type is consistent with that style (Fig. 35–3).

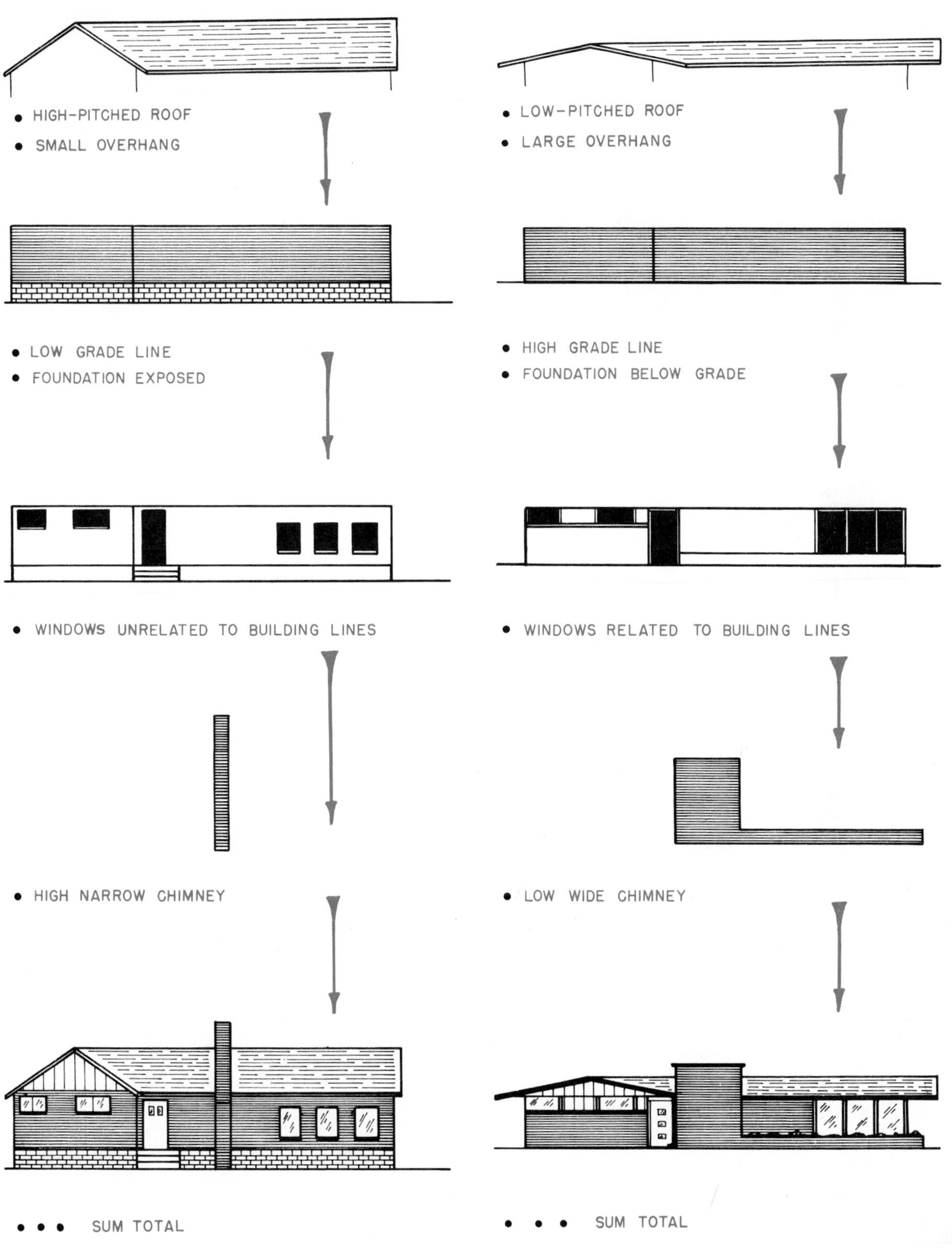

Fig. 35–1. Many factors affect the total appearance of the elevation.

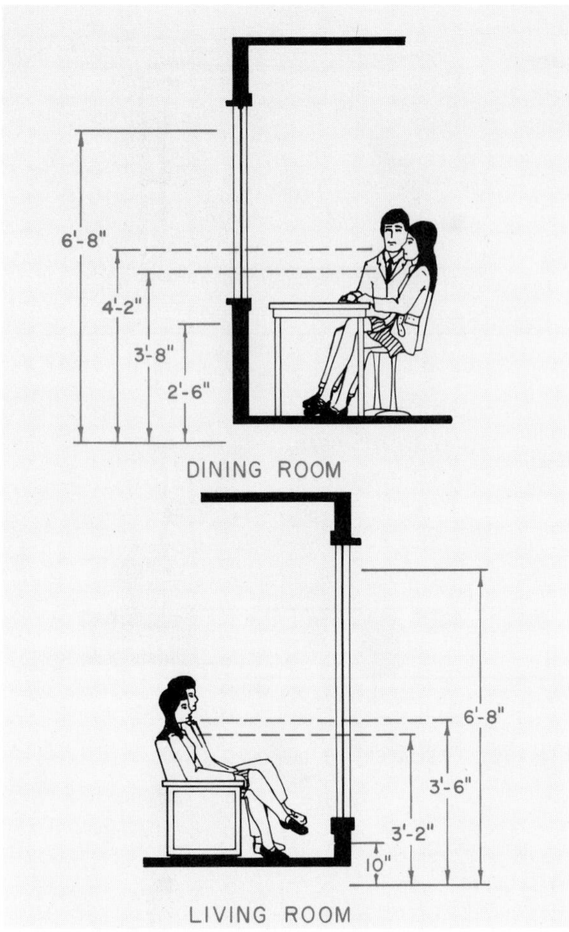

Small Homes Council

Fig. 35–2. Vertical distances, such as the heights of windows and doors, can be shown only on an elevation drawing.

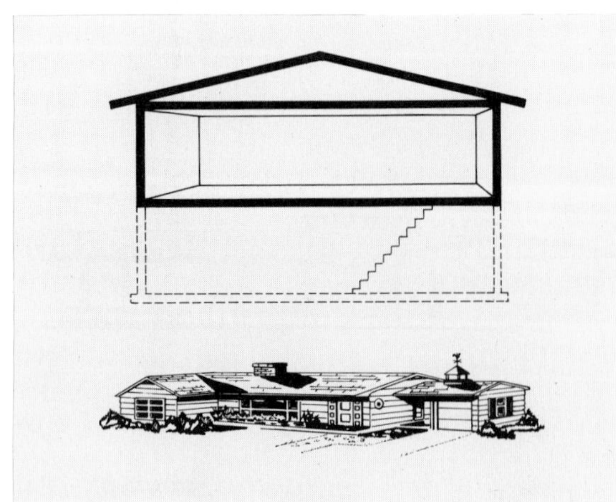

Fig. 35–4. Types of one-story structures.

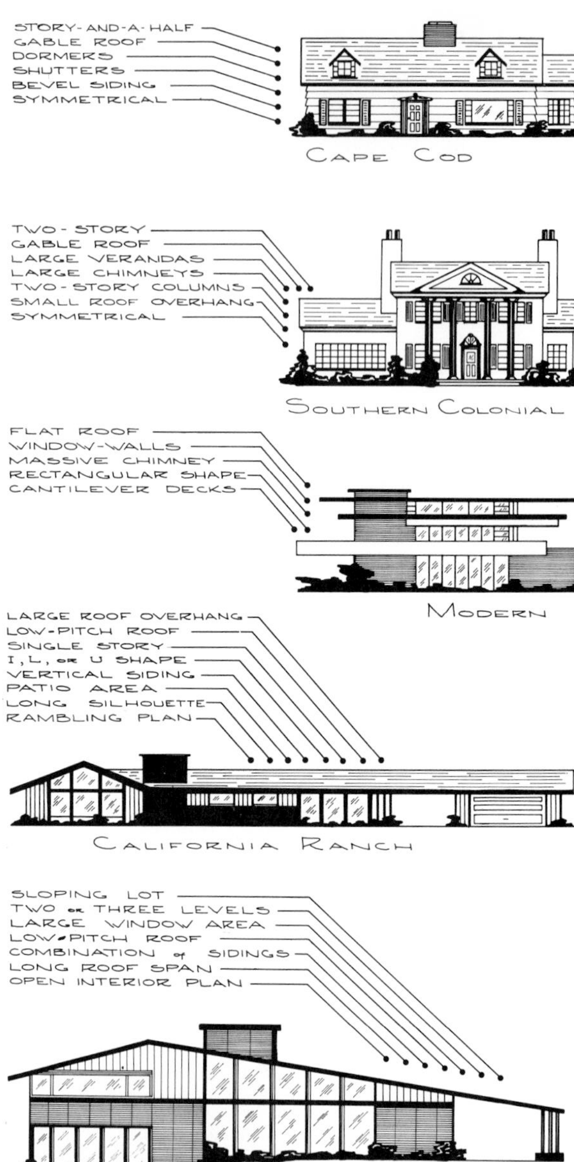

Fig. 35–3. The style of architecture will greatly determine the exterior appearance of the building.

Basic Types

Within basic styles of architecture there is considerable flexibility in the type of structure.

The basic types of structures include the one-story (Fig. 35–4), the one-and-one-half-story (Fig. 35–5), the two-story (Fig. 35–6), the split-level (Fig. 35–7), and the bilevel (Fig. 35–8).

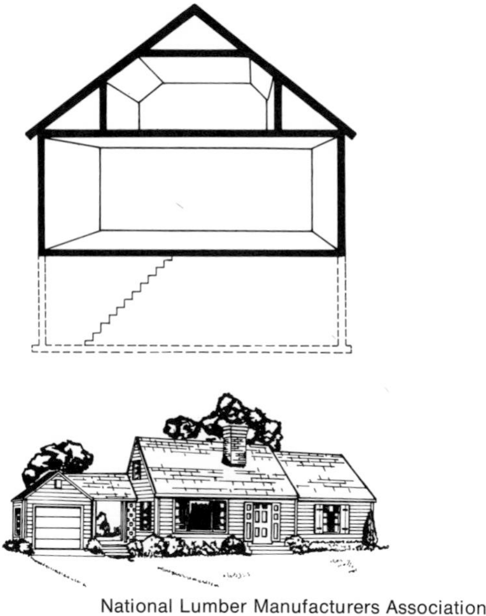

National Lumber Manufacturers Association

Fig. 35–5. A one-and-one-half-story home.

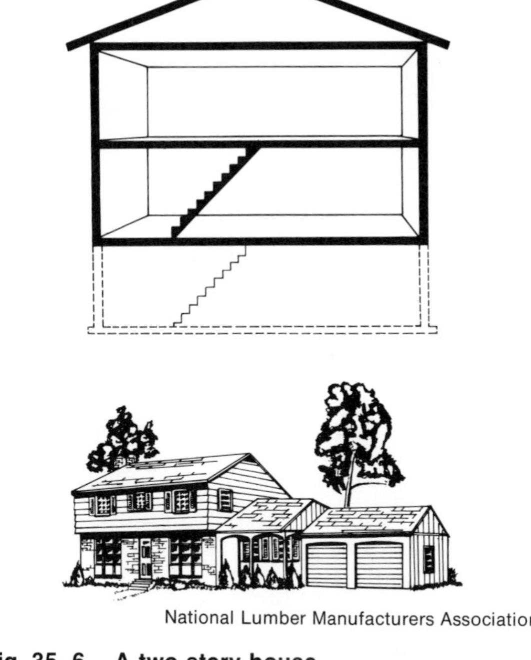

National Lumber Manufacturers Association

Fig. 35–6. A two-story house.

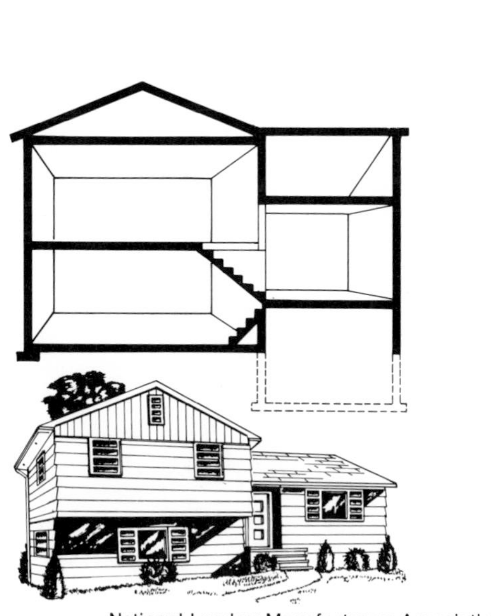

National Lumber Manufacturers Association

Fig. 35–7. A split-level home.

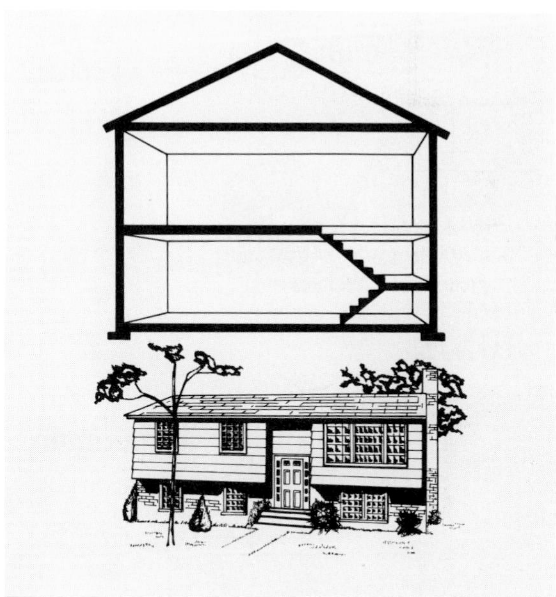

National Lumber Manufacturers Association

Fig. 35–8. The bilevel house.

Roof Styles

Nothing affects the silhouette of a house more than the roof line. The most common roofs are the gable roof, hip roof, flat roof, and shed roof (Fig. 35–9). A change in the roof style of a

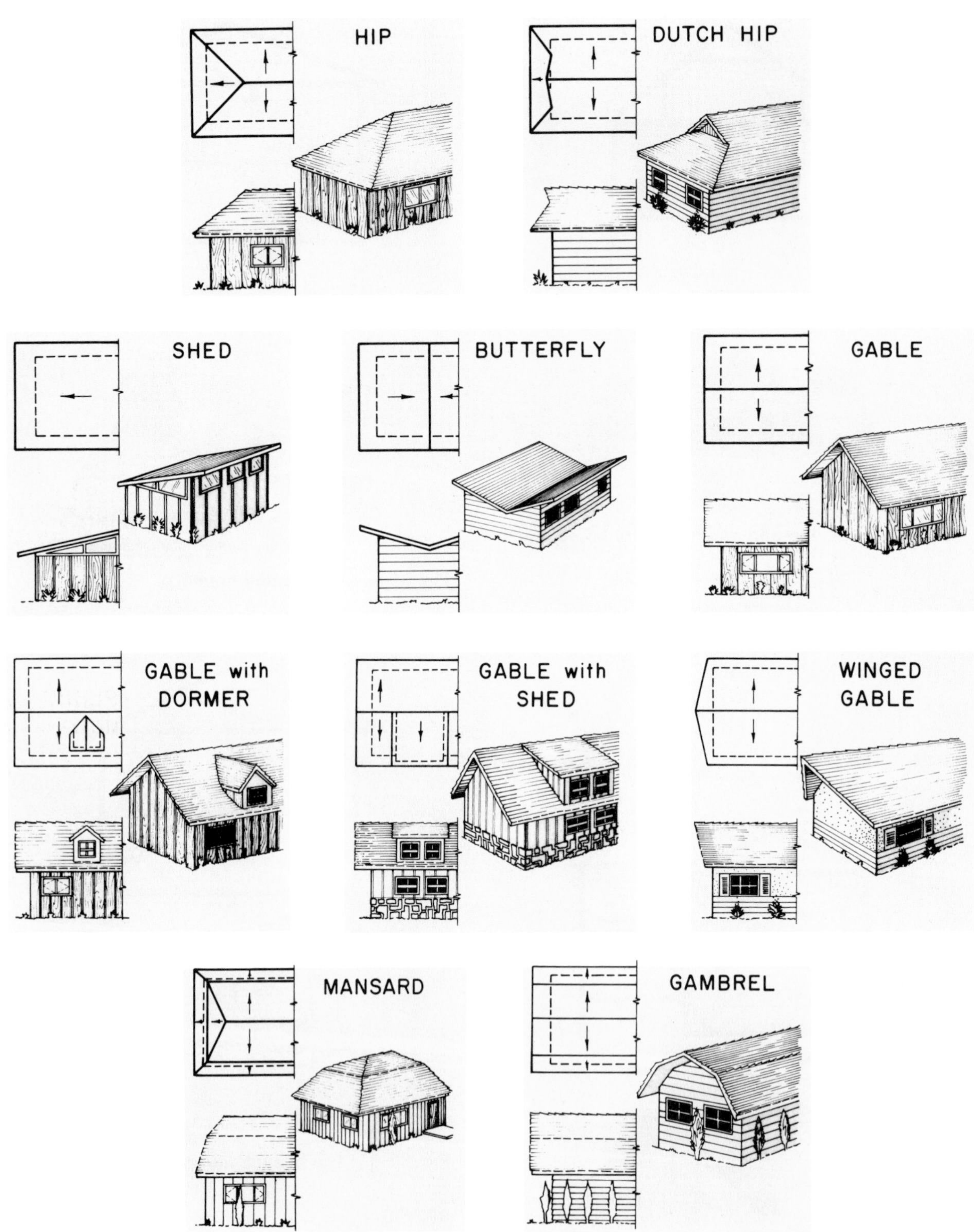

Fig. 35–9. Methods of drawing roofs and roof overhangs in plan, elevation, and pictorial views.

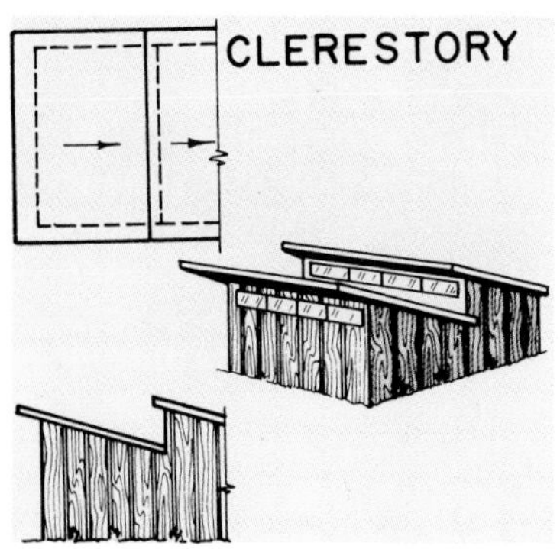
CLERESTORY

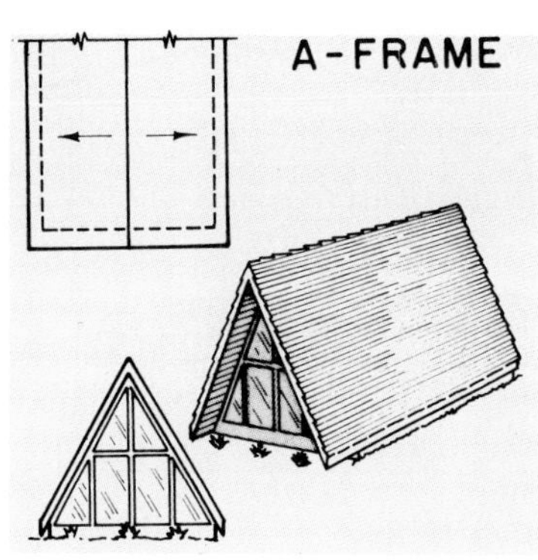
A-FRAME

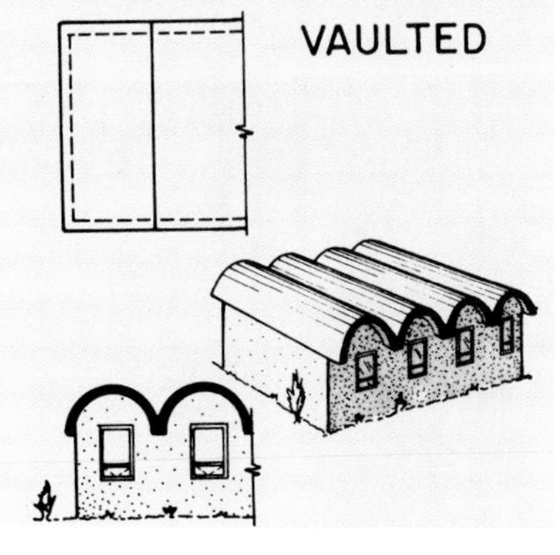
VAULTED

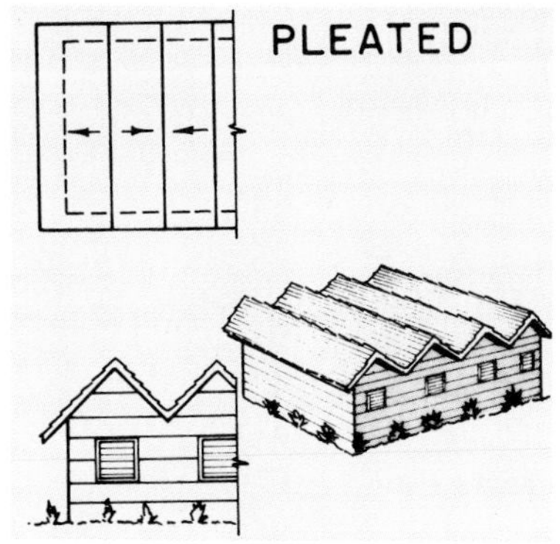
PLEATED

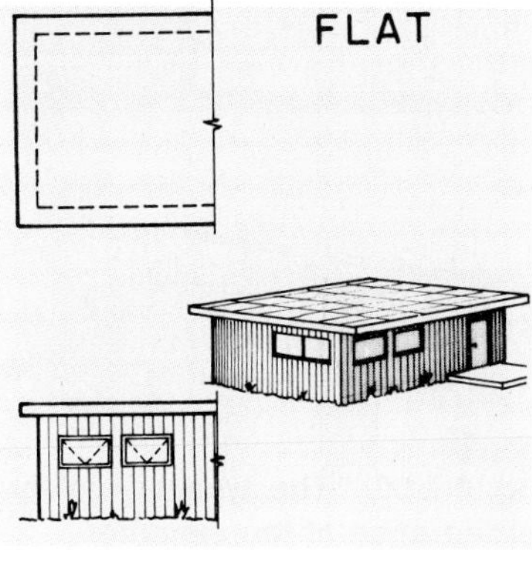
FLAT

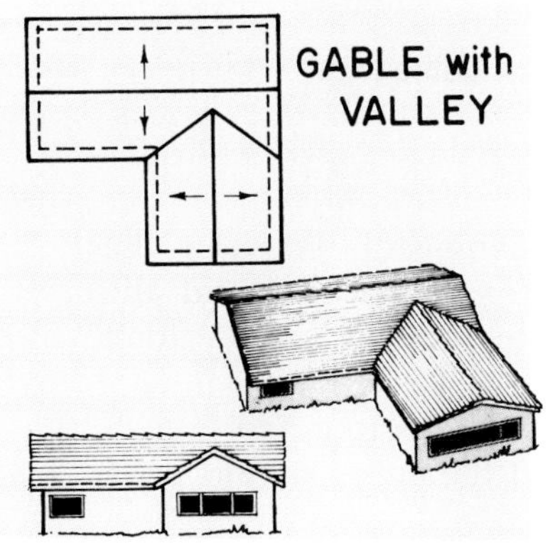
GABLE with
VALLEY

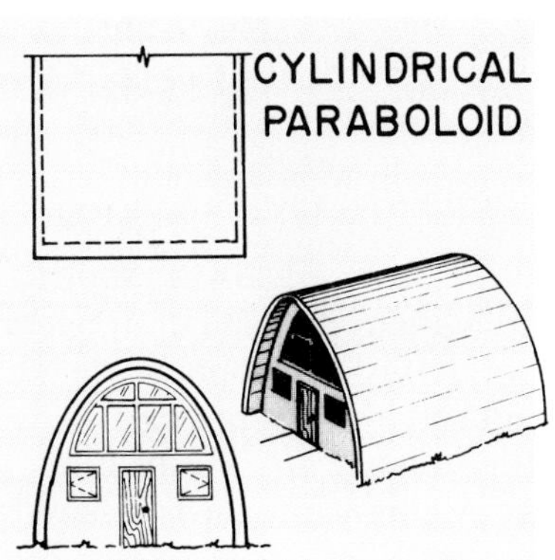
CYLINDRICAL
PARABOLOID

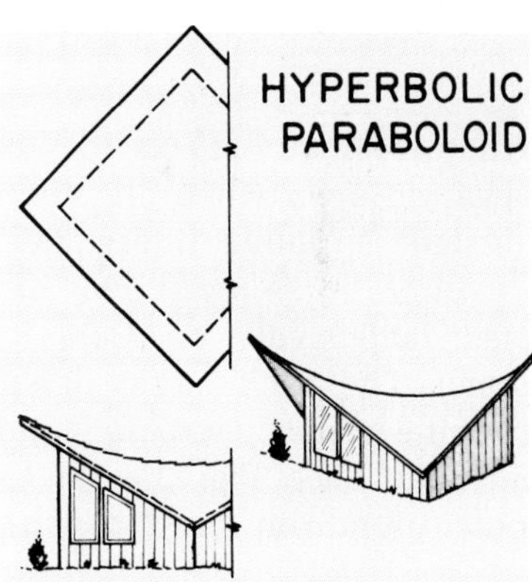
HYPERBOLIC
PARABOLOID

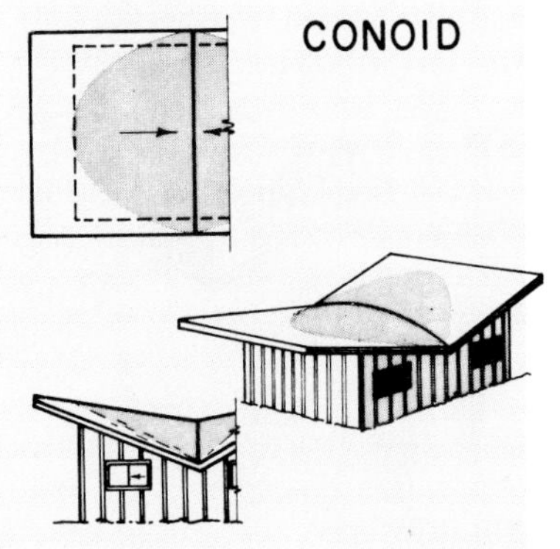
CONOID

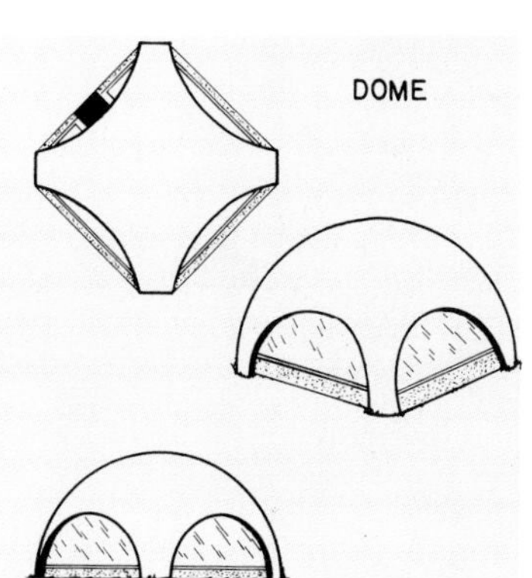
DOME

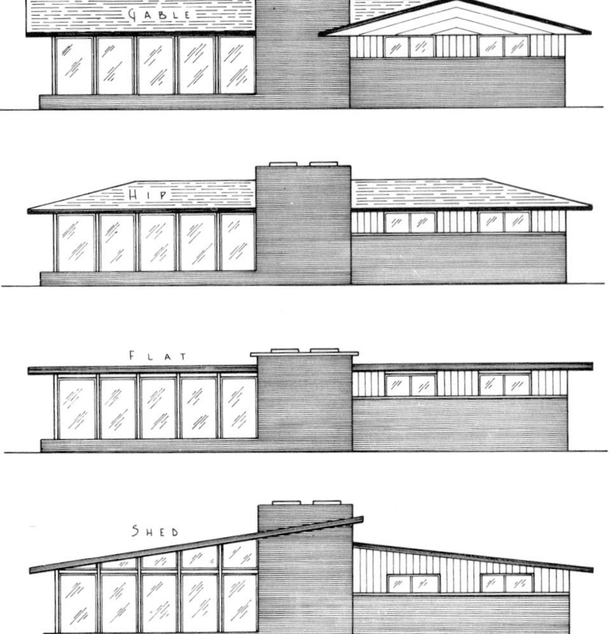

Fig. 35–10. The type of roof greatly affects the appearance of the elevation.

Home Planners, Inc.

Fig. 35-11. A house with a gable roof.

Master Plan Services, Inc.

Fig. 35–12. A high-pitch gable roof.

structure greatly affects the appearance of the elevation even when all other factors remain constant, as shown in Fig. 35–10.

Gable roofs, as shown in Fig. 35–11, are used extensively on Cape Cod and ranch homes. The pitch (angle) of a gable roof varies from the high-pitch roofs found on chalet style buildings (see Fig. 35–12) to the low-pitch roofs found on most ranch homes. Figure 35–13 shows the relationship between the actual appearance of a gable roof and the appearance of a gable roof on an elevation drawing.

Hip roofs are used when roof-line protection is desired around the entire perimeter of

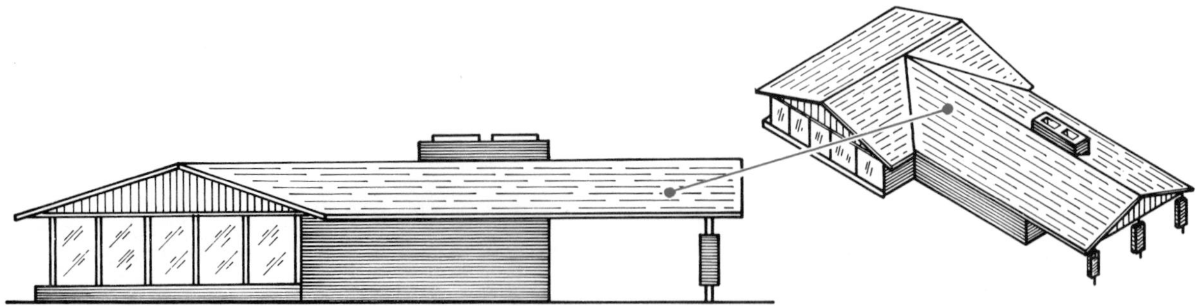

Fig. 35–13. The appearance of a gable roof on an elevation drawing.

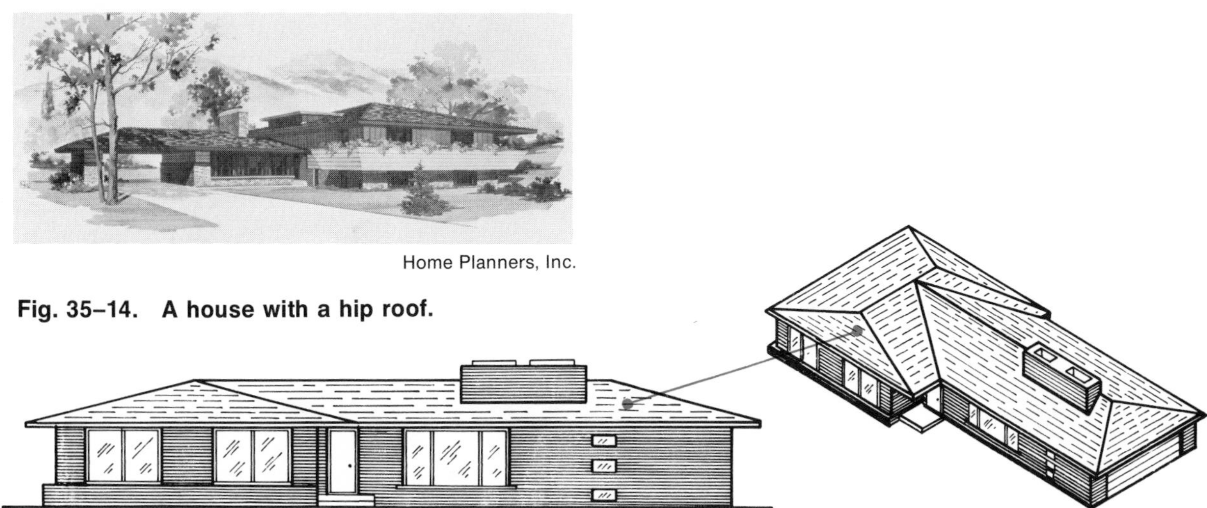

Fig. 35–14. A house with a hip roof.

Fig. 35–15. The appearance of a hip roof on an elevation drawing.

the building. Notice how the hip-roof overhang shades the windows of the house in Fig. 35–14. For this reason hip roofs are very popular in warm climates. Figure 35–15 shows the method of drawing hip roofs on elevation drawings. Hip roofs are commonly used on Regency and French Provincial homes.

Flat roofs are used to create a low silhouette on many modern homes (Fig. 35–16). Since no support is achieved by the leaning together of rafters, slightly heavier rafters are needed for flat roofs. Built-up asphalt construction is often used on flat roofs. Water may be used as an insulator and solar heater on flat roofs. Figure 35–17 illustrates the method of drawing flat roofs on elevations.

American Plywood Association

Fig. 35–16. A home with a flat roof.

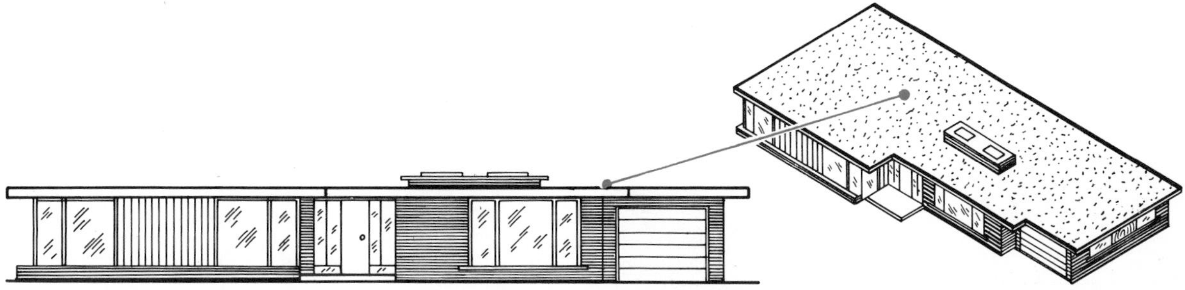

Fig. 35–17. The appearance of a flat roof on an elevation drawing.

Fig. 35–18. A shed roof with celestial windows.

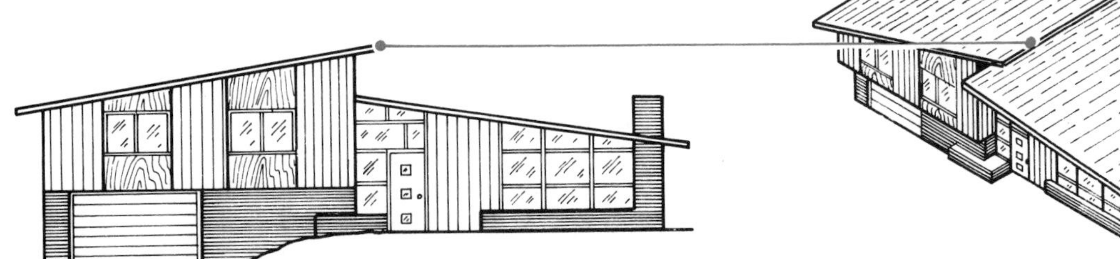

Fig. 35–19. The appearance of a shed roof on an elevation drawing.

Shed roofs are flat roofs that are higher at one end than at the other. They may be used effectively when two levels exist and where additional light is needed. The use of celestial windows between the two sheds (Fig. 35–18) provides skylight illumination. The double shed is really very advantageous on hillside split-level structures. Figure 35–19 shows a method of illustrating shed roofs on elevations.

The geodesic dome may constitute the roof (Fig. 35–20) or may extend completely to the ground and be part of the side wall structure as well.

Overhang

Sufficient roof overhang should be provided to afford protection from the sun, rain, and snow (Fig. 35–21). The length and angle of the

Kaiser Aluminum and Chemical Corp.

Fig. 35–20. A geodesic dome.

Fig. 35–21. Roof overhang is needed for protection from sun, rain, and snow.

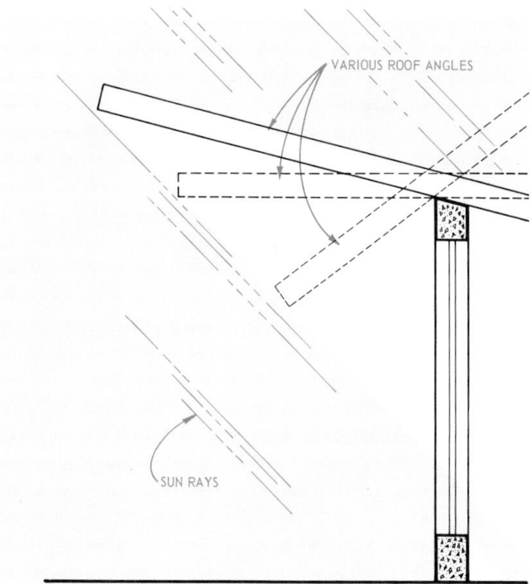

Fig. 35–22. The angle of the overhang determines its length.

overhang will greatly affect its appearance and its functioning in providing protection. Figure 35–22 shows that when the pitch is low, a larger overhang is needed to provide protection. However, with a high-pitch roof the overhang may be extended and block the view from the inside.

To provide protection and at the same time allow sufficient light to enter the windows, slatted overhangs similar to those shown in Fig. 35–23 may be used.

Figure 35–24 shows the effect of a small overhang. Figure 35–25 shows the protection afforded by a large overhang. The edge of the

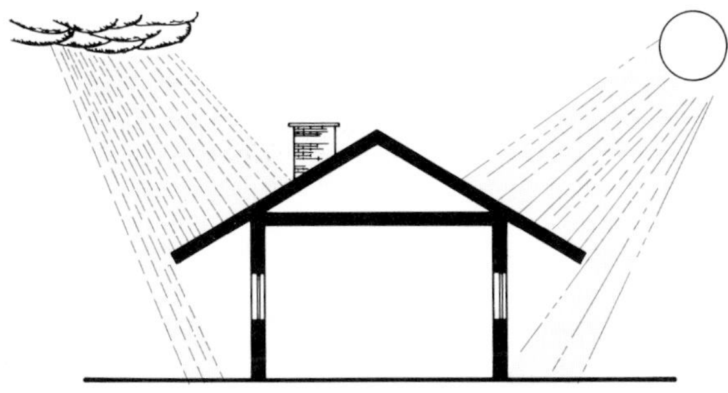

Fig. 35–25. The advantage of a large overhang.

Briar Hill Stone Company

Fig. 35–23. Slatted roof overhang.

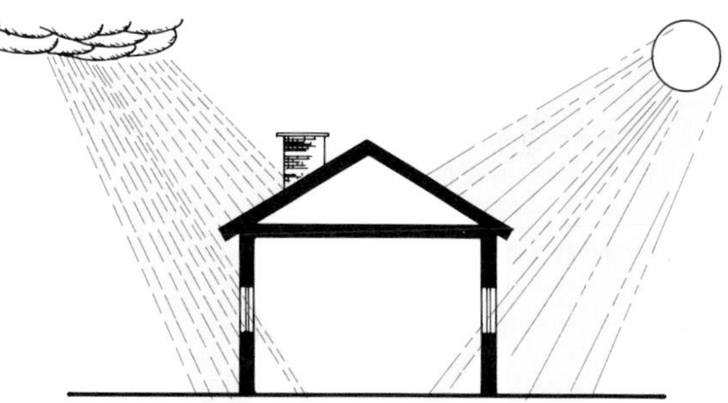

Fig. 35–24. The effect of a small overhang.

overhang does not always need to be parallel to the sides of the house. Notice how the roof line in Fig. 35–26 affords additional protection when the point of the overhang is extended from the outside wall.

This arrangement makes possible very large distances from wall to gutter.

Libby-Owens-Ford Company

Fig. 35–26. Additional protection can be achieved by changing the angle and overhang of the roof.

FORM AND SPACE

The total appearance of the elevation depends upon the relationship among the areas of the elevation such as surfaces, doors, windows, and chimneys. The balance of these areas, the emphasis placed on various components of the elevation, the texture, the light, the color, and the shadow patterns all affect greatly the general appearance of the elevation.

RELATED AREAS

The elevation should appear as one integral and functional facade rather than as a surface in which holes have been cut for windows and doors and to which structural components, such as chimneys, have been added without reference to the other areas of the elevation. Figure 35–27 shows a house with well-related lines and areas. Doors, windows, and chimney lines should constitute part of the general pattern of the elevation and should not exist in isolation. Figure 35–28 shows an elevation in which the windows and doors are related to the major lines of the elevation. Figure 35–29 shows the same elevation with unrelated doors and windows.

Windows

When the vertical lines of the windows are extended to the eave line from the ground line or planter line or some division line in the separation of materials, the vertical lines become related to the building. Horizontal lines of a window extending from one post to another, or from one vertical separation in the elevation to another, as between a post and a chimney, also help to relate the window to the major lines of the elevation. For example, the windows in Fig. 35–30 were related by being extended to fill the area between posts and between the door and eave line.

Doors

Doors can easily be related to the major lines of the house by extending the area above the door to the ridge line, or divider, and making the side panels consistent with the door size, as shown in Fig. 35–31. A comparison between Fig. 35–32 and Fig. 35–33 shows the effect of extending the door lines vertically and horizontally to integrate the door with the window line and the overall surface of the elevation.

Home Planners, Inc.

Fig. 35–27. A house with well-related lines and areas.

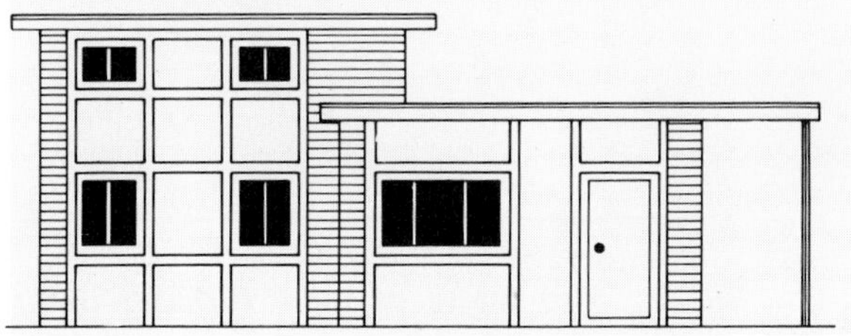

Fig. 35–28. An elevation drawing, showing related lines.

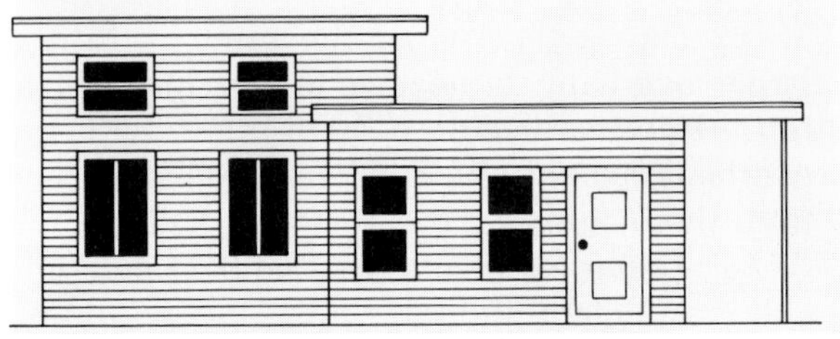

Fig. 35–29. Unrelated elevation lines.

SHAPE

Although it is important to relate the lines of the elevation to each other, nevertheless, the overall shape of the elevation should reflect the basic shape of the building. Do not attempt to camouflage the shape of the elevation. An example of such camouflage is the old Western store (Fig. 35–34), whose builder tried to

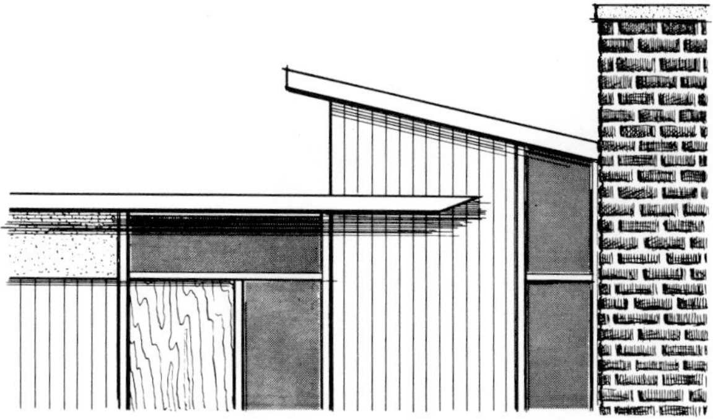

Home Planners, Inc.

Fig. 35–30. Effective relationships between roof, windows, siding, and chimney.

Fig. 35–31. A door unit related to the other lines of the elevation.

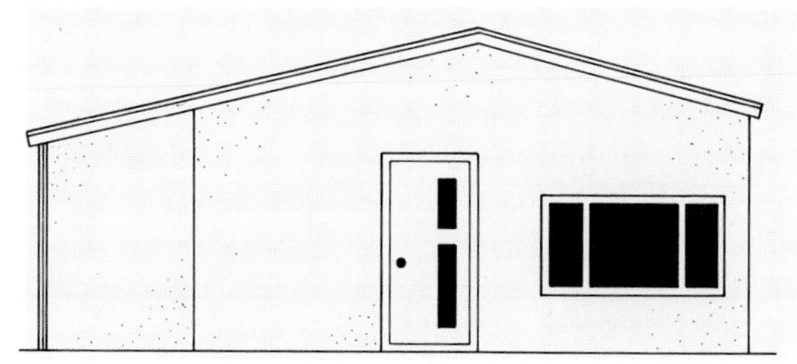

Fig. 35–32. Unextended door and window lines.

Fig. 35–33. Door and window lines extended horizontally and vertically.

Fig. 35–34. Avoid elevation camouflage.

disguise the actual elevation by constructing a false front.

Patio walls, fences, or other structures may block the view of the elevation wall. If such blocking occurs, it is advisable to draw the elevation with the wall in position, to show how the elevation will appear when viewed from a distance (Fig. 35–35 at A). It is advisable also to draw the elevation as it will exist inside the wall (Fig. 35–35 at B).

The American Home Magazine

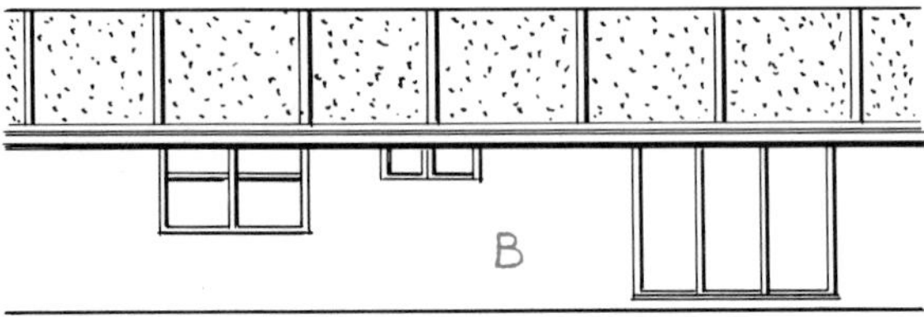

Fig. 35–35. It is sometimes necessary to draw an elevation with an obstructing feature (A) and without it (B).

Balance

The term *balance* refers to the symmetry of the elevation. An elevation is either *formally* or *informally* balanced (Fig. 35–36). Formal balance is used extensively in colonial and period styles of architecture. Informal balance is more widely used in modern residential architecture. Informally balanced elevations are frequently used in modern designs such as ranch and split-level styles.

Emphasis

Elevation emphasis, or accent, can be achieved by several different devices. An area may be accented by mass, by color, or by material. Every elevation should have some point of emphasis. Compare the two elevations in Fig. 35–37. Note that in the second example the chimney and the roof have been accented to provide a focal point.

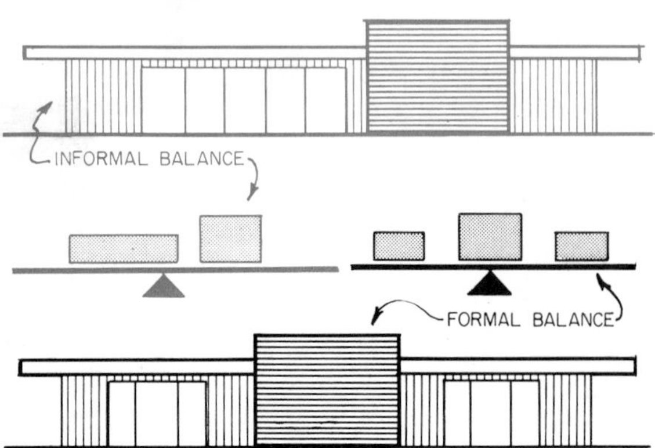

Fig. 35–36. A formally and an informally balanced elevation.

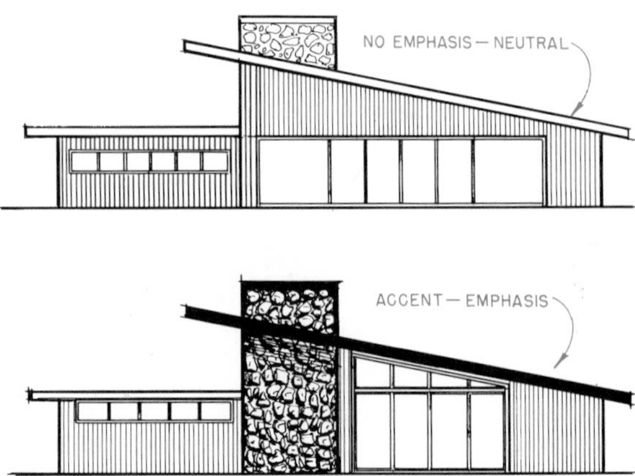

Fig. 35–37. Every elevation should have some point of emphasis.

Home Planners, Inc.

Fig. 35–38. Light, shade, and color should be balanced on every elevation.

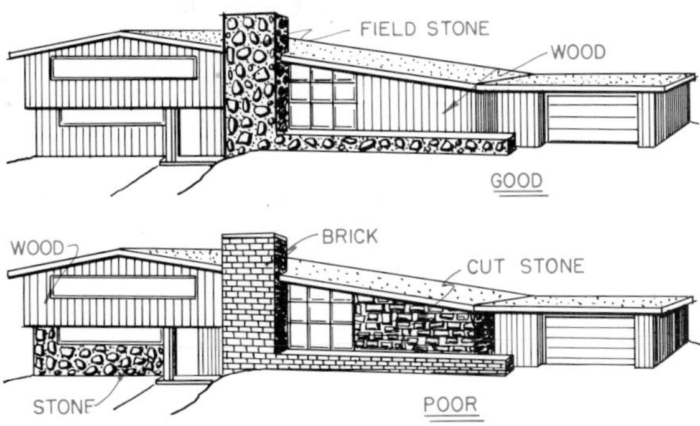

Fig. 35–39. The effect of combining too many materials.

Home Planners, Inc.

Fig. 35–40. Emphasis placed on the horizontal eave line.

Home Planners, Inc.

Fig. 35–41. Horizontal emphasis.

Light and Color

An elevation that is composed of all light areas or all dark areas tends to be uninteresting and neutral. Some balancing of light, shade, and color is desirable in most elevations. This can be achieved through developing shadow patterns by depressing areas, by using overhang, by grading, and by color variation, as shown in Fig. 35–38.

Texture

An elevation contains many kinds of materials such as glass, wood, masonry, and ceramics. These must be carefully and tastefully balanced to be effective. An elevation comprised of too few materials is ineffective and neutral. Likewise an elevation which uses too many materials, especially masonry, is equally objectionable.

In choosing the materials for the elevation, the designer should not mix horizontal and vertical siding or different types of masonry. If brick is the primary masonry used, brick should be used throughout. It should not be mixed with stone. Similarly, it is not desirable to mix several types of brick or several types of stone. Figure 35–39 shows the effect of mixing too many materials in an elevation.

LINES

The lines of an elevation are the *ground line, eave line,* and *ridge line.* These are horizontal lines. One of these lines should be emphasized. In Fig. 35–40, the horizontal eave line has been accented by being extended over the porch. The lines of an elevation can help to create horizontal or vertical emphasis. If the ground line, ridge line, and eave line are accented, the emphasis will be placed on the horizontal, as shown in Fig. 35–41. If the emphasis is placed on vertical lines such as corner posts and columns, the emphasis will be vertical. Figure 35–42 shows a comparison between placing the emphasis on horizontal lines and placing the emphasis on vertical lines. In general, low buildings will usually appear longer and lower if the emphasis is placed on horizontal lines.

Lines should be consistent. The lines of an elevation should appear to flow together as one integrated line pattern. It is usually better to continue a line through an elevation for a long distance than to break the line and start it again. Figure 35–43 shows the difference between a building with consistent lines and a building with inconsistent lines. Rhythm can be developed by the use of lines, and lines can be repeated in various patterns. When a line is repeated, the basic consistency of the elevation is considerably strengthened.

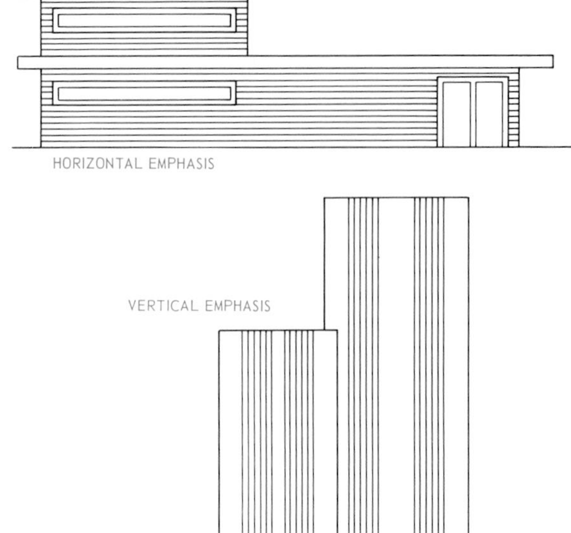

Fig. 35–42. Emphasis on vertical and on horizontal lines.

PROBLEMS

1. **Sketch an elevation of your own design. Trace the elevation, adding a flat roof, gable roof, shed roof, and butterfly roof. Choose the one you like best and the one that is most functional for your design.**
2. **Sketch the front elevation of your home. Vary the roof style, making it consistent with the major lines of the elevation. Redesign the elevation, relating the door and window lines to the major lines of the building.**
3. **Too many materials are used in the building shown in Fig. 35–44. Sketch an elevation of this house and change the building materials to be consistent with the design.**
4. **State as many facts as you can about the elevation design of the home in Fig. 35–11.**
5. **Sketch the elevation shown in Fig. 35–17 with a hip roof, double-shed roof, and gable roof. Resketch this illustration, using different siding materials.**
6. **Identify the roof shown in Fig. 35–41.**
7. **Resketch the bottom elevation shown in Fig. 35–37. Place the emphasis on an area of the elevation other than the chimney.**
8. **Resketch the formally balanced elevation shown in Fig. 35–36. Convert this elevation to an informally balanced elevation.**
9. **Resketch the elevation shown in Fig. 35–19. Change the roof style and siding materials.**
10. **Resketch the elevation shown in Fig. 35–17, using a gable roof.**
11. **Sketch the elevation shown in Fig. 35–15, using a double-shed roof.**
12. **Define the following terms: *one-story house, one-and-one-half-story house, bilevel, split-level, hip roof, flat roof, gable roof, shed roof, high pitch, low pitch, celestial windows, gambrel roof, mansard roof, butterfly roof, overhang, related lines, unrelated lines, ridge lines, eave lines, ground lines, formal balance, informal balance, texture emphasis.***

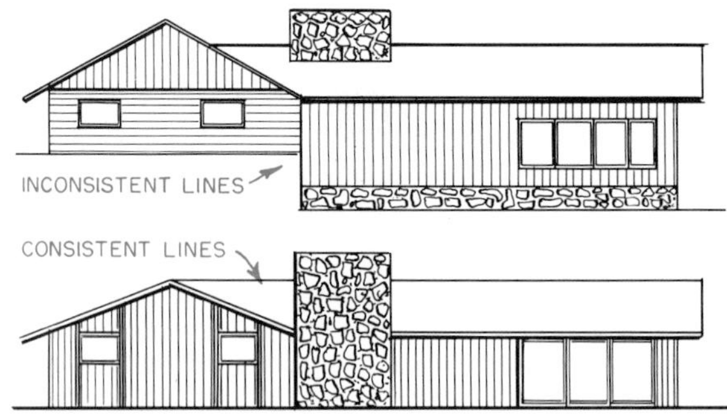

Fig. 35–43. Consistent lines are essential for good elevation design.

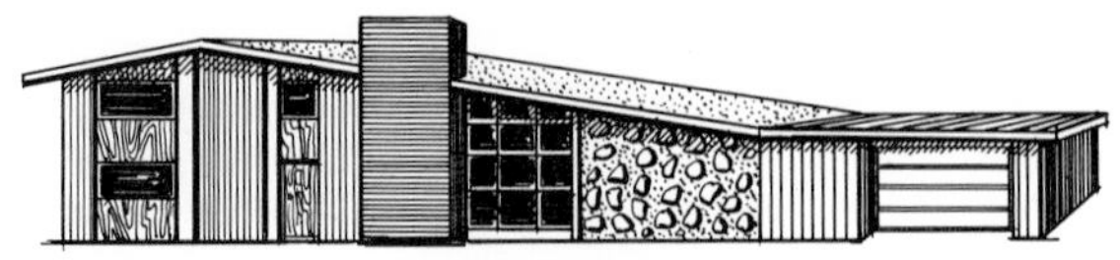

Fig. 35–44. Resketch this elevation to eliminate the inconsistent use of materials.

UNIT 36

Elevation Projection

Elevation drawings are projected from the floor plan of an architectural drawing just as the side views are projected from the front view of an orthographic drawing. Figure 36–1 shows how elevations are projected from the floor plan. The positions of the chimney, doors, windows, overhang, and building corners are projected directly from the floor plan outward to the elevation plane. If you trace the projection of the chimney from the plan to each of the elevations shown in Fig. 36–1, you will see the relative position of the chimney as you view the house from four different directions which correspond to the four normal elevations.

ELEVATION PLANES

You may think of the elevation as a drawing placed on a vertical plane. Figure 36–2 shows how this vertical plane is related to the floor-plan projection.

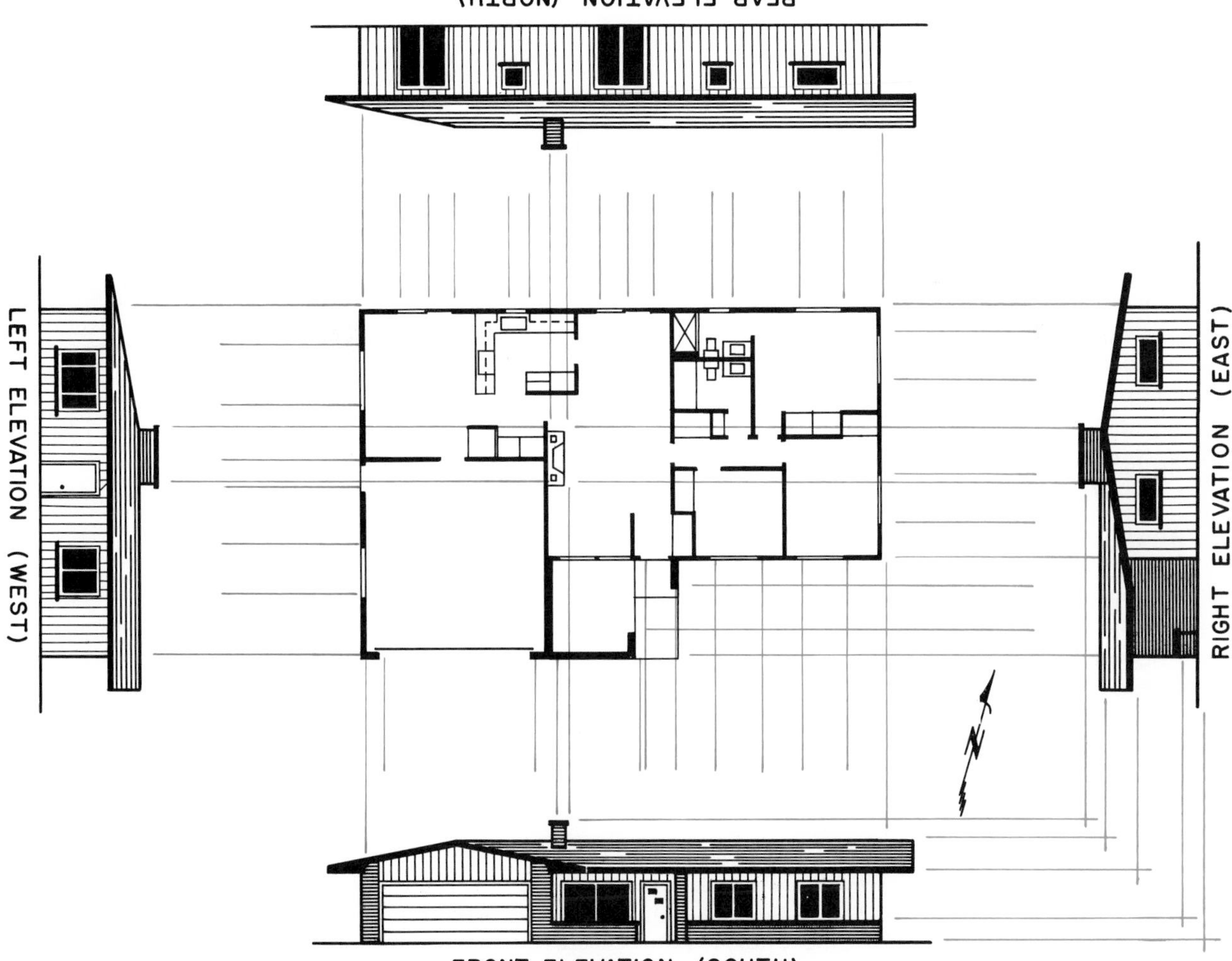

Fig. 36–1. Projection of the basic elevations from the floor plan.

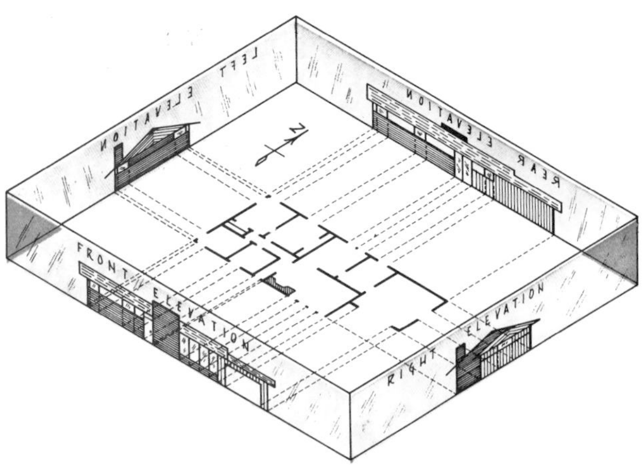

Fig. 36–2. **Elevation planes of projection.**

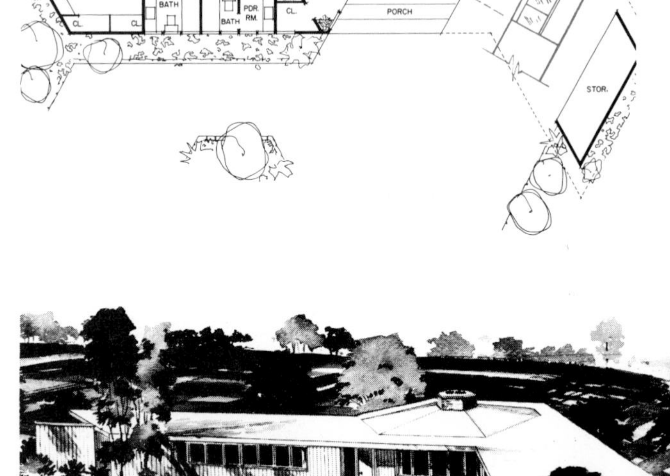

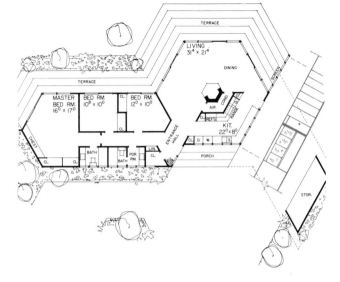

Home Planners, Inc.

Fig. 36–3. Auxiliary elevation projection.

Functional Orientation

Four elevations are normally projected from the floor plan. When these elevations are classified according to their function, they are called the front elevation, the rear elevation, the right elevation, and the left elevation. The front view of the house is known as the *front elevation.* The view projected from the rear of the house is known as the *rear elevation.* The view projected from the right side of the house is known as the *right elevation,* and the view projected from the left side of the house is known as the *left elevation.* When these elevations are all *projected* on the same drawing sheet, the rear elevation appears to be upside down and the right and left elevations appear to rest on their sides. Owing to the large size of most elevation drawings, and because of the desirability of drawing elevations as we normally see them, each elevation is usually drawn with the ground line on the bottom and the roof on the top.

Compass Orientation

The north, east, south, and west compass points are often used by architects to describe and label elevation drawings. This method is preferred when there is no so-called front or rear view to a structure. When this method is used, the north arrow on the floor plan is the key to the designation of the elevation title. For example, in Fig. 36–2 the rear elevation is facing north. Therefore the rear elevation could also be called the north elevation. Here the front elevation is the south elevation, and the left elevation is the west elevation.

Auxiliary Elevations

When a floor plan has more than four sides, or sides that deviate from the normal 90° projection, an auxiliary elevation view is often necessary. To project an auxiliary elevation, follow the same rules for projecting orthographic auxiliaries. Project the auxiliary elevation perpendicular to the wall of the floor plan from which you are projecting, as shown in Fig. 36–3. When an auxiliary elevation is drawn, it is usually prepared in addition to the standard elevations and does not replace them. It merely clarifies the foreshortened lines of the major elevations caused by the receding angles.

STEPS IN PROJECTING ELEVATIONS

The major lines of an elevation are derived by projecting vertical lines from the floor plan and measuring the position of horizontal lines from the ground line.

Vertical-Line Projection

Vertical lines representing the main lines of the building should first be projected as shown in Fig. 36–4. These lines show the overall length and width of the building. They also show the length of the major parts or offsets of the building.

Horizontal-Line Projection

Horizontal lines which represent the height of the eave line, ridge line, and chimney line above the ground line are projected to intersect with the vertical lines drawn from the floor plan, as shown in Fig. 36–4. The intersection of these lines provides the overall outline of the elevation.

Roof-Line Projection

The ridge line and eave line cannot be accurately located until the *roof pitch* (angle) is established. On a high-pitch roof there is a greater distance between the ridge line and the eave line than on a low-pitch roof. Figure 36–5 shows a high-pitch roof and a low-pitch roof.

Pitch is the angle of the roof and is described in terms of the ratio of the *rise over the run* (rise/run). *Run* is the horizontal distance covered by a roof. *Rise* is the vertical distance. The run is always expressed in units of 12. Therefore, the pitch is the ratio of the rise to 12.

When the roof pitch is established, the rise and the run should be drawn to scale and the roof angle established by connecting the extremities of these lines, as shown in Fig. 36–6. Next, the roof angle can be extended and the

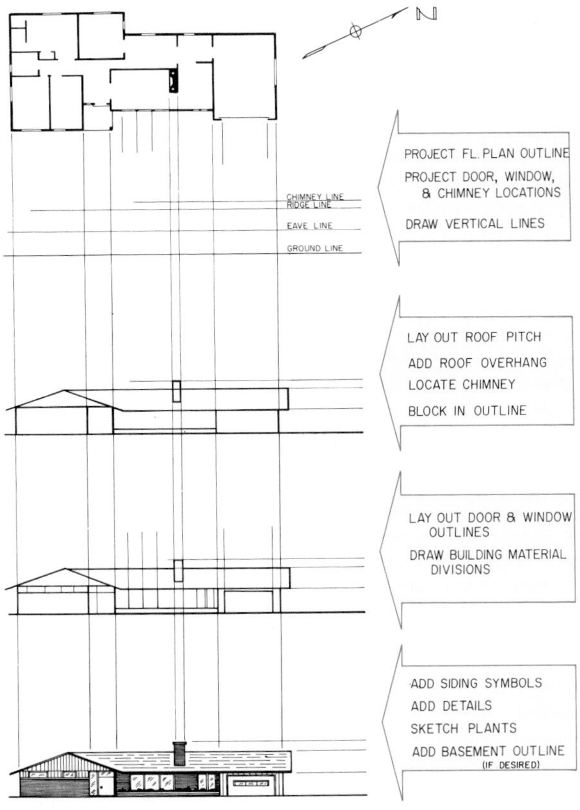

Fig. 36–4. The sequence of projecting elevations.

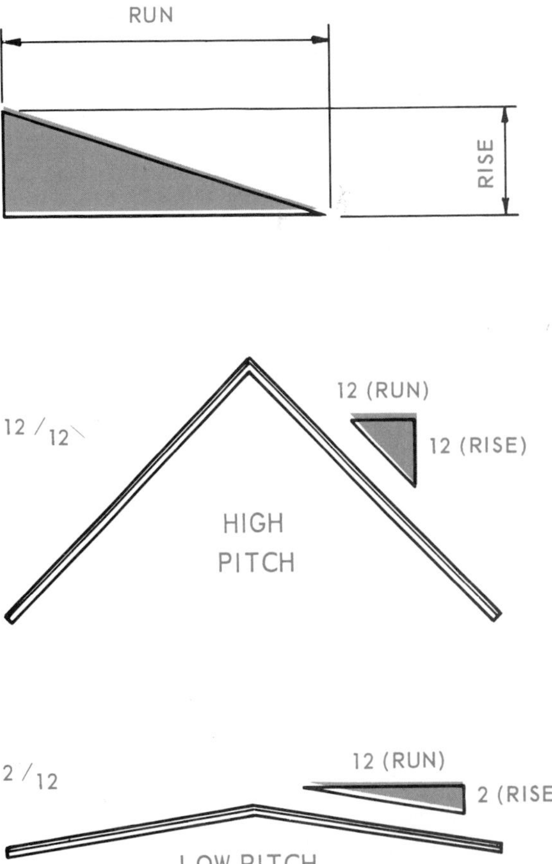

Fig. 36–5. A high-pitch and a low-pitch roof.

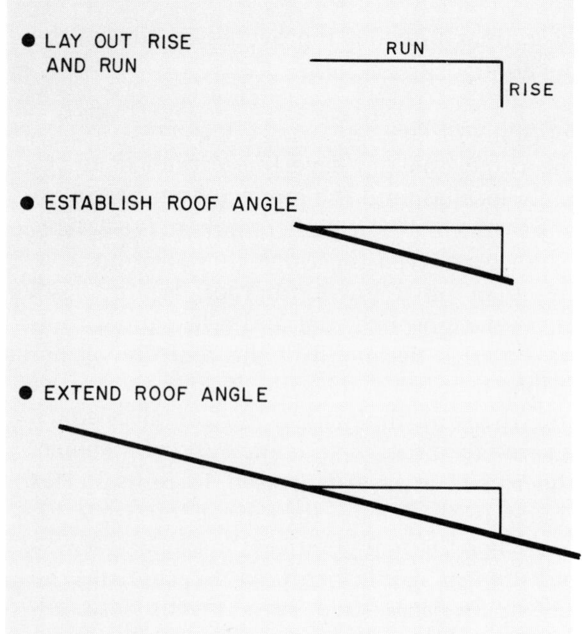

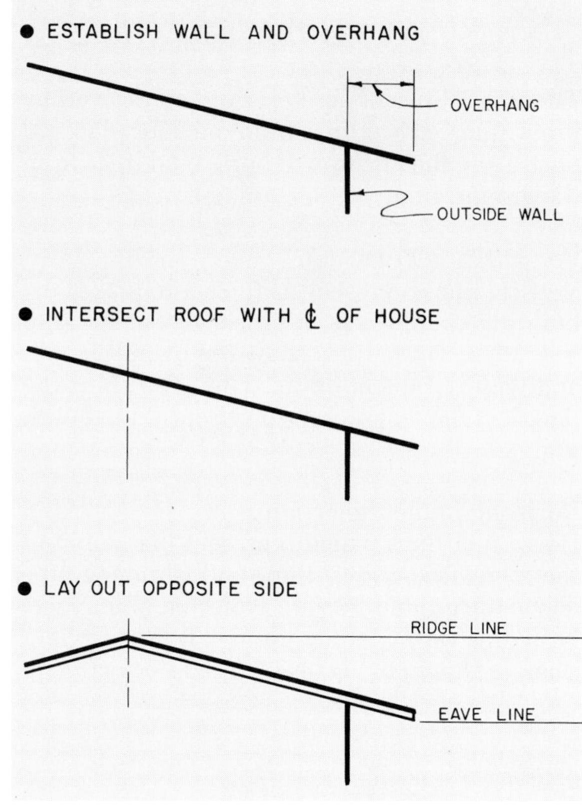

Fig. 36–6. The sequence of projecting roof outline.

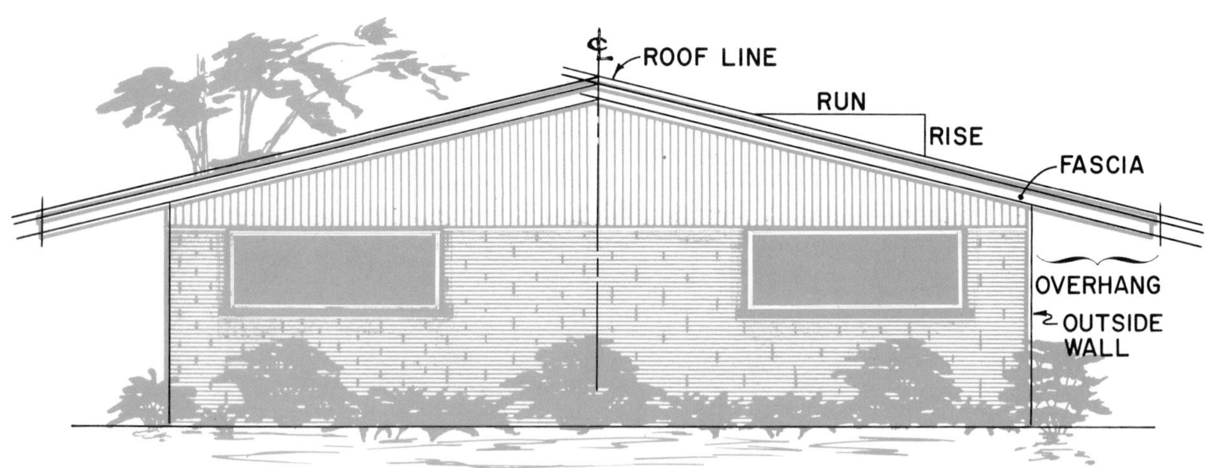

1. Lay out rise and run to establish roof angle.
2. Extend angle to show roof line.
3. Draw parallel line to show fascia.
4. Draw vertical line for outside wall.
5. Measure width of overhang and draw vertical line.
6. Measure distance from top of outside wall to grade line.
7. Draw and extend grade line.
8. Measure from outside wall to center line of roof; draw vertical center line.
9. Draw opposite side of roof showing outside wall and width of overhang.
10. Darken all object lines.
11. Add siding symbols and door or window symbols.
12. Add gutter or cornice details.
13. Dimension if necessary.
14. Add landscaping if desired.

Fig. 36–7. Symbols added to elevation.

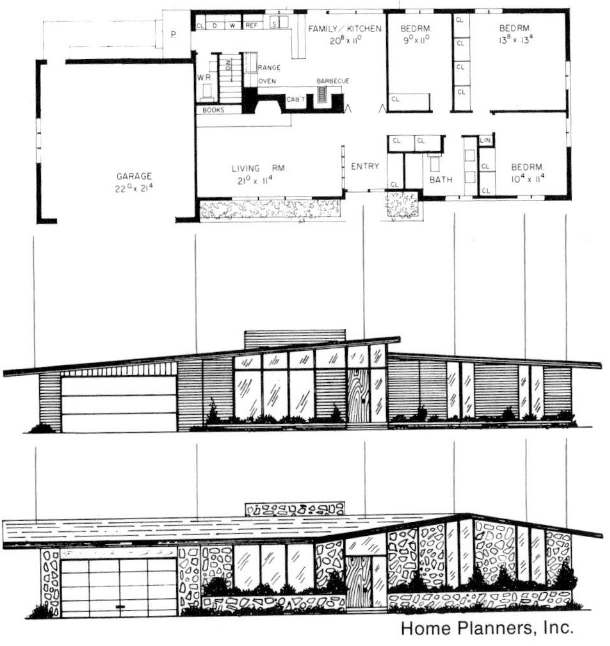

Home Planners, Inc.

Fig. 36–8. Two different elevation styles projected from one floor plan.

overhang measured from the outside wall to the eave. When the center line of the house is established, the exact positions of the ridge line and eave line are established, and the eave line and ridge line are projected and blocked-in as shown in Fig. 36–4.

Blocking-In the Outline

After the roof outline has been established, the major lines of the house are drawn. This drawing is made by following the outline developed from the intersection of horizontal and vertical lines, as shown in Fig. 36–4. The outlines of materials, doors, windows, chimney, and roof are drawn in their final line weight.

Adding Elevation Symbols

The next step is to add the elevation symbol for each material and feature on the elevation, as shown in Fig. 36–7.

FLEXIBILITY

It is possible to project many different elevation styles from one floor plan. The pitch, size of overhang, position of the grade line, window position and style, chimney size and style, and the door style and position all can be manipulated to create different effects. Figure 36–8 shows two different elevations projected from the same floor plan. Here the change was accomplished primarily by varying the distances between the major lines of the elevation.

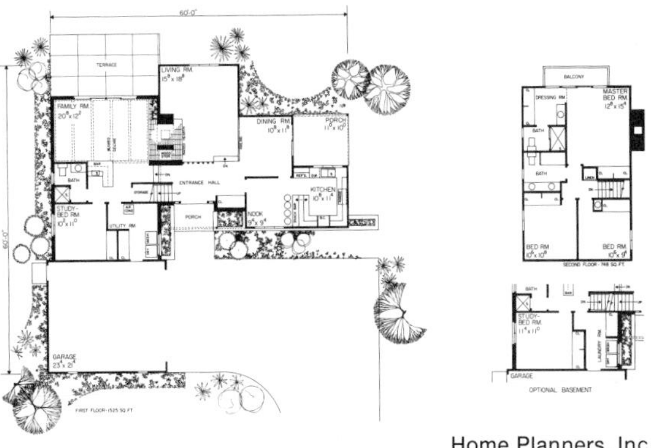

Home Planners, Inc.

Fig. 36–9. Draw the front elevation of this plan.

PROBLEMS

1. **Project the front, rear, right, and left elevations of a floor plan of your own design.**
2. **Sketch the front elevation of your home.**
3. **Project and sketch or draw the front elevation suggested in the pictorial drawing and floor plan in Fig. 36–9.**
4. **Complete the elevation-projection problem shown in Fig. 36–10 by drawing the elevation on the terrain as shown.**
5. **Sketch the front and left elevations of the house shown in Fig. 36–11.**
6. **Define the following terms: *front elevation, rear elevation, right elevation, left elevation, north elevation, east elevation, south elevation, west elevation, auxiliary elevations, pitch, rise, run.***

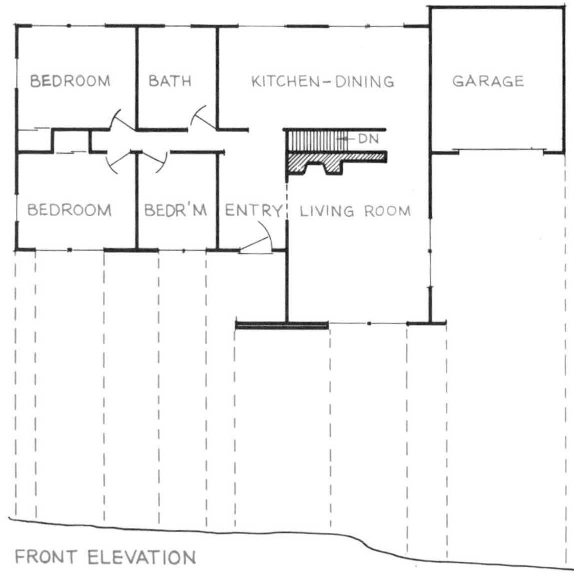

Fig. 36–10. Complete the front elevation on the terrain, as shown.

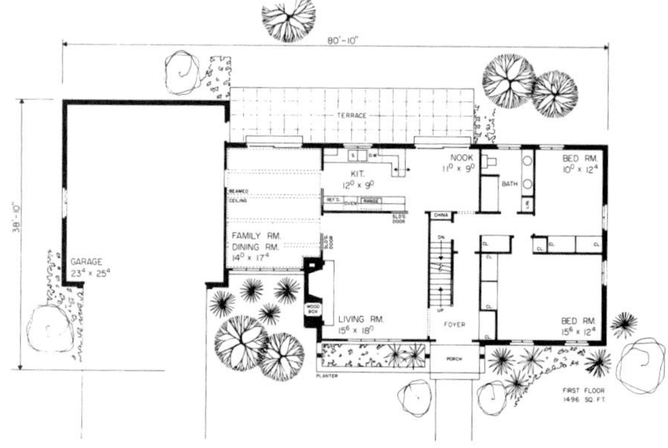

Home Planners, Inc.

Fig. 36–11. Sketch the front and left elevations of this house.

UNIT 37

Elevation Symbols

Symbols are needed to clarify and simplify elevation drawings. Symbols help to describe the basic features of the elevation. They show what building materials are used, and they describe the style and position of doors and windows. Symbols also help to make the elevation drawing look realistic. Some of the most common elevation symbols are shown on the elevation drawing in Figs. 37–1 and 37–2.

MATERIAL SYMBOLS

Figure 37–3 shows the relationship between material symbols used on an elevation and the actual material as it is used in construction. Most architectural symbols look very similar to the material they represent. However, in many cases the symbol does not show the exact appearance of the material. For example, the symbol for brick, as shown in Fig. 37–3, does not include all the lines shown in the pictorial drawing. Representing brick on the elevation drawing exactly as it appears is a long, laborious, and unnecessary process. Therefore, many elevation symbols are simplifications of the actual appearance of the material. The symbol often resembles the appearance of the material at a distance. Figures 37–4 and 37–5 show the relationship between elevation symbols and floor-plan symbols.

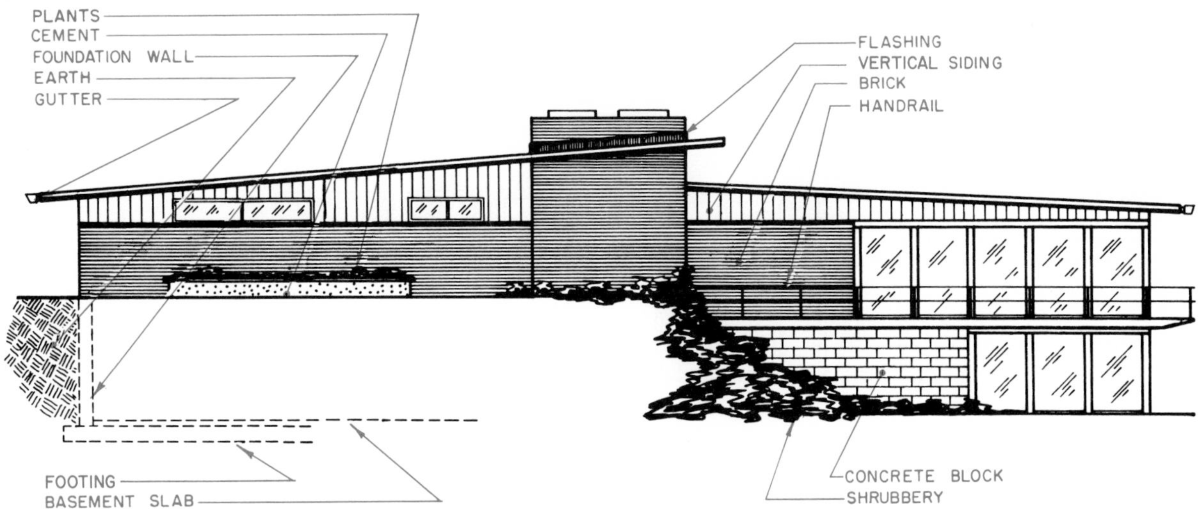

Fig. 37–1. Symbols help make the elevation look more realistic.

Fig. 37–2. Some common elevation symbols in use.

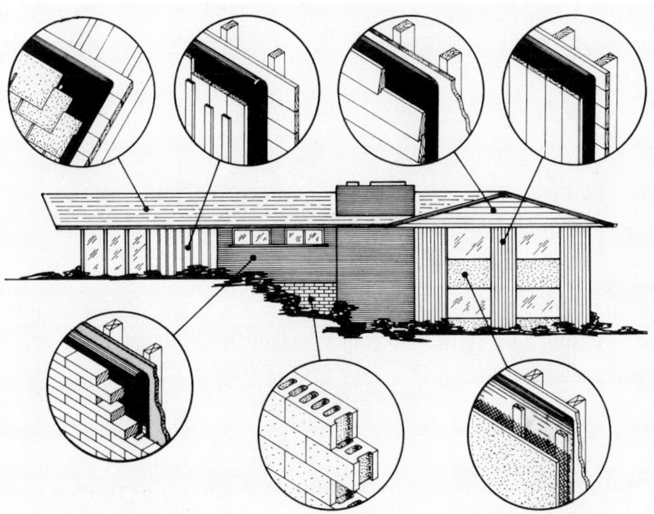

Fig. 37–3. The relationship between material symbols and materials used in construction.

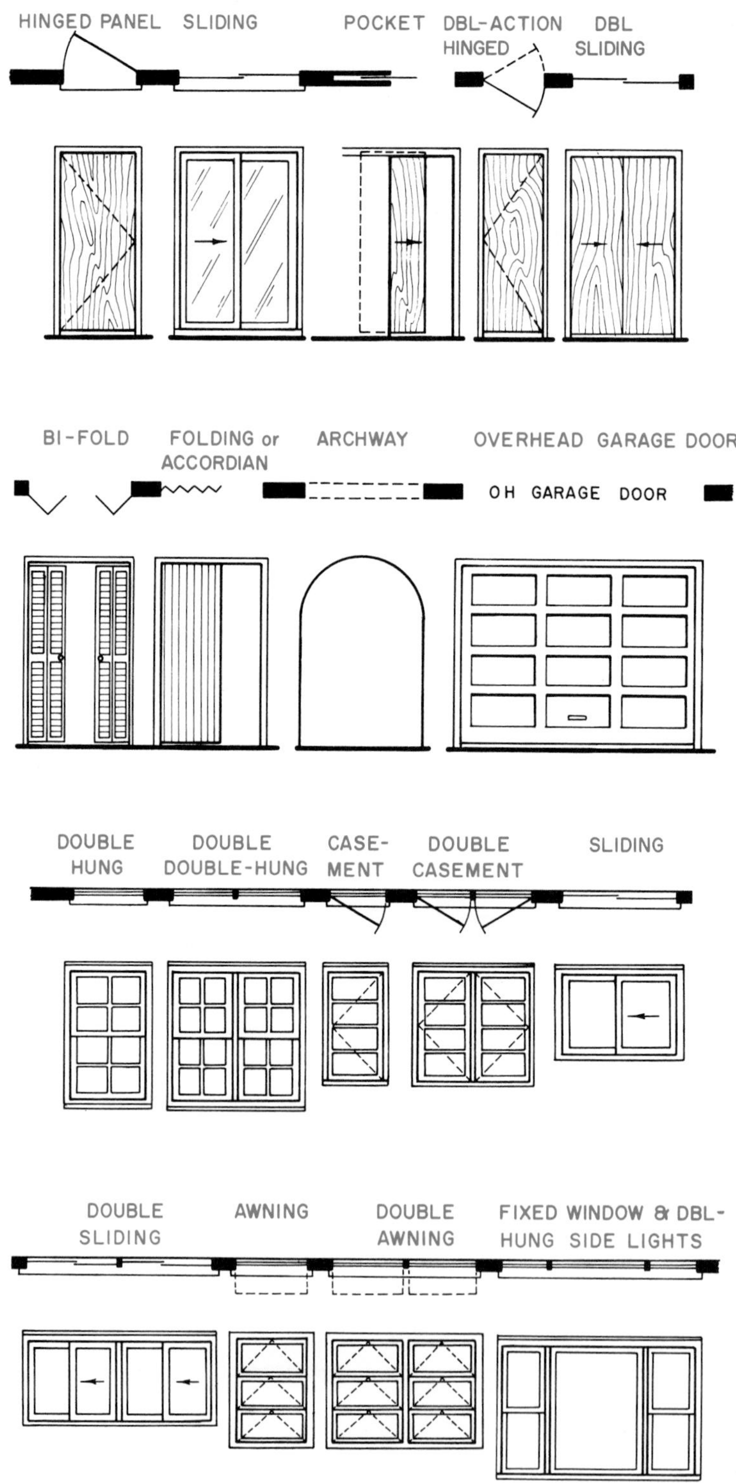

Fig. 37–4. The relationship between floor-plan and elevation door and window symbols.

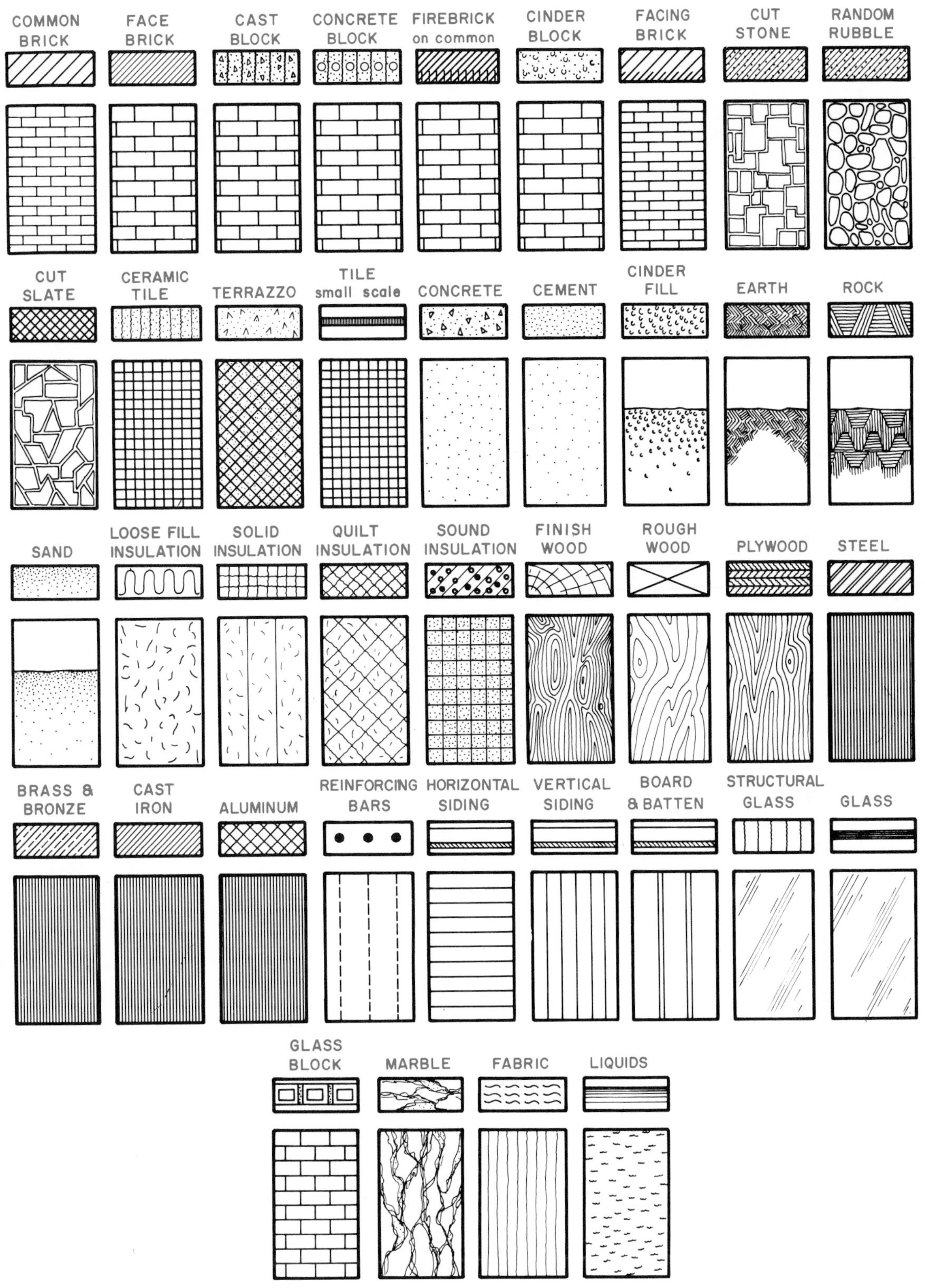

Fig. 37–5. Elevation and plan symbols for various materials.

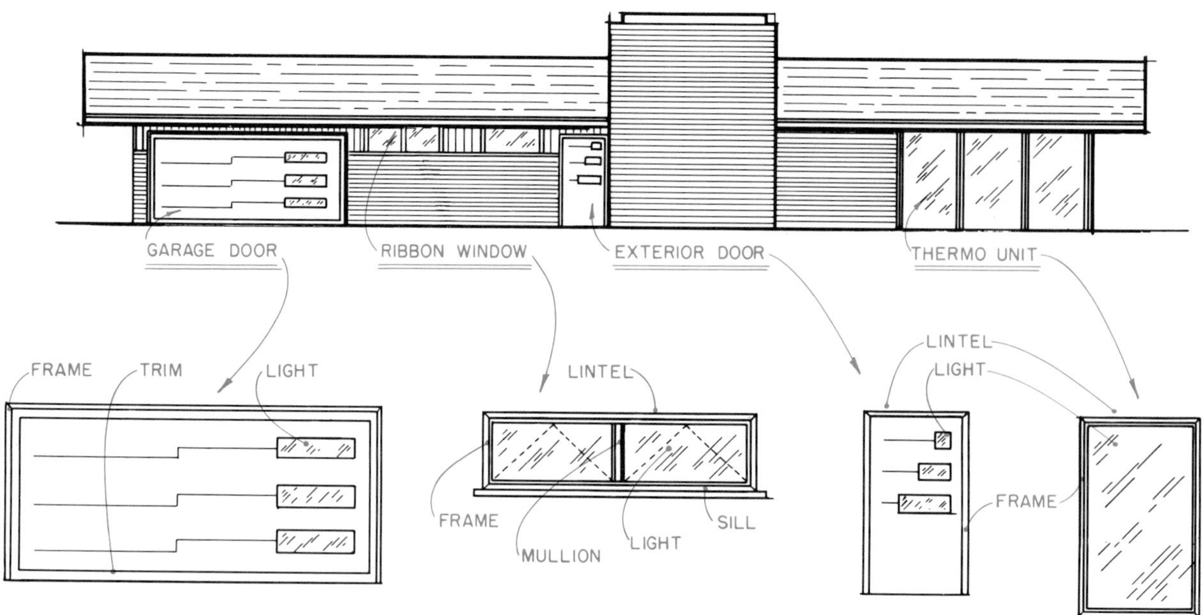

Fig. 37–6. Window symbols as they appear on elevation drawings.

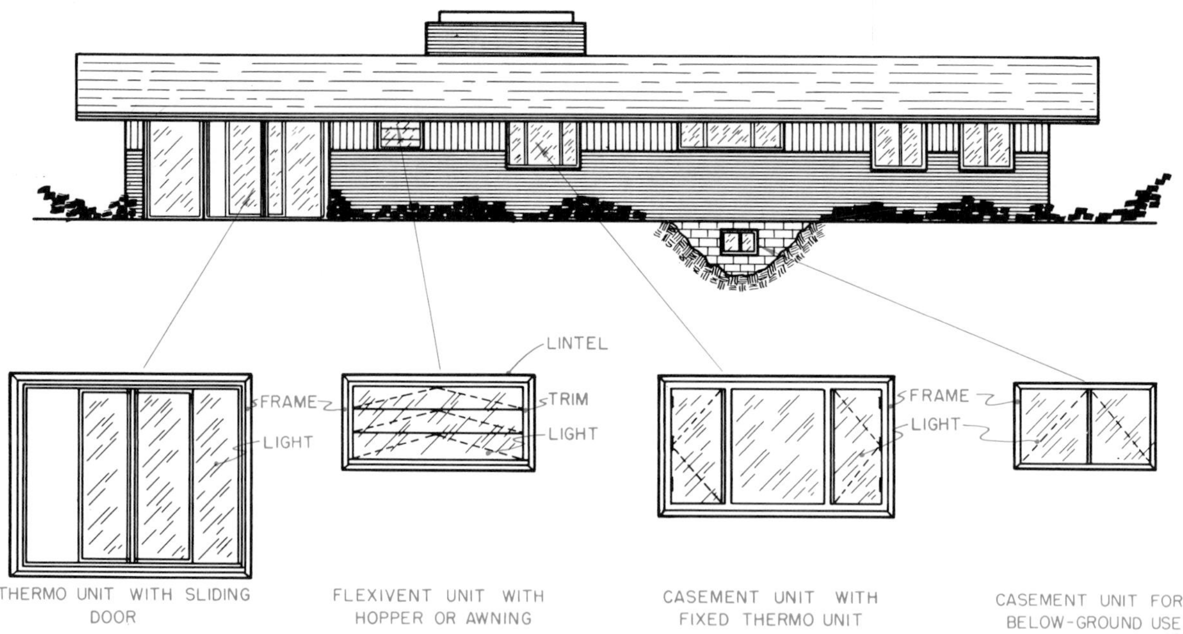

Fig. 37–7. Often it is not possible to show all details of windows on elevation drawings.

WINDOW SYMBOLS

The position and style of windows greatly affect the appearance of the elevation. Windows are therefore drawn on the elevation with as much detail as the scale of the drawing permits. Parts of windows that should be shown on all elevation drawings include the sill, sash, mullions, and muntins (Fig. 37–6). Figure 37–7 shows the method of illustrating casement, awning, and sliding windows.

In addition to showing the parts of a window, it is also necessary to show the direction of the hinge for casement and awning windows. Figure 37–8 shows the method of indicating the direction of the hinge on elevation drawings. The direction of the hinge is shown by dotted lines. The point of the dotted line shows the part of the window to which the hinge is attached.

Many different styles of windows are available, as shown in Fig. 37–9. Figure 37–10 shows the methods of illustrating some of these window styles on elevation drawings.

Fig. 37–8. **The placement of the hinge is shown by the dotted line.**

Architects often use an alternative method of showing window styles on elevation drawings. In this alternative method, the draftsman prepares a window-detail drawing, as shown in Fig. 37–11, to a rather large scale. He or she prepares a window drawing in different detail for each different style of window to be used. When the elevation is drawn, only the position of the window is shown. The style

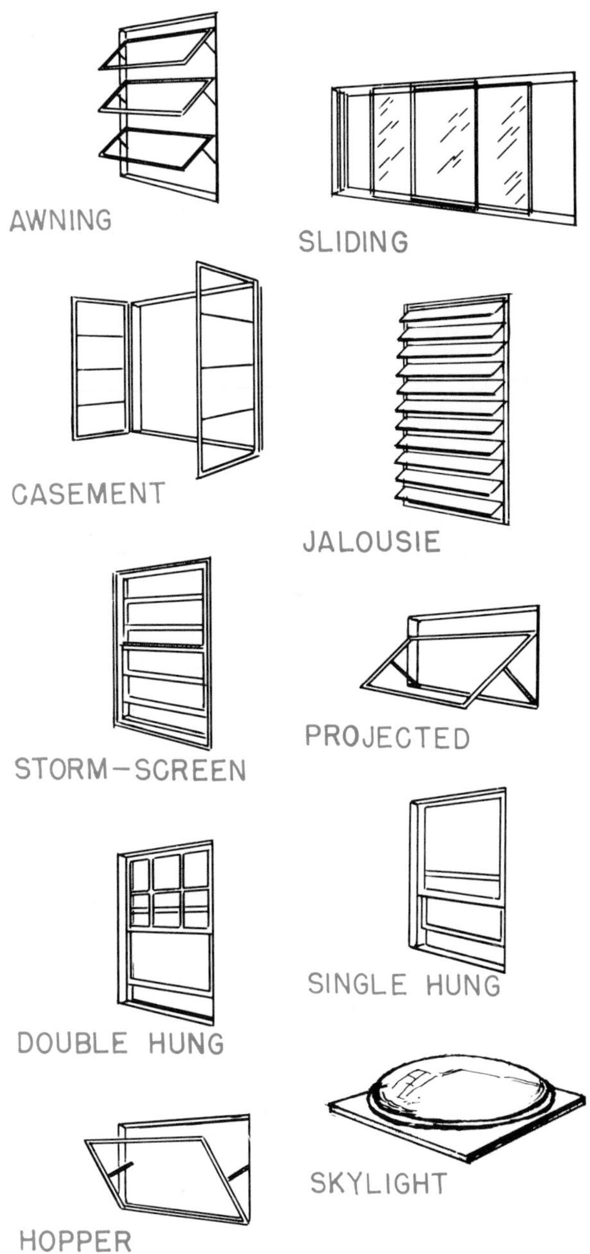

Fig. 37–9. **Common window styles.**

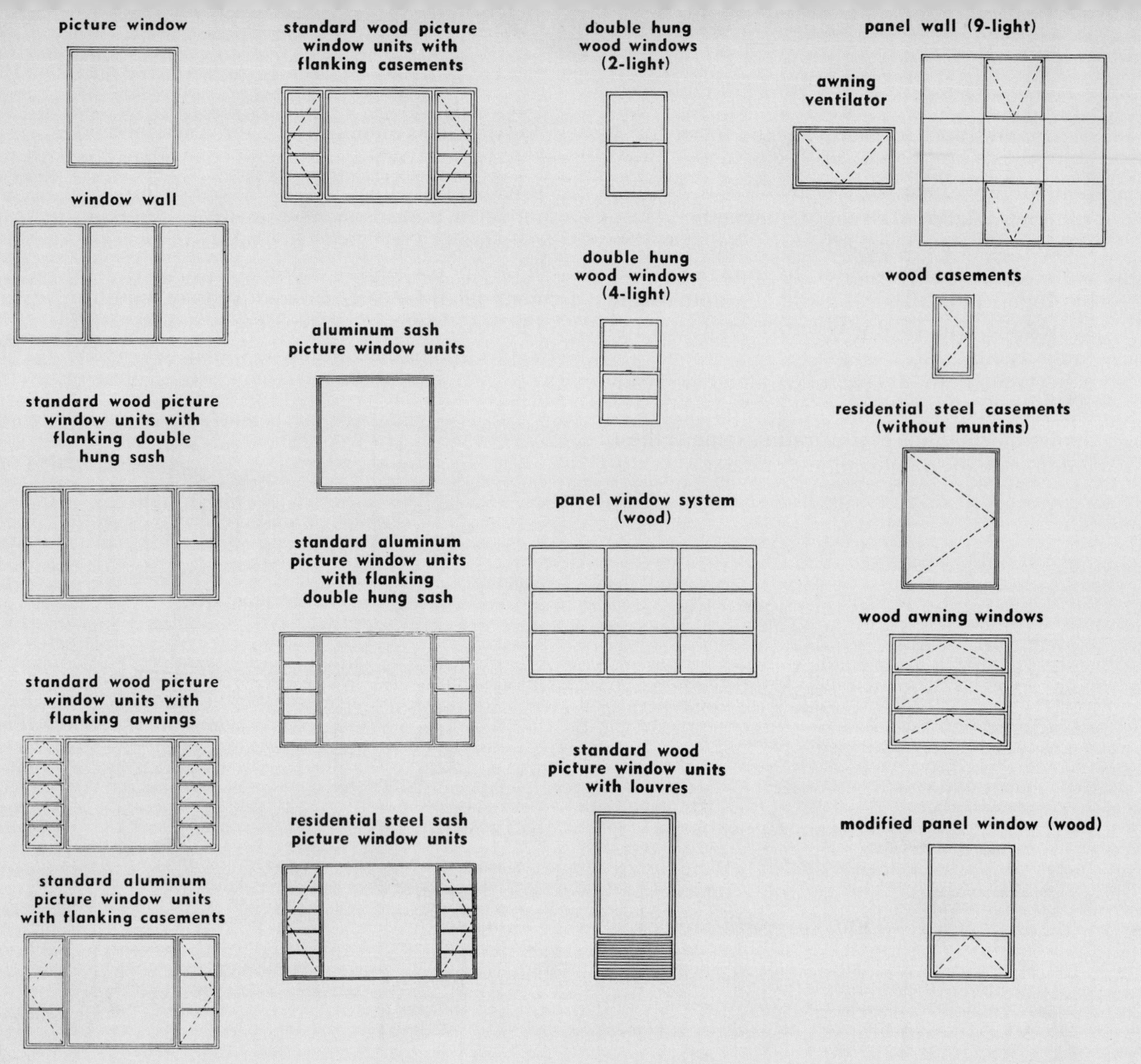

Fig. 37–10. Methods of drawing window styles on elevations.

of window to be included in this opening is then shown by a letter or number indexed to the letter or number used for the large detail drawing. Sometimes the window symbol is abbreviated and indexed in the same way to a more complete detail. Unit 70 contains further treatment of door and window schedules.

DOOR SYMBOLS

Doors are shown on elevation drawings by methods similar to those used for illustrating window style and position. They are either drawn completely if the scale permits or shown in abbreviated form. Sometimes the outline is indexed to a door schedule. The complete drawing of the door, whether shown on an elevation or on a separate detail, should show the division of panels and lights, sill, jamb, and head-trim details.

Many exterior door styles are available (Fig. 37–12). The total relationship of the door and trim to the entire elevation cannot be seen unless the door trim is also shown (Fig. 37–13).

Exterior doors are normally larger than interior doors. They must provide access for larger amounts of traffic and be sufficiently

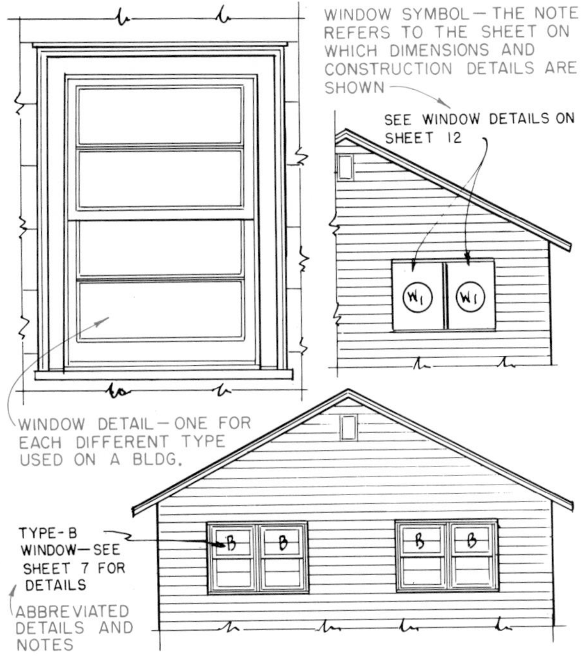

Fig. 37-11. The use of symbols and notes identifies window style.

Fig. 37-12. Examples of exterior door styles.

large to permit the movement of furniture. They must also be thick enough to provide adequate insulation and sound barriers. Common exterior door sizes include widths of 2′—8″, 3′—0″, and 3′—6″ (0.8, 0.9 and 1.1 m). Common exterior door heights range from 6′—8″ to 7′—6″ (2.0 to 2.3 m).

PROBLEMS

1. **Draw and add symbols to the elevation outline shown in Fig. 37-14.**
2. **Redesign the front elevation of your home. Change siding materials and door and window styles.**

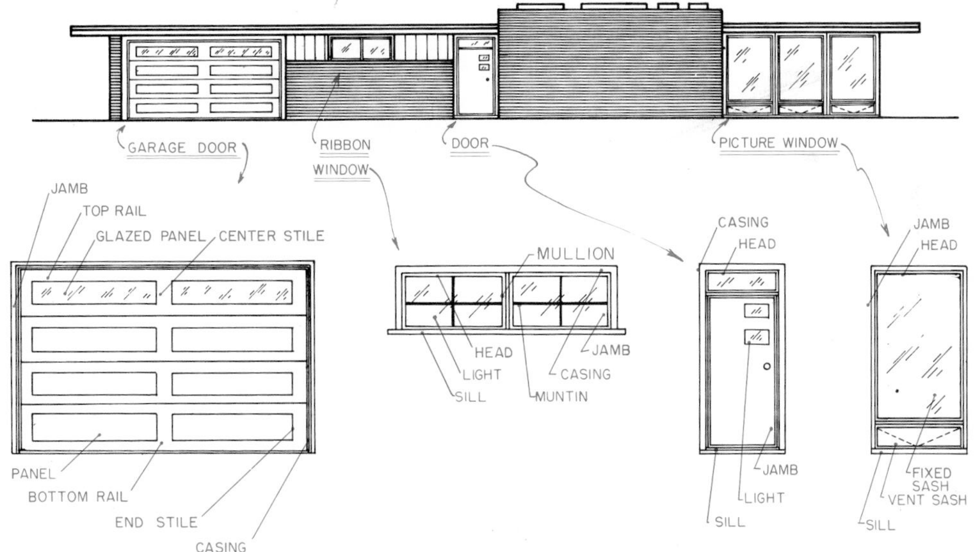

Fig. 37-13. Methods of drawing door and window trim.

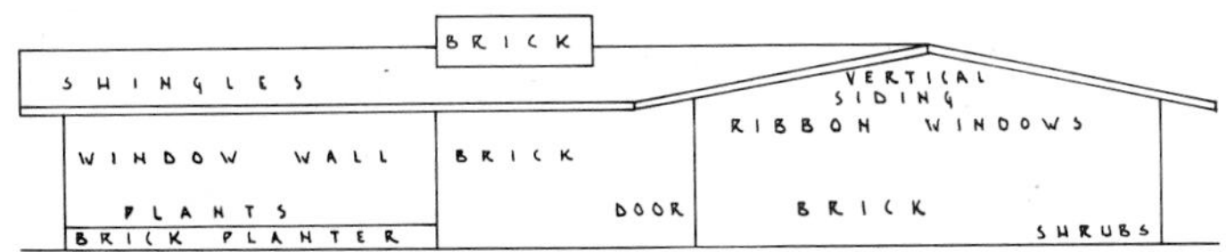

Fig. 37-14. Add symbols to this elevation.

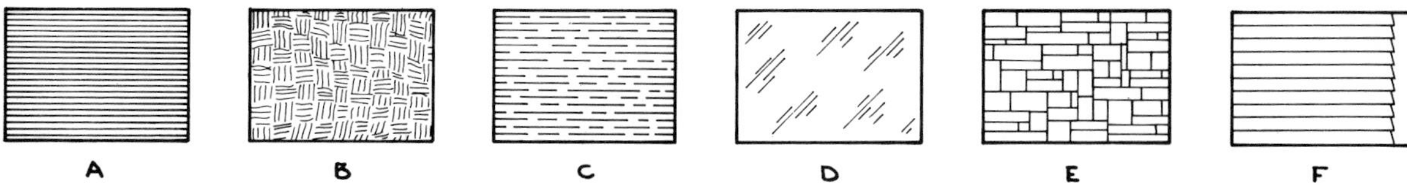

Fig. 37–15. Identify these elevation symbols.

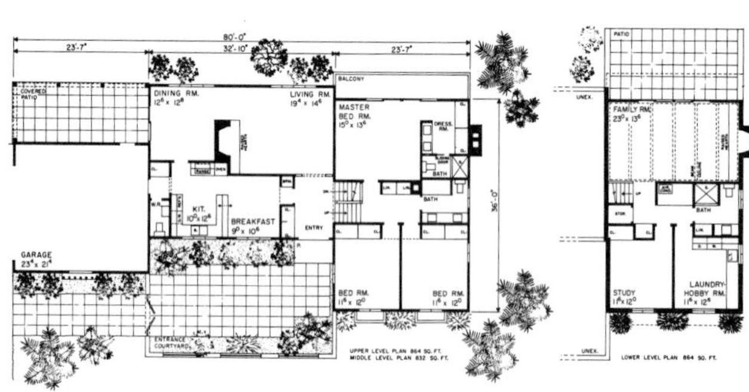

Home Planners, Inc.

Fig. 37–16. Draw the front elevation of this house, complete with symbols.

3. Add elevation symbols to an elevation of your own design.
4. Identify the elevation symbols shown in Fig. 37–15.
5. Draw the front elevation of the house shown in Fig. 37–16. Show elevation symbols.
6. Redesign and finish the front elevation of the house shown in Fig. 37–17, using brick as the basic siding material.
7. Draw the front and left-side elevations of the house shown in Fig. 37–18. Use symbols for the siding materials shown.
8. Draw the front and left-side elevations of the home shown in Fig. 37–19. Use the existing siding materials or redesign the elevation, changing the materials as you wish.

Home Planners, Inc.

Fig. 37–17. Redesign and finish this elevation.

Boise Cascade

Fig. 37–18. Draw a front and left-side elevation of this house.

Scholz Homes, Inc.

Fig. 37–19. Draw two elevations of this house.

UNIT 38

Elevation Dimensioning

Horizontal width and length dimensions are placed on floor plans. Vertical (height) dimensions are placed on elevation drawings.

Many dimensions on elevation drawings show the vertical distance from a datum line. The *datum line* is a horizontal plane that remains constant. Sea level is commonly used as the datum for many drawings, although any distance from sea level can be conveniently used.

Dimensions on elevation drawings show the height above the datum of the ground line. They also show the distance from the ground line to the floor, ceiling, and ridge and eave lines, and to the tops of chimneys, doors, and windows. Distances below the ground line are shown by dotted lines.

RULES FOR ELEVATION DIMENSIONING

Elevation dimensions must conform to basic standards to ensure consistency of interpretation. The arrows on the elevation drawing in Fig. 38–1 show the application of the following rules for elevation dimensioning:

1. Vertical elevation dimensions should be read from the right of the drawing.
2. Levels to be dimensioned should be labeled with a note, term, or abbreviation.
3. Room heights are shown by dimensioning from the floor line to the ceiling line.
4. The depth of footers (footings) is dimensioned from the ground line.
5. Heights of windows and doors are dimensioned from the floor line to the top of the windows or doors.
6. Elevation dimensions show only vertical distances. Horizontal distances are shown on the floor plan.
7. Windows and doors may be indexed to a door or window schedule, or the style of the windows and doors may be shown on the elevation drawing.
8. The roof pitch is shown by indicating the rise over the run.
9. Dimensions for small, complex, or obscure areas should be indexed to a separate detail.
10. Ground-line elevations are expressed as heights above the datum.
11. Heights of chimneys above the ridge line are dimensioned.
12. Floor and ceiling lines are shown by center lines that function as extension lines.
13. Heights of planters and walls are dimensioned from the ground line.

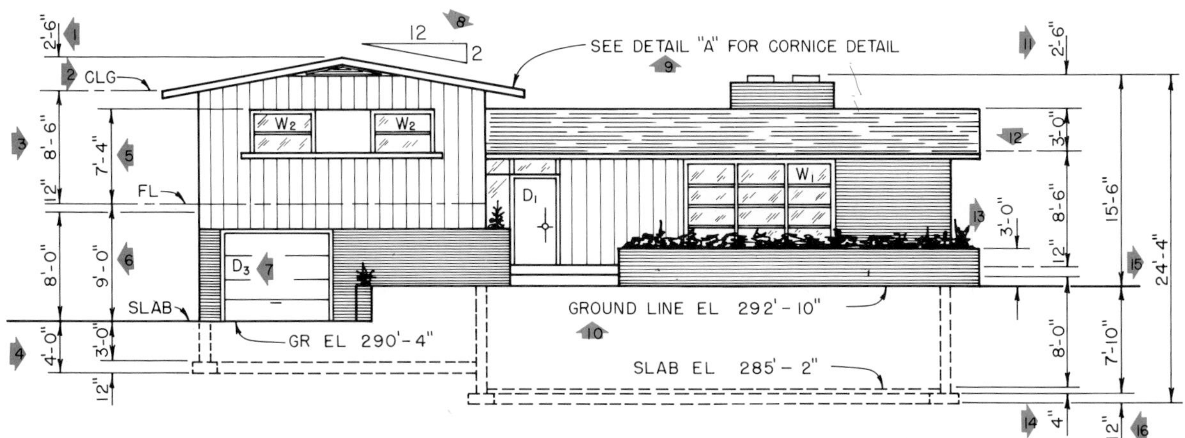

Fig. 38–1. Rules for elevation dimensioning.

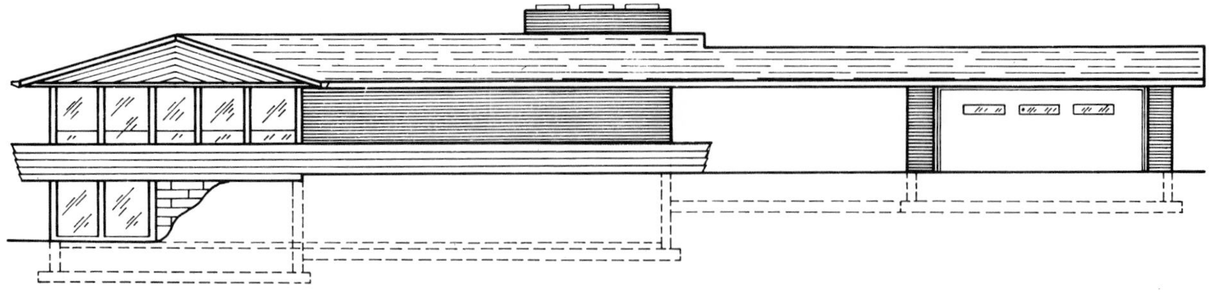

Fig. 38–2. Add dimensions to this elevation.

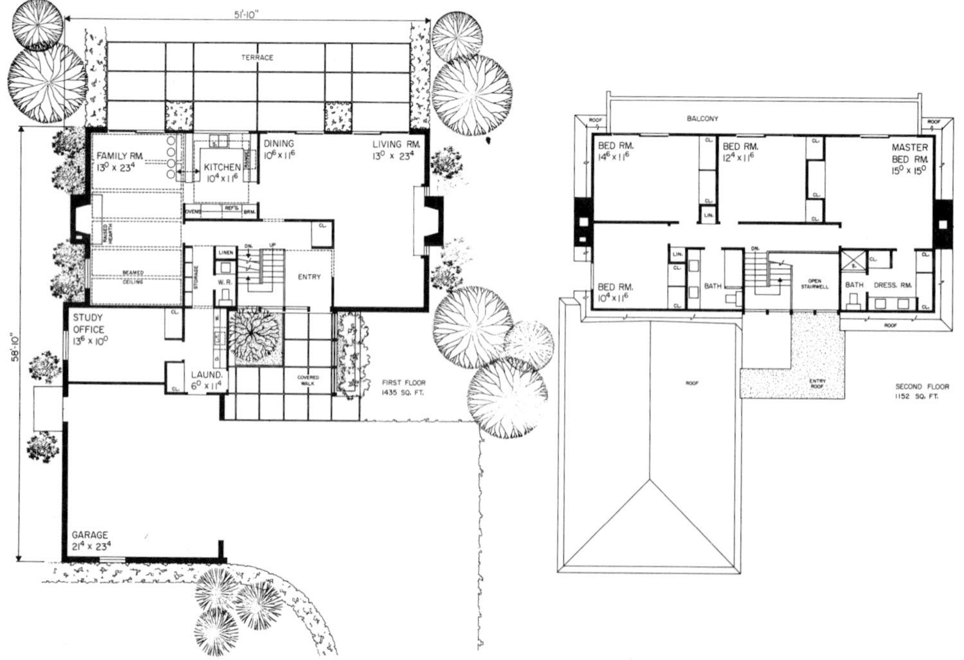

Home Planners, Inc.

Fig. 38–3. Draw and dimension one elevation of this two-story home.

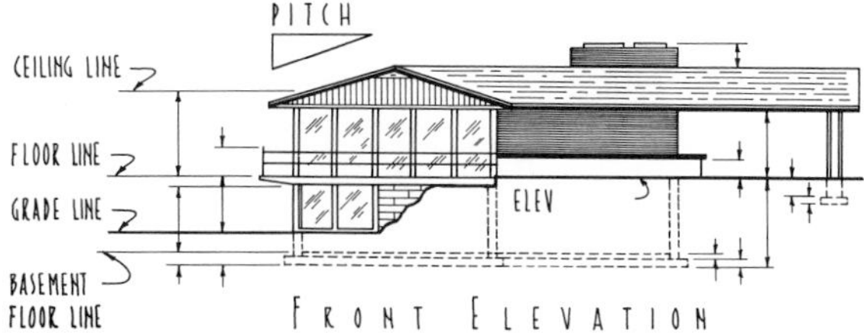

Fig. 38–4. Add dimensions to this elevation.

14. Thicknesses of slabs are dimensioned.
15. Overall height dimensions are placed on the outside of subdimensions.
16. Thicknesses of footers (footings) are dimensioned.

PROBLEMS

1. **Add the elevation dimensions to an elevation drawing of your own design.**
2. **Add dimensions to the elevation drawing shown in Fig. 38–2.**
3. **Dimension an elevation drawing of your home.**
4. **Draw an elevation of the home shown in Fig. 38–3. Completely dimension this elevation, following the rules for dimensioning outlined in this unit.**
5. **Enter the missing dimensions on the elevation shown in Fig. 38–4.**
6. **Finish and dimension the elevation shown in Fig. 38–5.**

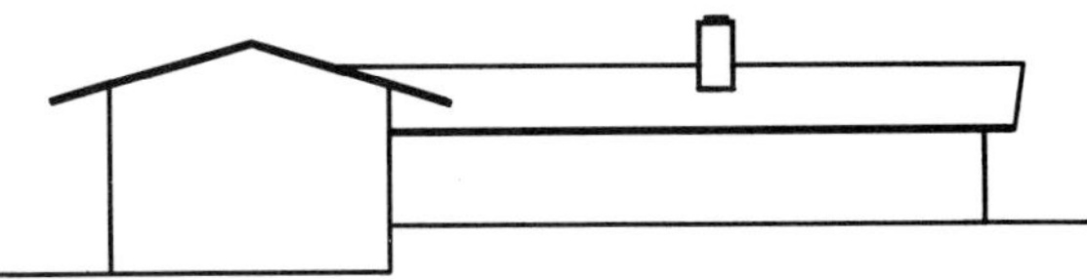

Fig. 38–5. Finish and dimension this elevation.

Home Planners, Inc.

Fig. 38–6. Draw and dimension four elevations of this house.

7. **Draw and dimension four elevations of the home in Fig. 38–6.**
8. **Define these terms: *datum line, sea level, vertical dimensions, ground line, ceiling line, ridge line, eave line, chimney line, room height, door schedule, window schedule, slab thickness, footer thickness, overall dimensions, subdimensions.***

UNIT 39

Landscape Rendering

Elevation drawings, although accurate in every detail, do not show exactly what the house will look like when it is complete and landscaped. The reason is that elevation drawings do not show the position of trees, shrubbery, and other landscape features that would be part of the total elevation design. Adding these landscape features to the elevation drawing creates a more realistic drawing of the house.

INTERPRETIVE DRAWING

Figure 39–1 shows some of the advantages of adding landscape features to an elevation drawing. The elevation shown in Fig. 39–1 at A, when dimensioned, would be adequate for construction purposes. However, the illustration shown in Fig. 39–1 at B more closely resembles the final appearance of the house.

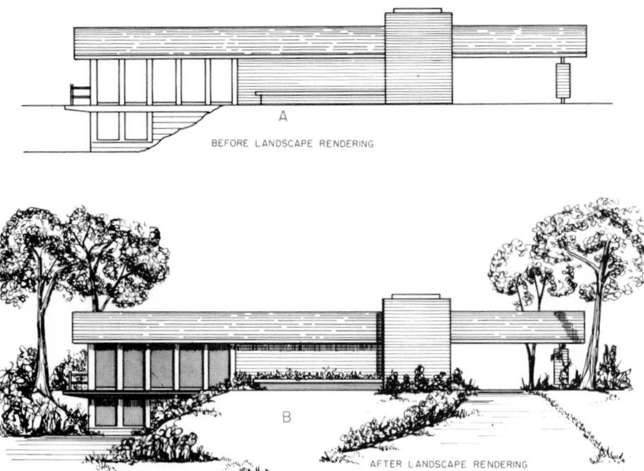

Fig. 39-1. An elevation drawing before (A) and after (B) landscape rendering.

Dimensions and hidden lines are omitted when landscape features are added to elevation drawings. Drawings of this kind are prepared only to interpret the final appearance of the house (Fig. 39–2). They are not used for construction purposes.

SEQUENCE

An elevation drawing is converted into a landscape elevation drawing in several basic steps, as shown in Fig. 39–3. After material symbols are added to the elevation, the positions of trees and shrubs are added. The elevation lines within the outlines of the trees and shrubs are erased, and details are added. Finally, shade

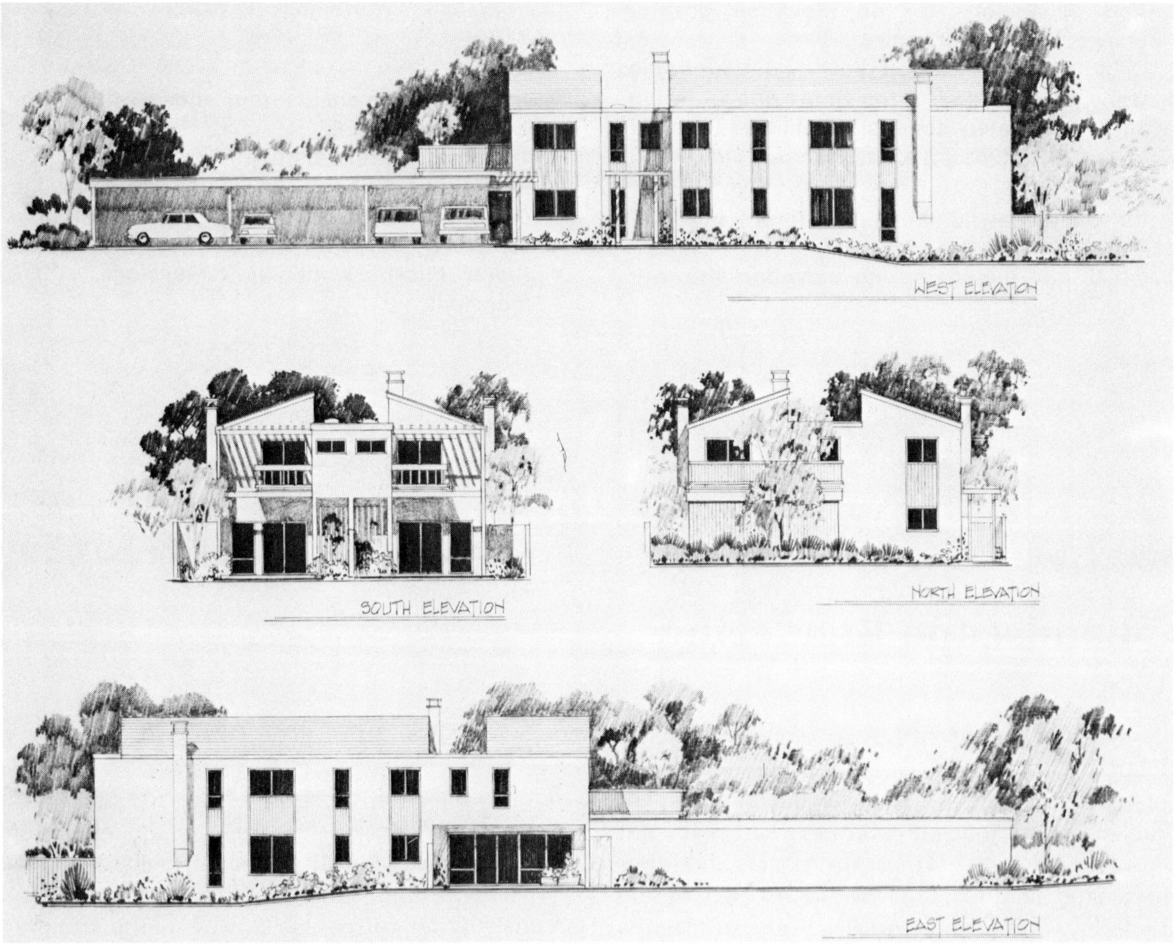

Karen and Seals Architects, Inc.

Fig. 39-2. Rendered elevations make the house appear complete and desirable.

Fig. 39–3. The sequence of adding landscape features to an elevation.

lines are added to trees, windows, roof overhangs, chimneys, and other major projections of the house. The addition of landscape features should not hide the basic lines of the house. If many trees or shrubs are placed in front of the house, it is best to draw them in their winter state.

Julius Shulman

Fig. 39–5. Landscaping greatly affects the appearance of the elevation.

Fig. 39–4 shows several methods of drawing trees and shrubs on elevation drawings. The draftsman should use the medium that best suits the elevation drawing to be rendered.

Fig. 39–4. Examples of sketches for drawing trees and shrubbery on an elevation.

Shakertown Corp.

Fig. 39-6. A house looks bare without landscaping.

Samuel Cabot, Inc.; Ralph W. Zimmerman, Architect

Fig. 39-8. Draw a front elevation of this house and add landscape features.

Fig. 39-7. Add landscape features to this elevation.

LANDSCAPE PLANNING

The importance of effective landscape design is obvious when the property shown in Fig. 39–5 is compared with the property shown in Fig. 39–6. Functional landscape planning not only enhances the appearance of the house but also provides shade from the sun and a baffle from the wind. When carefully planned, landscaping can provide area privacy and traffic control.

PROBLEMS

1. **Add landscape features to the elevation shown in Fig. 39–7.**
2. **Add trees, shrubs, plants, and shadows to an elevation of your own design.**
3. **Add landscape features to an elevation drawing of your home. Improve the present landscape treatment.**
4. **Draw a front elevation of the house shown in Fig. 39–8. Add landscape features to this drawing.**
5. **Define these terms: *landscape rendering, interpretive drawings, shade lines.***

SECTION 8

Pictorial Drawings

Pictorial drawings, both isometric and perspective, are picture-like drawings. They show several sides of an object in one drawing. Isometric drawings are used extensively in mechanical engineering work. The perspective drawing is more popular as an architectural pictorial drawing. Since the subject of most architectural pictorial drawings is much larger than that of most engineering drawings, perspective techniques are necessary to eliminate distortion of the object.

Bethlehem Steel Corporation

UNIT 40

Exteriors

In perspective drawings, the parts of a building that are furthest from your view appear to recede. For example, as you look down a railroad track, the tracks appear to come together and vanish at a point on the distant horizon. Similarly, the horizontal lines of the building shown in Fig. 40–1 appear to come together. A *perspective drawing,* more than any other kind of drawing, resembles a photograph of the exterior of a building. Notice the similarity of the perspective drawing of a building (Fig. 40–2A) and the photograph of the building (Fig. 40–2B).

On the perspective drawing, the receding lines of a building are purposely drawn closer together on one side or several sides of the building to create the illusion of depth. The point at which these lines intersect on a perspective drawing is known as the *vanishing point.* Just as railroad tracks would appear to come together at the horizon, the vanishing points in a perspective drawing are always placed on a horizon line. In preparing perspective drawings, the horizon line is the same as your line of sight. If the horizon line is placed through the building, the building will appear at your eye level. If the horizon line is placed

Libby-Owens-Ford Company

Fig. 40–1. Long horizontal lines appear to meet.

Haigh Jamgochian, Architect

Fig. 40–2A. Perspective drawing of the building shown in Fig. 40–2B.

Haigh Jamgochian

Fig. 40–2B. Photograph of the building shown in Fig. 40–2A.

below the building, it will appear to be above your eye level. If the horizon line is placed above the building, it will appear to be below your line of sight (Fig. 40–3). Applications of horizon-line placement are shown in Figs. 40–4 through the building, 40–5 below the building, and 40–6 above the building.

Perspective drawings do not reveal the true size and shape of the building. Perspective drawings are never used for working designs.

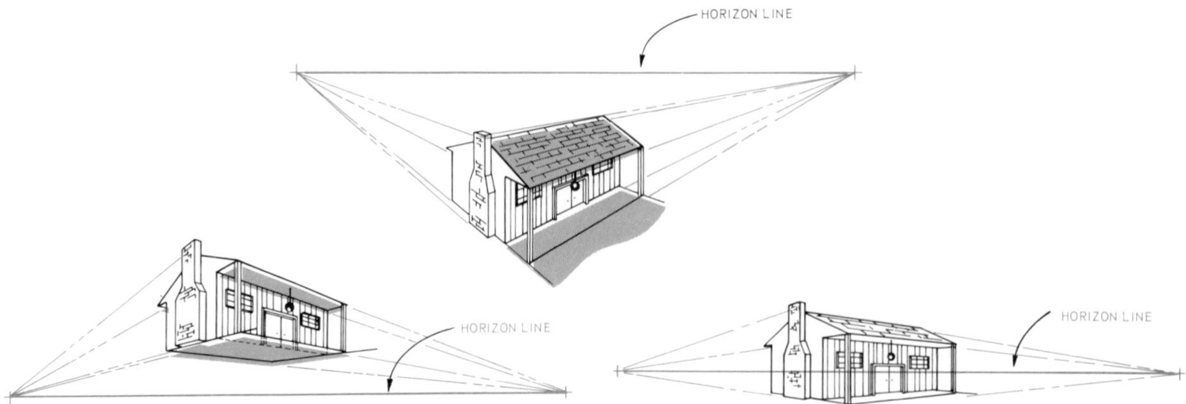

Fig. 40–3. The effect of horizon-line placement.

Steel Products News Bureau

Fig. 40–4. The horizon extends through this building.

To make the drawing appear more realistic, the actual length of the receding sides of the drawing are shortened. Figure 40–7 shows a perspective drawing with shortened sides and an *isometric drawing* which is prepared to the true dimension of the building. The two sides of the isometric drawing appear distorted because we are accustomed to seeing areas decrease in depth from our point of vision.

Boise Cascade

Fig. 40–5. The horizon is below this building.

Home Planners, Inc.

Fig. 40–6. The horizon line placed above a structure.

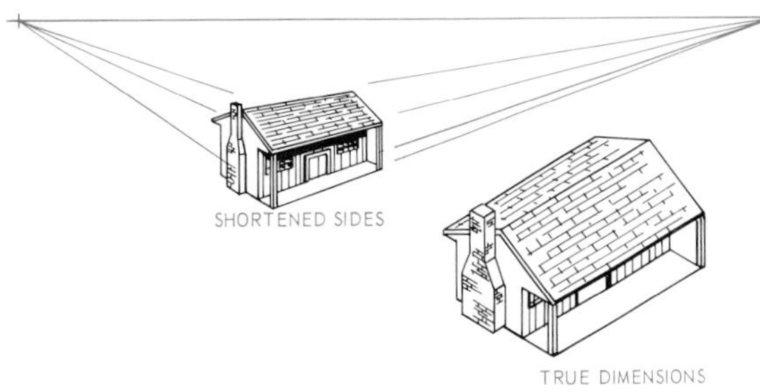

Fig. 40–7. The length of receding lines should be shortened on perspective drawings.

ONE-POINT PERSPECTIVE

A one-point perspective is a drawing in which the front view is drawn to its true scale and all receding sides are projected to a single vanishing point located on the horizon. If the vanishing point is placed directly behind the object, as shown in Fig. 40–8, no sides would show unless they were drawn with dashes (hidden lines). If the vanishing point is placed directly to the right or to the left of the object, with the horizon passing through the object, only one side (left or right) will show. If the object is placed above the horizon line and vanishing point, the bottom of the object will show. If the object is placed below the horizon line and vanishing point, the top of the object will show.

The one-point perspective is relatively simple to draw. The front view is drawn to the exact scale of the building. The corners of the front view are then projected to one vanishing point. Follow these steps in drawing or sketching a one-point perspective:

1. Draw the front view of the object (building). Draw the horizon line above, below, or through the building.
2. Mark the position of the vanishing point on the horizon line: to the left if you want to see the left side of the building; to the right if you want to see the right side of the building; to the rear if you want to see only the front.
3. Project all corners of the front view to the vanishing point, as shown in Fig. 40–9.
4. Estimate the depths of the receding sides, and draw a vertical line parallel with the vertical lines of the front view to indicate the back corner of the building.
5. Make all object lines heavy, and eradicate the horizon line and projection lines leading to the vanishing point.

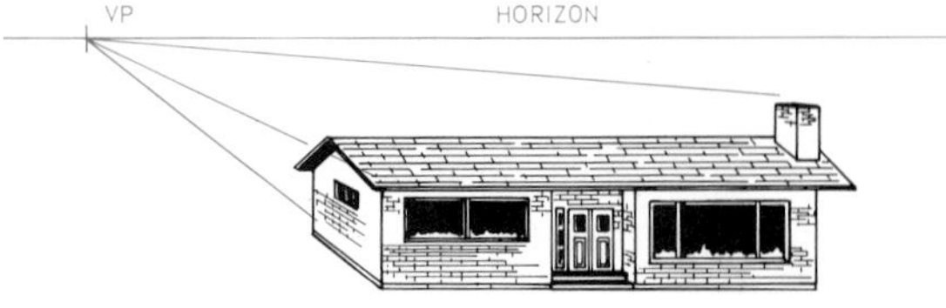

Fig. 40–9. Connect corners of the front view to the vanishing point.

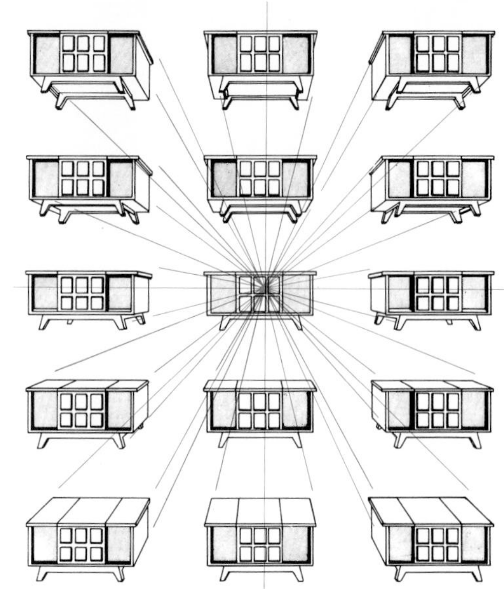

Fig. 40–8. A one-point perspective can show any three sides.

TWO-POINT PERSPECTIVE

A two-point perspective is a drawing in which the receding sides are projected to two vanishing points, one on each end of the horizon line (Fig. 40–10). In a two-point perspective, no sides are drawn exactly to scale. All sides recede to vanishing points. Therefore, the only true-length line on a two-point perspective is the corner of the building from which the sides are projected.

When the vanishing points are placed close together on the horizon line, considerable distortion results because of the acute receding angles (Fig. 40–11). When the vanishing points are placed further apart, the drawing looks more realistic. One vanishing point is often placed further from the building than the other van-

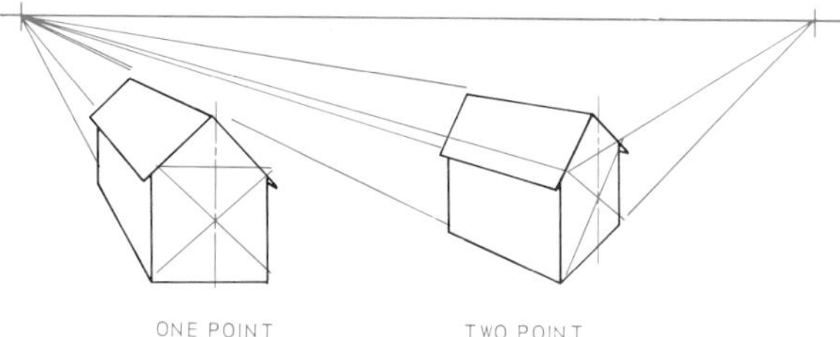

Fig. 40–10. **The use of two vanishing points on the horizon, compared to one.**

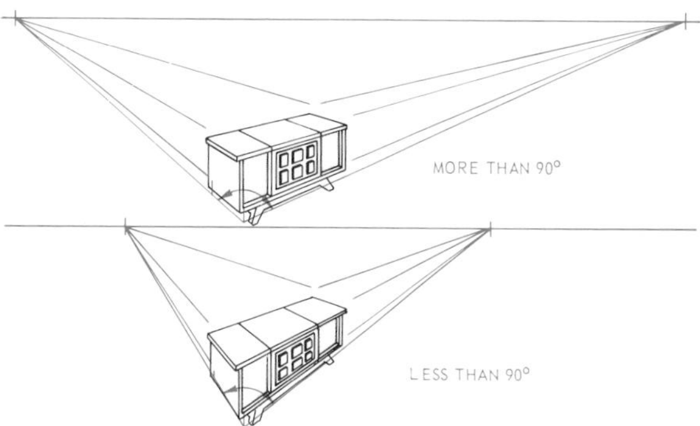

Fig. 40–11. The distance between vanishing points affects the angles of the object.

ishing point. This placement allows one side of the building to recede at a sharp angle and the front of the building to recede less sharply. The vanishing points for the perspective drawing shown in Fig. 40–12 have been placed closer to the left of the building than to the right. Consequently, the receding angle on the left is great, and the receding angle from the front of the building is slight.

VERTICAL PLACEMENT

The distance an object is placed above or below the horizon line also affects the amount of distortion in the drawing. Moving an object a greater distance vertically from the horizon line has the same effect as moving the vanishing points closer together. Objects placed close to the horizon line, either on it, above it, or below it, are less distorted than objects placed a great distance from the horizon (Fig. 40–13).

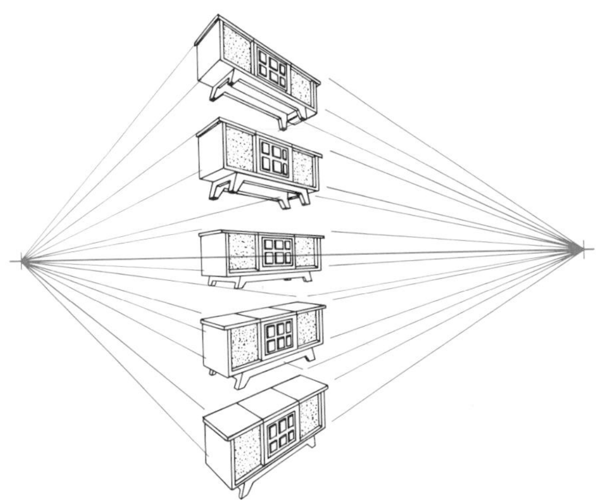

Fig. 40–13. Less distortion occurs close to the horizon.

New Homes Guide

Fig. 40–12. The effect of placing the left vanishing point closer to the building than the right vanishing point.

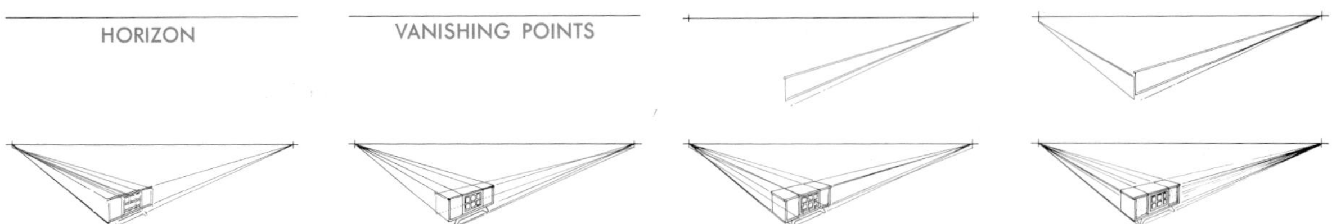

Fig. 40–14. Steps in preparing a two-point perspective.

SEQUENCE

In drawing or sketching a simple two-point perspective, the steps outlined in Fig. 40–14 can be followed. However, in projecting a two-point perspective from an established floor plan, the steps in Fig. 40–15 should be followed:

1. Draw a horizontal picture-plane line.
2. Position the floor plan 30° with the picture plane.

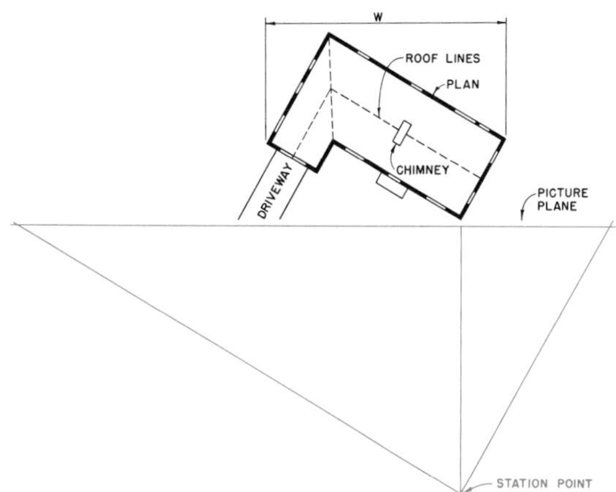

Fig. 40–15A. Establish the picture plane and station point.

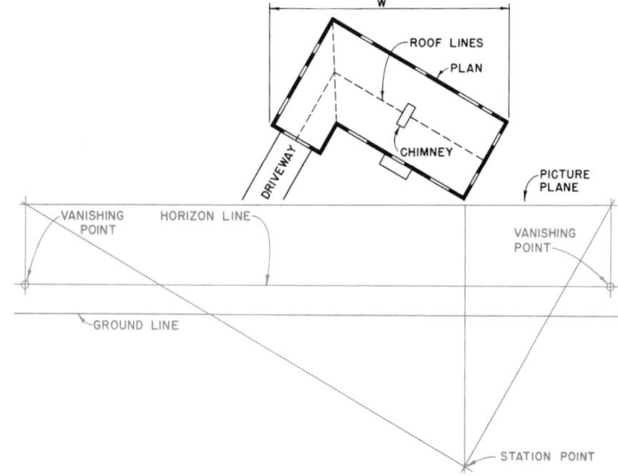

Fig. 40–15B. Locate the vanishing points and ground line.

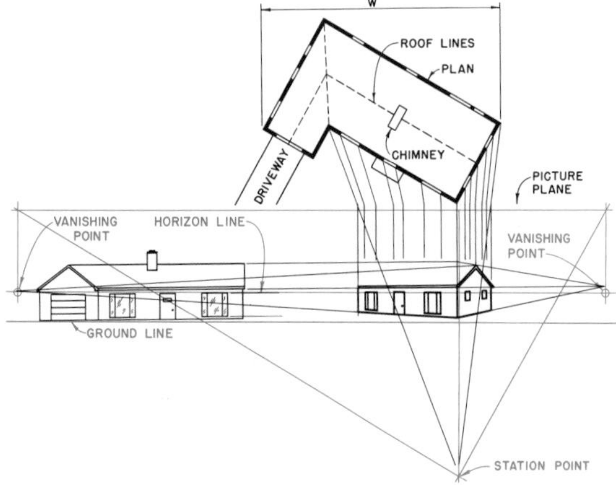

Fig. 40–15C. Project and intersect similar floor-plan and elevation lines.

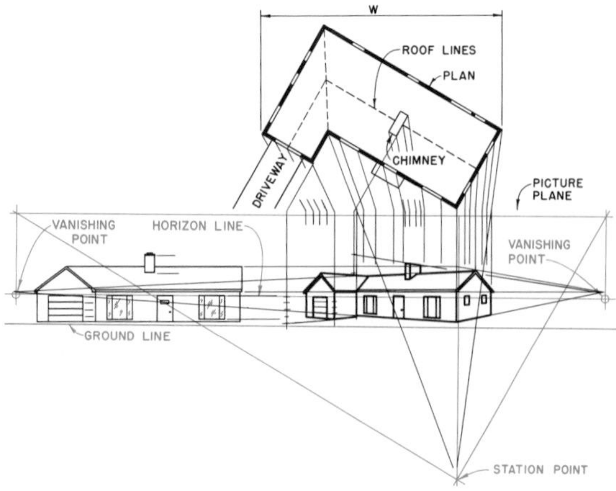

Fig. 40–15D. Project building extensions from the floor plan and elevation.

3. Locate the station point down from the picture plane about twice the width of the floor plan.
4. Project lines from the station point to the picture plane parallel to the front and end of the floor plan (Fig. 40–15A).
5. Draw the ground line.
6. Draw a horizon line about 6 feet or 2 m above the ground, depending on your scale.
7. Project lines down from the picture-plane intersection found in step 4 that intersect the horizon line to establish the vanishing points (Fig. 40–15B).
8. Position the elevation drawing on the ground line.
9. Extend key elevation lines horizontally.
10. Project key floor-plan lines to the station point.
11. Where the floor-plan lines intersect the picture plane, project lines down vertically.
12. Establish the corners of the building, the doors, and the windows at the points of intersection.
13. Connect intersections to the vanishing points to establish perspective outline (Fig. 40–15C).
14. Establish a secondary base line.
15. Add the building extensions.
16. Locate and draw the chimney (Fig. 40–15D).

THREE-POINT PERSPECTIVE

Three-point-perspective drawings are used to overcome the height distortion of tall buildings. In a one- or two-story building the vertical lines recede so slightly that, for practical purposes, they are drawn vertically. However, the top or bottom of extremely tall buildings appears smaller than the area nearest the viewer. A third vanishing point, as shown in Fig. 40–16, may be used to provide the desired recession. The smaller the vertical distance between the horizon and vanishing point 3, the more closely the vertical lines approach a parallel state and the less is the distortion. The farther vanishing point 3 is placed from the object, the more acute the angle and, therefore, the greater is the distortion. If vanishing point 3 is placed so far below or above the horizon that the angles are hardly distinguishable, then the advantage of a three-point perspective is lost, and a two-point perspective with parallel vertical lines would be desirable.

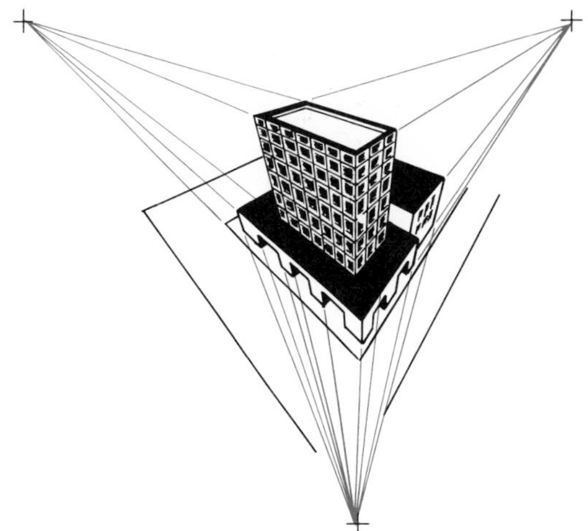

Fig. 40–16. The use of a third vanishing point.

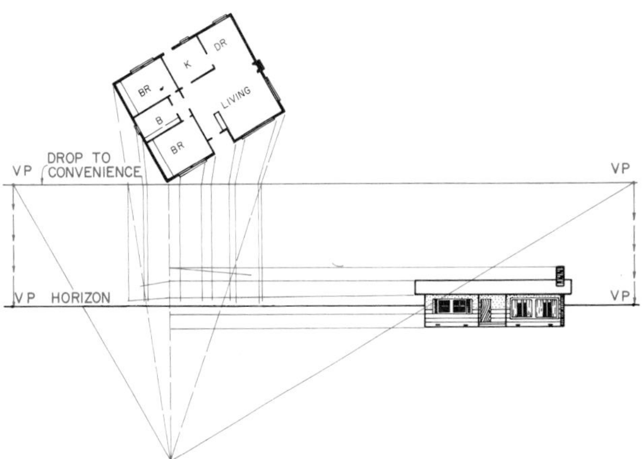

Fig. 40–17. Project a two-point perspective of this house.

PROBLEMS

1. **Project a two-point-perspective drawing from the floor plan and elevation shown in Fig. 40–17.**
2. **Draw a two-point perspective of the house shown in Fig. 40–18, using the scale ⅛″ = 1′—0″.**

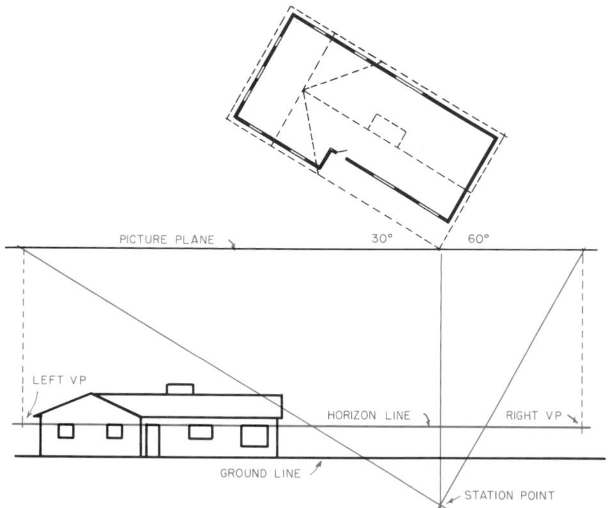

Fig. 40–18. **Draw a two-point perspective of this house.**

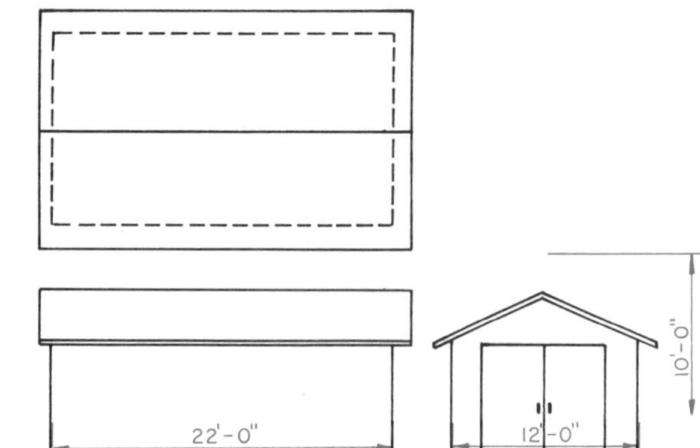

Fig. 40–20. **Draw a one- and a two-point perspective of this garage.**

Libbey-Owens-Ford Company

Fig. 40–19. **Find the vanishing points.**

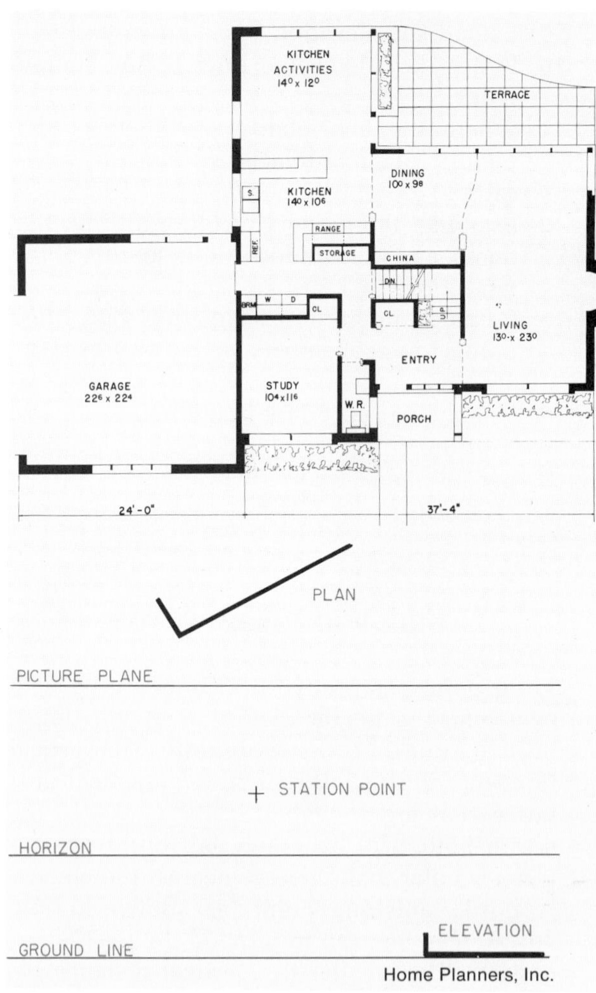

Home Planners, Inc.

Fig. 40–21. **Design an elevation and project a two-point perspective of this plan.**

3. **Trace the photograph shown in Fig. 40–19. Find the position of the vanishing point and the horizon.**
4. **Project a one- and two-point-perspective drawing of the garage shown in Fig. 40–20.**
5. **Use the layout and floor plan shown in Fig. 40–21 to project a two-point perspective. Sketch a design of the elevation prior to projection.**
6. **Draw a one-point and a two-point perspective of your own home.**
7. **Draw a two-point perspective of a building of your own design.**
8. **Sketch a three-point perspective of the tallest building in your community.**
9. **Define these terms: *pictorial, one-point perspective, two-point perspective, three-point perspective, isometric, vanishing point, horizontal, vertical, parallel, horizon, station point, base line.***

UNIT 41

Interiors

A pictorial drawing of the interior of a building may be an isometric drawing, a one-point-perspective drawing, or a two-point-perspective drawing. Pictorial drawings are prepared for the entire floor plan (pictorial floor plan). More commonly, however, pictorial drawings are prepared for a single room or living area.

ISOMETRIC DRAWINGS

Isometric drawings using constant angles of 30° from the horizontal are most effective for pictorial floor plans (Fig. 41–1). There are no receding lines on an isometric drawing. Isometric lines are always parallel and may be prepared to an exact scale.

Isometric drawings of room interiors are usually not desirable, because they lack receding lines.

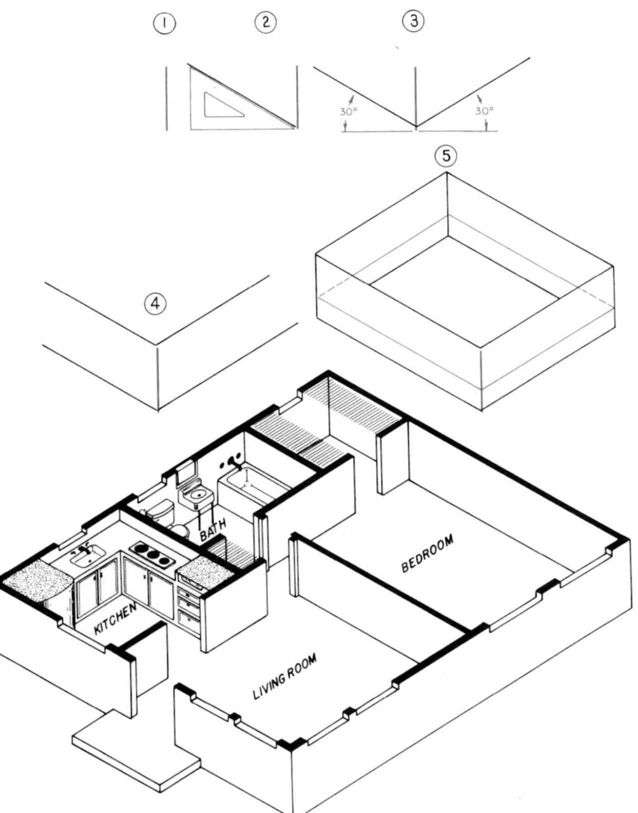

Fig. 41–1. An isometric drawing of a floor plan.

ONE-POINT PERSPECTIVE

A one-point perspective of a room is a drawing in which all the intersections between walls, floors, ceilings, and furniture may be projected to one vanishing point (Fig. 41–2). Drawing a one-point perspective of the interior of a room is similar to drawing the inside of a box with the front of the box removed. In a one-point interior perspective, walls perpendicular to the plane of projection, such as the back wall, are drawn to their proper scale and proportion. The vanishing point on the horizon line is then placed somewhere on this wall (actually behind this wall). The points of intersection where this wall intersects the ceiling and floor are then projected from the vanishing point to form the intersection between the side walls and the ceiling and the side walls and the floor.

Rendering by George A. Parenti for the Masonite Corporation

Fig. 41–2. A one-point perspective.

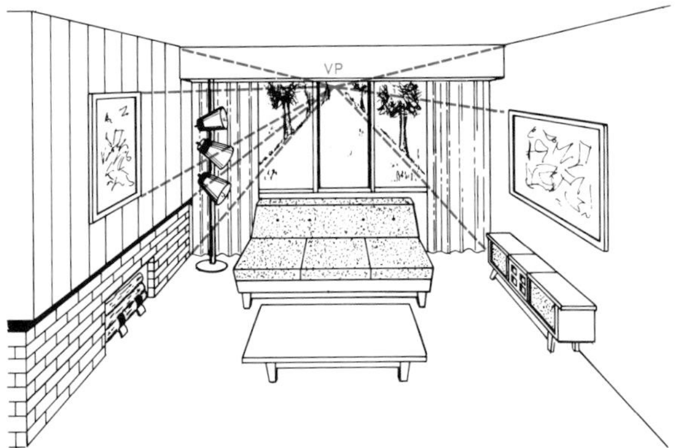

Fig. 41-3A. The effect of a high central vanishing point.

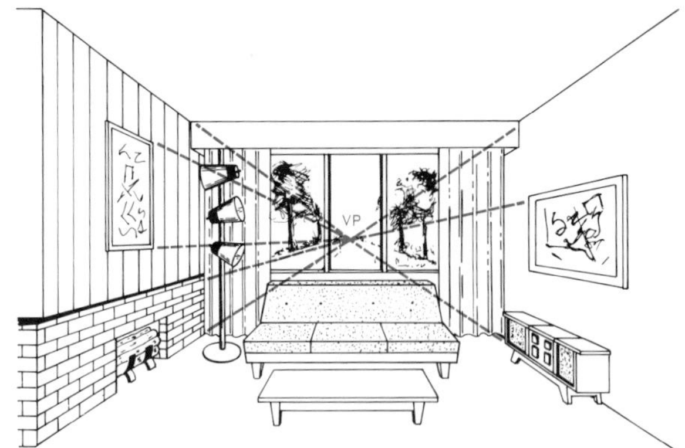

Fig. 41-3B. The effect of a centrally located vanishing point.

Fig. 41-3C. The effect of a low central vanishing point.

Vertical Placement

If the vanishing point is placed high, very little of the ceiling will show in the projection, but much of the floor area will be revealed (Fig. 41–3A). If the vanishing point is placed near the center of the back wall, an equal amount of ceiling and floor will show (Fig. 41–3B). If the vanishing point is placed low on the wall, much of the ceiling but very little of the floor will be shown (Fig. 41–3C). Since the horizon line and the vanishing point are at your eye level, you can see that the position of the vanishing point affects the angle from which you view the object.

Horizontal Placement

Moving the vanishing point from right to left on the back wall has an effect on the view of the side walls. If the vanishing point is placed to the left of the wall, more of the right wall will be revealed. Conversely, if the vanishing point is placed near the right side, more of the left wall will be revealed in the projection. If the vanishing point is placed in the center, an equal amount of right wall and left wall will be

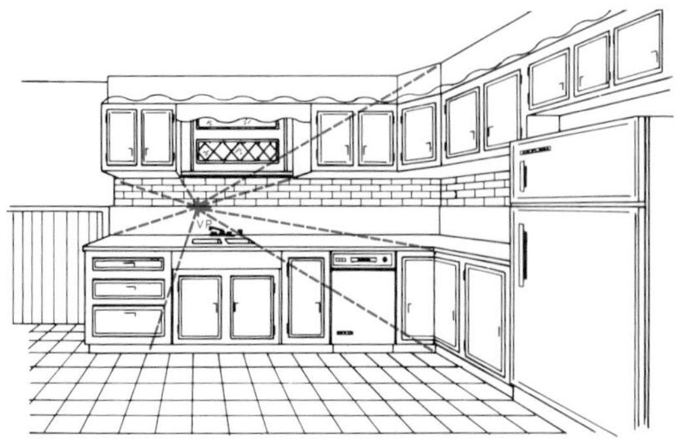

Fig. 41-4A. The effect of the horizontal placement of the vanishing point.

Home Planners, Inc.

Fig. 41-4B. Left-wall emphasis is obtained by placing the vanishing point to the extreme right.

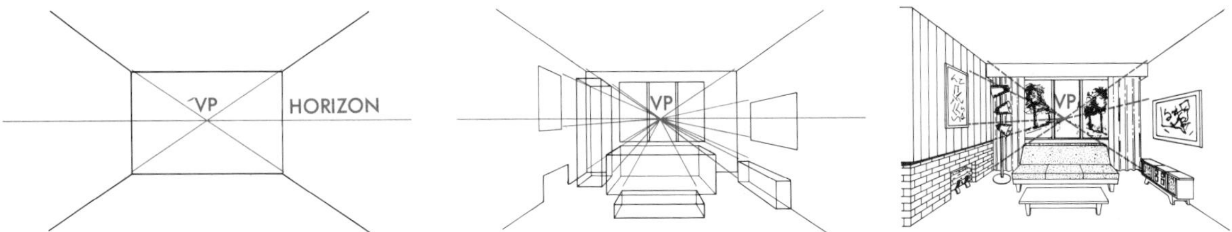

Fig. 41–5. Always block-in furniture and people.

shown (Fig. 41–4A). When one wall should dominate, place the vanishing point on the extreme end of the opposite wall, as shown in Fig. 41–4B.

When projecting wall offsets and furniture, always block-in the overall size of the item to form a perspective view, as shown in Fig. 41–5. The details of furniture or closets or even of persons can then be completed within this blocked-in cube or series of cubes.

TWO-POINT PERSPECTIVE

Two-point perspectives are normally prepared to show the final design and decor of two walls of a room. The base line on an interior two-point perspective is similar to the base line on an exterior two-point perspective. The base line in the drawing shown in Fig. 41–6 is the corner of the fireplace. Two rooms or an L-shaped room can then be shown projected to each vanishing point.

Once the walls are projected to the vanishing points in the two-point perspective, each object in the room can also be projected to the vanishing point as in external two-point perspectives. Projecting the coffee table shown in Fig. 41–7 to the vanishing point is the same as projecting a flat-roof house or building.

The sequence of steps in drawing two-point interior perspectives is shown in Fig. 41–8. Figure 41–9 shows the relationships between working drawings and perspective drawings.

Home Planners, Inc.

Fig. 41–6. A two-point interior perspective.

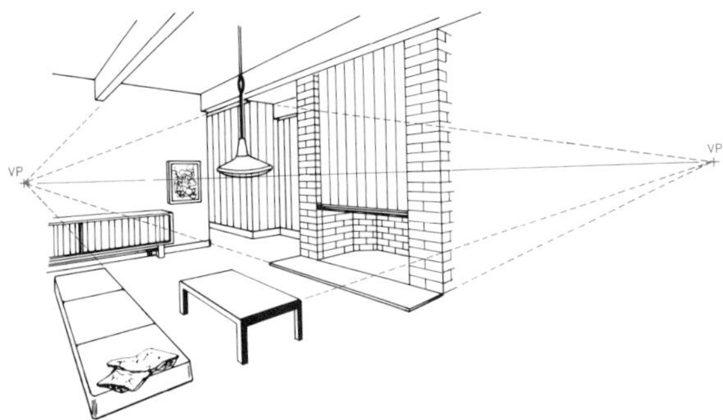

Fig. 41–7. Each object in a room is projected to the vanishing point.

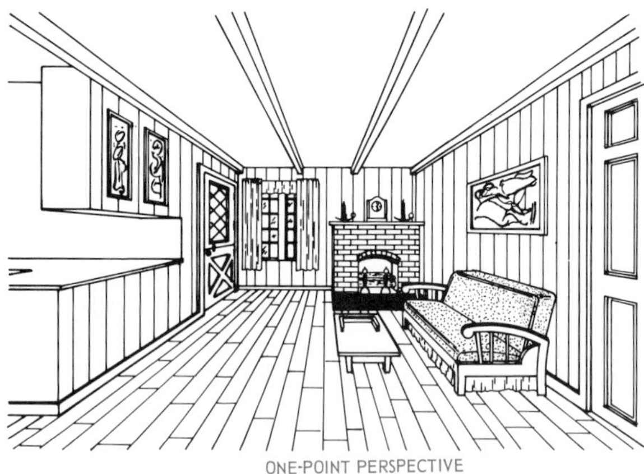

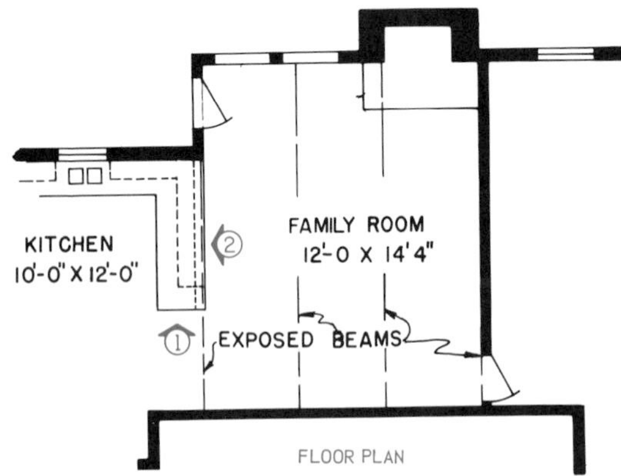

Fig. 41–9. A comparison of a plan and a perspective drawing.

PROBLEMS

1. Trace the drawing shown in Fig. 41–10. With a colored pencil, project the ceiling and floor lines to find the vanishing points and the horizon line.

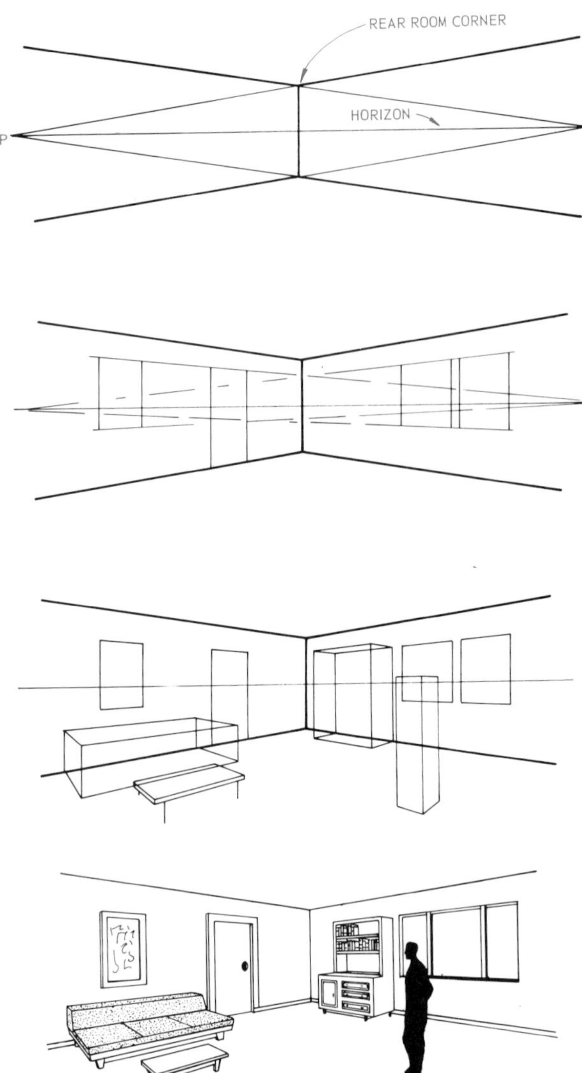

Fig. 41–8. The sequence used in drawing two-point interior perspectives.

2. Trace the perspective shown in Fig. 41–11. Find the position of the vanishing points. Extend the drawing to include the right wall of the living area.
3. Prepare a one-point interior perspective of your own room.
4. Prepare a one-point perspective of a room of your own design.
5. Draw a one-point interior perspective of a classroom. Prepare one drawing to show much of the ceiling and left wall. Prepare another drawing to show much of the floor and right wall.
6. Define these terms: *isometric, interior perspective.*

Rendering by George A. Parenti for the Masonite Corporation

Fig. 41–10. Find the vanishing points.

Rendering by George A. Parenti for the Masonite Corporation

Fig. 41–11. Extend the living area to include the right wall.

UNIT 42

Rendering

To render a pictorial drawing is to make the drawing appear more realistic. This may be done through the media of pencil, pen and ink, water colors, pastels, or air brush. Drawings are rendered by adding realistic texture to the materials and establishing shade and shadow patterns.

MEDIA

Soft pencils are one of the most effective media for rendering architectural drawings because tones can be greatly varied by the weight of the line used. Smudge blending can be accomplished by rubbing a finger over penciled areas to add tone.

Pen-and-ink renderings of architectural drawings vary greatly. Strokes must be placed further apart to create light effects and closer together to produce darker effects (Fig. 42–1).

SHADE

When you shade an object you lighten the part of the object exposed to the sun or other light sources and darken the part of the object not exposed to the sun or light source (Fig. 42–2). No-

General Motors Corporation; Signature Homes

Fig. 42–1. Two styles of renderings.

Fig. 42–2. The use of shading to show sunlight on high areas.

tice how the lower part of Fig. 42–3 is shaded darker and the top shaded lighter to show the different exposure to the sun. Likewise the right portion of Fig. 42–4 is shaded darker to denote distance and lack of direct sunlight. When objects with sharp corners are exposed to strong sunlight, one area may be extremely light and the other side of the object extremely dark. However, when objects and buildings have areas that are round (cylindrical), so that their parts move gradually from dark to light areas, a gradual shading from extremely dark to extremely light must be made.

SHADOW

In order to determine what areas of the building will be drawn darker to indicate shadowing, the angle of the sun in the illustration must be established. When the angle of the sun is established (Fig. 42–5), all shading should be consistent with the direction and angle of the shadow. On buildings that are drawn consider-

Port Authority of New York and New Jersey

Fig. 42–3. The use of shading to show depth and light angles.

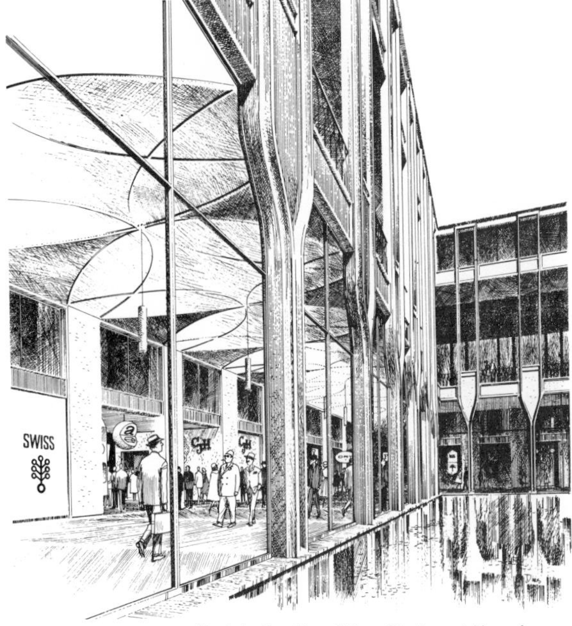

Port Authority of New York and New Jersey

Fig. 42-4. Methods of shading to show distance.

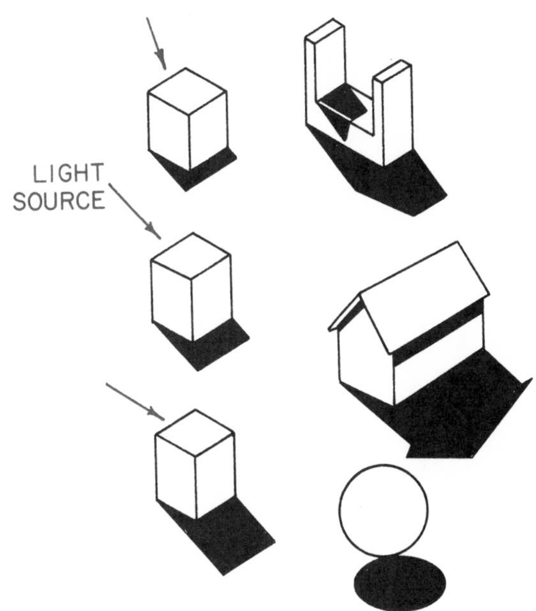

Fig. 42-5. Shadow the area opposite the light source.

ably below the horizon line, shadow patterns will often reveal more than the actual outline can reveal. Notice how the shadow patterns of the balconies in Fig. 42–6 reveal their shape and depth. Areas are shaded to show the shape of the entire house, the roof overhang, trees, fences, walls, and shrubbery. Notice the realism achieved in the house shown in Fig. 42–7 by providing projection of tree shadows and roof-overhang shadows on the house. Adding

Fig. 42-6. Shadows reveal hidden outlines.

Southern Mill Homes

Fig. 42–7. Shadows are needed to add realism.

shadows from structural features such as roof overhangs and columns, as shown in Fig. 42–8, helps show the building as it is usually viewed.

United States Steel Corporation

Fig. 42–8. The use of shadow to emphasize building features.

TEXTURE

Giving texture to an architectural drawing means making building materials appear as rough or as smooth as they actually are. Smooth surfaces are no problem since they are very reflective and hence are very light. Only a few reflection lines are usually necessary to illustrate smoothness of surfaces such as aluminum, glass, and painted surfaces. On rough surfaces, the thickness or roughness of the material can often be shown by shading.

SEQUENCE

In preparing pictorial renderings, proceed in the following sequence, as shown in Fig. 42–9.

1. Block-in with single lines the projection of the perspective (Fig. 42–9A).
2. Sketch the outline of building materials in preparation for rendering (Fig. 42–9B). This work can be done with a soft pencil, a ruling pen, or a crow-quill pen. Establish a semi-angle and sketch shadows and shading. Darken windows, door areas, and under-roof overhangs.
3. Add texture to the building materials. For example, show the position of each brick with a chisel-point pencil. Leave the mortar

Fig. 42–9A. Block in the basic outline.

Fig. 42–9B. Prepare the sketch for rendering.

Fig. 42–9C. Texture is added to building materials.

Home Planners, Inc.

Fig. 42–9D. The completed rendering.

space white and lighten the pressure for the areas that are in direct sunlight (Fig. 42–9C).

4. Complete the rendering by emphasizing light and dark areas and establishing more visible contrasts of light and dark shadow patterns (Fig. 42–9D).

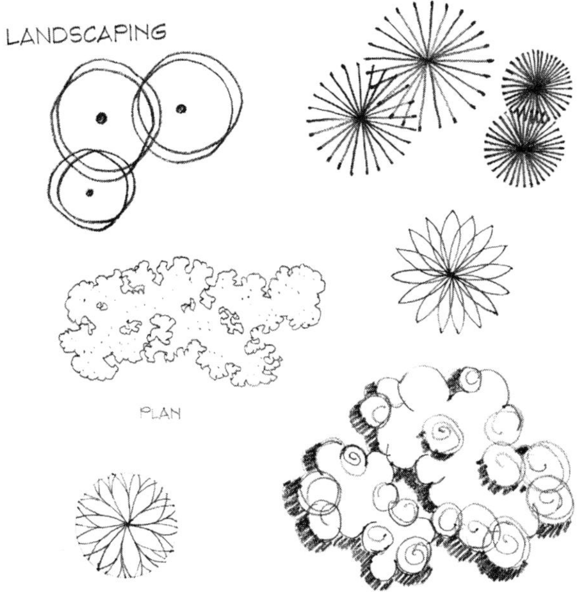

Fig. 42–10. Methods of rendering trees and shrubs on plan views.

TECHNIQUES

Figures 42–10 through 42–20 show the application of various rendering techniques to architectural drawings. Figure 42–10 shows some of the techniques used to draw trees and shrubs on plan views, and Fig. 42–11 shows some common methods of drawing trees on elevations. These methods are used to show tree placement without blocking out the view of the buildings. Figure 42–12 shows depth and shadows in rendering windows. Notice that some

Fig. 42–11. Methods of rendering trees and shrubs on elevations.

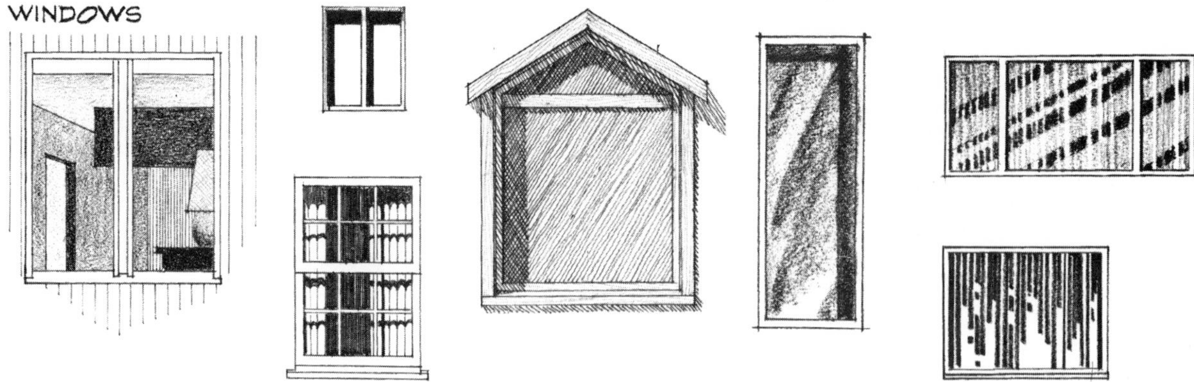

Fig. 42–12. Window-rendering techniques.

windows are rendered to show reflected light, and others are drawn to reveal the room behind, as though the window were open. Rendering fences and walls (Fig. 42–13) and rendering chimneys (Fig. 42–14) require a combination of shade, shadow, and texture techniques.

Sketches of people are often necessary to show the relative size of a building and to put the total drawing in proper perspective. Since people should not interfere with the view of the building, architects frequently draw people in outline or in extremely simple form (Fig. 42–15A). People are also used to show traffic

FENCES AND WALLS

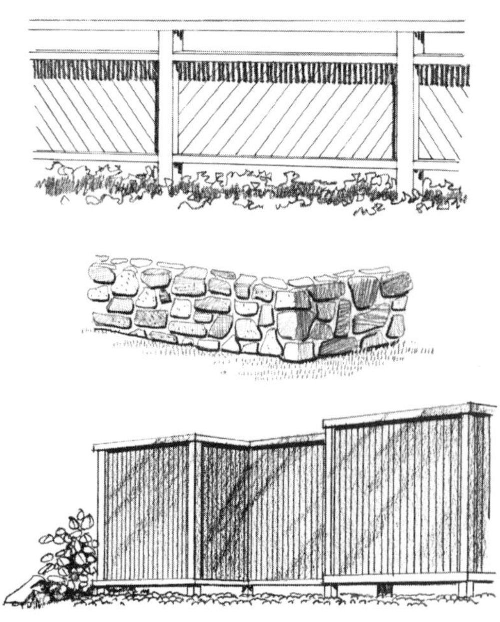

Fig. 42–13. Methods of rendering fences and walls.

CHIMNEYS

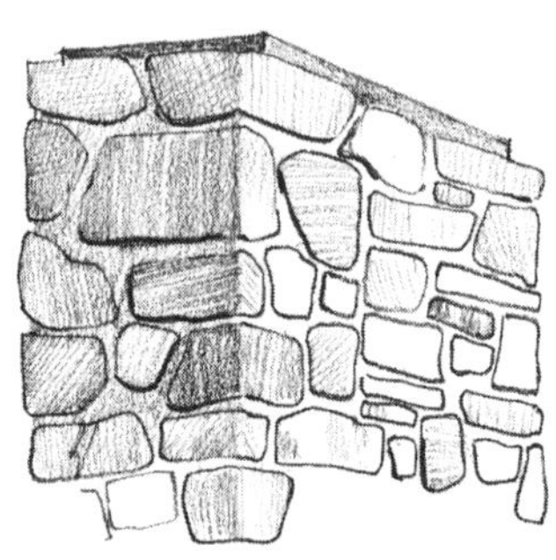

Fig. 42–14. Pencil renderings of chimneys.

Fig. 42–15A. Architectural sketches of people.

Port Authority of New York and New Jersey

Fig. 42–15B. The use of people to show traffic patterns.

Port Authority of New York and New Jersey

Fig. 42–15C. The use of people to show size comparisons.

patterns (Fig. 42–15B), size differences (Fig. 42–15C), and to provide a feeling of perspective and depth. Automobiles are added to architectural renderings (Fig. 42–16) to provide proper perspective and to give a greater feeling for external traffic patterns. It is also important to utilize proper rendering techniques to show texture and shadows on flat surfaces, such as

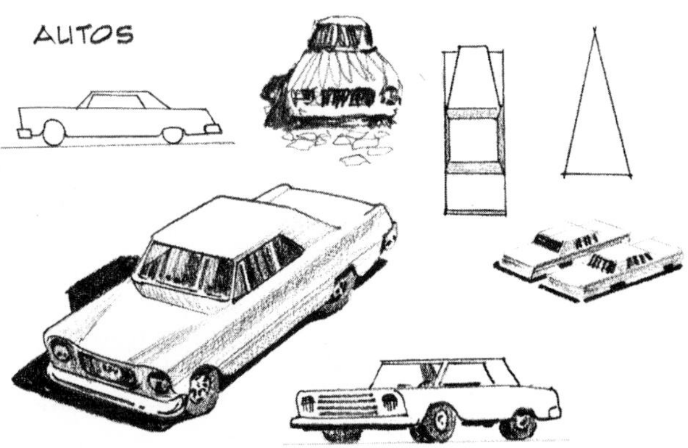

Fig. 42–16. Examples of automobile sketches for use on architectural drawings.

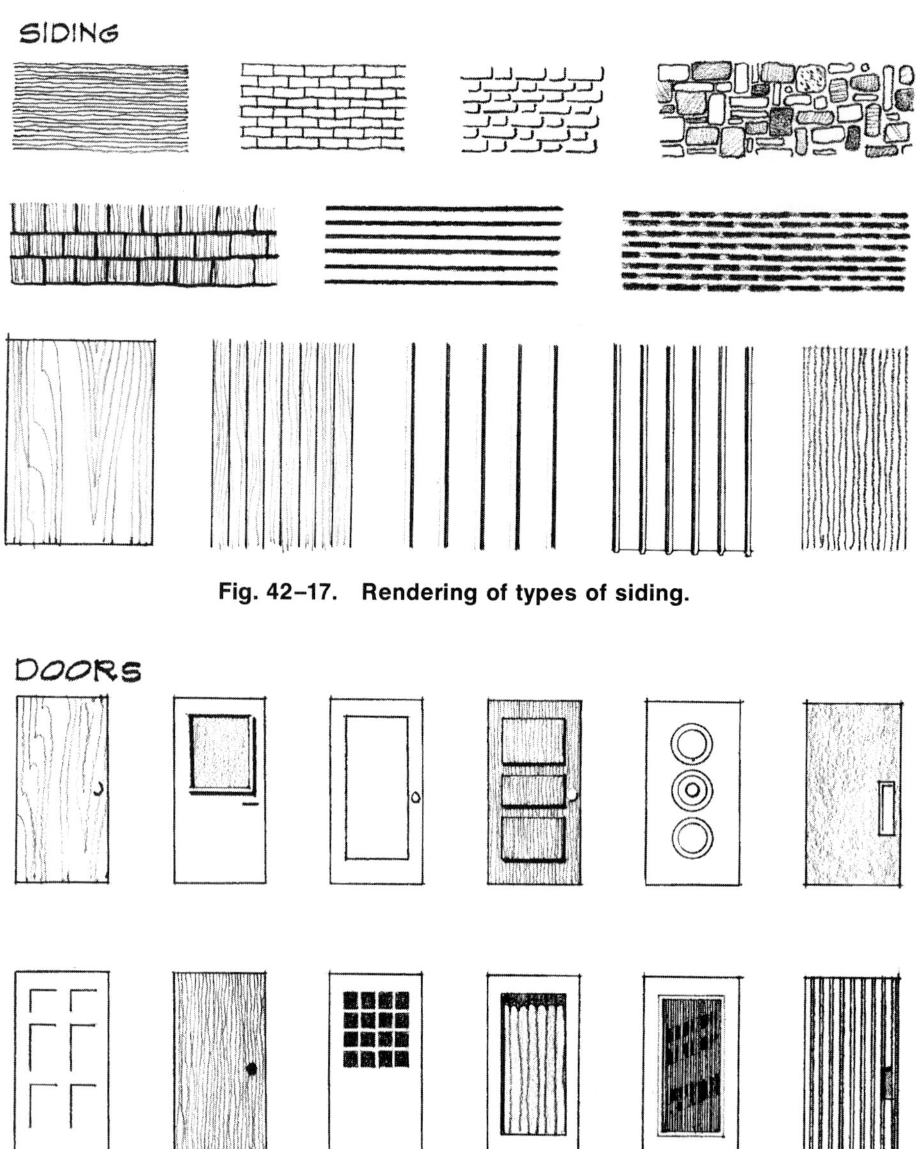

Fig. 42–17. Rendering of types of siding.

Fig. 42–18. Methods of rendering doors.

siding (Fig. 42–17) and doors (Fig. 42–18). Notice that most of this is done by light shading and also by variation of the pencil-stroke widths.

One popular technique that can be used to convert a perspective line drawing into a rendering is to apply screen tones. The drawings shown in Fig. 42–19 are simple line drawings with various shades of screens added to denote texture and shadow. The use of more realistic pencil technique to show texture and shadows is illustrated in Fig. 42–20.

ABBREVIATED RENDERING

Often it is necessary or desirable to render only one part of a building. In such cases, the other attached parts may be only outlined and the rendering gradually diminished, instead of abruptly stopped. Figure 42–21 was prepared to show only the porch of the house. However, the relationship to the remainder of the house is important and, therefore, the house is shown in outline.

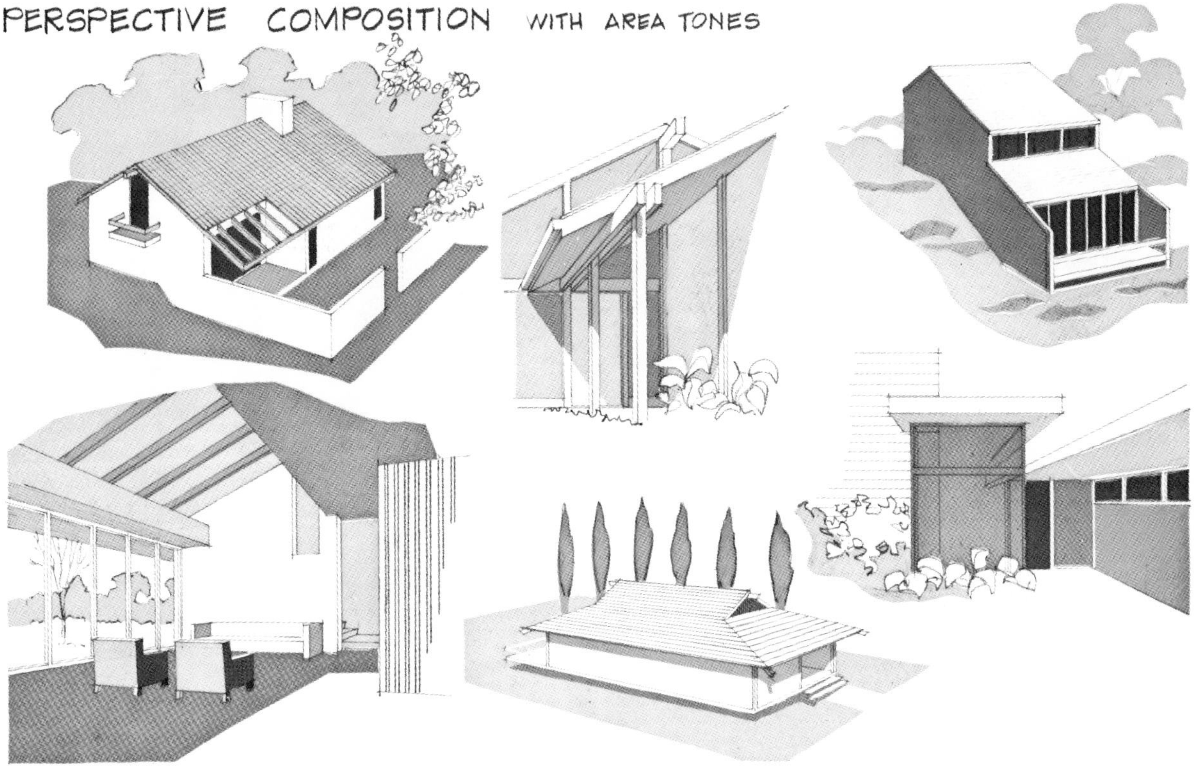

PERSPECTIVE COMPOSITION WITH AREA TONES

Fig. 42–19. The area-tone method of rendering.

PERSPECTIVE TECHNIQUES

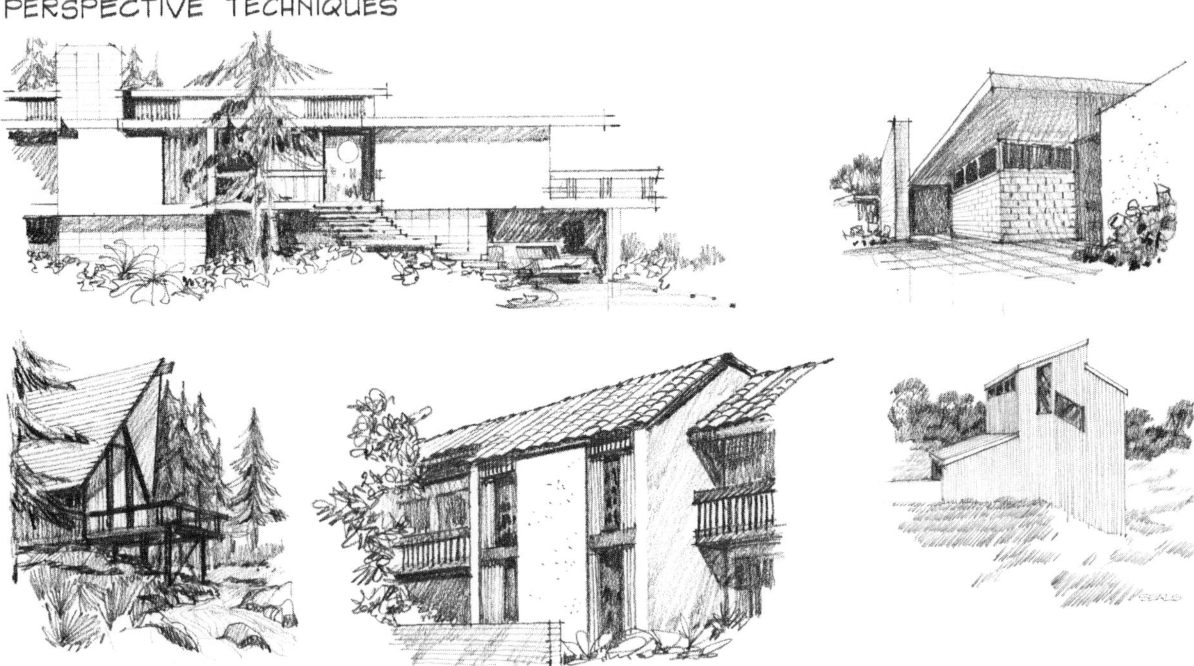

Fig. 42–20. A combination of pencil techniques showing shade, shadow, and texture.

Home Planners, Inc.

Fig. 42–21. A partial rendering.

Home Planners, Inc.

Fig. 42–22. Complete this rendering.

PROBLEMS

1. Render a perspective drawing of your own house.
2. Render a perspective drawing of a house of your own design.
3. Render a perspective sketch of your school. Choose your own medium: pencil, pen and ink, water colors, pastels, or air brush.
4. Complete the perspective shown in Fig. 42–22, and completely render the drawing in pencil.
5. Render the perspective drawing shown in Fig. 42–23.
6. Define these terms: *render, texture, shade, shadow, chisel-point, crow-quill.*

Fig. 42–23. Render this drawing.

PART THREE

Basic architectural plans, such as floor plans, elevations, and pictorial drawings, are adequate for describing the general design of a structure. However, to ensure that the building will be completed as specified, a more complete and detailed description of the construction features of the design must be prepared. Technical architectural plans are prepared for this purpose. These include location plans, sectional drawings, foundation plans, framing plans, specifications, building codes, electrical plans, air-conditioning plans, plumbing diagrams, and modular-construction plans. In Part Three you will learn the basic practices and procedures in preparing technical architectural plans.

Technical Architectural Plans

SECTION 9

Location Plans

Location plans are necessary to give the builder essential information about the property. They are of three types: the plot, the landscape, and the survey. The *plot plan* shows the location of all structures on the property. The *landscape plan* shows how the various features of the landscape will be used in the overall design. The *survey plan* shows the geographical features of the property.

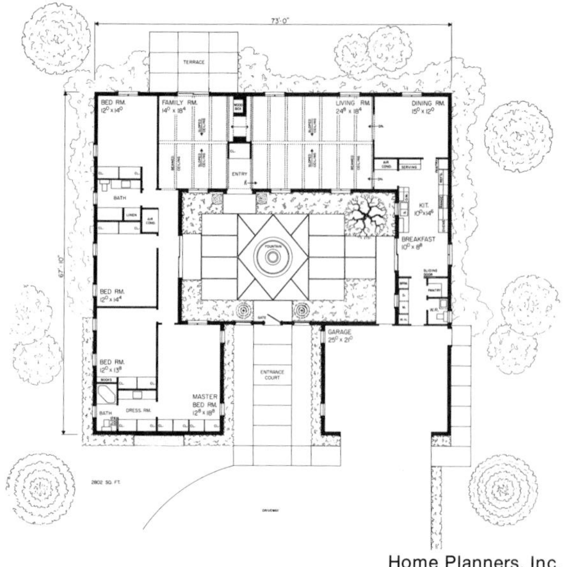

Home Planners, Inc.

UNIT 43

Plot Plans

Plot plans are used to show the location and size of all buildings on the lot. Overall building dimensions and lot dimensions are shown on plot plans. The position and size of walks, drives, patios, and courts are also shown. Compass orientation of the lot is given, and contour lines are sometimes shown. Figure 43–1 shows the key figures and the symbols commonly used on plot plans.

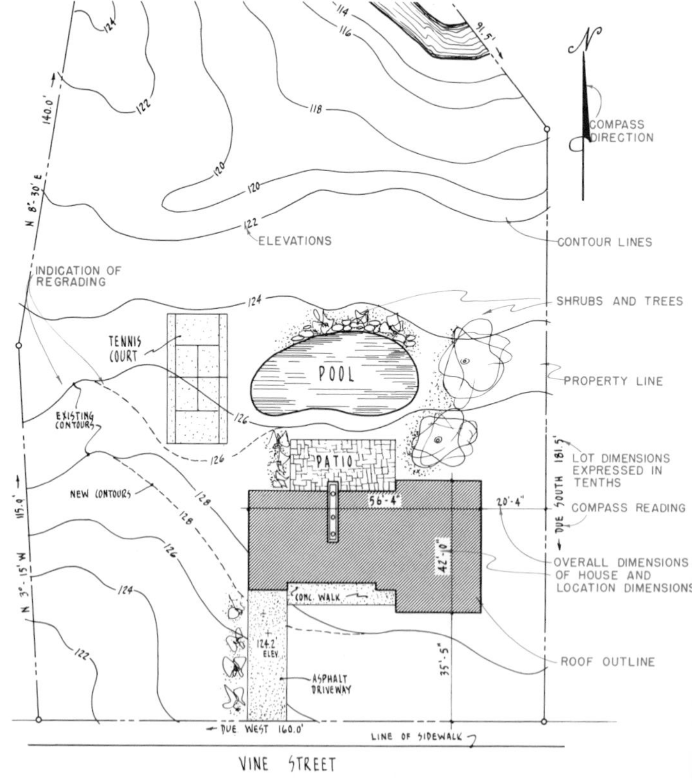

Fig. 43–1. Plot-plan symbols.

GUIDES FOR DRAWING PLOT PLANS

The numbered arrows in Fig. 43–2 illustrate the following guides for drawing plot plans:

1. Draw only the outline of the house. Cross-hatching is optional.
2. Draw the outlines of other buildings on the lot.
3. Show overall building dimensions. Figure 43–3 shows dimensional standards recommended for plot plans.
4. Locate each building by dimensioning from the property line to the building (Fig.

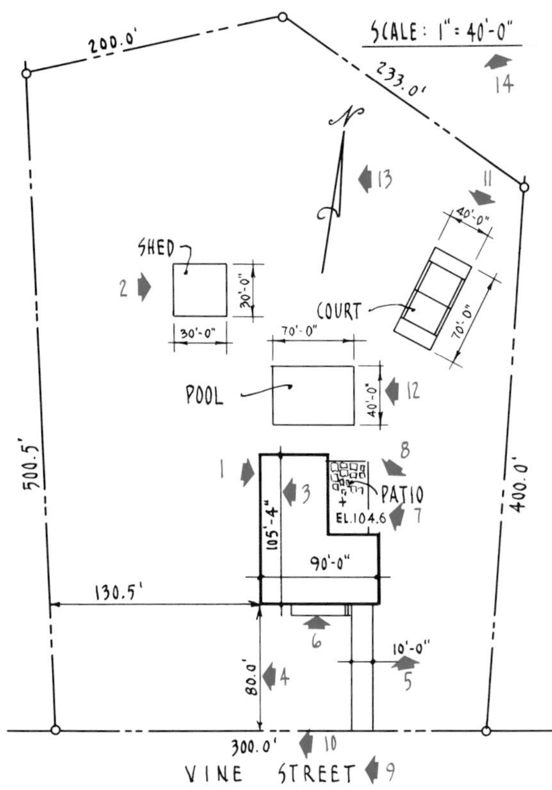

Fig. 43–2. Guides for drawing plot plans.

43–3). The property line shows the legal limits of the lot on all sides.

5. Show the position and size of driveways.
6. Show the location and size of walks.
7. Indicate grade elevation of key surfaces such as patios, driveways, and courts.
8. Outline and show the appropriate symbol for the surface material used on patios and terraces.
9. Label streets adjacent to the outline.
10. Place overall lot dimensions either on extension lines outside the property line or directly on the property line.
11. Show the size and location of courts.
12. Show the size and location of pools, ponds, or other bodies of water.
13. Indicate the compass orientation of the lot by the use of a north arrow.
14. Use a decimal scale such as 1/10″ = 1′—0″, or 1/20″ = 1′—0″ or a metric scale for preparing the plot plan.

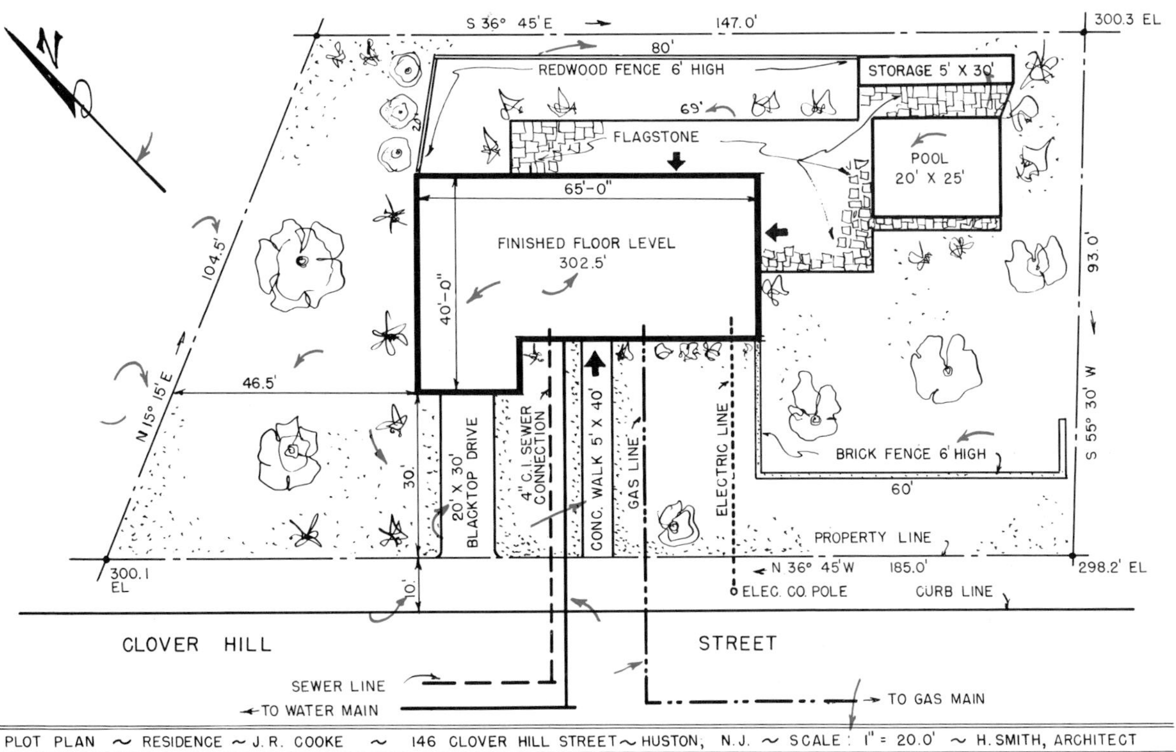

Fig. 43–3. Plot-plan dimensions.

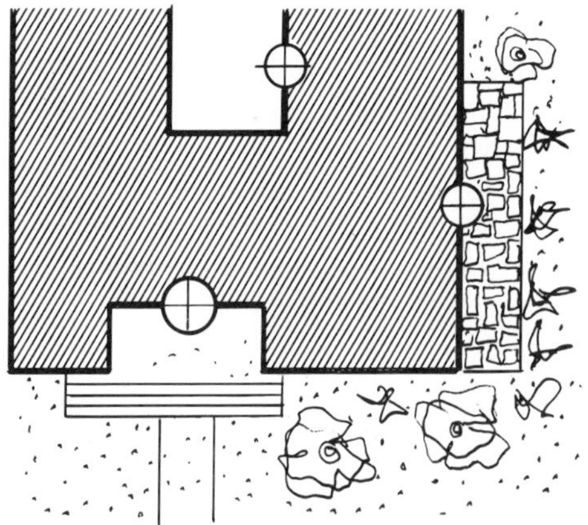

Fig. 43–4. Entrance symbols.

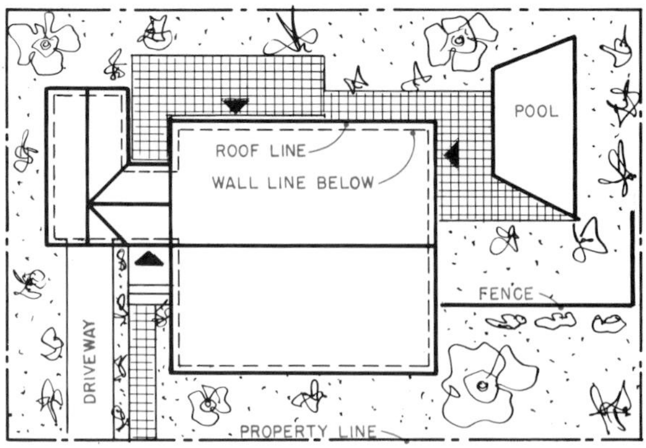

Fig. 43–5. The roof outline is often shown on plot plans.

ALTERNATIVE FEATURES

Although plot plans should be prepared according to the standards shown in Fig. 43–2, many optional features also may be included in plot plans. For example, sometimes the interior partitions of the residence are given to show a correspondence between the outside living areas and those inside. Some architects prefer to include only the outline of the building on the plot plan, while others favor crosshatching or shading the buildings.

The position of entrances to buildings are sometimes noted on plot plans, as shown in Fig. 43–4. This device provides an interpretation of the access to the house from the outside, without requiring a detailed plan of the inside.

Contour lines are another optional feature on plot plans. On lots that deviate greatly in contour, contour lines are sometimes almost mandatory.

The plot plan is also often used to show the outline of the roof, as in Fig. 43–5. When this outline is shown, the drawing gives the effect of looking down on the top of the lot.

VARIATION IN PLAN

There are more ways than one to place buildings on a lot. Sometimes alternative plot plans are developed to determine the best overall arrangement, as shown in Fig. 43–6. Variations are also possible in developing almost any detail of a plot plan. The steps for preparing a plot plan are shown in Fig. 43–7.

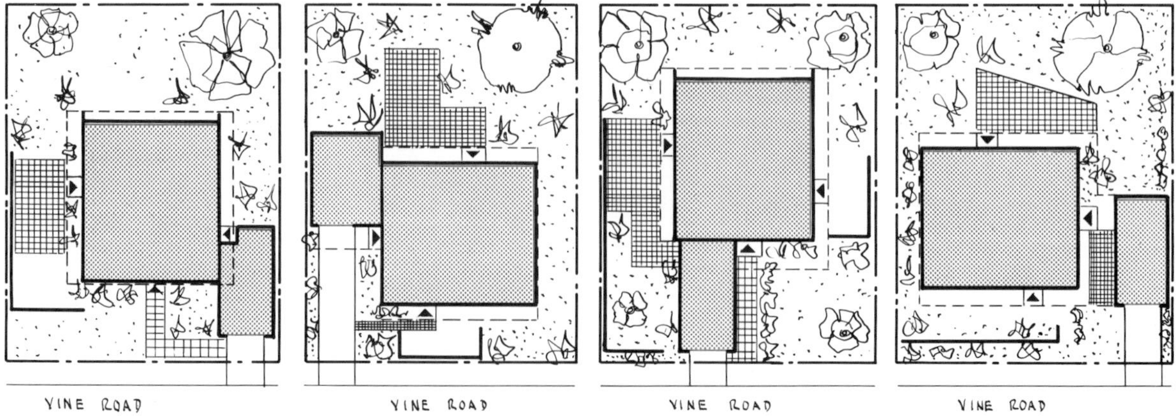

Fig. 43–6. Alternative plot plans.

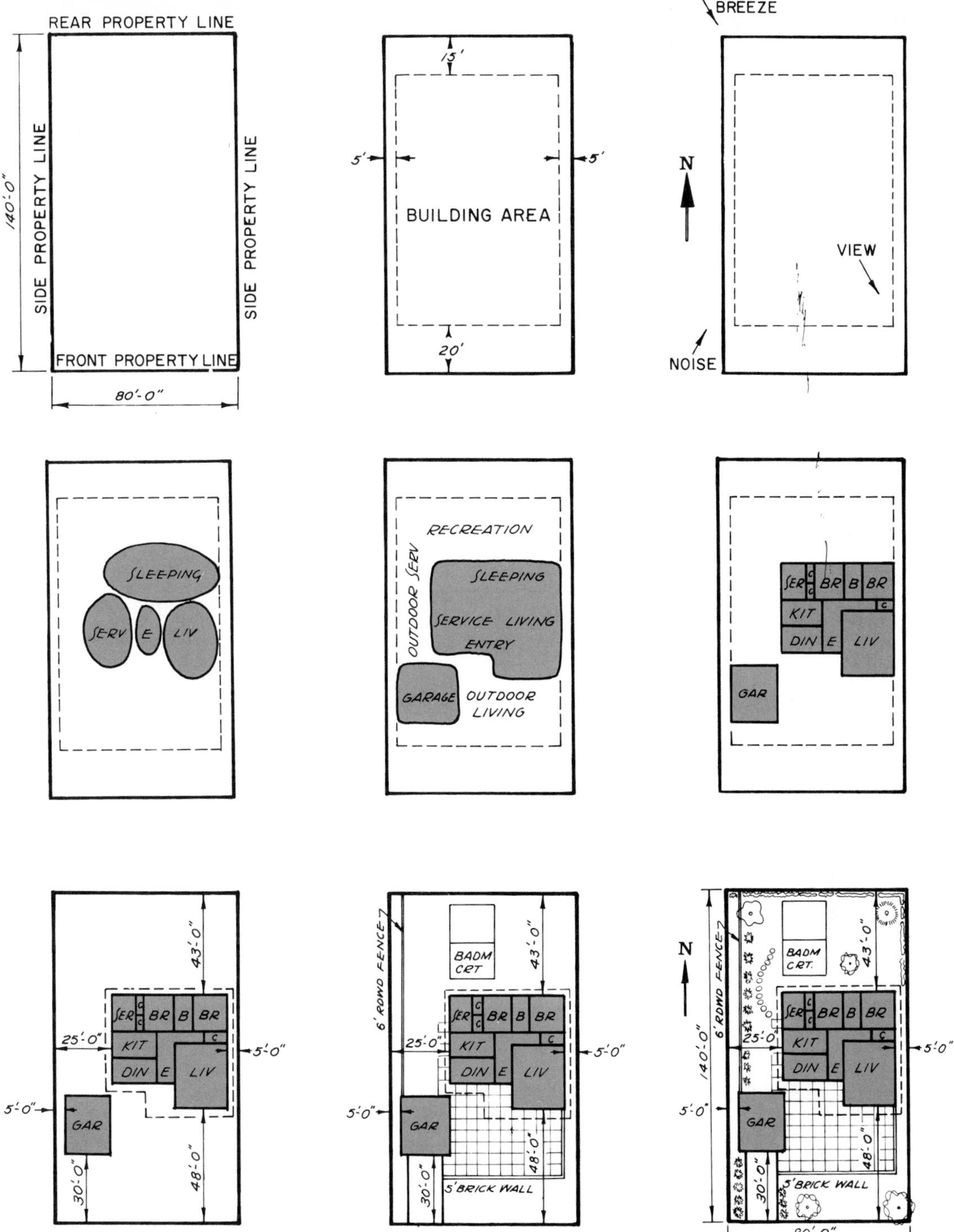

Fig. 43–7. Steps in drawing a plot plan.

PROBLEMS

1. Draw a plot plan of your own home.
2. From a survey plan you have developed, complete a plot plan showing the position of a residence.
3. Place the outline of a residence on the plot plan shown in Fig. 43-8. Include a two-car garage, swimming pool, and tennis court on this plan. Remember to take full advantage of existing landscape features.

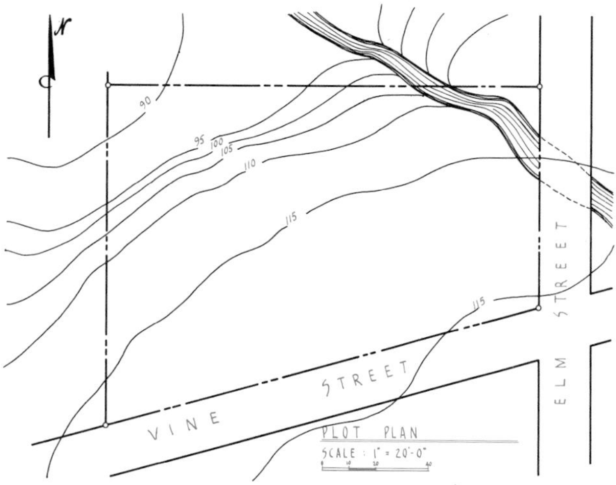

Fig. 43–8. Locate a residence on this lot.

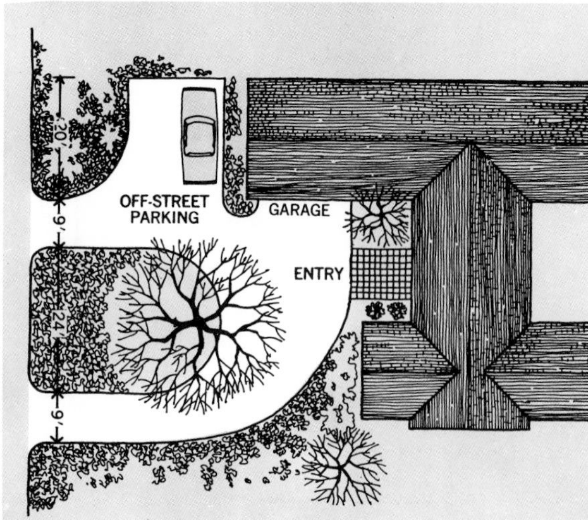

Fig. 43–9. Draw a plot plan for this home.

4. Draw a plot plan for the house shown in Fig. 43-9. Make the lot 100′ × 150′.

5. Define these terms: *plot plan, lot, compass orientation, contour lines, property line, grade elevation.*

UNIT 44

Landscape Plans

The primary function of the landscape plan is to show the types and location of vegetation for the lot. It may also show the contour of the land and the position of buildings. Such features are often necessary to make the placement of the vegetation meaningful.

Symbols are used on landscape plans to show the position of trees, shrubbery, flowers, vegetable gardens, hedgerows, and lawns. Figure 44–1 shows some common symbols used on a landscape plan.

A landscape architect or gardening contractor designs and prepares the landscape plan in cooperation with the designing architect. The landscape architect specifies the type and location of all trees, shrubs, flowers, hedge, and ground cover. He or she often proposes changes in the existing contour of the land to enhance the site appearance and function.

GUIDES FOR PREPARING LANDSCAPE PLANS

The following guides in preparing landscape plans are illustrated by the numbered arrows shown in Fig. 44–2:

1. The elevation of all trees is noted to show the datum level.
2. Vegetable gardens are shown by outlining the planting furrows.
3. Orchards are shown by outlining each tree in the pattern.
4. The property line is shown to define the limits of the lot.
5. Trees are located to provide shade and windbreaks and to balance the decor of the site.

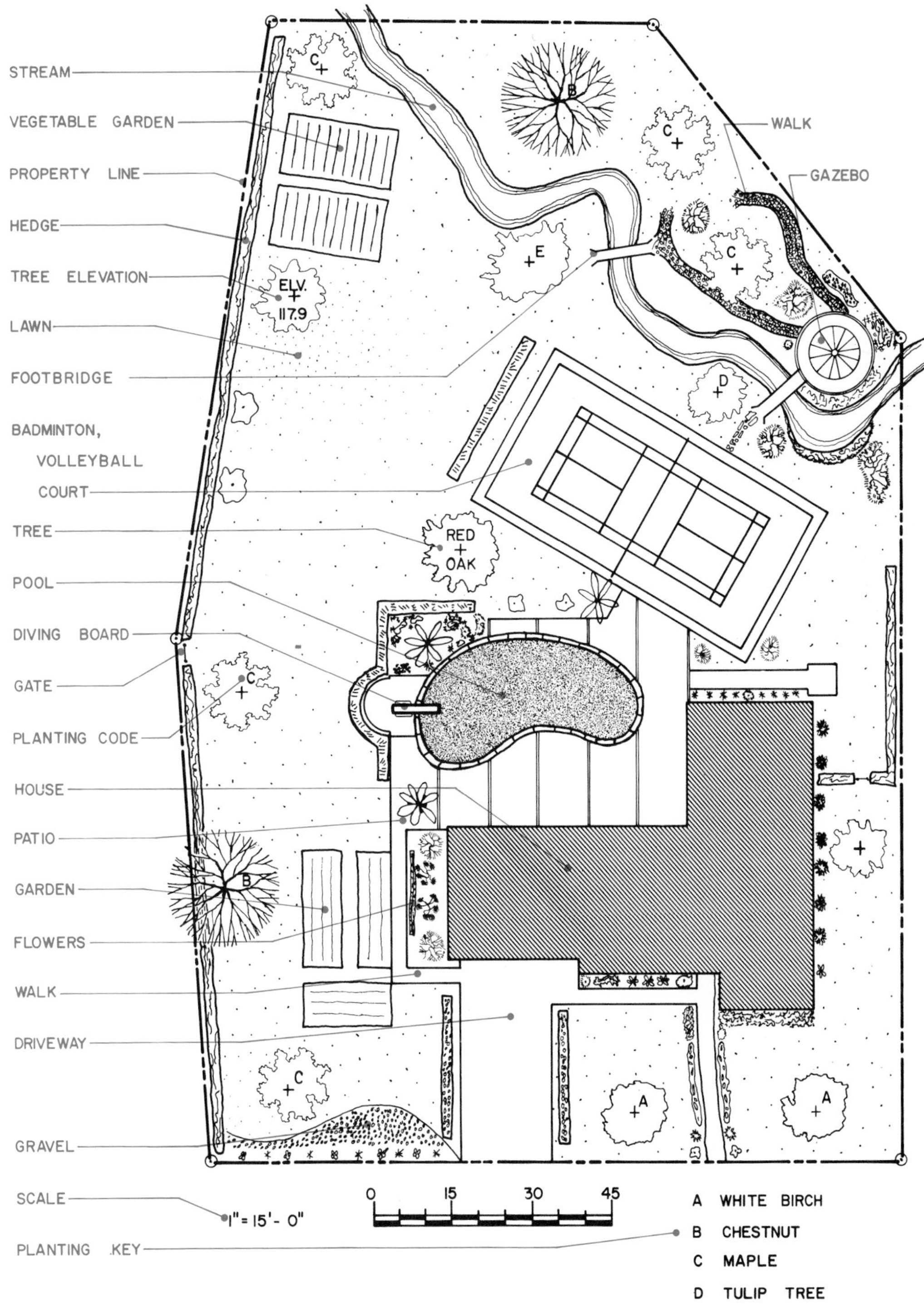

Fig. 44–1. Landscape-plan symbols.

6. Shrubbery is used to provide privacy, define boundaries, outline walks, conceal foundation walls, and balance irregular contours.
7. The outline and subdivisions of courts are shown.
8. Flower gardens are shown by the outline of their shapes.

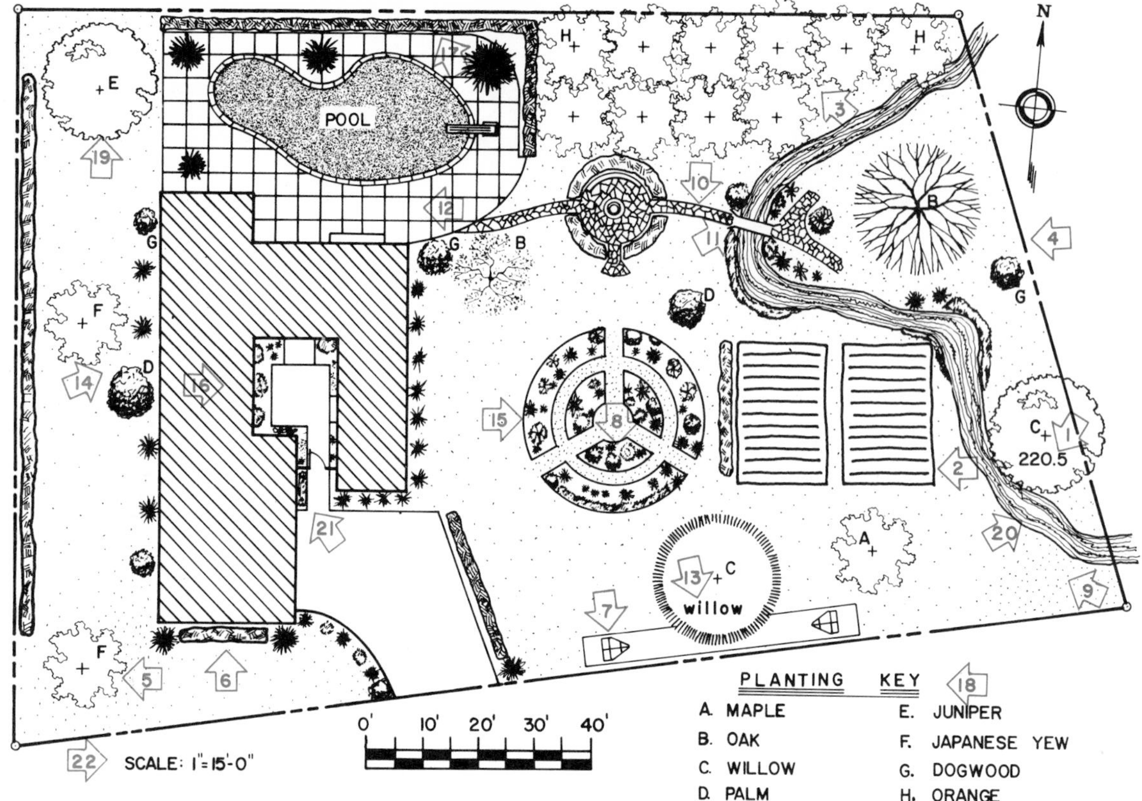

Fig. 44–2. Guides for preparing landscape plans.

9. Lawns are shown by small, sparsely placed dots or vertical lines.
10. The outlines of all walks and planned paths are shown.
11. Conventional map symbols are used for small bridges.
12. The outline and surface covering of all patios and terraces are indicated.
13. The name of each tree and shrub is labeled on the symbol.
14. All landscaping should enhance the function and appearance of the site.
15. Flowers should be located to provide maximum beauty and ease of maintenance.
16. The house is outlined, crosshatched, or shaded. In some cases, the outline of the floor plan is shown in abbreviated form. This helps to show the relationship of the outside to the inside living areas.
17. Hedge is used as a screening device to provide privacy, to divide an area, to control traffic, or to serve as a windbreak.
18. Each tree or shrub is indexed to a planting schedule, if there are too many to be labeled on the drawing, as suggested in 13.
19. A tree is shown by drawing an outline of the area covered by its branches. This symbol varies from a perfect circle to irregular lines representing the appearance of branches. A plus sign (+) indicates the location of the trunk.
20. Water is indicated by irregular parallel lines.
21. Shrubbery in front of the house should be low in order not to interfere with traffic or with window location.
22. An engineer's scale is used to prepare landscape plans. This is because surveyors use this measure.

PHASING

The complete landscaping of a lot may be prolonged through several years. This procedure is sometimes followed because of a lack of time to accomplish all the planting necessary, or for financial reasons. Figure 44–3 shows a landscape plan divided into three different phases for completion. When a landscape plan is phased, the total plan is drawn, and then dif-

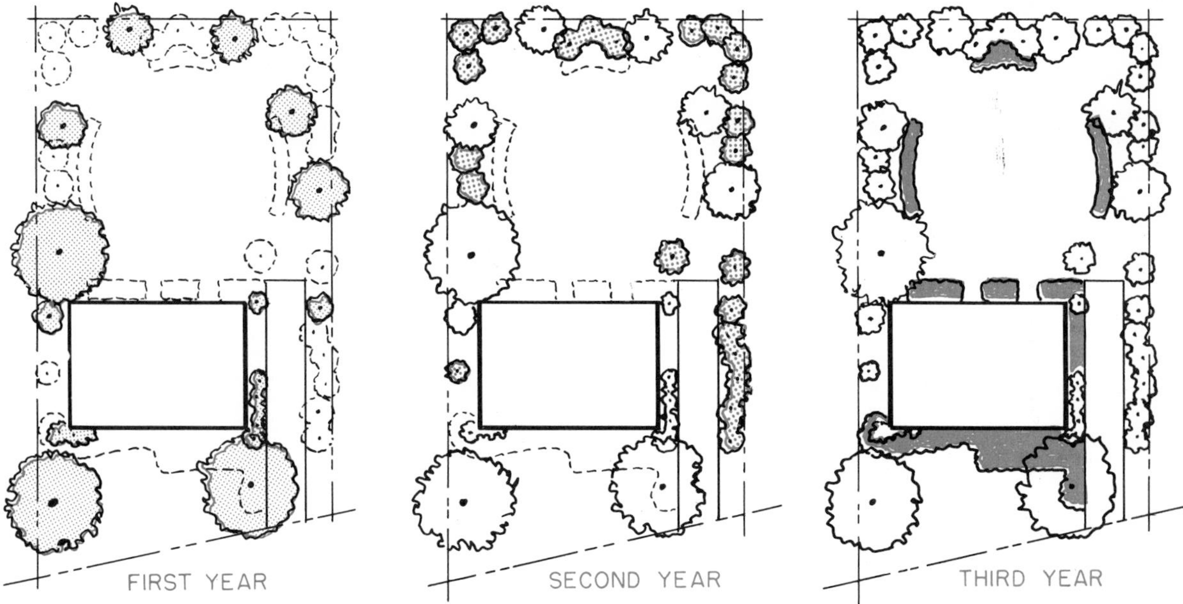

Fig. 44–3. A phased landscape plan.

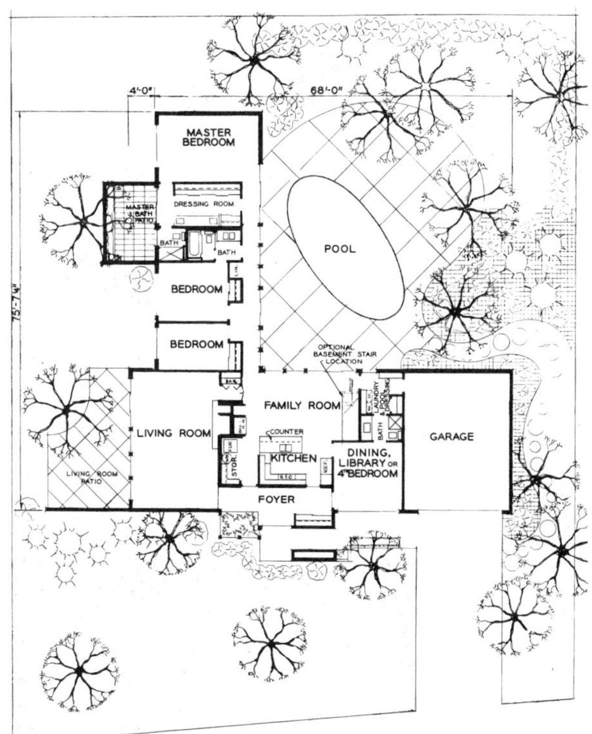

Secor Landscape Co.

Fig. 44–4. An interpretive landscape plan without detail dimensions.

ferent shades or colors are used to designate the items that will be planted in the first year, in the second year, and in the third year. A plan can be phased over many years or several months, depending on the schedule for completion of the landscaping.

VARIATIONS

Many landscape plans, such as the one shown in Fig. 44–4, are strictly interpretive and contain few or no dimensions. The plan shown in Fig. 44–5 contains no dimensions. The position from which the photograph was taken in Fig. 44–5B is shown by the arrow in Fig. 44–5A.

Combination Plans

Often the lot or estate is too large to be shown accurately on a standard landscape plan. A scale such as 1″ = 20′—0″ may not show the entire estate; or a scale must be used that is so small that the features cannot be readily identified, labeled, and dimensioned. One solution to such a problem is to prepare a total plan of the large estate to a large scale. This is indexed to a drawing of the immediate area around the house. Figure 44–6 shows the total estate plan

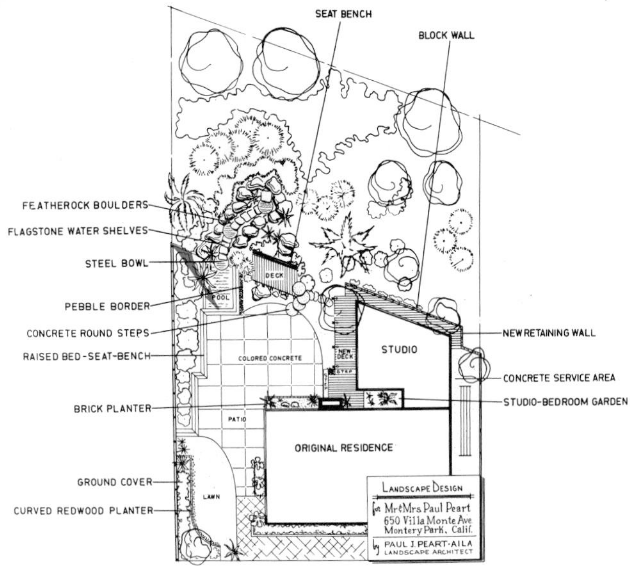

Paul J. Peart, AILA

Fig. 44–5A. A landscape plan with all materials labeled.

Paul J. Peart, AILA

Fig. 44–5B. A picture of the area shown in Fig. 44–5A.

as an insert in the drawing showing the lower right-hand corner of the estate developed in more detail.

It is sometimes desirable or necessary to combine all the features of the survey, plot plan, and landscape plan in one plan. In such a combination, all the symbol dimensions are incorporated in one location plan, as shown in Fig. 44–6. This includes contour lines and the exact position of vegetation and buildings.

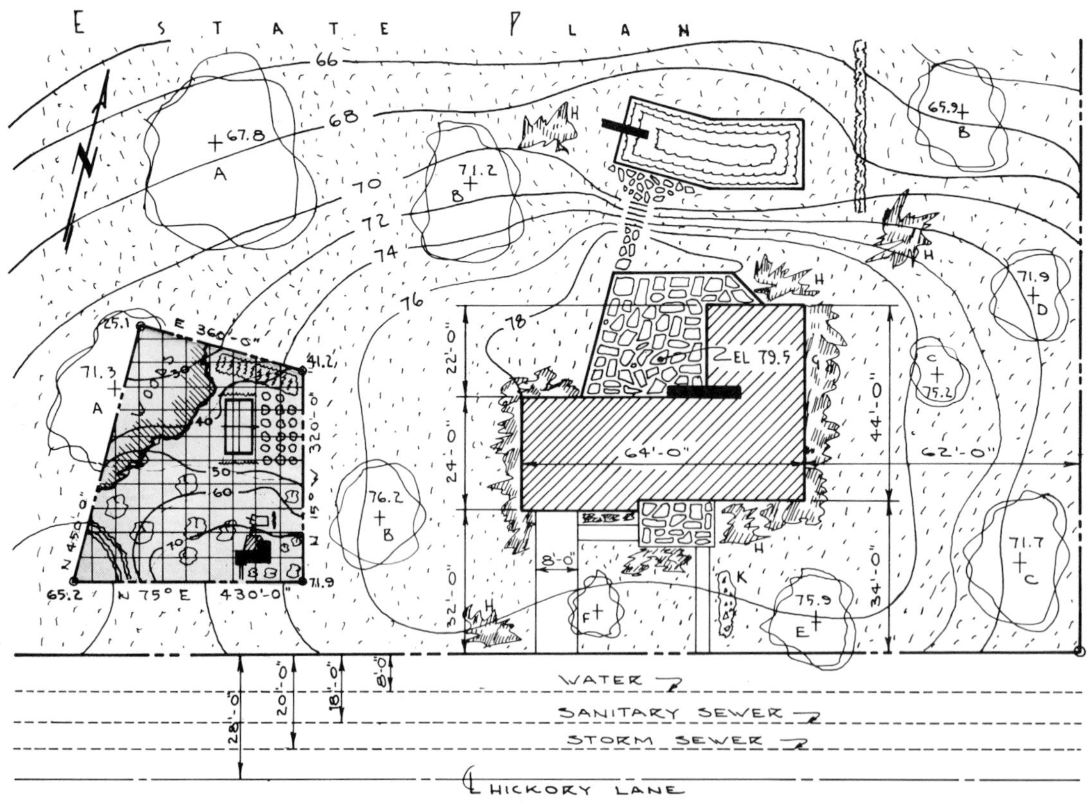

Fig. 44–6. An estate plan with a partial detail.

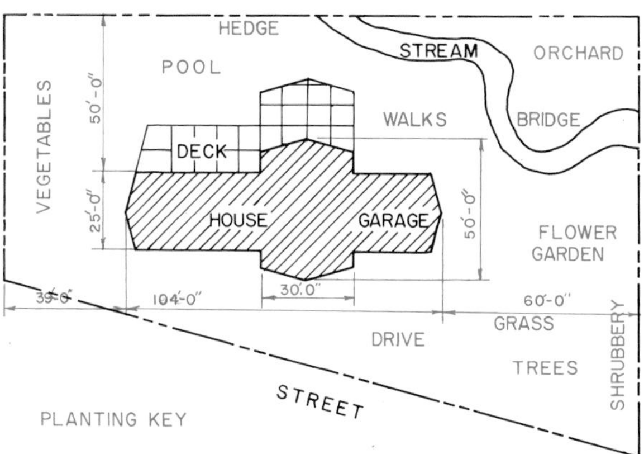

Fig. 44–7. Add landscape symbols to this plan.

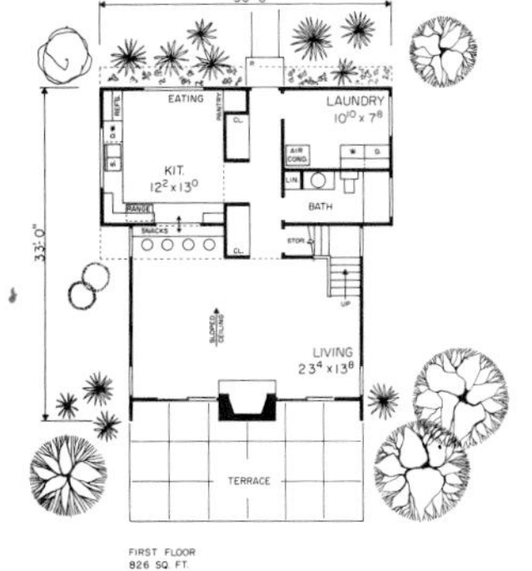

Home Planners, Inc.

Fig. 44–8. Place this house on a 100′ × 200′ lot.

PROBLEMS

1. **Add landscape features to your own plot plan.**
2. **Sketch the landscape plan in Fig. 44–7 and add the landscape symbols where named.**
3. **Place the house shown in Fig. 44–8 on a 100′ × 200′ lot. Prepare a landscape drawing of the lot according to your own taste.**
4. **Define these terms: *landscape plan, landscape symbol, landscape architect, gardening contractor, datum level, orchards, tree-location symbol, map symbols.***

UNIT 45

Survey Plans

A *survey* is a drawing showing the exact size, shape, and levels of a lot. When prepared by a licensed surveyor, the survey can be used as a legal document. It is filed with the deed to the property. The lot survey includes the length of each boundary, tree locations, corner elevations, contour of the land, and position of streams, rivers, roads or streets, and utility lines. It also lists the name of the owner of the lot and of the owner or title of adjacent lots.

A survey drawing must be accurate and must communicate a complete description of the features of the lot. Symbols are used extensively to describe the features of the terrain. Figure 45–1 shows the survey symbols most frequently used. Some symbols depict the appearance of a feature. Most survey symbols are *schematic* representations of some feature.

GUIDES FOR DRAWING SURVEYS

The numbered arrows in Fig. 45–2 correspond to the following guides for preparing survey drawings:

1. Record the elevation above the datum of the lot at each corner.
2. Represent the size and location of streams and rivers by wavy lines (blue lines on geographical surveys).

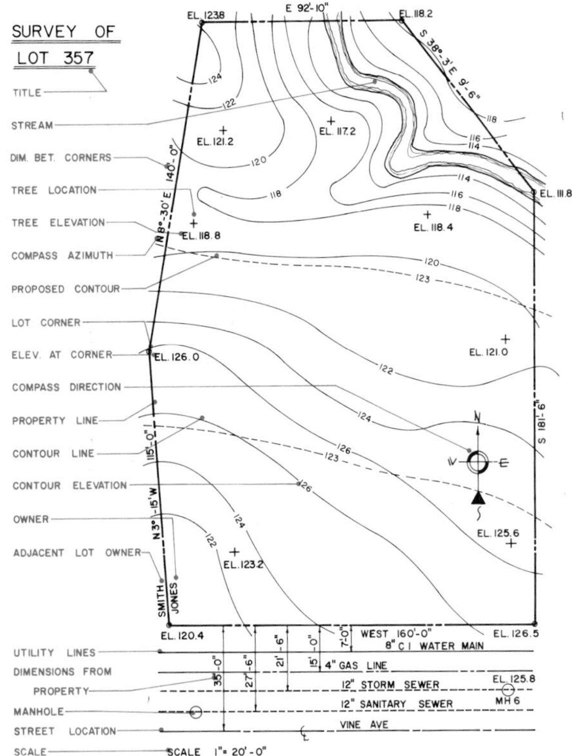

Fig. 45–1. Survey-plan symbols.

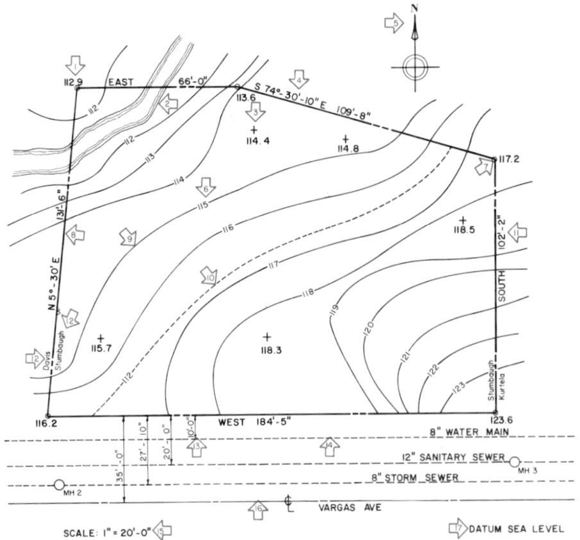

Fig. 45–2. Guides for preparing survey plans.

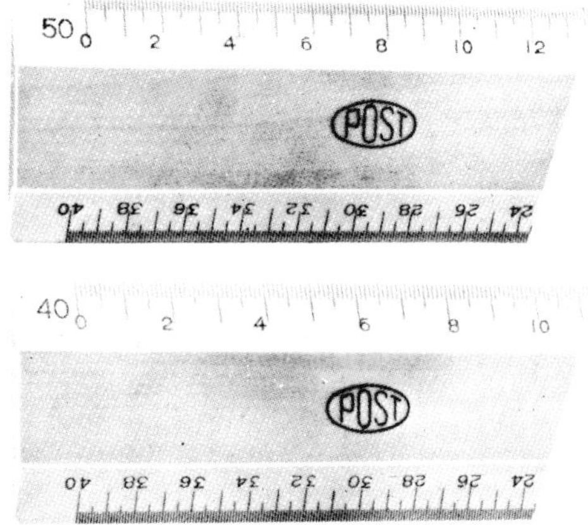

Fig. 45–3. An engineer's scale.

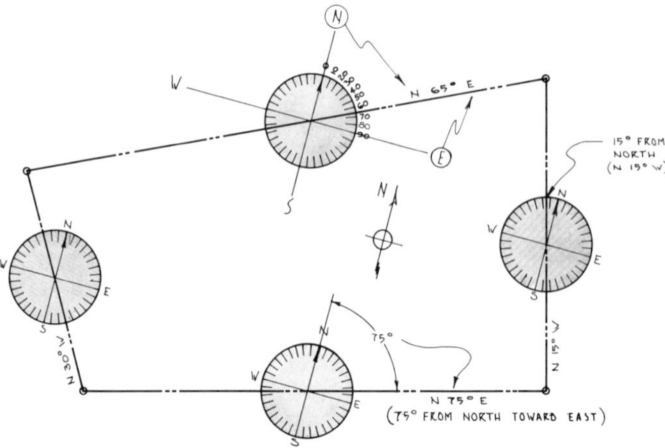

Fig. 45–4. An azimuth projection.

3. Use a cross to show the position of existing trees. The elevation of existing tree positions at the base of the trunk is shown.
4. Indicate the compass direction of each property line by degrees, minutes, and seconds (see Fig. 45–4).
5. Use a north arrow to show compass direction.
6. Break contour lines to insert the height of contour above the datum.
7. Show lot corners by small circles.
8. Draw the property line by using a repeated short line with two dots.
9. Show elevations above the datum or sea level by contour lines (brown lines on geographical survey maps—see Fig. 45–14).
10. Show any proposed change in grade line by dotted contour lines.
11. Show plot dimensions by indicating the distance between corners (dots) and the property line.
12. Give the names of owners of adjacent lots outside the property line. Place these names outside the property line. The name of the owner of the property is shown inside the property line.

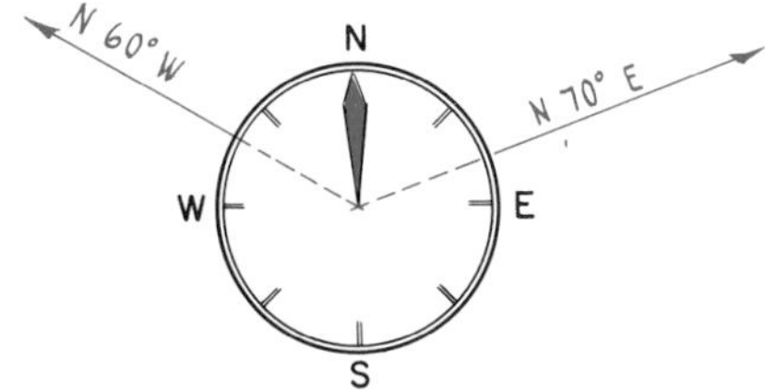

Fig. 45–5. Property-line angles are read on the circumference of the compass.

13. Dimension the distance from the property line to all utility lines.
14. Show the position of utility lines by dotted lines. Utility lines are labeled according to their function.
15. Draw surveys with an engineer's scale (decimal scale, Fig. 45–3). Common scales for surveys are $^1/_{10}'' = 1'—0''$ and $^1/_{20}'' = 1'—0''$.
16. Show existing streets and roads either by center lines or by curb or surface outlines.
17. Indicate the datum level used as reference for the survey.

LOT LAYOUT

The size and shape of lots can be determined by several different methods. However, the methods of dimensioning lots are the same.

Lot Dimensions

The exact shape of the lot is shown by the property line. The property line is dimensioned by its length and angle. The angle of each property line from north is known as an *azimuth*. Figure 45–4 shows how the azimuth of each line is determined with a compass or protractor. In Fig. 45–4, **N** indicates that the bearing of the property line reads from north; 65° means that the property is 65° from north; **E** means that the line is between north and east. Hence, **N** 65° **E** means 65° from north heading east.

The angle of the property line is established by intersecting the property line with the center of the compass when the compass needle is aligned with north. The degree of the angle of this property line is then read on the circumference of the compass, as shown in Fig. 45–5.

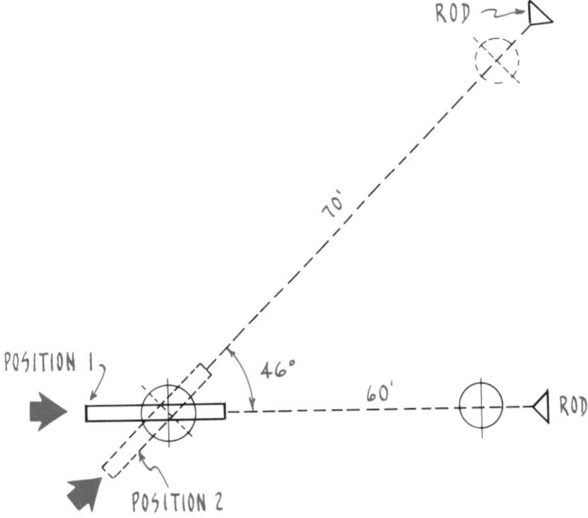

Fig. 45–6. A line can be projected to a rod at any visible distance.

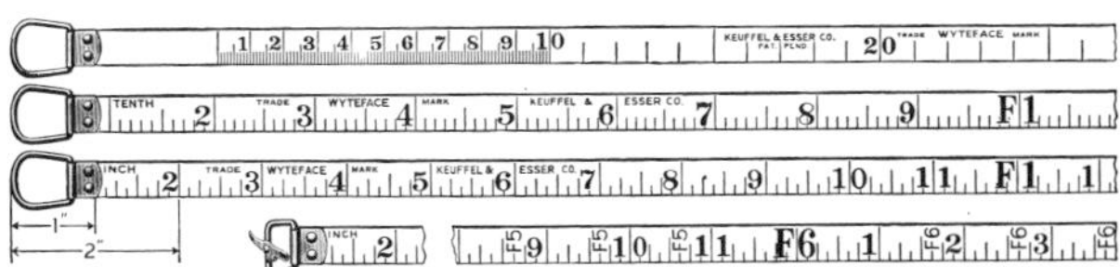

Fig. 45–7. Steel tape is used by surveyors to measure the length of property lines.

Transit Method

Surveyors use a transit to establish the angle (azimuth) of each property line. The *transit* is a telescope which can be set at any desired angle. Once an angle is set, the line may be projected to a rod at any visible distance, as shown in Fig. 45–6. A second line can then be projected by rotating the transit to the desired angle between the property lines. The rotation and projection are shown in position 2, Fig. 45–6.

In measuring the length of each property line, surveyors use a steel tape or chain (Fig. 45–7). Figure 45–8 shows the sequence of using the transit and chain to establish the angle and the length of each property line. Step 1 shows the projection of a line 50′ long. Step 2 shows the rotation of an angle 45° from this line. Step 3 shows a line projected 85° from the other end of the first line at a distance of 25′. Step 4 shows the projection to intersect the line established in step 2. This is called *closing*.

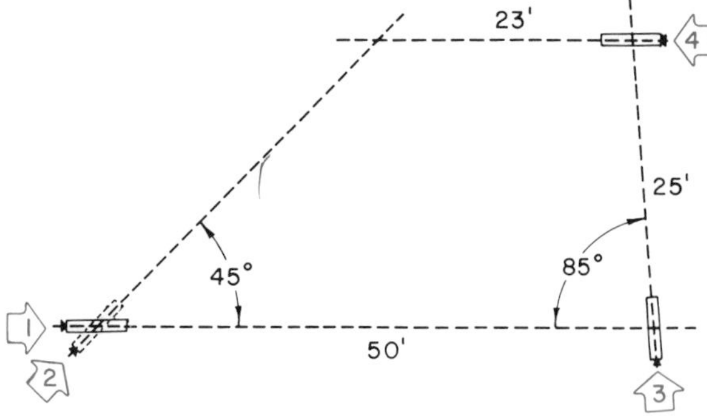

Fig. 45-8. The sequence of establishing the angle and length of each property line.

Fig. 45-9A. Establishing height with a level.

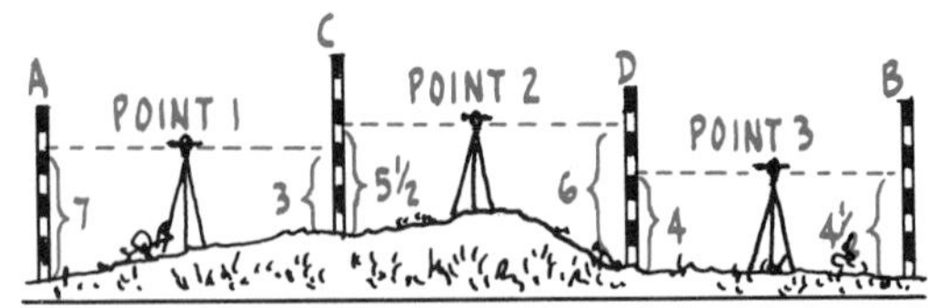

Fig. 45-9B. Projecting several elevations from one point.

Fig. 45-9C. A view of a rod through a level.

Heights of various parts of the line are established by sighting through a level from a known to an unknown distance. Figure 45–9 shows how a level is used to measure a distance from the known to an unknown distance. In Fig. 45–9A, position A is ½′ higher than position B. Figure 45–9B shows how several elevations can be projected from one known point. For example, if position A is a known value above the datum, a level line can be projected to position C. By measuring any distance up on point C, a level line can be established between C and D, and likewise between D and B. Figure 45–9C shows what the surveyor sees as he looks through the level and determines the elevation on a rod.

To establish levels with the transit, the surveyor sets up the instrument so that all points can be seen through the telescope. The reading from the rod on the cross hairs is recorded. The rod is then moved to the second position to be established. The rod is raised or lowered until the original reading is located. The bottom of the rod is then on the same level with the original point.

To obtain the difference in elevation between two points, such as points A and B in Figure 45–9A, sight on a rod held over point A. Note the reading where the horizontal cross hairs of the telescope cut the graduation on the rod. Then with the rod held at point B, rotate the telescope in a horizontal plane. Again sight on the rod. Note where the horizontal cross hairs cut the graduation on the rod (Fig. 45–9C). The difference between reading A (6′) and reading B (6½′) will give the difference in elevation between the two points. The ground at point B is ½′ lower than at point A.

When for any reason, such as irregularities in the ground or large differences in elevation, the two points whose difference in elevation is to be found cannot be determined from a single point, intermediate points must be used, as shown in Fig. 45–9B.

Plane-Table Method

The plane-table method is an alternative method of plot layout. This method is less accurate than the transit method since it relies on the naked eye and not on a graduated telescope. Furthermore, this method is generally

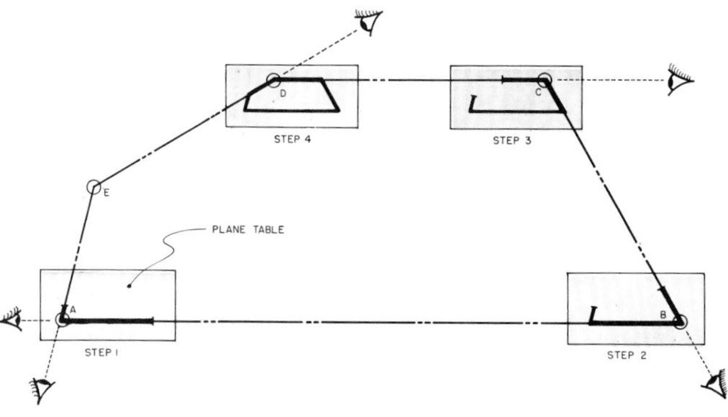

Fig. 45–10. The plane-table method of property-line layout.

Fig. 45–12. The projection of a profile from contour lines.

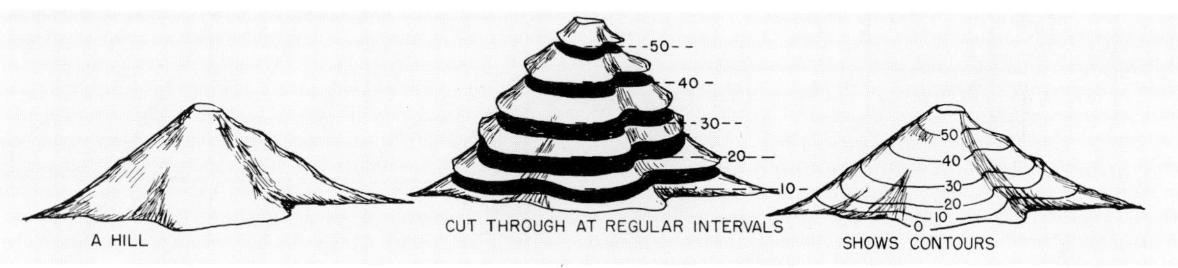

Fig. 45–11. Contour lines result from imaginary cuts made through the terrain.

used to draw a lot that has been established rather than to lay out a lot.

The *plane table* is a drawing board mounted on a tripod. The plane table is placed on a starting point, as shown in step 1, Fig. 45–10. The first line is established by sighting from corner A to corner B. The distance from corner A to corner B is then measured and drawn to scale on the plane table. Next the line AE is drawn by sighting from the starting point A to corner E.

In step 2, the plane table is moved over corner B, with line AB in the same position. Line BC is then established by sighting from corner B to corner C and measuring this distance. Step 3 establishes line CD by moving the plane table to corner C and sighting to corner D. Step 4 completes the layout by sighting from corner D back to corner E.

Contour lines show the various heights of the lot above an established plane known as the *datum*. Sea level is the universal datum line, although many municipalities have established datum points to aid surveyors. The datum is always zero.

Contour lines result from an imaginary cut made through the terrain at regular intervals. Figure 45–11 shows how this cut forms contour lines. The *contour interval*, or the vertical distance between contour lines, can be any convenient distance. It is usually an increment of 5. Contour intervals of 5′, 10′, 15′, and 20′ are common on large surveys. The use of smaller contour intervals provides a more accurate description of the slope and shape of the terrain than does the use of larger intervals.

Land on any part of a contour line has the same altitude, or height, above the datum. Contour lines are therefore always continuous. The area intersected by contour lines may be so vast that the lines may go off the drawing. However, if a larger geographical area were drawn, the lines would ultimately meet and close. Figure 45–12 shows how contours are projected from a profile through a hill. Contour lines that are very close together indicate a very steep slope.

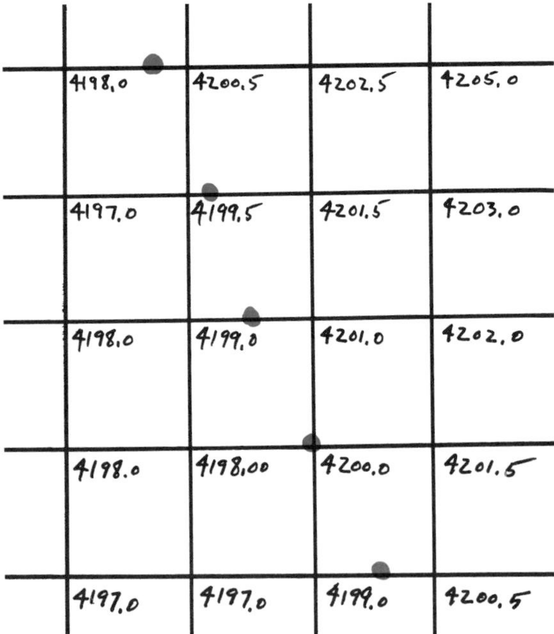

Fig. 45–13A. Elevations located on a grid.

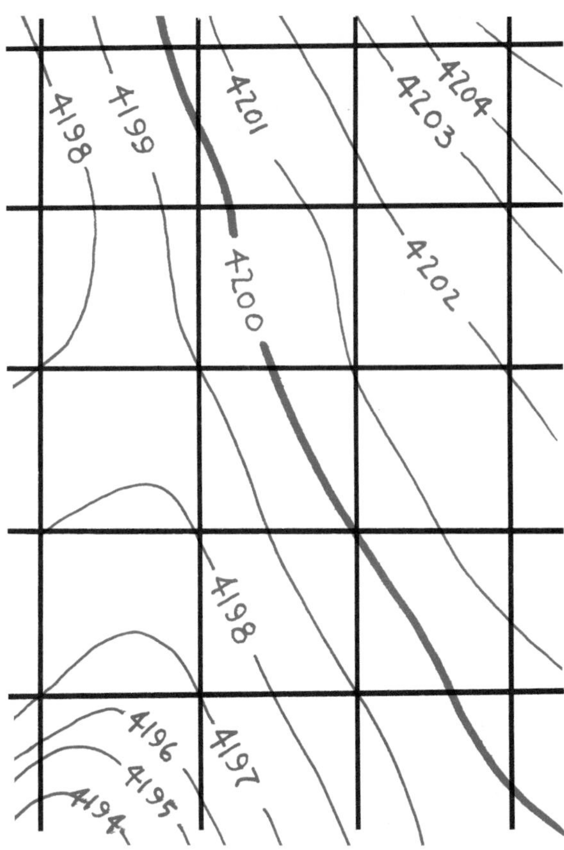

Fig. 45–13B. Grid elevations converted to contour lines.

Contour lines that are far apart indicate a more gradual slope.

Surveyors often note elevation heights on a grid, as shown in Fig. 45–13A. This can be done easily in the field. A draftsman can then use these grid heights to prepare a contour map, as shown in Fig. 45–13B. For example, the 100-foot contour line (see Fig. 45–13B) represents the location on the drawing that is at a level 100 feet above the datum. Follow the 100-foot intersection points shown in Fig. 45–13A and you will see how the contour map was developed.

GEOGRAPHICAL SURVEYS

Geographical survey maps are similar to surveys except that they cover extremely large areas. The entire world is divided into geographical survey regions. However, not all these regions have been surveyed. When large areas are to be covered, a small scale is used. When smaller areas are to be covered, a larger scale, such as 1 to 25,000, can be used. Figure 45–14A shows a typical portion of a geographical survey map. Geographical survey maps show the general contour of the area, natural features of the terrain, and constructed features. Figure 45–14B shows an aerial photograph of the same area shown in the survey map in Fig. 45–14A. Figure 45–14C shows the use of an automatic contour-line plotting machine.

PROBLEMS

1. **Make a survey of a lot in your neighborhood using the plane-table method.**
2. **Use a compass to find the azimuth of streets that surround your home.**
3. **Select a lot in your community suitable for a home site and prepare a survey of this property.**
4. **Find what the established datum for your community is.**

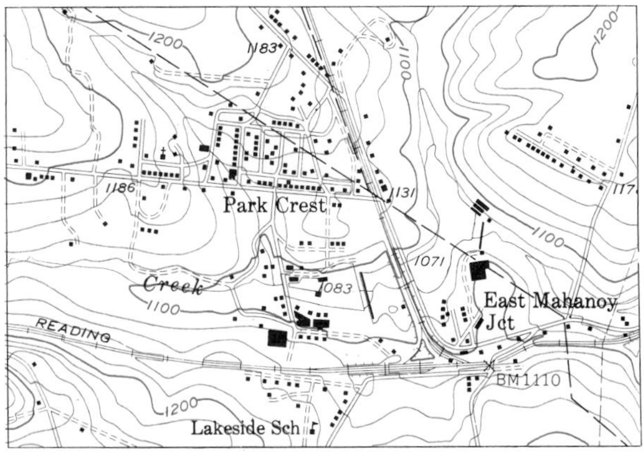

Fig. 45–14A. A segment of a geographical survey map.

Fig. 45–14B. An aerial photograph of the same area shown in Fig. 45–14A.

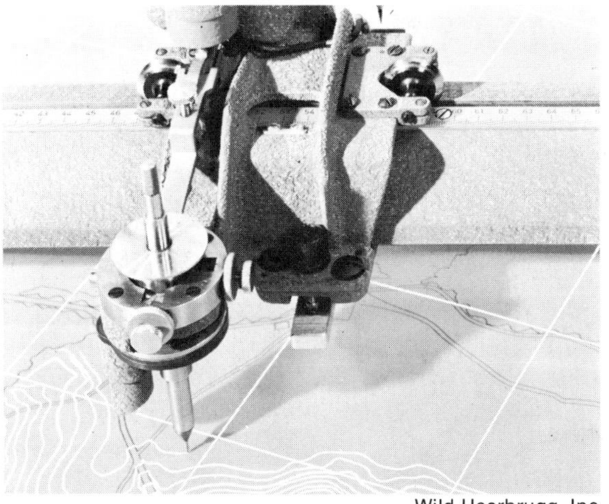

Wild Heerbrugg, Inc.

Fig. 45–14C. Contour lines drawn by a computer.

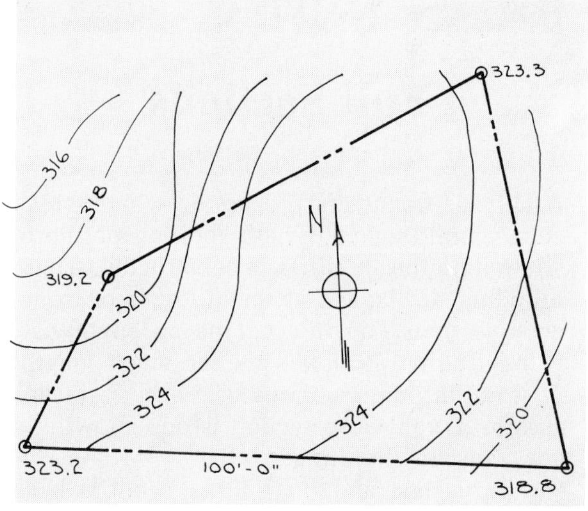

Fig. 45–15. Determine the azimuth of each property line.

5. Determine the azimuth of each property line shown in Fig. 45–15. Use a protractor or compass.
6. What is the contour interval used in Fig. 45–15?
7. Find identical features in the geographical survey map shown in Fig. 45–14A and those shown in Fig. 45–14B, the aerial photograph.
8. Draw a survey of the ideal property on which you would like to build a home.
9. Identify the following terms: *survey, contour lines, lot cornice, dotted contour lines, utility lines, azimuth bearing, transit, angle, surveyor, plane table, contour interval, geographical surveys.*

SECTION 10

Sectional Drawings

Sectional drawings reveal the internal construction of an object. Architectural sectional drawings are prepared for the entire structure (full sections), or are prepared for specific parts of the building (detail sections). The size and complexity of the part usually determines the type of section.

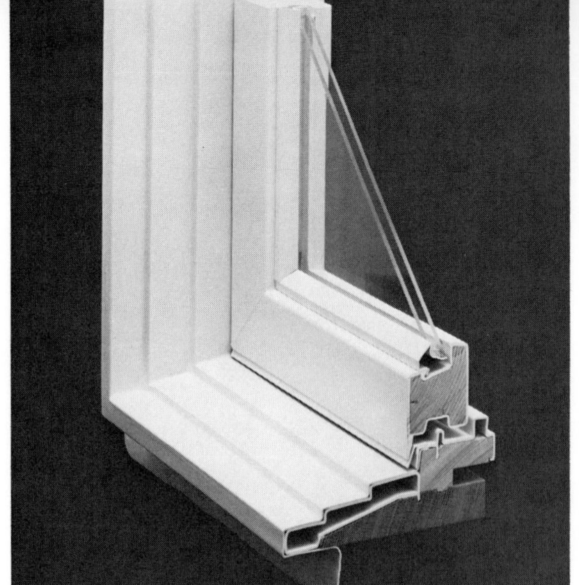

Anderson Corp.

UNIT 46

Full Sections

Architects frequently prepare drawings which show a building cut in half. Their purpose is to show how the building is constructed. These drawings are known as *longitudinal* or *transverse sections. Longitudinal* means lengthwise. A longitudinal section is one showing a lengthwise cut through the house. *Transverse* means across. A transverse section is one showing a cut across the building.

Transverse and longitudinal sections have the same outlines as the elevation drawings of the building. Figure 46–1 is a section cut parallel to the short axis of the building. Figure 46–2 is a section cut parallel to the major axis of the building.

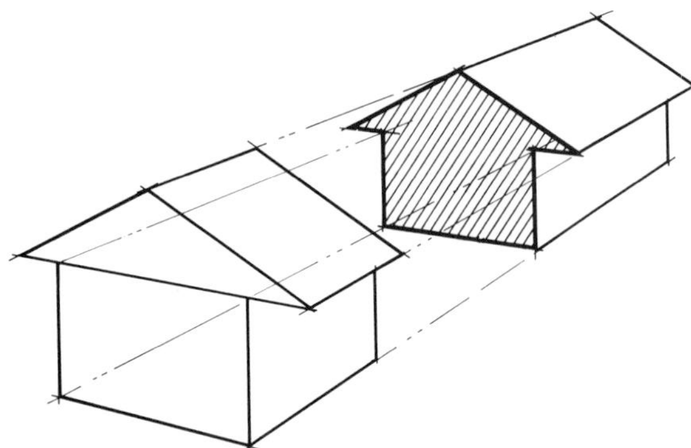

Fig. 46–1. A transverse section through the minor axis of the building.

THE CUTTING PLANE

The cutting plane is an imaginary plane which passes through the building. The position of the cutting plane is shown by the cutting-plane line. The cutting-plane line is a long heavy line with two dashes. Figure 46–3 shows a cutting-plane line and the cutting plane it represents. The cutting-plane line is placed in the part to be sectioned, and the arrows at its extremes show the direction from which the section is supposed to be viewed. For example, in Fig.

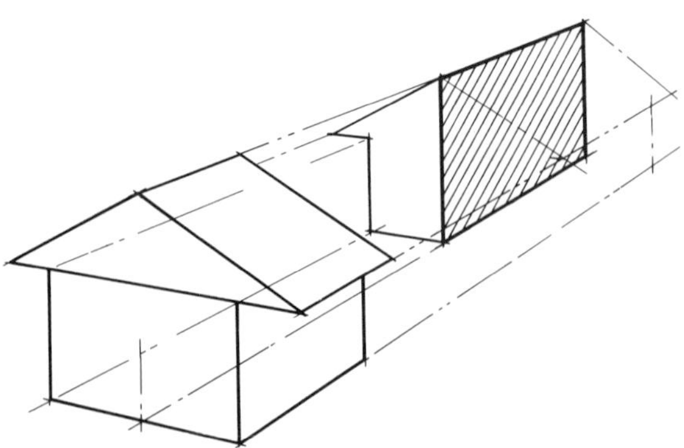

Fig. 46–2. A longitudinal section through the major axis of the building.

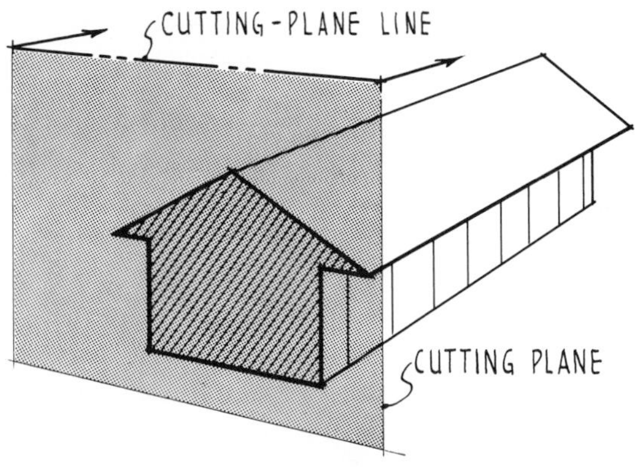

Fig. 46–3. The cutting plane and cutting-plane line.

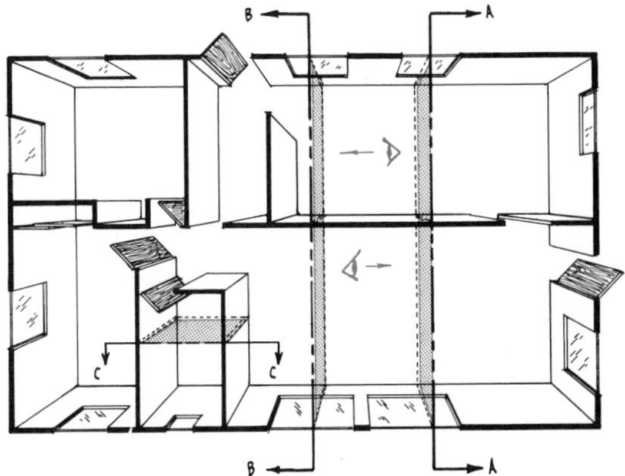

Fig. 46–4. Arrows on the cutting-plane line determine the position from which these sections are viewed.

46–4, section BB would be viewed from the right; section AA would be viewed from the left.

The cutting-plane line often interferes with many dimensions, notes, and details. An alternate method of drawing cutting-plane lines is used to overcome this interference. The alternate method is shown in Fig. 46–5. Notice that only the extremes of the cutting-plane line are used. The cutting-plane line is then *assumed to be in a straight line* between these extremes.

When a cutting-plane line must be offset to show a different area, the corners are illustrated as shown in Fig. 46–6. The *offset cutting plane* is often used to show different wall sections on one sectional drawing.

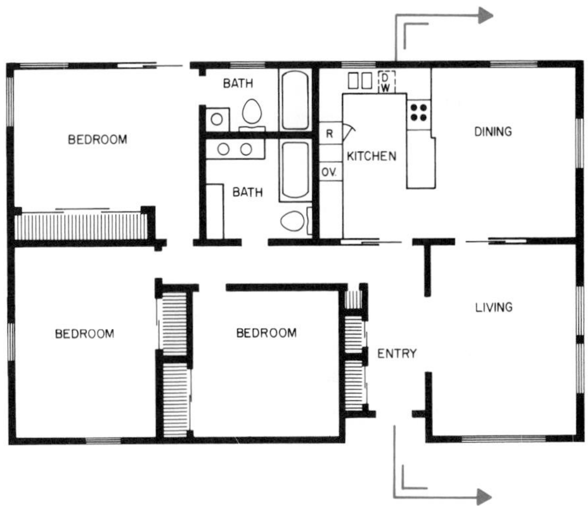

Fig. 46–5. The alternative method of drawing cutting-plane lines.

Fig. 46–6. The use of an offset cutting-plane line.

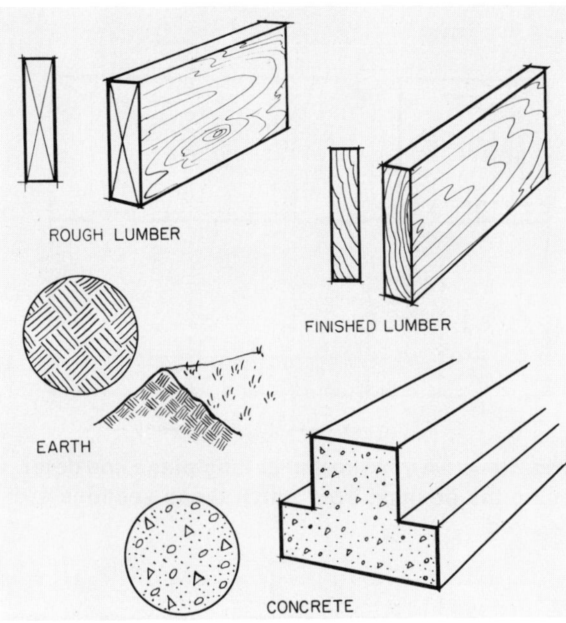

Fig. 46–7. Some common sectional symbols.

SYMBOLS

Section-lining symbols represent the way building materials look when they are cut through. A floor-plan drawing is actually a horizontal section. Many of the symbols used in floor plans also apply to longitudinal sections. However, there are some materials that are only found in longitudinal sections. The symbols for these materials are shown in Fig. 46–7. Even though an attempt is made to have section-lining symbols look like the material they represent, many are purely symbolic in order to conserve time on the drawing board.

A building material is only sectioned when the cutting-plane line passes through the material. However, the outline of all other materials visible behind the plane of projection must also be drawn in the proper position and scale.

Figure 46–8 shows the various building materials as they appear in a transverse section across the gable end of a residence. Figure 46–9 shows the same building materials as they appear when the cutting-plane line is placed parallel with the beam and a ridge of the house.

Because longitudinal sections show the construction method used in the entire building, they must be drawn to a relatively small scale. The use of this small scale often makes the drawing and interpretation of minute details extremely difficult or impossible. Removed sections of details such as the cornice, sill, and footer are often used to eliminate this problem (Fig. 46–10).

STEPS IN DRAWING LONGITUDINAL SECTIONS

In drawing the longitudinal section, the architect actually constructs the framework of a house on paper. Figure 46–11 shows the progressive steps in the layout and drawing of a gable-end section:

1. Lightly draw the floor line approximately at the middle of the drawing sheet.
2. Measure the thickness of the subfloor and of the joist and draw lines representing these under the floor line.

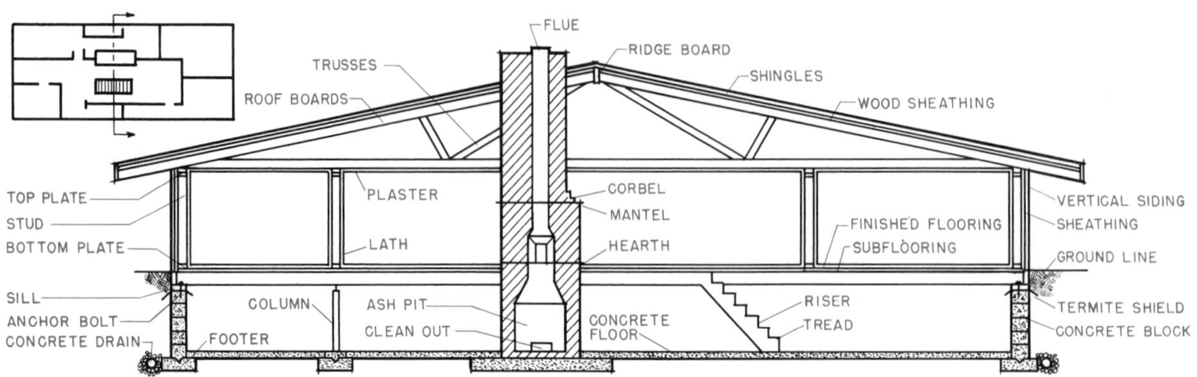

Fig. 46–8. A section of a house, perpendicular to the roof ridge.

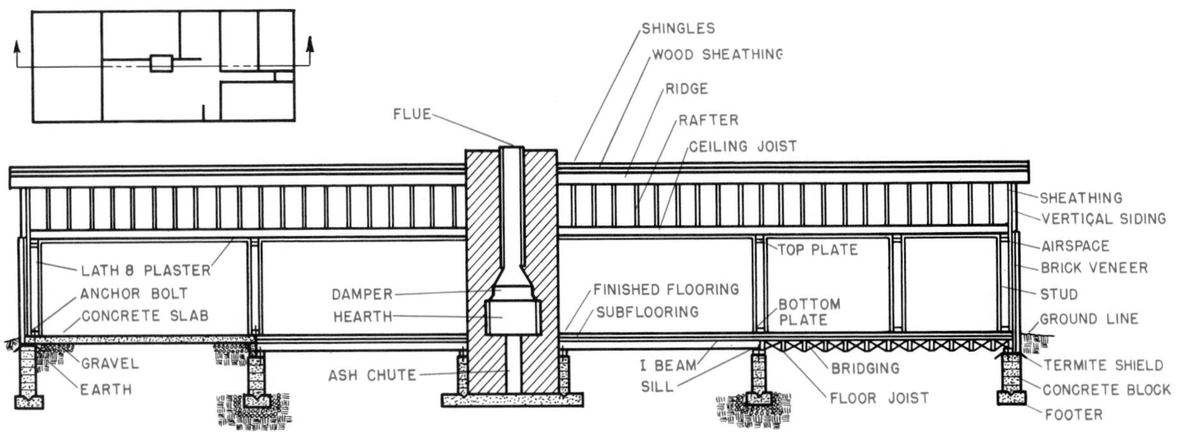

Fig. 46–9. A section through a house, parallel with the roof ridge.

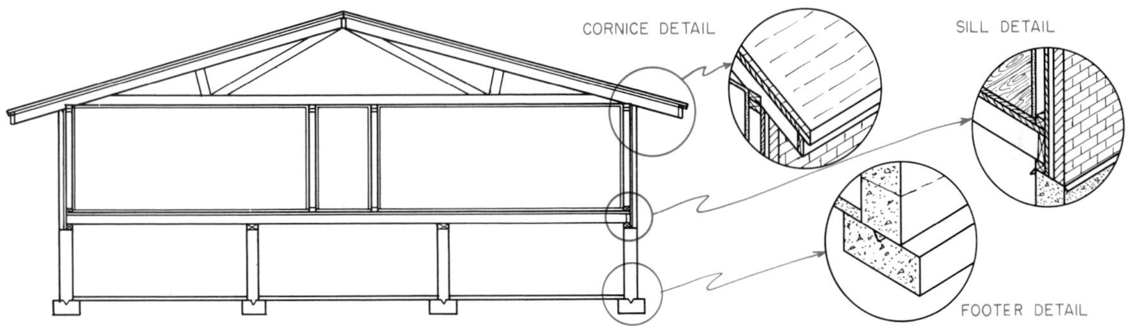

Fig. 46–10. Three common sectional details are the cornice, sill, and footer.

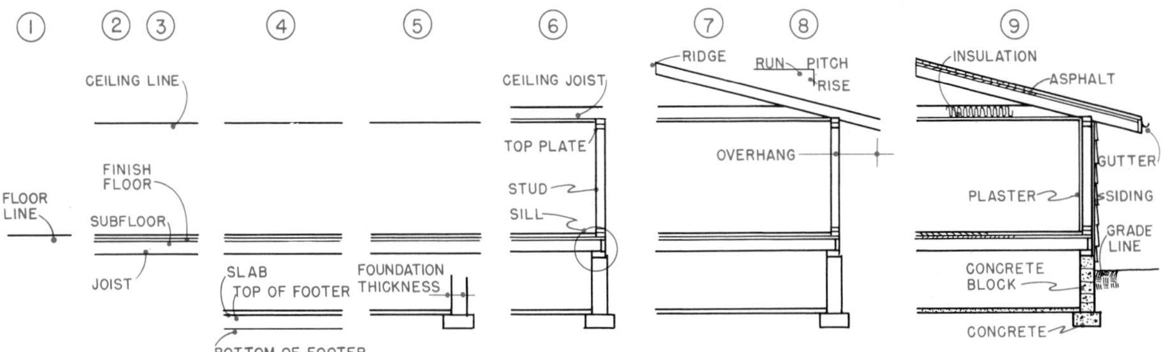

Fig. 46–11. The sequence of projecting an elevation section.

3. From the floor line measure up and draw the ceiling line.
4. Measure down from the floor line to establish the top of the basement slab and footer line, and draw in the thickness of the footer.
5. Draw two vertical lines representing the thickness of the foundation and the footer.
6. Construct the sill detail and show the alignment of the stud and top plate.
7. Measure the overhang from the stud line and draw the roof pitch by projecting from the top plate on the angle which represents the rise over the run.
8. Establish the ridge point by measuring the distance from the outside wall horizontally to the center of the structure.
9. Add details and symbols representing siding and interior finish.

SECTIONAL DIMENSIONING

Since longitudinal sections expose the size and shape of building materials and components not revealed on floor plans and elevations, the longitudinal section is an excellent place on which to locate many detail dimensions. Longitudinal-section dimensions primarily show specific elevations, distances, and the exact size of building materials.

Figure 46–12 shows some of the more important dimensions that can be placed on longitudinal sections. The rules for dimensioning elevation drawings apply also to longitudinal elevation sections (see Unit 38).

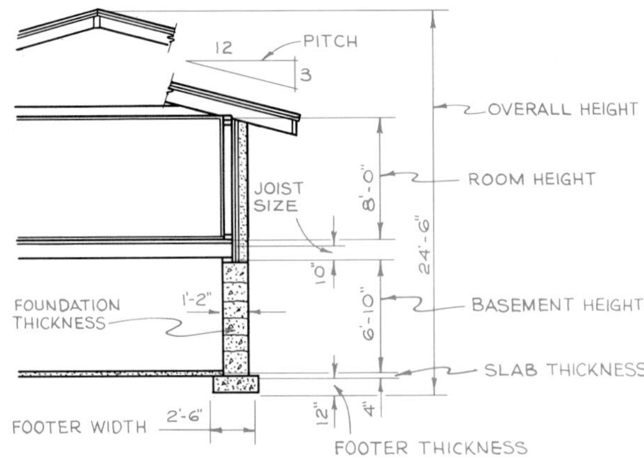

Fig. 46–12. Methods of dimensioning elevation sections.

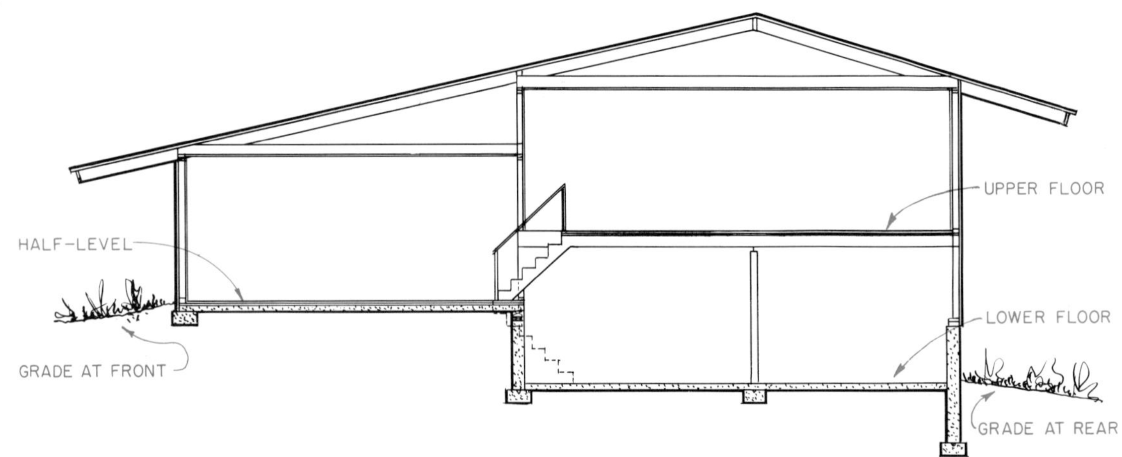

Fig. 46–13. A section through a split-level home.

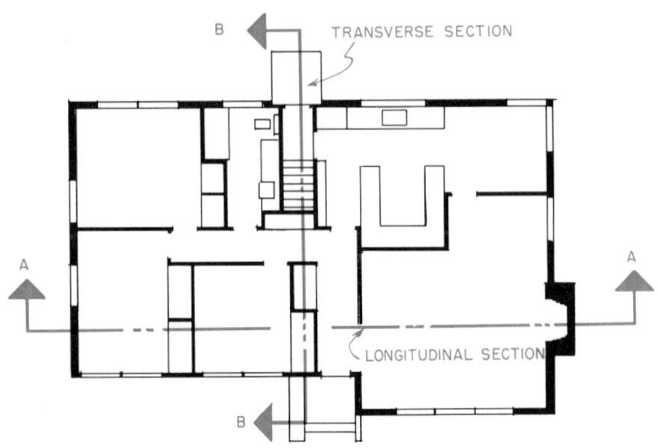

Fig. 46–14. Draw and dimension sections AA and BB.

MULTILEVEL SECTIONS

Longitudinal sections are especially effective and necessary for showing the various methods of constructing multilevel buildings, since footers, grade lines, slabs, and floor lines vary greatly. Figure 46–13 shows a section of a split-level home. It is difficult to show the relationship of the various levels and the construction of each without using this type of section.

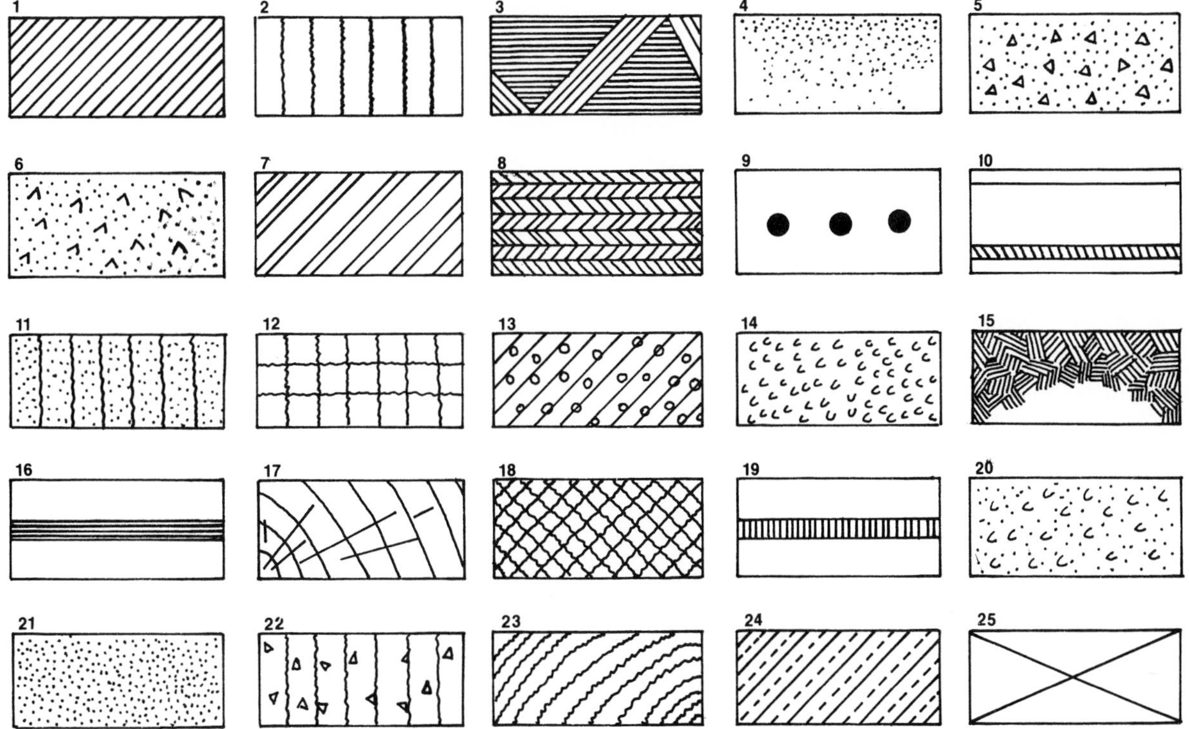

Fig. 46–15. Identify these materials.

PROBLEMS

1. Draw a longitudinal section of a house you have designed.
2. Draw a longitudinal section of your home.
3. Draw a longitudinal section of your school building.
4. Draw and dimension a longitudinal section AA of the plan indicated in Fig. 46–14.
5. Draw section BB, Fig. 46–14.
6. Identify the symbols found in Fig. 46–15.
7. Define these terms: *longitudinal section, whole section, cutting plane, offset cutting plane, section lining, transverse section.*

UNIT 47

Detail Sections

Because longitudinal sections are usually drawn to a small scale (1/8″ = 1′—0″ or 1/4″ = 1′—0″), many parts are difficult to interpret and dimension. In order to reveal the exact position and size of many small members, the draftsman needs an enlarged section.

VERTICAL-WALL SECTIONS

One method of showing sections larger than is possible in the longitudinal section is through the use of *break lines* to reduce vertical distances on exterior walls. Using break lines

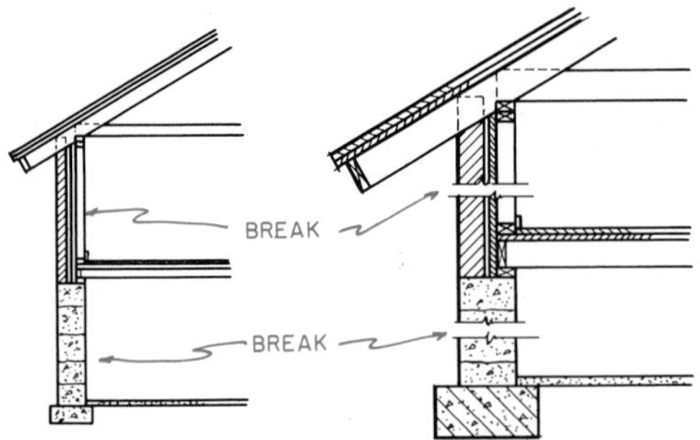

Fig. 47–1. Sections can be drawn larger when break lines are used.

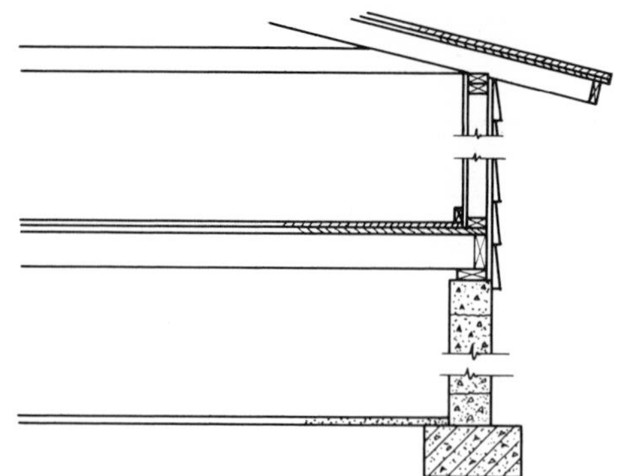

Fig. 47–2. The use of break lines on a frame-wall section.

allows the draftsman to draw the area larger than is possible when the entire length is included in the drawing. Break lines are placed where the material does not change over a long distance. Figure 47–1 shows the difference between a brick-veneer wall drawn completely to a small scale and the same wall enlarged by the use of break lines. Figure 47–2 shows the use of break lines to enlarge a frame-wall section.

When a very large section is needed for interpretation or dimensioning purposes, it is sometimes impossible to draw the entire wall section even with the use of break lines. In this case a *removed section* is prepared. Removed sections are frequently drawn for the ridge, cornice, sill, footer, and beam areas, as shown in Fig. 47–3.

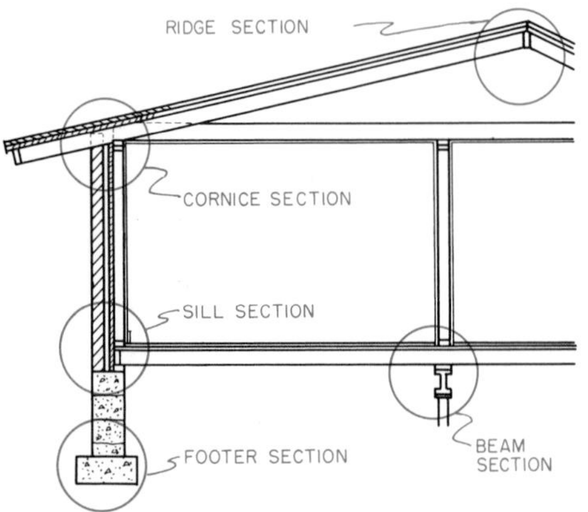

Fig. 47–3. Removed sections are often drawn of the ridge, cornice, sill, footer, and beam areas.

Cornice Sections

Figure 47–4 shows several typical cornice sections and the pictorial interpretation of each. Cornice sections are used to show the relationship between the outside wall, top plate, and rafter construction. Some cornice sections show gutter details.

Sill Sections

Sill sections, as shown in Fig. 47–5, explain graphically how the foundation supports and intersects with the floor system and the outside wall.

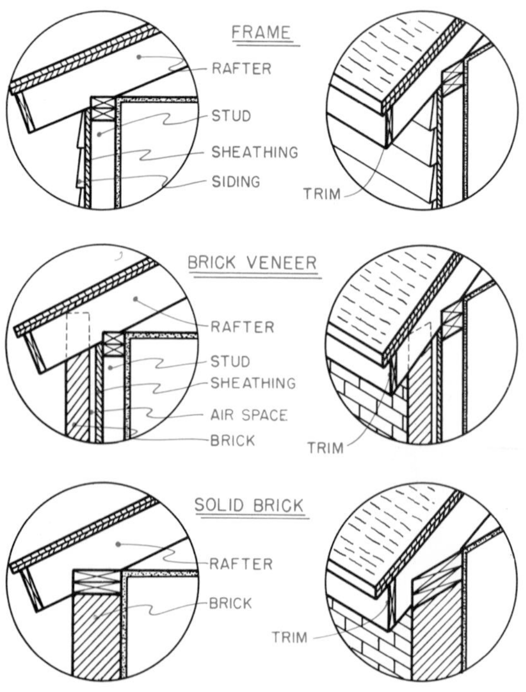

Fig. 47–4. Compare the pictorial section with the orthographic section.

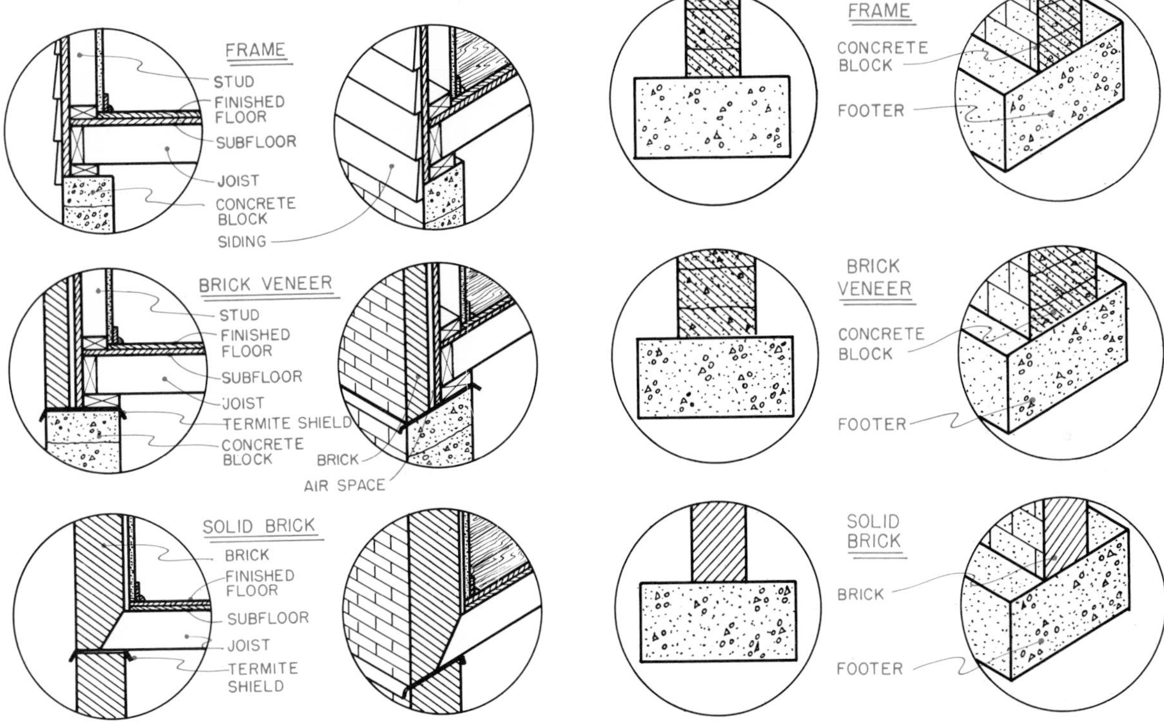

Fig. 47–5. A comparison of sill sections and the sill constructions they represent.

Fig. 47–6. A comparison of pictorial and orthographic footer sections.

Footer Sections

A footer section is needed to show the width and length of the footer, the type of material used, and the position of the foundation wall on the footer. Figure 47–6 shows several footer details and the pictorial interpretation of each type.

Beam Details

Beam details are necessary to show how the joists are supported by beams and how the beams support columns or foundation walls. As in all other sections, the position of the cutting-plane line is extremely important. Figure 47–7 shows two possible positions of the

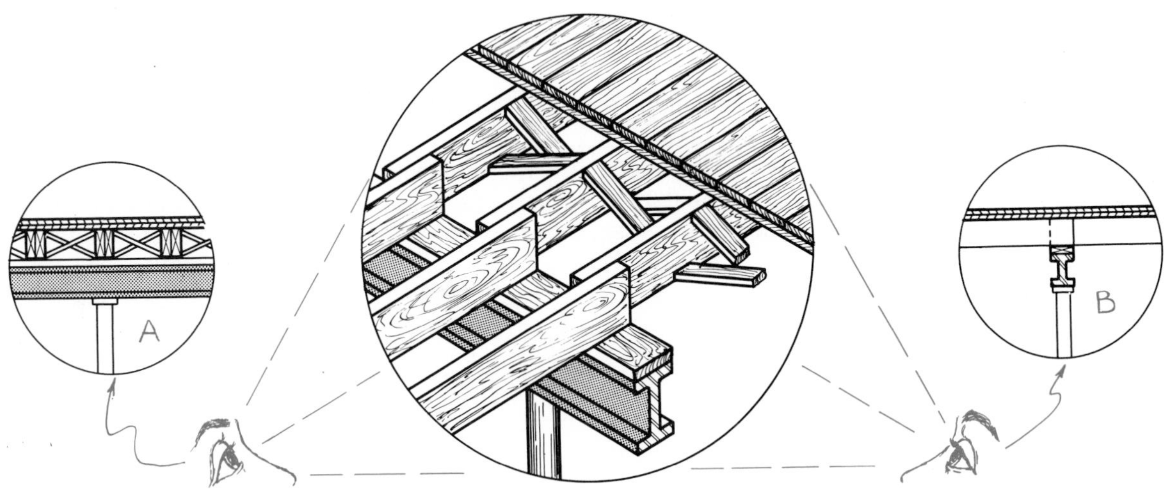

Fig. 47–7. Beam sections can be drawn from two angles.

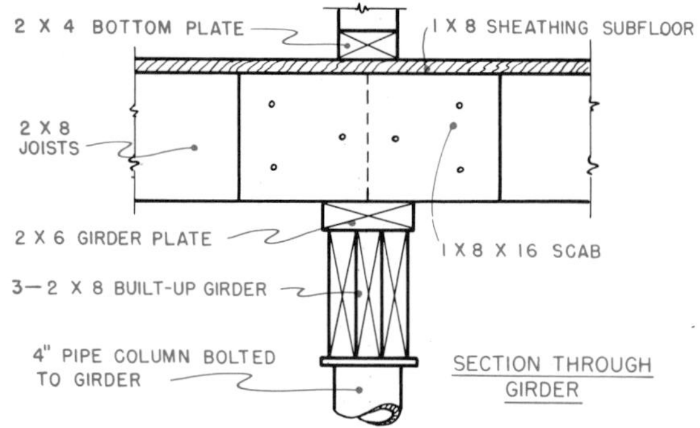

Fig. 47–8. A section through a built-up wood girder.

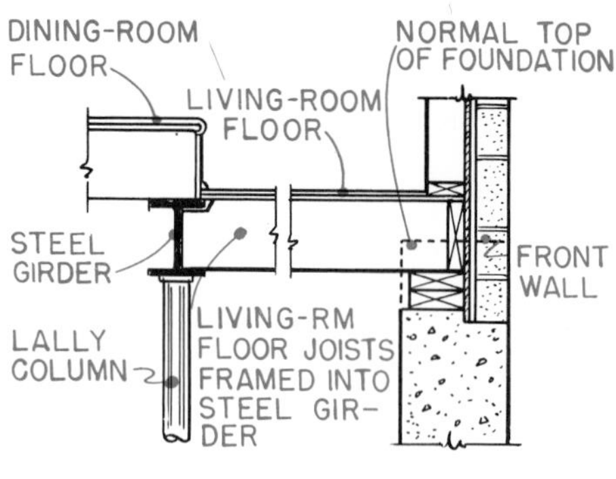

Fig. 47–9. The beam section and sill section can be shown on the same drawing by use of break lines.

cutting plane. If the cutting-plane line is placed parallel to the beam, you see a cross section of the joist, as shown in A. If the cutting-plane line is placed perpendicular to the beam, you see a cross section of the beam, as shown in B. Figure 47–8 shows a similar section through a built-up wood girder.

Sometimes it is desirable or necessary to show the relationship between the beam detail and a detail of the sill area. This relationship is especially needed when a room is sunken or elevated. In Fig. 47–9 the beam and sill areas on one sectional drawing are shown by breaking the area between the sill and the beam.

Interior-Wall Sections

To illustrate further the methods of constructing inside partitions, sections are often drawn of interior walls at the base and at the ceiling. *Base sections* (Fig. 47–10) show how the wall-finishing materials are attached to the studs and how the intersection between the floor and wall is constructed. The section at the ceiling, as shown in Fig. 47–11, is drawn to show the intersection between the ceiling and the wall and to show how the finishing materials of the wall and ceiling are related.

HORIZONTAL-WALL SECTIONS

Horizontal-wall sections are drawn of interior and exterior walls.

Exterior Walls

A floor plan is a horizontal section. However, many details are omitted from the floor plan because of the small scale used. Very few construction details are necessary to interpret adequately the floor plan. If the floor plan is drawn exactly as a true horizontal section, it will appear similar to the sections shown in Fig. 47–12. When more information is needed to describe the exact construction of the outside corners and the intersections between interior partitions and outside walls, horizontal sections of the type shown in Fig. 47–12 are prepared.

Interior-Wall Sections

Typical sections are often drawn of interior-wall intersections. Unusual wall-construction methods are *always* sectioned. For example, a horizontal section is needed to show the inside

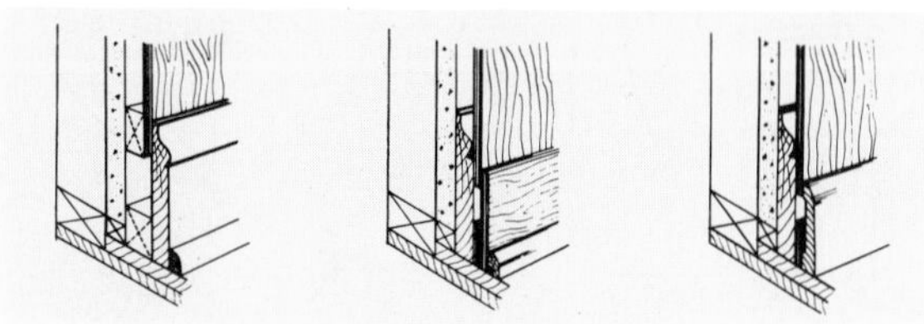

Fig. 47–10. Pictorial sections through the base of an interior partition.

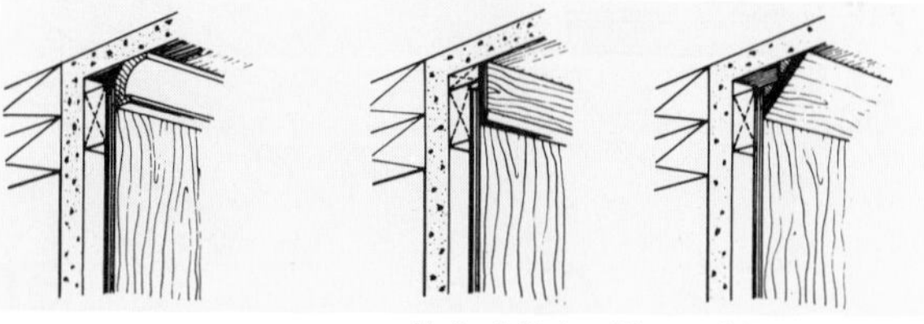

United States Plywood Corporation

Fig. 47–11. Pictorial sections at the intersection of interior wall and ceiling.

corner construction of a paneled wall (Fig. 47–13). An outside corner section of the same type of paneling construction is shown in Fig. 47–14. Horizontal sections are also used extensively to show how paneled joints and other building joints are constructed (Fig. 47–15).

Horizontal sections are also very effective in illustrating the various methods of attaching building materials together. For example, the sections shown in Fig. 47–16 illustrate the various methods for attaching furring and paneling to interior walls.

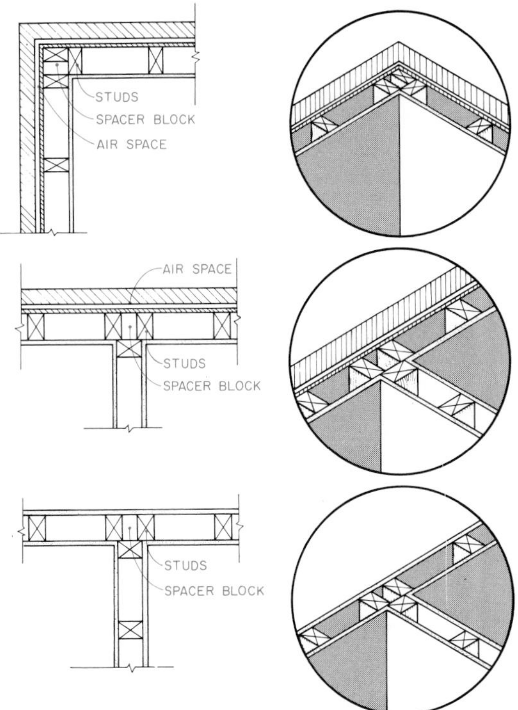

Fig. 47–12. Horizontal sections through exterior-wall intersections.

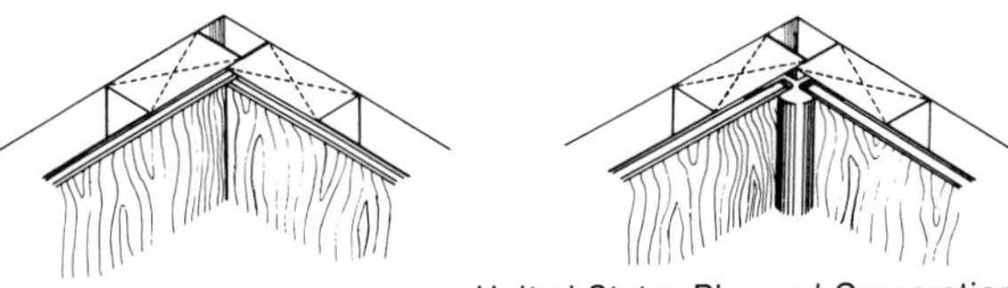

United States Plywood Corporation

Fig. 47–13. Two sections of an inside paneled-wall corner.

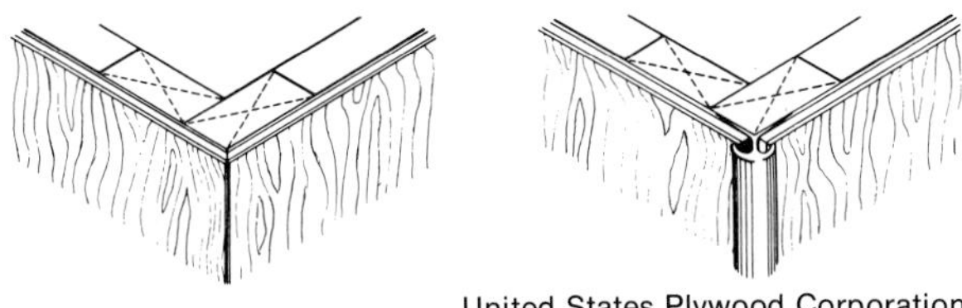

United States Plywood Corporation

Fig. 47–14. Two sections of an outside paneled-wall corner.

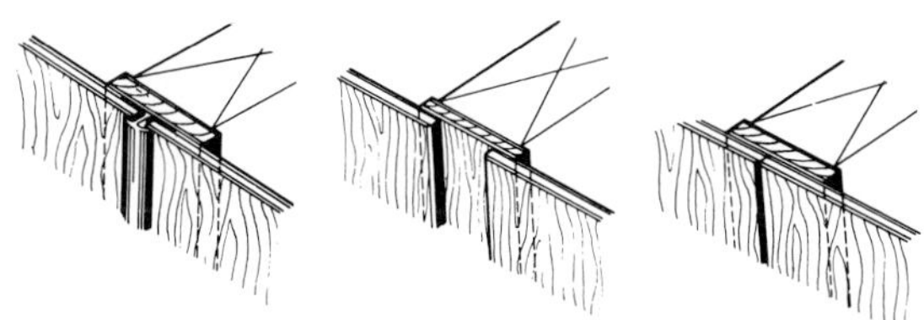

Fig. 47–15. Panel-joint details.

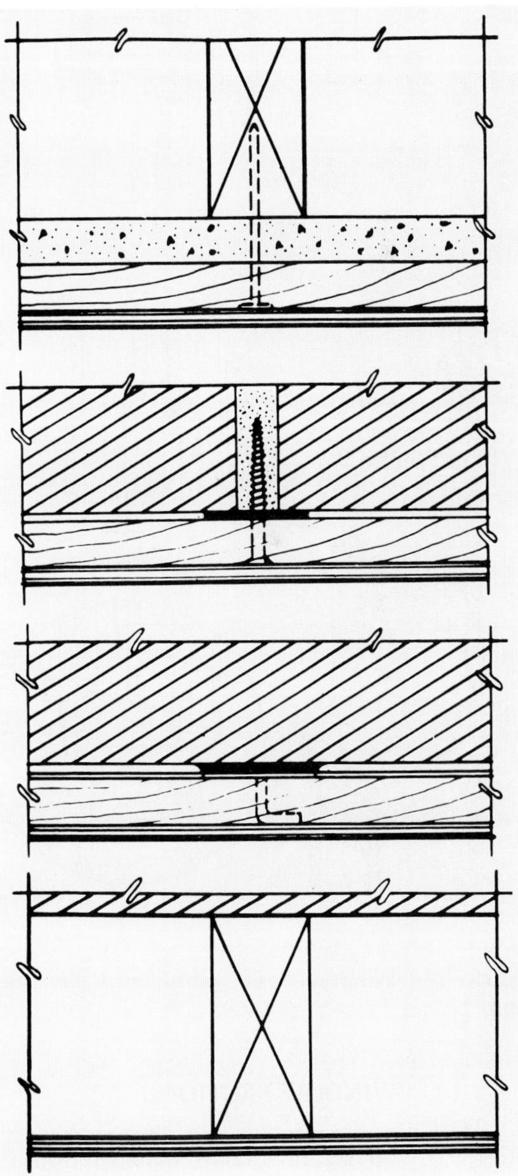

Fig. 47–16. Sections of methods of attaching paneling.

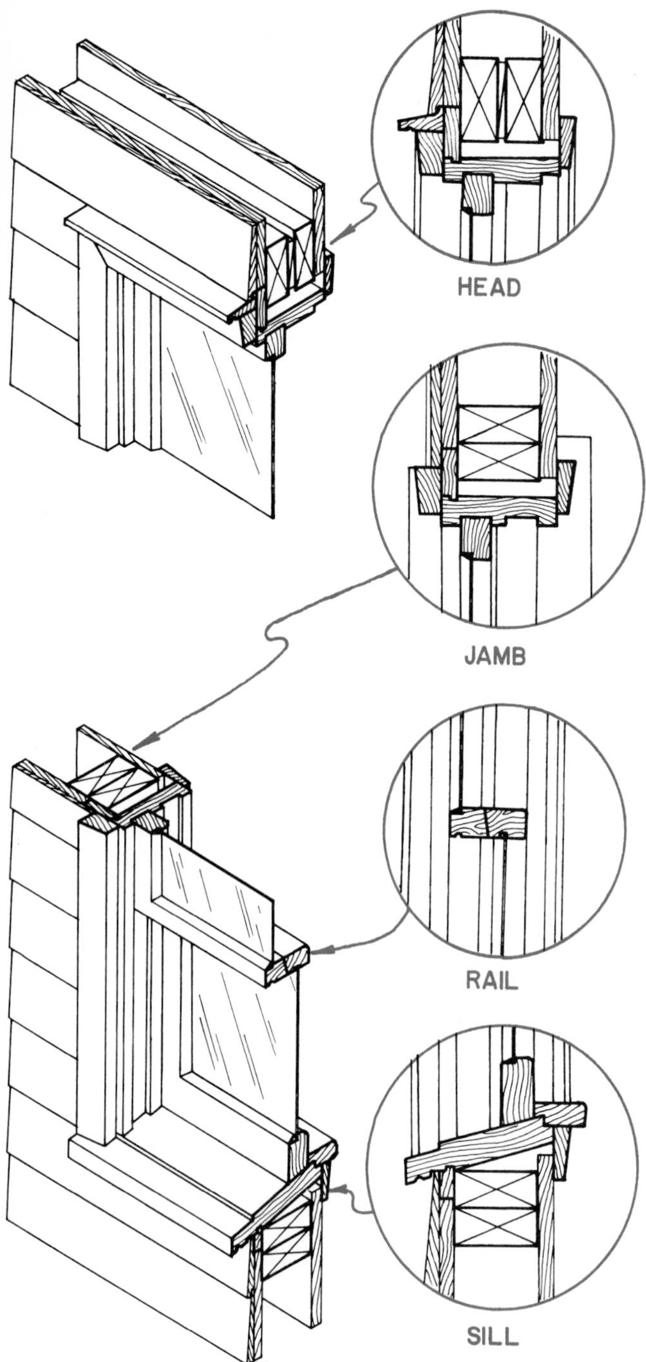

Fig. 47–17. Window head, jamb, and sill sections.

WINDOW SECTIONS

Because much of the actual construction of most windows is hidden, a section is necessary for the correct interpretation of most window-construction methods. Figure 47–17 shows the areas of windows that are commonly sectioned. These include sections of the head, jamb, and sill construction.

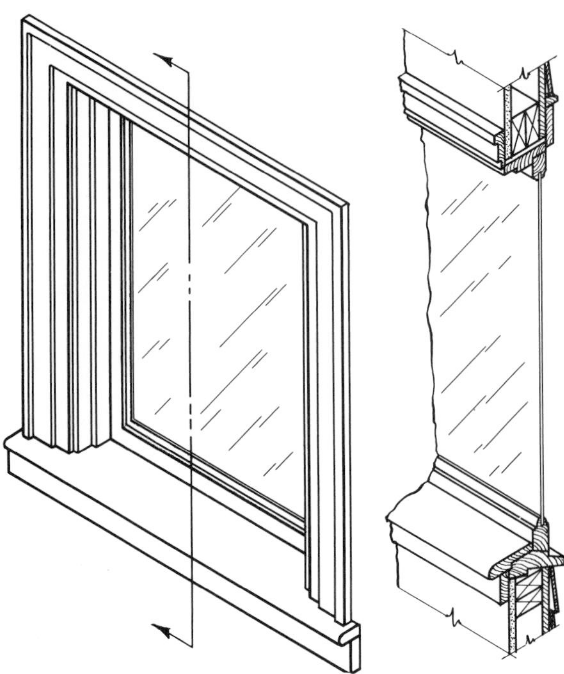

Fig. 47–18. Head and sill sections are in the same plane.

Vertical Sections

Sill sections and head sections are vertical sections and are sometimes prepared on the same sectional drawing. Preparing sill and head sections on the same drawing is possible only when a small scale is used. If a larger scale is needed, the sill and head must be drawn independently, or a break line must be used. Figure 47–18 shows the relationship between the cutting-plane line and the sill and head sections. The circled areas in Fig. 47–19 show the areas that are removed when a separate head and sill section is prepared.

Horizontal Sections

When a cutting-plane line is extended horizontally across the entire window, the resulting sections are known as *jamb sections.* Figure 47–20 shows the derivation of the jamb section from a horizontal cutting-plane line. Figure 47–21 shows the method of projecting the jamb details from the window-elevation drawing.

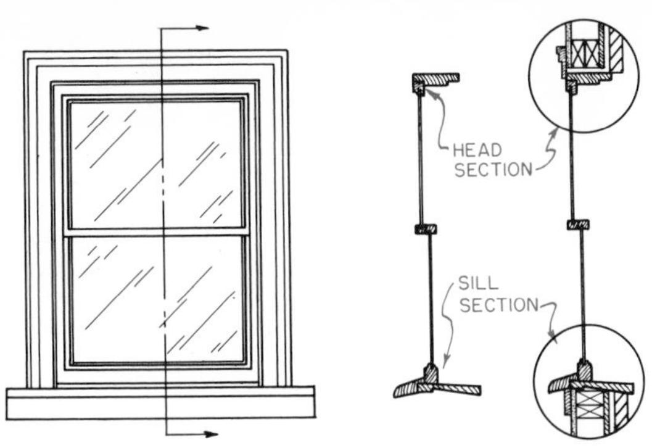

Fig. 47–19. The projection of the head and sill section.

Since the construction of both jambs is usually the same, the right jamb drawing is the reverse of the left. Only one jamb detail is normally drawn. The builder interprets the right jamb or left jamb as the reverse of the other.

Commercial Details

Many window manufacturers use pictorial sectioning techniques to show the correct installation of windows. The relationship between a commercially manufactured window and the framing methods necessary for correct fitting is shown in Fig. 47–22. Notice that this section shows the head, sill, and jamb construction in one pictorial view.

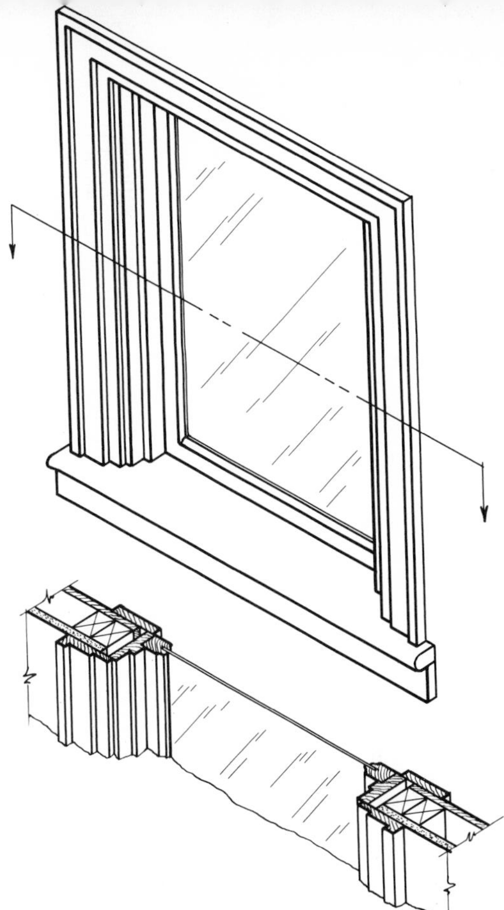

Fig. 47–20. The right and left jamb are in the same plane.

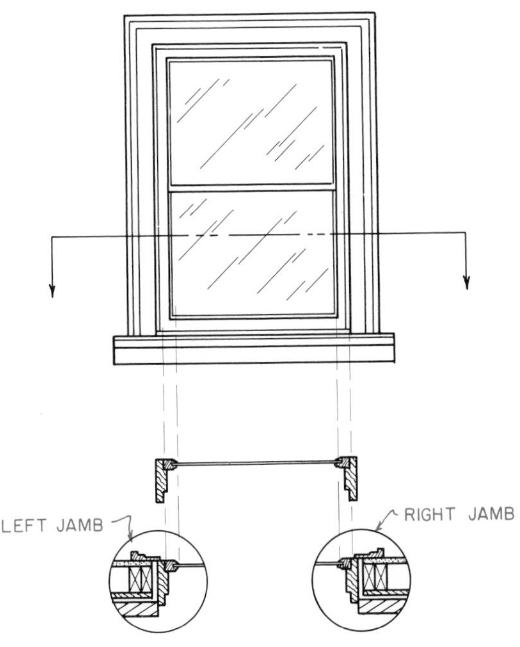

Fig. 47–21. The projection of the left- and right-jamb section.

Ceco Steel Products Corporation

Fig. 47–22. A pictorial section showing sill, jamb, and head details.

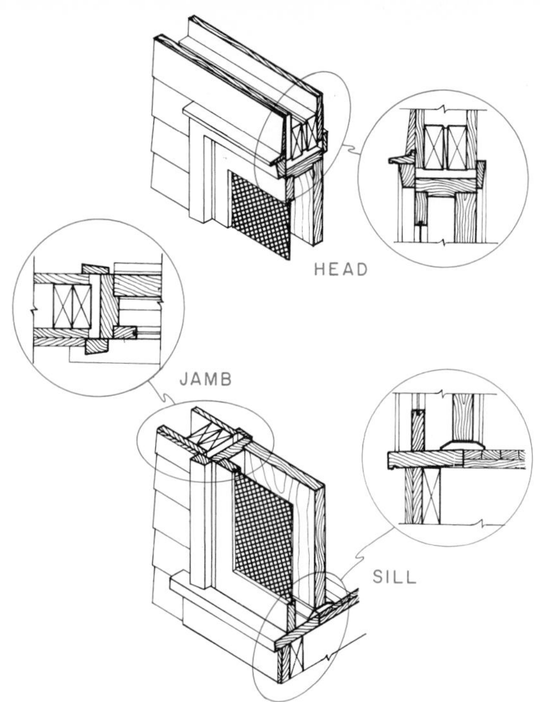

Fig. 47–23. Head, jamb, and sill details can be removed or drawn pictorially.

Fig. 47–24. The head and sill sections of a door, in the same plane.

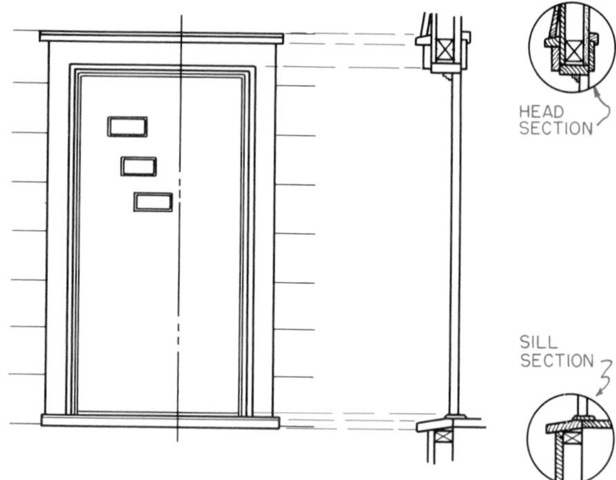

Fig. 47–25. The projection of the head and sill sections of a door frame.

DOOR SECTIONS

A horizontal section of all doors is shown on a floor plan. However, this section is almost completely symbolic and lacks sufficient detail. An enlarged jamb, head, and sill section, as shown in Fig. 47–23, is necessary to describe completely the door-construction methods used. When a cutting-plane line is extended vertically through the sill and head, a section similar to the one shown in Fig. 47–24 is revealed. However, these sections are often too small to show the desired degree of detail necessary for construction. A removed section, as shown in Fig. 47–25, is drawn to show the enlarged head and sill sections. A break line is used to reduce the distance between head and sill sections.

Since doors are normally not as wide as they are high, an adequate jamb detail can be projected, as shown in Fig. 47–26, without the use of break lines or removed sections. Figure 47–27 shows the method of projecting the left and right jamb sections from the door elevation drawing. Occasionally architectural draftsmen prepare sectional drawings of the rough framing details of the door head, sill, and jamb, exclusive of the door and door frame assembly. In such drawings, the draftsman draws the framing section with the door frame and door removed. Usually, however, door sections are prepared with the framing trim and door in their proper locations.

Drawings of garage doors and industrial size doors are usually prepared with sections of the brackets and apparatus necessary to house the door assembly, as shown in Fig. 47–28. This is done even when stock doors are used.

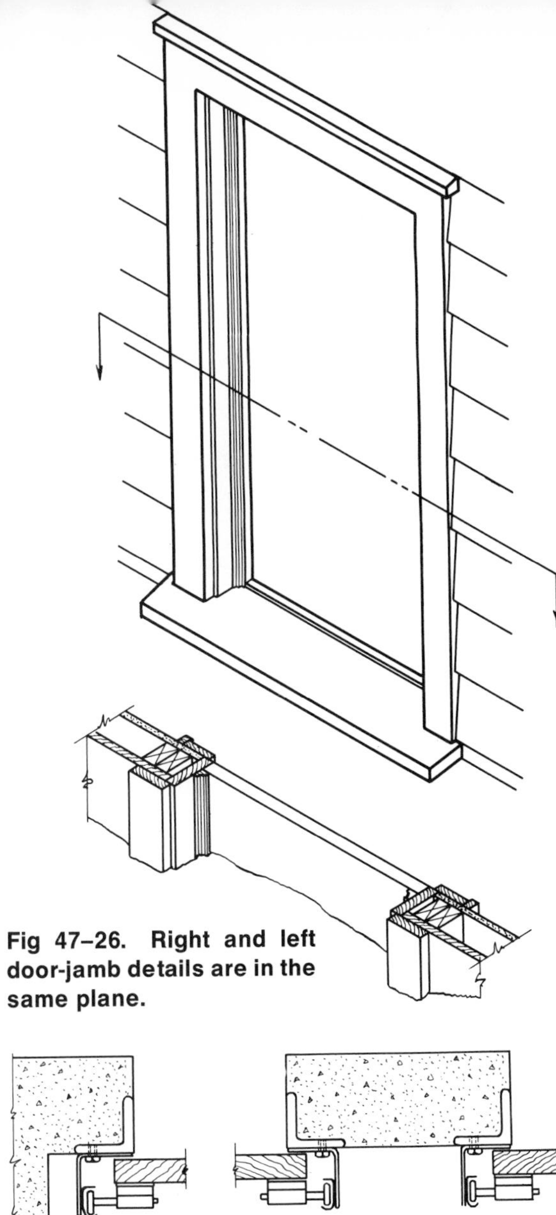

Fig 47–26. **Right and left door-jamb details are in the same plane.**

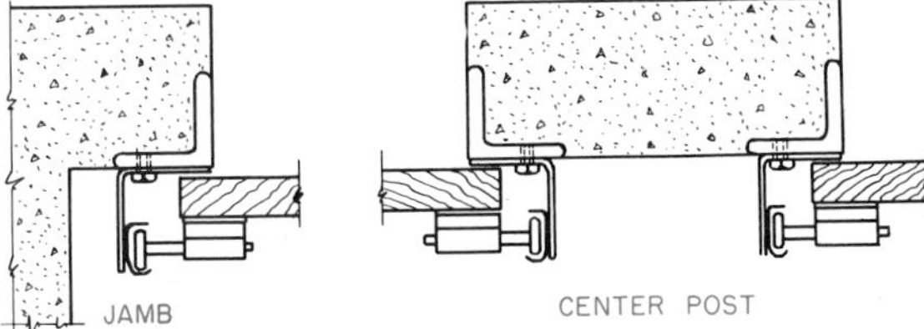

Fig. 47–28. **Special brackets and devices often require detailed sectional drawing.**

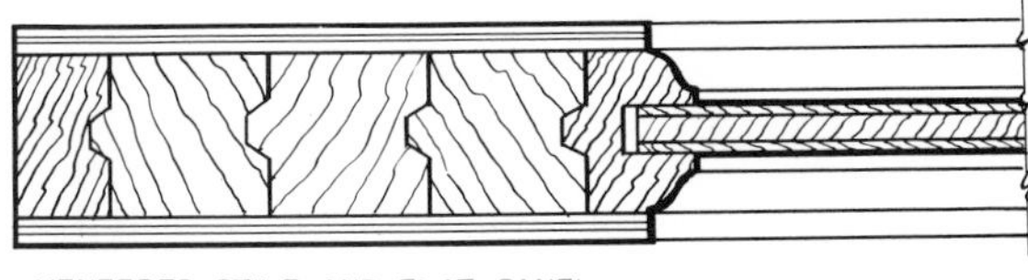

Fig. 47–29. **Interior door construction is shown by a sectional drawing.**

Rarely is the architectural draftsman called upon to prepare sectional drawings of internal door construction details. Most doors are purchased from manufacturers' stock.

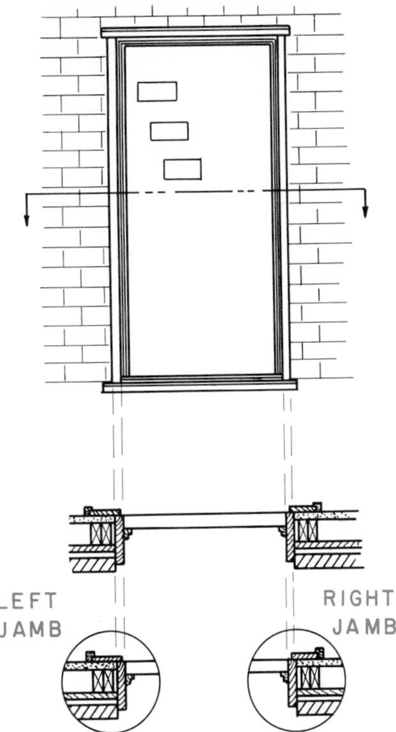

Fig. 47–27. **The projection of the left and right door-jamb section.**

Occasionally doors are supplied by the manufacturer specifically for a building. Only when a special door is to be manufactured is a sectional drawing prepared of the internal detail of the door construction (Fig. 47–29).

PROBLEMS

1. **Draw a large cornice, sill, and footer section from the circled sections shown in Fig. 47–3.**
2. **Draw a section through the girder, as shown in Fig. 47–8, revolving the cutting plane line 90°.**
3. **Draw a head, jamb, and sill section of the window shown in Fig. 47–22.**
4. **Draw a sill, cornice, and footer section of a house you have designed.**
5. **Draw a sill, cornice, and footer section of your home.**
6. **Prepare an interior-wall section at the ceiling and at the floor line to accompany the section shown in Fig. 47–8.**
7. **Draw a detail section of the intersection of the inside foundation-support wall, I beam, and interior partition, as shown in Fig. 47–9.**
8. **Define these terms: *break line, removed section, interior-wall sections, vertical-wall sections, horizontal-wall sections, jamb sections, head sections, sill sections.***

SECTION 11

Foundation Plans

The methods and materials used in constructing foundations vary greatly in different parts of the country and are continually changing. The basic principles of foundation construction are the same, regardless of the application.

Every structure needs a foundation. The function of a foundation is to provide a level and uniformly distributed support for the structure. The foundation must be strong enough to support and distribute the load of the structure, and sufficiently level to prevent the walls from cracking and the doors and windows from sticking. The foundation also helps to prevent cold air and dampness from entering the house. The foundation waterproofs the basement and forms the supporting walls of the basement.

U. S. Army Photograph

UNIT 48

Foundation Members

The structural members of the foundation vary according to the design and size of the foundation.

FOOTING

The footing, or footer (Fig. 48–1), distributes the weight of the house over a large area. Concrete is commonly used for footers because it can be poured to maintain a firm contact with the supporting soil. Concrete is also effective because it can withstand heavy weights and is a relatively decay-proof material. Steel reinforcement is sometimes added to the concrete footer to keep the concrete from cracking and to provide additional support (Fig. 48–2). The footer must be laid on solid ground to support the

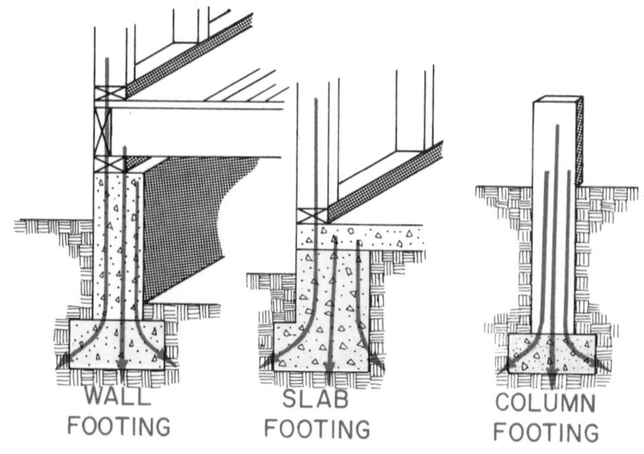

Fig. 48–1. Footers distribute the weight of the building over a wide area.

Fig. 48–2. Steel reinforcing rods add strength to the footer.

weight of the building effectively and evenly. In cold climates the footer must be placed below the frost line.

FOUNDATION WALLS

The function of the foundation wall is to support the load of the building above the ground line and to transmit the weight of the house to the footing. Foundation walls are normally made of concrete, stone, brick, or concrete block (Fig. 48–3). When a complete excavation is made for a basement, foundation walls also provide the walls of the basement (Fig. 48–4).

PIERS AND COLUMNS

Piers and columns are vertical members, usually made of concrete, brick, steel, or wood, which are used to support the floor systems (Fig. 48–5). Piers or columns may be used as the sole support of the structure. They also may be used in conjunction with the foundation wall and provide only the intermediate support between girders or beams.

ANCHOR BOLTS

Anchor bolts are embedded in the top of the foundation walls or piers (Fig. 48–6). The exposed part of the bolt is threaded so that the first wood member (the sill) can be bolted onto

Fig. 48–3. Foundation walls are constructed of concrete, stone, brick, or concrete block.

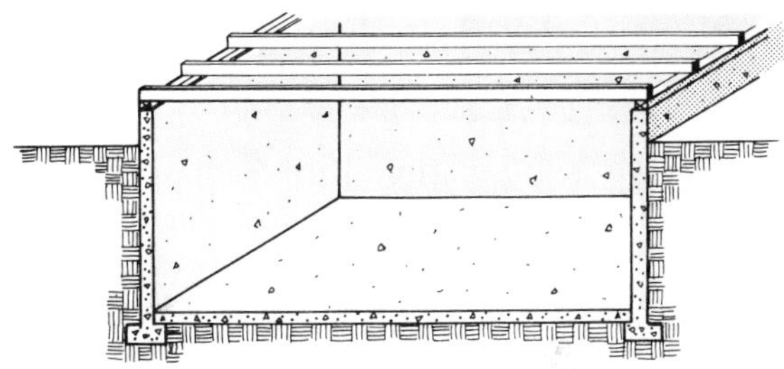

Fig. 48–4. A foundation wall can also be a basement wall.

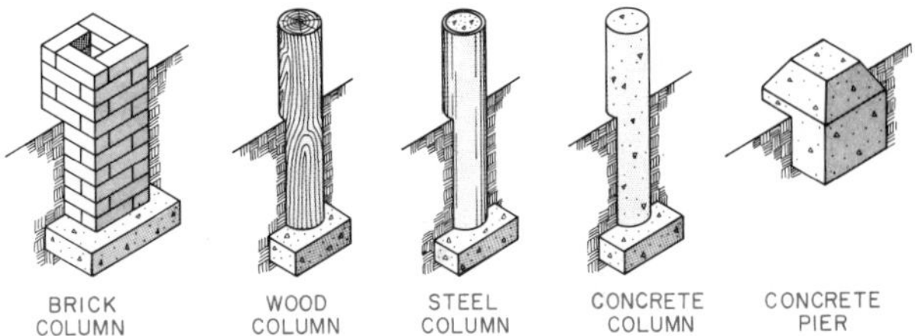

Fig. 48–5. Piers and columns are made of concrete, brick, steel, or wood.

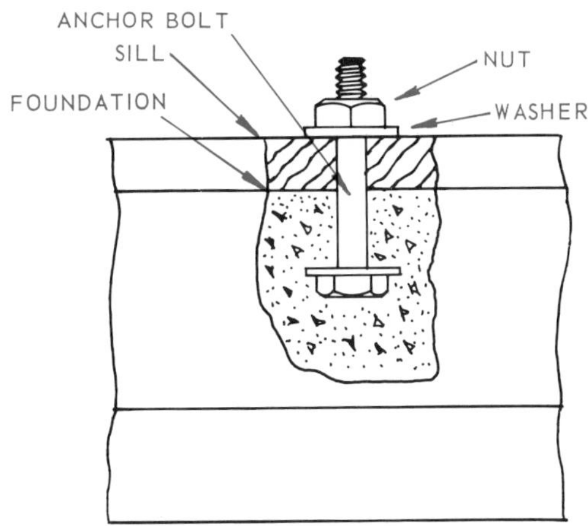

Fig. 48–6. Anchor bolts hold the sill to the foundation.

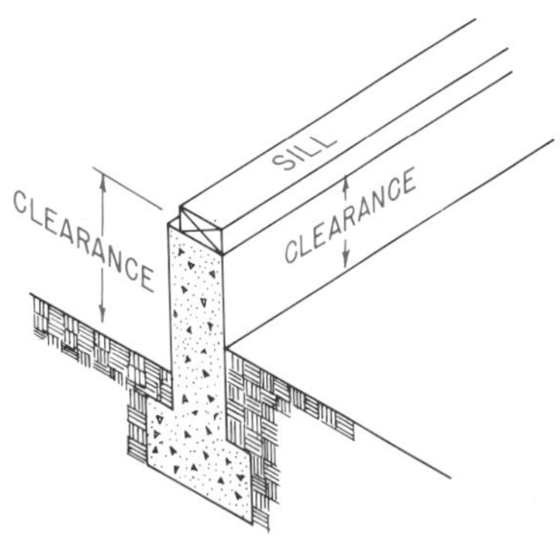

Fig. 48–7. The sill is the point of contact between the foundation and the framework of the building.

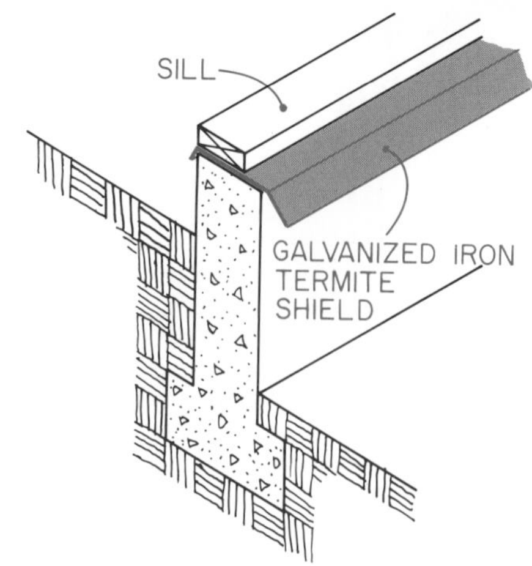

Fig. 48–8. Placement of a termite shield between the foundation and the sill protects the wood from termites.

the top of the foundation wall. Anchor bolts for residential use are ½″ (12.7 mm) in diameter and 10″ (254 mm) long. They are spaced at approximately 6′ (1.8 m) intervals, starting 1′ (0.3 m) from each corner.

SILLS

Sills are wood members that are fastened with anchor bolts to the foundation wall (Fig. 48–7). Sills provide the base for attaching the exterior walls to the foundation.

A galvanized iron sheet is often placed under the sill to check termites (Fig. 48–8), since the sill is normally the lowest wood member used in the construction. Building laws specify the distance required from the bottom of the sill to the grade line inside and outside the foundation.

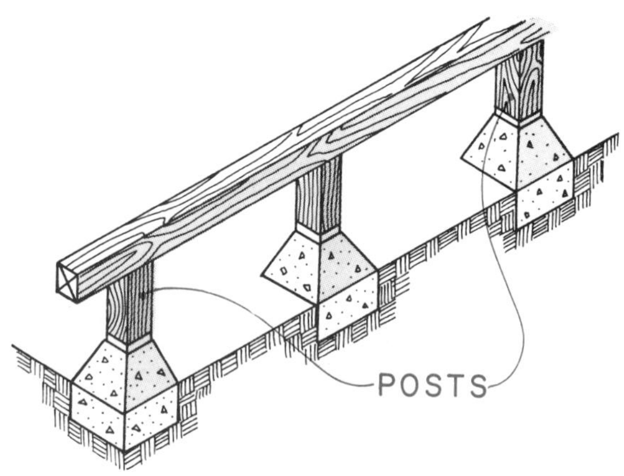

Fig. 48–9. Posts transmit the weight of girders and beams to the footings.

POSTS

Posts are wood members that support the weight of girders or beams and transmit the weight to the footings (Fig. 48–9).

CRIPPLES

Cripples are used to raise the floor level without the use of a higher foundation wall (Fig. 48–10). Since the load of the structure must be transmitted through the cripples, these are usually heavy members, often four-by-fours (4 × 4's) and spaced at close intervals.

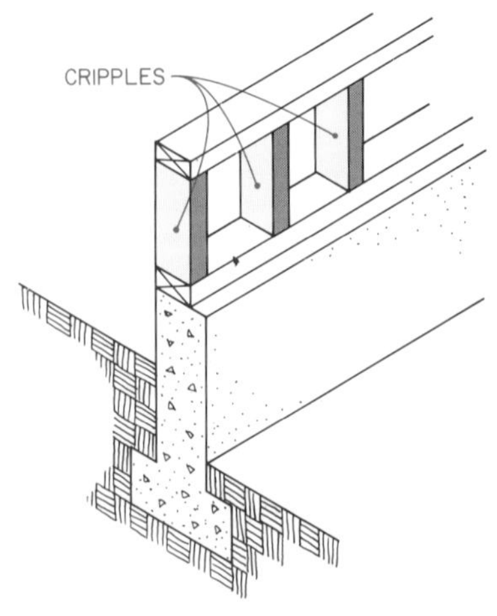

Fig. 48–10. Cripples raise the height of a floor without raising the foundation height.

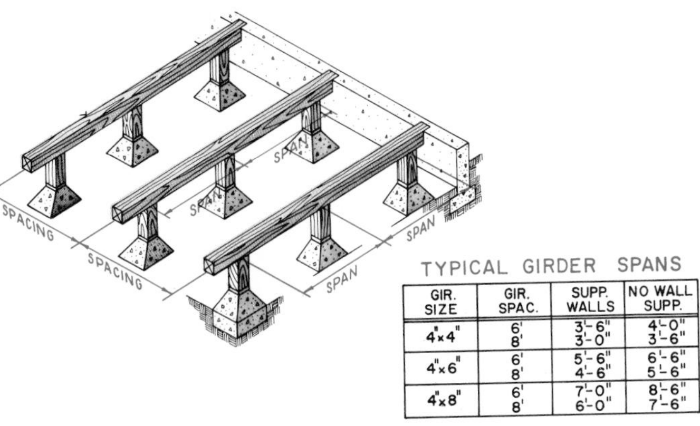

TYPICAL GIRDER SPANS

GIR. SIZE	GIR. SPAC.	SUPP. WALLS	NO WALL SUPP.
4"x4"	6' 8'	3'-6" 3'-0"	4'-0" 3'-6"
4"x6"	6' 8'	5'-6" 4'-6"	6'-6" 5'-6"
4"x8"	6' 8'	7'-0" 6'-0"	8'-6" 7'-6"

Fig. 48–11. Girders are major horizontal support members.

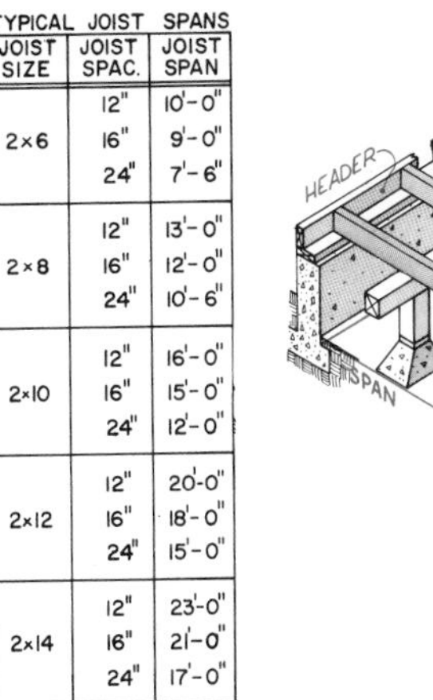

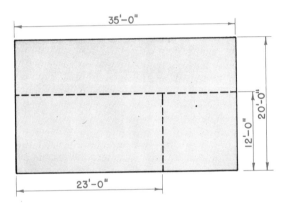

TYPICAL JOIST SPANS

JOIST SIZE	JOIST SPAC.	JOIST SPAN
2×6	12" 16" 24"	10'-0" 9'-0" 7'-6"
2×8	12" 16" 24"	13'-0" 12'-0" 10'-6"
2×10	12" 16" 24"	16'-0" 15'-0" 12'-0"
2×12	12" 16" 24"	20'-0" 18'-0" 15'-0"
2×14	12" 16" 24"	23'-0" 21'-0" 17'-0"

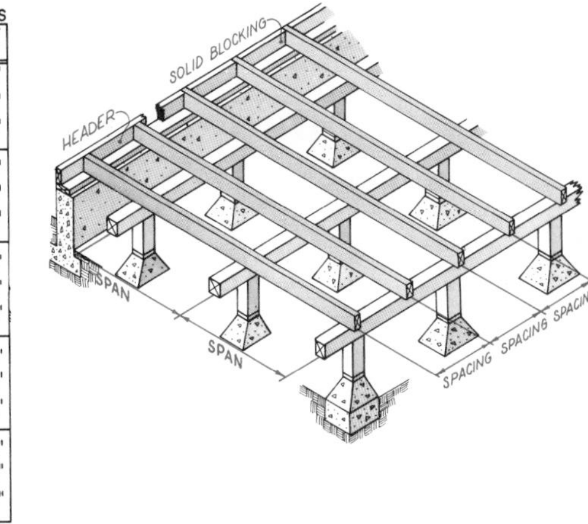

Fig. 48–12. Joists support the floor and rest on girders.

GIRDERS

Girders are major horizontal support members upon which the floor system is laid. They are supported by posts and piers and are secured to the foundation wall as shown in Fig. 48–11. Girder sizes are closely regulated by building codes. The allowable span of the girder depends on the size of the girder. A decrease in the size of a girder means that the span must be decreased by adding additional column supports under the girder. Built-up wood girders for residential construction are normally made from 2 × 8's or 2 × 10's spiked together.

STEEL BEAMS

Steel beams perform the same function as wood girders. However, steel beams can span larger areas than can wood girders of an equivalent size.

JOISTS

Joists are the part of the floor system that is placed on the girders. Joists span either from girder to girder or from girder to the foundation wall. The ends of the joists butt against a header or extend to the end of the sill, with blocking placed between them as shown in Fig. 48–12.

35'-0"
20'-0"
12'-0"
23'-0"

Fig. 48–13. Draw a T foundation for this plan.

PROBLEMS

1. Draw a slab-foundation plan to the scale ½" = 1'—0" for the floor plan shown in Fig. 6–2.
2. Draw a T-foundation plan for Fig. 48–13, using the scale ¼" = 1'—0".
3. Draw a slab foundation for Fig. 48–13, using the scale ¼" = 1'—0".
4. Know these architectural terms: *foundation, structural members, footing, concrete, foundation wall, pier, column, anchor, sill, post, cripple, girder, span, spacing, joists.*

UNIT 49

Foundation Types

The type of foundation the architect selects for a structure depends on the nature of the soil, the size and weight of the structure, the climate, building laws, and the relationship of the floor to the grade line (Fig. 49–1). Foundations are divided into three basic types: the T foundation, the slab foundation, and the pier and column foundation (Fig. 49–2).

T FOUNDATIONS

The T foundation consists of a trench footer upon which is placed a concrete wall or a concrete-block wall. The combination of the footer and the wall forms an inverted T. The T foundation is popular in structures with basements or when the bottom of the first floor must be accessible (Fig. 49–3).

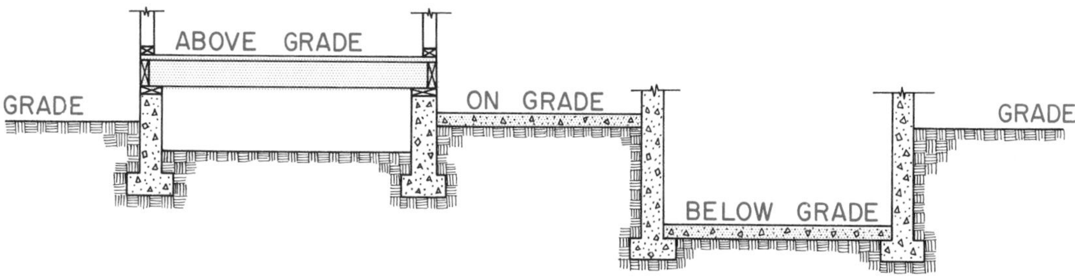

Fig. 49–1. Foundation positions.

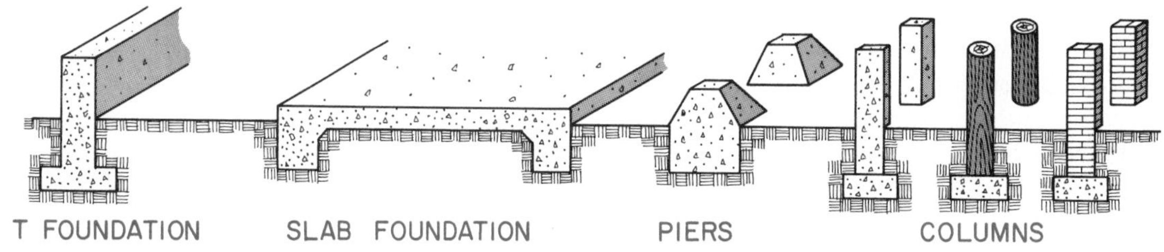

Fig. 49–2. Types of foundations.

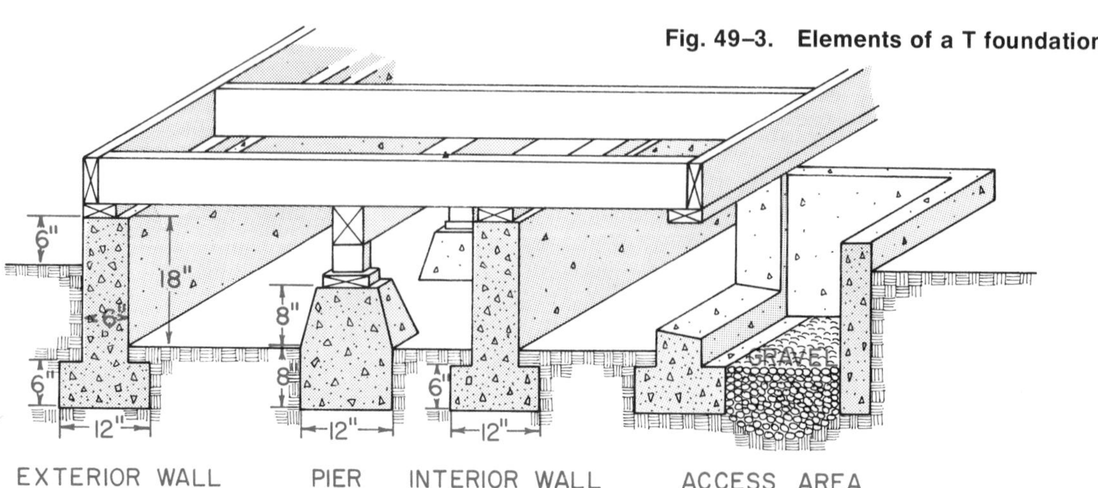

Fig. 49–3. Elements of a T foundation.

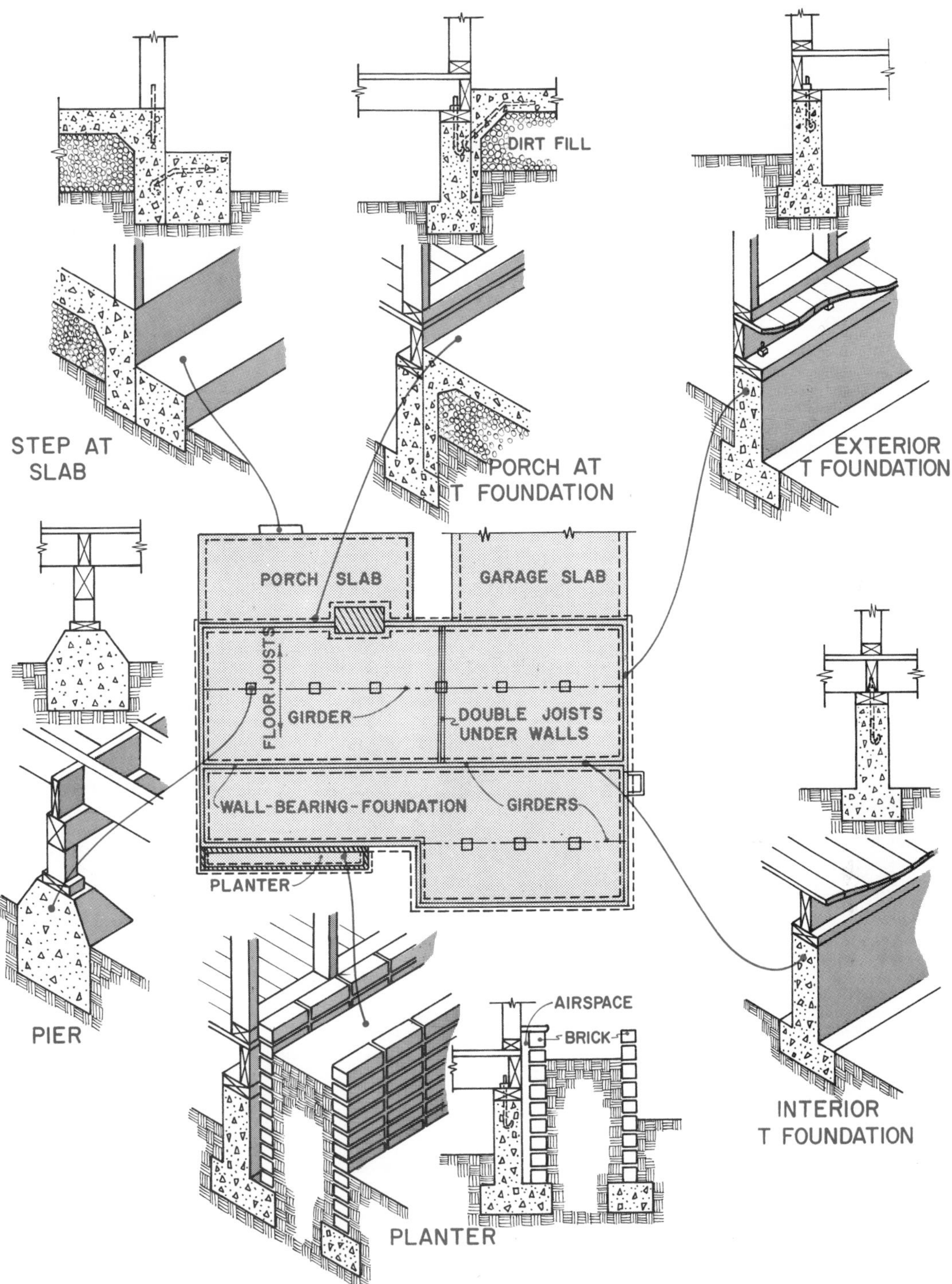

Fig. 49–4. Methods of drawing T-foundation details.

The details of construction relating to the T foundation and the methods of representing this construction on the foundation plan are shown in Fig. 49–4.

SLAB FOUNDATIONS

A slab foundation is a poured solid slab of concrete. The slab is poured directly on the ground, with footers placed where extra sup-

HOUSE SLAB
3½"
GARAGE OR PORCH SLAB
6"
6"
9"
6"
12"
12"
8"
8"
6"
EXTERIOR WALL
INTERIOR WALL
EXTERIOR WALL AT PORCH OR GARAGE
EXTERIOR WALL AT PORCH OR GARAGE

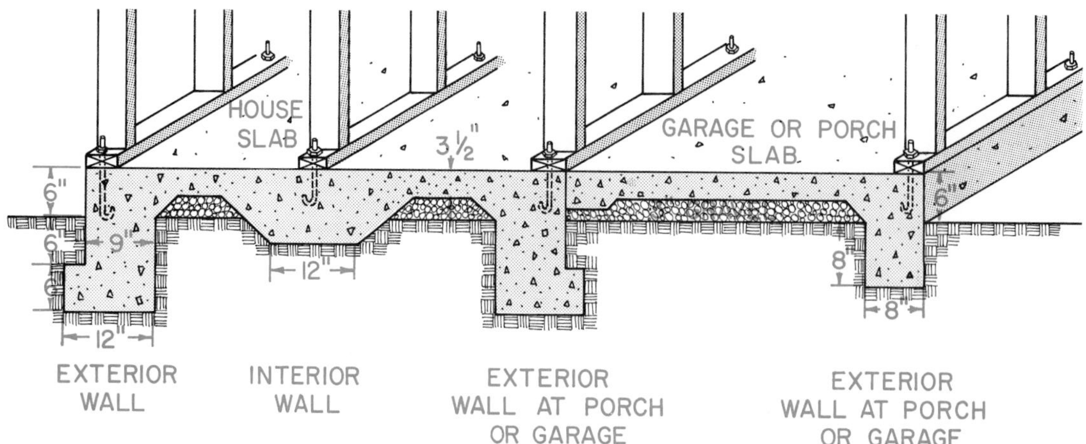

Fig. 49–5. Slab-foundation support methods.

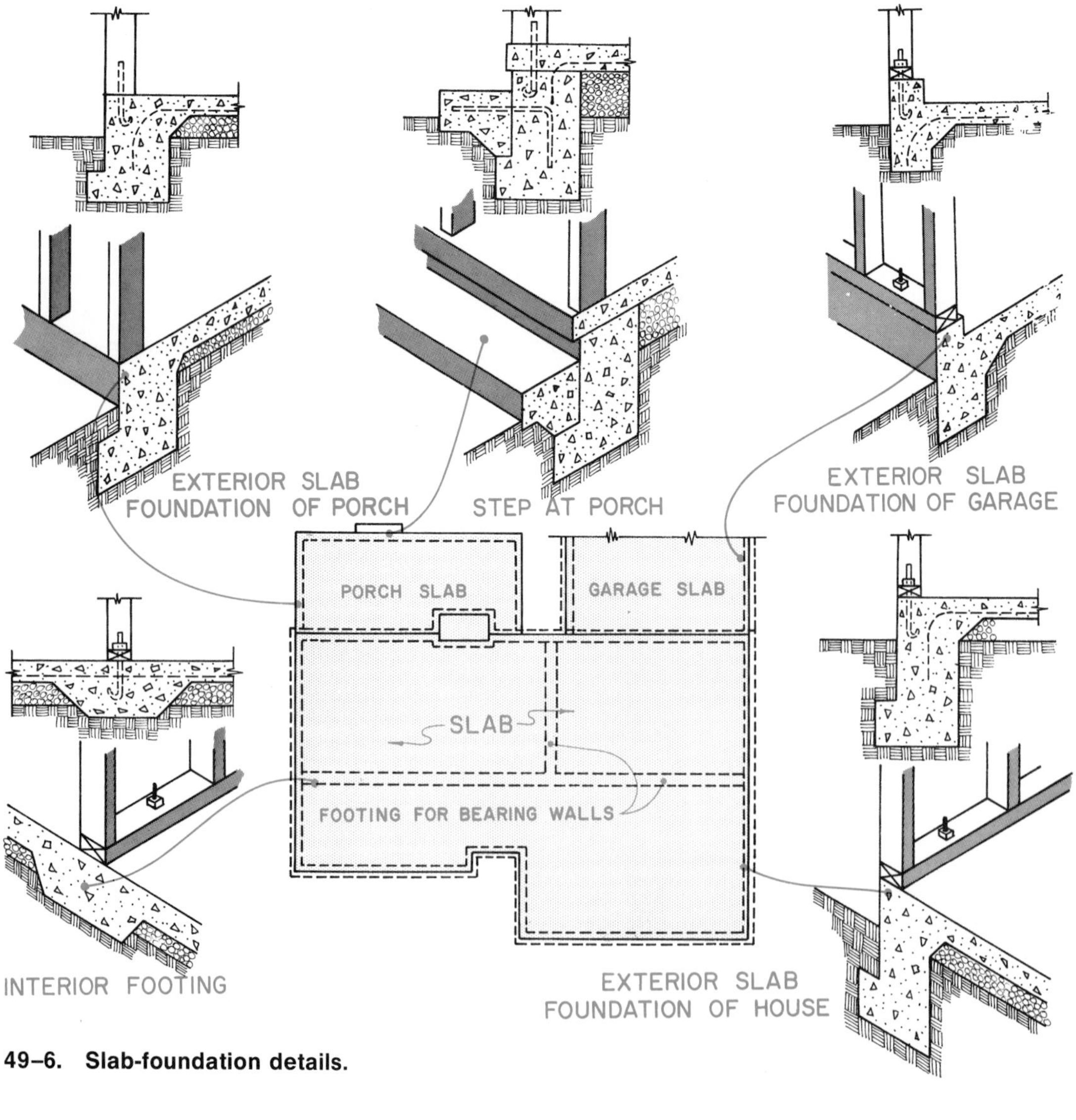

EXTERIOR SLAB FOUNDATION OF PORCH
STEP AT PORCH
EXTERIOR SLAB FOUNDATION OF GARAGE
PORCH SLAB
GARAGE SLAB
SLAB
FOOTING FOR BEARING WALLS
INTERIOR FOOTING
EXTERIOR SLAB FOUNDATION OF HOUSE

Fig. 49–6. Slab-foundation details.

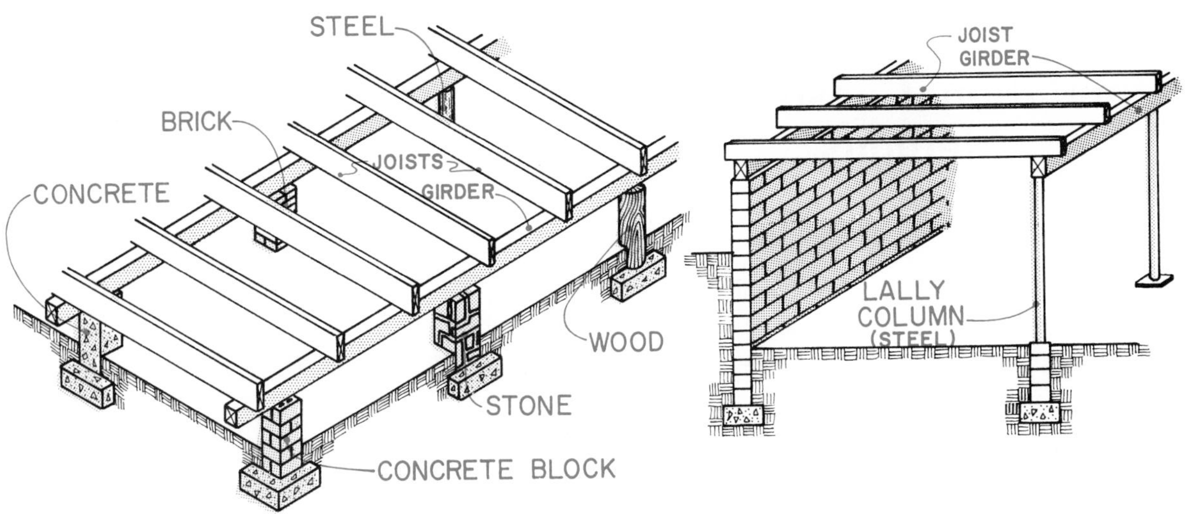

Fig. 49–7. Pier and column construction.

port is needed (Fig. 49–5). A slab foundation requires considerably less labor to construct than do most other foundation types. Details of the slab foundation and methods of drawing slab foundations are shown in Fig. 49–6.

PIER AND COLUMN FOUNDATIONS

The pier and column foundation consists of individual footers upon which columns are placed. Fewer materials and less labor are needed for the pier and column foundation (Fig. 49–7). The main objection to using pier and column foundations for most residence work is that a basement is not possible when this construction is used.

PROBLEMS

1. **Sketch Fig. 49–8, using the scale 1/4″ = 1′—0″ for a T foundation.**
2. **Sketch Fig. 49–8, using the scale 1/4″ = 1′—0″ for a slab foundation.**
3. **Sketch Fig. 49–8, using the scale 1/4″ = 1′—0″ for a pier foundation.**
4. **Know these architectural terms: *contractor, grade, slab, T foundation, column, frost depth.***

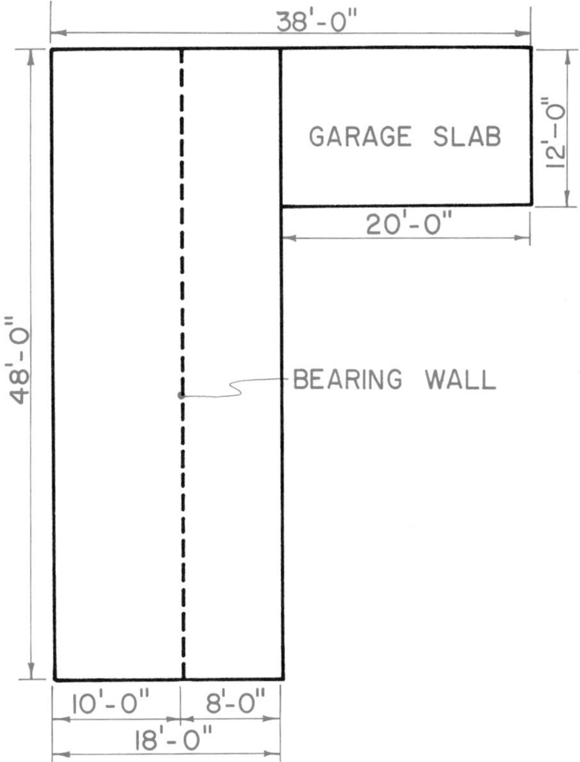

Fig. 49–8. Sketch a T-foundation, slab-foundation, and pier-foundation detail for this plan.

UNIT 50

Foundation Construction Methods

The designer must be familiar with all methods of foundation construction in order to design the most practical and economical foundation (Fig. 50–1). When the designer has chosen the most appropriate foundation for the type of soil, climate, and structure to be supported, he or she must prepare working drawings that will facilitate the layout, excavation, and construction of the foundation.

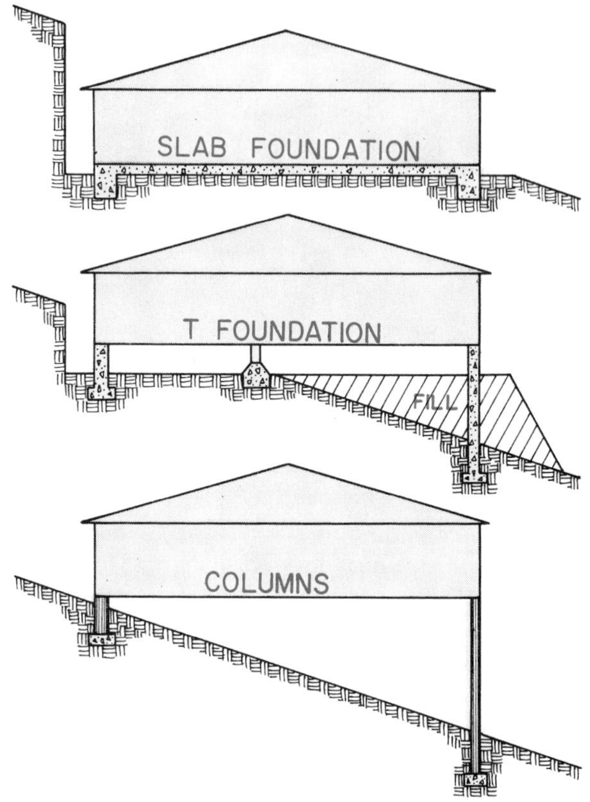

Fig. 50–1. Conditions of the terrain determine the type of foundation used.

LAYOUT

The size and shape of the foundation are normally laid out with a transit and measuring tape. String is then used with batter boards to indicate the exact position of the excavation line, footer line, and foundation wall line, as shown in Fig. 50–2. The angle of the corners can be set with a transit, as described in Unit 45, or square corners can be laid out by the 8–6–10 unit method of obtaining a right angle, as shown in Fig. 50–3.

EXCAVATIONS

Foundation plans should clearly show what parts of the foundation are to be completely excavated, partly excavated for crawl space, or unexcavated. The depth of the excavation should be shown also on the elevation drawings. If a basement is planned, the entire excavation for the basement is dug before the footers are poured. If there is to be no basement, a trench excavation is made.

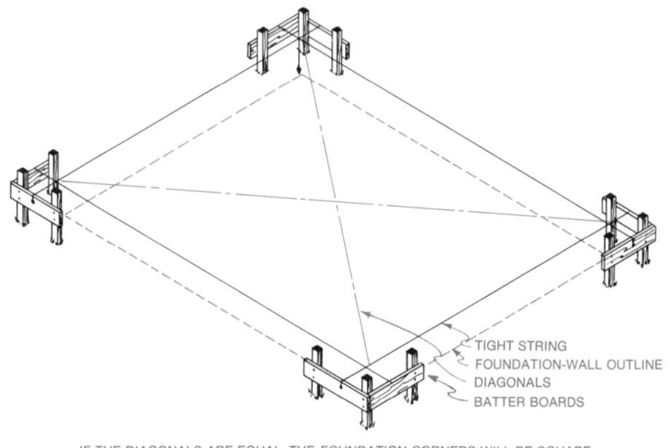

Fig. 50–2. The batter-board layout method.

T FOUNDATIONS

The T foundation is prepared by pouring the footer in an excavated trench, leveling the top of the footer, and erecting a concrete block or masonry wall on top of the footer. If concrete

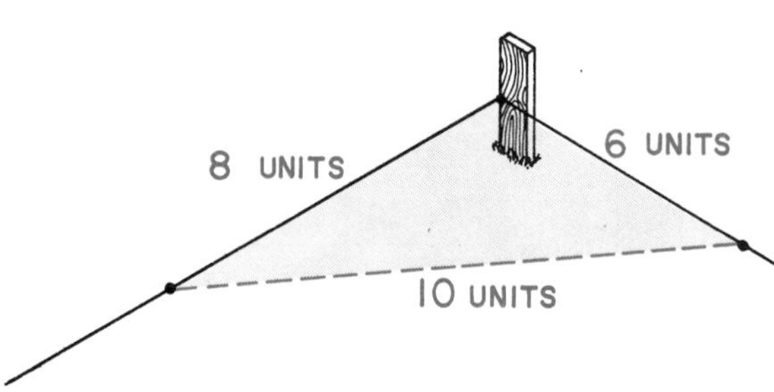

Fig. 50–3. Establishing right angles by the 8-6-10 unit method.

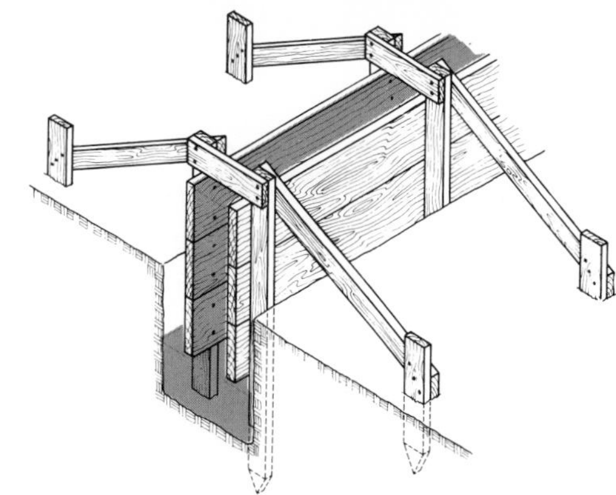

Fig. 50–4. Forms for a poured T foundation.

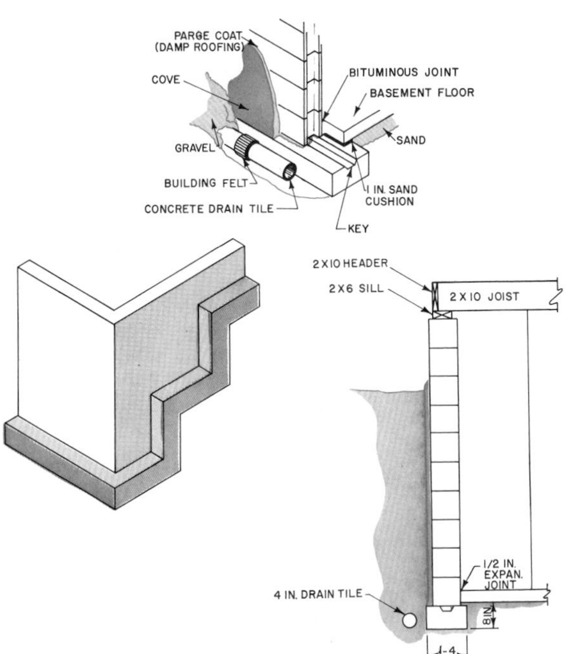

Fig. 50–5. Extending the length of a T foundation forms basement walls.

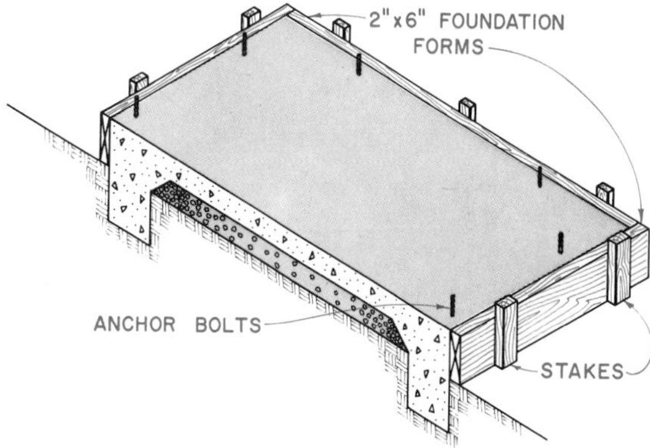

Fig. 50–6. Slab-form construction.

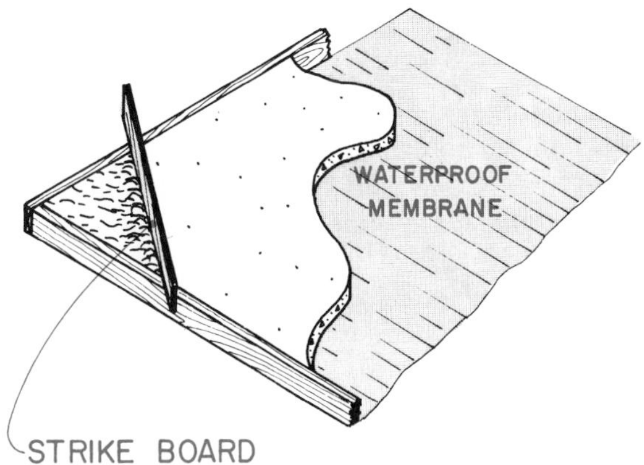

Fig. 50–7. Leveling the slab.

foundation walls are to be used, building forms are erected on top of the footer. Concrete is poured into these forms (Fig. 50–4). After the concrete dries, the wood is removed and may be reused for other forms. When a poured foundation wall is to be used, the concrete mix is sand, gravel, water, and cement. After the forms are filled, the concrete is leveled with a strike board so that it has a rough, nonslip surface. By continuing the depth of the T foundation, a basement area is formed (Fig. 50–5).

SLAB FOUNDATIONS

The excavation for a slab foundation is made for the footings only. Two-by-sixes are used to construct the forms for the slab, as shown in Fig. 50–6. The entire foundation is then poured, and the top of the slab is leveled with a strike board (Fig. 50–7). Slab foundations and

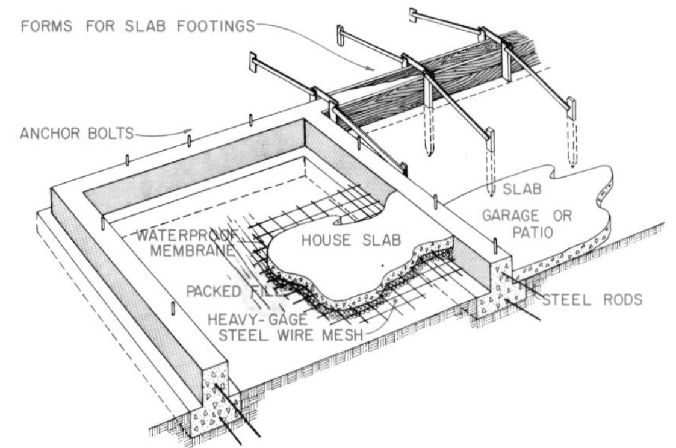

Fig. 50-8. A reinforced slab foundation.

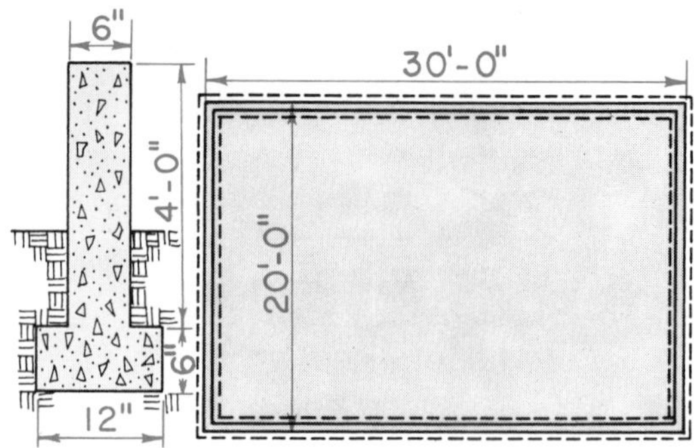

Fig. 50-9. Determine the size of excavation and the amount of concrete needed for this foundation.

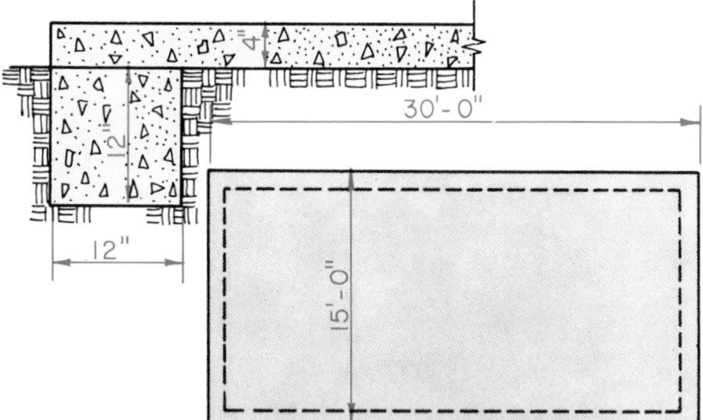

Fig. 50-10. Determine the size of the excavation and the amount of concrete needed for this foundation.

basement floors in T foundations should be waterproofed. This can be done by putting a waterproof membrane between the slab and the ground. Slabs are often reinforced with steel-wire mesh placed inside the slab before pouring, as shown in Fig. 50–8.

Types and sizes and mixtures of materials for foundations are rigidly controlled by most building codes. The designer must check the building code for the area.

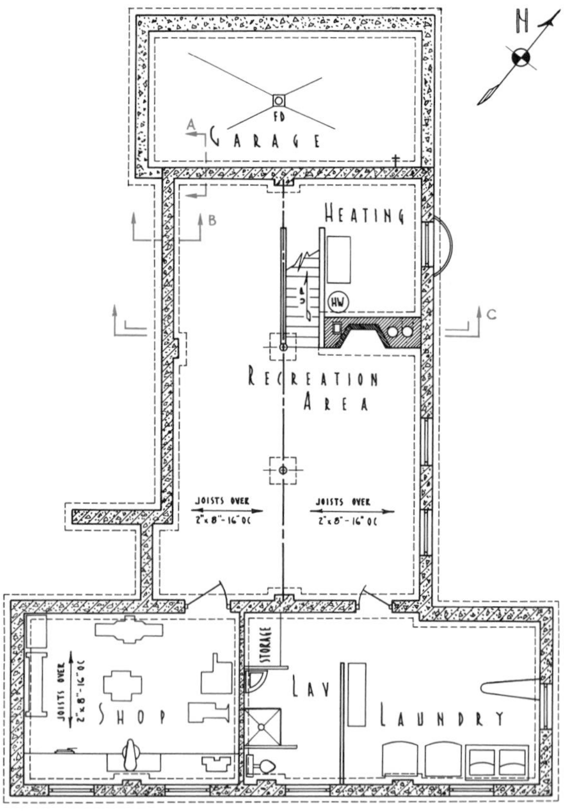

Fig. 50-11. Draw sections A, B, and C of this foundation.

PROBLEMS

1. **In Fig. 50–9, how many cubic feet of dirt must be excavated? How many cubic yards? How many cubic feet of concrete must be poured for the footing? How many cubic yards for the slab?**
2. **In Fig. 50–10, how many cubic yards of dirt must be excavated for the footings? How many cubic yards of concrete will be used?**
3. **What is the concrete mix for foundations in your community? Check your building code.**
4. **List several different types of foundations and materials used in your community.**
5. **Draw sections of this foundation plan as shown in Figs. 50–11A, B, and C.**
6. **Define these architectural terms: *excavations, foundation forms, steel-wire mesh, strike board, waterproof membrane.***

UNIT 51

Fireplaces

Provision must be made in the foundation plans to support the weight of the fireplace and chimney (Fig. 51–1). A solid reinforced concrete footer is used in most plans. This footer is usually 12″ (305 mm) thick and extends at least 12″ (305 mm) past the perimeter of the chimney.

Fireplaces are designed in three types: those constructed totally on the site (Fig. 51–1), those using a manufactured firebox and flue system (Fig. 51–2), and free-standing units (Fig. 51–3).

FIREPLACE

The main part of the fireplace is the firebox. The firebox reflects heat and draws smoke up the chimney. Included in the firebox are the sides, back, smoke chamber, flue, throat, and damper (Fig. 51–1). Most fireboxes are constructed in a factory. The mason places the firebox in the proper location in the chimney construction and lines it with firebrick. Figure 51–2 shows the installation of a manufactured unit prior to the addition of masonry covering.

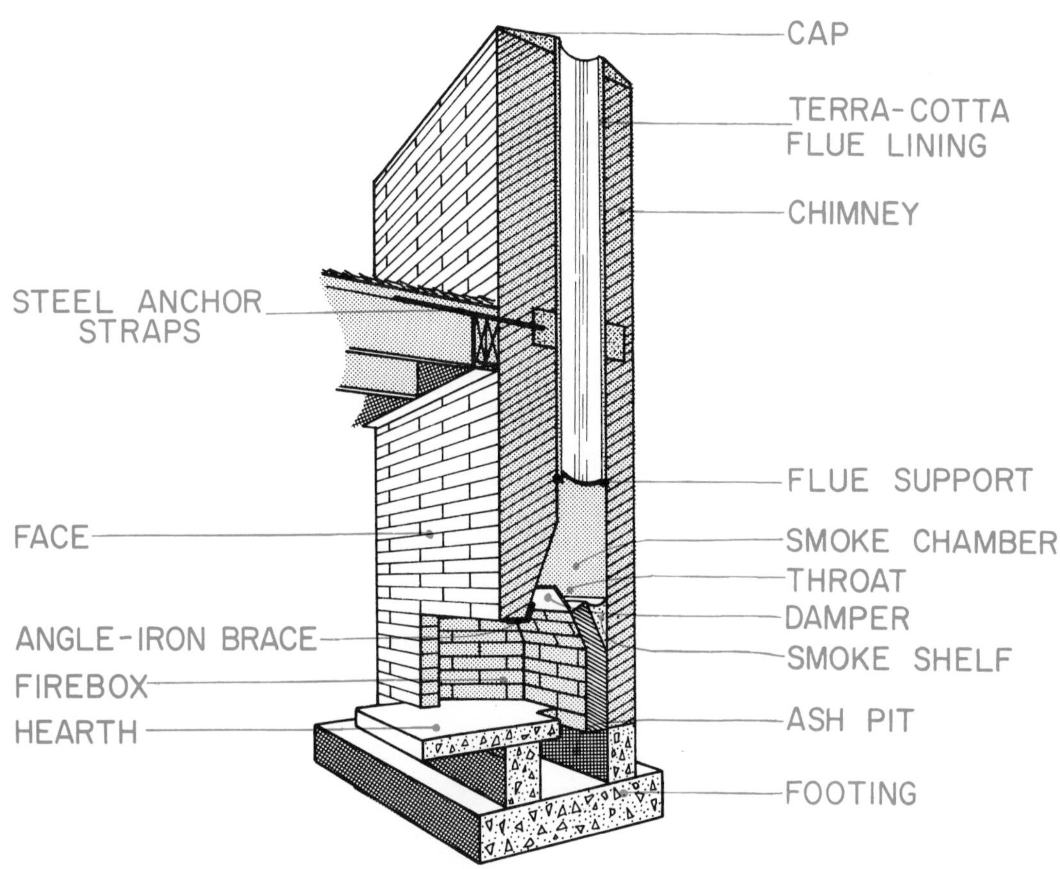

Fig. 51–1. The major components of fireplace and chimney structure.

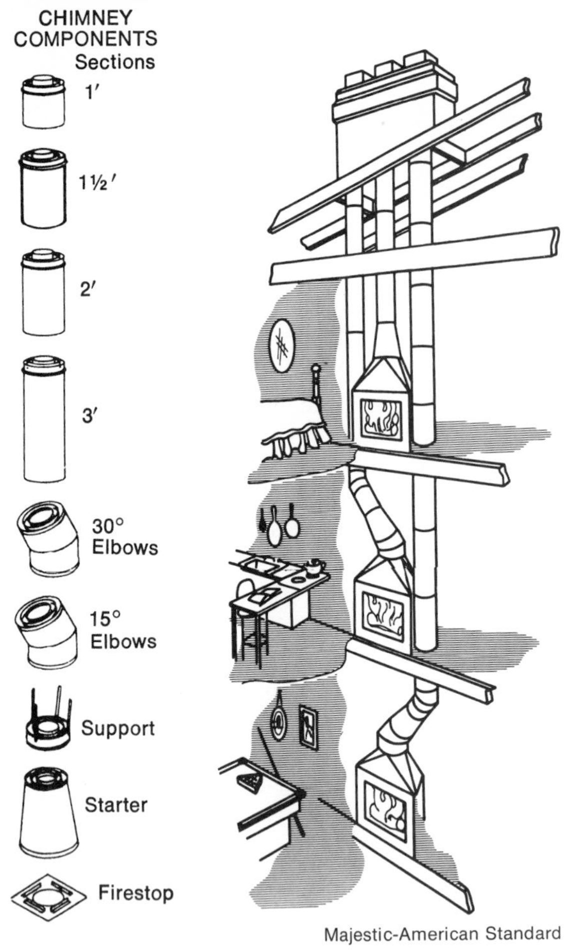

Fig. 51–2. The use of manufactured fireplace components.

Masonry used in fireplaces and chimneys is usually of brick, stone, or concrete. Firebrick is used to line the firebox. The hearth also should be constructed of fire-resistant material such as brick, tile, marble, or stone.

The best method of drawing construction details of a fireplace is to prepare a sectional drawing, as shown in Fig. 51–4. This gives the position of the firebox and the size of materials used in the footer, hearth, face, flue, and cap of the chimney. It also shows the relationship of the chimney to the floor and ceiling lines of the structure.

CHIMNEY

A chimney extends from the footer through the roof of the house. The footer should be of sufficient size to support the entire weight of the chimney. The chimney extends above the roof line to provide a better draft for drawing the smoke and to eliminate the possibility of sparks igniting the roof.

The height of the chimney above the roof line varies somewhat, according to local building codes. In most areas the minimum distance is 2′ (610 mm).

Fig. 51–3. A freestanding fireplace.

Olson-Spencer & Associates; Southern California Edison Company

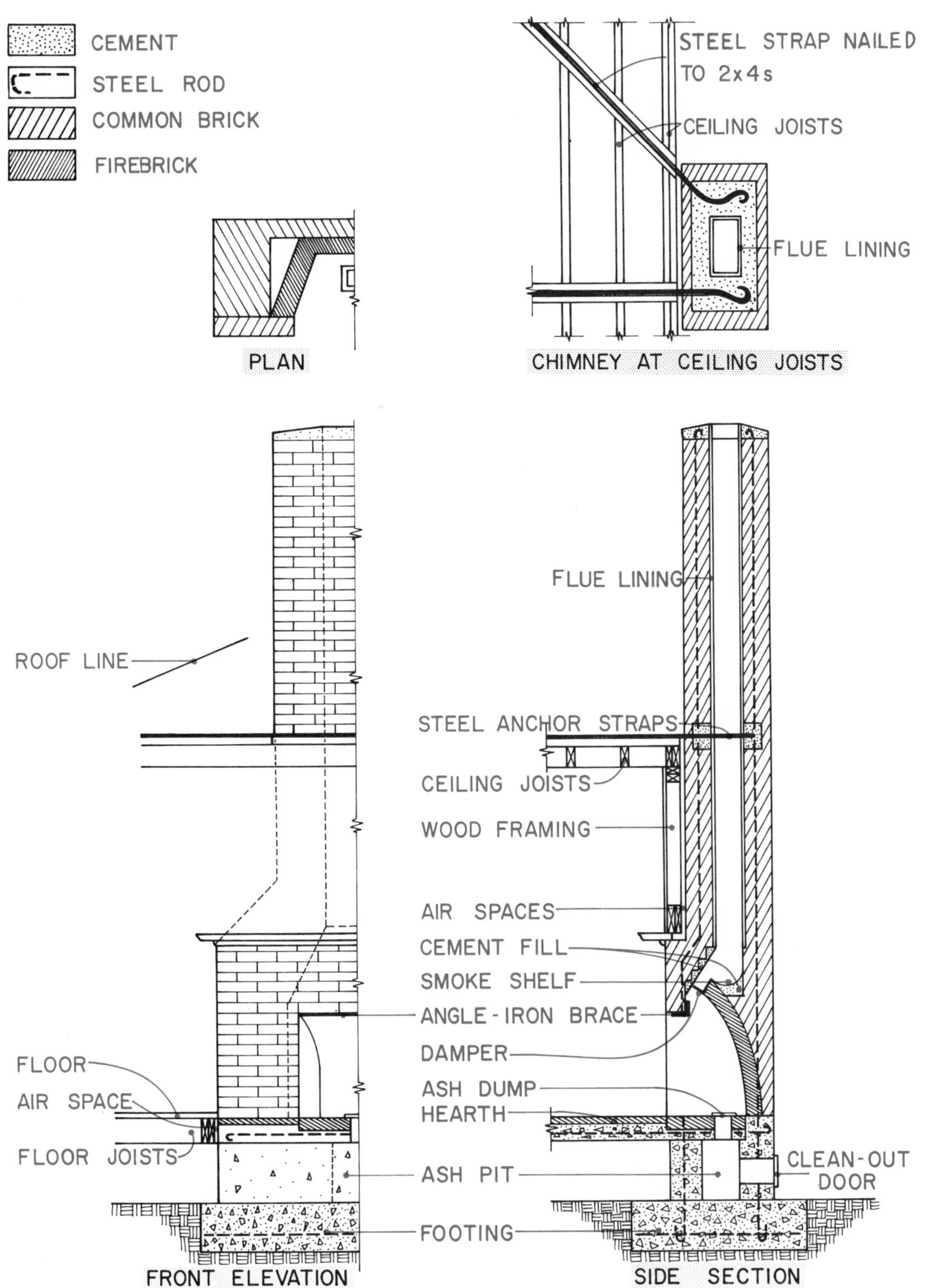

Fig. 51-4. A sectional drawing of a fireplace and chimney.

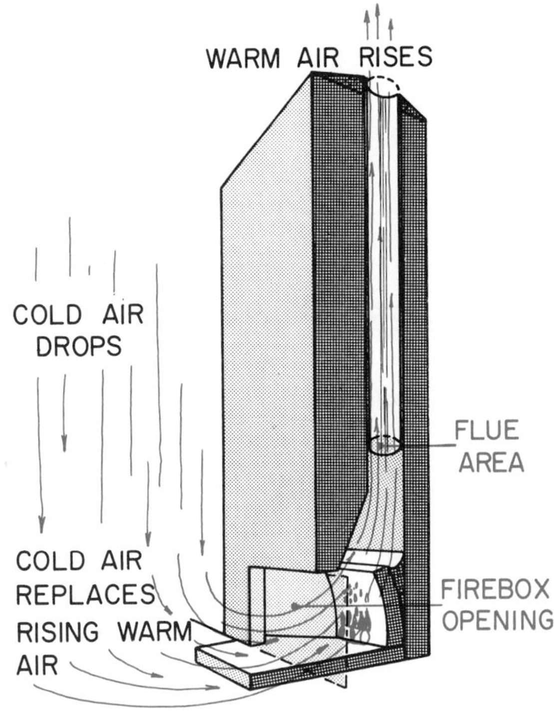

Fig. 51–5. The functioning of a fireplace flue.

The chimney is secured to ceiling and floor joists by iron straps embedded in the brickwork. Floor joists and ceiling joists around the chimney and fireplace and hearth should have sufficient clearance to protect them from the heat. Most building codes specify this distance.

The designer must also indicate the type and size of flues to be inserted in the chimney. One flue is necessary for each fireplace or furnace leading into the chimney. Note the three flues serving the three fireplaces in Fig. 51–2. The flue from the fireplace or from the furnace in the basement extends directly to the top of the chimney, completely bypassing the first-floor fireplaces. The first-floor fireplace flues completely bypass the second-floor fireplace flues, and so forth. The size of each flue must be at least one-tenth the opening of the fireplace to accommodate the rise of warm air (see Fig. 51–5). Designing for adequate warm-air rise is critical to the effective operation (draw) of the fireplace. Inadequate draw, either from using too small a flue or from improper chimney placement, can result in smoke leading into the room rather than being drawn up the chimney. Figure 51–6 shows the operation of this thermosiphoning principle in a manufactured unit. This insulating air-flow system utilizes triple-walled chimney components with positive spaced concentric pipes. Cool outside air is circulated down and around the firebox and up between the middle chamber to initiate a siphoned draft system that controls the burning process, with minimum room air needed for proper combustion.

Many fireplaces are constructed by using some manufactured components and constructing the remainder on the site. The design of the fireplace usually determines the degree to which manufactured components can be used. The more unconventional the fireplace, usually the fewer the standard components that can be used. Figure 51–7A shows elevation and plan drawings for a fireplace using a manufactured flue unit but a site-constructed firebox area. Figure 51–7B shows the plan, elevation, and section of a fireplace constructed on site.

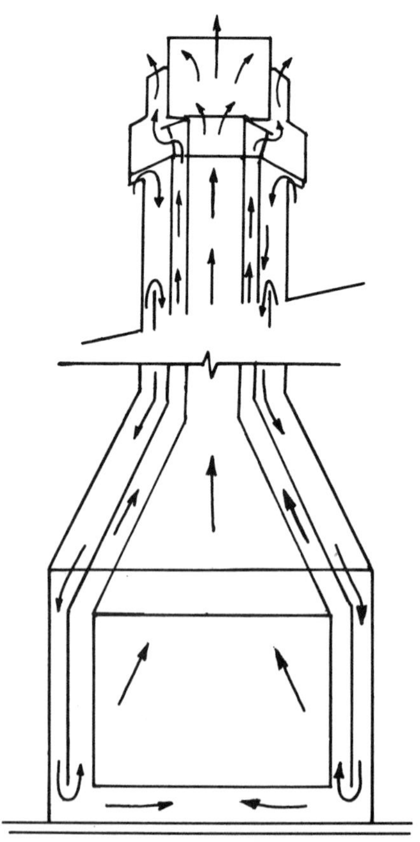

Majestic-American Standard

Fig. 51–6. The thermosiphoning principle.

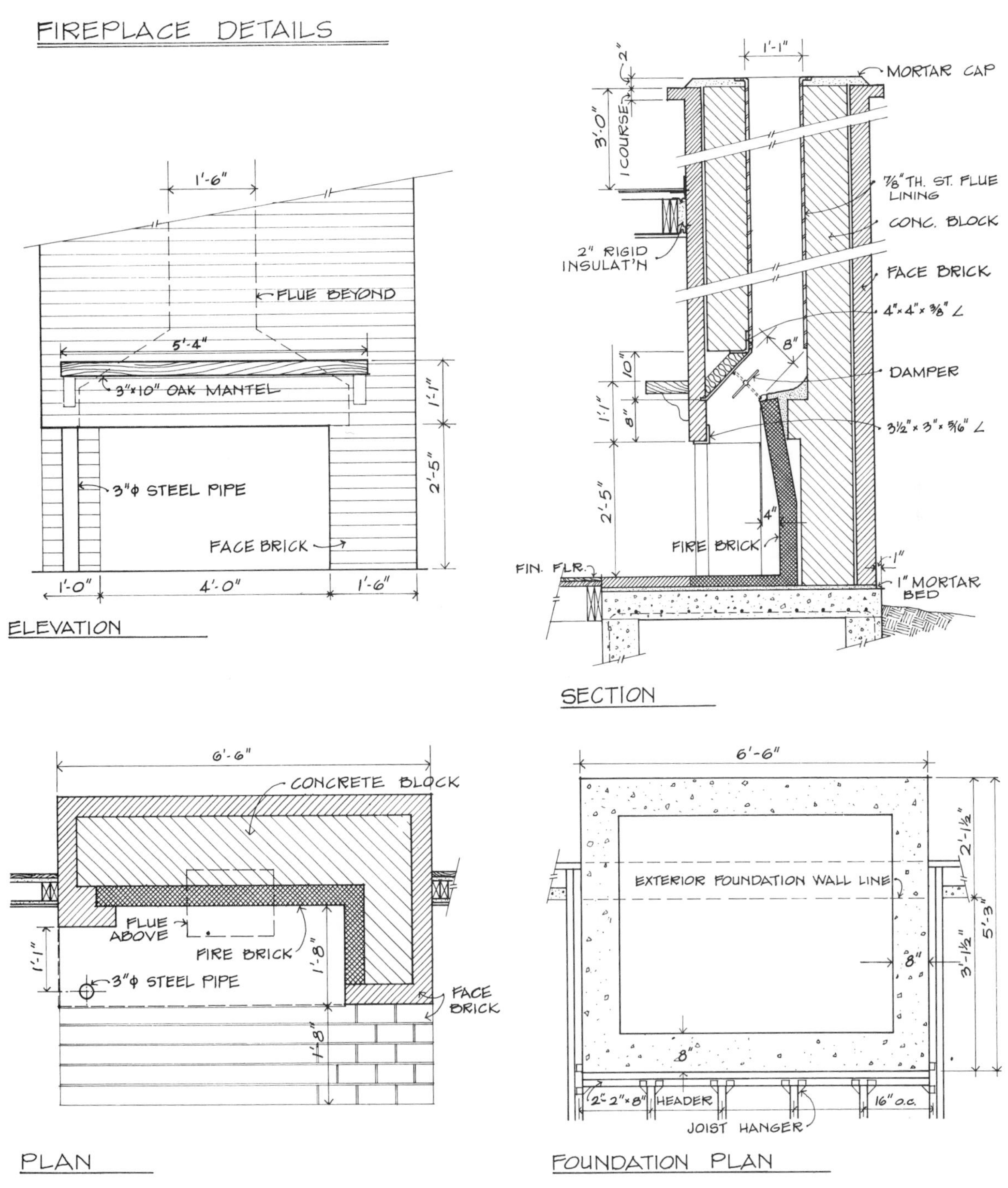

Fig. 51–7A. A fireplace with a manufactured flue in elevation, section, plan, and foundation-plan views.

Fireplaces add warmth and atmosphere to a room; however, most of the heat produced by some fireplaces goes up the chimney. To reduce this heat loss and redirect some of this heat, warm-air outlets, balanced by cold-air outlets, can be installed, as shown in Fig. 51–8.

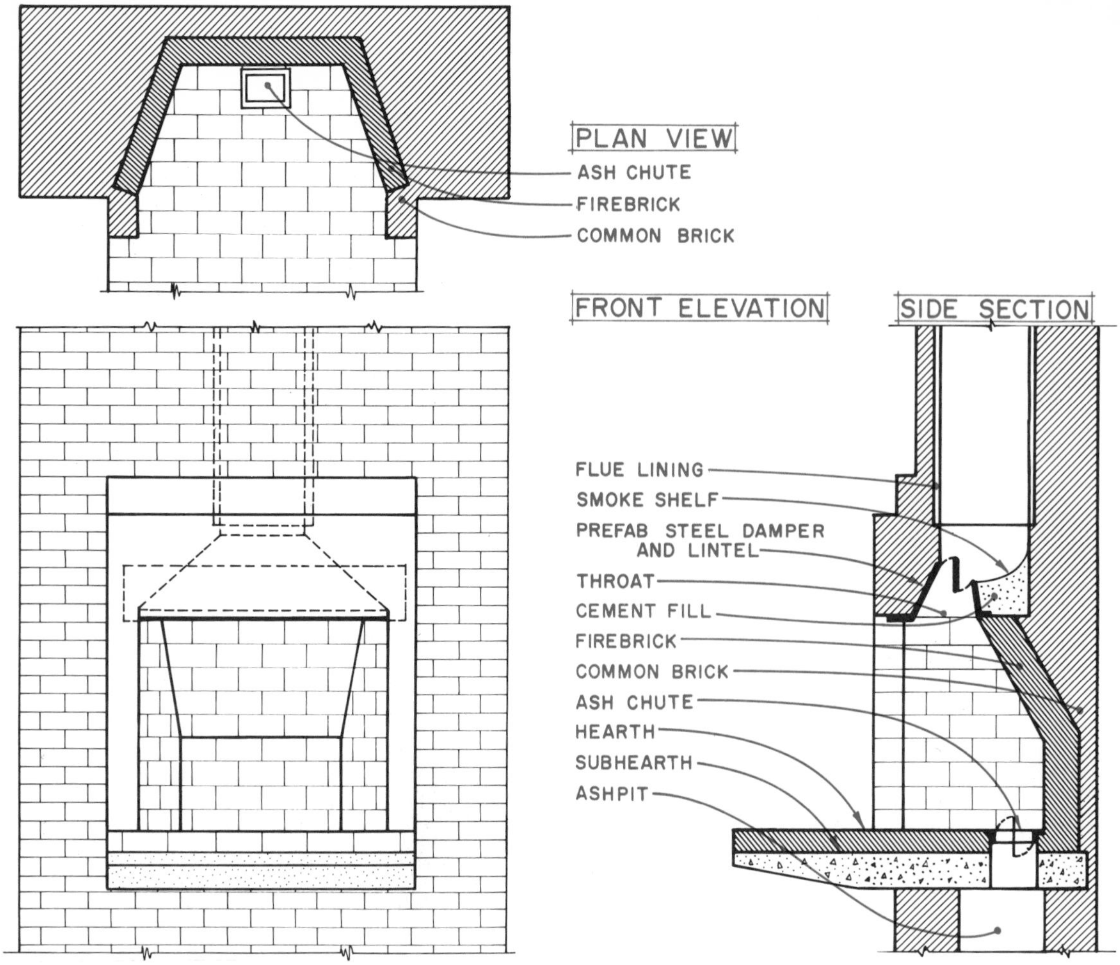

Fig. 51–7B. The plan, elevation, and section of a conventionally constructed fireplace.

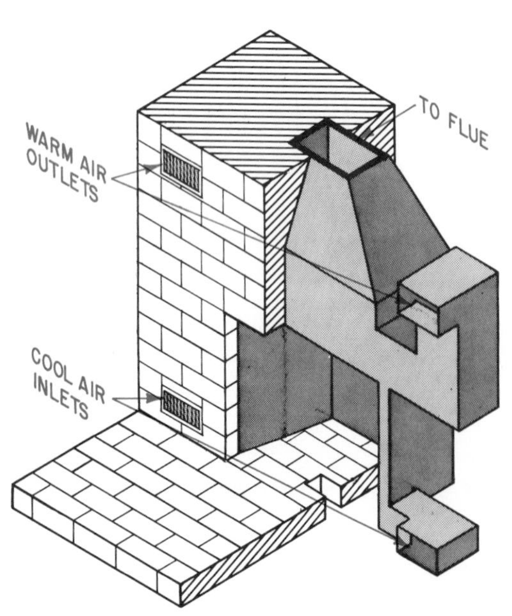

Fig. 51–8. The placement of warm-air ducts.

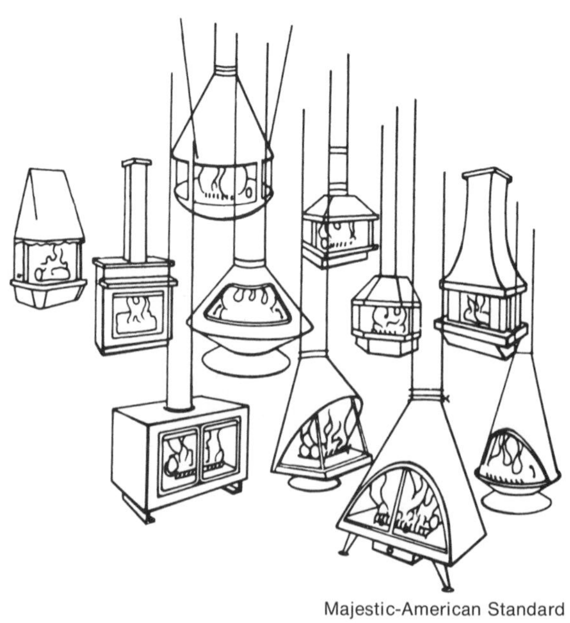

Majestic-American Standard

Fig. 51–9. Free-standing fireplaces come in a variety of shapes and sizes.

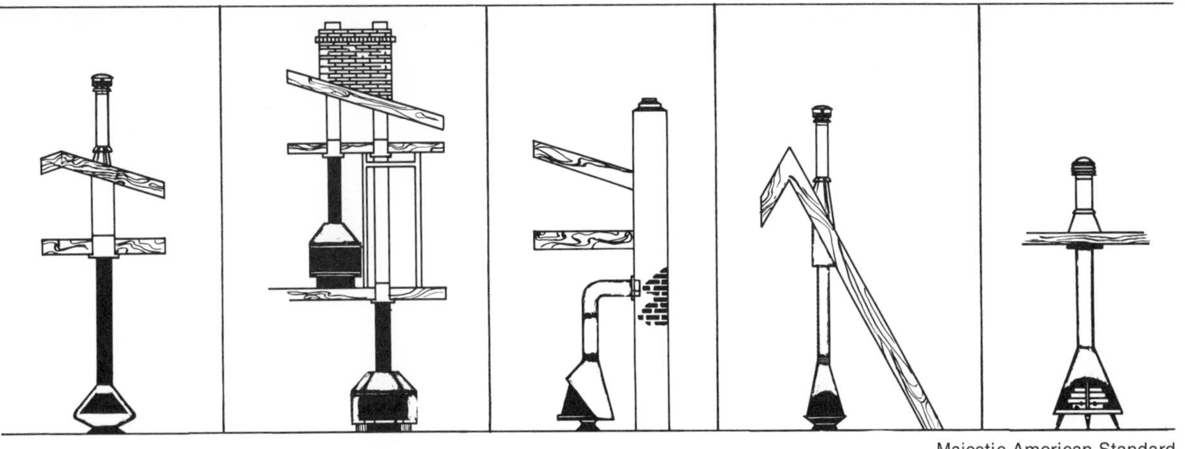

Majestic-American Standard

Fig. 51–10. Some fireplace exhaust-system design options.

Home Planners, Inc.

Fig. 51–11. Redesign this fireplace.

PREFABRICATED FIREPLACES

Free-standing metal fireplaces constructed of heavy-gage steel, as shown in Fig. 51–2, are available in a variety of shapes (Fig. 51–9). They are relatively light woodburning stoves and therefore need no concrete foundation for support. A stovepipe leading into the chimney provides the exhaust flue. Figure 51–10 shows several methods of designing the exhaust system. Since metal units reflect more heat than masonry, the metal fireplace is much more efficient, especially if centrally located. These fireplaces can be mounted on the walls or on legs, or they can be built into the chimney. Prefabricated fireplaces do not require a foundation to support their weight. They are complete, ready-to-install fireplaces. Nevertheless a fire-resistant material such as concrete, brick, stone, or tile must be used beneath and around these fireplaces (Fig. 51–2).

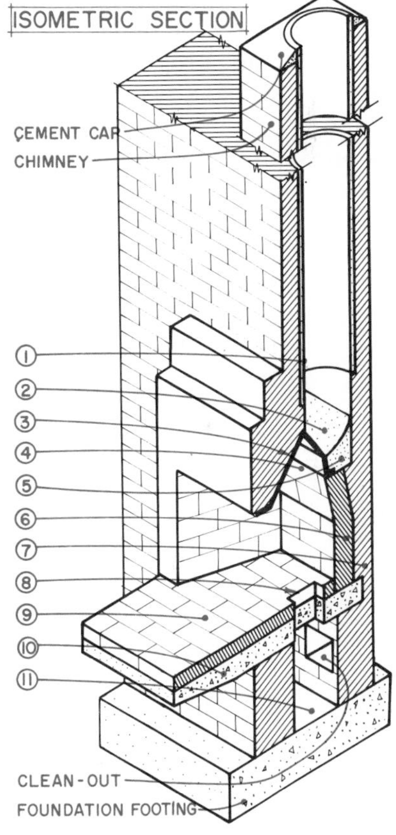

Fig. 51–12. Identify the numbered parts.

PROBLEMS

1. **Redraw the fireplace in Fig. 51–1, using the scale ½″ = 1′—0″.**
2. **Redesign the front of the fireplace in Fig. 51–11.**
3. **Identify the parts of the fireplace shown in Fig. 51–12.**
4. **Define these architectural terms: *firebox, chimney, smoke chamber, flue, throat, damper, draft, draw, ceiling joist, firebrick, prefabricated fireplace, chimney sections.***

SECTION 12
Framing Plans

Most of the basic engineering principles upon which modern framing methods are based have been known for centuries. However, it has not been until recent years that the development of materials and construction methods has allowed the full use of these principles. Today's architect can choose among many basic materials in the design of the basic structural framework of a building. New and improved methods of erecting structural steel, new developments in laminating and processing preformed wood structural members, developments and refinements in the use of concrete and masonry products such as prestressed concrete slabs, and continual progress in standardization in the design of structural components all provide the architect with the flexibility to design the most appropriate structural system for a building at the lowest possible cost and with the smallest waste of materials and time.

American Plywood Association

UNIT 52
Types of Framing

New construction materials and new methods of using conventional materials provide the architect with much flexibility in framing design.

Stronger buildings can now be erected with lighter and fewer materials.

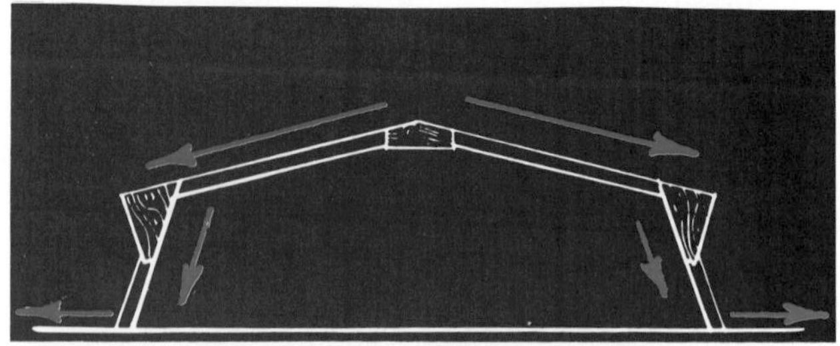

Fig. 52–1. Major lines of support.

PRINCIPLES OF FRAMING

Regardless of the materials used and the methods employed, the physical principles upon which structural design is based remain constant. In most structures the roof is supported by the wall framework and interior partitions or columns. Each exterior wall and bearing partition is supported by the *foundation*, which, in turn, is supported by a *footing*. The footing distributes this load over a wide area of load-bearing soil and thus ties the entire structural system to the ground (Fig. 52–1).

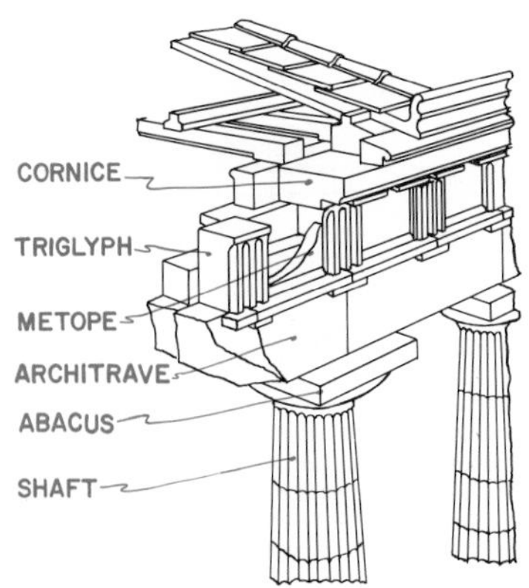

Fig. 52–2. The column support of the Doric order of architecture.

Early Framing Methods
In earlier centuries, people did not have strong, light framing materials such as structural steel, aluminum, or sized and seasoned lumber. Therefore, extremely heavy material such as stone was used to support the great weight of a building. Foundations were large and footers enormous, to support and spread the heavy load. Walls were frequently constructed larger at the base than at the top, and a very elaborate system of column support was developed, as shown in the Doric order in Fig. 52–2.

Current Framing Methods
Today most buildings are constructed with a basic skeleton framework. A structural tie, such as *sheathing* or *diagonal bracing,* is covered with protective siding. The structural system is somewhat related to the structure of most vertebrates. The framework functions like the skeleton in providing the basic rigid frame. The structural tie, whether it be sheathing on a wooden structure or cross-bracing on a steel framework, acts like the muscles in holding the framework in the desired position. The protective covering, which is similar to the skin, provides the necessary protection from the weather (Fig. 52–3).

LOADS

Loads that must be supported by the structure are divided into two types, live loads and dead loads.

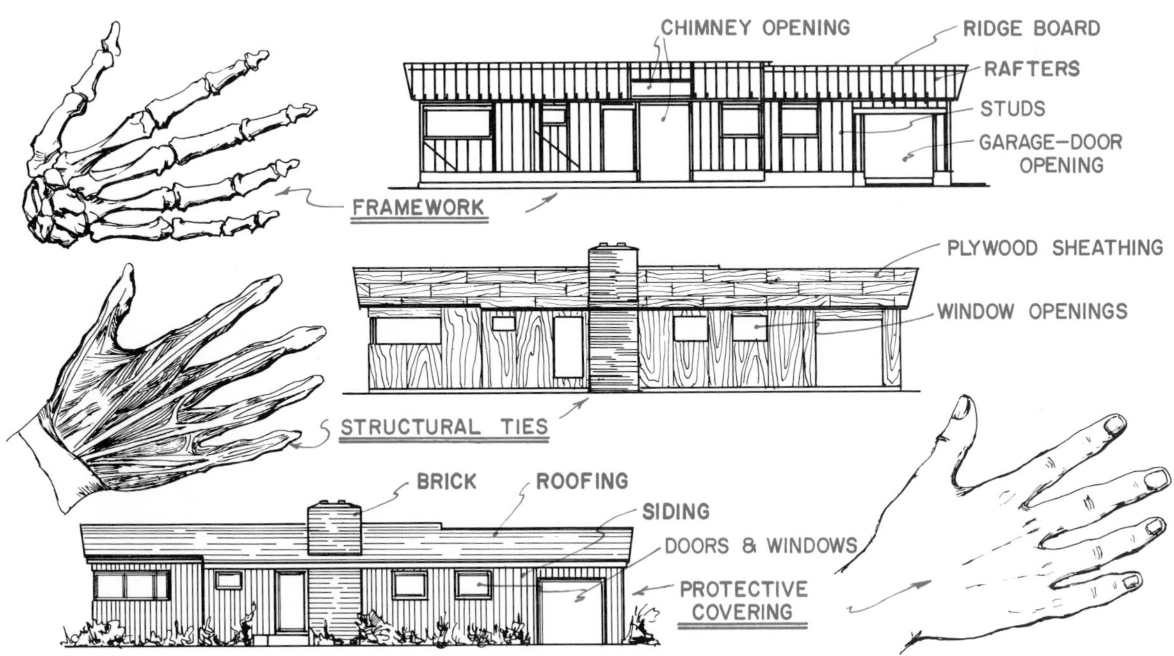

Fig. 52–3. The skeleton of a building is similar to the skeleton of a person.

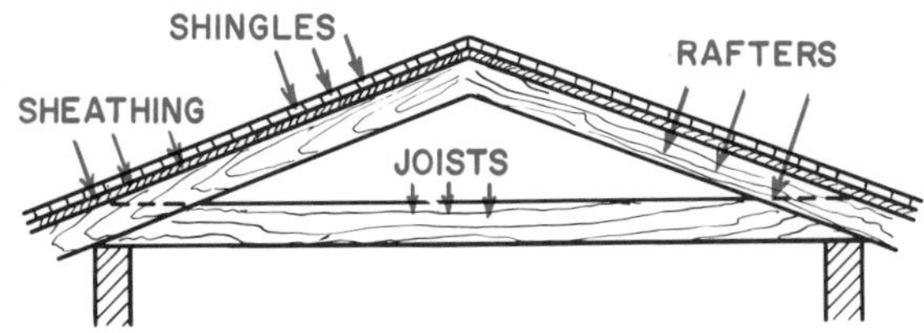

Fig. 52–4. Dead loads.

Fig. 52–5. Live loads.

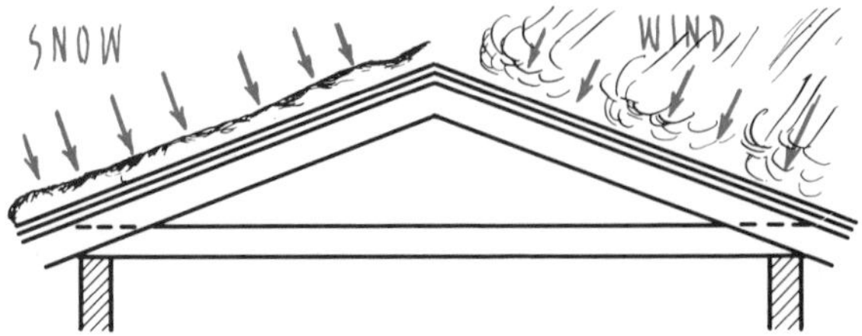

Fig. 52–6. Live loads acting upon a roof.

Dead Loads

Dead loads are those loads caused by the weight of the construction materials. The dead loads of the roof (Fig. 52–4) must be supported by the walls or bearing partitions. The dead loads of the walls must be supported by the foundation. Every piece of lumber, plywood, glass, and sheetmetal, and every nail and brick adds to the total dead load of the structure.

Live Loads

Live loads are those loads that may vary from structure to structure. Live loads of a floor include furniture and people, as shown in Fig. 52–5. Live loads of a roof include such variables as wind, snow, and even rain when the roof is flat (Fig. 52–6). As you learn more about the construction of roofs, floors, and walls in the succeeding units you will learn how to design these structurally so that they will withstand normal live and dead loads.

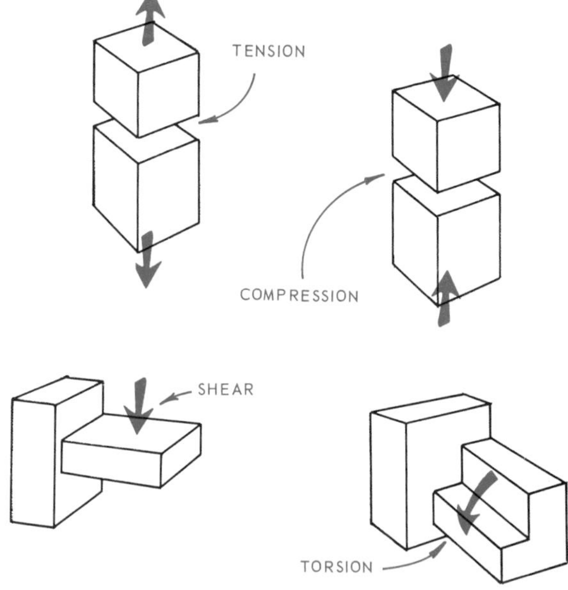

Fig. 52–7. The framework of a building is designed to overcome tension, compression, shear, and torsion.

STRENGTH OF MATERIALS

The stability of the building depends on the strength of the material used and the connection of members to overcome *tension, compression, shear,* and *torsion* (Fig. 52–7). The strength of the building material is irrelevant if the building is not structurally stable. Likewise, the building will be inadequate if the building materials are weak, regardless of the stability of the design (Fig. 52–8).

The strength of building material is significant only when related to the structure. Most lumber and even steel are relatively flexible until tied into the structure. Grasp a piece of paper between your thumb and forefinger, as shown in Fig. 52–9. The other end of the paper

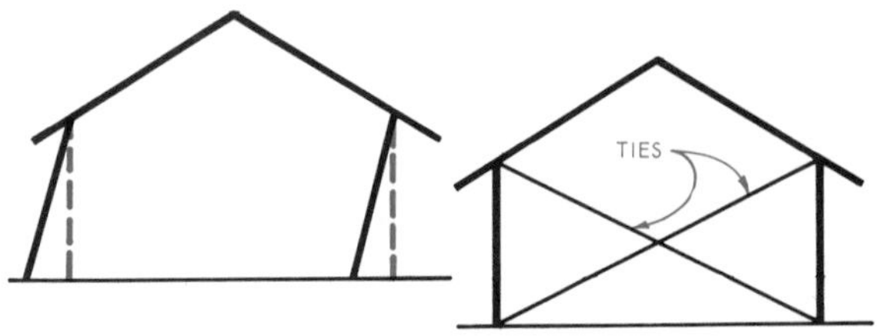

Fig. 52–8. The stability of a structure is determined by its design.

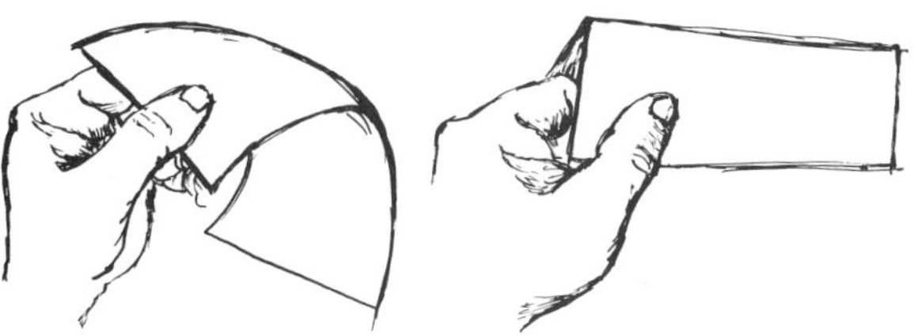

Fig. 52–9. The strength of a material is related to its shape.

will drop. If you fold this same piece of paper, you will be able to support it from one end easily. This principle is applied to the use of structural members in building design.

Figure 52–10 shows that turning a member on its side will reduce the *vertical deflection* (bending) significantly but that *horizontal deflection* will be unaffected. Combining the horizontal and vertical components of the member (to make a channel) reduces both the vertical and horizontal deflection. Combining two horizontal members with one vertical member (as in an I beam) provides even more stability.

It would seem that the design of structures is a relatively simple matter. The materials must be strong enough and the structure rigid enough. But it is not that simple. Care must be taken not to overdesign the structure. A beam that is one size too large will not support the structure any better than will a member of the right size. Overdesigning (except for allowing safety margins) a few items of this kind can cost thousands of dollars on a large job. For example, the member used to support the loads in Fig. 52–11 at A is considerably overdesigned. The support used in Fig. 52–11 at B is satisfactory. The support used in Fig. 52–11 at C is inadequately designed. Achieving the perfect balance, as shown in Fig. 52–11 at B, is the goal of every structural designer.

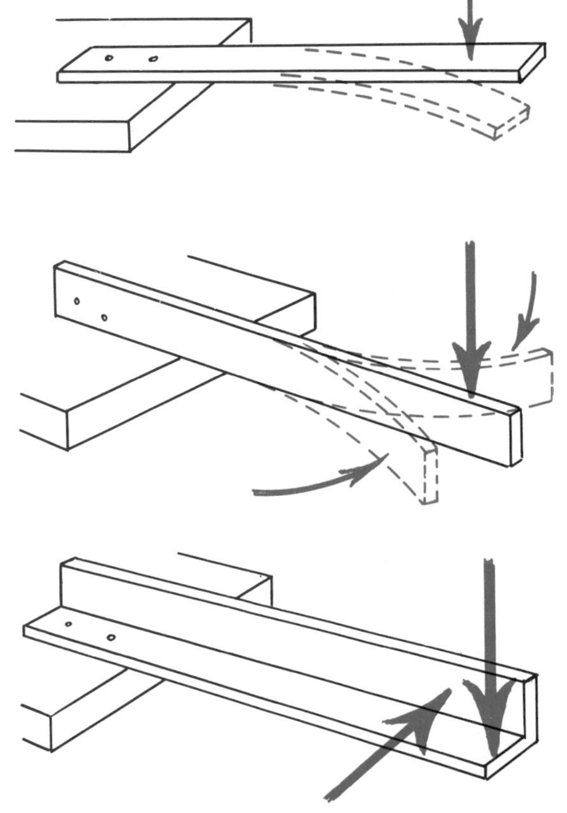

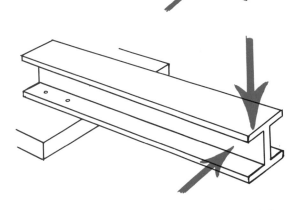

Fig. 52–10. Deflections can be eliminated by combining members.

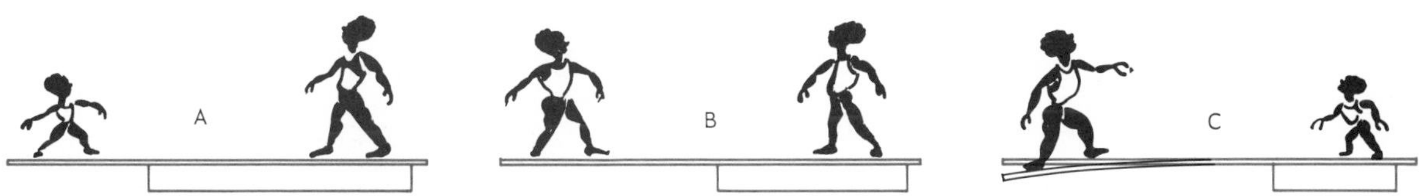

Fig. 52–11. Structural stability depends on the support and the spacing of support members.

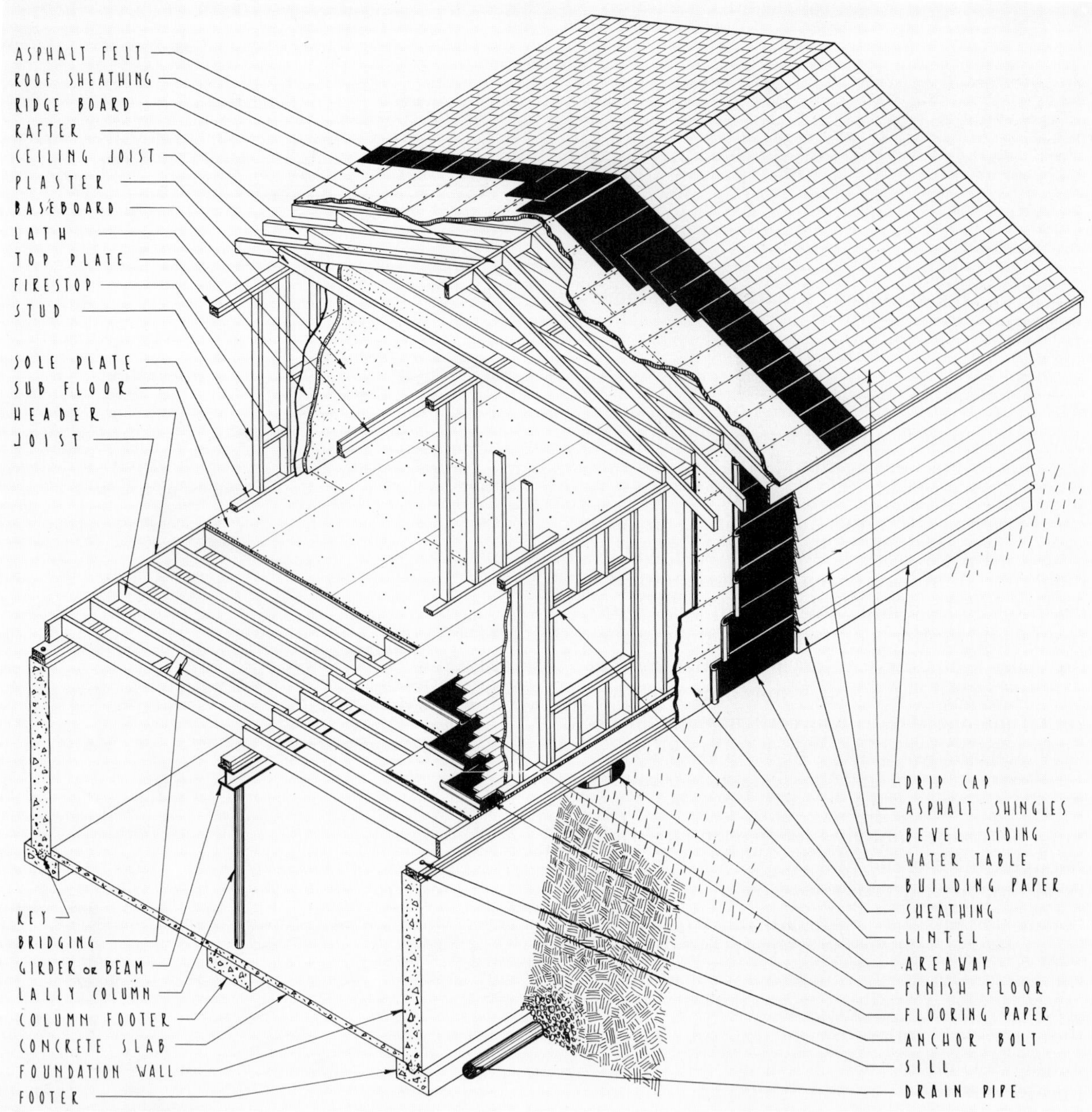

Fig. 52–12. Residential skeleton framing.

WOOD FRAMING

Early pioneers used wood as the basic construction material in building log cabins. Wood was used in its raw form to make the entire solid wall.

Conventional Framing

With the passing of the log cabin from the American scene, *skeleton-frame* construction was developed. This was made possible through the development of machinery capable of mass-producing sized and seasoned lumber that could be used interchangeably for framing purposes. However, limits on the size of lumber that could be processed effectively on the job led to the use of relatively small structural members placed at close intervals. Figure 52–12 shows the anatomy of a house constructed by this method. The framing methods

Scholz Homes, Inc.

Fig. 52–13. Application of the post and beam construction method and the use of large windows.

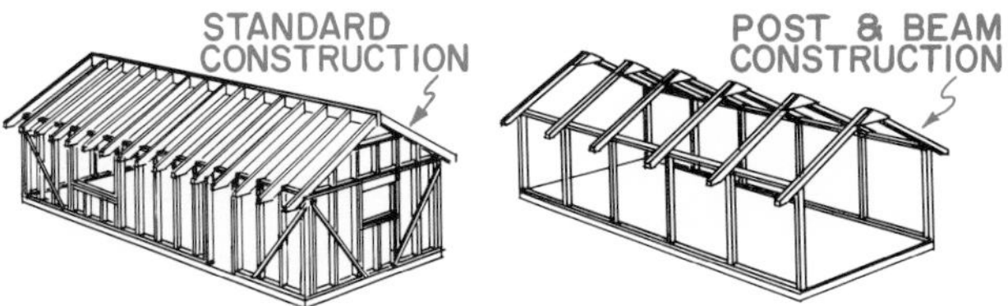

Fig. 52–14. Post and beam construction compared to conventional construction.

shown here have been in use practically from the end of the log-cabin period to the present day.

Post and Beam Construction

The use of post and beam construction methods has been increased by the popularity of indoor-outdoor living. The practicality of manufacturing large heat-resistant windows and window walls (Fig. 52–13) and the accessibility of larger wood members have popularized the post and beam method of construction. This method is based on the use of larger members spaced at greater intervals. This spacing accommodates large windows and sliding doors that unite the indoors and outdoors in a single living space.

Figure 52–14 shows a comparison of the post and beam method of construction and the conventional method. Figure 52–15 shows some of the basic details of post and beam construction. The preparation of the various framing plans using both the post and beam and the conventional wood-framing method will be presented in succeeding units.

STEEL FRAMING

Steel framing is similar in principle to post and beam framing. Figure 52–16 shows a comparison between the use of posts, beams, and planks in post and beam construction and the use of columns, beams, and slabs in steel construction.

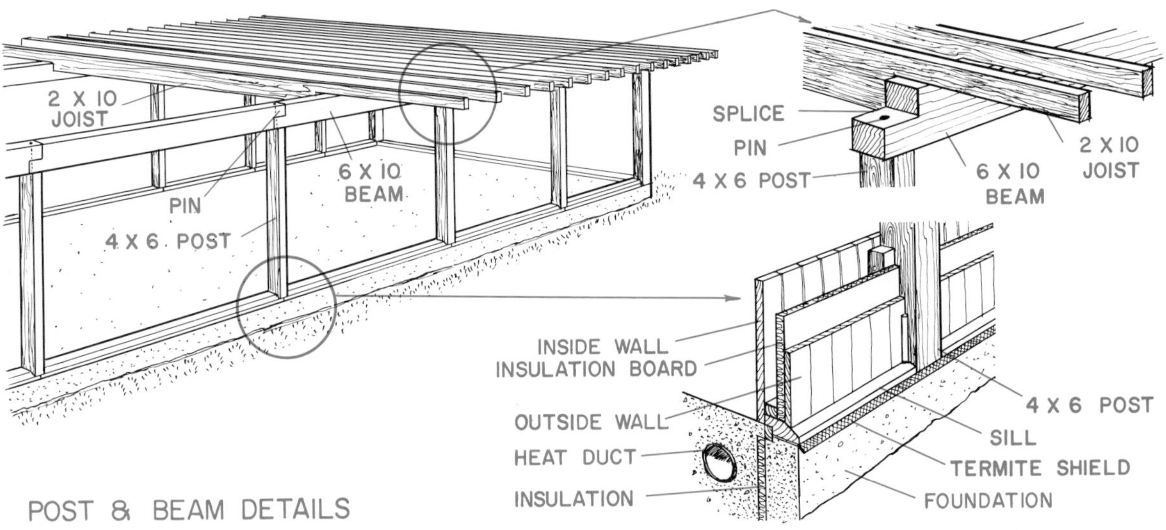

Fig. 52–15. Basic details of post and beam construction.

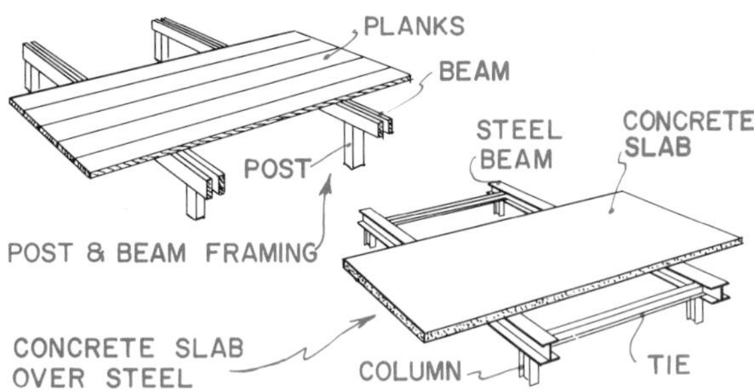

Fig. 52–16. Comparison of post and beam construction with steel and concrete slab construction.

Bethlehem Steel Corp.; American Iron and Steel Institute

Fig. 52–17. Steel framing permits the use of large spans.

Steel columns perform the same function as wooden posts in providing the vertical support. Steel beams, like wood girders, support the floor or roof system. Steel framing, however, can support and span longer distances because of the rigidity of structural steel members. For this reason, steel framing is used to erect tall multiple-story buildings. In fact, the greatest utilization of structural-steel framing has been for large commercial and industrial buildings such as schools, churches, office buildings.

Steel has also gained popularity as a framing material for smaller structures. Large cantilever decks, as shown in Fig. 52–17, are possible because of the long distances that can be spanned by steel beams.

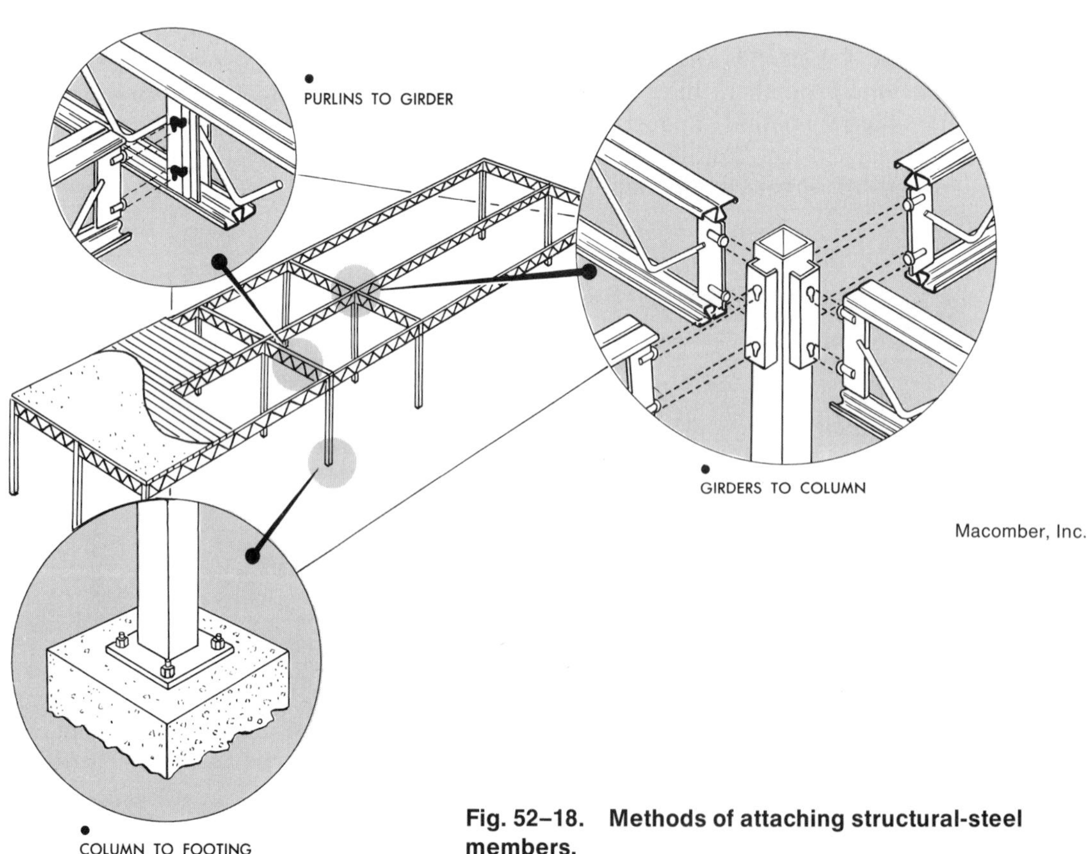

Macomber, Inc.

Fig. 52–18. Methods of attaching structural-steel members.

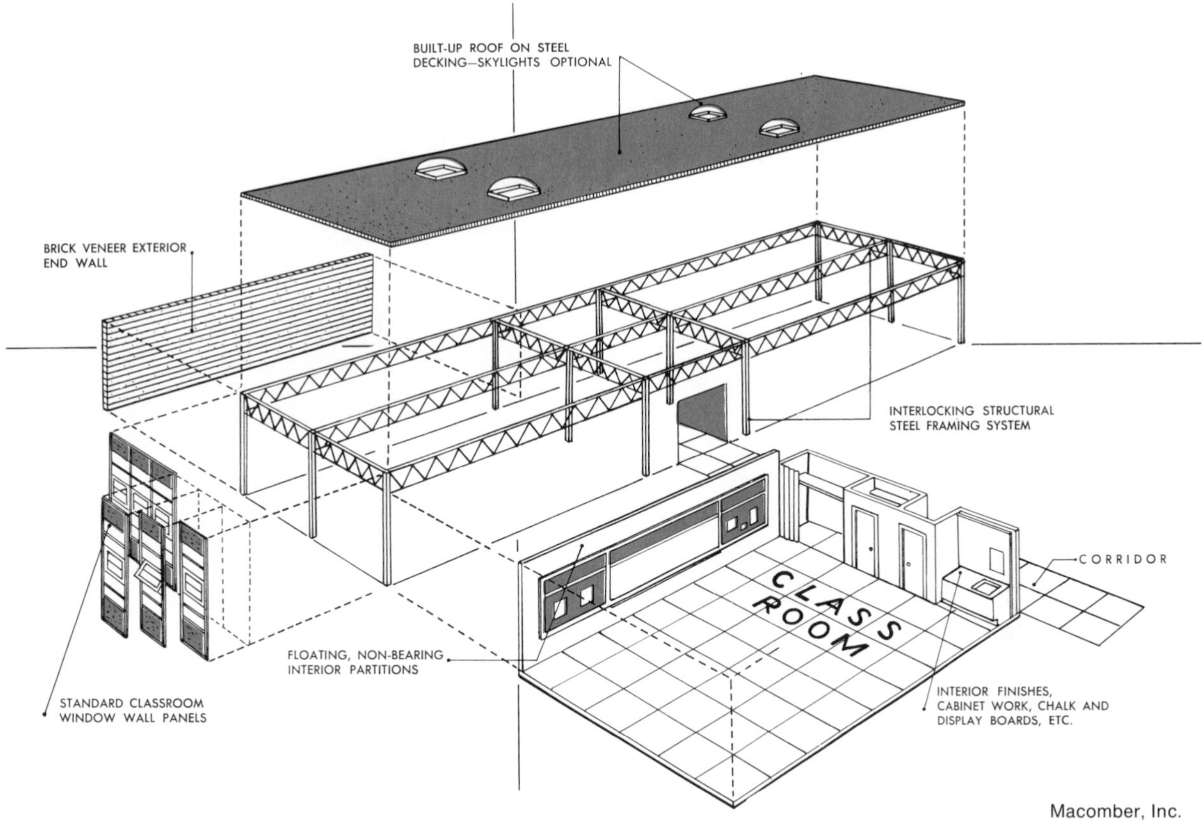

Fig. 52–19. Structural-steel framework permits flexibility in design.

Because of the rigid attachment of steel members to each other and to footers and walls, a minimum of crossbracing is needed (Fig. 52–18). Structural-steel framework can be designed to span long distances without intervening support. Longer spans create large unobstructed areas by eliminating the need for columns or bearing partitions. These large clear-span areas provide the designer with considerable flexibility in the design and location of interior partitions. Figure 52–19 shows some of the flexibilities in the interior design and in the placement of the exterior-wall treatment in steel construction.

Structural-steel members are available in a variety of shapes and sizes. Figure 52–20 shows some of the standardized shapes used in architectural work. Structural aluminum members are also used for house framing (Fig. 52–21).

PREFABRICATION

From the time of the construction of the Pyramids, men have been building with prefabricated component parts. The word *fabricate* simply means to put together. The combination of *pre* and *fabricate* indicates that the parts of the structure are put together prior to erection, at a place permitting more controlled and more desirable conditions than are possible at a building site.

Beginnings

In its simplest form, prefabrication dates back to the time when primitive people cut and trimmed wood and tanned skins before building a shelter (Fig. 52–22). Hannibal carried prefabricated huts across the Alps in a war with the Romans. Portable buildings were used by the Army in the 1800s for barracks and small

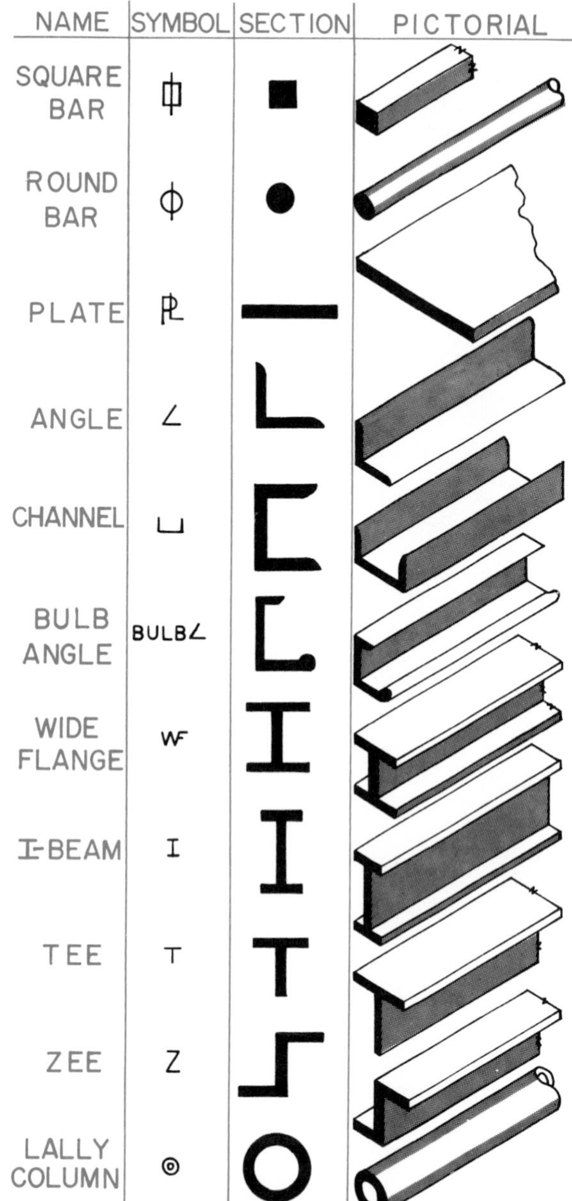

NAME
SYMBOL
SECTION
PICTORIAL
SQUARE BAR
ROUND BAR
PLATE
ANGLE
CHANNEL
BULB ANGLE
BULB∠
WIDE FLANGE
WF
I-BEAM
I
TEE
T
ZEE
Z
LALLY COLUMN

Fig. 52–20. Standard structural-steel shapes.

Aluminum Company of America

Fig. 52–21. Use of structural aluminum for house framing.

field hospitals. The Union Army used these structures for its troops during the Civil War (Fig. 52–23).

Throughout the early twentieth century, 1900 to about 1940, prefabrication became more popular for precut houses. Its use was a modified do-it-yourself approach to home building. A few companies then ventured into prefabrication of a more complete house package including ceiling panels, wall panels, and floor panels, complete with plumbing and electrical work installed in the walls. At the same time, conventional builders were accepting prefabrication to a great extent. They recognized, for example, that a better and less expensive window sash could be produced in a plant than could be handmade on the job site. As builders became more aware of the time, labor, and materials that could be saved by prefabrication, they began to use preassembled

Fig. 52–22. An early application of the principle of prefabrication.

Fig. 52–23. Prefabrication techniques were used in the Civil War.

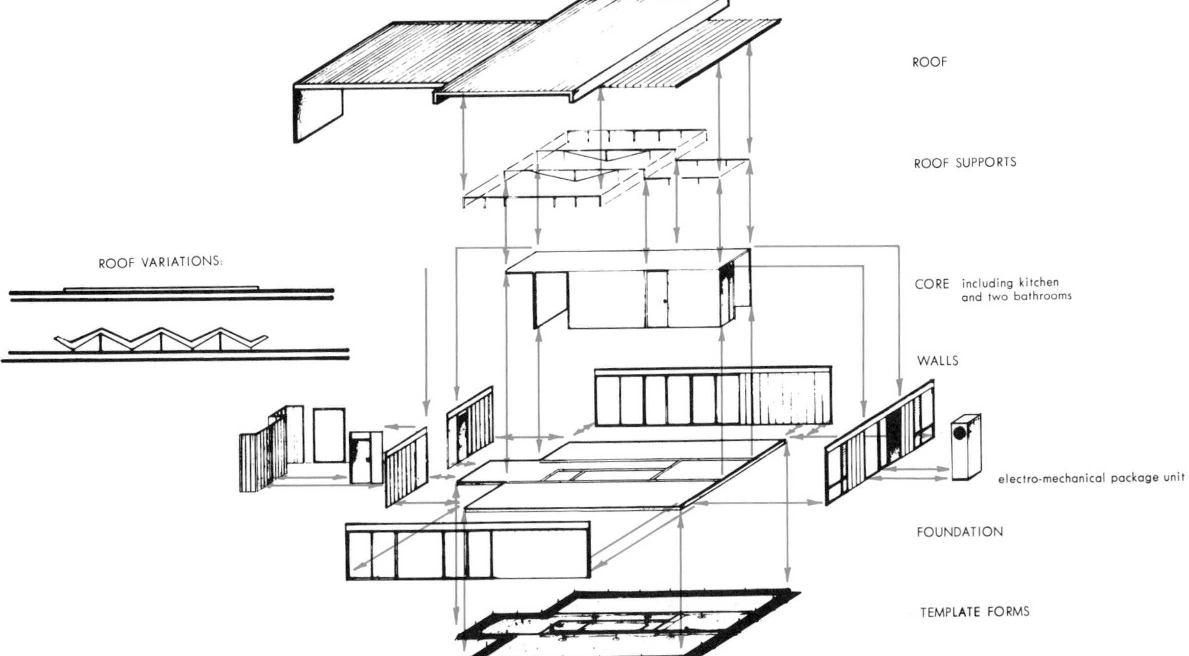

Steelways Magazine; American Iron and Steel Institute

Fig. 52–24. The maximum utilization of factory components.

cabinets, prefitted doors, prefinished sink tops, prefinished floors, and other prefabricated parts.

Prefabrication Today

Today, the most successful companies producing factory-made homes rely on constructing building panels, exterior panels, partitions, and floor systems by conventional framing methods. They simply apply the techniques of mass production to their production methods. The goal is to minimize custom-job work without sacrificing the quality of the construction.

The National Association of Home Builders has sponsored the design and construction of an experimental house to determine to what extent factory-finished materials can be applied throughout the house. Figure 52–24 shows some of the basic components of this prefabricated house.

Factory-Built Structures

All structures are factory built to some extent; that is, not all the materials or components are manufactured or put together on the site. Some structures are simply precut. This means that all the materials are cut to specification at the factory, and then assembled on the site by conventional methods.

With the most common type of factory-built (prefabricated) homes, the major components, such as the walls, trusses, decks, and partitions, are assembled at the factory. The utility work, such as installation of electrical, plumbing, and heating systems, is completed on site. The final finishing work, such as installation of floors, roof coverings, and walls, is also done on site.

There are some factory-built homes, however, that are constructed in complete modules at the factory and require only final electrical-outlet, roof-overhang, and assembly fastening on site to complete the job. A factory-built home of this kind is shown in Figs. 52–25A through G. Figures 52–25A and B show part of the factory fabrication process of assembling a wall component. Figures 52–25C and D show the unloading of a module on site. Figures 52–25E and F show the completion of electrical hookup and roof overhang. It takes only two weeks from receipt of order at the factory to completion of the finished product shown in Fig. 52–25G. This time factor is a major advantage of this kind of construction. However, the size of the modules is limited to only 12′ (3.7 m) widths. This restriction is due to highway limits for transportation.

Designaire Home Corporation

Fig. 52–25A. Wall prefabrication at a factory.

Designaire Home Corporation

Fig. 52–25B. The fastening of framing in a factory.

Fig. 52–25C. Unloading a module at the site.

Designaire Home Corporation

Designaire Home Corporation

Fig. 52–25D. Setting the module on a foundation.

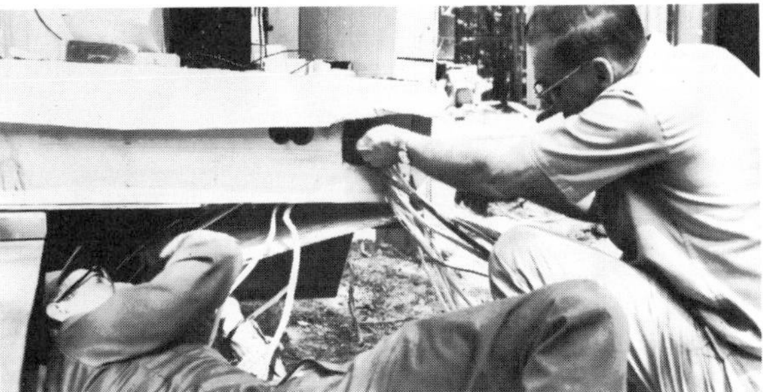
Designaire Home Corporation

Fig. 52–25E. Making final electrical connections at the site.

Designaire Home Corporation

Fig. 52–25F. Installation of roof overhang components.

Designaire Home Corporation

Fig. 52–25G. The completely assembled house.

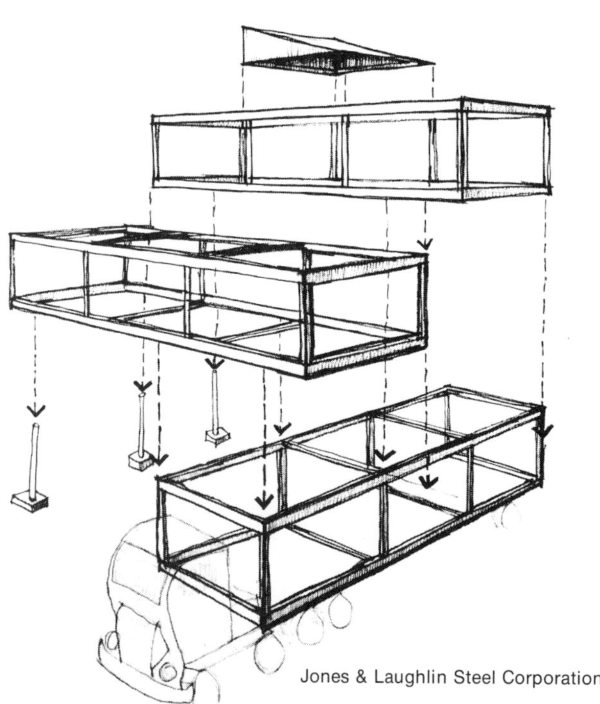

Jones & Laughlin Steel Corporation

Fig. 52–26A. Cross-stacking of structural steel members.

Jones & Laughlin Steel Corporation

Fig. 52–26B. Module can be stacked to produce variety.

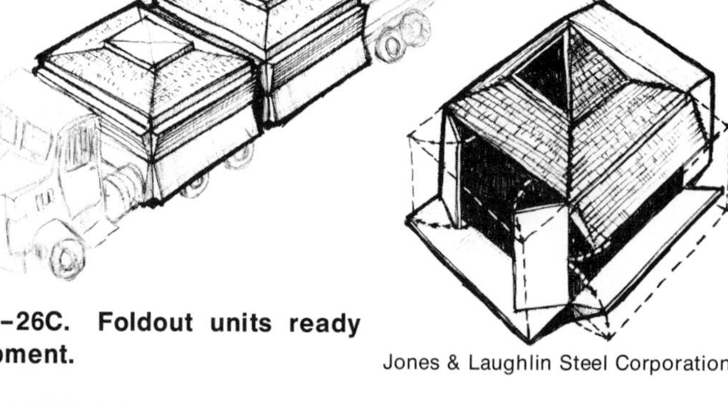

Jones & Laughlin Steel Corporation

Fig. 52–26C. Foldout units ready for shipment.

Jones & Laughlin Steel Corporation

Fig. 52–26D. Completed foldout modules.

Another new steel-construction technique developed within the steel industry is shown in Figs. 52–26A through D. Figure 52–26A shows the basic framing members made of lightweight structural steel, which can be cross stacked at the site and fitted into place. Figure 52–26B shows the several lightweight steel-frame units stacked at right angles in this design. Three units shown here yield a total area of 1200 square feet (111.5 m^2). Upper units are connected to form a double-wide living room, kitchen, and dining area. The lower unit employs a foldout wall section in the bedroom area. Its roof forms a sundeck.

Another steel building innovation is the utilization of foldout sections, as shown in Figs. 52–26C and D. Figure 52–26C shows three units that can be fitted together for transportation on one trailer. Figure 52–26D shows a model of the completed units after foldout sections are placed in position.

With the exception of mobile homes, most factory-built homes require some on-site preparation. Designers have been working for years to develop residential designs that would eliminate or greatly curtail the amount of on-site preparation. The only site preparation necessary for the home shown in Fig. 52–27 is the installation of concrete piers to which the legs of the steel tubing are bolted. This type of installation requires few, if any, landscape changes. Factory-built steel structures like this one make ideal vacation homes, since they can easily be brought to the site by a variety of means, including helicopter.

Mobile Homes

The first completely factory-built homes were trailers, or mobile homes. The mobile-home buyer, unlike the buyer of a conventional factory-built home, has little option to adjust or customize the design of his residence. He or

Fig. 52–27. This complete home will fit any lot without much site preparation.

Futro Corporation

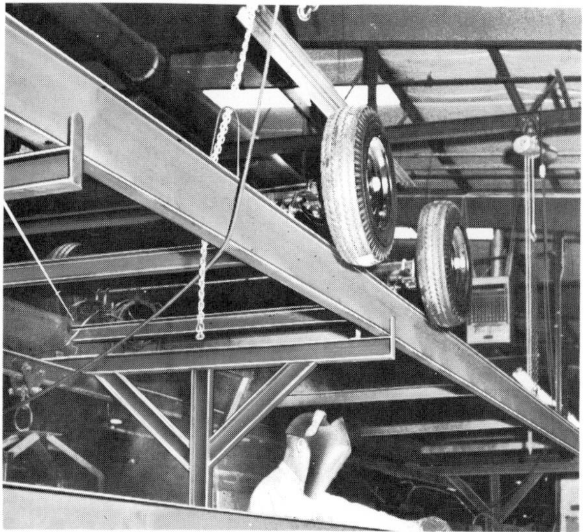

Champion Home Builders Co.

Fig. 52–28A. Welding a mobile-home frame.

she does have opportunities to select from many different sizes, models, and interior components.

The mobility of our population and the increasing cost of real estate and real-estate taxes have contributed to the growth of the mobile-home industry. It is now estimated that approximately 25 percent of all one-family houses in the United States are mobile homes.

Thus, the mobile-home designer must plan homes that can be mass-produced, but which also provide a variety of options for the prospective buyer. Also, a variety of sizes must be designed to span the price range of various consumers.

Figures 52–28A through H show the steps in the construction of a mobile home. These steps lead from the fabrication of the basic frame through the installation of walls, partitions, mechanical equipment, insulation, and furnishings to the finished product.

Research and development in all phases of our technology will contribute to the increased use of factory-produced and factory-finished materials for architectural purposes.

Champion Home Builders Co.

Fig. 52–28B. Assembly of a floor system.

Champion Home Builders Co.

Fig. 52–28C. Wall and partition assembly.

Champion Home Builders Co.

Fig. 52–28D. Attachment of mechanical equipment.

Champion Home Builders Co.

Fig. 52–28E. Assembling the roof rafters.

Champion Home Builders Co.

Fig. 52–28F. Attaching insulation to the walls.

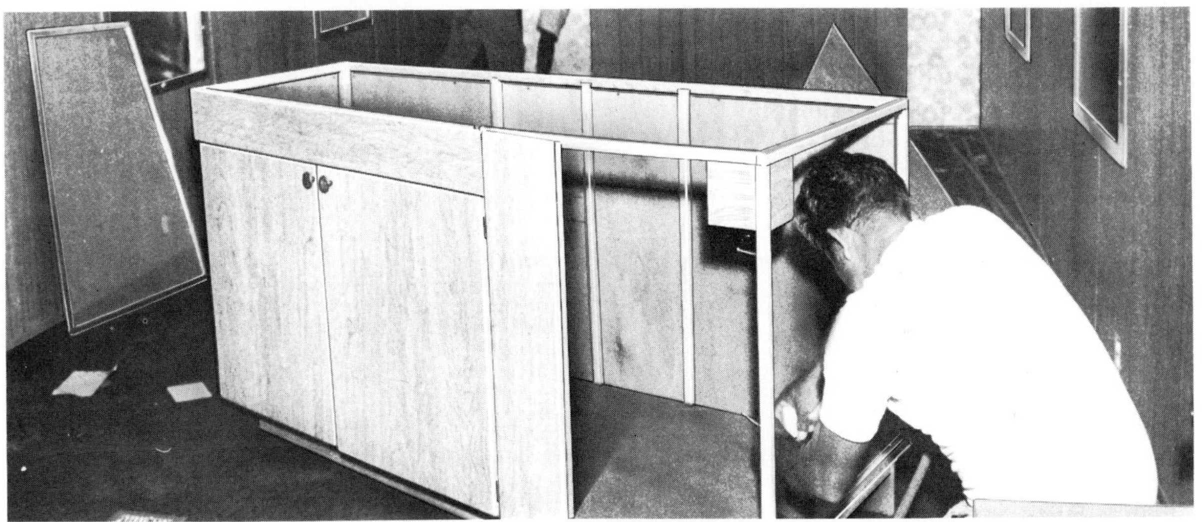

Champion Home Builders Co.

Fig. 52–28G. The installation of built-in components.

Champion Home Builders Co.

Fig. 52–28H. A completed mobile home.

PROBLEMS

Define the following architectural terms: *span, framework, skeleton frame, structural tie, sheathing, live load, dead load, tension, compression, shear, torsion, deflection, equilibrium, conventional wood framing, post and beam framing, column, beam, post, plank, cantileverage, bearing partition, nonbearing partition.*

UNIT 53

Floor-Framing Plans

Platform-floor systems are those systems that are suspended from foundation walls and/or beams.

METRICATION FOR UNIT 53

The tables in this unit are concerned with joist spans and safe loads for various members. They all use customary units. As the construction industry becomes metric, new lumber sizes will probably become standard. New tables similar to those found in this unit will then become available in metric units for those new standards. To make the metric equivalent of the tables available would not be a practical approach to metrication and would give a false impression of metric standards. For individual assignments the appropriate data from any of the tables may be converted to metric by using Table 25–4.

TYPES OF PLATFORM-FLOOR SYSTEMS

Platform-floor systems are divided into three types: the conventional floor-framing systems, plank and beam floor systems, and panelized floor systems. These types are shown in Fig. 53–1.

Conventional Systems

The conventionally framed platform system provides a most flexible method of floor framing for a wide variety of design conditions. Floor joists are spaced at 16″ (406 mm) intervals and are supported by the side walls of the foundation or by beams.

Plank and Beam Systems

The plank and beam (post and beam) method of floor framing utilizes individual framing members that are much larger and less numerous than conventional framing members. Because of the size and rigidity of the members

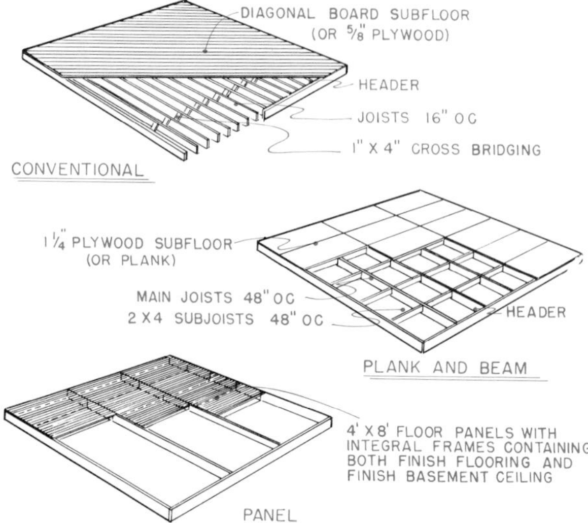

Fig. 53–1. Types of platform-floor systems.

the necessity for bridging for stability between joists is eliminated.

Panelized Systems

Panelized floor systems are composed of preassembled sandwich panels of a variety of skin and core materials. Core-panel systems are used for long clear spans over basement construction and for shorter spans in nonbasement houses.

Other experimental methods of core-component design and construction are continually being developed and refined to reduce the on-site construction costs. Research in engineering and wood technology is continually extending the use of components for support systems.

DESIGN

The design of the floor system depends on load, type of material, size of the members, spacing of the support members, and distance between the major support members (span).

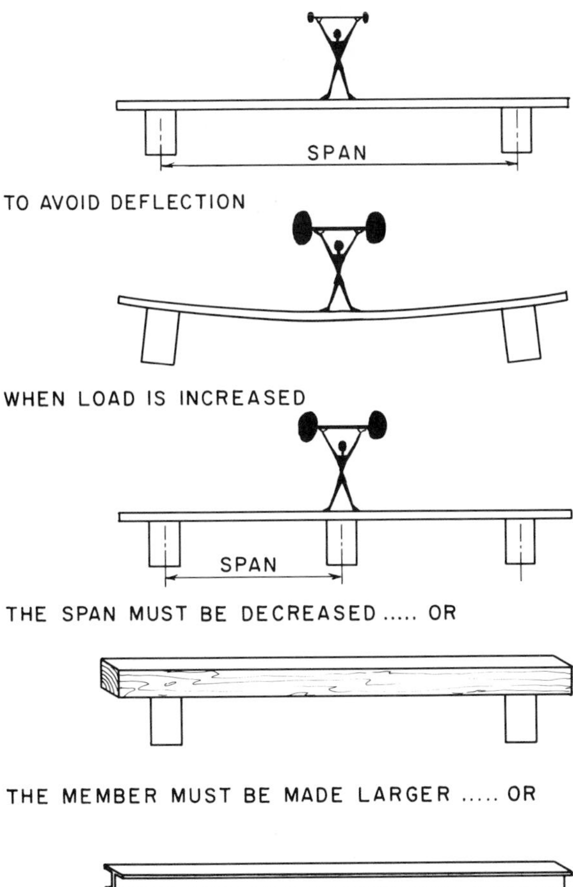
SPAN
TO AVOID DEFLECTION
WHEN LOAD IS INCREASED
SPAN
THE SPAN MUST BE DECREASED ..... OR
THE MEMBER MUST BE MADE LARGER ..... OR
MADE OF STRONGER MATERIAL

Fig. 53–2. The design of the floor system depends on many factors.

Figure 53–2 shows that as the load is increased, the span must be decreased to compensate for the increase, or the member must be made larger or of a stronger material. The design of floor systems, therefore, demands very careful calculation in determining the live and dead loads acting on the floor. The most appropriate material for posts, beams or girders, and blocking must be selected. The design also requires determination of the exact size of the posts, beams, and deck materials and joists and establishment of the exact spacing between posts, girders, and joists.

The parts of a floor system that must be selected on the basis of loads, material, size, and spacing include the deck, joist, girders or beams, and posts or columns.

DECK

The deck of a floor system is composed of a subfloor and a finished floor. A *subfloor* is a floor usually made of dressed sheathing lumber or plywood, which is laid over the floor joist and over which the finished floor is laid. The functions of the subfloor are as follows:

1. It increases the strength of the floor and provides a surface for the laying of a thin finished floor.
2. It helps to stiffen the position of the floor joist.
3. It serves as a working surface during construction.
4. It helps to deaden sound.
5. It prevents dust from rising through the floor.
6. It helps to insulate.

The *finished floor* provides a wearing surface over the subfloor, or over the joist if there is no subfloor. Hardwood, such as oak, maple, beech, and birch, is used for finished floors. Tile is often used as a finished floor. It may be laid directly on the subflooring.

JOISTS

To determine the proper type of joists, the load, spacing, and strength of the joists must be considered.

Loads

Only live loads bear directly on the decking and joists. Therefore, the total live loads for the room having the heaviest furniture and the heaviest traffic should be used to compute the total load for the entire floor. To find the live load in pounds per square foot, divide the total room loads in pounds by the number of square feet supporting the load. To find the live load in kilograms per square meter, divide the total room loads in kilograms by the number of square meters supporting the load.

Spacing

When the live load is determined, the size and spacing of joists can be established by referring to Table 53–1. This table is based on #1 Southern white pine with a fiber stress of 1200

Table 53-1. MAXIMUM SPANS FOR JOISTS

LIVE LOAD—POUNDS PER SQUARE FOOT	SPACING	2 INCHES WIDE BY DEPTH OF—					3 INCHES WIDE BY DEPTH OF—				
		6	8	10	12	14	6	8	10	12	14
	12	12- 9	16- 9	21- 1	24- 0	—	14- 7	19- 3	24- 0	—	—
10	16	11- 8	15- 4	19- 4	23- 4	24- 0	13- 6	17- 9	22- 2	24- 0	—
	24	10- 3	14- 6	17- 3	20- 7	24- 0	11-11	15- 9	19-10	23- 9	24- 0
	12	11- 6	15- 3	19- 2	23- 0	24- 0	13- 3	17- 6	21- 9	24- 0	—
20	16	10- 5	13-11	17- 6	21- 1	24- 0	12- 0	16- 1	20- 2	24- 0	—
	24	9- 2	12- 3	15- 6	18- 7	21- 9	10- 6	14- 2	17-10	21- 6	24- 0
	12	10- 8	14- 0	17- 9	21- 4	24- 9	12- 4	16- 4	20- 5	24- 5	—
30	16	9- 9	12-11	16- 3	19- 6	22- 9	11- 4	14-11	18- 9	22- 7	26- 4
	24	8- 6	11- 4	14- 4	17- 3	20- 2	10- 0	13- 2	16- 8	19-11	23- 4
	12	10- 0	13- 3	16- 8	20- 1	23- 5	11- 8	15- 4	19- 3	23- 1	26-11
40	16	9- 1	12- 1	15- 3	18- 5	21- 5	10- 8	14- 0	17- 8	21- 3	24-10
	24	7-10	10- 4	13- 1	15- 9	18- 5	9- 4	12- 4	15- 7	18- 9	22- 1
	12	9- 6	12- 7	15-10	19- 1	22- 4	11- 0	14- 7	18- 4	22- 0	25- 8
50	16	8- 7	11- 6	14- 7	17- 6	20- 5	10- 0	13- 4	16-10	20- 3	23- 8
	24	7- 3	9- 6	12- 1	14- 7	17- 0	8-10	11- 9	14-10	17-10	20-10
	12	9- 0	12- 0	15- 2	18- 3	21- 4	10- 6	14- 0	17- 7	21- 1	24- 7
60	16	8- 1	10-10	13- 8	16- 6	19- 3	9- 7	12-10	16- 1	19- 4	22- 7
	24	6- 8	8-11	11- 3	13- 7	15-11	8- 5	11- 3	14- 1	17- 0	20- 0
	12	8- 7	11- 6	14- 6	17- 6	20- 6	10- 1	13- 5	16-11	20- 5	23- 9
70	16	7- 8	10- 2	12-10	15- 6	18- 3	9- 3	12- 3	15- 5	18- 7	21-10
	24	6- 5	8- 5	10- 7	12- 9	15- 0	8- 0	10- 7	13- 4	16- 1	18-10

pounds per square inch and a modulus of elasticity (ratio of stress and strain) of 1 600 000 pounds per square inch. For other materials, such as redwood or Douglas fir lumber, with different fiber stresses and different moduli of elasticity, a different chart should be used. For example, if the live loads are approximately 40 pounds per square foot and 16″ spaces are desired between joists, you can see that a 2 × 8 is good for a spacing of only 12′—1″. For a span larger than 12′—1″, a joist of larger cross section is necessary.

Fig. 53-3. A floor-framing plan with blocking shown.

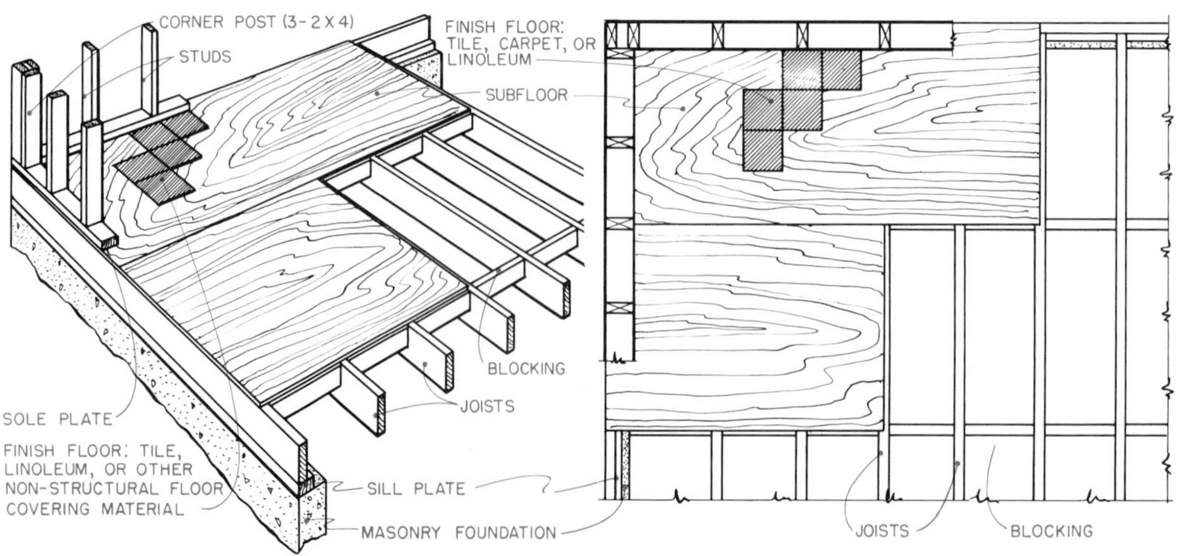

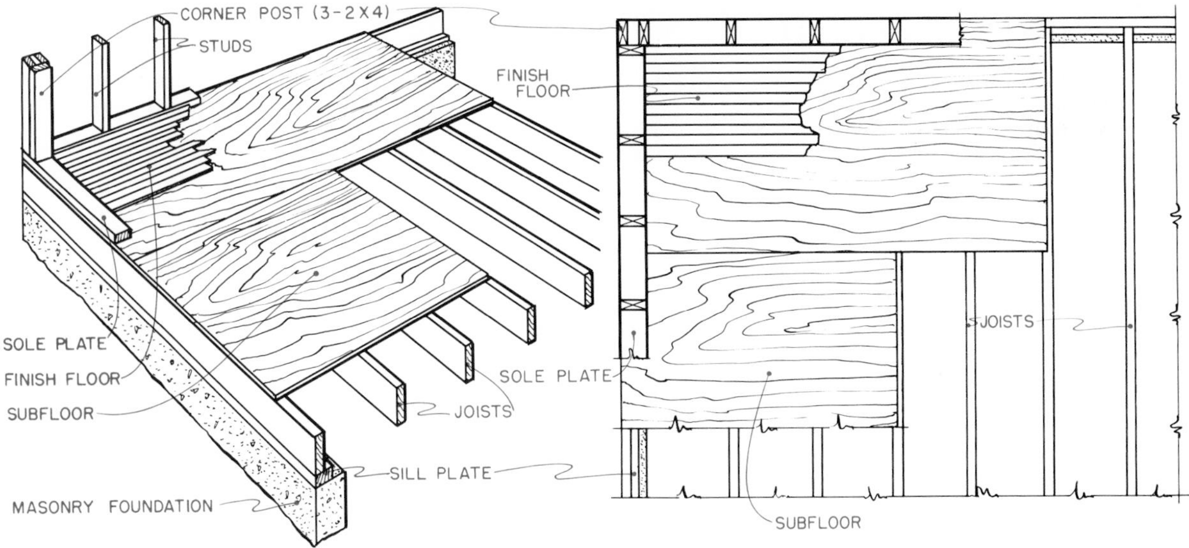

Fig. 53–4. A floor-framing plan without blocking.

SIZE

You can see, therefore, that as the size, spacing, and load vary, the spans must vary accordingly. Or if the span is changed, the dimensions of the spacing of the joist must change accordingly. Figure 53–3 indicates the method of drawing part of the floor-framing plan which shows the size and position of joists and the blocking between joists. In this particular detail, the relative position of the subfloor, finished floor, sill, and exterior walls is also shown. In Fig. 53–4 there is an alternative floor system showing the relationship between the joists of the floor and the finished floor and sill.

In some systems the floor system may appear to have no joists, as shown in Fig. 53–5. However, in this system the girder and blocking perform the function of the joist. The girders rest directly on posts, and the sub-

Fig. 53–5. A method of drawing floor-framing systems without joists.

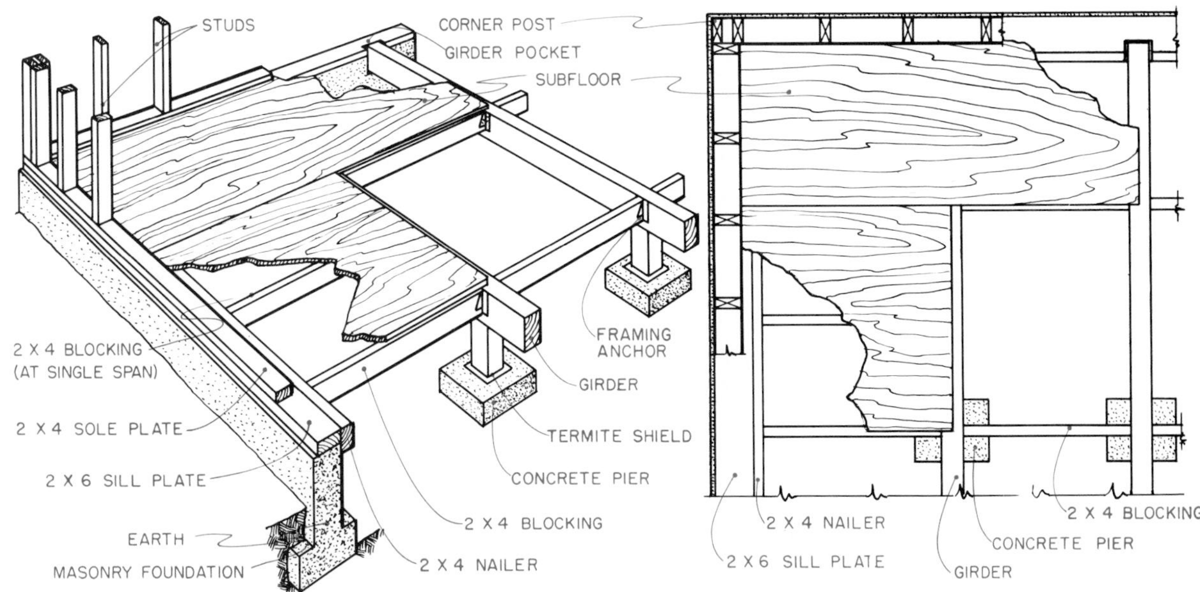

Fig. 53–6. Subfloor application.

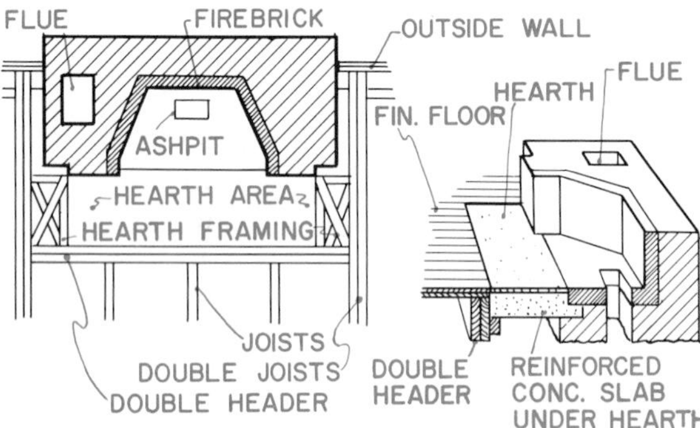

Fig. 53–7. Double headers are used around fireplaces.

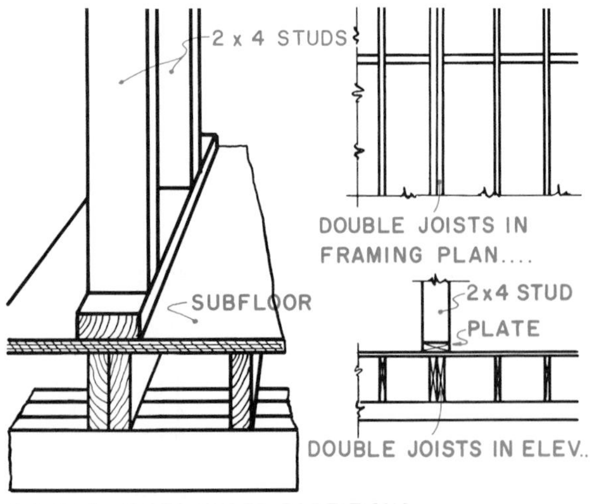

Fig. 53–8. Double joists are used under partitions.

flooring rests directly on the girders, which are spaced more closely than most girders which support joists. The subflooring can be nailed or glued with adhesives to bond structural members together (Fig. 53–6).

HEADERS

Whenever it is necessary to cut regular joists to provide an opening for a stairwell or a hearth, it is necessary to provide auxiliary joists called *headers*. Headers are placed at right angles to the regular joists, to carry the ends of joists that are cut. A header cannot be of greater depth than any other joist; hence, headers are usually doubled (placed side by side) to compensate for the additional load. Figure 53–7 shows the use of the double header as compensation for the joists that are cut to provide space for the fireplace.

Additional support is also needed under bearing partitions. Figure 53–8 shows the use of double joists under partitions. The method of drawing the double joists both on the floor-framing plan and on the floor-framing elevation drawing is also shown.

GIRDERS AND BEAMS

All the weight of the floor system, including the live loads and the dead loads, are transmitted to bearing partitions. These loads are then transmitted either to the foundation wall or to horizontal supports known as *girders* or *beams*. To determine the exact spacing, size, and type of beam to support the structure, follow these steps:

1. Determine the total load acting on the entire floor system in pounds per square foot. Divide the total live and dead loads by the number of square feet of floor space. For example, if the combined load for the floor system shown in Fig. 53–9 is 48,000 pounds, then there are 50 pounds per square foot of load acting on the floor (48,000 pounds divided by 960 square feet equals 50 pounds per square foot).
2. Lay out the proposed position of all columns and beams. It will also help to sketch the po-

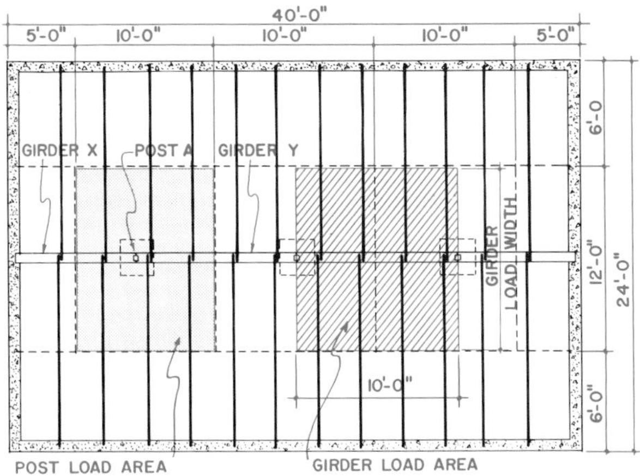

Fig. 53–9. The area supported by a girder is known as the tributary area.

American Plywood Association

Fig. 53–10. The use of box beams.

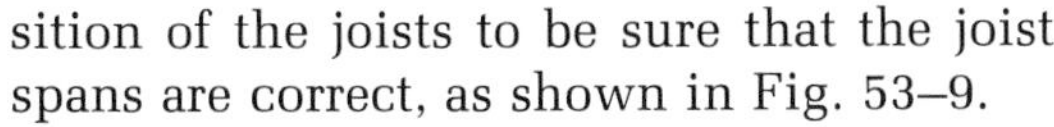

sition of the joists to be sure that the joist spans are correct, as shown in Fig. 53–9.

3. Determine the number of square feet supported by the girder (girder load area). The *girder load area* is determined by multiplying the length of a girder from column to column by the girder load width. The *girder load width* is the distance extending on both sides of the center line of the girder, halfway to the nearest support, as shown in Fig. 53–9. The remaining distance from a girder load area to the outside wall is supported by the outside wall.
4. To find the load supported by the girder load area, multiply the girder load area by the load per square foot. For example, the girder load in Fig. 53–9 is 6000 pounds (120 square feet × 50 pounds per square foot).
5. Select the most suitable material to carry the load at the span desired. Built-up wood girders are equivalent to steel I beams in many respects. However, I beams will span a greater length without intervening support.
6. Select the exact size and classification of the beam or girder. Use Table 53–2 to select the most appropriate wood girder. For example, to support 6000 pounds over a 10′ span, either an 8 × 8 solid girder or a 6 × 10 built-up girder would suffice. The girder should be strong enough to support the load, but any size larger is a waste of materials. The only alternative to increasing the size of the girder is to decrease the size of the span.

An alternate kind of beam is shown being used in Fig. 53–10. It is a constructed box beam.

Table 53–2. SAFE LOADS FOR WOOD GIRDERS

GIRDER SIZE	SAFE LOAD IN POUNDS FOR SPANS FROM 6 TO 10 FEET				
	6 FT	7 FT	8 FT	9 FT	10 FT
6 x 8 SOLID	8 306	7 118	6 220	5 539	4 583
6 x 8 BUILT-UP	7 359	6 306	5 511	4 908	4 062
6 x 10 SOLID	11 357	10 804	9 980	8 887	7 997
6 x 10 BUILT-UP	10 068	9 576	8 844	7 878	7 086
8 x 8 SOLID	11 326	9 706	8 482	7 553	6 250
8 x 8 BUILT-UP	9 812	8 408	7 348	6 544	5 416
8 x 10 SOLID	15 487	14 732	13 608	12 116	10 902
8 x 10 BUILT-UP	13 424	12 768	11 792	10 504	9 448

Table 53-3. SAFE LOADS FOR I BEAMS, SHOWING NUMBER OF KIPS (1000 POUNDS) A BEAM WILL SUPPORT AT A GIVEN SPAN

	4 INCHES DEEP BY—				5 INCHES DEEP BY—			6 INCHES DEEP BY—			7 INCHES DEEP BY—		
WEIGHT PER FOOT	7.7	8.5	9.5	10.5	10.0	12.25	14.75	12.5	14.75	17.25	15.3	17.5	20.0
SPAN IN FEET													
4	9.0	9.5	10.1	10.7	14.5	16.2	18.0	21.8	23.8	26.0	31.0	33.4	36.0
5	7.2	7.6	8.0	8.5	11.6	13.0	14.4	17.4	19.0	20.8	24.8	26.7	28.7
6	6.0	6.3	6.7	7.1	9.7	10.8	12.0	14.5	15.9	17.3	20.7	22.2	24.0
7	5.1	5.4	5.7	6.1	8.3	9.3	10.3	12.5	13.6	14.9	17.7	19.1	20.5
8	4.5	4.7	5.0	5.3	7.3	8.1	9.0	10.9	11.9	13.0	15.5	16.7	18.0
9	4.0	4.2	4.5	4.7	6.5	7.2	8.0	9.7	10.6	11.6	13.8	14.8	16.0
10	3.6	3.8	4.0	4.3	5.8	6.5	7.2	8.7	9.5	10.4	12.4	13.3	14.4
11	—	—	—	—	5.3	5.9	6.5	7.9	8.7	9.5	11.3	12.1	13.1
12	—	—	—	—	—	—	—	7.3	7.9	8.7	10.3	11.1	12.0
13	—	—	—	—	—	—	—	6.7	7.3	8.0	9.5	10.3	11.1
14	—	—	—	—	—	—	—	6.2	6.8	7.4	8.9	9.5	10.3
15	—	—	—	—	—	—	—	—	—	—	8.3	8.9	9.6
16	—	—	—	—	—	—	—	—	—	—	7.7	8.3	9.0
17	—	—	—	—	—	—	—	—	—	—	—	—	—
18	—	—	—	—	—	—	—	—	—	—	—	—	—
19	—	—	—	—	—	—	—	—	—	—	—	—	—
20	—	—	—	—	—	—	—	—	—	—	—	—	—

	8 INCHES DEEP BY—				9 INCHES DEEP BY—					10 INCHES DEEP BY—		
WEIGHT PER FOOT	18.4	20.5	23.0	25.5	21.8	25.0	30.0	35.0	25.4	30.0	35.0	40.0
SPAN IN FEET												
4	42.7	45.2	48.2	51.1	56.6	60.9	67.6	74.2	73.3	80.1	87.5	94.8
5	34.1	36.1	38.5	40.9	45.3	48.7	54.1	59.4	58.6	64.1	70.0	75.8
6	28.5	30.1	32.1	34.1	37.7	40.6	45.1	49.5	48.8	53.4	58.3	63.2
7	24.4	25.8	27.5	29.2	32.3	34.8	38.6	42.4	41.9	45.8	50.0	59.2
8	21.3	22.6	24.1	25.5	28.3	30.5	33.8	37.1	36.6	40.1	43.7	47.4
9	19.0	20.1	21.4	22.7	25.2	27.1	30.0	33.0	32.6	35.6	38.9	42.1
10	17.1	18.1	19.3	20.4	22.6	24.4	27.0	29.7	29.3	32.0	35.0	37.9
11	15.5	16.4	17.5	18.6	20.6	22.2	24.6	27.0	26.6	29.1	31.8	34.5
12	14.2	15.1	16.1	17.0	18.9	20.3	22.5	24.7	24.4	26.7	29.2	31.6
13	13.1	13.9	14.8	15.7	17.4	18.7	20.8	22.8	22.5	24.6	26.9	29.2
14	12.2	12.9	13.8	14.6	16.2	17.4	19.3	21.2	20.9	22.9	25.0	27.1
15	11.4	12.0	12.8	13.6	15.1	16.2	18.0	19.8	19.5	21.4	23.3	25.3
16	10.7	11.3	12.0	12.8	14.2	15.2	16.9	18.6	18.3	20.0	21.9	23.7
17	10.0	10.6	11.3	12.0	13.3	14.3	15.9	17.3	17.2	18.8	20.6	22.3
18	9.5	10.0	10.7	11.4	12.6	13.3	15.0	16.5	16.3	17.8	19.4	21.1
19	9.0	9.5	10.1	10.8	11.9	12.8	14.2	15.6	15.4	16.9	18.4	20.0
20	8.5	9.0	9.6	10.2	11.3	12.2	13.5	14.8	14.7	16.0	17.5	19.0

STEEL BEAMS

The method for determining the size of steel beams is the same as for determining the size of wood beams. As wood beams vary in width for a given depth, steel beams vary in weight, depth, and thickness of webs and flanges; and classifications vary accordingly. Table 53–3 shows the relationship of the span, the load, the depth, and the weight of standard I beams and channels. A steel beam may be selected by referring to the desirable span and load and then choosing the most appropriate size (depth and weight) for the I beam. For example, a

5″ × 12.25-pound I beam will support 6.5 kips per given span of 10 feet. A kip is equal to 1000 pounds.

COLUMNS

When girders or beams do not completely span the distance between foundation walls, then wood posts, steel-pipe columns, masonry columns, or steel-beam columns must be used for intervening support. To determine the most appropriate size and classification of posts or columns to support the girders or beams, follow these steps:

1. Determine the total load in pounds per square foot for the entire floor area by multiplying the total load by the number of square feet of floor space.
2. Determine the spacing of posts necessary to support the ends of each girder. Great distances between posts should be avoided because great weight would concentrate on one footing. Long spans also require extremely large girders. For example, it is possible to span a distance of 30′, but to do so, a 15″ I beam would be needed. The extreme weight and cost of this beam would be prohibitive. On the other hand, if only a 6′ span were used, the close spacing might greatly restrict the flexibility of the internal design. As a rule, use the shortest span that will not interfere with the design function of the area.
3. Find the number of square feet supported by each post. A post will carry the load on a girder to the midpoint of the span on both sides. For example, post A in Fig. 53–9 carries half the load of girder X and girder Y in the direction of the joist. The post also carries half the load to the nearest support wall on either side of the post. The number of square feet supported by post A in Fig. 53–9 is therefore 120 square feet (10′ × 12′).
4. Find the load supported by the post support area. Multiply the number of square feet by the load per square foot (120 × 50).
5. Determine the height of a post. The height of the post is related to the span of a beam. The 4 × 4 post shown in Fig. 53–11 may be more than adequate to support a given weight if the height of the post is 6′. However, this same 4 × 4 post may be totally inadequate to support the same weight when the length is increased to 20′.
6. Determine the type of column needed to support the load at the anticipated height.
7. Select the thickness and width of the post needed to support the load at the given height.
   Use Table 53–4 for lumber posts. Use Table 53–5 for I-beam columns. Use Table 53–6 to determine the correct diameter of steel-pipe column supports.

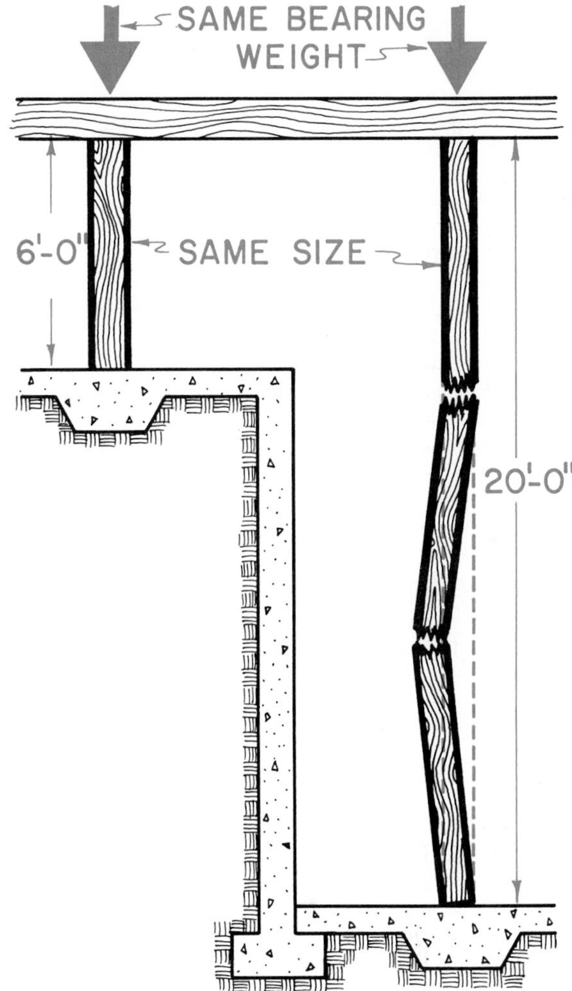

Fig. 53–11. A heavier post is needed to support the same load when the height is increased.

Table 53-4. MAXIMUM LOADS FOR LUMBER POSTS

NOMINAL SIZE, INCHES	3 BY 4	4 BY 4	4 BY 6	6 BY 6	6 BY 8	8 BY 8
ACTUAL SIZE, INCHES	2⅝ BY 3⅝	3⅝ BY 3⅝	3⅝ BY 5⅝	5½ BY 5½	5½ BY 7½	7½ BY 7½
AREA IN SQUARE INCHES	9.51	13.14	20.39	30.25	41.25	56.25
HEIGHT OF COLUMN:						
4 FEET	8 720	12 920	19 850	30 250	41 250	56 250
5 FEET	7 430	12 400	19 200	30 050	41 000	56 250
6 FEET	5 630	11 600	17 950	29 500	40 260	56 250
6 FEET 6 INCHES	4 750	10 880	16 850	29 300	39 950	56 000
7 FEET	4 130	10 040	15 550	29 000	39 600	55 650
7 FEET 6 INCHES	—	9 300	14 400	28 800	39 000	55 300
8 FEET	—	8 350	12 950	28 150	38 300	55 000
9 FEET	—	6 500	10 100	26 850	36 600	54 340
10 FEET	—	—	—	24 670	33 600	53 400
11 FEET	—	—	—	22 280	30 380	52 100
12 FEET	—	—	—	19 630	26 800	50 400

Table 53-5. SAFE LOADS FOR I-BEAM COLUMNS IN KIPS (1000 POUNDS)

DEPTH IN INCHES	10	9	8	7	6	5	4	3
WEIGHT PER POUND PER FOOT	25.4	21.8	18.4	15.3	12.5	10.0	7.7	5.7
EFFECTIVE LENGTH:								
							33.3	24.6
3 FEET	110.7	94.8	80.1	66.5	54.2	43.1	33.0	23.5
4 FEET	110.7	94.8	80.1	65.9	52.1	39.7	29.1	20.3
5 FEET	109.5	91.2	74.9	60.0	46.9	35.1	25.3	17.2
6 FEET	101.7	83.9	68.3	54.1	41.8	30.7	21.8	14.6
7 FEET	93.8	76.7	61.8	48.5	37.0	26.8	18.7	12.3
8 FEET	86.0	69.7	55.7	43.3	32.7	23.4	16.1	10.5
9 FEET	78.7	63.2	50.1	38.6	28.9	20.4	13.9	—
10 FEET	71.8	57.2	45.0	34.5	25.5	17.9	—	—
11 FEET	65.5	51.8	40.5	30.8	22.6	—	—	—
12 FEET	59.7	47.0	36.5	27.6	20.2	—	—	—
AREA IN SQUARE INCHES	7.38	6.32	5.34	4.43	3.61	2.87	2.21	1.64

Table 53-6. SAFE LOADS FOR STEEL-PIPE COLUMNS IN KIPS (1000 POUNDS)

NOMINAL SIZE, INCHES	6	5	4½	4	3½	3	2½	2	1½
EXTERNAL DIAMETER, INCHES	6.625	5.563	5.000	4.500	4.000	3.500	2.875	2.375	1.900
THICKNESS, INCHES	.280	.258	.247	.237	.226	.216	.203	.154	.145
EFFECTIVE LENGTH:									
5 FEET	72.5	55.9	48.0	41.2	34.8	29.0	21.6	12.2	7.5
6 FEET	72.5	55.9	48.0	41.2	34.8	28.6	19.4	10.6	6.0
7 FEET	72.5	55.9	48.0	41.2	34.1	26.3	17.3	9.0	5.0
8 FEET	72.5	55.9	48.0	40.1	31.7	24.0	15.1	7.4	4.2
9 FEET	72.5	55.9	46.4	37.6	29.3	21.7	12.9	6.6	3.5
10 FEET	72.5	54.2	43.8	35.1	26.9	19.4	11.4	5.8	2.7
11 FEET	72.5	51.5	41.2	32.6	24.5	17.1	10.3	5.0	—
12 FEET	70.2	48.7	38.5	30.0	22.1	15.2	9.2	4.1	—
AREA IN SQUARE INCHES	5.58	4.30	3.69	3.17	2.68	2.23	1.70	1.08	0.80
WEIGHT PER POUND PER FOOT	18.97	14.62	12.54	10.79	9.11	7.58	5.79	3.65	2.72

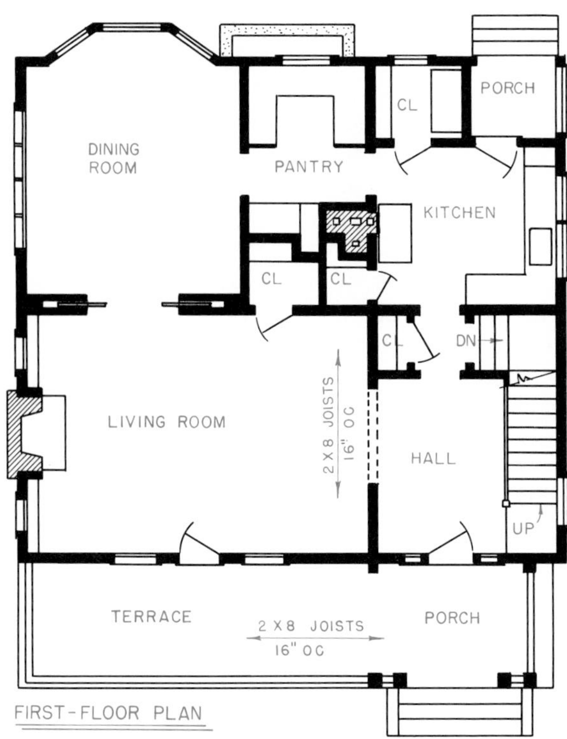

Fig. 53–12A. A method of showing joist direction on floor plan.

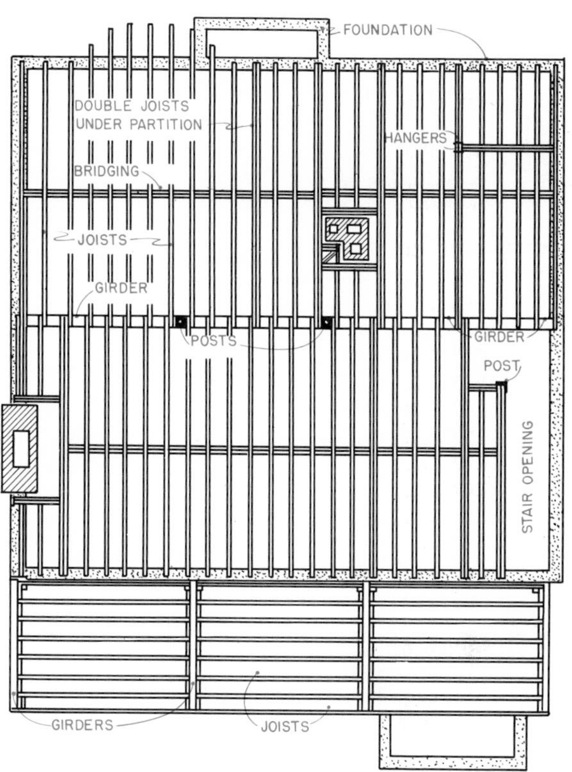

Fig. 53–12B. A floor-framing plan showing material thicknesses.

PLANS

The more complete the architectural plan, the better the chances are that the building will be constructed exactly as designed. If a floor-framing plan is not prepared to accompany the basic architectural plans, then the framing of the floor system is left entirely to the desires of the builder. Some architectural plans do not include a floor-framing plan. Only the direction of joists and the possible location of beams or girders are shown on the floor plan. Figure 53–12A shows a plan of this type on a floor plan. Figures 53–12B and C show other methods of drawing floor-framing plans. All are related to the basic floor plan shown in Fig. 53–12A.

The most complete and most acceptable method of drawing floor-framing plans is shown in Fig. 53–12B. Each structural member is represented by a double line which shows its exact thickness.

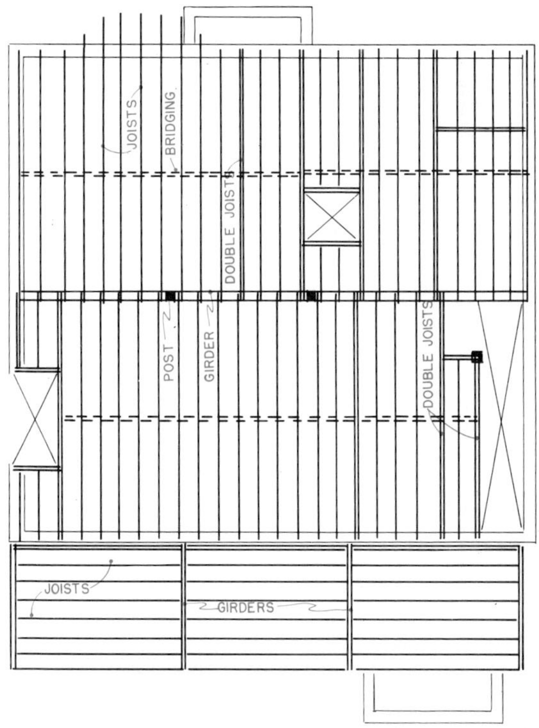

Fig. 53–12C. A simplified method of drawing floor-framing plans.

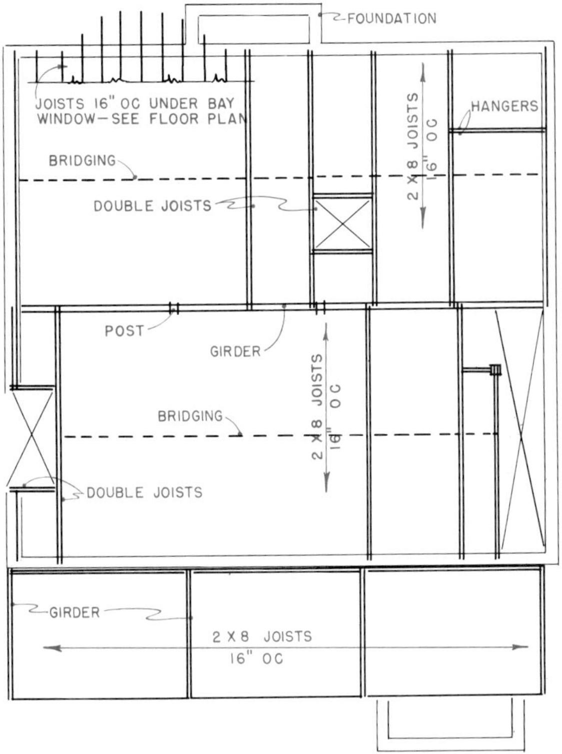

Fig. 53–12D. An abbreviated method of drawing floor-framing plans.

The more abbreviated plan shown in Fig. 53–12C is a short-cut method of drawing floor-framing plans. A single line is used to designate each member. Chimney and stair openings are shown by diagonals. Only the outline of the foundation and post locations is shown. The abbreviated floor-framing plan given in Fig. 53–12D uses a technique similar to the one used in floor plans to show the entire area where uniformly distributed joists are placed. The direction of joists is shown by an arrow. The size and spacing of joists are shown by notes placed on the arrow. This type of framing plan is usually accompanied by numerous detail drawings such as the ones shown in Figs. 53–3 and 53–4.

DETAILS

Although many floor-framing plans are completely interpretable for the experienced builder, others may require that the detail of some segment of the plan be prepared separately to explain more clearly the construction methods recommended. The detail is drawn to eliminate the possibility of error in interpretation or to explain more thoroughly some unique condition of the plan. Details may be merely enlargements of what is already on the floor-framing plan. They may be prepared for dimensioning purposes, or they may show a view from a different angle to reveal the underside or elevation view for better interpretation.

Figure 53–13 shows a floor-framing plan and several details that have been removed for clarity. Detail 1 shows the position of cross-bridging. Detail 2 shows the relationship of the built-up beam, the double joist under the partition, and the solid bridging. Detail 3 shows the sill construction in relation to the floor joist and rough flooring, and to the foundation. Detail 4 shows the method of supporting the built-up beam by the *lally* (steel) *column* and the joist position on the beam. Detail 5 shows several alternative methods of supporting the joist over a built-up beam or an I beam; thus the builder is given an option. Detail 6 shows the attachment of the typical box sill to the masonry foundation. Detail 7 shows the method of supporting the built-up beam with a pilaster, and the tie-in with the box sill and joist.

Depending on the size, material, and relative floor heights, there are many methods of attaching joists to girders or beams. The representation of these intersections on floor-framing plans is sometimes misinterpreted because the lines of the floor plan do not reflect differences in heights; the lines show only that they pass over other members. Figure 53–14 shows the method of illustrating these intersections on the floor-framing plan. A pictorial detail is often drawn to reinforce the interpretation of the floor-framing plan.

In addition to pictorial drawings, elevation sections are also used extensively to aid in the interpretation of floor-framing plans. An elevation section reveals a relationship of the construction members exactly 90° from the projection of the plan. The construction of the floor systems given in Fig. 53–15 is better shown by elevation drawings than by floor-framing plans.

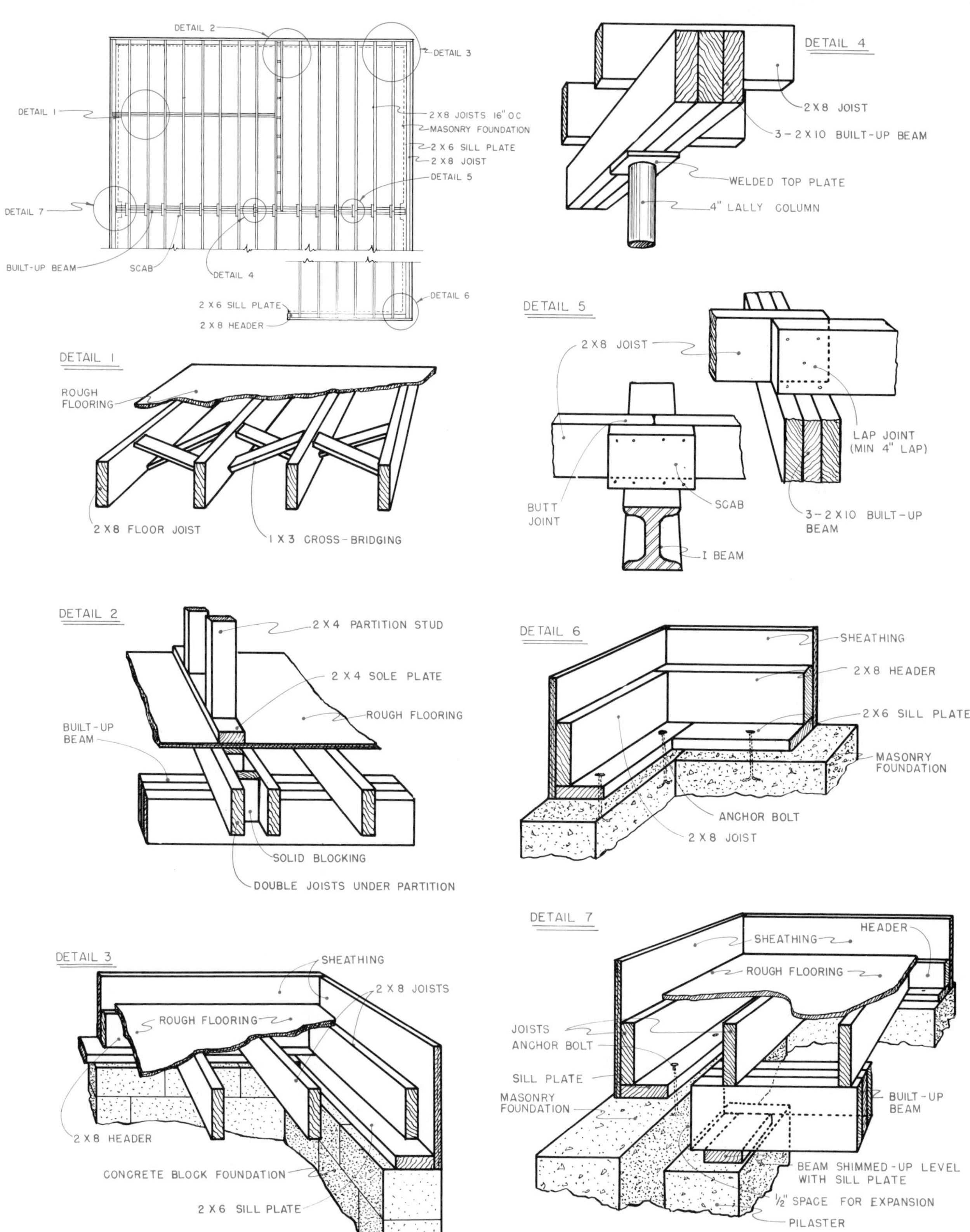

Fig. 53–13. Floor-framing plan details.

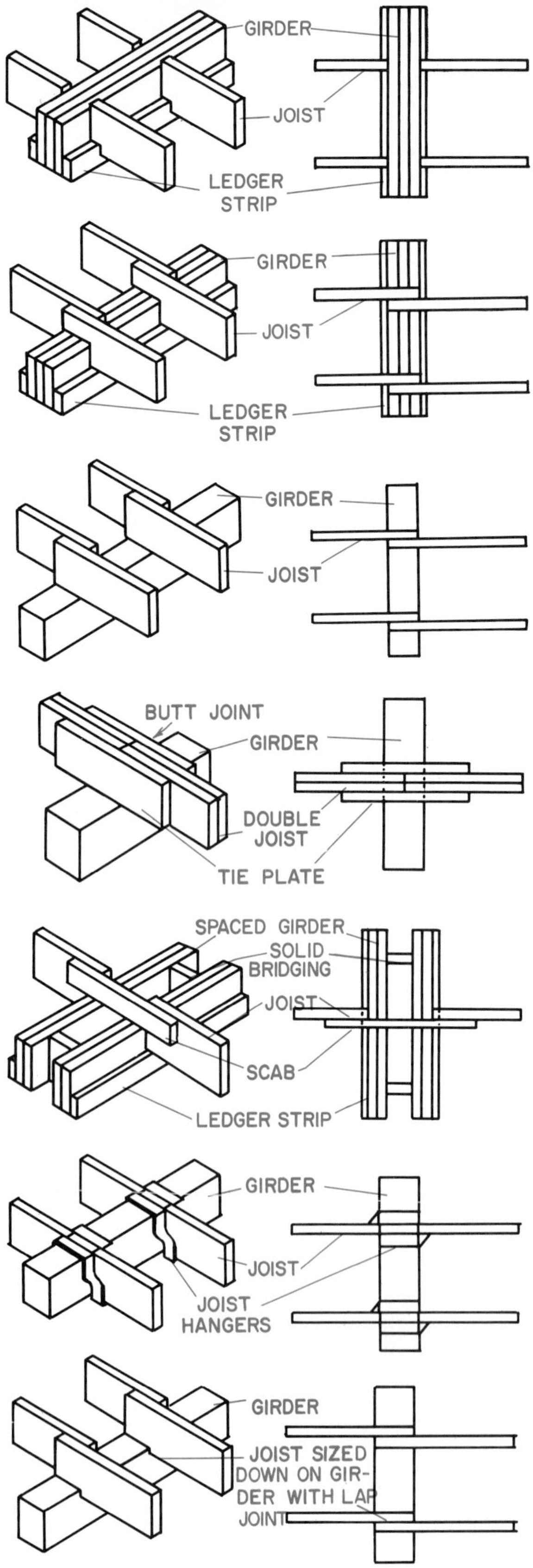

GIRDER
JOIST
LEDGER STRIP
GIRDER
JOIST
LEDGER STRIP
GIRDER
JOIST
BUTT JOINT
GIRDER
DOUBLE JOIST
TIE PLATE
SPACED GIRDER
SOLID BRIDGING
JOIST
SCAB
LEDGER STRIP
GIRDER
JOIST
JOIST HANGERS
GIRDER
JOIST SIZED DOWN ON GIRDER WITH LAP JOINT

Fig. 53–14. Methods of drawing intersections.

VAPOR BARRIER
EXTERIOR BRICK
SLEEPER
SHEATHING
CONCRETE SLAB
AIR SPACE
GRAVEL
STUD
FINISH FLOOR
GYPSUM BD
BASEBOARD
SECTION–OAK FLOOR ON CONCRETE SLAB

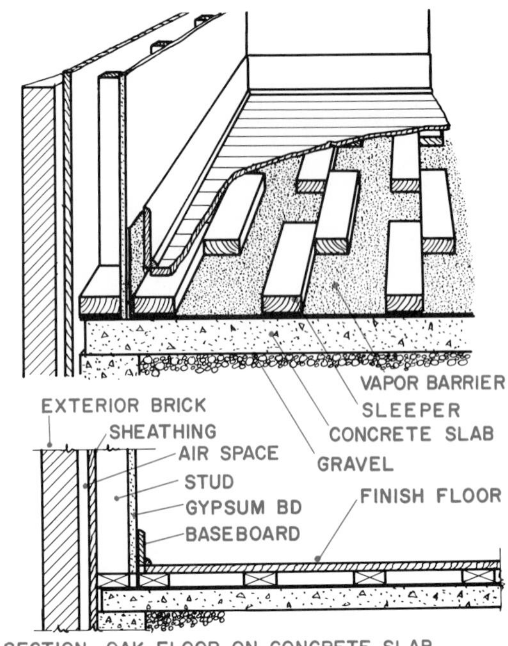

Fig. 53–15. An elevation section showing floor-framing construction.

Recommended methods of splicing lumber when necessary, so that spliced members will be as strong as single members, should also be detailed to eliminate building failures. The splices shown in Fig. 53–16 will resist compression, tension, and bending.

STAIRWELL FRAMING

The stairwell opening as drawn on the floor-framing plan shows the relative position of the double joists and headers. Frequently more information is needed concerning the relationship of the other parts of the stair assembly to the stairwell opening shown in Fig. 53–17. Information concerning the size and position of the various parts of the stair assembly is shown in Fig. 53–18. Such information is often shown in a separate detail.

Since the stairwell opening must be precisely shown on the floor-framing plan, a complete design of the stair system should precede the preparation of the floor-framing plan. The steps outlined in Figs. 53–19A through G show the sequences necessary for determining the exact dimensions of the entire stair structure.

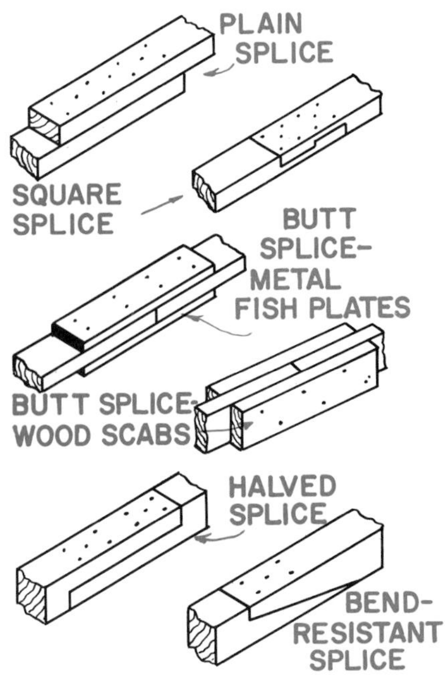

Fig. 53–16. Splices that resist compression, tension, and bending.

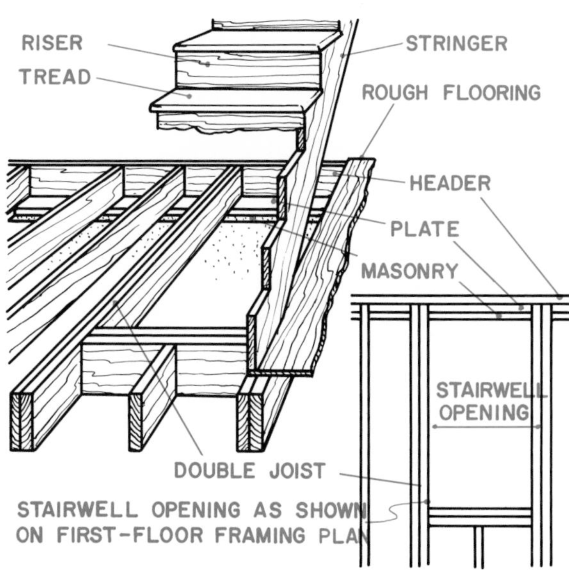

Fig. 53–17. Methods of drawing a stairwell opening.

1. Lay out the distance from the first-floor level to the second-floor level exactly to scale (Fig. 53–19A). Convert this distance to inches and add the position of the ceiling line. If working in the metric system no conversion is necessary.
2. Determine the most desirable riser heights (7½″, or 190 mm, is normal). Divide the number of inches (millimeters) between floor levels by the desired riser height to find the number of risers needed (Fig. 53–19B). Divide the area between the floors into spaces equaling the number of risers needed. This work can be done by inclining the scale.
3. Extend the riser-division lines lightly for about an inch, or 25 mm.

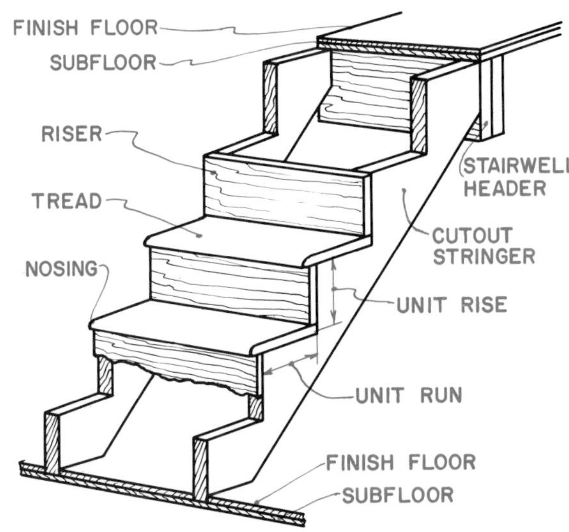

Fig. 53–18. Parts of the stair assembly.

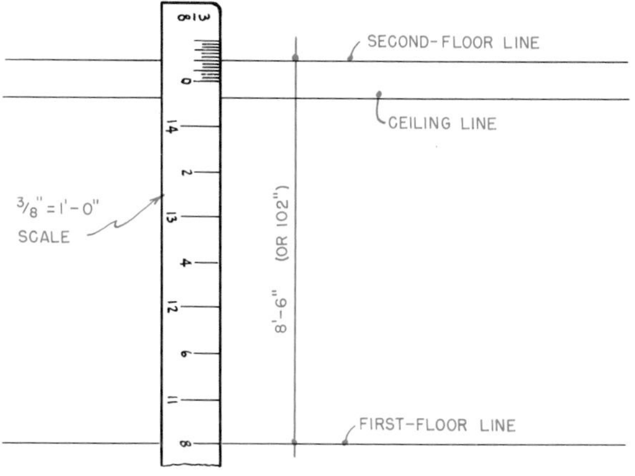

Fig. 53–19A. Lay out the distance from the first-floor level to the second-floor level.

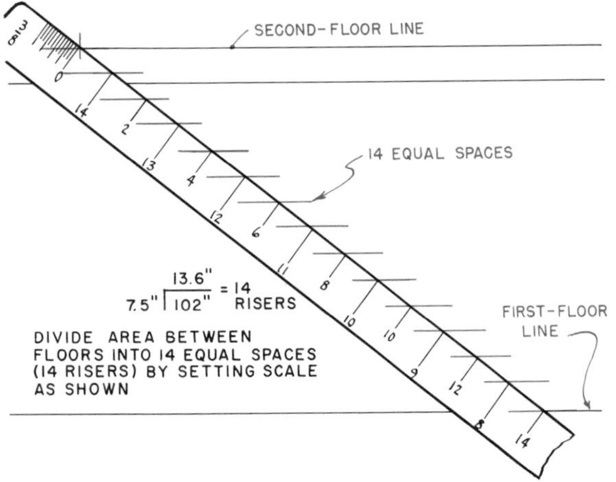

Fig. 53–19B. Determine the number of risers and extend the riser lines.

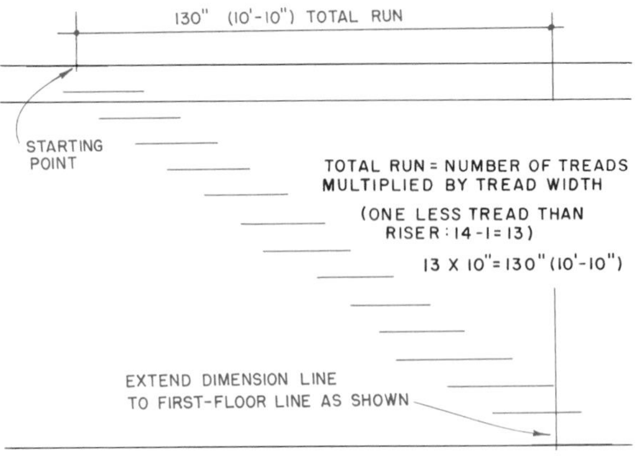

Fig. 53–19C. Lay out the total run.

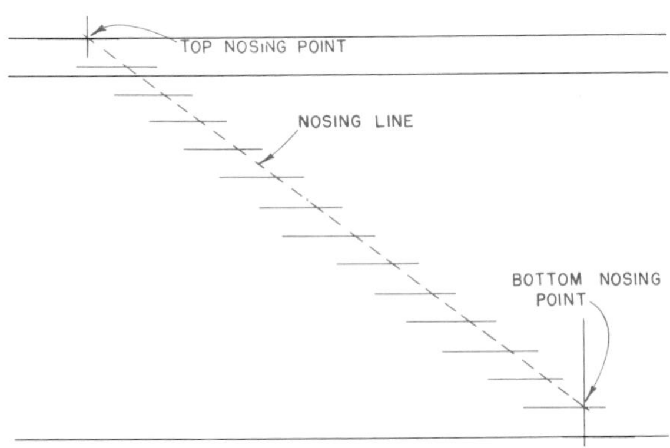

Fig. 53–19D. Locate the nosing points and draw the nosing line.

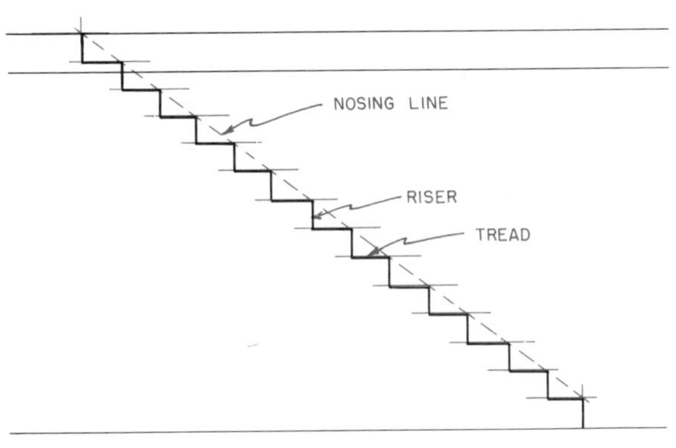

Fig. 53–19E. Draw the riser lines and the tread lines.

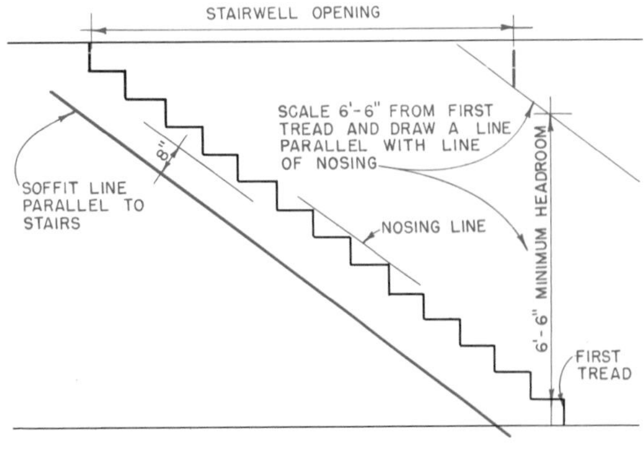

Fig. 53–19F. Establish the headroom clearance, stairwell opening, and soffit line.

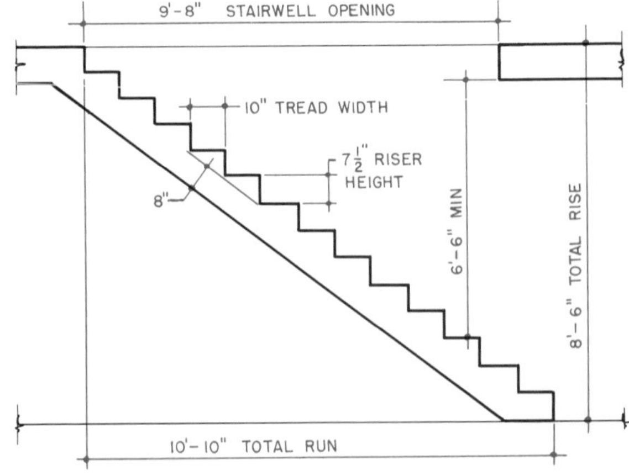

Fig. 53–19G. Erase guidelines and add dimensions.

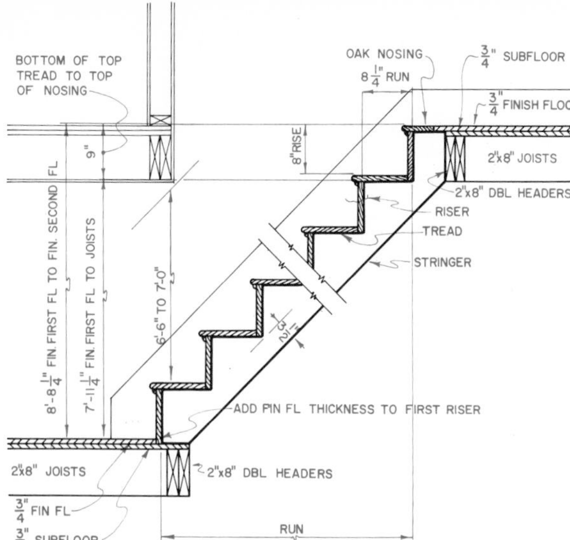

Fig. 53–20. Sectional drawing of a stair assembly.

4. Determine the total length of the run (Fig. 53–19C). Lay out this distance from a starting point near the top riser line and measure the total run horizontally. Extend this line vertically to the first-floor line. The total run is the number of treads multiplied by the width of each tread. There is always one less tread than riser.
5. Locate the top and bottom nosing points (Fig. 53–19D). Mark the intersection between the starting point of the total run and the intersection between the end of the total run and the first riser line.
6. Draw the nosing line by connecting the bottom nosing point with the top nosing point.
7. Draw riser lines intersecting the nosing points and the light riser lines (Fig. 53–19E).
8. Make the tread lines and the riser lines heavy.
9. Draw the soffit line the same as the thickness of the stringer. Establish headroom clearances. Draw a parallel line 6′—6″ (1.980 m) above the nosing line (Fig. 53–19F). Establish the stairwell opening by cutting the joists where the headroom clearance line intersects the bottom of the joist.
10. Show the outline of the carriage or stringer assembly.
11. Erase all layout lines and make all object lines heavier (Fig. 53–19G).
12. Add dimensions to describe the length of the stairwell opening, the size of the tread widths, the riser height, the minimum headroom, the total rise, and the total run.

When the basic information pertaining to the overall dimensions and relationships of the stair assembly is established, a complete sectional drawing showing thicknesses and floor-framing tie-ins can be prepared, as shown in Fig. 53–20. In this sectional drawing, the headers and the position of the bearing walls are shown.

STEEL

Floor-framing plans for steel construction (Figs. 53–21A through C) are prepared like other floor-framing plans. The exact positions of columns, beams, and *purlins* (horizontal

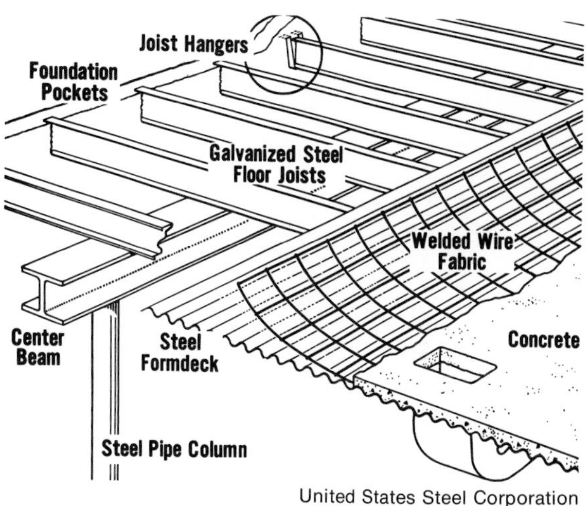

United States Steel Corporation

Fig. 53–21A. Steel floor framing.

Fig. 53–21B. Applying steel formdeck.

United States Steel Corporation

United States Steel Corporation

Fig. 53–21C. Adding the layer of welded wire fabric.

Douglas Fir Plywood Assoication

Fig. 53–22. Pouring lightweight concrete.

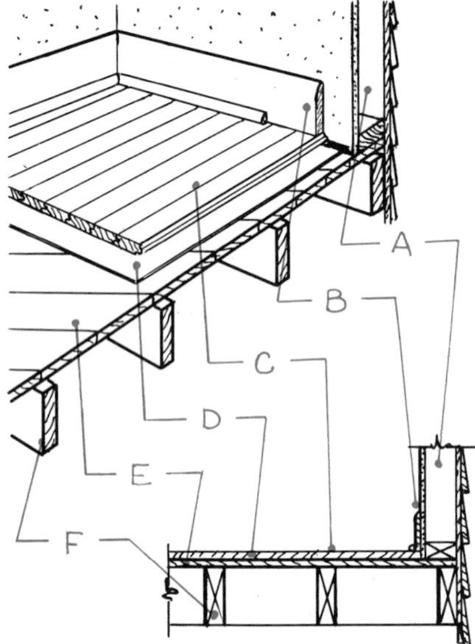

Fig. 53–23. Identify these floor-framing members.

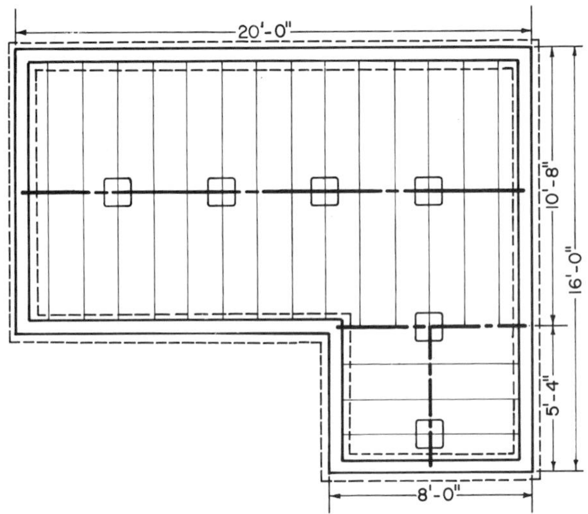

Fig. 53–24. Determine the size of the girder needed.

member) are dimensioned and the classification of each member indicated on the plan. Details should accompany steel-framing drawings to indicate the method of attaching steel members to each other. Lightweight concrete can be poured over steel or wood subfloors (Fig. 53–22).

PROBLEMS

1. **Identify the floor-framing terms illustrated in Fig. 53–23.**
2. **Determine the size of joists for the floor-framing plan shown in Fig. 53–24. Base your calculations on a combined load of 80 pounds per square foot.**
3. **Determine the size of the wood girder needed to support 80 pounds per square foot in the plan shown in Fig. 53–24. What size of steel beam would be needed to carry the same load?**
4. **Define the following architectural terms: *panel framing, deflection, load, spacing, modulus of elasticity, fiber stress, maximum span, blocking, bridging, girder pocket, girder, built-up girder, pier, post, column, beam, header, double header, double joists, girder load area, post-load area, lally column, I beam, channel, joist hanger, scab, ledger strip, butt joint, square splice, butt splice, halved splice, bent splice. stairwell opening, tread, riser, nosing, unit run, unit rise, stringer, top nosing point, bottom nosing point, nosing line.***

UNIT 54

Exterior-Wall Framing Plans

Exterior walls for most residential buildings are of either conventional or post and beam construction. The typical method of erecting walls for most conventional buildings follows the braced-frame system and has changed little since its introduction in this country. Prefabrication methods have led to variations in the erection of exterior walls, ranging from the panelization of just a basic frame to the complete panelized exterior wall, including plumbing, electrical work, doors, and windows, as shown in Fig. 54–1.

Large commercial structures usually use the curtain wall for their exterior wall. In this type of construction, nonstructural wall panels cover a steel framework. Figure 54–2 shows types of steel framework structures and their relationship to height.

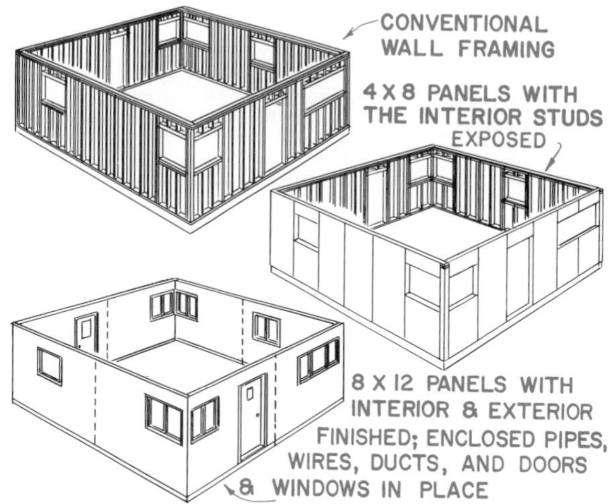

Fig. 54–1. Methods of wall paneling.

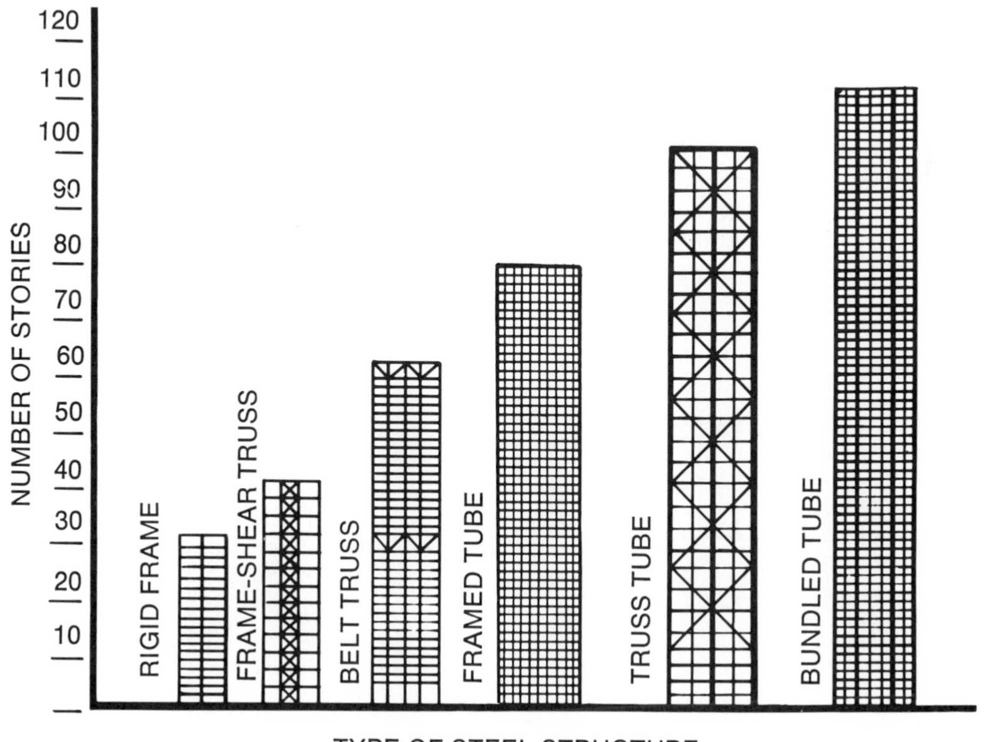

Iron and Steel Institute

Fig. 54–2. Types of steel framework compared to height.

Fig. 54–3A. Erection of an exterior wood-wall frame panel.

Regardless of the method of construction or fabrication, the preparation of exterior-panel drawings is relatively the same, whether they are prepared for factory use or for field use.

FRAMING ELEVATIONS

Exterior-wall framing panels, such as those shown being erected in Figs. 54–3A and B, are best constructed by using a framing elevation drawing as a guide. The wall-framing elevation drawing is the same as the north, south, east, or west elevation of the building, with all the building materials removed except the basic framing. Figure 54–4 shows a wall-framing elevation compared with a pictorial drawing of the same wall. Notice that the framing elevation is an orthographic projection and does not reveal a second dimension or angle of projection. Figure 54–5 shows some of the basic framing members included in framing elevations.

The framing elevation is projected from the floor plan and elevation, as shown in Fig. 54–6. Since floor-plan wall thicknesses normally include the thickness of siding materials, care should be taken to project the outside of the framing line to the framing drawing and

Fig. 54–3B. Erection of an exterior steel-wall frame panel.

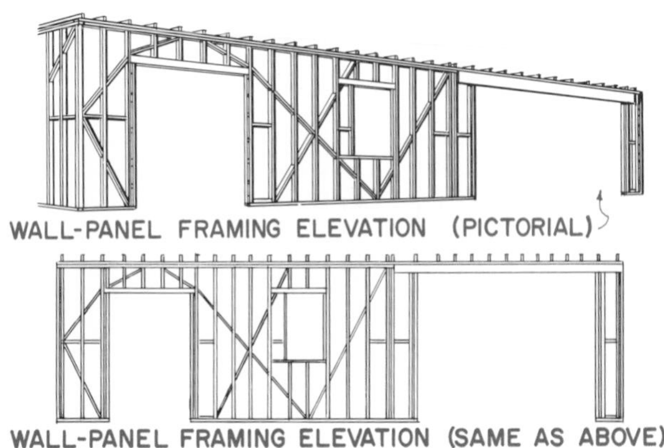

Fig. 54–4. Wall-framing elevation.

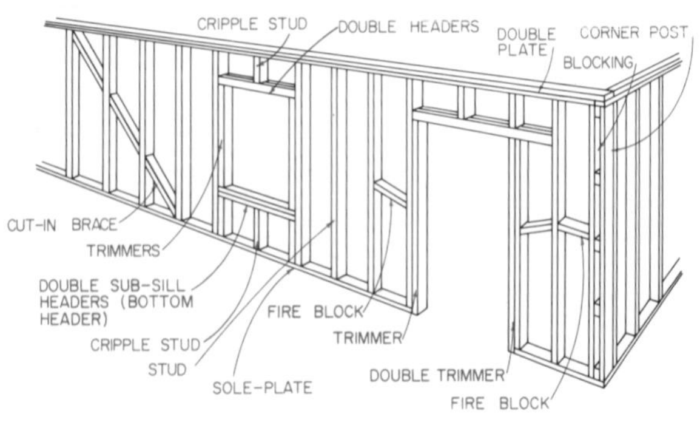

Fig. 54–5. Basic framing members shown in framing elevations.

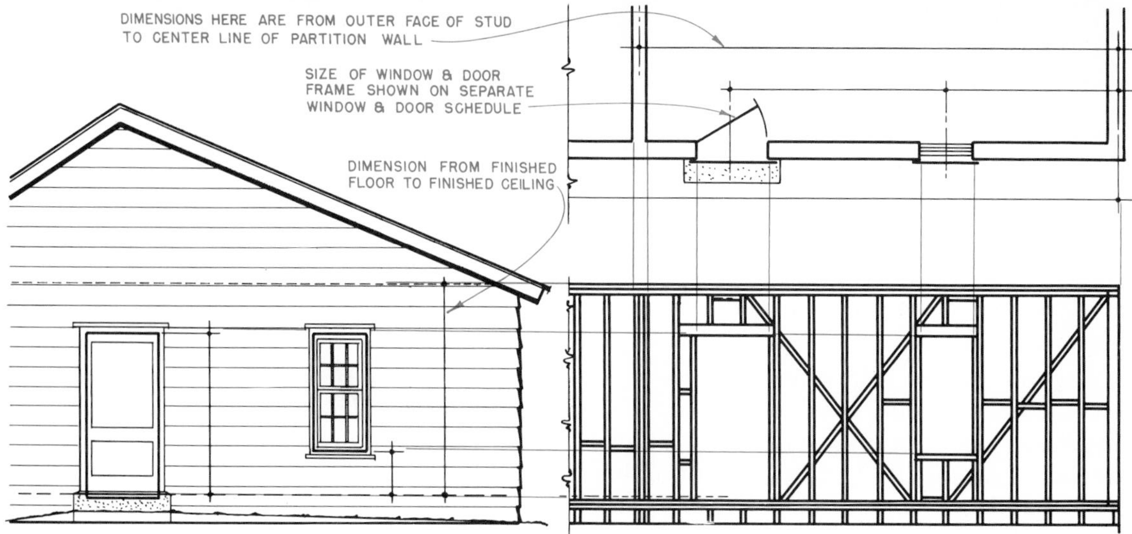

Fig. 54–6. Projection of an exterior-framing elevation from the floor-plan and elevation drawing.

not the outside of the siding line. In projecting door and window openings, the framing opening as outlined on the manufacturing specifications or on the door-window schedule should be rechecked when the final openings for doors and windows are projected both from the floor plan and from the elevation.

If aligned correctly, the elevation will supply all the projection points for the horizontal framing members, and the floor plan will provide all the points of projection for the location of vertical members.

COMPLETE SECTIONS

Another method of illustrating the framing methods used in wall construction is shown in Fig. 54–7. In this drawing, the elevation-

Fig. 54–7. A framing elevation incorporated in a complete section of the building.

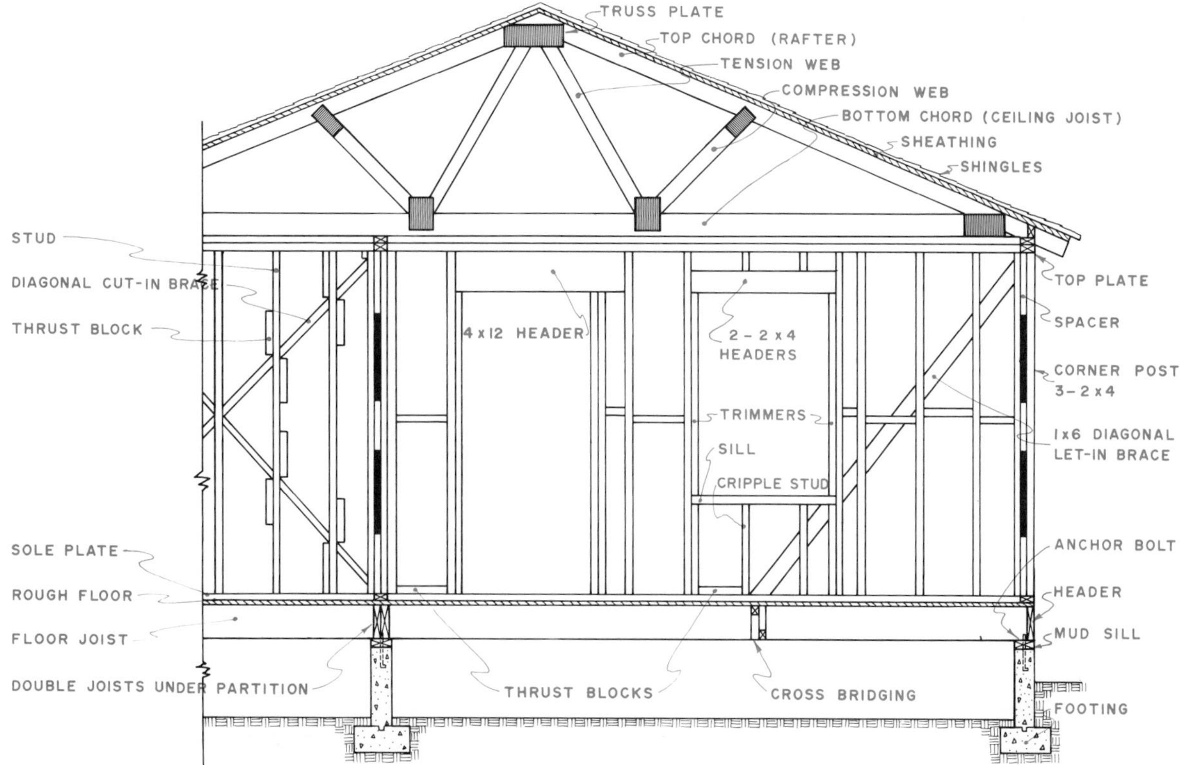

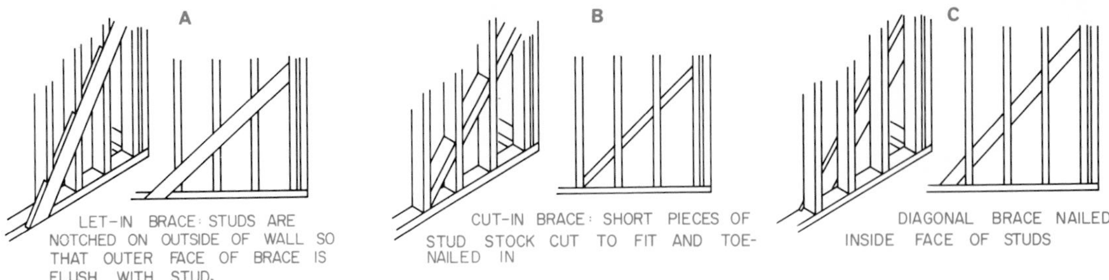

Fig. 54-8. Methods of illustrating braces.

framing information is incorporated in a complete sectional drawing of the entire structure. The advantage of this drawing is that it shows the relationship of the elevation-panel framing to the foundation-floor system and roof construction. Since this is a sectional drawing, blocking, joists, or any other member that is intersected by the cutting-plane line is shown by crossed diagonals.

BRACING

One of the problems in preparing and interpreting framing-elevation drawings is to determine whether bracing is placed on the inside of the wall, on the outside of the wall, or between the studs. Figure 54–8 at A shows the methods of illustrating *let-in* braces that are notched on the outside of the wall so that the outer face of the brace is flush with the stud. Figure 54–8 at B shows the method of illustrating *cut-in* braces that are nailed between the studs; and Fig. 54–8 at C shows the methods of illustrating diagonal braces that are on the inside faces of the studs.

Similar difficulties often occur in interpreting the true position of headers, cripple studs, plates, and trimmers. Figure 54–9 shows the method of illustrating the position of these members on the framing-elevation drawing to eliminate confusion and to simplify the proper interpretation.

Fig. 54-9. Methods of illustrating the positions of headers and cripples.

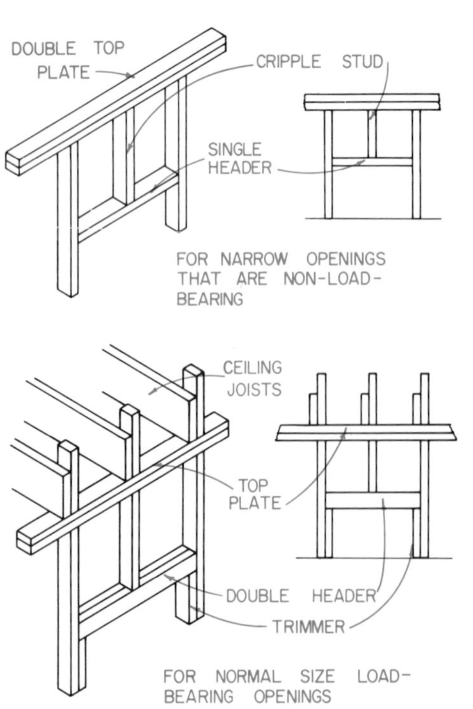

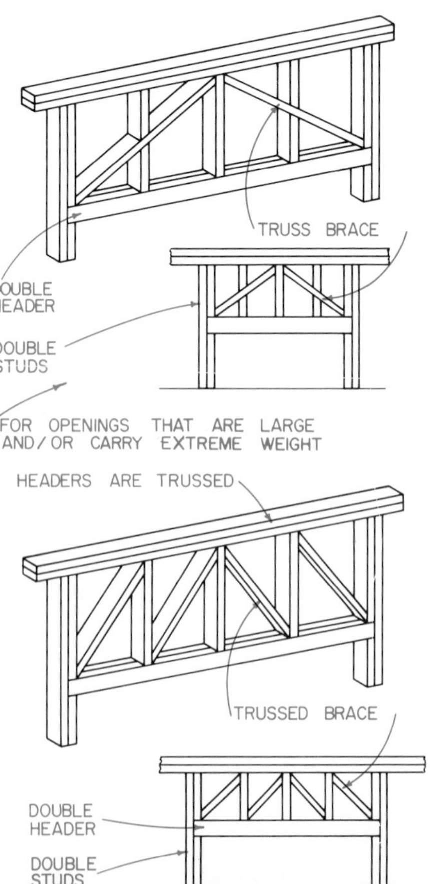

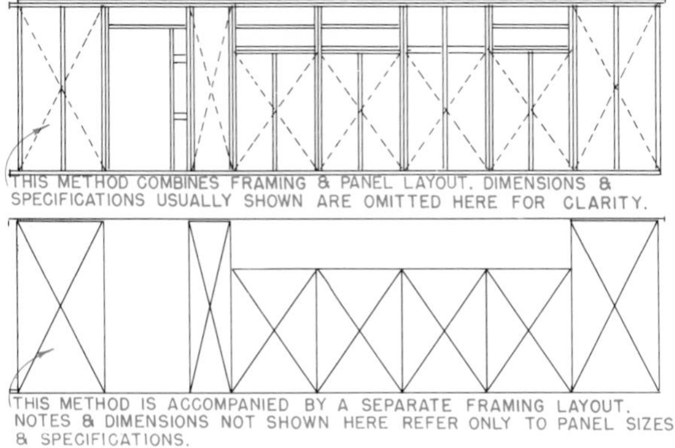
THIS METHOD COMBINES FRAMING & PANEL LAYOUT. DIMENSIONS & SPECIFICATIONS USUALLY SHOWN ARE OMITTED HERE FOR CLARITY.
THIS METHOD IS ACCOMPANIED BY A SEPARATE FRAMING LAYOUT. NOTES & DIMENSIONS NOT SHOWN HERE REFER ONLY TO PANEL SIZES & SPECIFICATIONS.

Fig. 54–10. Diagonal lines are used to show the positions of panels.

PANEL ELEVATIONS

Panel elevations show the attachment of sheathing to the framing. It is often desirable or necessary to show the relationship between the *panel layout* and the *framing layout* of an elevation when the panel drawing and the framing drawing are combined in one drawing. The diagonals which indicate the position of the panels are drawn with dotted lines, as shown in Fig. 54–10. When only the panel layouts are shown, the outline of the panels and diagonals are drawn solid, as shown in Fig. 54–10. In this case, a separate framing plan must also be prepared and correlated with the panel elevation.

DIMENSIONS

The method of dimensioning panel and framing-elevation drawings is shown in Fig. 54–11. Overall widths, heights, and spacing of studs should be given. Control dimensions for the heights of horizontal members and *rough openings* (framing openings) for windows should also be included. If the spacing of studs does not automatically provide the rough opening necessary for the window, the rough-opening width of the window should also be dimensioned.

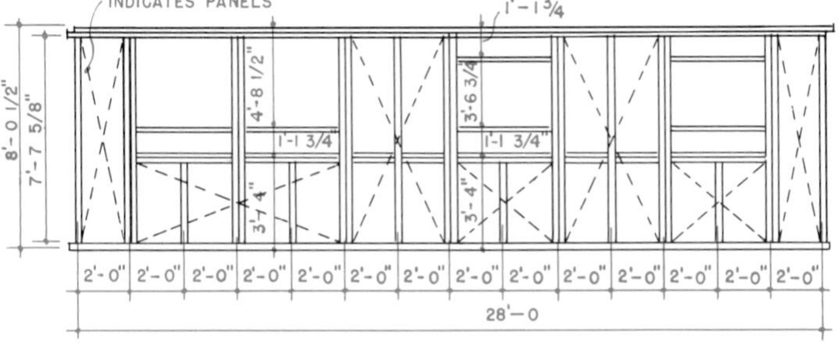
INDICATES PANELS
1'-1 3/4"
8'-0 1/2"
7'-7 5/8"
4'-8 1/2"
1'-1 3/4"
3'-4"
3'-6 3/4"
1'-1 3/4"
3'-4"
2'-0" 2'-0" 2'-0" 2'-0" 2'-0" 2'-0" 2'-0" 2'-0" 2'-0" 2'-0" 2'-0" 2'-0" 2'-0" 2'-0"
28'-0

Fig. 54–11. Methods of dimensioning panel and framing elevations.

DETAILS

Not all the information needed to frame an exterior wall can be shown on the elevation drawing. One of the most effective means of showing information at right angles to the elevation drawing is by removed sections.

REMOVED SECTIONS

Removed sections may be indexed to the floor plan or elevation, as indicated in Section 10. They may be removed sections from a pictorial drawing, as shown in Fig. 54–12. In this example, Section A describes the framing method employed on the wall and roof intersections, using break lines to expose the framing. Section B shows a wall section at the sill, revealing the intersection between the foundation-floor system and the exterior wall. These sections also show the inside wall treatment, insulation, sheathing, and exterior siding. Removed sections are effective in showing enlarged details.

SECTIONAL BREAKS

A larger scale is used on wall sections if the use of break lines is employed. Figure 54–13 shows the sequence of steps used to lay out and draw a typical external wall section.

1. Determine the width of the walls, foundation, and footer.
2. Lay out the angle of the roof and point of intersection of the roof and top plate. Lay out the width of the joist and sill.
3. Block in the position of roof rafters, top plates, sole plate, and roof floor lines.
4. Draw vertical lines to indicate the width of stud, insulation, air space, and brick.

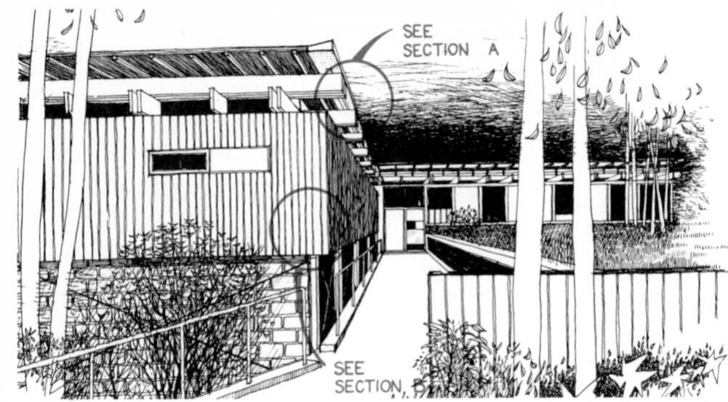

Rendering by George A. Parenti for Masonite Corporation

5. Add details of the outlines of roof boards and shingles. Show outlines of roof boards and shingles. Show outline of cornice construction.
6. Draw horizontal lines representing break lines. Add section-lining symbols.

Fig. 54–12. Removed sections may be indexed to a floor plan and to elevation or pictorial drawings.

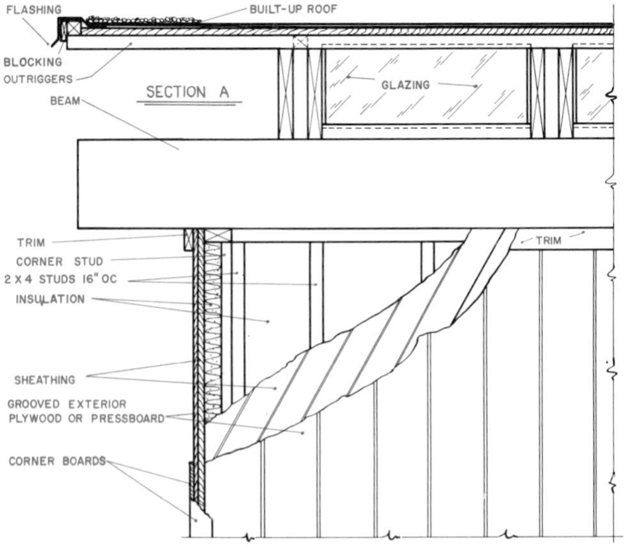

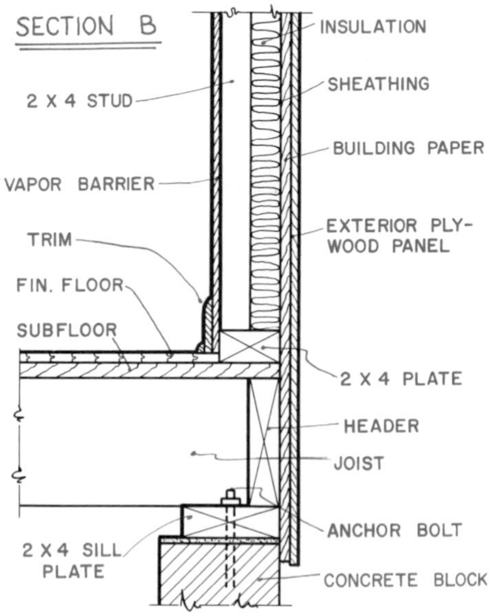

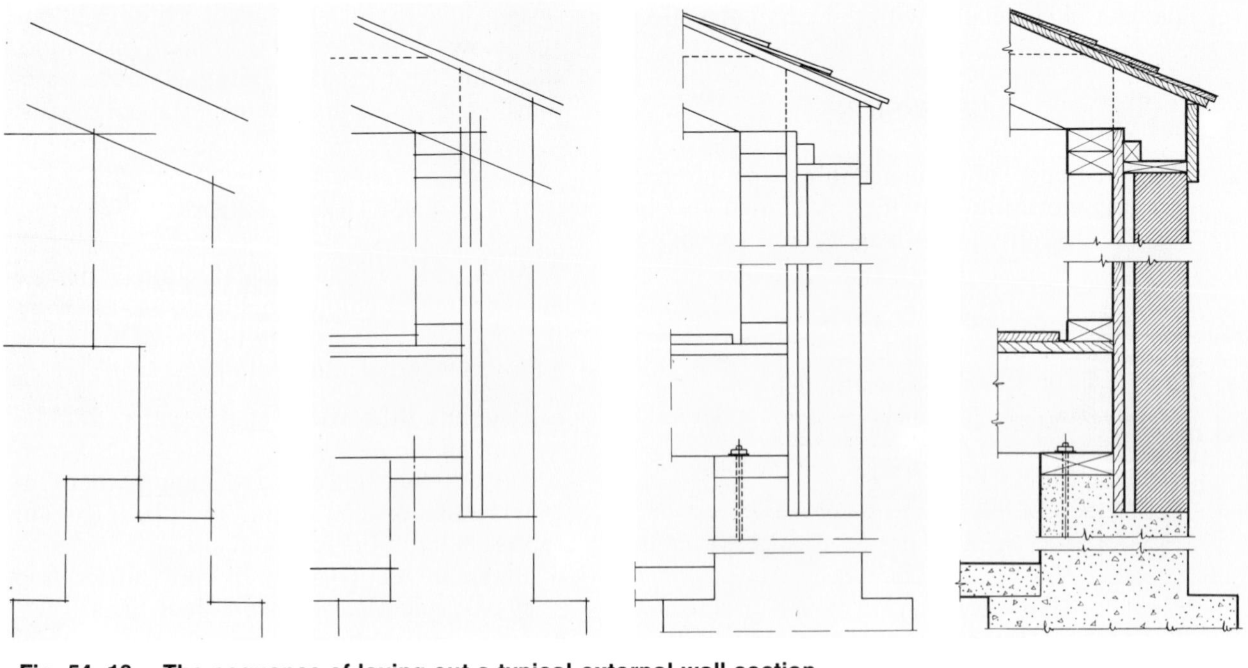

Fig. 54–13. The sequence of laying out a typical external wall section.

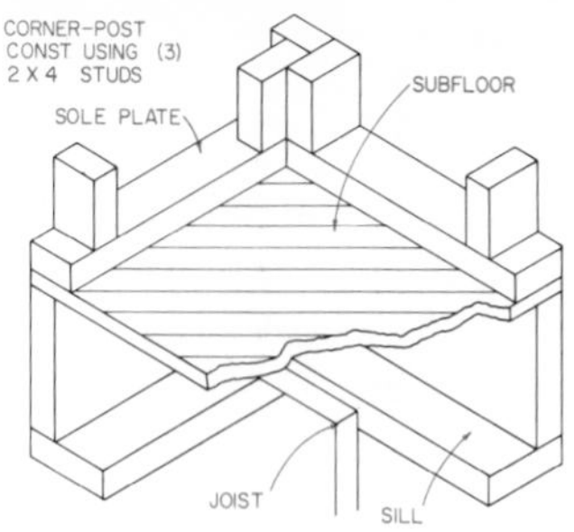

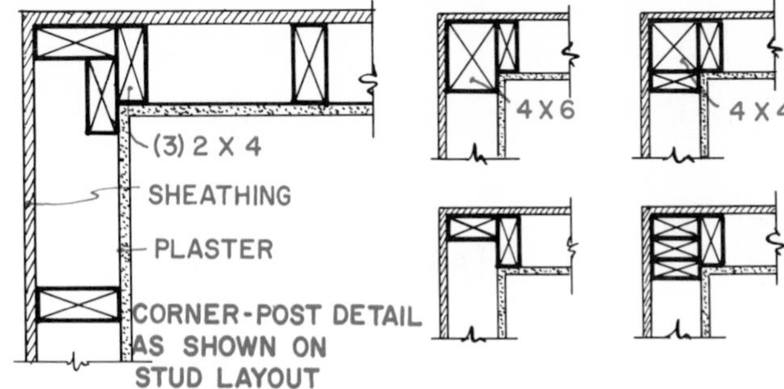

Fig. 54–14. Pictorial and horizontal sections showing corner-post construction.

PICTORIAL DETAIL

A pictorial detail or horizontal section of a wall is often used to clarify the relationship of framing members. This method is especially helpful in describing the layout of corner posts, as shown in Fig. 54–14. The horizontal section is more accurate in showing exact size and position of studs, but the pictorial drawing is more effective in showing the total relationship among sole plate, corner-post studs, and box-sill construction.

EXPLODED VIEWS

Exploded views are most effective in showing internal construction that is hidden when the total assembly is drawn in its completed form. Figure 54–15 shows an exploded view of a corner-post construction, which reveals the position of the corner post on the sole. It shows also the construction and position of the top plate on the corner post. This method of detailing is also extensively used in cabinet work.

SIDING DETAILS

New siding materials are constantly being developed and new applications found for existing materials. Aluminum is a good example. Today the residential use of aluminum is most common for door and window frames, gutters and downspouts, and siding (Fig. 54–16). Growing emphasis on the use of siding-panel components designed to modular limits increases the necessity for carefully describing the relationship between the basic framing and exterior-wall coverings (Fig. 54–17).

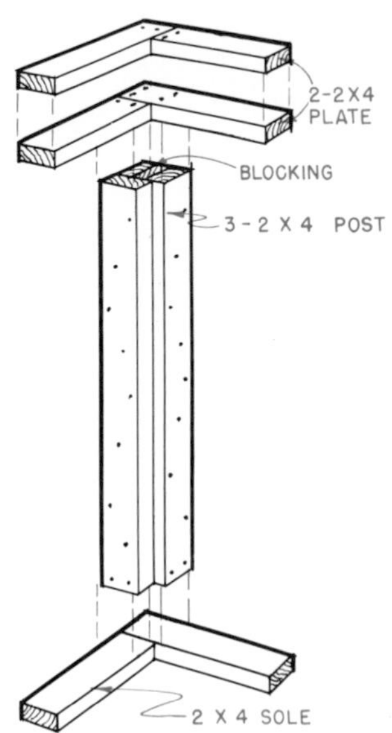

Fig. 54–15. An exploded view of corner-post construction.

Aluminum Company of America

Fig. 54–16. Installation of aluminum siding.

Normal F. Carver, Designer

Fig. 54–17. The relationship between siding materials and framing materials is important.

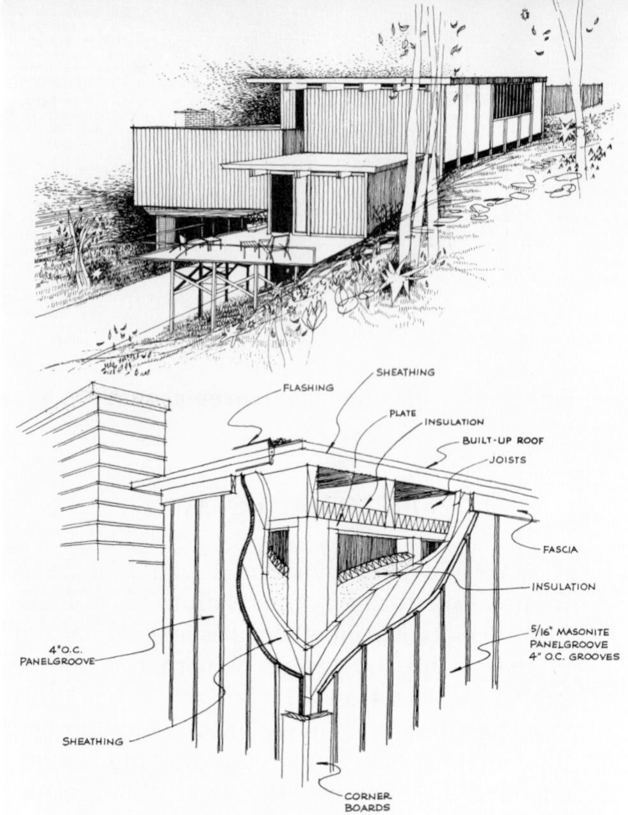

Rendering by George A. Parenti for the Masonite Corporation

Fig. 54–18. The use of a breakaway pictorial section to show construction details.

One method of showing the relationship between the basic framing and siding materials is the *breakaway pictorial drawing,* as shown in Fig. 54–18. This kind of drawing can be most effectively interpreted by the layman. However, it is most difficult to dimension for construction purposes. A more effective method of showing the exact position of siding materials is the *vertical* or *horizontal section.* Figure 54–19 shows the *sectional method* of representing a typical brick veneer wall. Compare the plan section and the elevation section with the related pictorial drawing. Follow the relationship of each material as it exists in each drawing. You should be able to visualize the pictorial drawing by studying the sectional drawings of the plan and elevation. Figure 54–20 shows the same relationship of sectional to pictorial drawings for a stucco wall. Figure 54–21 shows how a board and batten wall appears in pictorial, plan, and elevation sections.

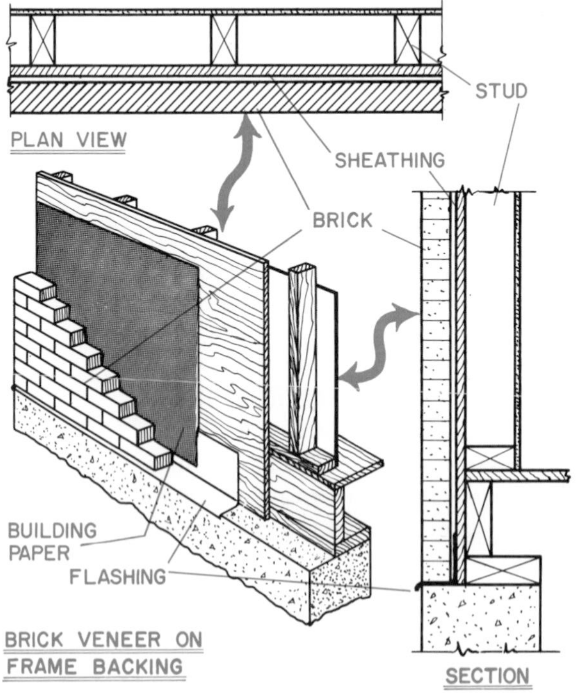

Fig. 54–19. Construction details can be shown on a plan section or on an elevation section.

WINDOW-FRAMING DRAWINGS

One of the most effective methods of showing window-framing details is the head, jamb, and sill sections, as described in Section 10 (Figure 54–22). Most windows are factory-made components ready for installation. Therefore, the

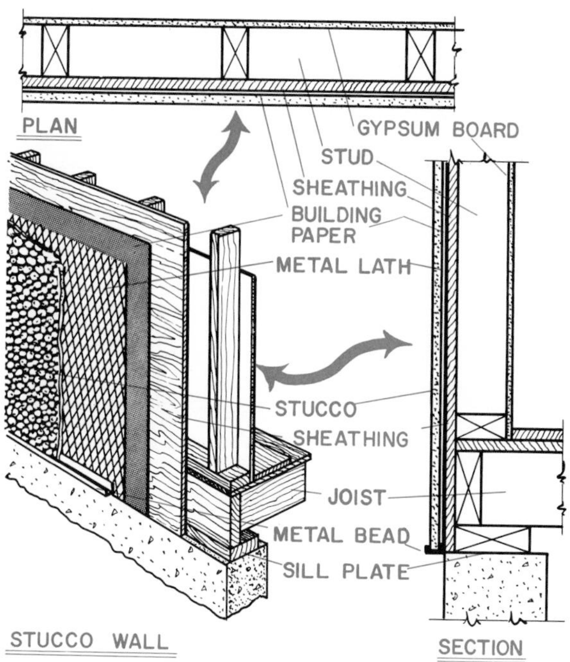

Fig. 54–20. The relationship between a plan and an elevation section of a stucco wall.

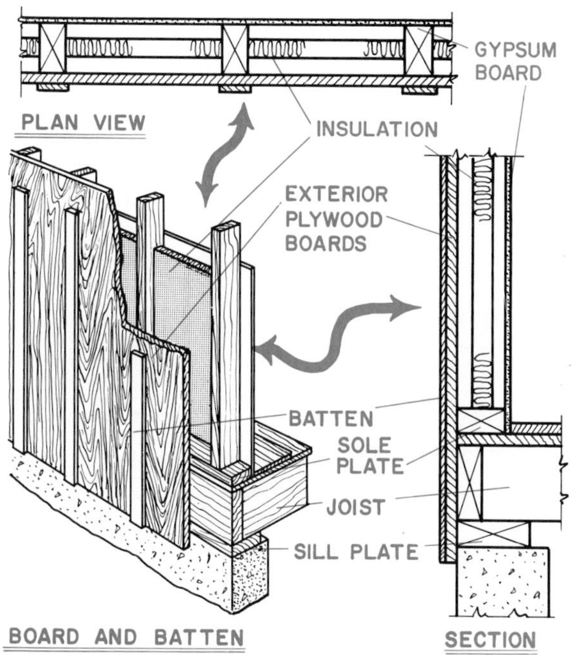

Fig. 54–21. The relationship between a plan and an elevation section of a board and batten wall.

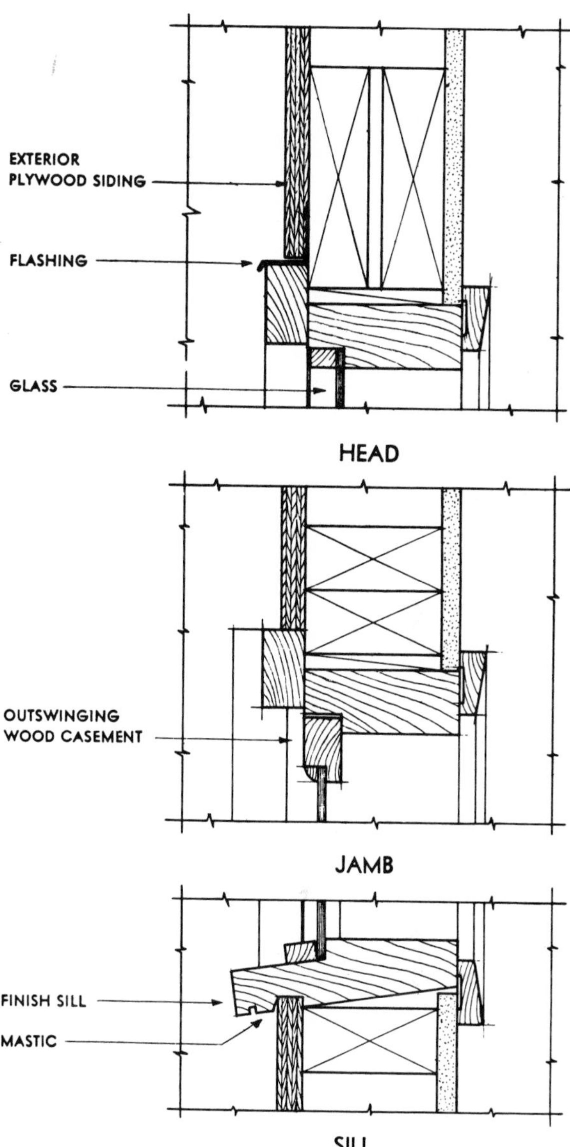

Fig. 54–22. Head, jamb, and sill sections are most commonly used to show window-framing details.

most critical framing dimensions are those that describe the exact size of the framing opening. Window-framing drawings should include the dimensions of the rough framing-opening in addition to the dimensions of the sash openings or windows that may be found on the door and window schedule (Fig. 54–23).

Figure 54–24 shows rough stud openings and sash openings for some of the more common sizes of windows.

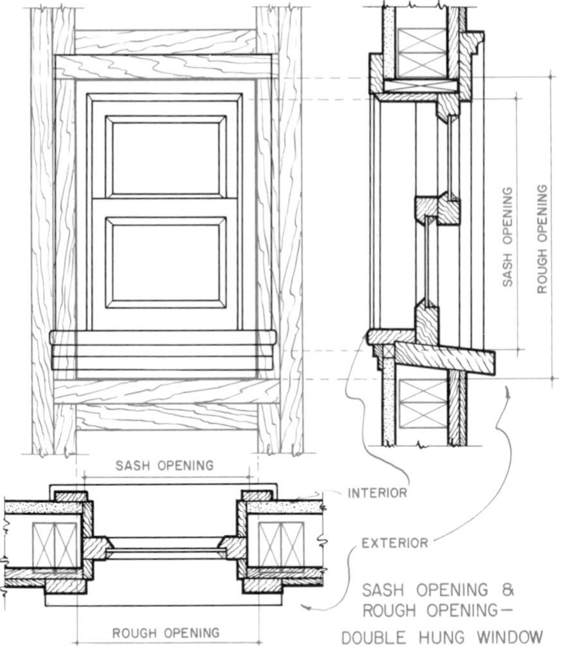

Fig. 54–23. Details are often needed to show the rough openings for doors and windows.

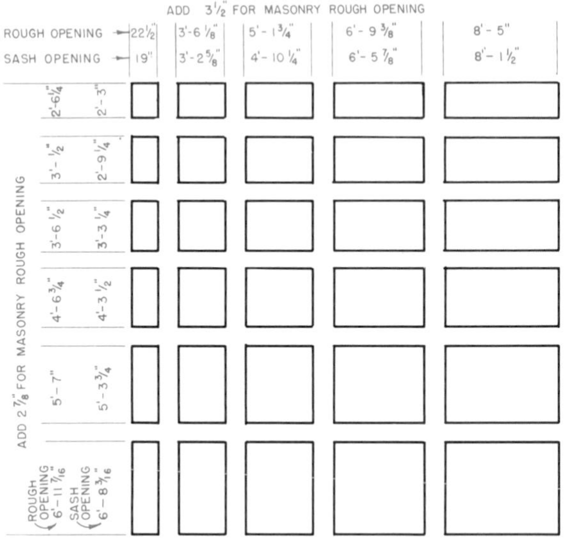

Fig. 54–24. Rough-opening dimensions for common sizes of windows.

Rendering by George A. Parenti for the Masonite Corporation

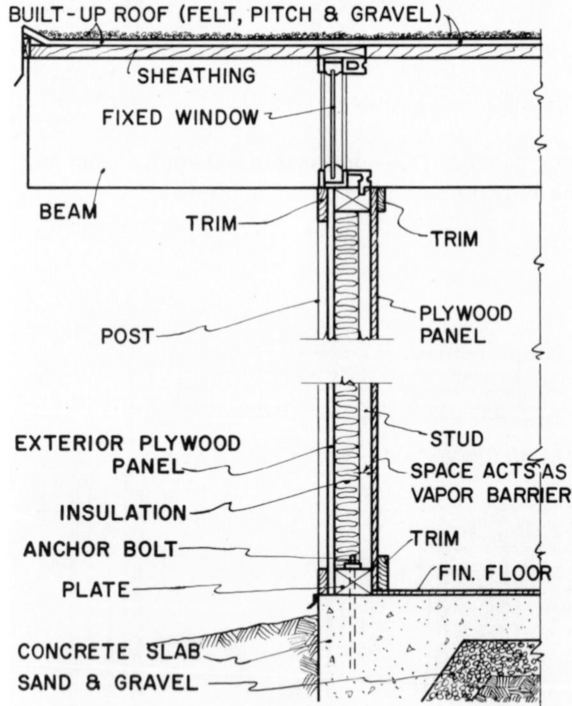

Fig. 54–25. Details are always needed for fixed-window construction.

When fixed windows or unusual window treatments are constructed in the field or even at the factory for a specific building, complete framing details must be drawn similar to the detailed drawing shown in Fig. 54–25.

The more unusual the use of nonstandard sizes and components, the more complete must be the detail framing drawings that accompany the design. Figure 54–26 shows a Japanese *shoji* window assembly that would require complete detailing of the shutters, screening glass, and shoji construction. Complete construction details for the fabrication of the track and for the installation of the track in the wall would also be necessary to ensure proper operation of the shoji.

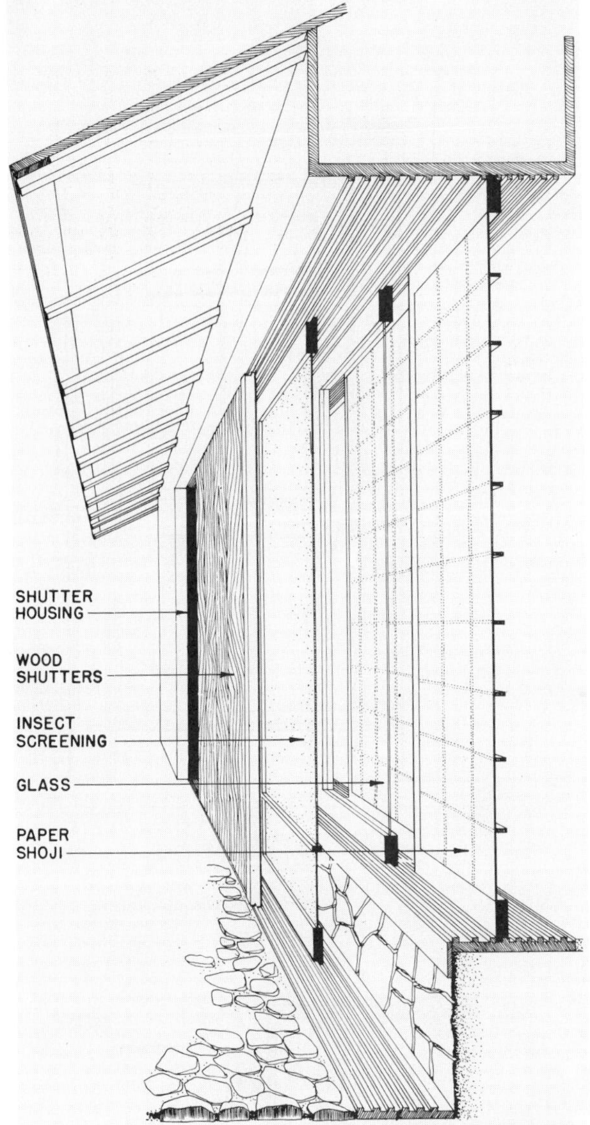

Fig. 54–26. A Japanese shoji window assembly.

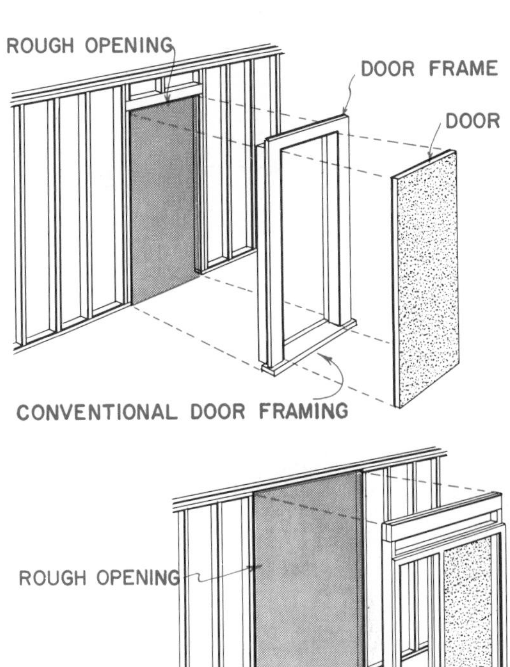

Fig. 54–27. Modular-component door assembly.

DOOR-FRAMING PLANS

The use of modular-component door units, as shown in Fig. 54–27, is increasing throughout the home-building industry. Maintaining accurate rough-opening dimensions for these units is most critical to their installation. Whether the door framing is conventional or of a component design, the exact position of the opening and the dimensions of the rough opening must be clearly illustrated and labeled on the framing drawing. Figure 54–28 shows some rough-opening dimensions for standard-sized doors that are used in various locations throughout a residence.

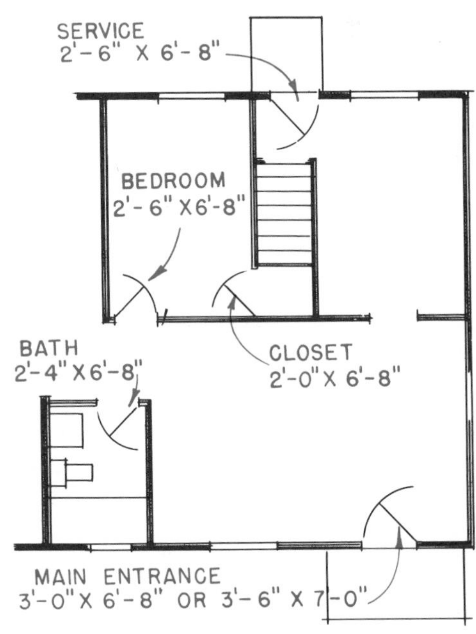

Fig. 54–28. Rough-opening dimensions for standard-sized doors.

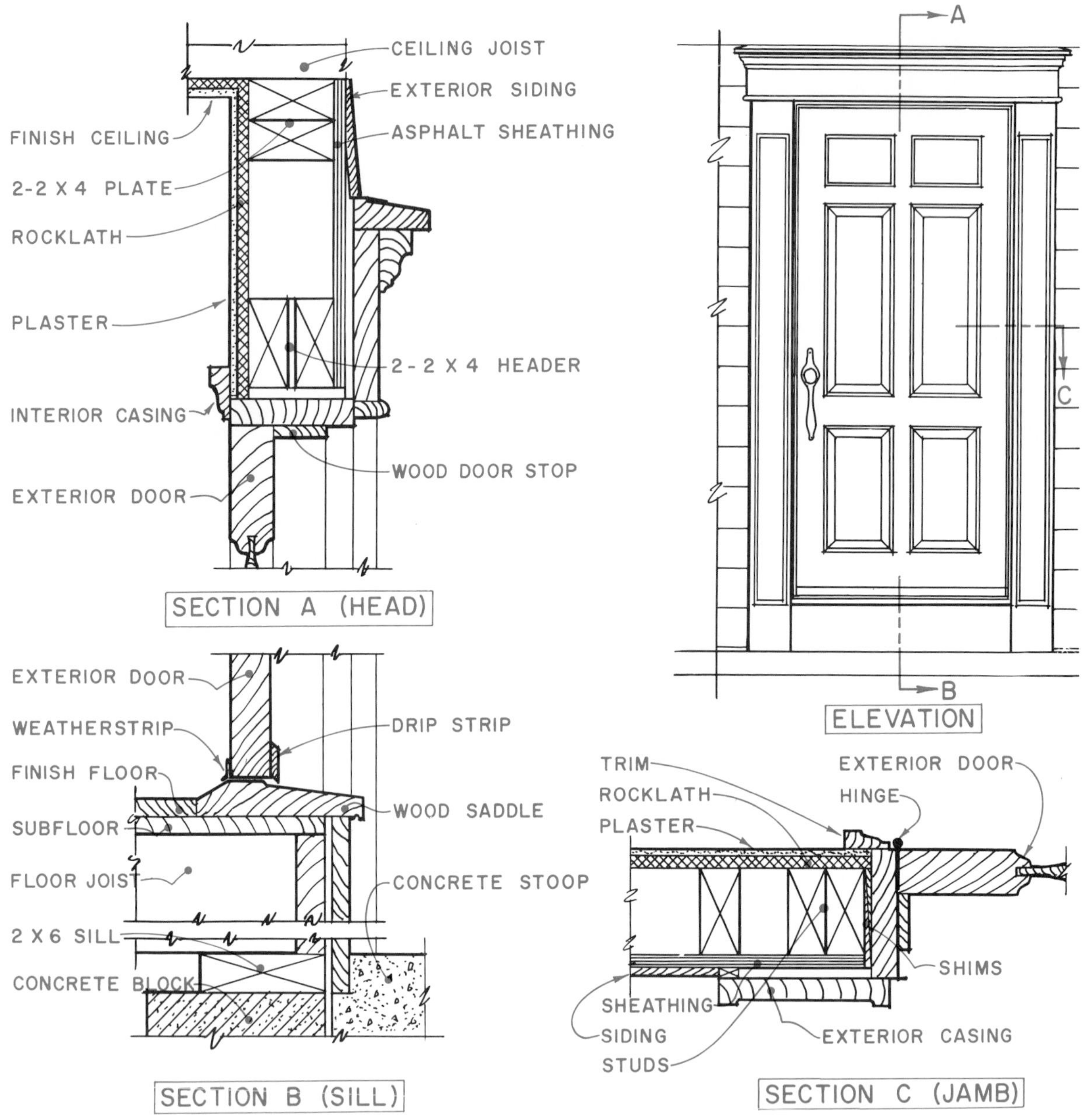

Fig. 54–29. The relationship between the door assembly and the wall-framing method.

Head, sill, and jamb sections, as shown in Section 10, are as effective in describing the door-framing construction as they are in showing window-framing details. Since the door extends to the floor, the relationship of the floor-framing system to the position of the door is critical. The method of intersecting the door and hinge with the wall framing, as shown in Fig. 54–29, is also important. Section A (head) shows the intersection of the door and the header framing. Section B (sill) shows how the door relates to the floor framing. Section C (jamb) shows how the hinged side is constructed.

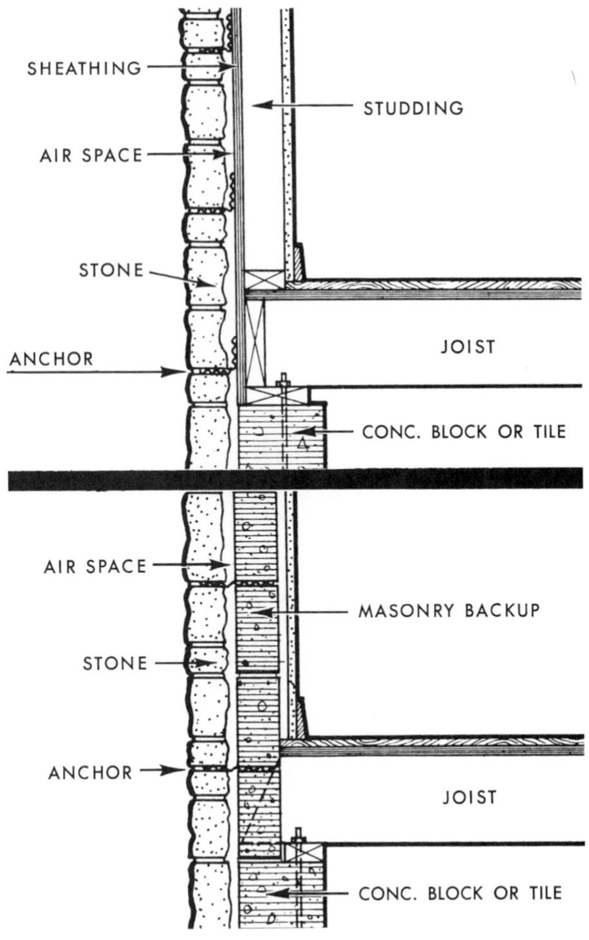

Fig. 54-30. Draw a plan section of these walls.

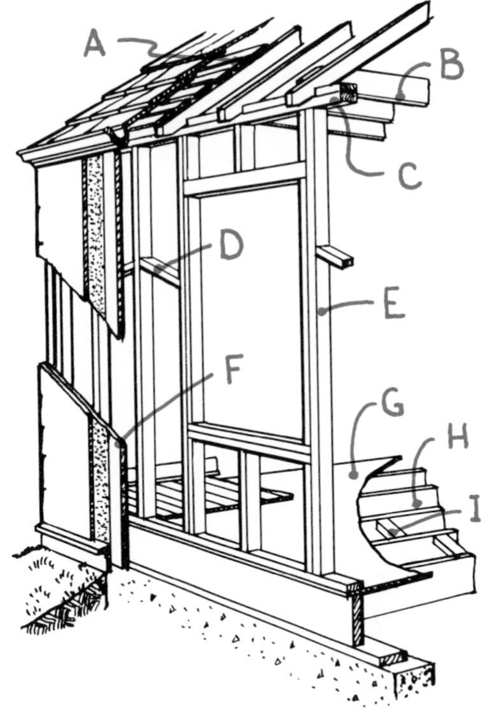

Fig. 54-31. Identify these framing members.

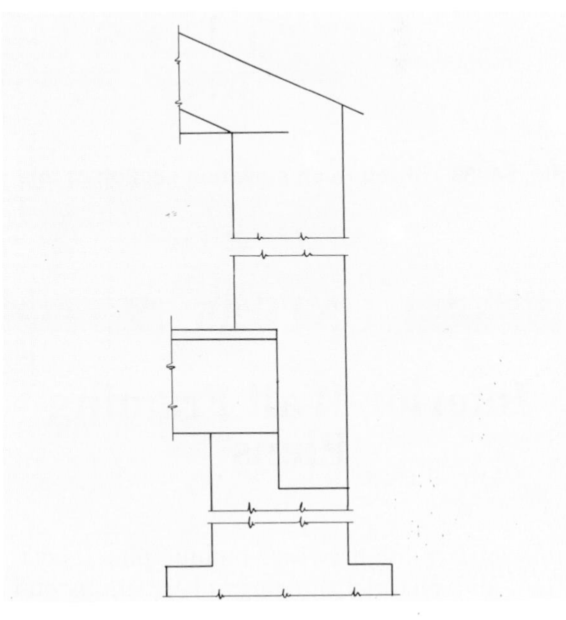

Fig. 54-32. Complete a sectional drawing of this wall, using stone veneer.

PROBLEMS

1. Draw a plan section view of the walls shown in Fig. 54-30.
2. Identify the framing members shown in Fig. 54-31.
3. Draw a wall section, using Fig. 54-32 as a guide. Plan to use stone veneer.
4. Prepare an elevation section of the wall shown in Fig. 54-33.
5. Prepare an exterior panel-framing plan for a home of your own design.
6. Prepare an exterior panel-framing plan for your own home.
7. Define the following terms: *framing elevation, bracing, let-in, panel elevation, removed sections, exploded view, rough opening, sash opening, sectional breaks.*

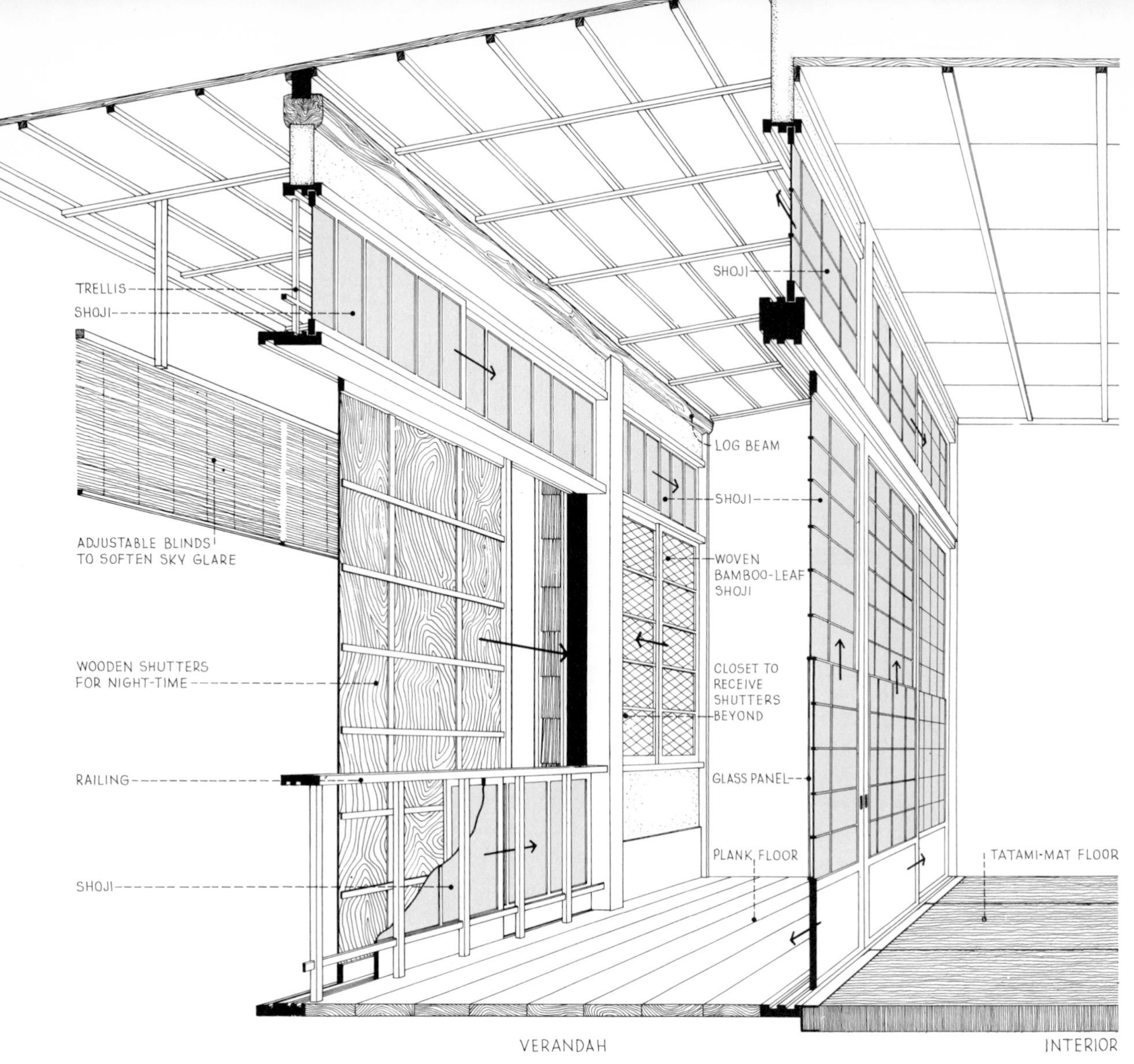

Fig. 54–33. Prepare an elevation section of this wall.

UNIT 55

Interior-Wall Framing Plans

Interior-framing drawings include plan, elevation, and pictorial drawings of partitions and wall coverings. Detail drawings of interior partitions are also prepared to show intersections between walls and ceilings, floors, windows, and doors.

PARTITION-FRAMING PLANS

Interior partition-framing elevations are most effective in showing the construction of interior partitions. Interior partitions are projected from the partition on the floor plan in a manner

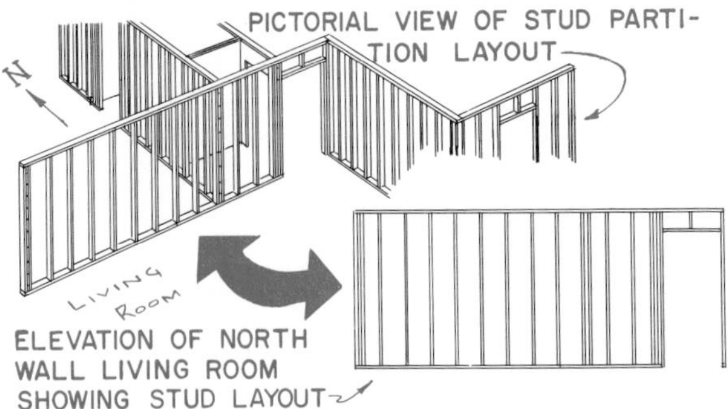

Fig. 55–1. Panel elevation of an interior wall.

similar to the projection of exterior partitions. To ensure the correct interpretation of the partition elevation, each interior elevation drawing should include a label indicating the room and compass direction of the wall. For example, the elevation shown in Fig. 55–1 should be labeled *North Wall Living Room.* If either the room name or the compass direction is omitted, the elevation may be misinterpreted and confused with a similar wall in another room. The elevation drawing is always projected from the room it represents.

A complete study of the floor plan, elevation, plumbing diagrams, and electrical plans should be made prior to the preparation of the interior wall-framing drawings. Provision must be made in the framing drawings for soil stacks and other large plumbing facilities and for special electrical equipment (Fig. 55–2).

When a stud must be broken to accommodate an item such as the cabinets shown in Fig. 55–3, the framing drawing must show the recommended construction.

Southern California Gas Company

Fig. 55–2. Space must be allowed for plumbing and electrical equipment.

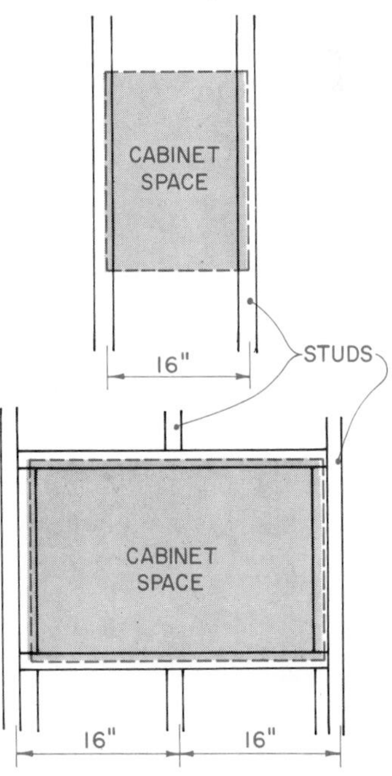

Fig. 55–3. Framing-elevation details shown provisions for built-in items.

WALL-COVERING DETAILS

Basic types of wall-covering materials used for finished interior walls include plaster, dry-wall construction, paneling, tile, and masonry.

Plaster

Plaster is applied to interior walls by using wire lath or gypsum sheet lath, as shown in Fig. 55–4. Plaster walls are very strong and sound-absorbing. Plaster is also decay-proof and termite-proof. However, plaster walls crack

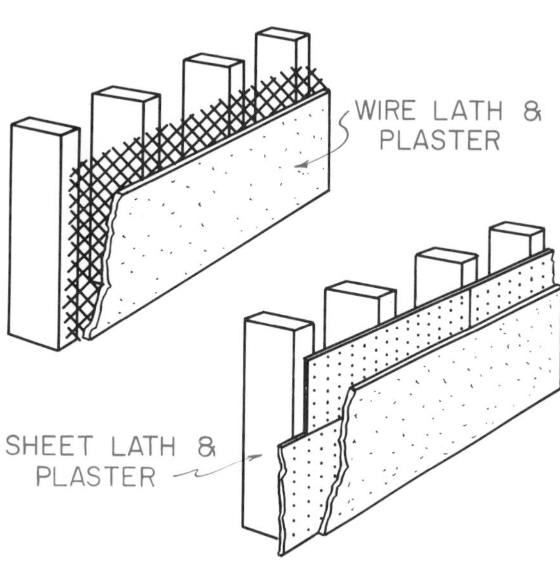

Fig. 55–4. The application of plaster to interior walls.

easily and take months to dry. Also, installation costs are rather high.

Dry-Wall Construction

Materials applicable to dry-wall construction include fiber boards, gypsum wallboards, plywood, and asbestos wallboard. The most popular dry-wall construction is gypsum wallboards nailed directly to the studs, as shown in Fig. 55–5. When this construction is used, furring strips may be placed over the joints and nail holes. However, the more common practice is to camouflage the joints by sanding a depression in the wallboard and applying a perforated tape covered with Swedish putty and sanded smooth, as shown in Fig. 55–6.

Paneling

When paneling is used as an interior finish, horizontal furring strips should be placed on the studs to provide a nailing or gluing surface for the paneling (Fig. 55–7). Determining the type of joint that should be used between panels is a design problem that should be solved through the use of a separate detail, as shown in Fig. 55–8. The joint may be exposed by use of the butt joint or cross-lap joint. A series of furring strips can be used between the joints or on the outside of them.

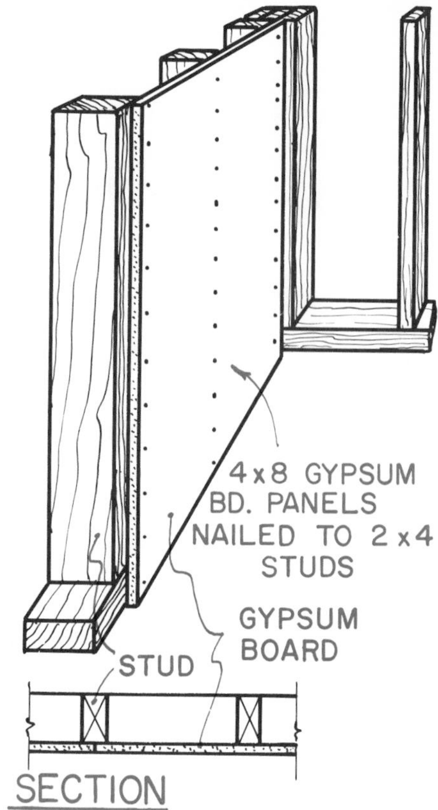

Fig. 55–5. Dry-wall construction.

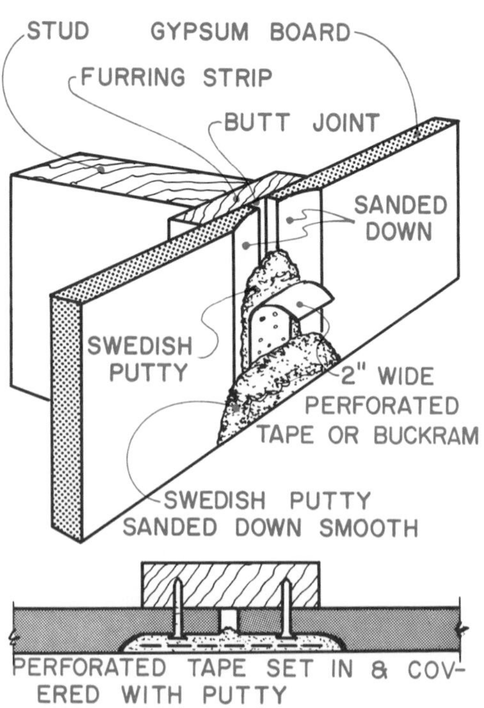

Fig. 55–6. The most common method of concealing dry-wall joints.

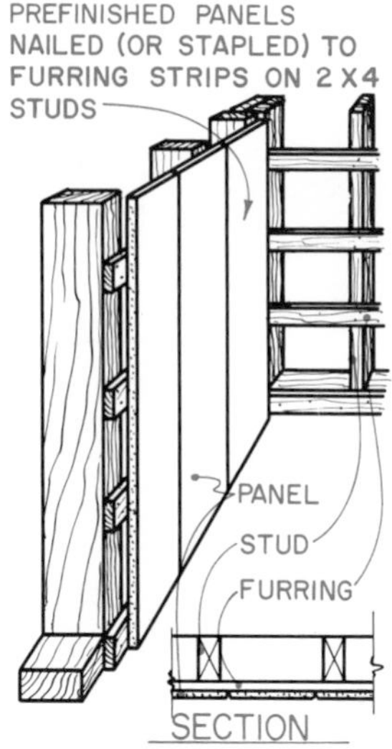

Fig. 55–7. Furring strips provide a horizontal surface for attaching paneling.

The method of intersecting the outside corners of paneling must also be detailed. Outside corners can be intersected by mitering or overlapping and exposing the paneling. Corner boards, metal strips, or molding may be used on the intersection (Fig. 55–9).

Inside-corner intersections can be drawn as shown in Fig. 55–10.

BASE INTERSECTIONS

The method of intersecting the finished wall materials and the floor should be detailed. The details may be a section or a pictorial drawing, as shown in Fig. 55–11. The position of the sole plate, wallboard or lath and plaster, baseboard, and molding should be shown.

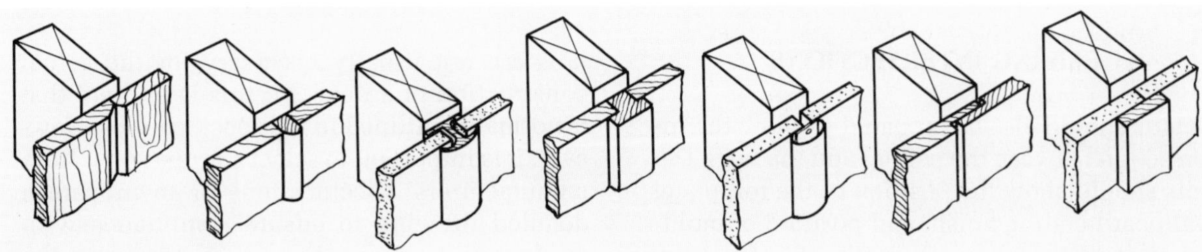

Fig. 55–8. Panel-joint details.

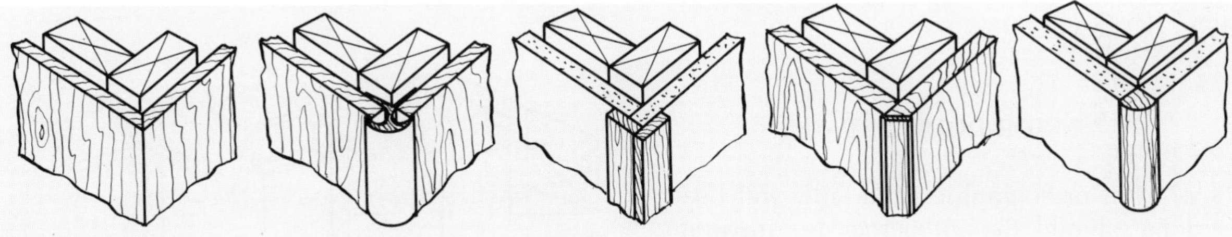

Fig. 55–9. Outside-corner panel joints.

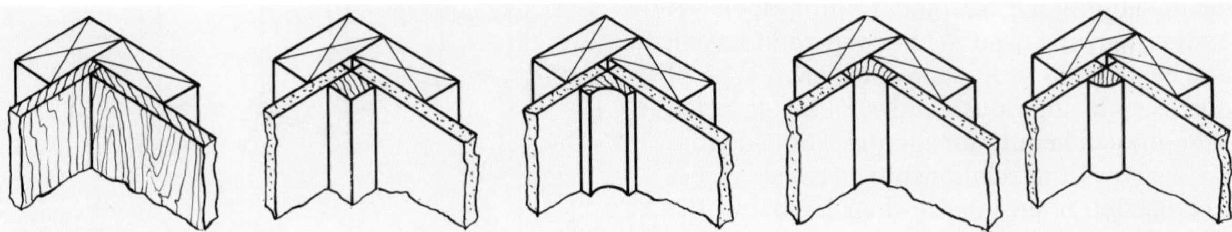

Fig. 55–10. Inside-corner panel joints.

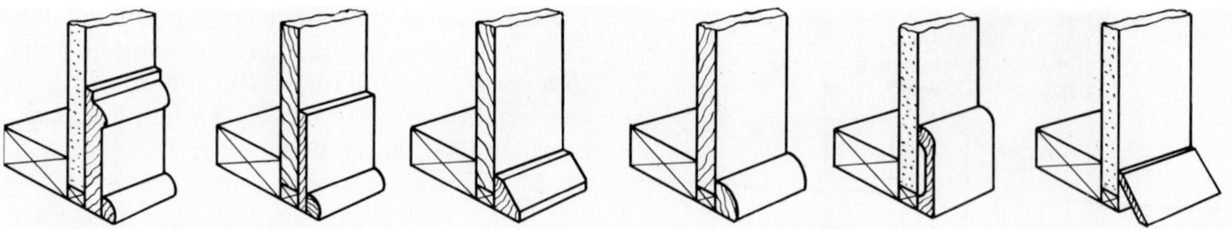

Fig. 55–11. A method of intersecting the panel wall with the floor.

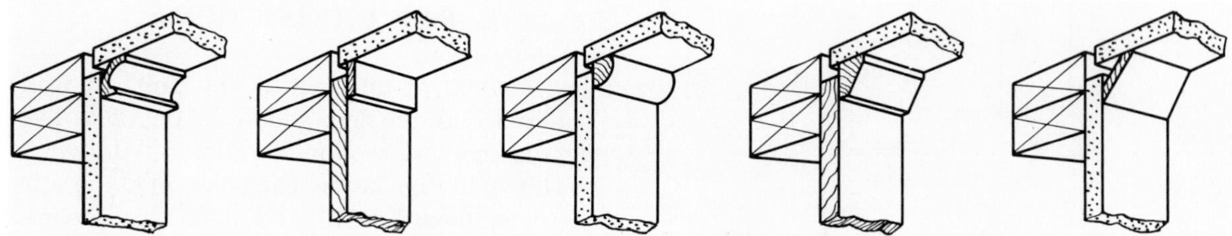

Fig. 55–12. A method of intersecting the panel wall with the ceiling.

CEILING INTERSECTIONS

Details should also be prepared to show the intersection between the ceiling and the wall. Details should show the position of the top plate, wallboard-ceiling finish, and position of molding used at the intersection (Fig. 55–12). Care should be taken when designing the base treatment and ceiling-intersection treatment to ensure that the intersections are consistent in style, as shown in Fig. 55–13.

INTERIOR-DOOR DETAILS

Pictorial or orthographic jamb, sill, and head sections should be prepared to illustrate methods of framing used around interior doors. Figure 55–14 shows the methods of framing split-jamb, surface-mounted, bifolding, sliding-pocket, sliding-bypass, and folding-doors. A detailed drawing need not be prepared for each door but should be prepared for each type of door used in the house and should be keyed to the door schedule for identification. Figure 55–15 shows the relationship between a pictorial section of an interior-door jamb and the variations of this section necessary for plaster, gypsum-board, or paneled wall coverings. Details are not usually necessary for the actual construction of a door, for this is an item that is normally outlined in the specifications. However, it is important to select a proper door from manufacturers' specifications or to prepare a detailed drawing to ensure compliance with minimum standards. Figure 55–16 shows the cutaway drawing and section of two types of solid doors. Hollow-core doors are generally used on interior partitions.

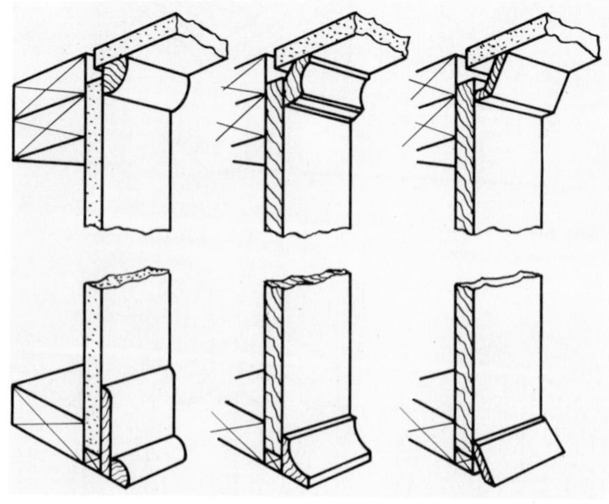

Fig. 55–13. Base and ceiling intersections should be consistent.

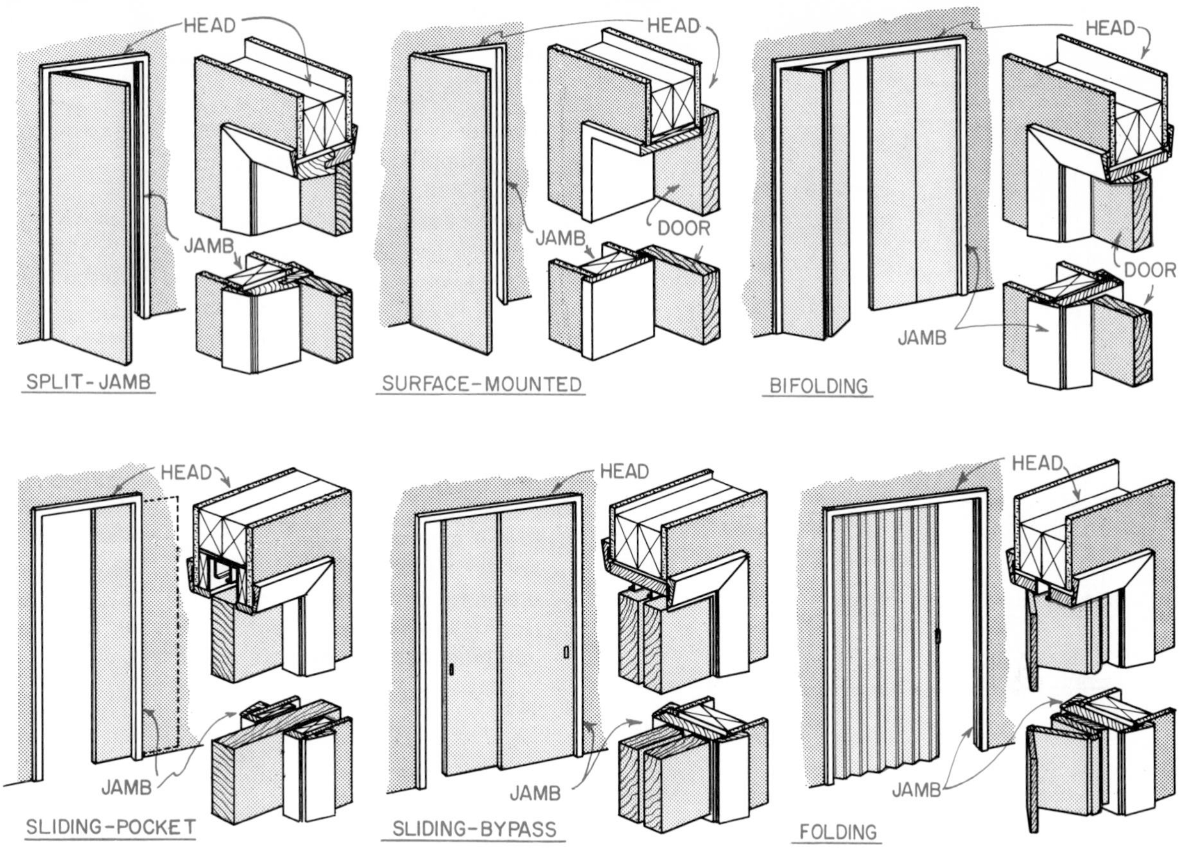

National Lumber Manufacturers Association

Fig. 55–14. The framing methods used for different types of interior doors.

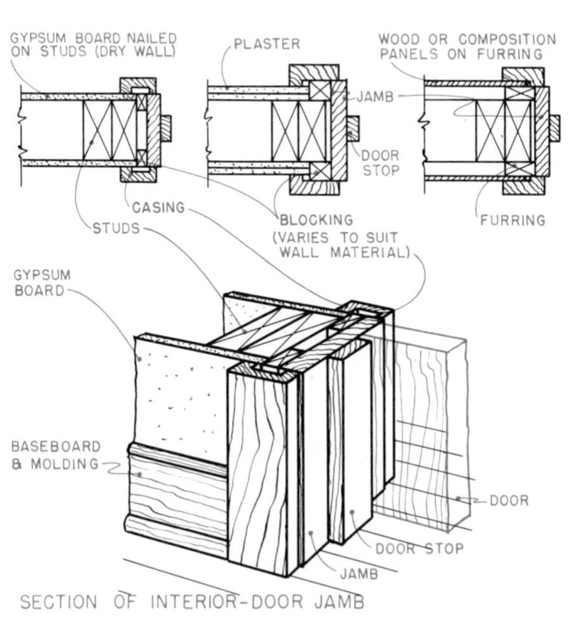

Fig. 55–15. The door-framing methods needed for different types of construction.

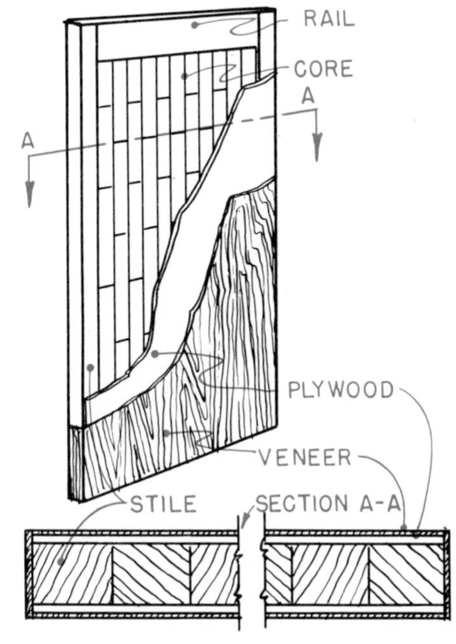

Fig. 55–16A. A solid-core door construction.

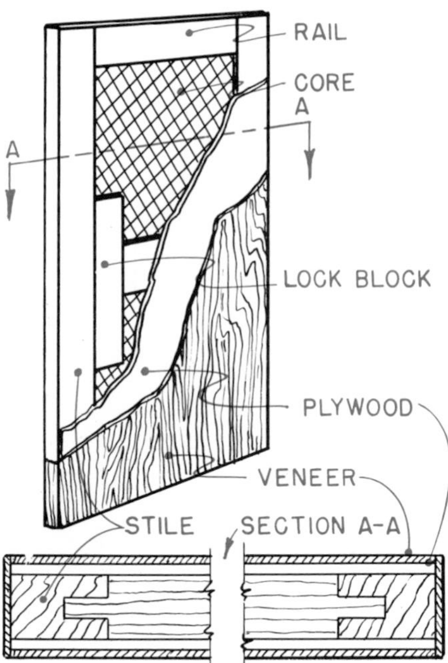

Fig. 55–16B. Another solid-core door construction.

PROBLEMS

1. Project a panel-framing elevation drawing of the plumbing wall of bathroom #1, as shown in Fig. 37–16.
2. Draw a vertical section of the wall shown in Fig. 55–7.
3. Draw plan and elevation sections of one of the joints shown in Fig. 55–8.
4. Draw plan sections for one of the intersections shown in Fig. 55–9 and Fig. 55–10.
5. Draw a complete horizontal wall section of the front living room wall shown in Fig. 6–4. As part of the fireplace treatment, plan to make the entire wall brick from the fireplace to the door opening.
6. Prepare a plan section similar to the plan shown in Fig. 55–15. Show the position of brick, blocking, casing, and jamb.
7. Define the following terms: *dry wall, plaster, paneling, base detail, interior partition.*

UNIT 56

Stud Layouts

A stud layout is a plan similar to a floor plan, showing the position of each wall-framing member. The stud layout is a section through each panel elevation, as shown in Fig. 56–1. The cutting-plane line for purposes of projecting the stud layout is placed approximately at the midpoint of the panel elevation. Figure 56–2 shows a stud layout which represents the framing plan of the panel.

STUD DETAILS

Stud layouts are of two types: the *complete plan,* which shows the position of all framing members on the floor plan, and the *stud detail,* which shows only the position and relationship of several studs or framing intersections. Figure 56–3 shows the relationship of a stud detail, a section through the elevation, and a pictorial framing of the same wall.

CORNER POST

The position of each stud in a corner-post layout is frequently shown in a plan view, as illustrated in Fig. 56–4. Occasionally, siding and inside-wall covering materials are shown on this plan. Preparing this type of detail without covering materials is the easiest and quickest way to show corner-post construction.

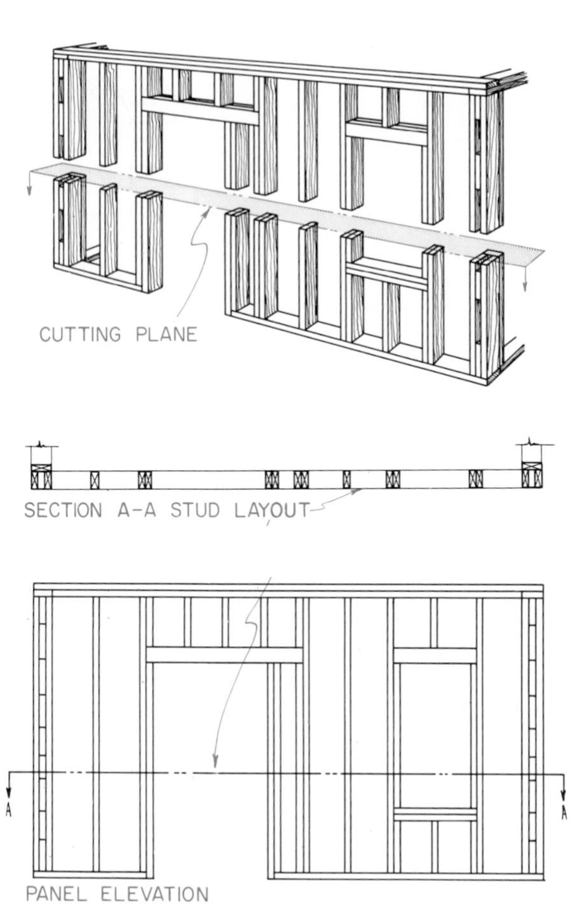

Fig. 56–1. The stud layout is a plan section taken through the panel elevation.

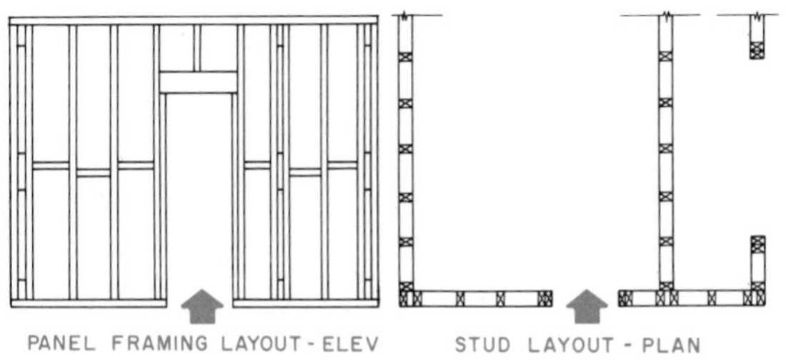

Fig. 56–2. The relationship of a stud layout to a panel elevation.

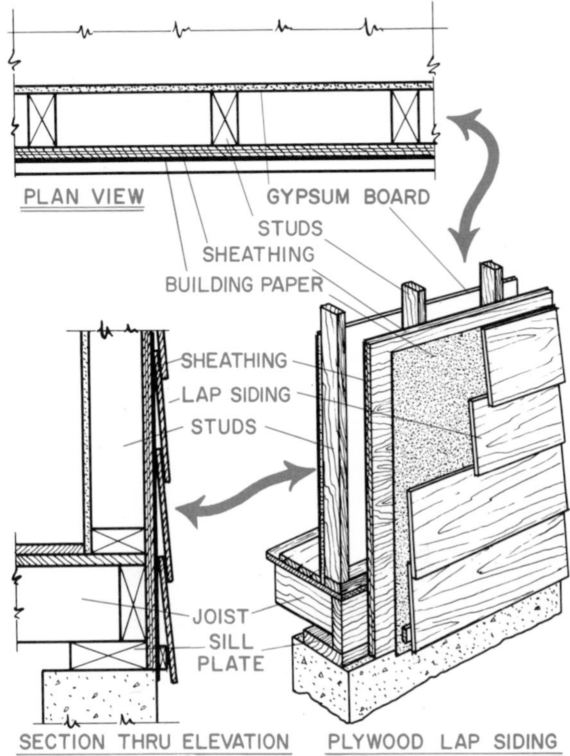

Fig. 56–3. The stud layout is a plan view.

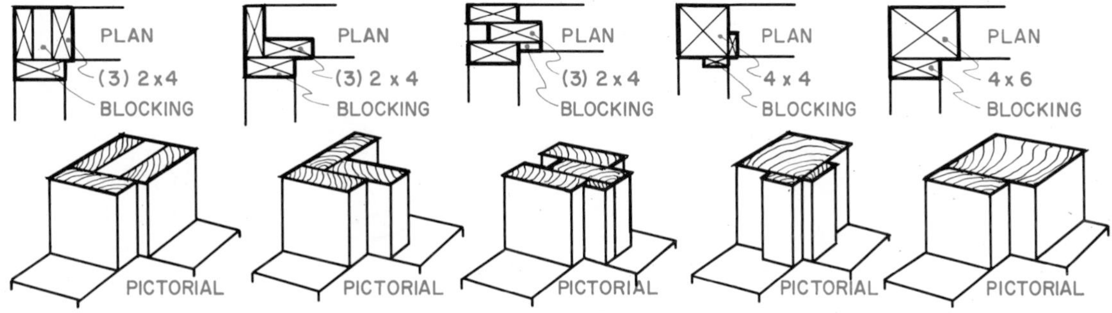

Fig. 56–4. Stud details of several corner-post layouts.

PARTITION INTERSECTIONS

Details of the exact position of each stud and blocking in an intersection are shown by a plan section (Fig. 56–5). If wall coverings are shown on the detail, the complete wall structure can be drawn (Fig. 56–6). In preparing the plan section, care should be taken to show the exact position of blocking or short pieces of stud stock that may not pass through the cutting-plane line. Blocking should be labeled to prevent the possibility of identifying the blocking as a full-length stud. When laying out the position of all studs, remember that the finished dimensions of a 2×4 are actually $1\frac{1}{2} \times 3\frac{1}{2}$. The exact dressed sizes of other rough stock are as follows:

Rough	Dressed
2×3	$1\frac{1}{2} \times 2\frac{1}{2}$
2×4	$1\frac{1}{2} \times 3\frac{1}{2}$
2×6	$1\frac{1}{2} \times 5\frac{1}{2}$
2×8	$1\frac{1}{2} \times 7\frac{1}{4}$
2×10	$1\frac{1}{2} \times 9\frac{1}{4}$
2×12	$1\frac{1}{2} \times 11\frac{1}{4}$
1×6	$\frac{3}{4} \times 5\frac{1}{2}$
1×8	$3\frac{1}{4} \times 7\frac{1}{4}$

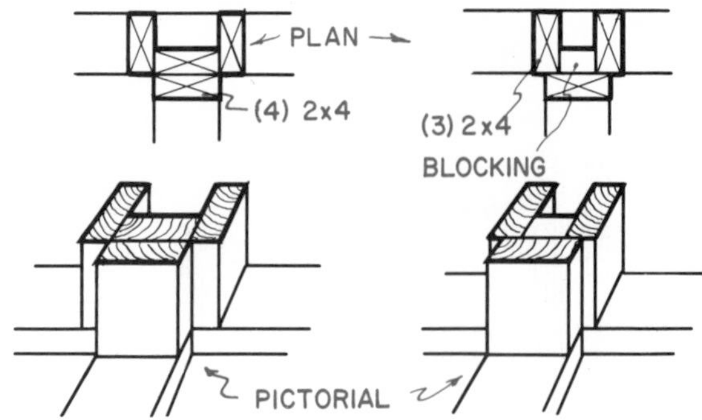

Fig. 56–5. Position of studs in a partition intersection.

COMPLETE PLAN

The main purpose of a stud layout is to show how interior partitions fit together and how studs are spaced on the plan. Figure 56–7 shows part of a stud layout. The outline of the plate and the exact position of each stud that falls on an established center (16″, 20″, 24″, or 400 mm) are normally identified by diagonal lines. Studs other than those that are on regular centers are shown by different symbols. Studs that are short, blocking, or different in size are

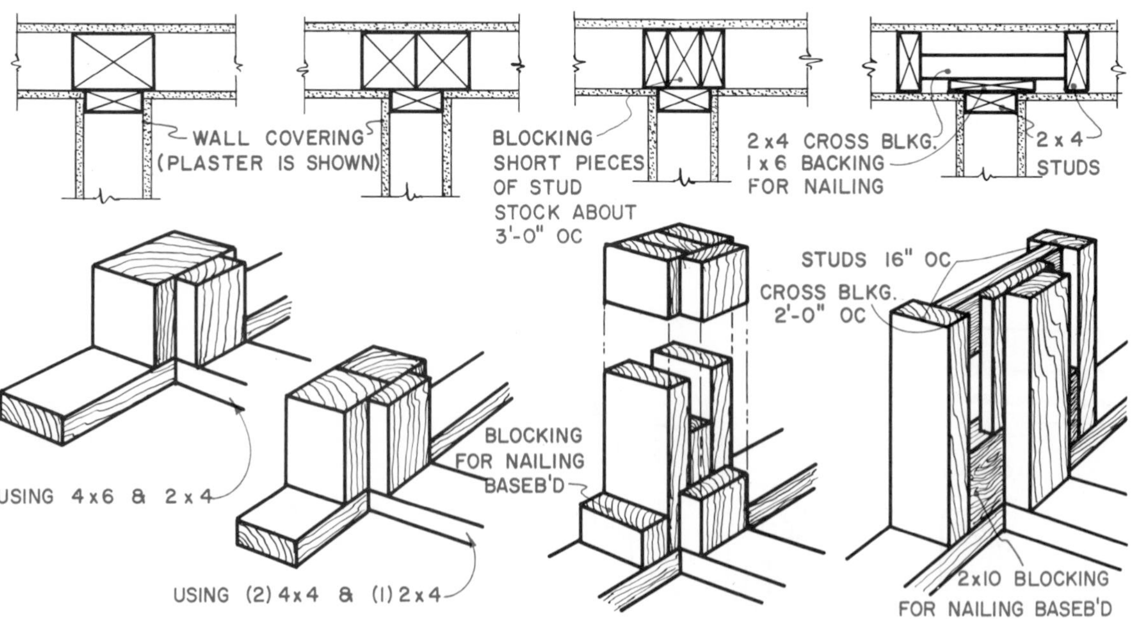

Fig. 56–6. Wall covering and blocking can be shown on intersection details.

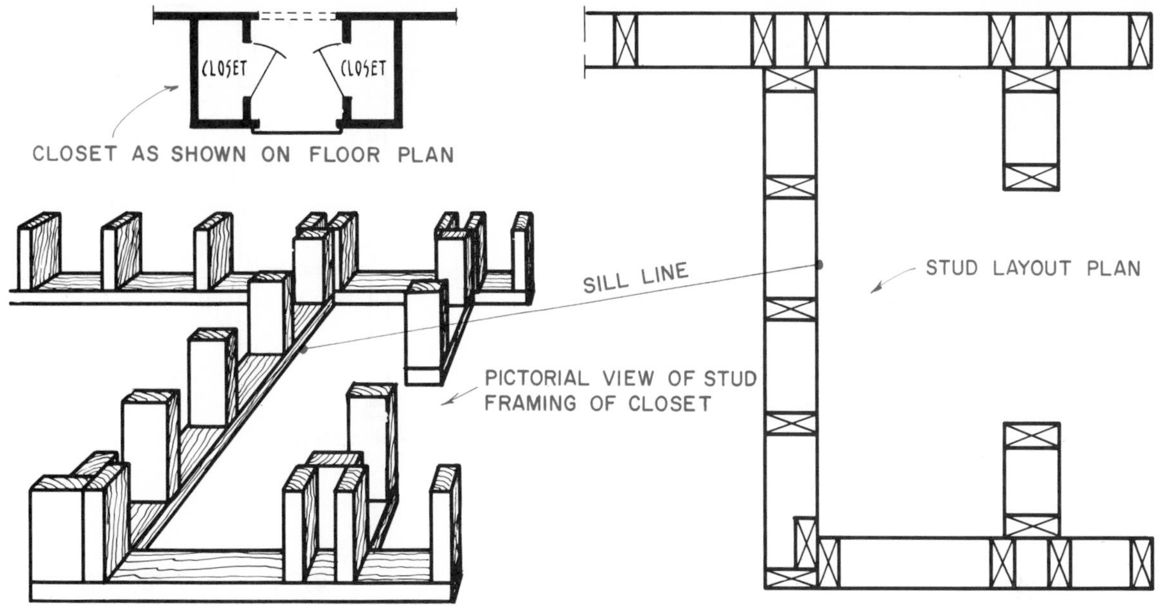

Fig. 56–7. The outline of the sill is shown in a stud layout.

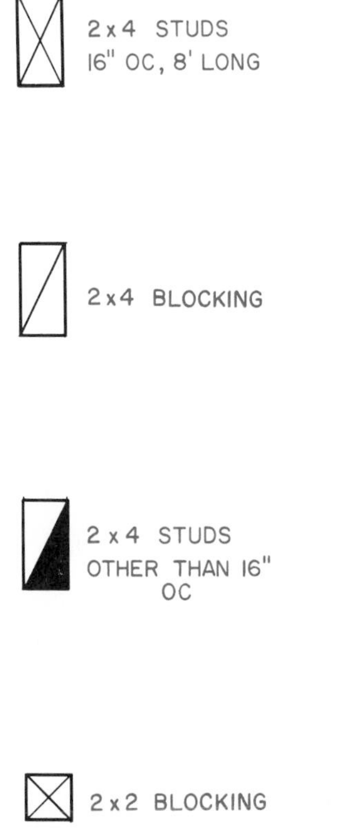

Fig. 56–8. Stud-layout symbols.

identified by a different key (Fig. 56–8). Using a coding system of this type eliminates the need for dimensioning the position of each stud if it is part of the regular partitioned pattern. The practice of coding studs and other members shown on the stud plan also eliminates the need for showing detailed dimensions of each stud.

Detailed dimensions are normally shown on the key or on a separate enlarged detail.

Distances that are dimensioned on stud layout include the following:

1. Inside framing dimensions of each room
2. Framing width of the halls
3. Rough openings for doors and arches
4. Length of each partition
5. Width of partition where dimension lines pass through from room to room (This provides a double check to ensure that the room dimensions plus the partitioned dimensions add up to the overall dimension.) When a stud layout is available it is used on the job to establish partition positions.

Figure 56–9 shows the application of these dimensional practices to a typical stud layout plan.

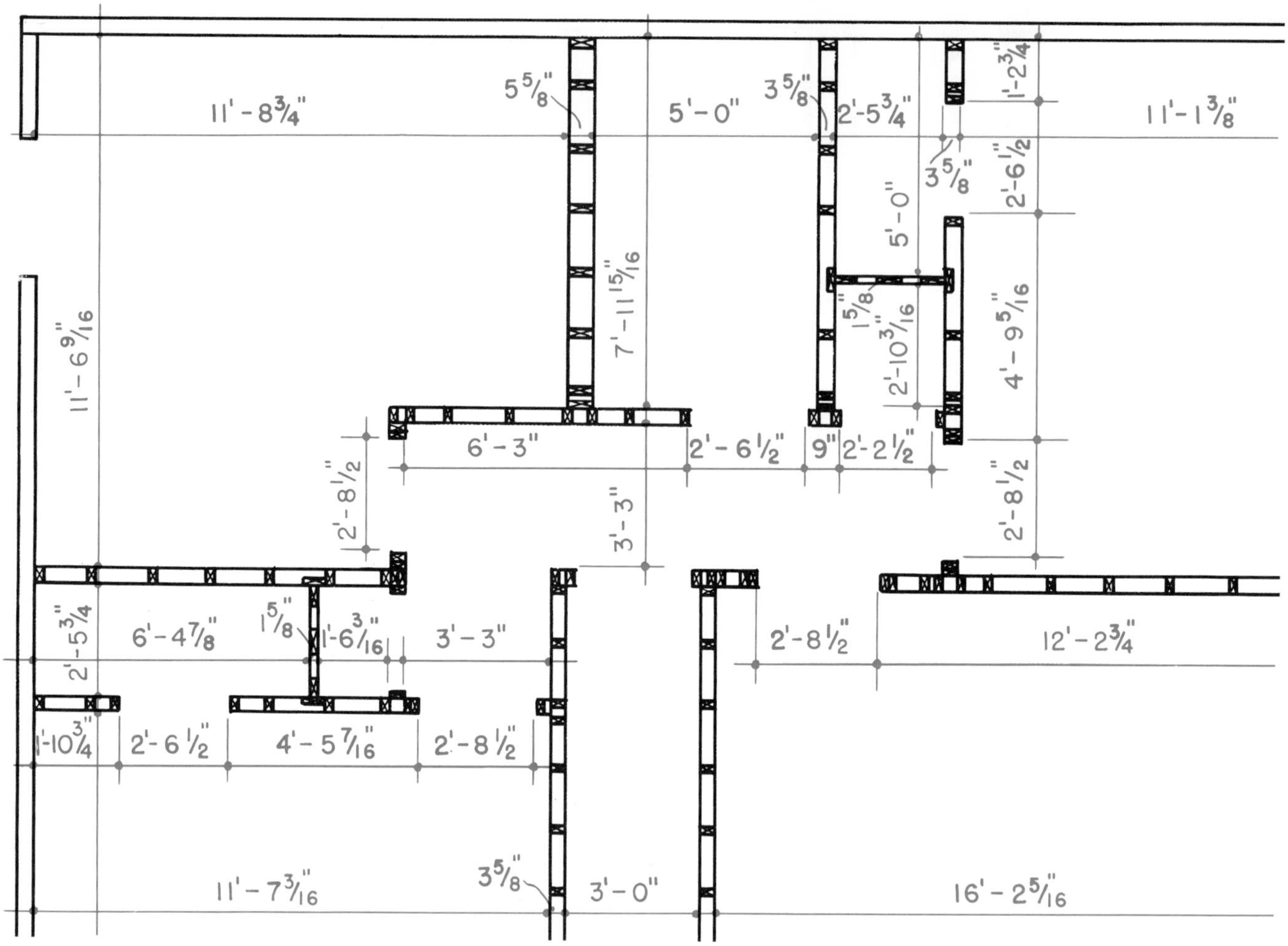

Fig. 56–9. Stud-layout dimensioning.

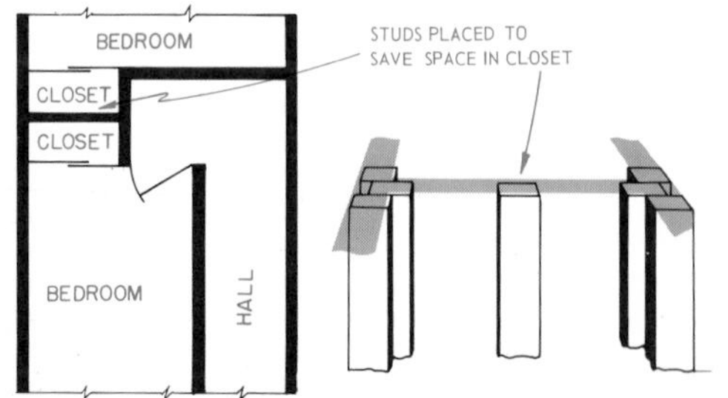

Fig. 56–10. Studs are placed flat to conserve space.

To conserve space where full partition width is not important, as between closets, studs are sometimes turned so that they are flat. This rotation should be reflected in the stud layout (Fig. 56–10).

PROBLEMS

1. **Prepare a stud layout for the floor plan shown in Fig. 33–15.**
2. **Prepare a corner-post detail for the corner posts shown in Fig. 33–19.**
3. **Prepare a stud layout for the home in which you now reside.**
4. **Prepare a stud layout (¼″ = 1′ – 0″) for a home of your own design.**
5. **Draw a stud layout of the east living-room partition shown in Fig. 33–15.**
6. **Define the following terms: *stud layout, stud detail, corner post, rough lumber, dressed lumber, blocking, inside framing dimensions.***

UNIT 57

Roof-Framing Plans

The first structure made for shelter was probably a lean-to roof supported by posts. As structures became larger and more complex, the composition and shape of the roof also changed.

The main function of a roof is to provide protection from rain, snow, sun, and various degrees of temperature. The roof of a northern building is designed to withstand heavy snow loads. The thatched roof of a tropical native hut provides protection only from sun and rain.

As roof styles developed through the centuries, pitches (angles) were changed, gutters and downspouts were added for better drainage, and overhangs were extended to provide more protection from the sun. As the size of roofs changed, the size and types of material changed accordingly. In any modern residence the roof is an integral part of the design of the whole house.

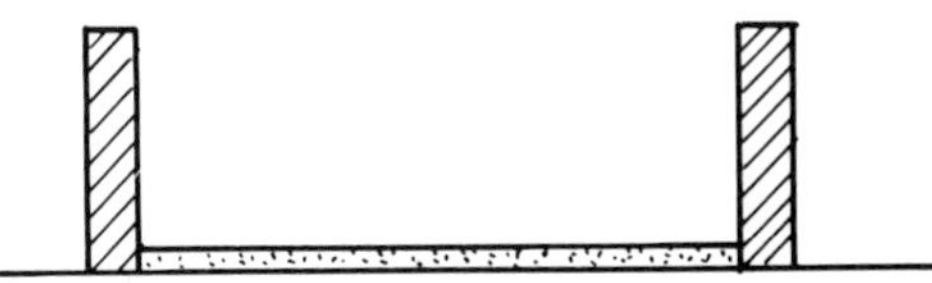

A STRUCTURE IS NOT COMPLETE
WITHOUT A ROOF.

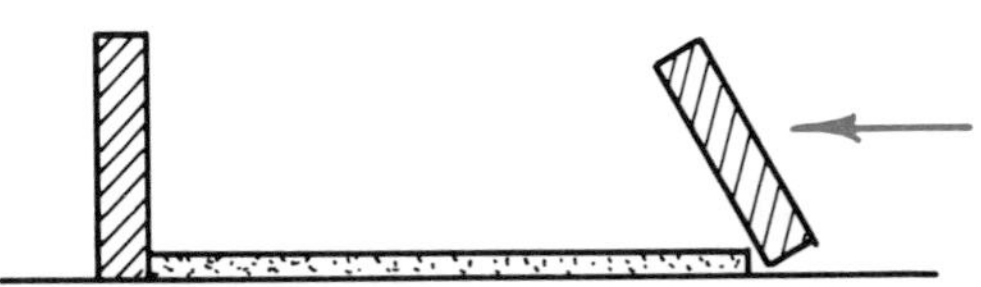

WALLS CANNOT RESIST FORCES—
FORCE FROM OUTSIDE..

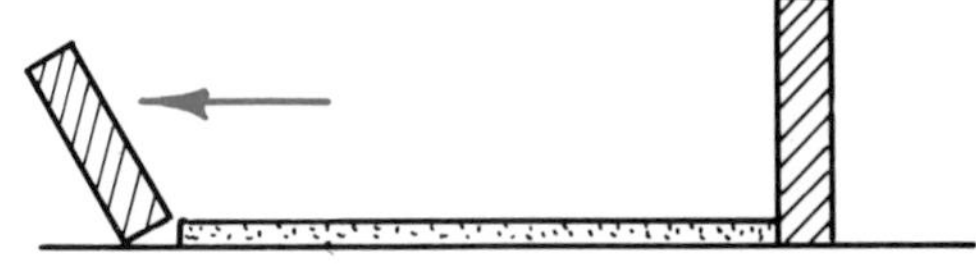

FORCES FROM INSIDE...

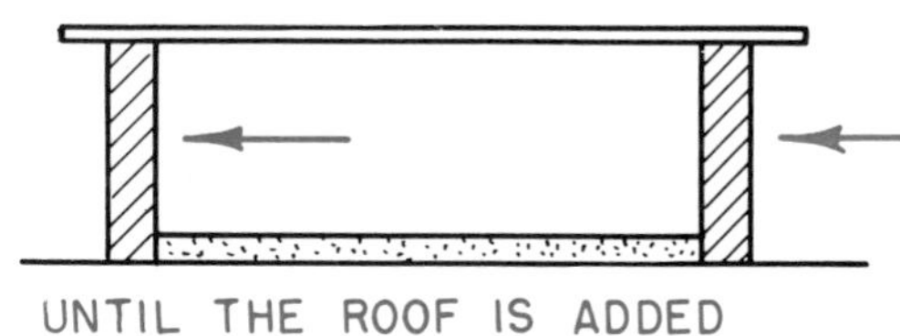

UNTIL THE ROOF IS ADDED

Fig. 57–1. A roof adds stability to a structure.

STRUCTURAL DESIGN

The walls of the structure are given stability by their attachment to the ground and to the roof. Most buildings are not structurally sound without roofs. Walls cannot resist forces from the outside or forces from the inside unless some horizontal support (roof) is given to the upper part of the wall. This principle is shown in (Fig. 57–1).

SUPPORT

The weight of the roof is normally supported by the exterior walls of the structure (Fig. 57–2). Roofs may be supported by a combination of the exterior walls plus the load-bearing partitions or beams (Fig. 57–3). In a frame or continuous-arch design, the roof is supported by direct connection with the foundation (Fig. 57–4).

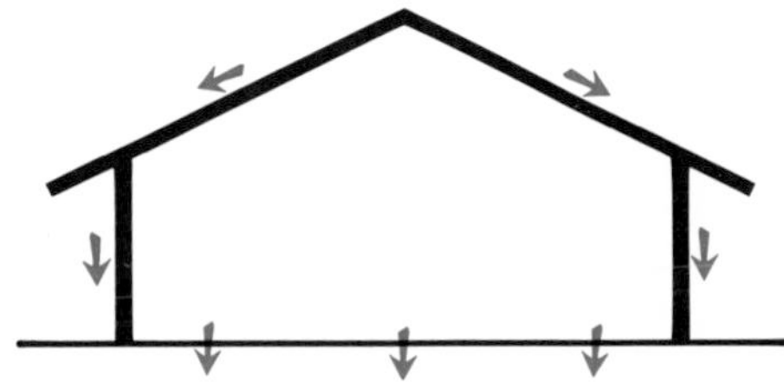

Fig. 57–2. The weight of the roof is transmitted to the outside walls.

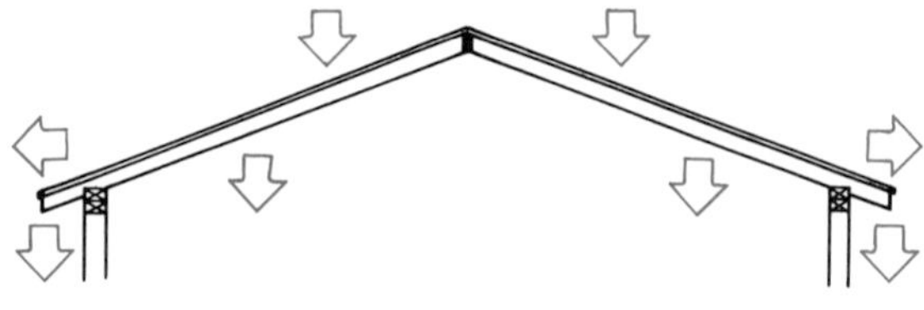

Fig. 57–3. Interior load-bearing partitions help support roofs.

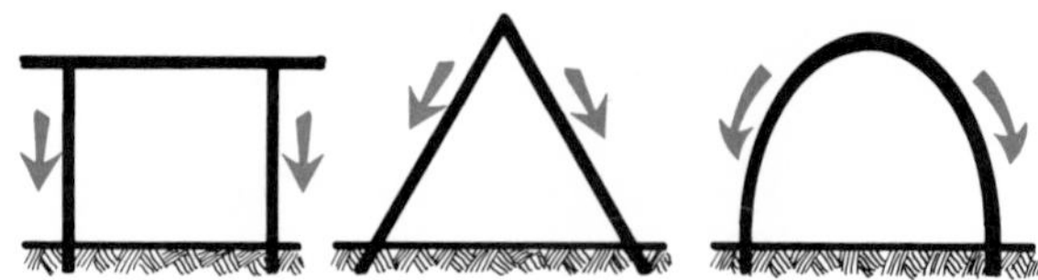

Fig. 57–4. A roof can be connected directly to the foundation.

LOADS

The structural members of a roof must be sufficiently strong to withstand the loads which bear upon it.

Dead Loads

Dead loads that bear upon most roofs include the weight of shingles, sheathing, and rafters.

All loads are computed on the basis of pounds per square foot, or kilograms per square meter if using metric measurements. The typical asphalt-shingle roof weighs approximately 10 pounds per square foot (Fig. 57–5), and a typical asbestos roof weighs approximately 12 pounds per square foot. A Spanish tile roof weighs 17 pounds per square foot. Thus a 40′ × 20′ (800 square feet) asphalt-shingle roof would be designed to carry an 8000 pound load (800 square feet × 10 pounds per square foot).

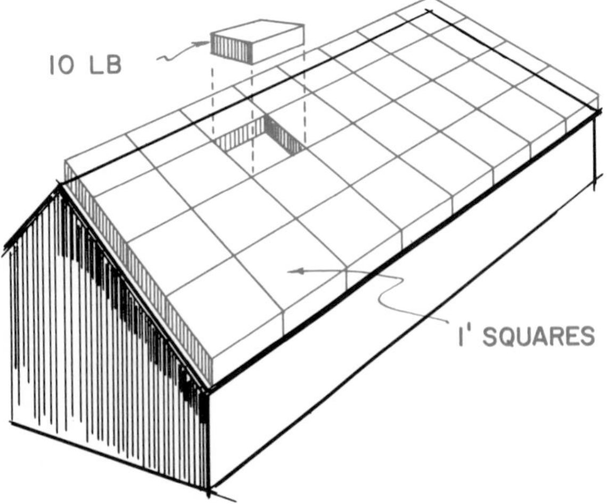

Fig. 57–5. Roof loads are measured in pounds per square foot.

Live Loads

Live loads that act on the roof include wind loads and snow loads, which vary greatly from one geographical area to another. For example, the combined wind and snow loads in the South Pacific are approximately 20 pounds per square foot. In the central and western parts of the United States, these loads are 30 pounds

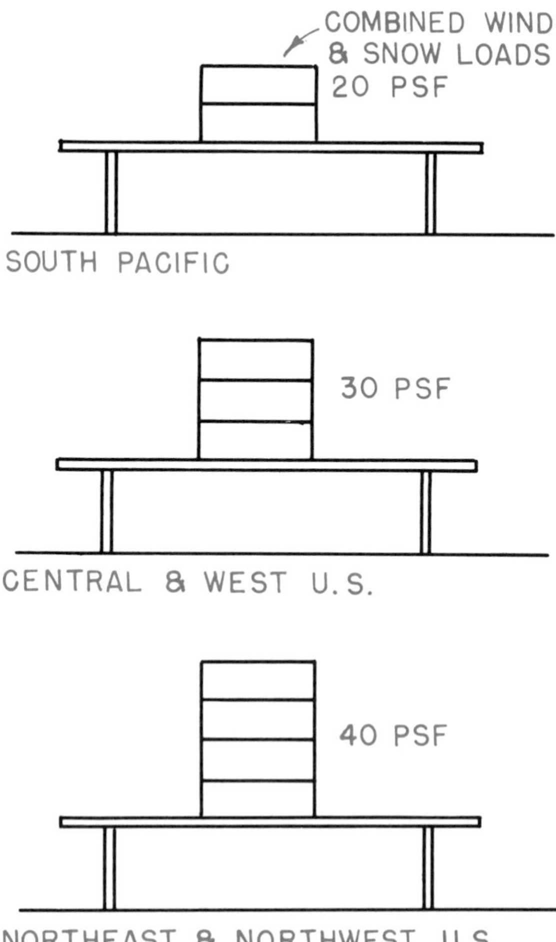

Fig. 57–6. Live roof loads vary from region to region.

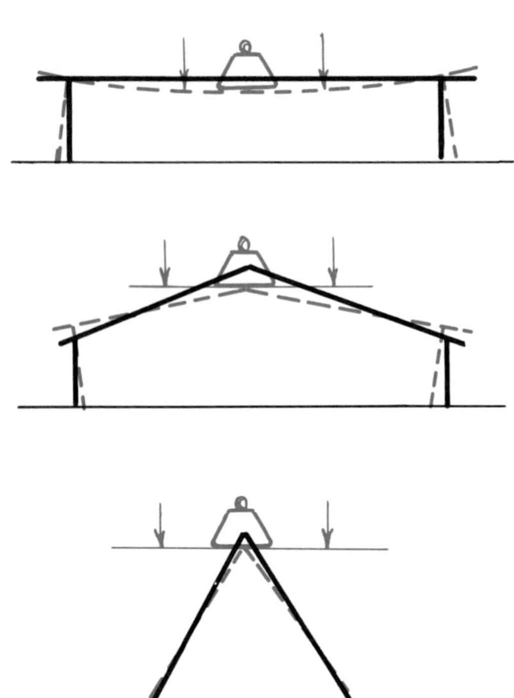

Fig. 57–7. Low-pitch roofs need heavier supports or shorter spans to withstand snow and wind loads.

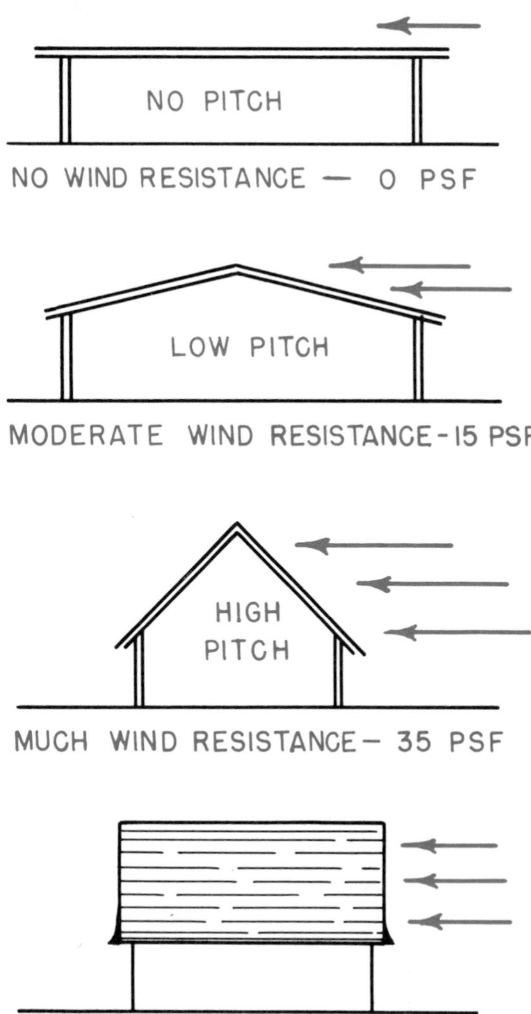

Fig. 57–8. High-pitch roofs contribute to high wind loads.

per square foot, and in the northeastern and northwestern parts of the United States, they are 40 pounds per square foot (Fig. 57–6).

Snow and wind loads vary greatly as the pitch of the roof is changed. Snow loads are exerted in a vertical direction; wind loads are exerted in a horizontal direction. A high-pitch roof will withstand snow loads better than a low-pitch roof (Fig. 57–7). The reverse is true of wind loads. There is virtually no wind load exerted on a flat roof, and moderate wind loads (15 pounds per square foot) are exerted on a low-pitch roof. Approximately 35 pounds per square foot is exerted on a high-pitch roof. An excessively resistant wind load is exerted on a completely vertical wall, approximately 40 pounds per square foot, which is equivalent to hurricane force, as shown in Fig. 57–8. For all practical purposes, snow and wind loads are combined in one total live load. Live loads and dead loads are then combined in the total load acting on the roof.

SIZE OF MEMBERS

The size of all structural members used for roof framing depends on the combined loads bearing on the member and the spacing of each member. If the load is increased, either the spacing must be decreased or the size of the member increased to compensate for the increased load. Consequently, if the size of a member is decreased, the members must be spaced more closely or the span must be decreased. If the length of the span is increased, the size of the members must be increased or the spacing made closer.

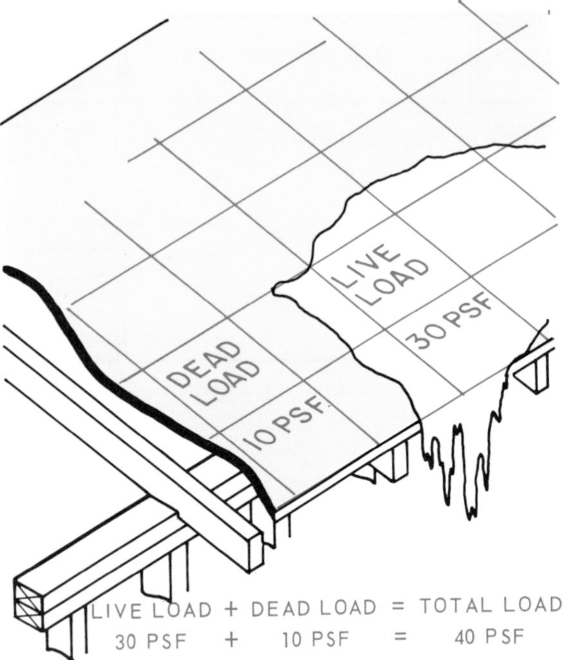

Fig. 57–9. Determining the total load per square foot.

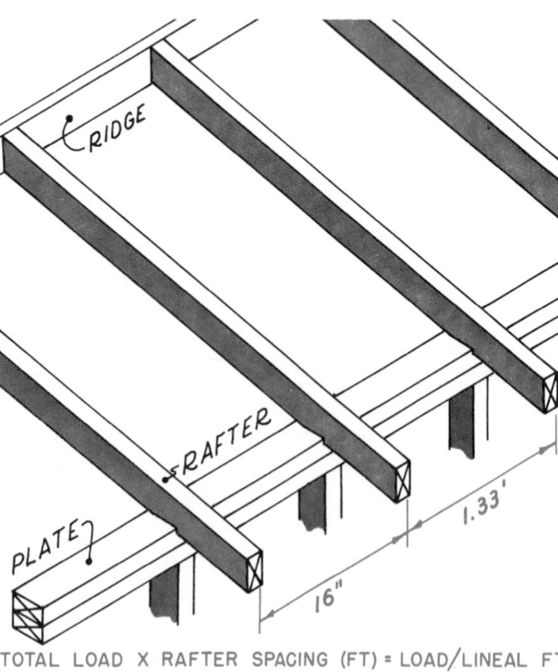

Fig. 57–10. Determining the load per lineal foot on each rafter.

To compute the most appropriate size of roof rafter for a given load, spacing, and span, follow these steps:

1. To determine the total load per square foot of the roof space, add the live load and the dead load (Fig. 57–9).
2. To determine the load per lineal foot on each rafter, multiply the load per square foot by the spacing of the rafters (Fig. 57–10). If rafters are spaced at 12″ intervals, then the load per square foot and the load per lineal foot will be the same. However, if the rafters are spaced at 16″ intervals, then each lineal foot of rafter must support 1⅓ of the load per square foot (Fig. 57–11).
3. To find the total load each rafter must support, multiply the load per lineal foot by the length of the span in feet (Fig. 57–12).
4. To compute the bending moment in inch-pounds, multiply the total load supported by each rafter by the length of the span in feet by 12. Divide this figure by 8. The *bending moment* is the force needed to bend or break the rafter. When the length of the span in pounds is multiplied by the length of the span in feet, the result is expressed in foot-pounds. The span must be multiplied by 12 to convert the bending moment into inch-pounds (Fig. 57–13).
5. Set up the equation to determine the resisting moment. The *resisting moment* is the strength or resistance the rafter must possess to withstand the force of the bending moment. The resisting moment must therefore

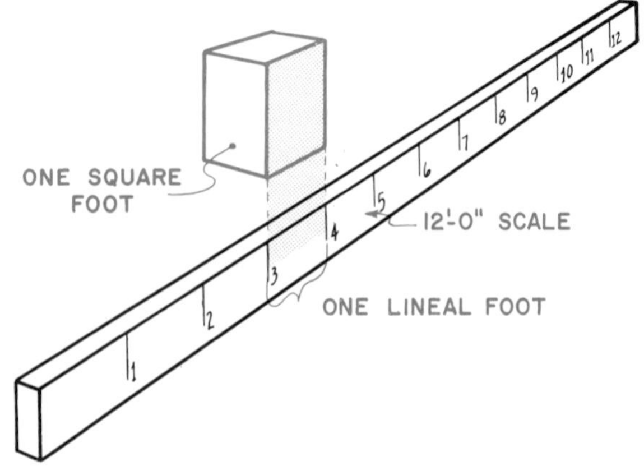

Fig. 57–11. Rafter loads are expressed in lineal feet.

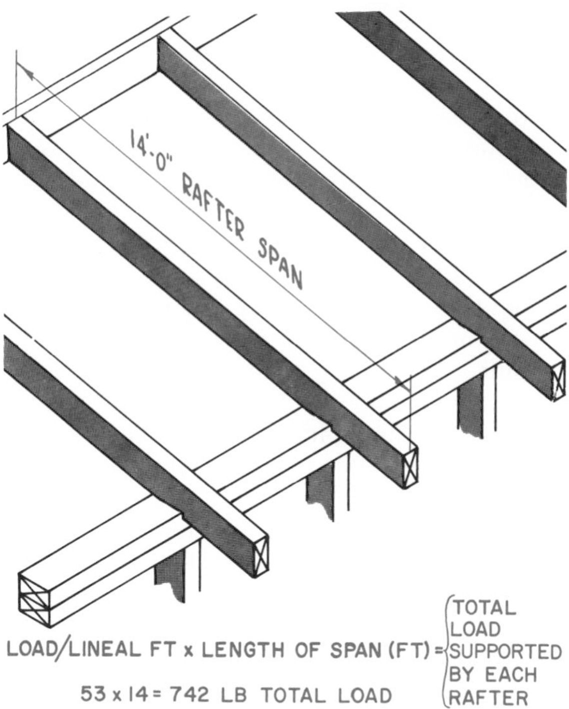

14'-0" RAFTER SPAN
LOAD/LINEAL FT x LENGTH OF SPAN (FT) = {TOTAL LOAD SUPPORTED BY EACH RAFTER
53 x 14 = 742 LB TOTAL LOAD

Fig. 57–12. Finding the total load each rafter must support.

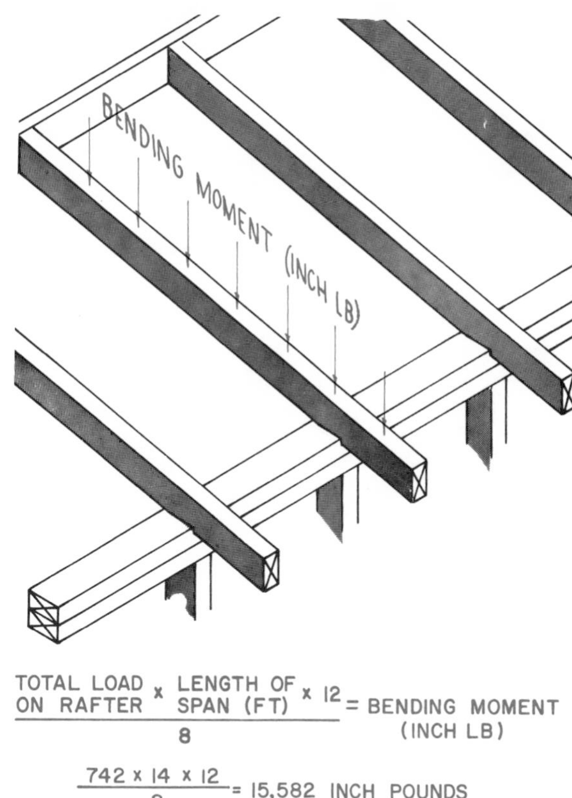

BENDING MOMENT (INCH LB)
(TOTAL LOAD ON RAFTER x LENGTH OF SPAN (FT) x 12) / 8 = BENDING MOMENT (INCH LB)
(742 x 14 x 12) / 8 = 15,582 INCH POUNDS

Fig. 57–13. Computing the bending moment.

be equal to or greater than the bending moment of the rafter (Fig. 57–14). The resistance moment is determined by multiplying the fiber stress by the rafter width by the rafter depth squared. This figure is divided by 6. Rafter widths should be expressed in the exact dimensions of the finished lumber (Fig. 57–15). The *fiber stress* is the tendency of the fibers of the wood to bend and stress

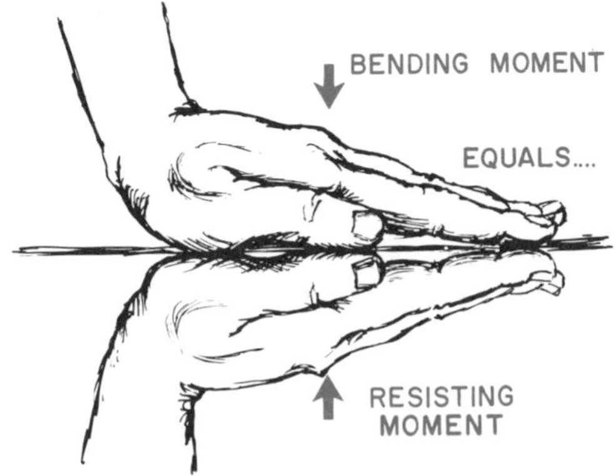

Fig. 57–14. The resisting moment must be equal to or greater than the bending moment.

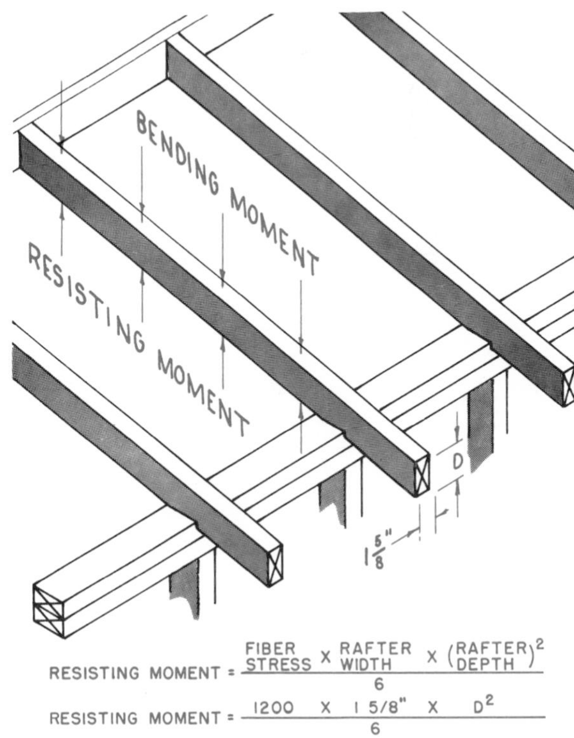

Fig. 57–15. Determining the resistance moment.

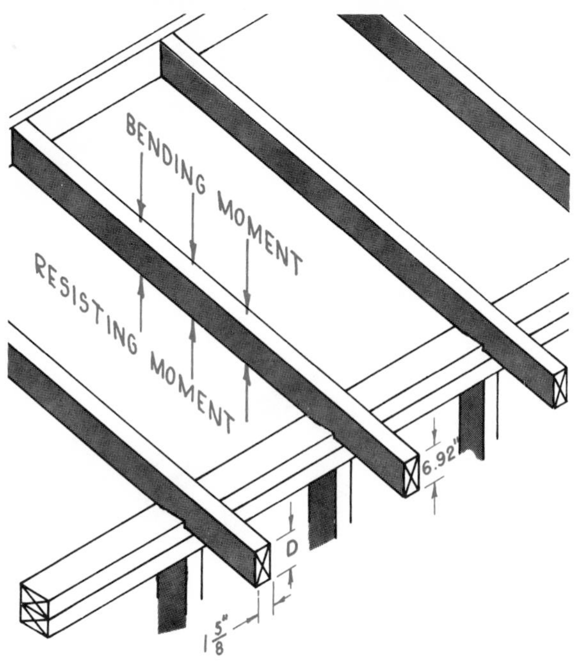

BENDING MOMENT = RESISTING MOMENT

$$\frac{742 \times 14 \times 12}{8} = \frac{1200 \times 1\frac{5}{8} \times D^2}{6}$$

$$15{,}582 = 325\ D^2$$

$$6.92 = D$$

Fig. 57–16. Combining the bending-moment and resistance-moment formulas.

as the member is loaded. Fiber stresses range from 1750 pounds per square inch for Southern dense pine select to 600 pounds per square inch for red spruce. Dense Douglas fir and Southern pine possess average fiber stresses of 1200 pounds per square inch. The rafter depth is squared, since the strength of the member increases by squares. For example, a rafter 12″ deep is not three times as strong as a rafter 4″ deep. It is nine times as strong.

6. Since the bending moment equals the resistance moment, the formulas can be combined, as shown in Fig. 57–16. The formula can then be followed for any of the variables, preferably the depth of the rafter, since varying the depth will alter the resisting moment more than any other single factor.

Care should be taken in establishing all sizes to ensure that the sizes of materials conform to manufacturers' standards and building-code allowances. Table 57–1 shows a typical space-span chart based on common lumber sizes and spacing. Table 57–2 shows common truss specifications based on normal loading for residential work.

Table 57–1. MAXIMUM RAFTER SPANS FOR 5/12 PITCH, 40 PSF LOAD

PITCH: 5/12
LOAD: 40 PSF

LUMBER SIZE	SPACING, IN INCHES	FIBER STRESS, 1200 POUNDS, FOR DOUGLAS FIR AND SOUTHERN YELLOW PINE
2 x 4	24	6′—6″
	20	7′—3″
	16	8′—1″
	12	9′—4″
2 x 6	24	10′—4″
	20	11′—4″
	16	12′—6″
	12	14′—2″
2 x 8	24	13′—8″
	20	15′—2″
	16	16′—6″
	12	18′—4″

Table 57–2. COMMON TRUSS SPECIFICATIONS

		SPAN	26′			28′		
			0″	4″	8″	0″	4″	8″
TOP CHORDS	OVERHANG A	2/12	33½″	31½″	29½″	45½″	43½″	41½″
		3/12	30¼″	28¼″	26¼″	42¼″	40¼″	38¼″
		4/12	26⅛″	24⅛″	22⅛″	36⅞″	34⅞″	32⅞″
BOTTOM CHORD	B		13′-0″	12′-8″	14′-0″	14′-0″	14′-4″	14′-8″

		SPAN	30′			32′		
			0″	4″	8″	0″	4″	8″
TOP CHORDS	OVERHANG A	2/12	33½″	31½″	29½″	45½″	43½″	41½″
		3/12	30¼″	28¼″	26¼″	42¼″	40¼″	38¼″
		4/12	24⅞″	22⅞″	20⅞″	34¾″	32¾″	30¾″
BOTTOM CHORD	B		14′-0″	14′-4″	14′-8″	16′-0″	16′-4″	16′-8″

ROOF-FRAMING TYPES

The conventional method of roof framing consists of roof rafters or trusses spaced at small intervals such as 16″ (406 mm) on center. These roof rafters align with the partition studs placed on the same centers (Fig. 57–17). The second method is the post and beam or plank and beam (Fig. 57–18). The plank and beam roof consists of planks placed on longitudinal (transverse) beams. Regularly spaced posts serve as load bearers for the roof members. A *ridge beam* is the center of a gable roof, and intermittent beams directly support the roof planking. Roof planking can then be used as a ceiling and a base for roofing that will shed water. Exposed plank and beam ceilings achieve a distinctive and pleasing architectural effect. When planks are selected for appearance, the only ceiling treatment needed is a desired finish. Longitudinal beam sizes vary with the span and spacing of the beams. Design variations of end walls are achieved by an extensive use of glass and protecting roof overhangs.

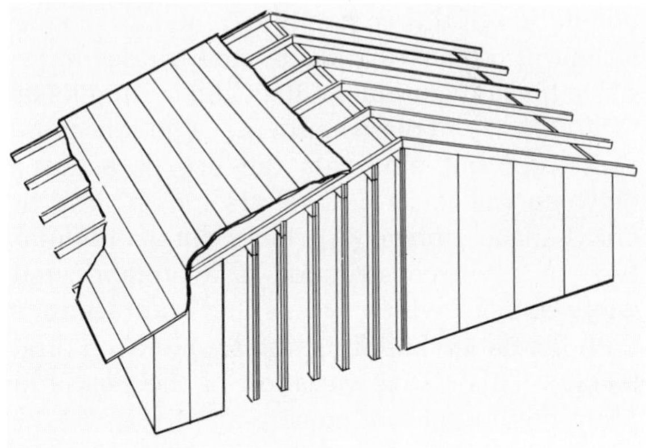

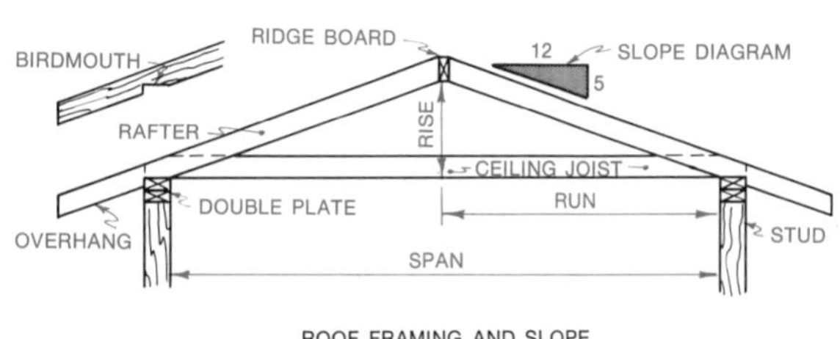

Fig. 57–17. Conventional roof framing.

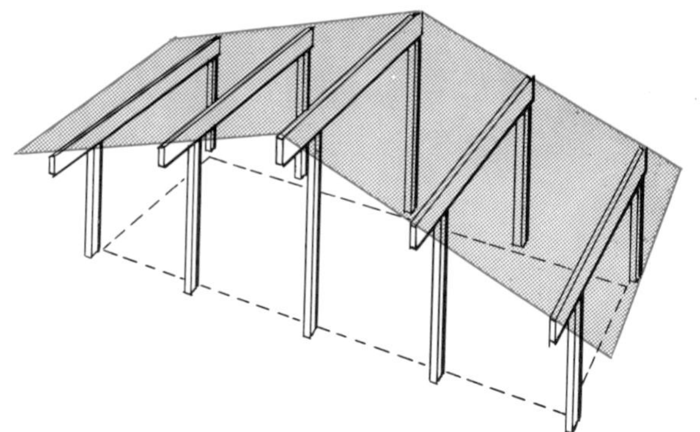

Fig. 57–18. **Plank and beam framing.**

Scholz Homes, Inc.

Fig. 57–19. Post and beam framing allows for larger open areas.

The use of larger members in post and beam construction allows the designer to plan larger open areas unobstructed by bearing partitions (Fig. 57–19).

GABLE ROOFS

Gable roofs are constructed by the use of the conventional rafters and ceiling joists usually spaced 16″ on center and covered with sheathing felt and shingles (Fig. 57–20). An adaptation of this conventional method of constructing roofs is the use of roof trusses to replace the conventional rafters and ceiling joists (Fig. 57–21). Trusses provide a much more rigid roof but eliminate the use of a space between the joists and rafters for an attic or crawl-space storage. An increasingly popular type of gable construction is a prefabricated gable end, to which beams and roof sections with insulation and finishing are attached (Fig. 57–22). This is one variation of the post and beam method of roof construction.

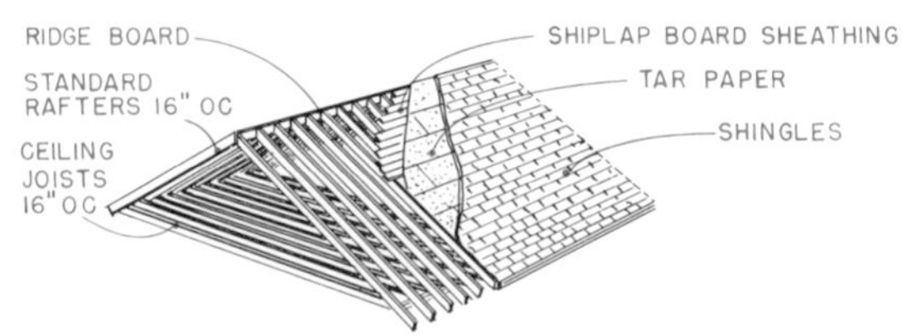

Fig. 57–20. A conventionally framed gable roof.

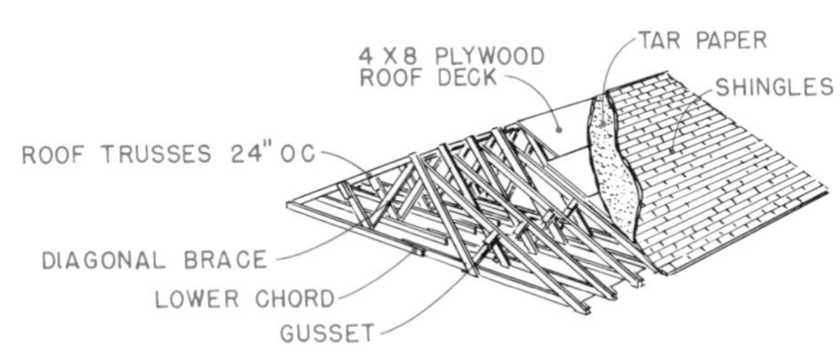

Fig. 57–21. A trussed gable roof.

PITCH

A gable roof has pitch on two sides but no pitch on the ends (gable ends). The *pitch* is the angle between the top plate and the ridge board. *Rise* is the vertical distance from the top plate to the ridge. *Run* is the horizontal distance from the ridge to the top plate. The *pitch* is referred to as the *rise over the run*. In a gable roof with the ridge board in the exact center of the building,

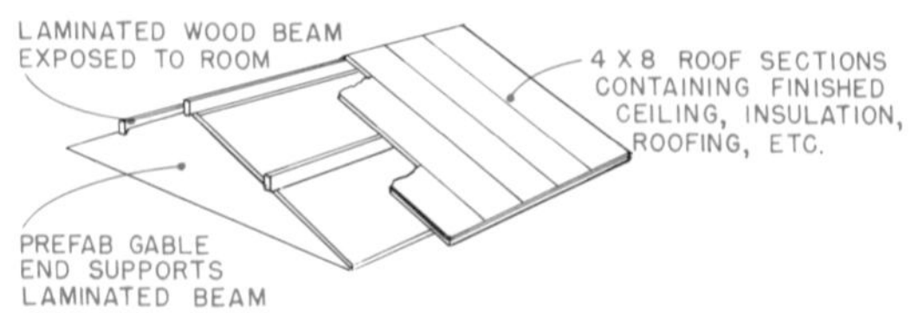

Fig. 57–22. A prefabricated post and beam gable roof.

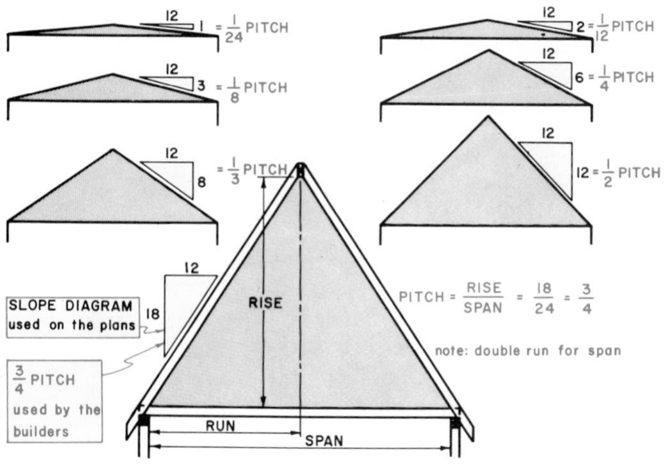

Fig. 57–23. Roof pitch can be expressed as rise over run or as the fraction rise over span.

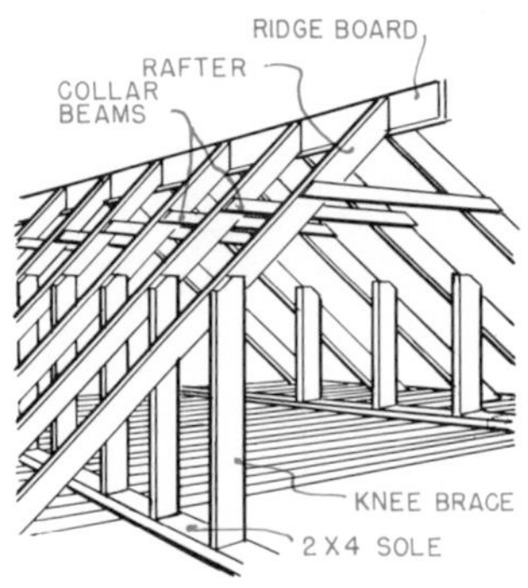

Fig. 57–24. The ridge board is the top member in the roof assembly.

the run is one-half the span (Fig. 57–23). The run is always expressed in units of 12. Therefore, the rise is the number of inches the roof rises as it moves 12″ horizontally. A 6/12 pitch means that the roof rises 6″ for every 12″ of horizontal distance (run).

Gable-roof pitches vary greatly. The 1/12 pitch shown in Fig. 57–23 is almost a flat roof. The 8/12 pitch however is a moderately steep roof. The angle of a roof with a 12/12 pitch is 45°. Metric pitch sizes are not yet established.

RIDGE BEAMS

The ridge board or ridge beam as shown in Fig. 57–24 is the top member in the roof assembly. Rafters are fixed in their exact position by being secured to the ridge board. The ridge beam in a cathedral ceiling of post and beam construction may be part of the top plate assembly (Fig. 57–25).

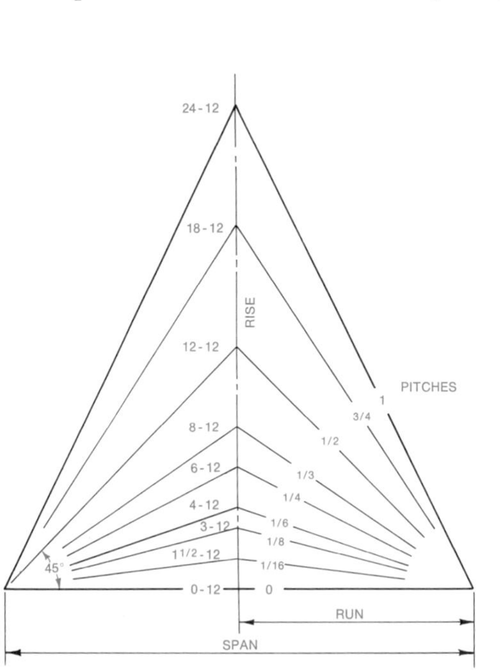

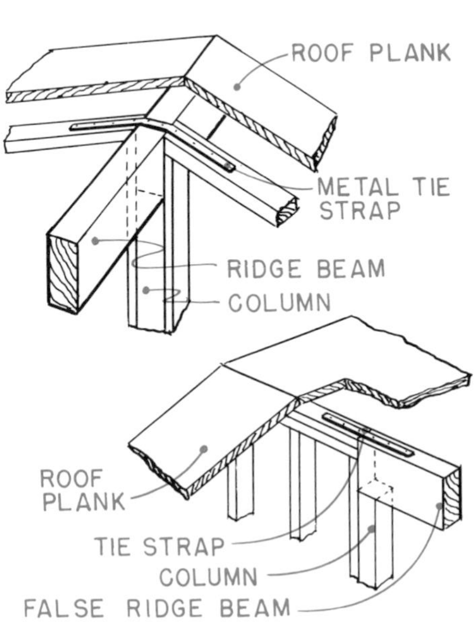

Fig. 57–25. Ridge-beam assemblies.

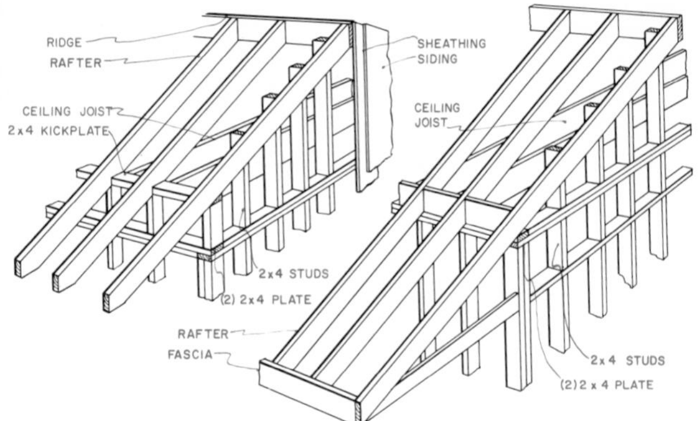

Fig. 57–26. Gable-end construction.

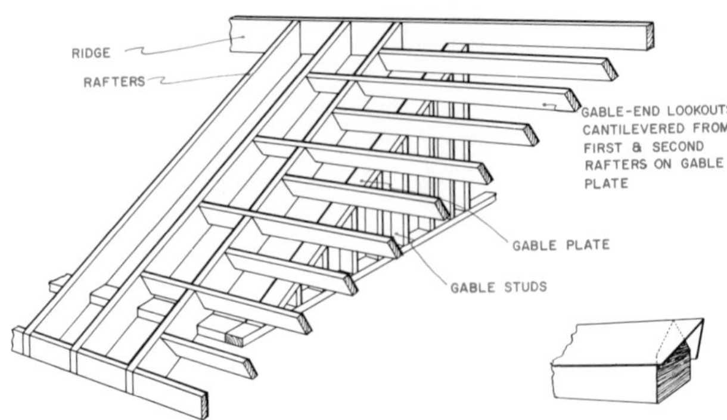

Fig. 57–27. Winged-gable lookout construction.

GABLE END

The gable end is the side of the house that rises to meet the ridge (Fig. 57–26). In some cases, especially on low-pitch roofs, the entire gable-end wall from the floor to the ridge can be panelized with varying lengths of studs. However, it is more common to prepare a rectangular wall panel and erect separate studs that project from the top plate of the panel to the rafter. Sheathing and siding are then added to the entire gable end of the house. When post and beam construction is used, celestial windows in the gable end can be utilized, since studs are unnecessary on the gable end.

An increased use of windows in gable ends has necessitated the use of larger overhangs on the gable end. Gable-end lookouts can be framed from the first or second rafters on the gable plate, as shown in Figs. 57–27 and 57–38.

OVERHANGS

Post and beam construction allows for larger overhangs since larger members are used and rafters can quite often be exposed. Several variations of cuts are used to finish the rafter end. A comparison of the plumb, level, combination, and square cuts is given in Fig. 57–28. Notice also that the rafters are notched with a seat (birdmouth) cut, to provide a level surface for the intersection of the rafters and top plates. The area bearing on the plate should not be less than 3″ (75 mm) (Fig. 57–29).

Overhangs are normally larger on the side walls than on gable ends. Overhangs should be

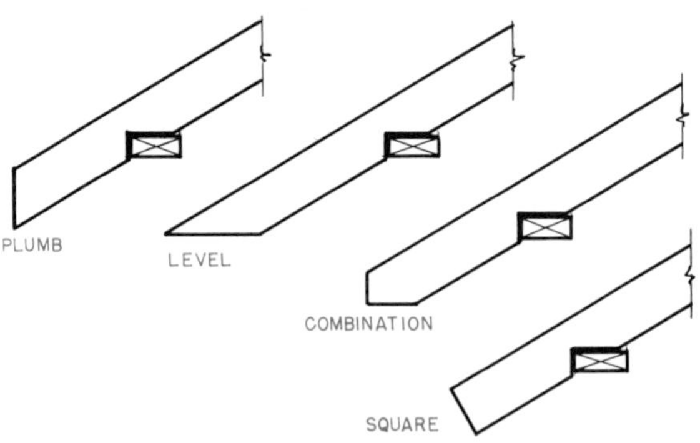

Fig. 57–28. Types of tail-rafter cuts.

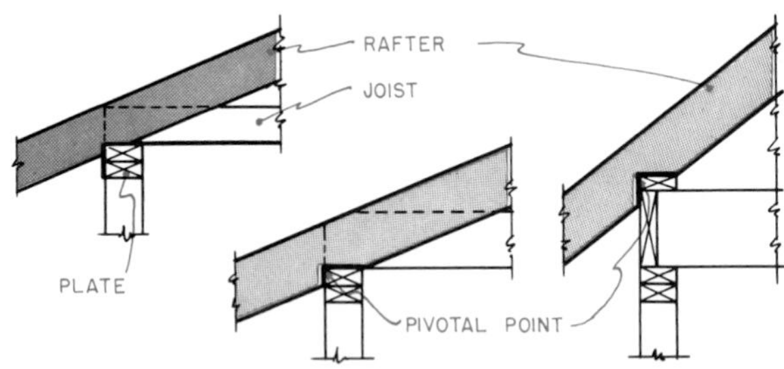

Fig. 57–29. Method of intersecting rafters and top plates.

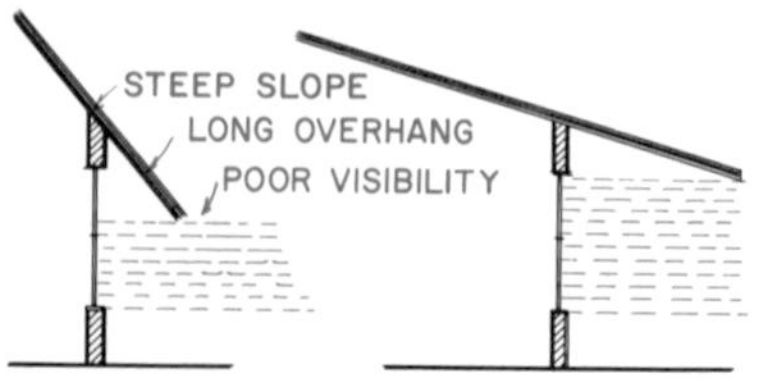

Fig. 57–30. Large overhangs are desirable only if designed correctly.

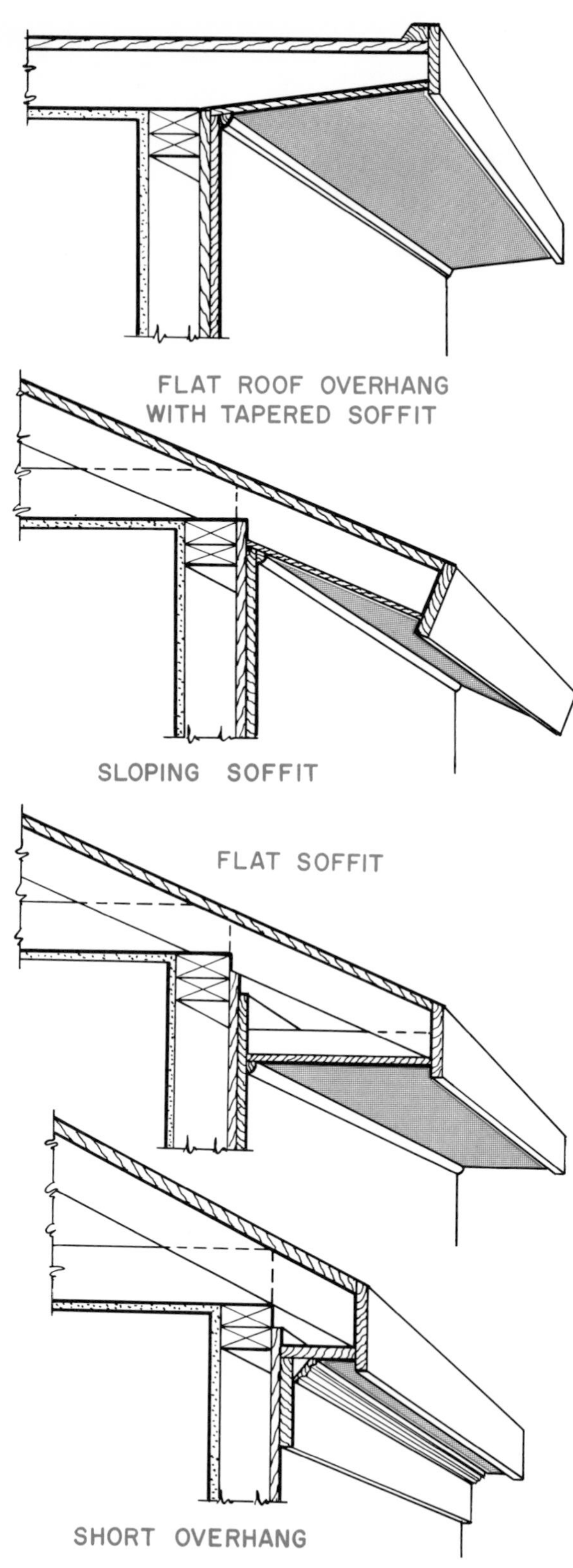

National Lumber Manufacturers Association

Fig. 57–31. Types of soffit design.

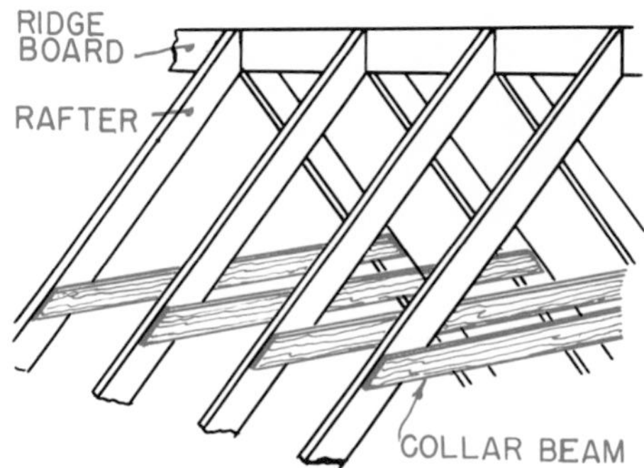

Fig. 57–32. Collar beams reduce rafter stress.

designed to provide maximum protection from sun and rain without restricting the light and view. Figure 57–30 shows some of the difficulties in designing large overhangs. On a low-pitch roof the problem is not acute since the rise is relatively small compared with the run. But on a steep pitch roof, where the rise is large, the light might be completely shut off if the same amount of overhang were used. Furthermore, when the end of the overhang extends below the level of the window, there is no possibility of using a flat soffit. Figure 57–31 shows several alternative soffits.

COLLAR BEAMS

Collar beams provide a tie between rafters. They may be placed on every rafter or only on every other rafter. Collar beams are used to reduce the rafter stress that occurs between the top plate and the rafter cut. They also act as ceiling joists for finished attics (Fig. 57–32).

KNEE WALLS

Knee walls are vertical studs which project from an attic floor to the roof rafters, as shown in Fig. 57–33. Knee walls add rigidity to the rafters and also provide wall framing for finished attics.

TRUSSES

Figure 57–34 shows lightweight wood trusses that have become increasingly popular for homes and small buildings. Roof trusses allow complete flexibility for interior spacing. They

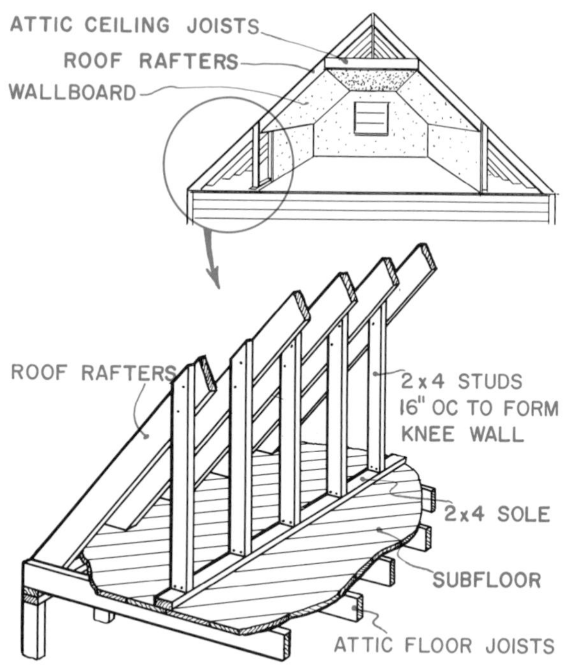

Fig. 57–33. Knee walls add rigidity to the rafters.

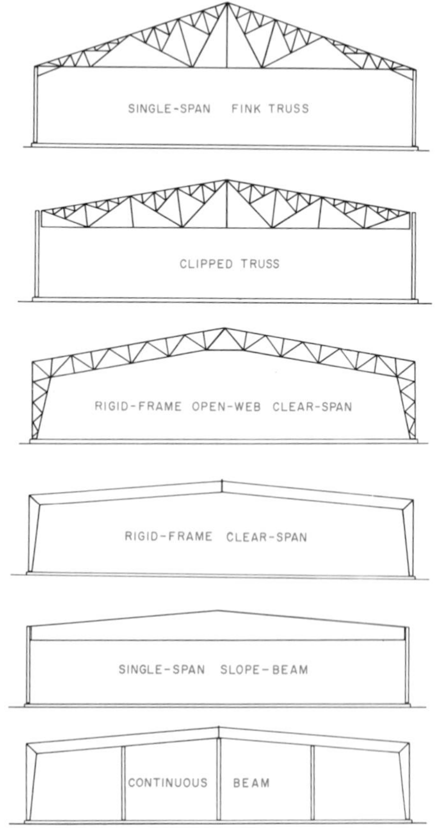

Fig. 57–35. Standard types of trusses.

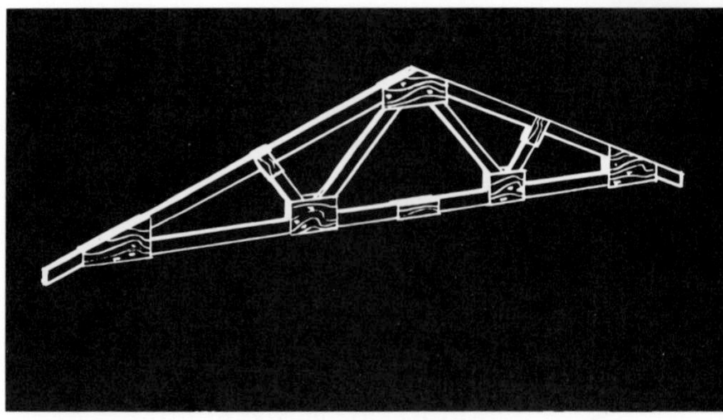

Fig. 57–34. Lightweight wood trusses.

save approximately 30 to 35 percent on materials, compared with the requirements of conventional framing methods. Trusses can be fabricated and erected in one-third of the time required for rafter and ceiling-joist construction. Truss construction helps to put the building under cover almost immediately. The use of trusses saves material and erection time and eliminates normal interior load-bearing partitions. Trusses save construction foundations and footings required for load-bearing partitions. Standard types of trusses are shown in Fig. 57–35. Truss-construction methods are as applicable to large steel-framed buildings (Fig. 57–36) as to small wood-framed buildings (Fig. 57–37).

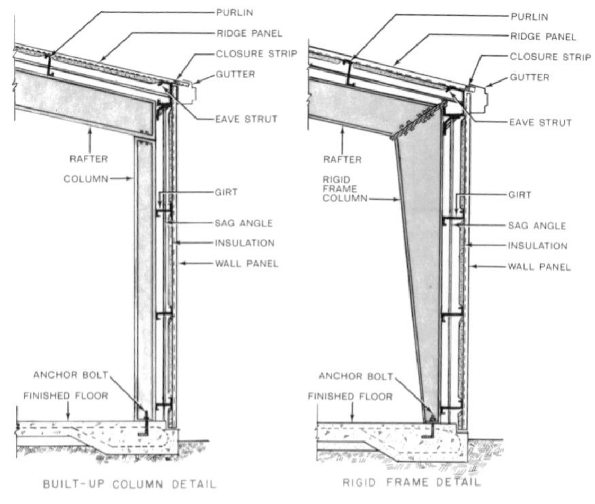

Macomber, Inc.

Fig. 57–36. A structural-steel truss.

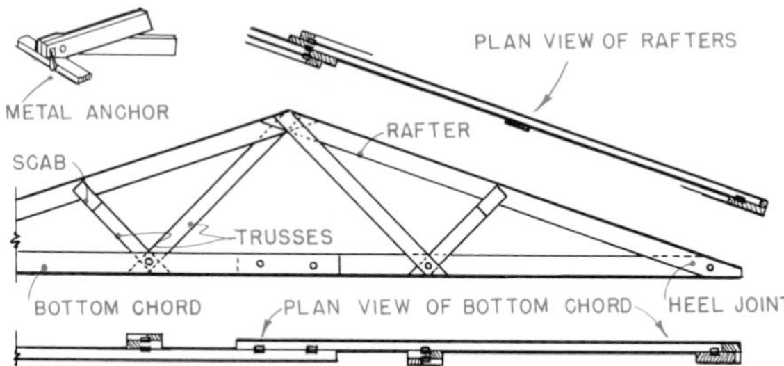

Fig. 57–37. A wood-frame truss.

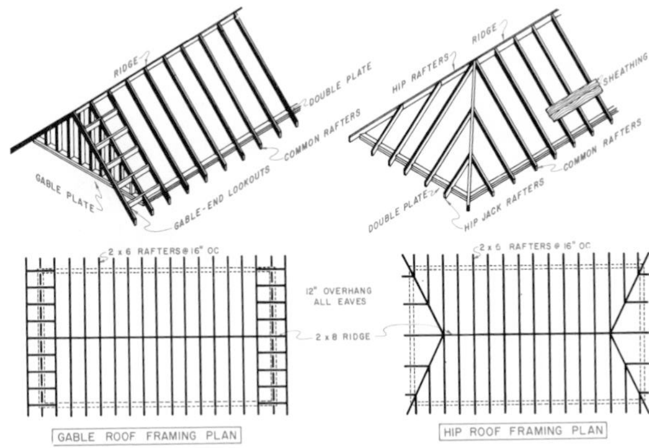

Fig. 57–38. Hip and gable roof construction.

HIP ROOF

Hip-roof framing is similar to gable-roof framing except that the roof slopes in two directions instead of intersecting a gable-end wall. The hip roof may be pyramid-shaped on square buildings.

Where two adjacent slopes meet, a *hip* is formed on the external angle. A *hip rafter* extends from the ridge board over the top plate to the edge of the overhang. The hip rafter performs the same function as the ridge board.

The internal angle formed by the intersection of two slopes of the roof is known as the *valley*. A *valley rafter* is used on the internal angle as a hip rafter is used on the external angle. Hip rafters and valley rafters are normally 2″ (50 mm) deeper or 1″ (25 mm) wider than the regular rafters, for spans up to 12′ (3.658 m). For spans of over 12′ (3.658 m) the rafter should be doubled in width.

Jack rafters are rafters that extend from the wall plate to the hip or valley rafter. They are always shorter than *common* rafters. Figure 57–38 illustrates the use of these various framing members in hip- and gable-roof construction.

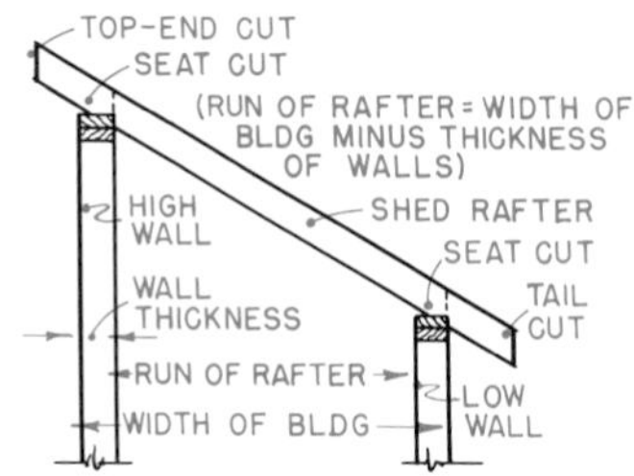

Fig. 57–39. Shed-roof framing.

SHED ROOF

A shed roof is a roof which slants in only one direction (a gable roof is actually two shed roofs, sloping in opposite directions). Shed-roof rafter design is the same as rafter design for gable roofs, except that the run of the rafter is the same as the span. The shed rafter differs from the common rafter in the gable roof in that the shed rafter has two seat cuts, a tail cut, and a top-end cut (Fig. 57–39).

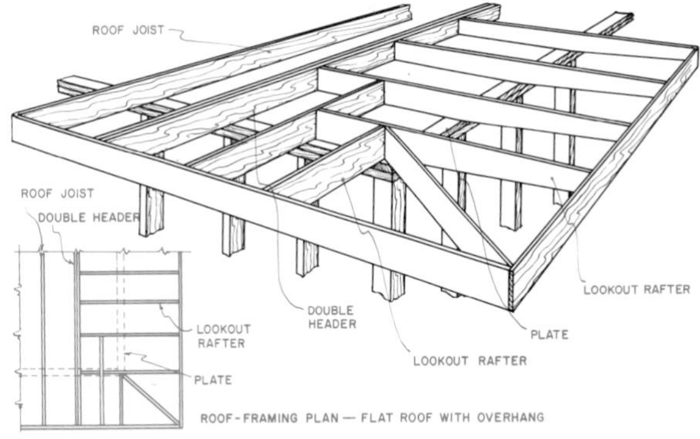

Fig. 57–40. Lookout rafters are used to extend the overhand perpendicular to the common rafters.

FLAT ROOF

A flat roof has no slope. Therefore the roof rafters must span directly from wall to wall or from wall to bearing partition. When rafters also serve as ceiling joists, the size of the rafter must be computed on the basis of both the roof load and the ceiling load (Fig. 57–40).

Southern California Edison Company

Fig. 57–41. Post and beam roof beams also function as exposed ceiling beams.

OVERHANG

Large overhangs are possible on flat roofs. The roof joists can be extended past the top plate far enough to provide sun protection and yet not block the view. This extension is possible because there is no slope. When overhangs are desired on all sides, *lookout rafters,* as shown in Fig. 57–40, are used to extend the overhang on the side of the building perpendicular to the rafter direction.

Republic Steel Corp.

Fig. 57–43. A steel flat-roof structure.

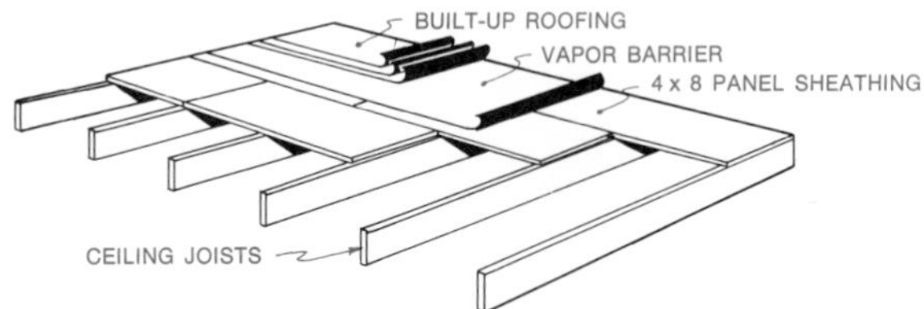

Fig. 57–42. Built-up roof construction.

In post and beam construction, roof beams are used to support the roof construction. They also function as exposed ceiling beams (Fig. 57–41).

DRAINAGE

Since there is no slope to a flat roof, drainage must be provided for by downspouts extending through the overhang. Flat roofs must be designed for a maximum snow load, since snow will not slide off the roof but must completely melt and drain away. A built-up roof consisting of sheathing, roofing paper, and crushed gravel can be used (Fig. 57–42). If a flat roof is so designed, a gravel stop and cant strip can be made high enough to hold water at a specific level. Water will then lie on the roof at all times and provide additional insulation.

STEEL

Steel-construction methods are especially applicable to flat roofs (Fig. 57–43). The simplicity of erecting a steel roof results from the great strength of steel joints (Fig. 57–44). The cross-

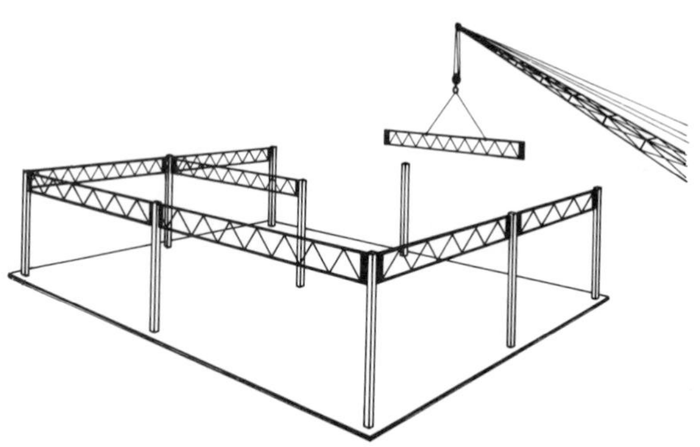

American Bridge Division of United States Steel Corporation

Fig. 57–44. Erecting a steel roof.

Mitchell Construction Company

Fig. 57–45. Typical steel-roof construction.

Macomber, Inc.

Fig. 57–46. A lightweight steel truss.

bracing between widths of a steel *purlin* (horizontal member), as shown in Fig. 57–45, provides the purlin with a strength comparable to that of a truss. Lightweight steel trusses used on a flat roof are shown in Fig. 57–46.

PLAN DEVELOPMENT

A *roof plan* (Fig. 57–47) is a plan view of the roof showing the outline of the roof and the major object lines indicating ridges, valleys, hips, and openings. The roof plan is not a framing plan. To develop a roof-framing plan, a roof must be stripped of its covering to expose the position of each structural member and each header (Fig. 57–48). The roof plan can be used as the basic outline for the roof-framing plan. The roof-framing plan must show the exact position and spacing of each member. Figure 57–49 shows a comparison of a roof plan and a roof-framing plan of the same roof.

SINGLE-LINE PLANS

In the roof-framing plan shown in Fig. 57–49, each member is represented by a single line. This method of preparing roof-farming plans is acceptable when only the general relationship and center spacing are desired.

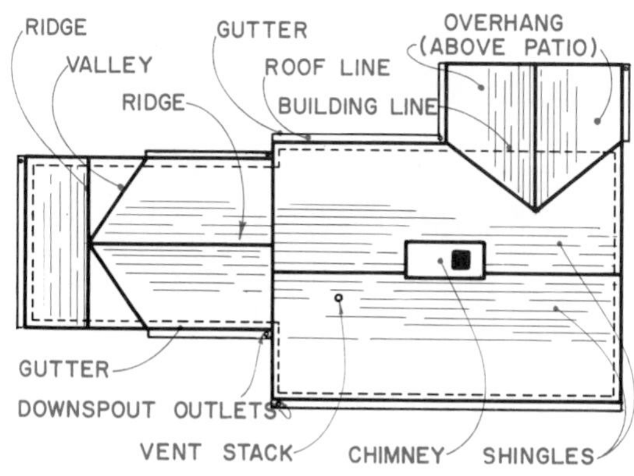

Fig. 57–47. A roof plan.

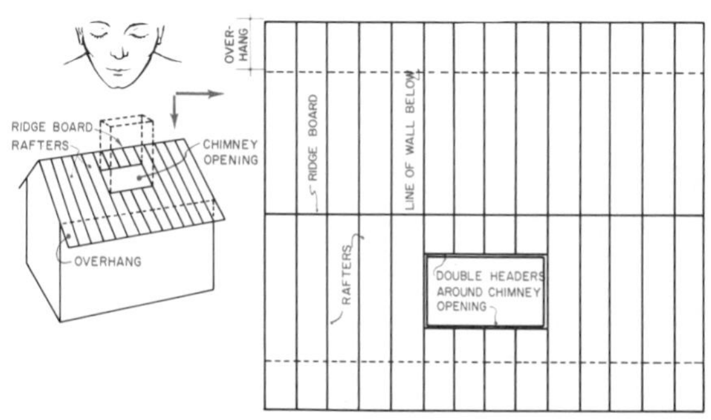

Fig. 57–48. A roof-framing plan.

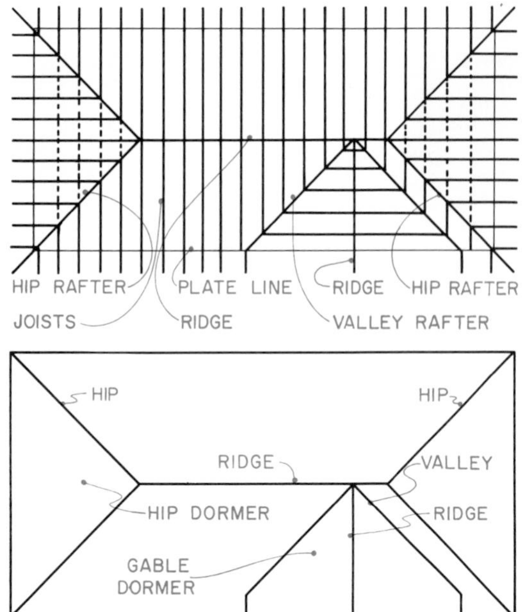

Fig. 57–49. Comparison of a roof plan (bottom) and a roof-framing plan (top).

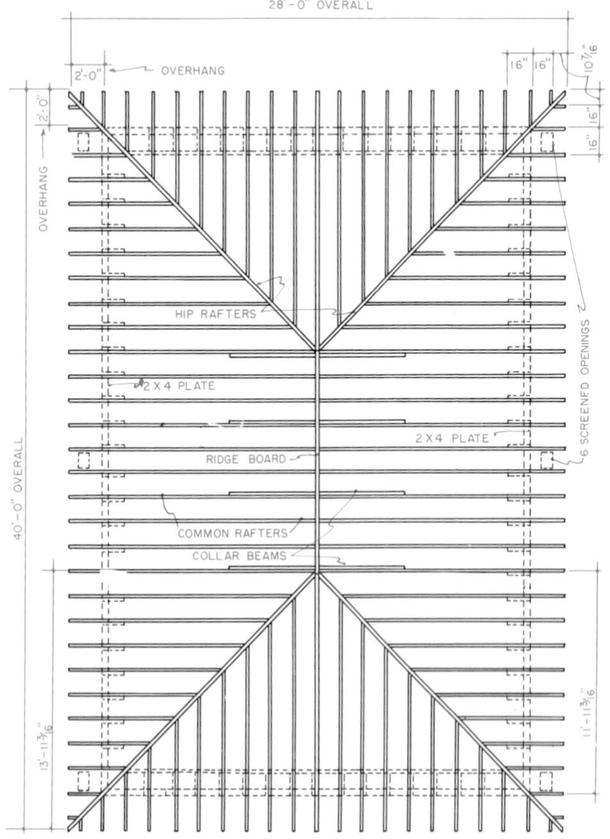

Fig. 57–50. A roof-framing plan showing the thickness of each member.

COMPLETE PLAN

When more details concerning the exact construction of intersections and joints are needed, a plan showing the thickness of each member, as shown in Fig. 57–50, should be prepared. This type of plan is necessary to show the relative height of one member compared with another; that is, to determine whether one member passes over or under another. In this plan the width of ridge boards, rafters, headers, and plates should be shown to the exact scale.

When a complete roof-framing plan of this type cannot fully describe construction framing details, then additional removed pictorial or elevation drawings should be prepared, as shown in Fig. 57–51. A similar technique of removing details can also be used to increase the size of a particular area in detail for dimensioning purposes.

On roof-framing plans, only the outline of the top of the rafters is shown. All areas underneath, including the gable-end plate, are shown by dotted lines. When a gable-end lookout slopes, a true orthographic projection of the plan would indicate three lines—two lines for the top of the rafter and one line for the bottom. However, roof-framing plans are normally simplified to show only the outline of the top of each member (Fig. 57–52). The angle or vertical position of any roof-framing member should be shown on a roof-framing elevation.

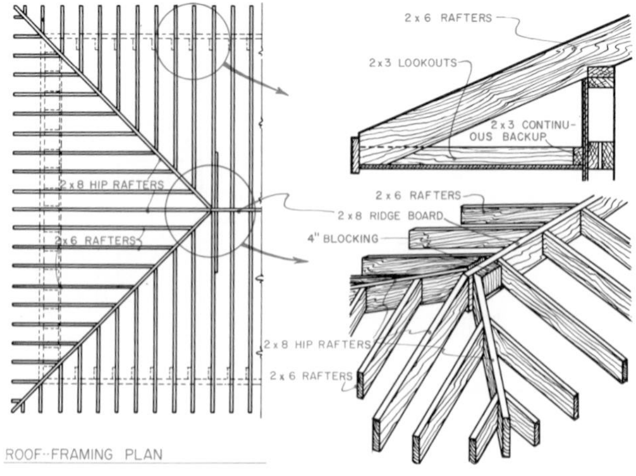

Fig. 57–51. Roof-framing plan details.

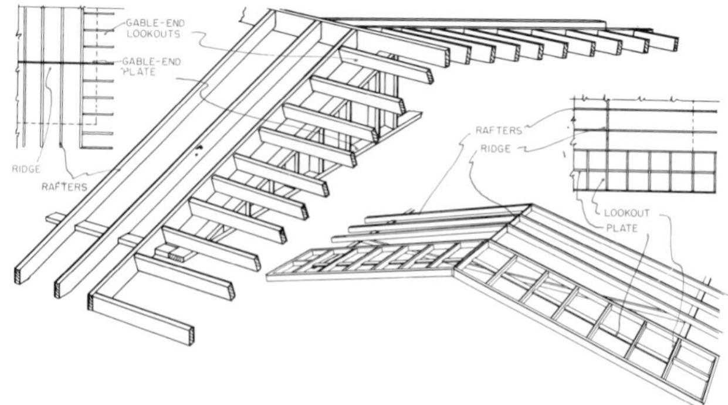

Fig. 57-52. Roof-framing plans show only the outline of the top of each member.

DORMERS

Parts of the roof-framing plan which extend above the normal plane of projection, such as dormer rafters, are drawn with dotted lines. This device indicates that the parts do not directly intersect with the other framing members shown on the plan. It is quite common to show the position of dormer rafters or ridge as illustrated in Fig. 57–53. The details of intersecting the dormer-roof framing with dormer walls should be shown on roof-framing elevations or other details.

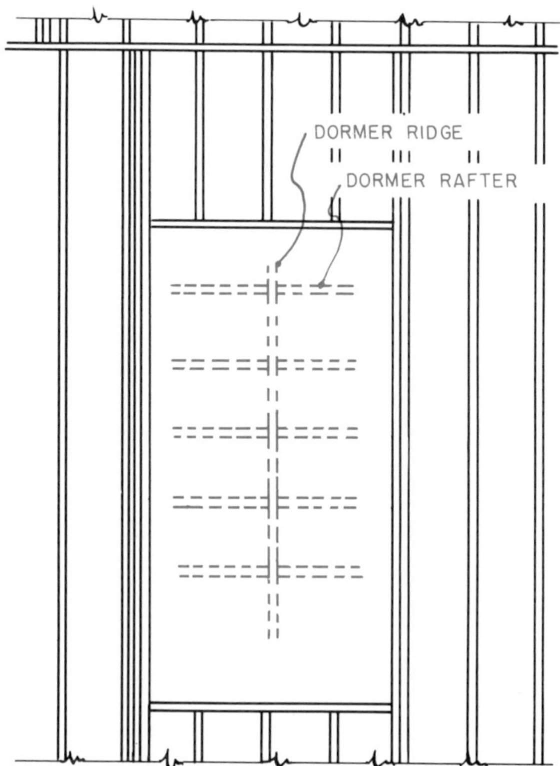

Fig. 57-53. A method of drawing dormer rafters.

STEEL CONSTRUCTION

Roof-framing plans for steel construction are prepared like those for wood construction. However, in plans for structural steel, single-line drawings are almost universally used. A complete classification of each steel member is shown on the drawing. This includes the size, type, and weight of the beams and columns. Each different type of member is shown by a different line weight, which relates to the size of the member. Structural-steel roof-framing plans frequently show *bay areas* (areas between columns) indicating the number of spaces and the spacing of each purlin between columns. Bays are frequently shown in circles: numerically in one direction and alphabetically in the other direction (Fig. 57–54).

ROOF-FRAMING ELEVATIONS

Roof-framing plans show horizontal relationships of members such as width, length, and horizontal spacing. In a top view (plan), you cannot show vertical dimensions such as pitch,

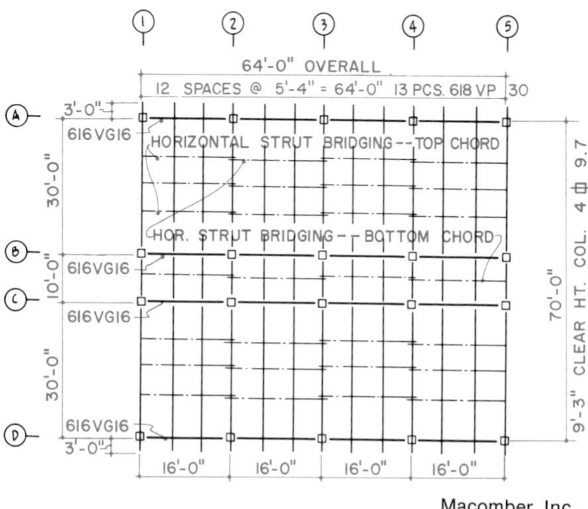

Macomber, Inc.

Fig. 57-54. Steel roof-framing plan areas are often identified by numbers and letters.

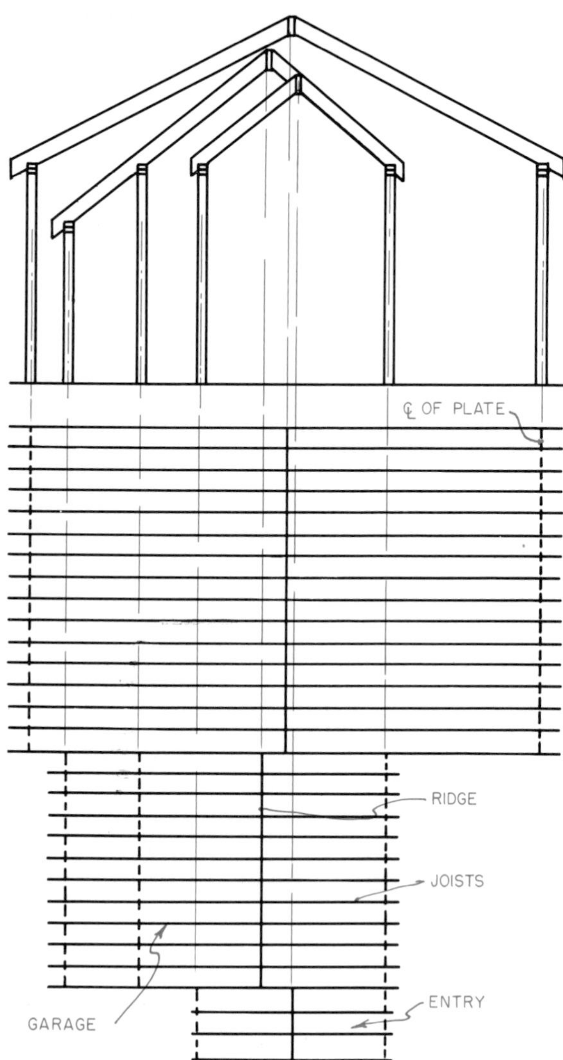

Fig. 57–55. A method of projecting roof-framing elevations.

ridge height, plate height. The transverse sections supply information of this type through one part of the structure. However, if a comparison of different heights and pitches is desired, a composite framing-elevation drawing should be prepared. This elevation can be projected from the roof-framing plan and corresponding lines on the elevation drawings, as shown in Fig. 57–55.

Dormer rafters and walls do not lie in the same plane as the remainder of the roof rafters. A framing-elevation drawing is therefore advantageous in illustrating the exact position of the dormer members and their tie-in with the common roof rafters. Figure 57–56 illustrates a side-framing elevation of an individual dormer and shows how it is structurally related to other roof-framing members. Figure 57–57 shows the side-wall framing of a shed dormer, in which the position of the dormer studs is revealed by the elevation drawing.

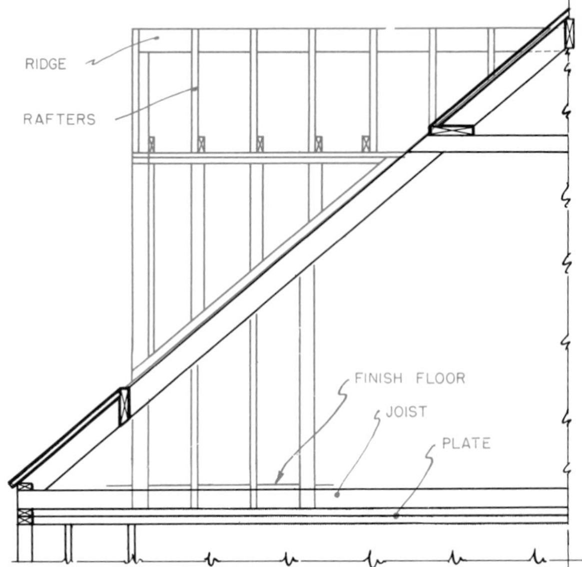

Fig. 57–56. A frame elevation of an individual dormer.

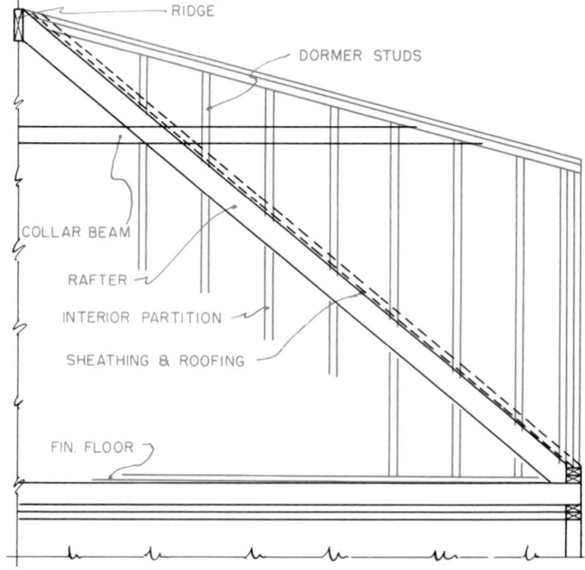

Fig. 57–57. A side-wall framing elevation of a shed dormer.

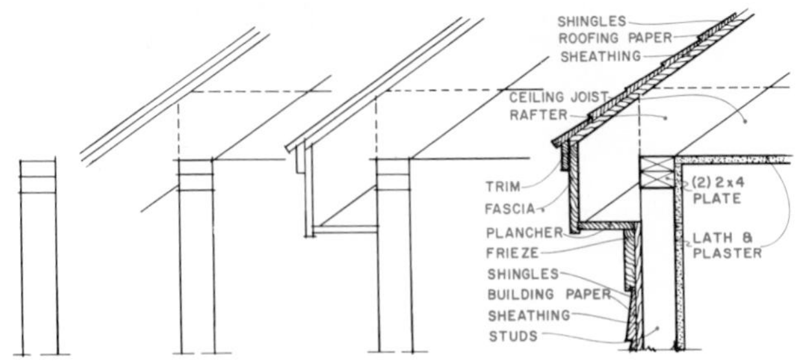

Fig. 57–58. Steps in laying out a cornice detail.

Parts of roof-framing elevations are actually parts of transverse sections. They are used to show the basic relationship between major framing members and the roof-covering and trim details. Figure 57–58 shows the steps in laying out one of the most widely used drawings of this type, a cornice detail. Other cornice details that show the relationship among roof-framing members and trim materials are shown in Fig. 57–59.

BEAMS

The beams are the major support of the roof. Many types of beams have been developed for light weight or more strength when compared to the solid beam (Fig. 57–60). The laminated beam or the built-up beam adds great strength (Fig. 57–61) and can be formed into graceful arches as shown in Fig. 57–62. Other shapes of laminated beams that can be produced are shown in Fig. 57–63.

The box beam offers lightness, low cost, and good supporting strength (Fig. 57–64). Figure 57–65 shows the use of the box beam in construction.

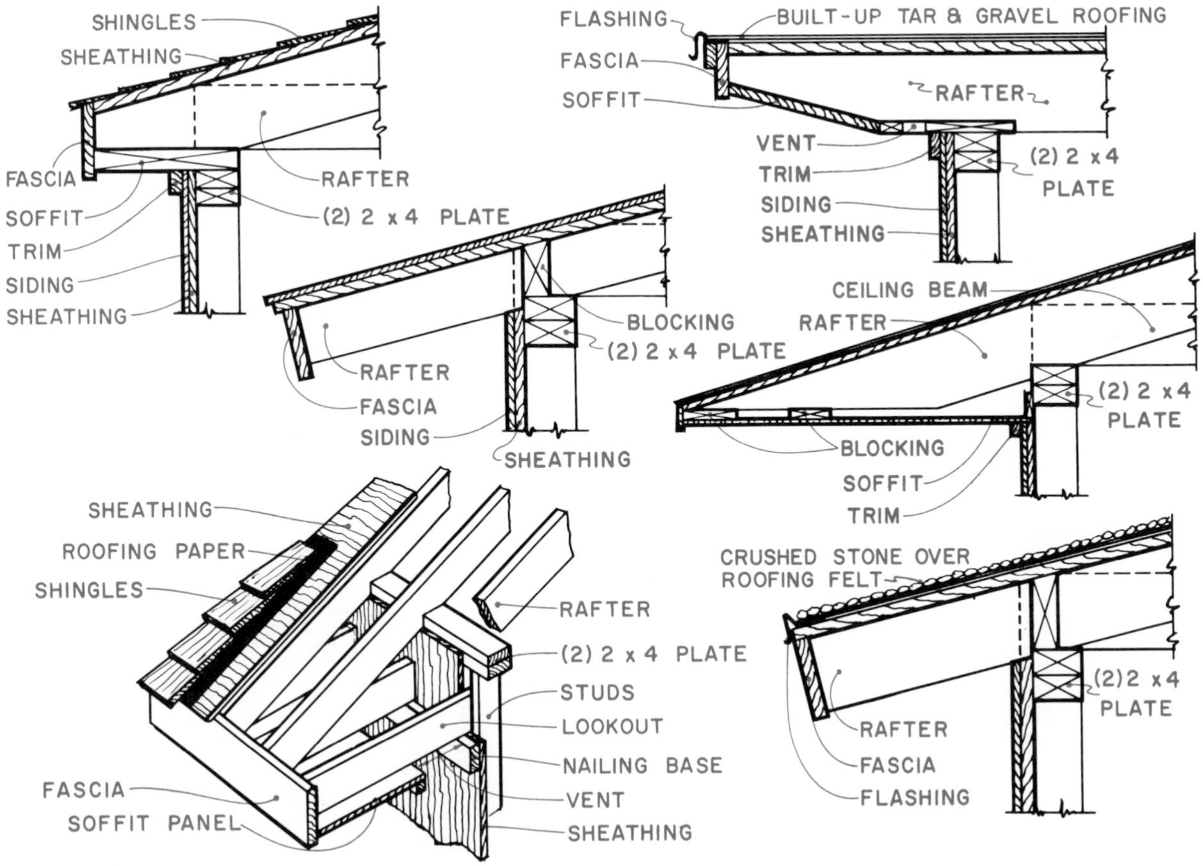

Fig. 57–59. Cornice-framing details.

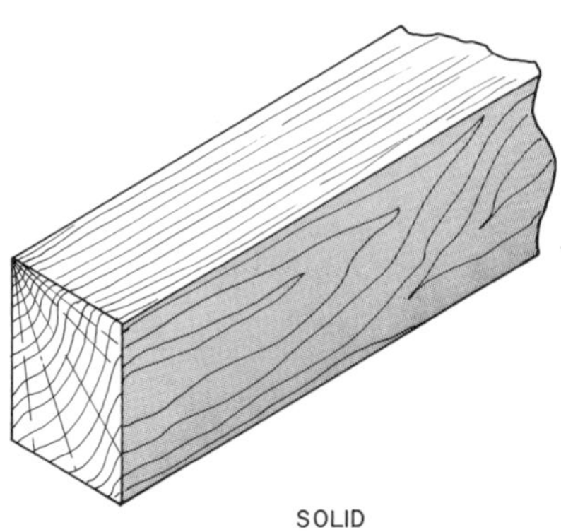

Fig. 57–60. A solid beam.

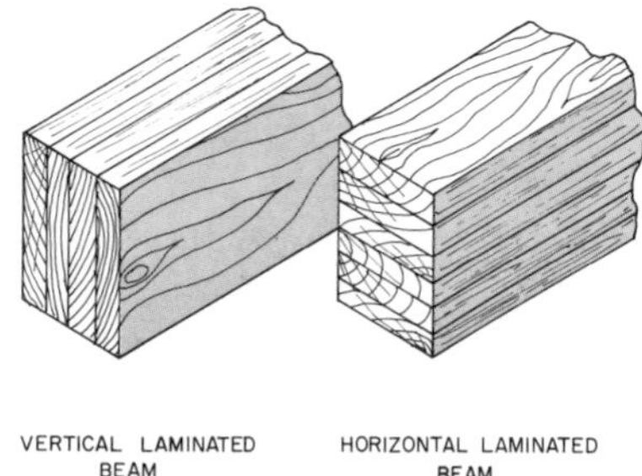

Fig. 57–61. Laminated beams.

Fig. 57–62. The use of specially formed laminated beams.

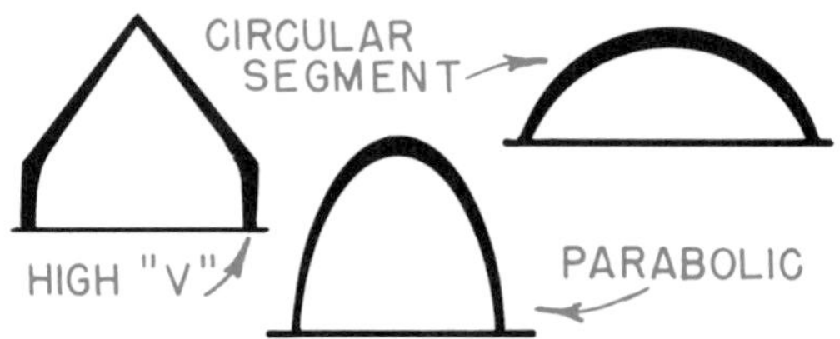

Fig. 57–63. Various shapes of laminated beams and arches.

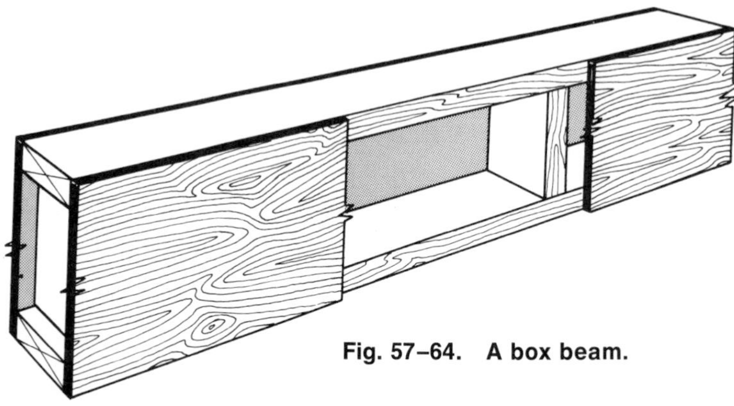

Fig. 57–64. A box beam.

American Plywood Association

Scholz Holmes, Inc.

Fig. 57–65. An example of the use of box beams.

The strongest of the built-up beams is the steel-reinforced beam (Fig. 57–66). It can support heavy weights and span long distances.

ROOF PANELS

Many forms of lightweight, prefabricated roof units have been developed. Some of the more commonly used units are described.

Stressed Skin Panels

Stressed skin panels are constructed of plywood and seasoned lumber. The simple framing and the plywood skin act as a unit to resist loads. Glued joints transmit the shear stresses, making it possible for the structure to act as one piece. Stressed skin panels (Fig. 57–67) are used in floors, walls, and roofs. Figure 57–68 shows the use of stressed skin panels in construction.

Fig. 57–66. Steel-reinforced beams.

Fig. 57–67. A stressed skin panel (below) and its application (above).

American Plywood Association

Fig. 57–68. Installing stressed skin panels.

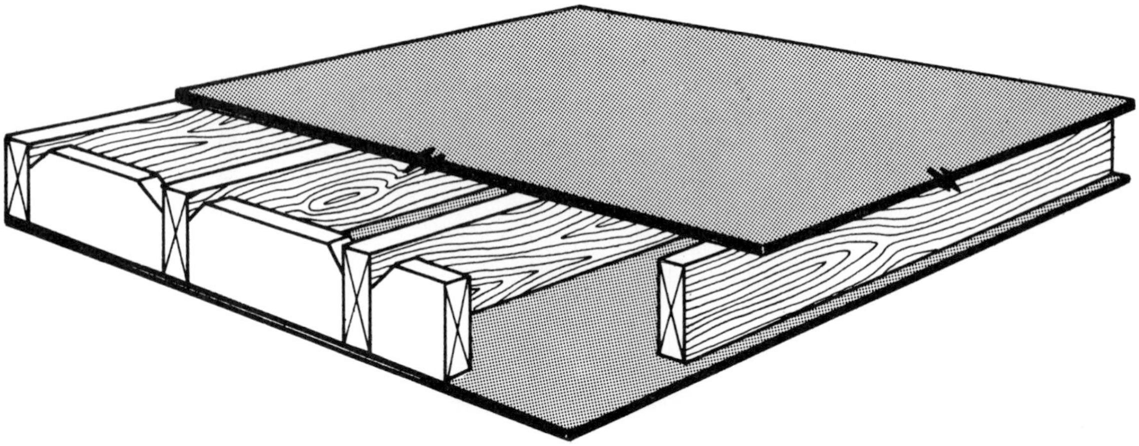

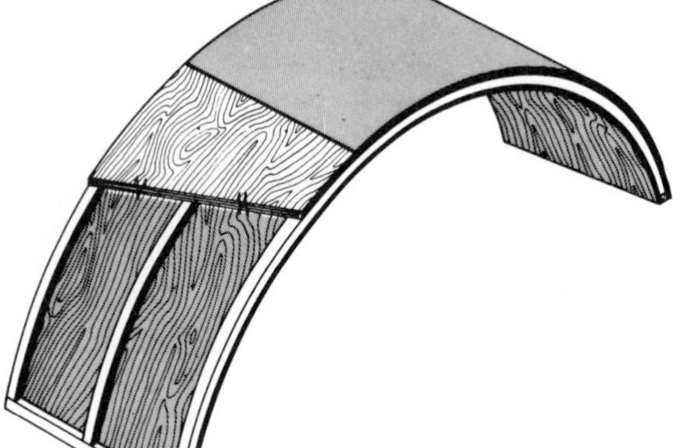

Fig. 57–69. Curved sandwich panels.

Curved Panels

Curved panels are constructed in three types: the sandwich, or honeycomb papercore, panel; the hollow-stressed end panel; and the solid-core panel. The arching action of these panels (Fig. 57–69) permits the spanning of great distances with a relatively thin cross section. Figure 57–70 shows the use of lightweight curved panels in construction.

American Plywood Association

Fig. 57–70. The use of curved panels.

Folded Plate Roofs

Folded plate roofs are thin skins of plywood reinforced by purlins to form shell structures that can utilize the strength of plywood. The use of folded plate roofs eliminates trusses and other roof members. The tilted plates lean against one another, acting as giant V-shaped beams supported by walls or columns.

Figure 57–71 shows the construction and use of lightweight folded plates, panels, and beams. Figure 57–72 shows the use of plywood to produce low-cost housing units that expand on site like an accordian. The designer calls this system *plydom*.

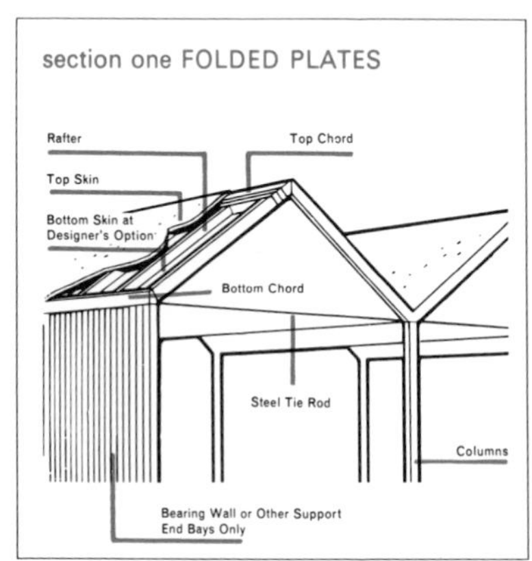

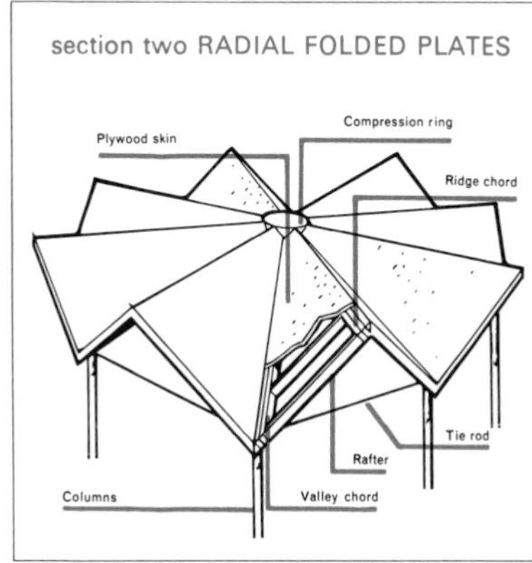

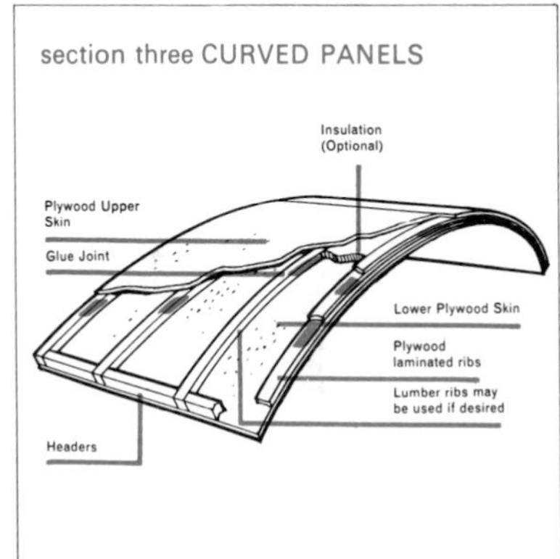

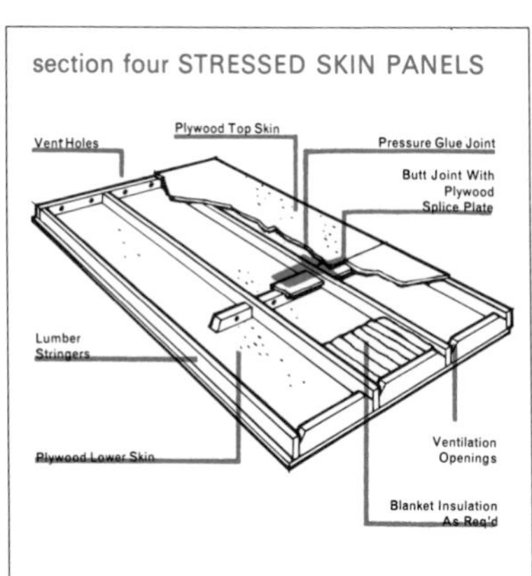

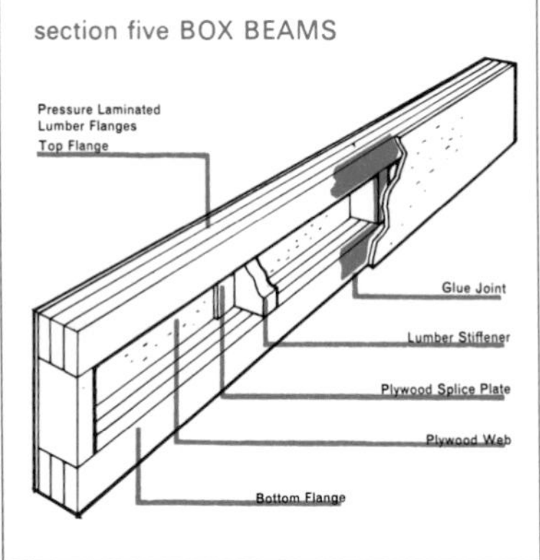

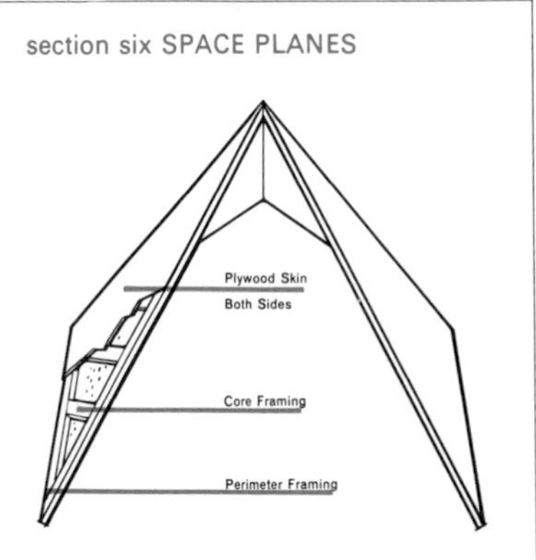

Douglas Fir Plywood Association

Fig. 57–71. Construction and use of lightweight wood components.

Hishen & Van Der Ryn, Architects

Fig. 57–72. Plywood housing units.

Fig. 57–73A. Structural equilibrium is possible with lightweight materials.

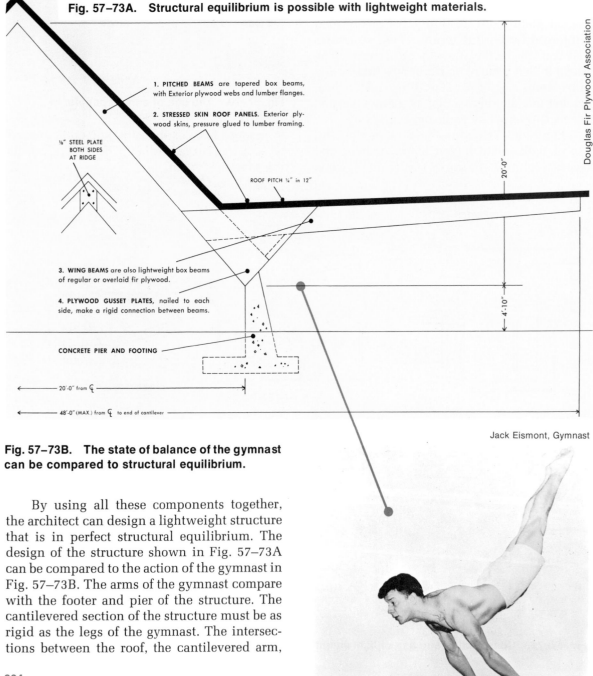

Douglas Fir Plywood Association

1. PITCHED BEAMS are tapered box beams, with Exterior plywood webs and lumber flanges.

2. STRESSED SKIN ROOF PANELS. Exterior plywood skins, pressure glued to lumber framing.

¼" STEEL PLATE BOTH SIDES AT RIDGE

ROOF PITCH ¼" in 12"

20'-0"

3. WING BEAMS are also lightweight box beams of regular or overlaid fir plywood.

4. PLYWOOD GUSSET PLATES, nailed to each side, make a rigid connection between beams.

4'-10"

CONCRETE PIER AND FOOTING

20'-0" from ℄

48'-0" (MAX.) from ℄ to end of cantilever

Jack Eismont, Gymnast

Fig. 57–73B. The state of balance of the gymnast can be compared to structural equilibrium.

By using all these components together, the architect can design a lightweight structure that is in perfect structural equilibrium. The design of the structure shown in Fig. 57–73A can be compared to the action of the gymnast in Fig. 57–73B. The arms of the gymnast compare with the footer and pier of the structure. The cantilevered section of the structure must be as rigid as the legs of the gymnast. The intersections between the roof, the cantilevered arm,

American Plywood Association

Fig. 57–74. The use of folded plates.

New York Telephone Co.

Fig. 57–75. The use of concrete to reduce radiation.

and the footer are all controlled and held in a state of equilibrium by plywood panels. These panels can be compared to the gymnast's shoulders, which keep him in a rigid, fixed position, falling neither forward nor backward. Figure 57–74 shows the use of lightweight folded plates.

CONCRETE

Pouring concrete into forms is certainly not new to the building industry. But the preparation of concrete building components away from the site is relatively new. The use of reinforced and prestressed concrete for floors, roofs, and walls, and the fabrication of concrete into shells account for an increase in the use of concrete as a building medium. For example, a New York Telephone Company building in Manhattan uses 10′ × 10′ (3 × 3 m) concrete slabs that are 1′ (0.3 m) thick to protect sensitive electronic equipment from the effects of radiation and other outside disturbances (Fig. 57–75).

Prestressed Concrete

When a beam carries a load it bends, and its center sags lower than the ends. The bottom fibers are stretched and the top fibers are compressed. Concrete can be prestressed to eliminate sag. In prestressing concrete, steel wires are strung through the concrete beam. The wires are stretched and anchored at the ends of the beam. When the concrete is hard, the protruding wires spring back to their original shape because the stress is relieved. This return to their original shape acts as a wedge to hold the wires bonded to the concrete. The wires inside are held under stress.

Prestressing can be compared to holding a row of blocks or books between your hands. As long as sufficient pressure can be exerted, as shown in Fig. 57–76, no sag can occur. The use of prestressed concrete prevents cracks because this concrete is always in compression. Prestressing permits less depth of beams as related to the span. Prestressed concrete has remarkable elastic properties and develops considerable resistance to shear stresses.

Precast Concrete

Precast concrete is concrete that has been poured into molds prior to its use in construction. When high stresses will not be incurred, precasting without prestressing will suffice.

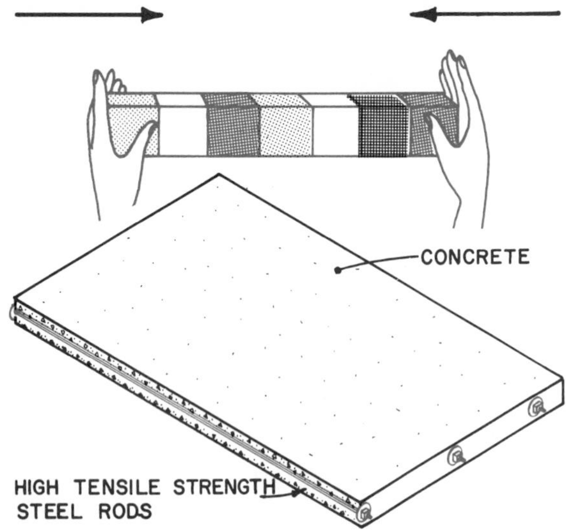

Fig. 57–76. The principle of prestressing concrete.

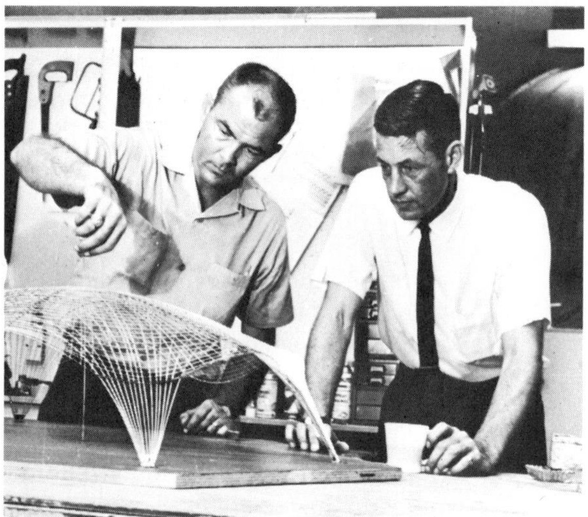

Texas A&M University; American Builder

Fig. 57–78. Model of the framework for a concrete-lift building.

Reinforced Concrete

Reinforced concrete is precast or poured-on-site concrete with steel reinforcing rods inserted for stability and rigidity. The rods are not placed under stress as are the wires in prestressed concrete. Reinforced concrete slabs are used extensively for floor systems where short spans make prestressing unnecessary.

Concrete Shells

Concrete shells are curved, thin sheets of concrete usually poured or sprayed on some material, such as steel rods, that provides temporary rigidity until the concrete hardens (Fig. 57–77). One of the latest innovations in the design and construction of concrete shells is the use of reinforcing mats that are laid flat on the ground. The structure is then lifted into the desired position, as shown in the model in Fig. 57–78. The mat is then sprayed with a coating of concrete, which holds the steel rods in place after the concrete solidifies. Concrete-shell construction is becoming increasingly popular in the design of air terminals, auditoriums, and gymnasiums (Fig. 57–79).

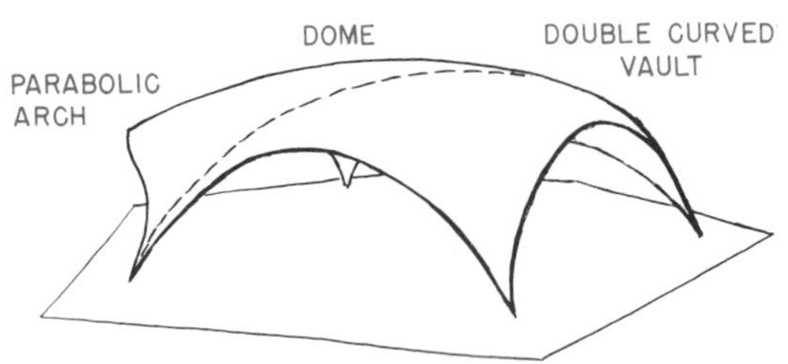

Fig. 57–77. A concrete shell.

Ezra Stoller; Raymond International, Inc.

Fig. 57–79. The concrete-shell construction used on the TWA Terminal at the John F. Kennedy International Airport.

Lightweight Concrete

New developments in concrete technology now enable the designer to specify lightweight concrete to be poured directly over a plywood base. The application of concrete, which has excellent acoustical properties, is extremely fast and relatively inexpensive.

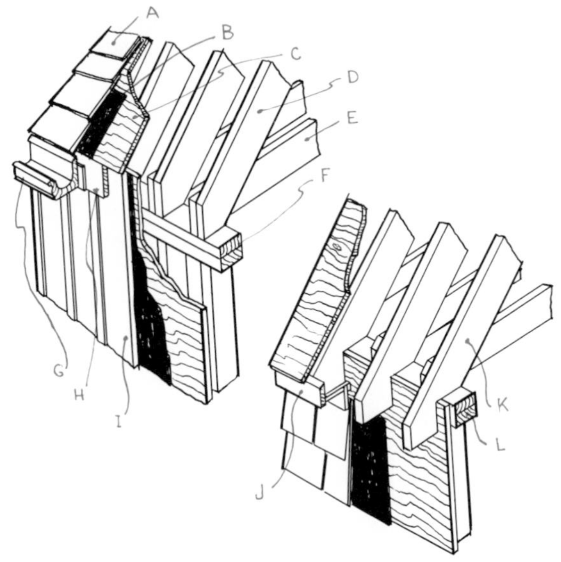

Fig. 57–80. Identify these roof-framing members.

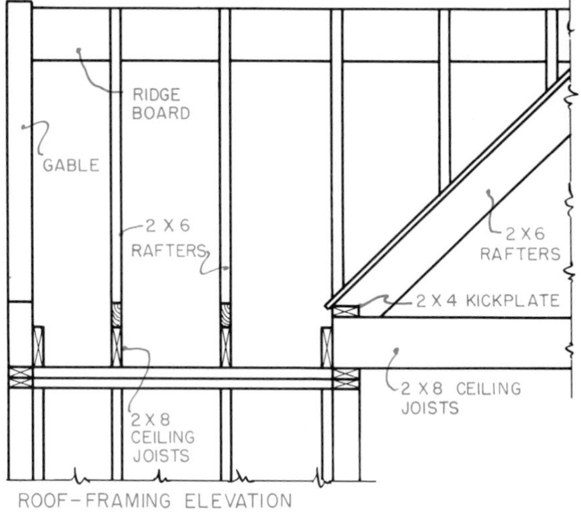

Fig. 57–81. Draw a roof-framing plan of this dormer.

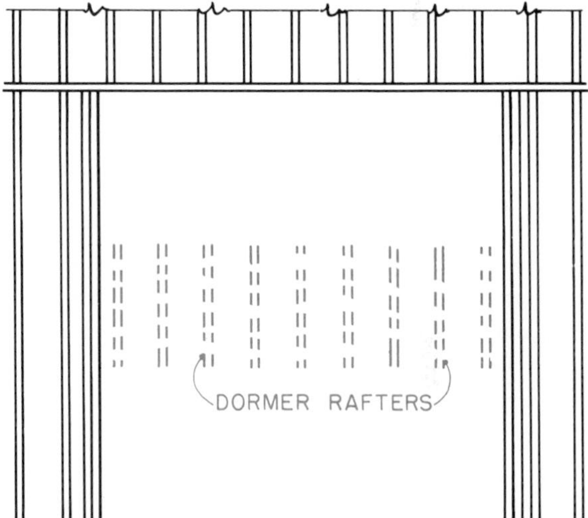

Fig. 57–82. Draw a framing elevation of this dormer.

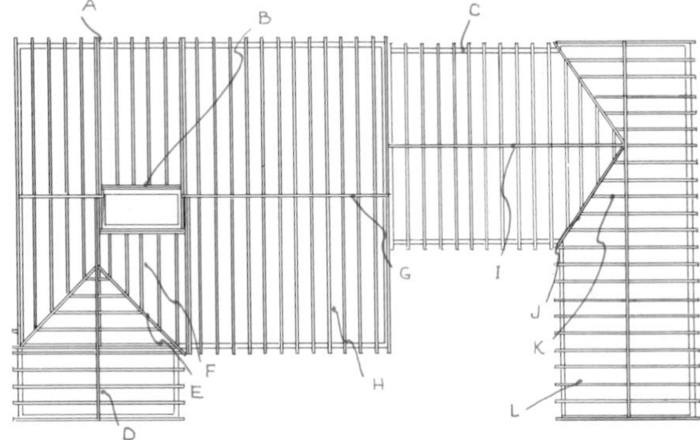

Fig. 57–83. Identify these roof-framing members.

PROBLEMS

1. Identify the roof-framing members shown in Fig. 57–80.
2. Draw a roof-framing plan for the dormer shown in the roof-framing elevation in Fig. 57–81. Use the dormer shown in Fig. 57–57 as a guide.
3. Draw a framing elevation of the dormer shown in Fig. 57–82. Use the dormer shown in Fig. 57–57 as a guide.
4. Identify the roof-framing members shown in Fig. 57–83.
5. Prepare a roof-framing plan for the house shown in Fig. 33–2. First prepare a roof plan for a gable roof or a hip roof and project the roof-framing plan from this.
6. Prepare a roof-framing plan for the house shown in Fig. 46–8.
7. Draw a roof-framing plan for the house shown in Fig. 67–12.
8. Prepare a roof-framing plan for your own house.
9. Prepare a roof-framing plan for a house of your own design.
10. Define the following terms: *wind load, snow load, bending moment, resisting moment, fiber stress, truss, transverse beam, gable end, rise, run, seat cut, collar beam, knee wall, valley, hip, cornice, jack, downspout, roof plan, roof-framing plan, dormer, bay.*

UNIT 58

Roof-Covering Materials

Roof covering protects the building from rain, snow, wind, heat, and cold. Materials used to cover pitched roofs include wood shingles, asphalt shingles, and asbestos shingles. On heavier roofs, tile or slate may also be used. Roll roofing or other sheet material, such as galvanized iron, aluminum, copper, and tin, may also be used for flat or low-pitched roofs. A built-up roof consisting of layers of roofing-felt covered with gravel topping may also be used on low-pitched or flat roofs. If a built-up roof is used on highpitched roofs, the gravel will weather off.

SHEATHING

Roof sheathing consists of 1 × 6 lumber or plywood nailed directly to the roof rafters. Sheathing adds rigidity to the roof and provides a surface for the attachment of waterproofing materials. In humid parts of the country, sheathing boards are sometimes spaced slightly apart to provide ventilation and to prevent shingle rot.

ROLL ROOFING

Roll roofing may be used as an *underlayment* for shingles or as a finished roofing material (Fig. 58–1). Roll roofing used as an underlayment includes asphalt and saturated felt. The underlayment serves as a barrier against moisture and wind. Mineral surface and selvage roll-roofing can be used as the final roofing surface.

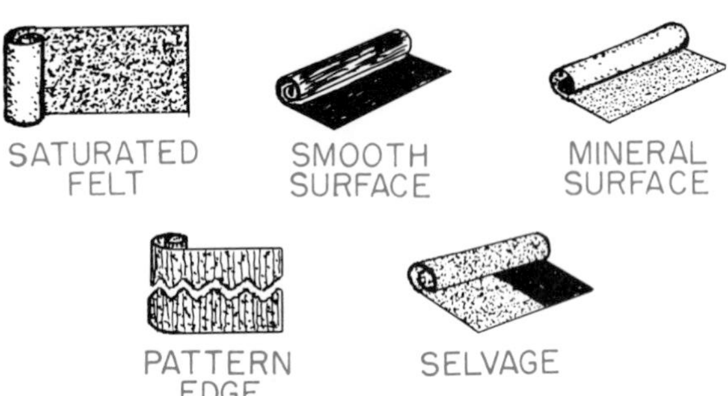

Fig. 58–1. Types of roll roofing.

WEIGHT

The weight of roofing materials is important in computing dead loads. A heavier roofing surface makes the roof more permanent than does a lighter surface. Generally, heavier roofing materials last longer than lighter materials. Therefore, heavy roofing, such as strip or individual shingles, is superior. Roof-covering materials are classified by their weight per 100 square feet (100 square feet equals 1 *square*). Thus 30-pound roofing-felt weighs 30 pounds per 100 square feet. Although metric identification has not become standard it would be easy to convert the classification to kilograms per square meter.

SHINGLES

Shingles are commonly made from asphalt, asbestos, wood, tile, and slate and are available in a variety of patterns and shapes. Shingles and underlayment are overlapped when applied, as shown in Fig. 58–2. Shingles are best for pitches steeper than 4/12. For pitches less than 4/12, roll roofing is better. Shingles may be laid flat or, if extra shingles are added, patterns may be produced (Fig. 58–3).

BUILT-UP ROOFS

Built-up roof coverings are used on flat or extremely low-pitched roofs. Because rain or snow may not be immediately expelled from these roofs, complete waterproofing is essential. Built-up roofs may have three, four, or five layers of roofing-felt, sealed with tar or asphalt,

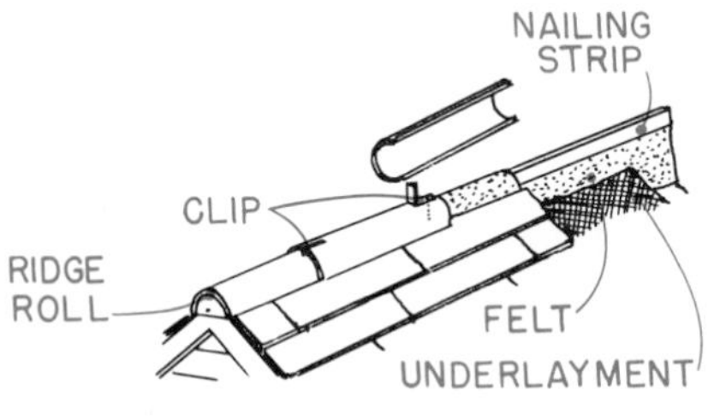

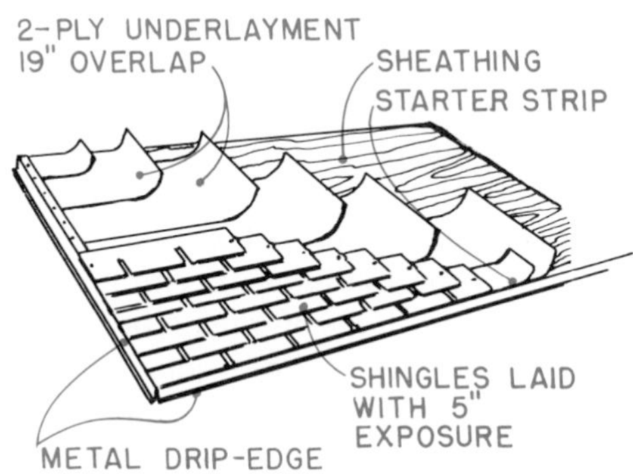

Fig. 58–2. Methods of shingle application.

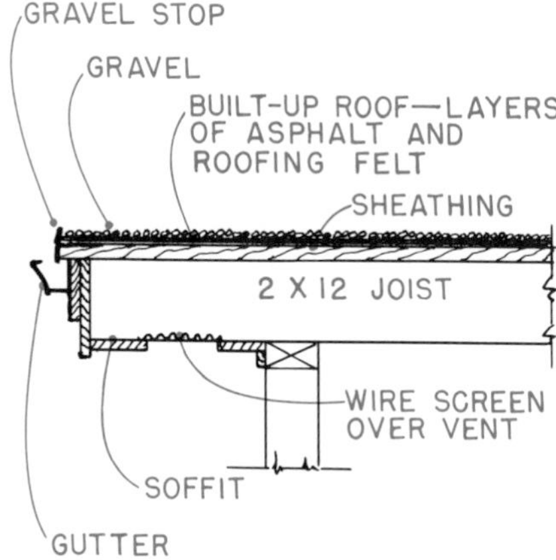

Fig. 58–4. Built-up roof construction.

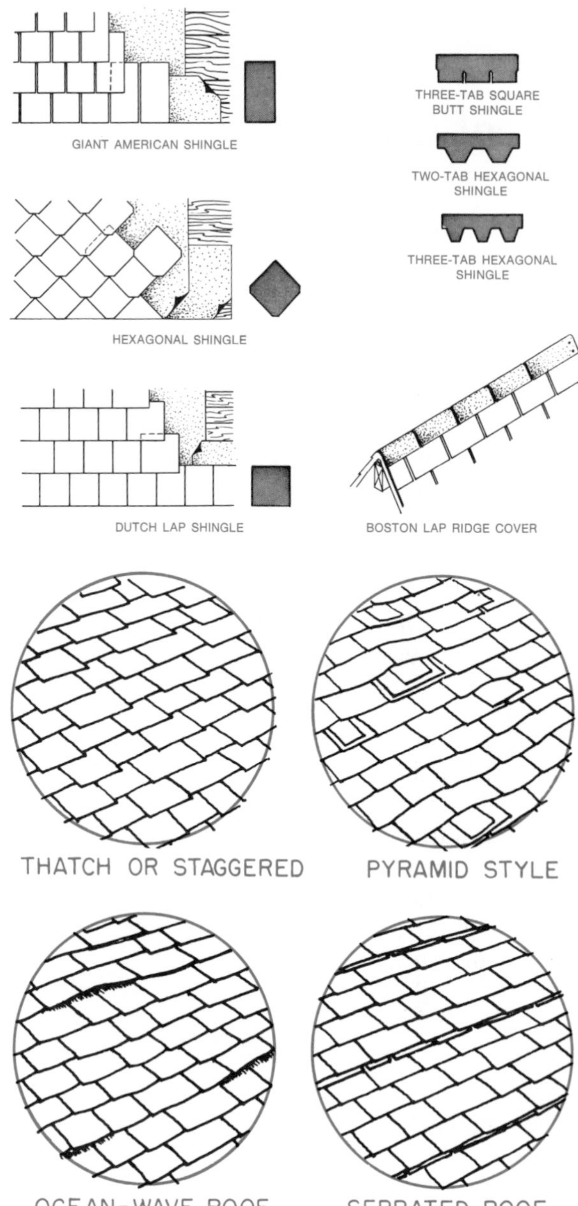

Fig. 58–3. Shingle patterns.

between each two coatings. The final layer of tar or asphalt is then covered with roofing gravel or a top sheet of roll roofing (Fig. 58–4).

FLASHING

Joints where roof-covering materials intersect at the ridge, hip, valley, chimney, and parapet joints must be flashed. *Flashing* is additional

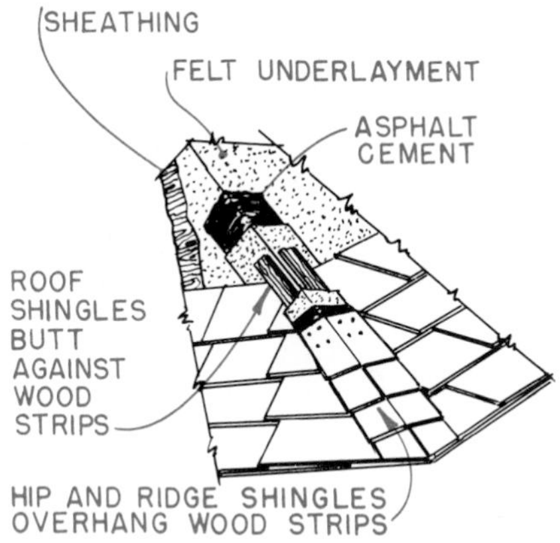

Fig. 58–5. One method of flashing corners.

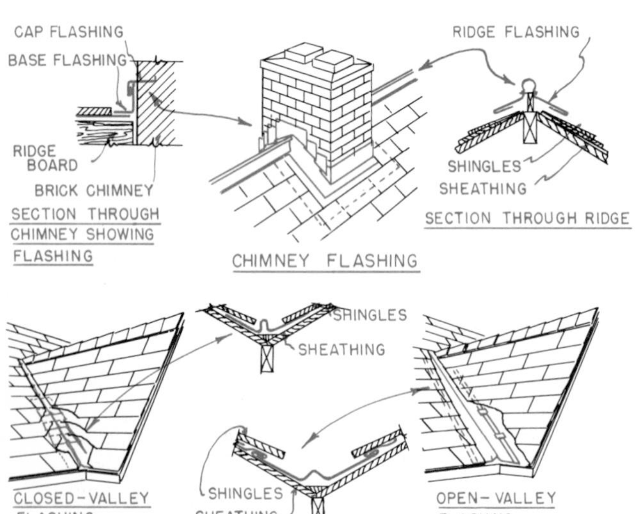

Fig. 58–6. Application of sheet-metal flashing.

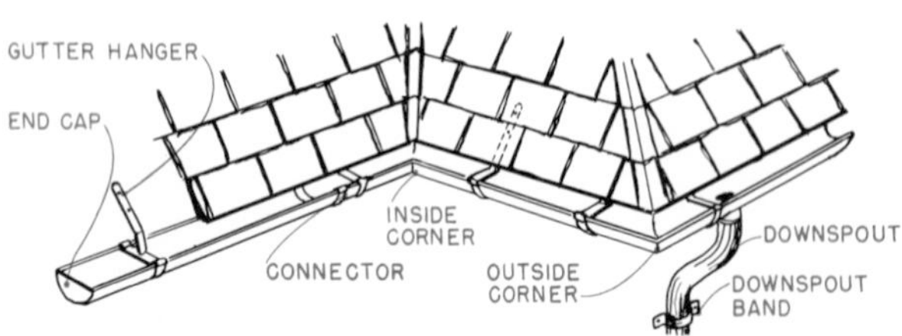

Fig. 58–7. Gutter-assembly terminology.

covering used on a joint to provide complete waterproofing. Roll-roofing shingles or sheet metal is used as the flashing material. For flashing hip and valley joints, shingle flashing is best; it may be attached by nails to wood strips applied over asphalt, cement, and felt underlayment (Fig. 58–5).

When sheet-metal flashing is used, watertight sheet-metal joints should be used, as shown in Fig. 58–6. Chimney flashing is frequently bonded into the mortar joint and under shingles and is caulked to provide completely waterproof joints.

GUTTERS

Gutters are troughs designed to carry water to the downspouts, where it can be emptied into the sewer system (Fig. 58–7). The two materials used most commonly for gutters are sheet metal and wood such as red cedar and redwood (Fig. 58–8). Gutters may be built into the roof structure, as shown in the fascia-board gutter and the pole gutter in Fig. 58–9. Gutters may be made of additional sheet metal or wood attached or hung from the fascia board. All gutters should be pitched sufficiently to provide for drainage to the downspout. In selecting gutters and downspouts, care must be taken to ensure that their size is adequate for the local rainfall.

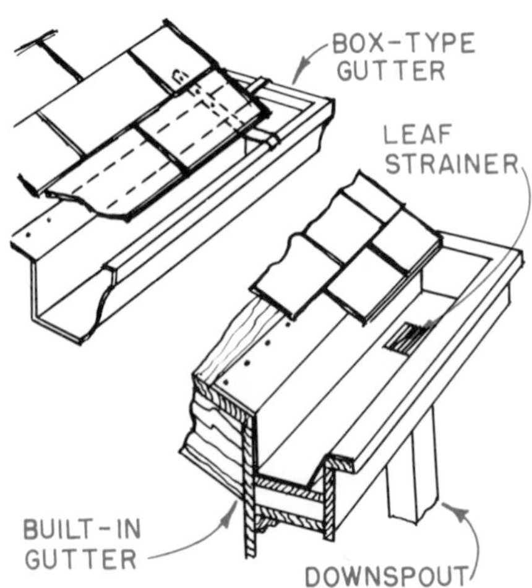

Fig. 58–8. Common types of gutters.

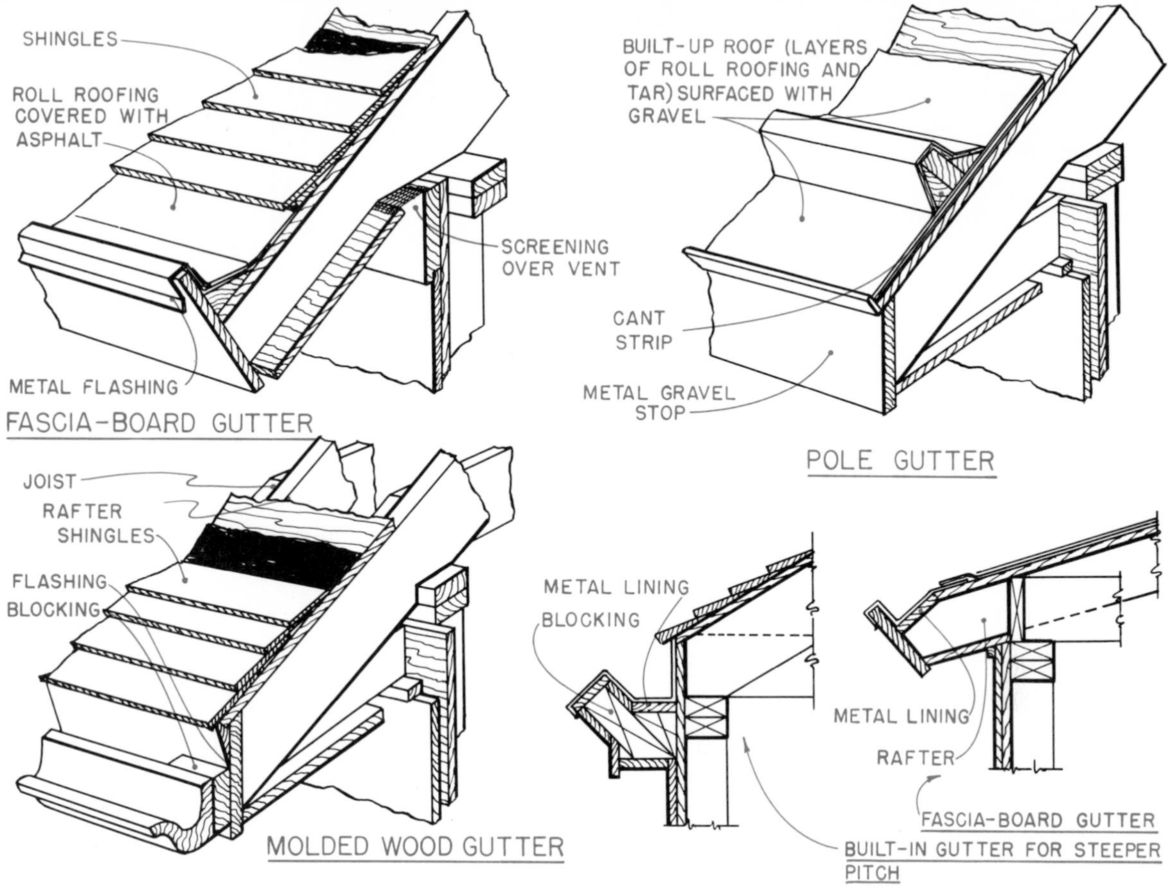

Fig. 58–9. Built-in gutters.

SUN SCREENS

The design of the roof overhang must be sufficient to provide complete protection from the direct rays of the sun. Such protection is especially important in large areas such as patio and porches. The basic problem is to block the direct rays of the sun without impairing the illumination. Often a completely solid covering would produce an area so dark that the advantages of outdoor living would be eliminated. The sunshade shown on the building in Fig. 58–10 does not completely block illumination from the window or obstruct the view. It does block the direct rays of the sun from reaching the window.

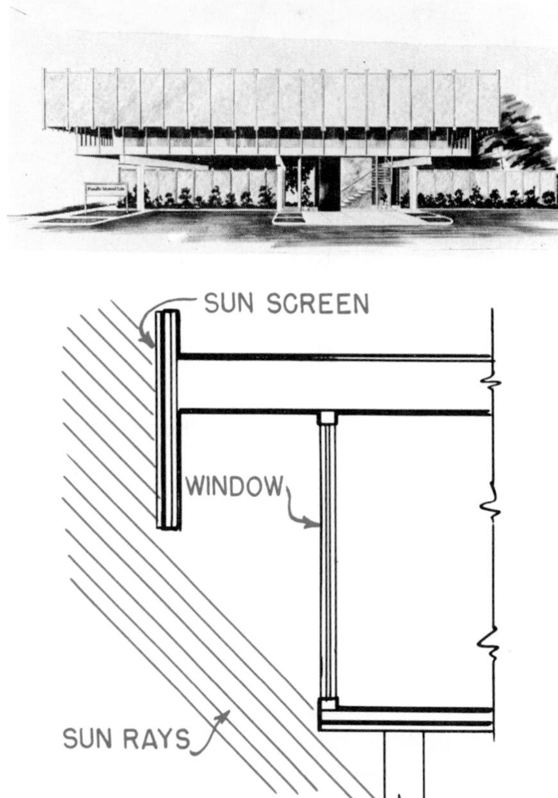

Fig. 58–10. An effective sun-screening device.

On many patios it is desirable to admit the rays of the sun when it is high and block the rays of the sun when it is lower in the sky. To accomplish this, the angle of the sun should be measured at several times during the day. The spacing and angle of louvers are then set to block the rays at the appropriate time (Fig. 58–11). There are many methods that can be used to construct sun shields of this type (Fig. 58–12). Louvers placed only in one direction will block the rays of the sun from the side perpendicular to the louvers. Louvers placed in egg-crate patterns will block the rays of the sun at all angles.

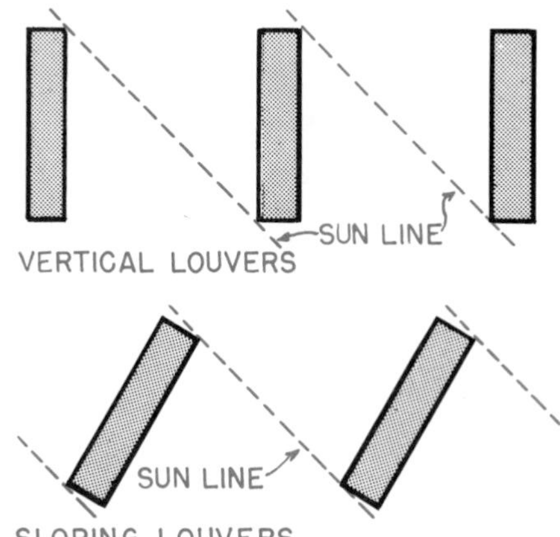

Fig. 58–11. The angle and spacing of louvers is important in sun screening.

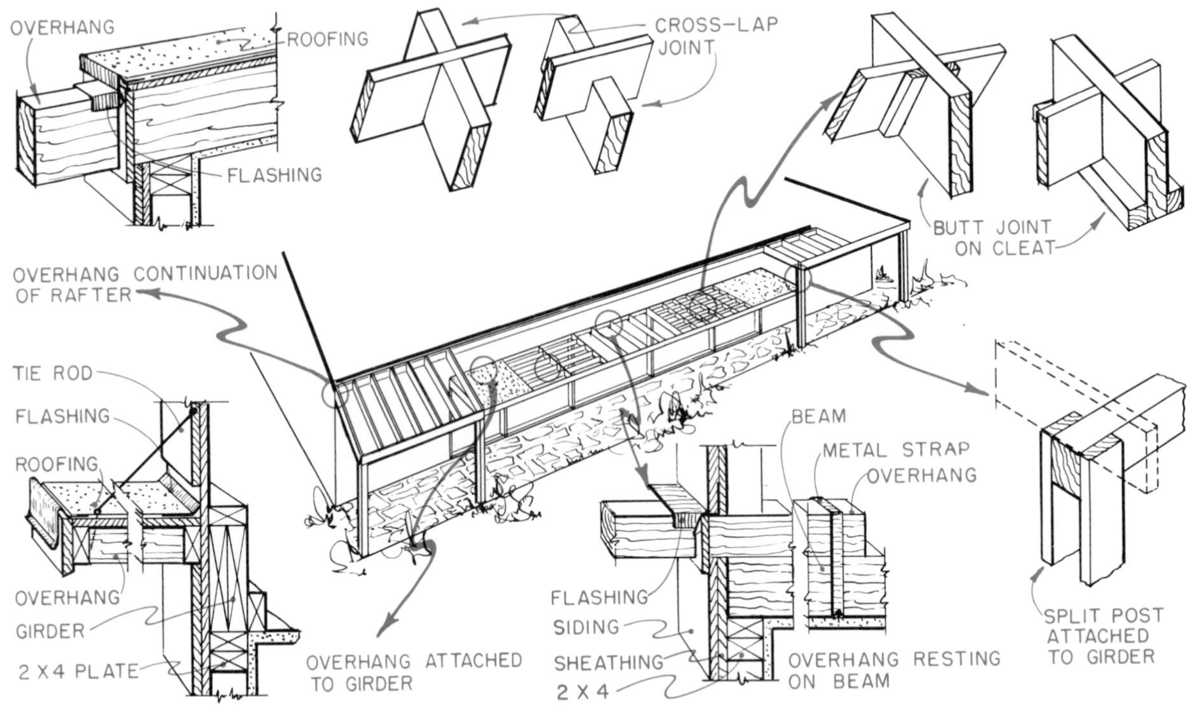

Fig. 58–12. There are many methods of screening out the sun's rays.

PROBLEMS

1. **Name three types of roll roofing suitable for finished roof covering.**
2. **Name two types of roll roofing suitable for underlayment.**
3. **Name three shingle patterns.**
4. **Name the materials used in a built-up roof.**
5. **Design a sun screen for the house shown in Fig. 10–9.**
6. **Define these terms: *roof sheathing, roll roofing, slate, shingles, underlayment, square, roofing-felt, flashing, pole gutter, fascia board, louvers.***

SECTION 13

Electrical Plans

Electricity is the major source of energy for the home. Electricity cooks, washes, cleans, heats, air-conditions, lights, preserves, and entertains. But the finest home is not practical if the wiring is not adequate to bring power to the appliances and lighting fixtures. The most important problem in planning the electrical wiring system is to keep up with all the new requirements for energy.

UNIT 59

Lighting

Planning for adequate lighting involves the eyes, the object, and the light (Fig. 59–1). Planning to light the home involves three questions: How much light is needed? What is the best quality of light? How should this light be distributed? Whether planning lighting for a large commercial building, as shown in Fig. 59–2, or for a residence, the same design factors must be considered.

Fig. 59–1. Lighting needs vary according to three factors.

TYPES OF LIGHT

Candles and oil and natural gas lamps were once the major sources of light. Today's major source of light in the home comes from the incandescent lamp and the fluorescent lamp.

Incandescent Lighting

The use of incandescent lamps is shown in Fig. 59–3. A filament inside the bulb provides a small, concentrated glow of light when an electric current heats the filament to the glowing point. Following are some of the many types of incandescent bulbs:

Inside-frosted bulbs to spread out the light

White bulbs for softer light for exposed bulbs

Silver-bowl bulbs that direct the light upward

Outdoor projector bulbs for spotlight or floodlight

Haigh Jamgochian, Architect

Fig. 59–2. Commercial lighting.

Colored bulbs for decorative effects
Sun-lamp bulbs for sun tanning
Infrared bulbs for instant heat
Reflector bulbs that are used to display with a spot or floodlight
Outdoor yellow bulbs that do not attract insects
Night-light bulbs

Fluorescent Lighting

Fluorescent lamps (Fig. 59–4) give an unbroken line of light, a uniform glareless light which is ideal for large working areas. Fluorescent lamps give more light per watt than incandescent lamps and last as much as seven times longer.

Fig. 59–4. An example of the use of fluorescent lighting.

Consoweld Corp.

Fig. 59–3. Uses of incandescent lighting.

In the fluorescent lamp, current flows through mercury vapor and activates the light-giving properties of the coating inside the tube.

LIGHT MEASUREMENTS

You can read in bright sunlight or in a dimly lit room because your eyes are adaptable to varying intensities of light (Fig. 59–5). However, you must be given enough time to adjust slowly to different light levels. Sudden extreme changes of light cause great discomfort.

Light is measured in customary units called *footcandles*. A footcandle is equal to the amount of light a candle throws on an object 1′ away (Fig. 59–6). Ten footcandles equal the amount of light that 10 candles throw on a surface 1′ away. A 75-watt bulb provides 30 footcandles of light at a distance of 3′. It provides 20 footcandles at a distance of 6′.

In the metric system the standard unit of illumination is the *lux* (lx). One lux is equal to 0.093 footcandles. To convert footcandles to lux, multiply by 10.764.

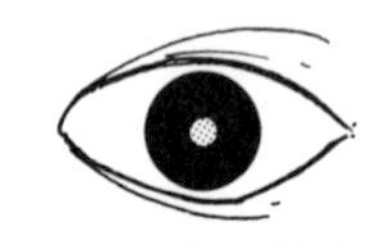

LOW LIGHT LEVEL HIGH LIGHT LEVEL

Fig. 59–5. Eyes will adjust to extreme intensities of light.

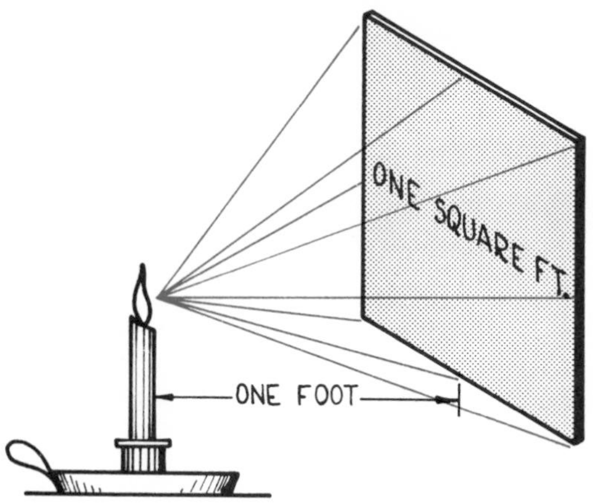

Fig. 59–6. One footcandle of light (candela) is equal to the amount of light thrown on a surface 1 foot away.

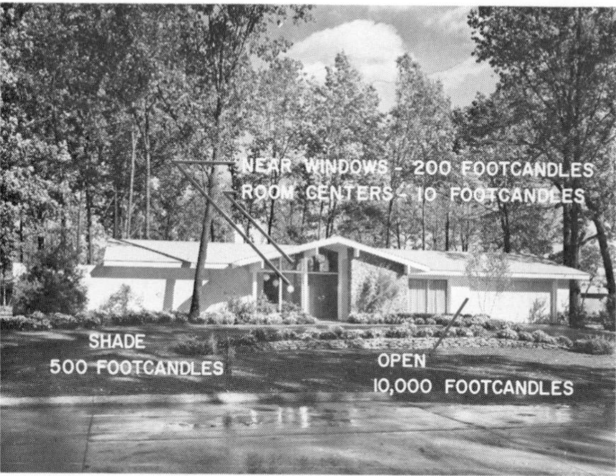

Scholz Homes, Inc.

Fig. 59–7. Light distribution on a sunny day.

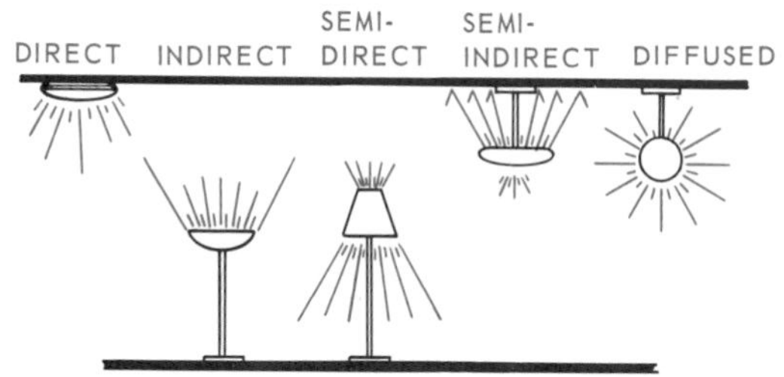

Fig. 59–8. Methods of light dispersement.

On a clear summer day the sun delivers 10 000 footcandles (107 640 lx) of light to the earth (Fig. 59–7). This is found at the beaches and in open fields. In the shade of a tree there will be 1000 footcandles (10 764 lx). In the shade on an open porch there will be 500 footcandles (5382 lx). Inside the house a few feet from the window there will be 200 footcandles (2153 lx); and in the center of the house, 10 footcandles (108 lx).

Accepted light levels for various living activities are as follows:

10 to 20 footcandles (108 to 215 lx): casual visual tasks, card playing, conversation, television, listening to music

20 to 30 footcandles (215 to 320 lx): easy reading, sewing, knitting, house cleaning

30 to 50 footcandles (320 to 540 lx): reading newspapers, doing kitchen and laundry work, typing

50 to 70 footcandles (540 to 750 lx): prolonged reading, machine sewing, hobbies, homework

70 to 200 footcandles (750 to 2150 lx): prolonged detailed tasks such as fine sewing, reading fine print, drafting

DISPERSAL OF LIGHT

After the necessary amount of light is known, the method of spreading, or dispersing, the light through the rooms must be determined.

Types of Lighting

There are five types of lighting dispersement (Fig. 59–8): direct, indirect, semidirect, semi-indirect, and diffused. *Direct* light shines directly on an object from the light source. *Indirect* light is reflected from large surfaces. *Semidirect* light shines mainly down as direct light, but a small portion of it is directed upward as indirect light. *Diffused* light is spread evenly in all directions.

Reflectance

All objects absorb and reflect light. Some white surfaces reflect 94 percent of the light. Some black surfaces reflect 2 percent of the light. The rest of the light is absorbed. The proper amount of reflectance is obtained by the color and type of finish. The amounts of reflectance that are recommended are from 60 percent to 90 per-

Potlach Corp.

Fig. 59–9A. The use of a skylight.

Southern California Edison

Fig. 59–9B. The use of translucent panels.

cent for the ceiling, from 35 to 60 percent for the walls, and from 15 to 35 percent for the floor.

All surfaces in a room will act as a secondary source of light when the light is reflected. Glare can be eliminated from this secondary source of light by having a dull, or matte, finish on surfaces and by avoiding strong beams of light and strong contrasts of light. Eliminating excessive glare is essential in designing adequate lighting.

LIGHTING METHODS

Good lighting in a home depends upon three methods. *General lighting* spreads an even, low-level light throughout a room. *Specific (local) lighting* directs light to an area used for a specific visual task. *Decorative lighting* makes use of lights to develop different moods and to accent objects for interest.

General lighting

General lighting is achieved by direct or indirect methods of light dispersement, as shown in Fig. 59–8. In addition to artificial general light sources, skylights as shown in Fig. 59–9A can be used to admit light during the day. If the skylight is covered with translucent panels, it can contain an artificial light source, usually fluorescent, for nighttime use (Fig. 59–9B). General light can also be produced by many portable lamps, ceiling fixtures, or long lengths of light on the walls (Fig. 59–10). In the living and sleeping areas, the intensity of general lighting should be between 5 and 10 footcandles (54 to 108 lx) A higher level of general lighting should be used in the service area and bathrooms.

Specific Lighting

Specific (local) lighting (Fig. 59–11A) for a particular visual task is directed into the area in which the task will be done. The specific light in a room will add to the general lighting level. Figure 59–11B shows the use of specific lighting in a den.

Decorative Lighting

Decorative lighting (Fig. 59–12) is used for atmosphere and interest when activities do not require much light. Bright lights are stimu-

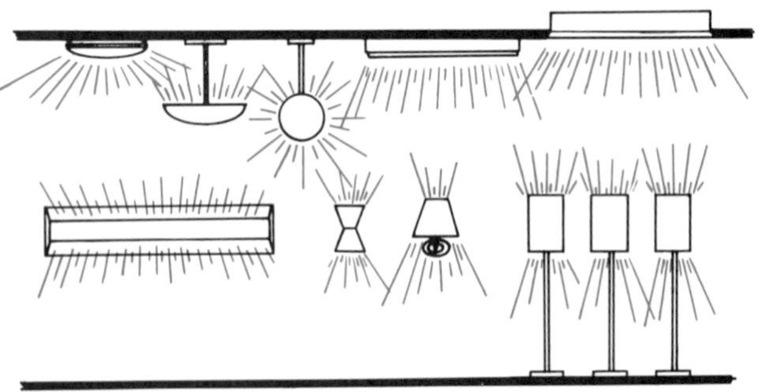

Fig. 59–10. Types of general lighting.

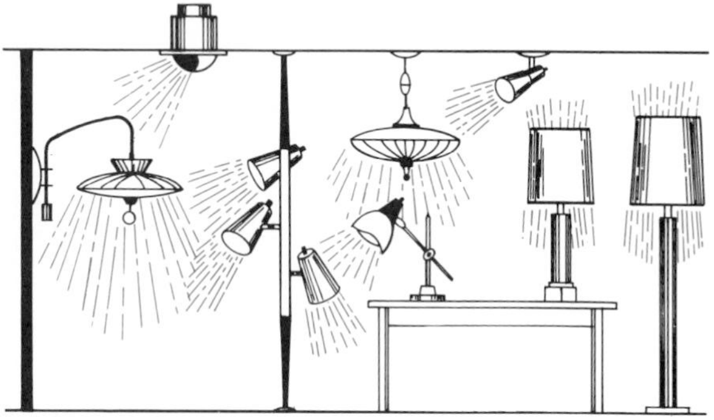

Fig. 59–11A. Types of specific lighting.

Fig. 59–11B. Specific lighting.

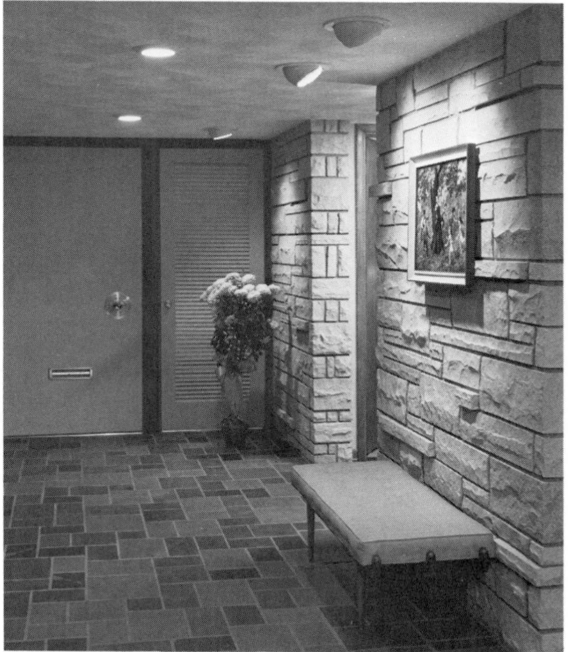

General Electric Company

Fig. 59–12. Decorative lighting.

lating; low levels of lighting are quieting. Decorative lighting strives for unusual effects. Some of these can be obtained with candlelight, lights behind draperies, lights under planters, lights in the bottoms of ponds, controlled lights with a dimmer switch, and different types of cover materials over floor lights and spotlights.

ELECTRICAL FIXTURES

The average two-bedroom home should have between 24 and 35 light fixtures (Fig. 59–13). It should also have from 16 to 20 floor, table, or wall lamps. Yet most homes average only one-third of the fixtures they should have for quality lighting.

Light fixtures fall into three groups: ceiling fixtures (Fig. 59–14), wall fixtures (Fig. 59–15), and portable plug-ins (Fig. 59–16).

A *valance* is a covering over a long source of light over a window. Its light illuminates the wall and draperies for the spacious effect that daylight gives a room.

A *wall bracket* balances the light of a valance. It gives an upward and downward wash of light difficult to obtain on an inner wall.

A *cornice* is attached to the wall and can be used with or without drapes. All light from this fixture is directed downward, to give an impression of height to the room.

Lamps provide light needed for a seeing task. The bottom of the shade must be below the level of the eyes doing the visual task (Fig. 59–17). The source of light for a lamp should be a short distance at one side of the work area.

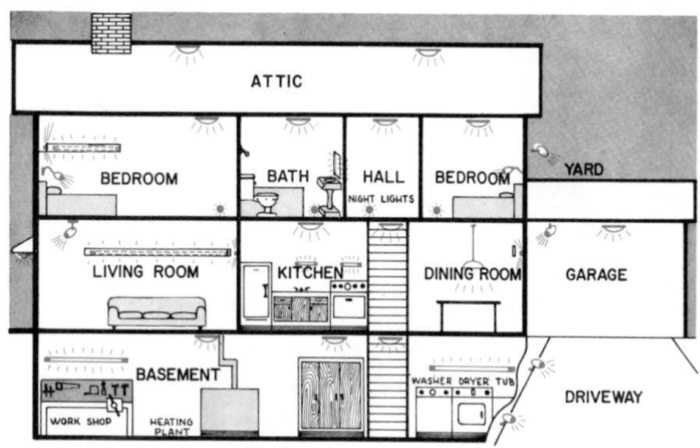

Fig. 59–13. Locations of lighting fixtures throughout the home.

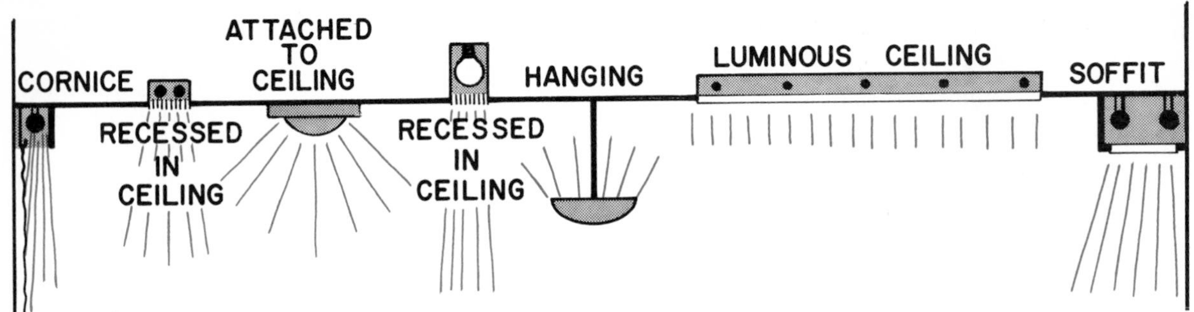

Fig. 59–14. Examples of ceiling fixtures.

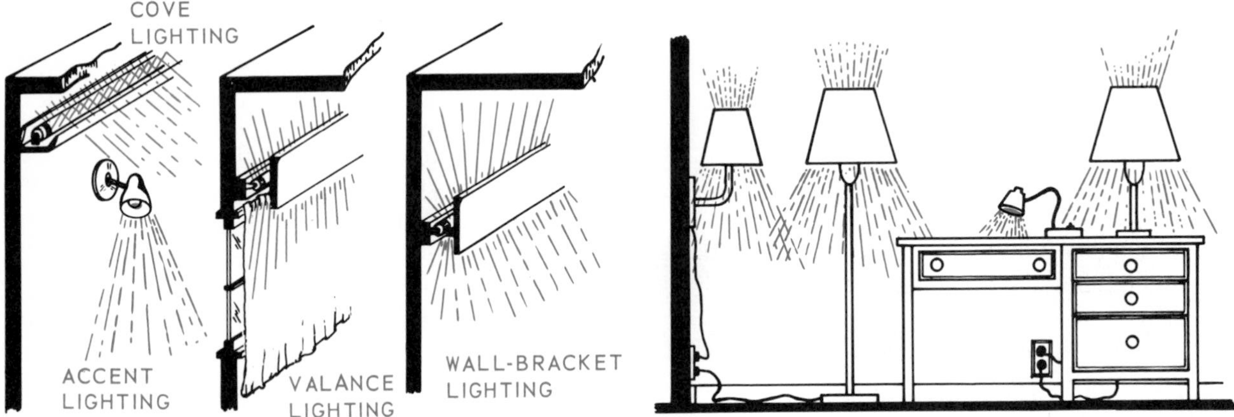

Fig. 59–15. Examples of wall fixtures.

Fig. 59–16. Examples of portable plug-in lamps.

Fig. 59–17. The bottom of a lamp shade should be lower than the eyes.

General Electric Company

Fig. 59–18. Kitchen lighting.

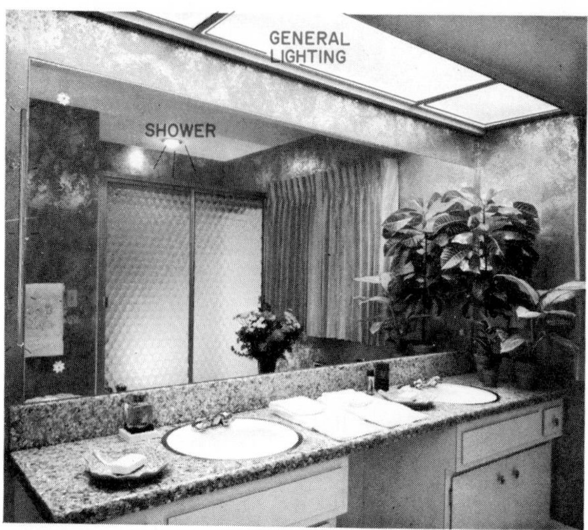

General Electric Company

Fig. 59–19. Bathroom lighting.

Armstrong Cork Company

Fig. 59–20. Living-room lighting.

ILLUMINATION PLANNING

Following are general rules to observe when planning the lighting of each room.

The kitchen (Fig. 59–18) requires a high level of general lighting from ceiling fixtures. Specific lighting for all work areas—range, sink, tables, and counters—is also recommended.

The bathroom (Fig. 59–19) requires a high level of general lighting from ceiling fixtures. The shower and water closet, if compartmented, should have a recessed, vaporproof light. The mirror should have lights on two sides.

The living room (Fig. 59–20) requires a low level of general lighting but should have specific lighting for areas for reading and other visual tasks. Decorative lighting should be used.

The bedroom (Fig. 59–21) requires a low level of general lighting but should have specific lighting for reading in bed and on both sides of the dressing-table mirror. The dressing area requires a high level of general lighting. Children's bedrooms require a high level of general lighting. Closets should have a fixture placed high at the front.

The dining area (Fig. 59–22) requires a low level of general lighting, with local lighting over the dining table.

Armstrong Cork Company

Fig. 59–21. Bedroom and den lighting.

Fig. 59–22. Dining-room lighting.

Thomas Industries, Inc.

Fig. 59–23A. Entry lighting.

Fig. 59–23B. Foyer lighting.

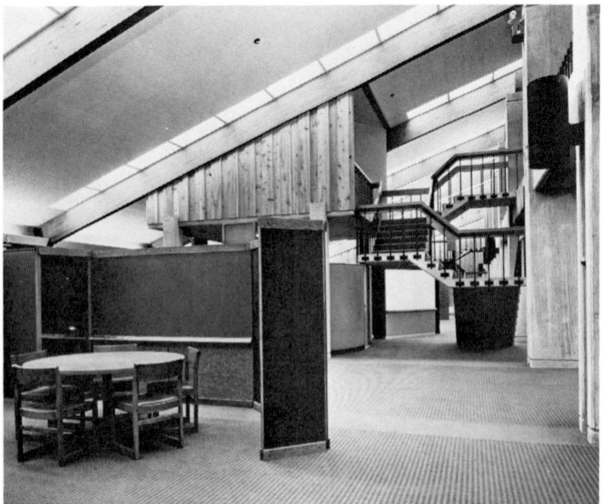

Armstrong Cork Company

Fig. 59–24. Traffic-area lighting.

General Electric Company

Fig. 59–25. Lighting for reading and studying.

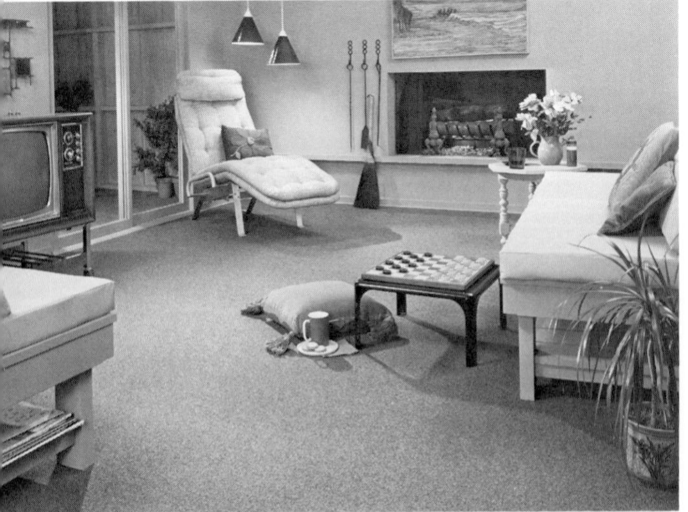

Armstrong Cork Company

Fig. 59–26. Lighting for television viewing.

The entrance and foyer (Figs. 59–23A and B) require a high level of general and decorative lighting.

Traffic areas (Fig. 59–24) require a high level of general lighting for safety.

Reading and desk areas require a high level of general light and specific light that is diffused and glareless. There should be no shadows (Fig. 59–25).

Television viewing (Fig. 59–26) requires a very low level of general lighting. Television should not be viewed in the dark because the strong contrast of dark room and bright screen is tiring to the eyes.

Outdoor lighting (Fig. 59–27) is accomplished by waterproof floodlights and spotlights. Extensive outdoor lighting will provide convenience, beauty, and safety. Areas which

Scholz Homes, Inc.

Fig. 59–27. Outdoor lighting.

Simpson Timber Company

Fig. 59–28. Outdoor lights should be shielded from windows.

could be illuminated are the landscaping, game areas, barbecue area, patio, garden, front of picture window, pools, and driveways.

Outdoor lights should not shine directly on windows. Lights near the windows should be placed above the windows to eliminate the glare. Ground lights should be shielded by bushes to keep them from shining into the windows (Fig. 59–28).

PROBLEMS

1. **List several artificial light sources.**
2. **List several natural light sources.**
3. **List several methods to obtain general lighting.**
4. **List several sources for specific lighting.**
5. **List several methods for decorative lighting.**
6. **On a floor plan of your home, show the lighting as it now exists.**
7. **On a floor plan of your home, show how you would plan the lighting.**
8. **Plan the lighting for the floor plan in Fig. 33–20.**
9. **Plan the lighting for the floor plan in Fig. 70–1.**
10. **Define these terms: *incandescent bulb, fluorescent tube, filament, direct light, indirect light, semidirect light, diffused light, reflectance, valance lighting, wall bracket lighting, cornice lighting.***

UNIT 60

Electrical Principles

An average home has 45 different electrical appliances. In addition to new appliances, the existing ones are being improved to provide more efficient use of electrical energy. The demand for energy makes it necessary to have larger wiring systems in the home for safety and convenience. Electrical appliances cannot effectively serve the homemaker unless the wiring system that supplies the power is adequate.

Electrical power is generated by a utility company and sent through wires to the home by means of a transmission-line system (Fig. 60–1). The correct amount of electricity sent over the wires is regulated by transformers.

WIRING TERMS

Understanding the home electrical system begins with the basic terms used in home wiring.

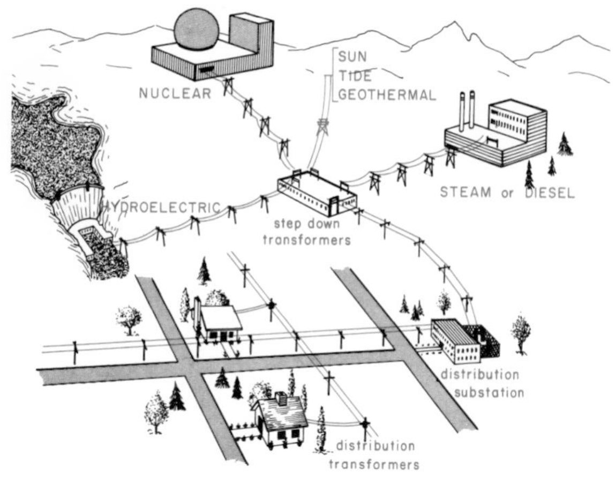

Fig. 60–1. **Sources of electrical energy for the home.**

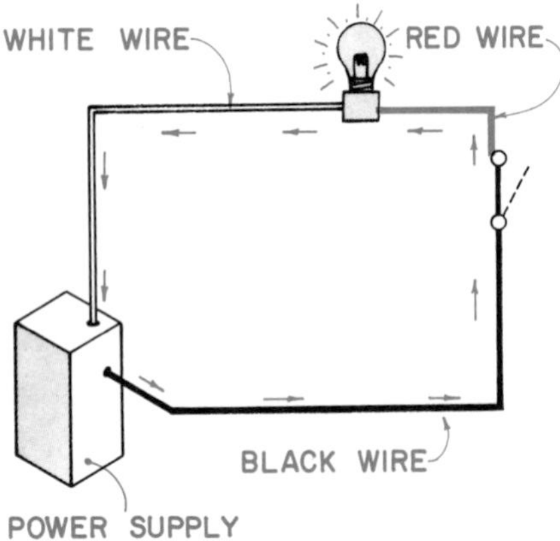

Fig. 60–3. **A simple electric circuit.**

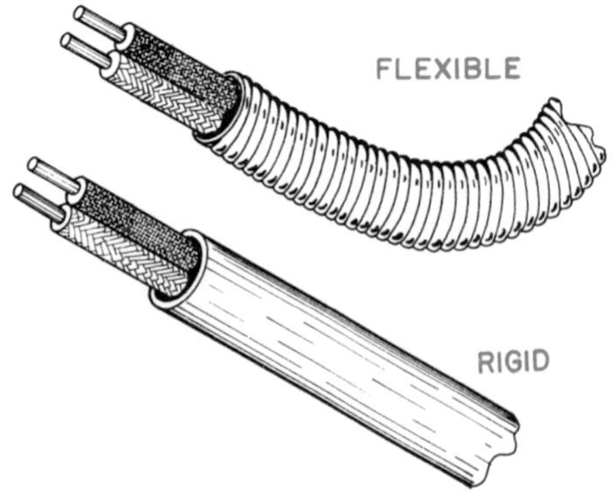

Fig. 60–4. **A conduit is a hard shield which protects electric wires.**

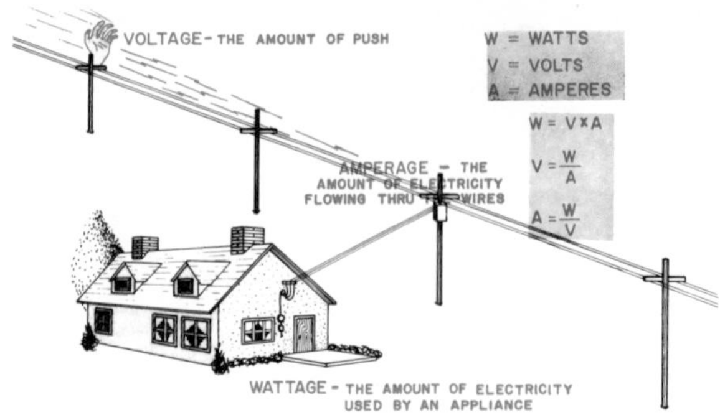

Fig. 60–2. **Properties of electric circuits.**

Voltage is an electrical pressure that is produced by a generator. It is this pressure that makes the electricity move from the generator to the home. Electrical energy can also come from small generators, batteries, photoelectric cells that convert light energy to electrical energy, and a thermocouple of two different metals that generate a low voltage when heated.

Note that the following units are common to both the metric and the customary system.

Ampere is the unit by which the electricity that passes through a wire is measured. The number of amperes determines the size of wire and circuit breakers or fuses that should be used in the wiring system.

Watt is the unit by which the amount of electricity needed for the operation of an electric appliance is measured. The wattage can be obtained by multiplying the amperage by the voltage (Fig. 60–2). Watts measure the amount of electric power used.

A *kilowatt* is 1000 watts.

A *kilowatthour* is 1000 watts used per hour. A *watthour* is 1 watt used for one hour. For convenience, the utility companies charge by every 1000 watthours, or 1 kilowatthour. The total kilowatthours used determines the amount of the electricity bill.

A *circuit* is a path for electricity to follow from the power supply to the source and back to the power supply (Fig. 60–3).

A *conduit* is a pipe containing the wires that connect the lights and convenience outlets throughout the house. The conduits may be flexible or rigid, depending on where they are to be used (Fig. 60–4).

Los Angeles Dept. of Water and Power

Fig. 60–5. The watthour meter records the amount of electricity used.

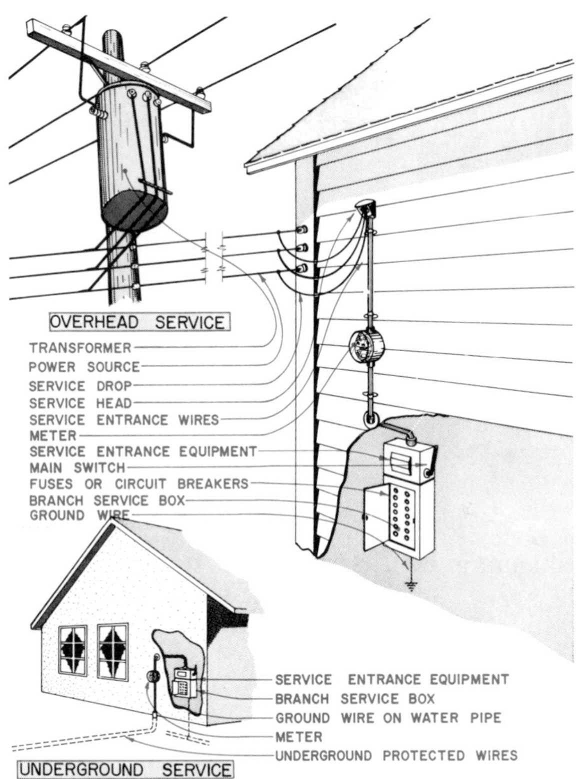

Fig. 60–6. Service entrance equipment.

Electric current is the moving electricity that is carried by a wire. By applying an electrical pressure (voltage) with a generator, the *electrons* (negative electrical charge) are forced along a wire to an appliance that will use the energy. Current is measured in amperes.

Overloading occurs if too much current moves through the wires leading to the electrical appliances. In this condition the wires will become overheated. Proper wiring design and installation will minimize the chance of fire.

Resistance is an electrical friction that tends to prevent electrical current from passing through wires. All materials have some resistance to electricity. Materials that offer little resistance are *conductors*. Copper is one of the best conductors. Materials that offer great resistance are *nonconductors*, or *insulators*. Glass, rubber, and many plastics are excellent insulators.

A *short circuit* will occur when a faulty appliance or exposed wires touch a conductor. The wires heat rapidly and cause a fire.

Service is all the equipment used to bring the electricity to the home from the power lines.

SOURCE

The electrical energy is brought to the home by the service entrance wires. The size of the service entrance wires determines the amount of electricity that can enter the wiring system safely. The heavy service wires are connected to the watthour meter (Fig. 60–5), then to the service entrance equipment, with the same heavy wire (Fig. 60–6). At the service entrance equipment is a distribution panel (Fig. 60–7) that sends the electricity throughout the house with branch circuits (Fig. 60–8).

Between the meter and the branch circuit box is a main fuse or circuit breaker. If too much current is drawn from the outside source and heats the wires, the fuse will burn out (Fig. 60–9). If there is a circuit breaker instead of a fuse, it will trip itself and open the circuit. In addition to the protection of the main source of power, each branch circuit is protected with fuses. Branch circuits become hot when too

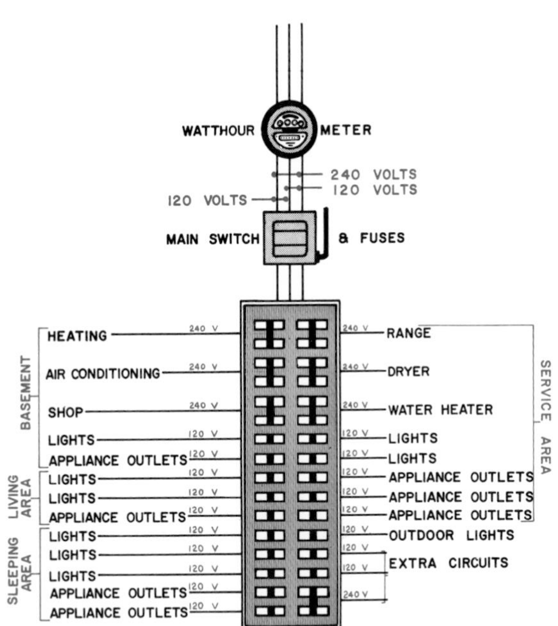

Fig. 60–7. The branch circuit distribution panel.

many appliances draw too much current. The fuse then blows or the circuit breaker trips.

BRANCH CIRCUITS

Each branch circuit delivers electricity to one or more outlets. It is necessary to divide the electricity that enters the house into branch circuits so that one line will not have to carry all the energy. If the whole house were on one circuit, a short circuit or an overloading would leave the entire house without power.

The size of the service entrance wires determines the total amount of electricity the home can use at one time. The homeowner should plan for more power than needed at the time of building, to allow for future demands from new and improved appliances. The minimum wire size for service entrance wires is No. 2 gage.

Electricity is delivered at pressures of about 120 volts and 240 volts. Major electrical appliances such as the electric range, water heater, clothes dryer, and large air conditioners are usually operated on a 240-volt system. Higher voltage systems are used where the power requirements are high, in order to reduce the number of amperes, and therefore the size of wire, in these circuits (Fig. 60–10).

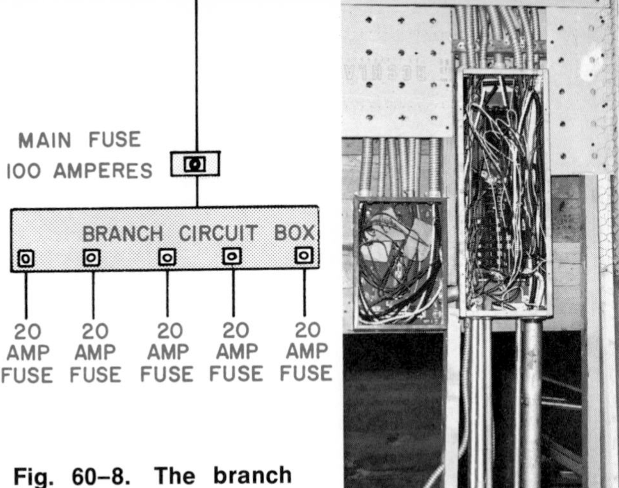

Fig. 60–8. The branch circuit box.

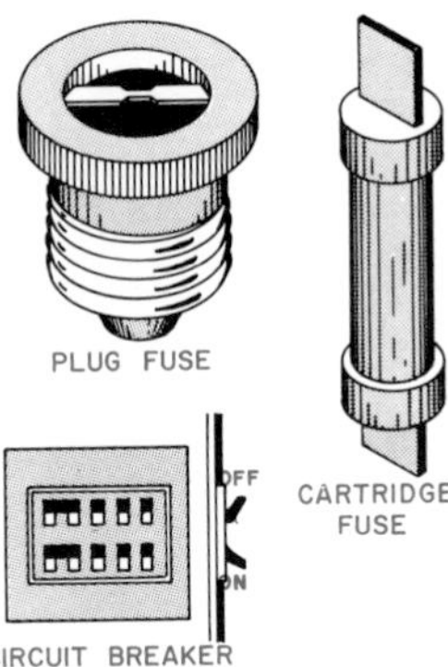

Fig. 60–9. Fuses and circuit breakers provide safety from fires.

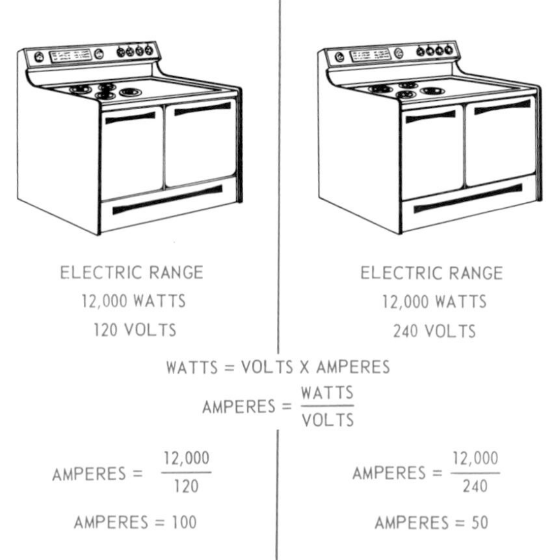

Fig. 60–10. Two identical ranges may use a different number of amperes on different power lines.

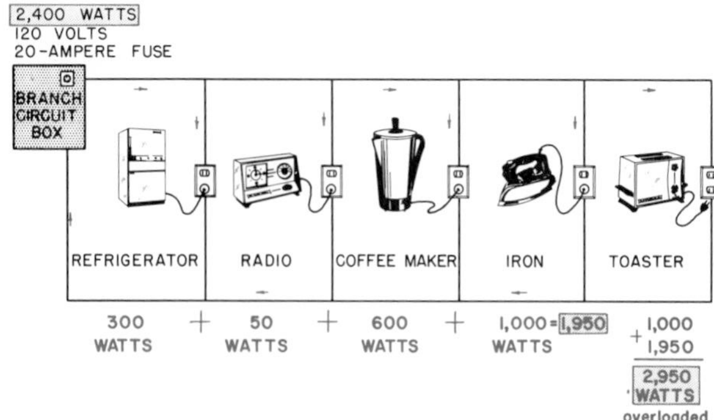

Fig. 60–11. Drawing too much current will overload a circuit.

To determine the size of service entrance wires needed, the homeowner should know how much current will be needed. In the older-style home, a 60-ampere electric service was sufficient. Today the size should be selected from the following guidance list for homes:

100-ampere service: appliance circuits, lighting circuits, electric cooking, electric water heater, electric laundry. 100 amperes @ 120 volts = 12 000 watts. 100 amperes @ 240 volts = 24 000 watts.

150-ampere service: appliance circuits, lighting circuits, electric cooking, electric water heater, electric laundry, electric heating, air conditioning for small home. 150 amperes @ 120 volts = 18 000 watts. 150 amperes @ 240 volts = 36 000 watts.

200-ampere service: appliance circuits, lighting circuits, electric cooking, electric water heater, electric laundry, electric heating, air conditioning for large home. 200 amperes @ 120 volts = 24 000 watts. 200 amperes @ 240 volts = 48 000 watts.

To plan the size of a branch circuit, add all the wattages of the appliances to be placed on the circuit. The total wattage determines the size of the wire and fuses or circuit breakers

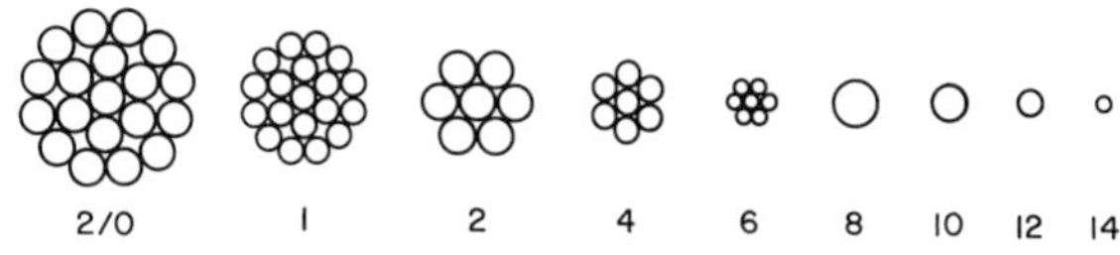

Fig. 60–12. Wire gage sizes.

(Fig. 60–11). A 120-volt circuit has one fuse. A 240-volt circuit has two fuses.

The wires of the branch circuits are smaller than the wires of the service entrance (Fig. 60–12). Minimum requirements for branch circuit wires in many areas still are a No. 14 wire with a 15-ampere fuse for safe delivery up to 1800 watts. It is more convenient and less expensive to use a No. 12 wire with a 20-ampere fuse for safe delivery of 2400 watts. The smaller wires create heat which wastes energy.

TYPES OF BRANCH CIRCUITS

The branch circuits are divided into three groups.

Lighting circuits (Fig. 60–13) provide for the lighting outlets in the home. Multiple lights in one room should be on different circuits. If one fuse blows, the room will not be in total darkness. Use a No. 12 wire with a 20-ampere fuse for 2400 watts for lighting circuits. Lighting requires about 6000 watts of power. Have a minimum of four 15-ampere fuse circuits for 1800 watts each or three 20-ampere fuse circuits for 2400 watts each.

Small-appliance circuits serve only convenience outlets (Fig. 60–14). Use No. 12 wire with a 20-ampere fuse for 2400 watts on each circuit. For more power, use a double-branch circuit with three wires and two fuses for 240 volts. With a 20-ampere fuse, this circuit will safely carry up to 4800 watts (Fig. 60–15).

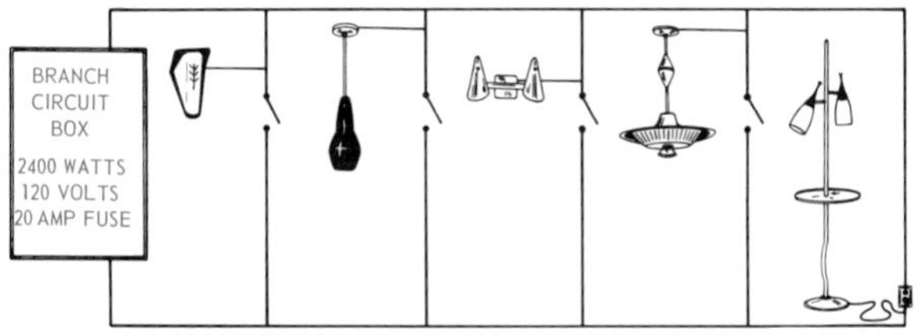

Fig. 60–13. A typical lighting circuit.

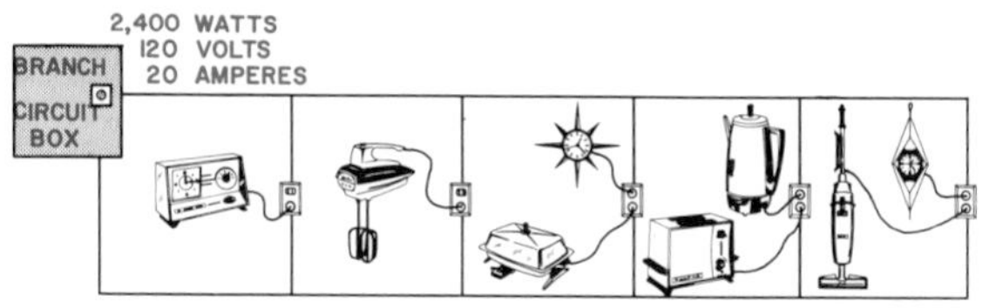

Fig. 60–14. A small-appliance circuit.

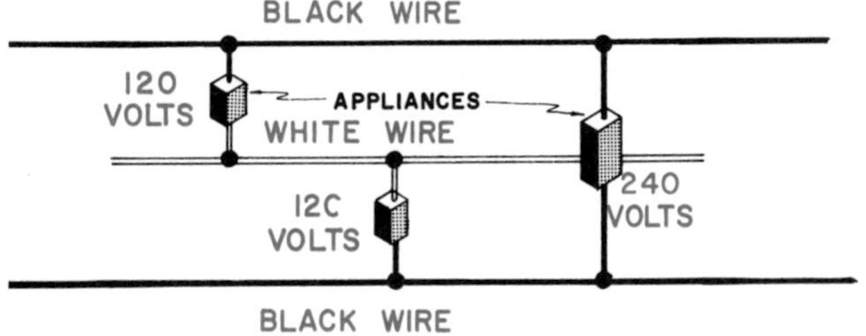

Fig. 60–15. A method of obtaining 120 volts or 220 volts from a three-wire system.

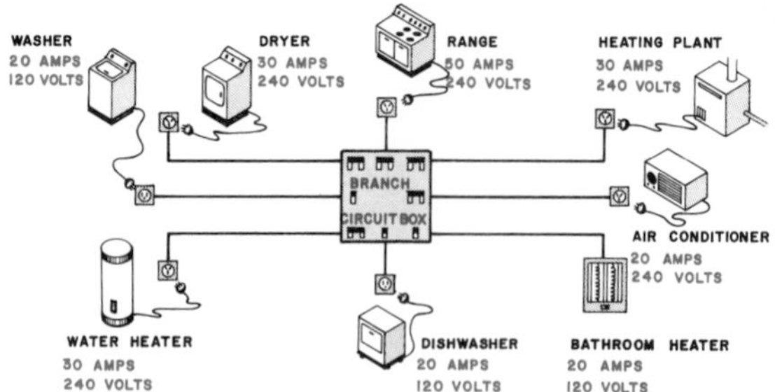

Fig. 60–16. Examples of individual circuits.

A general rule to follow for wire sizes in each circuit is:

20 amp—No. 12 wires
30 amp—No. 10 wires
40 amp—No. 8 wires
50 amp—No. 6 wires

Individual circuits serve one piece of electrical equipment (Fig. 60–16). Appliances that require individual circuits are the electric range, automatic heating units, water heater, clothes dryer, air conditioner, built-in electric heater, shop bench, and large motor-driven appliances such as washers, disposals, and dishwashers. When a motor starts, it needs an extra surge of power. This is called the *starting load.*

Allow extra circuits and outlets for future addition of appliances. Well-planned wiring gives more power throughout the home for appliances, and makes the lighting more efficient.

Table 60–1 shows acceptable electrical loads and circuits for residential wiring systems.

Table 60–1. LOAD REQUIREMENTS FOR ELECTRICAL APPLIANCES **(continued on next page)**

	TYPICAL CONNECTED WATTS	VOLTS	WIRES	CIRCUIT BREAKER OR FUSE	OUTLETS ON CIRCUIT	OUTLET	NOTES
	KITCHEN						
RANGE	12 000	120/240	3 #6	50A	1	Special purpose	Use of more than one outlet is not recommended.
OVEN (BUILT-IN)	4500	120/240	3 #10	30A	1	Special purpose	May be direct connected.
RANGE TOP	6000	120/240	3 #10	30A	1	Special purpose	May be direct connected.
RANGE TOP	3300	120/240	3 #12	20A	1	Special purpose	May be direct connected.
DISHWASHER	1200	120	2 #12	20A	1	Parallel grounding	These appliances may be direct connected on a single circut. Grounded receptacles required otherwise.
WASTE DISPOSER	300	120	2 #12	20A	1	Parallel grounding	These appliances may be direct connected on a single circuit. Grounded receptacles required otherwise.
BROILER	1500	120	2 #12	20A	1 or more	Parallel grounding Parallel	Heavy-duty appliances regularly used at one location should have a separate circuit. Only one such unit should be attached to a single circuit at the same time.
FRYER	1300	120	2 #12	20A	1 or more	Parallel grounding Parallel	Heavy-duty appliances regularly used at one location should have a separate circuit. Only one such unit should be attached to a single circuit at the same time.

Table 60–1. LOAD REQUIREMENTS FOR ELECTRICAL APPLIANCES (continued on next page)

	TYPICAL CONNECTED WATTS	VOLTS	WIRES	CIRCUIT BREAKER OR FUSE	OUTLETS ON CIRCUIT	OUTLET	NOTES
COFFEEMAKER	1000	120	2 #12	20A	1 or more	Parallel grounding Parallel	Heavy-duty appliances regularly used at one location should have a separate circuit. Only one such unit should be attached to a single circuit at the same time.
REFRIGERATOR	300	120	2 #12	20A	1 or more	Parallel grounding Parallel	Separate circuit serving only refrigerator and freezer is recommended.
FREEZER	350	120	2 #12	20A	1 or more	Parallel grounding Parallel	Separate circuit serving only refrigerator and freezer is recommended.
				LAUNDRY			
WASHING MACHINE	1200	120	2 #12	20A	1 or more	Parallel grounding	Grounding type receptacle required. Separate circuit is recommended.
DRYER	500	120/240	3 #10	30A	1	Special purpose	Appliance may be direct connected—must be grounded.
IRONER	1650	120	2 #12	20A	1 or more	Parallel grounding	
HAND IRON	1000	120	2 #12	20A	1 or more	Parallel	Consider possible use in other locations.
WATER HEATER	3000					Special purpose	Consult utility company for load requirements.
				LIVING AREAS			
WORKSHOP	1500	120	2 #12	20A	1 or more	Parallel grounding	Separate circuit recommended.
PORTABLE HEATER	1300	120	2 #12	20A	1	Parallel	Should not be connected to circuit serving other heavy-duty loads.
TELEVISION	300	120	2 #12	20A	1 or more	Parallel	Should not be connected to circuit serving appliances.
PORTABLE LIGHTING	1200	120	2 #12	20A	1 or more	Parallel	Provide one circuit for each 500 sq. ft. Divided receptacle may be switch controlled.
				FIXED UTILITIES			
FIXED LIGHTING	1200	120	2 #12	20A			Provide at least one circuit for each 1200 watts of fixed lighting.
AIR CONDITIONER ¾ HP	1200	120	2 #12	20A	1	Parallel grounding	Consider 4 kw 3-wire circuits to all window or console type air conditioners. Outlets may then be adapted to individual 120- or 240-volt machines. Connection to general purpose or appliance circuits is not recommended.
CENTRAL AIR CONDITIONER	5000	240				Special purpose	Consult manufacturer for recommended connections.
HEAT PUMP	* 14 000	240				Special purpose	Consult manufacturer for recommended connections.

* Maximum connected load (range varies from 6000 to 14 000, depending on season).

Table 60–1. LOAD REQUIREMENTS FOR ELECTRICAL APPLIANCES (continued)

	TYPICAL CONNECTED WATTS	VOLTS	WIRES	CIRCUIT BREAKER OR FUSE	OUTLETS ON CIRCUIT	OUTLET	NOTES
SUMP PUMP	300	120	2 #12	20A	1 or more	Parallel grounding	May be direct connected.
HEATING PLANT	600	120	2 #12	20A	1		Direct connected. Some local codes require separate circuit.
FIXED BATHROOM HEATER	1500	120	2 #12	20A	1		Direct connected.
ATTIC FAN	300	120	2 #12	20A	1 or more	Parallel grounding	May be direct connected. Individual circuit is recommended.

PROBLEMS

1. **Figure 60–17 represents a four-circuit system for a one-bedroom apartment. Draw the floor plan to ¼″ scale. List the rooms on each circuit; draw all lighting outlets; draw all convenience outlets; draw all special outlets; draw all circuits; and label the wire size, the line voltage, the maximum watts on each circuit, and the fuse size.**
2. **Draw Fig. 34–3 and complete the electrical plan. Show all the circuits and label each type. Label the voltage, wattage, wire size, and fuse size for each circuit.**
3. **Define these terms: *wiring system, generator, transformer, voltage, battery, photoelectric cell, light energy, thermocouple, ampere, watts, circuit, electric current, electrons, overloading, short circuit, conductor, resistance, nonconductor, transmission-line system, insulators, kilowatt, kilowatthour, conduit, service entrance, service meter, distribution panel, branch circuits, fuse, circuit breaker, outlet, lighting circuit, small-appliance circuit, starting load.***

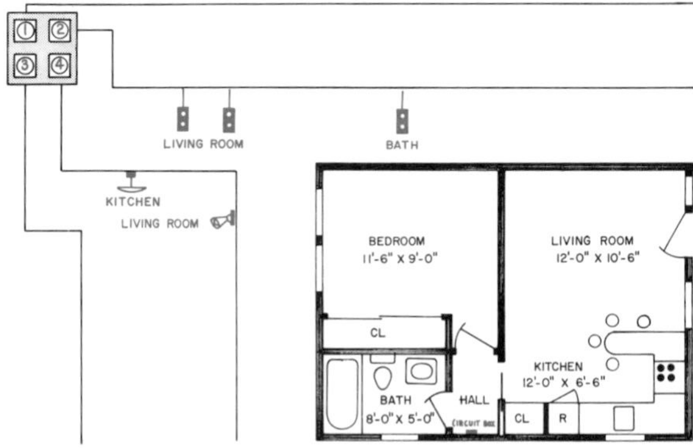

Fig. 60–17. Complete the four circuits by sketching outlets and fixtures.

UNIT 61

Planning with Electricity

Wiring methods are controlled by building codes. The job of wiring is performed by licensed electricians. However, the wiring plans for a building are prepared by the architect. For large structures a consulting electrical contractor may aid in the preparation of the final plans. Electrical plans must include information concerning the type and location of all switches, fixtures, and controls.

PLANNING RULES

Basic rules to follow when planning the electrical system are listed below.

1. The main source of light in a room should be controlled by a wall switch located on the latch side of the room's entrance. It should

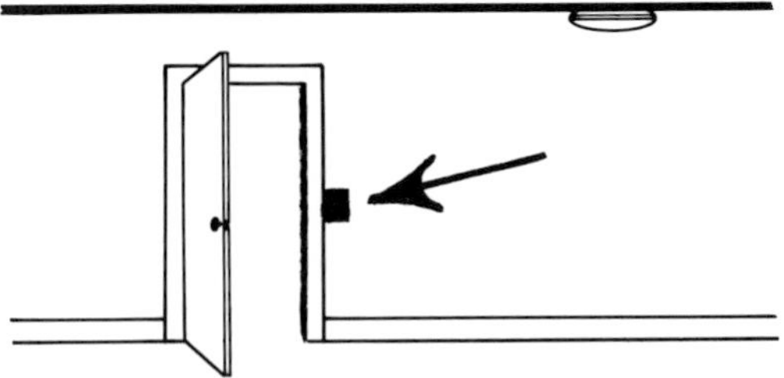

Fig. 61-1. The light switch should be conveniently located near a door.

not be necessary to walk into a dark room to find the light switch (Fig. 61–1).

2. Electrical outlets (except in the kitchen) should average one for every 6′ (1.8 m) of wall space.
3. Electrical outlets in the kitchen should average one for every 4′ (1.2 m) of wall space.
4. Walls between doors should have an outlet, regardless of the size of the wall space (Fig. 61–2).
5. Each room should have in the ceiling or wall a light outlet that will be a major source of light for the whole room (Fig. 61–3).
6. Each room should have adequate lighting for all visual tasks.
7. Each room should have at least one easy-to-reach outlet for the vacuum cleaner or other appliances which are often used.
8. Not all the lights in one room should be on the same circuit.
9. List the height of all outlets in the house (Fig. 61–4) on the plans.

SWITCH LOCATION

Switches should be located according to the following guides.

1. Plan what switches are needed for all lights and electrical equipment. Toggle switches are available in several different types: single-pole, double-pole, three-way, and four-way (Fig. 61–5).
2. Show location and height of switches.
3. Select the type of switches, type of switch-plate cover, and type of finish.

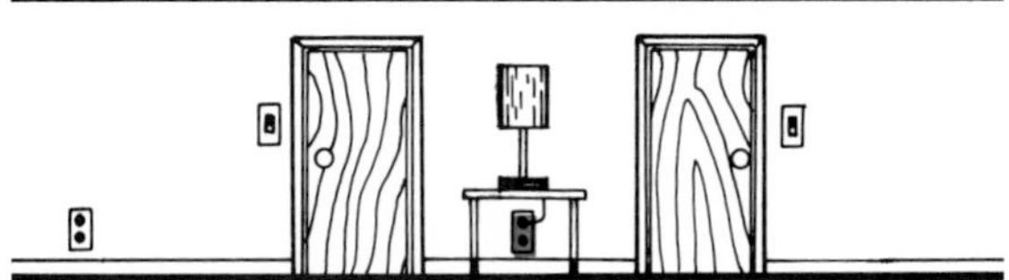

Fig. 61–2. Wall spaces between doors should have a convenience outlet.

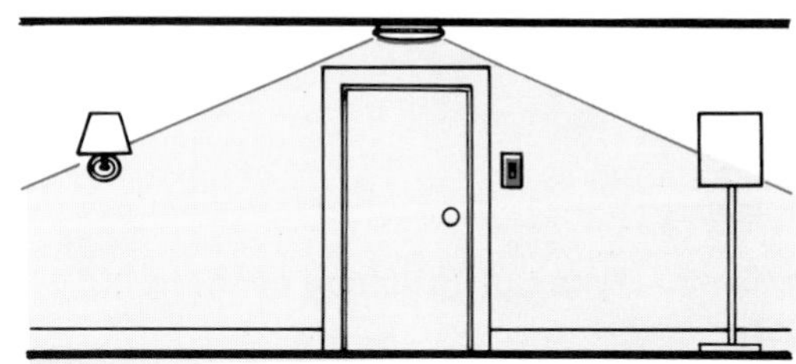

Fig. 61–3. A switch by a door should control the main source of light.

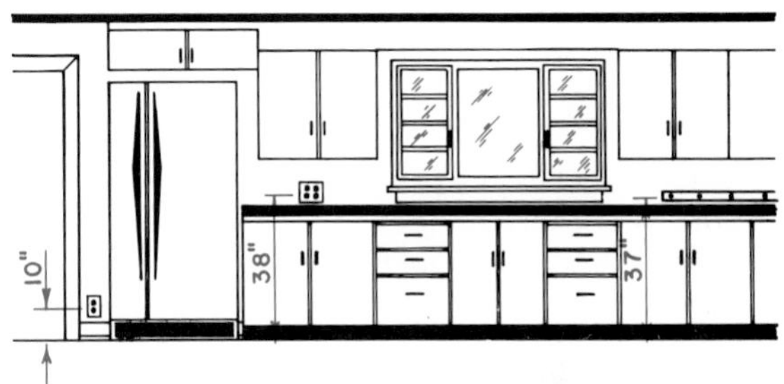

Fig. 61–4. The height of all outlets should be noted on wall elevations or in the specifications.

4. If there are only lamps in a room, the entry switch should control the outlet into which the lamps are plugged.
5. Lights for stairways and halls must be controlled from both ends (Fig. 61–6).
6. Bedroom lights should be controlled from bedside and entrance with a three-way switch.
7. Outside lights must be controlled with a three-way switch from the garage and from the exit of the house.
8. Basement lights should be controlled by a switch and a pilot light in the house at the head of the basement stairs (Fig. 61–7).
9. Install wall switches in preference to pullstring switches in closets.
10. Describe all special controls to be used.

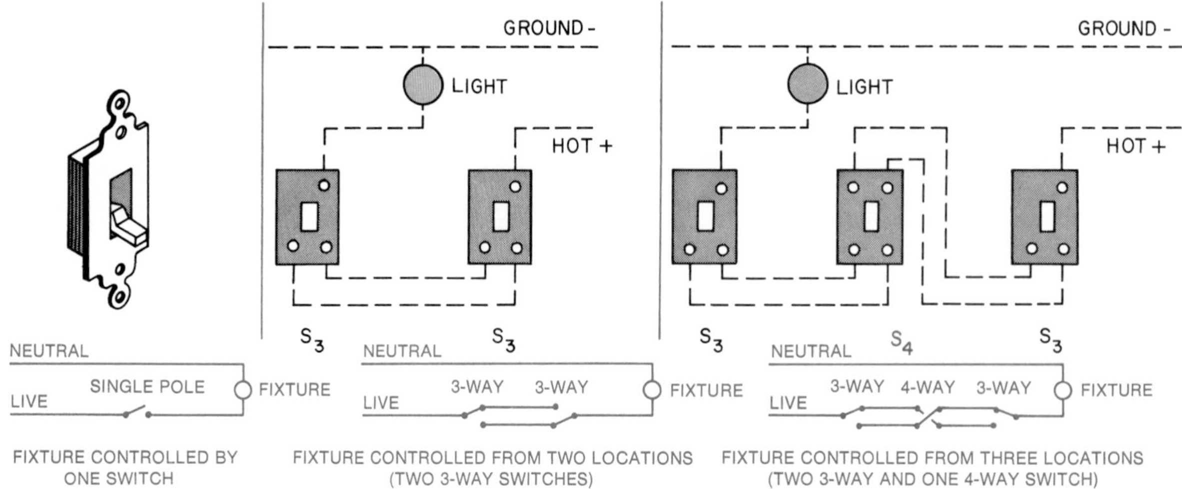

Fig. 61–5. Types of switching controls.

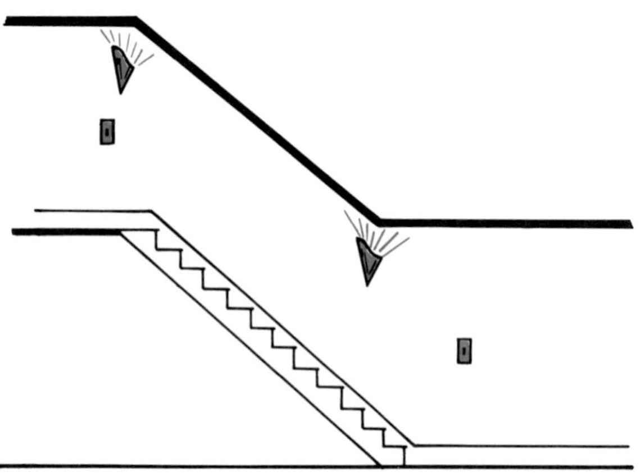

Fig. 61–6. Three-way switches should be used on stairway lights.

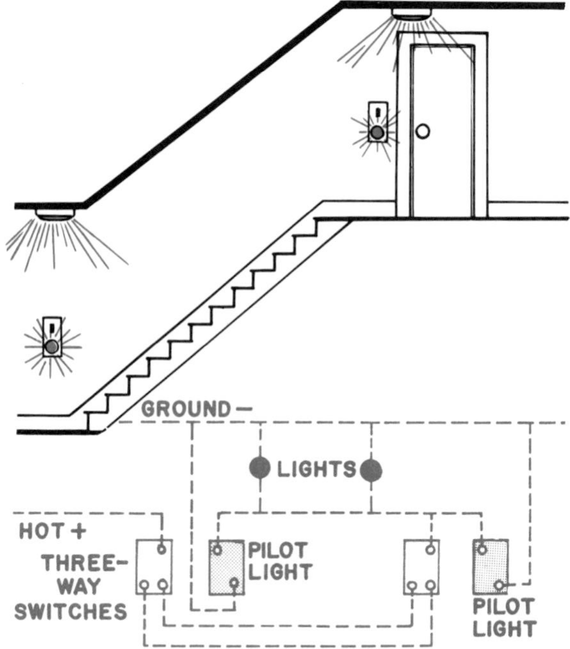

Fig. 61–7. Three-way switches with pilot lights should be used on basement stairs.

SPECIAL CONTROLS

Special controls make appliances and lighting systems more efficient. Some special controls for electrical equipment include the following:

Mercury switches are silent, shockproof, easy to wire and install, and last longer than a regular toggle switch.

Automatic cycle controls, as on washers, can be installed on appliances to make them perform their functions on a time cycle.

Photoelectric cells control switching at a wave of the hand.

Automatic controls adjust heating and cooling systems.

Clock thermostats adjust heating units for day and night.

Aquastats keep water heated to selected temperatures.

Dimmers control intensity of light.

Time switches control lights or watering systems.

Safety alarm systems activate a bell when a circuit on a door or window is broken.

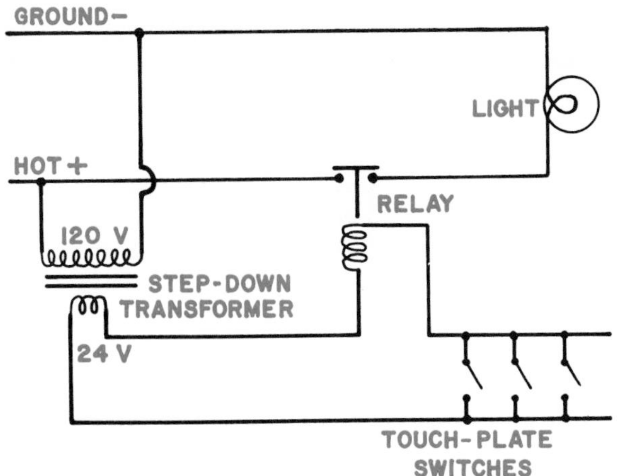

Fig. 61–8. A low-voltage control system.

Master switches control switching throughout the home from one location.

Low-voltage switching systems (Fig. 61–8) provide economical long runs.

The low-voltage method of switching offers convenience and flexibility. A *relay* isolates all switches from the 120-volt system. The voltage from the switch to the appliance is only 24 volts. At the appliance a *magnetic-controlled switch* opens the full 120 volts to the appliance. The magnetic-controlled switch is more commonly called a *touch switch*. The low, 24-volt system permits long runs of inexpensive wiring that is easy to install and safe to use. This makes it ideal for master-control switching from one location in the house.

ELECTRICAL OUTLETS

There are several types of electrical outlets. The *convenience outlet* (Fig. 61–9) is the plug-in, receptacle type. It is available in single, double, triple, or strip outlets.

Lighting outlets (Fig. 61–10) are for the connection of lampholders, surface-mounted fixtures, flush or recessed fixtures, and all other types of lighting fixtures.

The *special-purpose outlet* (Fig. 61–11) is the connection point of a circuit for one special piece of equipment.

The wires that hook up the whole electric system are installed during the construction of the building, in the walls, floors, and ceilings. In a finished house, the entire system is hidden (Fig. 61–12). The conventional wiring system

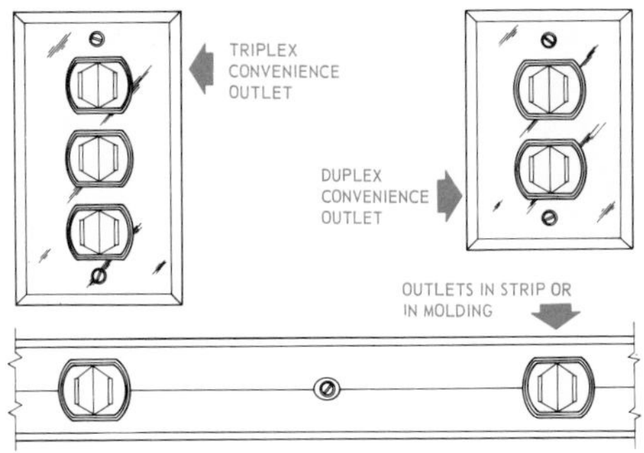

Fig. 61–9. Examples of convenience outlets.

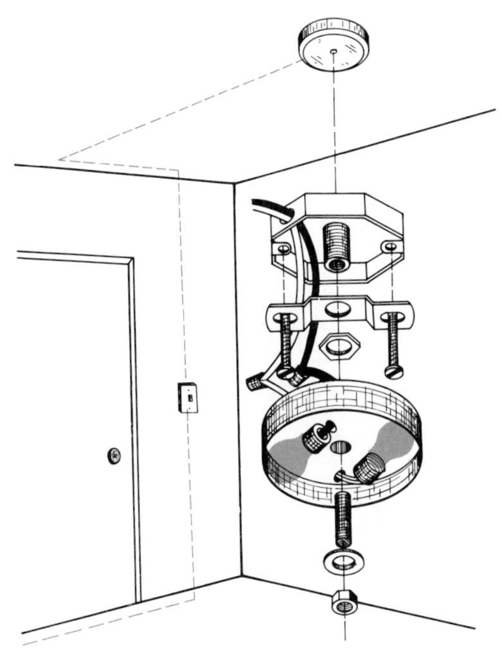

Fig. 61–10. A ceiling lighting outlet.

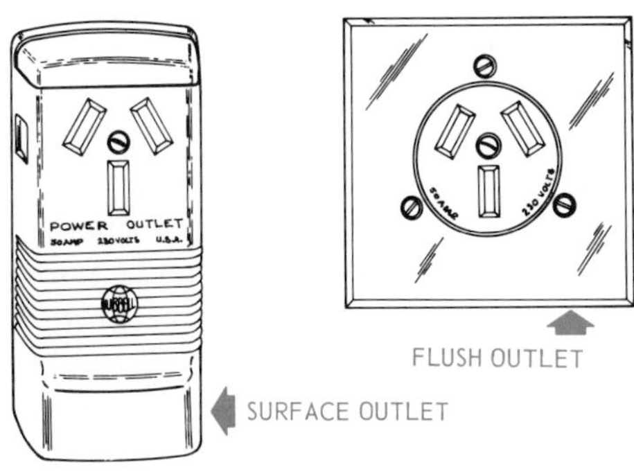

Fig. 61–11. Special-purpose outlets.

Los Angeles Dept. of Water and Power

Fig. 61–12. Conduits should be installed before wall coverings are attached.

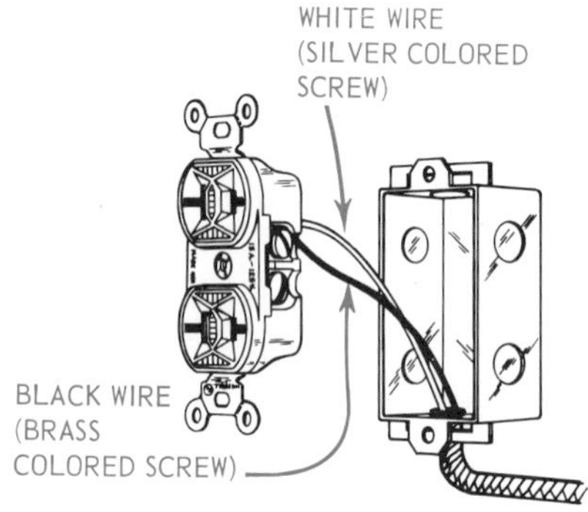

Fig. 61–13. Convenience-outlet wiring.

used for outlets, lights, and small appliances consists of a black wire (the hot wire) and a white wire (the neutral or common wire), as shown in Fig. 61–13. A third, green, wire is a grounding wire. For large appliances the wiring consists of a black wire and a red wire both of which are hot wires, and a white wire. All three wires connect through a switch to the appliance.

If the wire is too long or too small, there will be a voltage drop because of the wire's resistance. Another cause of voltage drop is the drawing of too much current from the branch circuit. This will cause heating appliances such as toasters, irons, and electric heaters to work inefficiently. Motor-driven appliances will overwork and possibly burn out.

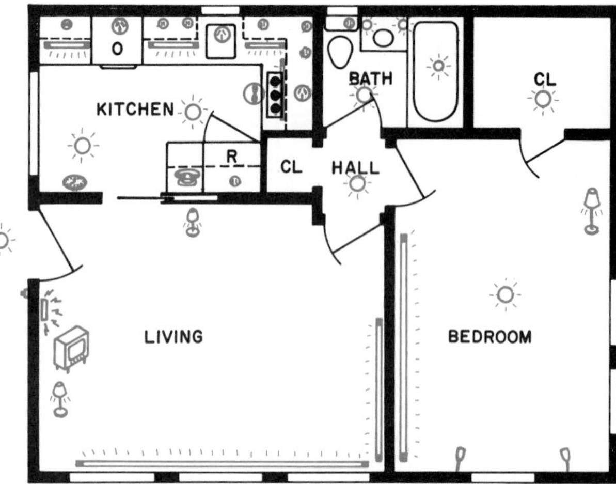

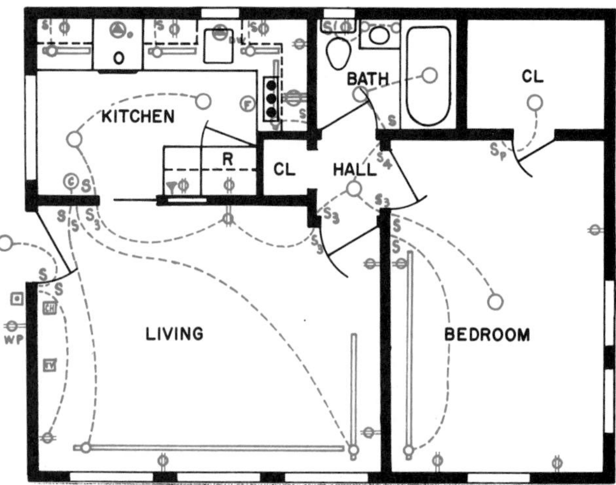

Fig. 61–14. Planning home wiring to anticipated needs.

ELECTRICAL WORKING DRAWINGS

Complete electrical plans will ensure the installation of electrical equipment and wiring exactly as planned. If electrical plans are incomplete and sketchy, the completeness of the installation is largely dependent upon the judgment of the electrician. The designer should not rely upon the electrician to design the electrical system, only to install it.

Preparing the Electrical Plan

After the basic floor plan is drawn, the designer should determine the exact position of all appliances and lighting fixtures on the plan, as shown in Fig. 61–14. The exact position of

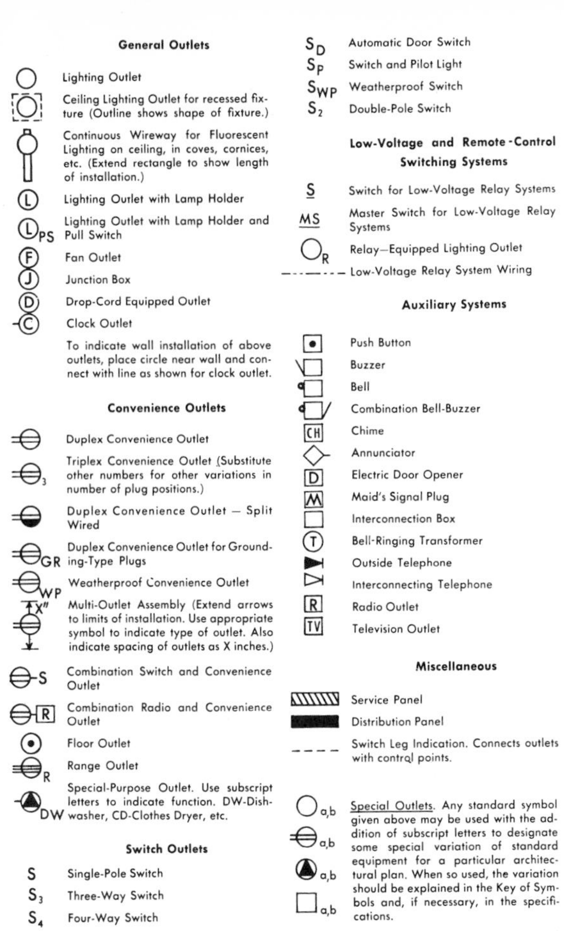

Fig. 61–15. Graphic symbols for electrical and layout diagrams used in architecture and building construction.

switches and outlets to accommodate these appliances and fixtures should be determined. Next, the electrical symbols representing the switches, outlets, and electrical devices should be drawn on the floor plan. A line is then drawn from each switch to the connecting fixture. Figure 61–15 shows electrical symbols used for residential wiring plans. The exact position of each wire is determined by the electrician. The designer indicates only the position of the fixture and the switch and the connecting line.

Figure 61–16 shows a typical electrical plan of a residence. The circuits for this plan are also shown. The architectural method as shown in Fig. 61–17 is used on this plan because of its simplicity. Compare the architectural method with the true wiring diagram and you will see that it would be virtually impossible to complete a true wiring diagram for the entire structure.

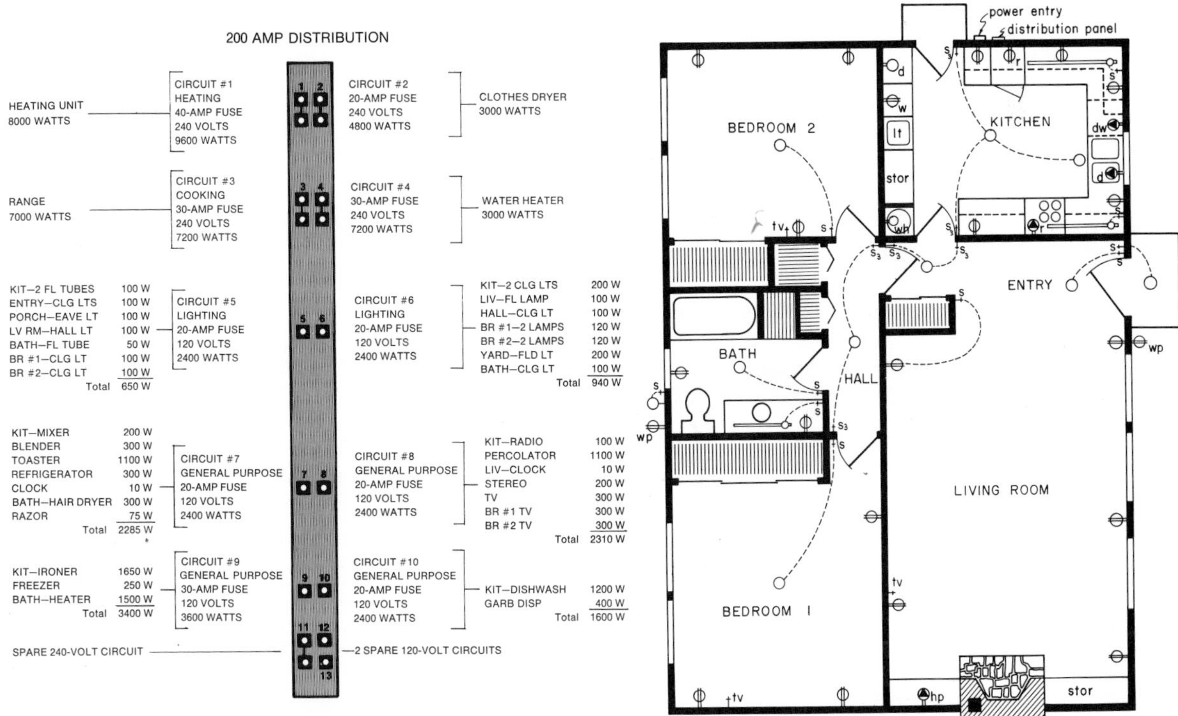

Fig. 61–16. A floor plan complete with electrical symbols and the circuits for this plan.

Room Wiring Diagrams

Figure 61–18 through 61–25 show some typical wiring diagrams of various rooms in the home. Refer to the symbols shown in Fig. 61–15 to identify the various symbols. You will notice you can trace the control of each fixture to a switch. You will notice how much more involved the electrical appliances for the kitchen and laundry are than those in the other rooms in the house. Notice also the use of three-way and four-way switches in halls and other traffic areas to provide flexibility and control.

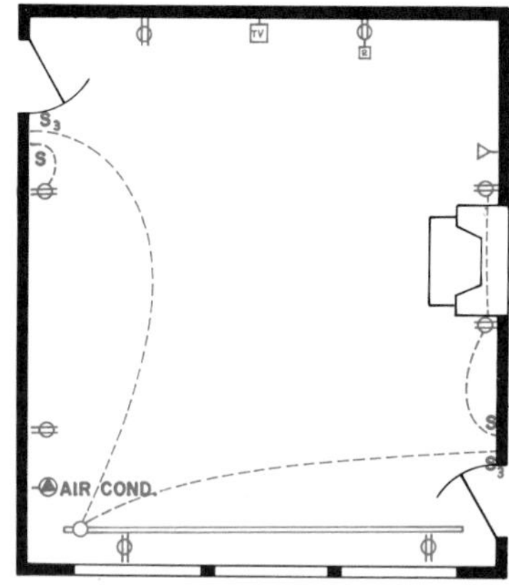

Fig. 61–18. The wiring plan for a living room.

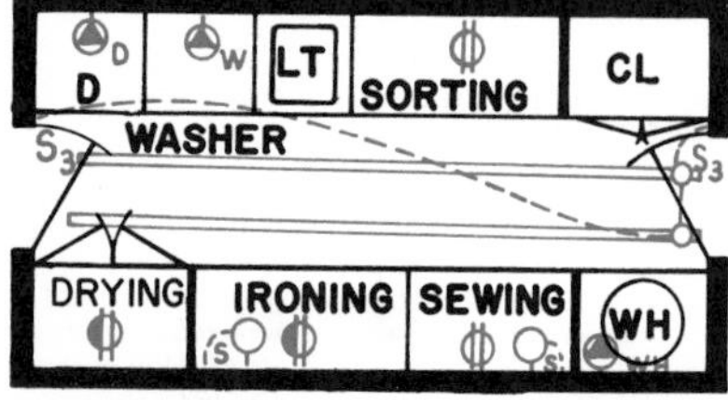

Fig. 61–20. The wiring plan for a utility room.

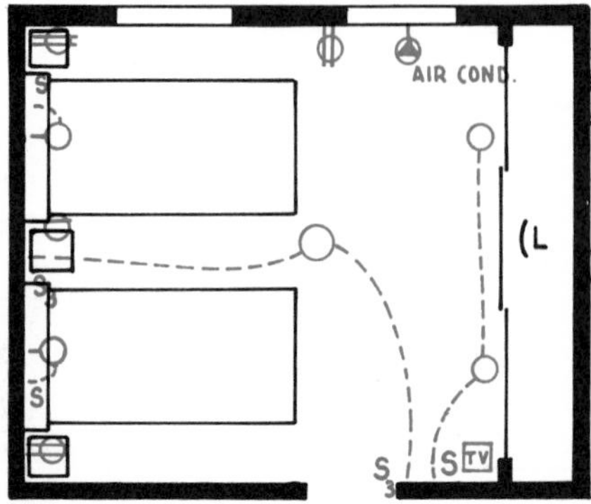

Fig. 61–21. The wiring plan for a bedroom.

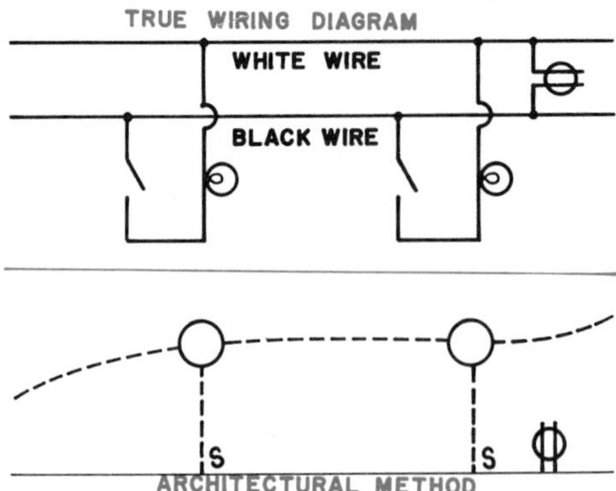

Fig. 61–17. Architectural wiring plans do not show the position of each separate wire.

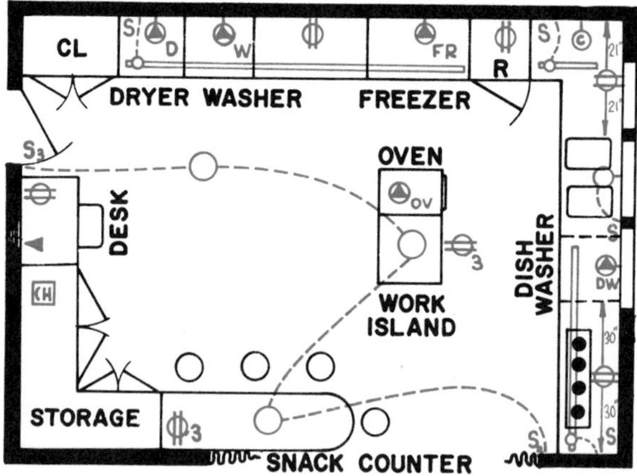

Fig. 61–19. The wiring plan for a kitchen.

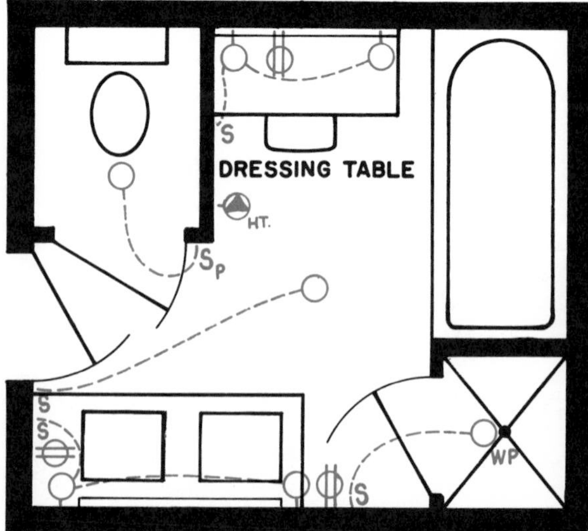

Fig. 61–22. The wiring plan for a bathroom.

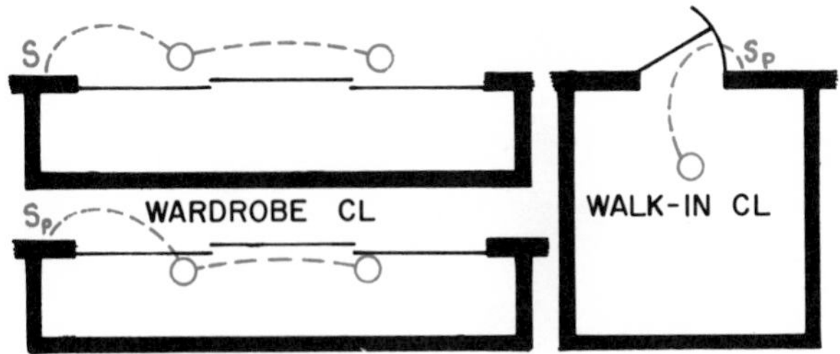

Fig. 61–23. A wiring plan for closets.

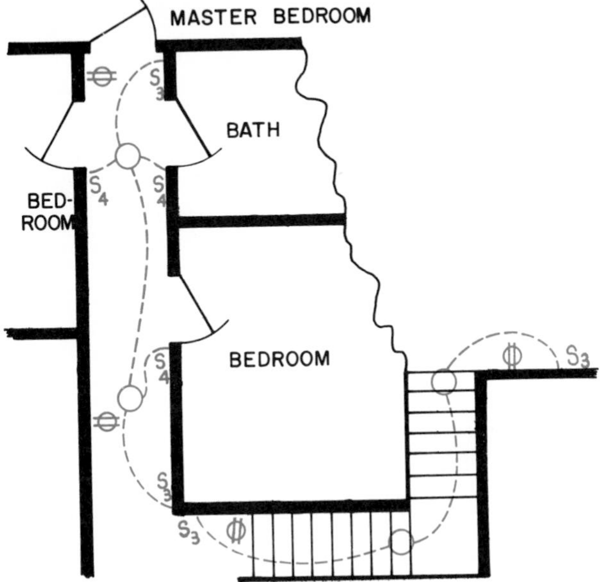

Fig. 61–25. The wiring plan for hall and stairs.

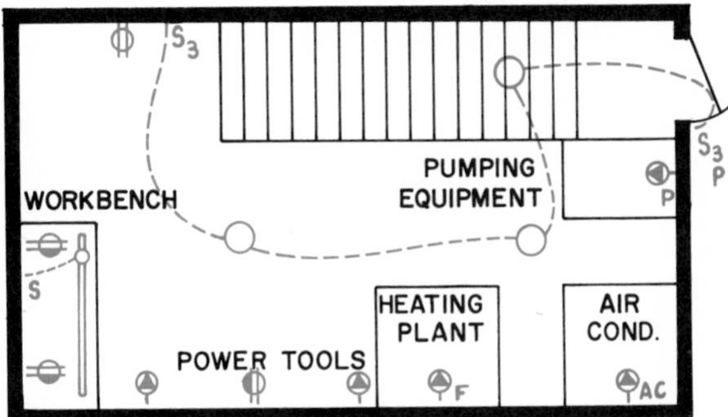

Fig. 61–24. The wiring plan for a basement.

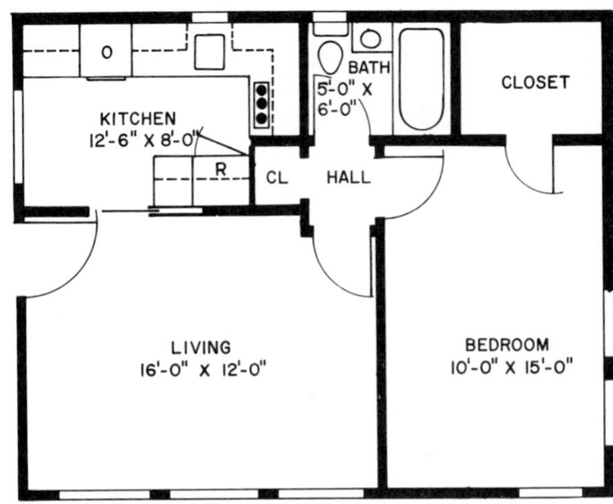

Fig. 61–26. Complete a wiring plan for this floor plan.

Fig. 61–27. Add electrical symbols to this floor plan.

PROBLEMS

1. Make a complete electrical drawing of your classroom.
2. Complete with symbols an electrical plan of your home.
3. Complete the electrical plan for Fig. 61–26.
4. Complete the electrical plan for Fig. 61–27.
5. Go to a store and compile a list of new lighting fixtures, and fixtures and parts of the wiring system.
6. Define these terms: *switch, outlet, toggle switch, single-pole switch, double-pole switch, three-way switch, four-way switch, switch plate, switch and pilot light, mercury switch, automatic cycle control, photoelectric cells, clock thermostats, aquastats, dimmers, time switch, master control switch, low-voltage switching system, hot wire, black wire, red wire, white wire, strip outlets, special-purpose outlets, convenience outlets, lighting outlets.*

SECTION 14

Air-Conditioning Plans

Comfort requires more than having enough control to keep warm in the winter and cool in the summer. True comfort means a correct temperature, a correct amount of moisture in the air (humidity), and clean, fresh, odorless air. The achievement of this ideal comfort, or air conditioning, is achieved through the use of a heating system, a cooling system, air filters, and humidifiers.

Libbey-Owens-Ford Company

UNIT 62

Air-Conditioning Methods

Many different systems can be used to heat and cool a building. The effective use of insulation, ventilation, roof overhang, caulking, weather stripping, and solar orientation helps to increase the efficiency of the air-conditioning system (Fig. 62–1).

·VENTILATION
·INSULATION
·ROOF OVERHANG
·CAULKING
·WEATHER STRIPPING
·ORIENTATION TO SUN

Fig. 62–1. Many factors affect the efficiency of air-conditioning systems.

HEAT TRANSFER

Heat is transferred from a warm to a cool surface by three methods: radiation, convection, and conduction.

Radiation

In radiation, heat flows to a cooler surface through space in the same way in which light travels. The air is not warm but the cooler object it strikes becomes warm. The object in turn, warms the air that surrounds it (Fig. 62–2).

Convection

In convection, a warm surface heats the air about it. The warmed air rises and cool air moves in to take its place, causing a convection current (Fig. 62–3).

Conduction

In conduction, heat moves through a solid material. The denser the material, the better it will conduct heat. For example, iron conducts heat better than wood (Fig. 62–4).

Fig. 62–2. Radiation is one method of heat transfer.

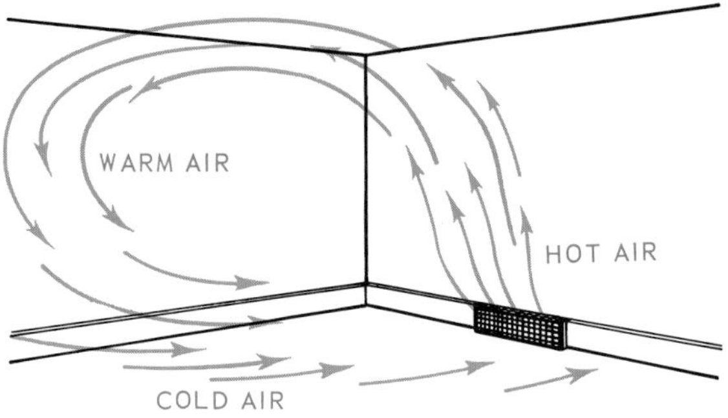

Fig. 62–3. Heating by convection.

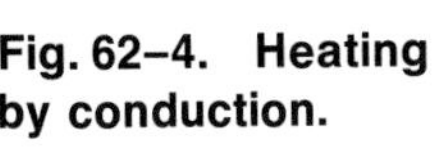

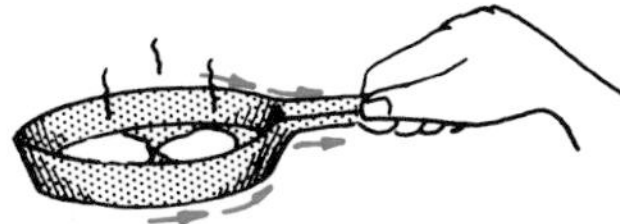

Fig. 62–4. Heating by conduction.

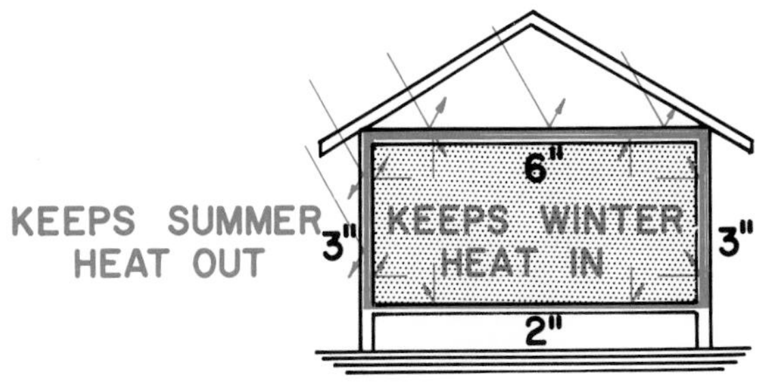

Fig. 62–5. Insulation stops or retards the transfer of heat.

INSULATION

Insulation is a material used to stop the transfer of heat. Thus, insulation can be used to limit the area to be heated or cooled. It helps keep heat inside the house in the winter and outside in the summer.

Without insulation, a heating or cooling system must work harder to overcome the loss of warm air or cool air through the walls, floors, and ceilings. Full insulation—6″ (150 mm) in the roof, 3″ (75 mm) in the walls, and 2″ (50 mm) in the floors—can save 40 percent of heating and cooling costs (Fig. 62–5).

Properly insulating walls and floors, as shown in Fig. 62–6, alone can reduce 25 percent of the heat transfer.

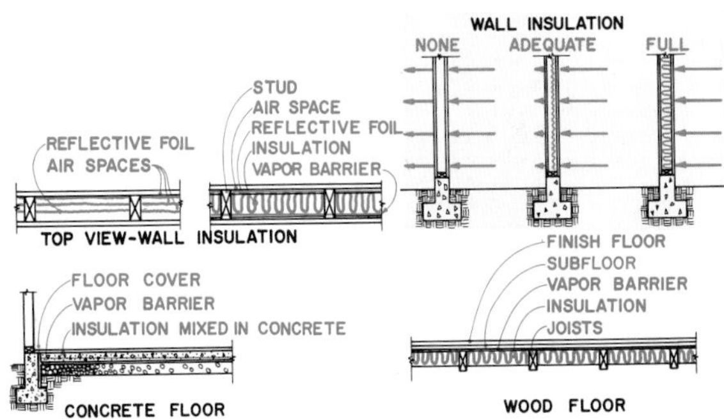

Fig. 62–6. Types of wall and floor insulation.

ROOF

Because most roofs cannot be sheltered from the sun, 40 percent of all heat transfer is through the roof. Six-inch insulation with an area for ventilation above the insulation, as shown in Fig. 62–7, is most effective. The use of light-colored roofs also helps in reflecting the heat and preventing the absorption of excessive heat (Fig. 62–8).

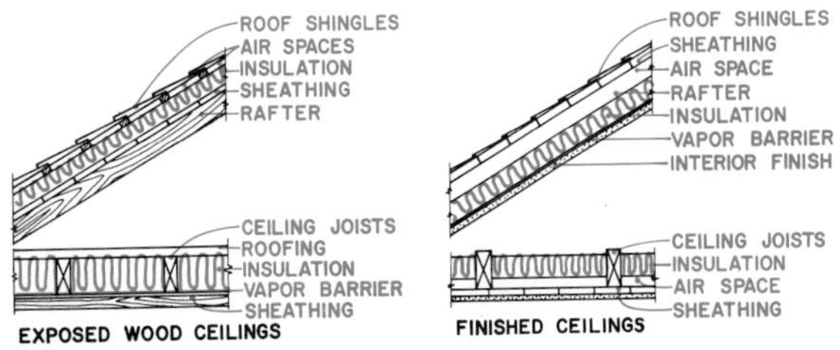

Fig. 62–7. Examples of ceiling and roof insulation.

LIGHT ROOF
DARK ROOF

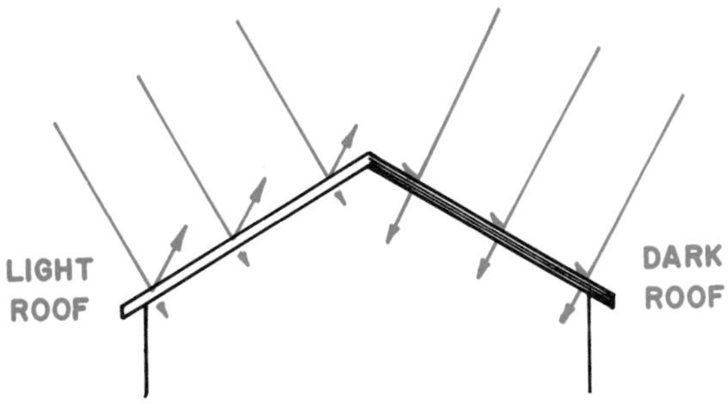

Fig. 62–8. **Roofs should reflect some heat.**

ROOF OVERHANG
CURTAINS
BLINDS
DOUBLE-PANED
LANDSCAPING
INSULATION

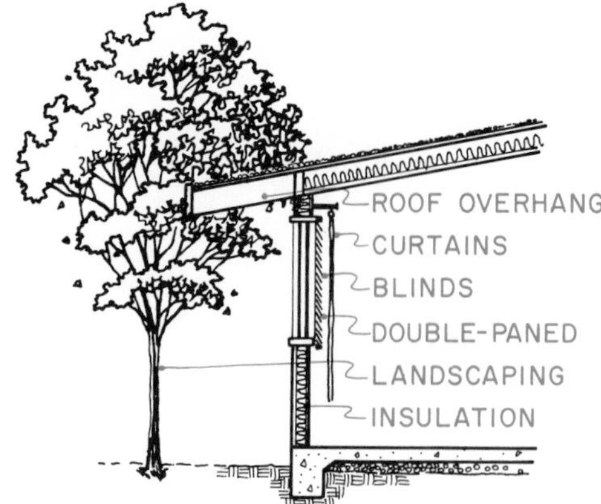

Fig. 62–9. **Deterrents to heat transfer through windows.**

Fig. 62–10. **Types of insulation.**

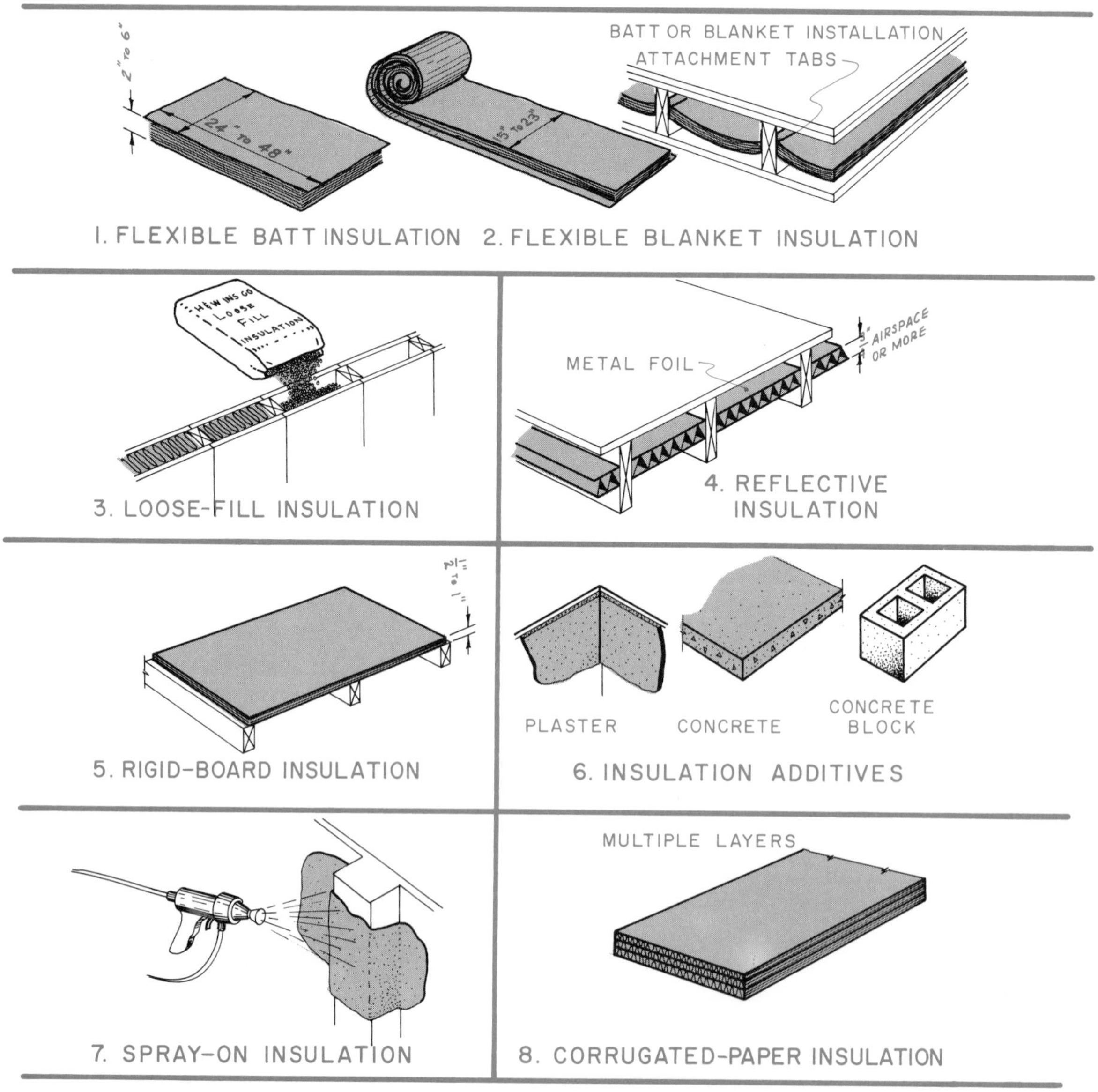

2" TO 6"
24" TO 48"
15" TO 23"
BATT OR BLANKET INSTALLATION
ATTACHMENT TABS
1. FLEXIBLE BATT INSULATION
2. FLEXIBLE BLANKET INSULATION
LOOSE FILL INSULATION
3. LOOSE-FILL INSULATION
METAL FOIL
AIRSPACE OR MORE
4. REFLECTIVE INSULATION
5. RIGID-BOARD INSULATION
PLASTER
CONCRETE
CONCRETE BLOCK
6. INSULATION ADDITIVES
7. SPRAY-ON INSULATION
MULTIPLE LAYERS
8. CORRUGATED-PAPER INSULATION

WINDOWS AND DOORS

Windows alone can allow 25 percent of the heat within a house to transfer to the outside. Some deterrents to this transfer are the use of large roof overhangs, trees and shrubbery, drapes, and window blinds. Double-paned glass is also effective (Fig. 62–9).

In an imperfectly constructed house, cracks around doors, windows, and fireplaces can combine to make a hole of sufficient size to lose all internal heat in less than an hour. Weather stripping and caulking can prevent this heat loss.

INSULATION MATERIALS

Insulation is available in different forms (Fig. 62–10). Insulation is made from a wide variety of vegetable, mineral, plastic, and metal materials. Their purpose is to stop heat transfer, block moisture (Figs. 62–11 and 62–12), stop sound, resist fire, and resist insects.

The different types of insulation are:

1. *Flexible batt:* paper-covered insulating materials that are attached between structural members. The batts are 2″ to 6″ (50 to 150 mm) thick.
2. *Flexible blanket:* paper-covered insulating materials that are attached between structural members. The blankets are long sheets 1″ to 3″ (25 to 75 mm) thick.
3. *Loose fill:* poured or blown into walls or attic floors.

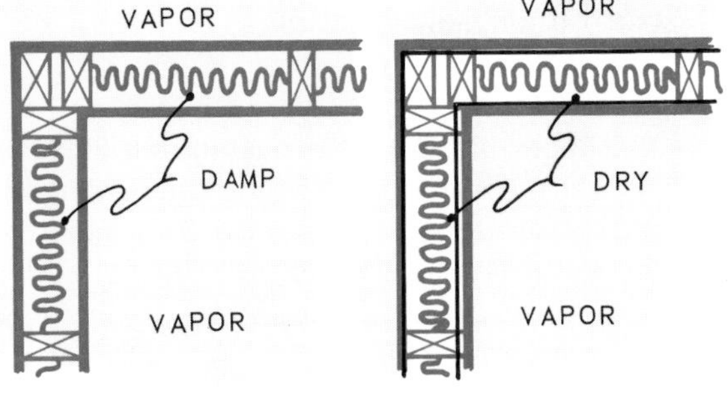

Fig. 62–12. Vapor barriers prevent condensation.

Fig. 62–11. Plastic moisture insulation.

4. *Reflective:* multiple spaces of reflecting metal attached between construction members (Fig. 62–13). Reflective is often mounted on other types of insulation. It is excellent for reflecting heat and for retarding fire, decay, and insects.
5. *Rigid board:* thin insulating sheathing cover that is manufactured in varying sizes.

Reynolds Metal Co.

Fig. 62–13. Reflective insulation.

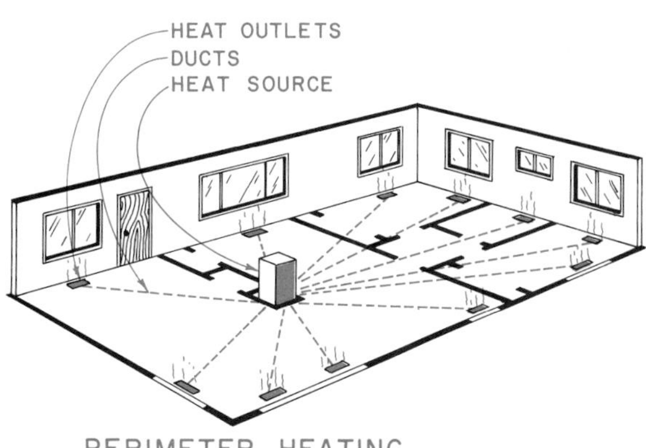

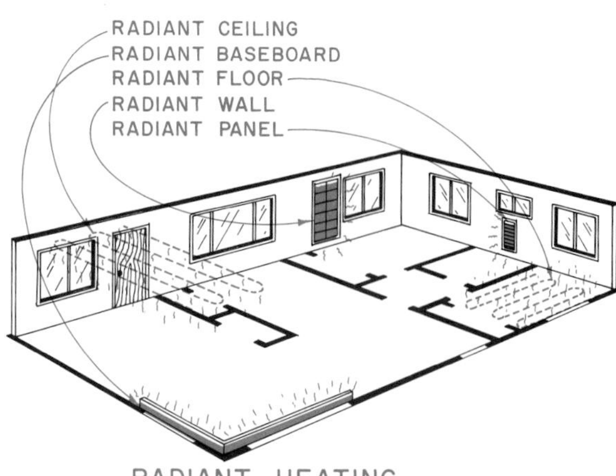

National Warm Air Heating and Air Conditioning Association

Fig. 62–14. Two types of heating systems.

6. *Additives:* lightweight aggregates are mixed with construction materials to increase their insulating properties.
7. *Spray on:* insulating materials mixed with an adhesive and sprayed on.
8. *Corrugated paper:* multiple layers of corrugated paper that are easy to cut and install.

HEATING SYSTEMS

The two most flexible types of heating systems are perimeter heating and radiant heating (Fig. 62–14).

Perimeter Heating
In perimeter heating, the heat outlets are located on the outside walls of the rooms. The heat rises and covers the coldest areas in the house. In this system the main loss of the heat is through the windows and outside walls. Warm air rises, passes across the ceiling, and returns in an *air return* while still warm. Baseboards, convectors, and radiators can be used to project the heat in the perimeter system.

Radiant Heating
Radiant heating functions by heating an area of the wall, ceiling, or floor. These warm surfaces in turn radiate heat to cooler objects. The heating surfaces may be lined with pipes containing hot water or hot air, or with electric resistance wires covered with plaster.

HEATING DEVICES

Devices that produce the heat used in the various heating systems include the following: warm-air units, hot-water units, steam units, electrical units, solar heating.

Warm-Air Units
In a warm air unit the air is heated in a furnace (Fig. 62–15). Air ducts distribute the heated air to outlets throughout the house (Fig. 62–16). The air supply can be taken from the outside, from the furnace room, or from return-air ducts in heated rooms (Fig. 62–17). Warm-air units can operate either by gravity or by forced air. Warm air (often called *hot air*) provides almost instant heat. Air filters and humidity control

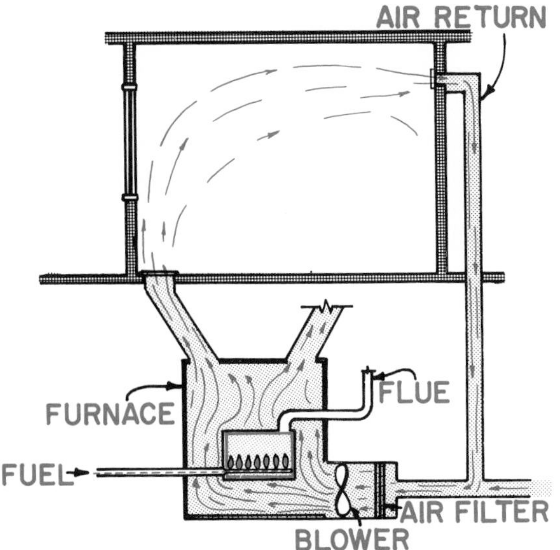

Fig. 62–15. A warm-air heating system.

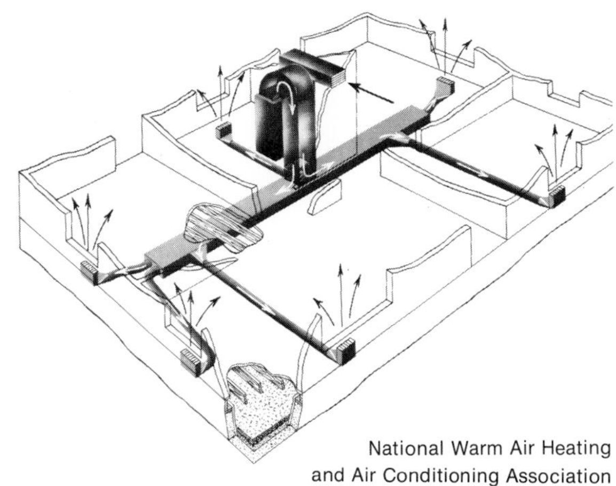
National Warm Air Heating and Air Conditioning Association

Fig. 62–16. Air ducts distribute heated air.

can be combined with the heating unit, and the cooling system can use the same ducts as the heating system, if the ducts are rustproof.

Hot-Water Units

A hot-water unit uses a boiler to heat water and a water pump to send the heated water to radiators, thin tubes, convectors, or baseboards (Figs. 62–18 and 62–19). Forcing the water through the pipes with a pump is faster than allowing gravity to make it flow. If a radiant heating system is used with a hot-water unit,

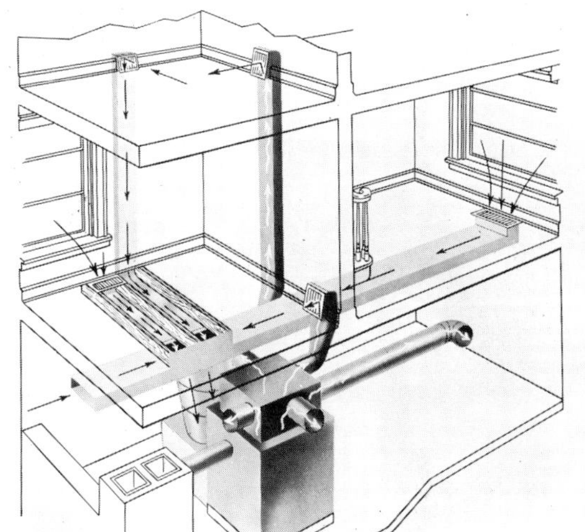
National Warm Air Heating and Air Conditioning Association

Fig. 62–17. Circulation of the air supply.

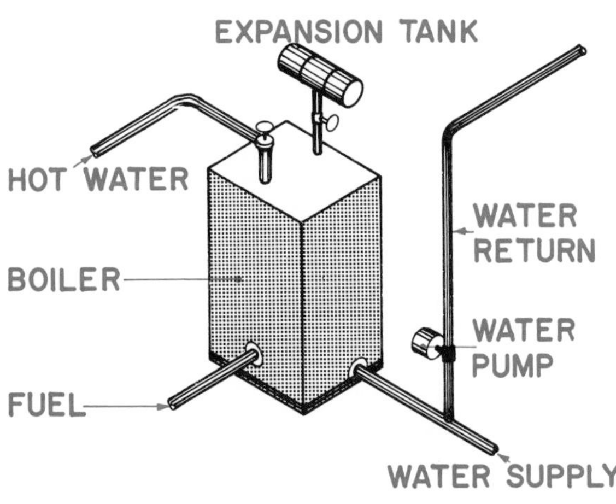

Fig. 62–18. A hot-water unit.

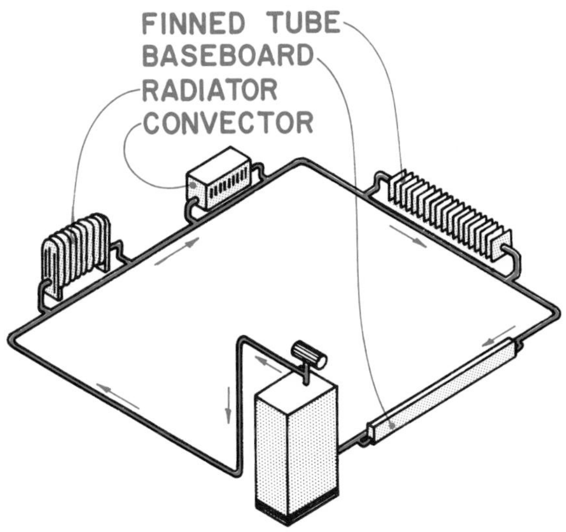

Fig. 62–19. A hot-water system.

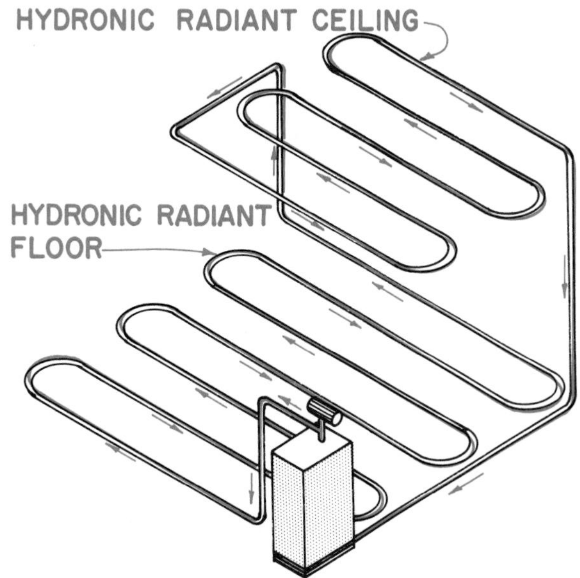

Fig. 62–20. A radiant heating system.

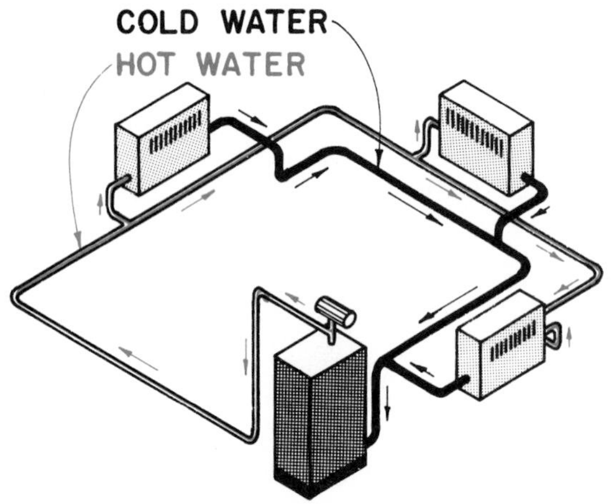

Fig. 62–21. Hot and cold water distribution in a hot-water system.

Electromode

Fig. 62–22. Resistance wires can be placed in the ceiling for radiant heat.

hot-water pipes are placed either in the ceiling or in the floor, as shown in Fig. 62–20. The ceiling is the best location for radiant heating since furniture and rugs may restrict the distribution of heat from the floor. The balance of hot-water and cold-water lines in a hot-water unit is shown in Fig. 62–21. Hot-water heating provides even heat. It keeps heat in the outlets longer than warm-air units. The hot-water boiler is smaller than the warm-air furnace. The hot-water pipe is smaller than the warm-air ductwork.

Steam Units

The steam-heating unit operates by a boiler used to make steam. The steam is then transported by pipes to radiators or convectors and baseboards which give off the heat. The steam condenses to water, which returns to the boiler to be reheated to steam. The boiler must always be located below the level of the rooms being heated. For this reason, steam heat is generally not used for residences but for larger buildings.

Electric Heat

Electric heat is produced when electricity passes through resistance wires. This heat is usually radiated or it could be fan blown (convection). Resistance wires can be placed in panel heaters built into the wall or ceiling (Fig. 62–22) or placed in baseboards or set in plaster to heat the walls, ceilings, or floors. Electric heaters use very little space and require no air for combustion. Electric heat is very clean. It requires no storage or fuel and no duct work.

Complete ventilation and humidity control should accompany electric heat, since it provides no air circulation. Consequently, it tends to be very dry.

Another use of electricity and air conditioning is the *heat pump* (Fig. 62–23). The heat pump is a year-round air conditioner. In winter it takes the heat from the outside and pumps it into the house. There is always some heat in the air regardless of the temperature. In summer the pump is reversed and the heat in the house is pumped outside. Thus the pump works like a reversible refrigerator (Fig. 62–24).

Solar Heat

Solar heating is simply the use of the sun to its fullest possible extent to help the heating

National Warm Air Heating and Air Conditioning Association

Fig. 62–23. A heat pump.

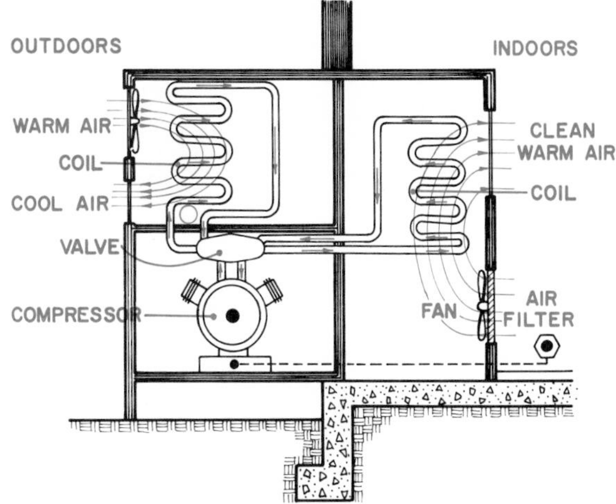

Fig. 62–24. The operation of a heat pump.

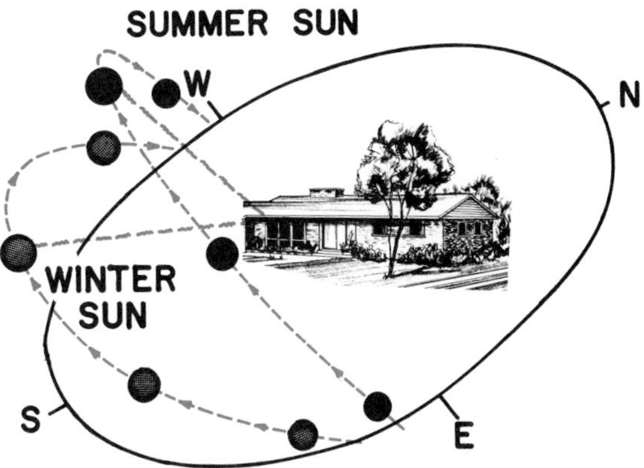

Fig. 62–25. Solar heat should be used to its greatest possible advantage.

Fig. 62–26. Trees provide shade in summer and allow sun to enter the house in the winter.

system. One method of solar heating takes advantage of the relationship between the roof overhangs and large glass areas on the south side of the building. Overhangs should be designed so that the summer sun, which is more directly overhead, is blocked off and the winter sun, which is lower on the southern horizon, is allowed to heat the large window area (Fig. 62–25). Summer control on the east and west sides of the building can also be provided through the use of protective window coverings and trees and shrubbery. In summer the trees provide shade and in winter they lose their leaves and allow the sun to enter the house (Fig. 62–26).

A second method is the harnessing of the sun's energy to heat and cool homes. This can be accomplished in several ways. One procedure is the use of a coated aluminum plate under two transparent covers that would absorb thermal energy and transfer it to a fluid stored in an insulated tank. The fluid would be pumped throughout the house for heating, cooling, or water-heating.

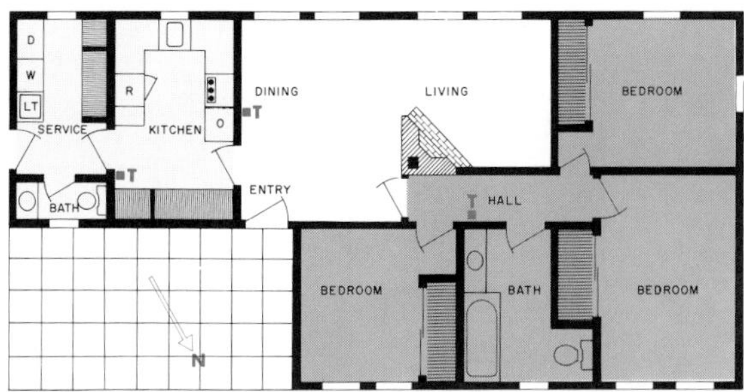

Fig. 62–27. Large homes may require thermostats to control different zones.

A second solar procedure uses the sun's heat for heating and cooling and for converting sunlight into electricity to run home appliances. This is accomplished by two large panels or collectors. They consist of a number of solar cells, which are made of sandwiches of cadmium sulfide and copper sulfide between thin layers of glass. These solar cells produce electrical current on exposure to sunlight. Part of the current produced in this manner is fed immediately into the home's electrical system, to run lights and appliances. The remainder is used to charge a series of batteries. The batteries provide energy when the sun is not shining on the panels.

A third procedure is the use of a solar furnace. The solar furnace is a collection of mirrors that focuses the sun's heat on a concentrated area. Temperature as high as 3500 degrees Fahrenheit (1926 degrees Celsius) can be attained and its energy used.

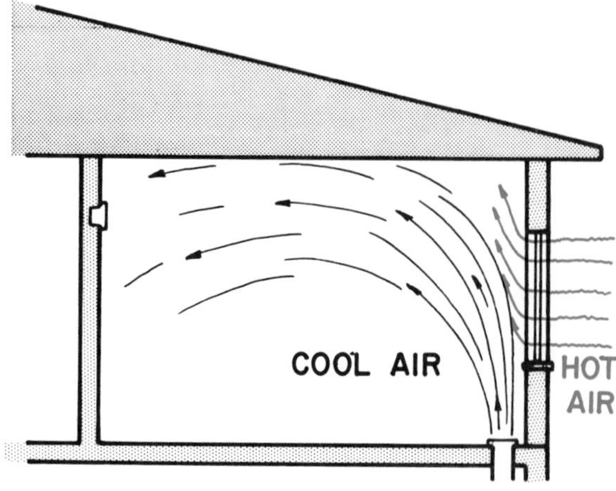

Fig. 62–29. Circulation of cool air.

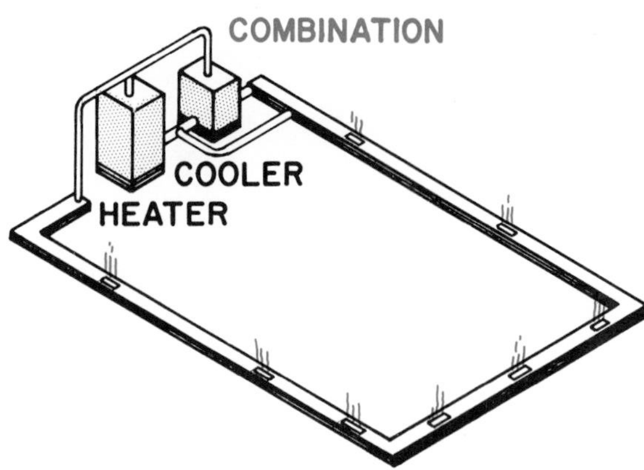

Fig. 62–28. A cooling unit can be part of the heating unit.

With the shortage of fossil fuels for energy, more experimentation, time, and money is being put into this pollution free, inexhaustible supply of energy.

THERMOSTAT

A thermostatic control keeps the house at a constant temperature regardless of the loss of heat and the temperature outside. Thermostatic controls may be used with any heating system. The automatic thermostat control should be located on an interior wall away from any sources of heat or cold such as fireplaces or windows. Larger homes may require zoning controls in which two or more separate heating areas work on separate thermostats (Fig. 62–27). One advantage of electrical heating is

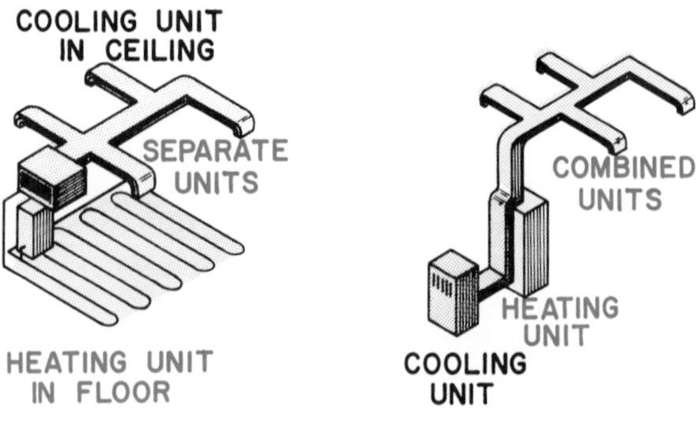

Fig. 62–30. Heating and cooling units may be either separate or combined.

National Warm Air Heating and Air Conditioning Association

Fig. 62–31. One ton of refrigeration, defined.

the fact that each room may be thermostatically controlled. This is especially important in regulating the temperature of children's rooms.

COOLING

A building is air-conditioned by removing the heat. Heat can be transferred in one direction only, from the warmer object to the cooler object. Therefore, to cool a building comfortably, the central air-conditioning system absorbs the heat from the house and transfers it to a liquid refrigerant, usually freon.

COOLING UNITS

The cooling unit can be part of the heating unit using the same blower and vent. In this arrangement, the cooling unit can also use the perimeter ducts (Fig. 62–28). In this system the cool air rises against the warm walls in the summer and cools the house, as shown in Fig. 62–29. The cooling system can also be separate from the heating system (Fig. 62–30).

AIR-CONDITIONING CAPACITY

The size of air-conditioning equipment is usually rated in *tons of refrigeration. A ton of refrigeration* is equal to the amount of cooling that would be produced by melting 1 ton of ice in 24 hours (Fig. 62–31). This amount is equivalent to removing heat at the rate of 12 000 British thermal units per hour (BTU). Air conditioners are also classified by British thermal units. Although metric standards for air-conditioning units have yet to be established,

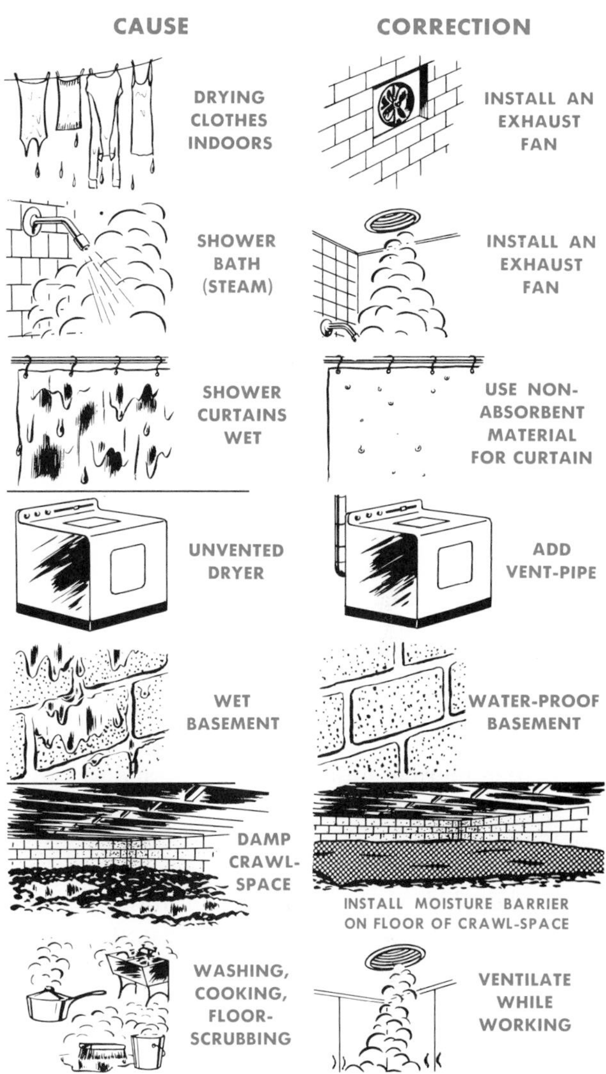

Fig. 62–32. Methods of controlling excessive moisture in the home.

Fig. 62–33. Effective ventilation helps control moisture.

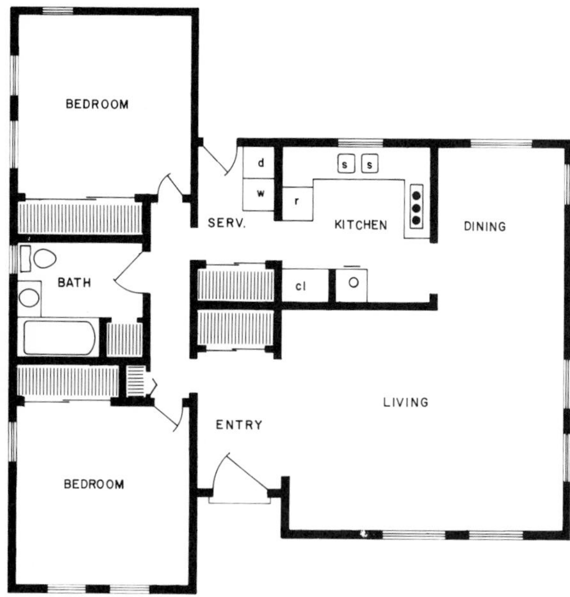

Fig. 62–34. Locate the position of a heating unit and heating outlets on this plan.

Fig. 62–35. Locate the positions of all duct work for a forced-air perimeter system on this plan.

British thermal units can be converted to joules (J). Multiply BTU by 1055 to obtain J approximately.

The average small house can be comfortably cooled with central air-conditioning units of 2- or 3-ton capacities. A 2-ton unit extracts 24 000 BTU per hour. A 3-ton unit extracts 36 000 BTU per hour. Larger homes may require a 5-ton unit which can remove 60 000 BTU per hour.

Because 1 horsepower of electricity is needed per ton of refrigeration, air-conditioning equipment is sometimes referred to by the number of horsepower used to drive the unit.

HUMIDITY CONTROL

The proper amount of moisture in the air is important for good air conditioning. Excessive moisture in the home comes from many sources, such as cooking, cleaning, and washing, and from the outside air. To remove excessive moisture from the air, adequate ventilation and a humidification system is necessary (Fig. 62–32). A *humidification* system takes the moisture from the damp air and passes it over cold coils. When the moisture-laden air passes over these coils, it deposits excess moisture on the coils by condensation. Conversely, if the air is too dry, the humidification system adds moisture to the air. A device used only to remove the humidity from the air is known as a *dehumidifier.* A device used only to add humidity to the air is a *humidifier.*

VENTILATION

Ventilation is necessary to keep fresh air circulating. In the summer it circulates warm and damp air out of the house. Effective ventilation also controls moisture and keeps air relatively dry (Fig. 62–33). The simplest type of ventilation system is cross-ventilation through open windows. However, exhaust fans should be provided in the kitchen, bathroom, and attic to remove moisture, fumes, and warm air. Since large appliances tend to raise the heat of the house by 15 percent, vents also should be provided.

PROBLEMS

1. **Sketch the floor plan shown in Fig. 62–34. Sketch a warm-air heating unit in the most appropriate location and locate the outlets for this system.**
2. **Sketch the floor plan shown in Fig. 62–35. Indicate the thermostatic zones for this house by using different colored pencils to shade the areas.**
3. **Sketch the house shown in Fig. 62–35. Locate the position of all duct work for a forced warm-air perimeter system.**
4. **Define these terms: *air conditioning, humidity, air filter, humidifier, humidification, radiation, convection, conduction, insulation, perimeter, radiant heating, warm air, hot water, steam, electric heating, thermostat, solar heating, tons of refrigeration.***

UNIT 63

Air-Conditioning Symbols

Heating and ventilating equipment is drawn on floor plans using symbols (Fig. 63–1). They show the location and type of equipment, and also the movement of hot and cold air.

The location of horizontal ducts on a heating and ventilating duct plan is shown by outlining the position of the ducts. Since vertical ducts pass through the plane of projection,

LINES

AIR PRESSURE LINE FLOW
AIR PRESSURE LINE RETURN
COLD WATER
DRAIN — D —
FUEL OIL FLOW — FOF —
FUEL OIL RETURN — FOR —
GAS — G — G —
HUMIDIFICATION LINE — H —
HOT WATER HEATING RETURN
HOT WATER HEATING SUPPLY
ICE WATER RETURN
ICE WATER SUPPLY
REFRIGERANT
REFRIGERANT DISCHARGE — RD —
STEAM — MEDIUM PRESSURE
STEAM RETURN—MED. PRESS.

DUCTS

DIRECTION OF FLOW
DUCT SIZE — 10×15
DUCT SECTION RETURN — 10x15
DUCT SECTION FLOW — 10x15
EXHAUST DUCT
FILTER LINE
PIPE COIL
PIPES & JOINTS
VANES

INSULATION

BLANKET INSULATION
GENERAL INSULATION
LOOSE INSULATION
RIGID BOARD INSULATION
REFLECTIVE FOIL

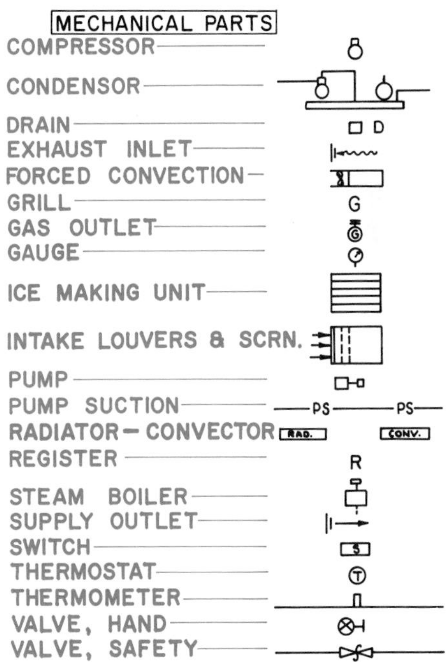

Fig. 63–1. Heating and ventilating symbols used on floor plans.

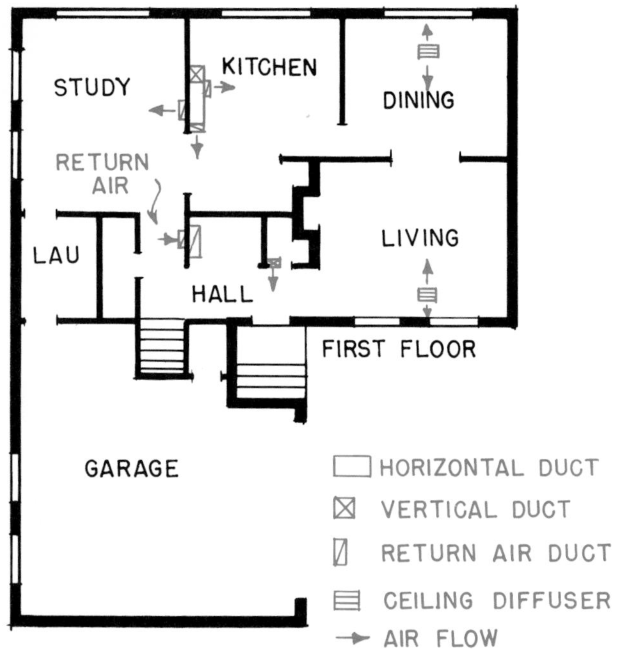

Fig. 63–2. A heating and ventilating duct plan.

diagonal lines are used to indicate the position of vertical ducts. The flow of air through the ducts can be easily traced. The direction of air flow is shown by an arrow pointing in the direction of the air flow (Fig. 63–2).

Air flow emanating from the heating-cooling unit is shown by an arrow pointing out from the diffusers. Return air is indicated by an arrow pointing into the duct.

In preparing heating and ventilating duct plans for multiple-story buildings, the position of second-story ducts can be determined by placing the second-floor plan on top of the first-floor plan.

PROBLEMS

1. **Draw a floor plan and insert those symbols which apply to your heating unit.**
2. **Draw a floor plan and insert the symbols which apply to your complete air-conditioning unit.**
3. **What type of heating unit is best for your community? Consider the weather and the price of fuel.**
4. **What type of cooling system is best for your community?**
5. **Would a separate or a combined heating and cooling unit be more satisfactory in your home?**

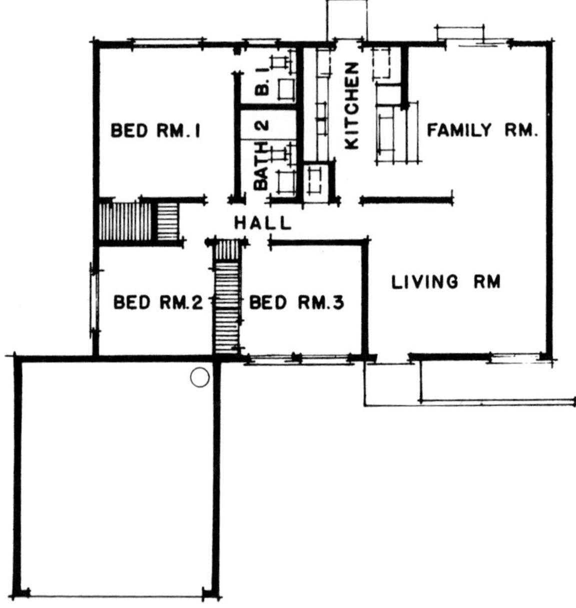

Signature Homes

Fig. 63–3. Add heating and ventilation symbols to this plan.

6. **Draw an air-conditioning plan for the house shown in Fig. 63–3.**
7. **Define these terms: *duct, diffusers, return air, air flow.***

SECTION 15

Plumbing Diagrams

Plumbing **refers to the water supply and drainage of waste water and sewage. A plumbing system consists of supply pipes that carry fresh water under pressure from a public water supply or individual wells to fixtures. The water is then disposed of through pipes which carry waste to the disposal system by gravity drainage.**

Prefabricated plumbing walls installed at the factory save the builder installation time by having part of the labor done on an assembly line. If fixtures are placed close together, many feet of pipelines can be saved. The kitchen and bathrooms can also be placed back to back or over each other in a two-story house to eliminate long runs of pipe. However, it is important to put the kitchen and bathrooms where they would be most convenient, even if they are at opposite ends of the house

Owens-Corning Fiberglas Corporation

UNIT 64

Plumbing Lines

Two types of plumbing lines (pipes)—water supply lines and waste lines (Fig 64–1)—carry the water to and from the fixtures.

Chase Brass & Copper Company

Fig. 64–1. Plumbing lines are of two types, water supply lines and waste lines.

WATER SUPPLY

Fresh water is brought in to all plumbing fixtures under pressure. This water is supplied from a public water supply or from private wells. Because the water is under pressure, the pipes may be run in any convenient direction after leaving the main control valve (Fig. 64–2).

Water lines require a shutoff valve at the property line and at the foundation of the

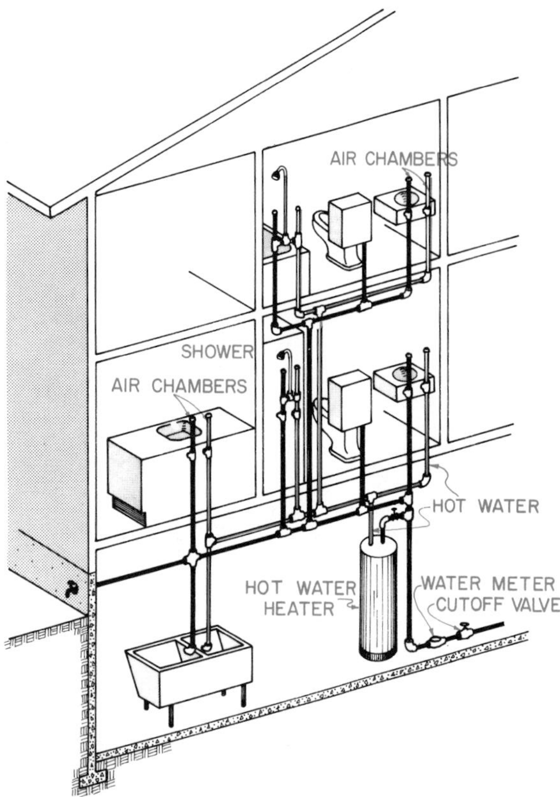

Fig. 64–2. The position of basic plumbing lines.

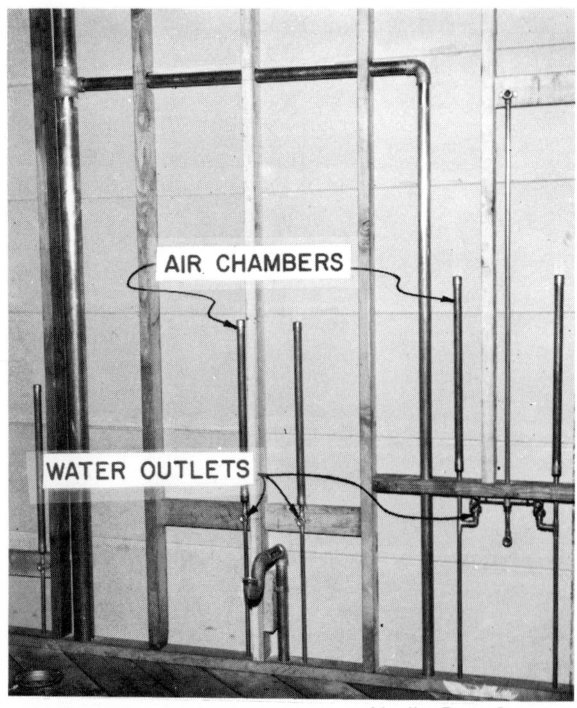

Mueller Brass Company

Fig. 64–4. Air-cushion chambers stop hammering noises.

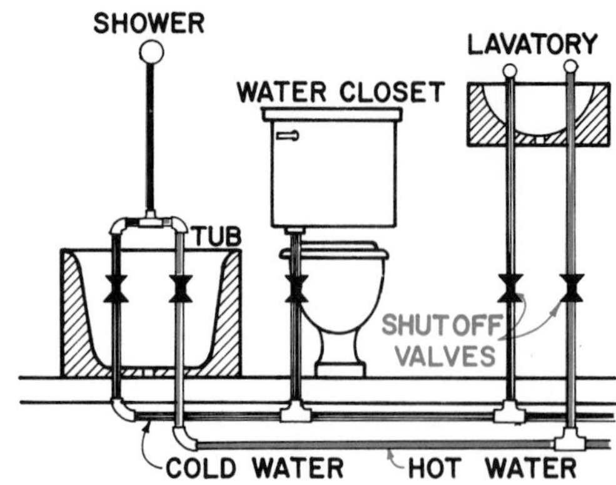

Fig. 64–3. Each fixture should have a shutoff valve.

house. The water meter is located at the shutoff valve near the house. The size of all water supply lines for a house ranges from 3/4″ to 1″ (19 to 25 mm). Each fixture has a shutoff valve on the pipe to allow repairs (Fig. 64–3).

All fixtures have a free-flowing supply of water if the lines are the correct size. Lines that are too small cause a whistling as the water flows through at high speeds. Air-cushion chambers stop hammering noises caused by closing valves (Fig. 64–4). Too many changes of direction of pipe cause friction that reduces the water pressure.

Hot water is obtained by routing cold water through a water heater (Fig. 64–5). The hot water is then directed, under pressure, to all fixtures needing it. The hot-water valve is on the left of the fixture as you face it. Placing insulation around hot-water lines conserves hot water and reduces the total cost of fuel for heating water.

WASTE LINES

Waste water is discharged through the disposal system by gravity drainage (Fig. 64–6). All pipes in this system must slant down toward the main disposal so that the weight of the waste will cause it to flow toward the main disposal system and away from the house. Because of the gravity flow, the waste lines that run to the city sewage system must be much larger than the water supply lines, in which there is pressure (Fig. 64–7).

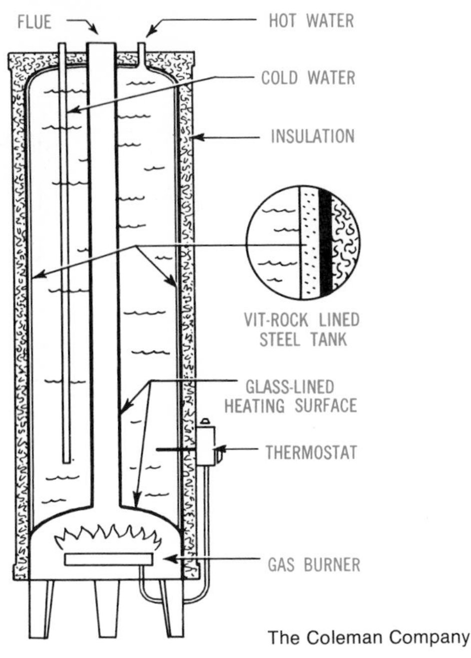

The Coleman Company

Fig. 64–5. Glass-lined steel hot-water heater.

In the house, the waste lines are concealed in the walls and under floors. The vertical lines are called *stacks*, and the horizontal lines are called *branches*. Also needed are the *vents* for circulation of air. Vents permit sewer gases to escape through the roof to the outside, equalizing air pressure in the drainage system. The *fixture traps* stop the gases from entering the house. Each fixture must have a separate seal to prevent backflow of sewer gas into the house. The fixture traps are exposed for easy maintenance. The water-closet trap is built in.

The flow of waste water starts at the fixture trap. It flows through the fixture branches to the soil stack. It continues through the house drain, house sewer, and finally reaches the main sewer.

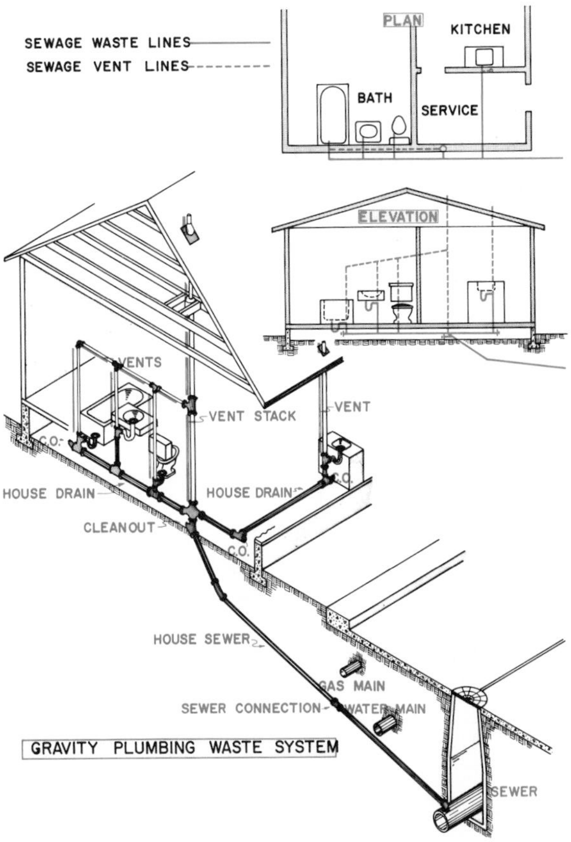

Fig. 64–6. Waste is discharged through gravity drainage.

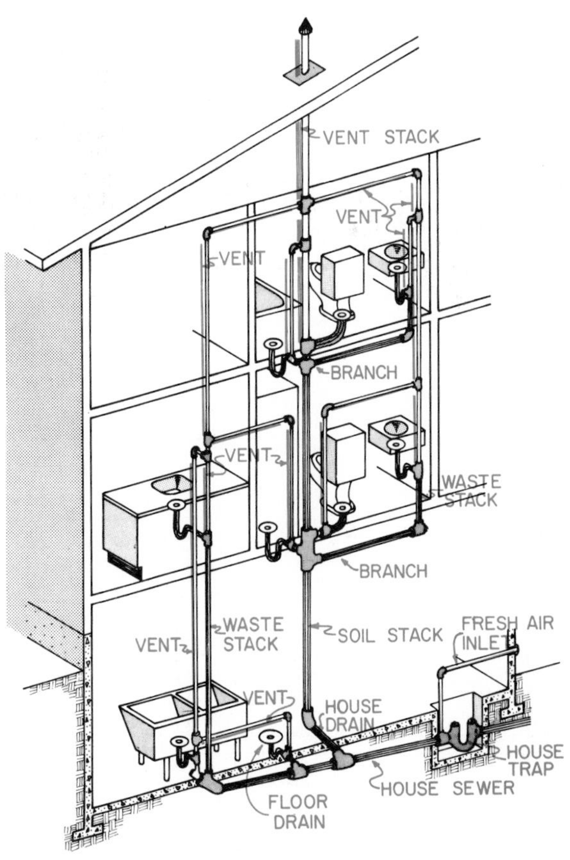

Fig. 64–7. Waste lines must be larger than water supply lines.

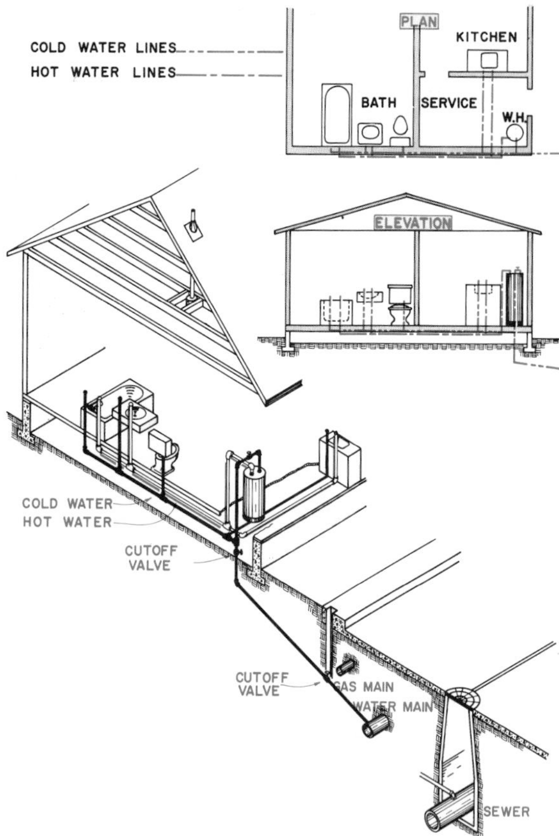

Fig. 64–8. A pressure plumbing and supply system.

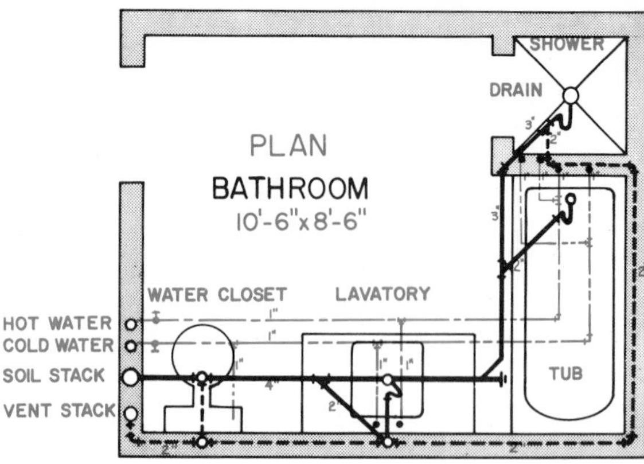

Fig. 64–9. A schematic plan of bathroom plumbing lines.

Waste stacks carry only water waste. The lines taking the wastes from the water closet are called the *soil lines.* Because of the solid waste materials, soil lines are the largest in the system. Each time the soil lines are used, they are flushed.

The fresh-water supply pipes are wet pipes, full of water under pressure at all times. The waste and soil pipes are wet pipes having water in them only when waste water is being disposed of. The vent-pipe system is composed of dry pipes which never have water in them.

Figure 64–8 shows the plumbing and supply system. The systems are usually shown on a pictorial drawing, elevation, or plan. Figures 64–9 and 64–10 show the working drawings for a bathroom.

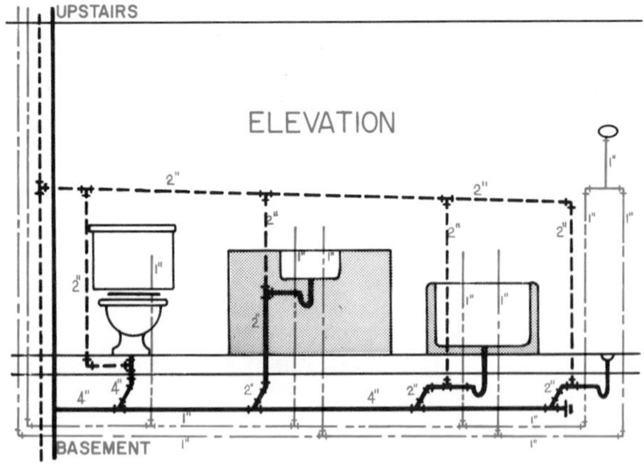

Fig. 64–10. A schematic elevation of bathroom plumbing lines.

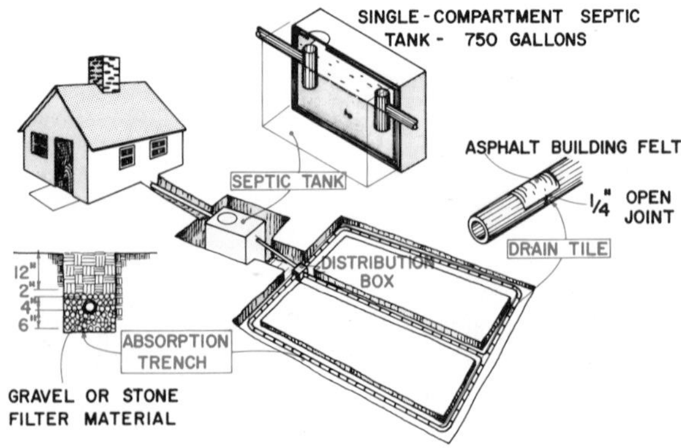

Fig. 64–11. A complete plumbing system.

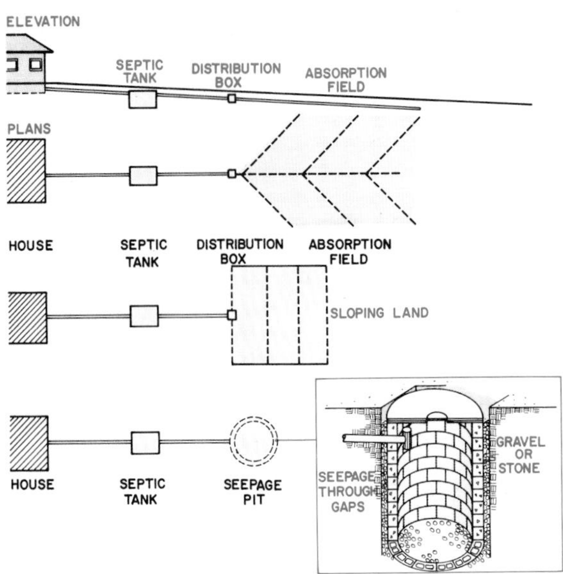

Fig. 64–12. Plumbing symbols.

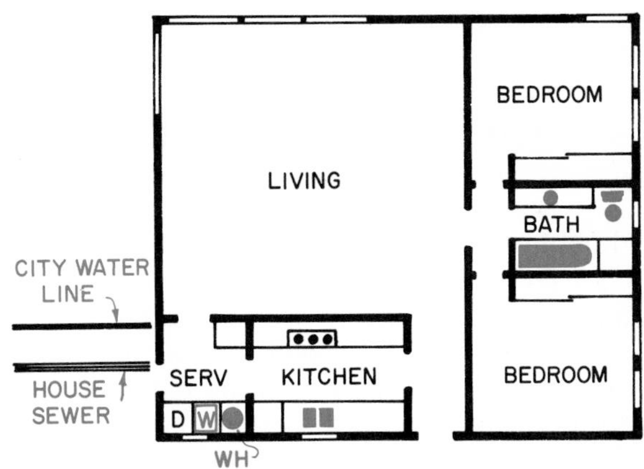

Fig. 64–13. Add water supply lines to this plan.

Fig. 64–14. Add plumbing symbols to this plan.

SEPTIC SYSTEM

When a city sewer is not available, a private sewer, called a *septic system,* must be used (Fig. 64–11). The septic system converts waste solids into liquid by bacterial action. The house wastes go to a septic tank buried outside. The lighter part of the liquid flows out of the septic tank into the *drainage field,* which is made up of porous pipes spread over an area to allow distribution of water (Fig. 64–12).

The size of the septic system varies according to the number of occupants of the house. The size of the lines and the distance of the septic tank and drainage field from the house depend on the building codes of the community.

PROBLEMS

1. **Make a sketch of Fig. 64–13 and add the water supply system, using the proper plumbing symbols. Use examples in Figs. 64–9 and 64–10.**
2. **Make a sketch of Fig. 64–14 and indicate a water supply system, using the proper plumbing symbols.**
3. **Add the waste lines to the sketch you made for Problem 2.**
4. **Define these terms: *gravity drainage, stack, branch, vent, fixture trap, soil stack, house drain, house sewer, waste stack, septic system, septic tank, drainage field, shutoff valve, air chambers, waste lines.***

UNIT 65

Plumbing Fixtures

Plumbing fixtures are available in a variety of sizes, colors, and materials. Since they are used continually for many years, durability is extremely important. Good fixtures are more convenient than poorer ones and require fewer repairs. The following fixtures represent the most common kinds available for the bathroom and the kitchen.

Fig. 65–1. Types of showers.

BATHROOM FIXTURES

Bathroom fixtures are divided into four kinds, as follows:

Water closets: tank and bowl in one piece, separate tank and bowl, wall-hung tank and bowl
Showers (Fig. 65–1): prefabricated, built on the job, placed over bathtub
Bathtubs (Fig. 65–2): recessed, square, free-standing, sunken
Lavatories (Fig. 65–3): wall-hung, cabinet, built-in counter-top, corner

KITCHEN FIXTURES

Kitchen fixtures are divided into five kinds, as follows:

Sinks (Fig. 65–4): sink and drainboard unit, single sink, double sink
Laundry tubs: single, double, triple
Dishwashers (Fig. 65–5): built-in, free-standing
Hot water heater: electric, gas
Washing machine (Fig. 65–6): top-loading, front-loading, wringer

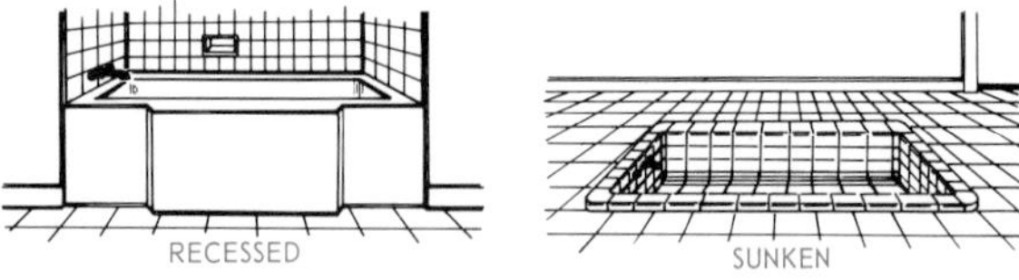

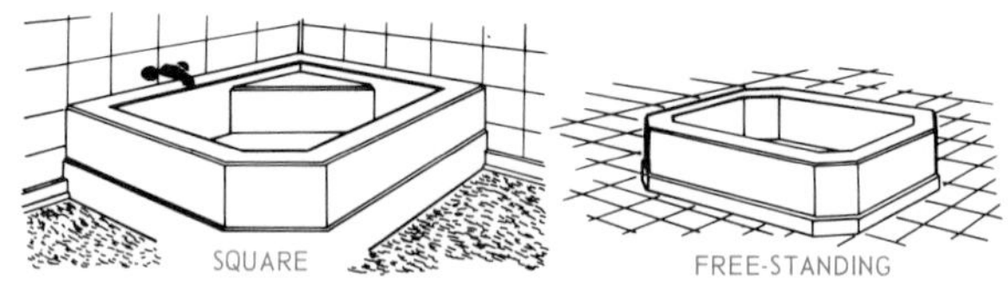

Fig. 65–2. Types of bathtubs.

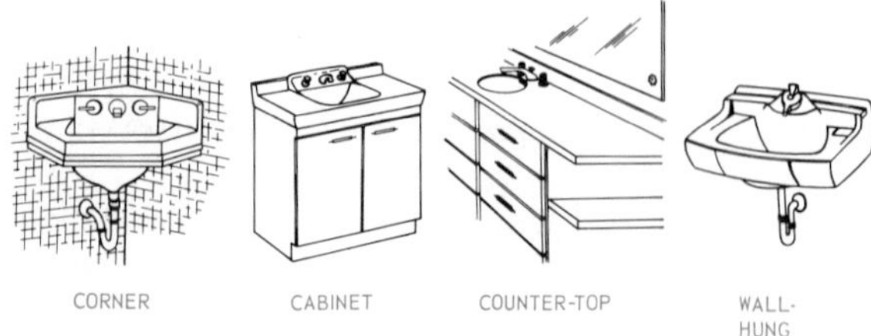

Fig. 65–3. Types of lavatories.

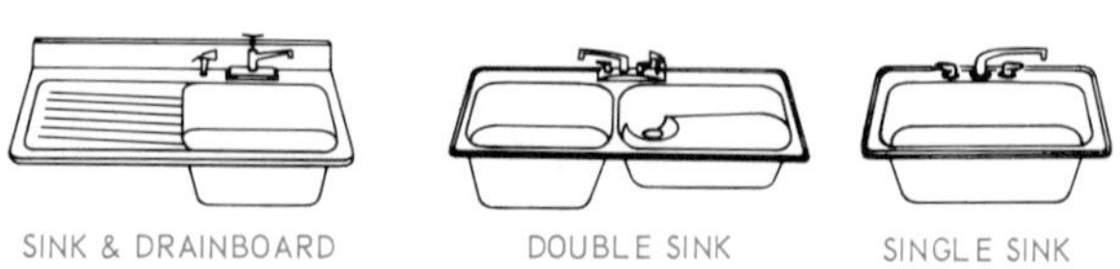

Fig. 65–4. Types of sinks.

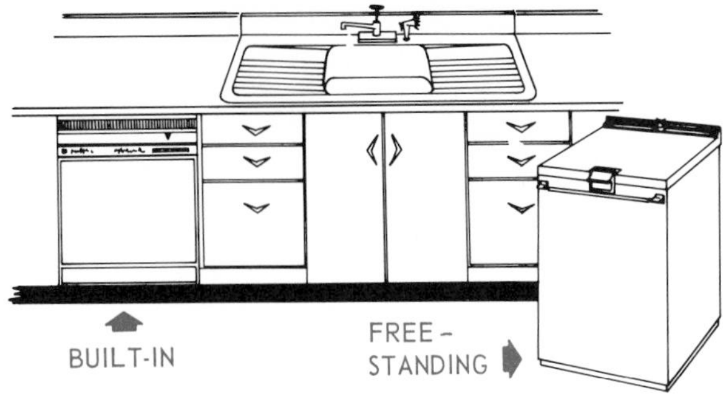

Fig. 65–5. Types of dishwashers.

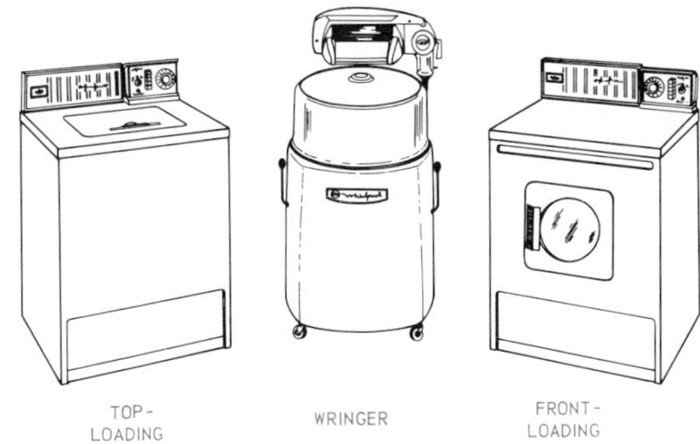

Fig. 65–6. Types of washing machines.

Fig. 65–7. Add plumbing fixtures and lines to this plan.

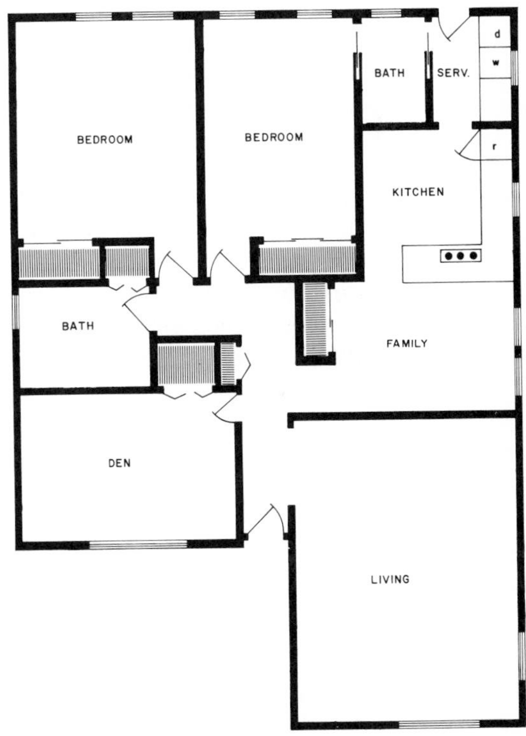

Fig. 65–8. Add plumbing lines to this plan.

PROBLEMS

1. Make a sketch to show the positions of the plumbing fixtures on the plan shown in Fig. 65–7 (water closet, shower, bathtub, lavatories, sinks, laundry tub, dishwasher, water heater, and washing machine).
2. Add the plumbing lines to the plan shown in Fig. 65–7.
3. Add the plumbing fixtures and lines to the plan shown in Fig. 65–8.
4. From your building code, give the sizes of the plumbing lines to be used in the plan shown in Fig. 65–7.
5. Define these terms: *plumbing fixture, water closet, wall-hung water closet, drainboard.*

SECTION 16

Modular Component Plans

Industrial automation methods have enabled manufacturers to produce high-quality and low-priced products more quickly than ever before. However, the home-building industry, which has constructed over 33 million homes for American families, has not industrialized or standardized its production methods to any great degree. Construction methods in the home-building industry continue to contribute to excessive waste of materials and time.

However, to standardize and automate more fully the home-building industry, lumber manufacturers have developed a program of coordinating dimensional standards and components on standard structural parts such as windows, doors, and trusses. This standardization enables the part to fit into the plan for any home designed according to a standard modular component.

Using a coordinated system of dimensioning for these components results in the most efficient use of materials and time.

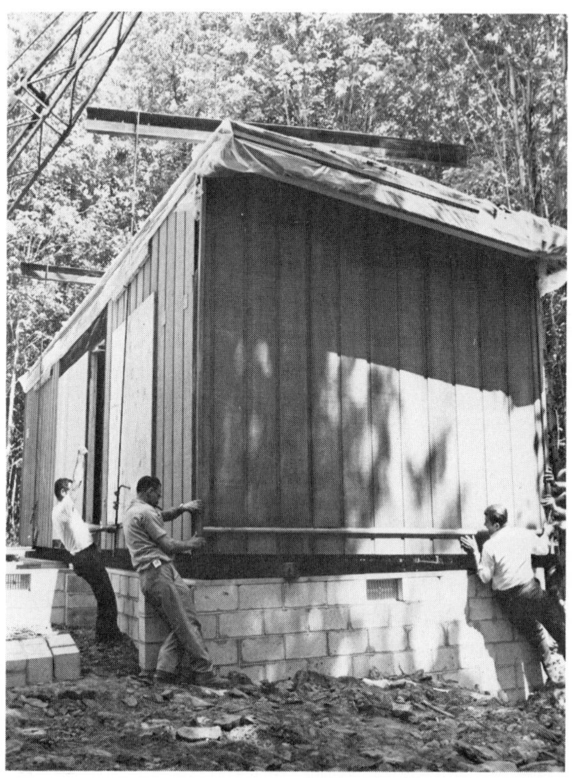

Designaire Home Corporation

UNIT 66

Modular System of Designing

The Unicom method of designing includes the use of modular components and the preparation of plans to a modular dimensional standard. *Unicom* means uniform manufacture of components. This modular system was developed by the National Lumber Manufacturers Association. Using this method, the designer must think of the home as a series of component parts. These component parts may be standard factory-made components or built on the job site. In either case, plans are prepared to be consistent with the size of these components. Plans must also be interchangeable and consistent with the Unicom method of dimensioning.

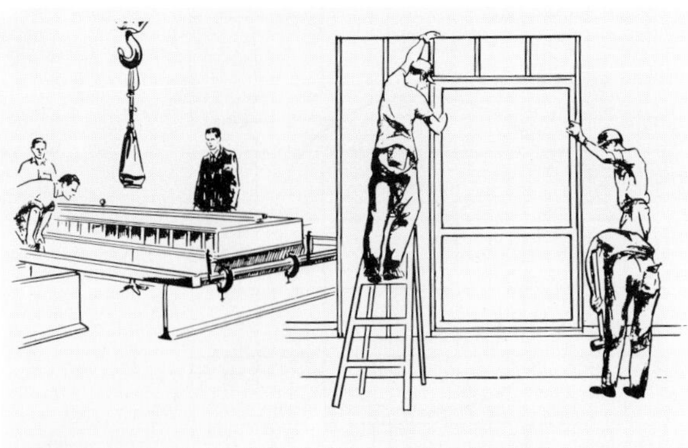

National Lumber Manufacturers Association

Fig. 66–1. Component parts may be factory-made or produced on the job site.

Without this dimensional standard the use of modular component parts is of no value (Fig. 66–1).

ADVANTAGES

The Unicom method is applicable to on-site or shop fabrication and is based on standard lumber sizes. Thus it may be used effectively by large builders or by the custom builder who erects only a few homes each year (Fig. 66–2).

Homes may be erected completely with factory-made parts (Fig. 66–3), or the house may be framed conventionally, or a combination method may be used. Faster planning and erection of the house benefit both builder and home buyer. This system makes possible the more efficient use of materials, thus reducing waste in conventional home construction.

Building inventory costs are cut because of the number of elements needed for maximum design flexibility. This saves considerable time. It also reduces the number of items that must be kept in inventory. Perhaps the most important advantage of the Unicom system is that it makes possible the use of modern mass-production techniques. These techniques provide great accuracy in the construction of components and superior quality control in their fabrication.

DESIGNING WITH MODULAR GRIDS

The coordination of modular components with the system of modular dimensions utilizes all three dimensions—length, width, and height. The overall width and length dimensions are most critical in the planning process, as shown in Fig. 66–4. The *modular planning grid* is a horizontal plane divided into equal spaces in length and width. It provides the basic control for the modular coordination system. The entire grid, shown in Fig. 66–5, is divided into equal spaces of 4″, 16″, 24″, and 48″ The Unicom system is not yet designed to metric standards. Composite dimensions are therefore all multiples of 4″. The 16″ unit is used in multiples for wall, window, and door panels to provide an increment small enough for flexible planning and optimum inventory of these components.

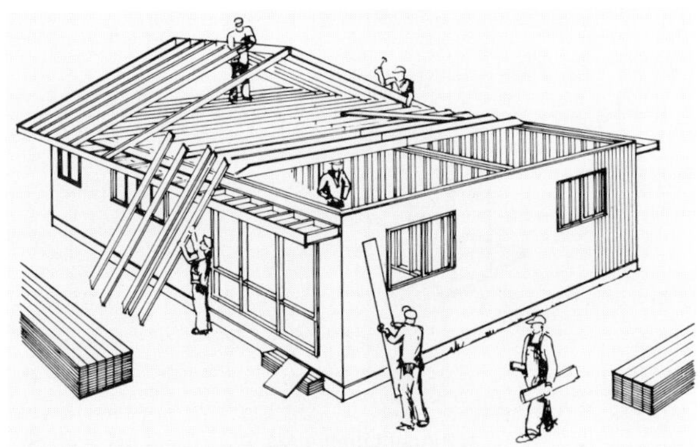

National Lumber Manufacturers Association

Fig. 66–2. On-site fabrication.

National Lumber Manufacturers Association

Fig. 66–3. Shop-fabricated components.

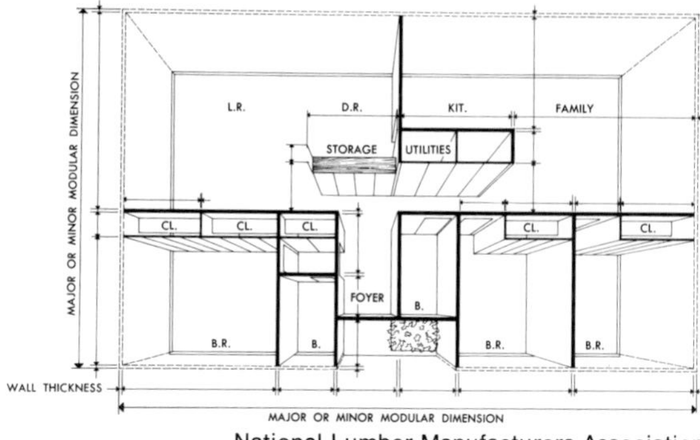

National Lumber Manufacturers Association

Fig. 66–4. The overall length and width must be modular dimensions.

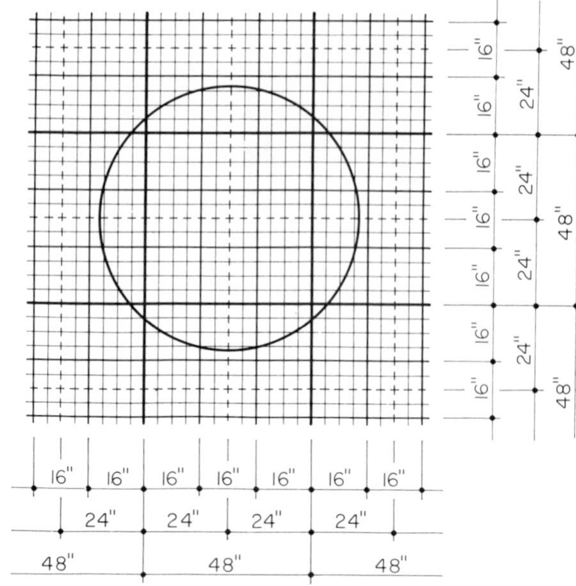

National Lumber Manufacturers Association

Fig. 66–5. Modular-component grid.

Increments of 24″ and 48″ are used for overall dimensions of the house. The 24″ module is called the *minor module*. The 48″ module is called the *major module*. Figure 66–6 shows the use of the 16″ module in design locations for window and door component panels. Figure 66–7 shows the use of the major and minor modules in establishing basic modular house length and width.

Since the Unicom method does not require the wall, floor, and roof elements to be tied to a large fixed panel size, there is no need for the designer to adhere to a fixed 4′ or larger increment in planning.

PREPARING THE MODULAR PLAN

When the basic floor-plan design is completed (Fig. 66–8), the plan should be sketched or drawn on the Unicom modular grid and all nonmodular dimensions converted to the nearest modular size (Fig. 66–9). Each square on the grid represents the basic 4″ module.

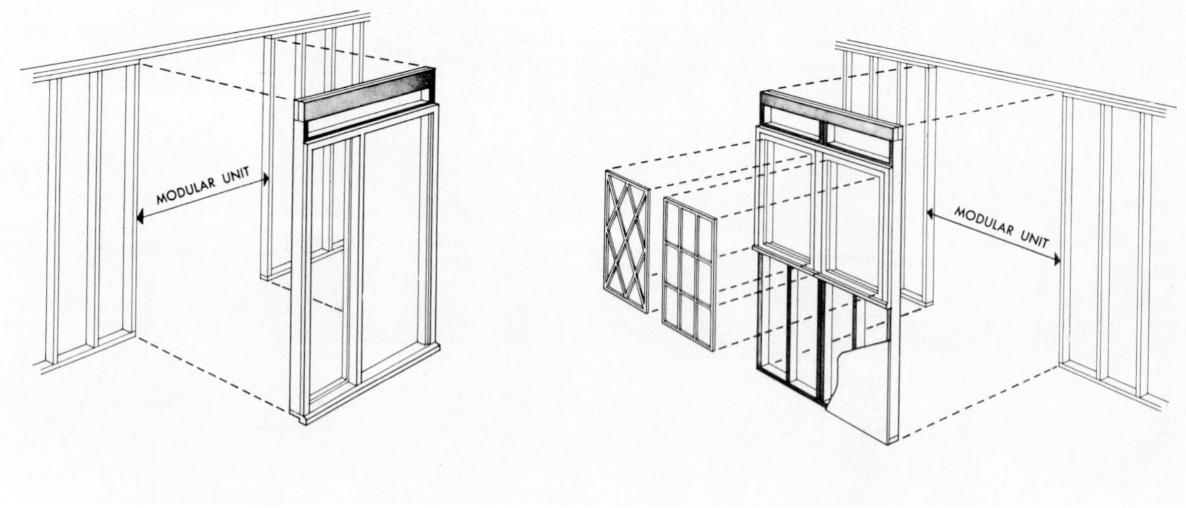

National Lumber Manufacturers Association

Fig. 66–6. Modular-component door and windows.

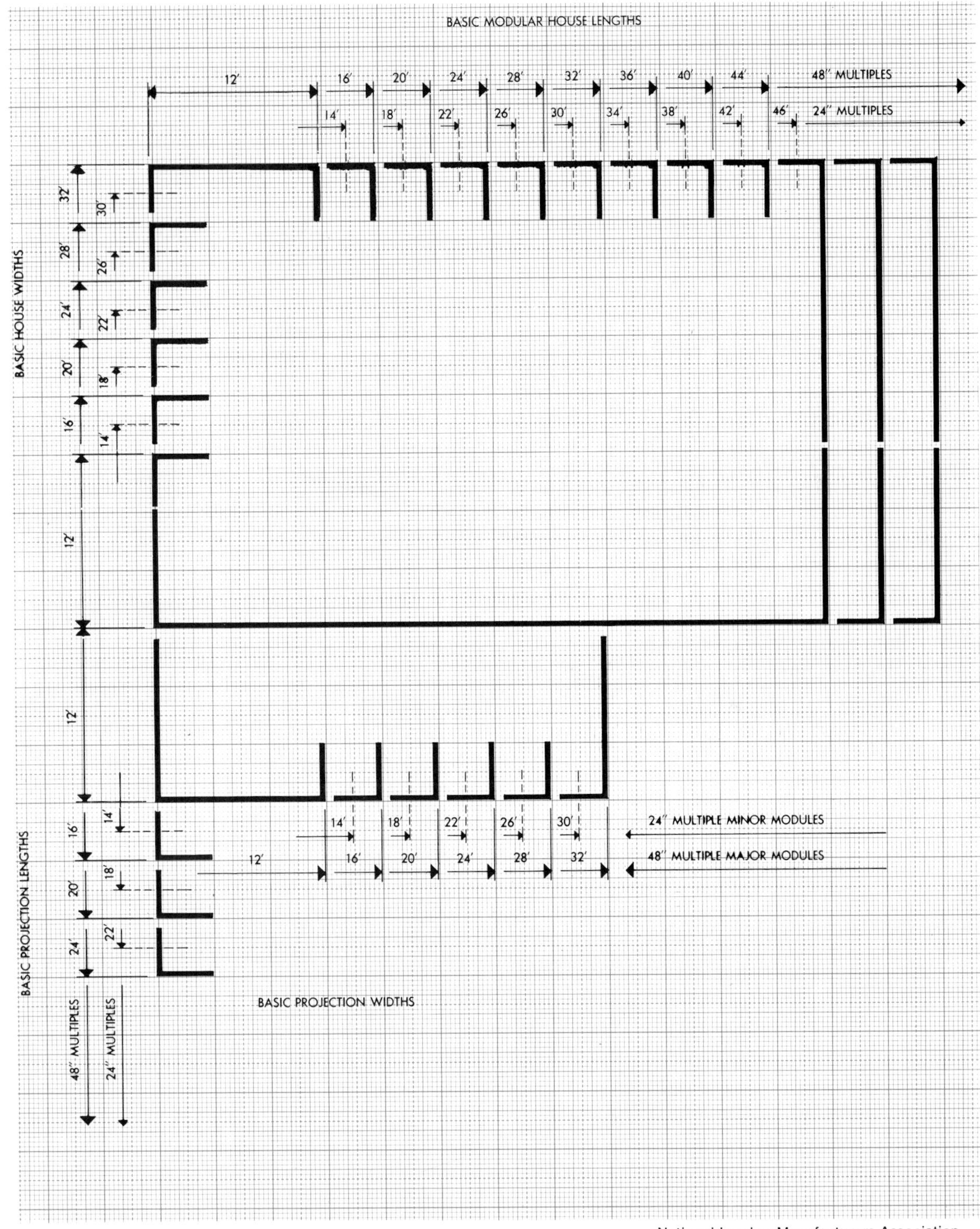

National Lumber Manufacturers Association

Fig. 66–7. Modular width and length increments.

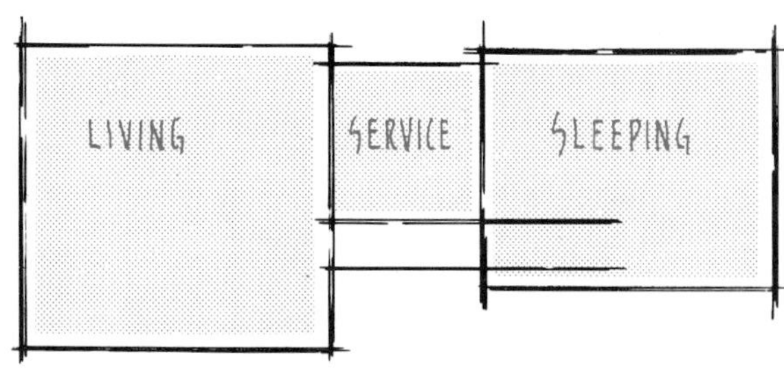

Fig. 66–8. Initial planning for modular construction is the same as in designing conventional buildings.

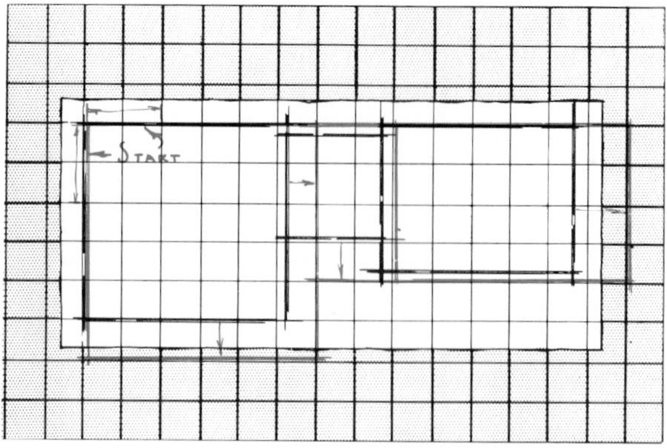

Fig. 66–9. Nonmodular dimensions must be converted to the nearest module.

Standard 16″ modules are represented by the intermediate heavy lines. Major 48″ module lines are indicated by the heaviest lines. Minor 24″ modules are represented by dotted lines. By employing modular dimensions in multiples of 2′ or 4′ for house exteriors, fractional spans for floor and roof framing are eliminated.

Variations in the thickness of exterior and partition walls interfere with true modular dimensioning; therefore, the total thicknesses of all of these walls must be subtracted from the overall modular dimension to obtain the net inside dimension, as shown in Fig. 66–10. Also nonmodular dimensions created by existing building laws or built-in equipment must be incorporated in the modular coordination system (Fig. 66–11). This end is accomplished by dimensioning conventionally the nonmodular distances where they exist.

After the overall dimensions are established and nonmodular dimensions incorpo-

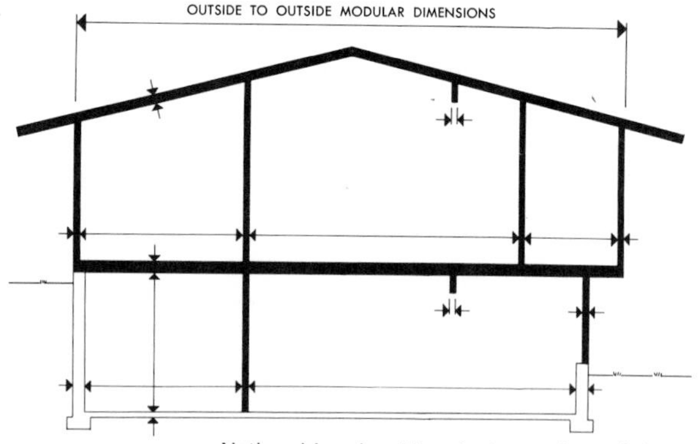

National Lumber Manufacturers Association

Fig. 66–10. The sum of the wall thicknesses must be subtracted from the overall modular dimension to obtain the net inside dimension.

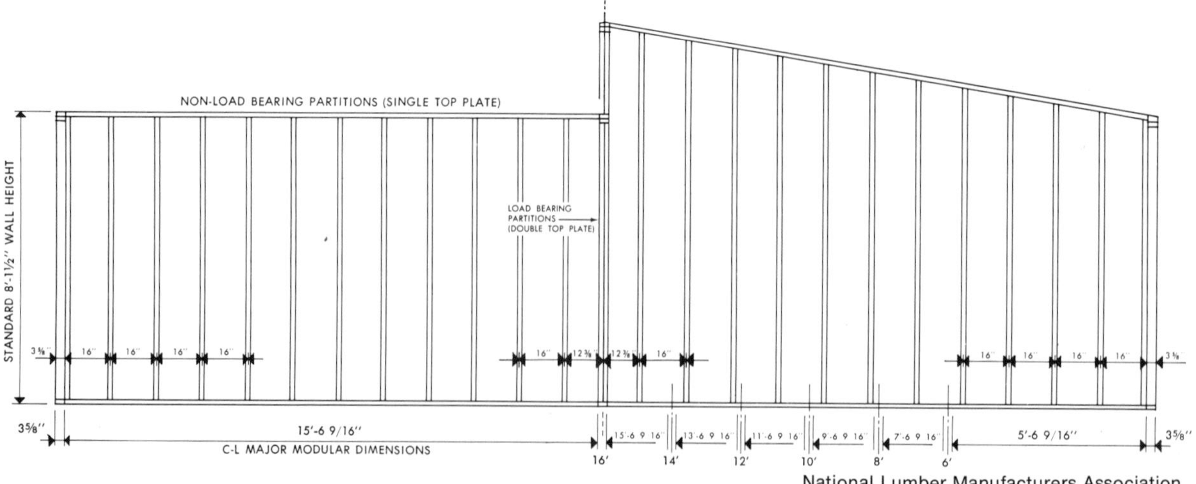

National Lumber Manufacturers Association

Fig. 66–11. Nonmodular dimensions must be incorporated into the Unicom system.

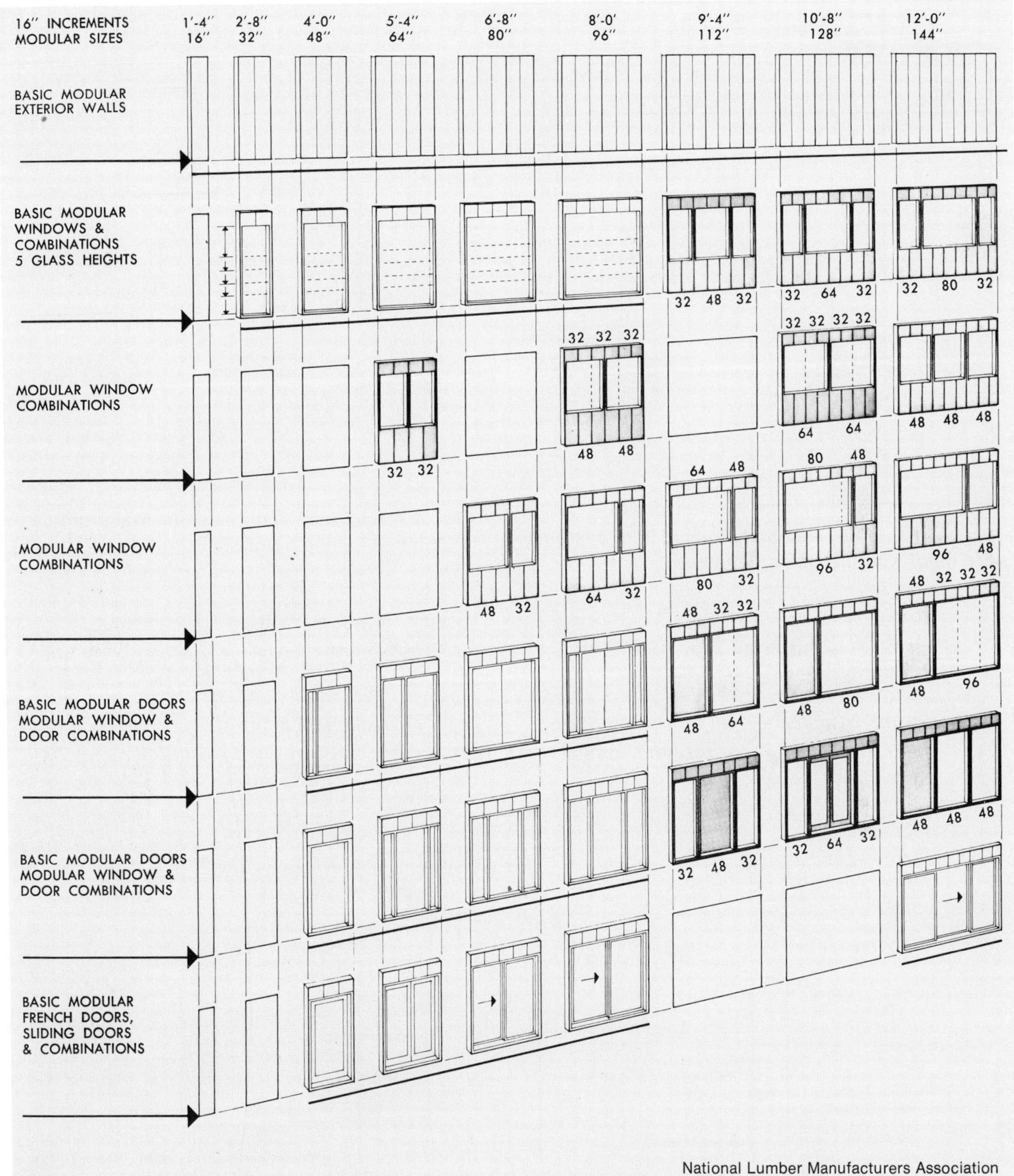

Fig. 66-12. Doors, windows, and panels should be located on the 16" module.

rated in the plan, the panels for exterior doors, and windows and for exterior walls should be established on the 16" module, as shown in Fig. 66-12. The precise location of wall openings on the 16" module also eliminates the extra wall framing commonly encountered in non-modular home planning; and the 16" spacing of structural members increases design flexibility by one-third, compared with spacing at the 24" minor module.

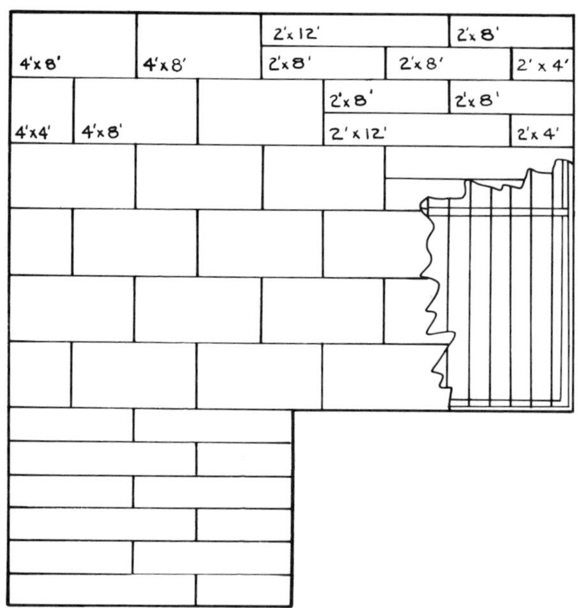

Fig. 66–13. Conventionally framed floor systems are used with the Unicom method.

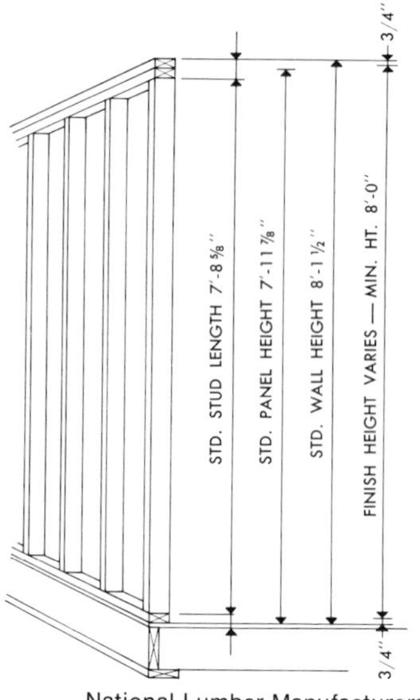

National Lumber Manufacturers Association

Fig. 66–14. Framing dimensions that produce an 8′ finished ceiling height.

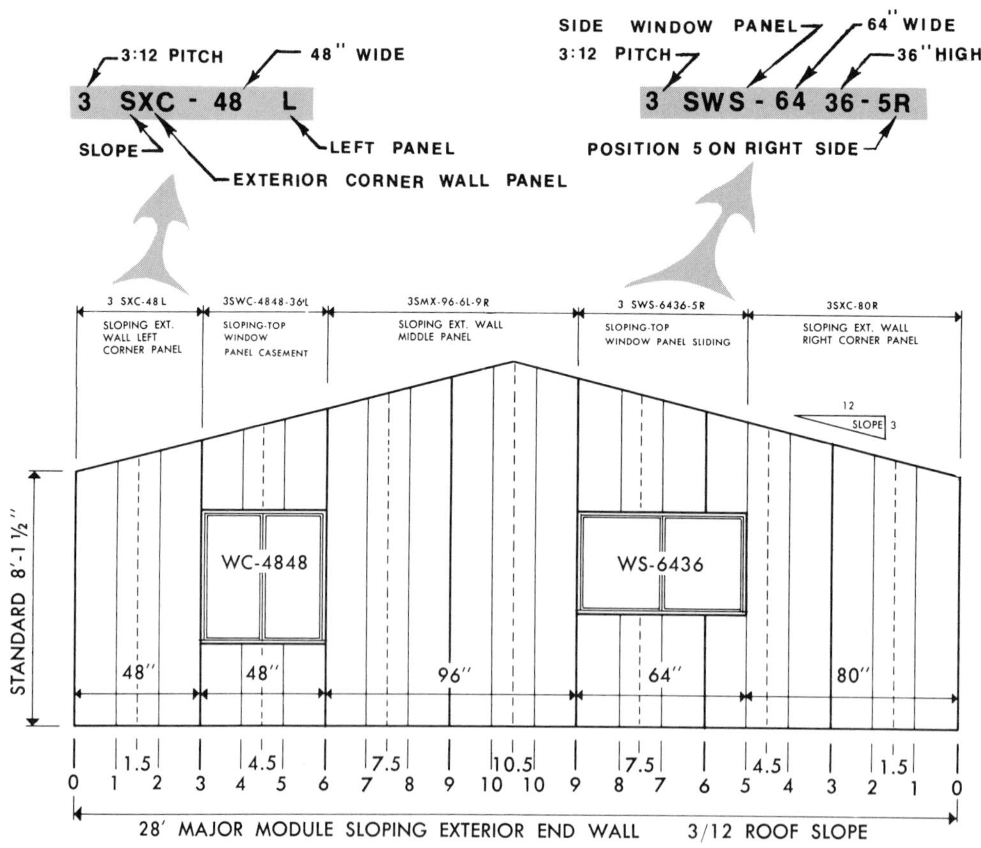

National Lumber Manufacturers Association

Fig. 66–15. The use of code numbers in describing components.

Conventionally framed platform floor systems (Fig. 66–13) provide the most flexible method of floor framing for the variety of design conditions encountered with the Unicom system. Modular sizes of floor sheathing materials are economically applied to the modular spacing of floor joists.

As previously stated, the Unicom method is based on modular coordination of all three dimensions—width, length, and height. Although width and length are the most critical dimensions, standard heights are necessary to eliminate much waste and to ensure the proper fitting of components. A standard height of 8′—1½″ for exterior-wall components allows for floor- and ceiling-finish applications with a combined thickness of 1½″. The result is a standard 8′ finished ceiling height, as shown in Fig. 66–14.

Table 66–1. ABBREVIATIONS USED TO IDENTIFY COMPONENTS

X	Exterior-wall panels
XC	Full-corner exterior-wall panels
XCBM	Cantilever-beam exterior-wall corner panels
XCA	Cut-back corner exterior-wall panels
RP	Roof panels
FP	Floor panels
P	Interior partition panel
WC	Casement window panels
WD	Double-hung window panels
WS	Sliding window panels
WAF	Fixed-awning window panels
WP	Fixed picture-window panels
WPP	Full-height, fixed, picture-window panels
GG	Glass gable panels
D	Door panels with one door
2D	Door panels with two doors
DS	Door panels with one side light
2DS2	Door panels with two doors and two side lights
DS2	Door panels with two side lights
DSL	Sliding door panels
DA	Garage door panels

IDENTIFICATION SYSTEM

A complete system of short-form identification for separate pieces and fabricated components simplifies the practical use of the modular coordination system of building. Table 66–1 shows some of the abbreviations used to identify components. In most cases, the basic identifying letter or combination is directly associated with the element. For example, J stands for joist and R stands for rafter.

The shorthand has been extended to include complete descriptions of wall panels, including information pertaining to the slope, window style, and position, as shown in Fig. 66–15.

Modular construction in industry is important because it eliminates individual constructed items, thereby reducing costs.

Architect Joseph Lombardo has designed portable modular units that can be transported to the site and be assembled with many different floor-plan arrangements (Figs. 66–16A, B, C, and D).

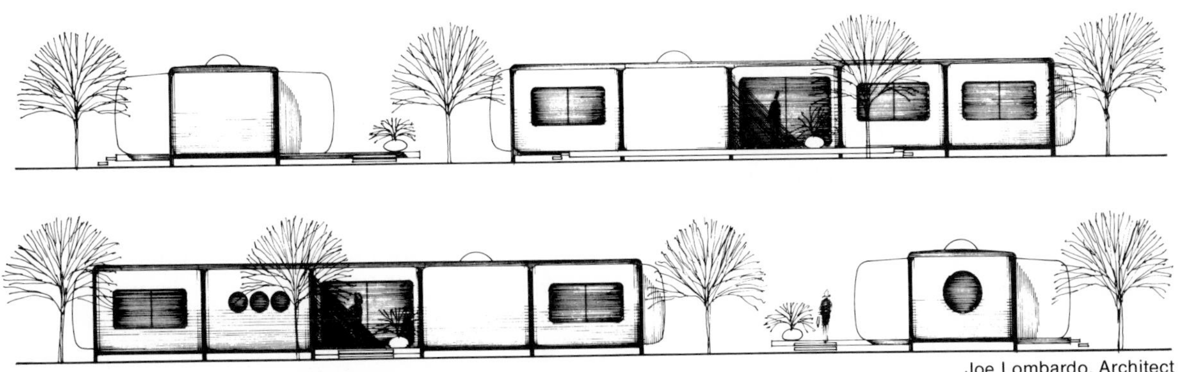

Joe Lombardo, Architect

Fig. 66–16A. Elevation of portable modular units.

Joe Lombardo, Architect

Fig. 66–16B. Pictorial drawing of modular units.

Joe Lombardo, Architect

Fig. 66–16C. An interior perspective of a modular unit.

Joe Lombardo, Architect

Fig. 66–16D. Floor-plan possibilities using portable modular units.

Modular on-site construction has undergone extensive changes in recent years. One of the many effective innovations was developed by architect Delp Johnson of San Francisco. Mr. Johnson developed a system which he calls *foldcrete,* in which walls and ceilings are poured on the ground and hinged together. As each unit is lifted, the walls drop down into position (Fig. 66–17). Then the foldcrete units are lifted by a crane and stacked on top of each other to form the building of the desired number of stories (Fig. 66–18).

Foldcrete International, Inc.

Fig. 66–17. A foldcrete panel is lifted to form a box.

Foldcrete International, Inc.

Fig. 66–18. A foldcrete unit being positioned on a building.

Architect Haigh Jamgochian has also developed a new method of construction involving the hanging of modular units from a central core (Figs. 66–19 and 66–20).

An innovation in modular steel construction has been used in Walt Disney World in Orlando, Florida. This is the world's first major use of a steel-framed, unitized construction system. Duplicating the model shown in Fig. 66–21, hotel rooms were built at an on-site facility designed for this purpose. Cranes then lifted the units into the structure.

All structures are built as modules to some extent. That is, not all the materials or components are manufactured or put together on the site. Some structures are simply precut. This means that all the materials are cut to modular specification at the factory and then assembled on the site by conventional methods.

With the most common factory-built (prefabricated) homes, the major modular components, such as the walls, trusses, decks, and partitions, are assembled at the factory. The

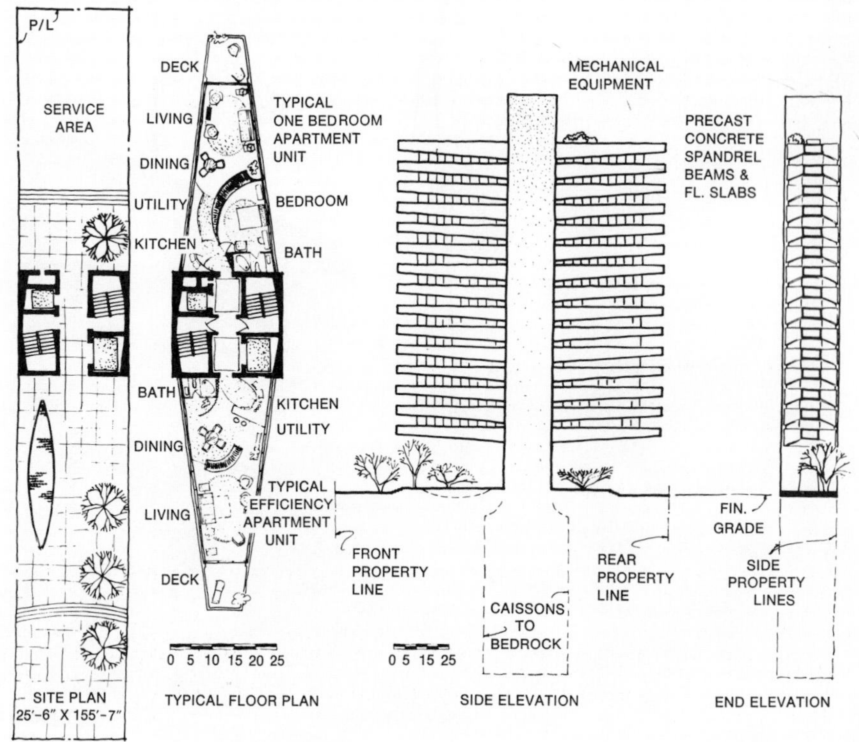

Haigh Jamgochian, Architect

Fig. 66–19. Core-supported construction.

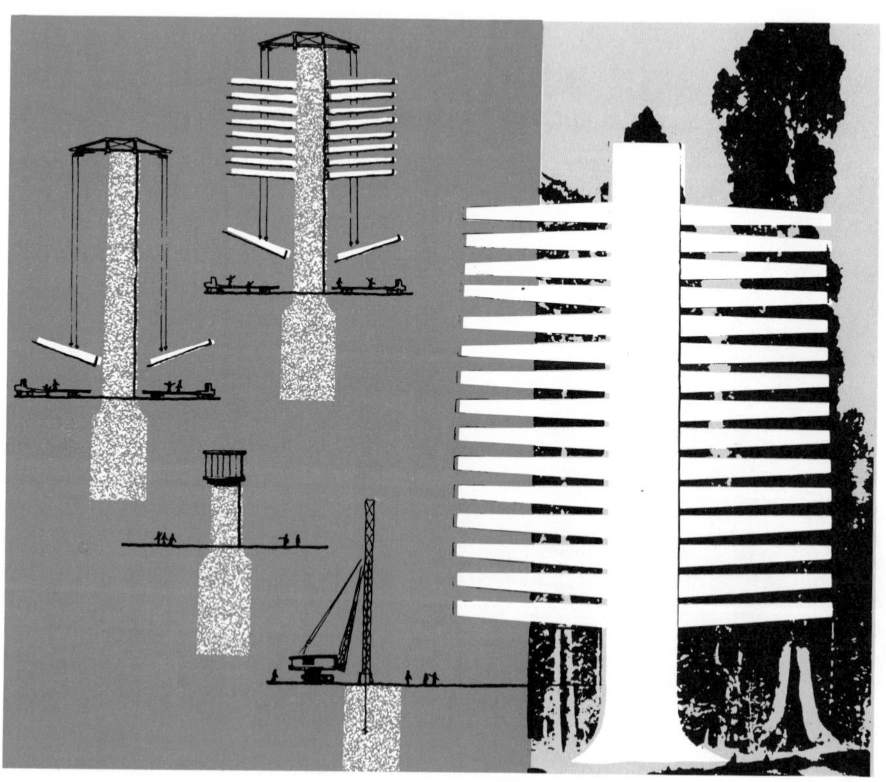

Haigh Jamgochian, Architect

Fig. 66–20. Erecting a core-supported building.

United States Steel Corporation

Fig. 66–21. The use of steel-framed, unitized construction.

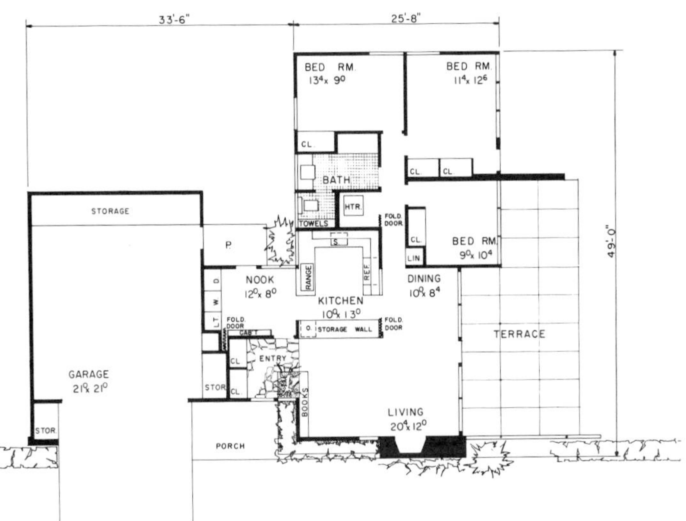

Home Planners, Inc.

Fig. 66–23. Convert this plan to a modular drawing.

utility work, such as installation of electrical, plumbing, and heating systems, is completed on site. The final finishing work, such as installation of floors, roof coverings, and walls, is also done on site.

There are some factory-built homes, however, that are constructed in complete modules at the factory and require only final electrical-outlet, roof-overhang, and assembly fastening on site to complete the job. A factory-built home of this kind is shown in Fig. 66–22. The

Intercontinental Industries, Inc.

Fig. 66–22. A factory-built home.

time factor is a major advantage of this type of construction. However, the size of the modules is limited to only 12′ widths. Twelve feet is the maximum width for a truck load on public roads. See Unit 52 for details of constructing this kind of module.

PROBLEMS

1. **Resketch the plan shown in Fig. 66–23 on modular grid paper and convert all nonmodular dimensions to the nearest modular size.**
2. **Define the following terms: *Unicom, modular components, modular planning grid, minor module, major module, nonmodular dimensions, modular dimensions, 16″ module.***

UNIT 67

Drawing Modular Plans

The floor plan shown in Fig. 67–1 has been fitted on the modular grid, and the designer has thus properly established the modular relationship of the foundation, floors, walls, windows, doors, partitions, and roof. Establishing the dimensions and components precisely on the 16″, 24″, and 48″ spaces of the modular grid assures accurate and less troublesome fitting of the components of the house at the time of its construction.

Fig. 67–1. A floor plan fitted on a modular grid.

Home Planners, Inc.

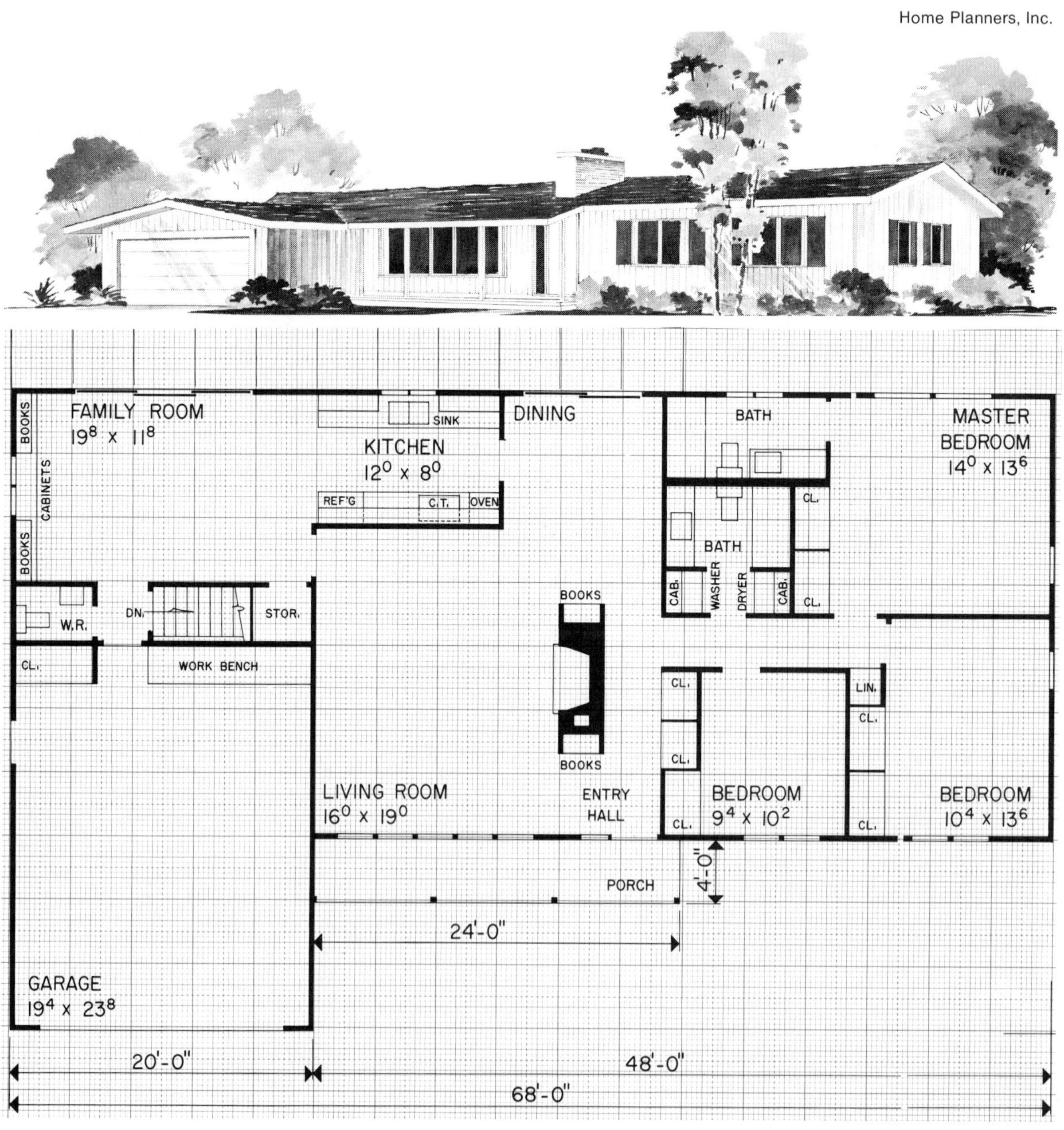

COMPONENT FLOOR PLANS

After completing the basic floor plan, a detailed component plan for fabrication and erection is prepared. Standard symbols are used to identify wall, window, door, and partition components by type and size (Fig. 67–2). The erection sequence for site assembly is also designated on this plan by ER 1, ER 2, and so on. This basic component floor plan for erection contains all basic dimensions necessary for layout work on the floor platform. Interior partitions may then be erected in varying sequences.

ELEVATION COMPONENT DRAWINGS

Just as the component floor plan for erection is prepared from the floor plan shown in Fig. 67–1, the elevation component drawings are prepared from standard elevations projected from the floor plan, as shown in Fig. 67–3. Elevation component drawings closely resemble conventional panel-framing elevations, except that wall, window, door, and roof components are identified and shown in their proper relationship, complete with standard Unicom nomenclature and erection sequences. Figure 67–4 shows the component elevation drawings prepared from standard elevations shown in Fig. 67–3.

FRAMING PLANS

From the basic floor plan, a floor-framing plan and stud layout, as shown in Fig. 67–5, are projected and dimensioned according to Unicom standards. Notice the precise rhythm of the 16″, on-center floor joists and the 48″ modular dimensions of the house perimeter (Fig. 67–6). The advantage of designing to these standards is the reduction of wasted material. Waste oc-

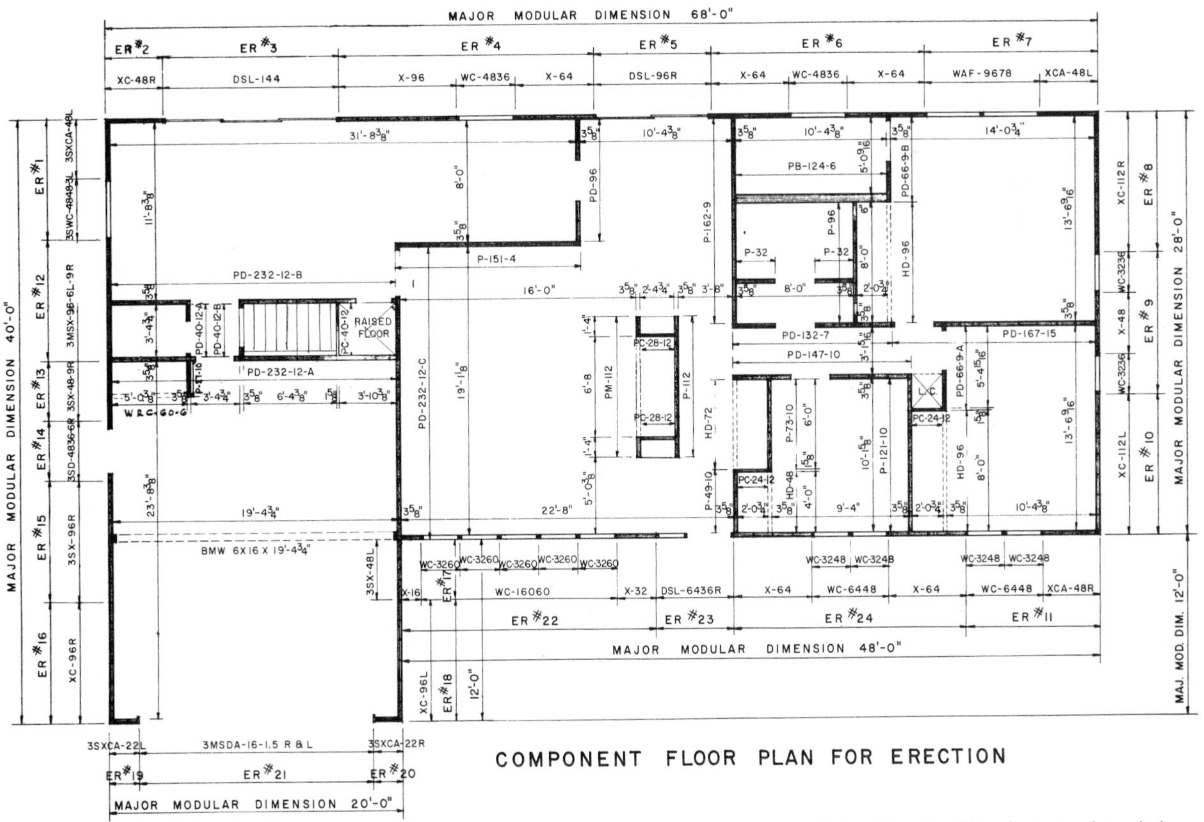

National Lumber Manufacturers Association

Fig. 67–2. Symbols are used to identify components on the floor plan.

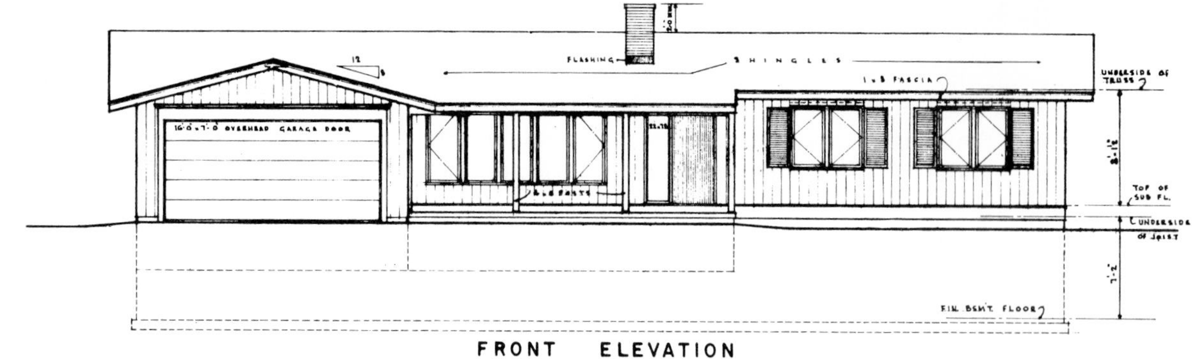

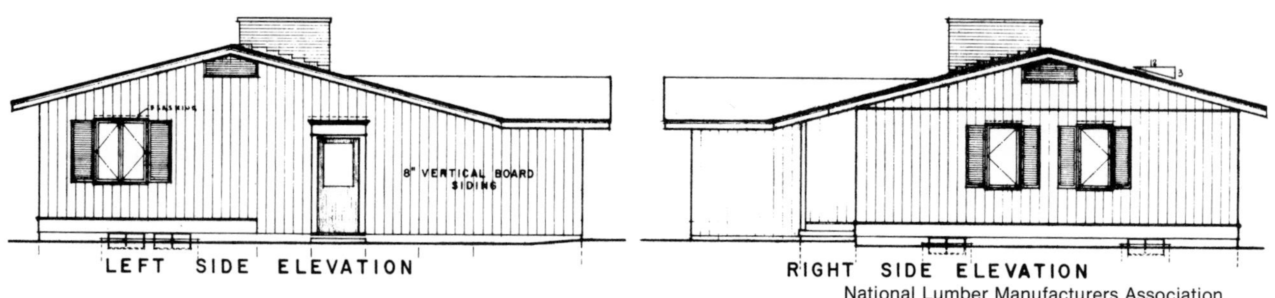

National Lumber Manufacturers Association

Fig. 67–3. Elevation component drawings are prepared from conventional elevations.

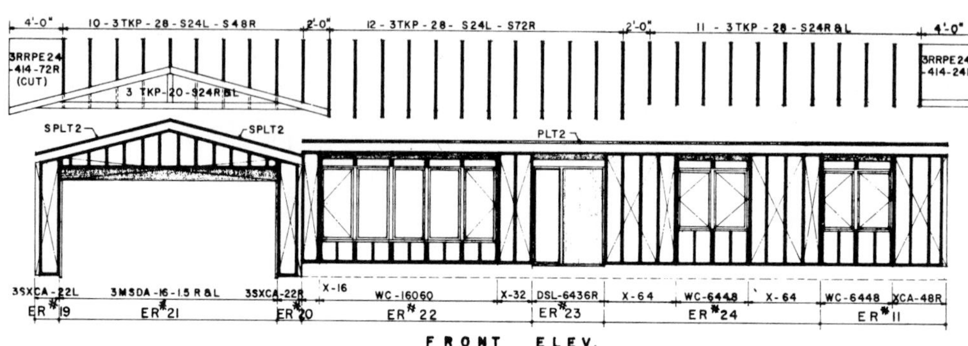

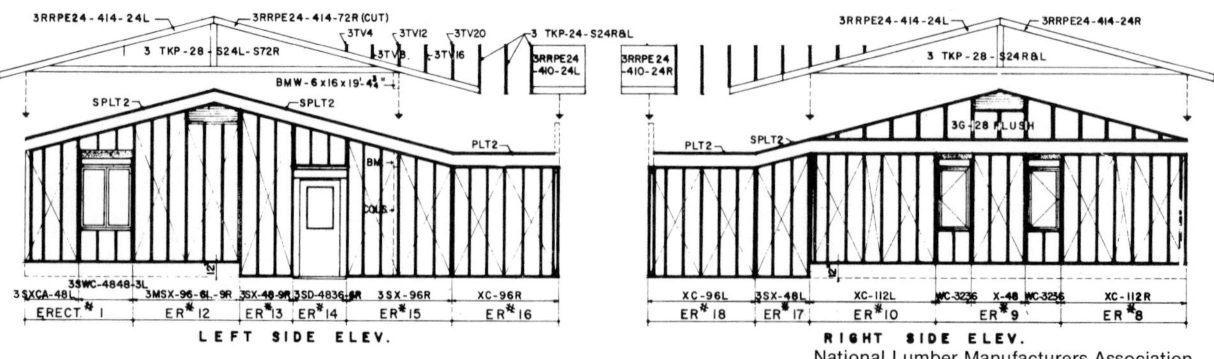

National Lumber Manufacturers Association

Fig. 67–4. An elevation component framing drawing.

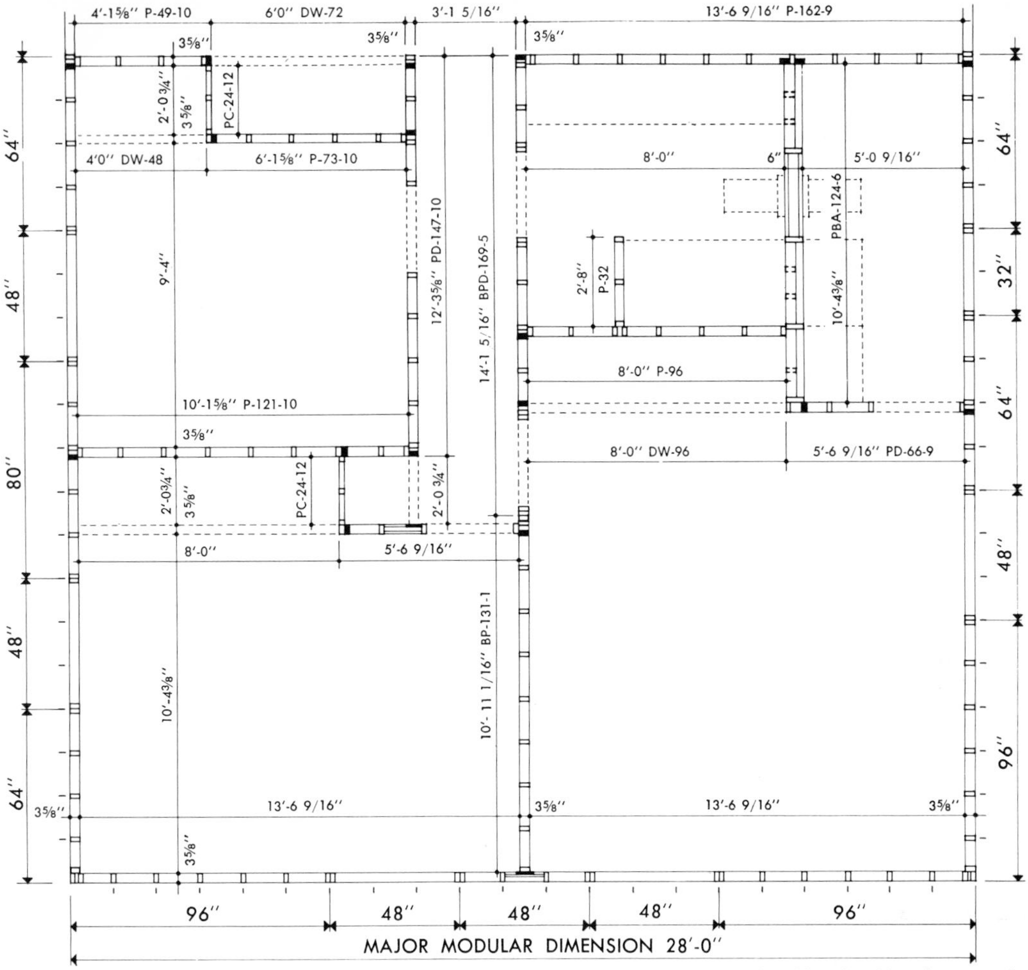

National Lumber Manufacturers Association

Fig. 67–5. **An example of a modular stud layout.**

Fig. 67–6. **Standard modular rhythms.**

National Lumber Manufacturers Association

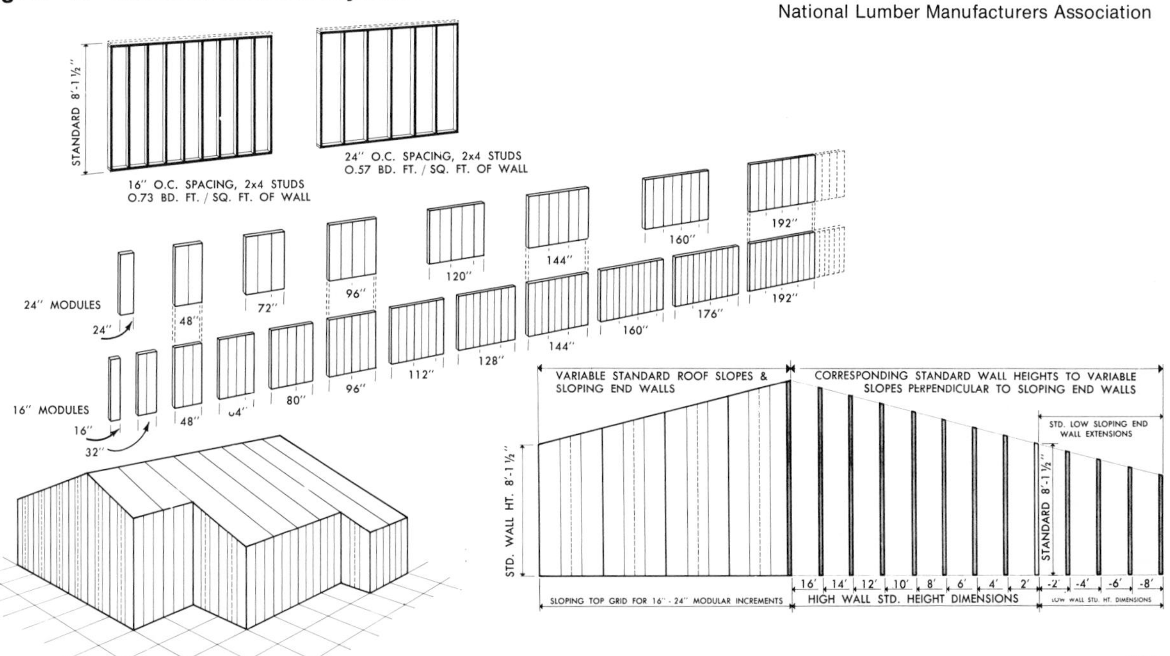

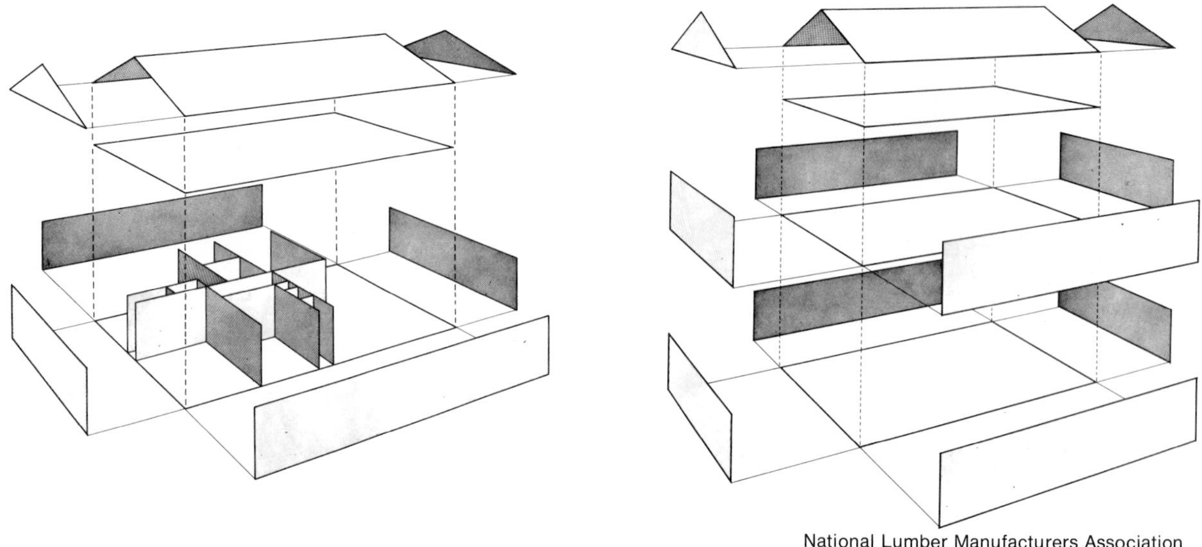

National Lumber Manufacturers Association

Fig. 67–7. Expansion possibilities designing in modular units.

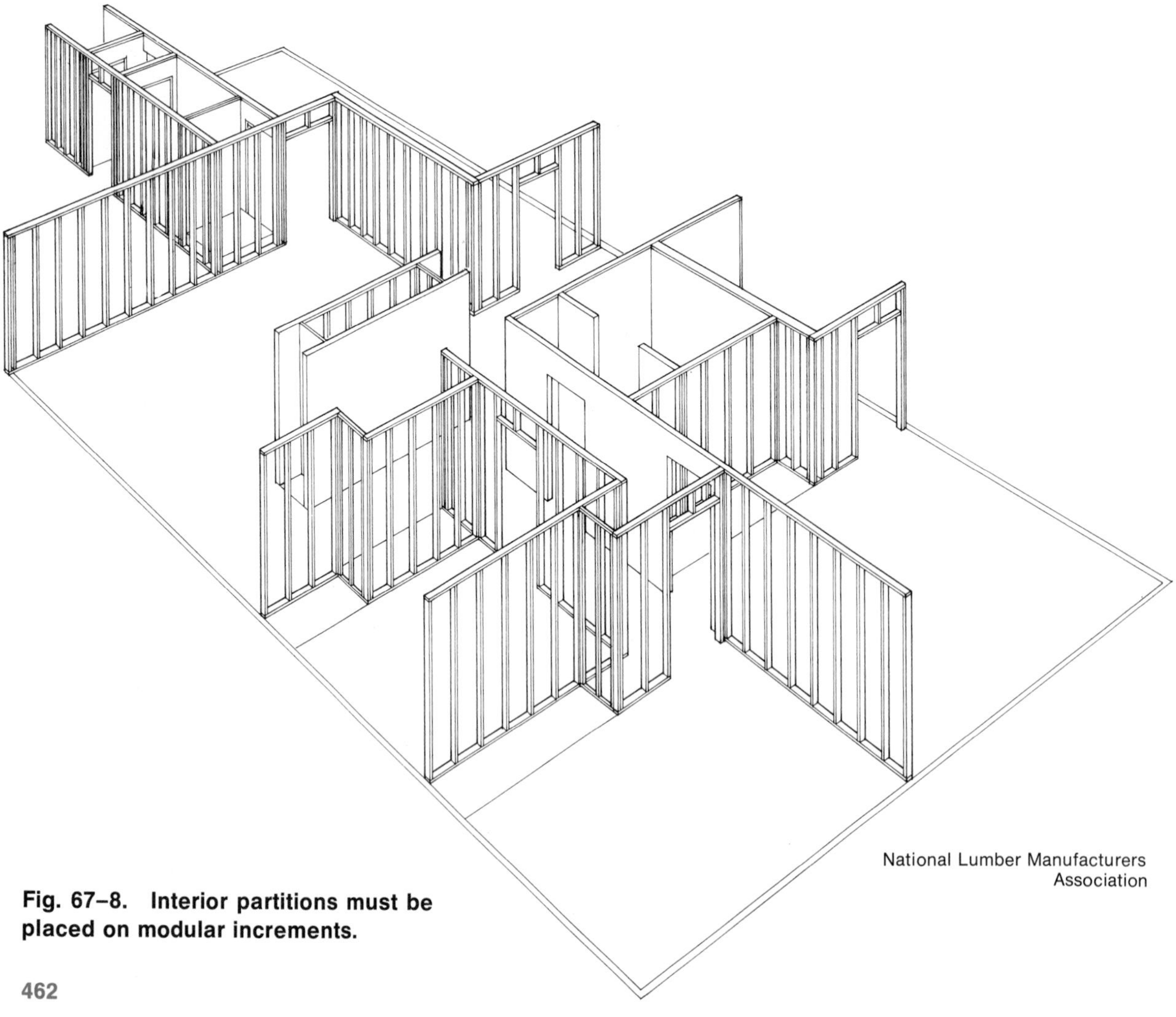

National Lumber Manufacturers Association

Fig. 67–8. Interior partitions must be placed on modular increments.

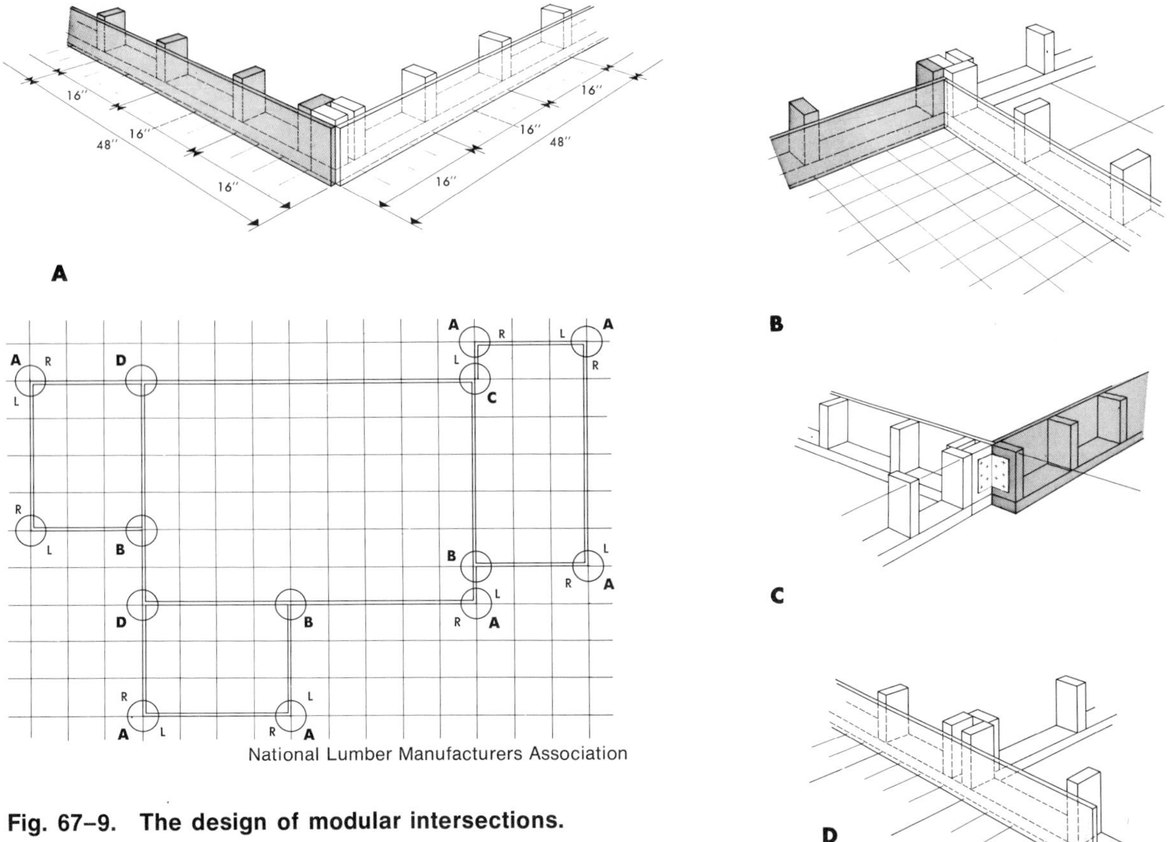

National Lumber Manufacturers Association

Fig. 67–9. The design of modular intersections.

curs only in cutting at the stairwell and fireplace openings or other areas which are different from modular dimensions. Modular dimensions and panel code numbers are indicated on all plans. Figure 67–7 illustrates the simplicity of controlled modular standards in effecting economies in the use of materials. It also suggests the endless possibilities for expansion.

INTERIOR PARTITION COMPONENTS

Partitions function as interior space separators for room privacy, traffic control, and storage. Their aesthetic value depends on decorative surface materials, doors, and trim designs. Partitions are a maze of intersecting planes which may carry the roof and ceiling loads, depending on the roof design. The illustration in Fig. 67–8 shows the partitions from the plan in Fig. 67–1 placed by modular standards. Figure 67–9 reveals some of the complexities of modular design of partition intersections. Partitions must fit between the basic exterior modular increments with allowance for exterior wall thicknesses. Space must be provided for intersecting partitions with backup members, proper door placement, vertical and horizontal plumbing runs, medicine cabinets, closets, fireplaces, and flexible room arrangements with varying designs. The partitions shown in Fig. 67–10 illustrate the method of dimensioning partitions to relate effectively modular and nonmodular dimensions. In addition to the dimensional designations, the identification code for the panel is also included on the partition drawing.

Many more modular drawings are needed to describe completely a Unicom plan in every detail. Just as in structures of conventional design, the more detailed the drawings are, the better the chance of achieving the desired outcome. Other plans which may become part of the complete Unicom design include transverse sections, truss and gable component drawings, roof-overhang details, and detailed

National Lumber Manufacturers Association

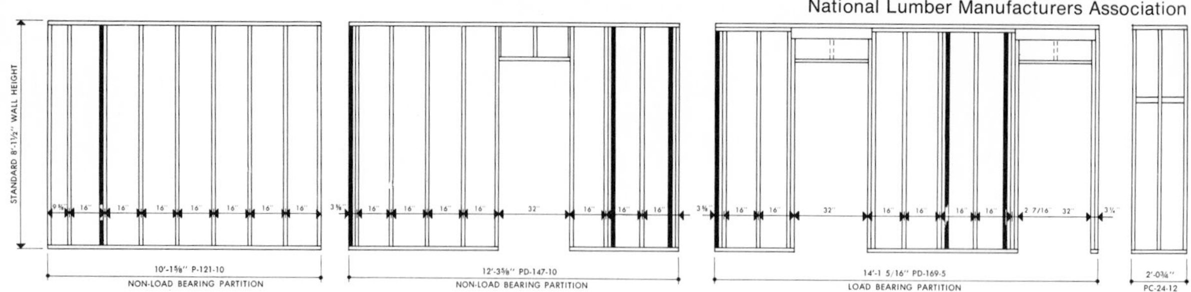

Fig. 67–10. Examples of panel elevation drawings.

National Lumber Manufacturers Association

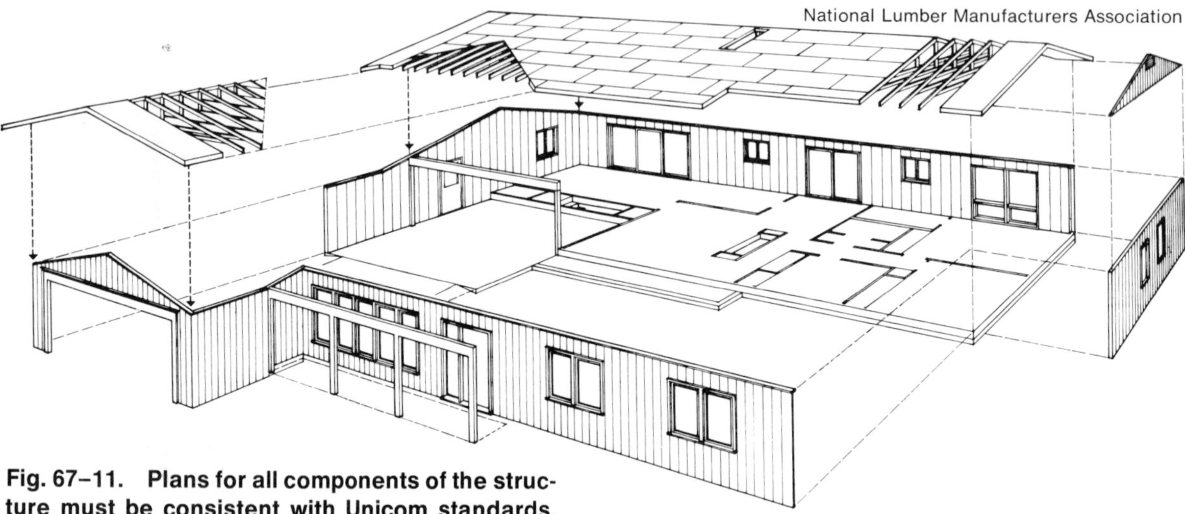

Fig. 67–11. Plans for all components of the structure must be consistent with Unicom standards.

Home Planners, Inc.

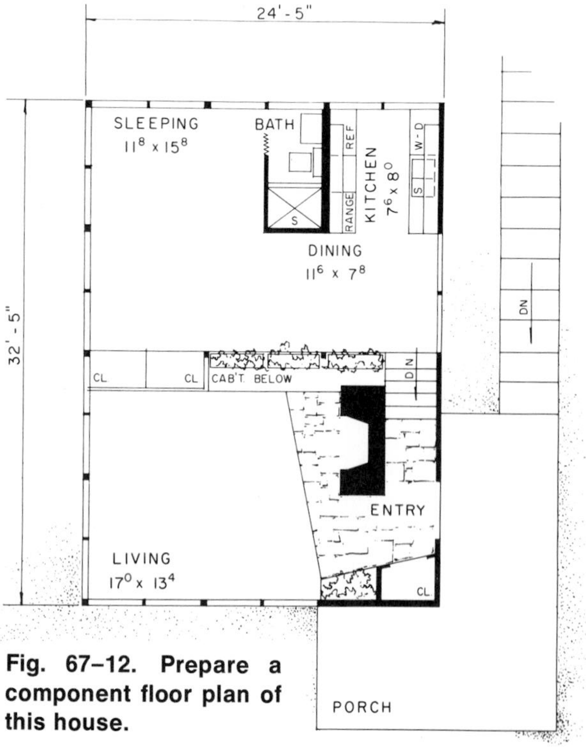

Fig. 67–12. Prepare a component floor plan of this house.

drawings of many nonstandard components. Figure 67–11 shows the relationship of basic components in a house designed by the modular system. With the Unicom method, all other basic house types may be designed and engineered in the same manner.

PROBLEMS

1. **Prepare a component floor plan for the floor plan shown in Fig. 67–12.**
2. **Prepare an elevation component drawing for the front elevation of the house shown in Fig. 67–12.**
3. **Prepare a floor-framing plan for the house shown in Fig. 67–12 and dimension it according to Unicom standards.**
4. **Prepare a roof-framing plan of the floor plan shown in Fig. 67–12 and dimension it to modular standards.**
5. **Define the following terms: *component floor plan, elevation component drawing, modular increment.***

SECTION 17

Architectual Set of Plans

Previous sections have covered the principles and practices involved in the preparation of each type of architectural drawing. In this unit the basic guidelines used in the preparation of a complete set of plans are developed. Special emphasis is placed on the relationship and consistency among plan features and dimensions.

Balthazar Korab Photo

UNIT 68

Set of Plans

Drawings used for construction vary from a simple floor plan to an entire set of plans complete with details, schedules, and specifications. The number of plans for a building depends on the complexity of the structure. The completeness of plans depends on the degree to which the designer needs or wants to control the various methods and details of construction. For example, if only a floor plan is prepared, the builder must create the elevation design. If only the floor plan and elevation drawings but no details or specifications are provided, the builder assumes responsibility for many construction details, including the selection of framing types, materials used, and many aspects of interior design. Therefore the more plans, details, and specifications developed for a structure, the closer the finished building will be to that conceived by the designer. Table 68-1 lists each type of architectural drawing included in a maximum, average, and minimum set of plans. However, the actual selection of drawings depends on the degree to which the designer wants to control various features of the building. Large sets of plans which include many different details require an indexing system. For large projects involving many buildings with many components, a much more detailed indexing system is needed to locate specific details on any building in a short period of time. In these cases a master index is prepared which shows the sheet number where each drawing for each building is found. Figure 68–1 shows a title

Home Planners, Inc.

Fig. 68–1. A little block with a simple indexing system.

block with a simple indexing system. It includes a design number, sheet number, and the total number of drawings in the set.

The Northern California Chapter of the American Institute of Architects (AIA) has developed a numbering system which gives access to the information in a set of drawings. The description of their system is adapted from a report titled *Recommended Standards on Production Procedure* and is used with permission.

Drawings are numbered for ease of referencing. The system is specific without being cumbersome. It is easy for everyone to comprehend at first glance. A standard system such as this must fulfill the need of the user. It will ultimately provide a more efficient set of documents and, consequently, a saving in production cost.

For example, an alphabetical designation is used to identify the work phases of the project:

- SK Sketches (used through all phases)
- PR Programming
- MP Master planning
- SC Schematics
- DD Design development

A readily identifiable alphabetical prefix is used to denote the specific discipline of work covered by a group of working drawings:

- A Architectural
- C Civil
- D Interior design (color schemes, furniture, furnishings)
- E Electrical
- F Fire protection (sprinkler, standpipes, CO_2, etc.)
- G Graphics
- K Dietary (food service)
- L Landscape
- M Mechanical (heating, ventilating, air conditioning)
- P Plumbing
- S Structural
- T Transportation/conveying systems

Table 68-1. DRAWINGS NECESSARY FOR SETS OF PLANS

DRAWINGS	SIZE OF SET OF PLANS		
	Min.	Aver.	Max.
FLOOR PLANS	X	X	X
FRONT ELEVATION	X	X	X
REAR ELEVATION		X	X
RIGHT ELEVATION	X	X	X
LEFT ELEVATION		X	X
AUXILIARY ELEVATIONS			X
INTERIOR ELEVATIONS		X	X
EXTERIOR PICTORIAL RENDERINGS		X	X
INTERIOR RENDERINGS			X
PLOT PLAN		X	X
LANDSCAPE PLAN			X
SURVEY PLAN	X	X	X
FULL SECTION	X	X	X
DETAIL SECTIONS		X	X
FLOOR-FRAMING PLANS			X
EXTERIOR-WALL FRAMING PLANS			X
INTERIOR-WALL FRAMING PLANS			X
STUD LAYOUTS			X
ROOF-FRAMING PLAN			X
ELECTRICAL PLAN		X	X
AIR-CONDITIONING PLAN			X
PLUMBING DIAGRAM			X
SCHEDULES			X
SPECIFICATIONS			X
COST ANALYSIS			X
SCALE MODEL			X

SYSTEM CODE:

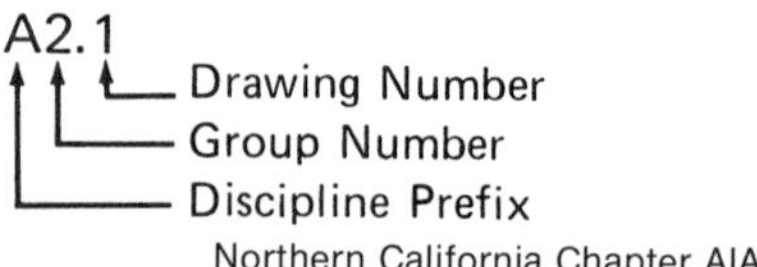

Northern California Chapter AIA

Fig. 68–2. An explanation of the use of the system code on drawings.

In this system architectural drawings are divided into 10 specific groups, A0 through A9. The group number will always remain the same no matter how large the project. Additional drawings may be added within groups without interrupting the alphanumerical order. Figure 68–2 explains the coding system as it would appear in use on a drawing. Figure 68–3 shows a listing of these groups and their symbols.

ARCHITECTURAL DRAWINGS

A0.1,2,3 – General (Index, Symbols, Abbrev. notes, references)
A1.1,2,3 – Demolition, Site Plan, Temporary Work
A2.1,2,3 – Plans, Room Material Schedule, Door Schedule, Key Drawings
A3.1,2,3 – Sections, Exterior Elevations
A4.1,2,3 – Detailed Floor Plans
A5.1,2,3 – Interior Elevations
A6.1,2,3 – Reflected Ceiling Plans
A7.1,2,3 – Vertical Circulation, Stairs (Elevators, Escalators)
A8.1,2,3 – Exterior Details
A9.1,2,3 – Interior Details

STRUCTURAL DRAWINGS

S0.1,2,3 – General Notes
S1.1,2,3 – Site Work
S2.1,2,3 – Framing Plans
S3.1,2 – Elevations
S4.1,2 – Schedules
S5.1,2 – Concrete
S6.1,2 – Masonry
S7.1,2 – Structural Steel
S8.1,2 – Timber
S9.1,2 – Special Design

MECHANICAL DRAWINGS

M0.1,2 – General Notes
M1.1,2 – Site/Roof Plans
M2.1,2 – Floor Plans
M3.1,2 – Riser Diagrams
M4.1,2 – Piping Flow Diagram
M5.1,2 – Control Diagrams
M6.1,2 – Details

PLUMBING DRAWINGS

P0.1.2 – General Notes
P1.1,2 – Site Plan
P2.1,2 – Floor Plans
P3.1,2 – Riser Diagram
P4.1,2 – Piping Flow Diagram
P5.1,2 – Details

ELECTRICAL DRAWINGS

E0.1,2 – General Notes
E1.1,2 – Site Plan
E2.1,2 – Floor Plans, Lighting
E3.1,2 – Floor Plans, Power
E4.1,2 – Electrical Rooms
E5.1.2 – Riser Diagrams
E6.1,2 – Fixture/Panel Schedules
E7.1,2 – Details

Northern California Chapter AIA

Fig. 68–3. A coding system for drawings.

PROBLEMS

1. **Prepare an index for a set of plans you have developed.**
2. **List the minimum number of and the kind of drawings necessary to build the home shown in Fig. 33–1.**
3. **Identify these terms: *plan set, index, title block, master index.***

UNIT 69

Relationship of Plans

In previous units, samples of architectural drawings were shown to illustrate principles and practices related to the creation of each plan. However, these drawings did not relate to the same structure. Drawings in this unit are of the same building; therefore the interrelationship and agreement among plans can be studied.

SEQUENCE

The floor plan which is prepared first relates to most other drawings. The second and successive floor plans are prepared by tracing the first floor-plan outline. Bearing partitions, plumbing wall, stairwells, fireplace and chimney openings, and other components can then be aligned vertically. The basement, floor, and roof-framing plans are prepared in the same way. Stud layouts and the length of interior partition panel layouts are also derived from the floor plan. Horizontal distances on elevation drawings are also projected from the four sides of the floor plan. Because the floor plan functions as a base for so many other drawings, errors on the floor plan can easily be transferred to other drawings. For this reason the floor plan must be carefully checked for accuracy before other drawings in the set are prepared. The usual sequence in preparing architectural drawings is as follows:

1. Floor plan
2. Foundation plans
3. Front elevation
4. Rear elevation
5. Right elevation
6. Left elevation
7. Auxiliary elevation
8. Plot plans
9. Landscape plans
10. Survey plans
11. Full sections
12. Detail sections
13. Electrical plans
14. Air-conditioning plans
15. Plumbing diagrams
16. Exterior pictorial rendering
17. Interior pictorial rendering
18. Landscape elevation
19. Floor-framing plans
20. Exterior-wall framing plans
21. Interior-wall framing plans
22. Stud layouts
23. Roof-framing plans
24. Fireplace details
25. Foundation details
26. Checking and checklists
27. Architectural models
28. Door and window schedules
29. Finish schedules
30. Specifications
31. Building cost and estimates

AGREEMENT AMONG DRAWINGS

Selected areas of each plan in this unit have been marked with circles, rectangles, hexagons, crosses, or diamonds. By studying the positions of these symbols you can observe how a specific area appears on each marked drawing in the set. For example, the position of the colored circle on the main-level floor plan represents the area covered with the same colored circle on the right elevation, lower level plan, and rear pictorial or any plan so marked. Likewise the part of each drawing covered by a grey hexagon represents that same area on those drawings. The same is true for areas covered by colored rectangles, crosses, or diamonds. The relationship between sectional views and basic drawings can be followed by the use of these geometric symbols and by locating the position of the appropriate cutting-plane line as marked on the basic plan.

DIMENSIONS

If a building is to be conconstructed as designed, it is extremely critical that dimensions describing the size of each component of a building agree on each drawing. If the dimensions of a basement plan do not match related dimensions on the floor plan, prefabricated wall panels may not fit, or the position of stairwell openings and fireplace footers may not align. Whether a dimension describes the overall length or width of a structure or only indicates the size of a subdimension of a detail, like dimensions must agree on each drawing in a set. For this reason dimensional accuracy is verified by locating one dimension at a time throughout the entire set until each has been checked and agreement is determined.

PROBLEMS

1. List the order in which you would prepare each of the following drawings: stud layout, foundation plan, specifications, floor plan, front elevation, left elevation, exterior rendering, basement plan, second-floor plan.

2. Pick an area on the floor plan shown in Fig. 69–2 not covered by a circle or square. Locate that same area on the other drawings in this unit.

3. Pick a dimension not circled on the floor plan shown in Fig. 69–2. Find that dimension on other drawings in this unit.

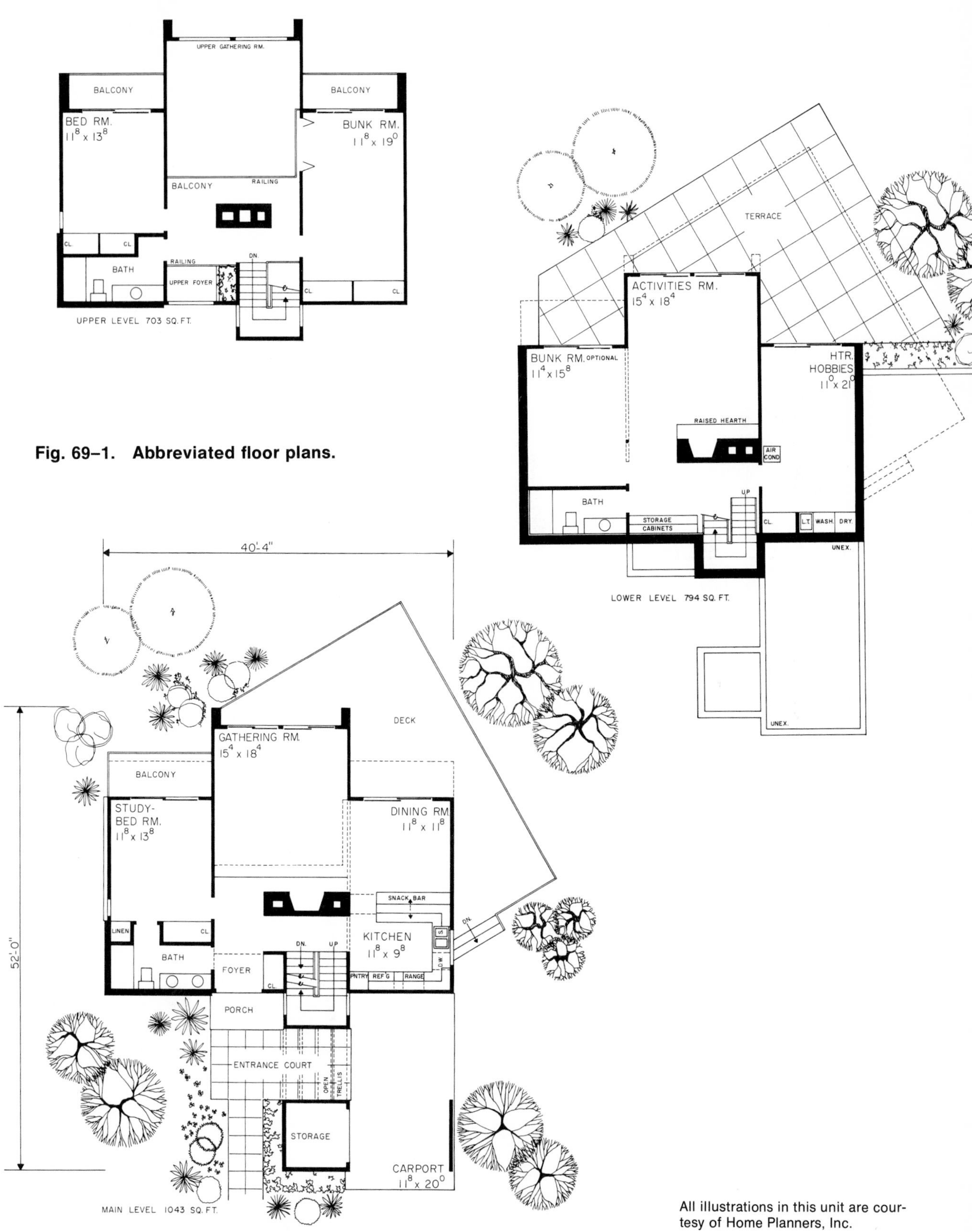

Fig. 69–1. Abbreviated floor plans.

All illustrations in this unit are courtesy of Home Planners, Inc.

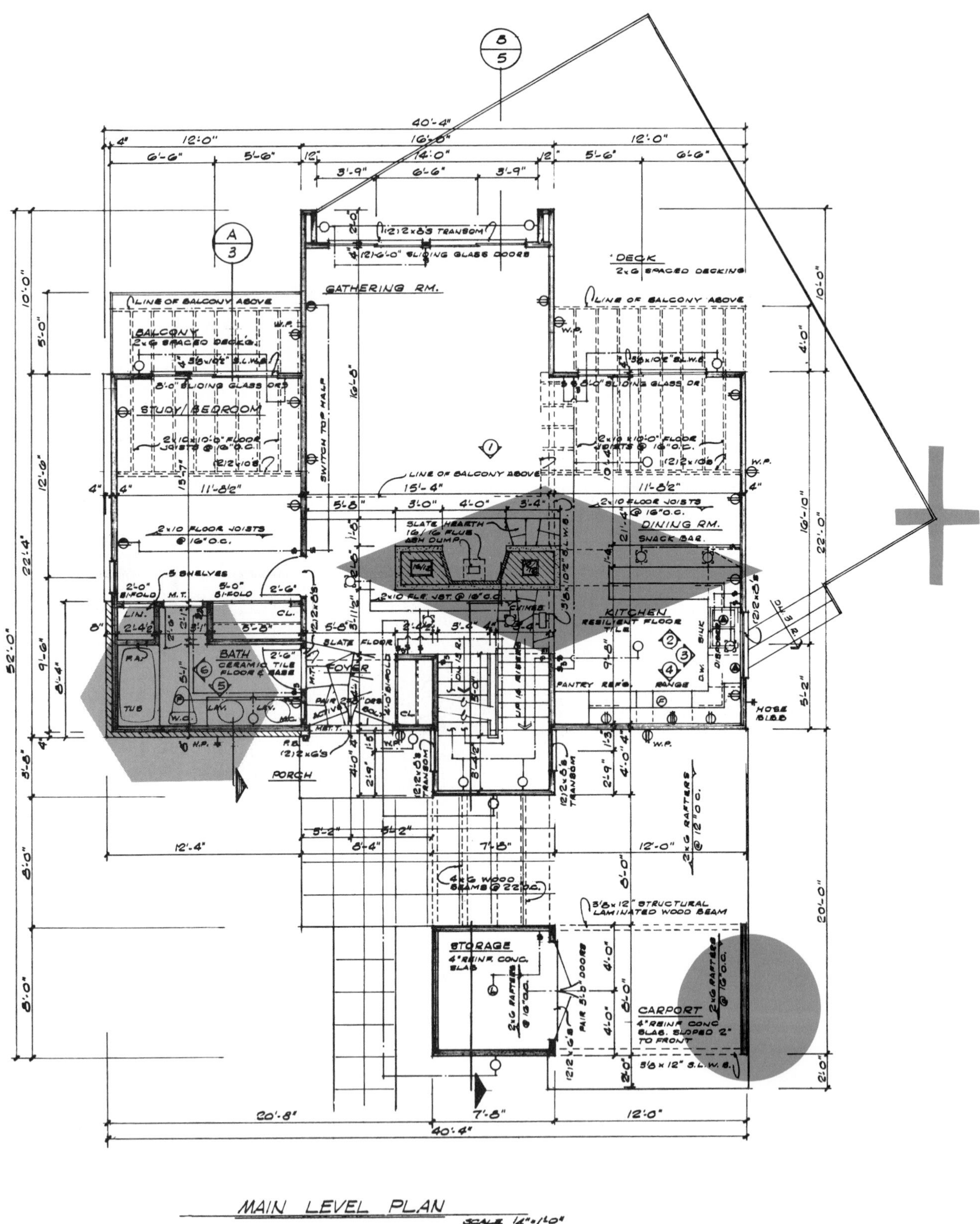

Fig. 69–2. A complete main level floor plan.

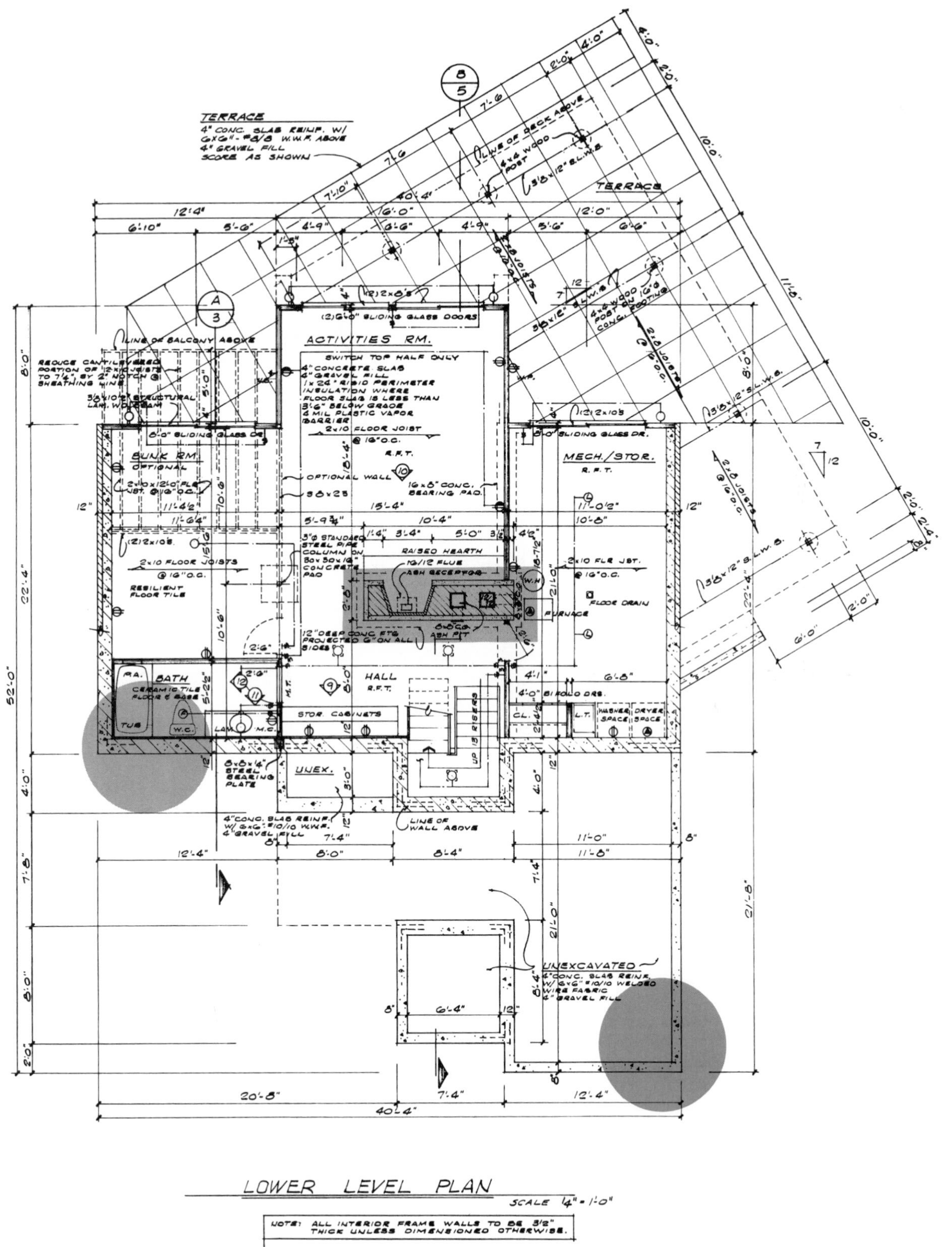

Fig. 69–3. A complete lower level (basement) floor plan.

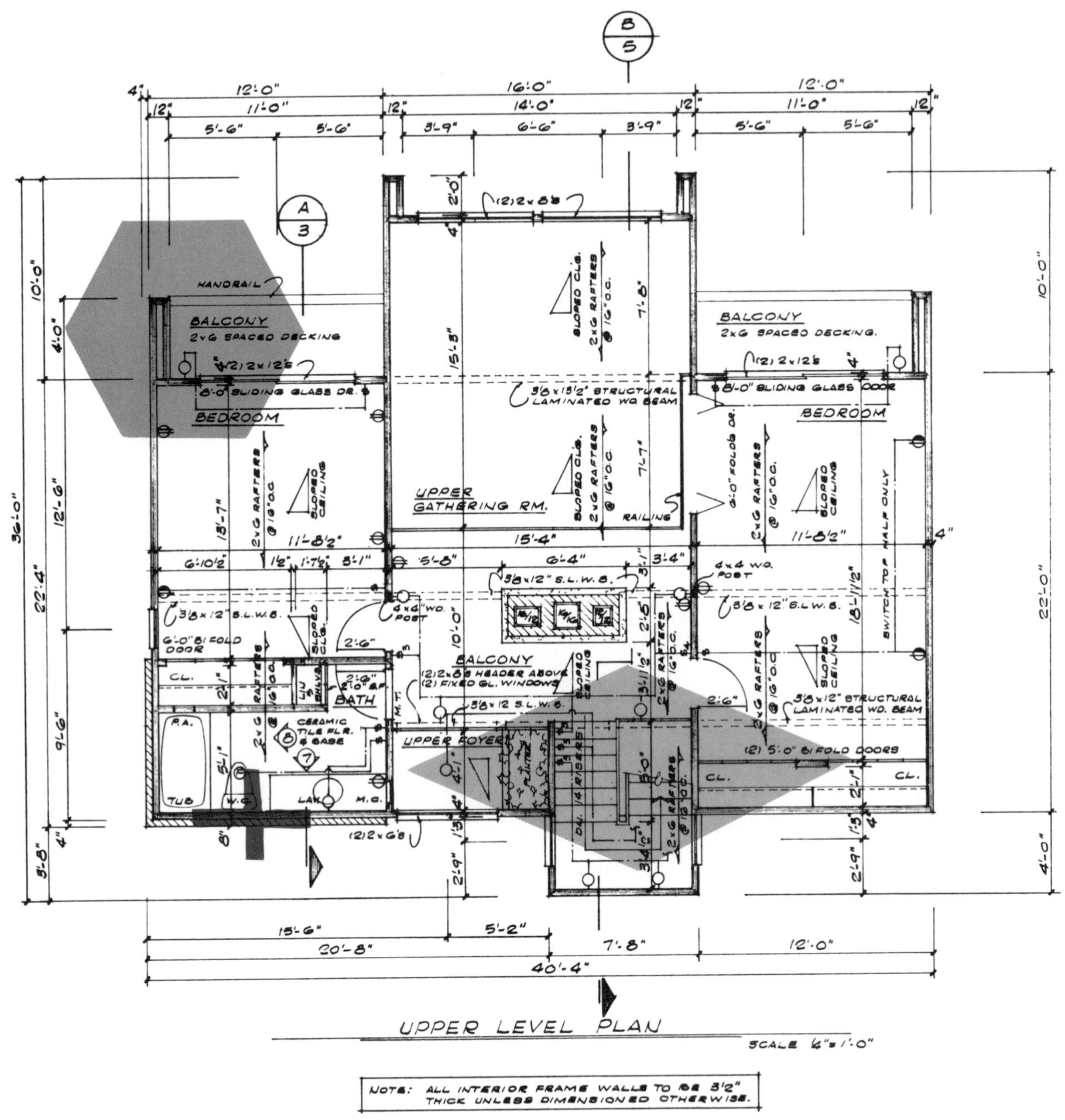

Fig. 69–4. An upper level floor plan.

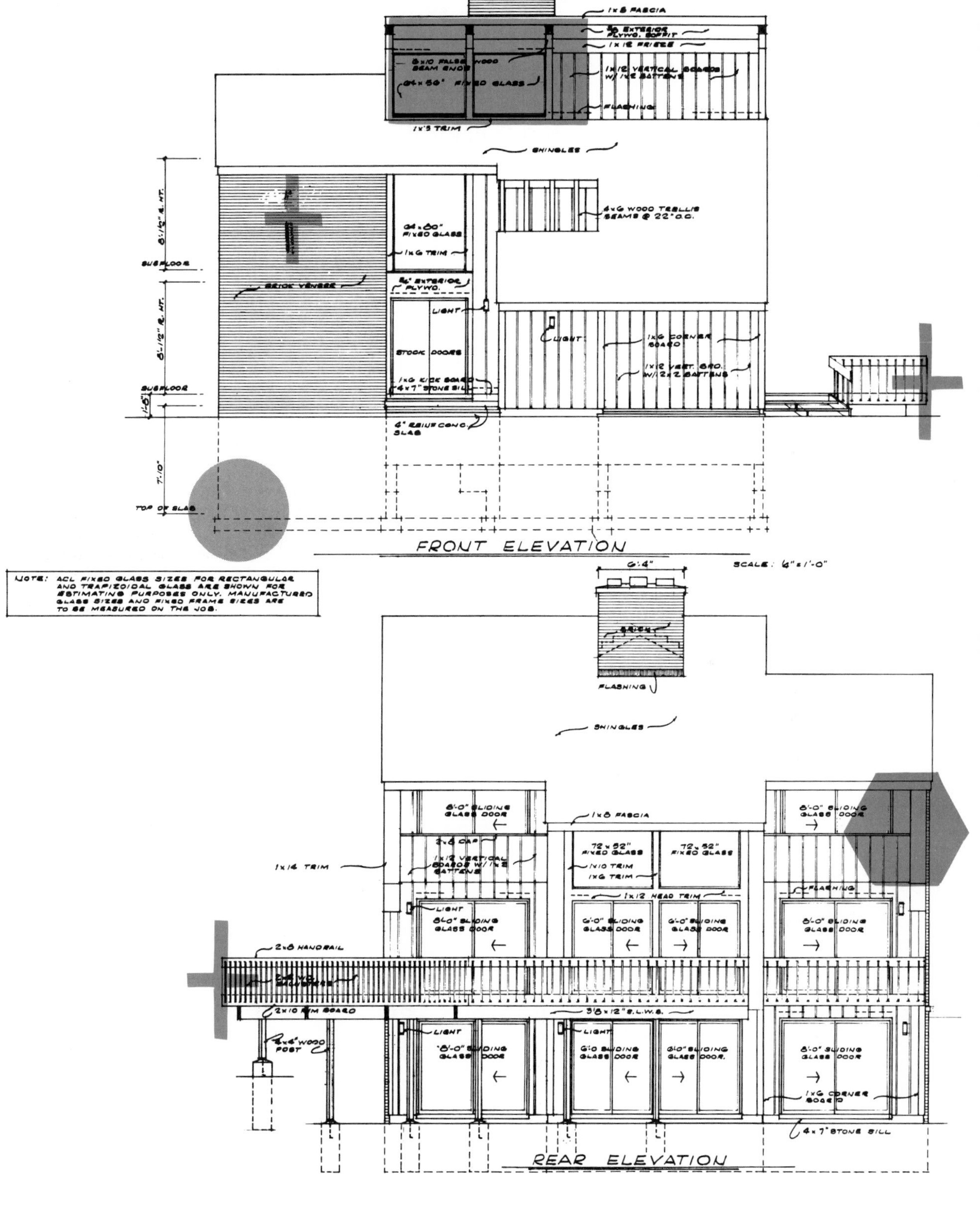

Fig. 69–5. A front and a rear elevation.

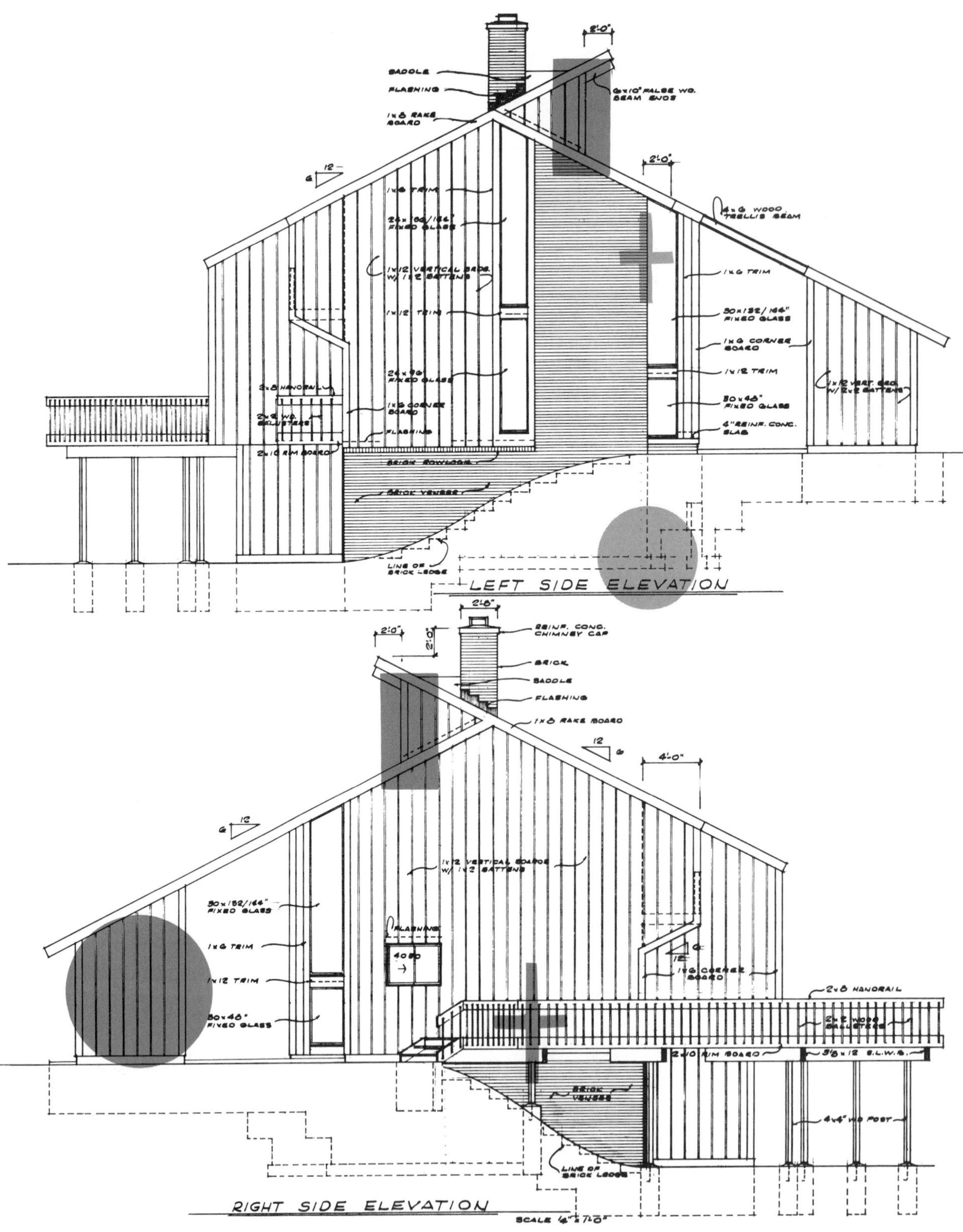

Fig. 69–6. A right and a left elevation.

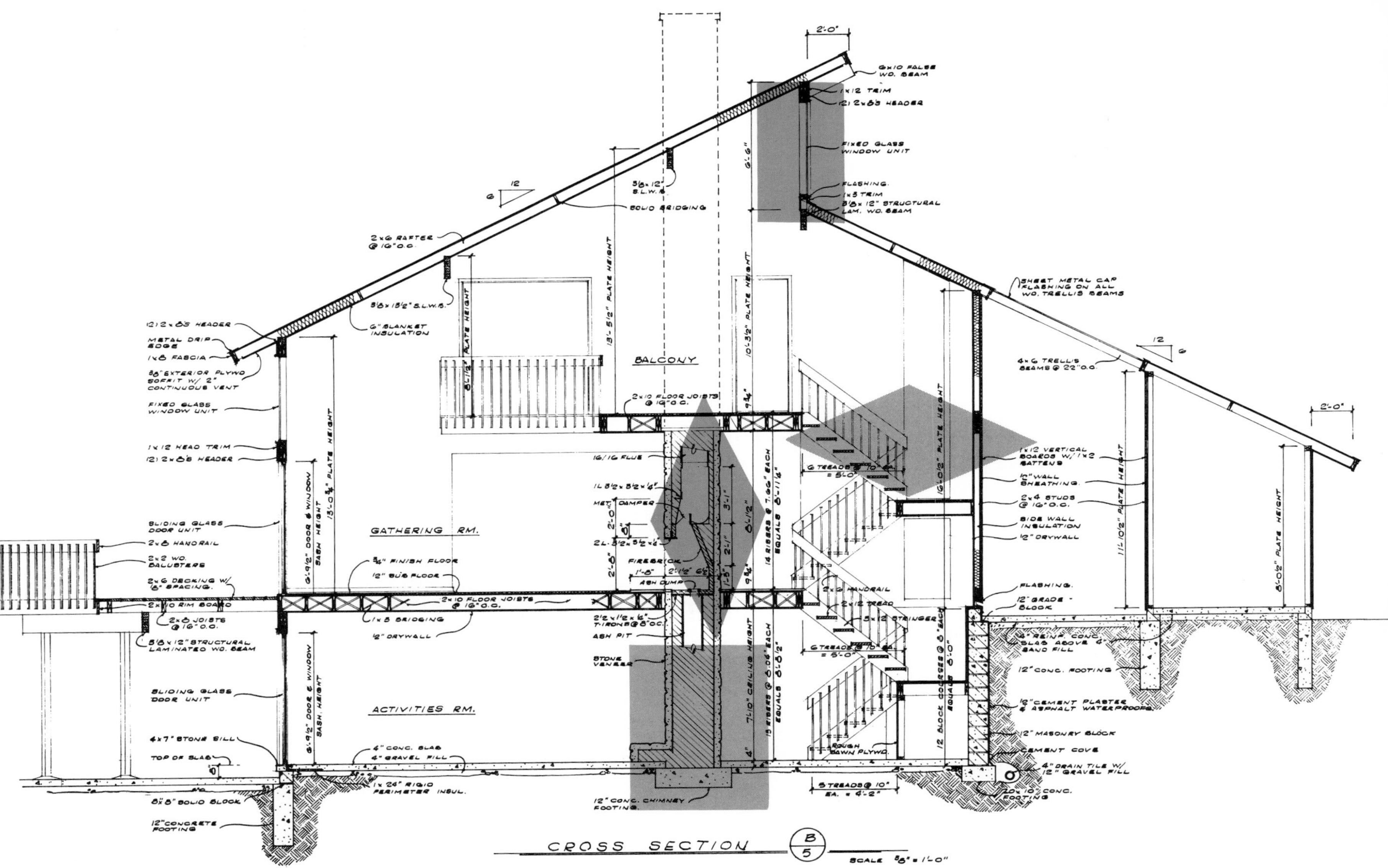

Fig. 69–7. The complete section through the center of the house.

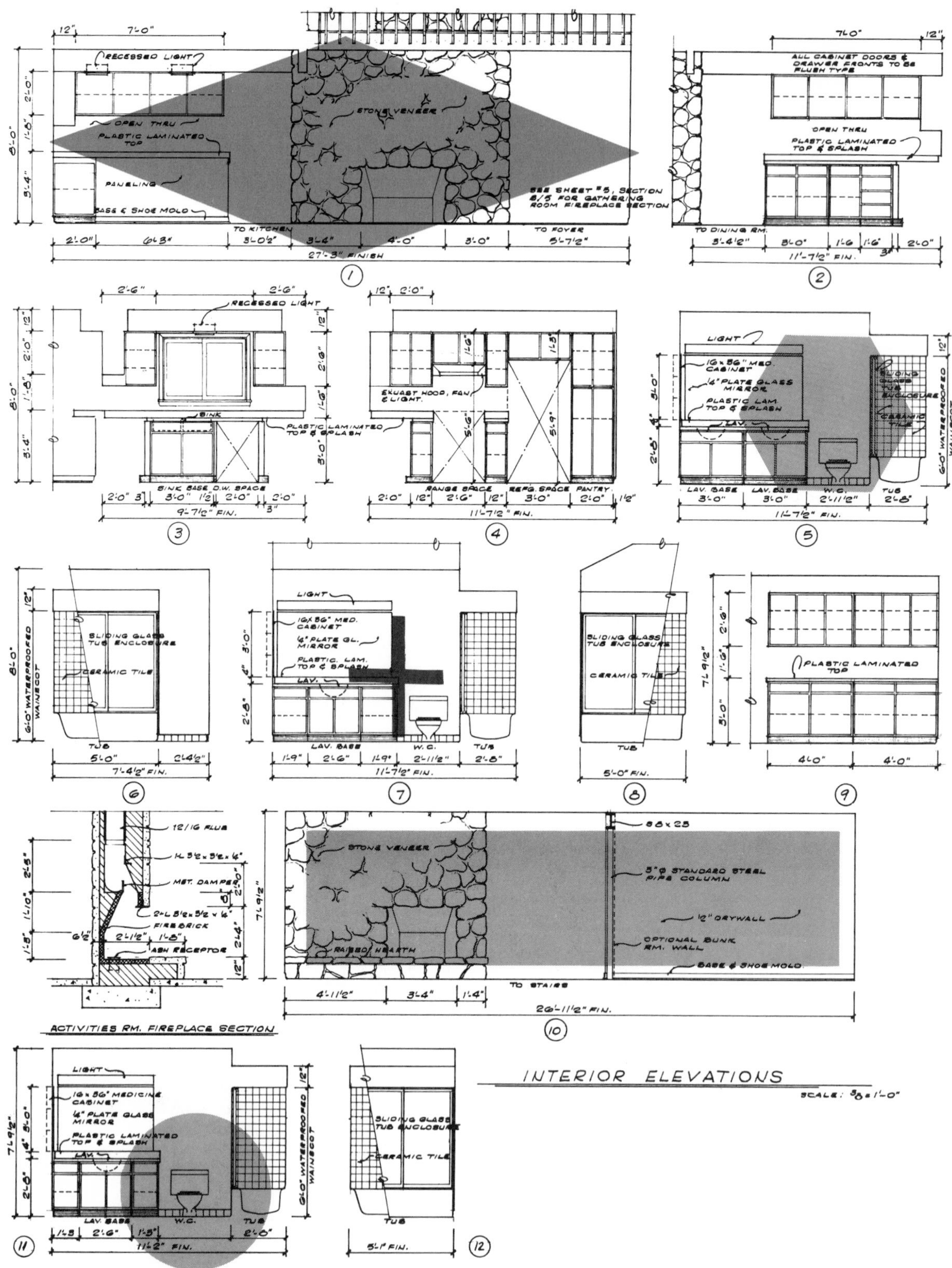

Fig. 69–8. Interior wall elevations.

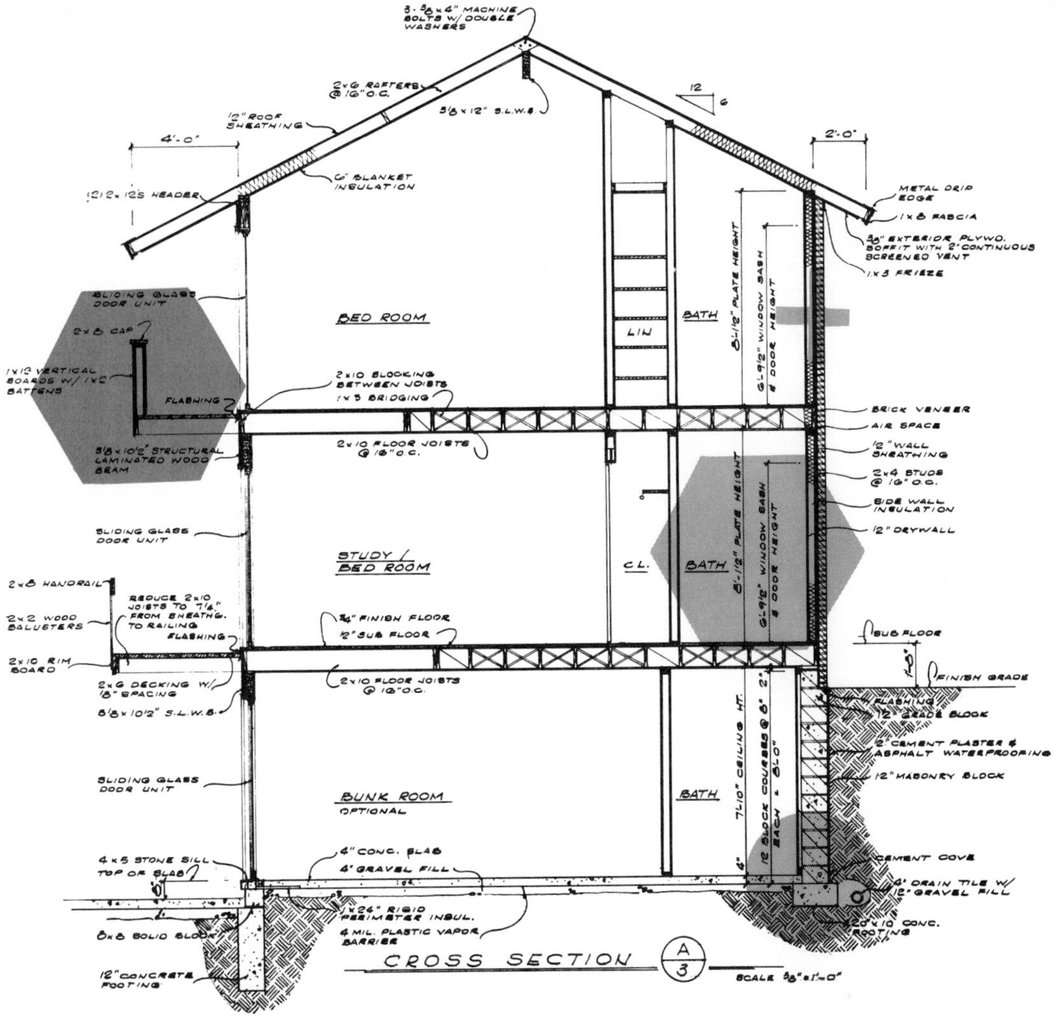

3-5/8 x 4" MACHINE BOLTS W/ DOUBLE WASHERS
2x6 RAFTERS @ 16" O.C.
1/2" ROOF SHEATHING
5 1/8 x 12" S.L.W.B.
6" BLANKET INSULATION
4'-0"
2'-0"
(2) 2 x 12'S HEADER
METAL DRIP EDGE
1 x 8 FASCIA
3/8" EXTERIOR PLYWD. SOFFIT WITH 2" CONTINUOUS SCREENED VENT
1 x 3 FRIEZE
SLIDING GLASS DOOR UNIT
2x8 CAP
BED ROOM
LIN
BATH
8'-1 1/2" PLATE HEIGHT
6'-9 1/2" WINDOW SASH & DOOR HEIGHT
1x12 VERTICAL BOARDS W/ 1x2 BATTENS
FLASHING
2x10 BLOCKING BETWEEN JOISTS
1 x 3 BRIDGING
BRICK VENEER
AIR SPACE
1/2" WALL SHEATHING
2x4 STUDS @ 16" O.C.
SIDE WALL INSULATION
1/2" DRYWALL
5 1/8 x 10 1/2" STRUCTURAL LAMINATED WOOD BEAM
2x10 FLOOR JOISTS @ 16" O.C.
SLIDING GLASS DOOR UNIT
STUDY / BED ROOM
CL.
BATH
8'-1 1/2" PLATE HEIGHT
6'-9 1/2" WINDOW SASH & DOOR HEIGHT
2x8 HANDRAIL
REDUCE 2x10 JOISTS TO 7 1/4" FROM SHEATHG. TO RAILING
2x2 WOOD BALUSTERS
FLASHING
3/4" FINISH FLOOR
1/2" SUB FLOOR
SUB FLOOR
FINISH GRADE
2x10 RIM BOARD
2x6 DECKING W/ 1/8" SPACING
5 1/8 x 10 1/2" S.L.W.B.
2x10 FLOOR JOISTS @ 16" O.C.
FLASHING
12" GRADE BLOCK
1/2" CEMENT PLASTER & ASPHALT WATERPROOFING
12" MASONRY BLOCK
SLIDING GLASS DOOR UNIT
BUNK ROOM
OPTIONAL
BATH
7'-10" CEILING HT.
12 BLOCK COURSES @ 8" EACH = 8'-0"
4 x 5 STONE SILL TOP OF SLAB
4" CONC. SLAB
4" GRAVEL FILL
CEMENT COVE
4" DRAIN TILE W/ 12" GRAVEL FILL
1 x 24" RIGID PERIMETER INSUL.
4 MIL. PLASTIC VAPOR BARRIER
20" x 10" CONC. FOOTING
8x8 SOLID BLOCK
12" CONCRETE FOOTING
CROSS SECTION A/3
SCALE 3/8" = 1'-0"

Fig. 69-9. The complete section through the left portion of the house.

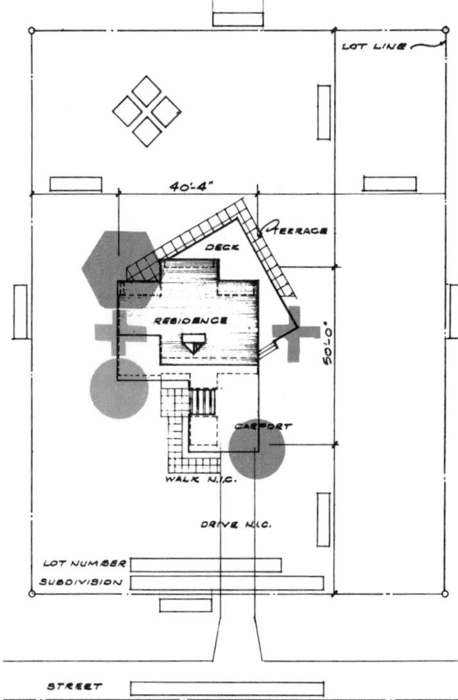

Fig. 69-10. A plot plan.

FRONT

REAR

Fig. 69–11. Exterior pictorial renderings.

PART FOUR

The development of a total architectural design does not stop with the completion of a set of drawings. There is additional information needed by contractors, financial institutions, and governmental agencies which is not found on architectural drawings. The preparation and use of this information is presented in this part.

Architectural Support Services

SECTION 18

Schedules and Specifications

The plans and drawings of a building are documents prepared to ensure that the building will be constructed as planned. It is sometimes difficult or impossible to show on the drawings all details pertaining to the construction of a building. All features not shown on a drawing should be listed in a schedule or in the specifications.

A *schedule* is a chart of materials and products. Most plans include a window, door, and interior-finish schedule. Schedules are also prepared for exterior finishes, electrical fixtures, and plumbing fixtures. Schedules can also be prepared for equipment and furnishings specified for the building.

***Specifications* are lists of details and products to be included in the building. Specifications may be rather brief descriptions of the materials needed, or they may be complete specifications which list the size, manufacturer, grade, color, style, and price of each item of material to be ordered.**

Eastman Kodak Co.

UNIT 70

Door and Window Schedules

Door and window schedules conserve time and space on a drawing. Rather than include all the information about a door or window on the drawing, a key number or letter is attached to each door and window (Fig. 70–1). This symbol is then keyed to the door and window schedule, which includes the width, height, material, type, quantity, and other general information about each window or door (Table 70–1). Window schedules eliminate space-consuming notes on drawings.

Figure 70–2 shows some of the basic information included in a door schedule. In addition to the information shown in chart form on the door and window schedule, the door or window design is often drawn separately and indexed to the schedule. Figure 70–3 shows exterior door designs, which may be drawn sep-

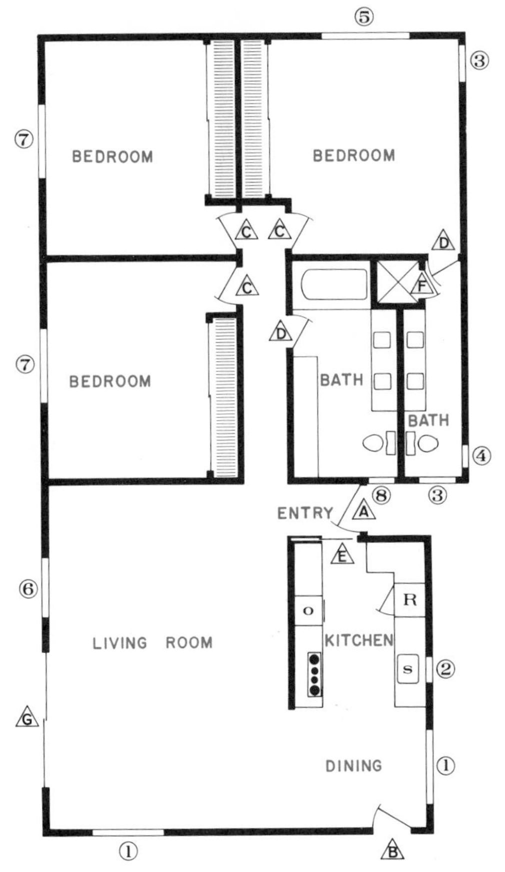

Fig. 70–1. Key numbers.

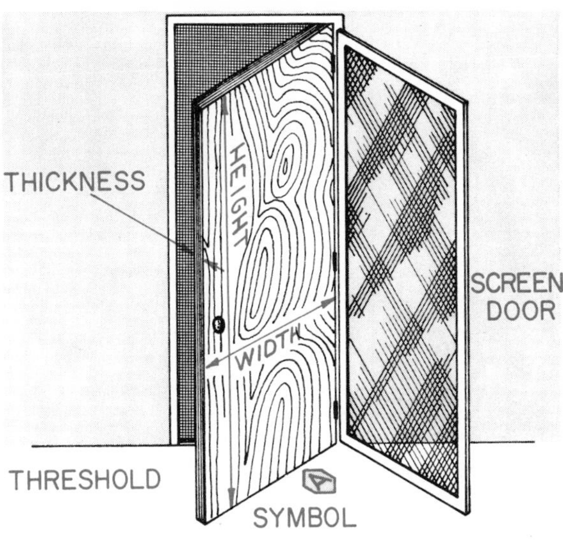

Fig. 70–2. Basic information included on a door schedule.

Table 70–1. THE KEY SYMBOL IS INDEXED TO A DOOR AND WINDOW SCHEDULE

DOOR SCHEDULE

SYMBOL	WIDTH	HEIGHT	THICKNESS	MATERIAL	TYPE	SCREEN	QUANTITY	THRESHOLD	REMARKS	MANUFACTURER
A	3′-0″	7′-0″	1¾″	Wood—Ash	Slab core	No	1	Oak	Outdoor varnish	A. D. & D. Door, Inc.
B	2′-6″	7′-0″	1¾″	Wood—Ash	Slab core	Yes	1	Oak	Oil stain	A. D. & D. Door, Inc.
C	2′-3″	6′-8″	1⅜″	Wood—Oak	Hollow core	No	3	None	Oil stain	A. D. & D. Door, Inc.
D	2′-0″	6′-8″	1⅜″	Wood—Ash	Hollow core	No	2	None	Oil stain	A. D. & D. Door, Inc.
E	2′-3″	6′-8″	1¼″	Wood—Fir	Plywood	No	1	None	Sliding door	A. D. & D. Door, Inc.
F	1′-9″	5′-6″	½″	Glass & metal	Shower door	No	1	None	Frosted glass	A. D. & D. Door, Inc.
G	4′-6″	6′-6″	½″	Glass & metal	Sliding	Yes	2	Metal	1 sliding screen	A. D. & D. Door, Inc.

WINDOW SCHEDULE

SYMBOL	WIDTH	HEIGHT	MATERIAL	TYPE	SCREEN	QUANTITY	REMARKS	MANUFACTURER	CATALOG NUMBER
1	5′-0″	4′-0″	Aluminum	Stationary	No	2		A & B Glass Co.	18BW
2	2′-9″	3′-0″	Aluminum	Louver	Yes	1		A & B Glass Co.	23JW
3	2′-6″	3′-0″	Wood	Double Hung	Yes	2	4 Lites—2 High	A & B Glass Co.	141PW
4	1′-6″	1′-6″	Aluminum	Louver	Yes	1		Hampton Glass Co.	972 BW
5	6′-0″	3′-6″	Aluminum	Louvered Sides	Yes	1		Hampton Glass Co.	417CW
6	4′-0″	6′-6″	Aluminum	Stationary	No	1		H & W Window Co.	57DH
7	5′-0″	3′-6″	Aluminum	Sliding	Yes	2	Frosted Glass	H & W Window Co.	22DH
8	1′-9″	3′-0″	Aluminum	Awing	Yes	1		H & W Window Co.	1711JB

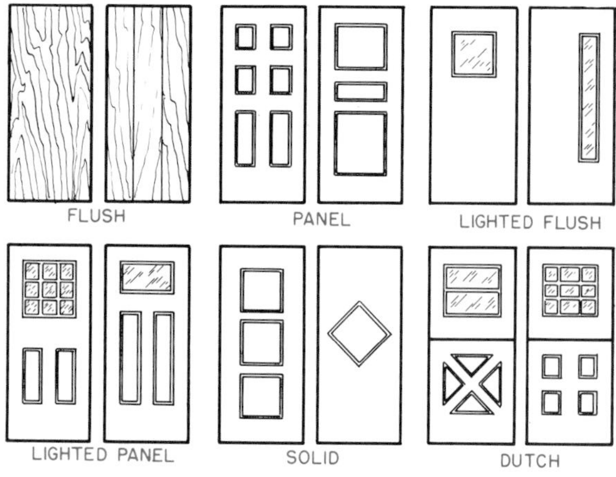

Fig. 70–3. Exterior door designs.

arately, thus eliminating the need for this detail on the elevation. Unless an interior wall elevation is prepared for every wall in the house, it is impossible to determine the style of interior doors from the floor-plan drawing. Figure 70–4 shows drawings of interior door styles which may be indexed to the door schedule.

Window styles are normally depicted on the elevation drawing and complete information included in the window schedule. However, to conserve time many architectural draftsmen draw a separate window detail and show only the window outline and the schedule key for that window on the elevation drawing.

Fig. 70–4. Interior door designs.

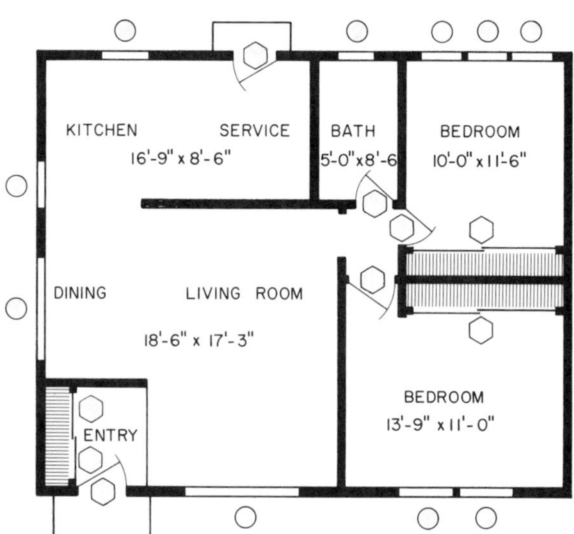

Fig. 70–5. Prepare a door and window schedule for this plan.

PROBLEMS

1. **Prepare a door schedule for the plan shown in Fig. 70–5.**
2. **Prepare a separate drawing showing the several styles of doors you would recommend for the exterior doors shown in Fig. 70–5.**
3. **Draw the designs you would recommend for the interior doors shown in Fig. 70–5.**
4. **Prepare a window schedule for the windows shown in Fig. 70–5.**
5. **Prepare a drawing of each of the window styles you would recommend for the windows shown in Fig. 70–5. Give the manufacturer's name and catalog number for each door and window in your schedule.**
6. **Prepare a door and window schedule for the windows and doors in your classroom.**
7. **Prepare a door and window schedule for the doors and windows in your home.**
8. **Define these architectural terms: *schedule, specifications, sliding window, awning window, double-hung window, panel door, flush door, French door, Dutch door.***

UNIT 71

Finish Schedules

Many types of finishes are used on the interior and the exterior of a building.

PAINT SCHEDULE

To describe the type of finish enamel, paint, and stain, and the amount of gloss and color of each finish for each room would require an exhaustive list with many duplications. A *finishing schedule* is a chart which enables the designer to condense all this information. The interior-finish schedule shown in Table 71–1 includes, in the horizontal column, the parts of each room and the type of finish to be applied. In the vertical column is information pertaining to the application of the finish and the room to which it is to be applied. The exact

Table 71–1. PAINT SCHEDULE

ROOMS	FLOOR			CEILING					WALL					BASE					TRIM					REMARKS
	FLOOR VARNISH	UNFINISHED	WAXED	ENAMEL GLOSS	ENAMEL SEMI-GLOSS	ENAMEL FLAT	FLAT LATEX	STAIN	ENAMEL GLOSS	ENAMEL SEMI-GLOSS	ENAMEL FLAT	FLAT LATEX	STAIN	ENAMEL GLOSS	ENAMEL SEMI-GLOSS	ENAMEL FLAT	FLAT LATEX	STAIN	ENAMEL GLOSS	ENAMEL SEMI-GLOSS	FLAT LATEX	ENAMEL FLAT	STAIN	
ENTRY			√				Off Wht					Off Wht			Off Wht					Off Wht				Two coats
HALL			√					Lt Brn		Tan					Drk Brn					Drk Brn				Two coats
BEDROOM 1	√						Off Wht					Off Wht				Grey				Grey				One coat primer & sealer —painted surface
BEDROOM 2	√						Off Wht				Lt Yel					Yel						Yel		One coat primer & sealer —painted surface
BEDROOM 3		√					Off Wht						Lt Brn					Drk Brn					Tan	One coat primer & sealer —painted surface
BATH 1				Wht					Wht					Lt Blue					Lt Blue					Water-resistant finishes
BATH 2				Wht					Wht					Lt Blue					Lt Blue					Water-resistant finishes
CLOSETS	√						Brn					Brn					Brn					Brn		
KITCHEN			√		Wht				Yel					Yel					Yel					
DINING			√					Tan		Yel					Yel				Yel					Oil stain
LIVING		√						Tan					Lt Brn					Lt Brn					Lt Brn	Oil stain

color classification has been noted in the appropriate intersecting block. The last column, headed "Remarks," is used for making notes about the finish application.

MATERIALS SCHEDULE

To ensure that all floor, wall, and ceiling coverings blend with the overall decor in each room, an interior-finish schedule can be prepared. All the possible materials for each part of the room should be listed in the horizontal column. The rooms are listed in the vertical column. The appropriate block can be checked for the suitable material for the ceiling, wall, wainscoting, base, and floor of each room (Table 71–2). When a schedule is prepared in this manner, it is easy to read and facilitates checking the color scheme of each room and of the overall decor. This kind of schedule condenses pages of unrelated material lists for each room into one chart, thus enabling the designer to see at a glance all the material that should be ordered for each room.

SPECIAL SCHEDULES

To ensure that appliances and fixtures will blend with the decor of each room, a separate schedule can be prepared for them (Table 71–3). Similar schedules are sometimes prepared for furniture and built-in components. By preparing schedules of these kinds, the designer can control every aspect of the overall design, including colors, materials, and styles.

USES OF SCHEDULES

Schedules not only are useful in designing and ensuring that the finishing is completed as planned, but also are valuable as aids in ordering manufactured items, such as appliances and fixtures.

Table 71–2. MATERIALS SCHEDULE

ROOMS	FLOOR									CEILING					WALL			WAINSCOT					BASE					REMARKS
	ASPHALT TILE	CERAMIC TILE	CORK TILE	LINOLEUM TILE	WOOD STRIP—OAK	WOOD SQS.—OAK	PLYWOOD PANEL	CARPETING	SLATE	TERRAZZO	PLASTER	WOOD PANEL	ACOUSTICAL TILE	EXPOSED BEAM	PLASTER	WOOD PANEL	WALL PAPER	WOOD	CERAMIC TILE	PAPER	ASPHALT TILE	STONE VENEER	LINOLEUM	WOOD	RUBBER	TILE—CERAMIC	ASPHALT	
ENTRY									✓	✓		✓				✓								✓				Terrazzo-step covering
HALL			✓								✓				✓					✓				✓				
BEDROOM 1					✓								✓		✓			✓									✓	Mahogany wainscot
BEDROOM 2					✓								✓		✓		✓	✓									✓	Mahogany wainscot
BEDROOM 3							✓	✓					✓			✓									✓			See owner for grade carpet
BATH 1		✓									✓				✓				✓							✓		Water seal tile edges
BATH 2	✓										✓				✓				✓							✓		Water seal tile edges
KITCHEN				✓									✓		✓						✓		✓					
DINING				✓										✓	✓		✓				✓		✓					
LIVING							✓	✓						✓		✓						✓		✓				See owner for grade carpet

Table 71–3. FIXTURE AND APPLIANCE SCHEDULES

APPLIANCE SCHEDULE

ROOM	APPLIANCE	TYPE	SIZE	COLOR	MANUFACTURER	MODEL NO.
KITCHEN	Electric stove	Cook top	4 Burner	Yellow	Ideale Appliances	341 MG
KITCHEN	Electric oven	Built-in	30″ × 24″ × 24″	Yellow	Zeidler Oven Mfg.	27 Mg
SERVICE	Hot-water heater	Gas	50 Gal	White	Oratz Water Htr.	249 KG

FIXTURE SCHEDULE

ROOM	FIXTURE	TYPE	MATERIAL	MANUFACTURER	MODEL NUMBER
LIVING	2 Electric lights	Hanging	Brass reflectors	Hot Spark Ltd.	1037 IG
BEDROOM 1	2 Spot lights	Wall bracket	Flexible neck—aluminum	Gurian & Barris Inc.	1426 SG
BATHS 1 & 2	2 Electric lights	Wall bracket	Aluminum—water resistant	Marks Electrical Co.	2432 DG

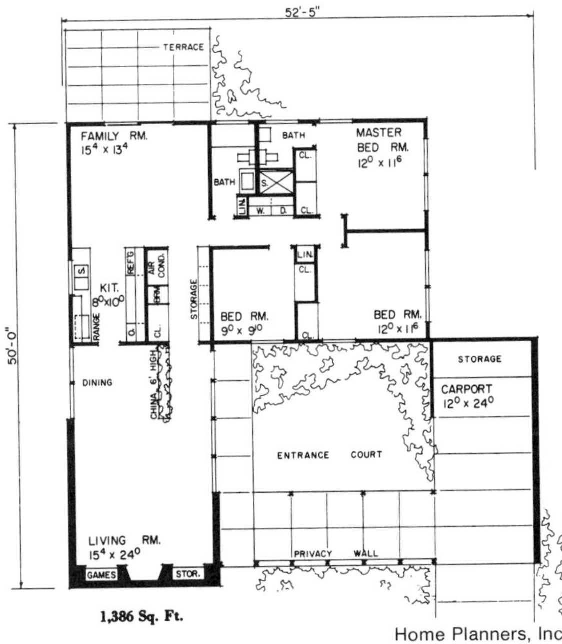

Home Planners, Inc.

Fig. 71–1. Make a finish schedule for this plan.

Home Planners, Inc.

Fig. 71–2. Make an appliance schedule for this plan.

PROBLEMS

1. Make a finish schedule for Fig. 71–1.
2. Make a paint schedule for Fig. 70–5.
3. Add to each item on your schedules the name of a manufacturer and the catalog number.
4. Make an appliance schedule for Fig. 71–2.
5. Make a fixture schedule for Fig. 70–5.
6. Complete all the schedules for your own home. List the types of fixtures, finishes, and doors that you prefer.
7. Know these architectural terms: *finish schedule, trim, base, wainscot, fixture schedule, appliance schedule, flat latex, enamel, primer, sealer, asphalt tile, slate, diato, acoustical tile, veneer, ceramic tile.*

UNIT 72

Specifications

Specifications are written instructions describing the basic requirements for constructing a building. Specifications describe sizes, kinds, and quality of building materials. The methods of construction, fabrication, or installation are also spelled out explicitly. Specifically they tell the contractor, "These are the materials you must use, and this is how you must use them, and these are the conditions under which you undertake this job." Specifications guarantee the purchaser that the contractor will deliver the building when it is finished exactly as specified.

Information that connot be conveniently included in the drawings, such as the legal responsibilities, methods of purchasing materials, and insurance requirements, is included in the specifications. In order to make an accurate construction estimate, contractors refer to the material lists that are included in the specifications (Fig. 72–1).

Specifications help ensure that the building will be constructed according to standards that the building laws require. Specifications are used frequently by banks and federal agencies in appraising the marker value of a building.

Since many specifications are similar, the use of a fill-in form is often desirable. Fill-in forms include all the major classifications included in most specifications. The designer adds the exact size and kind of material required. Figure 72–2 shows a standard form used by the FHA and VA for describing materials to secure FHA or VA loan approval.

The following specifications outline shows the major divisions and subdivisions of a typical set of specifications. This outline does not include the exact size and kind of material included under each category, as these would vary with each building. You will notice that the sequence of the outline roughly approximates the sequence of actual construction.

SPECIFICATIONS OUTLINE

Owner's name and address
Contractor's name and address
Location of new structure

1. **General information**
   - List of all drawings, specifications, legal documents
   - Allowances of money for special orders, such as wallpaper, carpeting, fixtures
   - Completion date
   - Contractor's bid
   - List of manufactured items bought for the job
   - Guarantees for all manufactured items

2. **Legal responsibilities—contractor**
   - Good workmanship
   - Adherence to plans and specifications
   - Fulfillment of building laws
   - Purchase of materials
   - Hiring and paying all workers
   - Obtaining and paying for all permits
   - Providing owner certificate of passed inspection
   - Responsibility for correction of errors
   - Responsibility for complete cleanup
   - Furnish all tools and equipment
   - Providing personal supervision
   - Having a foreman on the job at all times
   - Providing a written guarantee of work

3. **Legal responsibilities—homeowner**
   - Carrying fire insurance during construction
   - Paying utilities during construction
   - Specifying method of payment

#1575

LINE NO.	ITEM COLUMN NO. 2	QUANTITY & UNIT MEAS.	MATERIAL (TYPE and/or SIZE)	UNIT COST	TOTAL COST
1	Interior Partitions				
2		195 Pcs.	2 x 4 x 8'-0" Studs		
3		30 Pcs.	2 x 4 x 10'-0" Studs		
4		34 Pcs.	2 x 4 x 12'-0" Studs		
5		870 Lin. Ft.	2 x 4 Plates		
6		48 Lin. Ft.	2 x 6 Headers		
7		3 Pcs.	2 x 8 x 10'-0" Headers		
8		2 Pcs.	2 x 8 x 14'-0" Headers		
9		2 Pcs.	2 x 12 x 12'-0" Headers		
10		7 Pcs.	2 x 8 x 8'-0" Studs		
11		3 Pcs.	2 x 8 x 6'-0" Plates		
12					
13	Ceiling Framing				
14		26 Pcs.	2 x 6 x 12'-0" Ceiling Joist		
15					
16	Roof Framing				
17		16 Units	24'-0" 3/12 Pitch 2 x 6 Trusses		
18		76 Pcs.	2 x 6 x 16'-0" Rafters		
19		24 Pcs.	2 x 6 x 12'-0" Rake Rafters		
20		2800 Sq. Ft.	Roof Sheathing		
21		5600 Sq. Ft.	15# Felt		
22		9 Pcs.	2 x 6 x 10'-0" Rafters		
23	Balcony Framing				
24		24 Lin. Ft.	2 x 6 Joist Trimmers		
25		230 Lin. Ft.	2 x 6 S 4 S Plank Flooring		
26					
27	Roofing & Sheet Metal				
28		1 Square	Asphalt Ridge Shingles		
29		28 Squares	Asphalt Self Sealing Shingles		
30		284 Lin. Ft.	Metal Drip Edging		
31		90 Pcs.	5" x 7" Metal Drip Edging		
32		16 Lin. Ft.	Window Head Flashing		
33		24 Lin. Ft.	Roof to Wall Flashing		
34		13 Lin. Ft.	Chimney Counter Flashing		
35		140 Lbs.	Roofing Nails		
36					
37	Windows				
38		15 Single	4'-0"x3'-0" Aluminum Gliding Windows-Loose Casing		
39		4 Single	44x80" Fixed Plate Glass - Loose Casing		
40		1 Each Right			
41		& Left	48x24"-36" Fixed Plate Glass 3/12 Pitch		
42			Sloping Head - Loose Casing		
43		1 Each Right			
44		& Left	26"x104"-110½" Fixed Plate Glass 3/12 Pitch		
45			Sloping Head - Loose Casing		
46		2 Singles	26"x92" Fixed Plate Glass - Loose Casing		
47		1 Single	8"x80" Fixed Plate Glass - Loose Casing		
48		4 Single	4[illegible]78" Fixed Plate Glass - Loose Casing		
49	Door Frames	1 Fr[illegible]nt	[illegible]7'-0" Rabbeted 1-3/4" Loose Casing		
5[illegible]		[illegible]	[illegible]-8" Rabbeted 1-3/4" 5/4 x 6" [illegible]ing		
			[illegible] Glass Slidi[illegible]		
			[illegible] Casing		

Fig. 72–1. Part of a contractor's materials list.

4. **Earthwork**
   Excavation, backfills, gradings
   Irregularities in soil
   Location of house on lot
   Clearing of lot
   Grading for water drainage
   Preparation of ground for foundation

5. **Concrete and cement work**
   Foundation sizes
   Concrete and mortar mix
   Cement, sand, and gravel
   Curing the concrete
   Finishing-off concrete flatwork
   Vapor seals and locations
   Type and size of reinforcing steel and locations
   Outside concrete work, sizes and locations
   Cleaning of masonry work
   Porches, patios, terraces, walks, driveways: sizes and locations

6. **Carpentry, rough**
   Required types of wood grades
   Maximum amount of moisture in wood
   List of construction members, sizes, and amount of wood needed
   Special woods, mill work
   Nail sizes for each job

7. **Floors**
   Type, size, and finish of floor
   Floor coverings

8. **Roofing**
   Type of coverings
   Amount of coverings
   Methods to bond coverings
   Color of final layer

9. **Sheet metal**
   List of flashing and sizes
   List of galvanized iron and sizes
   Protective metal paint and where to use
   Size and amount of screens for vents, doors, and windows

10. **Doors and windows**
    Sizes
    Material
    Type
    Quantity
    Manufacturer and model number
    Window and door trims
    Frames for screens
    Amount of window space per room
    Amount of openable window space per room
    Types of glass and mirrors
    Types of sashes
    Window and door frames
    Weather stripping and caulking

11. **Lath and plaster**
    Type, size, and amount of lath needed
    Type, size, and amount of wire mesh, felt paper, and nails
    Types of interior and exterior plaster
    Instructions of manufacturer for mixing and applying
    Number of coats
    Finishing between coats
    Drying time

12. **Dry walls**
    Wall covering—types, sizes, manufacturer's model number

13. **Insulation**
    List of types, makes, sizes, model number
    Instructions for applying

14. **Electrical needs**
    Electrical outlets and their locations
    Electrical switches and their locations
    Wall brackets and their locations
    Ceiling outlets and their locations
    Signed certificate that electrical work has passed the building inspection
    Guarantee for all parts

List of all electrical parts with name, type, size, color, model number, and lamp wattage
Locations for television outlet and aerial, telephone outlet, main switches, panel board, circuits, and meter
Size of wire used for wiring
Number of circuits

15. **Plumbing**
List of fixtures with make, color, style, manufacturer, and catalog number
List of type and size of plumbing lines—gas, water, and waste
Vent pipes and sizes
Inspection slips on plumbing
Guarantees for plumbing
Instructions for installing and connecting pipelines

16. **Heating and air conditioning**
List of all equipment with make, style, color, manufacturer's name, catalog number
Guarantee for all equipment
Signed equipment inspection certificate
List and location of all sheet metal work for heat ducts
List of fuels, outlets, exhausts, and registers
Types of insulation
Location for heating and air-conditioning units

17. **Stone and brickwork**
List and location of all stone and brickwork (fireplace, chimney, retaining walls)
Concrete and mortar mix
Reinforcing steel
Kind, size, and name of manufacturer of any synthetic stone

18. **Built-ins**
List of all built-ins to be constructed on the job
Dimensions
Kinds of materials
List of all manufactured objects to be built in
Model number
Make
Color
Catalog number
Manufacturer

19. **Ceramic tile**
List of types, sizes, colors, manufacturers, catalog numbers
Mortar mix

20. **Painting**
List of paints to be used—type, color, manufacturer's name, catalog number
Preparation of painted surface
Number of coats and preparation of each
Instructions for stained surfaces or special finishes (type of finish, color, manufacturer, and catalog number)

21. **Finish hardware**
List of hardware—type, make, material, color, manufacturer's name, catalog number

22. **Exterior**
List of types of finishes for each exterior wall
Instructions for each type
Color, manufacturer, and catalog number

23. **Miscellaneous**
List and location of all blacktop areas

PROBLEMS

1. **Make a specifications list for a single garage.**
2. **Make a specifications list for Fig. 70-5.**
3. **Obtain a specifications list from a set of plans.**
4. **Define these terms: *specifications, guarantee, documents, contractor.***

FHA Form 2005
VA Form 26-1852
Rev. 3/68

For accurate register of carbon copies, form may be separated along above fold. Staple completed sheets together in original order.

Form approved.
Budget Bureau No. 63-R055.11.

☐ Proposed Construction

☐ Under Construction

DESCRIPTION OF MATERIALS

No. ________ (To be inserted by FHA or VA)

Property address ________ City ________ State ________

Mortgagor or Sponsor ________ (Name) ________ (Address)

Contractor or Builder ________ (Name) ________ (Address)

INSTRUCTIONS

1. For additional information on how this form is to be submitted, number of copies, etc., see the instructions applicable to the FHA Application for Mortgage Insurance or VA Request for Determination of Reasonable Value, as the case may be.
2. Describe all materials and equipment to be used, whether or not shown on the drawings, by marking an X in each appropriate check-box and entering the information called for in each space. If space is inadequate, enter "See misc." and describe under item 27 or on an attached sheet.
3. Work not specifically described or shown will not be considered unless required, then the minimum acceptable will be assumed. Work exceeding minimum requirements cannot be considered unless specifically described.
4. Include no alternates, "or equal" phrases, or contradictory items. (Consideration of a request for acceptance of substitute materials or equipment is not thereby precluded.)
5. Include signatures required at the end of this form.
6. The construction shall be completed in compliance with the related drawings and specifications, as amended during processing. The specifications include this Description of Materials and the applicable Minimum Construction Requirements.

1. EXCAVATION:

Bearing soil, type ________

2. FOUNDATIONS:

Footings: concrete mix ________; strength psi ________ Reinforcing ________

Foundation wall: material ________ Reinforcing ________

Interior foundation wall: material ________ Party foundation wall ________

Columns: material and sizes ________ Piers: material and reinforcing ________

Girders: material and sizes ________ Sills: material ________

Basement entrance areaway ________ Window areaways ________

Waterproofing ________ Footing drains ________

Termite protection ________

Basementless space: ground cover ________; insulation ________; foundation vents ________

Special foundations ________

Additional information: ________

3. CHIMNEYS:

Material ________ Prefabricated *(make and size)* ________

Flue lining: material ________ Heater flue size ________ Fireplace flue size ________

Vents *(material and size)*: gas or oil heater ________; water heater ________

Additional information: ________

4. FIREPLACES:

Type: ☐ solid fuel; ☐ gas-burning; ☐ circulator *(make and size)* ________ Ash dump and clean-out ________

Fireplace: facing ________; lining ________; hearth ________; mantel ________

Additional information: ________

5. EXTERIOR WALLS:

Wood frame: wood grade, and species ________ ☐ Corner bracing. Building paper or felt ________

Sheathing ________; thickness ________; width ________; ☐ solid; ☐ spaced ________" o. c.; ☐ diagonal; ________

Siding ________; grade ________; type ________; size ________; exposure ________"; fastening ________

Shingles ________; grade ________; type ________; size ________; exposure ________"; fastening ________

Stucco ________; thickness ________"; Lath ________; weight ________ lb.

Masonry veneer ________ Sills ________ Lintels ________ Base flashing ________

Masonry: ☐ solid ☐ faced ☐ stuccoed; total wall thickness ________"; facing thickness ________"; facing material ________

Backup material ________; thickness ________"; bonding ________

Door sills ________ Window sills ________ Lintels ________ Base flashing ________

Interior surfaces: dampproofing, ________ coats of ________; furring ________

Additional information: ________

Exterior painting: material ________; number of coats ________

Gable wall construction: ☐ same as main walls; ☐ other construction ________

6. FLOOR FRAMING:

Joists: wood, grade, and species ________; other ________; bridging ________; anchors ________

Concrete slab: ☐ basement floor; ☐ first floor; ☐ ground supported; ☐ self-supporting; mix ________; thickness ________

reinforcing ________; insulation ________; membrane ________

Fill under slab: material ________; thickness ________". Additional information: ________

7. SUBFLOORING: *(Describe underflooring for special floors under item 21.)*

Material: grade and species ________; size ________; type ________

Laid: ☐ first floor; ☐ second floor; ☐ attic ________ sq. ft.; ☐ diagonal; ☐ right angles. Additional information: ________

8. FINISH FLOORING: *(Wood only. Describe other finish flooring under item 21.)*

Location	Rooms	Grade	Species	Thickness	Width	Bldg. Paper	Finish
First floor							
Second floor							
Attic floor ________ sq. ft.							

Additional information: ________

Fig. 72–2. An FHA and VA description of materials.

9. PARTITION FRAMING:

Studs: wood, grade, and species ______ size and spacing ______ Other ______

Additional information: ______

10. CEILING FRAMING:

Joists: wood, grade, and species ______ Other ______ Bridging ______

Additional information: ______

11. ROOF FRAMING:

Rafters: wood, grade, and species ______ Roof trusses (see detail): grade and species ______

Additional information: ______

12. ROOFING:

Sheathing: wood, grade, and species ______; ☐ solid; ☐ spaced ______" o.c.

Roofing ______; grade ______; size ______; type ______

Underlay ______; weight or thickness ______; size ______; fastening ______

Built-up roofing ______; number of plies ______; surfacing material ______

Flashing: material ______; gage or weight ______; ☐ gravel stops; ☐ snow guards

Additional information: ______

13. GUTTERS AND DOWNSPOUTS:

Gutters: material ______; gage or weight ______; size ______; shape ______

Downspouts: material ______; gage or weight ______; size ______; shape ______; number ______

Downspouts connected to: ☐ Storm sewer; ☐ sanitary sewer; ☐ dry-well. ☐ Splash blocks: material and size ______

Additional information: ______

14. LATH AND PLASTER

Lath ☐ walls, ☐ ceilings: material ______; weight or thickness ______ Plaster: coats ______; finish ______

Dry-wall ☐ walls, ☐ ceilings: material ______; thickness ______; finish ______

Joint treatment ______

15. DECORATING: ***(Paint, wallpaper, etc.)***

Rooms	Wall Finish Material and Application	Ceiling Finish Material and Application
Kitchen ______		
Bath ______		
Other ______		

Additional information: ______

16. INTERIOR DOORS AND TRIM:

Doors: type ______; material ______; thickness ______

Door trim: type ______; material ______ Base: type ______; material ______; size ______

Finish: doors ______; trim ______

Other trim *(item, type and location)* ______

Additional information: ______

17. WINDOWS:

Windows: type ______; make ______; material ______; sash thickness ______

Glass: grade ______; ☐ sash weights; ☐ balances, type ______; head flashing ______

Trim: type ______; material ______ Paint ______; number coats ______

Weatherstripping: type ______; material ______ Storm sash, number ______

Screens: ☐ full; ☐ half; type ______; number ______; screen cloth material ______

Basement windows: type ______; material ______; screens, number ______; Storm sash, number ______

Special windows ______

Additional information: ______

18. ENTRANCES AND EXTERIOR DETAIL:

Main entrance door: material ______; width ______; thickness ______". Frame: material ______; thickness ______"

Other entrance doors: material ______; width ______; thickness ______". Frame: material ______; thickness ______"

Head flashing ______ Weatherstripping: type ______; saddles ______

Screen doors: thickness ______"; number ______; screen cloth material ______ Storm doors: thickness ______"; number ______

Combination storm and screen doors: thickness ______"; number ______; screen cloth material ______

Shutters: ☐ hinged; ☐ fixed. Railings ______, Attic louvers ______

Exterior millwork: grade and species ______ Paint ______; number coats ______

Additional information: ______

19. CABINETS AND INTERIOR DETAIL:

Kitchen cabinets, wall units: material ______; lineal feet of shelves ______; shelf width ______

Base units: material ______; counter top ______; edging ______

Back and end splash ______ Finish of cabinets ______; number coats ______

Medicine cabinets: make ______; model ______

Other cabinets and built-in furniture ______

Additional information: ______

20. STAIRS:

Stair	Treads		Risers		Strings		Handrail		Balusters	
	Material	Thickness	Material	Thickness	Material	Size	Material	Size	Material	Size
Basement ______										
Main ______										
Attic ______										

Disappearing: make and model number ______

Additional information: ______

Fig. 72–2. Continued.

21. SPECIAL FLOORS AND WAINSCOT:

	Location	Material, Color, Border, Sizes, Gage, Etc.	Threshold Material	Wall Base Material	Underfloor Material
Floors	Kitchen				
	Bath				

	Location	Material, Color, Border, Cap. Sizes, Gage, Etc.	Height	Height Over Tub	Height in Showers (From Floor)
Wainscot	Bath				

Bathroom accessories: ☐ Recessed; material ______; number ______; ☐ Attached; material ______; number ______

Additional information: ______

22. PLUMBING:

Fixture	Number	Location	Make	Mfr's Fixture Identification No.	Size	Color
Sink						
Lavatory						
Water closet						
Bathtub						
Shower over tub△						
Stall shower△						
Laundry trays						

△☐ Curtain rod △☐ Door ☐ Shower pan: material ______

Water supply: ☐ public; ☐ community system; ☐ individual (private) system.★

Sewage disposal: ☐ public; ☐ community system; ☐ individual (private) system.★

★*Show and describe individual system in complete detail in separate drawings and specifications according to requirements.*

House drain (inside): ☐ cast iron; ☐ tile; ☐ other ______ House sewer (outside): ☐ cast iron; ☐ tile; ☐ other ______

Water piping: ☐ galvanized steel; ☐ copper tubing; ☐ other ______ Sill cocks, number ______

Domestic water heater: type ______; make and model ______; heating capacity ______

______ gph. 100° rise. Storage tank: material ______; capacity ______ gallons.

Gas service: ☐ utility company; ☐ liq. pet. gas; ☐ other ______ Gas piping: ☐ cooking; ☐ house heating.

Footing drains connected to: ☐ storm sewer; ☐ sanitary sewer; ☐ dry well. Sump pump; make and model ______

______; capacity ______; discharges into ______

23. HEATING:

☐ Hot water. ☐ Steam. ☐ Vapor. ☐ One-pipe system. ☐ Two-pipe system.

☐ Radiators. ☐ Convectors. ☐ Baseboard radiation. Make and model ______

Radiant panel: ☐ floor; ☐ wall; ☐ ceiling. Panel coil: material ______

☐ Circulator. ☐ Return pump. Make and model ______; capacity ______ gpm.

Boiler: make and model ______ Output ______ Btuh.; net rating ______ Btuh.

Additional information: ______

Warm air: ☐ Gravity. ☐ Forced. Type of system ______

Duct material: supply ______; return ______ Insulation ______, thickness ______ ☐ Outside air intake.

Furnace: make and model ______ Input ______ Btuh.; output ______ Btuh.

Additional information: ______

☐ Space heater; ☐ floor furnace; ☐ wall heater. Input ______ Btuh.; output ______ Btuh.; number units ______

Make, model ______ Additional information: ______

Controls: make and types ______

Additional information: ______

Fuel: ☐ Coal; ☐ oil; ☐ gas; ☐ liq. pet. gas; ☐ electric; ☐ other ______; storage capacity ______

Additional information: ______

Firing equipment furnished separately: ☐ Gas burner, conversion type. ☐ Stoker: hopper feed ☐; bin feed ☐

Oil burner: ☐ pressure atomizing; ☐ vaporizing ______

Make and model ______ Control ______

Additional information: ______

Electric heating system: type ______ Input ______ watts; @ ______ volts; output ______ Btuh.

Additional information: ______

Ventilating equipment: attic fan, make and model ______; capacity ______ cfm.

kitchen exhaust fan, make and model ______

Other heating, ventilating, or cooling equipment ______

24. ELECTRIC WIRING:

Service: ☐ overhead; ☐ underground. Panel: ☐ fuse box; ☐ circuit-breaker; make ______ AMP's ______ No. circuits ______

Wiring: ☐ conduit; ☐ armored cable; ☐ nonmetallic cable; ☐ knob and tube; ☐ other ______

Special outlets: ☐ range; ☐ water heater; ☐ other ______

☐ Doorbell. ☐ Chimes. Push-button locations ______ Additional information: ______

25. LIGHTING FIXTURES:

Total number of fixtures ______ Total allowance for fixtures, typical installation, $ ______

Nontypical installation ______

Additional information: ______

Fig. 72–2. Continued.

26. INSULATION:

Location	Thickness	Material, Type, and Method of Installation	Vapor Barrier
Roof			
Ceiling			
Wall			
Floor			

HARDWARE: *(make, material, and finish.)* ______

SPECIAL EQUIPMENT: *(State material or make, model and quantity. Include only equipment and appliances which are acceptable by local law, custom and applicable FHA standards. Do not include items which, by established custom, are supplied by occupant and removed when he vacates premises or chattles prohibited by law from becoming realty.)* ______

27. MISCELLANEOUS: *(Describe any main dwelling materials, equipment, or construction items not shown elsewhere; or use to provide additional information where the space provided was inadequate. Always reference by item number to correspond to numbering used on this form.)* ______

PORCHES:

TERRACES:

GARAGES:

WALKS AND DRIVEWAYS:

Driveway: width ______ ; base material ______ ; thickness ______"; surfacing material ______ ; thickness ______"
Front walk: width ______ ; material ______ ; thickness ______". Service walk: width ______ ; material ______ ; thickness ______"
Steps: material ______ ; treads ______"; risers ______". Cheek walls ______

OTHER ONSITE IMPROVEMENTS:

(Specify all exterior onsite improvements not described elsewhere, including items such as unusual grading, drainage structures, retaining walls, fence, railings, and accessory structures.)

LANDSCAPING, PLANTING, AND FINISH GRADING:

Topsoil ______" thick: ☐ front yard; ☐ side yards; ☐ rear yard to ______ feet behind main building.
Lawns *(seeded, sodded, or sprigged)*: ☐ front yard ______ ; ☐ side yards ______ ; ☐ rear yard ______
Planting: ☐ as specified and shown on drawings; ☐ as follows:

______ Shade trees, deciduous, ______" caliper.
______ Low flowering trees, deciduous, ______' to ______'
______ High-growing shrubs, deciduous, ______' to ______'
______ Medium-growing shrubs, deciduous, ______' to ______'
______ Low-growing shrubs, deciduous, ______' to ______'
______ Evergreen trees. ______' to ______', B & B.
______ Evergreen shrubs. ______' to ______', B & B.
______ Vines, 2-year ______

IDENTIFICATION.—This exhibit shall be identified by the signature of the builder, or sponsor, and/or the proposed mortgagor if the latter is known at the time of application.

Date ______ Signature ______

Signature ______

FHA Form 2005
VA Form 26-1852

GPO 1068 o48—16—80081-1 296-152

Fig. 72–2. Continued.

SECTION 19

Building Codes

A building code is a collection of laws listed in book or pamphlet form for a given community. It outlines restrictions which will maintain minimum standards set up by the Building Department of the community for safeguarding life and health. These laws help to control design, construction, materials, maintenance, location of structure, use of structure by the occupants, quality of materials, and use of materials. To stay within the law, designers and builders must observe the code.

Before anything is built, altered, or repaired, a building permit must be obtained from the Building Department. This permit ensures the appearance of an inspector to inspect the work. The inspections usually made for a house are the plans, grading of land, excavations, foundation forms, foundations, carpentry, plumbing, heating, ventilation, and electrical work.

Building laws have lessened the loss of life and property from earthquakes, storms, and fires. The homeowner knows that when his home is finished, it will be a secure and well-constructed dwelling. It will be free from shoddy materials and poor workmanship. He knows that his home will have a good resale value and that he will be able to obtain a mortgage loan on it.

Other advantages of the building codes are that they allow an amateur craftsman to build his own home by supplying all the engineering information necessary for building a family dwelling. Since he does not need a complete version of the building code, many communities print a condensed copy for the family dwelling.

The codes of some communities are better than others because the laws are continually being revised to keep pace with new types of construction and materials. These codes accept any material and method of construction that does the job safely. Using newer methods may save the owner money through efficiency of construction.

Simpson Lumber Company

Building codes also vary in different communities because of the geographical differences. However, a problem arises concerning such differences. The codes vary in their make-up as well as in their methods of construction, which leads to confusion among builders. A method of construction used in one community is barred in another because of a different interpretation of the law. What is needed is a uniform code that has a simple interpretation of each law. Each community would have this law adjusted to fit the physical conditions of the area. For example, the foundation footings need to be deep in the ground in cold climates. It must be below the frost line where the earth does not freeze. In warm climates there is no need for such depth. The law concerning foundation footings should be stated and cataloged in the same way in all building codes, except that the specification for distance beneath the ground should vary according to the community. Required sizes, classifications, and kinds of materials are shown in building codes.

UNIT 73

Required Sizes

Each municipality formulates its own building code requirements. Building codes are necessary to ensure that substandard, unsafe, and unattractive buildings are not built in the area. Building codes also help to regulate the kinds of structures that can be built in a specific area by zoning. Zones are classified as residential, commercial, and industrial. Size restrictions are a vital part of every code.

Building code information is presented in printed material, charts, sectional drawings, specifications, and pictorial drawings (Fig. 73–1). Building codes also contain regulations pertaining to building permits, fees, inspection requirements, drawings, property location, zoning, and general legal implications connected with building.

Some of the more common items included in family dwelling building codes are as follows:

Minimum room sizes
Ceiling heights
Window areas
Foundations (Fig. 73–2)
Retaining walls
Concrete mix
Girders (Fig. 73–3)

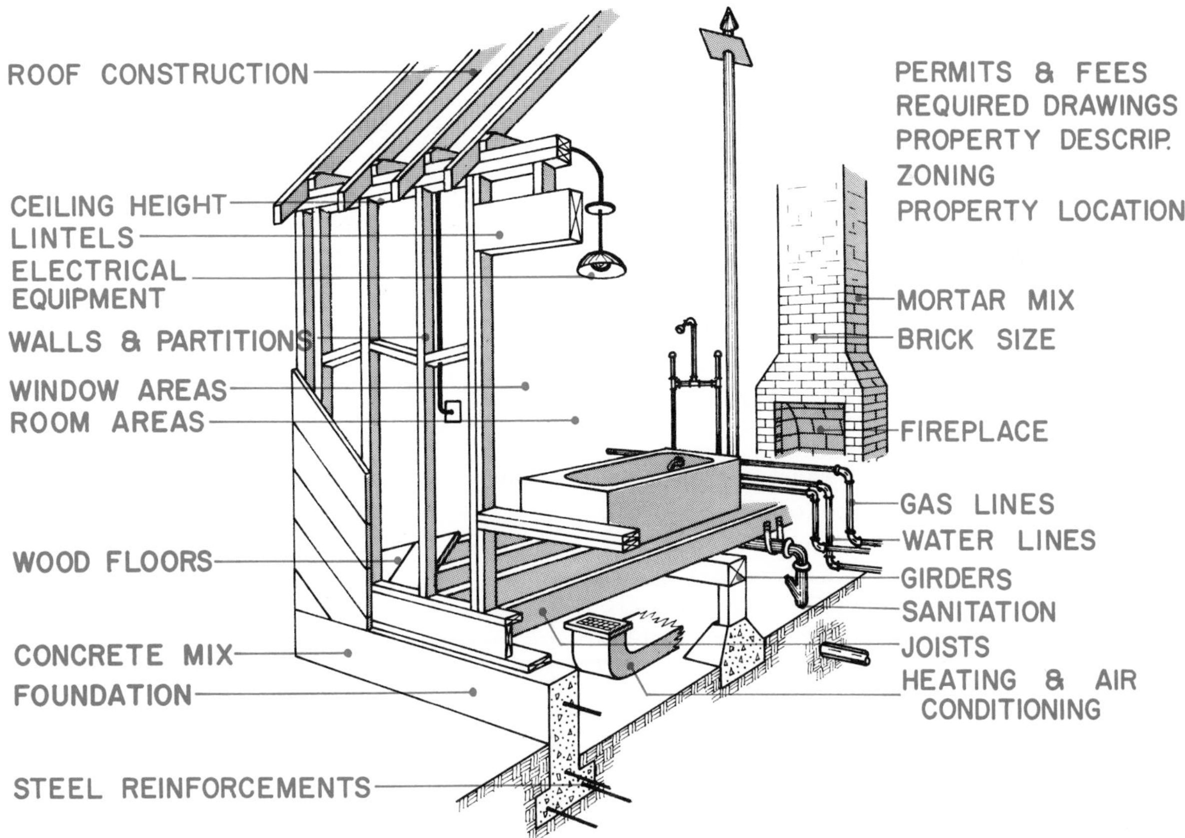

Fig. 73–1. The common items controlled by building codes.

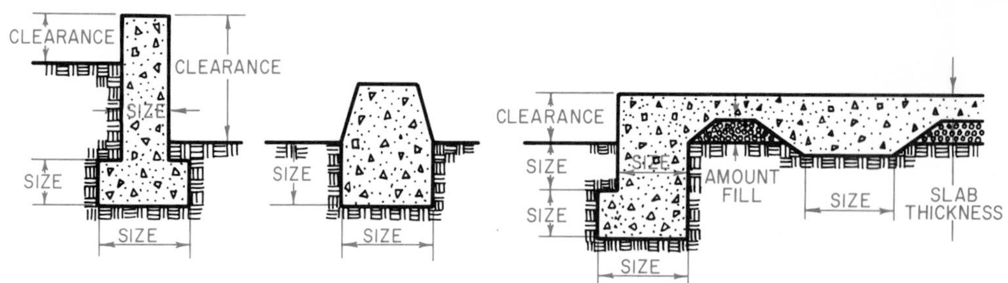

Fig. 73–2. Size, clearance, and composition of foundations are determined by building codes.

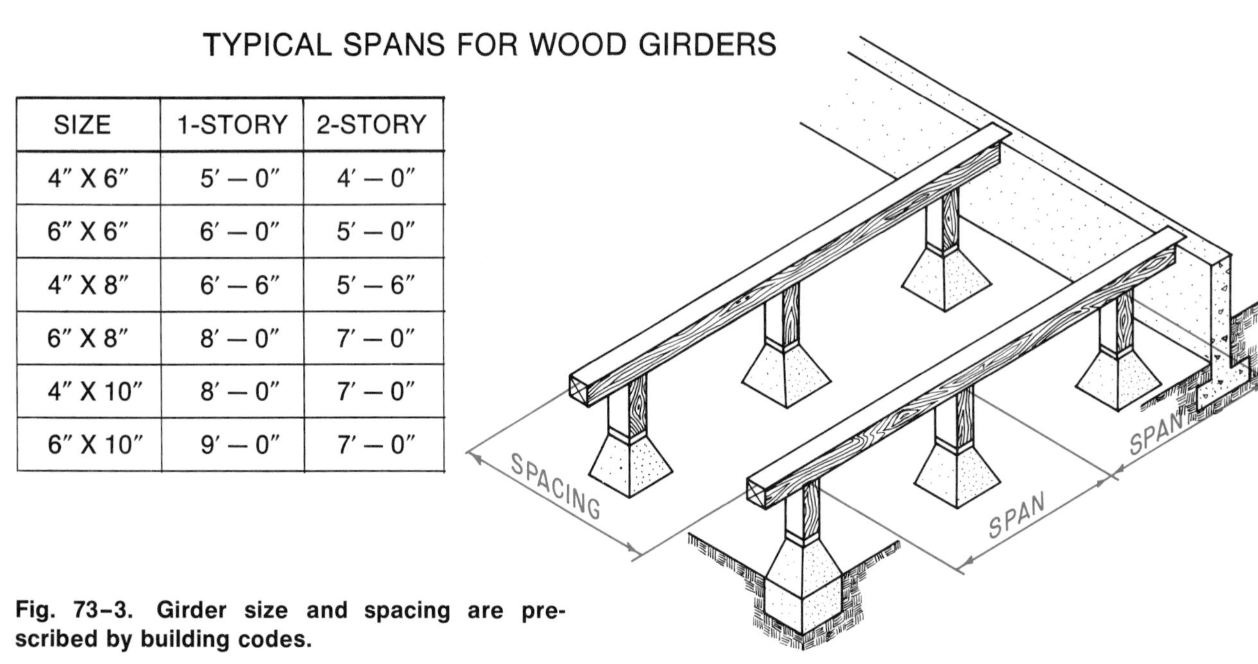

TYPICAL SPANS FOR WOOD GIRDERS

SIZE	1-STORY	2-STORY
4″ X 6″	5′ — 0″	4′ — 0″
6″ X 6″	6′ — 0″	5′ — 0″
4″ X 8″	6′ — 6″	5′ — 6″
6″ X 8″	8′ — 0″	7′ — 0″
4″ X 10″	8′ — 0″	7′ — 0″
6″ X 10″	9′ — 0″	7′ — 0″

Fig. 73–3. Girder size and spacing are prescribed by building codes.

Fig. 73–4. The size and span of lintels are outlined in building codes.

LINTEL SPANS

SUPPORTING ROOF & CEILING ONLY		SUPPORTING FLOOR, ROOF & CEILING ONLY	
SIZE	SPAN	SIZE	SPAN
4 x 4	3′ – 0″	4 x 4	3′ – 6″
4 x 6	4′ – 0″	4 x 6	5′ – 0″
4 x 8	6′ – 0″	4 x 8	5′ – 6″
4 x 10	8′ – 0″	4 x 10	7′ – 0″
4 x 12	9′ – 0″	4 x 12	8′ – 0″
4 x 14	10′ – 0″	4 x 14	9′ – 0″
4 x 16	12′ – 0″	4 x 16	10′ – 0″

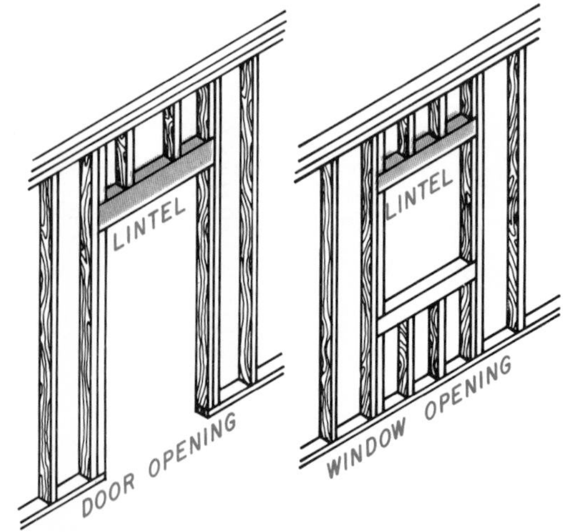

JOIST SPANS

JOIST SIZE	JOIST SPACING	JOIST SPAN
2 x 4	12"	10'-0"
	16"	9'-0"
	24"	7'-0"
2 x 6	12"	13'-0"
	16"	12'-0"
	24"	10'-6"
2 x 10	12"	16'-0"
	16"	15'-0"
	24"	12'-0"
2 x 12	12"	20'-0"
	16"	18'-0"
	24"	15'-0"
2 x 14	12"	23'-0"
	16"	21'-0"
	24"	17'-0"

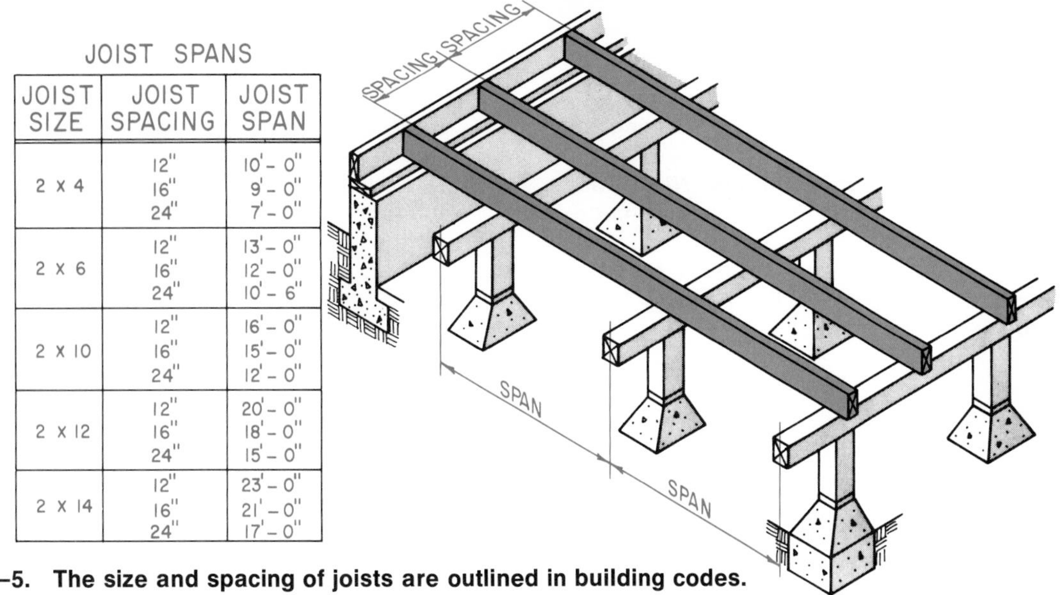

Fig. 73–5. The size and spacing of joists are outlined in building codes.

Lintels (Fig. 73–4)
Walls and partitions
Joists (Fig. 73–5)
Wood floors
Concrete blocks
Steel reinforcing
Fireplaces
Chimneys
Roof construction (Fig. 73–6)
Stairways
Electrical equipment
Gas piping
Heating
Air conditioning
Plumbing
Sanitation
Garages

RAFTER SPANS

SIZE	RAFTER SPACING	SPAN·ROOF PITCH LESS THAN 4:12	SPAN·ROOF PITCH MORE THAN 4:12
2 X 4	12"	9'-0"	10'-0"
	16"	8'-0"	8'-6"
	24"	6'-6"	7'-0"
	32"	5'-6"	6'-0"
2 X 6	12"	14'-0"	16'-0"
	16"	12'-6"	13'-6"
	24"	10'-6"	11'-0"
	32"	9'-0"	9'-6"
2 X 8	12"	19'-0"	21'-6"
	16"	17'-0"	18'-6"
	24"	13'-6"	15'-0"
	32"	11'-6"	13'-0"
2 X 10	12"	23'-0"	25'-0"
	16"	21'-0"	22'-6"
	24"	17'-6"	19'-0"
	32"	15'-0"	16'-6"

CEILING JOIST SPANS

SIZE	JOIST SPACING	SPAN
2 X 4	12"	10'-0"
	16"	9'-0"
	24"	8'-0"
2 X 6	12"	16'-0"
	16"	14'-6"
	24"	12'-6"
2 X 8	12"	21'-6"
	16"	19'-6"
	24"	17'-0"

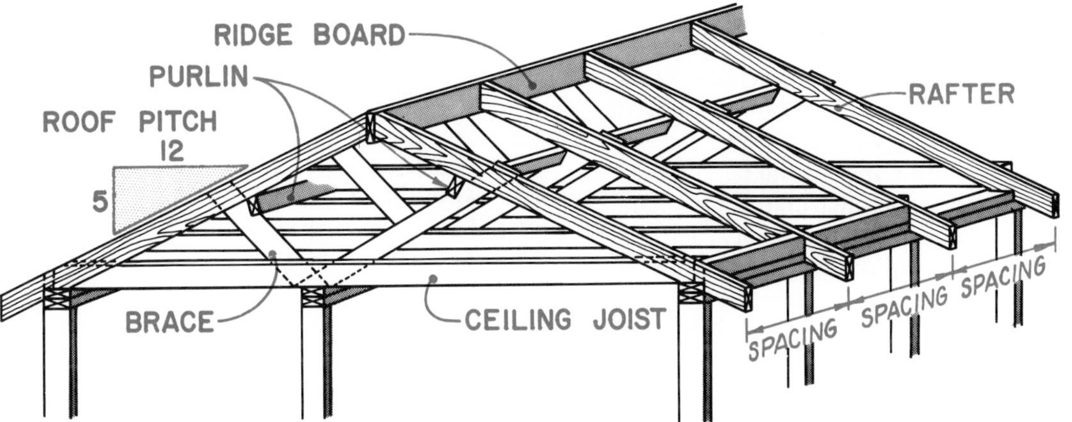

Fig. 73–6. Roof types, pitches, size of materials, and spacing of rafters and joists are determined by building codes.

PROBLEMS

1. **Determine the distance between the posts shown in Fig. 73-3, using the building code of your community.**
2. **Sketch the joists shown in Fig. 73-3. Dimension them according to the building code in your community.**
3. **Draw Fig. 73-2 and put in the T foundation members according to the building laws of your community.**
4. **From study of your building code, what other parts of construction can be added to the list of building requirements in this unit?**
5. **Does your building code permit the use of prefabricated materials?**
6. **Define these architectural terms: *building code, building permit, cutaway view, legal description, zoning.***

UNIT 74

Building Loads

The weight of all the materials used in the construction of a building, including all permanent structures and fixtures, constitutes the *dead weight* of a building. All movable items, such as the occupants and furniture, are the *live weight*. The total weight of the live load plus that of the dead load is called the *building load*.

MAXIMUM ALLOWANCES

The maximum amount of load permissible for each kind of structure is always listed in the building code. The size of the various structural members to support the various loads is also included in the code.

When material-size regulations are compiled for the building codes, they are computed on the basis of maximum allowable loads. Engineers who are drawing up the code determine the correct size of construction members for carrying a maximum load. A safety factor is then added to the size of the materials to eliminate any possibility of building failure.

Structural sizes required by building codes not only provide for the support of all weight in a vertical direction but also allow for all possible horizontal loads, such as come from winds and earthquakes (Fig. 74–1).

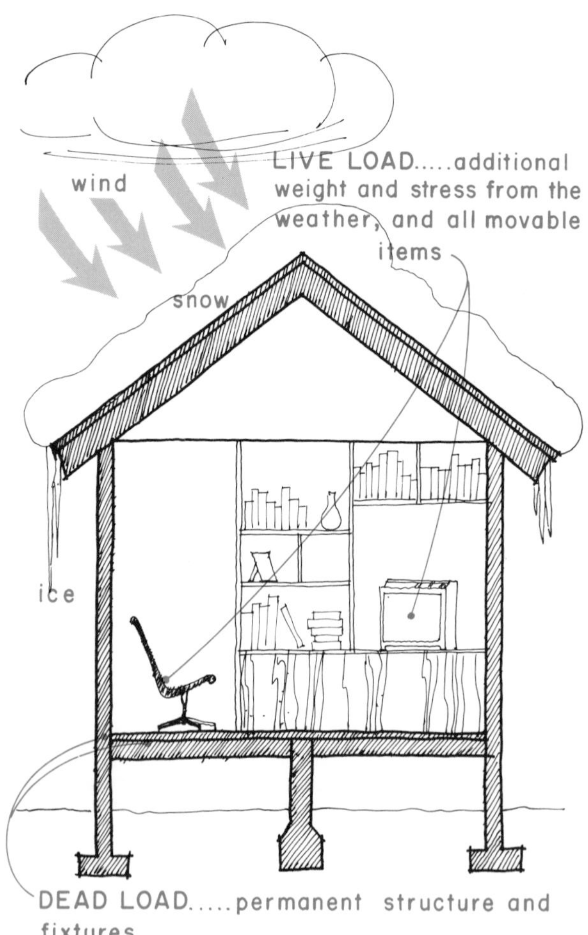

Fig. 74–1. Building codes help ensure that the structure will resist and support all loads.

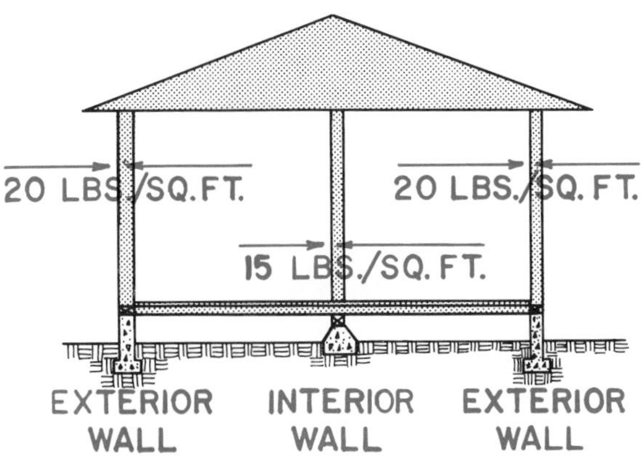

Fig. 74–2. The horizontal load acting on exterior walls is greater than the load acting on interior walls.

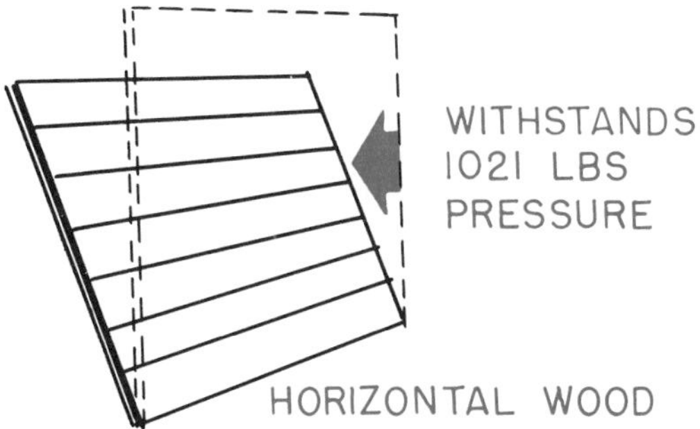

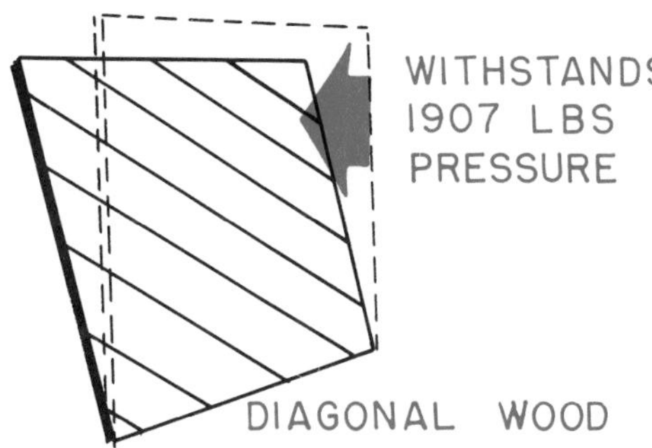

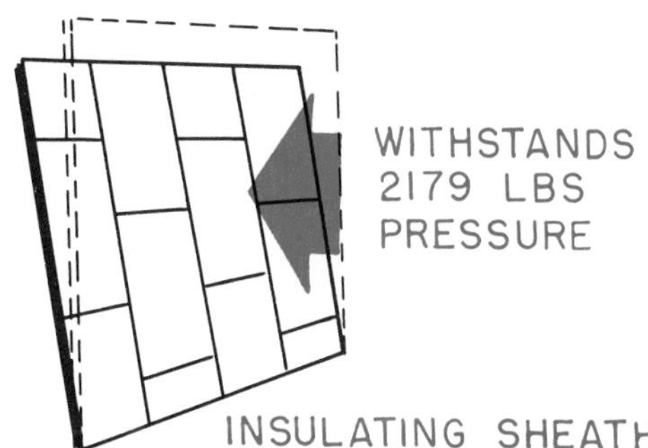

Fig. 74–3. Ability of sheathing to resist horizontal loads in pressure (pounds per square inch).

LIVE LOADS

Live loads include the weight of any movable object on the floors, roofs, or ceilings. Live loads acting on floors include persons and furniture. Live loads acting on roofs include wind and snow loads. Live loads acting on walls are wind loads. Lateral loads from earthquakes may also be considered.

Because of the additional wind load that acts on exterior walls, the horizontal load acting on exterior walls is considerably greater than the horizontal load acting on the interior walls (Fig. 74–2). Most exterior walls must be designed to withstand a load of 20 pounds per square foot (958 pascals), whereas interior walls need withstand a load of only 15 pounds per square foot (718 Pa). In the metric system force is measured in pascals (Pa). Multiply pounds per square foot by 47.88 to obtain pascals approximately. The type of exterior-wall sheathing differs greatly in its ability to withstand horizontal loads (Fig. 74–3). Figure 74–3 shows that horizontal sheathing will withstand only 1021 pounds per square foot (49 kPa). Diagonal sheathing will withstand 1907 pounds per square foot (91 kPa), and insulation-board sheathing will withstand up to 2179 pounds per square foot (104 kPa).

DEAD LOADS

A building must be designed to support its own weight (dead load). Building codes specify the size and type of materials that are used in foundations to support maximum live loads. The size and spacing and type of materials used in walls that support the roof load is also specified. Loads become greater as the distance from the footing diminishes. For example, the load on the attic shown in Fig. 74–4 is only 25 pounds per square foot (1197 Pa). The load on the first floor is 45 pounds per square foot (2155 Pa). However, the typical floor load for an average room will vary from 30 to 40 pounds per square foot (1436 to 1915 Pa).

Roof loads are comparatively light, but vary according to the pitch of the roof. Flat roofs offer more resistance to loads than do pitch roofs. Low-pitched roofs—those below 3/12 pitch—must often be designed to support

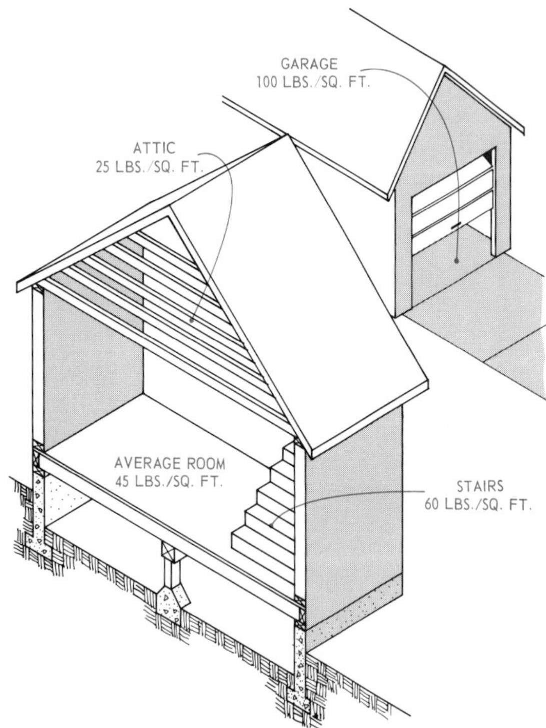

Fig. 74–4. Loads increase closer to the foundation.

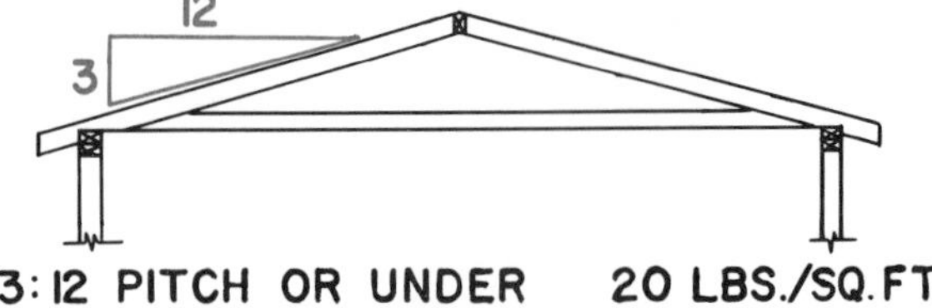

Fig. 74–5. Roofs must be designed to support load limits established by local building codes.

wind and snow loads of 20 pounds per square foot (958 Pa). High-pitched roofs—those over 3/12 pitch—need be designed to support only 15 pounds per square foot (718 Pa). Since these loads, especially snow loads, vary greatly from one part of the country to another, local building codes establish the amount of load a roof must be designed to support at any given pitch (Fig. 74–5).

PROBLEMS

1. **List 20 items used in the construction of a home that are part of the dead load.**
2. **List 20 objects that are part of the live load.**
3. **Why is load specified in pounds per square foot?**
4. **Why is a low-pitched roof constructed to support more weight per square foot than a roof of steeper pitch?**
5. **A room has 600 square feet. How much load should it be designed to support?**
6. **An exterior wall is 8′ high and 30′ long and is sheathed with diagonal sheathing. How much vertical load will the entire wall support?**
7. **Define these terms: *maximum allowance, live loads, dead loads, building load, wind load, snow load.***

SECTION 20

Methods of Checking

The appropriateness of the size and layout should be completely checked by the architect, designer, builder, and occupant before a completed architectural plan is used for actual construction purposes. The technical authenticity of the drawing should first be checked by the draftsman and/or by a checker. He or she should be certain that all dimensions and symbols are correct and that each detail drawing agrees with the basic plan

It is sometimes difficult for people without technical training to interpret engineering and architectural drawings adequately. For this reason, it is sometimes advisable to construct an architectural model which represents more closely the appearance of the finished building or groups of buildings.

Another concept that is sometimes difficult for untrained people to grasp is the relationship of the size of rooms to the furniture and equipment that will actually be placed in these rooms. Checking the adequacy of room size can be done by placing furniture, equipment, and even people in the rooms through the use of templates.

Welton Becket and Associates

UNIT 75

Architectural Models

The use of an architectural model is the only way to actually see the finished design in all three dimensions. A model is also the only representation of a building that can be viewed from any angle.

FUNCTION

Models may be used in planning cities or parts of city redevelopments, as shown in Fig. 75–1. Models are often used to check the design of

General Motors

Fig. 75–1. Models may be used for planning cities.

Haigh Jamgochian, Architect

Fig. 75–2. Models are often used to check the designs of commercial buildings.

Designaire Homes Corporation

Fig. 75–3. The use of a model to check the design of a home.

large commercial buildings, as shown in Fig. 75–2. They also may be used to check the design of a residence (Fig.75–3).

The appropriateness of size and layout can be seen better on a model than through any other device. The relationship to other objects, such as people, cars, trees, and other buildings, becomes more apparent when the structure is viewed in three-dimensional form. For these reasons, it is advisable to include within the overall model as many scale models of furniture, equipment, cars, and people as possible. Fig. 75–4 shows a model with cutaway walls, revealing the relationship among furnishings, room size, and layout. It is sometimes advisable to prepare basic outline blocks representing adjacent buildings in order to compare their rela-

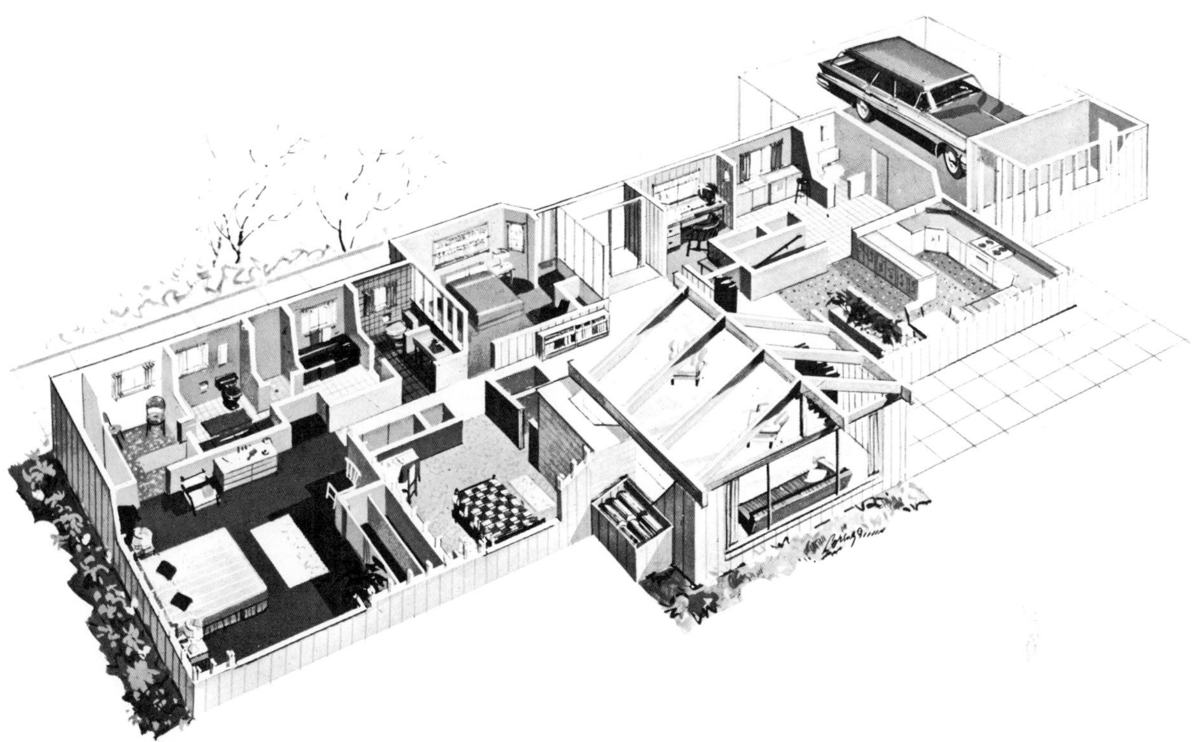

Fig. 75–4. Cutaway walls help show space relationships.

tive size and position with those of the building being designed (Fig. 75–1). The model can also be used to design effectively or to check the color scheme of the entire house or of individual rooms since the entire house can be seen at a glance.

Some models are prepared to check only the structural qualities of the building. An example is the structural model of a convention center exhibit hall shown in Fig. 75–5. When a structural model of this type is prepared, balsa wood strips are used to represent sills, studs, rafters, and beams. These structural members are prepared to the exact scale of the model, and the balsa wood members are attached together with modelmakers' glue or with small pins, to approximate the methods used in nailing the full-sized house. Pre-cut model lumber is often used.

MODEL CONSTRUCTION

Since the materials used in full-size buildings are too large for model construction, they must be simulated by other materials and other products. For example, coarse sandpaper may be used to simulate a built-up gravel roof.

United States Steel Corporation

Fig. 75–5. The use of a model to check structural qualities.

Table 75-1. MATERIALS USED ON ARCHITECTURAL MODELS

PART	MODEL MATERIALS	METHODS OF CONSTRUCTION
WALLS	Soft wood; cardboard	Cut wall to exact dimensions of elevations. Allow for overlapping of joints at corners. Have wall thicknesses to scale.
ROOFS	Thin, stiff cardboard; paint-colored sand; sandpaper; wood pieces	Cut out roof patterns and assembly. For sand or gravel roof, paint with slow-drying enamel the color of roof. Sprinkle on sand. For shingle roof, cut sandpaper or thin wood pieces, and glue on as if laying shingle roof.
BRICK & STONE	Commercially printed paper	Glue paper in place; cut grooves in wood, and paint color of bricks or stones.
WOOD PANELING	Commercially printed paper; 1/32″ veneer wood	Glue paper in place; with veneer wood, rule on black lines for strip effect, and glue in place. Mahogany veneer equals redwood.
STUCCO	Plaster of Paris	Mix and dab on with brush.
WINDOWS & DOORS	Preformed plastic; wood strips and clear plastic	Purchase ready-made windows to scale in model store; or frame openings with wood strips and glue in clear plastic for windows or wood panel for door.
FLOORS	Flocked carpet; commercially printed paper; 1/32″ veneer wood	Paint area with slow-drying colored enamel, and apply flock, removing excess when dry. With paper, glue in place. With veneer, rule on black lines for strip effect, and glue in place.
FURNITURE	Cardboard, nails, flock, wood, clay	Fashion furniture to scale. Paint and flock to give effect of material.
SITE AREAS	Wood slab, wire screen, paper mâché	Build up hilly areas with sticks and wire. Place paper mâché over wire.
GRASS	Green enamel paint and flock	Paint grass area. Apply flock, removing excess when dry.
TREES & BUSHES	Sponge; lichen	Grind up sponges and paint different shades of green. Use small pieces for bushes. Glue small pieces to tree twigs for trees. Lichen may be purchased in model stores and used in the same manner as sponges.
AUTOS & PEOPLE	Toys and miniatures	If time permits, carve from soft wood.

Sponges may be used to simulate trees, and green flocking may be used for grass. In addition to such substitute materials, a great variety of commercially prepared model materials is now available. Table 75–1 shows some of the special materials used to make various parts of architectural models.

Methods of constructing models vary greatly, just as methods of constructing full-sized structures vary, according to the building materials used. Nevertheless, the following procedures represent the normal sequence of constructing models, even though some of the techniques may vary with the use of different materials.

1. A floor plan and elevation outline should be prepared to the size to which the model will be built (Fig. 75–6). Small structures such as houses can be built conveniently at the scale ½″ = 1′—0″. Larger structures such as commercial office buildings should be built to the scale ¼″ = 1′—0″ or even smaller.

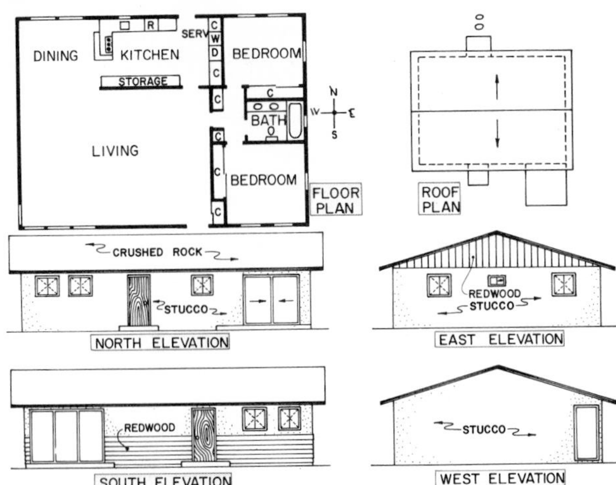

Fig. 75-6. Models should be built from floor plans and elevations.

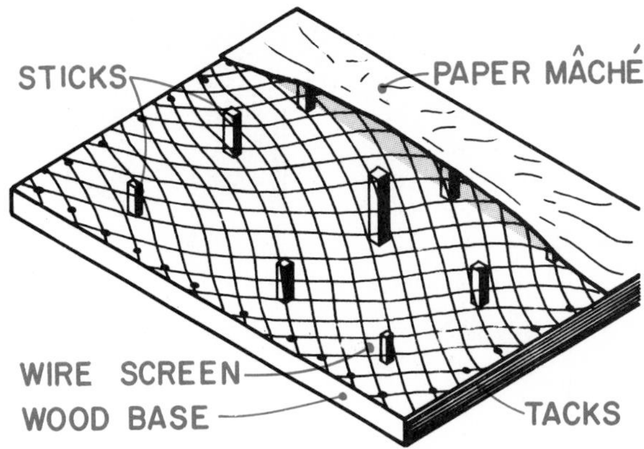

Fig. 75-7. Developing the contour of a lot.

2. The contour of the lot should be developed, as shown in Fig. 75–7.
3. Glue or trace the floor-plan outline on a ¼″-(6-mm) thick pad, and tack or glue this pad to a base, as shown in Fig 75–8.
4. Cut exterior walls from balsa wood or heavy cardboard. Carefully cut out the openings for windows and doors with a razor blade, as shown in Fig. 75–9. When cutting side walls, cut them long to allow overlapping of the front and back walls.
5. Glue small strips of wood or paper around the windows to represent framing and trim, as shown in Fig. 75–10. Glue clear plastic inside the window openings to represent window glass and cover the joint with trim. Cut out doors and hang them on the door openings, using transparent tape, as shown in Fig. 75–11. Add siding materials to the exterior of the wall panels to simulate the materials that will be used on the house, as shown in Fig. 75–12.

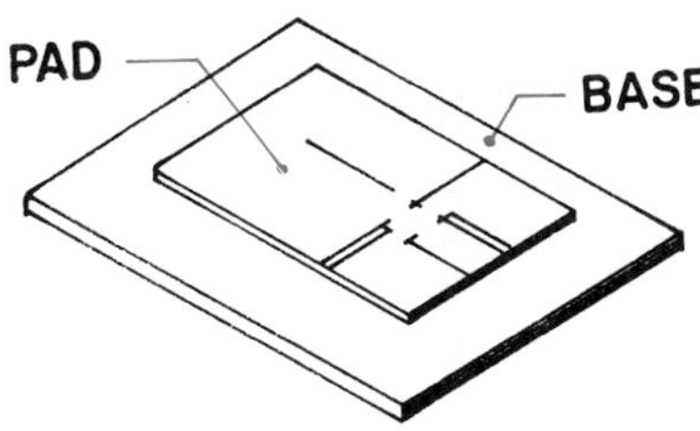

Fig. 75-8. A pad attached to a base.

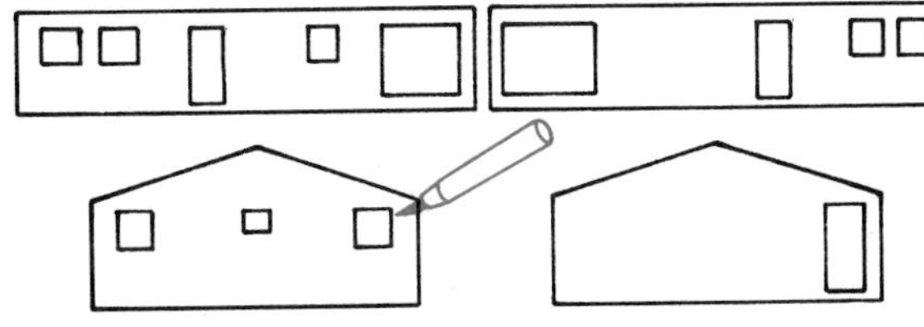

Fig. 75-9. Cutouts of exterior walls.

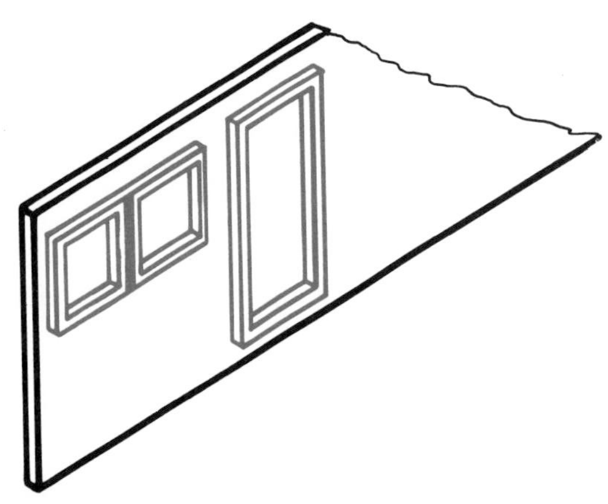

Fig. 75-10. Small strips of wood or paper can represent framing and trim around windows and doors.

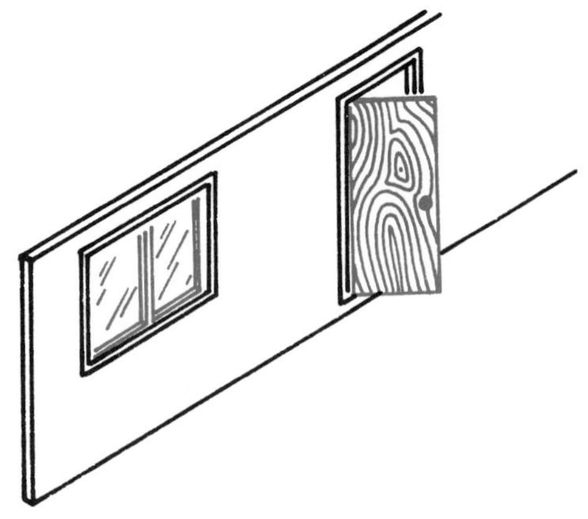

Fig. 75–11. **Doors can be hung with transparent tape.**

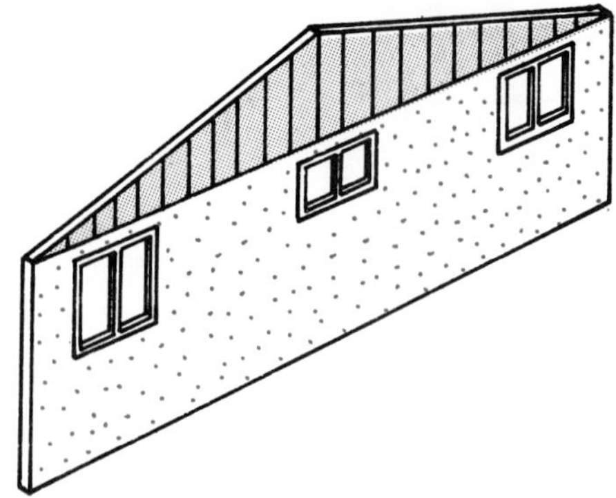

Fig. 75–12. **Siding materials are added to the exterior panels.**

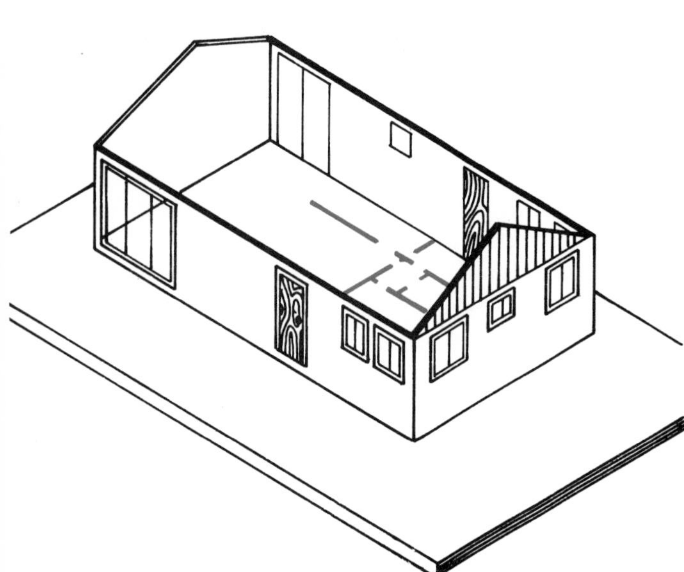

Fig. 75–13. **Exterior walls are glued to the pad.**

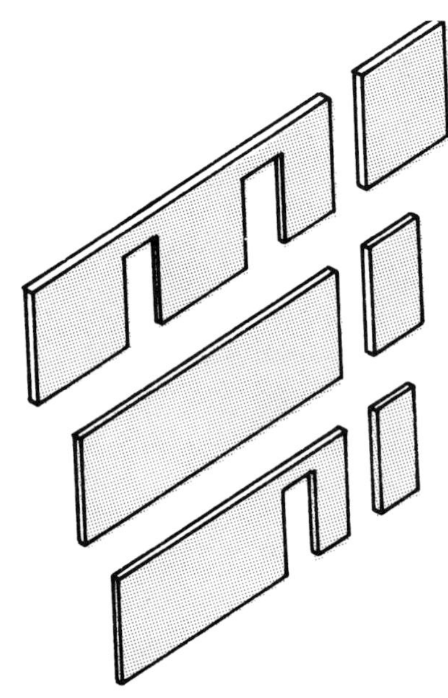

Fig. 75–14. **Openings in interior walls are cut out.**

6. Glue the exterior walls to the pad and to each other at the corners (Fig. 75–13).
7. Cut out openings in interior walls for doors, arches, and fireplaces, as shown in Fig. 75–14.
8. Glue interior walls to the partition lines of the floor plan (Fig. 75–15).
9. Add interior fixtures such as built-in cabinets, kitchen equipment, bathroom fixtures. Paint the interior surfaces to determine the color scheme and add furniture if desired (Fig. 75–16).
10. Cut out roof parts, join roof parts together, and brace them so that the roof will lift off. Add material to simulate the roof treatment on the exterior of the roof (Fig. 75–17).
11. Add landscaping features such as trees, shrubs, grass, patios, walkways, and outdoor furniture to add to the authentic appearance of the model (Fig. 75–18).

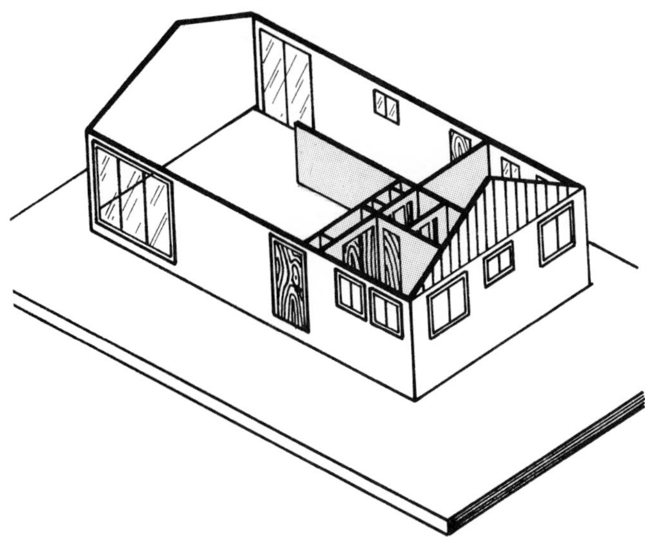

Fig. 75–15. Interior walls are glued to exterior walls and to the pad.

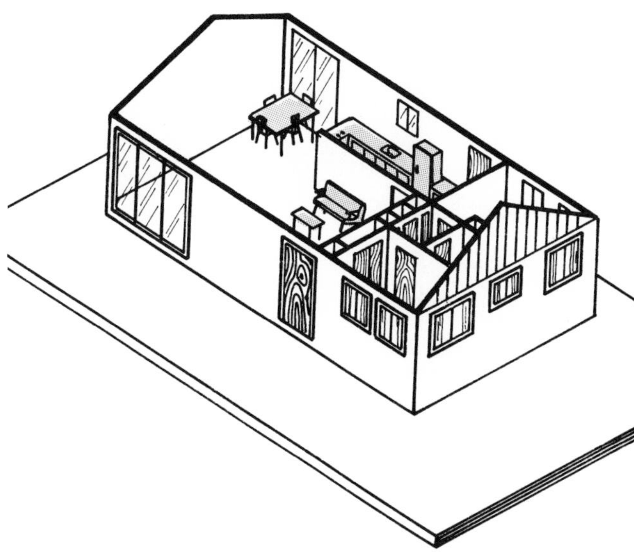

Fig. 75–16. Furniture, fixtures, and color schemes are added.

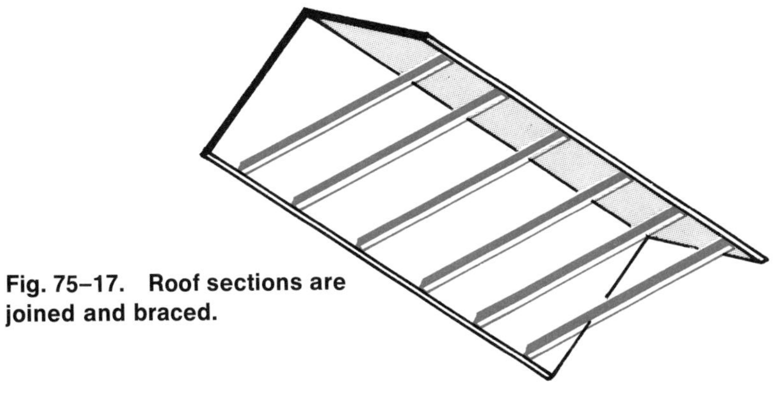

Fig. 75–17. Roof sections are joined and braced.

Fig. 75–18. Landscaping features are added.

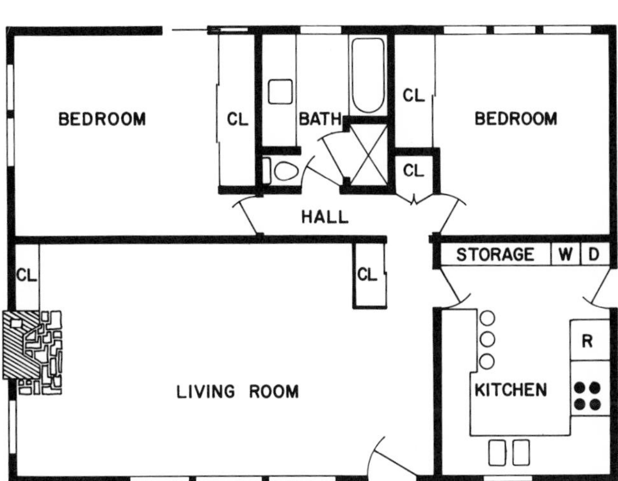

Fig. 75–19. Make a model of this plan.

Designaire Homes Corporation

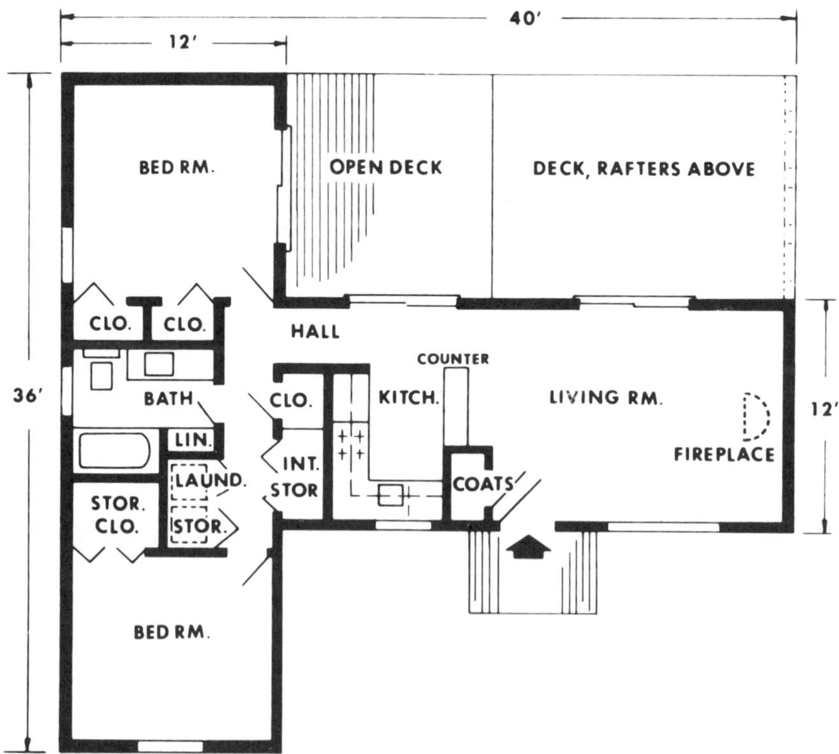

Fig. 75–20. Make a model of this plan.

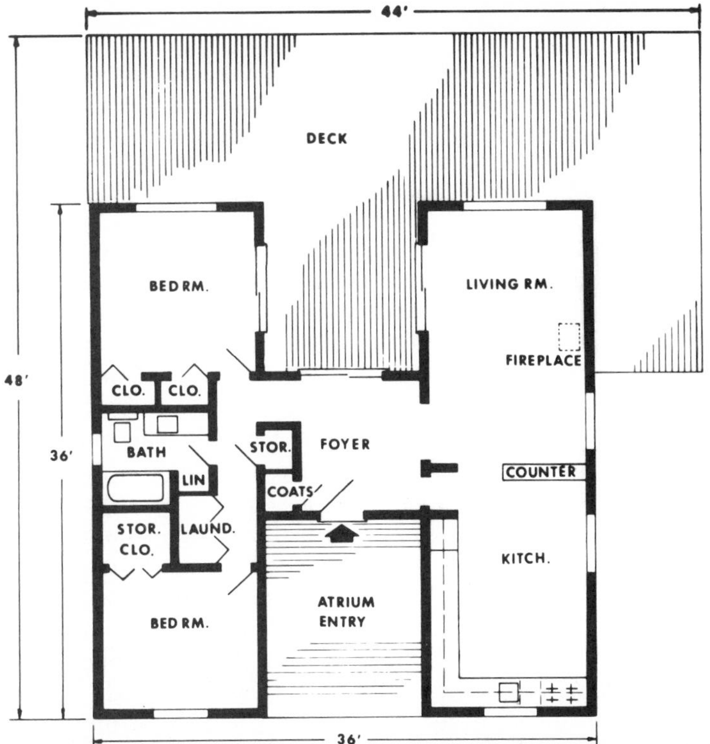

Designaire Homes Corporation

Fig. 75–21. Make a model of this plan.

PROBLEMS

1. **Construct a model similar to the one shown in Fig. 75–16.**
2. **Construct a model of your own home. Make any design adjustments you would recommend in the basic plan.**
3. **Construct a model of a home you have designed.**
4. **Construct models of the houses shown in Figs. 75–19, 75–20, 75–21.**
5. **Define these terms: *scale model, structural model, balsa wood, flocking.***

UNIT 76

Template Checking

Room sizes often appear adequate on the floor plan, but when furniture is placed in the rooms, the occupants may find them too small or proportioned incorrectly. After the house is built, it is too late to change the sizes of most rooms. Therefore, extreme care should be taken in the planning stage to ensure that the plan as designed will accommodate the furniture, fixtures, and traffic anticipated for each area.

TEMPLATE PREPARATION

One method of determining the adequacy of room sizes and proportions is to prepare templates of each piece of furniture and equipment that will be placed in the room. These templates should be on the same scale as the floor plan. Placing the templates on the floor plan (Fig. 76–1) will show graphically how much floor space is occupied by each piece of furniture. The home planner can determine whether there is sufficient traffic space around the furniture, whether the room must be enlarged, whether the proportions should be changed or whether, as a last resort, smaller items of furniture should be obtained.

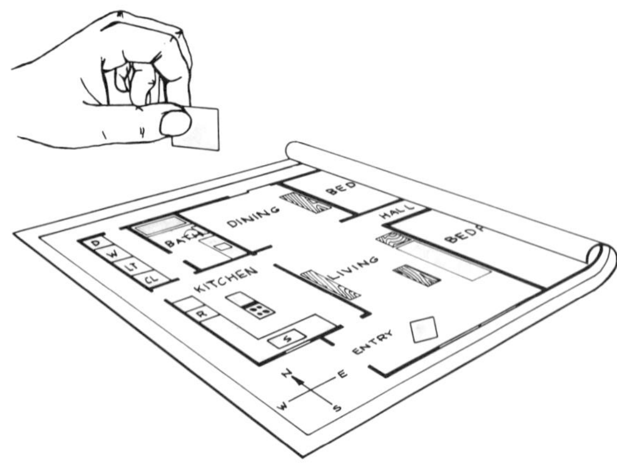

Fig. 76–1. Placing templates on a floor plan.

The placement of the templates on the plan in Fig. 76–2 indicates that some rearrangement or adjustment should be made in the furniture placement in bedroom No. 3, and that the dining room might be inadequate if the table is expanded.

Checking by templates can be significant only if the templates are carefully prepared to the same scale as the floor plan and if the actual furniture dimensions are used in the preparation of the templates. Figure 76–3 shows some typical furniture sizes that may be used in the preparation of templates for checking purposes. The floor-plan design can be checked much more quickly by the template method than it can by a model. Furthermore, if templates are used while the plan is still in the sketching stage, adjustments can be made easily and rooms rearranged to produce a more desirable plan.

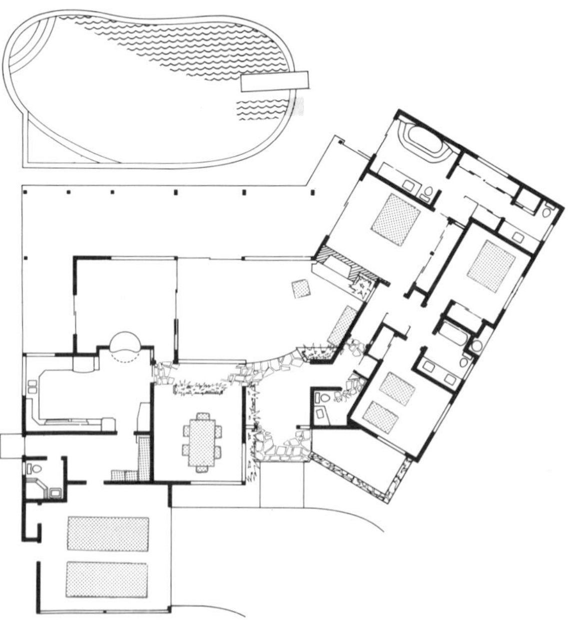

Southern California Gas Company

Fig. 76–2. Space requirements can be determined by placing furniture templates on the floor plans.

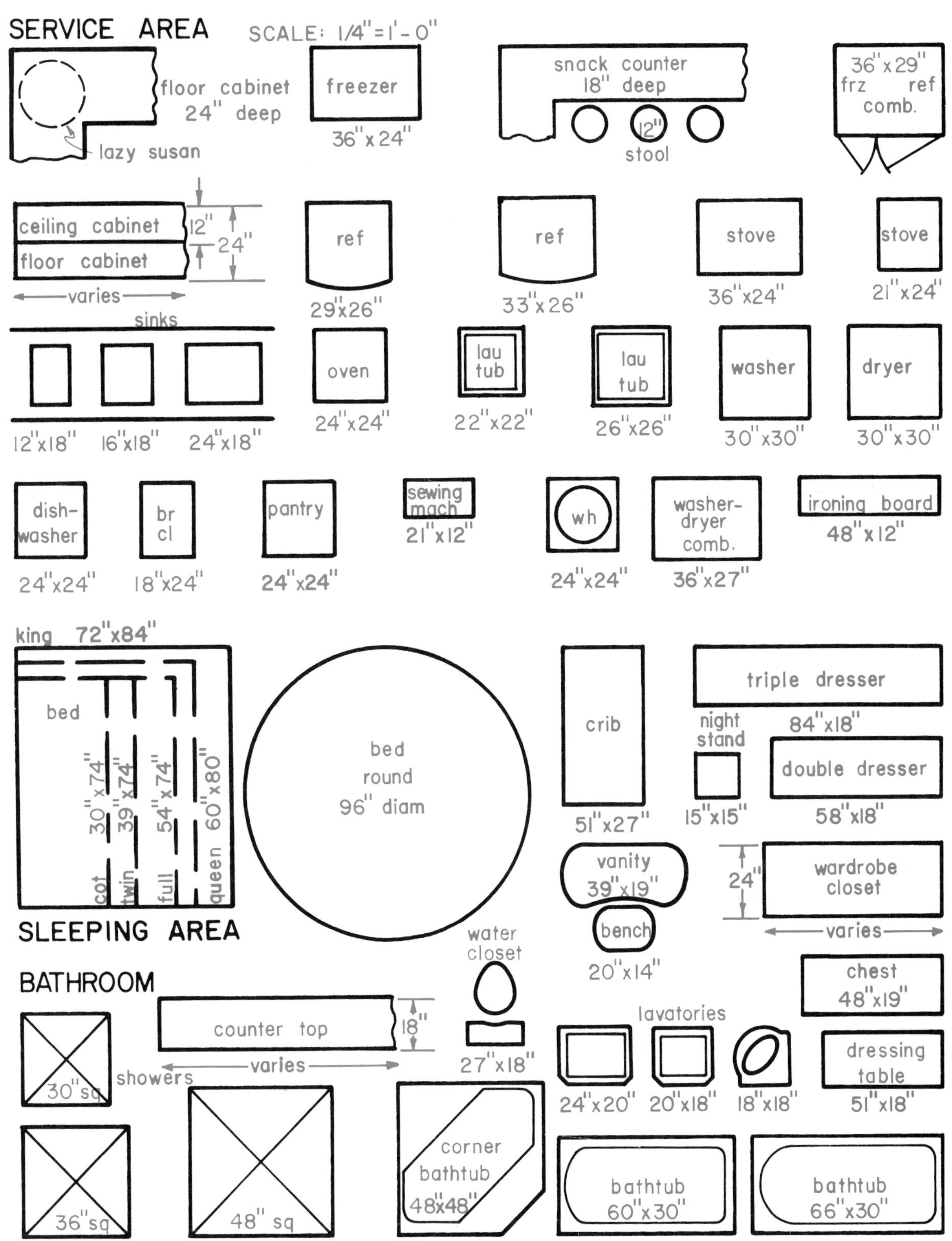

Fig. 76–3. Typical furniture sizes used for templates.

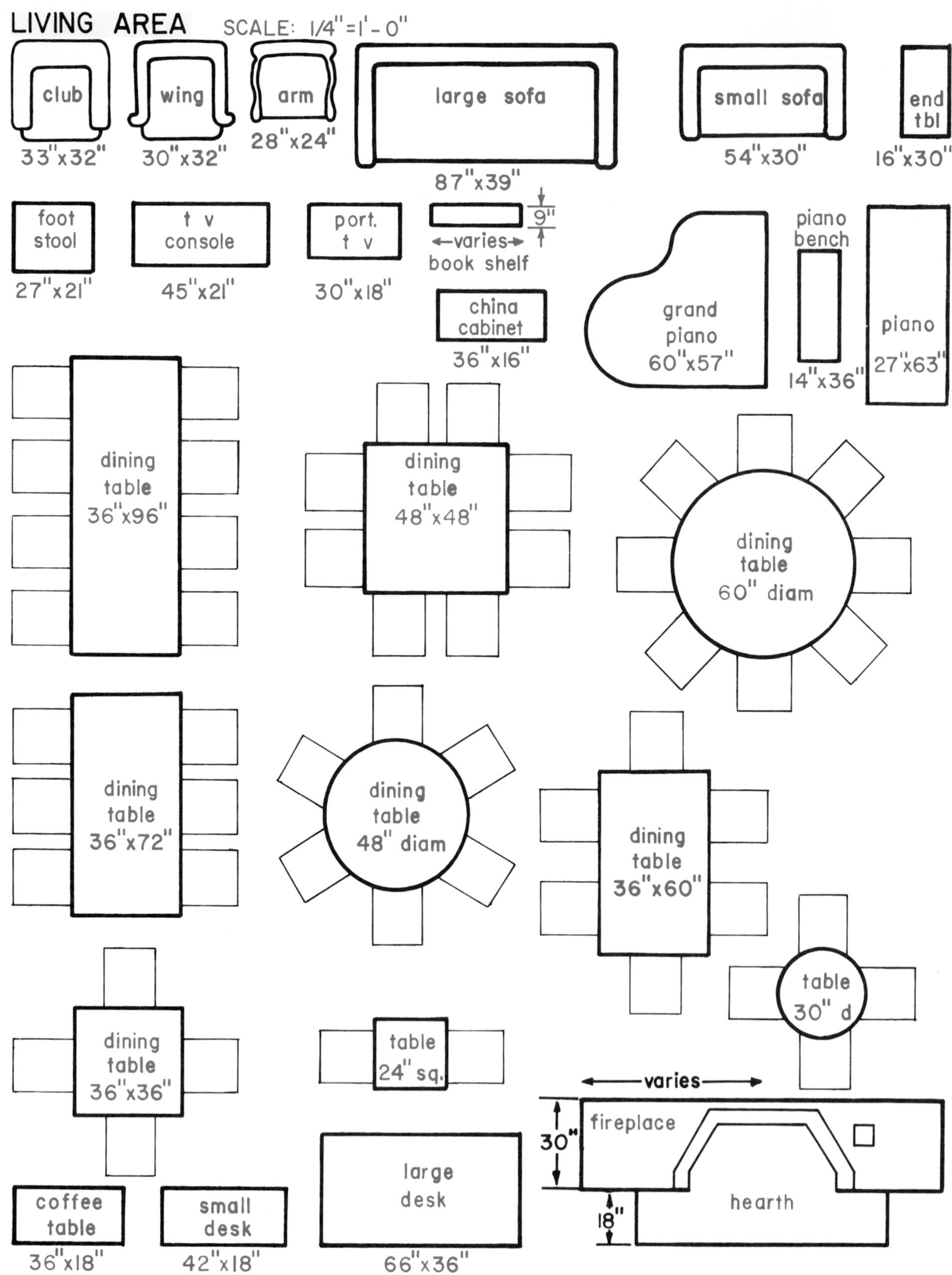

LIVING AREA SCALE: 1/4"=1'-0"
club
33"x32"
wing
30"x32"
arm
28"x24"
large sofa
87"x39"
small sofa
54"x30"
end tbl
16"x30"
foot stool
27"x21"
t v console
45"x21"
port. t v
30"x18"
9"
varies
book shelf
china cabinet
36"x16"
grand piano
60"x57"
piano bench
14"x36"
piano
27"x63"
dining table
36"x96"
dining table
48"x48"
dining table
60" diam
dining table
36"x72"
dining table
48" diam
dining table
36"x60"
table
30" d
dining table
36"x36"
table
24" sq.
varies
fireplace
30"
hearth
18"
coffee table
36"x18"
small desk
42"x18"
large desk
66"x36"

Fig. 76–3. Continued.

THREE-DIMENSIONAL TEMPLATES

The template method of checking room sizes does not reveal the three-dimensional aspect of space planning as a model does. One compromise between the model method and the template method of checking drawings is the preparation of three-dimensional templates. Three-dimensional templates not only have width and length but also height, as shown in Fig. 76–4. This method of checking is essentially the same as placing furniture on a model, except that the walls do not exist and adjustments can be made much more easily. Figure 76–5 shows the height of typical pieces of furniture for use in preparing three-dimensional templates. These dimensions are typical and may vary slightly with different manufacturers.

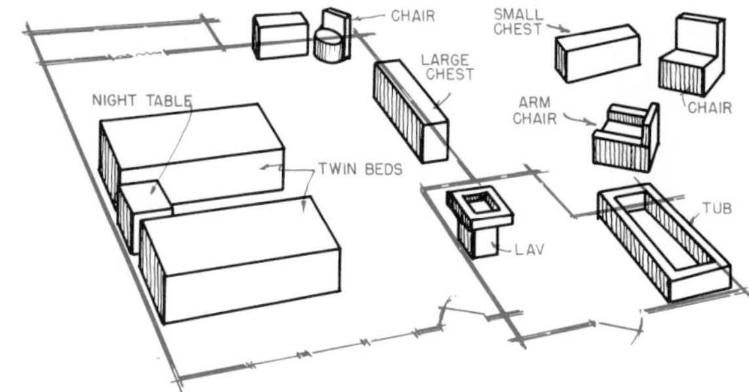

Fig. 76–4. Three-dimensional templates.

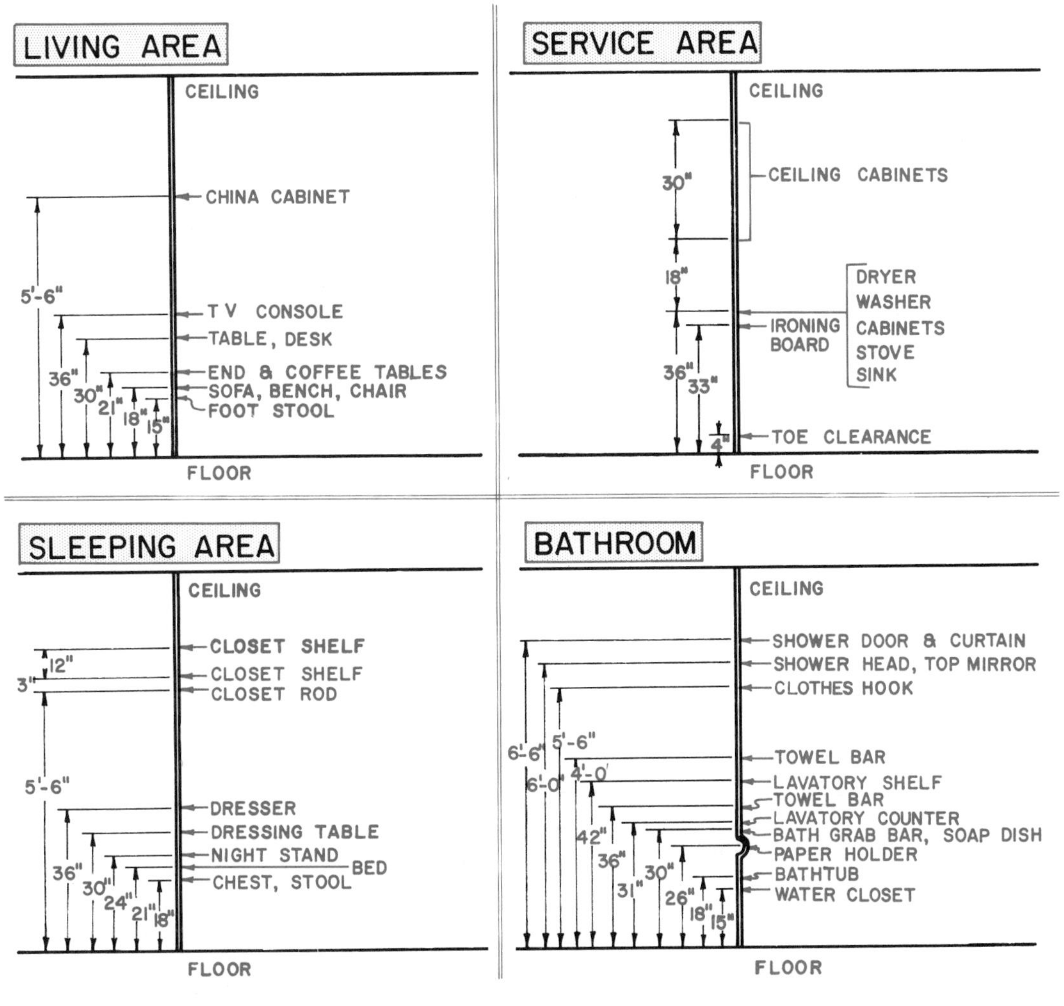

Fig. 76–5. Typical heights of cabinets, furniture, and fixtures.

TRAFFIC PATTERNS

A well-designed structure must provide for efficient and smooth circulation of traffic. Traffic patterns must be controlled, and yet sufficient space must be allowed for adequate passage and flexibility in the traffic pattern. Rooms should not be used as hallways or access areas to other rooms. Any room should be accessible from the front entrance or the service entrance without the necessity of passing through other rooms. The length of halls should be minimized because halls provide only traffic access and do not contribute livable space.

One method of checking the traffic pattern is to use a scale drawing and trace, with a pencil, the movements of your daily routine, as shown in Fig. 76–6. If you prepare a template of a person (an overhead view of yourself with arms outstretched), you will be able to determine the effectiveness of the traffic pattern as it relates to the size of each room and the layout of the entire plan. Table 76–1 is a checklist of traffic-pattern adequacies.

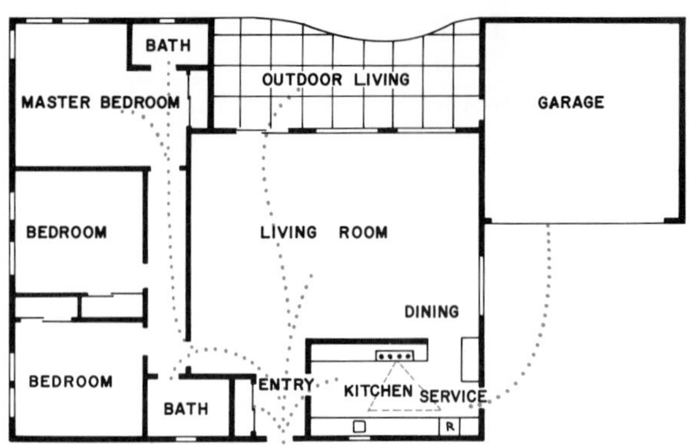

Fig. 76–6. Checking traffic patterns.

Table 76–1. A CHECKLIST FOR TRAFFIC PATTERNS

SERVICE CIRCULATION	EXCELLENT	FAIR	POOR	DISTANCE
Service door to kitchen	X			5′
Service door to living area	X			12′
Service door to bathroom			X	30′
Service door to bedrooms			X	36′
Kitchen to bathrooms		X		14′
Paths around work triangle			X	24′
GUEST'S CIRCULATION				
Front door to closet	X			3′
Front door to living room	X			10′
Front door to bathroom	X			16′
Front door to outdoor living		X		33′
Living room to bathroom	X			8′
OCCUPANTS' CIRCULATION				
Front door to kitchen	X			6′
Kitchen to bedrooms		X		15′ to 35′
Kitchen to children's play area		X		15′
Kitchen to children's sleeping area		X		17′
Bedrooms to bathrooms	X			4′ to 10′
Outdoor living area to bathroom			X	25′
Living room to outdoor living area	X			3′

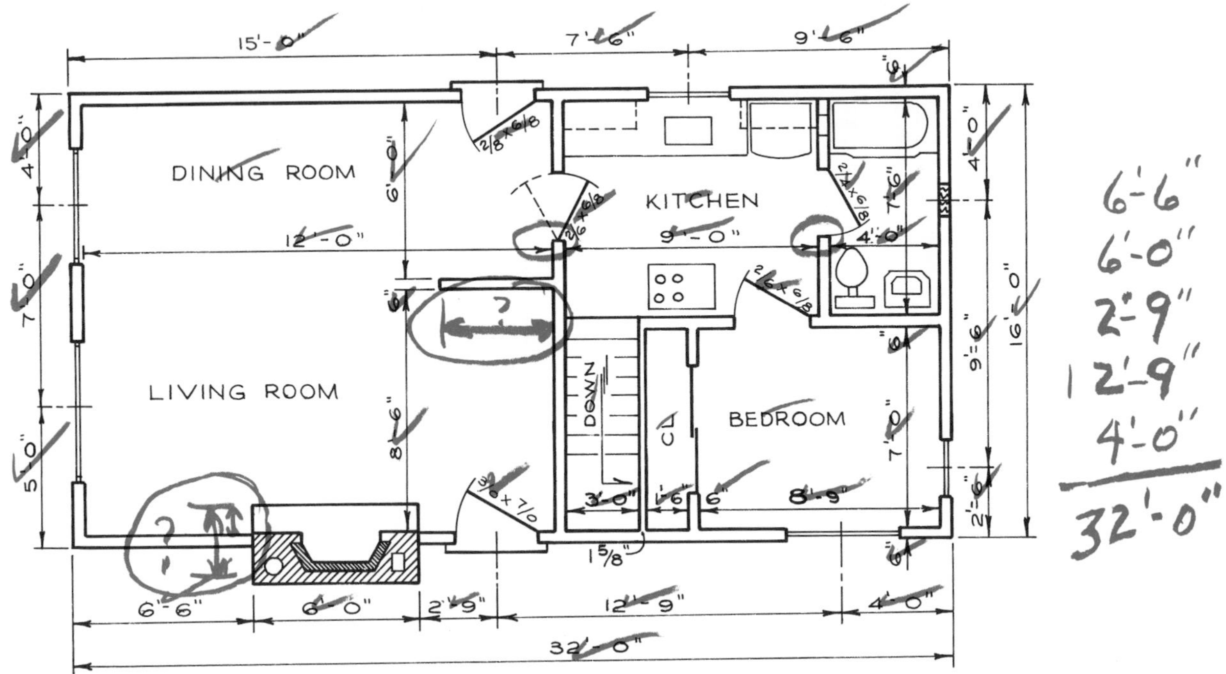

Fig. 76–7. Checking architectural drawings by using a colored pencil.

TECHNICAL CHECKING

The draftsman should always check dimensions, labels, and symbols before the drawing is removed from the board. A more formal check of these factors should be made on a print prepared for checking purposes (check print). After the draftsman has made this check, another draftsman, architect, or checker should also scrutinize the drawing for dimensional accuracy, proper labeling, and correctness of symbols.

One of the most effective methods of checking architectural drawings is the use of a colored pencil, as shown in Fig. 76–7. A checker draws a line through each dimension, label, and symbol as it is checked. Otherwise the result is rechecking the same dimensions and missing many others. Many architectural offices use a color-coding system to indicate the checker's reaction to the drawing. In one system a yellow pencil is used for checking items that are correct, a red pencil for checking errors, and a blue pencil for marking recommended changes.

Regardless of the checking method used, one of the most important items to check on architectural drawings is the correctness of dimensions. Dimensioning errors cause more difficulty on the construction job than any other single factor relating to architectural drawings. Dimensions must be added to ensure that they total the overall dimension. Interior dimensions must be added to ensure that they agree with the exterior dimensions.

PLAN AGREEMENT

An important relationship that must be very carefully checked on architectural drawings is the agreement of plans with each other. The design and dimensions of the floor plan must be compared with the design and dimensions of the elevation. The floor plan must also be compared with the foundation to ensure complete alignment on the perimeter, over the beams, and through the chimney. The foundation plan must also be compared with the elevation. Sectional drawings and all details must be compared with the floor-plan and elevation drawing to which they relate. It is therefore mandatory that a complete system of checking be established and carefully followed in the preparation of all architectural plans.

Fig. 76–8. Rearrange this plan to improve the traffic pattern.

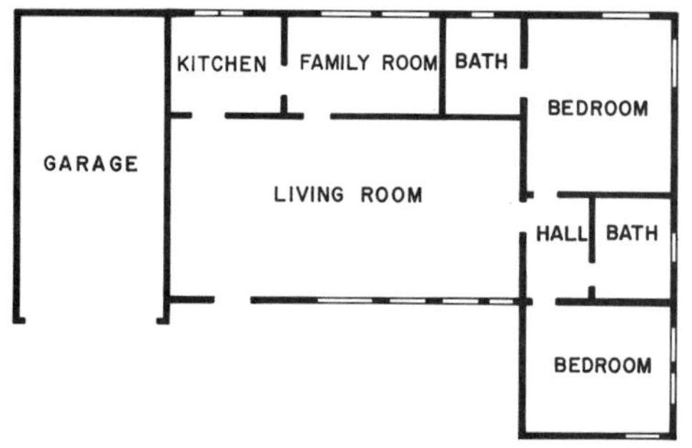

Fig. 76–10. Redesign this plan to produce a better traffic pattern.

Fig. 76–9. Check the adequacy of these rooms by using templates.

PROBLEMS

1. Prepare a set of templates, using Fig. 76–3 as a guide. Sketch the floor plan of your own home and check its adequacy with these templates.
2. Use the templates you have prepared to check a floor plan of your own design.
3. Check the traffic pattern of the plan shown in Fig. 76–8. What recommendations would you make to improve the traffic pattern?
4. Sketch the plan shown in Fig. 76–9 and determine the adequacy of room sizes by the use of templates.
5. Redesign the plan shown in Fig. 76–10 to produce a better traffic pattern.
6. Define these architectural terms: *template, two-dimensional template, three-dimensional template, traffic pattern, checker, check print.*

UNIT 77

Architectural Checklists

The number and type of architectural drawings prepared for any structure depend on the amount of control the designer demands. The more control the designer wants, the more drawings must be prepared. For example, if a designer prepares only a floor plan, the contractor is allowed to specify and build the exterior of the structure. Thus the amount and type of drawings determine the degree of control the designer achieves. For maximum control, a complete set of architectural plans should include the following drawings and schedules:

- Preliminary sketches
- Presentation drawing
- Specifications
- Plot plan
- Landscape plan
- Floor plan
- Foundation and basement plan
- Exterior elevations
- Interior elevations
- Electrical plan
- Plumbing plan
- Floor-framing plan
- Roof-framing plan
- Heating and air-conditioning plan
- Wall details
- Stair details
- Cabinet details
- Window schedule
- Door schedule

Architectural drawings are prepared for a variety of purposes. They show dimensions of a lot, types of siding material, sizes and shapes of the floor plan, types and styles of exteriors, and so forth. Because each drawing must agree with all other drawings in a set, the designer must be sure that each drawing includes all the information for which it was intended. The following checklist should be used to ensure the completeness of each drawing:

PRELIMINARY SKETCHES

Floor plan—freehand scale drawings
Plot plan—freehand scale drawings
Elevations—freehand scale drawings

PRESENTATION DRAWINGS

Title block:
  Names of drawings
  Scale
  Architect's name
  Draftsman's name
  Owner's name
  Owner's address
Floor plan
Overall dimensions
Pictorial renderings

SPECIFICATIONS

Written list of information not on drawings

PLOT PLAN

Property lines
Building lines—setback
House
All structures
Overall dimensions
Setback dimensions
Roof overhang
Patios
Walks
Driveway
Fences
Pools
Public utilities—gas, water, sewer, electricity, telephone
Curb line
Street center
Street name
Street elevation
House elevation
Elevations of walks and driveway
Tree elevations
Contour lines
Property-line compass orientation
North arrow
Land cuts
Landscape
Drainage
Retaining walls
Datum reference
Radius of curves
Outdoor living area

Outdoor service area
Title block:
- Title of drawings
- Scale
- Owner's name
- Firm's name and address
- Architect's name
- Draftsman's name
- House number and street
- Lot number
- Block number
- Subdivision's name
- City, county, and state
- Sheet number

LANDSCAPE PLAN

Title block (see plot plan)
Property lines
House and all structures
Overall dimensions
Setback dimensions
Patios
Walks
Driveway
Fences
Pools
Curb line
Street
Compass direction
Land contours
Land cuts
Drainage
Trees and elevations
Plants
Gardens
Ground cover
Common and scientific names for plantings
Tree trunk diameters

FLOOR PLAN

Rooms and sizes
Overall dimensions
Location dimensions of all structural members
Closets
Storage
Partition thicknesses
Windows
Doors
Ceiling joists—size, spacing, direction
Lintels
Beams
Fireplace and hearth
Patios
Walks
Landings
Garage
Garage drainage
Stairs—number, size, and direction
Major appliances
Major fixtures
Heating and air-conditioning unit
Hose bib
Window and door callout symbols
Arches and openings
Balconies
Decks
Attic
Additional floors
Medicine cabinets
Built-ins
Compass orientation
Square footage
Clipped ceilings
Scuttle
Title block:
- Title of drawings
- Scale
- Owner's name
- Firm's name and address
- Architect's name
- Draftsman's name
- House number and street
- Sheet number

FOUNDATION AND BASEMENT

Title block (see floor plan)
Footings
Foundation outline
Overall dimensions
Location dimensions for all structural members
Size, spacing, spans for all structural members
Pilasters
Posts
Piers
Columns
Girders
Sills
Anchor bolts
Plates
Solid blocking
Bridging
Double floor joists
Floor joists
Headers
Slabs
Drainage
Waterproofing
Fireplace footing
Access area
Crawl space
Garage slab and details
Excavated areas
Fills
Steel dowels
Wire mesh
Concrete patios and walks
Concrete stairs
Foundation sections:
- Footings
- Slabs
- Piers
- Areaways
- Floor systems
- Fireplace

Vents
Basement:
- Partitions
- Doors
- Window wells
- Stairs

EXTERIOR ELEVATIONS

Title block (see floor plan)
Elevation for each side of house
Foundation outline
Overall dimensions
Dimension floor line to ceiling

Dimension floor line to top of windows and doors
Dimension finish grade to floor line
Dimension eave to ridge
Dimension ridge to chimney top
Window-opening symbols
Grade line
Vents
Access areas
Finish materials for roof
Finish materials for walls
Stairs
Porches
Balconies
Decks
Drawing callouts
Exterior trim
Exterior lights
Gutters
Downspouts
Fascia
Flashing
Roof pitch
Hose bibs
Chimney

INTERIOR ELEVATIONS

Title block (see floor plan)
Elevations of selected rooms
Overall dimensions
Location dimensions
Elevation callouts
Windows
Doors
Cabinets
Shelves
Drawers
Stairs
Cabinet sections
Furred-out ceilings
Closets—rods and shelves
Built-ins
Mirrors
Major appliances
Range hood
Fireplace
Finish materials
Lights
Switches
Convenience outlets
Registers
Trim
Floor line
Ceiling line
Walls
Exposed beams
Counter tops
Splashes
Soap dishes
Hand guards
Medicine cabinets
Planters

ELECTRICAL PLAN

Title block (see floor plan)
Lighting outlets
Outdoor lighting
Convenience outlets
TV and radio antennas
Bells, buzzers, and chimes
Push buttons
Special outlets
Outdoor outlets
Switches
Panel board
Meter
Telephone
Telephone jacks
Intercom system
Electric heating system
Alarm system

PLUMBING PLAN

Title block (see floor plan)
Plumbing fixtures
Plumbing lines and sizes
Plumbing fittings and sizes
Soil pipes
Vent pipes
Waste lines
Cleanouts
Water pipes
Gas meter
Gas lines
Gas outlets
Water meter
Water lines
Private water supply
Sprinkler system
Fire control system
Hot-water heater
Valves

FLOOR-FRAMING PLAN

Title block (see floor plan)
Foundation outline
Overall dimensions
Location dimensions for structural members
Structural members' sizes and spacing
Floor joists
Headers
Bridging
Blocking
Piers
Posts
Girders
Subfloor
Double headers
Double floor joists
Concrete areas
Stairwell openings
Fireplace openings

ROOF-FRAMING PLAN

Title block (see floor plan)
Roof outline
Overall dimensions
Locations for structural members
Structural members' sizes and spacing
Rafters
Ceiling joists
Ridge board
Overhang
Sheathing
Roof cover
Chimney opening
Skylight openings
Double headers

HEATING AND AIR-CONDITIONING PLAN

Title block (see floor plan)
Floor plan
Location of heating plant
Location of cooling plant
Rating and sizes of plants
Ducts and sizes
Registers and sizes
Blowers
Fans
Vents
Radiators
Convectors
Controls
Radiant systems
Thermostats
Humidifying system
Insulation

WALL DETAILS

Title block (see floor plan)
Section callout
Overall dimensions
Location dimensions of structural members
Structural members—sizes and spacing
Plates
Sills
Headers
Lintels
Studs
Thresholds
Subfloor
Finish floor
Ceiling line
Windows
Doors
Finish materials
Sheathing
Termite protection
Insulation
Waterproofing
Furred ceilings

STAIR DETAILS

Title block (see floor plan)
Section callouts
Overall dimensions
Location dimensions of structural members
Plan
Elevation
Sections
Pitch
Rails
Structural members—sizes and spacing
Risers
Treads
Strings
Nosing
Trim
Head clearance

CABINET DETAILS

Title block (see floor plan)
Section callouts
Overall dimensions
Location dimensions of structural members
Plan
Elevations
Sections
Doors
Drawers
Shelves
Hardware
Toe clearance

WINDOW SCHEDULE

Title block (see floor plan)
Location callouts
Width
Height
Material
Kind
Screen
Quantity
Manufacturer
Catalog number
Special installation instructions
Glass type
Shutters

DOOR SCHEDULE

Title block (see floor plan)
Location callouts
Width
Height
Thickness
Material
Kind
Screen
Quantity
Threshold
Manufacturer
Catalog number
Special installation instructions
Finish
Trim
Hardware

SECTION 21

Cost Analysis

Architects would welcome the opportunity to design a structure free from financial limitations. Such a condition, however, rarely exists. Budgets are the necessary framework within which architects must design most buildings, ranging from the smallest residence to the largest office building. There is of course more flexibility in some budgets than in others, but in every design problem the designer must strive to create a design that will provide optimum facilities and keep within the budget.

UNIT 78

Building Costs

Approximately 40 percent of the cost of the average home is for materials. Labor costs account for another 40 percent. The remaining 20 percent is taken up by the price of the lot. As labor and material costs rise, the cost of homes increases proportionately.

TOTAL COST

Many factors influence the total cost of the house. The location of the site is extremely important. An identical house built on an identical lot can vary several thousand dollars in cost, depending on whether it is located in a city, in a suburb, or in the country. Labor costs also vary greatly from one part of the country to another and from urban to rural areas (Table 78–1). Normally labor costs are lower in rural areas. The third important variable contributing to the difference in housing costs is the cost of materials. Material costs vary greatly, depending upon whether materials native to the region are used for the structure. In some areas, brick is a relatively inexpensive building material. In other parts of the country, a brick home may be one of the most expensive. Climate also has some effect on the cost of building. In moderate climates many costs can be eliminated by excluding heating plants and frost-deep foundations. In other climates air conditioning is mandatory.

ESTIMATING COSTS

There are two basic methods of determining the cost of a house. One is adding the total cost of all the materials to the hourly rate for labor multiplied by the anticipated number of hours it will take to build the home. The cost of the lot, landscaping, and various architects' and surveyors' fees must also be added to this figure. This process involves much computation and adequate techniques for estimating construction costs.

Table 78–1. APPROXIMATE COST BREAKDOWN FOR A $40 000 HOME

LOT $8000 (20%)	
LABOR $16 000 (40%)	**MATERIALS $16 000 (40%)**
plans and specs	building permits
utilities installation	insurance
survey	drain tiling
excavating, grading	concrete materials
foundation work	paving materials
paving	rough lumber
sodding	millwork and trim
rough carpentry	sash and doors
finish carpentry	screens
window installation	windows
glazing	cabinets
door installation	counter tops
sanding floors	hardwood floors
finishing floors	roofing materials
roofing	sheet metal
plumbing	iron and steel
heating	lath and plaster
air conditioning	dry-wall material
sewer connection	plumbing fixtures
masonry	plumbing lines
two-car garage	heating plant
closed-in porch	air conditioner
hardware installation	shower door
electrical	masonry materials
insulation	two-car garage
weatherproofing	closed-in porch
painting	rough hardware
sheet-metal work	finish hardware
sprinkling system	electrical fixtures
landscaping	electrical wiring
basement	lighting fixtures
fences	insulation
clean-up	weather-stripping
fixture installation	caulking
	shades and blinds
	linoleum
	tile
	paints
	sprinkling system
	landscaping
	fence and trellis materials
	fireplace materials
	floor covers
	composition

Two quicker, rule-of-thumb methods for estimating the cost of the house are the square-foot method and the cubic-foot method. These methods are not as accurate as itemizing the cost of all materials, labor, and other items. However, they do provide a quick estimate for speculative purposes.

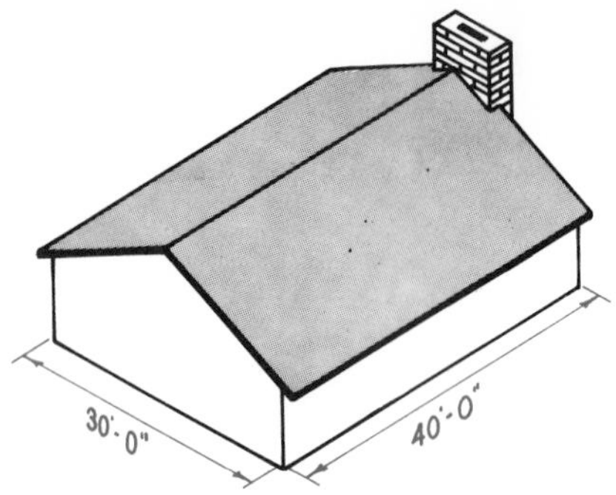

CONSTRUCTION COST: $30 PER SQ FT
SQUARE FOOTAGE: 30' x 40' = 1200 SQ FT
COST: 1200 x $30 = $36 000

Fig. 78–1. The square-foot method of determining costs.

Square-Foot Method

In general, the cost of the average home ranges from $20 to $30 per square foot of floor space, depending on the geographical location (Fig. 78–1). Each local office of the Federal Housing Administration can supply current estimating information peculiar to the locale.

Cubic-Foot Method

The cubic-foot method of estimating is slightly more accurate than the square-foot method and is more appropriate for multiple-story dwellings (Fig. 78–2).

Metric Measurements

If you have been using metric measurements, a cost estimate would be figured using square meters or cubic meters. The cost for the average home would be between $215 and $322 per square meter. If conversion from square feet to square meters is desired, multiply square feet by 0.0929 for an approximate answer.

Using a cubic-meter method of estimating costs, the average home would cost between $58.66 and $88.34 per cubic meter. If conversion from cubic feet to cubic meters is desired, multiply cubic feet by 0.0283 for an approximate answer.

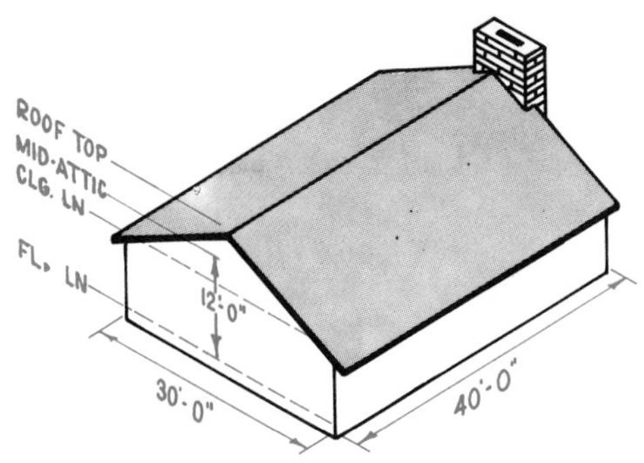

CONSTRUCTION COST: $2.50 PER CU FT
CUBIC VOLUME = FLOOR AREA x HEIGHT
CUBIC VOLUME: 1200 x 12 = 14 400 CU FT
TOTAL COST: CUBIC VOLUME x COST PER CU FT
TOTAL COST: 14 400 x $2.50 = $36 000

Fig. 78–2. The cubic-foot method of determining costs.

Building Materials Method

The square-foot and cubic-foot methods are at best rough estimates. The final cost of a building will depend upon the quality of building materials used. Table 78–2 shows the percentage of total cost of each material in a typical building. A 2000-square-foot home constructed with inexpensive materials may vary in cost several thousand dollars from a 2000-square-foot home constructed with more expensive materials.

Lots

The cost of the lot and landscaping must be added to the total cost of the materials.

The cost of residential lots in the United States varies considerably, as does the cost of landscaping a typical residence (Table 78–3). Other costs in addition to the cost of the home

Table 78–2. A METHOD OF DETERMINING THE COST OF A COMMERCIAL BUILDING BY COMPUTING THE COST OF BUILDING MATERIALS

PRINCIPAL ITEMS	COST	PERCENTAGE OF TOTAL COST
Excavation and site improvements	$ 65 524	4.45%
Foundations	107 101	7.28
Structural frame	140 080	9.52
Cement finish	80 018	5.44
Exterior masonry	96 776	6.58
Interior partitions	71 956	4.89
Carpentry and millwork	71 184	4.84
Sash and glazing	70 213	4.77
Roofing	36 374	2.47
Insulation	33 562	2.28
Waterproofing and dampproofing	1 700	0.12
Metal lath, furring, and plastering	52 424	3.56
Hollow metal work	16 730	1.14
Miscellaneous iron and ornamental metal	27 955	1.90
Tile, terrazzo, and marble	22 068	1.50
Floor covering	15 284	1.04
Painting	25 154	1.71
Finish hardware	22 825	1.55
Acoustical ceiling	53 040	3.60
Plumbing	109 335	7.43
Heating, ventilating, and air conditioning	220 585	14.99
Electrical work and light fixtures	131 560	8.94
TOTAL	$1 471 448	100%

Engineering News-Record

Table 78-3. COST OF LANDSCAPING

Item	Cost
Fine grading	$ .05 per sq ft
Site clean-up	15.00 per hour
Medium trees	
15 gal container	50.00
20″ box container	100.00
Small trees and shrubs	
5 gal container	15.00
1 gal container	5.00
1 qt container	1.00
Redwood header boards	.60 per lineal ft
Boulders—24″ to 36″	20.00 each
Crushed rock	.20 per sq ft
Ground cover	
Ivy	.10 per sq ft
Ice plant	.12 per sq ft
Strawberry	.12 per sq ft
Lawns	
Top quality	.16 per sq ft
Medium	.12 per sq ft
Inexpensive	.10 per sq ft

must also be considered. These include service charges, title search, insurance costs, and transfer taxes. These are called *closing costs.* Table 78–4 shows a breakdown of typical closing costs.

The lawyer's, architect's, and surveyor's fees are sometimes included in the closing costs. Lawyers' fees range between $150 and $400, and surveys cost between $100 and $200. Architects usually work on a 7 percent commission basis—10 percent if they supervise construction in addition to designing.

CUTTING COSTS

Some construction methods and material utilization that may greatly affect the ultimate cost of the home are listed as follows:

1. Square or rectangular homes are less expensive to build than irregular-shaped homes.
2. It is less expensive to build on a flat lot than on a sloping or hillside lot.
3. Using locally manufactured or produced materials cuts costs greatly.

Table 78-4. CLOSING COSTS FOR A $55 000 HOME

Item	Cost
Loan charges	$250
(Mortgage service charge)	
(Loan origination fee)	
(Points on loan)	
Notary fee	2
Recording deed	5
Title search	100
Title insurance	200
Household insurance	40
Appraisal fee	50
Credit report	25
Federal revenue stamps	15
State revenue stamps	15
Conveyacing fee	20
Lawyers' fee	300
Survey	180
Total	$952

4. Using stock materials and stock sizes of components takes advantage of mass-production cost reductions.
5. Using materials that can be quickly installed cuts labor costs. Prefabricating large sections or panels eliminates much time on the site.
6. Using prefinished materials saves labor costs.
7. Using prehung doors cuts considerable time from the finishing process.
8. Designing the home with a minimum amount of hall space increases the usable square footage and provides more living space for the cost.
9. Using prefabricated fireboxes for fireplaces cuts installation costs.
10. Investigating existing building codes before beginning construction eliminates unnecessary changes as construction proceeds.
11. Refraining from changing the design or any aspect of the plans after construction begins reduces costs.
12. Minimizing special jobs or custom-built items keeps costs from increasing.
13. Designing the house for short plumbing lines saves on materials.
14. Proper insulation saves heating and cooling costs.

PROBLEMS

1. **At $20 a square foot, how much will the home shown in Fig. 33–20 cost?**
2. **At $2.00 per cubic foot, how much will the home shown in Fig. 34–3 cost?**
3. **Resketch the elevation of the building shown in Fig. 36–9. Substitute building materials that will reduce the cost of this home.**
4. **Resketch the plan shown in Fig. 11–1 to reduce the cost.**
5. **Compute the cost of your present home based on the existing cost per square foot or cubic foot in your area.**
6. **Define these architectural terms: *real-estate survey, square footage, cubic footage.***

UNIT 79

Financing

Few people can accumulate sufficient funds to pay for the entire cost of the home at one time. Therefore, most home buyers pay a percentage —10, 20, 30 percent—at the time of occupancy, and arrange a loan (mortgage) for the balance.

MORTGAGE

A mortgage is obtained from a mortgage company, bank, savings and loan association, or insurance company. The lending institution pays for the house, and through the mortgage loan agreement collects this amount from the home buyer over a long period of time: 10, 20, or even 30 years.

INTEREST

In addition to paying back the lending institution the exact cost of the house, the home owner must also pay for the services of the institution. Payment is in the form of a percentage of the total cost of the home and is known as *interest*. Normal interest rates range from 6 to 10 percent. Rates of 8 and 9 percent, however, are most common. The interest payments increase with the length of time needed to pay back the loan. On a long-term loan—for example, 30 years—the monthly payments will be smaller but the overall cost will be much greater because the interest is higher. A long-term loan can, over the life of the loan, accumulate 200 percent interest.

A comparison of the time factor, amount of payment, and number of payments on a $10 000 loan at 9 percent interest is shown in Table 79–1. Table 79–2 shows similar information for a $20 000 loan, and Table 79–3 shows the same information for a $30 000 loan.

TAXES

In addition to the principal (amount paid back that is credited to the payment for the house), and the interest, the taxes on the house must be added to the total cost of the home. Taxes on residential property vary greatly. Taxes on a $20 000 home in many residential suburban communities range between $500 and $1000 per year.

INSURANCE

The purchase of a home is a large investment and must be insured for the protection of the home buyer and for the protection of the lending institution. Insurance rates vary greatly, depending on the cost of the home, location, type of construction, and availability of fire fighting equipment (Table 79–4). The home should be insured against fire, public liability, property damage, vandalism, natural destruction, and accidents to trespassers and workers.

Table 79–1. PAYMENTS ON A $10 000 MORTGAGE AT 9 PERCENT INTEREST

TIME IN YEARS	MONTHLY PAYMENTS	NUMBER OF PAYMENTS	TOTAL COST
10	$126.68	120	$15 201.60
15	101.43	180	18 257.40
20	89.98	240	20 785.20
25	83.92	300	25 176.00
30	80.47	360	28 969.20

Table 79–2. PAYMENTS ON A $20 000 MORTGAGE AT 9 PERCENT INTEREST

TIME IN YEARS	MONTHLY PAYMENTS	NUMBER OF PAYMENTS	TOTAL COST
10	$253.36	120	$31 403.20
15	202.86	180	36 518.80
20	179.95	240	43 188.00
25	167.84	300	50 252.00
30	160.93	360	57 934.80

Table 79–3. PAYMENTS ON A $30 000 MORTGAGE AT 9 PERCENT INTEREST

TIME IN YEARS	MONTHLY PAYMENTS	NUMBER OF PAYMENTS	TOTAL COST
10	$380.04	120	$45 604.80
15	304.29	180	54 772.20
20	269.93	240	64 783.20
25	251.76	300	75 528.00
30	241.40	360	86 904.00

BUDGETS

Since most household budgets are established on a monthly basis, the monthly payments needed to purchase and maintain a residence are more significant than the total cost of the home. Monthly payments are broken into four categories: principal, interest, taxes, and insurance (PITI). Table 79–5 shows the amortization for a 10-year, 20-year, and 30-year loan.

The prospective home buyer and builder should consider the following factors before selecting a particular institution for a mortgage. He or she should know the interest rate, the number of years needed to repay, prepayment penalties, total amount of monthly payment, conditions of approval, placement fees, amount of down payment required, service fees, and closing fees. Typical closing costs on a home would include lawyers' fees, transfer taxes, escrow deposit, insurance, and survey fees.

Table 79–4. INSURANCE RATES PER THREE-YEAR PERIOD

TYPE OF INSURANCE	$10 000 HOME	$20 000 HOME	$50 000 HOME
MINIMUM COVERAGE: FIRE, PUBLIC LIABILITY	$100	$200	$315
AVERAGE COVERAGE: FIRE, PUBLIC LIABILITY, PROPERTY DAMAGE, THEFT	$135	$235	$350
MAXIMUM COVERAGE: FIRE, PUBLIC LIABILITY, PROPERTY DAMAGE, THEFT, MEDICAL, PERSONAL LIABILITY, LANDSCAPE INSURANCE, WIND, FLOOD, EARTHQUAKE	$250	$350	$450

Table 79–5. PRINCIPAL, INTEREST, TAXES, AND INSURANCE COSTS FOR A $20 000 LOAN AT 9 PERCENT INTEREST

	10-YEAR LOAN—AMORTIZATION $253.36			20-YEAR LOAN—AMORTIZATION $179.95			30-YEAR LOAN—AMORTIZATION $160.93		
PAYMENT BREAKDOWN	FIRST PAYMENT	5TH YEAR PAYMENT	LAST PAYMENT	FIRST PAYMENT	10TH YEAR PAYMENT	LAST PAYMENT	FIRST PAYMENT	15TH YEAR PAYMENT	LAST PAYMENT
PRINCIPAL	$103.36	$161.86	$251.47	$ 29.95	$106.50	$178.61	$ 10.93	$119.10	$159.93
INTEREST	150.00	91.50	1.89	150.00	73.45	1.34	150.00	41.83	1.00
TAXES (VARIES)	40.00	40.00	40.00	40.00	40.00	40.00	40.00	40.00	40.00
INSURANCE (VARIES)	10.00	10.00	10.00	10.00	10.00	10.00	10.00	10.00	10.00
TOTAL MONTHLY PAYMENT	$303.36	$303.36	$303.36	$229.95	$229.95	$229.95	$210.93	$210.93	$210.93

SALARY AND HOME COSTS

If the home buyer considers the purchase or the building of a home as an investment, he or she should take steps to ensure the maximum return on investment. If the home buyer purchases a home that costs considerably less than he or she can afford, he or she is not investing adequately. On the other hand, if the home buyer attempts to buy a home that is more expensive than he or she can afford, the payments will become a drain on the family budget and undue sacrifices will have to be made to compensate.

Family budgets vary greatly, and a house that may be a burden for one person to purchase may be quite suitable for another, even if

Fig. 79–1. Compute the monthly mortgage payments for this house.

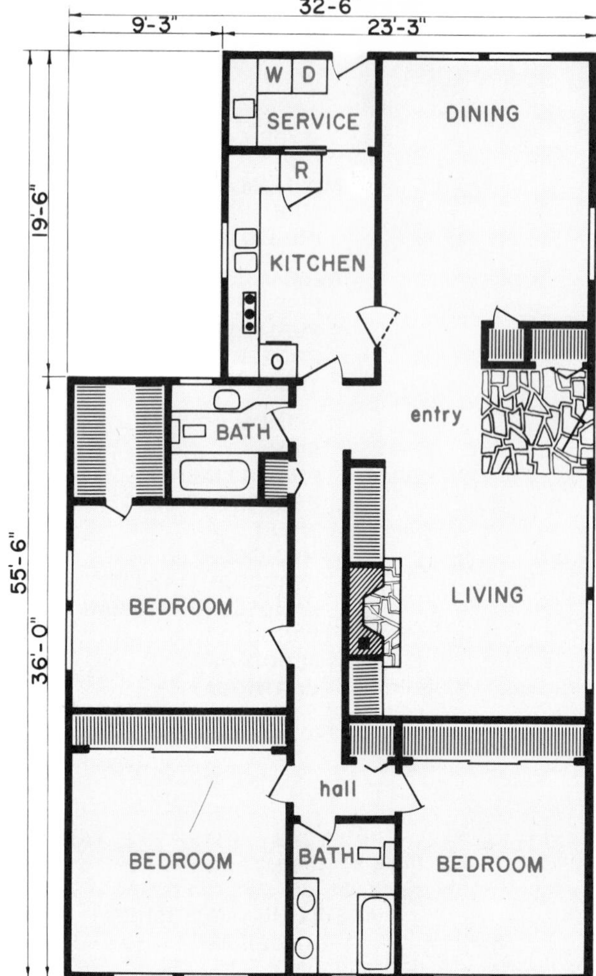

the two owners are earning the same relative salary. In general, the cost of the house should not exceed two and one-half times the annual income.

PROBLEMS

1. **What is the cost of the home you could afford if you were earning $10 000 a year? $20 000 a year? $30 000 a year?**
2. **You purchase a home valued at $40 000 and make a 10 percent down payment. Your interest rate is 9 percent. What amount of interest will you pay over the life of a 25-year mortgage?**
3. **What will be your total monthly payment on an $38 000 home if you have made a 10 percent down payment and are paying an interest rate of 10 percent? Your yearly taxes are $1000, and your insurance is $150.**
4. **What will your monthly mortgage payment be if you buy the house shown in Fig. 79–1 for $20 per square foot? Your interest is 9 percent for 25 years. You make a down payment of 9 percent of the total price. Your closing costs total $1000.**
5. **Define these terms: *interest, principal, escrow, mortgage, closing costs, taxes, insurance.***

PART FIVE

Information frequently used in the preparation of architectural drawings and documents is repeated in the appendix, consisting of a glossary, which is an alphabetical list of terms and their meanings; architectural synonyms, which are a matchup of terms that have the same meaning; and architectural abbreviations, which are used to conserve space on drawings. The appendix begins with a section about major careers for which a background in architectural drawing is necessary or helpful and a section of basic mathematical formulas most commonly used in architectural drafting and design.

Appendix

SECTION 22

Careers Related to Architecture

A career in one of the many architecture-related fields is rewarding, involves hard work, and offers good to excellent financial returns. The greatest satisfaction, whether you become a blueprinter or a structural engineer, is the reward of seeing your creations and efforts take form in structures that become part of our physical environment. Architecture-related professional and technical careers, including educational requirements, are described in this unit.

RECOMMENDED SUBJECTS FOR PREARCHITECTURAL STUDENTS

The following subjects are listed according to their importance:

- math
- physics
- English
- social studies
- chemistry
- mechanical drafting
- architectural drafting
- art
- physical education
- foreign language elective
- industrial arts elective

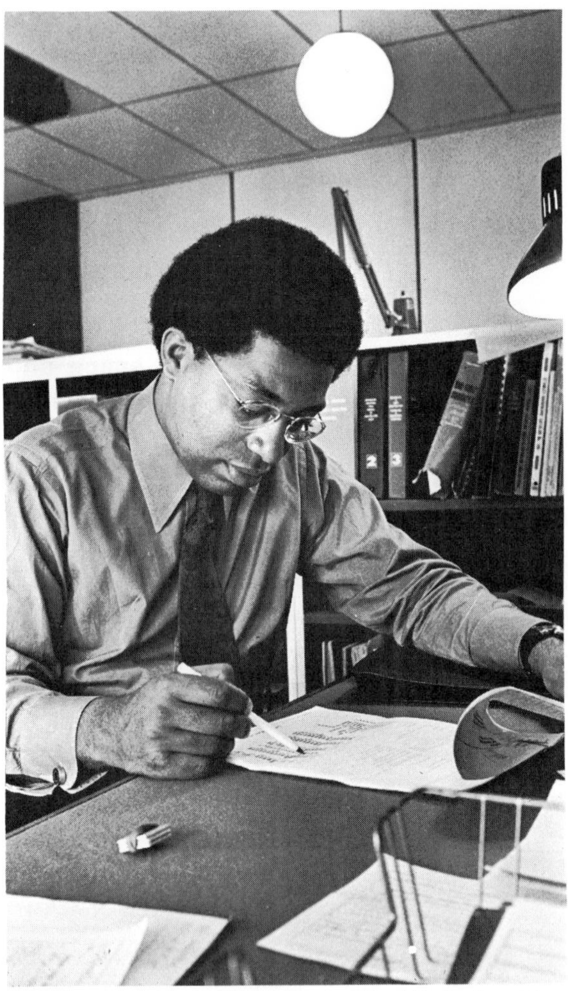

Bond Ryder Associates

Fig. 80–1. Architect.

ARCHITECT

Architecture is a rewarding and demanding profession. The architect (Fig. 80–1) must be an artist, engineer, and businessman combined. Special qualities are required of the architect. He or she must understand people. She or he must have a talent for creative design and have skill in math and science. And he or she must be able to graphically communicate ideas and designs.

The architect is trained in school and then must serve an internship before entering practice. High school preparation is the first step in becoming an architect. The outline below indicates the courses needed at this stage. All accredited architectural colleges have the same general requirements, although it is a good idea to write to the college of your choice for exact information. If you are planning to attend a junior or community college first, check with your prospective university concerning what courses will be accepted for transfer of credit.

Practical experience is invaluable. Some architects will hire students for summer or part-time work if the students are known to be responsible and are interested in becoming architects. Take any job which will enable you to work near practicing architects.

PROBABLE COURSES IN THE UNIVERSITY FRESHMAN YEAR FOR ARCHITECTURAL STUDENTS

architectural design
analytical geometry
calculus
physics
materials of construction
surveying
English and public speaking
architectural rendering
history of architecture
psychology
physical education

For further information write to:
American Institute of Architects
1735 New York Avenue, NW
Washington, DC 20006

ARCHITECTURAL DRAFTSMAN

The architectural draftsman (Fig. 80–2) is the channel of communication between the architect and the builders. She or he translates the ideas, sketches, and designs of an architect into sets of drawings from which a structure can be built. The work includes drawings, sketching, tracing, computation, and detailing.

The architectural draftsman must be able to get along with people. He or she must be able to take criticism and follow instructions carefully and must be able to work as a member of a team.

An architectural draftsman may become an architect by gaining architectural drafting and design experience, by obtaining letters of recommendation, by additional education, and by passing a state examination.

Dynecourt Mahon, Photo

Fig. 80–2. Architectural draftsman.

For further information write to:
American Federation of Technical Engineering
1126 16th Street, NW
Suite 28
Washington, DC 20036

CITY PLANNER

The city planner (Fig. 80–3) studies and plans the development or redevelopment of large areas such as cities, communities, housing projects, commercial projects, and so forth. The planning takes into account the utilities and necessities required for today's living. After designs are completed, the individual buildings may be designed by other architects. The other facets of the planner's overall design are handled and completed by other engineering specialists. With the growth of our country, the construction of new cities and the renovating of slum areas in older cities will require much new personnel in this area.

Bond Ryder Associates

Fig. 80–3. City planner.

The planner's college degree should be in architecture, planning, engineering, or landscaping, with further training for a master's degree in planning.

For further information write to:
American Institute of Planners
917 15th Street, NW
Washington, DC 20005

LANDSCAPE ARCHITECT

The landscape architect (Fig. 80–4) controls the development of the site, which includes earthwork, planting, layout of streets and walks, and the orientation of the structure. She or he should have an understanding of plant life and a background in math, art, architectural drafting, and rendering.

A college degree in landscape architecture is required.

For further information write to:
American Society of.Landscape
Architects, Inc.
2000 K Street, NW
Washington, DC 20006

STRUCTURAL ENGINEER

The structural engineer (Fig. 80–5), through the use of calculations, designs the structural part of buildings. He or she is usually a civil engineer who specializes in structures. Of all the professional areas in the building trades, this is considered one of the most difficult, because of the high competence it requires in physics and math.

For further information write to:
American Society of Civil Engineers
345 East 47th Street
New York, NY 10017

CIVIL ENGINEER

The civil engineer (Fig. 80–6) handles the calculating and designing also done by the structural engineer. In addition, he or she may survey, or may conduct large-scale planning of utilities, roads, structures, harbors, airfields, tunnels, bridges, and sewage plants. The field of civil engineering is so broad that a civil engineer has to specialize in one area, such as structures.

The civil engineer's college degree is in civil engineering.

For further information write to:
American Society of Civil Engineers
345 East 47th Street
New York, NY 10017

ELECTRICAL ENGINEER

Electrical engineers (Fig. 80–7) form the largest group of engineers. The need for them is great in the computer sciences and in the fields of aviation. The electrical engineer in the building trade designs the electrical components of structures. The electrical engineer's college degree is in electrical engineering.

For further information write to:
Institute of Electrical and Electronic
Engineers
345 East 47th Street
New York, NY 10017

Bond Ryder Associates

Fig. 80–4. Landscape architect.

American Plywood Association

Fig. 80–5. Structural engineer.

Inland-Ryerson Construction Products Company

Fig. 80–6. Civil engineer.

Henry Dreyfus Associates

Fig. 80–7. Electrical engineer.

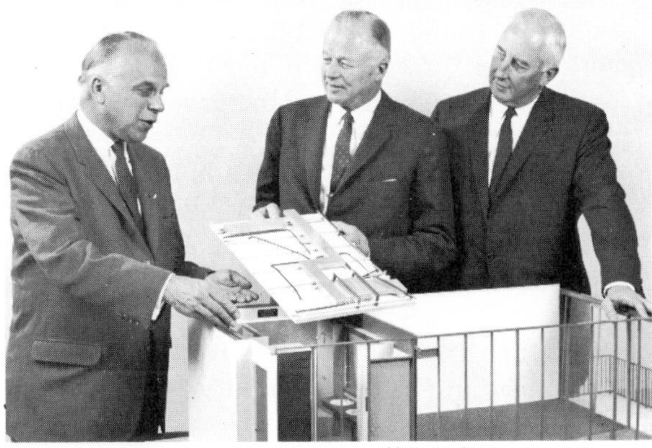

United States Steel Corp.

Fig. 80–8. Air-conditioning engineer.

AIR-CONDITIONING ENGINEER

The air-conditioning engineer (Fig. 80–8) designs the heating, ventilation, air-conditioning, and refrigeration systems for structures. This person's college degree is in mechanical engineering, and he or she will specialize in air conditioning.

For further information write to:

The American Society of Mechanical Engineers
United Engineering Center
345 East 47th Street
New York, NY 10017

ACOUSTICS ENGINEER

The acoustics engineer (Fig. 80–9) is responsible for controlling sound in the structure. However, this work is not confined to buildings; it can also be applied to noise suppression in machines, industrial factories, aircraft, and rockets. This field is very technical. The acoustics engineer needs a broad background in math and physics. Her or his college degree is in physics, engineering, architecture, or math.

For further information write to:
American Institute of Physics
335 East 45th Street
New York, NY 10017

MECHANICAL ENGINEER

The mechanical engineer (Fig. 80–10) is the engineer who does not specialize in one area. He or she works in production, the use of power, and machines which use power. The mechanical engineer who works in the building trades designs for operational parts of a structure.

The degree is in mechanical engineering.

For further information write to:
The American Society of Mechanical Engineers

ESTIMATOR

The estimator (Fig. 80–11) prepares estimates of the cost of building projects by figuring material requirements and labor costs. Her or his work must be accurate, because mistakes are expensive.

An estimator working in large construction should have a general or specialized college degree and a knowledge of construction and builders. His or her math skills must be good. An estimator for small construction, such as that of homes, can come from the ranks of the craftsman. The estimator's skills are largely learned in the office and in the field.

For further information write to:
Associated General Contractors of America, Inc.
1957 E Street NW
Washington, DC 20006

SPECIFICATION WRITER

The specification writer (Fig. 80–12) prepares specifications (a written description of exact materials, methods of construction, finishes, and tests and performances of everything required for the structure). A knowledge of all types of construction is needed, as is a technical background and experience in building.

His or her college degree can be general or specialized. Specification writers for small construction can come from the ranks of the craftsman. The specification writer's skills are learned in the office and in the field.

For further information write to:
Associated General Contractors of America, Inc.
1957 E Street, NW
Washington DC 20006

SURVEYOR

The surveyor (Fig. 80–13) defines in both words and pictures (usually maps) the specific space, position, and topography of a piece of land. The accuracy of the work is essential for proper foundations and construction. This work is the first step in the construction of roads, airfields, bridges, dams, and other structures.

Her or his college degree is in civil engineering. One may become a surveyor's aide with two years of junior college and on-the-job experience.

For further information write to:
American Congress on Surveying and Mapping
Woodward Building
Washington, DC 20005

Inland-Ryerson Construction Products Company

Fig. 80–9. Acoustics engineer.

Bond Ryder Associates

Fig. 80–10. Mechanical engineer.

Bond Ryder Associates

Fig. 80–11. Estimator.

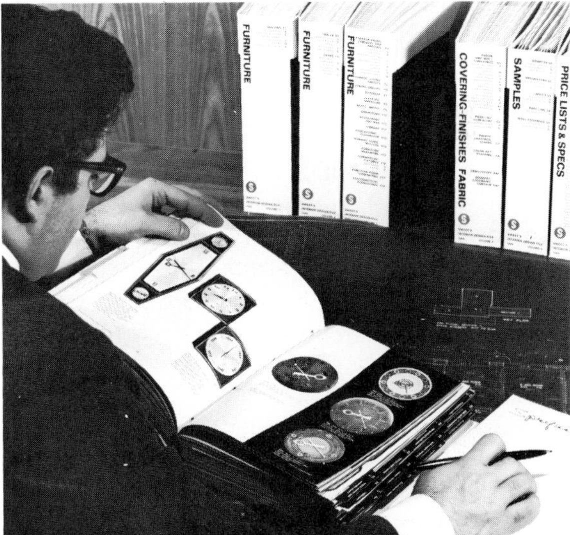

McGraw-Hill Information Systems Company

Fig. 80–12. Specification writer.

Steve Hamerman, Photo

Fig. 80–13. Surveyor.

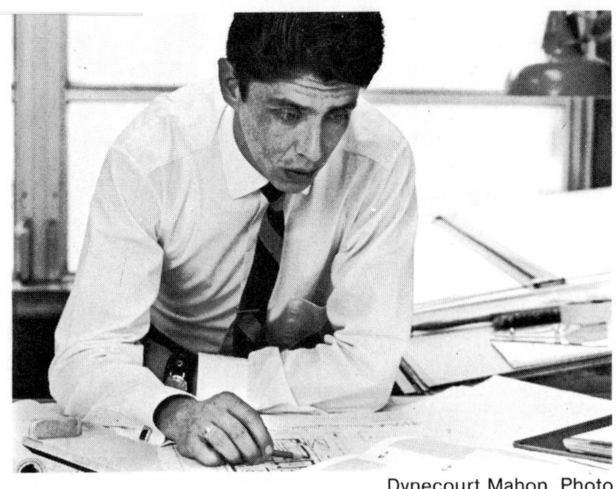

Dynecourt Mahon, Photo

Fig. 80–14. Architectural designer.

ARCHITECTURAL DESIGNER

The architectural designer (Fig. 80–14) designs and plans homes and other small buildings. She or he is usually an outstanding architectural draftsman but does not have a degree in architecture. The engineering for their structures is done by architects or structural engineers.

For further information write to:
American Institute of Building Design
2730 Arden Way, Suite 138
Sacramento, California 95825

CONTRACTOR

The contractor (Fig. 80–15) is a businessperson who is responsible for the construction and finishing of a structure. He or she can do this work either with his or her own employees or by subcontracting other workers. The contractor can work from his or her own plans, but usually builds from an architect's or a designer's plans. Several years' experience in the building trades and a state license are required to become a contractor.

For further information write to:
Associated General Contractors of America, Inc.
1957 E Street, NW
Washington, DC 20006

Associated Builders & Contractors
P. O. Box 8733
Baltimore Int'l Airport
Baltimore, MD 21240

National Association of Home Builders
15th and M Street, NW
Washington, DC 20005

General Building Contractors Association, Inc.
Suite 1212, 1 Penn Plaza
Philadelphia, PA 19102

CARPENTER

Carpenters form the largest group of building tradespeople. The carpenter is a skilled worker who constructs the wooden parts of a building. A rough carpenter (Fig. 80–16) works on the framing, floor, and roof system. The finish carpenter does the trim, cabinets, hardware, and floor cover.

Carpenters must be skilled with all hand and power tools used for wood and must be able to use all types of fasteners. The best way to enter this trade is through an apprenticeship program following vocational school training.

For further information write to:
United Brotherhood of Carpenters and Joiners of America
101 Constitution Avenue, NW
Washington, DC 20001

MASON

The mason (Fig. 80–17) works with stone of all kinds. The stone can be used either for the basic structure or as a veneer cover over another building structure.

National Warm Air Heating and Air Conditioning Association

Fig. 80–15. Contractor.

Weyerhaeuser Company

Fig. 80–16. Carpenter.

Bricklayer's, Mason's and Plasterer's International Union of America

Fig. 80–17. Mason.

The mason must be highly skilled in the use of specialized masonry tools, and must be familiar with the characteristics of natural stone, fired clay products, and artificial stone. The best way to enter this trade is through an apprenticeship program following some vocational school training.

For further information write to:
Bricklayer's, Mason's and Plasterer's
International Union of America
815 15th Street, NW
Washington, DC 20005

SECTION 23

Mathematics Related to Architecture

This unit contains basic rules and formulas commonly used in architectural computations. For more detailed instructional information refer to a text in descriptive geometry, trigonometry, or algebra.

The square of the hypotenuse of a right triangle is equal to the sum of the squares of the other two sides.

$$C^2 = A^2 + B^2$$

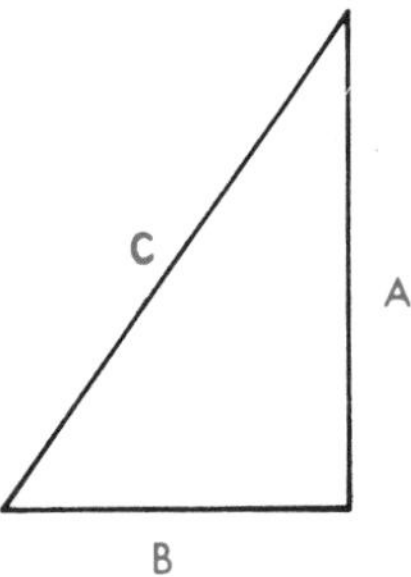

The square of one side of a right triangle equals the square of the hypotenuse minus the square of the other side.

$$A^2 = C^2 - B^2$$

The area of a triangle is equal to one-half the product of the base and height.

$$A = \frac{1}{2}(B \times H) \quad \text{or} \quad \frac{B \times H}{2}$$

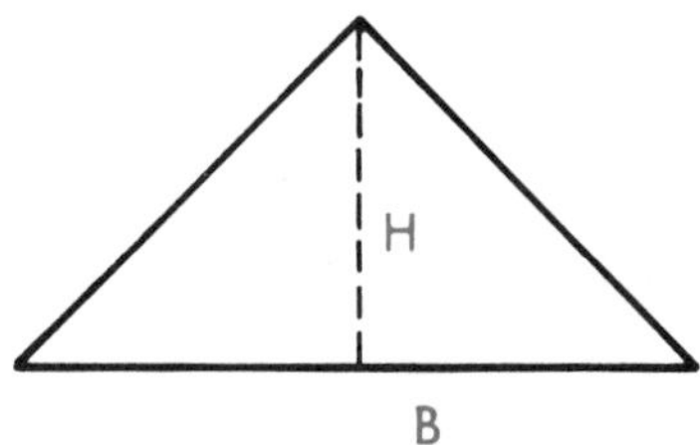

$$\pi = 3.1416 \quad \text{or} \quad \frac{22}{7}$$

The circumference of a circle is equal to π multiplied by the diameter.

$$C = \pi \times D$$

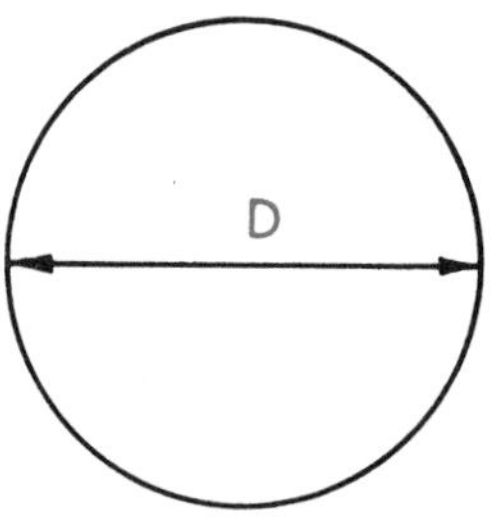

The area of a circle is equal to π multiplied by the radius squared.

$$A = \pi \times R^2$$

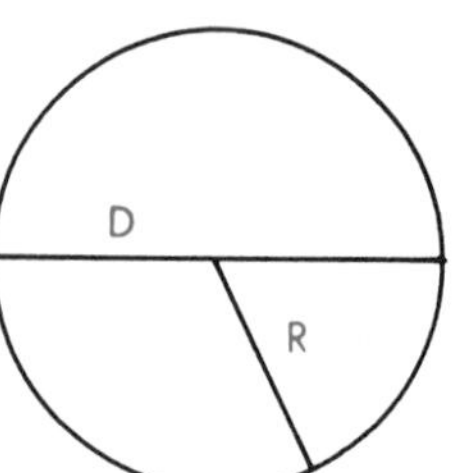

The area of a circle is equal to the circumference multiplied by one-half the radius.

$$A = C \times \frac{1}{2} R \quad \text{or} \quad \frac{C \times R}{2}$$

To find the area of a square or rectangle, multiply the length of one side by the length of an adjacent side.

$$A = S_1 \times S_2$$

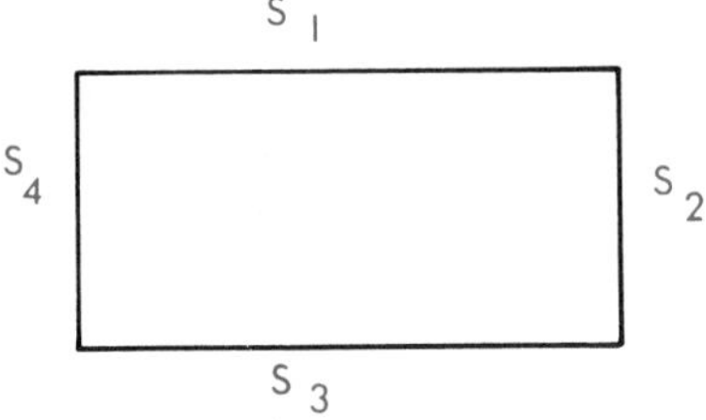

To find the perimeter of a polygon, add the length of all sides.

$$P = S_1 + S_2 + S_3 + S_4 + S_n \ldots$$

To find the area of a trapezoid, multiply its height by one-half the sum of the parallel sides.

$$A = \frac{1}{2}(L_1 + L_2) \times H \quad \text{or} \quad A = \frac{(L_1 + L_2) \times H}{2}$$

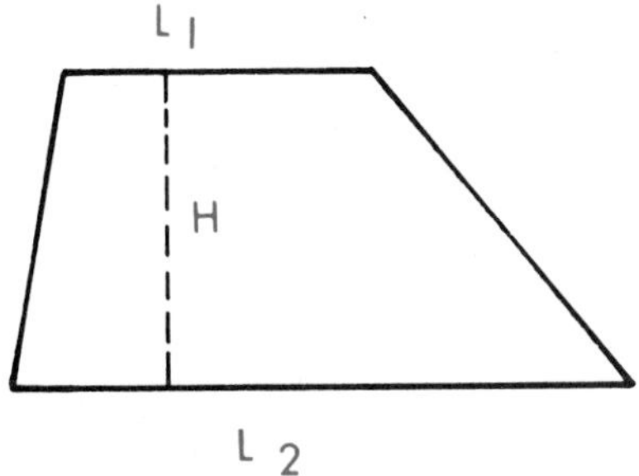

To find the volume of a square or rectangular solid, multiply the length by the height by the width.

$$V = L \times H \times W$$

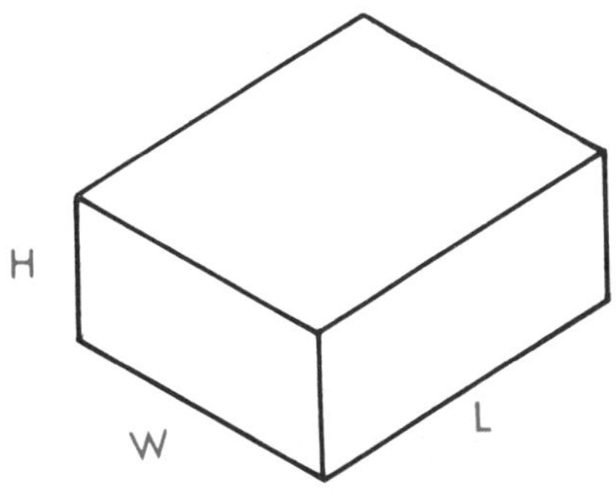

To find the volume of a sphere, multiply the diameter cubed by π by one-sixth.

$$V = \frac{1}{6} \times \pi \times D^3 \quad \text{or} \quad V = \frac{\pi \times D^3}{6}$$

To find the volume of a cylinder, multiply the area of its base by its height.

$$V = \pi R^2 \times H$$

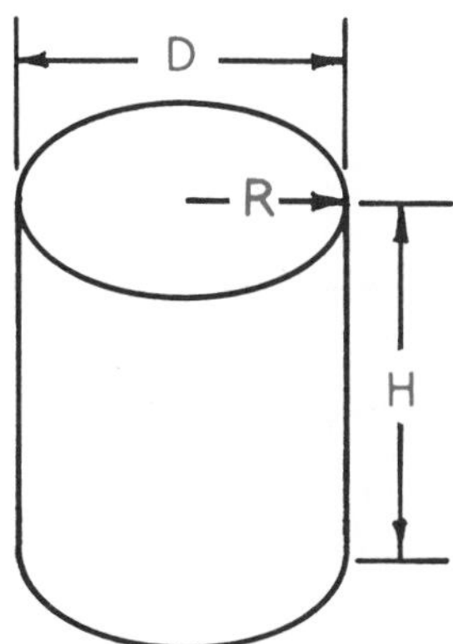

To find the volume of a pyramid, multiply the height by one-third its base area.

$$V = \frac{1}{3} H \times W \times D$$

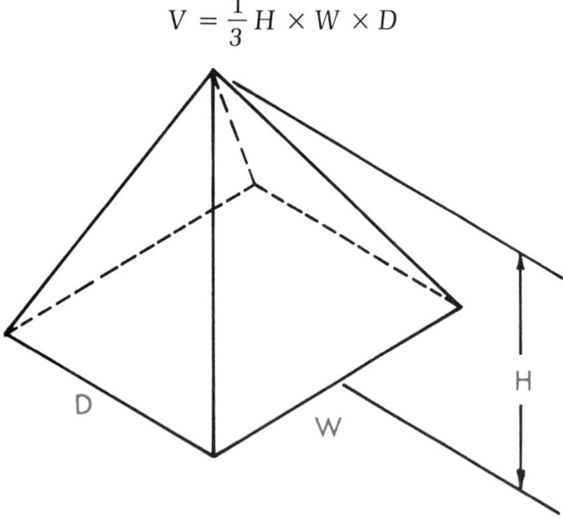

To find the volume of a cone, multiply one-third of the product of its base area by the height.

$$V = \frac{1}{3} \pi R^2 \times H$$

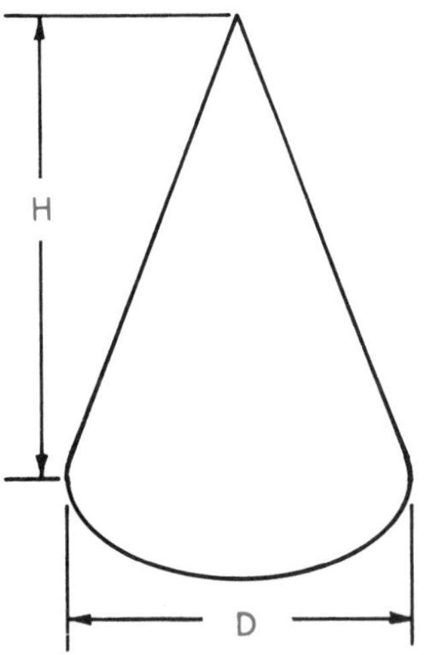

The diagonal of a square is equal to the square root of twice the area.

$$D = \sqrt{2A}$$

To find the tread width, divide the run of the stairs by the number of treads. This is always one less tread than riser.

$$\text{Tread width} = \frac{\text{Run of stairs}}{\text{Number of treads}}$$

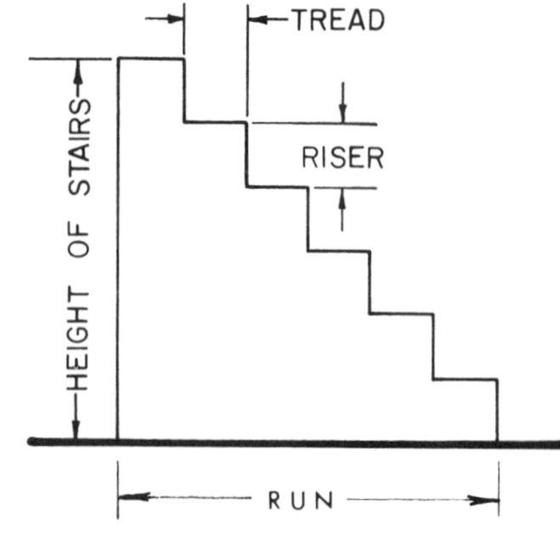

To find the height of a riser, divide the height of the stairs by the number of risers.

$$\text{Riser height} = \frac{\text{Height of stairs}}{\text{Number of stairs}}$$

To find the number of risers, divide the height of the stairs by the height of each riser.

$$\text{Riser number} = \frac{\text{Height of stairs}}{\text{Height of risers}}$$

To find the number of board feet in a piece of lumber, multiply the length in feet by the width in inches by the thickness in inches, divided by 12.

$$BF = \frac{L \times W \times T}{12}$$

To find the electrical resistance in a circuit, divide the voltage (E) by the amperage (I).

$$R = \frac{E}{I}$$

To find the electric current in amperes (I) in a circuit, divide the voltage (E) by the resistance in ohms (R).

$$I = \frac{E}{R}$$

To find the voltage in an electric circuit, multiply the current in amperes (I) by the resistance in ohms (R).

$$E = I \times R$$

SECTION 24

Architectual Glossary

Abstract of title A summary of all deeds, wills, and legal actions to show ownership.
Acoustics The science of sound. In housing, acoustical materials used to keep down noise within a room or to prevent it from passing through walls.
Adobe construction Construction using sun-dried units of adobe soil for walls; usually found in the southwestern United States.
Air conditioner An apparatus that can heat, cool, clean, and circulate air.
Air-dried lumber Lumber that is left in the open to dry rather than being dried by a kiln.
Air duct A pipe usually made of sheet metal that conducts air to rooms from a central source.
Air trap A U-shaped pipe filled with water and located beneath plumbing fixtures to form a seal against the passage of gases and odors.
Alcove A recessed space connected at the side of a larger room.
Alteration A change in, or addition to, an existing building.
Amortization An installment payment of a loan, usually monthly for a home loan.
Ampere The unit used in the measure of the rate of flow of electricity.
Anchor bolt A threaded rod inserted in masonry construction for anchoring the sill plate to the foundation.
Angle iron A structural piece of rolled-steel shaped to form a 90° angle.
Appraisal The estimated price of a house which a buyer would pay and the seller accept for a property. An appraisal is a detailed evaluation of the property.
Apron The finish board immediately below a window sill. Also the part of the driveway that leads directly into the garage.

Arcade A series of arches supported by a row of columns.
Arch A curved structure that will support itself by mutual pressure and the weight above its curved opening.
Architect A person who plans and designs buildings and oversees their construction.
Areawall A wall surrounding an areaway to admit light and air to a basement.
Areaway A recessed area below grade around the foundation to allow light and ventilation into a basement window or doorway.
Asbestos A soft, fibrous, fireproof mineral fiber used in fireproofing building materials.
Asbestos board a fire-resistant sheet made from asbestos fiber and portland cement.
Ashlar A facing of squared stones.
Ashpit The area below the hearth of a fireplace which collects the ashes.
Asphalt Bituminus sandstones used for paving streets and waterproofing asbestos roof and wall covering.
Asphalt shingles Composition roof shingles made from asphalt-impregnated felt covered with mineral granules.
Assessed value A value set by governmental assessors to determine tax assessments.
Atrium An open court within a building.
Attic The space between the roof and the ceiling.
Awning window An outswinging window hinged at the top.

Backfill Earth used to fill in areas around exterior foundation walls.
Backhearth The part of the hearth inside the fireplace.
Baffle A partial blocking against a flow of wind or sound.
Balcony A deck projecting from the wall of a building above the ground.
Balloon framing The building-frame construction in which each of the studs is one piece from the foundation to the roof.
Balustrade A series of balusters or posts connected by a rail, gen-

erally used for porches, and balconies.

Banister A hand rail.

Base The finish of a room at the junction of the walls and floor.

Baseboard The finish board covering the interior wall where the wall and floor meet.

Base course The lowest part of masonry construction.

Baseline A located line for reference control purposes.

Basement The lowest story of a building, partially or entirely below ground.

Base plate A plate, usually of steel, upon which a column rests.

Base shoe A molding used next to the floor in interior baseboards.

Batt A blanket insulation material usually made of mineral fibers and designed to be installed between framing members.

Batten A narrow strip of board, used to cover cracks between the boards in board and batten siding.

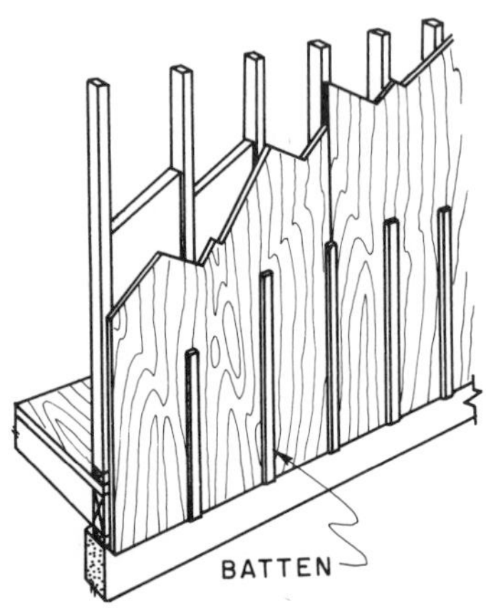

Batter Sloping a masonry or concrete wall upward and backward from the perpendicular.

Batter boards Boards at exact elevations nailed to posts just outside the corners of a proposed building. Strings are stretched across the boards to locate the outline of the foundation.

Bay window A window projecting out from the wall of a building to form a recess in the room.

Beam A horizontal structural member that carries a load.

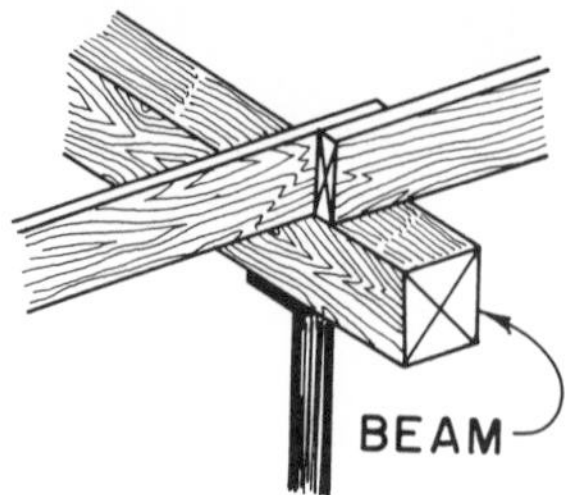

Beam ceiling A ceiling in which the ceiling beams are exposed to view.

Bearing plate A plate that provides support for a structural member.

Bearing wall or partition A wall supporting any vertical load other than its own weight.

Bench mark A metal or stone marker placed in the ground by a surveyor with the elevation on it. This is the reference point to determine lines, grades, and elevations in the area.

Bending moment A measure of the forces that break a beam by bending.

Bent A frame consisting of two supporting columns and a girder or truss used in vertical position in a structure.

Bevel siding Shingles or other siding board thicker on one edge than the other. The thick edge overlaps the thin edge of the next board.

Bib A threaded faucet allowing a hose to be attached.

Bill of material A parts list of material accompanying a structural drawing.

Blanket insulation Insulation in rolled-sheet form, often backed by treated paper which forms a vapor barrier.

Blocking Small wood framing members that fill in the open space between the floor and ceiling joists to add stiffness to the floors and ceiling.

Blueprint An architectural drawing used by workers to build from. The original drawing is transferred to a sensitized paper that turns blue with white lines when printed.

Board measure A system of lumber measurement having as a unit a board-foot. One board-foot is the equivalent of 1 foot square by 1 inch thick.

Brace Any stiffening member of a framework.

Braced framing Frame construction with posts and braces used for stiffening. More rigid than balloon framing.

Breezeway A roofed walkway with open sides. It connects the house and garage. If large enough it can be used as a patio.

Broker An agent in buying and selling property.

BTU Abbreviation for British thermal unit, a standard unit for measuring heat gain or loss.

Buck Frame for a door, usually made of metal, into which the finished door fits.

Building code A collection of legal requirements for buildings designed to protect the safety, health, and general welfare of people who work and live in them.

Building line An imaginary line on a plot beyond which the building cannot extend.

Building paper A heavy, waterproof paper used over sheathing and subfloors to prevent passage of air and water.

Building permit A permit issued by a municipal government authorizing the construction of a building or structure.

Built-up beam A beam constructed of smaller members fastened together.

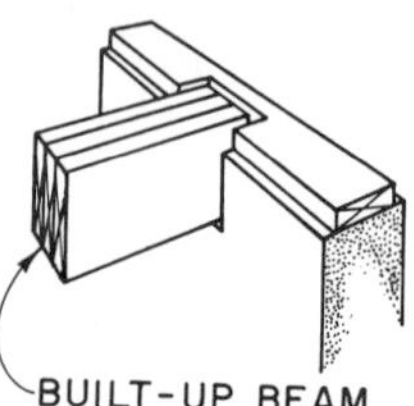

Built-up roof A roofing material composed of several layers of felt and asphalt.

Butterfly roof A roof with two sides sloping down toward the interior of the house.

Butt joint A joint formed by placing the end of one member against another member.

Buttress A mass of masonry projecting beyond a wall to take thrust or pressure. A projection from a wall to create additional strength and support.

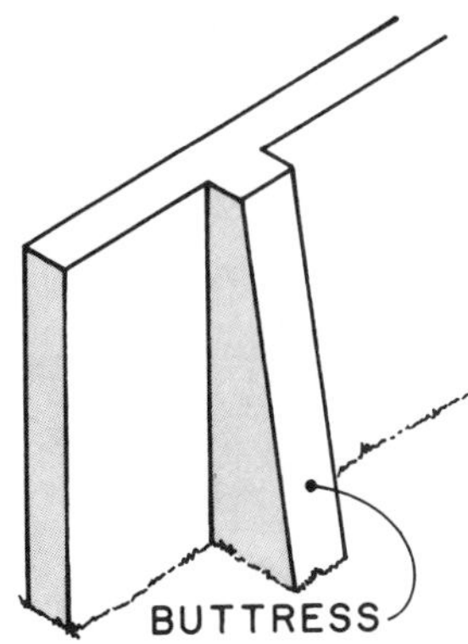

BX cable Armored electric cable wrapped in rubber and protected by a flexible steel covering.

Cabinet work The finish interior woodwork.

Canopy A projection over windows and doors to protect them from the weather.

Cantilever A projecting member supported only at one end.

Cant strip An angular board used to eliminate a sharp, right angle on roofs or flashing.

Carport An automobile shelter not fully enclosed.

Carriage The horizontal part of the stringers of a stair that supports the treads.

Casement window A hinged window that opens out, usually made of metal.

Casing A metal or wooden member around door and window openings to give a finished appearance.

Catch basin An underground structure for drainage into which the water from a roof or floor will drain. It is connected with a sewer or drain.

Caulking A waterproof material used to seal cracks.

Cavity wall A hollow wall usually made up of two brick walls built a few inches apart and joined together with brick or metal ties.

Cedar shingles Roofing and siding shingles made from western red cedar.

Cement A masonry adhesive material purchased in the form of pulverized powder. Any substance used in its soft state to join other materials together and which afterward dries and hardens.

Central heating A single source of heat which is distributed by pipes or ducts.

Certificate of title A document given to the home buyer with the deed, stating that the title to the property named in the deed is clearly established.

Cesspool A pit or cistern to hold sewage.

Chalk line A string that is heavily chalked, held tight, then plucked to make a straight guideline against boards or other surfaces.

Chase A vertical space within a building for ducts, pipes, or wires.

Checks Splits or cracks in a board, ordinarily caused by seasoning.

Check valve A valve that permits passage through a pipe in only one direction.

Chimney A vertical flue for passing smoke and gases outside a building.

Chimney stack A group of flues in the same chimney.

Chord The principal members of a roof or bridge truss. The upper members are indicated by the term upper chord. The lower members are identified by the term lower chord.

Cinder block A building block made of cement and cinder.

Circuit The path of an electric current. The closed loop of wire in which an electric current can flow.

Circuit breaker A device used to open and close an electrical circuit.

Cistern A tank or other reservoir to store rain which has run off the roof.

Clapboard A board, thicker on one side than the other, used to overlap an adjacent board to make house siding.

Clearance A clear space to allow passage.

Clerestory A set of high windows often above a roof line.

Clinch To bend over the protruding end of a nail.

Clip A small connecting angle used for fastening various members of a structure.

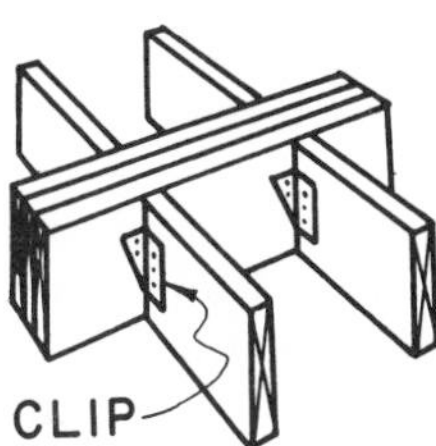

Collar beam A horizontal member fastening opposing rafters below the ridge in roof framing.

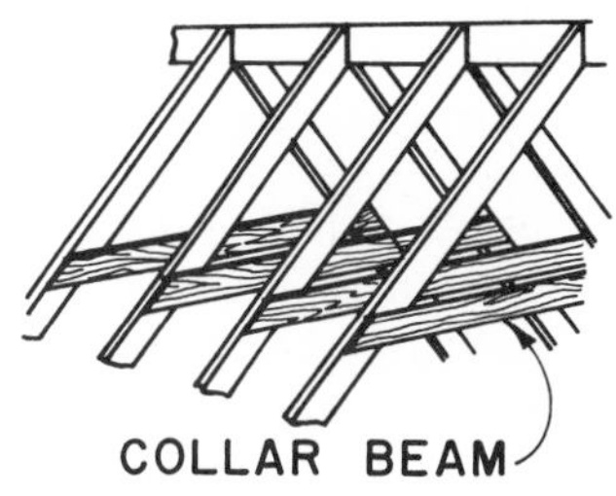

Column In architecture: a perpendicular supporting member, circular in section; in engineering: a vertical structural member supporting loads acting on or near and in the direction of its longitudinal axis.

Common wall A wall that serves two dwelling units.

Compression A force which tends to make a member fail because of crushing.
Concrete A mixture of cement, sand, and gravel with water.
Concrete block Precast hollow or solid blocks of concrete.
Condemn To legally declare unfit for use.
Condensation The formation of frost or drops of water on inside walls when warm vapor inside a room meets a cold wall or window.
Conductor In architecture: a drain pipe leading from the roof; in electricity: anything that permits the passage of an electric current.
Conductor pipe A round, square, or rectangular metal pipe used to lead water from the roof to the sewer.
Conduit A channel built to convey water or other fluids; a drain or sewer. In electrical work, a channel that carries wires for protection and for safety.
Construction loan A mortgage loan to be used to pay for labor and materials going into the house. Money is usually advanced to the builder as construction progresses and is repaid when the house is completed and sold.
Continuous beam A beam that has three or more supports.
Contractor A person offering to build for a specified sum of money.
Convector A heat-transfer surface which uses convection currents to transfer heat.
Coping The top course of a masonry wall which projects to protect the wall from the weather.

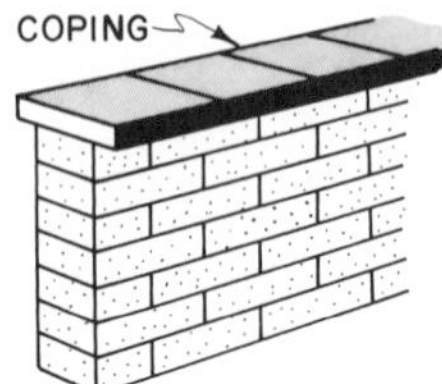

Corbel A projection in a masonry wall made by setting courses beyond the lower ones.

Corner bead A metal molding built into plaster corners to prevent the accidental breaking off of the plaster.
Cornice The part of a roof that projects out from the wall.
Counterflashing A flashing used under the regular flashing.
Course A continuous row of stone or brick of uniform height.
Court An open space surrounded partly or entirely by a building.
Crawl space The shallow space below the floor of a house built above the ground. It is surrounded by the foundation wall.
Cricket A roof device used at intersections to divert water.

Cripple A structural member that is cut less than full length, such as a studding piece above a window or door.

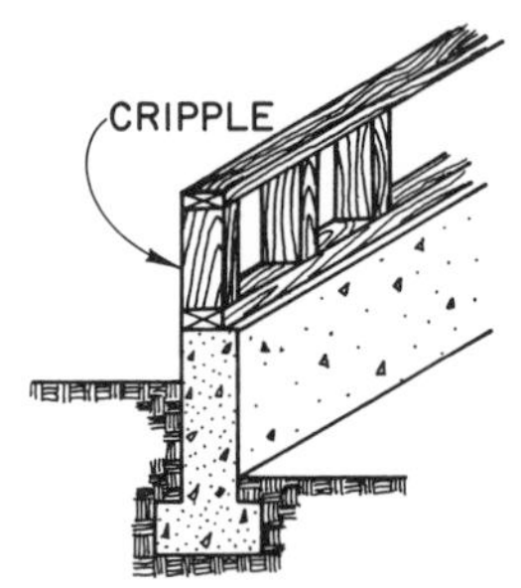

Cross bracing Boards nailed diagonally across studs or other boards to make framework rigid.
Cross bridging Bracing between floor joists to add stiffness to the floors.

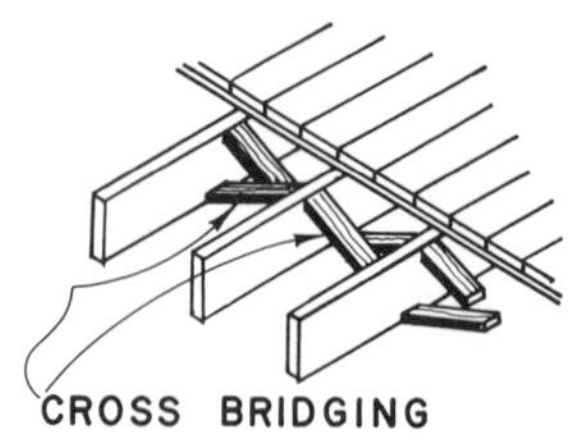

Crosshatch Lines drawn closely together at an angle of 45 degrees, to show a sectional cut.
Cull Building material rejected as below standard grade.
Culvert A passage for water below ground level.
Cupola A small structure built on top of a roof.

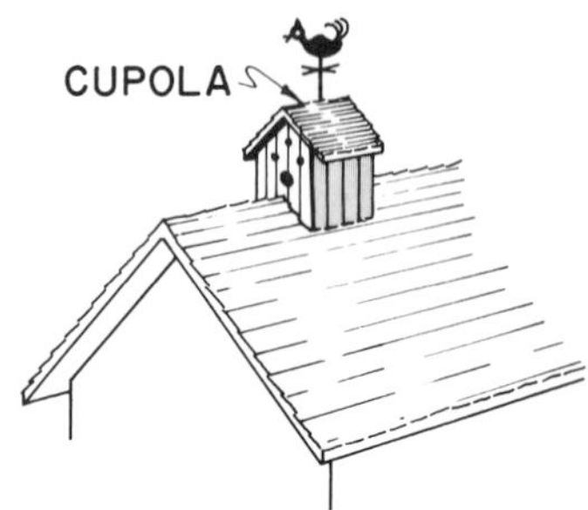

Curb A very low wall.
Cure To allow concrete to dry slowly by keeping it moist to allow maximum strength.
Curtain wall An exterior wall which provides no structural support.

Damp course A layer of waterproof material.
Damper A movable plate which regulates the draft of a stove, fireplace, or furnace.
Datum A reference point of starting elevations used in mapping and surveying.
Deadening Construction intended to prevent the passage of sound.
Dead load All the weight in a structure made up of unmovable materials. See also Loads.
Decay The disintegration of wood through the action of fungi.
Dehumidify To reduce the moisture content in the air.
Density The number of people living in a calculated area of land such as a square mile or square kilometer.
Depreciation Loss of value.
Designer A person who designs houses but is not a registered architect.
Detail To provide specific instruction with a drawing, dimensions, notes, or specifications.

Dimension building material Building material which has been precut to specific sizes.

Dimension line A line with arrowheads at either end to show the distance between two points.

Dome A hemispherical roof form.

Doorstop The strips on the doorjambs against which the door closes.

Dormer A structure projecting from a sloping roof to accommodate a window.

Double glazing A pane made of two pieces of glass with air space between and sealed to provide insulation.

Double header Two or more timbers joined for strength.

Double hung A window having top and bottom sashes each capable of movement up and down.

Downspout A pipe for carrying rainwater from the roof to the ground.

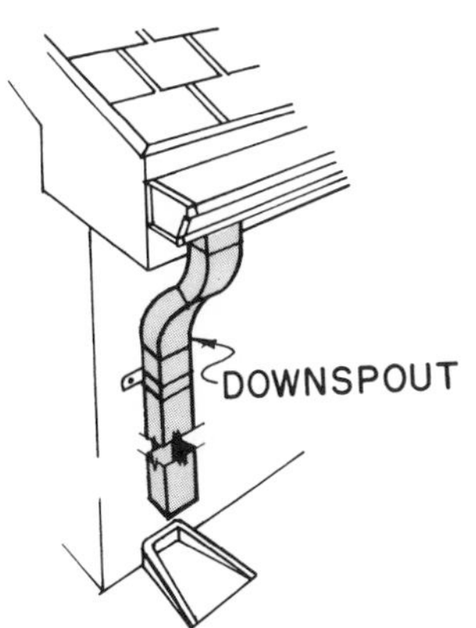

Drain A pipe for carrying waste water.

Dressed lumber Lumber machined and smoothed at the mill. Usually ½ inch less than nominal (rough) size.

Drip A projecting construction member or groove below the member to prevent rainwater from running down the face of a wall or to protect the bottom of a door or window from leakage.

Dry rot A term applied to many types of decay, especially an advanced stage when the wood can be easily crushed to a dry powder. The term is actually inaccurate because all fungi require considerable moisture for growth.

Dry-wall construction Interior wall covering other than plaster, usually referred to as gypsum-board surfacing.

Dry well A pit located on porous ground walled up with rock which allows water to seep through the pit. Used for the disposal of rainwater or the effluent from a septic tank.

Ducts Sheet-metal conductors for warm- and cold-air distribution.

Easement The right to use land owned by another, such as a utility company's right-of-way.

Eave That part of a roof that projects over a wall.

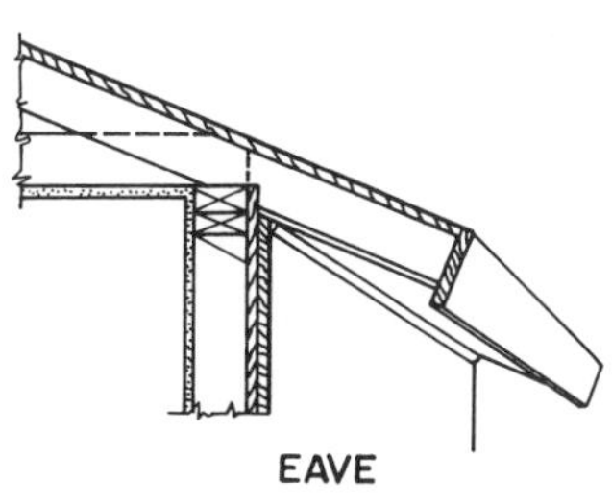

Efflorescence Whitish powder that forms on the surface of bricks or stone walls due to evaporation of moisture containing salts.

Effluent The liquid discharge from a septic tank after bacterial treatment.

Elastic limit The limit to which a material may be bent or pulled out of shape and still return to its former shape and dimensions.

Elbow An L-shaped pipe fitting.

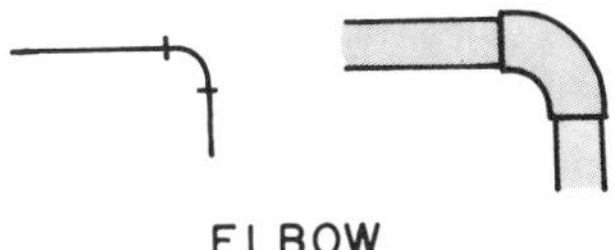

Elevation The drawings of the front, side, or rear face of a building.

Ell An extension or wing of a building at right angles to the main section.

Embellish To add decoration.

Eminent domain The right of the local government to condemn for public use.

Enamel Paint with a considerable amount of varnish. It produces a hard, glossy surface.

Equity The interest in or value of real estate the owner has in excess of the mortgage indebtedness.

Escutcheon The hardware on a door to accommodate the knob and keyhole.

Excavation A cavity or pit produced by digging the earth in preparation for construction.

Fabrication Work done on parts of a structure at the factory before delivery to the building site.

Facade The face or front elevation of a building.

Face brick A brick used on the outside face of a wall.

Facing A finish material used to cover another.

Fascia A vertical board nailed on the ends of the rafters. It is part of the cornice.

Fatigue A weakening of structural members.

Federal Housing Administration (FHA) A government agency that ensures loans made by regular lending institutions.

Felt papers Papers, sometimes tar impregnated, used on roofs and side walls to give protection against dampness and leaks.

Fenestration The arrangement of windows.

Fiberboard A building board made with fibrous material—used as an insulating board.

Filled insulation A loose insulating material poured from bags or blown by machines into walls.

Finish lumber Dressed wood used for building trim.

Firebrick A brick that is especially hard and heat-resistant. Used in fireplaces.

Fireclay A grade of clay that can withstand a large quantity of heat. Used for firebrick.

Fire cut The angular cut at the end of a joist designed to rest on a brick wall.

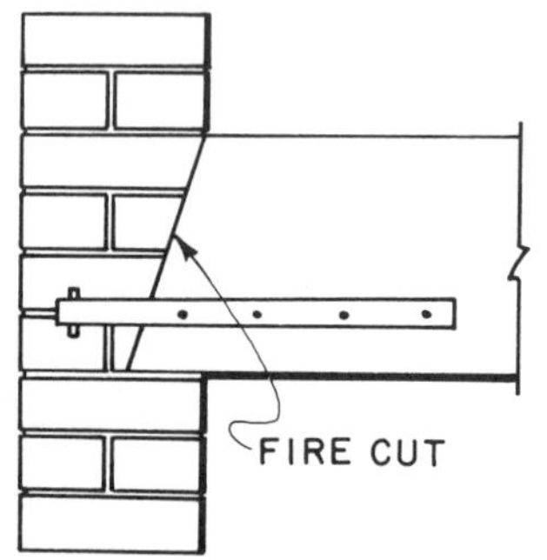

Fire door A door that will resist fire.

Fire partition A partition designed to restrict the spread of fire.

Fire stop Obstruction across air passages in buildings to prevent the spread of hot gases and flames. A horizontal blocking between wall studs.

Fished A splice strengthened by metal pieces on the sides.

Fixed light A permanently sealed window.

Fixture A piece of electric or plumbing equipment.

Flagging Cut stone, slate, or marble used on floors.

Flagstone Flat stone used for floors, steps, walks, or walls.

Flashing The material used for and the process of making watertight the roof intersections and other exposed places on the outside of the house.

Flat roof A roof with just enough pitch to let water drain.

Flitch beam A built-up beam formed by a metal plate sandwiched between two wood members and bolted together for additional strength.

Floating Spreading plaster, stucco, or cement on walls with use of a tool called a float.

Floor plan The top view of a building at a specified floor level. A floor plan includes all vertical details at or above windowsill levels.

Floor plug An electrical outlet flush with the floor.

Flue The opening in a chimney through which smoke passes.

Flue lining Terra-cotta pipe used for the inner lining of chimneys.

Flush surface A continuous surface without an angle.

Footing An enlargement at the lower end of a wall, pier, or column, to distribute the load into the ground.

Footing form A wooden or steel structure placed around the footing that will hold the concrete to the desired shape and size.

Framing (western) The wood skeleton of a building.

Frieze The flat board of cornice trim which is fastened to the wall.

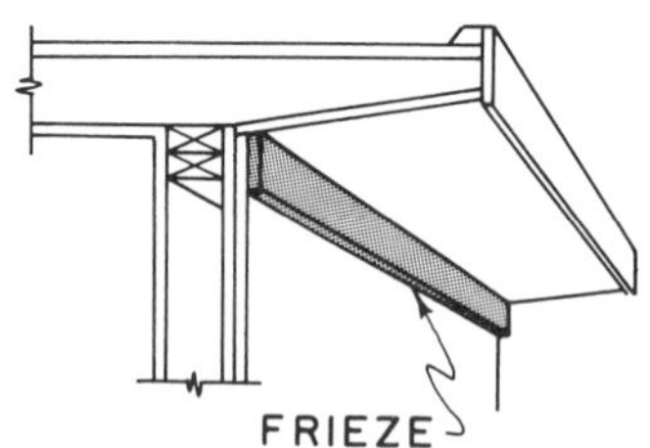

Frost line The depth of frost penetration into the soil.

Fumigate To destroy harmful insect or animal life with fumes.

Furring Narrow strips of board nailed upon the wall and ceilings to form a straight surface for the purpose of attaching wallboards or ceiling tile.

Fuse A strip of soft metal inserted in an electric circuit and designed to melt and open the circuit should the current exceed a predetermined value.

Gable The triangular end of an exterior wall above the eaves.

Gable roof A roof which slopes from two sides only.

Galvanize A lead and zinc bath treatment to prevent rusting.

Gambrel roof A symmetrical roof with two different pitches or slopes on each side.

Garret An attic.

Girder A horizontal beam supporting the floor joists.

Glazing Placing of glass in windows or doors.

Grade The level of the ground around a building.

Gradient The slant of a rod, piping, or the ground, expressed in percent.

Graphic symbols Symbolic representations used in drawing which simplify presentations of complicated items.

Gravel stop A strip of metal with a vertical lip used to retain the gravel around the edge of a built-in roof.

Green lumber Lumber that still contains moisture or sap.

Grout A thin cement mortar used for leveling and filling masonry holes.

Gusset A plywood or metal plate used to strengthen the joints of a truss.

Gutter A trough for carrying off water.

Gypsum board A board made of plaster with a covering of paper.

Half timber A frame construction of heavy timbers in which the spaces are filled in with masonry.

Hanger An iron strap used to support a joist beam or pipe.

Hardpan A compacted layer of soils.

Head The upper frame on a door or window.

Header The horizontal supporting member above openings as a lintel. Also one or more pieces of lumber supporting ends of joists. Used in framing openings of stairs and chimneys.

Headroom The clear space between floor line and ceiling, as in a stairway.

Hearth That part of the floor directly in front of the fireplace, and the floor inside the fireplace on which the fire is built. It is made of fire-resistant masonry.

Heel plate A plate at the ends of a truss.

Hip rafter The diagonal rafter that extends from the plate to the ridge to form the hip.

Hip roof A roof with four sloping sides.

House drain Horizontal sewer piping within a building which receives wastes from the soil stacks.

House sewer The watertight soil pipe extending from the exterior of the foundation wall to the public sewer.

Humidifier A mechanical device which controls the amount of water vapor to be added to the atmosphere.

Humidistat An instrument used for measuring and controlling moisture in the air.

I beam A steel beam with an I-shaped cross section.

Indirect lighting Artificial light that is bounced off ceiling and walls for general lighting.

Insulating board Any board suitable for insulating purposes, usually manufactured board made from vegetable fibers, such as fiber board.

Insulation Materials for obstructing the passage of sound, heat, or cold from one surface to another.

Interior trim General term for all the finish molding, casing, baseboard, etc.

Jack rafter A short rafter, usually used on hip roofs.

Jalousie A type of window consisting of a number of long, thin, hinged panels.

Jamb The sides of a doorway or window opening.

Jerry built Poor construction.

Joints The meeting of two separate pieces of material for a common bond.

Joist A horizontal structural member which supports the floor system or ceiling system.

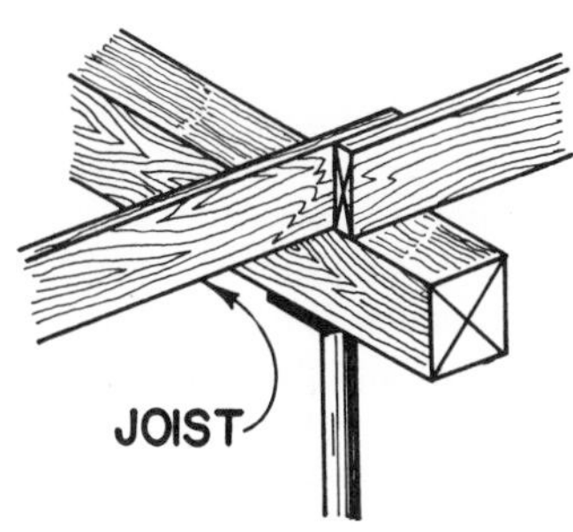

Kalamein door A fireproof door with a metal covering.

Keystone The top, wedge-shaped stone of an arch.

Kiln A heating chamber for drying lumber.

King post In a roof truss, the central upright piece.

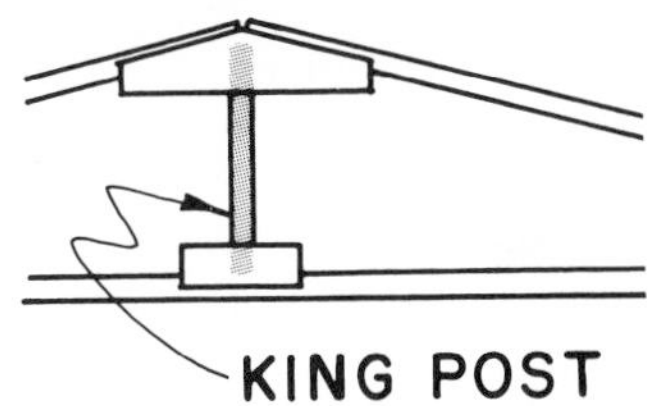

Knee brace A corner brace, fastened at an angle from wall stud to rafter, stiffening a wood or steel frame to prevent angular movement.

Knee wall Low wall resulting from one-and-one-half-story construction.

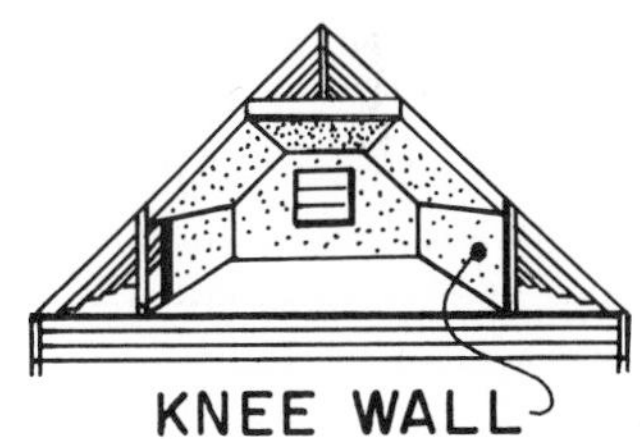

Knob and tube Electric wiring through walls where insulated wires are supported with porcelain knobs and tubes when passing through wood construction members.

Lally column A steel column used as a support for girders and beams.

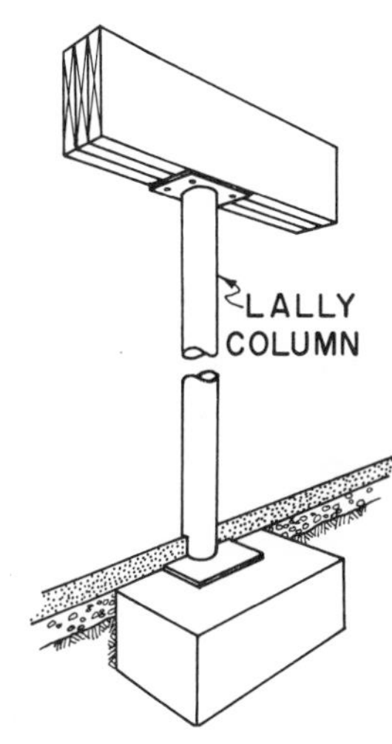

Laminated beam A beam made by bonding together several layers of material.

Landing A platform in a flight of steps.

Landscape architect A professional person who utilizes and adapts land for people's use.

Lap joint A joint produced by lapping two pieces of material.

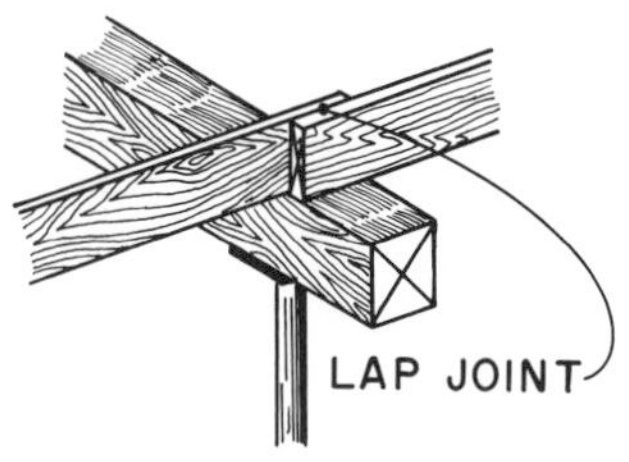

Lath (metal) Sheet-metal screening used as a base for plastering.

Lath (wood) A wooden strip nailed to studding and joists to which plaster is applied.

Lattice A grille or open work made by crossing strips of wood or metal.

Lavatory A washbasin or a room equipped with a washbasin.

Leaching bed A system of trenches that carries wastes from sewers. It is constructed in sandy soils or in earth filled with stones or gravel.

Leader A vertical pipe or downspout that carries rainwater from the gutter to the ground.

Lean-to A shed whose rafters lean against another building or other part of the same building.

Ledger A wood strip nailed to the lower side of a girder to provide a bearing surface for joists.

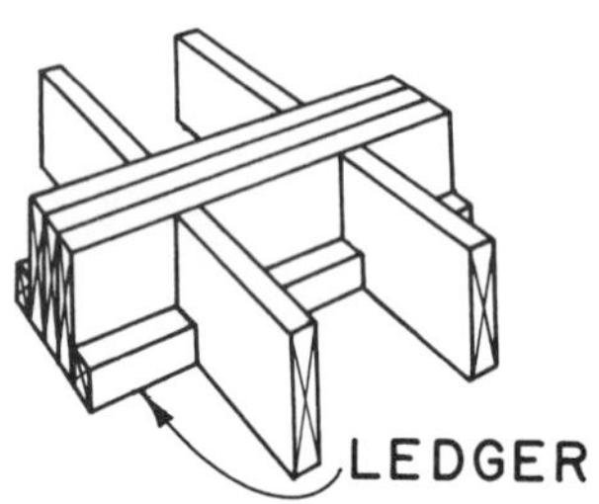

Lessee The one who leases.

Lessor The owner of leased property.

Lien A legal claim on a property, which may be exercised in default of payment of a debt.

Lineal foot A measurement of 1 foot along a straight line.

Lintel A horizontal piece of wood, stone, or steel across the top of door and window openings to bear the weight of the walls above the opening.

Loads Live load: the total of all moving and variable loads that may be placed upon a building. Dead load: the weight of all permanent, stationary construction including a building.

Load-bearing walls Walls that support weight from above as well as their own weight.

Loggia A roofed, open passage along the front or side of a building. It is often at an upper level, and it often has a series of columns on either or both sides.

Lookout A horizontal framing member extending from studs out to end of rafters.

Lot line The line forming the legal boundary of a piece of property.

Louver A set of fixed or movable slats adjusted to provide both shelter and ventilation.

Mansard roof A roof with two slopes on each side, with the lower slope much steeper than the upper.

Mantel A shelf over a fireplace.

Market price What property can be sold for at a given time.

Market value What property is worth at a given time.

Masonry Anything built with stone, brick, tiles, or concrete.

Meeting rail The horizontal rails of a double-hung sash that fit together when the window is closed.

Member A single piece in structure that is complete in itself.

Metal tie A strip of metal used to fasten construction members together.

Metal wall ties Strips of corrugated metal used to tie a brick veneer wall to framework.

Mildew A mold on wood caused by fungi.

Millwork The finish woodwork in a building, such as cabinets and trim.

Mineral wool An insulating material made into a fibrous form from mineral slag.

Modular construction Construction in which the size of the building and the building materials are based on a common unit of measure.

Moisture barrier A material such as specially treated paper that retards the passage of vapor or moisture into walls and prevents condensation within the walls.

Monolithic Concrete construction poured and cast in one piece without joints.

Monument A boundary marker set by surveyors to locate property lines.

Mortar A mixture of cement, sand, and water, used as a bonding agent by the mason for binding bricks and stone.

Mortgage A pledging of property, conditional on payment of the debt in full.

Mortgagee The lender of money to the mortgagor.

Mortgagor The owner who mortages property in return for a loan.

Mosaic Small colored tile, glass, stone, or similar material arranged on an adhesive ground to produce a decorative surface.

Mud room A small room or entranceway where muddy overshoes and wet garments can be removed before entering other rooms.

Mullion A vertical bar in a window separating two windows.

Muntin A small bar separating the glass lights in a window.

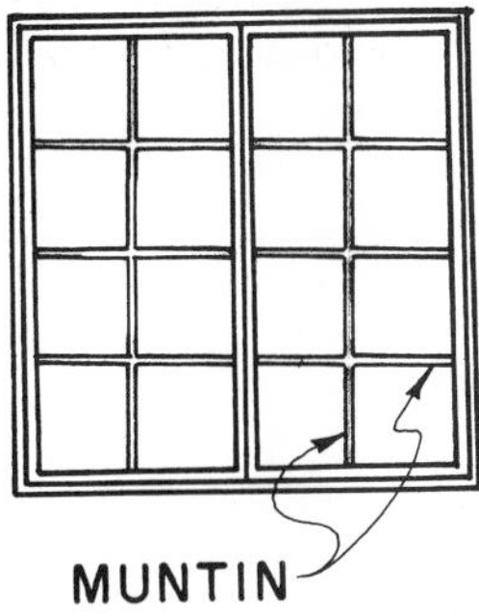

Newel A post supporting the handrail at the top or bottom of a stairway.

Nominal dimension Dimensions for finished lumber in which the stated dimension is usually larger than the actual dimension. These dimensions are usually larger by an amount required to smooth a board.

Nonbearing wall A dividing wall that does not support a vertical load other than its own weight.

Nonferrous metal Metal containing no iron, such as copper, brass, or aluminum.

Nosing The rounded edge of a stair tread.

Obscure glass Sheet glass that is made translucent instead of transparent.

On center Measurement from the center of one member to the center of another (noted oc).

Open-end mortgage A mortgage that permits the remaining amount of the loan to be increased, as for improvements, by mutual agreement of the lender and borrower, without rewriting the mortgage.

Orientation The positioning of a house on a lot in relation to the sun, wind, view, and noise.

Outlet Any kind of electrical box allowing current to be drawn from the electrical system for lighting or appliances.

Overhang The horizontal distance that a roof projects beyond a wall.

Panelboard The center for controlling electrical circuits.

Parapet A low wall or railing around the edge of a roof.

Parging A thin coat of plaster applied to masonry surfaces for smoothing purposes.

Parquet flooring Flooring, usually of wood, laid in an alternating or inlaid patter to form various designs.

Partition An interior wall that separates two rooms.

Party wall A wall between two adjoining buildings in which both owners share, such as a common wall between row houses.

Patio An open court.

Pediment The triangular space forming the gable end of a low-pitched roof. A similar form is often used as a decoration over doors in classic architecture.

Penny A term for the length of a nail, abbreviated d.

Periphery The entire outside edge of an object.

Perspective A drawing of an object in a three-dimensional form on a plane surface. An object drawn as it would appear to the eye.

Pier A block of concrete supporting the floor of a building.

Pilaster A portion of a square column, usually set within or against a wall for the purpose of strengthening the wall. Also a decorative column attached to a wall.

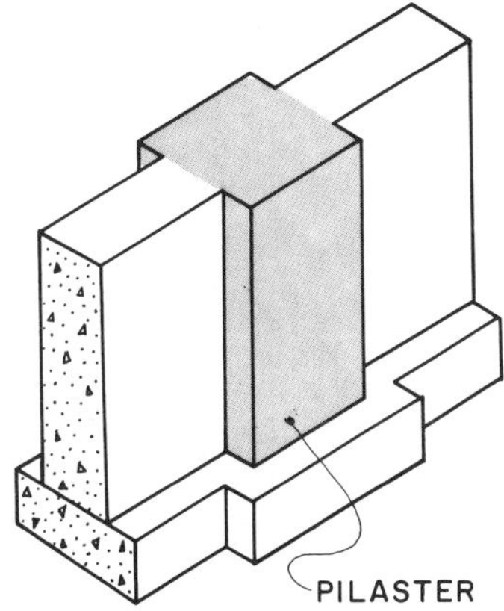

Piles Long posts driven into the soil in swampy locations, or whenever it is difficult to secure a firm foundation, upon which the foundation footing is laid.

Pillar A column used for supporting parts of a structure.

Pinnacle Projecting or ornamental cap on the high point of a roof.

Plan A horizontal, graphic representational section of a building, showing the walls, doors, windows, stairs, chimneys, and surrounding objects as walks and landscape.

Planks Material 2 or 3 inches (50 or 75 mm) thick and more than 4 inches (100 mm) wide, such as joists, flooring, and the like.

Plaster A mortarlike composition used for covering walls and ceilings. Usually made of portland cement mixed with sand and water.

Plasterboard A board made of plastering material covered on both sides with heavy paper. It is often used instead of plaster. Also called gypsum board.

Plaster ground A nailer strip included in plaster walls to act as a gage for thickness of plaster and to give a nailing support for finish trim around openings and near the base of the wall.

Plat A map or chart of an area showing boundaries of lots and other pieces of property.

Plate The top horizontal member of a row of studs in a frame wall to carry the trusses of a roof or to carry the rafters directly. Also a shoe or base member, as of a partition or other frame.

Plate cut The cut in a rafter which rests upon the plate. It is also called the seat cut or birdmouth.

Plate glass A high-quality sheet of glass used in large windows.

Plenum system A system of heating or air conditioning in which the air is forced through a chamber connected to distributing ducts.
Plot The land on which a building stands.
Plow To cut a groove running in the same direction as the grain of the wood.
Plumb Said of an object when it is in true vertical position as determined by a plumb bob.
Plywood A piece of wood made of three or more layers of veneer joined with glue and usually laid with the grain of adjoining plies at right angles.
Porch A covered area attached to a house at an entrance.
Portico A roof supported by columns, whether attached to a building or wholly by itself.
Portland cement A hydraulic cement, extremely hard, formed by burning silica, lime, and alumina together and then grinding up the mixture.
Post A perpendicular supporting member.
Post and beam construction Wall construction consisting of posts rather than studs.
Precast Concrete shapes made separately before being used in a structure.
Prefabricated houses Houses that are built in sections or component parts in a factory, and then assembled at the site.
Primary coat The first coat of paint.
Principal The original amount of money loaned.
Purlin A structural member spanning from truss to truss and supporting the rafters.

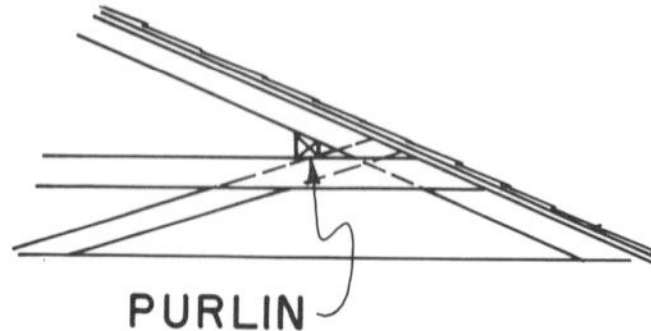

Quad An enclosed court.
Quarry tile A machine-made, unglazed tile.
Quoins Large squared stones set in the corners of a masonry building for appearance.

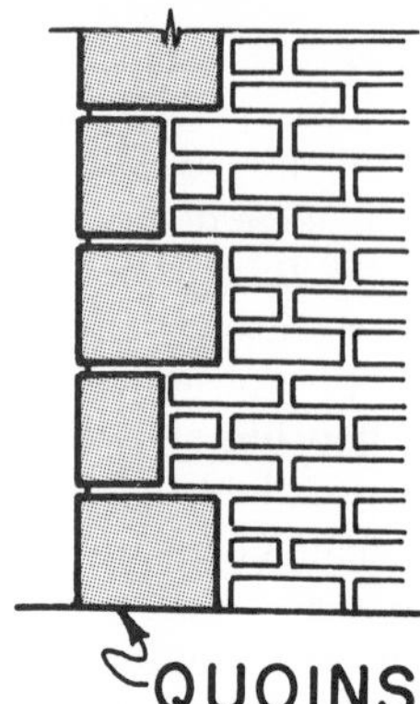

Radiant heating A system using heating elements in the floors, ceilings, or walls to radiate heat into the room.
Rafters Structural members used to frame a roof. Several types are common, hip, jack, valley, and cripple.
Raglin The open joint in masonry to receive flashing.
Realtor A real estate broker who is a member of a local chapter of the National Association of Real Estate Boards.
Register The open end of a duct in a room for warm or cool air.
Reinforced concrete Concrete in which steel bars or webbing has been embedded for strength.
Rendering The art of shading or coloring a drawing.
Restoration Rebuilding a structure so it will appear in its original form.
Restrictions Limitations on the use of real estate as set by law or contained in a deed.
Retaining wall A wall to hold back an earth embankment.

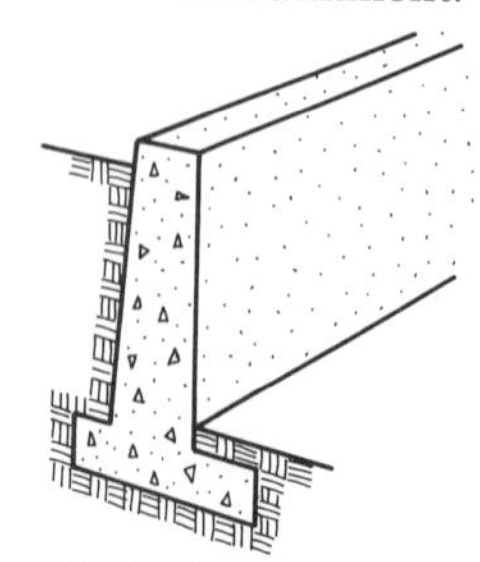

Rheostat An instrument for regulating electric current.
Ribbon A support for joists. A board set into studs that are cut to support joists.

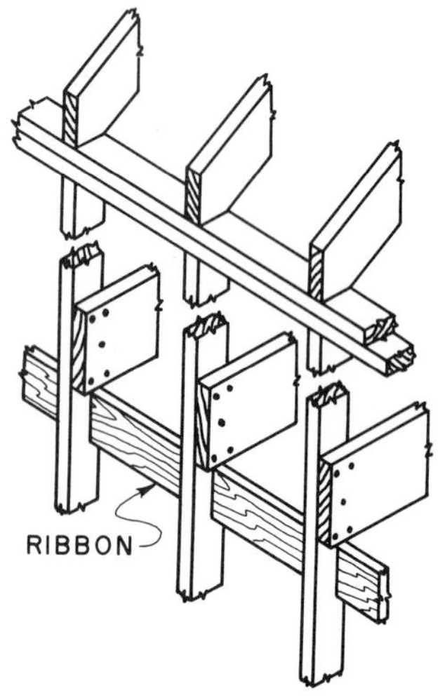

Ridge The top edge of the roof where two slopes meet.
Ridge cap A wood or metal cap used over roofing at the ridge.
Riprap Stones placed on a slope to prevent erosion. Also broken stone used for foundation fill.
Rise The vertical height of a roof.
Riser The vertical board in a stairway between two treads.
Rock wool An insulating material that looks like wool but is composed of such substances as granite or silica.
Rodding Stirring freshly poured concrete with a vibrator to remove air pockets.
Roll roofing Roofing material of fiber and asphalt.
Rough floor The subfloor on which the finished floor is laid.
Rough hardware All the hardware used in a house, such as nails and bolts, that cannot be seen in the completed house.
Roughing in Putting up the skeleton of the building.
Rough lumber Lumber as it comes from the saw.
Rough opening Any unfinished opening in the framing of a building.

Run Stonework having irregular-shaped units and no indication of systematic course work. The horizontal distance covered by a flight of stairs. The length of a rafter.

Saddle The ridge covering of a roof designed to carry water from the back of chimneys. Also called a cricket. A threshold.

Safety factor The ultimate strength of the material divided by the allowable working load. The element of safety needed to make certain that there will be no structural failures.

Sand finish A final plaster coat; a skim coat.

Sap All the fluids in a tree.

Sash The movable framework in which window panes are set.

Scab A small wood member used to join other members which is fastened on the outside face.

Scarfing A joint between two pieces of wood which allows them to be spliced lengthwise.

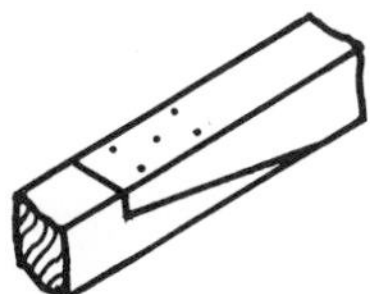

SCARFING

Schedule A list of parts or details.

Scratch coat The first coat of plaster. It is scratched to provide a good bond for the next coat.

Screed A guide for the correct thickness of plaster or concrete being placed on surfaces.

Scuttle A small opening in a ceiling to provide access to an attic or roof.

Seasoning Drying out of green lumber, either in an oven or kiln or by exposing it to air.

Second mortgage A mortgage made by a home buyer to raise money for a down payment required under the first mortgage.

Section The drawing of an object that is cut to show the interior. Also, a panel construction used in walls, floors, ceilings, or roofs.

Seepage pit A pit or cesspool into which sewage drains from a septic tank, and which is so constructed that the liquid waste seeps through the sides of the pit into the ground.

Septic tank A concrete or steel tank where sewage is reduced partially by bacterial action. About half the sewage solids become gases which escape back through the vent stack in the house. The other solids and liquids flow from the tank into the ground through a tile bed.

Service connection The electric wires to the building from the outside power lines.

Set The hardening of cement or plaster.

Set back A zoning restriction on the location of the home on a lot.

Settlement Compression of the soil or the members in a structure.

Shakes Thick hand-cut shingles.

Sheathing The structural covering of boards or wallboards, placed over exterior studding or rafters of a structure.

Sheathing paper A paper barrier against wind and moisture applied between sheathing and outer wall covering.

Shed roof A flat roof slanting in one direction.

SHED ROOF

Shim A piece of material used to level or fill in the space between two surfaces.

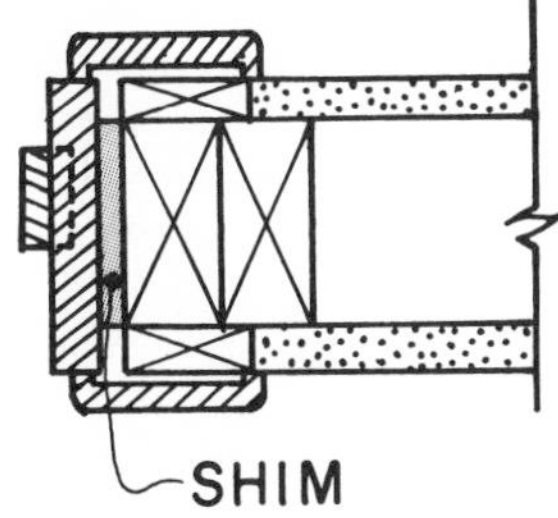

Shingles Thin pieces of wood or other materials which overlap each other in covering a roof. The number and kind needed depend on the steepness of the roof slope and other factors. Kinds of shingles include tile shingles, slate shingles, asbestos-cement shingles, and asphalt shingles.

Shiplap Boards with lapped joints along their edges.

Shoe mold The small mold against the baseboard at the floor.

Shoring Lumber placed in a slanted position to support the structure of a building temporarily.

Siding The outside boards of an exterior wall.

Sill The horizontal exterior member below a window or door opening. Also the wood member placed directly on top of the foundation wall in wood-frame construction.

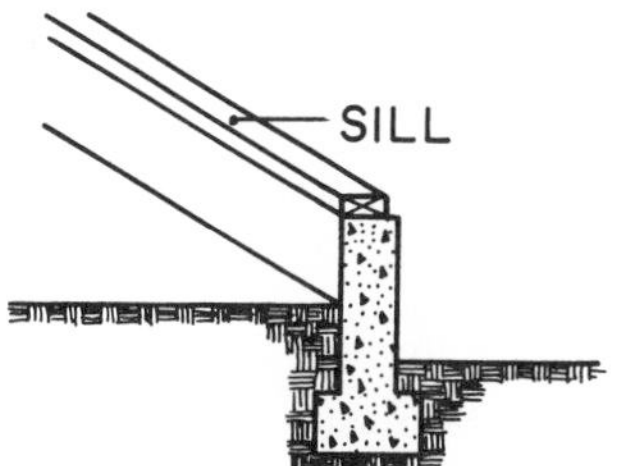

Skeleton construction Construction where the frame carries all the weight.

Skylight An opening in the roof for admitting light.

Slab foundation A reinforced concrete floor and foundation system.

Sleepers Strips of wood, usually 2 × 2's, laid over a slab floor to which finished wood flooring is nailed.

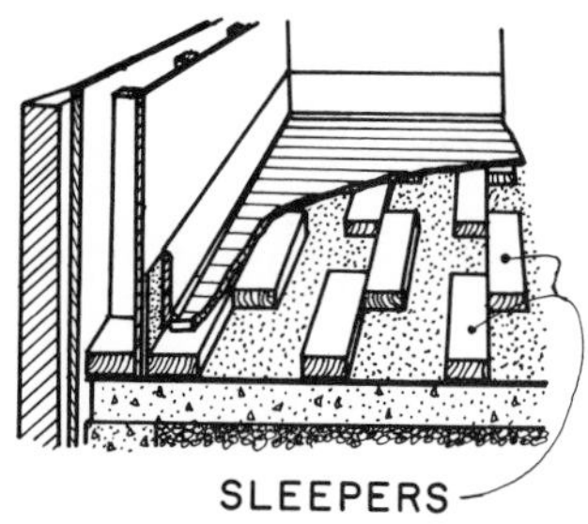

Smoke chamber The portion of a chimney flue located directly over the fireplace.

Soffit The undersurface of a projecting structure.

Softwood Wood from trees having needles rather than broad leaves. The term does not necessarily refer to the softness of the wood.

Soil stack The main vertical pipe which receives waste from all fixtures.

Solar heat Heat from the sun's rays.

Sole The horizontal framing member directly under the studs.

Spacing The distance between structural members.

Spackle To cover wallboard joints with plaster.

Span The distance between structural supports.

Specification The written or printed direction regarding the details of a building or other construction.

Spike A large heavy nail.

Splice Joining of two similar members in a straight line.

Stack A vertical pipe.

Stakeout Marking the foundation layout with stakes.

Steel-framing Skeleton framing with structural steel beams.

Steening Brickwork without mortar.

Stile A vertical member of a door, window, or panel.

Stirrup A metal U-shaped strap used to support framing members.

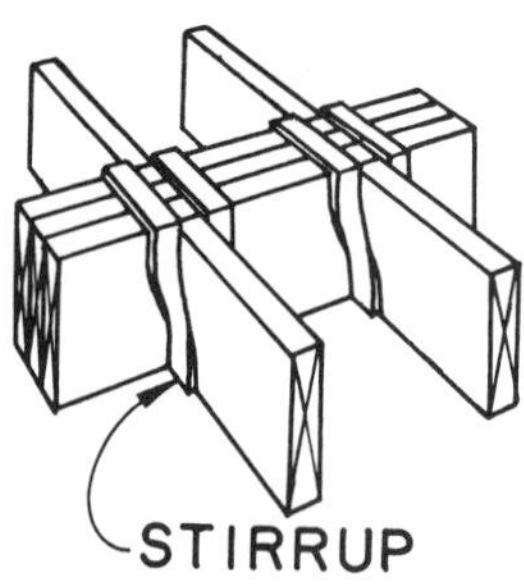

Stock Common sizes of building materials and equipment available from most commercial industries.

Stool An inside windowsill.

Stop A small strip to hold a door or window sash in place.

Storm door or window An extra door or extra window placed outside an ordinary door or window for added protection against cold.

Storm sewer A sewer that is designed to carry away water from storms, but not sewage.

Stress Any force acting upon a part or member used in construction.

Stress-cover construction Construction consisting of panels or sections with wood frameworks to which plywood or other sheet material is bonded with glue so that the covering carries a large part of the loads.

Stretcher course A row of masonry in a wall with the long side of the units exposed to the exterior.

Stringer The sides of a flight of stairs. The supporting member cut to receive the treads and risers.

Stripping Removal of concrete forms from the hardened concrete.

Stucco Any of various plasters used for covering walls, especially an exterior wall covering in which cement is used.

Stud Upright beams in the framework of a building. Usually referred to as 2 × 4's, and spaced at 16 inches from center to center.

Subfloor The rough flooring under the finish floor that rests on the floor joists.

Sump A pit in a basement floor to collect water, into which a sump pump is placed to remove the water through sewer pipes.

Surfaced lumber Lumber that is dressed by running it through a planer.

Surveyor A person skilled in land measurement.

Swale A drainage channel formed where two slopes meet.

Tamp To ram and concentrate soil.

Tar A dark heavy oil used in roofing and roof surfacing.

Tempered Thoroughly mixed cement or mortar.

Tensile strength The greatest stretching stress a structural member can bear without breaking or cracking.

Termite shield Sheet metal used to block the passage of termites.

Thermal conductor A substance capable of transmitting heat.

Thermostat A device for automatically controlling the supply of heat.

Threshold The beveled piece of stone, wood, or metal over which the door swings. It is sometimes called a carpet strip, or a saddle.

Throat A passage directly above the fireplace opening where a damper is set.

Tie A structural member used to bind others together.

Timber Lumber with a cross section larger than 4 by 6 inches (100 by 150 mm), for posts, sills, and girders.

Title insurance An agreement to pay the buyer for losses in title of ownership.
Toe nail To drive nails at an angle.
Tolerance The acceptable variance of dimensions from a standard size.
Tongue A projection on the edge of wood that joins with a similarly shaped groove.

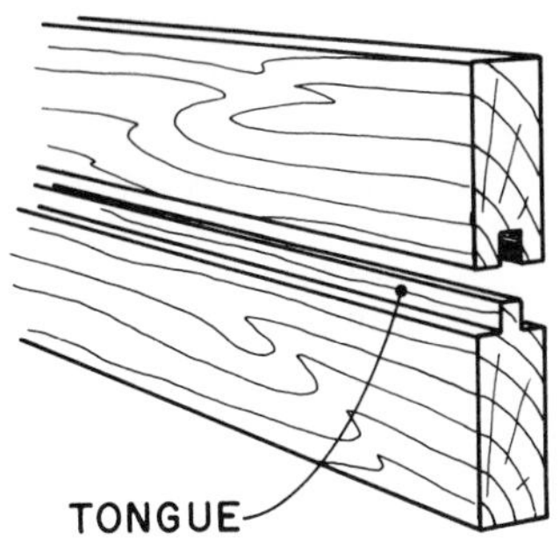

Total run The total of all the tread widths in a stair.
Transom A small window over a door.
Tread The step or horizontal member of a stair.
Trimmers Single or double joists or rafters that run around an opening in framing construction.
Truss A triangular-shaped unit for supporting roof loads over long spans.

Underpinning A foundation replacement or reinforcement for temporary braced supports.
Undressed lumber Lumber that is not squared or finished smooth.
Unit construction Construction which includes two or more preassembled walls, together with floor and ceiling construction, for shipment to the building site.

Valley The internal angle formed by the two slopes of a roof.
Valley jacks Rafters that run from a ridge board to a valley rafter.
Valley rafter The diagonal rafter forming the intersection of two sloping roofs.
Valve A device which regulates the flow of material in a pipe.

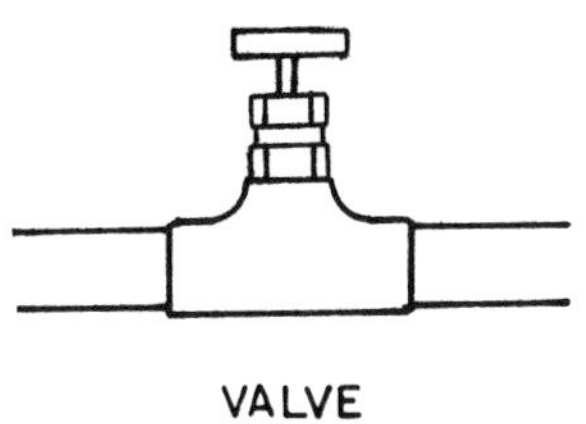

VALVE

Vapor barrier A watertight material used to prevent the passage of moisture or water vapor into and through walls.
Veneer A thin covering of valuable material over a less expensive material.
Vent A screened opening for ventilation.
Ventilation The process of supplying and removing air by natural or mechanical means to or from any space.
Vent pipes Small ventilating pipes extending from each fixture of a plumbing system to the vent stack.
Vent stack The upper portion of a soil or waste stack above the highest fixture.
Vergeboard The board which serves as the eaves finish on the gable end of a building.
Vestibule A small lobby or entrance room.
Vitreous Pertaining to a composition of materials that resemble glass.
Volume The amount of space occupied by an object. Measured in cubic units.

Wainscot Facing for the lower part of an interior wall.
Wallboard Wood pulp, gypsum, or similar materials made into large rigid sheets that may be fastened to the frame of a building to provide a surface finish.
Warp Any change from a true or plane surface. Warping includes bow, crook, cup, and twist.
Warranty deed A guarantee that the property is as promised.
Wash The slant upon a sill, capping, etc., to allow the water to run off.
Waste stack A vertical pipe in a plumbing system which carries the discharge from any fixture.
Waterproof Material or construction which prevents the passage of water.
Water table A projecting mold near the base on the outside of a building to turn the rainwater outward. Also the level of subterranean water.
Watt A unit of electrical energy.
Weathering The mechanical or chemical disintegration and discoloration of the surface of exterior building materials.
Weatherstrip A strip of metal or fabric fastened along the edges of windows and doors to reduce drafts and heat loss.
Weep hole An opening at the bottom of a wall to allow the drainage of water.
Well opening A floor opening for a stairway.

Zoning Building restrictions as to size, location, and type of structures to be built in specific areas.

SECTION 25

Architectural Synonyms

Architectural terms are standard. Nevertheless, architects, draftsmen, and builders often use different terms for the same object. Geographic location can influence a person's word choice. For instance, what is referred to as a faucet in one area of the country is called a tap in another area. What one person calls an attic, another calls a garret, and still another a loft. Each entry below is followed by a word or words which someone—somewhere—uses to refer to the entry.

Abutment: support
Acoustics: sound control
Adobe brick: firebrick, fireclay brick
Aeration: ventilation
Aggregate: cement matrix, concrete, mortar, plaster
Air-dried: air-seasoned, seasoned
Air-seasoned: air-dried, seasoned
Anchorage: footing, footer
Anchor bolt: securing bolt, sill bolt
Apartment: tenement, multiple dwelling, condominium
Arcade: corridor
Armored cable: conduit, tubing, metal casing, BX
Asbestos: fireproof material
Attic: garret, cot loft, half story, loft
Automatic heat control: thermostat
Auxiliary door: storm door
Auxiliary window: storm window
Awning: overhang, canopy

Backfill: fill, earth
Back plaster: parget
Baffle: screen
Baked clay: terra-cotta
Balcony: ledge, gallery, platform, veranda
Baseboard: mopboard, finish board, skirting
Basement: cellar, storm cellar, cyclone cellar, substructure
Base mold: shoe mold
Batten: cleat
Bead: thin molding
Beams: rafter, shaft, timber, girder, wood, spar, lumber
Bearing partition: support partition, bearing wall
Bearing plate: sill, load plate
Bearing soil: compact soil
Belvedere: gazebo, pavilion
Bermuda roof: hip roof
Beveled: mitered, chamfered
Bibs: faucets, taps
Birdmouth: plate cut, seat cut, seat of a rafter
Blanket insulation: sheet insulation
Blind: window shade
Blind nailing: secret nailing
Board insulation: heat barrier
Border: curb, parapet
Bracing: trussing
Breezeway: dogtrot
Brick: stone, masonry
Bridging: bracing, joining, cross supports, strutting
Buck: doorframe
Builder: contractor
Building area: setback, building lines
Building board: compo board, insulating board, dry wall, gypsum board, Sheetrock, wallboard, rocklath, plasterboard
Building code: building regulations
Building lines: setback, building area
Building paper: felt, tar paper, sheathing paper, construction paper, roll roofing
Building regulations: building code
Building steel: structural steel
Buttress: support, shield
BX: conduit, tubing, metal casing, armored cable

Candela: footcandle
Canopy: awning, overhang
Caps: coping

Carpenter's cloth: wire mesh, screen, wire cloth
Carport: car shed, open garage
Carriage: stringer
Carriage bolt: square bolt, threaded rod
Casement window: hinged window
Casing: window frame
Catch basin: cistern, dry well, reservoir
Caulking: sealer, oakum, pointing, masonry
Caulking compound: grout
Cavity wall: hollow wall
Ceiling clearance: headroom
Cellar: basement, storm cellar, cyclone cellar, substructure
Cement matrix: aggregate, concrete, mortar, plaster
Ceramic: porcelain, china
Cesspool: sewage basin, seepage pit
Chamber: bedroom
Chamfered: beveled, mitered
Chimney: flue, smokestack
Chimney pot: flue cap
China: ceramic, porcelain
Chute: trough
Cinder: rock, slag
Circuit box: fuse box, power panel, distribution panel
Circuit breaker: fuse
Cistern: catch basin, dry well reservoir
Cleat: batten
Clipped ceiling: hung ceiling, drop ceiling
Closet: cloakroom, storage area
Colonial: Early American
Colonnade: portico
Column: post, pillar, cylinder, pile, spile
Column base: plinth, wall base
Comb board: cricket, saddle
Common wall: party wall
Compact soil: bearing soil
Compo board: insulating board, building board, dry wall, gypsum board, Sheetrock, wallboard, rocklath, plasterboard
Composition board: fiberboard, particle board
Concrete: cement matrix, aggregate, mortar, plaster
Condominium: apartment, tenement, multiple dwelling
Conductor: heat transmission, transmitter
Conduit: tubing, metal casing, BX, armored cable
Connectors: splice
Construction paper: building paper, felt, tar paper, sheathing paper, roll roofing
Contemporary: modern
Contractor: builder
Coping: caps
Corridor: arcade, hallway, passageway, lanai
Cot loft: attic, garret, half story, loft
Court: yard, patio, quad
Cover: escutcheon, shield, plate, hood
Cricket: saddle, threshold, doorsill
Cripple stud: short stud
Cross supports: joining, bracing, bridging
Culvert: gutter, channel, ditch, waste drain
Curb: border, parapet
Curtain wall: filler wall
Cyclone cellar: basement, storm cellar, substructure, cellar

Damper: flue control
Deck: landing, platform
Decking: floor
Decorative: ornamental
Deed: ownership document
Dehydration: evaporation
Den: library, reading room, quiet room, sitting room
Disposal system: leach lines, sewage line
Distribution panel: power panel, fuse box, circuit box
Ditch: culvert, gutter, channel, waste drain
Dogtrot: breezeway
Domicile: home, house, dwelling, residence
Doorframe: buck
Doorsill: saddle, threshold, cricket
Dormer: gable window, projected window, eyebrow
Double hung: double sashed
Double plate: top plate
Downspout: drainage pipe, rain drainage
Drainage hole: weep hole
Drainage pipe: downspout, rain drainage
Drain line: flow line
Drop ceiling: clipped ceiling, hung ceiling
Drop support: hanger, iron strap
Dry wall: gypsum board, Sheetrock, wallboard, building board, rocklath, plasterboard, compo board, insulating board.
Dry well: cistern, catch basin, reservoir
Duct: pipeline, vent, raceway, plenum
Dumbwaiter: elevator, hoist, lift
Dwelling: domicile, home, house, residence

Early American: colonial
Earth: fill, backfill, topsoil
Easement: right-of-way
Eave overhang: roof projection, roof overhang
Egress: exit, outlet

Elevator: dumbwaiter, hoist, lift
Entrance: lobby, vestibule, stoop, porch, portal
Escalator: motor stairs
Escutcheon: shield, plate, cover
Evaporation: dehydration
Exit: egress, outlet
Exterior: facade, proscenium, facing
Exterior brick: face brick
Exterior wall: outside wall
Eyebrow: dormer

Facade: proscenium, facing, exterior
Face brick: exterior brick
Facing: facade, proscenium, exterior
Fan: blower
Faucets: taps, bibs
Felt: building paper, tar paper, sheathing paper, roll roofing, construction paper
Fiberboard: composition board, particle board
Fill: backfill
Fillers: shims
Filler stud: trimmer
Filler wall: curtain wall
Finish board: baseboard, mop board
Finish work: trim, millwork
Firebrick: adobe brick, fireclay brick
Fire door: resistance door
Fireplace: ingle
Fireproof material: asbestos
Flagstone: flagging
Flashing: vapor barrier
Flat roof: horizontal roof, shed roof, pent roof
Float valve: flush valve
Floor: decking
Flow line: drain line
Flue: chimney, smokestack
Flue cap: chimney pot
Flue control: damper
Flush plate: switch plate
Flush valve: float valve
Footcandle: candela
Footer: anchorage, footing
Footing: anchorage, footer
Foundation sill: mudsill
Framing: rough carpentry, skeleton
Fuse: circuit breaker
Fuse box: power panel

Gable window: dormer, projected window
Gallery: balcony, ledge, platform
Garret: attic, cot loft, half story, loft
Gazebo: pavilion, belvedere
Girder: beam, timber
Glazing bar: muntin, pane frames, sash bars
Glue: laminate
Grade: ground level, ground line, grade line
Granite: igneous rock, stone
Grate: spaced bars
Grease trap: U trap
Ground line: grade, grade line, ground level
Grout: caulking compound
Gutter: culvert, channel, ditch, waste drain
Gypsum: plaster
Gypsum board: dry wall, Sheetrock, wallboard, building board, insulating board, compo board, rocklath

Half story: loft, cot loft, garret, attic
Hallway: corridor, passageway, lanai
Handle: knob, pull
Handrail: newel
Hanger: drop support, iron strap
Hardboard: Masonite
Hatchway: opening, trapdoor, scuttle
Header: lintel
Headroom; ceiling clearance
Heat transmission: conductor, transmitter
Hinged window: casement window
Hip roof: Bermuda roof
Hoist: lift, elevator, dumbwaiter
Hollow-core door: veneer door
Hollow wall: cavity wall
Hood: cover
Horizontal roof: shed roof, flat roof, pent roof
Hung ceiling: drop ceiling, clipped ceiling

Igneous rock: stone, granite
Illumination level: light intensity
Ingle: fireplace
Insulating board: compo board, building board, dry wall, gypsum board, rocklath, Sheetrock, wallboard
Iron strap: drop support, hanger

Jalousies: louvers
Joining: bridging, bracing, cross supports

Knob: handle, pull

Lacing: lattice bars
Lambert: light unit, lumen
Laminate: glue
Laminated wood: plywood
Lanai: passageway, corridor, hallway

Landing: platform, deck
Larder: pantry
Lattice bars: lacing
Laundry: utility room, service porch
Laundry tray: slop sink, work sink
Lavatory: sink
Leach lines: disposal system, sewage line
Ledge: gallery, platform, balcony
Library: den, reading room, quiet room, sitting room
Lift: dumbwaiter, elevator, hoist
Light intensity: illumination level
Light unit: lumen, lambert
Lintel: header
Live load: moving load
Load: weight
Load plate: bearing plate, sill
Lobby: vestibule, stoop, porch, portal, entrance
Loft: half story, cot loft, garret, attic
Lot: plot, property, site
Louvers: jalousies
Lumen: light unit, lambert

Mantel: shelf
Masonite: hardboard
Masonry: stone, brick, pointing, caulking
Membrane: sheet, sisalkraft
Metal casing: tubing, conduit, BX, armored cable
Millwork: trim, finish work
Mitered: beveled, chamfered
Modern: contemporary
Module: standard unit
Moisture barrier: vapor barrier
Mop board: baseboard, finish board
Mortar: aggregate, cement matrix, concrete, plaster
Motor stairs: escalator
Moving load: live load
Mudsill: foundation sill
Mullion: window divider
Multiple dwelling: apartment, tenement, condominium
Muntin: glazing bar, pane frame, sash bar

Newel: handrail

Opening: trapdoor, scuttle, hatchway
Outside wall: exterior wall
Overhang: awning, canopy
Ownership document: deed

Pane frames: sash bar, glazing bar, muntin
Pantry: larder
Parapet: curb, border
Parget: back plaster
Particle board: composition board, fiberboard
Partition: wall
Party wall: common wall
Passageway: lanai, corridor, hallway
Patio: quad, court, yard, terrace
Pavement: paving, road surface, sidewalk
Pavilion: gazebo, belvedere
Paving: pavement, road surface
Pent roof: shed roof, flat roof
Pier: support, abutment
Pilaster: wall column
Pillar: post, column, pile, spile, cylinder
Pipeline: vent, raceway, duct, plenum
Pitch: slant, slope
Plank and beam: post and beam, post and lintel
Plaster: mortar, gypsum, concrete, cement matrix, aggregate
Plasterboard: dry wall, Sheetrock
Plastic membrane: vapor barrier, sisalkraft
Plate: escutcheon, shield, cover, shoe, scantling, sole
Plate cut: birdmouth, seat cut, seat of a rafter
Platform: balcony, ledge, gallery
Platform framing: western framing
Plenum: pipeline, vent, raceway, duct
Plinth: column base, wall base
Plot: lot, property, site
Plywood: laminated wood, veneer
Pointing: caulking, masonry
Porcelain: ceramic, china
Porch: stoop, lobby, entry, ingress, entrance, portal, gallery, lanai, terrace, veranda, vestibule
Portico: colonnade
Post: column, pillar, cylinder, pile, spile
Post and lintel: post and beam, plank and beam
Power and panel: distribution panel, fuse box, circuit box
Pressure: stress
Property: plot, lot, site
Proscenium: facade, facing, exterior
Pull: handle, knob

Quad: patio, court
Quiet room: sitting room, reading room, library, den
Quoins: stone coping

Raceway: duct, pipeline, plenum, vent
Rafter: beam, shaft, timber
Rain drainage: drainage pipe, downspout

Reading room: quiet room, sitting room, library, den
Recessed fluorescent fixture: troffer
Reservoir: catch basin, cistern, dry well
Residence: domicile, home, house, dwelling
Resistance door: fire door
Ridge: roof peak, ridge pole, ridge board
Right-of-way: easement
Rock: slab, cinder
Rocklath: compo board, insulating board, building board, dry wall, gypsum board, Sheetrock, wallboard
Roll roofing: construction paper, sheathing paper, tar paper, felt, building paper
Roof overhang: roof projection, eave overhang
Roof peak: ridge, ridge board, ridge pole
Rough carpentry: framing
Rough floor: subfloor
Rough lumber: undressed lumber

Saddle: threshold, doorsill, cricket
Sanitary sewer: storm sewer
Sash bar: pane frames, glazing bar, muntin
Scaffold: staging
Scantling: shoe, sole, plate
Screen: wire mesh, wire cloth, carpenter's cloth, baffle
Screw stairs: spiral stairs, winding stairs
Scupper: wall drain
Scuttle: hatchway, opening, trapdoor
Sealer: oakum, caulking
Seasoned: air-dried
Seat of a rafter: seat cut, plate cut, birdmouth
Secret nailing: blind nailing
Securing bolt: anchor bolt, sill bolt
Seepage pit: sewage basin, cesspool
Service porch: laundry, utility room
Setback: building lines, building area
Sewage basin: cesspool, seepage pit
Sewage line: leach lines, disposal system
Shaft: beam, rafter, timber
Sheathing paper: building paper, felt, tar paper, construction paper, roll roofing
Shed roof: flat roof, horizontal roof, pent roof
Sheet: sisalkraft, membrane
Sheet insulation: blanket insulation
Sheetrock: compo board, insulating board, building board, dry wall, gypsum board, wallboard, rocklath, plasterboard
Shelf: mantel
Shield: plate cover, escutcheon
Shims: fillers
Shoe: plate, scantling, sole
Shoe mold: base mold
Shoring: supporting, timber brace
Short stud: cripple stud
Sidewalk: pavement
Sill: bearing plate, load plate
Sill bolt: securing bolt, anchor bolt
Sink: lavatory
Sisalkraft: vapor barrier, plastic membrane, membrane, sheet
Site: plot, property, lot
Sitting room: quiet room, reading room, library, den
Skeleton: framing
Skirting: baseboard
Slag: cinder, rock
Slope: slant, pitch
Slop sink: work sink, laundry tray
Smokestack: flue, chimney
Soffit: underside
Solar energy: sun energy
Sole: shoe, plate, scantling
Sound control: acoustics
Spaced bars: grate
Spar: lumber, beam, wood, timber
Spile: pile, column, pillar, post
Spiral stairs: screw stairs, winding stairs
Splice: connectors
Square bolt: carriage bolt, threaded rod
Staging: scaffold
Standard unit: module
Steel connector: strap
Step: tread
Stiffener: tie
Stone: granite, igneous rock, brick, masonry
Stone coping: quoins
Stoop: porch, portal, vestibule, lobby, entrance
Storage area: cloakroom, closet
Storm cellar: basement, cyclone cellar, substructure, cellar
Storm door: auxiliary door
Storm sewer: sanitary sewer
Storm window: auxiliary window
Strap: steel connector
Strengthen: reinforce
Stress: pressure
Stringer: carriage
Strip insulation: weather stripping
Structural steel: building steel
Strutting: bridging
Subfloor: rough floor

Substructure: storm cellar, basement, cyclone cellar, cellar
Sun energy: solar energy
Support: shield, buttress, abutment, pier
Support partition: bearing partition
Surface drainage: surface flow
Switch plate: flush plate

Taps: faucets, bibs
Tar paper: building paper, felt, sheathing paper, construction paper, roll roofing
Tenement: apartment, multiple dwelling, condominium
Terrace: patio, passageway, corridor, hallway
Terra-cotta: baked clay
Thermostat: automatic temperature control
Thin molding: bead
Threaded rod: square bolt, carriage bolt
Threshold: saddle, doorsill, cricket
Tie: stiffener
Timber: shaft, rafter, beam, girder, lumber, wood
Timber brace: shoring, supporting
Top plate: double plate
Topsoil: earth
Tower: turret
Trapdoor: scuttle, hatchway, opening
Transmitter: conductor, heat transmission
Tread: step
Trim: finish work, millwork
Trimmer: filler stud
Troffer: recessed fluorescent fixture
Trough: chute
Trussing: bracing
Tubes: ducts, channels, air pipes
Tubing: BX, conduit, metal casing, armored cable

Underside: soffit
Undressed lumber: rough lumber
Utility room: service porch, laundry
U trap: grease trap

Vapor barrier: flashing, sisalkraft, plastic membrane, moisture barrier
Veneer: plywood
Veneer door: hollow-core door
Vent: duct, opening
Ventilation: aeration
Veranda: passageway, balcony
Vestibule: stoop, porch, portal, lobby, entrance

Wall: partition
Wall base: column base, plinth
Wallboard: compo board, insulating board, building board, dry wall, gypsum board, Sheetrock
Wall column: pilaster
Wall drain: scupper
Waste drain: gutter, culvert, channel, ditch
Water closet: toilet, W.C.
Water table: water level
W.C.: water closet, toilet
Weather stripping: strip insulation
Weep hole: drainage hole
Weight: load
Western framing: platform framing
Winding stairs: spiral stairs, screw stairs
Window divider: mullion
Window frame: casing
Window shade: blind
Wire cloth: screen, wire mesh, carpenter's cloth
Wood: beam, spar, lumber, timber
Work sink: laundry tray, slop sink

SECTION 26

Architectural Abbreviations

Architects and draftsmen print many words on a drawing. Often they use abbreviations. By using the standard abbreviations listed below, they ensure that their drawings are accurately interpreted.

Here are five points to remember:

1. Most abbreviations are in capitals.
2. A period is used only when the abbreviation may be confused with a whole word.
3. The same abbreviation can be used for both the singular and the plural.
4. Sometimes several terms use the same abbreviation.
5. Many abbreviations are very similar.

Access panel	AP
Acoustic	ACST
Actual	ACT.
Addition	ADD.
Adhesive	ADH
Aggregate	AGGR
Air condition	AIR COND
Alternating current	AC
Aluminum	AL
Ampere	AMP
Anchor bolt	AB
Apartment	APT.
Approved	APPD
Approximate	APPROX
Architectural	ARCH
Area	A
Asbestos	ASB
Asphalt	ASPH
At	@
Automatic	AUTO
Avenue	AVE
Average	AVG
Balcony	BALC
Basement	BSMT
Bathroom	B
Bathtub	BT
Beam	BM
Bearing	BRG
Bedroom	BR
Bench mark	BM
Between	BET.
Blocking	BLKG
Blower	BLO
Blueprint	BP
Board	BD
Boiler	BLR
Both sides	BS
Brick	BRK
British thermal units	BTU
Bronze	BRZ
Broom closet	BC
Building	BLDG
Building line	BL
Cabinet	CAB.
Caulking	CLKG
Cast concrete	C CONC
Cast iron	CI
Catalog	CAT.
Ceiling	CLG
Cement	CEM
Center	CTR
Centerline	CL
Center to center	C to C
Ceramic	CER
Circle	CIR
Circuit	CKT
Circuit breaker	CIR BKR
Circumference	CIRC
Cleanout	CO
Clear	CLR
Closet	CL
Coated	CTD
Column	COL
Combination	COMB.
Common	COM
Composition	COMP
Concrete	CONC
Conduit	CND
Construction	CONST
Continue	CONT
Contractor	CONTR
Corrugate	CORR
Courses	C
Cross section	X-SECT
Cubic foot	CU FT
Cubic inch	CU IN.
Cubic yard	CU YD
Damper	DMPR
Dampproofing	DP
Dead load	DL
Degree	(°) DEG
Design	DSGN
Detail	DET
Diagonal	DIAG
Diagram	DIAG
Diameter	DIA
Dimension	DIM
Dining room	DR
Dishwasher	DW
Ditto	DO.
Division	DIV
Door	DR
Double	DBL
Double hung	DH
Down	DN
Downspout	DS

Drain — DR
Drawing — DWG
Dryer — D

East — E
Electric — ELEC
Elevation — EL
Enamel — ENAM
Entrance — ENT
Equal — EQ
Equipment — EQUIP.
Estimate — EST
Excavate — EXC
Existing — EXIST.
Exterior — EXT

Fabricate — FAB
Feet — (′) FT
Feet board measure — FBM
Finish — FIN.
Fireproof — FPRF
Fixture — FIX.
Flashing — FL
Floor — FL
Floor drain — FD
Flooring — FLG
Fluorescent — FLUOR
Foot — (′) FT
Footcandle — FC
Footing — FTG
Foundation — FDN
Full size — FS
Furred ceiling — FC

Galvanize — GALV
Galvanized iron — GI
Garage — GAR
Gas — G
Gage — GA
Girder — G
Glass — GL
Grade — GR
Grade line — GL
Gypsum — GYP

Hall — H
Hardware — HDW
Head — HD
Heater — HTR
Height — HT
Horizontal — HOR
Hose bib — HB
Hot water — HW
House — HSE
Hundred — C

I beam — I
Impregnate — IMPG
Inch — (″) IN.
Incinerator — INCIN
Insulate — INS
Intercommunication — INTERCOM
Interior — INT
Iron — I

Joint — JT
Joist — JST

Kilowatt — KW
Kilowatt hour — KWH
Kip (1000 lb.) — K
Kitchen — KIT

Laminate — LAM
Laundry — LAU
Lavatory — LAV
Left — L
Length — LG
Length overall — LOA
Light — LT
Linear — LIN
Linen closet — L CL
Live load — LL
Living room — LR
Long — LG
Louver — LV
Lumber — LBR

Main — MN
Manhole — MH
Manual — MAN.
Manufacturing — MFG
Material — MATL
Maximum — MAX
Medicine cabinet — MC
Membrane — MEMB
Metal — MET.
Meter — M
Minimum — MIN
Minute — (′) MIN
Miscellaneous — MISC
Mixture — MIX.
Model — MOD
Modular — MOD
Motor — MOT
Molding — MLDG

Natural — NAT
Nominal — NOM
North — N
Not to scale — NTS
Number — NO.

Obscure — OB
On center — OC
Opening — OPNG
Opposite — OPP
Overall — OA
Overhead — OVHD

Panel — PNL
Parallel — PAR.
Part — PT
Partition — PTN
Penny (nails) — d
Permanent — PERM
Perpendicular — PERP
Piece — PC
Plaster — PL
Plate — PL
Plumbing — PLMB
Pound — LB
Precast — PRCST
Prefabricated — PREFAB
Preferred — PFD

Quality — QUAL
Quantity — QTY

Radiator — RAD
Radius — R
Range — R
Receptacle — RECP
Reference — REF
Refrigerate — REF
Refrigerator — REF
Register — REG
Reinforce — REINF
Reproduce — REPRO
Required — REQD
Return — RET
Riser — R
Roof — RF

Room — RM
Round — RD

Safety — SAF
Sanitary — SAN
Scale — SC
Schedule — SCH
Second — (″) SEC
Section — SECT
Select — SEL
Service — SERV
Sewer — SEW.
Sheet — SH
Sheathing — SHTHG
Shower — SH
Side — S
Siding — SDG
Similar — SIM
Sink — S
Soil pipe — SP
South — S
Specification — SPEC
Square — SQ
Stairs — ST
Steam — ST
Standard — STD
Steel — STL
Stock — STK
Street — ST
Storage — STG
Structural — STR
Supply — SUP
Surface — SUR
Switch — SW
Symmetrical — SYM
System — SYS

Tar and gravel — T & G
Tangent — TAN.
Tarpaulin — TARP
Tee — T
Telephone — TEL
Television — TV
Temperature — TEMP
Terra-cotta — TC
Terrazzo — TER
Thermostat — THERMO
Thick — THK
Thousand — M
Through — THRU
Toilet — T
Tongue and groove — T & G
Total — TOT.
Tread — TR
Tubing — TUB.
Typical — TYP

Unfinished — UNFIN
Urinal — UR

Valve — V
Vapor proof — VAP PRF
Vent pipe — VP
Ventilate — VENT.
Vertical — VERT
Vitreous — VIT
Volt — V
Volume — VOL

Washing machine — WM
Water closet — WC
Water heater — WH
Waterproofing — WP
Watt — W
Weather stripping — WS
Weatherproof — WP
Weep hole — WH
Weight — WT
West — W
Width — W
Window — WDW
With — W/
Without — W/O
Wood — WD
Wrought iron — WI

Yard — YD

Index

5 6 7 8 9 0 DODO 86 85 84 83 82 81